DEBATES

IN THE

CONVENTION

FOR THE

REVISION AND AMENDMENT OF THE CONSTITUTION

OF THE

STATE OF LOUISIANA.

ASSEMBLED AT LIBERTY HALL, NEW ORLEANS, APRIL 6, 1864.

BY

ALBERT P. BENNETT, *Official Reporter.*

H. A. GALLUP,
S. W. BURNHAM,
A. L. BARTLETT, } *Short-hand Reporters.*

NEW ORLEANS:
W. R. FISH, PRINTER TO THE CONVENTION.
1864.

DEBATES

IN THE

STATE CONSTITUTIONAL CONVENTION

FOR THE

REVISION AND AMENDMENT OF THE CONSTITUTION OF THE STATE OF LOUISIANA.

WEDNESDAY, April 6th, 1864.

This day being fixed by the General Order of Maj. Gen. Nathaniel P. Banks, commanding the United States forces in the Department of the Gulf, by virtue of the authority invested in him by the president of the United States, and also agreeably with the proclamation of his excellency Michael Hahn, governor of the State of Louisiana, ordering this Convention to assemble for the purpose of revising and amending the constitution of the State, the delegates from the several Representative Districts met in Liberty Hall, which had been prepared for their reception, in the Executive Building, New Orleans, at the hour of 12 o'clock M. The Hall was filled with delegates, and the lobbies and galleries overflowing with spectators.

Col. T. B. Thorpe, of Orleans, took the stand and said:

"I have been requested to call this Convention to order."

MR. TERRY, of Orleans—I nominate Alfred Shaw, Esq., as temporary president of the Convention.

Mr. Thorpe put the nomination to the House, and Mr. Shaw was declared unanimously chosen as temporary president, and took his seat.

Mr. Fish, of Orleans, then nominated Alfred C. Hills as secretary *pro tem.*, and he was unanimously elected, and took his seat.

On motion of Mr. Montamat, the proceedings were opened with prayer by the Rev. Dr. Newman, of the Methodist Church.

A communication from the secretary of state, enclosed the general order of Major General Nathaniel P. Banks, under which the election for delegates was held, as well as the proclamation of his excellency Michael Hahn, governor of the State of Louisiana, which were ordered to be read.

Also, the returns from the various districts and parishes in this city and State, of the election held for delegates.

A motion was made that the roll be called to ascertain the number of members present. The secretary read the names and the following gentlemen were present:

Joseph Gorlinski, John Stumpf, R. B. Bell, J. B. Schroeder, Geo. F. Brott, E. Murphy, W. T. Stocker, Terrance Cook, Alfred C. Hills, Joseph H. Wilson, T. B. Thorpe, John Henderson, Jr., J. J. Healy, J. H. Stiner, Geo. A. Fosdick, M. W. Murphy, W. H. Hire, P. K. O'Conner, Jno. W. Thomas, Jno. Foley, James Fuller, George Howes, John Sullivan, H. W. Waters, J. R. Terry, P. Harnan, O. W. Austin, Alfred Shaw, E. J. Wenck, R. King Cutler, Louis Gastinel, Judge E. H. Durell, Edmund Abell, J. B. Montamat, John Buckley, Jr., A. Mendiverri, Xavier Maurer, J. V. Bofill, Dr. M. F. Bonzano, F. M. Crozat, Adolphe Bailey, Judge R. K. Howell, M. Spellicy, J. K. Cook, O. H. Poynot, H. Maas, Edward Hart, E. Goldman, John Purcell, Geo. W. Geier, C. W. Stauffer, W.

R. Fish, James Duane, Benj. Campbell, Edmund Flood, J. L. Davies, J. T. Barrett, J. H. Flagg, W. H. Seymour, Joseph Dupaty, James Ennis, H. J. Heard, P. A. Kugler, Martin Schnurr, Robert Morris, Samuel Pursell, Christian Roselius, John Payne, J. B. Bromley, E. H. Knobloch, C. H. Gruneberg, Lewis Lombard, Thos. J. Decker, Thomas Ong, R. Beauvais, Young Burke, Charles Smith, R. W. Bennie, Adolphe Gaidry.

It was moved and seconded that a committee of three be appointed by the chair to examine credentials, which, after being amended by striking out "three" and substituting "five," was carried. The chair appointed the following gentlemen, with J. P. Montamat, Esq., chairman: Messrs. Thomas, Gruneberg, Bennie, Brott and S. Pursell.

Motions regarding the appointment of a committee to report rules and regulations for the government of the Convention, and to suggest officers for carrying out its business, were then offered; but these, as well as a resolution that all motions and resolutions be committed to writing and handed to the secretary, were considered premature, and lost, on the ground that no business could be transacted until the Committee on Credentials had made their report.

It was stated that the committee would require considerable time to make their report; and accordingly a motion was made and carried that the meeting adjourn until to-morrow at 12 o'clock.

THURSDAY, April 7, 1864.

At the appointed hour, 12 o'clock M., the president called the Convention to order, and decided that a quorum would consist of seventy-six members, for the purposes of organization.

The secretary was directed to call the roll, and it was announced that there was a quorum present, and the Convention then proceeded to business.

Mr. Montamat, chairman of the Committee on Credentials, rose and said that the Committee on Credentials would report, but that there were certain members claiming to be elected, in regard to whose merits no report could be made, inasmuch as no returns of their election had been received from the secretary of state.

Mr. Shaw, chairman, decided that it would be better to wait until the supposed fact was announced by the secretary of state, when Mr. Thomas informed the chair that a communication from the secretary was upon the speaker's desk, but upon search it was not to be found.

The Rev. Mr. Potter, at the request of the president, opened the proceedings with prayer.

The secretary then read the minutes of the preceding meeting, and no amendments being proposed, they were accepted.

MR. KAVANAGH—I would ask if the Committee on Credentials have made any report.

MR. MONTAMAT—In its behalf, I submit the following statement:

To the honorable the chairman and members of the Constitutional Convention:

The undersigned, Committee on Credentials, beg leave to submit the following report. Having examined the returns of election from the parishes hereinafter named, your committee find that the following named gentlemen were duly elected:

ORLEANS.

First Representative District— Joseph Gorlinski, R. B. Bell, Geo. F. Brott, W. T. Stocker, John Stumpf, J. B. Schroeder, E. Murphy.

Second Representative District—Terrance Cook, Joseph H. Wilson, John Henderson, Jr., J. H. Stiner, M. W. Murphy, P. K. O'Conner, Alfred C. Hills, T. B. Thorpe, J. J. Healy, Geo. A. Fosdick, W. H. Hire.

Third Representative District—John W. Thomas, James Fuller, John Sullivan, J. R. Terry, O. W. Austin, John Foley, George Howes, H. W. Waters, P. Harnan.

Fourth Representative District— Alfred Shaw, R. King Cutler, Judge E. H. Durell, E. J. Wenck, Louis Gastinel.

Fifth Representative District— Edmund Abell, John Buckley, Jr., Xavier Maurer, J. P. Montamat, A. Mendiverri.

Sixth Representative District—J. V. Bofill, F. M. Crozat, Dr. M. F. Bonzano, Adolphe Bailey.

Seventh Representative District—Judge R. K. Howell, J. J. Baum, M. D. Kavanagh, H. Millspaugh.

Eighth Representative District—J. A. Spellicy, O. H. Poynot, J. K. Cook.

Ninth Representative District—H. Maas, E. Goldman, Edward Hart.

Tenth Representative District—John Purcell, C. W. Stauffer, W. R. Fish, Benjamin Campbell, J. T. Barrett, Geo. W. Geier, R. S. Abbott, James Duane, Edmond Flood, J. L. Davies.

Right Bank of Mississippi (*Algiers*)—J. H. Flagg, W. H. Seymour.

ASSUMPTION.

Joseph Dupaty, Jas. Ennis, E. J. Pintado.

AVOYELLES.

L. P. Normand, H. C. Edwards.

BATON ROUGE (EAST.)

W. D. Mann, P. A. Kugler, H. J. Heard.

BATON ROUGE (WEST.)

Sidney A. Lobdell.

CONCORDIA.

Robert W. Taliaferro.

FELICIANA (EAST.)

Jansen T. Paine, Martin Schnurr.

JEFFERSON.

Robert Morris, Samuel Pursell, Christian Roselius, John Payne.

LAFOURCHE.

J. B. Bromley. E. H. Knobloch, C. H. L. Gruneberg.

MADISON.

R. V. Montague.

RAPIDES.

M. R. Ariail, A. Cazabat, J. H. Newell, Thomas M. Wells.

ST. BERNARD.

Thomas Ong.

ST. JAMES.

R. Beauvais.

ST. JOHN THE BAPTIST.

Young Burke.

ST. MARY.

Charles Smith.

TERREBONNE.

R. W. Bennie, Adolphe Gaidry.

Your committee find that in the parish of Ascension, Robert J. Duke received the highest number of votes, and was duly elected.

That Emile Collin and J. E. Richard each received an equal number of votes, and consequently neither of them was elected.

Your committee have thought proper, under such circumstances, to recommend that another election be ordered in said parish of one delegate.

Upon investigating the returns from the parish of Plaquemines, it appears that the sheriff thereof was guilty of the following acts of negligence, which, in the opinion of your committee, renders the election in that parish null and void:

First—He did not appoint deputies, or cause the polls to be opened at all the various precincts in that parish.

Second—He did not cause any return to be made of the result of the poll at Fort Jackson.

Third—He has made no official return whatever of the election in that parish.

Your committee would recommend that another election be ordered in that parish. All of which is respectfully submitted.

JOHN MONTAMAT, *Chairman.*

It was moved and seconded that the report be adopted.

MR. BROTT—Before we proceed to adopt that report, I wish to suggest that the last part of the report be set aside. A member having been elected, is entitled to represent that parish.

MR. LOMBARD, of Plaquemines—*Mr. Chairman:* Have I not protested against that election on account of the illegality and fraud which have prevailed in this and in every election of that parish since 1844? And did I not wish this in particular brought to light, my opponent would not have the benefit of all the evil, fraud and misdealing to change a vote he was not entitled to. I knew beforehand all this, and refused to accept the nomination from the citizens. I knew such practices would be made use of; but, notwithstanding, I faced this great discrepancy which was in my way, and I said that in case I should be defeated I should find those who would not give this their sanction. I call upon this Convention to decide whether I am entitled to my seat, and if not so, to some credit for having made a stand against the frauds. If you had observed the requisites of the law, you could not have had an election within a month. Is it to be said that the iniquities of old shall be prejudicial to this assembly? But is it rather not time to frown them down? Mr. President, I leave it to this House to decide, and call upon my opponent to come forward and state why it should not be so.

MR. DECKER—I was not a candidate, but was elected by the people. I am satisfied with the report of the committee, and with the will of the people, and am willing that the election should go back to them. I have no more to say.

The question was then called for.

MR. BELL—I would move that a special committee of five be appointed, to whom the matter may be referred.

Mr. Montamat moved that the motion be laid on the table.

The president stated that there was a motion already before the House to adopt the report of the committee. Mr. Bell having moved an amendment, the motion now would be to lay that amendment on the table.

The motion for amendment was lost.

Mr. Harnan—I move that every motion be presented in writing.

Motion decided to be out of order.

President—Shall the report on credentials be adopted?

Mr. Cazabat—Before the adoption of this motion, I beg leave most respectfully to suggest that there are now several parishes in Western Louisiana anxious and ready to participate in the proceedings of this Convention. In a few days the parishes of Natchitoches, Catahoula, St. Landry, Winn, Calcasieu, and adjoining parishes, will be represented. It seems to me, therefore, it would be proper and right, before we proceed any further, to adjourn this Convention, until next Monday, at 12 o'clock; therefore I move that this Convention, before going into permanent organization, or any further in these proceedings, shall adjourn until 12 o'clock on Monday next.

Mr. Montamat — The motion is out of order.

President—The motion now before the House is that the Convention shall adjourn.

The yeas and nays were called for.

During the calling of the roll it was decided that only the names of delegates which had been transmitted to the Convention by the secretary of state, and had been reported upon by the Committee on Credentials as duly elected, should be called.

The motion to adjourn was lost—nays 78; yeas 7.

President—The motion now before the House is to adopt the report of the committee.

Mr. Terry moved as an amendment, that the report be adopted with the exception of the portion referring to the contested seats.

Mr. Stocker moved to lay the amendment on the table, which motion being put to vote, was carried.

The report was then unanimously accepted.

Mr. Bell moved that the Convention go into permanent organization.

Mr. Comas—I offer as a substitute that a committee of five on permanent organization be appointed, which shall report the different officers necessary for the transaction of the business of the Convention, since it is necessary to know what officers are needful in this body.

Mr. Montamat moved that a sergeant-at-arms be appointed, which was put and unanimously carried.

Nominations for President were then made as follows:

Judge R. K. Howell, nominated by Mr. Campbell.

Judge E. H. Durell, nominated by Mr. Purcell.

Alfred Shaw, nominated by Mr. Brott.

Dr. Bonzano, nominated by Mr. Goldman.

T. B. Thorpe, nominated by Mr. O'Conner.

C. Roselius, nominated by Mr. Harnan.

J. R. Terry, nominated by Mr. Fuller.

Messrs. Terry and Shaw respectfully declined.

Mr. Stiner moved that the president be elected by ballot.

Mr. Montamat moved that the motion be laid on the table. Upon the nays appearing to have it, a division was called for.

Mr. Harnan—We call for the yeas and nays because we wish every man to vote openly, so that we may know how each one does vote.

The secretary stated it was difficult to call the name and register the vote of every member, and, wishing an assistant, he would suggest Mr. H. A. Gallup as assistant secretary, which was moved, seconded and carried.

Mr. Harnan moved that an assistant should be appointed to register the votes of each candidate, which was lost.

President—The question now before the House is whether the motion of the gentleman from the Second District (Mr. Stiner), shall be adopted.

The roll being called, it was decided to lay the motion to vote by ballot on the table. Yeas 56; nays 24.

President—You are about to elect a president. The candidates are Messrs. Howell, Durell, Roselius, Bonzano and Thorpe.

Mr. Balch—The delegates from the parish of Iberville desire to take their seats and cast their votes, as the elections were duly held and returns made to the secretary of state; but by some means they have been lost, and have not reached the secretary.

Since, as I have said, the elections were held according to the orders of Gen. Banks, and returns legally made, we would like to vote. I laid a communication on the desk, signed by the two delegates, in relation to this matter.

Mr. Thomas rose to a point of order.

PRESIDENT—These votes cannot be counted without the order of the Convention, and as no such permission has been given, the gentleman is out of order.

It was moved and seconded that the delegates be heard, and on being put was carried.

MR. BALCH—My object is that we may be permitted to take our seats previous to the organization of the Convention, so that we may vote. The fact is notorious that the election was legally held, and the other candidate and myself legally elected. By some mischance the returns of the provost marshal are lost, and have never reached the secretary of state. I dispatched a messenger yesterday to Capt. Cox, and requested him to send the certificate as soon as possible. Under these circumstances I consider it nothing but just we should have the privilege of voting in the organization. There was no opposition to this election, and we were elected beyond all question. Such being the facts, Mr. Chairman and gentlemen, we ask the privilege of taking our seats and voting.

Mr. Abell moved that the gentlemen be permitted to take their seats.

Mr. Waters moved that the matter be referred to the Committee on Credentials.

MR. THOMAS—Before the question is put I will state that it has already been referred to the Committee on Credentials. I do not doubt these gentlemen, neither do the committee, but there was no evidence brought before them other than the statement of the gentlemen themselves. Since there is no other evidence before them now, it would be useless to refer it back to them again, for the committee would be unable to make any different report, since it would not be based on any other evidence further than that body has already had.

The motion was then put and lost.

The original motion that the delegates be allowed to take their seats, was then put to vote and carried.

MR. BROTT—I notice that when the roll was called, three members answered from the parish of Ascension. This parish is entitled to but two, and only one is elected according to the report of the committee.

SECRETARY—I would state that those names were called through a mistake, but I did not deem it necessary to correct it, as none of them answered at the last call, and their names will not be read again.

The secretray then read the votes of the candidates for presidency as follows: T. B. Thorpe, one; Christian Roselius, seven; M. F. Bonzano, fifteen; Judge Howell, twenty-five; Judge Durell, thirty-five; and consequently there was no election.

The names of Messrs. Bonzano, Thorpe and Roselius were withdrawn.

Mr. Stocker moved that M. DeCoursey be requested to act as temporary sergeant-at-arms, which, being seconded, Mr. Montamat declared it to be out of order, and upon Mr. Stocker calling for a decision of the chair, it was ruled to be in order.

It was moved and carried that the motion be laid on the table.

There being no choice in the election of president, the secretary again called the roll. The following is a list of the votes for the candidates:

For Judge Durell—Messrs. Gorlinski, Bell, Brott, Stumpf, E. Murphy, Cook, M. W. Murphy, O'Conner, Thorpe, Healy, Hire, Sullivan, Thomas, Fuller, Terry, Waters, Shaw, Bofill, Crozat, Bailey, Howell, Maas, Goldman, Hart, J. Purcell, Stauffer, Fish, Campbell, Barrett, Geier, Duane, Davies, Flagg, Seymour, Schnurr, Roselius, Paine, Knobloch, Gruneberg, Smith, Bennie, Gaidry—43.

For Judge Howell—Messrs. Stocker, Wilson, Schroeder, Henderson, Fosdick, Austin, Foley, Harnan, Cutler, Durell, Wenck, Gastinel, Abell, Buckley, Maurer, Montamat, Mendiverri, Bonzano, Baum, Millspaugh, Kavanagh, Spellicy, Poynot, Cook, Flood, Dupaty, Ennis, Kugler, Heard, Morris, S. Pursell, Ong, Beauvais, Burke, Normand, Edwards, Cazabat, Newell, Balch, Dufresne, Hills—41.

Mr. Thorpe moved that Judge Durell be considered the choice of this Convention, which, being seconded, was put and unanimously carried.

It was moved and seconded that a com

mittee of three be appointed to escort Judge Durell to the chair, which being duly carried, the speaker appointed Messrs. Howell, Roselius and Bonzano.

Judge Durell was received with loud applause, and addressed the meeting as follows:

Gentlemen of the Convention—I thank you heartily for the honor you have conferred upon me in making me your president; and I thank you still more heartily for this proof of your confidence in my abilities and my patriotism. When, in presiding over your deliberations, I may show weakness, I know that you will give me of your strength; and that I shall not be disappointed in my expectation of finding with you that courtesy which is the best aid to an efficient business in every legislative body.

Gentlemen—In this time of great trouble, in this supreme hour of our country's battle for its life, you have been entrusted by your fellow-citizens with duties commensurate with those of the soldier in the field; you have been called upon to finish the labor which he, necessarily, leaves incomplete.

Gentlemen—On the 26th day of January, 1861, a few ambitious and bad men had assembled in convention, and representing a minority of the people of the State, declared "the connection between the State of Louisiana and the Federal Union dissolved;" you, gentlemen, have been chosen—the elect of the loyal people of Louisiana—to undo that work of folly and crime; to restore the State to its former legitimate position in the Union; to replace it under the protecting folds of that flag which, everywhere, upon the land and upon the seas, has been ever hailed as the symbol of liberty and equal rights.

Gentlemen—You are all familiar with the rise and progress of the grand drama which is being enacted in these days upon this continent, and of which we also are a part. With this knowledge, you will accept the progress of ideas; you will accept the changes which great convulsions in the opinions and in the societies of men make a necessity; you will willingly exchange a dead past for a living future.

Gentlemen—The first, chief cause of the present rebellion, is patent to all; you have been called together, invested with the plenary powers which, under our institutions, belong to an organic political body, not only for the purpose of restoring the State to the Union, but also for the equal purpose of removing that fatal cause of strife and rebellion from Louisiana forever. You will, I know, perform those and the many other duties confided to your charge boldly, with decision, looking only to the prosperity and happiness of your State and of our common country.

Mr. Bell moved to elect the secretary by ballot.

Mr. Montamat moved that the members cease from all motions relative to voting by ballot, as they were not there to vote by ballot, but to record their opinions and proceedings, and that the motion be laid on the table. The vote was put, and the motion of Mr. Bell was laid on the table.

The following gentlemen were then nominated for the office of secretary: Messrs. Neelis, McClellan, Girard, White, Reynolds, Derickson, Holland and Murphy.

The secretary read the names of the nominees, and the votes recorded were: for Neelis, 44; Derickson, 10; McClellan, 8; Holland, 6; White, 6; Girard, 4; Murphy, 2; Reynolds, none.

John E. Neelis was declared duly elected as secretary of the Convention.

Mr. Henderson moved, and it was seconded, that a committee of three be appointed by the chair to wait upon Mr. Neelis and inform him of his election, and conduct him to his seat.

The motion passed, and the chair appointed Messrs. Henderson, Thorpe and Campbell to wait upon Mr. Neelis. The committee reported that he could not be found, and Col. Hills, secretary *pro tem.*, continued to officiate.

A motion was made to ballot for sergeant-at-arms. This was laid on the table, and the following gentlemen were nominated: T. F. McGuire, C. Baumbach, Thomas K. Flanagan and M. DeCoursey. The roll was called, but there was no choice. Mr. Flanagan then withdrew, and the roll was again called, but with the same result. The secretary read the names again, and the following vote was cast: DeCoursey, 41; Baumbach, 36; McGuire, 1. Mr. DeCoursey was accordingly declared elected sergeant-at-arms.

It was moved by Mr. Brott that the committee appointed to wait on the secretary also wait upon the sergeant-at-arms, and inform him of his election. The motion was carried unanimously.

It was then moved and seconded that the Convention adjourn till to-morrow at 12 o'clock.

FRIDAY, April 8th, 1864.

The Convention was called to order at a quarter past 12 o'clock, Mr. Shaw in the chair.

The roll being called by the Secretary *pro tem.*, the following members answered to their names:

Messrs. Abell, Austin, Balch, Bailey, Barrett, Baum, Beauvais, Bell, Bennie, Bofill, Bonzano, Bromley, Brott, Buckley, Burke, Campbell, Cazabat, Cook J. K., Cook T., Crozat, Cutler, Davis, Dufresne, Duane, Dupaty, Durell, Edwards, Ennis, Fish, Flagg, Flood, Foley, Fosdick, Fuller, Gastinel, Geier, Goldman, Gorlinski, Gruneberg, Gaidry, Healy, Harnan, Hart, Heard, Henderson, Hills, Hire, Howell, Howes, Kavanagh, Knobloch, Kugler, Maas, Maurer, Mendiverri, Millspaugh, Montamat, Montague, Morris, Murphy E., Murphy M. W., Newell, Normand, O'Conner, Ong, Paine J. T., Pintado, Poynot, Purcell J., Pursell S., Schroeder, Schnurr, Seymour, Shaw, Smith, Spellicy, Stocker, Stumpf, Stiner, Stauffer, Sullivan, Terry, Thomas, Waters, Wenck, Wilson.

After the minutes had been read of the previous meeting, and before their adoption, Mr. Terry rose and requested that they might be amended in that portion in relation to the nomination of candidates for the speakership, so that he and Mr. Shaw might stand as having declined to become candidates for that office. No further objection being made, the minutes were adopted as corrected.

MR. HARNAN—I rise with some reluctance, but as I have been informed that some of our members have been grossly assaulted, I call upon the Convention to take into consideration the following resolution:

We are informed, from what appears to be good authority, that two members of this Convention have been assaulted, one for performing his duty as a member of this Convention; therefore,

Resolved, That said persons be reported to the proper authorities for merited punishment.

I came here to do justice to all, and to represent the minority as well as the majority. Therefore, I hope this resolution will be strictly enforced, since we claim nothing but what is right.

MR. STAUFFER—I think it is unnecessary to bring this matter before the Convention, for there are proper authorities to take care of any persons who may assault our members, and it is taking the time of the Convention unnecessarily; and therefore I move that the resolution be laid on the table.

The reading of the resolution was then called for.

The previous motion was amended by a motion that it be referred to a committee to report thereon; and this being stated by the chairman, it was announced that the majority had voted in the affirmative, when the yeas and nays were called for on the question and preference.

MR. STAUFFER—I will call the attention of the chair to the fact that the unfinished business of yesterday must be concluded before we take up any new business. At that time there was a resolution passed in regard to the election of president, secretary, sergeant-at-arms and doorkeeper. These have not all been chosen; and it therefore strikes me that this new matter is entirely out of order. I ask the decision of the chair on that point.

PRESIDENT—This is a question of privilege, and I believe it to be in order.

MR. BROTT—I request the privilege of changing my vote in regard to the question of reference to the affirmative.

No objections being made, Mr. Brott's vote was changed.

Upon calling the roll, 48 answered in the affirmative, and 30 in the negative; whereupon it was decided the matter should be referred.

As an amendment to Mr. Harnan's resolution, it was moved that the president appoint the committee, the number constituting it to be left to his discretion; which amendment being accepted, the chair appointed Messrs. Wilson, Roselius and Morris.

It was moved that Col. Thorpe should constitute a member of the committee; but Mr. Thorpe begged leave to decline.

Mr. Wilson was suggested as a member of this committee, when the chair announced that he had already been appointed as such.

MR. THOMAS—I move we now proceed to yesterday's unfinished business, which is the election of remaining officers.

This motion was seconded and carried.

MR. ENNIS—I now hold in my hand a resolution that I wish to lay before the Convention, and hope it will receive the attention its merits demand. Not being able to see myself, I request the secretary to read it.

MR. THOMAS—I move that we go on with the unfinished business of yesterday.

MR. CAZABAT—I move that the remainder of the officers be chosen by the appointment of the chair.

MR. MONTAMAT—I move that it be laid on the table.

Mr. Montamat's motion was seconded.

MR. STAUFFER—I offer as a substitute that a committee of five be appointed by the chair to report rules for the government of this Convention, and the additional number and character of the employés required for the transaction of the business of this Convention.

MR. HENDERSON—The gentleman is out of order.

MR. MONTAMAT—There is a doorkeeper yet to be elected, and I wish the resolution to be heard.

MR. HEARD—These debates are entirely out of order. It was moved to lay the motion of Mr. Cazabat on the table. That motion was not debatable. Other motions have subsequently been made, but that motion was never withdrawn. The first thing to be done is to settle that motion, for we ought to be governed by something like parliamentary law.

A motion was then made to proceed with the election of officers.

PRESIDENT—The first thing before the Convention is to lay upon the table the motion that the officers be appointed by the chair.

That question was disposed of by an affirmative vote.

The speaker then remarked that the motions were presented so rapidly that it was almost impossible to follow their sequence.

Mr. Stauffer withdrew his motion until after the election of doorkeeper and messenger.

PRESIDENT—The motion now is that the Convention proceed to the election of doorkeeper and messenger. All those in favor of it will answer yea; opposed, nay.

The motion was decided in the affirmative.

MR. FOLEY—I request that the names of candidates for doorkeeper be announced.

MR. HILLS—I not only request that the names of candidates be announced, but that as each member responds his choice be repeated by the assistant secretary.

The names of the candidates, Messrs. A. Martin, F. X. Martin, W. Martin, Maloy, Purcell, McCarthy, Coyle, Baumbach, Sullivan, Miller, Ernst and Freary, were then read and the roll called.

The result of the first call was as follows: A. Martin, 15; F. X. Martin, 1; W. Martin, none; Maloy, 3; Purcell, 4; McCarthy, 4; Coyle, 15; Baumbach, 29; Sullivan, 5; Miller, 1; Ernst, 1; Freary, 3.

Mr. Harnan withdrew Mr. Maloy's name.

MR. BAUM—I move that upon the next call the candidate receiving the highest vote shall be declared elected.

MR. HILLS—I move that the voting be confined to the three who have received the highest number of votes.

MR. FLAGG—I move that the election be confined to the two who have received the highest number of votes.

PRESIDENT—It has been moved and seconded that the choice of election be confined to the three who have received the highest number of votes.

No objection being made, the motion was accordingly adopted.

Upon calling the roll the second time, the result was as follows:

A. Martin, 14; Coyle, 22; Baumbach, 45.

Mr. Baumbach was declared elected.

MR. MONTAMAT—I move that Mr. Baumbach be considered the unanimous choice of this Convention.

No objection being made, Mr. Montamat's motion was adopted.

MR. FOLEY—I move we proceed to the election of messenger.

MR. TERRY—I move we proceed to elect two doorkeepers.

MR. STAUFFER—I think it would be proper that we should elect but one, and I have a motion before the House which should be afterwards brought up.

The following parties were then nominated as candidates for messenger: Messrs.

McLane, McDonald, Murphy, McGuire, McClair, Clark, Coyle, Newton.

Upon the first roll-call the result was as follows: McLane, 0; Newton, 0; McGuire, 2; Murphy, 3; McClair, 9; McDonald, 17; Clark, 21; Coyle, 25.

MR. WILSON—I move that only those two who have received the highest number of votes be considered as candidates.

The motion was carried.

MR. FOLEY—I would like to have the names of the candidates called now before the Convention.

The secretary then proceeded to call the roll the second time, when he was interrupted by Mr. Schroeder.

MR. SCHROEDER—There undoubtedly has been a confounding of the names of the candidates, the result of which has been that many members have answered to their names unadvisedly, and many votes have been cast for Mr. Clark when the intention of the members was to support Mr. McClair.

MR. FOLEY—I move that Mr. Wilson's motion be reconsidered and amended by striking out the word "two" and substituting "three."

It was moved that the last motion be laid upon the table, which being seconded by Mr. Cazabat, it was so ordered by the Convention.

MR. TERRY—We wish to understand who are the candidates.

The secretary announced that they were Messrs. Coyle and Clark.

MR. HILLS—Since there seems to have been some misunderstanding in regard to the names before the Convention, I move that the secretary begin and call the roll anew.

Mr. Hills's motion was seconded and carried; immediately after which the president remarked that there should be no mistake or misunderstanding, and hoped that in future no such difficulty would arise.

The second roll-call resulted as follows: Coyle 36, Clark 44.

MR. MONTAMAT—I move that Mr. Clark be considered the unanimous choice of the Convention.

Mr. Montamat's resolution was seconded and carried.

MR. STAUFFER—I will now present my resolution, heretofore referred to.

MR. HEARD—Mr. President, our organization will not be complete until we have elected an assistant secretary, for it is almost impossible for the secretary to perform the duties incumbent upon him, without such an assistant.

MR. GORLINSKI—I move we proceed to elect a postmaster, printer, and four reporters.

MR STAUFFER—I believe my resolution has precedence.

MR. MONTAMAT—I propose that the resolution of Mr. Gorlinski be referred to the Committee on Rules and Regulations.

MR. STAUFFER—I would like to have my resolution read.

MR. CAZABAT—I call for the resolution of Mr. Stauffer.

MR. MONTAMAT—I wish to hear the resolution read.

PRESIDENT—The resolution of Mr. Stauffer will now be read.

Mr. Stauffer's resolution:

Resolved, That a committee of five be appointed by the president to report rules for the government of the Convention, and in addition in regard to the character of the officers and employés, required for the transaction of business.

MR. HEARD—I offer this as a substitute:

Resolved, That a committee of five or seven be appointed by the president to prepare rules and orders for the government of the Convention, and that until said committee report, the proceedings be governed by Jefferson's Manual, and the rules and orders of the Senate and House of Representatives of the State of Louisiana as adopted in 1856.

MR. MONTAMAT—I move that the resolutions be laid on the table.

MR. STOCKER—I move that the original resolution and substitute be laid on the table.

Mr. Stocker's motion was carried.

Mr. Terry introduced the following resolution:

Resolved, That the status of every member of this Convention be, namely: that he be a legally qualified voter of the State, who has subscribed to the oath of the president's proclamation of the 8th of December, 1863; that each and every member produce the same to the secretary by 12 M., on the 9th of April, 1864, or be required to take the same before the president of the Convention.

It was moved to lay this motion on the

table, and upon a discussion arising as to the propriety of that motion, Mr. Thomas stated that the last motion was not debatable, and that he arose to a point of order.

The speaker then directed the roll to be called, to decide as to the disposition of the last motion; when it was decided not to lay it on the table by a vote of 55 nays to 26 yeas.

MR. HEARD—Since it was decided that the motion put before the House was not debatable, I will now explain why I voted against it. Every man who has been elected by a free and independent constituency, comes here as a man and to be respected as such. I for one am willing to resign my seat and go home, if we are to be trammeled and shackled, and if every man who has been elected here is to be an object of suspicion. It seems to me that the very fact that the gentlemen occupying seats on this floor, after the proclamations of General Banks and Governor Hahn, is *prima facie* evidence that he is entitled to a seat, the returns in pursuance of them having been made to the secretary of state. I took that oath when it first came out—on the very first week. Now, sir, this is what I suppose to be a Convention of the representatives of the great people of Louisiana, who have complied with the requisitions of the proclamation of President Lincoln. I am far from suspecting any gentleman who has taken his seat. What is the object of this resolution? I would like to hear the gentleman state if there is any member on this floor whose loyalty he suspects. If he can point any one out who has not complied with the requisitions of the president, I, for one, would be willing to vote for his expulsion, as being unworthy of a seat upon this floor. We have come here, as I understand it, to accomplish a great, a glorious, a noble purpose. We want to put our State in her former position—though I do not admit she has ever been out of the Union. They tried to put her out in 1861, but did not succeed in accomplishing it. Now, sir, let us go to work with calmness and deliberation. Let us all act as a band of brothers. I look upon every member of this Convention as a brother. We ought to act in harmony, and I, for one, will use all my feeble efforts to place our glorious State in her just position in the Union. Then, sir, I will be content to dedicate the last moments of my life to the care of my own interests.

MR. TERRY—I can see no harm in the resolution. It does not allude to any particular member or members of this Convention. I proposed this resolution because I have heard it asserted that one-half the members of this Convention were Copperheads, Now, sir, I do not wish this report to be circulated. I wish it put down, and this resolution simply asks for the confirmation that the delegation here have all concurred in the general order promulgated by the president of the United States and the general commanding this department. I not only wish that every citizen of this State, but the mass of people throughout the whole United States, may know that each member of this Convention is iron-clad. [Cheers.]

MR. THROPE—After the election of president, I believe it is customary that the members shall be sworn in before that officer; still I speak rather for information, and do not state it as a fact.

PRESIDENT—I believe that it is customary, and suppose every member is ready to do so.

MR. ROSELIUS—I have been a member of three conventions, and such a thing as requiring an oath of a member of a convention was never heard of until now.

PRESIDENT—Is the Convention ready for the question? The secretary will read the original resolution, and call the roll.

MR. CAZABAT—Mr. President: It may not have been customary in former conventions to require any oath on the part of its members. I do not suppose the Convention of 1861, which passed the ordinance of secession, required any oath of its members. But let it be known for the glory of Louisiana, that in the glorious and important work before us, each one took the iron-clad oath. [Applause.] I, for one, sir, raise my humble voice to require it from every member of this Convention who represents his respective parish. No harm can be done; no suspicion rests upon us, but it is a duty which we owe to our constituents—to our country. Let us proclaim to the world that every man who is to participate in the proceedings of this Convention has already complied with that important proclamation of December 8, 1863. [Applause.]

Sir, the eyes of the civilized world are upon us. This is a struggle between freedom and slavery, involving the salvation or the ruin of this country. In accordance with divine wisdom honest Abe Lincoln has been called to preside over the nation, and his name will be blessed not only by the American people but by the persecuted throughout the whole world. He will be known as the friend of the oppressed of every nationality, of all grades, and of all races and all colors. Therefore, to you, Mr. President and members of this Convention, I appeal honestly and conscientiously, that you allow no objection to be raised in relation to this question. Let every member of this Convention go forward and exhibit his passport at the doors of the Convention. If he has not already complied with the orders of the president of the United States let him go forward, before the president of this Convention, and take the oath. [Great applause,]

Mr. President, this question requires no further discussion. It should be in the heart of every member of this Convention to comply with the wishes of his constituents. Why, sir, the election was held under the order of the general commanding the Department of the Gulf. Was it not required of every member to take the iron-clad? Is it not proper—is it not right—is it not fair—that every one should be compelled to take it, and should any member upon this floor complain of it? No, sir. I hope, I trust, for God's sake, for the sake of my country, for the sake of Louisiana, that every one will take it, and will take it before the president of this Convention.

Mr. Thomas—Before the motion is put, I have a substitute for it which I would offer. I voted against the resolution, because I could not see any reason why we should require each other to take this oath. I could see none around me whose loyalty I suspected.

Inasmuch as the question in relation to the loyalty of some members has been raised, I move, as a substitute for the resolution now under consideration, that each and every member of this body be now required to come before the president and take the iron-clad.

Mr. Cazabat seconded the motion.

Still another resolution was offered as a substitute for the original, which Mr. Terry moved be laid upon the table, and the motion was seconded.

Mr. Waters—I move that we adjourn.

Mr. Cazabat—I move that motion be laid upon the table.

President—The motion to adjourn is always in order.

The vote on the question of adjournment was then taken, and it having been decided that the nays were preponderant, a division was called for, when the motion to adjourn was lost. Nays 54, yeas 24.

President—The question now is in regard to laying on the table the substitute last offered.

The question was put and lost.

President—The question now is the adoption of the amendment of Mr. Thomas.

Mr. Cazabat—I move that every member of this Convention stand before his desk, raising his right hand before Almighty God, and that the president read to each and every one of us the iron-clad oath required by the proclamation of Dec. 8th, 1863. This will settle the matter and end the work at once. [Applause.]

Mr. Davies—I would offer the following amendment.

President—But one amendment can be proposed at a time for the consideration of the House.

Mr. Harnan—How many times does the gentleman wish us to take the oath? It is quite unnecessary, and if the gentleman wishes to take it he can advance and do so.

Question called for.

Mr. Montamat moved that the Convention now adjourn till Saturday at 12 o'clock, which motion being seconded, a division was called for, and it was lost by a vote of nays 47, to yeas 35.

Mr. Hills—I wish to know what the question is before the House.

The president informed the House that the question was in relation to Mr. Cazabat's resolution, which that gentleman was reducing to writing.

Mr. Cazabat's resolution was :

Resolved, That the president of this Convention administer the iron-clad oath of December 8th, 1863, to each and every one of the members of this Convention.

PRESIDENT—A motion has been made to lay this on the table.

The question being put the Convention decided in the affirmative.

PRESIDENT—The next resolution is the substitute of Mr. Thomas. The substitute reads as follows:

That each and every member of the Convention take the iron-clad oath, in order to banish all suspicion.

And that motion has been seconded.

The Convention decided to lay the motion on the table.

MR. FOLEY—I move the original resolution (Mr. Terry's) be adopted.

The president then read the original resolution.

A motion to adjourn was decided to be out of order.

An amendment to the original resolution was offered to the effect that for the benefit of the House the secretary be requested to record the names of those who had already taken the "president's oath."

A motion that the amendment be laid on the table having been seconded, was carried.

A motion to adjourn was lost.

MR. STAUFFER—I move that the sergeant-at-arms be instructed to preserve order during the roll call.

The roll was then called on the original motion.

Mr. Thomas begged to be excused from voting; but that not being the pleasure of the House, he voted in the affirmative.

The chair announced that the Convention had adopted the resolution by a vote of 66 yeas, to 11 nays.

A motion to adjourn was made and withdrawn.

MR. AUSTIN—I beg leave to submit the following:

Resolved, That every member of this Convention of foreign birth be required to furnish evidence of his citizenship on or before Saturday, the 9th of April, at 12 M.

A motion to lay the resolution on the table was seconded.

MR. HILLS—I claim that this resolution is not in order, because the one already passed requires that the members shall prove themselves citizens.

MR. HARNAN—That is not embodied in that document.

MR. HILLS—Yes it is.

The motion to lay the resolution on the table was carried:

The following resolution was presented:

Resolved, That the governor be requested to issue his proclamation ordering an election, as early as possible, of one delegate from the parish of Plaquemines and one from the parish of Ascension, to represent the above named parishes in this Convention.

This motion was seconded and adopted.

A motion to adjourn was withdrawn.

The following resolution was then offered:

Resolved, That the proceedings of this Convention be published each day in the True Delta, Era and Times newspapers of this city.

The motion that this be laid on the table was seconded and carried.

MR. PURCELL—I beg leave to submit the following:

Resolved, That the clergymen of this city and environs be invited to meet together and furnish a list of those willing to act as chaplains to this Convention—one of them in rotation each day.

MR. HARNAN—I move to lay this on the table, and dispense with religious ceremonies altogether.

MR. CAZABAT—I move we now adjourn till to-morrow at 12 o'clock.

The motion being seconded, was put to vote and decided in the affirmative.

SATURDAY, April 9th, 1864.

At 12 o'clock the House was called to order by the president, and the proceedings were opened with prayer by the Rev. Mr. Strong.

The secretary then called the roll, and after some little delay it was announced that a quorum was present.

The minutes of the preceding day were then read by the secretary, and adopted.

The returns were received from the secretary of state confirming the election of Messrs. Balch and Dufresne, delegates from Iberville.

The secretary then read letters of resignation from Messrs. Abbott and Roselius.

Mr. Abbot's communication was as follows:

Mr. President and members of the Convention:

Pressing business requiring my unexpected absence from the city for some time, I hereby tender my resignation as a member of the Convention from the Tenth Representative District.

Yours, etc., R. S. Abbott.

Mr. Roselius's communication was then read:

To the president of the Convention:

I hereby resign my seat as a member of the Convention from the Parish of Jefferson.

I am, respectfully, your very obedient servant.

Christian Roselius.

Mr. Montamat—I move the resignations be accepted.

Mr. Hills—I offer as an amendment that Mr. Roselius be required to state the reasons why he resigns his seat in this Convention.

The nays appearing to carry the motion, the yeas and nays were taken, and it was decided not to accept the resignations, by an affimative vote of 44 to 32 nays.

Mr. Montamat—Is there a quorum voting?

President—I think so.

Mr. Buckley—I wish also to know whether a quorum voted.

Mr. Hills—The voting as announced shows there is a quorum present.

Mr. Mann—I call for the yeas and nays. I do not like to have any member forced to assign his reasons. Mr. Roselius is *required* to state his reasons. If he refuses to come forward and do so, which he certainly has a right to do, I would ask for information whether his seat is to remain vacant in this Convention.

Mr. Abell—If any person resigns, a proclamation is then issued for a new election to take place.

Mr. Hills—The majority having voted in favor of my motion, I respectfully beg leave to withdraw it.

Mr. Cazabat—I move it be laid on the table.

Leave was granted to withdraw the amendment.

A motion having been made to reconsider, it was decided in the affirmative.

Mr. Hills—I now move to lay that amendment on the table.

The motion was seconded and carried.

President—The original resolution now comes up to accept the resignations. Those in favor will say yea; contrary, nay.

The yeas and nays were called for.

While the yeas and nays were being called, the following interruption took place:

Mr. Stauffer—If I am compelled to vote, I would like to have my vote divided, as I am in favor of accepting Mr. Abbott's resignation and refusing that of Mr. Roselius.

President—That is not allowable.

Mr. Stauffer—Then I vote blank.

Mr. Duane being absent at the time his name was called, requested that his name might be again called, and voted in the affirmative.

It was decided to accept the resignations by a vote of 45 yeas to 25 nays.

A resolution was presented by Mr. Stauffer.

Mr. S. Purcell—I believe that my resolution of yesterday, in relation to the clergy, has the preference.

President—I think not. A resolution dies with the session.

Mr. Sullivan—I offer the following resolution:

Resolved, That no person shall be eligible to any office or employment whatever but duly qualified voters of this State, who shall present to the secretary of this Convention evidence that they have complied with the president's proclamation of December 8th, 1863.

The resolution was seconded.

Mr. Thomas—Before this resolution is adopted I beg leave to offer a few remarks. From the tenor of this resolution it would appear that a complaint has been entered by some person, in relation to the employment of young men under 21 years of age as messengers. One young man has already been elected as messenger who is not yet 21 years of age. One or two other messengers will probably be elected to-day. I, for one, Mr. President, think that the most fit persons for these offices are boys—young men; and that it is not necessary that we should have grown men—voters, to fill these offices. I would therefore move an amendment, that we exclude from the effect of the resolution the messengers of this body.

This motion was seconded and the yeas and nays called for.

Mr. Cazabat—I move that the motion be laid on the table.

Mr. Sullivan—I call for the yeas and nays.

President—The motion is to lay the original motion on the table.

Mr. Cazabat—My motion is to lay both motion and amendment on the table.

The yeas and nays were then called for, with a result of 66 in the affirmative and 13 in the negative.

Mr. Montamat—I offer the following resolution.

Mr. Thomas—I claim the precedence.

Mr. Foley—This is all entirely out of order, for the matter of yesterday, in relation to the iron-clad oath, has not been disposed of.

Mr. Thomas—I offer the following resolution:

Resolved, That this Convention proceed to elect an officer who shall be styled the Official Printer of the Convention, whose duty it shall be to print and publish the proceedings, to perform the necessary printing for the Convention, and to be responsible for the punctual and satisfactory execution of the work.

Mr. Heard—This is not in order. The next thing is to prepare rules for the government of this Convention.

A motion was made to lay Mr. Thomas's resolution on the table, and upon it appearing to be decided in the negative, the yeas and nays were called for.

The motion was put and decided in the negative.

The yeas and nays were called on the original motion of Mr. Thomas, and it was decided in the affirmative.

The following resolution was then offered.

Resolved, That a committee of five be appointed by the president to report rules for the government of this Convention, and the number and character of officers and employés required for the transaction of business.

An amendment was then proposed.

Mr. Thomas—I call for the question. I want to know what it is we are going to lay on the table.

Mr. Abell—The resolution was to lay that on the table.

President—That was lost.

Mr. Thomas—This is out of order. I nominate Mr. W. R. Fish, proprietor of the True Delta, for the official printer.

Mr. Fish's nomination was seconded.

Mr. Buckley—I think there is not a quorum present; therefore the resolution cannot be voted upon.

President—There was a quorum present, and those who did not vote were recorded blank.

Mr. Buckley—Then there was not a majority voting.

Mr. Mann—I would like to know what is a quorum of this body.

Mr. Montamat—I move we proceed to a second vote.

A motion was made to call the roll.

President—I think the resolution was properly carried on the first call.

An appeal was made from the decision of the chair, and the yeas and nays called for.

President—The yeas and nays are called for on the decision of the chair, which was that the resolution for printer was properly carried.

The decision of the chair was sustained by a vote of 65 yeas, to 10 nays.

Mr. Foley—I move that we see whether a quorum is present.

President—That is the proper motion. Secretary, call the roll.

The roll being called, it was found that there were but 75 members present, and consequently there was no quorum.

Mr. Purcell—I move we adjourn till Monday at 12 o'clock.

The motion was seconded.

President—It having been found there is no quorum present upon the vote for printer, the motion is now to adjourn.

The motion was lost.

Mr. Montamat—I move we take a recess of fifteen minutes.

Mr. Montague—I move, as an amendment, that the sergeant-at-arms be sent for members to make a quorum.

The motion as amended was carried.

At 2 o'clock the Convention came to order, and upon the roll being called, eighty-three members answered to their names, as follows:

Messrs. Abell, Bailey, Barrett, Baum

Beauvais, Bennie, Bofill, Bonzano, Bromley, Brott, Buckley, Burke, Balch, Campbell, Cazabat, Cook J. K., Cook T., Davies, Duane, Dupaty, Dufresne, Ennis, Fish, Flagg, Flood, Foley, Fosdick, Fuller, Gastinel, Geier, Goldman, Gorlinski, Goidry, Healy, Harnan, Hart, Heard, Henderson, Hills, Hire, Howell, Howes, Kavanagh, Knobloch, Kugler, Lobdell, Maas, Mann, Maurer, Mendiverri, Millspaugh, Montamat. Montague, Morris, Murphy E., Murphy M. W., Normand, O'Conner, Ong, Payne J., Paine J. T., Poynot, Purcell J., Pursell S., Schroeder, Schnurr, Seymour, Shaw, Smith, Spellicy, Stocker, Stumpf, Stiner, Stauffer, Sullivan, Terry, Thorpe, Thomas, Waters, Wenck, Wells, Wilson.

President—The question now comes on the resolution to elect an official printer.

The resolution was then carried, by 82 yeas to one in the negative.

The following nominations were then made:

Mr. Thomas nominated Mr. Fish.

Mr. Mann nominated Mr. Mills.

Mr. Brott nominated Mr. May.

Mr. Gorlinski nominated Fish and Hills.

The nominations were then closed.

Mr. Campbell—I move we vote by ballot.

A motion to lay it on the table was seconded and carried.

The secretary then proceeded to call the roll, with the following result:

For Fish—Messrs. Abbott, Abell, Ariail, Bailey, Barrett, Baum, Beauvais, Bell, Bennie, Bofill, Bonzano, Buckley, Burke, Campbell, Cazabat, Cook J. K., Cook T., Cutler, Davies, Duane, Edwards, Flagg, Foley, Fuller, Gastinel, Geier, Goldman, Gruneberg, Gaidry, Healy, Hart, Heard, Henderson, Hire, Howes, Kavanagh, Knobloch, Maas, Maurer, Mendiverri, Millspaugh, Montamat, Morris, Murphy E., Murphy M. W., Newell, Normand, O'Conner, Ong, Payne J., Poynot, Purcell J., Pursell S., Schroeder, Seymour, Spellicy, Stocker, Stumpf, Stiner, Stauffer, Sullivan, Terry, Thorpe, Thomas, Waters—64.

For Hills—Messrs. Dupaty, Dufresne, Flood, Fosdick, Harnan, Howell, Kugler, Mann, Montague, Paine J. T., Schnurr, Smith—10.

For May—Messrs. Bromley, Brott, Balch, Hills, Wilson—5.

For Fish and Hills—Messrs. Gorlinski and Wenck—2.

Mr. Hills—I move that Mr. Fish be unanimously declared the choice of this Convention.

Mr. Foley—I call for the resolution presented by Mr. Terry yesterday and unanimously adopted, that the members of this Convention show that they are citizens, and have taken the oath.

The motion was seconded.

President—The motion is made and seconded, that the secretary report to this body the nature of yesterday's resolution, in order to specify the members who have taken what is called the iron-clad oath.

The motion was put and carried.

The president then administered the oath to the following delegates, who advanced to his desk for the purpose: Messrs. Kugler, Normand, Balch, Dufresne, Thorpe, Bennie, Hire, Knobloch, Dupaty, Bromley and Gruneberg.

The roll being called, it was ascertained that all of the members had taken the oath required by the resolution, excepting the following: Messrs. Abbott, Ariail, Crozat, Ennis, Pintado, Wenck, Wells and Taliaferro.

Mr. Thorpe rose to speak, but was called to order.

Mr. Cazabat—I beg leave to state to the president and members of this Convention, that the two members of Rapides have not yet arrived in the city, but will be here today, or by to-morrow. They will come, I assure you, well prepared with the iron-clad.

President—Gentlemen of the Convention will offer their resolutions from their seats, and the first one catching the president's eye will have precedence.

Mr. Stauffer—I think my resolution has precedence over all others, as unfinished business.

President—Each day's resolutions expire with the session. Do you wish to call it up anew to-day?

Mr. Stauffer—I do, and offer the following:

Resolved, That a committee of five be appointed to draft rules and regulations for the government of this Convention, and that they report on Monday next.

The motion was seconded and carried.

Mr. Montamat—The resolution is not complete, since it does not state by whom the committee is to be appointed.

Mr. Thomas—I move it be appointed by the chair.

Seconded and carried.

MR. MONTAMAT—I offer the following:

Resolved, That the governor and the rest of the officers elected on the 22d of February last, and Capt. Hoyt, acting mayor of the city of New Orleans, be and are hereby invited to occupy seats within this room whenever the Convention may not be in secret session.

MR. HEARD—I approve of the motion, with the exception of the last clause in relation to secret session.

The amendment was laid on the table.

PRESIDENT—The question is on the resolution.

MR. THOMAS—If I understand the resolution it says that on the 22d February last Capt. Hoyt was elected mayor, which was not the case.

The resolution was adopted.

MR. THORPE—I move that the resolution accepting the resignations of Messrs. Abbott and Roselius be reconsidered, as there was not a quorum present at the time of the adoption of the resolution. I introduce this resolution for the reason that I do not consider that resignations ought to be accepted under any circumstances in such extreme haste. In accepting this office and running as candidates they made a bargain with the people of their districts to represent them here. Now, it may be possible that one of these gentlemen may have reasons for resigning; but business is not a reason for resigning. If it were so, you, Mr. President, would not have been here, and neither would I, nor many others; and I think that for such a reason none of us have a right to resign. I honor and respect Mr. Roselius. He is a gentleman whom we all delight to honor. We have reasons to respect him for his age and experience. It is barely possible that he left this House under a misapprehension; but when he comes to reflect upon the responsibility of having withdrawn from this Convention, he will perhaps think better of it, and he may return to conform to the rules adopted to-day. I see nothing in his compliance that would be inconsistent with his antecedents. It is simply this, "I will obey the laws of the United States until the Supreme Court says they are not laws."

Mr. Roselius cannot certainly object to taking the oath. I believe he will eventually take it, or at least I believe that this vote will be reconsidered.

The motion for reconsideration was seconded.

MR. SHAW—I believe the Convention has a perfect right to reconsider any resolution which has been passed. There is a part of this resolution which I disapprove; it contains an expression of opinion with which I do not concur. I believe that a quorum was present, but the resolution is offered on the ground that there was not a quorum present. We do not take any such ground as that. The quorum of this body means, if I understand it correctly, a majority of the members elected and returned, and not a majority of the number ordered to be elected. In the preliminary organization of this body, being temporary chairman, I adopted the number 76 as constituting a quorum, for the reason that no one knew how many had been elected, I could neither know nor decide upon hearsay evidence; but until the Committee on Credentials reported, the presumption was that the whole number had been elected. The presumption disappeared as soon as the committee reported and the facts were apparent. But 95 members have been elected and returned to this body; and I ask whether a majority of 95 does not constitute a quorum?

MR. THORPE—I accept the amendment.

MR. CAZABAT—The gentleman who has just resumed his seat, [Col. Thorpe,] has anticipated the motion which I now hold in my hand, for the purpose of reconsidering the vote of this Convention, in regard to the acceptance of the resignation of the Hon. Christian Roselius as a member of this august assembly. The motion which I intended to offer for the reconsideration of said vote does not specify any grounds or reasons whatsoever. I am actuated in this measure by motives of high personal regard and admiration for the Hon. Christian Roselius. I take it for granted that the prestige of his name, of his presence, and participaticipation here, would be beneficial to this Convention. By his experience, his learning, his influence, the power of his eloquent voice, his great reputation all over the State. his services would, I admit, be invaluable and highly creditable to this Convention. Sir, I admire and respect him for his well-known and appreciated talents as a lawyer, for his often tried honesty as a politician, for his undoubted and unsuspected loyalty as a citizen. No one here has a greater regard than I have for the private and public qualities of the "*Nestor of the Louisiana Bar.*"

No member of this Convention will regret more than I do the loss of his intellect and of the mighty influence of his voice in the great and important labors which we shall be called upon to perform. To be deprived of his needed assistance in our proceedings, will be a matter of deep regret to each and all of us. But, on the other hands if we consider seriously and impartially the sacred duty devolving upon us in the glorious work of the regeneration of our beloved Louisiana; if we intend to be true to ourselves, to our mission, and to our bleeding country, we are bound to stand by the *iron-clad oath* prescribed by the immortal proclamation issued on the 8th of December 1863, by the redeemer of the American republic.

The high and respected social standing of the Hon. Christian Roselius; his influence, his wisdom, his intellect, his powerful voice; all these personal attributes, which he possesses and deserves so well, fall into utter insignificance when compared with the principle now contended for.

If the gentleman declines to take or produce the oath prescribed by President Lincoln, in the name of justice, in the name of oppressed humanity, let him stand and remain outside of the portals of this Liberty Hall.

Mr. Abell—I concur in the remarks made by the last gentleman. When the people of these parishes, this State and this city, sent Mr. Roselius and the other members here, they elected them as delegates to form for them a new organic law. When Mr. Roselius came here he had already taken the requisite oaths. If he and others were not gratified upon coming here they can never be gratified. If the gentlemen here are so extremely fond of taking this oath, they should remember that it has already been looked upon as one of the most demoralizing things in the world.

I have already been under the necessity of taking five or six oaths, and I am now told that I must go forward and take another oath. I consider there is no necessity whatever for this movement. The people have selected their delegates and sent them here to transact their business. If Mr. Roselius had not taken the constitutional oath he would not have placed his foot in this House. I would have no objection if the gentlemen who are so fond of taking the oath should step forward every morning and take it, but I do not think they have a right to exact it of others. Mr. Roselius has been a practicing lawyer and knew this—that they cannot compel him to do it; therefore, he resigned and left the House. If they want him back let them rescind the resolutions, and then you will see him return and hear his eloquent voice on this floor.

Mr. Thomas—I think, for one, that it is bad policy for us to pass resolutions at one moment and rescind them the next. I think we ought to go to work and perform the duties for which we have been elected.

Mr. Roselius stated to this body yesterday the reason why he did not and would not take any oath. The oldest man in this body—a man whom the whole State of Louisiana looked up to, whose intellect, integrity and capacity they admire, informed us that he had already been in three different conventions, and had never known one in which the members were required to take *any* oath, and that he would not do so. That, I understand, Mr. President, to be the reason why Mr. Roselius declined, and left this hall, thinking you imposed illegally upon him, whom we know to stand high in the affections of the people and in the eyes of the municipal officers of the State and military officers of the department. I don't believe that he will consent to take any oath upon this floor. I understand that to be his reason. That was the reason why I hesitated in voting yes on the resolution yesterday. I thought it was directed against Mr. Roselius. Does, or can any member upon this floor question the loyalty of Mr. Roselius? The resolution offered by my friend from the

Second Ward does not go far enough, if we wish Mr. Roselius to return. He will not return if he be compelled to take any oath.

MR. THORPE—I did not introduce that resolution with any intention of occupying the time of the Convention. We admit that Mr. Roselius is a learned and patriotic man; but we wish to reconsider the resolution on the ground stated by our temporary chairman, (Mr. Shaw,) that there was not a quorum present. As regards taking oaths, I think that the gentleman from the Fifth District was a little out of place. I am willing to come into this Convention and take any oath that is prescribed to make me a fit representative.

Mr. Roselius never came into a convention that was the first-born child of liberty after a mighty rebellion; and, moreover, the circumstances under which we are assembled here never had any precedent in his experience.

The gentleman who makes remarks about taking oaths so freely, taxes the good sense of the Convention. I do not know of any man, nor can I conceive of any gentlemen, however high and exalted, whether in a political or any other situation, who is too great, grand and glorious to come here and take that oath. However, I still urge that my resolution be accepted—not on the ground that Mr. Roselius is not a proper gentleman to be in this Convention, because he is; nor because he has not taken the oath—but I do urge it on the ground that there was not a quorum present.

MR. HENDERSON—We have a quorum, if the proposition already asserted is true. As I understand, this Convention is composed of 150 members. Suppose a House to be composed of fifty members, and twenty-six be elected, does any member pretend to say that a majority of twenty-six constitutes a quorum? The ground was rightfully taken; 75 was an equal division of 150, and therefore 76 constitutes a quorum. Now, sir, it is necessary to understand our position. If the other parishes had conformed to their duty, they would have elected 150 members. As regards the question on which I voted in the negative, it was on the very point of qualification of members. I did so in conformity with the usage, and considering that when the committee examined the credentials the question of qualification would be settled. Their action is adopted, and since no member moves for a reconsideration, the decision is final and binding. Mr. Roselius has sent in his resignation, and the Convention has moved to accept it. I understand that in regard to a reconsideration there is no objection; but suppose we do reconsider, what action is then to be taken? Is it to give the gentlemen an opportunity to recall their resignations? Mr. Roselius thinks there is a conflict in regard to oaths, and therefore resigned.

The question was then called for.

Mr. Waters moved an adjournment, which he subsequently withdrew.

A *viva voce* vote was taken on the resolution.

A division being called for, it was decided in the affirmative—yeas 40, nays 26.

JUDGE HOWELL—I have not troubled this Convention so far with any attempts at speech-making, or presented any propositions: but I think it is time to go to work. With a view to that purpose, I offer the following resolutions, and when they have been read, I move that they be postponed until 1 o'clock on Monday;

Resolved, 1. That a committee of —— members be appointed by the president of this Convention, to whom shall be referred the subject of immediate and permanent abolition of slavery within the State of Louisiana, with instructions to report as early as practicable, ordinances and provisions in relation thereto, to be incorporated in the constitution of this State.

2. That a committee of —— members be appointed by the president, with instructions to recommend a preamble to the constitution of this State, and report as soon as possible.

3. That a committee of —— members be appointed to whom shall be referred the subject of the administration of the distribution of the powers of the government of the State of Louisiana, as set forth in the first title of the constitution of the State as adopted in 1852, with instructions to recommend changes, alterations and amendments, if any they may deem proper and expedient, and report thereon as soon as possible.

4. That a committee of —— members be appointed by the president, to whom shall be referred the subject of the legislative department, as set forth in the second title of the State constitution, with instructions to recommend changes, alterations and amend-

ments, if any they may deem proper and expedient, and report thereon as soon as possible.

5. That a committee of—— members be appointed by the president, to whom shall be referred the subject of the executive department, as set forth in the third title of said constitution, with instructions to recommend changes, alterations and amendments, if any they may deem proper and expedient, and report thereon as soon as possible.

6. That a committee of—— members be appointed by the president, to whom shall be referred the subject of the judiciary department, as set forth in the fourth title of said constitution, with instructions to recommend changes, alterations and amendments, if any they may deem proper and expedient, and report thereon as soon as possible.

7. That a committtee of—— members be appointed by the president, to whom shall be referred the subject of impeachments, as set forth in the fifth title of said constitution, with instructions to recommend changes, alterations and amendments, if any they may deem proper and expedient, and report thereon as soon as possible.

8. That a committee of—— members be appointed by the president, to whom shall be referred the subject of general provisions, as set forth in the sixth title of said constitution, with instructions to recommend changes, alterations and amendments, if any they may deem proper and expedient, and report thereon as soon as possible.

9. That a committee of—— members be appointed by the president, to whom shall be referred the subject of internal improvements, as set forth in the seventh title of said constitution, with instructions to recommend changes, alterations and amendments, if any they may deem proper and expedient, and report thereon as soon as possible.

10. That a committee of—— members be appointed by the president, to whom shall be referred the subject of public education, as set forth in the eighth title of said constitution, with instructions to recommend changes, alterations and amendments, if any they may deem proper and expedient, and report thereon as soon as possible.

11. That a committee of—— members be appointed by the president, to whom shall be referred the subject of the mode of revising the constitution, as set forth in the ninth title of said constitution, with instructions to recommend changes, alterations and amendments, if any they may deem proper and expedient, and report thereon as soon as possible.

12. That a committee of—— members be appointed by the president, to whom shall be referred the subject of the schedule, as set forth in the tenth title of said constitution, with instructions to recommend changes, alterations and amendments, if any they may deem proper and expedient, and report thereon as soon as possible.

13. That a committee of—— members be appointed by the president, to whom shall be referred the subject of the ordinance as set forth in the eleventh title of said constitution, with instructions to recommend changes, alterations and amendments, if any they may deem proper and expedient, and report thereon as soon as possible.

Mr. Montamat—I move as an amendment that a sufficient number of these resolutions be printed for the use of the members.

Mr. Waters—I move to lay all resolutions on the table.

Mr. Stauffer—I offer an amendment, subject to call.

The amendment was seconded and lost.

The motion of Mr. Montamat was put and carried.

It was moved and seconded that the Convention adjourn till Monday, which was put and carried.

Monday, April 11, 1864.

The Convention was called to order, prayer was offered by the Rev. Mr. DeOssey, of the Christian Commission, and upon the call of the roll, the following gentlemen answered to their names:

Messrs. Abell, Bailey, Barrett, Bell, Bofill, Bonzano, Bromley, Brott, Buckley, Burke, Campbell, Crozat, Dufresne, Davies, Durell, Edwards, Flagg, Flood, Foley, Fosdick, Geier, Goldman, Gorlinski, Gruneberg, Gaidry, Healy, Harnan, Heard, Henderson, Hills, Hire, Howell, Howes, Kavanagh, Knobloch, Kugler, Maas, Mann, Maurer, Millspaugh, Montamat, Montague, Morris, Murphy E., Murphy M. W., Newell, Normand, O'Conner, Ong, Schnurr, Seymour, Shaw, Smith, Spellicy, Stocker, Stumpf, Stiner, Stauffer, Sullivan, Terry, Thomas, Waters, Wenck, Wilson.

There being only 66 members present, it was announced there was not a quorum.

Mr. Mann—I offer the following resolution, which I would like to have read for the benefit of the House.

President—The gentleman is out of order.

The sergeant-at-arms having been instructed to proceed in quest of the members sufficient to form a quorum, the roll was called again.

When, in addition to the gentlemen already named, the following members were found to be present:

Messrs. Austin, Cazabat, Cook J. K., Cook T., Duane, Dupaty, Fish, Fuller, Gastinel, Hart, Mendiverri, Poynot, Purcell J. and Schroeder—14.

A quorum now being present, the secretary proceeded to read the minutes of Saturday.

MR. HENDERSON—I move we dispense with the reading of the votes of Saturday.

No objection being made, the motion was adopted.

MR. STAUFFER—I wish that portion of the minutes read, relating to the acceptance of Messrs. Roselius's and Abbott's resignation.

The reports of the papers read as follows:

"Mr. Stauffer—If I am compelled to vote, I would like to have my vote divided." Since this should be attributed to Mr. Stocker, if the minutes read in the same way, I would like to have them corrected.

MR. HILLS—The minutes are also incorrect in regard to the portion relating to Mr. Roselius's resignation. The motion was made accepting the resignations, when I moved as an amendment that Mr. Roselius be requested to give his reasons, which was declared to be carried; whereas the minutes read that it was laid on the table. I then moved to reconsider my amendment, which was also carried; whereas if it had been laid on the table, it could not have been carried.

MR. MONTAMAT—The gentleman who appealed from the decission of the chair at the last session was Mr. Gastinel, and not myself; and I would like to have the minutes corrected accordingly.

PRESIDENT—You have heard the minutes read and the corrections suggested. Shall the corrected record now be adopted?

The House so resolved, and the minutes were adopted.

Mr. Brott offered a resolution, which was declared out of order, the president remarking that, in accordance with the decision of the House at the last session, the report of the Committee on Rules and Regulations were now in order.

Mr. Stauffer, chairman of the Committee on Rules and Regulations for the Government of the Convention, then submitted the following report:

The committee appointed to draft Rules of Order for this Convention, beg leave to submit the following as their report:

RULES AND REGULATIONS OF THE CONVENTION OF THE PEOPLE OF LOUISIANA.

THE DUTIES AND RIGHTS OF THE PRESIDENT.

I. He shall take the chair every day at the hour to which the Convention shall have adjourned on the preceding day, and immediately call the members to order. If a quorum should be in attendance, he shall cause the journal of the preceding day to be read.

II. He shall preserve order and decorum; may speak to points of order in preference to members, rising from his seat for that purpose; he shall decide questions of order, subject to an appeal to the Convention, made by any two members, on which appeal no member shall speak more than once, unless by leave of the Convention.

III. He shall rise to put a question, but may state it while sitting.

IV. Questions shall be distinctly put in this form, to-wit: "As many of you as are of opinion that (as the question may be) say aye;" and, after the affirmative voice is expressed, "As many as are of contrary opinion, say no." If the president doubt, or if a division be called for, the Convention shall divide; those in the affirmative of the question shall rise from their seats, and afterwards those in the negative. The president shall then rise and state the decision of the Convention.

V. The president shall have the right to examine and correct the journal before it is read. He shall have general direction of the hall. He shall have a right to name any member to perform the duties of the chair, but such substitution shall not extend beyond an adjournment.

VI. In all cases of election by the Convention, the president shall vote; in other cases he shall not vote, unless the Convention be equally divided, or unless his vote, if given to the minority, will make the division equal; and in case of such equal division, the question shall be lost.

VII. All committees shall be appointed by the president, unless otherwise especially directed by the Convention, in which case they shall be elected by the Convention; and if, upon such vote, the number required shall not be elected by a majority of the votes given, the Convention shall proceed to a second ballot, in which a plurality shall prevail; and in case a greater number than are required to compose or complete a committee shall have an equal number of votes, the Convention shall take another vote.

VIII. All acts, addresses and joint resolutions shall be signed by the president; and all writs, warrants and subpœnas issued by order of the Convention shall be under his hand, and attested by the secretary.

IX. In case of any disturbance or disorderly conduct in the gallery or lobby, the president (or chairman) shall have power to order the same to be cleard.

RULES OF DECORUM AND DEBATE.

X. When any member is about to speak in debete, or deliver any matter to the Convention, he shall rise from his seat and respectfully address himself to "Mr. President."

XI. If any member, in speaking or otherwise, transgresses the rules of the Convention, the president shall, or any member may, call to order; in which case the member so called to order shall immediately sit down, unless permitted to explain; and the Convention shall, if appealed to, decide on the case, but without debate. If the decision be in favor of the member called to order, he shall be at liberty to proceed; if the decision be against him and the case require it, he shall be liable to the censure of the Convention.

XII. When two or more members happen to rise at once, the president shall name the one who is first to speak.

XIII. No member shall speak more than twice on the same question, nor more than an hour on each occasion, without leave of the Convention, nor more than once until every member choosing to speak shall have spoken. But the mover of any proposition shall have the right to open and close the debate; and in case the proposition comes from any committee, then the member making the report from the committee shall have the right to open and close the debate in like manner.

XIV. While the president is putting any question, or addressing the House, no member shall walk out of, or across, the House; nor shall any one, in such case, when a member is speaking, entertain private discourse or cross the hall between him and the speaker.

XV. No member shall vote on any question in the result of which he has a separate and distinct interest, nor in any case when he was not within the bar of the Convention when the question was put. And when any member shall ask leave to vote, the president shall propound to him the question: *Were you within the bar when the question was put?* But when the yeas and nays are taken, and any member ask leave to vote, the president shall enquire of him whether he was within the bar *when his name was called?*

XVI. Upon a division and a count of the Convention upon any question, no member without the bar shall be counted.

XVII. Every member who shall be in the Convention when a question is put, shall give his vote, unless the Convention, for reasons assigned, shall excuse him. No member shall be allowed to make any explanation of a vote he is about to give, or ask to be excused from voting, after the secretary, under order of the Convention, shall have commenced calling the yeas and nays.

XVIII. When a motion is made and seconded, it shall be stated by the president; or, being in writing, it shall be handed to the chair, and read aloud by the secretary, before debated.

XIX. Every motion should be reduced to writing, if the president or any member desire it.

XX. No person, except the commanding general of the department, the governor of any State, the heads of departments of this State, the mayor of the city, and such other persons as the Convention may see proper, shall be admitted within the bar of the Convention.

XXI. After a motion is stated by the president, or read by the secretary, it shall be deemad to be in possession of the Convention, but may be withdrawn by the mover with the consent of the member who may have seconded the proposition.

XXII. When a question is under debate, no motion shall be received but to adjourn; 2d, to lie on the table; 3d, for the previous question; 4th, to postpone to a certain day; 5th, to commit; 6th, to amend; or 7th, to postpone indefinitely—which several motions shall have precedence in the order in which they are arranged, and no motion to postpone to a day certain, to commit, or to postpone indefinitely being decided, shall be again allowed on the same day and at the same stage of the motion or proposition. A motion to strike out the enacting words of a motion shall have precedence of a motion to amend, and, if carried, shall be considered equivalent to its rejection.

XXIII. The previous question shall be put in this form: "Shall the main question now be put?" It shall only be amitted when seconded by a majority of the members present, and, when carried, its effects shall be to put an end to all debate, and to bring the Convention to a direct vote—1st, upon the pending amendment, and so on, back to the first amendment offered; 2d, upon amendments, reported upon by a committee, if any; and 3d, upon the main question.

On a motion for the previous question, and prior to the seconding of the same, a call of the Convention shall be in order; but after a majority shall have seconded such motion, no call shall be in order prior to a decision of the main question. On a motion for a previous question, there shall be no debate.

All incidental questions of order arising after a motion is made for the previous question, and pending such motion, shall be decided, whether on appeal or otherwise, without debate. After a call for the previous question has been sustained by the Convention, the question shall be put and determined in order as above, without debate on either amendments or the main question.

XXIV. Any member may call for a division of a question when the same will admit of it.

XXV. No new motion or proposition on a subject different from that under consideration shall be admitted under color of amendment, or as a substitute for the motion or proposition under debate.

XXVI. When a motion has been once made and carried in the affirmative or negative, it shall be in order for any member of the majority to move for a reconsideration thereof; provided, it is made on the same day or the next sitting day, before the order of the day is taken up. And a motion for immediate reconsideration shall supercede a notice that a reconsideration will be moved.

XXVII. When the reading of a paper is called for, and the same is objected to by any member, the Convention shall determine whether said paper shall be read or not.

XXVIII. If a pending question be not disposed of, owing to an adjournment of the Convention, and be revived on the succeeding day, no member, who has spoken twice on the day preceding, shall be allowed to speak again without leave.

XXIX. When motions are made for the reference of a subject to a select standing committee and to a standing committee, the question for the reference to a standing committee shall be first put.

ORDER OF BUSINESS FOR THE DAY.

XXX. As soon as the journal is read and the names of the members called, the president shall ask if there are any petitions, memorials, or resolutions to be presented. The petitions, memorials and resolutions having been presented and disposed of, reports, first from standing and then from select committees, shall be called for; after which the president shall dispose of the messages, communications, resolutions and ordinances on his table, and then proceed to call the order of the day, which shall always be taken up at 12 o'clock M.

XXXI. The unfinished business in which the Convention was engaged at the time of the last adjournment, shall have the preference in the orders of the day; and no motion, or any other business, shall have the preference in the orders of the day; and no motion or any other business, shall be received without special leave of the Convention until the former is disposed of. The order of the day shall be as follows:

1. The unfinished business in which the Convention was engaged at its last adjournment.
2. Special orders of the day.
3. Ordinances and resolutions, in the order in which they have been presented to the Convention.

XXXII. Petitions, memorials and other papers, addressed to the Convention, shall be presented by the president or a member in his place; a brief statement of the contents thereof shall be made verbally by the member introducing the same.

XXXIII. Any ten members, after organization of the Convention, are authorized to compel the attendance of absent members.

XXXIV. Upon calls for the Convention, and in taking the yeas and nays on any question, the names of the members shall be called alphabetically.

XXXV. All questions relating to the propriety of business shall be decided without debate.

XXXVI. A motion to adjourn, and a motion to fix the day to which the Convention shall adjourn, shall always be in order, except when the yeas and nays are being called, and when the question has just previously been put and negatived, these motions and the motion to lie on the table, shall be decided without debate.

XXXVII. No member shall absent himself from the service of the Convention, unless he have leave, or be unable from sickness to attend.

XXXVIII. No committee shall have the right to appoint a clerk without the consent of the Convention being first obtained, except the Committee on Enrollment.

XXXIX. It shall be in order for the Committee on Enrollment to report at any time.

XL. All officers appointed or elected by the Convention shall hold them during the pleasure of the Convention only.

XLI. All ordinances before the Convention shall be taken up and acted upon in the order in which they are numbered, and it shall be the duty of the secretary to number every ordinance in its regular order upon its first reading.

XLII. No standing rule or order of the Convention shall be rescinded or changed without one day's notice being given of the motion thereof. Nor shall any rule be suspended, except by a vote of two-thirds of the members present. Nor shall the order of business, as established by the rules of the Convention, be postponed or changed, except by a vote of at least two-thirds of the members present.

XLIII. After a resolution shall have been adopted by the Convention it shall be engrossed in a fair hand, and after examination and report by the Committee on Enrollment, shall be signed by the president and secretary.

XLIV. The proceedings of the Convention shall be entered on the journal as concisely as possible, care being taken to detail a true and accurate account of the proceedings.

XLV. Every vote of the Convention shall be entered on the journal with a concise statement of the question; and a brief statement of the contents of each petition, memorial or paper presented to the Convention, shall be also inserted on the journal.

XLVI. In case any secretary, sergeant-at-arms or door-keeper of the Convention fail to perform his duty, the secretary shall make a report thereof to the Convention without delay.

XLVII. The secretary shall read the journal daily from the sheet on which the minutes are written; and after being so read and corrected, the said minutes shall be recorded in the journal, and copies, authenticated by the signature of the secretary, shall be prepared for delivery at his desk to the printer by 10 o'clock on the day following that on which it shall have been read.

XLVIII. The secretary shall be responsible to the Convention for the accuracy of the journals and for the fidelity and prompt execution of all work ordered by the Convention; he shall keep the bill book in his own handwriting; he shall endorse all bills, joint resolutions, and all documents proper to be endorsed; he shall keep in his charge all bills and documents in the custody of the Convention, and keep them in proper order.

XLIX. The duties of the sergeant-at-arms shall be to attend the Convention during its sittings, to have the charge of the chamber of the Convention, and the committee rooms, and offices belonging thereto, to keep the same in order, and execute the commands of the Convention from time to time, together with all such process, issued by authority thereof, as shall be directed to him by the president.

L. The secretary or assistant secretary shall rise and remain standing whilst reading any document to the Convention.

LI. The assistant secretary of the Convention shall, in the event of the absence, resignation or death of the secretary, take charge of and attend to all the duties of his office until his successor shall be elected. It shall also be his duty to write with his own hand the journal of the Convention, when not acting as secretary.

LII. The duties of the door-keeper shall be to keep the door of the lobby, announce messages and perform such other duties as the president may require.

LIII. No less than one-fifth of the members present shall be entitled to call for the yeas and nays on any question.

LIV. A quorum shall consist of a majority of the members elected and admitted to this Convention.

LV. The officers of this Convention shall consist of a president, secretary, two assistant secretaries and as many clerks as may be required, an official printer, four reporters, a door-keeper, two messengers, a post-master, and such other officers as the Convention may deem necessary from time to time.

LVI. On any question of order or parliamentary practice, when these rules are silent or inexplicit, Jefferson's Manual, or Cushing's work on Parliamentary Law, shall be considered as authority.

The following committees shall be appointed by the chair as Standing Committees of this Convention:

1. A Committee on Elections, to be composed of five members.
2. A Committee on Preamble and Distribution of Powers, to consist of five members.
3. A Committee on the Legislative Department, to consist of seven members.
4. A Committee on Executive Department, to consist of seven members.
5. A Committee on Judiciary Department, to consist of seven members.
6. A Committee on Impeachment, to consist of three members.
7. A Committee on General Provisions, to consist of seven members.
8. A Committee on Internal Improvements, to consist of five members.
9. A Committee on Public Education, to consist of five members.
10. A Committee on Mode of Revising the Constitution, to consist of five members.
11. A Committee on Schedule, to consist of three members.
12. A Committee on Ordinances, to consist of five members.
13. A Committee on Enrollment, to consist of five members.
14. A Committee on Printing, to consist of three members.
15. A Committee on Finance, to consist of three members.

W. Stauffer, *Chairman.*

Mr. Montamat moved to print 300 copies for the use of the Convention, and that the report be made the order of the day for the 12th inst., at 2 o'clock.

President—Are you ready for the question? It is that the report of the committee be printed and be made the order of the day at 2 o'clock to-morrow, and that 300 copies of the report be printed.

The question was put and decided in the affirmative.

Mr. Wilson—The resignation of Mr. Roselius causes the Committee on Investigation to lack one member, and I therefore move that one be appointed to take his place.

The motion being seconded and carried, the president appointed Mr. Shaw to supply the deficiency.

Mr. Thomas—These (Judge Howell's) resolutions are in substance embodied in the report of the committee just read. There are, perhaps, one or two more standing committees needed than I mentioned in that report, and I move that the resolution be laid upon the table.

The motion was seconded.

President—The motion is to lay upon the table the action of the committee upon the resolution introduced yesterday, and made the order of to-day.

Mr. Brott—I move to amend by adding "subject to call."

Amendment accepted.

The decision of the Convention apparently was that the report of the committee should not be laid on the table.

A division was called for, and a rising vote taken, resulting in a vote of 47 nays to 29 yeas, and the motion was declared lost.

Mr. Mann—I move that the resolutions of Judge Howell be adopted, and that the chair proceed to appoint the committees.

Judge Howell—If the gentleman will withdraw his motion for a moment I will suggest the following number of members to fill the blanks.

Mr. Mann—I do so.

Mr. Abell—I move as a substitute--

President—There is a motion before the House.

Judge Howell--My motion is that the following numbers be inserted in the blanks: 5 in the first, 3 in the second, 3 in the third, 13 in the fourth, 7 in the fifth, 11 in the sixth, 5 in the seventh, 13 in the eighth, 3 in the ninth, 9 in the tenth, 15 in the eleventh, 5 in the twelfth and 5 in the thirteenth.

Judge Howell's motion was seconded.

Mr. Abell—I offer as a substitute—

President—The motion is upon filling up the blanks. Your motion will come in afterwards.

Mr. Harnan—I move an amendment to the 10th article of Judge Howell's resolution in regard to the subject of education, that one member be appointed from each Represntative District and each of the parishes. Since it is a subject that interests us all, it is right that it should be composed of such a number.

The amendment was seconded, and it was moved to lay it on the table.

Mr. Shaw—I move that the resolution of Judge Howell be taken up section by section, and be in that manner considered.

The motion was seconded, and decided in the affirmative.

Mr. Stauffer—Mr. Abell has offered a substitute, and I think that a substitute is always in order. If the chair decides that it is not, I shall appeal from that decision.

President—Order, gentlemen, order. The question before the Convention is in regard to filling the blanks.

Mr. Stauffer—I appeal from the decision of the chair; I wish to hear the substitute read.

Mr. Abell—Any action that may be taken in this matter will be proper.

President—We must dispose of one question at a time, and I have already stated what the question for consideration now is.

Mr. Stauffer—It seems there is a little misunderstanding.

President—There is no misunderstanding whatever. I know what I am about.

Mr. Stauffer—I appeal. I don't think that the Chair has a right to decide the question when an appeal is called for. The gentleman (Mr. Abell) was called to order when, in my opinion, he was in order. I appeal from the decision of the chair, and I desire to *know* whether his motion was in order or not. I do not believe that any member of this Convention should be *compelled* to sit down when he offers a motion that *is* in order. I appeal from the chair, and leave it to the Convention to decide in the matter.

Mr. Henderson—I move that the substitute be laid on the table.

[Cries of "there is already a question before the House."]

PRESIDENT—The question is upon the appeal from the decision of the chair, as to when a resolution to fill the blanks has been offered, and a substitute therefore presented, the motion to offer the substitute is in order or not.

The ayes and nays were called, and the chair was sustained by the following vote:

YEAS—Messrs. Austin, Barrett, Bell, Bromley, Buckley, Burke, Cazabat, Cook T., Crozat, Duane, Dupaty, Fish, Flagg, Flood, Foley, Fosdick, Fuller, Gastinel, Geier, Gorlinski, Gruneberg, Gaidry, Healy, Harnan, Hart, Henderson, Hills, Hire, Howell, Howes, Kavanagh, Knobloch, Kugler, Mann, Mendiverri, Millspaugh, Montamat, Montague, Murphy E., Murphy M. W., Newell, Normand, O'Conner, Payne, Poynot, Purcell J., Schroeder, Schnurr, Shaw, Smith, Spellicy, Stocker, Stumpf, Stiner, Sullivan, Terry, Thorpe, Waters, Wenck, Wilson—60.

NAYS—Messrs. Abell, Ariail, Bailey, Baum, Beauvais, Bonzano, Brott, Campbell, Cook J. K., Davies, Dufresne, Goldman, Maas, Maurer, Morris, Ong, Purcell S., Stauffer, Thomas—18.

PRESIDENT—We will now proceed to consider the resolution section by section.

A motion was then made to elect an assistant secretary.

PRESIDENT—The motion is not in order, as there is already a resolution before the House to fill up certain blanks.

The president being asked whether there was a quorum present, directed the roll to be called, and the following answered:

Messrs. Abell, Austin, Barrett, Beauvais, Bell, Bofill, Bonzano, Bromley, Brott, Buckley, Burke, Campbell, Cazabat, Cook T., Crozat, Davies, Duane, Dupaty, Durell, Dufresne, Edwards, Fish, Flagg, Flood, Foley, Fosdick, Fuller, Gastinel, Geier, Goldman, Gorlinski, Gruneberg, Gaidry, Healy, Harnan, Hart, Heard, Henderson, Hills, Hire, Howell, Howes, Kavanagh, Knobloch, Kugler, Maas, Mann, Maurer, Mendiverri, Millspaugh, Montague, Morris, Murphy, E., Murphy M. W., Newell, Normand, O'Conner, Ong, Payne J., Purcell J., Purcell S., Schroeder, Schnurr, Seymour, Shaw, Smith, Stauffer, Stiner, Stocker, Stump, Sullivan, Terry, Thomas, Thorpe, Waters, Wells, Wenck, Wilson-76.

A quorum was found to be present.

MR. THOMAS—Mr. President, I conceive that it is impossible for this body to transact business without adopting some code by which we may be governed. I think it is improper for us to proceed any further, until we have adopted such a code, and I now move that we adjourn till to-morrow, at 2 o'clock.

PRESIDENT—The vote will now be taken on the question of adjournment.

A *viva voce* vote being taken, the president stated he was unable to decide, and took a rising vote, and it was decided to adjourn until to-morrow, at 2 P. M., by a vote of yeas 43, nays 32.

TUESDAY, April 12th, 1864.

The House was called to order at 2½ o'clock, and the secretary proceeded to call the roll, when, after some delay, 76 members responded to their names.

The secretary then read the minutes of the preceding day.

MR. HENDERSON—I move that the calling of the names of the members present yesterday be dispensed with.

The question was put and carried.

MR. BROTT—I move that the secretary dispense with the reading of the report of the committee.

PRESIDENT—Gentlemen, you have heard the minutes of yesterday read—is there any objection to their adoption?

No objection being made, the minutes were adopted.

PRESIDENT—The report of the Committee on Rules and Regulations was made the order for to-day at 2 o'clock, and accordingly that matter now comes up.

MR. MONTAMAT—I move that the report of the Committee on Rules and Regulations be taken up section by section.

The motion was seconded and carried.

The secretary then proceeded to read the report of the committee, section by section, including the title.

MR. HILLS—I move to amend the title so that it read, "Rules and Regulations of the Convention for the revision and amendment of the Constitution of Louisiana," that being the official title adopted by Gen. Banks, and recorded in the minutes of the first day's proceedings.

The motion was carried.

The report of the committee being taken

up section by section, was adopted as read, with the exceptions hereinafter stated, interruptions, comments, &c.

It was moved that the first section be adopted.

MR. MANN—Before proceeding to vote, I would like to know what is a section? I believe that this document before me is so divided that the word "section" nowhere appears in it. I am in favor of adopting the whole report as it stands, but I nevertheless wish to know what is a section.

This was duly explained by the president.

MR. FOLEY—I move the word "ballot" be stricken out in the 5th line of section 7, and the word "vote" substituted.

The motion was seconded, and on being put was decided in the affirmative, and the amended section was then adopted.

Section 8 was then read.

MR. HILLS—I move to strike out the words "joint resolution."

The amendment was put and carried, and the section as amended was adopted.

Section 10 was read.

MR. BELL—I move that the section be amended by striking out the words "Mr. President," and substituting "Mr. President and members of the Convention."

It was moved and carried that the amendment be laid on the table.

The section was then adopted as read.

The 13th section was read.

MR. FOLEY—I move that the words "one hour" be stricken out, and the words "half an hour" substituted.

The motion was seconded, but on a *viva voce* vote being taken it was apparently lost.

A division was called for, and it was decided in the affirmative. Yeas 41, nays 34.

The section as amended was then adopted.

The 19th section was read.

MR. HILLS—I move that it be amended by striking out the word "should" in the first line, and substituting the word "shall."

The motion was seconded and carried.

MR. MONTAMAT—I move another amendment to section 19—that the word "motion" be stricken out, and "resolution" inserted.

Seconded and carried.

MR. GOLDMAN—I move as another amendment, that notice shall be given to the chair previous to the reading of such resolution.

Mr. Foley moved that the amendment be laid on the table, which was seconded and carried.

The resolution as amended was then adopted.

Section 22 was taken up.

MR. THORPE—I move to amend by striking out the words "but to adjourn" in the second line.

MR. MONTAMAT—I move to lay the amendment on the table. The motion being seconded, the amendment was tabled and the section adopted.

Section 24 was taken up.

MR. MONTAMAT—I move to strike out the words "when the same will admit of it."

MR. THOMAS—I move to lay it on the table.

The motion was seconded, and on a division being called for, Mr. Thomas's motion was carried. Yeas 44, nays 9.

The section, as amended, was adopted.

Section 25 was read.

MR. CAZABAT—I move as an amendment the word "resolution" be inserted before "motion."

MR. GOLDMAN—I move to lay it on the table.

The motion was seconded and carried.

The motion, as amended, was put and carried.

Section 26 was then read.

MR. GOLDMAN—I move to amend by striking out the third line.

MR. GORLINSKI—I move to amend by striking out "the same day or."

MR. FOLEY—I move the last motion be laid on the table.

The motion to lay the amendment on the table was seconded and carried.

MR. GOLDMAN—The next is my amendment. I move that the words "provided it be made on the same day, or the next sitting day before the order is taken up," be stricken out.

MR. THOMAS—I move to lay that amendment on the table.

Seconded and carried.

Section 29 was read.

A motion was made to strike out the

word "standing," upon which Mr. Thomas remarked that the word occurred twice, and was informed that it was the second one.

A motion to lay the amendment on the table was lost.

The vote being taken on the amendment it was adopted.

Mr. Shaw—I move to further amend the section by substituting "or" for "and" in the second line.

The amendment was seconded and carried, and the section, as amended, was adopted.

Section 30 was then read.

Mr. Montamat—I move that "one o'clock P. M." be substituted for "twelve o'clock M."

Mr. Goldman—I move it be laid on the table.

The motion was seconded.

Mr. Brott—Before that vote is taken I would state that I conceive it very difficult to proceed to our business at the time suggested in the report, since we do not meet until 12 o'clock.

President—We shall come to that motion in proper time. The motion now is to lay upon the table the amendment.

The motion was put and decided in the negative.

President—The question of the amendment now comes up.

Mr. Shaw—The rules, so far as we have adopted them, fix upon no hour for the assembling of this Convention. They assume that we shall have finished our preliminary business at 12 o'clock.

Mr. Hills—I move as an amendment to the amendment to strike out "12 o'clock" and substitute "— o'clock," and the Convention can fix upon such a time as it chooses.

The amendmeut was seconded and accepted by Mr. Montamat.

Mr. Wilson—I move as a further amendment to strike out "which shall always be taken up at 12 o'clock M."

The amendment was seconded and accepted, and the section was adopted as amended.

Section 31 was taken up.

Mr. Wilson—I move to strike out "No motion or any other business shall have the preference in the order of the day."

Mr. Stauffer—I move to lay it on the table.

The motion was put and lost.

The amendment was adopted, and afterwards the whole section as amended. was adopted.

Section 38 was read.

Mr. Stocker—I move to strike out the section.

The motion was seconded and carried.

Mr. Wilson—I move to amend section 38 by—

Mr. Brott—The gentleman is out of order.

President—The section has been striken out.

Section 40 was read,

Mr. Goldman—I wish to amend by striking out "them" and inserting "their offices."

A motion was made to lay the amendment on the table, and was seconded and carried.

Mr. Cazabat—I moved to amend by striking out "them" and inserting "their offices."

Mr. Goldman—That was my amendment.

The amendment was put and carried, and the section as amended was adopted.

Section 44 was read and taken up.

Mr. Wilson—I move to amend by substituting "president" for "secretary" and striking out "make a report thereof to" and inserting "shall inform the Convention without delay."

A motion was made to lay the amendment on the table, which being lost, the amendment was adopted.

The section as amended was then adopted.

Section 47 was read.

Mr. Cazabat—I move to strike out "by 10 o'clock."

Mr. Stauffer—I move to lay the motion on the table.

The motion was laid on the table, and the section adopted as read.

Section 48 was then read.

Mr. Montamat—I move to strike out "joint."

Motion seconded.

Mr. Hills—I move to amend further by striking out the word "bills" preceding "joint."

The amendment was accepted.

President—One motion at a time, gentlemen. The question is on the resolution to strike out the word "joint."

Mr. Hills—The gentleman accepted my amendment.

President—The question then is on the resolution to strike out the two words.

The amendment was carried and the section adopted as amended.

Section 49 was then read.

Mr. Wilson—I move a reconsideration of the adoption of section 48. The motion was seconded, and on being put lost.

Section 53 was taken up.

Mr. Montamat—I move to amend by strking out "no less than one-fifth of the" and inserting "any two." The motion was seconded.

Mr. Thomas—I move to lay it on the table.

Mr. Goldman—I move to strike out the whole section.

The motion to lay it on the table was carried by 39 yeas to 23 nays.

Mr. Montamat—I move to strike out the first seven words, and insert "any."

President—Is the motion seconded?

Mr. Shaw—I rise to a point of order. Has the gentleman a right to make such a motion, when his ameedment has just been laid upon the table. It seems to me that the greater number includes the less.

President—I think the member is in order. The question to make it two, is a very different one from that to make it one member.

The yeas and nays were called for on the adoption of the section as read. Adopted by a vote of yeas 49; nays 32.

Section 54 was read.

Mr. Montamat—I move that a quorum consists of 76 members, instead of a majority of the members present.

Mr. Gorlinski—I move to lay it on the table.

The motion was seconded, and it was announced as decided in the affirmative, when the yeas and nays were called for.

Judge Howell—I request the gentlemen who moved and seconded the last resolution, to withdraw for a moment.

As neither gentlemen withdrew, the roll was called and the motion lost—nays 59; yeas 23.

Mr. Hills—I offer the following additional amendment: If any member of this Convention, after having taken his seat, shall be absent at roll-call three successive days without furnishing to the Convention a reasonable excuse for such absence, his seat shall be declared vacant, and the election of a new member ordered.

A motion was made to lay it on the table.

Mr. Shaw—I think this is a subject of much importance—of more significance perhaps than any other rule reported by this committee. I would like to see it referred to a special committee, and for this reason I hope that the motion to lay it on the table will not prevail.

Mr. Hills's amendment was laid on the table.

President—The amendment as first offered now comes up.

Mr. Thomas—Before that is put I would ask for information, if I am in order, as to how many members have been returned and taken their seats in this Convention.

The president decided the inquiry to be in order, and the secretary announced that the number was ninety-three.

The amendment was then adopted and also the section as amended.

Section 55 was taken up.

Mr. Fuller—It seems to me that as far as the reporters are concerned, there should be a head, and I move to amend by stiking out "Four reporters" and inserting "One reporter and three assistants."

Mr. Wilson—I don't think we require four reporters.

Mr. Montamat—I move as an amendment to the amendment, that the word "two" be substituted.

Mr. Shaw—I think there should be a committee appointed to whom the matter can be referred. I move to lay the amendment on the table.

Mr. Shaw's motion was carried.

Judge Howell—I move, if it is in order, to substitute "one" for "four."

The motion was seconded and carried, and the section adopted as amended.

Section 56 was read.

Mr. Henderson—I move that all after the words "or Cushing's works on Parliamentary Law" be stricken out.

The motion was seconded.

A motion to lay it on the table was lost.

MR. HENDERSON—The two works named in the section are directly in conflict, and that is the reason why I made the motion.

The amendment was adopted.

MR. STOCKER—I desire to move a reconsideration of section 55, which provides for the officers of this Convention, by inserting among those enumerated sergeant-at-arms.

The motion was carried and the section adopted as amended.

A motion was made to strike out the remainder of the section, referring to committees.

MR. ABELL—I move that the committees be embraced in one grand committee, to be composed of one person for every five hundred votes cast at the election.

MR. CAMPBELL—I move to reconsider section 21, and that all after "more" be strcken out.

The motion was lost.

The section as amended was then put and adopted.

MR. SHAW—I move we take up the resolutions that were made the order of the day yesterday.

MR. HILLS—I move these resolutions be made the order of the day for to-morrow at 1 o'clock.

The motion was put and carried.

A motion was made to adjourn till to-morrow at 4 P. M., which was amended by insterting 12, and the Convention adjourned accordingly.

WEDNESDAY, April 13, 1864.

The president, Judge Durell, took the chair at 12 M., and the Convention was opened with prayer by the Rev. Mr. D'Ossey, of the Christian Commission.

On a call of the roll, the following members answered to their names:

Messrs. Abell. Ariail, Austin, Bailey, Balch, Barrett, Baum, Beauvais, Bell, Bonzano, Brott, Buckley, Burke, Campbell, Cazabat, Cook J. K., Crozat, Duane, Dufresne, Dupaty, Durell, Edwards, Ennis, Fish, Flagg, Flood, Foley, Fosdick, Geier, Goldman, Gorlinski, Gruneberg, Gaidry, Healy, Hart, Heard, Henderson, Hills, Hire, Howell, Howes, Kavanagh, Knobloch, Maas, Mann, Maurer, Mendiverri, Millspaugh, Montamat, Montague, Morris, Murphy E., Murphy M. W., Newell, Normand, O'Conner, Payne J., Paine J. T., Pintado, Poynot, Purcell J., Pursell S., Schroeder, Schnurr, Seymour, Shaw, Smith, Spellicy, Stumpf, Stiner, Stauffer, Sullivan, Thomas, Terry, Waters, Wilson—76.

A quorum being present, the journal of the previous day was read and approved without a dissenting voice.

The secretary read the minutes and they were adopted without objection.

MR. HENDERSON — The resignations of Messrs. Roselius and Abbott have not yet been acted upon, and I move they be accepted *viva voce.*

PRESIDENT—We will now proceed in order as directed by section 30, rules and regulations.

No petitions or memorials were presented,

MR. TERRY—I hold in my hand a preamble and resolution, which, on being passed, will wipe out the foul stain and damnable Ordinance of Secession which was passed in this very hall on the 26th of January, 1861, by traitors to God and their country. I present the following:

Whereas, At a Convention of delegates assembled in this hall on the 26th day of January, 1861, and purporting to represent the people of this State, it was ordained and declared in the words following—that is to say;

"An Ordinance to dissolve the union between the State of Louisiana and other States, united with her under the compact entitled 'The Constitution of the United States of America.'

"*We the people of the State of Louisiana, in Convention assembled, do declare and ordain, and it is hereby declared and ordained,* That the ordinance passed by us in Convention on the 22d day of November, in the year 1811, whereby the constitution of the United States of America and the amendments of the said constitution were adopted; and all laws and ordinances by which the State of Louisiana became a member of the Federal Union, be and the same are hereby repealed and abrogated; and that the Union now subsisting between Louisiana and other States, under the name of 'The United States of America,' is hereby resolved.

"*We do further declare and ordain,* That the State of Louisiana hereby resumes all rights and powers heretofore delegated to the government of the United States of America; that her citizens are absolved from all allegiance to said goverement; and that the is in full possession and exercise of all those rights of sovereignty which appertain to a free and independent State

"*We do further declare and ordain,* That all rights acquired and vested under the constitution of the United States, or any act of Congress, or treaty, or under any law of this State, and not incompatible with this ordinance, shall remain in force, and have the same effect as if this ordinance had not been passed."

Now we, the people of the State of Louisiana, loyal to the constitution of the government of the United States, do hereby announce, declare and ordain, that the said pretended ordinance of secession, so passed by disloyal traitors, without the authority of the people and in violation of the Federal constitution, together with all other ordinances, acts and proceedings of said secessionists in said Convention, and of the pretended State government instituted under the said ordinance of secession, are *utterly null* and *void.*

Resolved, That, representing the people of the State of Louisiana, we hereby declare her adherence and the adherence of the people of Louisiana to the Constitution of the United States, and that we will, by all our efforts, sustain the people and the government in all its efforts to end the present unjust and most wicked rebellion. [Applause.]

The resolution was seconded.

MR. HENDERSON—I move to lay it on the table.

The motion was laid on the table—vote, 42 ayes to 21 nays.

MR. MONTAMAT—I submit the following:

Resolved, That the members of the Convention shall receive from the public treasury compensation for their services, which shall be eight dollars per day during their attendance on, and going to and returning from the Convention.

And be it further resolved, That a committee of five be appointed by the president for the purpose of fixing the compensation of the several officers and employés of this Convention, and order such appropriation as is necessary for their expenses. The committee to report as early as possible.

The motion was seconded.

MR. HARNAN—I move as an amendment to that resolution that the members of this Convention shall attend gratuitously.

The motion was seconded.

A motion to lay the amendment on the table was seconded and carried.

MR. CAZABAT—I move to lay the original resolution on the table.

The motion was seconded and lost.

MR. MONTAMAT—I move that the original resolution be adopted.

The motion was seconded and apparently carried, when Messrs. Goldman and Cazabat called for the yeas and nays.

MR. HENDERSON—The yeas and nays cannot be called for unless one-fifth are in favor of so doing, and I wish to know whether that means one-fifth of the members elected or those present.

PRESIDENT—One-fifth of those present.

Upon calling the roll, there was a tie, which the president decided by casting his vote in the negative.

MR. SHAW—I move we take up the resolution made the order of to-day at 1 o'clock.

MR. MONTAMAT—I offer the following resolution:

Resolved, That the constitution which shall be framed by this Convention shall have no effect until the same shall have been ratified by the vote of the majority of the voters of Louisiana at the ballot-box qualified at the various election precincts of the State, under the regulations and laws in regard to the election of State officers. Those voting for the constitution shall endorse on their ticket "ratification," and those voting against it "no ratification."

The governor shall publish a proclamation duly notifying the people of this State of the holding of said election, and ordering the sheriffs of the several parishes of this State to cause an election to be held under the existing laws. Said election to take place twenty days after the adjournment of the Convention.

It was moved to lay it on the table, and the yeas and nays were called for.

PRESIDENT—Unless one-fifth so request.

A *viva voce* vote was taken, which being unsatisfactory, a rising vote was taken and the resolution adopted by a vote of 42 ayes to 38 nays.

MR. S. PURSELL—I submit the following:

Resolved, That the clergy of this city and environs be invited to come together and publish a list of those willing to act as chaplains to this Convention, and that one of the number officiate each day.

The motion to lay it on the table was seconded and carried.

MR. HENDERSON—I move to accept the resignations of Messrs. Roselius and Abbott.

MR. THORPE—I wish the gentleman would withdraw his motion for a moment.

The resolution was not withdrawn, nor was there any action taken thereon

MR. ABELL—I offer the following resolution:

Whereas, General Order No. 38, dated Headquarters, Department of the Gulf, New Orleans, March 22, 1864, the United States, through their proper officer, Major General Banks, has assumed to levy and collect taxes of the people of this State without their consent, and appropriate the same for domestic purposes, as will appear by the following taken from the Era, the official paper, and set forth in the words and figures of the Educational Order:

EDUCATION OF FREEDMEN.

HEADQUARTERS DEPARTMENT OF THE GULF,
New Orleans, March 22, 1864.

General Orders No. 38.

In pursuance of the provisions of General Orders No. 23, current series, for the rudimental instruction of the freedmen of this department, placing within their reach the elements of knowledge which give intelligence and greater value to labor, and reducing the provisions necessary therefor to an economical and efficient school system;

It is ordered that a Board of Education, consisting of three persons, be hereby constituted, with the following duties and powers:

1st. To establish one or more Common Schools in each and every school district that has been or may be defined by the parish provost marshals under orders of the provost marshal general.

2d. To acquire by purchase or otherwise, tracts of land, which shall be judged by the Board necessary and suitable for school sites, in plantation districts, to be not less than one-half acre in extent; to hold the same in trust to themselves until such schools shall have been established, when they shall transfer all the right and title thereto that may have vested in them to the superintendent of Public Institutions, or other competent State authority.

3d. To erect upon said plots of land such school-houses as they may judge necessary and proportioned to the wants of the population of the district, where there are no buildings available and proper for school purposes. And in this, as in all other duties, they shall exercise the strictest economy.

4th. To select and employ proper teachers for said schools, as far as practicable, from the loyal inhabitants of Louisiana, with power to require their attendance for the purpose of instruction in their duties, one week at least at a Normal School, to be conducted by the Board.

5th. To furnish and provide the necessary books, stationery and apparatus for the use of such schools, and in addition thereto to purchase and furnish an outfit of a well-selected library, &c., for each freed person in the several school districts who is above the age of attending school duty, at a cost to each, including a case to contain the same, not exceeding two and a half dollars, which sum shall be included in the general tax hereinafter provided, but shall be deducted from the laborer's wages by his employer, when such books are furnished.

6th. To regulate the course of study, discipline and hours of instruction for children on week days, and adults on Sundays; to require such conformity to their regulations and such returns and reports from their teachers as they may deem necessary to secure uniformity, thoroughness and efficiency in said schools.

7th. To have generally the same authority and perform the same duties that assessors, supervisors and trustees have in the Northern States, in the matter of establishing and conducting Common Schools.

And for the full accomplishment of these purposes and the performance of the duties enjoined upon them, the Board shall have full power and authority to assess, and levy a School Tax upon real and personal property, including crops of plantations, in each and every before mentioned School District. The said taxes so levied shall be sufficient in amount to defray the cost and expense of establishing, furnishing and conducting for the period of one year the school or schools so established in each and every of the said districts; and said taxes shall be collected from the person or persons in the occupation of the property assessed.

8th. The taxes so assessed and levied in and for each district shall be collected and paid over to the Board by the parish provost marshal, within thirty days after the tax list and schedule shall have been placed in his hands; and he shall forthwith report to the Board whether there are in the districts of his parish any buildings available and suitable for school-houses, and shall at all times, when required, assist by his authority the Board in carrying out the spirit of this order. The taxes, when collected, shall be forthwith deposited in the First National Bank of New Orleans, subject only to the order of the whole Board, which shall make a monthly exhibit of accounts and report of their doings to the commanding general.

9th. In the performance of all their duties the Board shall co-operate, as far as practicable, with the superintendent of Public Education, recently elected.

10th. The current school year shall be estimated from February 1st, 1864, to February 1st, 1865.

11th. The following officers and citizens are appointed upon this Board, and will be obeyed and respected accordingly:

Colonel H. N. Frisbie, Twenty-second Infantry, Corps d'Afrique.

Lieutenant E. M. Wheelock, Fourth Infantry, Corps d'Afrique.

Isaac G. Hubbs, New Orleans.

By command of Major General Banks,

RICHARD B. IRWIN.

And whereas, Taxes imposed without the consent of the people are unconstitutional and injurious to their rights and liberties, be it

Resolved, 1st. That the rights asserted in the order aforesaid are unconstitutional and in derogation of the honor of the State and the dearest rights of the people.

2d. That any legislation, or attempt to legislate, or any amendment or attempt to amend the Constitution of Louisiana, will be a partial admission of the right claimed, and an abandonment of the just rights of the people of Louisiana.

3d. That this Convention ought to adjourn until all the powers belonging to the people, supposed to be abridged by said order, be restored to them by their representatives.

Be it further Resolved, That the Convention do adjourn until ———, 1864, in order to go to or correspond with General Banks and the authorities of the General Government of the United States, before taking any further action, and that a day be appointed to ascertain the wish and purposes of the General Government in the premises; and

Be it further Resolved, That the foregoing resolutions are not intended to impair or controvert in any manner the right of the General Government to require the State of Louisiana to contribute by taxes or otherwise her just proportion of the expenses of the war.

MR. FISH—I move that the resolutions be laid indefinitely on the table.

The motion was seconded.

MR. HENDERSON—By referring to section 10, I find something in relation to a Committee on Public Schools, etc., therefore the matter is already before this body, and the gentleman is out of order.

MR. BROTT—I move to lay these resolutions on the table.

Messrs. Abell and Hills called for the yeas and nays.

The roll was called, and the resolutions laid on the table.

YEAS—Messrs. Ariail, Austin, Bailey, Barrett, Beauvais, Bell, Bonzano, Brott, Burke, Cazabat, Cook J. K., Cook Terrance, Crozat, Cutler, Duane, Dupaty, Edwards, Ennis, Fish, Flagg, Flood, Foley, Fosdick, Gastinel, Geier, Gorlinski, Gaidry, Harnan, Hart, Heard, Henderson, Hills, Hire, Howell, Howes, Kavanagh, Knobloch, Kugler, Mann, Maurer, Mendiverri, Millspaugh, Montague, Morris, Murphy E., Murphy M. W., Newell, Normand, O'Conner, Ong, Payne John, Paine J. T., Poynot, Purcell John, Pursell Sam., Schroeder, Schnurr, Seymour Shaw, Smith, Spellicy, Stocker, Stumpf, Stiner, Stauffer, Sullivan, Terry, Thorpe, Thomas, Waters, Wenck, Wilson—72.

NAYS—Messrs. Abell, Baum, Buckley, Campbell, Goldman, Gruneberg, Maas, Montamat, Pintado—9.

The Convention then proceeded to the business of the day—Judge Howell's resolutions.

MR. HILLS—I move they be taken up *seriatim.*

The motion was carried.

The first section was then read.

MR. ABELL—I present a substitute for that, which is as follows:

Whereas, Slavery having existed in this country, by custom, from its earliest settlements, by sanction of the constitution and laws of the United States, and by the constitution and laws of this State; and,

Whereas, The owners of slaves have improved property therein, by virtue of such custom, constitution and laws, and under the protection and guarantee thereof; and,

Whereas, All that is good and truly great, in individuals, or States, must have its foundation in good faith and justice;

Be it therefore Resolved, That no proposition for the abolition of slavery be entertained by this Convention, until ways and means are first provided for a full, fair and equitable compensation to all loyal owners, either by the future labor of the slaves, or out of the treasury of this State, or of the United States, and for the removal of all emancipated slaves out of the State.

The resolution was laid on the table.

MR. CAZABAT—I offer as an amendment to the original resolution that "unconditional" be inserted after "immediate."

Laid on the table.

MR. CUTLER—I move that "five" be inserted in the first blank.

MR. THOMAS—I would like to call the attention of the Convention to the fact that we are about to do the most important act of all, for the accomplishment of which we are assembled, when we proceed to adopt this resolution, while the State of Louisiana is not one-fourth represented, though the unrepresented districts have a direct interest in it.

From the city of New Orleans, of all the members elected, there is not a fourth, not a tenth, Mr. President, who did at the breaking out of this rebellion, or who ever will, own a slave. The country parishes will be soon represented in this body, and it is the country parishes that have the deepest interest in this question, and the members will soon be with us.

I, for one, am unwilling to adopt this resolution now. I am unwilling to proceed farther in this matter, believing that every one of those gentlemen, when elected, will go with us. When this resolution is then finally carried—when slavery is finally abolished in Louisiana—we shall have avoided all complaints of that party called Copperhead. If we do it now, sir, we do it mainly through the instrumentality of gentlemen from New Orleans.

I will therefore move, Mr. President, that that resolution be laid upon the table subject to call, that it may be taken up again when the State is properly represented.

Mr. Henderson—Every man in this Convention is here under the proclamation and the iron-clad, so that every one may speak his sentiments without being considered disloyal. The only question is, shall the people of Louisiana pay for those slaves, or shall the United States? I shall vote "yea" on the question of tabling. The question rather is, whether this matter shall be submitted to a committee of five, and on their report the question of compensation may or may not come up. We have seventy-six members here, more than one-half of the whole, and they are competent to pass upon the question. The country parishes have not seen fit to send delegates here, though required. It seems to me that this rather savors of Copperheadism. They want their pay in advance, before the delegation is sent here. I say that we come here for the purpose of freeing the slaves, and the only question is, whether this resolution shall be adopted or not.

Mr. Cazabat—Mr, President—

President—I think the gentleman has already spoken twice.

Mr. Cazabat—No, sir, I have not spoken on the subject, but think it open for discussion. I merely made a motion. I consider it almost useless to discuss the resolution which is now before this Convention. Its object is to place in the hands of a committee of five the most important and momentous question which will come before this Convention for discussion. I, for one, sir, coincide partly with the gentleman who has just taken his seat; but, on the other hand, I differ from him in regard to the insinuation which he has made against the country parishes. Let it be said for Western Louisiana, that, far from being "Copperhead," its inhabitants are as true, brave and loyal men as can be found even in the city of New Orleans.

Sir, if you do not see these seats filled by the country delegates, it is not their fault; for they are anxious, willing and ready to participate in the proceedings of this assembly. But let some of these city gentlemen go beyond our lines from Alexandria to Shreveport, and they will find a very good reason for this absence. Those remarks, sir, were uncalled for and very unjust.

As far as the question of compensation is concerned, I take the ground that the people of Louisiana have not a right to donate a dollar, not a single red cent from the public treasury to pay slaveholders. I, for one, sir, will, regardless of the consequences, raise my humble voice for the immediate, unconditional and permanent abolition of slavery in the State of Louisiana. [Applause.]

If compensation, however, is to be granted, in the name of justice, in the name of equity, let it be made by the United States government, and then only to loyal citizens who shall prove themselves to have been such from the beginning of this unholy rebellion. [Applause.]

Mr. President, I hope for the welfare of our country, for the benefit and honor of this Convention, that the committee which shall be appointed on this resolution, will bring in a report compatible with the progressive spirit of the age—in accordance with equity and justice. Reverse this and you will do a great injustice to all classes of citizens.

Mr. Cutler—This discussion is certainly entirely foreign to the issue before the Convention. As presented it is only to point out the manner in which the emancipation of slaves should take place in this State, not in relation to by whom they shall be paid for, whether by the Federal government, the State, or at all. Its only object is to appoint a committee to whom the whole matter may be referred. It seems to me that the resolution as it is read is in its terms clear and to the point. It seems to me, Mr. President, that in no other shape could it be so well presented. I do not agree with the gentleman, that we should wait until all the members elected have arrived, for it is not in contemplation to act upon this great and important subject, but it is only proposed to refer it to a proper committee. When that committee has reported then let this discussion come. It seems to me, Mr. President, that for seven days we have been working to very little purpose, and I think we should now go to work, avoiding all these discussions.

Mr. Abell—As I understand this debate, it is wished by some that this resolution should be deferred until certain members should have an opportunity of presenting themselves here. I think the remarks of the last gentleman very proper, but would like to make a little explanation of my own opinion.

Though my father and ancestors have been, I believe, slaveholders, and I have myself owned several slaves, since I have had the power to think I have not seen the day or moment when I believed in slavery in the abstract. But while I do not believe in slavery, I do believe that while we regard liberty, we must also look to justice, and should go back to see whether or no we are acting entirely justly. We must not confine ourselves to this day or to this country, but must take a retrospective glance and see how these individuals—our fellow-citizens—have acquired their rights.

How did they? Under the express language of the constitution of the United States, and the guaranty of this State, and the several laws of Congress, enacted under the clause of the constitutions giving that guarantee. These are, I say, matters that must and will be regarded by every good man before he can act rightly. We must do justice, and while I assume that there is no man here who is opposed to freedom, we should look the whole in the face and endeavor to act justly as well as to extend liberty.

Slavery is not a new thing. The Greeks had slaves in other Christian ages; Rome had slaves, with the power of life and death over them. Mr. President, we should look to our predecessors as much as we can, and unless we can do this, we may legislate ourselves into that which will meet neither the approbation of our own people nor of the world.

President—The question is on the motion to lay the first resolution on the table, subject to call.

The motion was lost and the first resolution immediately adopted.

Mr. Gastinel—I move to reconsider that portion of the resolution fixing the number of the committee at five.

The motion was adopted.

Mr. Buckley—I move that the number be seventeen.

The motion was tabled.

Mr. Montamat—I move to insert "eleven" in the blank.

The motion was adopted.

The blank of the second section was filled by inserting "seventeen."

Mr. Brott—I would like to inquire if resolutions were not passed fixing the number of members upon these committees at three?

President—No, sir.

The second section was then adopted.

The third section was taken up.

Mr. Smith—I move to fill the blank with "seven."

Motion was carried and the section adopted.

The fourth section was taken up.

Mr. Baum—I move that the blank be filled by "thirteen."

A motion to amend to "five" was called and tabled, and being declared lost a rising vote was taken and it was tabled, and the amendment lost by 29 ayes to 37 nays.

Mr. Thomas—I rise to a point of order,

and would ask whether, according to rule 17, every member present is not obliged to vote unless excused by the Convention, for I find that less than a quorum are voting now.

The motion to insert "thirteen" was put and lost, when "nine" having been moved was carried, and the section then adopted as a whole.

The blank of the fifth section was filled by "seven," and then, upon Mr. Goldman's motion, adopted.

The sixth section was read.

MR. BROTT—I move "nine" be inserted.

MR. MONTAMAT—I amend by suggesting "nine."

The amendment was carried.

MR. GORLINSKI—I amend to "eleven."

It was moved to lay all the amendments upon the table, and the motion was lost.

Mr. Montamat's amendment was carried, and the section then adopted as a whole.

The seventh section was taken up.

MR. HILLS—I move to fill the blank with "five."

MR. MONTAMAT—I amend to "three."

MR. BAUM—I amend to "seven."

Both amendments were seconded.

MR. GOLDMAN—I move to lay both of them on the table.

The motion was carried and the original motion prevailed, whereupon the section was adopted.

The secretary read the eighth section.

MR. BAUM—I move to insert "seven" in the blank.

The motion was carried and the section adopted.

The ninth section was taken up.

MR. SMITH—I move the blank be filled by "five."

The motion was carried and section adopted.

The tenth section was read.

MR. HENDERSON—I move to insert "seven."

MR. HARNAN—I move as an amendment "nineteen," representing one member from each representative district and parish.

The motion was seconded.

MR. BAUM—I amend to "nine."

"Eleven" was then suggested and carried, when the section was adopted.

The eleventh section was then read.

MR. BELL—I move to insert "five."

Motion carried and section adopted.

Section twelve was read.

MR. HENDERSON—I move to insert "five."

MR. BELL—I amend to "seven."

Mr. Bell's motion was carried, and the section as amended adopted.

Section thirteen was read.

The blank was filled by inserting "five" and the section adopted.

MR. MONTAMAT—I move that another section be added, and present the following:

Resolved, That the following Standing Committees be appointed by the chair: one on Enrollment, to consist of five members; one on Finance, of five members; one on Expenses, of five members; and one on Printing of three members.

The motion was adopted.

MR. MONTAMAT—I move that the resolution be adopted as a whole.

The motion was carried.

PRESIDENT—I would state to the Convention that I must have at least twenty-four and perhaps forty-eight hours in which to arrange the committees, and suggest that in the meantime we adjourn.

MR. GOLDMAN—I offer the following:

Resolved, That applause, pending discussions in this Convention, is out of order, and disallowable.

A motion to lay upon the table was lost, and the resolution on being put to vote was lost.

MR. SULLIVAN—I present the following:

Whereas, It is currently reported that many members of this Convention are not citizens of the United States, but owe allegiance to foreign powers; *And whereas,* it becomes the duty of this Convention to have its members placed above suspicion; be it

Resolved, That the members of this Convention, of foreign birth, be required to present to the president of this Convention evidence of their naturalization on or before 12 M., Thursday next.

HR. HARNAN—I hope none of us are not citizens of the United States, but should that be the case, no such persons should be admitted.

The president decided that the motion to lay upon the table was lost.

MR. GOLDMAN—I appeal from the decision of the chair.

Mr. Wenck—It seems to me very strange that at this stage of the proceedings such a resolution should be introduced. We have not a legislative power, but titles have not been called in question by any one. Must not a man be a citizen when he is elected and presented here? I do not speak for myself, but for the whole. Supposing any should not be citizens, what action could this Convention take to expel him from his seat? None at all, I think. It is a matter left entirely to the people, when they elect a man to defend their interests and to do what is right. I say that this is not a stage of the proceedings when such a resolution can be offered, and that it can reach no one; even if it did, no one could be rightfully expelled.

Mr. Waters—I would ask the gentleman what his action was in regard to the iron-clad? If these tests were right in that instance, they are in this.

Mr. Sullivan—I presented my resolution because it is reported through the city that there are several members here who are not naturalized citizens, though they have taken the iron-clad. I, as a citizen of foreign birth, feel hurt, and I wish to show to this Convention that all in my situation come here as *bona fide* citizens of the United States. Though I am foreign born, I owe allegiance to the United States, and am willing at any moment to go to the president's desk and exhibit my papers. I believe there is not a foreigner here but who is willing to do the same, and more than that, I will say that I do not believe there is one here who will object to it.

[Applause.]

Mr. Wilson—I think what papers have already been exhibited are sufficient. It seems to me a slander upon those of foreign birth to go on this way requiring proofs of this kind. Was not the production of the iron-clad sufficient? I move the matter be dropped.

Mr. Hire—If I am in order, I shall raise my feeble voice and ask that I may be heard. I hope to God that you will not insist upon testing this question beyond its proper bearings. It is well known that every man here must be a citizen, and so must every voter. I, for one, have voted here for fourteen years, and you have only to refer to the registry to find the names of *all* voters. I hope, Mr. President, that this matter will not be pressed by the opposition.

Mr. Goldman—I have heard that there are enemies here, but we do not exact from them any certificates, and why should we be required to exhibit our papers? I think it may be safely assumed that there are none among us but citizens.

Mr. Thorpe—I wish to record my vote against this resolution, because I consider it an outrage, both upon foreigners and every native born citizen.

Mr. Montamat—I will vote for this resolution, because I am informed that some members of this Convention, of foreign birth, took the iron-clad after their election, notwithstanding they had previously taken out British protection papers. No such gentlemen ought to be admitted as a member of this Convention. [Applause.]

Mr. Harnan—I would like to know whether the gentleman took the oath to the Southern Confederacy. [Laughter.]

Mr. Montamat—Yes, of course, we all did. [Cries of "No, no, not all."]

President—Are you ready for the question?

The yeas and nays were called for, and 39 members arose, whereupon the president directed the secretary to call the roll, and the following was the result:

Yeas—Messrs. Ariail, Austin, Barrett, Baum, Beauvais, Bell, Bennie, Brott, Buckley, Campbell, Cook T., Cutler, Duane, Dufresne, Flagg, Flood, Foley, Gastinel, Gorlinski, Gaidry, Healy, Harnan, Hart, Heard, Hills, Howes, Kavanagh, Knobloch, Mann, Maurer, Montamat, Montague, Murphy M. W., Newell, Normand, O'Conner, Ong, Payne J., Paine J. T., Pintado, Pursell S., Seymour, Shaw, Smith, Spellicy, Sullivan, Terry, Thomas, Waters—49.

Nays—Messrs. Bailey, Bonzano, Burke, Crozat, Dupaty, Ennis, Fish, Fosdick, Geier, Goldman, Gruneberg, Henderson, Hire, Howell, Kugler, Maas, Mendiverri, Millspaugh, Morris, Murphy E., Purcell J., Schnurr, Shaw, Stocker, Stiner, Stauffer, Thorpe, Wenck, Wilson—29.

The resolution was accordingly adopted.

Mr. Schroeder—I protest against these proceedings.

Mr. Goldman—I second the protest.

MR. WILSON—I move we adjourn.

MR. HOWELL—It seems to me that in accordance with the request, we should adjourn till to-morrow, at 5 o'clock, in order to give the president time to appoint the various committees, and I therefore make that motion.

MR. HARNAN—I amend to 7 o'clock.

MR. STAUFFER—If we are to adjourn, I move we go into an election of assistant secretary and reporter.

MR. MONTAMAT—I move we proceed to elect two assistant secretaries.

MR. HENDERSON—I move as an amendment to elect the number prescribed by the rules of this body.

MR. MONTAMAT—I accept the amendment.

MR. BELL—I offer the following resolution:

Resolved, That we proceed to elect two assistant secretaries, a postmaster, reporter and messenger.

MR. HENDERSON—I move we elect such numbers of these officers as are prescribed.

The resolution was carried.

The following gentlemen were nominated candidates for assistant secretaryship:

MR. AUSTIN—I am requested by Mr. Gallup to withdraw his name.

Messrs. H. A. Gallup, T. H. Murphy and Parker.

Several members stated that in consequence of the hasty mode of proceeding they had no opportunity of presenting several gentlemen as candidates.

The following were nominated: Messrs Carter, Hamilton, Winfree, Gordon and Cruise.

MR. HILLS—I move that the assistant secretaries be elected separately.

Upon the first roll-call the result was as follows:

Cruise	0
Carter	5
Parker	5
Winfree	11
Gordon	11
Hamilton	13
Murphy	35

No candidate having received a majority of all the votes cast, there was no election.

MR. MONTAMAT—I move the two receiving the highest number of votes cast be considered the candidates.

The motion was carried.

On calling the roll a second time, Mr. Murphy received 52, and Mr. Hamilton 24, and Mr. Murphy was accordingly declared elected.

MR. BROTT—I rise to a question of privilege, and offer the following:

Resolved, That Adjutant General Thomas be and is hereby invited to take a seat within the bar of this Convention.

The resolution was adopted.

Gen. Thomas entering the hall with Governor Hahn, was received with loud applause, to which he made the following acknowledgment:

Mr. President, I thank you most kindly for this compliment.

The following gentlemen were nominated for the second assistant secretaryship: Messrs. Gordon, Winfree, Hamilton, Cruise.

The roll was called with the following result: Hamilton, 38; Gordon, 19; Winfree, 19; Cruise, 0.

There was accordingly no election.

Upon a second call the vote was as follows: Gordon, 20; Winfree, 22; Hamilton, 35.

MR. HENDERSON—I move that the two highest only be voted for.

No objection being made, the roll was called, and Mr. Hamilton received 47 and Mr. Winfree 30, whereupon Hamilton was declared elected.

MR. WILSON—I move we proceed to the nomination of reporter.

The motion was carried, and Messrs. A. P. Bennett and H. A. Gallup were nominated for that position.

The roll being called, Mr. Bennett received 50 votes and Mr. Gallup 24.

MR. WILSON—I move Mr. Bennett be declared the unanimous choice of the Convention.

MR. THOMAS—It is evident that one man cannot perform all the duties that appertain to the office of reporter of this body. It is impossible that he should take down the proceedings and write them out, etc.; I therefore introduce the following:

Resolved, That the reporter be and he is hereby authorized to employ three assistants.

MR. MONTAMAT—I amend to two assistants.

MR. CAZABAT—I move to lay that motion on the table.

The motion was put and carried, and the original resolution was then put and carried.

MR. BROTT—I move we proceed to elect a postmaster.

Messrs. Toomy, Davis, Miller, Ganon, Gordon, Smith and Koch were nominated.

The roll was called with the following result: Toomy 3, Miller 7, Davis 7, Gordon 11, Smith 11, Ganon 15, Koch 21.

There was no election.

MR. HENDERSON—I move that the two highest only be voted for.

Upon the second vote Mr. Koch received 30 and Mr. Ganon 47 votes, and Mr. Ganon was declared elected.

MR. DUANE—I move we proceed to elect a messenger.

The motion was carried.

MR. BROTT—I move that Chas. Benedict be declared by acclamation the unanimous choice of this Convention.

The motion prevailed, and Chas. Benedict was elected messenger.

MR. THOMAS—If I am in order, I have a resolution to offer.

MR. BAUM—I move we adjourn till Friday, at 12 o'clock.

The motion was seconded and lost, nays 44, and yeas 26.

MR. THOMAS—My resolution is:

Resolved, That the sergeant-at-arms be authorized to employ two assistants.

MR. MONTAMAT—I move to lay it on the table.

The motion was lost, and the original motion put and carried.

A motion was made to adjourn till Friday, at 12 o'clock, and carried.

FRIDAY, April 15, 1864.

The Convention was called to order, and after prayer by the Rev. Mr. Mason, the secretary called the roll, and the following gentlemen answered to their names:

Messrs. Abell, Ariail, Austin, Bailey, Barrett, Beauvais, Bell, Bennie, Bonzano, Bromley, Brott, Buckley, Burke, Campbell, Cook J. K., Davies, Duane, Dufresne, Dupaty, Edwards, Ennis, Fish, Flagg, Flood, Foley, Fosdick, Geier, Goldman, Gorlinski, Gaidry, Healy, Harnan, Hart, Henderson, Hills, Howell, Howes, Maas, Mann, Mendiverri, Millspaugh, Montamat, Montague, Morris, Murphy E., Murphy M. W., O'Conner, Ong, Paine, Pintado, Poynot, Purcell J., Pursell S., Schroeder, Seymour, Shaw, Smith, Stumpf, Stiner, Stauffer, Sullivan, Terry, Thorpe, Thomas, Waters, Wenck, Wilson—66.

The secretary read the minutes of the preceding day.

MR. HILLS—I move that the reading of the Educational Order be dispensed with.

The motion was adopted.

PRESIDENT—Gentlemen, you have heard the minutes read. Is there any objection to their adoption?

MR. CAMPBELL—Before the adoption of the minutes, I request the secretary to read the names of the members voting yea on Mr. Montamat's resolution.

Mr. CAZABAT—I call for the same.

MR. CAMPBELL—I wish my name placed among the nays. I did not vote for the adoption of the resolution.

MR. CAZABAT—I request the same.

The minutes being accordingly corrected, and no further objection being made, they were accordingly adopted.

MR. HEARD—I rise to a question of privilege. I wish to ask for leave of absence for my colleague, Mr. Kugler, on account of serious illness in his family; he having received a telegram to that effect.

MR. FISH—I move that the request be granted.

The motion was seconded and carried.

PRESIDENT—If there are no petitions or memorials resolutions are in order.

MR. FISH—I offer the following resolution:

Resolved, That the governor of the State be requested to issue his proclamation, ordering an election as early as possible for one delegate from the Tenth Representative District of the parish of Orleans, to fill a vacancy in the representation from such district and parish.

PRESIDENT—The resolution is not seconded.

MR. HENDERSON—I have a resolution for the same purpose, to accept the resignations of Messrs. Abbott and Roselius, and that the governor be requested to issue his writs to fill the vacancy

MR. CAZABAT—I move to lay that on the table.

The motion was seconded and lost.

PRESIDENT—The question is on the original resolution.

The resolution was carried.

MR. STOCKER—

Resolved, That the official printer be authorized to print 300 copies of the Constitution of Louisiana of 1852, for the use of the members.

MR. MONTAMAT—I offer as a substitute, 200 copies.

MR. HOWELL—I would offer the following as a substitute, stating before I offer it, that the State librarian has informed me that he has a sufficient number of the Revised Statutes in the library for the use of the members, and in that volume are contained the constitutions of the State, of 1812, 1845 and 1852 ; therefore be it

Resolved, That the State librarian be requested to furnish each member of this Convention one volume of the Revised Statutes, for use during the session.

PRESIDENT—The original resolution is to print 300 copies ; the amendment is 200, and a substitute is offered. The question is on the substitute.

MR. HILLS—I would like to inquire whether the copies are to be furnished gratuitously.

MR. HOWELL—Certainly, during the sitting of the Convention.

The substitute was adopted.

MR. STOCKER—I have another resolution I wish to offer :

Resolved, That the rules and regulations be so amended as to require all orders and resolutions to lie over one day, unless referred to some committee before being acted upon by the Convention.

MR. MONTAMAT—Before you can amend them you must have the matter passed upon. We must be governed by the Art. XLII of Rules and Regulations, and regard must also be had to the rule in relation to altering our regulations.

MR. STOCKER—I did not propose to alter the rules, but merely to amend them. Rule XLII reads that "no standing rule or order of the Convention shall be rescinded or changed without one day's notice being given thereof," etc. This is not a standing rule. I give notice that I intend to offer that to-morrow.

MR. THOMAS—I have a resolution I desire to offer :

Resolved, That the printer of this Convention be ordered to print 300 copies of the Rules and Regulations of this body, as adopted.

We have now only the report of the committee. I don't know that that rule was adopted, or printed, as ordered, without reference to the clerk.

MR. MONTAMAT—I move as an amendment that the names of the members to be appointed on the several committees be also printed.

MR. HILLS—I move that the printer be instructed to insert the subject of each section in the margin.

The resolution as amended was carried.

MR. S. PURSELL—I present the following :

Resolved, That in consideration for and in just appreciation of the former services in the cause of the Union and the great respect entertained by the loyal people of the State of Louisiana for the Hon. Christian Roselius, and the fact of his election being a spontaneous action of the truly loyal people of the parish which he has served so long and faithfully, that he be invited to withdraw his resignation and resume his seat in this Convention.

MR. HENDERSON—I move to lay it on the table.

The motion was seconded and a *viva voce* vote taken, but the president being unable to decide, directed a rising vote. The result was, yeas 42, nays 31. It was accordingly laid on the table.

MR. HENDERSON—I offer the following :

Resolved, That the members of this Convention shall receive from the public treasury compensation for their services, which shall be ten dollars per day during their attendance on, going to, and returning from the session of this Convention.

Be it further Resolved, That a committee of five be appointed by the president to determine upon the compensation of officers and employés, and the mileage of members from the parishes, and report as early as possible.

MR. BROTT—I move that the resolution be divided, and that we vote on the first proposition.

The motion was seconded.

MR. FOLEY—I move to lay them both on the table, subject to call.

The last motion was negatived, as was the

6

preceding one, and the original resolution.

MR. THOMAS—I rise to a point of order, and call your attention to rule XXXII, which we adopted. This reading of resolutions and adopting them without knowing what they contain is, I think, prohibited by that rule.

MR. THORPE—I offer the following:

Resolved, That a committee of —— members be appointed by the president to whom all matters shall be referred to be brought before the Convention in regard to our relation with the Federal Union, and that the committee be called a Committee on Federal Relations.

MR. BROTT—I move to amend by saying that the committee shall consist of "five" members.

The amendment was accepted, and the resolution adopted.

MR. HOWELL—I rise to a question of privilege. When the motion of the gentleman was offered for fixing the compensation of members of this Convention, I arose, as I thought, in time to offer a substitute. I desire that this Convention and the people of Louisiana shall know that I was opposed to the resolutions as they were adopted. It was my wish, sir, to offer this resolution of mine as a substitute for those resolutions which were adopted:

Resolved, That the compensation of members of this Convention be the same that is allowed to the members of the General Assembly of this State.

I simply desire to have that appear on the minutes of the Convention.

MR. GOLDMAN—I rise to a question of privilege. I desire to be put down as having seconded that substitute, for I should most certainly have done so.

PRESIDENT—The whole of this conversation is out of order as well as the offered substitute. If the gentleman presents this matter to the Convention, and the Convention chooses to direct that the substitute be put upon the minutes, that will be done; otherwise not.

The Convention took no action in regard to the matter.

MR. MONTAMAT—I offer the following:

Be it Resolved, That the sum of one hundred thousand dollars be and the same is hereby appropriated out of the general funds for the purpose of paying the members, officers and employés of this Convention the mileage and *per diem* to which they are respectively entitled; the same to be paid by the treasurer of the State on a warrant of the President of this Convention.

MR. CAZABAT—I move to lay the resolution on the table.

The motion was lost.

MR. CAZABAT—I call for the yeas and nays on the adoption of the resolution.

In response to this, twenty-four members rose, and the president directed the roll to be called.

MR. ARIAIL—I understand the previous vote to have been on the adoption or rejection of the resolution, and should have voted yea, had I supposed that it was in regard to laying it on the table.

MR. FOLEY—I think the rule XV should be attended to.

SECRETARY—I am requested to state, by the president, that certain resolutions having been read, they must be brought before the house according to the rules.

The roll was then called on the adoption of the original resolution:

YEAS—Messrs. Abell, Austin, Bailey, Baum, Beauvais, Bell, Bennie, Bofill, Buckley, Cook J. K., Cook T., Crozat, Duane, Dufresne, Foley, Gorlinski, Gaidry, Healy, Heard, Henderson, Howes, Mann, Maurer, Mendiverri, Montamat, Montague, Murphy M. W., O'Conner, Poynot, Purcell S., Schroeder, Smith, Spellicy, Stiner, Sullivan, Terry, Waters, Wilson—37.

NAYS—Messrs. Barrett, Bonzano, Bromley, Brott, Burke, Campbell, Cazabat, Davies, Dupaty, Ennis, Fish, Flagg, Flood, Fosdick, Gastinel, Geier, Goldman, Harnan, Hart, Hills, Hire, Howell, Maas, Millspaugh, Morris, Murphy E., Ong, Paine, Pintado, Purcell J., Seymour, Shaw, Stocker, Stumpf, Stauffer, Thorpe, Thomas—37.

The secretary announced that there was a tie, upon which the president (Judge Durell) cast his vote in the negative, and the resolution was accordingly defeated by a vote of 38 nays to 37 yeas.

MR. CAZABAT—There is no quorum. I request that the name of Mr. Roselius be called.

PRESIDENT—The Secretary will call the roll.

Upon again calling the roll, the following gentlemen responded:

Messrs. Abell, Ariail, Austin, Bailey, Barrett, Beauvais, Bell, Bennie, Bofill, Bonzano, Bromley, Brott, Buckley, Burke, Campbell, Cazabat, Cook J. K., Cook T., Crozat, Davies, Duane, Dupaty, Dufresne, Edwards, Ennis, Fish, Flagg, Flood, Foley, Fosdick, Gastinel, Geier, Goldman, Gorlinski, Gruneberg, Gaidry, Healy, Harnan, Hart, Heard, Henderson, Hills, Hire, Howell, Howes, Maas, Mann, Maurer, Mendiverri, Millspaugh, Montamat, Montague, Morris, Murphy E., Murphy M. W., O'Conner, Ong, Payne J., Pintado, Poynot, Purcell J., Purcell S., Schroeder, Seymour, Shaw, Smith, Spellicy, Stocker, Stumpf, Stiner, Stauffer, Sullivan, Terry, Thorne, Thomas, Winters, Wenck, Wells, Wilson—79.

It was announced that 79 members had answered to their names.

PRESIDENT—A quorum is *now* present and the rule XVII must be enforced; call the roll again on the adoption of the resolution.

The roll was called, with the following result.

AYES---Messrs. Abell, Austin, Baum, Beauvais, Bell, Bennie, Bofill, Buckley, Burke, Cook J. K., Cook T., Crozat, Davies, Duane, Dufresne, Flagg, Foley, Fuller, Gorlinski, Geier, Gaidry, Healy, Heard, Henderson, Hire, Howes, Maurer, Mendiverri, Millspaugh, Montamat, Montague, Murphy M. W., O'Conner, Poynot, Purcell J., Purcell S., Schroeder, Spellicy, Stiner, Sullivan, Terry, Thorpe, Waters, Wilson—45.

NAYS---Messrs. Ariail, Bailey, Balch, Barrett, Bonzano, Bromley, Brott, Campbell, Cazabat, Dupaty, Ennis, Fish, Flood, Fosdick, Gastinel, Gorlinski, Harnan, Hart, Hills, Kavanagh, Maas, Mann, Morris, Murphy E., Ong, Paine, Pintado, Shaw, Stocker, Stumpf, Stauffer—31.

The resolution was accordingly adopted.

MR. MONTAGUE—I would ask a reconsideration of the question allowing ten dollars *per diem* to members of this Convention.

A motion was made to lay this on the table, and on taking the vote the president then announced it carried.

MR. THOMAS—I call for a division—for the yeas and nays. Let us see who votes, and how.

The yeas and nays being demanded by eighteen members, the president directed the roll to be called.

As several of the members had in the meantime left the hall, and others were about leaving the doors were closed, while the sergeant-at-arms was sent for absent members.

The roll being called, the resolution to reconsider was laid upon the table by the following vote.

YEAS—Messrs. Abell, Baum, Beauvais, Bell, Bofill, Buckley, Cook J. K., Cook T., Crozat, Duane, Dufresne, Flagg, Flood, Foley, Geier, Gorlinski, Gaidry, Healy, Heard, Henderson, Hills, Hire, Howes, Mendiverri, Montamat, Murphy E., Murphy M. W., O'Conner, Paine, Poynot, Purcell J., Schroeder, Seymour, Smith, Spellicy, Stocker, Stiner, Sullivan, Terry, Waters, Wilson—41.

NAYS—Messrs. Ariail, Bailey, Balch, Barrett, Bennie, Bonzano, Bromley, Brott, Campbell, Cazabat, Davies, Dupaty, Ennis, Fish, Fosdick, Gastinel, Goldman, Harnan, Hart, Howell, Maas, Mann, Maurer, Millspaugh, Montague, Morris, Ong, Paine, Pintado, Pursell S., Shaw, Stumpf, Stauffer, Thorpe, Thomas, Wenck—35.

MR. STAUFFER—I would like to have the following resolution laid over until to-morrow:

Resolved, That a committee of five members be appointed by the president, to wait upon the proper State officers, and ascertain if any and what amount of bonds have been issued, and what amount, if any, remains outstanding for the purpose of arming and keeping the State militia against the lawful authority of the United States.

PRESIDENT—If there are no further resolutions, we will proceed to the unfinished business of yesterday. The secretary will read the list of ommittees appointed by the chair. The secretary read the following list:

STANDING COMMITTEES.

I. *Emancipation*—Bonzano, chairman; Howell, Abell, Edwards, Goldman, Stocker, Cazabat, Bennie, Murphy E., Paine J. T., Schroeder—11.

II. *Preamble*--Heard, chairman; Montague, Sullivan, Cook T., O'Conner, Spellicy, Waters—7.

III. *Distribution of Powers*—Thomas, chairman; Kugler, Foley, Bofill, Stumpf, Ong, Bromley—7.

IV. *Legislative Department*—Fosdick, chairman; Thorpe, Stauffer, Cazabat, Hire, Knobloch, Schnurr, Taliaferro, Wells—9.

V. *Executive Department*—Fish, chairman; Austin, Gruneberg, Bromley, Crozat, Davies, Mann—7.

VI. *Judiciary Department*—Howell, chairman; Heard, Beauvais, Fuller, Henderson, Cutler, Seymour—7.

VII. *Impeachment*—Wilson, chairman; Bailey, Gastinel, Morris, Paine J. T., Smith—6.

VIII. *General Provisions*—Mann, chairman; Cook J. K., Foley, Geier, Maas, Wenck, Buckley—7.

IX. *Internal Improvements*—Gorlinski, chairman; Arial, Campbell, Flood, Healy—5.

X. *Public Education*—Hills, chairman; Howes, Lobdell, Burke, Hart, Murphy M. W., Terry, Wells, Gaidry, Balch, Edwards, Maurer—11.

XI. *Mode of Revising the Constitution*—Cutler, chairman; Knobloch, Baum, Stiner, Harnan—5.

XII. *Schedule*—Gruneberg, chairman; Dupaty, Shaw, Dufresne, Ennis, Flagg, Gaidry—7.

XIII. *Ordinance*—Shaw, chairman; Poynot, Kavanagh, Kugler, Mendiverri—5.

XIV. *Enrollment*—Thorpe, chairman; Brott, Millspaugh, Pintado, Crozat—5.

XV. *Finance*—Brott, chairman; Montamat, Normand, Schnurr, Sullivan—5.

XVI. *Expenses*—Pursell S., chairman; Bell, Duane, Newell, Payne J., of Jefferson—5.

XVII. *Printing*—Purcell J., chairman; Fuller, Barrett—3.

MR. CAZABAT—Can I rise to a question of privilege?

PRESIDENT—The question?

MR. CAZABAT—The names of Messrs. Roselius and Abbott were stricken from the rolls when there was no action upon the matter. I call now for the number of voters upon that question, upon the action of this Convention in regard to their resignations, the vote taken this morning.

PRESIDENT—Do you wish to reconsider?

MR. CAZABAT—Yes, sir.

PRESIDENT—Did you vote in the negative?

MR. CAZABAT—Yes, sir.

PRESIDENT—You are out of order.

MR. MONTAMAT—I move to have the rules suspended for the purpose of reconsideration.

The motion was lost.

MR. ABELL—I ask to be excused from sitting as one of the committee upon the first resolution, on the ground that nothing can move me to retract my substitute, since I am satisfied that nothing else is practicable.

MR. CAZABAT—I move that the gentleman's excuse be accepted, since he does not wish to make one of the Committee of Emancipation.

The motion was seconded.

[Cries of "out of order."]

MR. ABELL—I withdraw my request.

JUDGE HOWELL—I believe the gentleman has withdrawn.

MR. CAZABAT—He cannot do it without our consent, agreeably to rule XXI, adopted by this Convention; but I consent to waive the point.

MR. MONTAMAT—I wish to make a motion to suspend the rules for the purpose of introducing a resolution relating to the Enrollment Committee.

MR. DUANE—I move it be laid upon the table.

The motion to table was defeated, whereupon the original motion was carried.

MR. MONTAMAT—This is my resolution:

Resolved, That the Committee on Enrollment be and is hereby authorized to appoint one chief clerk and as many other enrolling clerks as may be necessary, subject to the approval of the Convention.

MR. STOCKER—I rise to offer an amendment, and move to strike out "subject to the approval of the Convention."

The amendment was accepted, and the resolution passed.

PRESIDENT—Now that we have gone through the regular order of business, as fixed by the rules, is there anything further?

MR. CAZABAT—A vote has been taken in regard to the resignations of Messrs. Roselius and Abbott. On counting that vote, it will be found that a quorum was not present, and therefore the sense of the Convention was not taken upon a fair vote. I rise to move a reconsideration of that action.

PRESIDENT—Did the gentleman vote in the affirmative?

MR. CAZABAT—I don't know. Reference to the minutes will determine.

PRESIDENT—If you voted in the affirmative, you are out of order.

MR. HILLS—In order to bring before this Convention the subject of fixing the hour of meeting, I move that when this Convention adjourns, it adjourn until 5 o'clock in the afternoon.

MR. STAUFFER—As an amendment, I would suggest 12 o'clock.

MR. WENCK—I move to lay that motion on the table.

MR. THOMAS—I offer, as an amendment, 1 o'clock.

MR. HARNAN—I move to amend by substituting 7 o'clock.

MR. STAUFFER—Is this matter debatable?

PRESIDENT—I think not.

MR. STAUFFER—I call for the yeas and nays on that question.

PRESIDENT—You are out of order.

MR. WENCK—I move that all the amendments be laid upon the table.

The original resolution was called for.

MR. MONTAMAT—Can I amend?

PRESIDENT—Any amendment not passed upon will be in order.

MR. MONTAMAT—I would amend to 1 o'clock.

PRESIDENT—Not in order; that has been passed upon.

PRESIDENT—The question recurs to Mr. Hills's motion.

A *viva voce* vote was taken.

PRESIDENT—I am unable to determine.

The ayes and nays were called.

PRESIDENT—Mr. Secretary call the ayes and nays.

The resolution was adopted by a vote of 43 ayes to 27 nays.

MR. GASTINEL—I offer the following:

Resolved, That a committee of five members of this body be appointed by the president to wait upon the governor and inform him that the Convention is organized and prepared to receive any communications he may have to make to this body.

MR. MONTAMAT—I move to lay that motion on the table.

MR. WENCK—I do not see that we require any instructions from the governor. We are assembled to do business, and there can be no instructions given to this body, but our consciences alone must tell us what we have to do. I think this resolution is entirely out of order. We are not a body for legislative purposes, but we only meet here, sent by the people to perform certain duties without instructions from anybody. I shall vote against the resolution.

The resolution was adopted.

PRESIDENT—I appoint Messrs. Gastinel, Shaw, Thomas, Goldman and Bofill.

MR. THORPE—I would like to have the following resolution lie over until to-morrow:

Cries of "there is no quorum."

The roll was again called, when 80 members responded.

PRESIDENT—The question is decided unless it is appealed. Those who fail to vote cannot be permitted to destroy the vote of the House. Some action on the part of the Convention is requisite.

MR. STOCKER—I offer the following:

Resolved, That a committee of five be appointed by the president, to inquire into the cause of the absence of Messrs. Wells of Rapides, and Taliaferro of Concordia. Also, to inquire into the expediency of ordering an election to fill their places.

MR. HEARD—Before the question is put, I would move to insert the name of Mr. Lobdell.

The amendment was accepted.

MR. CAZABAT—I move the motion be laid upon the table.

The motion was seconded and lost, and the original resolution was adopted.

PRESIDENT—I appoint Messrs. Stocker, Montague, Ariail, Heard and Mann to act upon this committee.

Resolved, That Section 54 of the Rules of this Convention shall read as follows: "A quorum shall consist of two-thirds of the members elected and admitted to this Convention."

SECRETARY—Before putting that question I will state that I am requested by the president to ask the members to remain after adjournment in order to organize the committees appointed this morning.

A motion to adjourn until to-morrow at five o'clock was carried, and the Convention dispersed to meet again at that hour.

SATURDAY, April 16, 1864.

Convention met at 5 o'clock P. M., pursuant to last adjournment, and came to order.

MR. HILLS—I move that Judge Howell be appointed president *pro tem.*

Motion seconded and carried.

Prayer was offered by Rev. Dr. Hopkins, and the secretary then called the roll, when the following gentlemen responded:

Messrs. Abbott, Abell, Ariail, Austin, Bailey, Beauvais, Bell, Bofill, Bonzano, Bromley, Brott, Buckley, Burke, Cazabat, Cook J. K., Cook Terrance, Crozat, Cutler, Davies, Duane, Edwards, Ennis, Fish, Flagg,

Flood, Foley, Fosdick, Fuller, Gastinel, Geier, Goldman, Gorlinski, Gaidry, Healy, Hart, Heard, Henderson, Hills, Hire, Howell, Howes, Kavanagh, Maas, Mann, Maurer, Mendiverri, Millspaugh, Montague, Morris, Murphy E., Murphy M. W., Newell, Normand, O'Conner, Payne Jno., Pintado, Poynot, Purcell Jno., Pursell Sam, Schroeder, Schnurr, Seymour, Shaw, Smith, Spellicy, Stocker, Stumpf, Stiner, Sullivan, Terry, Thorpe, Thomas, Wenck, Wilson—75.

The secretary proceeded to read the minutes of the second day.

MR. MONTAMAT—I move that the reading of the minutes be dispensed with.

Motion seconded.

MR. CAZABT—I move to lay that motion upon the table.

Mr. Goldman seconded.

The last motion was lost, and the original motion carried.

MR. THOMAS—I would like to call the attention of the House to the fact that *I* did *not* propose the printing of the constitutions. *My* proposition was to print three hundred copies of the rules and regulations adopted by the Convention.

The minutes were then adopted as read.

PRESIDENT—Are there any petitions?

None were presented.

PRESIDENT—Any memorials? If not, we will proceed to resolutions.

MR. MONTAMAT—I offer the following?

Resolved, That the sum of one hundred dollars be paid out of contingent funds of the Convention to Mr. H. A. Gallup, for his services as acting assistant secretary of this Convention before the same was organized.

The resolution was adopted.

MR. BELL—I offer the following:

Resolved, That the standing committees are hereby authorized to appoint and engage such clerks as are necessary for the duties of the committees.

Resolution seconded.

MR. CAZABAT—I move to lay on the table.

MR. PURCELL—I offer the following:

Resolved, That article 96 of the constitution of the State of Louisiana be so altered and amended as to read thus: "All civil officers for the State at large shall be voters of and reside in the State, and all district or parish officers shall be voters and reside whithin their districts or parish, and keep their offices in such places therein as may be required by law."

I wish it laid over or referred to a committee.

MR. HILLS—I move to refer it to the Committee on Legislation.

MR. HENDERSON—I move to lay it on the table.

The motion was carried.

MR. SULLIVAN—I wish to have the names of those delegates of foreign birth who have failed to produce their naturalization papers read to the Convention.

PRESIDENT—You are out of order.

MR. MONTAMAT—I present the following:

Resolved, That the Hon. A. A. Atocha, provost judge, Department of the Gulf, be and he is hereby invited to a seat within the bar of this Convention.

MR. GOLDMAN—I move to lay it on the table.

MR. MONTAMAT—I call for the ayes and nays.

Twenty-seven members rose, and the secretary proceeded to call the roll.

YEAS—Messrs. Bailey, Bonzano, Bromley, Ennis, Flagg, Goldman, Gaidry, Henderson, Hills, Maas, Mann, Millspaugh, Montamat, O'Conner—12.

NAYS—Messrs. Abell, Ariail, Austin, Barrett, Baum, Beauvais, Bell, Bennie, Bofill, Brott, Buckley, Burke, Cook J. K., Cook T., Crozat, Cutler, Cazabat, Dufresne, Davies, Duane, Edwards, Fish, Flood, Foley, Fosdick, Fuller, Gastinel, Geier, Healy, Harnan, Hart, Hire, Howell, Howes, Kavanagh, Maurer, Mendiverri, Montamat, Montague, Morris, Murphy E., Murphy M. W., Newell, Normand, O'Conner, Payne J., Pintado, Poynot, Purcell J., Purcell S., Schroeder, Seymour, Schnurr, Shaw, Smith, Spellicy, Stocker, Stumpf, Stiner, Stauffer, Sullivan, Terry, Thorpe, Thomas, Wenck, Wilson—67.

The motion to lay on the table was lost.

MR. THORPE—I offer the following amendment:

"That the resolution include all judicial officers of the parish of Orleans."

The amendment was accepted.

MR. FOLEY—I move to lay the amendment on the table.

The sense of the Convention upon the original resolution was taken *viva voce*, when the president, being unable to decide, ordered a rising vote, and the resolution was adopted as amended by 68 ayes to 8 nays.

MR. BROTT—I offer the following:

Resolved, That the attorney general of this State be and is hereby requested to give to this Convention his legal opinion as to the right of this body to exercise legislative powers and appropriate moneys from the public treasury, &c.

MR. BAUM—I move that it be laid on the table.

The motion was carried.

MR. BROTT—I call for the ayes and nays.

The call was not sustained.

MR. HENDERSON—I wish to have my vote changed on the vote to lay on the table Mr. Montamat's last resolution.

MR. MONTAMAT—I submit the following:

Resolved, That the journal and debates of this Convention be printed by the printer of this Convention in English and French separately, and each member of the Convention be furnished with three copies of the journal and debates for distribution among his constituents, each member to select copies in either language.

MR. THOMAS—I second that resolution.

MR. HILLS—I move to amend by striking out "French."

MR. MONTAMAT—I move to lay that on the table.

MR. S. PURSELL—I move to amend by adding "Spanish."

MR. MONTAMAT—I accept the amendment.

MR. STAUFFER—I move to lay on the table the resolution as amended.

MR. MONTAMAT—It is well known that in the parishes about the city of New Orleans there are a great many persons who do not understand, or even speak English. I infer that the gentleman has not been long in the State of Louisiana, and does not know her population. The parishes below are the same way, and if it is only published in English, they cannot and will not know the proceedings of this Convention. I move the amendment be laid on the table.

MR. HILLS—The gentleman who has just taken his seat has seen fit to intimate that I have not long been a resident of Louisiana. I am not aware that that has anything to do with the question before the Convention; whether I have been here for one year or twenty years, is not a matter in which this Convention is interested. I moved to strike from that resolution the words "and French," for I believe the English language is the official language of this country. I believe in a homogeneous people, in one language and one system of law, and I believe that the publication of the laws of this State, or the proceedings of any convention, or any English court, in the French language, is a nuisance and ought to be abolished in this State or any other.

Mr. President, I made that motion deliberately, and whether the Convention sees fit to adopt it or not, it is my belief that the English language alone should be the language of this State, and if there are any in the State who cannot speak, read or write the language, they should learn to do so before they reside in the country any longer.

MR. HENDERSON—It has been remarked that the majority of the people are French. Now I have just as much right to say, (having a knowledge of some of the parishes,) that the Germans and Irish preponderate over the Americans and French. I have just as good ground for asking an amendment in favor of the Germans, most of whom I know to be intelligent, but they cannot read the English language, or if they can, cannot speak it. Louisiana is behind in many points of view. Many American born citizens of French descent cannot read or write the English language. The provision of our constitution is, that the public records, and judicial and legislative proceedings of the State be promulgated, preserved, and conducted in the language in which the constitution of the United States is written. That language is my doctrine, and I never will vote for any other language but the American. I move that the German language be included, if the French is also used. It is no more right that this particu lar people ask to have our proceedings in French, than for me to go to another country and demand that the laws shall be published in my native language. I believe that the people should be educated in the English language. Our courts say that petitions, etc., may be in French or English, but the judgment must be rendered in English, the sense of which arrangement I do not understand. I do not believe in this half English half French mode of procedure, that we must have all written records in the

English language, while those printed may be in French and English.

Mr. Cazabat—For my part, sir, I coincide partly in these remarks, but we must remember there is a large class of our population—and native born population at that—which comprises the wealthy part of the State, and is deeply interested in its welfare, which is not unfrequently so unacquainted with the English language that they could know nothing in regard to our new constitution and the proceedings of this Convention unless they were written in French. The English is not the constitutional language of the State. I deny it, and cite article 129 of the constitution of 1852, which says the Constitution and laws of this State shall be promulgated in the English and French languages. Sir, I claim this not only as a matter of right to the Creole population, but as a matter of favor. We are here to frame a new constitution in accordance with the progressive spirit of the age. We have the law in our favor. The article states explicitly that the laws shall be promulgated in the English and French languages, and it is not yet repealed. We may repeal it in the constitution we are about to frame, but now it is the supreme law of the land, and therefore let our proceedings be promulgated in French and English.

Mr. Thomas—I think that there is some misapprehension as to the real meaning of these two articles. Ceriainly, sir, the law never required that the proceedings of a legislature or convention of this State should be in any other language than that in which the constitution is written; but in the promulgation of this law, it seems to me to be highly necessary and almost absolutely important. There are many parishes in this State where you cannot find ten men who are familiar with the English language; and how can you ask them to obey laws unless they know them? What expense would it be to have our fundamental law promulgated in French as well as in English? Trifling. We have spent money enough in this very body to have it done, which has been spent foolishly—if I may be permitted to express myself in that manner. The sum of $2500 will promulgate the constitution we adopt.

[Applause in the lobby.]

President—No applause will be allowed in the lobby.

Mr. Thomas—As an American and a man who knows no other language than the English, I view it as a matter not only of courtesy, and following in the footsteps of our ancesters and of ancient usages, but I deem it a matter of right that the French population of the State of Louisiana, born upon the soil and loyal to the government of it, should know what the laws of the land are. For one, I shall vote that they may be promulgated in both languages.

Mr. Bell—We have assembled here to debate upon the interests of the people at large—not one class alone—and it is right that we should, as representatives of the loyal people of Louisiana, give to them what they have a right to claim. It is inconsistent with true liberty that one class should be represented and not another. We profess to represent all classes, and all distinctions in this State, and we have assembled here to make their laws, and make them so they can read them. Many of our constituents are foreigners as well as native born, and they have a right to ask a report of our proceedings in their own language.

Mr. Montamat—I move the amendment be laid on the table.

The question was put, and decided by the chair to be lost.

Mr. Montamat—I call for the yeas and nays.

Twenty-five members acceding, the president directed the secretary to call the roll, with the following the result:

Ayes—Messrs. Abell, Austin, Bailey, Baum, Beauvais, Bell, Bofill, Bonzano, Bromley, Brott, Buckley, Cazabat, Cook J K., Cook T., Crozat, Cutler, Dufresne, Dupaty, Edwards, Ennis, Fish, Flagg, Foley, Fosdick, Fuller, Gastinel, Goldman, Gorlinski, Gaidry, Healy, Hart, Heard, Hire, Howes, Maas, Mann, Maurer, Mendiverri, Millspaugh, Montamat, Murphy M W., Newell, Normand, Pintado, Poynot, Purcell J., Schnurr, Seymour, Shaw, Stocker, Stumpf, Stiner, Sullivan, Terry, Thorpe, Thomas, Wenck—57.

Nays—Messrs. Ariail, Barrett, Burke, Campbell, Davies, Duane, Flood, Geier, Henderson, Hills, Howell, Montague, Morris, O'Conner, Ong, Payne J., Pursell S., Schroeder, Stauffer, Wilson—20.

The resolution was accordingly laid on the table.

MR. GOLDMAN—I wish to amend by adding the German language.

The motion was carried.

MR. STOCKER—I desire to offer a substitute:

Resolved, That the official printer be and he is hereby authorized to print, for the use of this Convention, the journals, in each of the following languages: English, German, French and Spanish.

MR. MONTAMAT—I move to lay it on the table.

MR. TERRY—Mr. President, I move to amend the resolution by adding the "Irish language."

MR. E. MURPHY—Mr. President, I move that it be printed in the English, German and French languages, and no other.

[The president put the question on the amendment of Mr. Terry, and it was carried with hardly a dissenting voice.]

MR. THOMAS—I call for the yeas and nays on the question to print the proceedings in the Irish language.

[The call being seconded by a fifth of the members present, the secretary proceeded to call the roll.]

MR. GOLDMAN—I desire to be excused, because I believe the motion was made for the purpose of casting ridicule on my motion to print the proceedings in the German language.

It appeared that there were sixty-eight nays and eleven ayes, and the amendment was lost.

[Voice—There is no quorum present.]

PRESIDENT—The secretary will call the roll.

[The roll was called and seventy-six members answered to their names.]

MR. GASTINEL—I move to strike out all languages except the English and French, which are now in use in the State.

MR. PRESIDENT—That will come up at the proper time. The question now is on the adoption of the substitute.

MR. MONTAMAT—I move to lay the substitute on the table.

[The motion was carried.]

PRESIDENT—The question is now upon the original motion.

7

MR. GOLDMAN—My amendment to print in German has been carried.

PRESIDENT—The question now is on the original motion to print in English and French.

The question was put to vote and carried.

MR. SULLIVAN—Mr. President, if I am in order, I should like to have the list of members of foreign birth—

PRESIDENT—That is not in order. It may come up at the proper time.

MR. GOLDMAN—Mr. President, I should like to call the attention of the chair to the fact that my amendment to publish the journals and debates in German, as well as in English was carried.

PRESIDENT—I do not understand what the gentleman is saying.

[Mr. Goldman repeated in a little louder tone.]

PRESIDENT—The gentleman is out of order.

MR. SULLIVAN—Mr. President, I should like to call now for the reading of the list of names of those members of foreign birth who have handed in their naturalization papers. Am I in order?

PRESIDENT—No.

MR. PURSELL, of Jefferson—Mr. President, I desire to offer a resolution:

Be it Resolved, That the following be adopted as an article in the constitution of the State of Louisiana: No profession, occupation, business or calling, requiring a license from any authority within this State, shall be exercised or carried on by any other than citizens of the United States, and those having made their legal declaration of becoming citizens.

MR. THOMAS—I move that the resolution be referred to the Committee on General Provisions.

PRESIDENT—It will take that course if no objections are made. [No objections were made.] Gentlemen, I consider these motions out of order. Committees have been appointed to take these matters into consideration and report. Until their report are made, I consider such resolutions out of order.

MR. MAURER—Mr. President, I have a resolution to offer:

Resolved, That the sergeant-at-arms be authorized to procure for each member of this Convention one copy each of five such daily newspapers as he may select.

Mr. Thomas—I move to strike out the word five and insert three.

Mr. Foley—I move to lay the amendment on the table.

[The motion to table the amendment was lost.]

[The amendment was carried and the resolution as amended was adopted.]

Mr. Sullivan—Mr. President, I have a resolution to offer:

Resolved, That the delegates of foreign birth who have not produced their naturalization papers, showing this Convention that they are citizens of the United States, agreeably to resolution passed on Wednesday last, shall produce their naturalization papers immediately, or their seats will de declared vacant in this body.

Mr. Foley—I move to amend so that it shall read that those who have not their papers shall step up and swear that they are naturalized citizens of the United States.

Mr. Bell—Mr. President, I move as a substitute that the secretary now read the names of those who have handed in their papers. Several members are here who have just come from the country. I therefore move to lay all the amendments on the table.

[The motion was put and carried.]

[The original motion was put and lost.]

Mr. Goldman—I now call for the reading of the minutes of to-day's proceedings. I wish to see about that motion of mine.

Mr. Seymour—Mr. President, I have a resolution to offer:

Whereas, The resolution adopted on the 9th inst., requiring the members of this Convention to produce evidence of having taken the oath prescribed by the president, in his proclamation of December 8th, 1863, was intended, and shall be so construed as to apply only to such members, if any, who had not up to that date (the 8th December, 1863,) taken the oath of allegiance to the United States under the previous military orders in the Department;

Be it Resolved, That the resignation of the Hon. Christian Roselius be set aside, and that he be invited to resume his seat as a member of this Convention.

Mr. Davies—I move to lay the resolution on the table.

[The resolution was carried.]

Mr. Fosdick—Mr. President, I have a resolution to offer:

Resolved, That when this Convention adjourns, it adjourns to meet at 3 o'clock P. M., in order to give the various committees time to make up their reports.

[A motion to lay the resolution on the table was carried.]

Mr. President—I move to adjourn to Monday, at 3 o'clock P. M.

Mr. Cazabat—I move to amend by striking out "three" and inserting "five."

Mr. Sullivan—I move to lay the motion on the table.

Mr. Hills—I move to amend.

President—The motion is—

Mr. Hills—I had the floor before the motion was made.

[The chair put the question and it was carried.]

Mr. Hills—I now move that this Convention when it adjourns, adjourn till next Saturday at 4 o'clock P. M. It must be apparent to every one in this hall that this will not be too much time to allow the committees to meet and make up their reports; and it must also be apparent that nothing futher can be done till their reports are made up.

[The question was put and lost.]

Mr. Montamat—I move that each of the committees announced be authorized to appoint and employ a clerk to aid them in carrying out their duties.

[The question was put and the motion carried.]

Mr. Healy—Mr. President, I move that we now adjourn until 3 o'clock P. M. on Monday.

Mr. Fosdick—I amend the motion by striking out "three P. M.," and inserting '12 M."

Mr. Foley—I believe these motions are out of order. It has already been resolved that when we adjourn we adjourn until four o'clock Saturday.

[The question on the amendment of Mr. Fosdick's motion was put, and on a division of the House lost—ayes 24, nays 36.]

[The motion of Mr. Healy was put and lost.]

Mr. Terry—I move that when this Convention adjourns it adjourn until 5 o'clock P. M. on Wednesday next.

[The question was put and on a division of the House carried—ayes 44, nays 20.]

MR. MONTAMAT—There was a resolution passed authorizing the president to appoint a committee.

PRESIDENT—That will come in its order after you get through with your numerous resolutions.

[A motion was made to suspend the rules.]

MR. GOLDMAN—I move to lay that motion on the table.

[The motion was carried.]

PRESIDENT—Are there any more resolutions?

[None were offered.]

The unfinished business, then, is in order. On the Committee on Federal Relations the president appoints Messrs. Thorpe, Brott, Montague, Howell and Henderson.

MR. MONTAMAT—There is another committee provided for in a resolution passed yesterday. I should like to know if it has been appointed.

PRESIDENT—What resolution?

MR. MONTAMAT—The resolution fixing the per diem and providing for the appointment of a committee to fix the compensation of employés and officers of this Convention.

PRESIDENT—Who was the mover of this resolution?

MR. MONTAMAT—Mr. M. W. Murphy.

PRESIDENT—I appoint on this committee Messrs. M. W. Murphy, Terry, Mann, Kugler and Cazabat.

SECRETARY—Mr. Kugler is absent from the city.

PRESIDENT—Then I appoint in his place Mr. Fosdick.

MR. CAZABAT—Mr. President, I ask to be excused from serving on that committee.

MR. HENDERRON—Mr. President, there is another committee to be appointed, to wait on the governor and inform him that the Convention is in session.

PRESIDENT—That committee has been appointed.

MR. AUSTIN—Mr. President, Mr. Cazabat has asked to be excused from serving on the committee on which he has just been named. I move that he be excused.

[The motion was carried.]

PRESIDENT—Mr. Cazabat is excused, and I will appoint Mr. Ennis.

MR. STOCKER—Mr. President, I wish to call up my resolution of yesterday:

Resolved, That the rules and regulations be so amended as to require all ordinances and resolutions to lie over one day (unless referred to some committee) before being acted upon by the Convention.

[The resolution was read.]

[A motion to lay on the table was lost, and the resolution was adopted.]

MR. GOLDMAN—I move that we now adjourn.

[The motion was lost.]

MR. THOMAS—Before we adjourn, I, as chairman of the Committee on Distribution of Powers, have a report to make.

PRESIDENT—That is in order at this time.

Mr. Thomas then read the following report:

Your committee have come to the unanimous conclusion that the constitution of 1852 should not be changed in any respect in the title which treats upon the subject of the distribution of powers, and submit the same to the consideration of the Convention.

MR. BROTT—Mr. President, I move that the report be referred back to the committee, and that they be instructed to incorporate that portion of the constitution of 1852 to which they refer in their report.

[The motion was carried.]

[A motion to adjourn was then made and carried, and the chair declared the Convention adjourned until 5 o'clock on Wednesday next.]

WEDNESDAY, April 20, 1864.

[The House was called to order at 5 P. M., and, after prayer by the Rev. Mr. Andrews, the following gentlemen answered to their names:

Messrs. Abell, Ariail, Austin, Balch, Barrett, Beauvais, Bell, Bonzano, Burke, Campbell, Cazabat, Cook J. K., Cook T., Davies, Dufresne, Duane, Durell, Edwards, Ennis, Flagg, Foley, Fosdick, Fuller, Gaidry, Gastinel, Geier, Goldman, Gorlinski, Gruneberg, Harnan, Hart, Healy, Heard, Henderson, Hills, Howell, Howes, Kavanagh, Knobloch, Mass, Mann, Maurer, Millspaugh, Montamat, Morris, Murphy M. W., Newell, Normand, O'Conner, Payne J., Pintado, Poynot, Purcell J., Pursell S., Schroeder, Shaw, Smith, Spellicy, Stumpf, Stiner, Stauffer, Sullivan, Terry, Thorpe, Thomas, Wilson—64.

The secretary announced that seventy-one members were present, and shortly after the president informed the Convention that seventy-nine were present, and accordingly a quorum.

The minutes of the last session were then read.]

MR. GEIER—I move that the reading of names be dispensed with.

[No objection being made, names were omitted.]

MR. HILLS—As I understand the secretary, he records that the substitute "be published in English, French, German and Spanish," was carried. According to my recollection it was not, and I wish that portion of the minutes read again.

MR. GOLDMAN—I rise to a question of order, and would like to know if, after an amendment has been put and carried, (as was the case in regard to my amendment relating to publication in the German language,) the original motion can be then put and carried, as was here done, when publication was ordered in English and French only?

[The secretary read the minutes again.]

MR. FOSDICK—I have no recollection of making a motion attributed to me by the secretary, and ask for correction.

MR. HILLS—If I understand the minutes, as now read, the substitute and original resolution were adopted. I do not understand—

PRESIDENT—According to the minutes, the final vote was on adopting the original resolution, striking out the amendment, which seems to be carried, that the proceedings shall be printed in the English and French only. In that respect I think that they are correct.

MR. GOLDMAN—I wish to call the attention of the chair to the fact that my amendment to print in German was carried.

PRESIDENT—The final resolution was to adopt the original resolution, which was tantamount to a reconsideration.

MR. FULLER—I cannot consider it so, for I find nothing of that kind in any work on parliamentary law or usage.

MR. STOCKER—I see by the newspaper report that I am reported to have voted against the amendment of the gentleman from New Orleans, (Mr. Goldman,) and if the minutes say the same, I should like to have them corrected, as I voted for it.

MR. GOLDMAN—May I call for the reading of the minutes again, to see if the voting was upon the original motion?

MR. HILLS—I ds not believe a substitute can be amended after adoption. According to those minutes, we are to publish our proceedings in English, German, French and Spanish. I distinctly recollect that the substitute was lost, whereas it appears upon the minutes as having been adopted, which, according to my recollection, is not correct.

MR. STOCKER—My recollection is, that the substitute was adopted.

MR. FOLEY—I move to reconsider the whole.

MR. MONTAMAT—I would like to ask the gentleman whether he voted for the reconsideration?

PRESIDENT—That question does not come up at this time. The question is upon the amendment to the minutes, and if any gentleman wishes to amend, he can so move.

MR. HILLS—I move to strike out "the substitute was adopted," and record it as lost.

PRESIDENT—The substitute?

MR. HILLS—The substitute of the gentleman from Orleans (Mr. Stocker).

MR. AUSTIN—That was laid upon the table.

PRESIDENT—We will settle that. Mr. Secretary, read the minutes again.

[This was done, and upon the question being put, the amendment proposed was carried.]

MR. STOCKER—I would like to know as to how my vote upon the amendment of the gentleman from Orleans (Mr. Goldman) is recorded.

SECRETARY—We have no yeas and nays recorded.

MR. STOCKER—I waive the point.

[The minutes, as amended, were then adopted.]

[No petitions or memorials were presented, and resolutions were accordingly offered.]

MR. HOWELL—I offer the following, to lie over until to-morrow:

Resolved, That hereafter this Convention shall meet at 11 o'clock A. M. and adjourn at 3 o'clock P. M., daily, (Sundays excepted,) and the order of the day shall be promptly taken up at the hour of 12 M. each day.

MR. SMITH—I have a resolution to present:

Resolved, That the Committee on General Provisions be instructed to embody in their report an article or articles, making it obligatory on the first Legislature to convene under the constitution to compel the several parishes, corporations, as well as private citizens throughout the State, that have issued sight drafts, notes or *shinplasters*, payable in Confederate money, or otherwise, to provide for the redemption of the same in current funds.

MR. MONTAMAT—I move this be referred.

PRESIDENT—Out of order.

MR. STOCKER—I wish to call the last gentleman's attention to the rule adopted at the last meeting, requiring all resolutions to lie over unless referred to a special committee; therefore I conceive the gentleman to be in order.

MR. THOMAS—I wish to call the attention of the Convention to rule XXXII according to which every member must make a brief, verbal statement of the matter he presents.

PRESIDENT—That does not apply to resolutions.

MR. MENDIVERRI—I offer the following:

Resolved, That the State auditor furnish this Convention, as soon as practicable, with a statement showing the receipts and expenditures of the State treasury under the administration of General G. F. Shepley, late military governor of the State, as far as the books and records in his possession may show, and expressing each item of receipt and expenditure in detail; also, if any balance was received from the late treasurer; and if so, the amount and the kind and description of funds.

MR. WILSON—I move to lay on the table.

[The motion was lost.]

MR. STOCKER—I wish to call attention again to section XXXII of our rules and regulations.

[The resolution was adopted.]

MR. HILLS—I beg leave to submit this resolution, which I wish to lie over:

Resolved, That the secretary be directed to obliterate from the records of this Convention the resolution inviting A. A. Atocha and the judicial officers of this parish to occupy a seat within the bar of this Convention.

[A motion to lay on the table was decided to be out of order.]

MR. THORPE—In behalf of the gentlemen upon the Enrollment Committee, I submit the following, which I wish handed to the president and then read.

MR. SULLIVAN—I think the gentleman is out of order.

MR. SULLIVAN—When the United States forces took possession of Baton Rouge, they captured the grand statue of Washington and sent it as a trophy to New York City. Now that the State has come back and shown its allegiance to the United States, I hope that the statue will be returned and offer the following in regard to it. [Applause.]

Resolved, That a committee consisting of five members be appointed by the president of this Convention for the purpose of corresponding with and requesting the authorities in Washington City for the return, to the State of Louisiana, of Powers's grand statue of Washington, taken from the Capitol building in Baton Rouge by the United States forces on the occupation of that place by the Federal army, and sent by them as a trophy to adorn the Central Park, in New York City, where it is now placed.

MR. HOWELL—I rise to correct in this resolution a statement of fact. The gentleman says the statue is in New York City. I think he is in error; for when I was in Washington last summer I saw it in the Patent Office, and was informed by the superintendent that as soon as the troubles in Louisiana were at an end, it would be returned to the State. I wish the gentleman would state this fact.

MR. MANN—I rose to state the same fact; and now will corroborate it.

MR. WILSON—I would ask for information. Is it certain that Louisiana was ever out of the Union, as the gentleman asserts? I have understood that never was the case.

[On a *viva voce* vote upon this resolution, the president was unable to decide, and thereupon a rising vote was taken, whereby the resolution was carried—yeas 49, nays 23.]

MR. WENCK—I submit the following:

I move for the reconsideration of the vote adopting the resolution requiring the journal and debates of this Convention to be published in the English and French languages, and furnishing each member with three copies thereof.

MR. MONTAMAT—I move to lay on the table.

MR. MONTAMAT—Did the gentleman vote in favor of the resolution at the last sitting?

Mr. Wenck—Yes, sir.

Mr. Howell—I call for the yeas and nays upon the question of laying on the table.

[The call was sustained and the secretary proceeded to call the roll, with the following result:]

Yeas—Messrs. Abell, Ariail, Austin, Balch, Bailey, Baum, Beauvais, Bell, Bofill, Brott, Buckley, Burke, Cazabat, Cook T., Crozat, Dufresne, Edwards, Ennis, Flagg, Fosdick, Fuller, Gastinel, Gaidry, Harnan, Hart, Hire, Howes, Knobloch, Maurer, Mendiverri, Montamat, Murphy E., Newell, Normand, O'Conner, Pintado, Purcell J., Seymour, Shaw, Sullivan, Terry, Thorpe, Thomas—43.

Nays—Messrs. Barrett, Bonzano, Campbell, Cook J. K., Davies, Duane, Fish, Flood, Foley, Geier, Goldman, Gorlinski, Gruneberg, Healy, Heard, Henderson, Hills, Howell, Kavanagh, Kugler, Maas, Mann, Millspaugh, Montague, Morris, Murphy M. W., Ong, Payne J., Poynot, Pursell S., Schroeder, Smith, Spellicy, Stocker, Stumpf, Stiner, Stauffer, Wenck, Wilson—39.

[The resolution was lost.]

Mr. Thomas—The question is now, I presume, open for discussion. If I understand the object of this reconsideration, it is to strike from the resolution that portion which requires our proceedings to be published in the French language. For one, Mr. President, I am entirely of opinion that the matter stands rightly upon the record now. Almost all of the territory of Louisiana, now under the control and loyal to the government of the United States, outside of New Orleans, is occupied by persons speaking the French language. They have ever been loyal; it is they who will pay the taxes for the support of this Convention, for the enactment of the laws we are about to frame, and yet a large portion of this population understand no other language than the French. Gentlemen who advocate so strongly this reconsideration, forget, Mr. President, that when the American race, the English race, the Anglo-Saxon race came upon the soil of Louisiana, they found here this very people, whom they are now blaming because they do not understand the English tongue. They were here, but because they have not yet learned our customs and government, shall we ostracise them from the knowledge of the laws? I for one would cheerfully have advocated the substitute offered by the gentleman from Orleans, (Mr. Stocker,) had the German race been as largely represented in Louisiana as the French. But that is not the case, and moreover they can almost all speak English, and besides they have never located in whole parishes as have the French. There are many, many of the most wealthy parishes of this State, who will pay very largely into the treasury for the support of the government, where scarcely any of the people can speak or read the English language. I say, Mr. President, that since this is the case, and since it is not proposed to enter and publish official minutes in the French language, that we ought in justice to this large class of people in our State to publish our proceedings in their native tongue for their information.

Mr. Henderson—This question is one of some little importance. The gentleman has stated that a large part of this population are French, but he did not state the fact that the constitution of 1812 nowhere provides for the publication of the proceedings in the French language. This resolution, in the year 1864, seems rather strange, when in the two constitutions of 1845 and 1852 we find nothing of the kind. In the day of Claiborne and Livingston, was it not required that the official proceedings should be published in the language of the American constitution? I ask gentlemen to answer one question, unbiased by prejudice—for I am not any more prejudiced against the Creole population than any other—why, in 1812, when there were only a few Americans upon this soil, the French themselves declared that the language of the Constitution should be American, and now the Americans wish to make French the language as well as English. I say it is a perfect humbug, brought about by the politicians. John Slidell was the great author of it.

I am not prejudiced against this people any more than against the Italians, Portuguese or Spanish; but at the same time I feel that we are an American people, and whatever race they may be, they should, upon American soil, learn to speak our langnage.

Lawyers and judges tell us that every man is bound to know the laws, and that ignorance of it is no plea. Therefore, it makes no difference whether that man understands the language in which the law is written.

I have been in this country twelve or fifteen years and do not understand French, because I am more among Americans. But is that any reason why a man, born upon the soil, can go into a court of justice and have judgment interpreted to him because he does not understand English? or why one-half of a legal proceeding should be in English and the other in French?

Suppose I was brought under French jurisdiction, would I not be compelled to learn the French language and customs? This people have lived here for a series of years, not when there have been but few Americans, but through two generations of them, and is it right for this third Creole generation to come here and say they do not understand the American language?

When you go into a court of justice you find that there is a French and an American side, and while the constitution says that if there is a conflict the American must decide, it practically depends upon the nationality of the judge.

These are my reasons for taking this position. If Frenchmen wish to have our proceedings published, they can do as do the Germans — start national papers; and so with the Spanish and Portuguese, and let them pay for it themselves. It is right that all these should be taxed to support themselves and that people who constitute the majority of the country's population. This population might, on the same principle, go to England and require the proceedings in Parliament to be published in French, and so if they were in Russia, Spain, and among the Choctaws, if you like. I say this is a mere matter of usage, not fit for the contemplation of a philosophic mind, and therefore I hope that a reconsideration may be moved, that our proceedings shall be published in one language, the American language, and nothing else.

Mr. Thorpe—I agree with the last gentleman in my desire for one language, and were it a question before the Legislature, I should oppose it; but the fact is nevertheless patent that we have met for the purpose of framing a constitution for the glory and honer of Louisiana. It is to be for the people of the State, more than one-half of the constituency of which are French. As for the question before this Convention, whether our proceedings should be published in French, I think that it should be done both in French and German.

I would, under no circumstances, support a resolution calculated to insult the intelligence of the people, but I think it will be unfair not to print our proceedings in French, and that it would be money well laid out to do so in German.

The French population have ever been loyal, not entered into this rebellion, but lived quietly under the United States government. I say that this constitution we are now engaged in making should be brought before the people, and that they will labor under a great disadvantage if it is published in a language they do not understand.

Mr. Howell—I shall vote for a reconsideration of this question on two general grounds: the first economy; secondly, that the conditions of the resolution tend to the perpetuation of a distinction which it should be the desire of all good citizens to break down—a local division—a sectional prejudice.

On the point of economy, I would call attention to the purport of the resolution we are seeking to reconsider. That resolution, sir, provides that the journal and debates of this Convention shall be printed in the English and French languages, three copies of which shall be furnished to every member of this Convention in the language which he may select.

The object, it is said, of this resolution is to communicate information to the people of this State, of all the proceedings of this Convention. Will the gentleman inform me, sir, how that is to be effected by this resolution? Are we to send copies of the journal and debates throughout the whole State in order that the people may read them?

If we undertake that, sir, is it possible in the conception of the mind of any gentleman here, that the people of the State will take those volumes and read them through in order to get the cream of what we are doing here? That is imposing upon the people a task they will never perform. Besides that, sir, it is futile, it is impracticable that the journals and debates shall be circulated throughout the State. That is something which has never been done in the history of civilization, nor in any of the States of this Union. We must look to the object of the resolutions and motions we adopt here.

Gentlemen should know that the proceedings here are known to the people of the State and throughout the country, only through the daily publications. They glance over the synopsis of our proceedings, and when they have done that, pass it from their attention. It is of very little consequence to the people of this or any other State, what I or any other gentleman may say in this room. I am not so vain as to desire my speeches circulated in this manner, for I do not believe that the people care enough for them.

I believe this is an enormous expense imposed upon the burdened people of this State, which is unnecessary, and let me say to the gentlemen, that every dollar unnecessarily imposed upon the tax-paying people of the State, will recoil upon the members of this Convention. Let gentlemen remember the condition of the people; let them go through the city, through the country parishes, and see how many of the tax-paying population are barely able to maintain themselves, and even those we burden. [Hear, hear.] Let them remember that the burdens of the people are now almost as many as any people can bear, and this may prove the last feather. [Hear.]

It is doubling the expenses of this Convention, which were already too great. We have even now dipped our hands so deep in the public treasury that we have well nigh reached its bottom. I believe that my resposibility goes beyond this Convention, beyond this great nation. It ascends to the Almighty throne, where I shall have to go and account for my work. I want not the tears, and poverty, and sufferings of the widows and orphans to meet me there and say, "you increased my burdens." [Hear, hear.]

Now, sir, upon the other consideration: it is simply pandering to a distinction unbecoming the people of any State. [Hear, hear.]

I do not believe, Mr. President, that there are any great number of the people of Louisiana incapable of reading the English language who can read French. I contend that whosoever can do the one can do the other, while those who cannot do either will not be benefited by the publication of our proceedings in French.

This tends to prevent the people educating their children in the English language; and the French, we must admit, have but a local habitation, within but a small territory of this country.

English is the national language, and why, then, shall we foster the continuance of a language—in a local sense—simply for the benefit of a people who cannot speak the national tongue? I have a higher respect for the descendants of the original French of this State than to believe they desire it, as I have a higher regard for the intelligence and patriotism of the Creoles of this State and city than to believe they do.

I do not believe, Mr. President, it is desired that the taxes of this State shall be increased doubly, simply to cater to a literary taste, for it is nothing but that.

Gentlemen do not believe in ostracism. I have yet to learn, sir, that such will be the fact. I have yet to learn, Mr. President, that the publication of the laws of Louisiana in the French language has been any benefit to any class of people, or preserved them from ostracism. The native-born population of Louisiana claim not that she shall be distinct from every other State in this nation.

I thank the Convention for their attention.

Mr. Abell—Mr. President, I rise for the purpose of making one or two observations, and I feel somewhat embarrassed when I am compelled to differ with gentlemen of the ability and judgment of those who have already expressed their opinion on this question; but, Mr. President, I have not come here with the intention of conducting the business of this Convention in a picayunish manner. Let us show the people that we appreciate ourselves, and that we are working upon a liberal scale. I cannot see how the printing of the journals and debates in French is going to double the expense of the Convention. It will certainly double the expense of publication. I do not know whether it will have much effect abroad, but I would like to see Louisiana, the first returning State, do the work on a grand scale. When I state to you that the gentleman who has just preceded me receives about thirteen dollars a day, and that my own book shows about double that, you might think it strange if we proposed to carry on the work in anything short of a manly, honorable way.

Were I not, however, from a district which is largely French, I might coincide with the gentleman who has just expressed his views on this question; but my constituents being nearly all French, I feel instructed to go for the publication in French.

Mr. Montamat—I call for the ayes and nays; I want the vote recorded on that question.

[The question was put by the chair and declared lost. A division was called for and the vote stood—ayes 33, nays 40.]

Mr. Montamat—There is no quorum voting; several members here did not vote.

Mr. Hills—I call for the yeas and nays.

[The call was sustained.]

Nays—Messrs. Abell, Austin, Balch, Bailey, Baum, Beauvis, Bell, Bofill, Buckley, Cazabat, Cook T., Crozat, Cutler, Dufresne, Dupaty, Durell, Edwards, Fish, Flagg, Foley, Fuller, Gastinel, Gruneberg, Gaidry, Healy, Hart, Hire, Knobloch, Lobdell, Maurer, Mendiverri, Millspaugh, Montamat, Murphy E., Murphy M. W., Newell, Normand, O'Conner, Pintado, Poynot, Seymour, Shaw, Terry, Thorpe, Thomas—44.

Yeas—Messrs. Ariail, Barrett, Bonzano, Brott, Burke, Campbell, Cook J. K., Davies, Duane, Ennis, Flood, Fosdick, Geier, Goldman, Gorlinski, Harnan, Heard, Henderson, Hills, Howell, Howes, Kavanagh, Kugler, Maas, Mann, Montague, Morris, Ong, Payne J., Pursell S., Schroeder, Smith, Spellicy, Stocker, Stumpf, Stiner, Stauffer, Sullivan, Wenck, Wilson—40.

Mr. Goldman—Mr. President, I wish to call attention to rule XV, which reads as follows:

XV. No member shall vote on any question in the result of which he has a separate and distinct interest, nor in any case when he was not within the bar of the Convention when the question was put. And when any member shall ask leave to vote, the president shall propound to him the question: *Were you within the bar when the question was put?* But when the yeas and nays are taken, and any member asks leave to vote, the president shall inquire of him whether he was within the bar *when his name was called?*

Mr. Fish voted on this question, and, as printer to the Convention, he is interested in it.

Mr. Fish—I desired to be excused from voting, but the chair insisted, and the Convention did not excuse me.

President—I do not think the case comes under the rule—ayes 40, nays 44. The resolution is lost.

Mr. Howell—Mr. President, I have two resolutions which I wish to have read and to be laid over till to-morrow.

Mr. Gorlinski—Mr. President, I have a resolution which I wish to offer.

[Secretary read:]

Resolved, That the regular hour for the meeting of this Convention, during the remainder of its sittings, shall be 12 o'clock M., and any member not answering to his name, when the roll is called, shall forfeit the sum of two dollars, to be deducted from his per diem, and any member who shall be absent from his seat an entire day, shall forfeit his per diem for each day he shall fail to attend, unless absent by permission of the Convention, or for sickness, either in his own person or family, the proof of which shall be a certificate from a regular physician.

Resolved, further, That the secretary keep a record of the names of all members not answering at roll-call, and the names of all members who shall be absent from their seats an entire day, and for each day so absent, unless they have leave of absence from the Convention, and to make a list of said members at the end of every week, a copy of which shall be furnished the Committee on Finance and a copy to the President of the Convention, who will strictly enforce the penalties as prescribed in the foregoing resolution.

Mr. Waters—Mr. President, I move to lay the resolution on the table.

Mr. Stocker—Mr. President, I do not

rise to debate this question, for I know it is not debatable, but I would like to have my resolution to amend the rules and regulations read, for the information of the Convention. I think that contains a provision applicable to such a case as this, and which will do away with so many motions.

PRESIDENT—Mr. Secretary, read the resolution.

[The secretary read :]

Resolved, That the rules and regulations be so amended as to require all orders and resolutions to lie over one day, unless referred to some committee before being acted upon by the Convention.

PRESIDENT—Under that rule the resolution must lie over.

MR. GAIDRY—Mr. President, I have a resolution to offer, to lie over under the rule.

[The secretary read :]

Whereas, All the constitutions ever framed in this State have decreed that all judicial and legislative proceedings should take place in the French and English language;

And whereas, Several members of this Convention, who are true republicans and loyal to the core, but are not very familiar with the English language, have been delegated to this Convention by constituents who are also unacquainted with the said language—which right to choose delegates as they please said constituents possessed and that to deny such supreme right would be tantamount to disfranchise said people;

Resolved, That all resolutions and motions to be presented in this Convention be translated into the French language, so that the members from the several parishes, who are not familiar with the English language, may be fully aware of what they are voting upon.

MR. SULLIVAN—Mr. President, I move to lay the resolution on the table.

PRESIDENT—Under the rules, it must lie over till to-morrow.

MR. MONTAMAT—Mr. President, I wish to give notice that I shall, at the next sitting of the Convention, move an amendment to the fifty-second section of the rules and regulations, relative to the ayes and noes.

MR. HOWELL—Mr. President, I call for the reading of my resolutions.

MR. CAZABAT—I see that a great deal of the time of this Convention has been wasted in discussing matters not immediately connected with the object for which the Convention was called. Instead of amending and revising the Constitution we are discussing the money in the public treasury, the administration of Goveronor Shepley, and a variety of other questions which I consider are not necessary to promote the object for which we were called together. I therefore offer this resolution for the purpose of preventing discussions on matters not applicable to the duties of the Convention, and not properly coming before us :

Whereas, This Convention assembled for the purpose only of *revising and amending the Constitution of Louisiana,* and for no other purpose,

Be it Resolved, That no resolution on any other subject than that above stated, shall be received or entertained by this Convention.

PRESIDENT—The resolution will lie over till to-morrow.

MR. HARNAN—Mr. President I call for the reading of Judge Howell's resolutions.

MR. WENCK—Mr. President I have a resolution to offer.

[The secretary read :]

Resolved, That the resolution adopted allowing each member of this Convention ten dollars a day be repealed.

PRESIDENT—Under the rule it lies over.

[The secretary read the resolutions of Mr. Howell, viz :]

Resolved, That the resolution adopted on Friday, 15th April, 1864, in the following words, to-wit:

"*Be it Resolved,* That the sum of one hundred thousand dollars be and the same is hereby appropriated out of the general fund, for the purpose of paying the members, officers and employés of this Convention, the mileage and per diem to which they are respectively entitled; the same to be paid by the treasurer of the State, on the warrant of the president of the Convention," be and the same is hereby repealed.

Resolved, first, That the resolution adopted on Friday, 15th April, 1864, in the following words, to-wit: "*Resolved,* That the members of this Convention shall receive from the public treasury a compensation for their services, which shall be ten dollars per day during their attendance on, going to and returning from the sessions of this Convention," be and the same is hereby rescinded.

Resolved, second, That the compensation for the services of the members of this Convention shall be the same as allowed to the members of the General Assembly by the constitution adopted in 1852.

MR. GOLDMAN—I second these resolutions.

MR. MONTAMAT—Mr. President, this has been introduced and voted down already.

PRESIDENT—Under the rule it lies over till to-morrow.

MR. AUSTIN—Mr. President, I rise to a point of order in regard to that last resolution.

PRESIDENT—The question will come up to-morrow, it is not subject to debate now.

MR. AUSTIN—I am aware that the question will come up to-morrow, but I ask for information.

PRESIDENT—Make your objection to-morrow.

MR. GOLDMAN—Mr. President, I offer the following resolution:

Resolved, That the amendment to publish an official report in the German language is hereby embodied in the original motion to publish in the English and French languages.

PRESIDENT—The resolution is out of order.

MR. CAZABAT—Mr. President, the resolution of Mr. Sullivan respecting Powers's statue of Washington was adopted against the rule. I ask now that the motion adopting it be reconsidered, in order that the resolution may lie over till to-morrow.

MR. SULLIVAN—I have no objection to having the resolution lie over.

[The secretary read.

The question, upon its acceptance, was put to the Convention and carried.]

PRESIDENT—I appoint on Statue Committee Mr. Mendiverri.

MR. MURPHY—Mr. President, I have a report to make.

PRESIDENT—The next business in order is the reports of standing committees. They will be called in their order. Committee on Emancipation.

MR. BONZANO—Mr. President, as chairman of the committee I would state that the committee has made progress, but is not ready to report.

PRESIDENT—Committee on Preamble.

MR. HEARD—Mr. President, as chairman of that committee I beg leave to submit the following report:

To the honorable the president and members of the Constitutional Convention :

The committee appointed by the president to prepare a preamble to the constitution which is to be framed by the Convention, beg leave to make the following report:

They have thought it best to adopt the preamble to the constitutions of eighteen hundred and forty-five and fifty-two—which read as follows: "We, the people of the State of Louisiana, do ordain and establish this constitution," and recommend its adoption.

Respectfully submitted,
H. J. HEARD, *Chairman*.

MR. HARNAN—I move that the report lie over till to-morrow.

[This motion not being seconded, a motion to adopt was made and carried.]

PRESIDENT—Committee on Distribution of Powers.

MR. THOMAS—As chairman of that committee I submit the following report:

REPORT OF COMMITTEE ON DISTRIBUTION OF POWERS.

Your Committee on Distribution of Powers respectfully submit the following report:

That Articles Nos. 1 and 2 of the constitution of 1852 ought not, in any manner, to be altered or changed, which articles read as follows:

Art. 1. The powers of the government of the State of Louisiana shall be divided into three distinct departments, and each of them be confided to a separate body of magistracy, to-wit: Those which are legislative to one, those which are executive to another, and those which are judicial to another.

Art. 2. No one of these departments, nor any person holding office in one of them, shall exercise power properly belonging to either of the others, except in the instances hereinafter expressly directed or permitted.

All of which is respectfully submitted,
JOHN W. THOMAS, *Chairman*.

[The report was adopted.]

PRESIDENT—Committee on Legislation.

MR. FOSDICK—I have to report that we have made some progress, but owing to the absence of several members in the country, we shall not be able to report for several days.

PRESIDENT—Committee on Executive Department.

MR. FISH—We have had one or two meetings, but are not yet ready to report.

PRESIDENT—Committee on the Judiciary.

MR. HOWELL—The committee reports progress.

PRESIDENT—Committee on Impeachment.

MR. WILSON—Mr. President, your committee respectfully report that the provisions of the constitution of 1852 upon this subject, which can easily be found, are fully up to the spirit of the age, and ought not in any manner to be changed.

The provisions are as follows, [read from the Revised Statutes :]

The power of impeachment shall be vested in the House of Representatives.

Impeachment of the governor, lieutenant governor, attorney general, secretary of state, state treasurer, and of the judges of the inferior courts, justices of the peace excepted, shall be held by the Senate; the chief justice of the Supreme Court, or the senior judge thereof, shall preside during the trial of such impeachment. Impeachments of the judges of the Supreme Court shall be tried by the Senate. When sitting as a court of impeachment the Senators shall be upon oath or affirmation, and no person shall be convicted without the concurrence of two-thirds of the senators present.

Judgment in cases of impeachment shall extend only to the removal from office and disqualification from holding any office of honor, trust or profit under the State; but the convicted parties shall, nevertheless, be subject to indictment, trial and punishment according to law.

All officers against whom articles of impeachment be preferred, shall be suspended from the exercise of their functions during the pendancy of such impeachment; the appointing power may make a provisional appointment to replace any suspended officer until the decison of the impeachment.

The Legislature shall provide by law for the trial, punishment, and removal from office of all other officers of the State by indictment or otherwise.

Mr. Hills—Mr. President, I move that the report be referred back to the committee, and that they be instructed to incorporate in their report such provisions of the constitution of 1852 as they recommend for adoption.

[The question on referring back was put and carried.]

President—Committee on General Provisions.

Mr. Mann—As chairman, I simply report progress. The committee is not yet ready to report.

President—Internal Improvements.

Mr. Gorlinski—I beg leave to report that the committee is not yet prepared to report.

President—Public Education.

Mr. Hills—Mr. President, I will report that four members of our committee are absent—at least, they have taken no part in our action. Seven of us have, however, held three meetings, and have made progress in the work, and will probably be ready to report very soon.

President—Committee on Mode of Revising the Constitution.

Mr. Cutler—As chairman, I can only report progress. It may be necessary for most of the other committees to report before our report is made.

President—Committee on Schedule.

Mr. Gruneberg—Mr. President, the committee is not ready to report.

President—Committee on Ordinance.

Mr. Shaw—This being the provision that puts the constitution in operation, we shall not be able to report until most of the other committees have reported, until we know what we have to put in operation.

President—Committee on Enrollment.

Mr. Thorpe—All enrolled bills are in the hands of the president.

President—Committee on Finance.

Mr. Brott—The committee have no finances on hand and have not had occasion to draw any warrants.

President—Committee on Expenses.

Mr. Pursell, of Jefferson—No report.

President—Committee on Printing.

Mr. Purcell, of Orleans—No report.

President—Committee on Federal Relations.

Mr. Thorpe—Mr. President, the committee has met several times, but is not prepared to report.

Mr. Wilson—I move that we adjourn till 5 o'clock P. M., on Monday next, in order to give the committees time to report.

Mr. Fosdick—Mr. President, I amend to 12 o'clock.

Mr. Montamat—I amend to 12 o'clock on Saturday.

Mr. Terry—Mr. President, I amend to to-morrow at 12 o'clock.

[The president put the question on the adjournment till Saturday, and declared it carried.]

Mr. Harnan—I move to adjourn till to-morrow at 12 o'clock.

[The question was put and lost.]

Mr. Harnan—I move to adjourn till to-morrow at 10 o'clock A. M.

Mr. Terry—I move to amend by substituting 12 M., for 10 o'clock A. M.

[The amendment was carried, and the motion as amended adopted, when the president declared the Convention adjourned.]

Thursday, April 21, 1864.

[At 12 o'clock the president called the Convention to order, and Rev. T. W. Gilbert opened the proceedings with prayer.]

Mr. Heard—Mr. President, I rise to a question of privilege, to ask a leave of absence for Mr. Schnurr, on account of sickness in his family.

President—That can come up after the roll is called. Mr. Secretary, call the roll.

[The roll was called, and the following members answered to their names:

Messrs. Abell, Ariail, Austin, Bailey, Balch, Barrett, Beauvais, Bell, Bofill, Bonzano, Brott, Buckley, Burke, Campbell, Cazabat, Cook J. K., Crozat, Davies, Duane, Dufresne Durell, Edwards, Ennis, Fish, Flagg, Flood, Foley, Fosdick, Fuller, Geier, Goldman, Gorlinski, Gruneberg, Gaidry, Healy, Harnan, Hart, Heard, Henderson, Hills, Hire, Howell, Howes, Kavanagh, Knobloch, Kugler, Maas, Mann, Maurer, Mendiverri, Millspaugh, Montamat, Montague, Murphy E., Murphy M. W., Newell, Normand, O'Conner, Poynot, Pursell S., Schroeder, Seymour, Shaw, Smith, Spellicy, Stumpf, Stiner, Stauffer, Sullivan, Terry, Thorpe, Thomas, Wenck—77.

The secretary read the minutes of the previous day's proceedings.]

Mr. Heard—Mr. President, I wish to resume my motion to grant a leave of absence to Mr. Schnurr, on account of sickness in his family.

Mr. Goldman—Mr. President, I wish to know before the minutes are adopted—I now ask the permission of the chair to appeal from its decision deciding my motion out of order yesterday. I did not understand the decision yesterday, or I should have appealed from it at the time.

President—The gentleman is out of order. The question is upon the adoption of the minutes.

[The minutes were then adopted.]

Mr. Thomas—Mr. President, I would ask to be excused from attendance to-day, as I am suffering severely from toothache.

[The question was put to the Convention, and Mr. Thomas was excused.]

Mr. Goldman—Mr. President, is my appeal now in order?

President—I think so.

Mr. Goldman—If it is in order, I would move that the decision of the chair be sustained.

Mr. Healy—Mr. President, I would like to have every gentleman addressing the chair speak loud enough so that all the members can hear him. In this part of the house we cannot hear half the motions that are made.

Mr. Heard—Mr. President, I have a resolution to offer.

President—Mr. Secretary, read the motion.

[The secretary read:]

I move that a leave of absence be granted to Mr. Schnurr, on account of illness in his family.

President—If there are no objections, it will be granted.

[No objections were made.]

President—Resolutions are now in order.

Mr. Shaw—Mr. President, I would ask, for information, whether new resolutions are in order now, or whether the resolutions offered yesterday are to be called up?

President—New resolutions are in order.

Mr. Gorlinski—Mr. President, I have a resolution to offer, as follows:

Whereas, On the evacuation of Baton Rouge, after the ever-memorable battle of the 5th day of August, 1862, Colonel Payne, of the Fourth Wisconsin Volunteers, then commanding the post of Baton Rouge, crowned his heroic deeds of that day by an act which has secured to the use of this Convention and the State a valuable public library, together with Thorpe's great painting of Gen. Zachary Taylor, and other paintings, which now adorn the hall of this Convention, and also saved Hiram Powers's statue of Washington, which is said now to be in the Patent Office at the national capital—all of which would have been stolen or destroyed by the fire, which demolished the State House, had not Colonel Payne caused the same to be removed to this city, where, by order of General Butler, they were protected as the property of the State; therefore, be it

Resolved, That the thanks of this Convention and of the people of Louisiana, are due and are hereby tendered to Major General B. F. Butler and Colonel Payne, for saving the above-mentioned valuable State property.

Resolved further, That the Governor be, and is hereby requested, to correspond with the authorities at Washington, and make suitable arrangements for the return and reception of the above-mentioned statue of Washington and its future disposition in this State.

Mr. Campbell—Mr. President, I have a resolution which I wish to offer, to lie over till to-morrow:

Whereas, The United States bounty paid to soldiers enlisting in the army cannot be paid to men enlisting in the First and Second Regiments of New Orleans Volunteers, now being raised under Colonels Killborn and Brown, because of their being organized for a specific purpose, that of the city defence alone, and wishing to aid in filling the same,

Resolved, That the sum of ——— dollars be, and the same is hereby appropriated by the State, to pay a bounty to each man who may hereafter enlist in the First and Second Regiments of New Orleans volunteers, and that the governor is hereby authorized to carry the same into effect according to his best judgment.

Mr. Seymour—Mr. President, I move to lay the resolution on the table.

Mr. Stocker—Mr. President, is it proper to make a motion that that proposition be printed and laid upon the desk of each member to-morrow morning?

[The president put the question, and declared it lost.]

Mr. Sullivan—Mr. President, I would like to hear the motion explained. Many of us could not hear it.

[A division was called for.]

President—Those in favor of the motion will rise and be counted by the secretary.

[The secretary counted twenty-seven ayes.]

Mr. Healy—I would like to have the resolution read, Mr. President; we could not hear it here.

President—Read the resolution, Mr. Secretary.

[The secretary read the resolution.]

Mr. Stocker—Mr. President, my object in making the motion is this: I desire to know and for the members to know what the resolution is, in order that we may act understandingly upon it; and in order to effect this object, I merely move to have the resolution printed and laid on the desks of the members in the morning, so that all may know what it is.

President—You will have it printed in the morning journals at any rate. The question is upon printing. Those in favor of it will rise and be counted by the secretary.

Secretary—Ayes, 34.

President—Contrary will rise.

Secretary—Nays, 36.

President—The motion is lost.

Mr. Hills—Mr. President, I offer the following resolution, to lie over under the rules:

Resolved, That rule XXXIV be so amended as to require members to read the same or explain them from their seats.

Mr. Stocker—Mr. President, I move a suspension of the rules in order that that resolution may be acted upon at once.

Mr. Stauffer—Mr. President, I ask for the reading of the resolution.

The secretary read the resolution.

Mr. Stauffer—I think that rule LII is almost entirely word for word like the resolution the gentleman offers.

Mr. Hills—Mr. President, I think that the chair has decided that that rule does not apply to resolutions.

President—It does not cover resolutions The question is upon a suspension of the rules.

[Upon taking the vote the chair announced the motion carried. A division was called for—ayes 54, nays 5.]

Mr. Stocker—I move the adoption of the resolution, Mr. President.

[The question was put and carried unanimously.]

Mr. Henderson—Mr. President, I believe that the rules have been suspended, and any party who has the floor can call up a motion at any time, and that a party who has the floor can make a motion.

President—The rule is suspended for the purpose of acting upon that resolution.

Mr. Stocker—That was my motion.

President—Reports of standing committees are now in order. They will be called in their order.

Committee on Emancipation.

MR. BONZANO—The committee can only report progress.

PRESIDENT—Judiciary Committee.

MR. HOWELL—The committee reports progress.

PRESIDENT—Committee on Impeachment.

MR. WILLSON—The committee is prepared to report.

[The secretary commenced to read the report.]

MR. HILLS—Mr. President, I rise to a point of order. I believe that rule XXXII requires the reading of that report by the member who presents it, or a statement of its contents.

MR. HENDERSON—I would like to have this question decided. I think it does not apply to the report of a committee.

PRESIDENT—I think you are right—the gentleman will do as he pleases.

[Mr. Wilson read:]

To the president and members of the Convention to "Revise and Amend the Constitution of Louisiana."

Your committee respectfully submit the following report:

The power of impeachment shall be vested in the House of Representatives.

Impeachments of the governor, lieutenant governor, attorney general, secretary of state, State treasurer, and the judges of the inferior courts, justices of the peace excepted, shall be held by the Senate; the chief justice of the Supreme Court, or the senior judge thereof, shall preside during the trial of such impeachment. Impeachments of the judges of the Supreme Court shall be tried by the Senate. When sitting as a Court of Impeachment the senators shall be upon oath or affirmation, and no person shall be convicted without the concurrence of two-thirds of the senators present.

Judgments in cases of impeachment shall extend only to removal from office and disqualification from holding any office of honor, trust or profit under the State; but the convicted parties shall, nevertheless, be subject to indictment, trial and punishment, according to law.

All officers against whom articles of impeachment may be preferred, shall be suspended from the exercise of their functions during the pendancy of such impeachment; the appointing power may make a provisional appointment to replace any suspended officer until the decision of the impeachment.

The Legislature shall provide by law for the trial, punishment and removal from office of all other officers of the State by indictment or otherwise.

JOS. H. WILSON, Chairman.
A. J. BAILEY,
CHARLES SMITH,
L. GASTINEL,
ROBT. MORRIS.

MR. FOLEY—I move that 200 copies be printed for the use of the Convention.

PRESIDENT—Committee on General Provisions.

MR. MANN—Not yet ready to report, Mr. President.

PRESIDENT—Committee on Internal Improvement.

MR. GORLINSKI—Not yet ready to report.

PRESIDENT—Committee on Public Education.

MR. HILLS—The committee have held three meetings, and will probably be ready to report to-morrow.

PRESIDENT—Enrollment.

No report.

PRESIDENT—Finances.

MR. BROTT—No report.

PRESIDENT—Expenses.

MR. PURSELL, of Jefferson—No report.

PRESIDENT—Printing.

MR. PURCELL, of Orleans—No report.

PRESIDENT—Federal Relations.

MR. THORPE—The committee will probably be ready to make their report to-morrow.

PRESIDENT—The next business in order will be the calling up of the resolutions offered yesterday.

MR. GASTINEL—Mr. President, I rise to a point of order. There are several special committees to report yet.

MR. M. W. MURPHY—Mr. President, I have a report of a special committee, which I wish to offer.

PRESIDENT—Reports of special committees are next in order.

MR. GASTINEL—Mr. President, as chairman of the committee appointed to wait upon the governor, and inform him that the Convention was in session, and ready to receive any communication he might have to make, I beg leave to submit the following report:

On behalf of the committee appointed to wait upon his excellency the governor, and inform him that the Convention was organized, and to inquire whether he had any communication to make to this body, I beg leave to report:

That the committee waited upon his excellency, who, in substance, replied that he did not consider that it would be becoming, nor within his province, to transmit a message or make suggestions or recommendations to the Convention, but that he would stand ready at any time to afford all facilities and information that may be required by this body from the executive department.

The committee having done their duty, beg leave to be discharged.

GASTINEL, *Chairman.*

MR. FOLEY—Mr. President, I move that the report be accepted and the committee discharged.

MR. STAUFFER—Mr. President, I rise to a point of order.

PRESIDENT—Mr. Secretary, read the other report.

[The secretary read :]

Mr. President—Your committee on fixing the compensation of officers and employés of the Convention, make the following report:

John E. Neelis, secretary	$14	per day
Thomas H. Murphy, assistant secretary	10	...
S. G. Hamilton, assistant secretary	10	...
Michael DeCoursey, sergeant-at-arms	10	...
Two assistant sergeants-at-arms, each	5	...
Two messengers, each	5	...
One postmaster	5	...
One doorkeeper	5	...
One reporter and three assistants, each	6	...
One warrant clerk	6	...
Enrolling clerks, each	6	...

In relation to the compensation of the printer of the Convention, your committee ask for further time to report.

The mileage of all members from the country parishes twenty cents per mile, going and coming.

All compensation to officers and employés shall commence from the day of their election or appointment.

(Signed) M. W. MURPHY, Chairman.
GEO. A. FOSDICK,
J. RANDALL TERRY,
W. D. MANN.

MR. HEARD—I move to recommit that report to the committee. I see several omissions in it. I have had the honor of representing constituencies in several deliberative bodies, and I never before saw the president omitted in that report. In 1852 the president received eight dollars per day, and the members but four. I think it is an oversight on the part of the committee to treat the president in such a manner, and that the matter needs further attention from the committee.

MR. FOSDICK—Mr. President, before that question is put, as a member of that committee, I would state that the question was raised in the committee room. We referred to the proceedings of the Convention of 1852, and found no mention made of the compensation of the president. In that Convention there was one reporter, who was paid $10 per day, the secretary was paid $14 per day, an assistant received $10, the sergeant-at-arms $8, and the other employés the rates elsewhere reported.

PRESIDENT—Gentlemen, the question is on the motion to recommit.

[The motion was carried.]

MR. STAUFFER—Mr. President, I rise to a point of order. At an early day of the session of this Convention, a committee was appointed to investigate and report the circumstances of an assault upon some of the members of this Convention; that committee, has failed to report progress. I now move that they be requested to report.

MR. WILSON—That committee will be able to report progress in a few days. It is a much more serious matter than we at first thought. It requires a great deal of investigation; some of the witnesses are at the barracks.

PRESIDENT—The next business in order will be the resolutions offered yesterday. Gentlemen will call them up from their seats.

MR. HOWELL—Mr. President, I call for the resolution in regard to fixing the hours for meeting. I believe it is the first in order.

PRESIDENT—Mr. Secretary read the resolution.

[The secretary read it.]

MR. STAUFFER—Mr. President, I move to amend so that it will read that hereafter this Convention shall meet at ten o'clock, and to strike out the words "adjourn at three o'clock P. M."

MR. WILSON—I move, as a substitute that it meet permanently at five o'clock P. M.

MR. GOLDMAN—Mr. President, I move to lay that motion on the table.

[The motion was carried.]

MR. STAUFFER—I will withdraw my amendment, except as to the words "adjourn at three o'clock."

MR. SULLIVAN—I move to substitute twelve o'clock.

PRESIDENT—The question is upon the amendment to twelve o'clock.

[The question was carried, and the President declared the amendment adopted.]

PRESIDENT—The motion, as adopted, is to meet at twelve o'clock, and take up the order of the day at twelve o'clock.

MR. BROTT—Mr. President, I move to amend by substituting "take up the order of the day at one o'clock."

MR. HOWELL—Mr. President, I move to amend by adding the words, "and adjourn regularly at four o'clock."

MR. BELL—I move to lay the amendment on the table.

[The motion was carried.]

MR. CAZABAT—Mr. President, I call for the resolution I offered yesterday. The character of that resolution is such that if it is adopted by the Convention much of this discussion will be avoided, and, it is to be hoped, more business done.

Secretary reads:

Whereas, This Convention is assembled for the purpose only of *revising and amending the constitution of Louisiana,* and for no other purpose;

Be it Resolved, That no resolution on any other subject but that above stated, shall be received or entertained by this Convention.

MR. BELL—I move to lay the resolution on the table.

[The motion was carried.]

MR. SULLIVAN—Mr. President, I call up my resolution, offered yesterday, in relation to Powers's statue of Washington.

MR. HENDERSON—Mr. President, my opinion is that our rules require the resolutions to be numbered and called up in their regular order, according to their numbers, and discussed or postponed accordingly.

PRESIDENT—Mr. Secretary, read the resolution.

Secretary read:

Resolved, That a committee, consisting of five members, be appointed by the president of this Convention for the purpose of corresponding with and requesting the authorities in Washington City for the return, to the State of Louisiana, of Powers's grand statue of Washington, taken from the Capitol building at Baton Rouge, by the United States, on the occupation of that place by the Federal army, and sent by them as a trophy to adorn the Central Park in New York City, where it is now placed.

MR. GORLINSKI—Mr. President, I offer a substitute.

PRESIDENT—It is out of order. The substitute should have been offered when the resolution was, yesterday.

MR. WILSON—Mr. President, I would like to have the resolution read again. I did not hear it. I expect it was my own fault, but I desire to know what it is before I vote on it.

[The secretary re-read the resolution.]

MR. BELL—Mr. President, I move to lay the resolution on the table.

[The motion to table was lost, and on putting the original motion the chair decided it carried.

A division was called, and a rising vote showed 51 ayes to 21 nays.]

PRESIDENT—I appoint on that committee Messrs. Sullivan, Stiner, Burke, Ennis and Waters.

MR. SMITH—Mr. President, I call up my resolution offered yesterday.

PRESIDENT—Mr. Secretary, read the resolution.

Secretary read:

Resolved, That the Committee on General Provisions be instructed to embody in their report an article, or articles, making it obligatory on the first Legislature to convene under the constitution, to compel the several parishes, corporations, as well as private citizens, throughout the State, that have issued sight drafts, notes or *shinplasters,* payable in Confederate money, or otherwise, to provide for the redemption of the same in current funds.

MR. HARNAN—I move the adoption of the resolution.

MR. HENDERSON—I believe it is open to debate.

MR. BAUM—I move to lay the resolution on the table.

MR. SMITH—I would like to say to the

member who moved to lay it on the table, that it involves a matter of more importance than most people are aware of. It is now in the hands of poor men, mechanics and laborers, who have earned it by hard labor; taken it because it was in a measure forced upon them—men who are loyal, and never had any faith in Confederate currency, and took it because they knew the men who issued it had property to redeem it. Under such circumstances, are they going to lose it? I say that if men here move to lay such a resolution on the table for the purpose of cutting off debate on it, their constituents will not bear them out in such action.

Mr. Montague—Mr. President, I would like to know if this is a legislative body? The question is clearly one for legislative action.

Mr. Stocker—Mr. President, I rise to a point of order. A resolution to lay on the table is not debatable.

[The president put the question, and on a rising vote it was lost. Ayes 32, nays 36.]

Mr. Wilson—I call for the ayes and noes on this question. This is a precedent, and I want to see how members vote on it.

Mr. Duane—Mr. President, I move that the question is open for debate.

President—The question is now open to debate on the motion to adopt the resolution.

Mr. Henderson—This question, sir, is of high importance to this Convention, for we are about to legislate on that which involves the fundamental law of the land, which appropriately is within the jurisdiction of another body. Every one understands that, according to military rule in Mississippi, trafficking in Confederate money is permitted within the Federal lines; whereas, in Louisiana, the money is not only forfeited, but the transaction is a criminal offence. What is to be the law of the land, the action of the State or of the military power? I say the latter. If we go on to-day and say that shinplasters, payable in Confederate money, shall be redeemed in Federal money, we are immediately in conflict with the Federal government.

Gen. Banks cares nothing for the decisions of our courts, and we might as well say to-day that there shall be a provision in the constitution by which the property of those persons who belong to the Confederate government is not that of enemies. We should not legislate upon a question involving a conflict with the constitution of the United States and the military power, or when the decision of that question belongs to another body, in times of peace, much less in these times of trouble. Even this case has been reasoned upon. If an auctioneer sells property and takes the currency of a *de facto* Confederate government, and is not called upon to pay them until the Federal government is restored, the money being in the meantime on deposit, there is an unsettled question as to his liability. You may put a valuation on it, but cannot order a note to be paid in Confederate money; and if you do you come in conflict with the military power, which is paramount now. As I said, this is a delicate question, which we should lay over to times of peace, when *we* can pass upon it.

Suppose a man owes me ten thousand dollars, and Confederate money is worth ten cents on the dollar, would he come into a court of justice as a Union man and pay me in Confederate money? No, the courts would oblige him to pay in Federal money. I say that such a debt cannot now be paid in Confederate money; *you* cannot do it. In other times such money *was* considered good, and if tendered you were bound to take it. Did not Congress judge that President Lincoln had no right to issue greenbacks? Yes; but that is a question of power. Let the Supreme Court decide that question; it is not for us to say. Judge Atocha, of the Provost Court, orders that Confederate money shall be delivered to the rightful owners, but they cannot pass it without committing a criminal offence if they do; they all become *particeps crimini* through violating a criminal law. I owe ten thousand dollars, and offer Confederate money in payment; my debtor states the case to Judge Atocha and I am put in prison, for military law is paramount.

Military law is the law of necessity, and because of that, civil law must yield when it conflicts with it.

I do not speak of any gentleman's motive, whether he be for or against this resolution. At some time we can, perhaps, consider this matter, but is *this* the time for action? I think we should not *now* consider or take action upon it.

MR. CAZABAT—I take it for granted that the members of this Convention are assembled here for one purpose, and for one purpose alone; that is to revise and amend the constitution of Louisiana. Our power so far is suprême; but I do not see how the position can be admitted, even for argument's sake, that we have a right to legislate on any other topic whatsoever. I, for my part, sir, firmly believe, right or wrong, that it would be the worst policy, and most insane and mischievous, to legislate upon matters which do not properly come before us.

We are here, sir, by what authority? By the military authority; by orders from the commanding general of this department. For what purpose? For the purpose I have already stated, to revise and amend the constitution of Louisiana.

MR. STOCKER—I, for one, sir, shall object to and vote against every resolution and motion that is not connected with the great object we have in view.

Sir, I have in my mind a few of the motives which induced Mr. Smith to introduce this resolution. I have no doubt but that he intends to do what is right, or that his sentiments and opinions are for the benefit of the people he represents, but this is not the time to discuss the merits or demerits of this resolution. Whether it is injurious or benefical to the people of Louisiana, it is not for me to say, for such discussion does not belong to this body. I think of it as I do of the resolution relating to Washington's statue and Gov. Shepley's administration.

I wish so to place myself before this Convention—not only before *it*, but my constituency— the people of Louisiana, the American people, the world and my conscience, that when I stand before Almighty God, I shall have to be answerable neither in word or action for anything which may be detrimental to the benefit of the people of Louisiana. With these remarks I leave the subject.

MR. CUTLER—I cannot see any good reason why the request of the gentleman from the parish of St. Mary should be granted. I see no reason why we should hesitate to act on any grave and important question that arises. All the gentleman desires, it seems to me is, that the Committee on General Provisions take into consideration the subject matter of his application, and report their deliberations thereon. Now, it is true that this body has assembled for no other purpose than to make the organic law of the State of Louisiana; in other words, to build a foundation for the Legislature of the State to build a great structure upon, and by recurring to the articles 118, 119, 120, and 121 of the constitution of 1852, we find this foundation is there laid for the Legislature to build a subsequent structure upon. It may be necessary even for this Committee on General Provisions as they necessarily have to consider those articles, to take into consideration any subject matter connected therewith that may be presented by any member of this Convention; at least, I suggest that there is nothing improper in it. Then, after the question has come before the committee for their careful deliberation, and is reported upon, seems to me it might be made the order of the day, and the merits or demerits of the subject matter discussed. By recurring to the article, you will find it is proper for this Convention to lay down the basis of the subsequent action of the Legislature.

MR. WILSON— I seconded the motion to lay the resolution on the table, because I think the agitation of the redemption of shinplasters, by this Convention, is a dangerous discussion. I think it has a much wider tendency than the previous speaker seems to imagine. In fact, it involves a principle, which, in my opinion, will give aid and comfort to the enemy. It is purely a matter for the Legislature, and should never have been introduced here. Although I honestly believe that the shinplasters were forced on many poor men without their will, and I am still in favor of sustaining a proposition of that sort embraces not one or ten thousand dollars, but a million even in this city ; for we cannot act upon the proposition in regard to the parish of St. Mary alone, and the question will ultimately arise on those who have made these issues in the city of New Orleans. Shall we indemnify men who issued and forced them on the poor and needy of New Orleans, without one dollar to back that issue? I think the question is a dangerous one, and one which we have no right to legislate upon or entertain for one moment.

MR. SMITH—I maintain that the non-redemption rather than the redemption of these shinplasters, gives aid and comfort to the enemy. According to the gentleman's own assertion, they have been forced in payment on the poorer classes, who refused to receive Confederate money, they had no confidence in it. The butchers, mechanics and working classes took this money, because they knew the men who issued it had property to redeem it; and now these men, with thousands of dollars in their pockets, say they will never redeem the shinplasters they have issued. The parish of St. Mary issued the money in good faith, to meet the wants of the people, and not to aid and comfort the rebellion or carry on the war, but simply because the laboring classes—the loyal people—would not receive Confederate money.

I maintain that this Convention, the first that has met since the commencement of the rebellion, has a right even to legislate in its sovereign power. The resolution only calls for the committee to report simply, not to legislate; and certainly they have a right to report articles.

MR. CUTLER—I move it be referred to the Committee on General Provisions.

MR. STOCKER—I wish the resolution read again. It strikes me that it instructs the committee to report in a particular way, and I would like to vote understandingly.

The resolution was read by the secretary.

MR. CUTLER—You will perceive the reading is, that the committee is instructed to report. I move it be referred to the Committee on General Provisions.

MR. CAZABAT—I move it be laid on the table.

[The motion was seconded, but on being put was declared lost.

The original motion of referring it to the committee was also lost.]

PRESIDENT—The question now is on the adoption of the original resolution.

MR. SMITH—I call for the yeas and nays.

[The call for yeas and nays was not responded to by the Convention, and a rising vote was taken and the resolution was declared lost; yeas 48, nays 13]

MR. HOWELL—I call my motion to rescind resolutions previously adopted.

The resolutions were read by the secretary as follows :

Resolved, That the resolution adopted on Friday, 15th April, 1864, in the following words, to-wit: "*Be it Resolved*, That the sum of one hundred thousand dollars be and the same is hereby appropriated out of the general fund, for the purpose of paying the members, officers and employés of this Convention, the mileage and *per diem* to which they are respectively entitled; the same to be paid by the treasurer of the State, on the warrant of the president of the Convention," be and the same is hereby rescinded.

Resolved, first, That the resolution, adopted on Friday, 15th April, 1864, in the following words, to-wit: "*Resolved*, That the members of this Convention shall receive from the public treasury a compensation for their services, which shall be ten dollars per day during their attendance on, going to and returning from the sessions of this Convention," be and the same is hereby rescinded.

Resolved, second, That the compensation for the services of the members of this Convention shall be the same as allowed to the members of the General Assembly by the constitution adopted in 1852.

MR. SULLIVAN—I move to lay it on the table.

[The motion was put and carried.]

MR. GORLINSKI—I call for the reading of my resolutions of yesterday.

The secretary read the resolutions as follows :

Resolved, That the regular hour for the meeting of this Convention, during the remainder of its sittings, shall be 12 o'clock

M., and any member not answering to his name when the roll is called, shall forfeit the sum of two dollars, to be deducted from his *per diem*, and any member who shall be absent from his seat an entire day, shall forfeit his *per diem* for each day he shall fail to attend, unless absent by permission of the Convention, or for sickness, either in his own person or family, the proof of which shall be a certificate from a regular physician.

Resolved, further, That the secretary keep a record of the names of all members not answering at roll-call, and the names of all members who shall be absent from their seats an entire day, and for each day so absent, unless they have leave of absence from the Convention; and to make a list of said members at the end of every week, a copy of which shall be furnished the Committee on Finance, and a copy to the President of the Convention, who will strictly enforce the penalties as prescribed in the foregoing resolution.

MR. DAVIES—I move to lay it on the table.

[The motion was carried.]

MR. CAZABAT—I move a reconsideration of the resolution adopted yesterday, requiring the State auditor to furnish a statement of the receipts and expenditures of the treasury under the administration of Gen. Shepley, on the ground that all resolutions are required to lie over one day before being acted upon by the Convention.

MR. MAURER—I move to lay the motion to reconsider on the table.

PRESIDENT—How did the gentleman vote on the original resolution?

Mr. CAZABAT—I voted in the affirmative.

PRESIDENT—Then you cannot make a motion to reconsider.

Mr. STOCKER—At the time the resolution was introduced I called the attention of the chair to the fact that, according to the rule adopted all resolutions and ordinances must lie over one day before being acted upon, but the matter having escaped the memory of the chair, my motion was not regarded at the time, and the resolution was adopted, but it was adopted in opposition to the rules, and I now ask the chair to decide whether that resolution is in fact complete.

PRESIDENT—I think the resolution was properly adopted.

MO. THROPE—The rules were suspended in that particular case.

MR. SHAW—I move we adjourn till to-morrow at 12 o'clock.

The motion was carried, and the Convention adjourned accordingly.

FRIDAY, April 22, 1864.

The proceedings were opened with prayer by the Rev. Mr. Jones, and the roll was called and the following gentlemen responded to their names:

Messrs. Abell, Ariail, Balch, Baum, Barrett, Bell, Bofill, Bonzano, Buckley, Burke, Campbell, Cazabat, Cook J. K., Crozat, Cutler, Davies, Dufresne, Duane, Durell, Edwards, Ennis, Fish, Flagg, Flood, Fosdick, Foley, Fuller, Gaidry, Geier, Goldman, Gorlinski, Gruneberg, Harnan, Hart, Healy, Heard, Henderson, Hills, Hire, Howell, Howes, Kavanagh, Knobloch, Kugler, Maurer, Maas, Mann, Mendiverri, Millspaugh, Montamat, Montague, Morris, Murphy E., Murphy M. W., Newell, Normand, O'Conner, Payne J., Poynot, Purcell J., Pursell S., Schroeder, Seymour, Shaw, Smith, Spellicy, Stocker, Stumpf, Stiner, Stauffer, Sullivan, Terry, Wenck, Wells, Wilson—75.

The secretary then proceeded to read the minutes.

Mr. Harnan moved to dispense with the reading of the names. Carried.

MR. HILLS—I move to dispense with the reading of resolutions which are the order of the day.

[The reading of the reports of the Committee on Impeachment and the Special Committees, were also dispensed with.

The minutes were adopted as read.

There being neither petitions nor memorials, resolutions were next in order.]

MR. GORLINSKI—I offer the following, to lie over till to-morrow:

Resolved, That the following be adopted as an additional standing rule of the Convention:

Rule LVI. It shall be in order for any member to propose, without previous notice, any amendment or substitute for an original proposition which may be under consideration, provided the same does not conflict with rule XXV.

MR. MONTAMAT—I wish to be informed if the secretary of state has sent to the Convention anything in relation to new members.

PRESIDENT—That will come up in course.

MR. TERRY—I offer the following:

Resolved, That no person is eligible for State or municipal office who has not the qualifications required in a voter for members of this Convention; and if there are any persons holding office under the State or municipal authorities, not so qualified, they shall be promptly removed.

Mr. Abell—I desire to offer a resolution in regard to the laying over of the reports of the committees:

Resolved, That the reports of the several committees on amendments be printed, and required to lie over at least two days.

Mr. Montamat—I move that the rules be suspended, in order to adopt that resolution immediately.

Mr. Hills—I second the motion.

[The question was put and carried.]

Mr. Montamat—I move the adoption of the resolution.

[The resolution was adopted.]

The reports of the Standing Committees were then in order.

Mr. Bonzano,—As chairman of the Committee on Emancipation, Mr. President, I report progress.

Mr. Fosdick—Mr. President, the chairman of the Committee on Legislative Department reports progress.

Mr. Fish, chairman of Committee on Executive Department, announced they had no report to make.

Mr. Howell, chairman of Committee on Judiciary Department, stated they would be able to report during the day.

Mr. Mann, chairman of the Committee on General Provisions, requested that Mr. Foley, a member of the committee, be allowed to read the report.

Mr. Foley then read the following:

Mr. President — Your Committee upon General Provisions beg leave to make the following report:

Article 1. Members of the General Assembly, and all officers, before they enter upon the duties of their offices, shall take the following oath or affirmation: "I (A B) do solemnly swear (or affirm) that I will support the constitution and laws of the United States and of this State, and that I will faithfully and impartially discharge and perform all the duties incumbent on me as ———, according to the best of my abilities and understanding, so help me, God."

Art. 2. Treason against the State shall consist only in levying war against it, or in adhering to its enemies, giving them aid and comfort. No person shall be convicted of treason, unless on the testimony of two witnesses to the same overt act, or his own confession in open court.

Art. 3. The Legislature shall have power to declare the punishment of treason; but no attainder of treason shall work corruption of blood or forfeiture, except during the life of the person attainted.

Art. 4. Every person shall be disqualified from holding any office of trust or profit, in this State, and shall be excluded from the right of suffrage, who shall have been convicted of treason, perjury, forgery, bribery, or other crimes or misdemeanors.

Art. 5. All penalties shall be proportioned to the nature of the offence.

Art. 6. The privilege of free suffrage shall be supported by laws regulating elections, and prohibiting, under adequate penalties, all undue influence thereon from power, bribery, tumult, or other improper practice.

Art. 7. No money shall be drawn from the treasury but in pursuance of specific appropriation made by law, nor shall any appropriation of money be made for a longer term than two years. A regular statement and account of the receipts and expenditures of all public moneys shall be published annually, in such manner as shall be prescribed by law.

Art. 8. It shall be the duty of the General Assembly to pass such laws as may be proper and necessary to decide differences of arbitration.

Art. 9. All civil officers for the State at large shall reside within the State, and all district or parish officers within their districts or parishes, and shall keep their offices at such places therein as may be required by law.

Art. 10. All civil officers, except the governor, and judges of the Supreme and Inferior Courts, shall be removable by an address of two-thirds of the members of both Houses, except those the removal of whom has been otherwise provided for by this constitution.

Art. 11. In all elections by the people, the vote shall be taken by ballot, and in all elections by the Senate and House of Representatives, jointly or separately, the vote shall be given *viva voce.*

Art. 12. No member of Congress, nor person holding or exercising any office of trust or profit under the United States, or either of them, or any foreign power, shall be eligible as a member of the General Assembly, or hold or exercise any office of trust or profit under the State.

Art. 13. None but citizens of the United States shall be appointed to any office of trust or profit or be employed on the *public works* in this State, providing the same be paid from the public funds, except the compensation be less than nine hundred dollars ($900) per annum.

Art. 14. The laws, public records, and the judicial and legislative written proceedings of the State, shall be promulgated, preserved, and conducted in the language in which the constitution of the United States is written.

Art. 15. That no power of suspending the laws shall be exercised, unless by authority of the Legislature.

Art. 16. Prosecutions shall be by indictment or information. The accused shall have a speedy public trial by an impartial jury of the parish in which the offence shall have been committed. He shall not be compelled to give evidence against himself; he shall have the right of being heard by himself or counsel; he shall have the right of meeting the witnesses face to face, and shall have compulsory process for obtaining witnesses in his favor; he shall not be twice put in jeopardy for the same offence.

Art. 17. All persons shall be bailable by sufficient sureties, unless for capital offences, where the proof is evident or the presumption great, and the privilege of the writ of *habeas corpus* shall not be suspended, unless when in cases of rebellion or invasion the public safety may require it.

Art. 18. Excessive bail shall not be required; excessive fines shall not be inflicted, nor cruel and unusual punishments inflicted.

Art. 19. The right of the people to be secure in their persons, houses, papers and effects, against unreasonable searches and seizures, shall not be violated, and no warrant shall issue but upon probable cause, supported by oath or affirmation, and particularly describing the place to be searched and the persons or things to be seized.

Art. 20. No ex-post facto law, nor any law impairing the obligations of contracts, shall be passed, nor vested rights be divested, unless for purposes of public utility, and for adequate compensation previously made.

Art. 21. That all courts shall be open, and any person, for any injury done him, in his lands, goods, person or reputation, shall have remedy by due course of law, and right and justice administered without denial or unreasonable delay.

Art. 22. The press shall be free; every citizen may freely speak, write and publish his sentiments on all subjects; being responsible for an abuse of this liberty.

Art. 23. The Legislature shall have power to grant aid to companies or associations of individuals, formed for the exclusive purpose of making works of internal improvement, wholly or partially within the State, to the extent only of one-fifth of the capital of such companies, by subscription of stock or loan in money or public bonds; but any aid thus granted shall be paid to the company only in the same proportions as the remainder of the capital shall be actually paid in by the stockholders of the company; and, in case of loan, such adequate security shall be required as to the Legislature may seem proper. No corporation or individual association, receiving the aid of the State as herein provided, shall possess banking or discounting obligations.

Art. 24. No liability shall be contracted by the State as above mentioned, unless the same be authorized by some law for some single object or work, to be distinctly specified therein, which shall be passed by a majority of the members elected to both Houses of the General Assembly, and the aggregate amount of debts and liabilities incurred under this and the preceding article shall never, at any one time, exceed eight millions of dollars.

Art. 25. Whenever the Legislature shall contract a debt exceeding in amount the sum of one hundred thousand dollars, unless in case of war to repel invasion or suppress insurrection, they shall, in the law creating the debt, provide adequate ways and means for the payment of the current interest and of the principal when the same shall become due. And the said law shall be irrepealable until principal and interest are fully paid and discharged, or unless the repealing law contains some other adequate provision for the payment of the principal and interest of the debt.

Art. 26. The Legislature shall provide by law for all change of venue in civil and criminal cases.

Art. 27. No lottery shall be authorized by this State, and the buying and selling of lottery tickets within the State is prohibited.

Art. 28. No divorce shall be granted by the Legislature.

Art. 29. Every law enacted by the Legislature shall embrace but one object, and that shall be expressed in the title.

Art. 30. No law shall be revived or amended by reference to its title; but in such case the act revived or section amended, shall be re-enacted and published at length.

Art. 31. The Legislature shall never adopt any system or code of laws by general reference to such system or code of laws, but in all cases shall specify the several provisions of the law he may enact.

Art. 32. Corporations with discounting privileges, may be either created by special acts or framed under general laws. But no corporation or individu:.l shall have the privilege of issuing notes or bills except those which are already chartered.

Art. 33. In case of the insolvency of any bank or banking association, the bill holders thereof shall be entitled to preference in payment over all other creditors of such bank or association.

Art. 34. No person shall hold or exercise at the same time, more than one civil office of trust or profit, except that of justice of the peace.

Art. 35. Taxation shall be equal and uniform throughout the State. All property on which taxes may be levied in this State, shall be taxed in proportion to its value, to be ascertained as directed by law. No one species of property shall be taxed higher than another species of property of equal value, on which taxes shall be levied; the Legislature shall have power to levy an income tax, and to tax all persons pursuing any occupation, trade or profession.

Art. 36. The citizens of the city of New Orleans shall have the right of appointing the several public officers necessary for the administration of police of the said city, pursuant to the mode of election which shall be prescribed by the Legislature; *Provided*, That the mayor and recorder shall be ineligible to a seat in the General Assembly, and the mayor and recorders shall be commissioned by the governor as justices of the peace, and the Legislature may vest in them such criminal jurisdiction as may be necessary for the punishment of minor crimes and offences.

Art. 37. The Legislature may provide by law in what case officers shall continue to perform the duties of their offices until their successors shall have been inducted into office.

Art. 38. The Legislature shall have power to extend this constitution and the jurisdiction of this State over any territory acquired by compact with any State, or with the United States, the same being done by consent of the United States.

Art. 39. None of the lands granted by Congress to the State of Louisiana for building or constructing the necessary levees and drains, to reclaim the swamp and overflowed lands in the State, shall be diverted from the purposes for which they were granted.

Art. 40. The Legislature shall pass no law excluding citizens of this State from office for not being conversant with any language except that in which the constitution of the United States is written.

Respectfully submitted,

W. D. MANN, Chairman.
ERNEST WENCK,
JOHN FOLEY,
J. K. COOK,
JOHN BUCKLEY, JR.,
GEO. GEIER,
H. MAAS.

MR. ABELL—I move it be received, and made the special order of the day for next Thursday, at 1 o'clock.

[The motion was carried.]

MR. HILLS—Mr. President, the Committee on Public Education submits the following:

To the president and members of the Convention for the Revision and Amendment of the Constitution of Louisiana:

The undersigned, members of the Committee on Public Education, have the honor to submit the following report:

Aticle —. There shall be elected a superintendent of public education, who shall hold his office for the term of two years. His duties shall be prescribed by law, and he shall receive such compensation as the Legislature may direct, provided that the General Assembly shall have power, by a vote of the majority of the members elected to both Houses, to abolish the said office of superintendent of public education, whenever, in their opinion, said office shall be no longer necessary.

Art. —. The General Assembly shall establish free public schools throughout the State for all children, and shall provide for their support by general taxation on property or otherwise, and all moneys so raised or provided shall be distributed to each parish in proportion to the number of children between such ages as shall be fixed by the General Assembly; but all schools for colored children shall be separate and distinct from schools for white children.

Art. —. In order to promote the more extensive diffusion of knowledge, the General Assembly shall make annual appropriation for the encouragement of private schools throughout the State, but the General Assembly shall not be required to make such appropriation for private schools in the parish of Orleans that do not number two hundred pupils, and in other parishes the General Assembly shall determine what private schools are sufficiently large to deserve such appropriations.

Art. —. The English language only shall be taught in the common schools in this State.

Art. —. An university shall be established in the city of New Orleans. It shall be composed of four faculties, to-wit: one of law, one of medicine, one of the natural sciences, and one of letters. The Legislature shall provide by law for its organization, but shall be under no obligation to contribute to the establishment or support of said university by appropriations.

Art. —. The proceeds of all lands heretofore granted by the United States to this State for the use or support of schools, and of all lands which may hereafter be granted or bequeathed for any other purpose, which hereafter may be disposed of by the State, and the proceeds of the estates of deceased persons to which the State may become entitled by law, shall be held by the State as a loan, and shall be and remain a perpetual fund on which the State shall pay an annual interest of six per cent., which interest together with the interest of the Trust Funds, deposited with this State by the United States, under the act of Congress approved June 23, 1836, and all the rents of the unsold lands, shall be appropriated to the interest of such schools, and this appropriation shall remain inviolable.

Art. —. All moneys arising from the sales which have been, or may hereafter be made, of any lands heretofore granted by the United States to this State for the use of a seminary of learning, and from any kind of donation that may hereafter be made for that purpose, shall be and remain a perpetual fund, the interest of which, at six per cent. per annum, shall be appropriated to the support of a seminary of learning, for the promotion of literature and the arts and sciences, and no law shall ever be made diverting said fund to any other use than to the establishment and improvement of said seminary of learning, and the General Assembly shall have power to raise funds for the organization and support of said seminary of learning, in such manner as it may deem proper.

ALFRED C. HILLS, Chairman.
M. W. MURPHY,
X. MAURER,
J. RANDALL TERRY,
T. M. WELLS,
GEORGE HOWES.

Edward Hart signs the above, intending to offer an amendment to the third clause.

H. C. Edwards signs, dissenting entirely from third clause in said report.

I coincide with Mr. Edwards.

YOUNG BURKE.

MR. HART—As a member of that committee, I will read my amendment:

In order to promote the more extensive diffusion of knowledge, it shall be the duty of the General Assembly to make annual appropriations for the encouragement of all private schools throughout the State, which are, or may hereafter be, incorporated by legislative enacted.

MR. BALCH—I was a member of that committee, but through indisposition was unable to attend its sittings. I wish that the consideration of the report be postponed until Saturday, and accordingly make that motion, as I intend to discuss several of its provisions.

[The motion was carried.]

MR. STOCKER—I arose, as I believed, in time for the purpose of objecting to the adoption of that motion, since, as I understand, the amendment must be offered at the time the report was made.

PRESIDENT—The amendments are a minority report.

MR. CUTLER—Mr. President, the Committee on the Mode of Revising the Constitution will be able to report to-morrow.

MR. GRUNEBERG—Mr. President, the Committee on Schedule are not ready to report.

MR. SHAW—Mr. President, the Committee on Ordinance report progress.

MR. BROTT—Mr. President, the Committee on Finance have no report.

MR. S. PURSELL—Mr. President, the Committee on Expenses report progress.

MR. J. PURCELL—Mr. President, the Committee on Printing have no report.

MR. HOWELL—As a member of the Committee on Federal Relations, I beg leave to state, in the absence of the chairman, that we have not yet prepared the report. With the permission of the Convention and president, I will now submit the report of the Committee on Judiciary Department:

To the president and members of the Convention to Revise and Amend the Constitution of the State of Louisiana:

The Committee on the Judiciary Department beg leave to report the following articles, and recommend their adoption as a portion of the constitution of this State on the subject of the Judiciary, to-wit:

TITLE IV—JUDICIARY DEPARTMENT.

Article 1. The Judiciary power shall be vested in a Supreme Court, in such inferior courts as the Legislature may, from time to time, order and establish, and in justices of the peace.

Art. 2. The Supreme Court, except in cases hereinafter provided, shall have appellate jurisdiction only; which jurisdiction shall extend to all cases when the matter in dispute shall exceed three hundred dollars; in all cases in which the constitutionality or legality of any tax, toll or import whatsoever, or of any fine, forfeiture or penalty imposed by a municipal corporation, shall be in contestation; and to all criminal cases on questions of law alone, whenever the offence charged is punishable with death or imprisonment at hard labor, or when a fine exceeding three hundred dollars is actually imposed.

Art. 3. The Supreme Court shall be composed of one chief justice and four associate justices, a majority of whom shall constitute a quorum. The chief justice shall receive a salary of ten thousand dollars, and each of the associate justices a salary of nine thousand dollars annually, until otherwise provided by law. The court shall appoint its own clerks.

Art. 4. The Supreme Court shall hold its sessions in New Orleans from the first Monday of the month of November to the end of the month of June inclusive. The Legislature shall have power to fix the sessions elsewhere during the rest of the year; until otherwise provided, the sessions shall be held as heretofore.

Art. 5. The Supreme Court, and each of the judges thereof, shall have power to issue writs of *habeas corpus*, at the instance of persons in actual custody under process, in all cases in which they may have appellate jurisdiction.

Art. 6. No judgment shall be rendered by the Supreme Court without the concurrence of a majority of the judges comprising the court. Whenever the majority cannot agree, in consequence of the recusation of any member or members of the court, the judges not recused shall have power to call upon any judge or judges of the inferior courts, whose duty it shall be, when so called upon, to sit in the place of the judge or judges recused, and to aid in determining the case.

Art. 7. All judges, by virtue of their office, shall be conservators of the peace throughout the State. The style of all process shall be "the State of Louisiana." All prosecutions shall be carried on in the name and by the authority of the State of Louisiana, and conclude against the peace and dignity of the same.

Art. 8. The judges of all courts within the State shall, as often as it may be possible so to do, in every definite judgment, refer to the particular law in virtue of which such judgment may be rendered, and in all cases adduce the reasons on which their judgment is founded.

Art. 9. The judges of all courts shall be liable to impeachment; but for any reasonable cause, which shall not be sufficient ground for impeachment, the governor shall remove any of them, on the address of three-fourths of the members present of each House of the General Assembly. In every such case the cause or causes for which such removal may be required shall be stated at length in the address, and inserted in the journal of each House.

Art. 10. The judges, both of the Supreme and inferior courts shall, at stated times, receive a salary which shall not be diminished during their continuance in office; and they are prohibited from receiving any fees of office or other compensation than their salaries for any civil duties peformed by them.

Art. 11. The judges both of the Supreme and inferior courts, shall be appointed by the governor, by and with the advice and consent of the Senate, and they shall hold their offices during good behavior.

Art. 12. The clerks of the superior courts shall be appointed by the judges thereof, and they shall hold their offices during good behavior, subject to removal by the judges respectively, with the right of appeal in all such cases to the Supreme Court.

Art. 13. The Legislature shall have power to vest in clerks of courts authority to grant such orders and do such acts as may be deemed necessary for the furtherance of the administration of justice, and in all cases the power thus granted shall be specified and determined.

Art. 14. The jurisdiction of justices of the peace shall not exceed, in civil cases, the sum of one hundred dollars, exclusive of interest, subject to appeal in such cases as shall be provided for by law. They shall be appointed by the governor, with the advice and consent of the Senate, and shall hold their offices during good behavior. They shall have such criminal jurisdiction as shall be provided by law.

Art. 15. There shall be an attorney general for the State, and as many district attorneys as may be hereafter found necessary. They shall be appointed by the governor, with the advice and consent of the Senate, and shall hold their offices during the term for which the governor shall have been elected. Their duties shall be determined by law.

Art. 16. A sheriff and coroner shall be appointed in each parish by the governor, with the advice and consent of the Senate, and they shall hold their offices for the term for which the govenor shall have been elected, unless sooner removed. The Legislature shall have power to increase the number of sheriffs in any parish.

All of which is respectfully submitted.

R. K. Howell, Chairman.
H. J. Heard,
R. King Cutler,
John Henderson, Jr.,
R. Beauvais,
Wm. H. Seymour,
James Fuller.

Mr. Harnan—I move that report be made the order of the day for Friday, the 29th.

[The motion was carried.

Reports of special committees were then declared in order.]

Mr. Montamat—Mr. President, the Committee on Credentials report progress.

Mr. Wilson—Mr. President, the Committee on Assault of Members report progress.

PRESIDENT—Committee on Absent Members.

MR. STOCKER—We have diligently tried to make our report, but have not received such information as will justify us in doing so at present, and therefore ask for further time.

MR. M. W. MURPHY—Mr. President, the Committee on Compensation of Officers submitt the following report:

Mr. President—Your committee, appointed to fix the compensation of the officers and employés of this Convention, beg leave to present the following, viz:

President of the Convention	$20	per day.
John E. Neelis, secretary	18	"
S. G. Hamilton, assistant secretary	10	"
Thomas H. Murphy, assistant secretary	10	"
M. DeCoursey, sergeant-at-arms	15	"
Two assistant sergeants-at-arms	6	"
Two messengers, each	5	"
One postmaster	8	"
One doorkeeper	8	"
Chief reporter	12	"
Three assistant reporters, each	10	"
One warrant clerk	10	"
Enrolling clerks, each	5	"

The mileage of each member from the country parishes, twenty cents per mile, going and coming.

All compensation to officers and employés shall commence from the date of their election or appointment.

All of which is respectfully submitted.

M. W. MURPHY, Chairman,
W. D. MANN,
J. RANDALL TERRY,
JAMES ENNIS.

MR. FOSDICK—Mr. President, as a member of that committee, I desire to submit the following minority report:

To the president and members of the Convention:

The undersigned, one of the committee appointed to fix the compensation of the officers and employés of the Convention, begs leave to submit the following report, that they shall receive as follows:

Secretary	$15	per day.
Assistant secretaries, each	10	"
Sergeant-at-arms	10	"
Two assistant sergeants-at-arms, each	6	"
Two messengers, each	3	"
One postmaster	5	"
One doorkeeper	5	"
One reporter	8	"
Three assistant reporters, each	8	"
One warrant clerk	6	"
Enrolling clerks, each	$6	per day.
Translating clerks, each	8	"

The mileage of each member from the country parishes 20 cents per mile, coming and returning to ———. All compensation to officers and employés to commence from the date of their election or appointment.

All of which is respectfully submitted.

GEO. A. FOSDICK.

MR. TERRY—I move it be made the order of the day next Tuesday.

MR. HILLS—I amend to to-morrow at one o'clock.

MR. BELL—I rise to a point of order. We have just adopted a resolution that the reports of committees shall lie over at least two days.

PRESIDENT—That applies to standing committees.

[Mr. Hills's motion was then carried.]

The following communication from the secretary of state was then read:

STATE OF LOUISIANA,
Office Secretary of State,
New Orleans, April 22.

To the honorable president of the Constitutional Convention of Louisiana:

SIR—I have the honor of transmiting you, herewith, the official return of the election for *one delegate* from the parish of Ascension, to represent that parish in the Constitutional Convention of Louisiana, held on the 18th ultimo, and stating that Emile Collin obtained 85 votes of 131, and was consequently elected *as such*.

Very respectfully, your obedient servant,

S. WROTNOWSKI.

MR. HIRE—I move that the report be adopted, and that Mr. Collin be received as a member of this Convention.

PRESIDENT—The proper motion is to refer it to the Committee on Credentials.

MR. GASTINEL—I make that motion.

[The motion was adopted without objection.

The unfinished business of yesterday was next in order.]

MR. GORLINSKI—I call for the reading of my resolution of yesterday.

The resolution was read by the secretary:

Whereas, On the evacuation of Baton Rouge, after the ever-memorable battle of the 5th day of August, 1862, Col. Payne, of the Fourth Wisconsin Volunteers, then commanding the post of Baton Rouge, crowned his heroic deeds of that day by an act which has secured to the use of this Convention and the State a valuable public library, together with Thorpe's great painting of Gen. Zachary Taylor, and other paintings, which now adorn the hall of this Convention, and also saved Hiram Powers's statue of Washington, which is said now to be in the Patent Office at the national capital—all of which would have been stolen or destroyed by fire, which demolished the State House, had not Col. Payne caused the same to be removed to this city, when, by order Gen. Butler, they were protected as the property of the State; therefore, be it

Resolved, That the thanks of this Convention and of the people of Louisiana are due and are hereby tendered to Major Gen. B. F. Butler and Col. Payne for saving the above mentioned State property.

Resolved, further, That the governor be and is hereby requested to correspond with the authorities at Washington, and make suitable arrangements for the ruturn and reception of the above mentioned statue of Washington and its future disposition in this State.

MR. SULLIVAN—I move to lay it on the table.

[The motion was carried.]

Mr. Campbell called for the reading of the following:

Whereas, The United States bounty paid to soldiers enlisting in the army, cannot be paid to men enlisting in the First and Second regiments of New Orleans Volunteers, now being raised under Cols. Killborn and Brown, bacause of their being organized for a special purpose, that of the city defence alone and wishing to aid in filling the same,

Resolved, That the sum of——dollars be and the same is hereby appropriated by the State, to pay a bounty to each man who may hereafter enlist in the First and Second regiments of New Orleans Volunteers, and that the government is hereby authorized to carry the same into effect according to its best judgment.

MR. MONTAMAT—I move that be referred to the next Legislature; we have nothing to do with it.

[A motion to lay on the table was carried.]

MR. GORLINSKI—I move to adjourn.

[The motion was lost.]

Mr. Schroeder offered the following, to lie over until to-morrow:

Resolved, That the resolution adopted on Friday, April 15, 1864, in the following words, to-wit:

"*Resolved*, That the members of the Convention shall receive from the public treasury a compensation for their services, which shall be ten dollars, during their attendance on, going to and returning from the sessions of this Convention," be and the same is hereby rescinded.

Resolved, second, That the compensation for the services of the members of this Convention shall be referred to a special committee.

MR. STOCKER—Mr. President, a resolution to the same effect was offered and acted upon yesterday, and I wish to know if this was properly presented.

PRESIDENT—The Convention may pass a resolution one day and rescind it the next; but, in any event, it will probably administer a proper rebuke to any member who unnecessarily delays business.

MR. KAVANAGH—I move to adjourn until 12 o'clock Saturday, the 23d instant.

[The motion was carried.]

SATURDAY, April 23, 1864.

[The House was called to order a few minutes past 12 o'clock, and the proceedings opened with prayer by the Rev. Mr. Thomas.

The secretary then called the roll, and the following gentlemen answered to their names:

Messrs. Abell, Ariail, Austin, Balch, Bailey, Barrett, Beauvais, Bell, Bofill, Buckley, Burke, Campbell, Cazabat, Collin, Cook J. K., Cook T., Davies, Duane, Dufresne, Duke, Dupaty, Edwards, Ennis, Fish, Flagg, Flood, Foley, Fosdick, Fuller, Gastinel, Geier, Goldman, Gorlinski, Gruneberg, Gaidry, Healy, Harnan, Hart, Heard, Henderson, Hills, Howes, Kavanagh, Knobloch, Kugler, Maas, Mann, Maurer, Mendiverri, Millspaugh, Montamat, Morris, Murphy E., Murphy M. W., Newell, Normand, O'Conner, Payne J., Pintado, Poynot, Purcell J., Pursell S., Schroeder, Seymour, Shaw, Smith, Spellicy, Stumpf, Stiner, Stauffer, Terry, Thomas, Thorpe, Wells, Wilson—78.

The secretary then read the minutes of the preceding session, dispensing, on Mr. Stiner's motion, with calling the votes, etc., on Mr. Hills's motion with resolutions, the order of the day and the reports.]

MR. CAMPBELL—I would make a correction. The minutes as read state that my resolution of yesterday came up. I wish the secretary to correct by saying the chair ordered it up.

MR. CAZABAT—My attention has been called to the passage in the minutes, which states that the members whose credentials were referred to the committee were from the parishes of Plaquemines and Ascension. I wish to amend by striking out "Plaquemines," both members being from the parish of Ascension.

MR. GORLINSKI—I called for the yeas and nays on my resolution, and not Mr. Goldman.

[The minutes, as amended, were then adopted.]

There being no petitions or memorials, new resolutions were in order.

MR. S. PURSELL—I have a resolution to offer, in regard to which I hope the summary process will not be adopted. Let things be considered on their merits.

[Mr. Pursell's resolution was then read.]

Resolved, That the following be offered as a substitute for article 35 of the report of the Committee on General Provisions, and that it be made the order of the day and taken up with said report:

Art. —. Taxation shall be equal and uniform throughout the State. All property shall be taxed in proportion to its value, to be ascertained as directed by law. The General Assembly shall have power to exempt from taxation property actually used for church, school, or charitable purposes. The General Assembly shall levy an income tax upon all persons pursuing any profession, occupation, trade or calling, and all such persons shall obtain a license, as provided by law. All tax on income shall be *pro rata* on the amount of income or business done.

MR. HILLS—In order to save the time of the Convention, I offer the following, and move to suspend the rules in order to act upon it at once:

Resolved, That in reading the minutes of this Convention the secretary shall dispense with the reading of all roll-calls, giving simply the results, all resolutions that lie over under the rules, and all that were laid on the table, and all printed reports, unless otherwise directed by the Convention.

[The rules were suspended and the resolution adopted.]

MR. ABELL—I offer the following:

Resolved, That when a report of a standing committee is taken up, it shall be considered section by section (*seriatim*), and that no section shall be finally adopted until it has undergone three readings on separate days.

MR. FULLER—I offer the following in regard to amendments and substitutes, since several of the most important committees have reported:

Resolved, That one day's notice shall be given of any amendment or substitute to be proposed to the report of any of the standing committees.

MR. FOLEY—I offer the following, and move to suspend the rules and adopt it immediately:

Resolved, That the secretary be directed to cause the various reports of the committees of the Convention to be printed in such form as will admit of amendments therein; and that the secretary be directed to cause the same to be printed without delay by the printer of this Convention.

[The motions were carried.]

The reports of standing committees were next in order.

No report was offered from the Committee on Emancipation.

The chairman of Committee on Legislative Department, and the chairman of the Committee on Internal Improvement, reported progress.

No report was received from the Committee on Executive Department.

MR. CUTLER—As chairman of Committee on Mode of Revising the Constitution, I present the following:

To the president and members of the State Constitutional Convention:

Your committee, to whom was referred the "Mode of Revising the Constitution," beg leave to submit the following report, and recommend the adoption of the following instead of article 141 of the constitution of 1852.

Art. —. Any amendment or amendments to this constitution may be proposed in the Senate or House of Representatives, and if the same shall be agreed to by two-thirds of the members elected to each House, such proposed amendment or amendments shall be entered on their journals with the yeas and nays taken thereon. Such proposed amendment or amendments shall be submitted to the people at an election to be ordered by said Legislature, and held within ninety days after the adjournment of the same, and after thirty day's publication according to law; and if a majority of the voters at said election shall approve and ratify such amendment or amendments, the same shall become a part of the constitution. If more than one amendment be submitted at a time, they shall be submitted in such manner and form that the people may vote for or against each amendment separately.

Respectfully submitted,
R. KING CUTLER, Chairman.
E. A. KNOBLOCH,
JOS. G. BAUM,
J. H. STINER,
PATRICK HARNAN.

MR. STOCKER—I move that the report be received, 200 copies printed, and that it be made the order of the day for May 3d.

MR. HILLS—I amend to next Tuesday.

[The motion was seconded.]

MR. HARNAN—The report of another committee is made the order of that day ; therefore this should not also be.

[Mr. Hills's motion was carried.]

MR. GRUNEBERG—Mr. President, the Committee on Schedule reports progress.

MR. SHAW—The Committee on Ordinance reports progress.

Neither the Committee on Enrollment, nor that on Finance, had any report.

MR. S. PURSELL—The Committee on Expenses reports progress.

MR. J. PURCELL—The Committee on Printing reports progress.

No report was received from the Committee on Federal Relations.

Reports of special committees were then called for.

MR. MONTAMAT—The Committee on Credentials will report in a few minutes.

MR. WILSON—The Committee on Assault of Members reports progress.

MR. STOCKER—As chairman of Committee on Absent Members, I would state that we are not yet prepared to make such a report as will be satisfactory.

[The secretary read a communication from the secretary of state, enclosing credentials of Mr. T. J. Decker, returned from the parish of Plaquemines.]

MR. HILLS—I move that the matter be referred to the Committee on Credentials.

[The motion was carried.]

MR. MONTAMAT—As chairman of the Committee on Credentials, I submit a report in favor of the admission of new members, which was received, and Mr. Collin admitted.

[Unfinished business was next in order.]

MR. TERRY—I call for the reading of my resolution.

[Mr. Terry's resolution was read :]

Resolved, That no person is eligible for State or municipal office who has not the qualifications required in a voter for members of this Convention ; and if there are any persons holding office under the State or municipal authorities not so qualified, they shall be promptly removed.

MR. HARNAN—I move its adoption.

MR. THOMAS—I move to lay it on the table.

[The motion was lost by a vote of 7 to 37. The yeas and nays were called.]

YEAS — Messrs. Ariail, Austin, Cutler, Flagg, Henderson, Maas, Mann, Newell, Payne J., Seymour, Wells—11.

NAYS—Messrs. Abell, Bailey, Barrett, Baum, Beauvais, Bell, Bofill, Burke, Campbell, Cazabat, Cook J. K., Cook T., Crozat, Davies, Dufresne, Duane, Dupaty, Edwards, Flood, Foley, Fosdick, Gastinel, Geier, Goldman, Gorlinski, Gruneberg, Gaidry, Healy, Harnan, Hart, Hills, Hire, Howell, Howes, Kavanagh, Knobloch, Kugler, Maurer, Mendiverri, Millspaugh, Montamat, Montague, Morris, Murphy E., Murphy M. W., Normand, O'Conner, Ong, Pintado, Poynot, Purcell J., Pursell S., Shroeder, Shaw, Spellicy, Stocker, Stumpf, Stiner, Stauffer, Sullivan, Terry, Thorpe, Wenck, Wilson, Collin, Duke—68.

[The motion to lay on the table was consequently lost.

The motion to adopt the resolution was stated by the chair.]

MR. HENDERSON—I suppose the motion is debatable. I oppose the resolution now before the Convention upon the same ground that I did one of yesterday—on the ground that it is retroactive. We have nothing to do with officers appointed by either Governor Shepley or Governor Hahn, whether we approve or disapprove of the respective appointees. We have come here to make a constitution for the people of Louisiana. When the consttitution goes into effect, and not till then, can we call in question the qualifications of officers already appointed. This resolution covers two propositions—first, the eligibility of any man to an office ; secondly, the eligibility of those now incumbent. When this constitution goes into effect it can operate upon those henceforth holding offices, but not upon those previously appointed ; for these last may, or may not, have taken a certain oath. I am opposed to any action of this Convention in regard to governor, scretary of state, treasurer, or any other officer already appointed. Our action should be prospective from the time the constitution takes effect, when all officials must have certain qualifications prescribed by it.

Gentlemen of the Convention, if you go back to the time of the first great convention of 1776, you will find that certain members of it were born upon foreign soil. Two of those members—Hamilton and Wilson—the one a delegate from New York, and the other from Pennsylvania, were *leading* men. The action of that convention was prospective, for the constitution then framed declared that only native born citizens should be eligible to the offices of president and vice-president, except those who were then on the soil fighting for it, thereby rendering Hamilton and Wilson, who were foreigners, as eligible as George Washington. The very men who wished to make ineligible to those offices all except native born citizens, did not sustain their own proposition, but, to a man, voted against it, rightly feeling that Hamilton, though born in the Highlands, was fighting our battles, and was as much an American as Washington, born in Virginia.

You may by your schedule decide what shall be the qualifications of the officers we are to have in future, and more than that, you may say that no man shall hold an office between the time of the adoption of the constitution, or any period thereafter, unless he possesses certain qualifications. That is our power, but we know nothing in regerd to present appointees. I am, therefore, in favor of the first clause of the resolution but opposed to the second, because with it we have no concern. We have elected a governor and that governor is bound to see that every officer appointed by himself, or by Gov Shepley, is duly qualified, and if he think him disqualified may remove him. I think we have sufficient confidence in our governor and the powers that be to believe that all officers appointed either by him or the military power are properly in their places; still, if we adopt the first clause there may be a conflict of powers, whereas any qualifications prescribed for future officers will be right, and all will act in concert.

Whose duty is it to appoint and remove the officials of either the State or city? The governor and mayor are the two who possess the power, and that is right; but if we make laws to act retrospectively, we may cause discord, since this would be the first time that this has been done by any convention, State or national, from that of 1776 to the present time. The existing laws must remain as they are till the new constitution goes into effect.

It may be I have spoken too long on this question, but I desire that the members of this Convention shall understand my position.

MR. MONTAMAT—I would like to have the gentleman explain if he intends this resolution to apply to both civil and military officers. I do not like to vote on the question without being well aware what I am doing.

MR. TERRY—The resolution applies to civil officers only—State and municipal. The question in regard to what we have to do in the future, has nothing to do with the present. The only question is, whether we are delegates of the people or not; whether we are sent here by them or the military power. We are here as the sovereign and supreme power of Louisiana; but since we have first to show our qualifications which enable us to hold our seats in this Convention, is it right that men should receive pay from the State and city who are not qualified as well as we? This is, I think, the only question.

MR. HOWELL—Mr. President, I voted against laying the resolution on that table for the reasons, first, because I desired to oppose the habit which has obtained in this Convention of throwing everything upon the table as soon as it is proposed; secondly, in order to obtain the opinion of some of the members of this Convention upon the question. I have no objection to having the Convention express an opinion as to what shall be the qualifications for officeholders in this State at this early period of the session, but I am opposed to any attempt of the Convention to vacate any office now filled, because I think this is not a part of our duty.

Mr. Abell—Mr. President, I think this Convention has no such power. I should like to know how it is to be done, unless we send out a *posse* to remove them? That question belongs more properly to the Legislature. It may be well for the Convention to express its opinion on the qualifications of office-holders, but it has no power to remove from office.

Mr. Thomas—Before the question is put, Mr. President, I desire to give my reasons for voting against its adoption. I think that we have come here for a single purpose, to revise and amend the constitution, and that this question is not in the line of our duty. I shall therefore vote against it, because it is foreign to the purpose and object of the Convention; and I shall vote against all similar resolutions on the same ground, and upon the ground, too, that the doings of this Convention are not the law of the land, until they are submitted to the people. Suppose we should remove men from office, and then when our acts are submitted to the people they should not be accepted. I think that when the question of the adoption of section XIII comes before the convention will be the proper time to introduce this question.

Mr. Fosdick—Mr. President, I fully agree with the views expressed by Judge Howell, and at the same time I think this Convention ought to express its opinion on the subject. I therefore move to amend by striking out the words "shall be removed" and substituting "in the opinion of this Convention ought to be removed."

[The amendment was not seconded.]

Mr. Shaw—Mr. President, before this question goes to the Convention, I think it ought to be explained to the Convention what the reasons are that have called for such action. I think we could hardly expect such a resolution to be presented unless there was some occasion to render such action necessary or expedient; and if there is any particular necessity for the measure, the Convention has the right to know it before voting on the question.

Mr. Thorpe—Mr. President, the resolution simply calls for the iron-clad from every man in office, State or municipal. We all of us have been required to take it, and I see no objection to requiring it from every office-holder. I therefore move to lay the resolution on the table, subject to call.

[The motion was seconded.]

Mr. Stocker—Mr. President, I rise to a point of order. The question has already been decided by this Convention.

President—The motion is not debatable. You will sit down. A motion to lay on the table, subject to call, is not decided by a motion to lay on the table merely.

[The motion was put and lost.]

Mr. Stocker — Mr. President, I voted against laying the resolution on the table for two reasons; one was, that I wanted to have the expression of the Convention on the question itself, and another reason was because I believed it a matter not in the province of the Convention to decide, and I wish to record my vote against it.

Mr. Hills—Mr. President, I wish to say that I am in favor of the resolution as a general principle, but if it has any application to any military officers or appointments, I should vote against it; understanding that it has no such application, I shall vote for it.

Mr. Austin—Mr. President, I wish to call the attention of the Convention for a moment to the resolution and its effects. Who are the officers which it is designed to affect? It certainly includes the mayor, the chief of police and the lieutenants. We have no right to call these appointments in question. It is simply absurd, and I shall vote against it.

Mr. Cazabat—Mr. President, in regard to this question, I am somewhat in the dark. I voted against laying it on the table as a matter of principle. My views have been expressed by Mr. Stocker. I believe it is a matter with which this Convention has nothing to do.

I am in favor of the principle involved in this resolution, because I want every man in office in Louisiana to show the evidence that he has taken the oath prescribed by the president in his proclamation of December 8th, 1863. If this was the object of this resolution, and it was a matter within the province of the Convention, I should vote for it. I know little of the officers now in position in New Orleans. I take it for granted they are all loyal men, and worthy their position. I take it for granted that our worthy governor has not appointed any one unless he was satisfied that he was a citizen of the United States. I take it for granted that he has ascertained, in every case, that every man was qualified as required by the proclamation of the commanding general. On these grounds, therefore, and because I think we have nothing to do with the matter—although I voted not to lay the resolution on the table—I vote against its adoption.

MR. CUTLER—Mr. President, I have no doubt the question has already been sufficiently discussed, but I desire to add a few remarks, inasmuch as I heard a voice or two in favor of its adoption.

Nearly all the speakers on the question are correct in taking the ground that it is a matter with which this Convention has nothing to do. We should keep in mind the difference between the duties of this Convention and of a legislative body. This is clearly a legislative act, and it will not be merely an act of legislation, but an act of great injustice to that class of men now in office. I do not question the motive of the mover, but it was certainly unwise to introduce such a resolution.

The argument of the gentleman from the Third District (Mr. Thomas) is conclusive, that this body cannot pass any law, nor can it pass a public law that can have a retrospective action; and if, by this resolution, we remove any officers now holding their positions, we do it in violation of fundamental law.

I voted to lay this resolution on the table. I did it in a spirit of candor, because I thought it was time to stop this discussion by laying all such motions on the table, and to come to the work before us. With these views, I must vote for such action on all similar questions that may be proposed here.

If a man who is not properly qualified takes the oath of office in violation of law, he is responsible by law, and the law should be enforced. It is not, however, in the province of this Convention to remove an officer; that duty devolves upon the governor and the heads of departments.

MR. THOMAS—I call for the yeas and nays.

[The call was sustained, and the roll was called with the following result:]

YEAS—Messrs. Bailey, Baum, Campbell, Flood, Foley, Fosdick, Gastinel, Harnan, Healy, Hills, Howes, Murphy E., Murphy M. W., Sullivan, Taliaferro, Terry, Thorpe, Wilson—18.

NAYS—Messrs. Abell, Ariail, Austin, Barrett, Balch, Beauvais, Bell, Bofill, Buckley, Burke, Cazabat, Cook J. K., Cook T., Crozat, Cutler, Davies, Dufresne, Duane, Dupaty, Edwards, Ennis, Fish, Fuller, Gaidry, Geier, Goldman, Gorlinski, Gruneberg, Hart, Henderson, Heard, Hire, Howell, Kavanagh, Knobloch, Kugler, Maas, Mann, Maurer, Mendiverri, Millspaugh, Montamat, Morris, Montague, Newell, Normand, O'Conner, Ong, Payne J., Pintado, Poynot, Purcell J., Pursell S., Schroeder, Seymour, Shaw, Smith, Spellicy, Stocker, Stumpf, Stiner, Stauffer, Thomas, Wenck, Wells, Collin, Duke—68.

MR. STOCKER — Mr. President, the hour having passed for taking up the order of the day, I move we take it up.

MR. MONTAMAT—By request of the member from Terrebonne, I call up his resolution laid over from yesterday.

MR. STOCKER—I submit to the decision of the chair the hour has passed.

PRESIDENT — The unfinished business always has precedence, unless the order of the day is specially called up by the Convention. Mr. Secretary, read the resolution of Mr. Gaidry.

[The secretary read:]

Whereas, All the constitutions ever framed in this State have decreed that all judicial and legislative proceedings should take place in the French and English languages;

And whereas, Several members of this Convention, who are true republicans and loyal to the core, but are not very familiar with the English language, have been delegated to this Convention by constituents who are also unacquainted with the said language—which right to choose delegates as they please said constituents possessed, as they are the sovereign people, and that to deny such supreme right would be tantamount to disfranchise said people;

Resolved, That all resolutions and motions to be presented in this convention be translated into the French language, so that the members from the several parishes, who are not familiar with the English language, be fully aware of what they are voting upon.

Mr. Henderson—Mr. President, I move to lay the resolution on the table.

Mr. Hills—I second the motion.

[The question was put, and the resolution tabled.]

ORDER OF THE DAY.

President—If there are no other resolutions the secretary will read the special order of the day.

[The secretary read the majority report made yesterday by the Committee on Compensation of Officers and Employés.]

Mr. Bell—Mr. President I have a substitute to offer.

Mr. Henderson—Mr. President—

President—There is a minority report.

[The secretary read the minority report of same committee.]

Mr. Henderson—I move to amend so that instead of being from the date of appointment or election, they all be paid from the commencement of the session; they have done back work, and should receive the pay.

Mr. Hills—I move to take up the report offered by officer.

Mr. Bell—Mr. President, my amendment was first, but I did not have an opportunity to have it acted upon.

Mr Stauffer—I move to lay the amendments on the table, because I think we have already paid the reporter extra.

[The motion to lay on the table was lost.

The question was then put on Mr. Henderson's motion, and it was adopted.]

Mr. Hills—Mr. President, I now renew my motion to take up the report officer by officer.

[The question was put and carried.

The first part of the report was read fixing the compensation of the president at $20 per day.]

Mr. Hills—Mr. President, I move to strike out that portion of the report. My reasons are, that it is eminently a position of honor, and I do not believe that the president would wish to have extra compensation.

Mr. Montamat—I move to amend by substituting "fifteen dollars" for twenty dollars.

Mr. Goldman—I move to lay that amendment on the table.

Mr. Terry—I amend, subject to call.

[The amendments were tabled.]

President—The question is on the motion to strike out.

Mr. Henderson—I move to lay Mr. Hills's motion on the table.

Mr. Hills—I call for the yeas and nays.

[The roll was called, with the following result:

Yeas—Messrs. Abell, Austin, Barrett, Beauvais, Bell, Burke, Campbell, Cook T., Crozat, Cutler, Ennis, Fish, Fuller, Geier, Goldman, Heard, Henderson, Kugler, Maas, Mann, Maurer, Mendiverri, Montague, Murphy M. W., O'Conner, Payne J., Purcell J., Shaw, Stocker, Stumpf, Stiner, Sullivan, Terry, Thorpe, Thomas, Wilson—36.

Nays—Messrs. Ariail, Bailey, Baum, Balch, Bofill, Buckley, Cook J. K., Collin, Davies, Duane, Dupaty, Duke, Edwards, Flagg, Flood, Foley, Fosdick, Gastinel, Gorlinski, Gruneberg, Gaidry, Healy, Harnan, Hart, Hills, Hire, Howell, Howes, Kavanagh, Knobloch, Millspaugh, Morris, Montague, Murphy E., Newell, Normand, Ong, Pintado, Poynot, Schroeder, Seymour, Smith, Spellicy, Stauffer, Wenck, Wells—46.

The motion to lay on the table was lost.

The question upon the adoption of the original motion to strike out was then put by the chair and declared adopted. A division was called and the vote stood: ayes 39, nays 31, as follows:

Yeas—Messrs. Arial, Bailey, Baum, Beauvais, Bofill, Buckley, Burke, Campbell, Cook J. K., Crozat, Collin, Duane, Dufresne, Duke, Flagg, Fosdick, Foley, Gastinel, Goldman, Gruneberg, Gaidry, Harnan, Hart, Hills, Howell, Howes, Kavanagh, Maas, Maurer, Mendiverri, Millspaugh, Morris E., Newell, Normand, Ong, Pintado, Poynot, Pursell S., Seymour, Smith, Stumpf, Stauffer, Sullivan, Wenck, Wells—46.

Nays—Messrs. Abell, Austin, Barrett, Bell, Cazabat, Cook T., Cutler, Davies, Dupaty, Edwards, Ennis, Fish, Flood, Fuller, Geier, Gorlinski, Healy, Heard, Henderson, Hire, Knobloch, Kugler, Mann, Montamat, Montague, Murphy M. W., O'Conner, Spellicy, Stocker, Stiner, Terry, Thorpe, Thomas, Wilson—34.

The motion to strike out was carried.

The second clause, fixing compensation of the secretary at $15 per day, was then read.

A motion was made to amend to $12 per day, and, on motion, tabled, and the report adopted.

The question on the adoption of the portion referring to Mr. S. G. Hamilton, assistant secretary, was then put.]

Mr. Stocker—I move to amend to twelve dollars and a half.

[The amendment was lost and the report adopted.

The portion of the report referring to Mr. Murphy, assistant secretary, was then adopted without remark.

The portion of the report fixing the compensation of the sergeant-at-arms, Michael DeCoursey,at $15 per day, was next read.]

Mr. Fosdick—I move to amend to $10 per day.

Mr. Henderson—I move to lay that amendment on the table.

[The motion to table was carried, and the report adopted.

The secretary read "two assistants, each, six dollars per day."]

Mr. Healy—I move to amend by making it ten dollars per day.

[A motion was made to lay the amendment on the table.

The president put the question and declared it lost; but, upon a call for a division the vote showed that it was carried—yeas 51, nays 20.

A motion to amend to eight dollars was made.]

Mr. Montamat—I move to lay the motion on the table.

[The motion was tabled and the report adopted.

The report fixing the salaries of messengers at five dollars per day, was read by the secretary.]

Mr. Fosdick—I move to amend to three dollars per day.

Mr. Henderson—I move to lay the motion on the table.

[The amendment was tabled.]

Mr. Healy—I move to amend to six dollars per day.

[A motion to table this amendment was carried, and the report adopted.

The compensation for postmaster then came up.]

Mr. Fosdick—I move to amend to five dollars.

[The amendment was tabled and the report adopted.

To fix compensation for door-keeper was next in order.]

Mr. Montamat—I move to amend to ten dollars.

Mr. Fosdick—I move to amend to five dollars.

[The amendments were tabled and the report adopted.

The salary of A. P. Bennett, chief reporter, now came up.]

Mr. Stocker—I move to amend to fifteen dollars per day. The most laborious portion of the work is that performed by the reporters, and they ought to be well compensated for it.

[A motion to table the amendment was lost, and the amendment was carried, and the report as amended adopted.

The compensation of the assistant reporters, Messrs. Gallup, Bartlett and Burnham, next came up.]

Mr. Bell—I move to amend to twelve dollars and a half per day.

[The amendment was tabled and the report adopted.

To fix the salary of the warrant clerk was next in order.]

Mr. Stocker—I move to amend to six dollars per day.

Mr. Goldman—I move to lay the amendment on the table.

[The motion was carried and the report adopted.

The next question was on compensation of enrolling clerks.]

Mr. Harnan—How many enrolling clerks? We want to know how many we are to pay. I move to make it one chief clerk and ten assistants.

Mr. Goldman—I move to lay the amendment on the table.

Mr. Gastinel—I move that the chief of the enrolling clerks shall receive twelve dollars and a half per day.

President—The motion is out of order.

[The question on the adoption of the report was put, and the report adopted.

The report fixing the mileage of members at 20 cents, was next in order.]

Mr. Fosdick—I move to amend to 15 cents per mile.

Mr. Maurer—Mr. President, I wish to

inquire whether the members receive their per diem for the time occupied in coming and going as well as their mileage; if they do, I shall oppose the adoption of the report.

Mr. Heard—The words per diem going and coming are mere surplussage. I have been a member of two Legislatures, and I never knew members to draw for the time occupied in going and coming. They never do it. The distance from Baton Rouge is calculated at 140 miles in round numbers, and the mileage is something like fifty-four dollars.

[The question on the adoption of the report was put and carried.

A motion was made to adopt the report, as amended, as a whole.]

Mr. Stocker—I move to amend so that it shall read, instead of saying that they shall receive pay from the date of their election or appointment, it shall read that they shall receive pay from the 6th day of April.

Mr. Hills—Mr. President, I rise to a point of order; that amendment has already been adopted.

President—The question is on the adoption of the amendment offered by Mr. Stocker.

Mr. Hills—Mr. President, I think it will be seen, by referring to the secretary's minutes, that that amendment has already been adopted.

Mr. Stocker—Mr. President, I think that the gentleman is in error. A resolution to that effect was introduced, which, under the rules, must lie over till to-morrow. Now, I move this as an amendment to the report.

[The question on the adoption of the report as a whole was then put and carried.]

Mr. Montamat—Mr. President, I think we have omitted translating clerks altogether; we have two translating clerks; I move that they receive eight dollars per day.

Mr. Davies—I amend to six dollars.

[A motion to lay the amendment on the table was lost.]

Mr. Stauffer—Mr. President, is the question now debatable?

President—Yes.

Mr. Stauffer—I wish, then, Mr. President, to enquire what necessity there is to employ translating clerks, or what authority there is to have them employed? There has been no resolution passed authorizing their employment. If our proceedings are to be translated into French, it is done by the printer, and they are published in French in the official paper. I think that is all that is necessary in the premises.

Mr. Howell—I move to adjourn.

[The motion was carried, and the Convention adjourned till 12 o'clock on Monday.]

Monday, April 25, 1864.

[The house was called to order a few minutes past 12 o'clock, and after prayer by the Rev. Mr. Hopkins, the secretary proceeded to call the roll, and after some delay the following members answered to their names:

Messrs. Bell, Arial, Austin, Bailey, Barrett, Baum, Bennie, Bofill, Bonzano, Bromley, Burke, Campbell, Cook T., Crozat, Cutler, Duke, Davies, Dufresne, Duane, Edwards, Ennis, Fish, Flagg, Flood, Foley, Fosdick, Fuller, Gastinel, Geier, Goldman-Gorlinski, Gruneberg, Gaidry, Healy, Harnan, Hart, Heard, Henderson, Hills, Hire-Howell, Howes, Kavanagh, Knobloch, Kugler, Maas, Mann, Maurer, Mendiverri, Mills. paugh Montamat, Murphy E., Murphy M. W., Newell, Normand O'Conner, Ong, Payne J., Pintado, Poynot, Purcell, J., Pursell, S., Schroeder, Seymour, Shaw, Smith, Spellicy, Stocker, Stumpf, Stiner, Stauffer, Sullivan, Terry, Thorpe, Thomas, Wells, Wilson and Mr. President—78 members present.

The minutes of Saturday were then read by the secretary.]

Mr. Fosdick—There is an error in the minutes. They state the minority report of the Committee on Compensation presented by myself was taken up, which was not the case.

President—The secretary will make the correction.

[The minutes were then adopted without objection.]

Mr. Crozat—I beg leave to reconsider my vote on the resolution to strike out the compensation of president.

President—It is not in order.

Mr. Goldman—I rise to a question of privilege. Two years ago to-day the citizens of New Orleans beheld the stars and stripes for ihe first time since the commencement of the rebellion. To render appropriate honor to Admiral Farragut, I move we go into a Committee of the Whole and adjourn till to-morrow.

PRESIDENT—Not in order.

Mr. GOLDMAN—I thought a motion to adjourn was always in order. I move we adjourn till to-morrow.

Mr. MONTAMAT—I move to lay it on the table.

[The motion was carried.

Petitions, memorials and resolutions were declared in order.]

Mr. CROZAT—I beg leave to reconsider my vote on the amendment of Mr. Hills to strike out of the report of the committee the compensation of president.

Mr. MONTAMAT—I second it.

Mr. FOSDICK—I amend by reconsidering the vote on the whole.

Mr. FOLEY—I move that we reconsider the vote on the resolution to strike out the compensation of the president.

Mr. GOLDMAN—I move to lay it on the table.

[The motion was put and declared lost.]

Mr. GOLDMAN—I call for a division.

[A rising vote showed yeas 59, nays 9.]

PRESIDENT—The motion now is on the reconsideration.

Mr. HARNAN—I move it lay over under the rules.

[The motion was lost, and the question to reconsider carried by *viva voce* vote.]

Mr. MONTAMAT—I move the adoption of the report.

Mr. GOLDMAN—I move to lay it on the table.

Mr. HILLS—I second the motion.

[The motion to lay on the table was lost.]

Mr. HILLS—I believe the question is open to debate. Mr. President, I should very much regret to see this Convention recede from its action of last Saturday on this question. There is an opinion abroad in the community that this Convention is very wasteful of the public money, and I am not sure it is altogether unfounded. In the beginning the Convention voted its members each $10 per day. It may be that is not too much. I will not say, but I repeat what I have previously stated, that the honor of occupying the seat as president of this Convention is a sufficient remuneration for all the duties belonging to that office. It is pre-eminently a position of honor—a position which any gentleman might well be proud of, and I think it would be degrading to that office to give it additional compensation. I think the president should receive the same compensation as the other members of the Convention, and no more. I would not have any member swayed in his action by the fear of public opinion; but at the same time, I believe that in these matters we should carry out the wishes of our constituents, and it seems to me we have done several things in this Convention which were not economical, and were against the interests of our constituency. For one thing, we voted the salaries of the employés of the Convention back to the 6th of April, thus disposing of hundreds of dollars for services never rendered to the Convention. It seems to me to be wasteful, unnecessary and unjust. I for one am in favor of the Convention adhering to its action of Saturday last, making the remuneration of the president the same as that of the other members of the Convention.

Mr. HENDERSON—This question has already been decided by public usage, since you will find that in all the various conventions the president has received double the pay of the members. I refer the gentleman to the distinguished positions of the president and vice-president of the United States. The vice president is ordinarily the president of the Senate, and he has larger compensation than any member, but not as large as that of the president. When any member of that body is called to the chair to supply the place of the vice president, who, in case of the death of the President, is called to fill that office, the compensation of that member is increased from that which he received as senator to the salary of the vice-president. This was the case at the time of the death of President Harrison. Had we fixed the pay of members at four dollars per day, the president would be entitled to $8. This is partly a matter of deference to the gentleman occupying that position, while at the same time it is due to him on account of the duties of his office, as he has to direct the calling of the ayes and nays, put the resolutions, rise from his seat, etc., while any member may retain his seat from the beginning to the end of the session without speaking a word and yet receive his ten dollars per day. I regard this as a question of principle, and therefore am in favor of reconsideration; and as for honor, I am in favor of compensation in proportion. Since honors are not always easy, although it is often remarked that the greater the honor the less the pay; my will is the reverse. I wish in an officer who fills this position, talent and integrity, and one capable ot commanding respect; and therefore I shall from this time forward, vote for compensation in proportion to the distinction of the office, irrespective of the man who fills it. Why should the president and vice-president receive different salaries? Simply because of the distinction, since it is very seldom that a vice president is called upon to act as president. In conventions this is always allowed as a tribute of respect to the president, whether individually they are for or against him; and for that reason I voted for it the other day.

Mr. Fosdick—Before the question is put, Mr. President, I consider that it is but due that I, as a member of the committee, having made a minority report, should have something to say upon it. I take issue with the gentleman who has just spoken upon the question upon the custom of paying the president a per diem double that of the members in Louisiana. It is not mentioned in the proceedings of the convention of 1852. The custom, if it exists anywhere, is not known in the reports of former conventions in Louisiana. It is entirely a different affair from the speakership of the House of Representatives. In fact, he is not president, and no precedent can be found in Louisiana for making him a higher rate of compensation than that of other members.

Mr. Goldman—I move that it be postponed indefinitely.

[The motion was not seconded.

The motion was then put and the report adopted.]

Mr. Hills—I call for the ayes and nays.

[The call was sustained, and the roll was called, with the following result:

Yeas—Messrs. Abell, Austin, Baily, Barrett, Beauvais, Bell, Bennie, Bofill, Burke, Cazabat, Cook, T., Crozat, Cutler, Davies, Duane, Dupaty, Durell, Ennis, Fish, Fuller, Gaidry, Heard, Henderson, Hire, Kugler, Maas, Mann, Maurer, Mendiverri, Montamat, Montague, Murphy M. W., O'Conner, Payne J., Pintado, Purcell J., Pursell S., Shaw, Smith, Stocker, Stiner, Terry, Thorpe, Thomas, Wilson—44.

Nays—Messrs. Ariail, Balch, Baum, Bonzano, Bromley, Collin, Duke, Dufresne, Edwards, Flagg, Flood, Foley, Fosdick, Gastinel, Geier, Goldman, Gorlinski, Gruneberg, Healy, Harnan, Hart, Hills, Howes, Kavanagh, Knobloch, Millspaugh, Murphy E., Normand, Ong, Poynot, Schroeder, Seymour, Spellicy, Stumpf, Stauffer, Sullivan Wells—38.]

Mr. Kavanagh—Mr. President, I am informed by the mayor of the city that the police officers on duty have been dropped from the police pay roll. I therefore offer a resolution to pay them:

Resolved, That all the police officers on duty at this hall receive four dollars per day each for their services.

Mr. Campbell—Mr. President, I move to so amend the resolution that it shall read:

Resolved, That all the police officers of the city receive four dollars each for their services.

President—Amendments are not in order. The resolution lies over under the rules.

Mr. Foley—Mr. President, I move to suspend the rules, in order to take it up now.

[The question on the adoption of the motion was put and carried.]

Mr. Campbell—Mr. President, I now move to amend the resolution so as to extend it to all the police of the city.

Mr. Thomas—Mr. President, I move to amend by striking out four dollars per day, substituting "the same as they receive on the police pay roll."

[A motion to lay the motion on the table was lost.]

Mr. Montague—I move to amend by adding that the number be restricted to four.

[The question was put and declared lost. A division was called for, when a dozen members sprung to their feet inquiring, "What is the question?" "What are we voting on?" "I don't what the question is!" "We don't know what we are voting for!" etc. Upon counting the votes, the secretary reported 12 yeas and 33 nays, and the president declared the amendment lost.]

Mr. FOLEY—I now move the adoption of the original resolution.

PRESIDENT—The question is on the adoption of the original resolution.

Mr. AUSTIN—Mr. President, is that motion debatable?

PRESIDENT—No; it has been debated already.

[The question was put, and the chair declared it carried. A division was called for, and showed a vote of 46 ayes to 34 nays.]

PRESIDENT—The next business in order is the reports of standing committees: Emancipation.

Mr. BONZANO—Progress.

PRESIDENT—Legislative.

Mr. FOSDICK—Progress.

PRESIDENT—Executive.

Mr. FISH—The committee have agreed to adopt Art. III of the constitution of 1852 as it stands.

Mr. GOLDMAN—Mr. President, I rise to a question of privilege. I will ask the Convention to excuse me to-day, because I look upon this as a holiday, and I wish to observe it as such.

PRESIDENT—The gentleman is out of order.

Mr. GOLDMAN—I think this is a question of privilege.

PRESIDENT—There is a report before the House; the gentleman will take his seat until that is disposed of.

[Mr. Fish read the article from the Revised Statutes.]

Mr. HEALY—Mr. President, I move that the report be accepted.

Mr. FOSDICK—I move that the report be referred back to the committee, and that they be instructed to make their report in writing.

Mr. HILLS—I second that motion.

[The question was put and carried.]

PRESIDENT—Internal Improvements.

Mr. GORLINSKI—The committee can only report progress; it will be ready to report soon.

PRESIDENT—Schedule.

Mr. GRUNEBERG—Progress.

PRESIDENT—Enrollment.

Mr. THORPE—I would report that the Committee on Compensation of Officers and Employés, have left off two officers from their report—the chief clerk of the Enrollment Committee and the translators. They are not on the majority report at all, but are on the minority report.

PRESIDENT—What shall we do with the report?

Mr. WILSON—I move that they be added to the report.

Mr. BAILEY—I move that the compensation of translators be fixed at twelve dollars per day.

PRESIDENT—That is out of order. The question is that they be added to the report of the Committee on Enrollment.

Mr. MONTAGUE—Committee on Compensation, he means.

Mr. WILSON—That they be added to the report of the Committee on Compensation.

Mr. HILLS—I move to amend that their names be added to the pay roll.

Mr. FOLEY—I make a motion that their compensation be referred to the proper committee.

Mr. BAILEY—I move that it be referred to the Committee on Finance.

Mr. FOLEY—I accept the amendment.

Mr. HILLS—I move to refer it to the Committee on Compensation.

PRESIDENT—There is no such committee.

Mr. HILLS—It is a special committee.

Mr. MONTAMAT—I move to refer it to the Committee on Enrollment.

[The motion of Mr. Hills was put and carried.]

PRESIDENT—Committee on Finance.

Mr. MONTAMAT—No report.

PRESIDENT—Expenses.

Mr. PURSELL, of Jefferson—Progress.

PRESIDENT—Printing.

Mr. PURCELL, of Orleans—No report.

PRESIDENT—Federal Relations.

Mr. THORPE—I will make a report, with a statement, that there will probably be a minority report not differing in sentiment from this, but in language:

To the president and members of the Conven-

tion for Revision and Amendment of the Constitution of Louisiana:

Your committee beg leave to report that the constitution and laws of the United States shall be the supreme law of the land, anything in the constitution of this State to the contrary notwithstanding.

PRESIDENT—Credentials.

[MR. MONTAMAT read :]

NEW ORLEANS, April 13, 1864.

To the honorable the president and members of the Constitutional Convention:

Gentlemen—Your Committee on Credentials, having examined the returns of elections from the parish of Plaquemines for one delegate to represent the said parish in this Convention, respectfully beg leave to report that Mr. Thomas J. Decker was duly elected, and is entitled to a seat in this Convention.

Respectfully submitted,

JOHN T. MONTAMAT, *Chairman.*

[A motion for the adoption of the report was made and carried without debate or remark.]

Mr. MONTAMAT—I move that the secretary be instructed to add his name to the roll.

PRESIDENT—That will be done as a matter of course. Assault of Members.

Mr. WILSON—The committee will be ready to report to-morrow.

PRESIDENT—Statue of Washington.

Mr. SULLIVAN—No report.

PRESIDENT—If there are no other reports, gentlemen can call up their resolutions laid over from yesterday.

Mr. THOMAS—Mr. President, I call up the resolution offered by Mr. Fuller on Saturday.

[The secretary read :]

Resolved, That one day's notice shall be given of any amendment or substitute to be proposed to the report of any of the standing committees.

Mr. FOLEY—I move to lay the resolution on the table.

[The question was put and the resolution tabled, by a vote of 49 yeas to 26 nays.]

Mr. ABELL—Mr. President, there is a resolution that I offered on Saturday, which I wish to call up.

[The secretary read :]

Resolved, That when a report of a standing committee is taken up, it shall be considered section by section (*seriatim*), and that no section shall be finally adopted until it has undergone three readings on separate days.

Mr. MONTAMAT—I move its adoption.

[The question was put and the resolution adopted.]

Mr. POYNOT—Mr. President, I move that the newly elected members be requested to present their iron-clads to the president.

Mr. MONTAMAT—I beg leave to inform the gentleman that they have already produced them to the Committee on Credentials.

Mr. KAVANAGH—I move we adjourn.

[The motion was carried.]

TUESDAY, April 26, 1864.

[The Convention met at 12 M., pursuant to adjournment, and after prayer by the Rev. Mr. Newman, the secretary called the roll and the following gentlemen responded :

Messrs. Abell, Ariail, Austin, Balch, Bailey, Barrett, Beauvais, Bell, Bonzano, Bromley, Brott, Buckley, Burke, Cazabat, Cook T., Collin, Crozat, Davies, Dufresne, Duane, Dupaty, Duke. Decker, Edwards. Ennis, Fish, Flagg. Flood, Foley, Fosdick, Gastinel, Geier, Goldman, Gorlinski, Gruneberg, Gaidry, Healy, Harnan, Hart, Heard, Henderson, Hills, Hire, Kavanagh, Knobloch, Kugler, Maas, Maurer, Mendiverri, Millspaugh, Montamat, Montague, Murphy E., Murphy M. W., Newell, Normand, O'Conner, Ong, Payne J., Pintado, Poynot, Purcell J., Pursell S., Schroeder, Seymour, Shaw, Smith, Spellicy, Stumpf, Stiner, Stauffer, Sullivan, Thomas, Wenck, Wells, Wilson—76 members present.

A quorum being present, the minutes of the preceding session were read.]

Mr. STAUFFER—I notice that the secretary omitted to give the report of the Committee on Federal Relations; but as there was such a report, I desire to have it put upon the minutes.

SECRETARY—I beg leave to state that Mr. Thorpe, the chairman, specially requested that it should be delayed.

Mr. STAUFFER—The secretary has no right to leave out the report of a committee without leave of the Convention.

Mr. BALCH—In regard to rescinding the resolution of Saturday, in regard to compensation of president, I am reported as having voted on both sides, when I was not present at all.

Mr. GOLDMAN—My motion was to go into a Committee of the Whole, in honor of Admiral Farragut, and then adjourn. It is said that motion to adjourn was laid on the table, but this could not be done, being unparliamentary.

[The minutes were adopted.

No petitions or memorials were presented.]

Mr. EDWARDS—I offer the following preàmble and resolutions :

Whereas, Positive information has been received by members of this Convention, that all kinds of depredations are daily committed in the parish of Avoyélles and other western portions of Louisiana, within the Federal lines, by guerrillas and other bands of disorganized men ; that there is neither safety nor protection for the life and property of loyal citizens, who are driven away from their homes and families on account of their devotion to the sacred cause of Union and liberty ; that no respect is shown by those bands of guerrillas to either age, sex or condition ; therefore, be it

Resolved, That the attention of the adjutant general of this State be called to the actual deplorable condition of affairs in the parish of Avoyelles, in order that proper and necessary means be put in force for the protection and safety of loyal citizens from the guerrillas, raids or attacks from the enemy.

Be it further resolved, That a committee of three be appointed by the president of this Convention to wait on the adjutant general of this State, and furnish him the necessary information in regard to this matter.

Mr. CAZABAT—I move to suspend the rules in order to act on it immediately.

Mr. ABELL—I move to refer it to General Banks.

[Mr. Cazabat's motion was carried.]

Mr. HILLS—I move to lay the resolution on the table.

[The motion was carried.]

Mr. HILLS—I beg leave to offer the following ; believing it to be a shame that sixty or seventy members should be kept waiting for an hour every morning for six or seven.

Resolved, That members of this Convention not absent with leave, who do not answer to the first roll-call of the secretary, shall forfeit one-half of their per diem allowance for every day of such absence.

Mr. CAZABAT—I move to lay it on the table.

Mr. FOLEY—I move to suspend the rules, for its immediate adoption.

[The motion was lost.]

PRESIDENT—It lies over.

12

PRESIDENT—Reports of Standing Committees are now in order.

Mr. BONZANO—The Committee on Emancipation reports progress.

Mr. FOSDICK—Mr. President, the Committee on Legislative Department reports progress.

Mr. FISH—Mr. President, the Committee on the Executive Department is ready to report.

Mr. AUSTIN—I move to dispense with the reading of that report.

[The motion was carried.]

Mr. SULLIVAN—I move it be made the order of the day for Monday next.

[The motion was carried.]

Mr. THORPE—The Committee on Enrollment reports progress.

Mr. GRUNEBERG—The Committee on Schedule has no report.

Mr. BROTT—The Committee on Finance reports progress.

Mr. S. PURSELL—The Committee on Expenses has no report.

Mr. J. PURCELL—The Committee on Printng has no report.

PRESIDENT—Reports of Special Committees are in order.

Mr. WILSON—The Committee on Assault of Members beg leave to report as follows, viz :

MR. WENCK'S STATEMENT.

On the second day of the session (April 7th, 1864,) as I came down the steps from the hall of the Convention, after its adjournment, I saw John McClelland, Mr. Girodias and others standing together on the banquette. Passing by the side of McClelland, I said, "How are you, John?" He said, pointing his finger at me, "You damned loafer." I answered him, "John, you're wrong in saying so." Then he slapped me in the face, and said, "I'll give you more if you're not satisfied ;" then he went ahead about half a block, and waited again ; when I came near, with other gentlemen, he went ahead again about a block, and waited ; seeing that I was in the company of ten or twelve friends, he again went on, and so continued, until he, with Gerodias and others, went into the Washington coffeehouse, nearly opposite the True Delta office.

On the evening before the occurrence, about five o'clock, I met him for the first time in several weeks ; he called me and said, "Have you ten dollars to loan me?" I told him I had only about five or six dollars small change, or otherwise I would give it to him; then he took a ring from his finger, and said, "I will give you this ring as security."

I told him, "I don't want your ring. If I had the money I would give it to you without the ring." As I was about leaving him, he turned round and said, "Wenck, I'm a candidate for secretary of the Convention, are you going to vote for me?" I answered him, "I have promised, but if my man has no chance after the first ballot, I'll vote for you." This is all that has passed between us for several months.

On, or about the 8th instant I made an affidavit before Recorder Vennard, charging McClelland with assault and battery. He was arrested, and gave bail. Three days after, I was informed that the case had been fixed by Recorder Vennard for a hearing on the 30th of April.

(Signed) ERNEST J. WENCK.

MR. JOHN BUCKLEY, JR.'S STATEMENT.

As I left the Convention I met Mr. McClelland, and a few other gentlemen conversing. I stopped, and said, "Mr. McClelland, I am sorry that my vote did not elect you;" whereupon he replied, "But there are some that are not gentlemen," or something to that effect. As Mr. Wenck came, I turned my back to the parties, and conversed with Mr. Gerodias and Maurer, when I heard Mr. McClelland say, "You know me, and you know where to find me," and I looked around and saw Mr. Wenck's hand on his hat, and Mr. McClelland walked off, and Mr. Wenck a few steps behind him. When Mr. Wenck asked me if I saw "that." I said "no, I did not. I had my back turned talking to Mr. Gerodias and Mr. Maurer," and I walked home slowly with Mr. Maurer. Mr. Wenck came with us as far as Canal and St. Charles streets.

JOHN BUCKLEY, JR.

MR. M'CLELLAND'S STATEMENT.

On day of election for chief clerk of Convention, met some of the members after adjournment; among others met Mr. Buckley, who remarked "that he had done his best for me, but that those members who had voluntarily pledged themselves to vote for me had not kept their promise." I asserted "that all such were not gentlemen;" whereupon Mr. Wenck came up, and asked me "if my remarks were intended for him?" I replied "yes." He then told me he did not care a d—n. Having the True Delta in my hand at the time, I tapped him on the cheek with it; I then moved on. Wenck then came up, making a demonstration as if to strike me; I told him "I did not want to have anything to do with him, to let me alone;" I then went away, and on arriving at corner of St. Charles and Common, I saw that he had followed me; I told my friends that I feared a difficulty with Wenck, I would leave, and I left. Wenck has made an affidavit before Recorder Vennard against me for the alleged offence, and I am now awaiting trial—said trial to come off on the 30th inst.

(Signed) JOHN MCCLELLAND.

The committee have thought it best to report the facts of the case as presented before them in evidence, and leave it to the good sense of the Convention to suggest what action shall be taken in the case.

All of which is respectfully submitted.

J. H. WILSON, Chairman.
ALFRED SHAW,
ROBERT MORRIS.

Mr. DUANE—I move the statement of the accused be stricken out; as he is a prisoner he has no right to make a statement in his own behalf.

Mr. MONTAMAT—I move the report be laid on the table. The case is in the hands of the proper authorities, and—

Mr. STAUFFER—I call the gentleman to order; he has no right to discuss a motion to lay on the table.

PRESIDENT—I must say, as president of this Convention, I consider the motion to lay the report on the table a very extraordinary motion, but, as the motion has been seconded, I shall put it.

[The motion was lost.]

Mr. STAUFFER—I call for the reading of the report by the secretary.

[The report was read again by Mr. Wilson.]

Mr. FOLEY—I move it be received, but not inserted in the minutes of the Convention.

Mr. DUANE—I move the report of the accused be stricken out.

Mr. GORLINSKI—I move the report be laid over to await the decision of the court.

[The motion was lost.]

Mr. THORPE—Is the question debatable?

PRESIDENT—It is.

Mr. THORPE—I think it is our business to attend to the punishment of these parties, if they are guilty, and not leave it to the court. The fact that two members of this Convention have been assaulted, while in the performance of their duties, is a very serious, and to me a very alarming state of things; and I agree with the president that the gentleman who moved to lay the whole thing on the table made a very extraordinary proposition. It is undoubtedly the fact that the great mass of the people of New Orleans have been always among the best disposed and most excellent citizens of the whole country. They were excellent under the Union, and excellent as a general thing under the Confederate rule; but it is also true that this city has been for thirty-five years, to my personal knowledge, disgraced by a species of rowdyism that has made it undeservedly notorious beyond any city in the United States. I believe that New York, Philadelphia, or Boston, to-day, have more outrages committed than the city of New Orleans; but here these matters particularly are brought before the public in such a way as to exaggerate the facts and give the city an unenviable notoriety. We are here in Convention to form a State constitution, and the position of a delegate is one of the most responsible and honorable duties that has been performed since our fathers made the Declaration of Independence. We have high duties to perform, and are thrown upon our sense of honor and dignity. Here two members elected to the Convention, and only a day or two afterwards, in this hall, a member is assaulted because he presumed to use his independence and vote for whom he pleased to fill one of the offices of the Convention. He was assaulted, and I do not care whether it was a mere laying on of the finger or a rude assault, it was an outrage on the members of this Convention and on the dignity of this body, and if we permit it to go unpunished and unnoticed, I do not know where it is to end. I am for taking the matter in hand and making an example that will strike terror to those who would take the law into their own hands. I say, without fear of contradiction, that while I have been in New Orleans I have seen no crime committed in Louisiana—not even the pulling down of the Union flag by Mumford—that is more censurable than these assaults of members.

Now, let us set an example and for all time, and pass sentence on this individual to-day, and pass some resolution that will put a stop to this personal Thugism that is a disgrace to the city of New Orleans, and if allowed to rise again, I ask, what will honorable men say?

Mr. HARNAN — Mr. President, that report does not embody the second assault. It merely refers to one. I move that it be referred back, and that the committee be instructed to report on both assaults.

Mr. WILSON—The committee did not think it right or proper to embody the other assault in their report. It did not grow out of, or have any connection with the action of the party assaulted in this Convention, who although he is a member of the Convention, was not assaulted as such. We did not think it proper to bring every member's private grievances before this Convention. We thought it sufficient to lay before the Convention the case in which the action of a member in the Convention was the occasion of the assault.

Mr. HILLS—Mr. President, it seems to me that the committee has failed to perform its duty fully. They have simply set forth facts. They should have stated what action they thought it necessary for the Convention to take in the matter. I therefore move the appointment of a special committee of three, with Col. Thorpe as chairman, to take into consideration the facts, and report what action they deem it best for the Convention to take.

Mr. BROTT—Before the question is put, I wish to remark that I consider the question, as it now stands, as an indignity to the committee who have had the matter under consideration, and, therefore, I move to amend the resolution so that the report shall be referred back to the same committee.

Mr. HILLS—I accept the amendment, Mr. President. No reflection was intended against that committee when I made my motion.

Mr. FOLEY—Mr. President, I move that the name of Mr. Thorpe, as chairman, be added to that committee.

Mr. HILLS—I accept that amendment, too.

Mr. MORRIS—I was one of that committee, and was in favor of reporting a resolution but it was not considered necessary by the other members, and was not done.

[The question was put, and the motion, as amended, was adopted.]

Mr. PURSELL, of Jefferson—Mr. President, I have a resolution, offered on Saturday, which I wish to call up.

PRESIDENT—It should have been called up yesterday. It cannot be called up to-day.

Mr. PURSELL—What, then, can be done with it?

PRESIDENT—It may be offered again as a new resolution, and will have to lie over one day under the rules.

Mr. PURSELL—I wish, then, to offer it to day. The secretary has it.

PRESIDENT—The Convention cannot wait Gentlemen must attend to these things in time. Offer it to-morrow.

Mr. PURSELL—But it is a substitute to a part of a report that is the order of the day for to-morrow, and that will be too late to offer it.

PRESIDENT—If there are no other resolutions, the order of the day will now be taken up. Mr. Secretary, what is the order of the day?

SECRETARY—The report of the Committee on Public Education.

Mr. BALCH—The secretary is in error. I made the motion myself to make it the order of the day for Saturday, and the motion was carried.

PRESIDENT—Read again, Mr. Secretary, the order of the day for to-day.

[Secretary read—April 26th, special order of the day, report of the Committee on Public Education.

Half a dozen members sprung to their feet, denying the correctness of the secretary's minutes, among which could be distinguished the voice of—]

Mr. MONTAMAT—It is a mistake. I made the motion myself to make it the order of the day for Tuesday, and it was amended to Saturday and the amendment adopted.

Mr. HILLS—Mr. President, if the secretary will take the trouble to examine the minutes, he will find that the report of the Committee on Public Education is ordered for Saturday, and that the report of the Committee on the Mode of Revising the Constitution was made the order for to-day.

PRESIDENT—How is it that the secretary has made such a mistake as this? Read the report, Mr. Secretary, section by section.

[The president called Mr. Brott to the chair and left the hall.

The Secretary read:]

To the president and members of the State Constitutional Convention:

Your committee, to whom was referred the "Mode of Revising the Constitution," beg leave to submit the following report, and recommend the adoption of the following, instead of article 141 of the constitution of 1852:

Article —. Any amendment or amendments to this constitution may be proposed in the Senate or House of Representatives, and if the same shall be agreed to by two-thirds of the members elected to each House, such proposed amendment or amendments shall be entered on their journals, with the yeas and nays taken thereon. Such proposed amendment or amendments shall be submitted to the people at an election to be ordered by said Legislature, and held within ninety days after the adjournment of the same, and after thirty days' publication, according to law, and, if a majority of the voters at said election shall approve and ratify such amendment or amendments, the same shall become a part of the constitution. If more than one amendment be submitted at a time, they shall be submitted in such manner and form that the people may vote for or against each amendment separately.

Respectfully submitted,

R. KING CUTLER, Chairman.
JOSEPH G. BAUM,
J. H. STINER,
PATRICK HARNAN,
E. A. KNOBLOCH.

Mr. HENDERSON—I move the adoption of the entire report of the committee.

[The question was put by the chair, and the report declared adopted.]

Mr. ABELL—Mr. President, this is all out of order.

Mr. GOLDMAN—I call for the reading of the report.

Mr. MONTAMAT—Mr. President, there is a rule that no report of one of these committees shall be adopted until it has been read, section by section, on three several days.

Mr. THOMAS—Mr. President, I call for the reading of the report.

PRESIDENT—Mr. Secretary, read the report section by section.

[The secretary read the report again.]

PRESIDENT—That report seems to have but one section, and therefore comes within the rule.

Mr. SULLIVAN—Mr. President, according to Mr. Abell's resolution, which has been adopted, a report must be read three times, on different days, before it can be adopted.

PRESIDENT (to the secretary)—What do you do in such a case? (To the Convention)—It lies over under the rule; this will be the first reading.

Mr. HILLS—I do not understand it in that manner. I understand that it must be voted on, on each of the several readings, but that its adoption is not final until after the third reading. The Convention may receive it to-day and reject it to-morrow.

Mr. STOCKER—If the gentleman wishes to go contrary to the decision of the chair, he must go it about in a different way. The chair has already decided that the report must lie over for a second and third reading. If the gentleman is not prepared to abide by the decision, he must appeal from it.

Mr. HILLS—If the chair has so decided, I appeal from the decision.

Mr. HEARD—The proper course would be, if gentlemen are anxious to act on the report at once, to move a suspension of the rules in order to put it upon its passage. I therefore move a suspension of the rules for that purpose.

Mr. BEAUVAIS—I second that.

Mr. ABELL—Mr. President, the object of the resolution I introduced was to prevent hasty action on any of these reports, and to allow time for due deliberation, and I hope the Convention will not abandon the rule.

[The chair put the question on Mr. Heard's motion and declared it carried. A division being called for, a rising vote showed 28 ayes to 42 nays. The resolution was therefore lost.]

Mr. MONTAMAT—I move that we adjourn till to-morrow at 12 o'clock.

Mr. WELLS—I have a resolution to offer.

Mr. MONTAMAT—Then I withdraw my motion.

[Mr. Wells read:]

Whereas, It is right and proper that sufficient time be allowed for the calm consideration of the perplexing and important questions now before this Convention and in order to give ample opportunity and further time for the country parishes to send their delegates, by which the State at large may be more fully represented and heard;

Be it Resolved, That this Convention adjourns on Saturday, the 30th instant, until the 1st June, 1864, at 12 o'clock M., or until such time as called by order of the president of this Convention.

Mr. HILLS—I move that the resolution be referred to Gen. Banks.

Mr. DUANE—I move that the resolution be read by the secretary.

Mr. GOLDMAN—I move to adjourn till 12 o'clock to-morrow.

[Five or six other motions to adjourn to various times specified, were made, simultaneously with that of Mr. Goldman.]

PRESIDENT—The secretary will read the resolution.

[The secretary read Mr. Wells's resolution.]

Mr. MONTAMAT—I move to adjourn.

Mr. PURSELL, of Jefferson—Mr. President, I have a resolution to offer.

PRESIDENT—The motion is to adjourn.

[The president put the motion and decided it carried.

A division being called for, a rising vote showed 29 ayes to 42 nays.]

Mr. CAZABAT—I move a suspension of the rules in order to take up the resolution of Mr. Wells.

Mr. THOMAS—I move to adjourn till to-morrow at 12 o'clock.

Mr. CAZABAT—The motion is out of order. I had the floor when the gentleman offered it.

PRESIDENT—The motion to adjourn is in order.

[The resolution was put and lost.]

Mr. CAZABAT—I renew my resolution to suspend the rules in order to take up the resolution of Mr. Wells.

Mr. BELL—I move to lay the motion on the table.

Mr. MURPHY—I wish to offer a report of the Committee on Compensation.

Resolved, That the compensation of the

chief clerk of the bureau of enrollment be fixed at twelve dollars per day, and two translating clerks each ten dollars per day.

Mr. Cazabat---I move to adjourn.

Mr. Pursell, of Jefferson, (at the same time)—I wish to give notice that I shall offer a substitute for the first five articles of the report of the Committee on Public Education. If gentlemen wish to force me to relinquish my purpose by moving an adjournment, when they see me standing with the paper in my hand, they can perhaps do so, but—

Mr. Cazabat---I beg the gentleman's pardon and withdraw my motion. I should not have offered it had I seen him at the time.

Mr. Pursell read:

Art. —. There shall be elected a superintendent of public education, who shall hold his office for the term of four years. His duties shall be prescribed, and compensation fixed by the General Assembly.

Art. —. The General Assembly shall establish free public schools throughout the State for white children, and shall provide for their support by general taxation on property or otherwise, and all moneys so raised or provided shall be distributed to each parish or incorporated city, in proportion to the number of children of such ages as shall be fixed by the General Assembly.

Art. —. The General Assembly shall establish free public schools for colored children between the ages of six and sixteen, who shall be taught the primary branches of an English education; the means of support and the distribution shall be the same as provided for other public schools.

Art. —. The English language only shall be taught in the primary departments of the public schools of this State.

Art. —. The General Assembly shall establish an university in New Orleans, and shall have power to pass such laws as may be necessary for its regulation and the promotion of law, medicine, literature and science.

Mr. Harnan---I move it lie over.

President---That will be done, of course.

Mr. Stocker—Mr. President, in regard to that substitute, I move that it be printed and laid upon the tables of the members.

[The motion was carried.]

Mr. Sullivan---I move we adjourn till to-morrow at 12 o'clock.

President---The motion is not in order; it has been voted on once and lost.

Mr. Abell---I move to adjourn till Thursday at 12 o'clock.

President---That motion is out of order; it has been put once and lost.

Mr. Durell---Mr. President, a motion to adjourn is always in order, if it is made fifty times in fifteen minutes.

Mr. Stocker---Mr. President, I think if you examine Jefferson's Manual, which lies on your desk, you will find that a motion to adjourn is not always in order. It is not in order when the yeas and nays have been called for, when a question has been put, nor when a member has the floor.

Mr. Henderson---A motion to adjourn is not always in order. It is not in order when a member has the floor, and you will find that, when it is made in such cases, it is always by his permission. It is not in order, either, when a question is before the House.

President—The decision of the chair is, that when a motion to adjourn to a certain specified time has been put and lost once, it cannot be put again on the same day.

Mr. Hills---Mr. President, I move that this Convention do now adjourn.

[The question was put and the motion carried.]

Wednesday, April 27th, 1864.

[The Convention was called to order at 12 o'clock m., and after prayer by the Rev. Mr. D'Ossy, of the U. S. Christian Commission, the secretary called the roll and the following gentlemen answered to their names:

Messrs. Abell, Ariail, Balch, Barrett, Bell, Bofill, Bonzano, Buckley, Burke, Campbell, Cazabat, Cook J. K., Cook T., Crozat, Collin, Davies, Dufresne, Decker, Dupaty, Edwards, Ennis, Fish, Flagg, Foley, Fosdick, Geier, Goldman, Gorlinski, Gruneberg, Gaidry, Healy, Harnan, Hart, Heard, Hills, Kavanagh, Kugler, Maas, Maurer, Millspaugh, Murphy E., Murphy M. W., Newell, Normand, O'Conner, Ong, Payne J., Pintado, Poynot, Purcell J., Seymour, Shaw, Smith, Spellicy, Stumpf, Stiner, Sullivan, Wells, and Mr. President—59.

There being no quorum present the president directed the sergeant-at-arms to procure the attendance of absent members.

Messrs. Austin, Bromley, Brott, Gastinel, Hire, Howell, Knobloch, Mendiverri, Montamat, Montague, Morris, Pursell S., Schroeder, Stocker, Stauffer, Wilson and Beauvais, having entered the hall and taken their seats, the president announced that a quorum was present.

PRESIDENT—Mr. Secretary, read the minutes.

[Secretary read the minutes. When he reached the resolution of Mr. Edwards, tabled yesterday, he was interrupted by]

Mr. E. MURPHY—Mr. President, that resolution was laid on the table yesterday, and under our rules cannot be read again. I move, therefore, that the reading be dispensed with.

PRESIDENT—Is there any objection to dispensing with reading of the resolution?

PRESIDENT—The reading of the resolution is dispensed with.

[The minutes were adopted.]

PRESIDENT—The next thing in order is petitions. Are there any petitions?

[None.]

PRESIDENT—Memorials?

Mr. BONZANO—I hold in my hand a memorial from Dr. A. Vallas, who was for some time superintendent of the State Seminary at Alexandria, a gentleman of large experience, and I think the memorial will be found one of interest to the Convention.

[Read.]

NEW ORLEANS, April 27, 1864.

To the honorable president and members of the Constitutional Convention of Louisiana:

GENTLEMEN—The undersigned begs leave to offer a few remarks on the report of your Committee on Public Education.

The report in question is a work that reflects much credit, in general, on the members of the Committee on Public Education, although there are minor points in which it might be perfected and brought nearer to what the public have a right to expect.

The committee propose, in their report, that a University shall be established in the city of New Orleans; said University to be composed of four faculties, to-wit: one of law, one of medicine, one of natural sciences and one of letters. The word faculty signifying the body of teachers, it would be well to replace it by department, which includes teachers and students. The committee recommend a faculty of natural sciences and another of letters. Now, all over the continent of Europe, with the sole exception of France, letters and natural sciences—that is everything that relates to general erudition—is thrown into one department, just as in English colleges and those of this country, and there is no weighty reason for departing from this time-honored practice, particularly if the grammar school fully answers its purpose and the higher collegiate classes comprise two courses of study—a literary and a scientific one.

A collegiate department comprises properly five different branches of human knowledge, to-wit: Those of the philological, historical, strictly philosophical, mathematical and physical science. A knowledge of much of all these branches constitute what we call liberal education. And it does not only suit all the capacities, but is regarded as necessary for the harmonious development of the mental faculties of the students. The deeper and more abstruse portion cannot be imparted to all, but must be left to the choice of those who have a particular leaning for them, and this may be done, very properly, in the two collegiate courses of study above mentioned. The splitting into two different departments would not only imperfectly answer the purpose, as it would lead to the neglect of either of them, and would awaken the idea that they are not equally worthy of being embraced.

A despot may withhold his favor from the cultivation of the circle of historical science, and frown down upon those who devote their time to what he pleases to call *idealogy;* he may also countenance the cultivation of the exact science; but a free people, and one that is determined to be free, will do well to embrace, with equal ardor, all the different branches of a liberal education; giving prominence to none, nor divide what, by its very nature, ought to be mixed.

The undersigned accordingly proposes that the University should comprise a law department, a medical department and a collegiate department.

The committee recommend further: "That the Legislature shall be under no obligations to contribute to the establishment or support of said University by appropriations." If this is meant of the two first faculties or departments, as professional schools, which ought to be self-supporting, no one will object to it; but a collegiate department cannot be left to its own resources, because it does not impart any knowledge or skill which might be immediately available in life, although it might justly vindicate to itself the production of the material out of which the great statesman, philosopher, lawyer, etc., is to be formed. Similar institutions are liberally endowed all over the world, and even poor but talented youth are aided by stipends in order to secure the best talent to the service of the State and public. If the collegiate department is to be left to itself, one of two things will certainly happen. Either it will fail, as other schools have failed under similar circumstances, or it will become an aristocratic institution for the exclusive benefit of the few who are able to pay high fees.

The last article of the report of the Committee of Public Education relates to the Seminary of learning. The United States have donated to this, as well as to other States, several townships of land for the establishment of a Seminary of learning. Other States have thought to fulfil the intention of the donor by establishing State Universities with the funds arising from such donation. The people of Louisiana—that is, the dominant party of former times—kept the Seminary apart from the University; and as soon as symptoms of the impending civil war were perceptible, they endeavored to convert it into a *Military Academy*, for resisting and defeating the authority of the donor. (See report of the Board of Supervisiors of the State Seminary, 1860.) This plan, indeed, proved abortive, and the Seminary never went beyond company drill, by the self-sacrificing resistance of a few loyal men; but the intention was manifest, and may be easily understood from the report just alluded to, and the act of organization subsequent to it.

The past, with its prejudices, with its views and tastes, with its plans and schemes, has rolled down into the abyss of eternity. On the ruins of an almost mediaeval society the edifice of modern civilization is to be erected. Among the fragments of the past we find a University, without endowment and funds, without a proper object. Have not the disenthralled people of Louisiana a right to see the two united? Particularly as there is no need any more of a separate institution for the benefit of a higher class of citizens, all differences, all pretensions, having been obliterated by the victorious progress of the armies of the United States.

The undersigned, led by these views, begs leave to propose that all the property and revenues of the State Seminary be transferred to the collegiate department of the University, and that the last article of the report of the Committee on Public Education be amended accordingly.

Respectfully submitted by
A. Vallas, Ph. D.,

Late Acting Superintendent and Professor at the State Seminary of Louisiana.

I now move, Mr. President, that a sufficient number of copies be printed for the use of the Convention, and that the memorial be referred to the Committee on Public Education.

Mr. Sullivan—Mr. President, I wish to offer a substitute for the report of the Committee on Judiciary.

President—The substitute will be in order when the report comes up. Reports of committees.

Mr. Bonzano—Mr. President, the Committee on Emancipation is ready to report.

To the president and members of the Convention for the Revision and Amendment of the Constitution of the State of Louisiana:

Your Committee, to whom was referred the subject of Emancipation, respectfully beg leave to report the following ordinance and recommend its adoption:

AN ORDINANCE TO ABOLISH SLAVERY AND INVOLUNTARY SERVITUDE.

We, the people of the State of Louisiana, in Convention assembled, do hereby declare and ordain as follows:

Section 1. Slavery and involuntary servitude, except as a punishment for crime, whereof the party shall have been duly convicted, are hereby forever abolished and prohibited throughout the State.

Sec. 2. The Legislature shall make no law recognizing the right of property in man.

Sec. 3. The code of laws, known as the Black Code, and legislation and jurisprudence on the subject of slavery, are hereby declared annulled and abolished.

Sec. 4. No penal laws shall be made against persons of African descent, different from those enacted against white persons.

Sec. 5. The Legislature shall, at its first session under this constitution, enact laws providing for the indenture of minors of African descent, as apprentices, to citizens of the State, on the same terms and conditions as those prescribed, or which may hereafter be prescribed, for the apprenticing of white minors.

Adopted in Convention, at the city of New Orleans, this——day of——, in the year of our Lord one thousand eight hundred and sixty-four, and of the Independence of the United States eighty-eight.

M. F. Bonzano, Chairman;
A. Cazabat,
H. C. Edwards,
Edmund Goldman,
E. Murphy,
T. B. Schroeder,
W. T. Stocker,
R. K. Howell.

I now move that the report be made the special order of the day for Saturday.

Mr. Austin—I ask that the report be read by the secretary, in a tone that we can all hear. I have not been able to hear it, and I don't think any gentleman on this side of the house has.

[The secretary read the report.]

Mr. ABELL—Mr. President, I hold in my hand a minority report, which, as a member of that committee, I wish to present to the Convention; and as I do not think that I shall be able to read it so as to be heard all over the house, perhaps it will be as well for the secretary to read it at once.

Mr. FOLEY—I move that the gentleman presenting it read it himself.

[The secretary read.]

To the president and members of the Convention for the Revision and Amendment of the Constitution of Louisiana:

The undersigned having failed to arrive at the same conclusion with the majority of your committee, begs leave to submit the following minority report:

Your committee would gladly acquiesce in any proposition for the emancipation of slaves in this State, that would be consistent with the honor, the integrity and safety of the State, the rights of the master, and the future welfare, safety and happiness of the slave, and their final removal from the State.

He could not view as just to the master, honorable to the State, or advantageous to the slave, any proposition which has for its object the immediate emancipation of the slave without the consent of the master, or a fair compensation for his property.

The master having acquired a vested right in his property, by virtue of the customs of the country, guaranteed by the constitutions of this and the United States, the various acts of the Legislature of the several States and the Congress of the United States, confirmed by numerous decisions of the highest courts in the land, and assented to and acted upon by the wisest statesmen, perhaps, of the world, your committee does not believe that this Convention could divest the master of his property without doing a flagrant injustice.

Were he to consider the interest of the slave, without reference to the right of the master, or advantage or detriment to the State, it would not be their interest to be immediately emancipated. Their tendency to idleness, their general ignorance and want of skill to provide for themselves, would leave them the prey of their vices and dissipation, and of disease and death; and any law that would force them to a different system of labor than is required of the white race, would be a violation of their rights as free men, and only a change from the present system of servitude or slavery to that of another.

The money-making speculator would be substituted for the kind and interested owner. The object of the sharper would be to make money; the kind master's interest to preserve and improve his property.

But, above all considerations, your committee believe that the State has the deepest interest in preserving its safety and forwarding the interests of the white race. With the lights now before this Convention, emanating from our sister States, New York, Pennsylvania, Ohio, and the Western States generally, with free white labor this State would rise in population, wealth and grandeur; but in competition with 312,000 negroes, with a natural increase unparalleled in the history of any people, surrounded by millions who would make Louisiana their asylum, the Convention cannot be blind to the fact that a system of peonage or slavery would be established, all inducement for white labor overridden, and the safety of the State menaced.

Mr. PURSELL, of Jefferson—Mr. President, I desire to know whether that is a report the secretary is reading, or an argument.

PRESIDENT—It is a minority report.

Mr. PURSELL, of Jefferson—It sounds to me more like an argument than like a report.

[The secretary read:]

The Convention cannot be insensible to the already demoralized state of the slave, and the disorganized state of their labor and the terrible havoc of mortality among them; nor should the Convention be unmindful of the fact that of all the Northern States that have rid themselves of slavery, not one of them have freed a single slave. They adopted a system of laws which provided, prospectively, that all children born of slaves within their jurisdiction, after certain specified dates, should be held free when they attained a given age. As early as 1774, it was provided by a law in Rhode Island "that all offspring born of slaves after 1784, should be free." Pennsylvania in 1780 passed an act declaring "that all children born of slaves after the passage of the act free at a given age." [Stroud's Digest, 789.] New York, in 1783, passed a similar act, and the New England States generally pursued a similar mode of ridding themselves of slavery, by inducing owners to remove their slaves to the Southern States.

Your committee is informed that little if any more than 2000 out of 40,000 votes were cast in the country parishes, they being the principal slaveholding portions of the State.

Your committee has been forced to the conclusion that the adoption of the majority report would be unconstitutional, in violation of the first principles of right, and unjust to the loyal owner; ruinous, demoralizing and destructive to the best interests of the slave; dishonorable and dangerous to the safety of the State.

Your committee, in view of the philanthrophy of our Northern brethren, could not deem it just to withhold from them the opportunity of contributing largely to the freedom of the slave.

Your committee, therefore, earnestly recommend the indefinite postponement of any action on the subject until such time as any future Legislature of this State, conjointly with the Congress of the United States, shall provide ways and means to pay all loyal owners for their slaves, and for their permanent removal from the State; and that, in the meantime, the State do take possession of all unclaimed slaves, and hire or employ them to the best advantage, the proceeds of their labor to be paid into the treasury of this State, to be disposed of as the Legislature may direct.

Most respectfully submitted.

EDMUND ABELL.

Mr. GOLDMAN—Did nobody else sign that report?

Mr. HILLS—Mr. President, I move that the reports be printed and made the order of the day for Monday.

Mr. STAUFFER—As the order for Monday is already fixed, I amend to Wednesday.

Mr. HILLS—I accept the amendment.

[The question was put and carried.]

PRESIDENT—Committee on Execetive Department?

Mr. FISH—The committee reported yesterday. There is no report to-day.

PRESIDENT—Committee on the Judiciary?

Mr. SULLIVAN—Mr. President, I have some substitutes which I wish to offer to some of the articles of the report of that committee.

PRESIDENT—What disposition shall be made of the substitute?

Mr. WILSON—Mr. President, I move that it be printed and made the order of the day for Friday.

[The motion was put and carried.]

PRESIDENT—Committee on Internal Improvement?

Mr. GORLINSKI—Progress.

PRESIDENT—Schedule?

Mr. GRUNEBERG—No report.

PRESIDENT—Ordinance?

Mr. SHAW—Progress.

PRESIDENT—Enrollment?

Mr. THORPE—The committee reports as duly enrolled the following resolutions, to-wit:

Resolution allowing one hundred dollars to H. A. Gallup, for services as assistant secretary before the organization of this Convention.

Resolution requesting the State librarian to furnish each member with a copy of the Revised Statutes.

Resolution fixing the compensation of the members of this Convention, and also appointing a committee of *five* to fix the salary of the officers and employés of this Convention.

Resolution inviting the governor to issue his proclamation to fill a vacancy for a delegate in the Tenth Representative District.

PRESIDENT—What shall be done with the report?

Mr. BELL—I move that it be received.

PRESIDENT—The proper motion is whether it shall be received and signed by the president.

Mr. MONTAMAT—I move that it be received and signed by the president.

[The question was put and the motion carried.]

PRESIDENT—Committee on Finance?

Mr. BROTT—The committee make the following report:

STATEMENT OF WARRANTS ISSUED AND PAID, AND OF THE BALANCE ON HAND OUT OF THE APPROPRIATION OF $100,000.

1864.

Date	Item	Amount	Subtotal	Total
April 15,	Appropriation			$100,000 00
" 21,	Warrant No. 1,	$1440 00		
" "	" " 2,	2240 00		
" "	" " 3,	1220 00		
			4900 00	
" 22,	" " 4,	2891 85		
" "	" " 5,	2040 00		
" "	" " 6,	510 00		
			5441 85	
" 23,	" " 7,	2448 00		
" "	" " 8,	432 00		
" "	" " 9,	1620 00		
" 25,	" " 10,	920 00		
			5420 00	15,761 85
April 26,	Bal. on hand in State Treas.			$84,238 15

New Orleans, April 26th, 1864.

A true copy from the Warrant Book.

L. C. MAUREAU, Warrant Clerk.

GEO. F. BROTT, Chairman.

PRESIDENT—Committee on Printing?

Mr. J. PURCELL—No report.

PRESIDENT—Federal Relations?

Mr. THORPE—As chairman of that committee I made a report a day or two ago which was adopted. I was afterwards informed that it had to be read on three several days. I am not aware how it can be brought up again, nor whether it has been properly adopted; but, if in order, Mr. President, I call for a second reading of that report.

Mr. BROTT—I would state, that as a member of that committee, I was necessarily compelled to be absent from some of its sessions, and did not know what the report was.

[The secretary read:]

The constitution and laws of the United States shall be the supreme law of the land, anything in the constitution and laws of the State to the contrary notwithstanding.

Mr. PURSELL, of Jefferson—Mr. President, would I be in order to offer a substitute for that.

PRESIDENT—Yes.

Mr. PURSELL, of Jefferson read:

The United States is one government, the several States auxiliary thereto with local powers.

Mr. FOLEY—I move to lay the resolution on the table.

[The question was put and the motion lost.]

Mr. SHAW—I move that the substitute be referred to the Committee on Federal Relations.

Mr. MONTAMAT—Mr. President, I move that the rules be suspended in order to put it upon its passage at once.

Mr. HEALY—Mr. President, I move the substitute be referred to the Committee on Preamble.

Mr. CAZABAT—Mr. President, I rise to a point of order. I do not see how a substitute can be referred to a Committee on a Preamble which has already been reported, received and adopted.

Mr. THOMAS—Mr. President, I wish merely to call attention to the fact, that the reports of the committees on the Preamble and on Distribution of Powers are in the same condition as the report of the Committee on Federal Relations, of which Col. Thorpe is chairman. They have been received and adopted, but have not passed through the second reading yet. I would, therefore, ask that they now be called for their second reading.

Mr. WILSON—They were received and adopted before the adoption of Mr. Abell's resolution, which requires three readings, and consequently cannot in any way be affected by it. It seems to me that if this is the way business is to be done here, we are going backward rather than forward.

PRESIDENT—The gentleman has a right to make the motion. That point may come up in the debate.

PRESIDENT—Committee on Assault of Members?

Mr. WILSON—No report to-day, Mr. President.

PRESIDENT—Unfinished business. Gentlemen will call up their resolutions from yesterday.

Mr. HILLS—Mr. President, I call for my resolution of yesterday.

[The secretary read:]

Resolved, That members of this Convention, now absent without leave, who do not answer to the first roll-call of the secretary, shall forfeit one-half their per diem for every day of such absence.

Mr. HILLS—Mr. President, I now move the adoption of the resolution.

Mr. MONTAMAT—I move to lay it on the table.

PRESIDENT—I have not heard the motion seconded yet.

Mr. FOLEY—I second the motion of Mr. Hills.

Mr. HILLS—My motion was seconded.

[The question was put, and the chair unable to decide, directed a division.]

Mr. HILLS—I call for the ayes and nays.

Mr. GOLDMAN—The ayes and nays.

[One-fifth of the members sustained the call, and the vote was taken, with the following result:

AYES—Messrs. Austin Balch, Baum, Beauvais, Bofill, Bromley, Buckley, Burke, Campbell, Crozat, Cutler, Davies, Dufresne, Decker, Dupaty, Edwards, Fish, Gastinel, Gruneberg, Harnan, Heard, Hire, Kavanagh, Knobloch, Kugler, Mendiverri, Montamat, Morris, Murphy M. W., Newell, Normand, O'Conner, Ong, Payne J., Pintado, Purcell J., Pursell S., Seymour, Stocker, Sullivan, Thorpe—41.

NAYS—Messrs. Abell, Ariail, Barrett

Bell, Bonzano, Brott, Cook J. K., Cook T., Collin, Ennis, Foley, Fosdick, Goldman, Gorlinski, Gaidry, Healy, Hart, Hills, Howell, Maas, Maurer, Millspaugh, Montague, Murphy E., Poynot, Schroeder, Shaw, Smith, Spellicy, Stumpf, Stiner, Stauffer, Thomas, Wenck, Wells, Wilson—37.]

Mr. M. W. MURPHY—Mr. President, I call up my report of yesterday.

[The secretary read :]

Resolved, That the compensation of the chief clerk of the Bureau of Enrollment be fixed at twelve dollars per day, and two translating clerks, each ten dollars per day.

Mr. MONTAMAT—I move that the translating clerks receive eight dollars each per day, and the chief clerk ten dollars per day.

Mr. FOSDICK—The resolution was referred to the committee to fix the compensation of members. The committee has not as yet taken the matter under consideration and made a report.

Mr. MONTAMAT—That is the report of the committee.

Mr. M. W. MURPHY—The only gentleman who objects to it is the gentleman on my right, who made the minority report the other day.

PRESIDENT—The order of the day.

[The secretary read the report of the Committee on the Mode of Revising the Constitution.]

Mr. HOWELL—Mr. President, I move to strike out in the 3d line the word "two-thirds" and insert instead the word "three-fourths."

Mr. HARNAN—I move that the amendment be laid on the table.

[The question was put on Mr. Harnan's motion. The president being unable to decide directed a rising vote, which showed 18 yeas and 42 nays. The motion was therefore lost.]

PRESIDENT—The question is on the adoption.

Mr. CUTLER—Mr. President——

[The vote was taken, and the chair decided the amendment carried.]

Mr. CUTLER—Mr. President——

PRESIDENT—The amendment is adopted.

Mr. CUTLER—Mr. President, I think this is a little too fast. The question should be stated, and then it is open to debate. I rose in time, but was unable to get the attention of the chair.

PRESIDENT—I did not hear you.

Mr. CUTLER—I believe that I speak tolerably loud.

PRESIDENT—Will some one move a reconsideration, in order to allow the gentleman to debate the question ?

[A reconsideration was moved and carried.]

Mr. CUTLER—My object simply was this, not that I desire to discuss the question at all, but, as chairman of the committee, I deemed it my duty to advocate the report.

You all know that this report reads two-thirds, and that the change by amendment suggested by the gentleman from the Fifth Representative District (Judge Howell) is "three-fourths."

The deliberations of the committee were confined to this material part of the question presented, that is, whether the people of the State of Louisiana, when it becomes necessary to make a change in the organic law, should be detained in making that change for a period of years, or whether they should do so at once.

According to the constitution of 1812, it required a great period of time for the purpose of revising any particular article of that constitution. There were no inroads made upon the provisions therein contained until 1845. By the action of the Convention of 1845, we find that there was a change, lessening the period of time in which the constitution could be revised, and changing the mode and manner of revision. *Since* the constitution of 1845, there has been no material change. I believe that even the rebel Convention of 1861 coincided with the views taken in 1852 by the committee that reported on that constitution and made no amendment. *Then* the subject matter under the consideration of the committee, or, rather, the graver portion of it, was the speedy revision of the constitution.

We agreed unanimously that it was certainly proper, under the peculiar and existing circumstances that surround this Convention ; under the peculiar circumstances, I say, both military and civil, that surround us, that it might suggest itself to the people of Louisiana, in the short future, that a speedy amendment to some portion of the constitution might be absolutely necessary.

Hence, we thought it proper in that committee to report to this Convention the propriety of revising the constitution, or any portion of it therein contained, in as speedy a manner as possible. Therefore, instead of prolonging the term to the June election next following the adjournment of the Legislature, or to that election which takes place for the election of representatives to the General Assembly, as was the case in the constitution of 1845 or 1852, we thought it proper, in our judgment, to present to the consideration of this Convention a different mode of revision,—that is to say, within sixty days; that an election should take place within ninety days after the adjournment of the Legislature wherein the proposed amendment was made, after giving thirty days' publication to the entire people of the State that an election to that effect should be held—giving them fair warning, that they may come up and vote for the proposed amendment or amendments previously voted upon by two-thirds. Now, if you confine it to a three-fourths vote, you go behind the constitution of 1845, to those times when we had just emerged from the Territory of Orleans, and when our legislation was in its dark ages.

It struck our minds that it was proper to keep pace with the times, with the progress of the times; and if the great people of Louisiana deemed it necessary to make amendments, that the power be not wrested from their hands, but be given to them within a short period of time. If you leave the question to three-fourths of both Houses, you require such a vote as may destroy the ends and purposes of the provisions.

If you refer it to a two-thirds vote, you have over a majority vote, and that is all that could be required by the constituency and the people at large in this State. Two-thirds, then, we considered a sufficient vote to settle the question, whether any amendment should be proposed or not, and whether it meets the approbation of this Convention or not, it is for your votes to determine; whether three-fourths of the vote of both Houses, taking into consideration all the circumstances which cause this Convention to act, is absolutely necessary for the purpose of making one or more amendments to this constitution remains to be seen. I did not feel disposed, as chairman, nor did any members of the committee, to vote simply for a majority; we thought it proper not to reduce to a *mere* majority, but asked before it was left to the consideration of a vote, for at least two-thirds, but when you come to "three-fourths," you come to a vote that the people may disapprove.

It was the result of our deliberations, that a two-thirds vote was a sufficient vote upon an amendment, when the people could cast their votes for or against.

It was upon this consideration, I desire to state to the president, that when a question is stated, it should be announced by the chair that it is open for debate, inasmuch as there is a disposition upon the part of some members to make an effort that might thwart the desires of the people.

Now, in conclusion, permit me to say, I am inclined to think that there is but one mode parliamentary in which this report should be presented to this Convention, and that is this: when put upon either reading, it should afterwards be voted upon, and must be voted upon three times in the affirmative before it becomes a law.

Mr. HOWELL—I will state that it was with no disposition to oppose the report of any committee that might be presented to this Convention that I offered the amendment. My object was simply to bring to the mind of the Convention the important subject that is now under consideration. I am willing, sir, that every proper means should be adopted to avoid the cumbersome and expensive process of holding conventions to revise and amend the constitution; but in adopting that plan, we should be careful not to go to the other extreme, and open the door of amendment so wide that the people may have to act every year upon some proposed amendment to their organic law. When an event of that kind shall have occurred the republican form of government becomes unsettled, and the institutions of the country unsafe. It is the duty of wise men to guard against any system which may in its tendency produce such a result. It may be, my proposition to amend this report appears to restrict, but I am inclined to the opinion that if the gentlemen of this Convention will reflect for a time, they will agree with me in the propriety at least of being very careful in adopting a mode of revising the constitution. The Legislature is the creature of the constitution, and when you give the creature power to destroy the creator, you adopt almost an anomaly.

I do not contend, sir, that my amendment affects at all the real merits of the report now under consideration. It does not con template prolonging the time for amending the constitution; it only gives the people a guarantee that there shall be some deliberation—some consideration before their fundamental law shall be interfered with, and those familiar with legislation in this or any other State, will bear me out in the statement that it is not always difficult to get a vote of two-thirds in any body of a legislative character. The object of putting the number at three-fourths is simply to effect the proper consideration of every subject before it is submitted to the people for their adoption. It assumes more of the character of a deliberative assembly, formed and organized for business of that kind, than for mere law-making, which may be repealed at any succeeding session. Make it three-fourths, and you then require of the representatives of the people to be satisfied that the amendments proposed are required by the demands of the country. Two-thirds is but a small number beyond a majority; and three-fourths is but a small number beyond two-thirds; but it is a greater number than the majority, and the higher the number you fix upon when you shorten the time, gives a greater guarantee to the people against constant changes in their organic law. It is to avoid these frequent changes that I proposed the amendment, and not to prolong the time. I have no objection to having it done within the time proposed, but would have suggested a longer period. I think amendments to the constitution should be presented under such restrictions as would require deliberation—not only in those who propose them, but give those who pass finally upon them an opportunity to consider them also. According to the report of the committee, an amendment may be proposed by the Legislature during the last week of its term, and within sixty days it may become the organic law of the State. It is seldom that the attention of the whole people of the State can be aroused in that time. To secure that, in some respeet, or guard them in some measure, I am of opinion that the requirement of a three-fourths vote in the Legislature will make it so very apparent that the people will be aided at least in their deliberations.

Mr. Cazabat—I seconded the amendment of the gentleman from New Orleans (Judge Howell) which he has so ably discussed.

What may have been suitable under the constitution of 1812–'45 and '52 or '61, may be now considered a serious ill and source of mischief to the rights of the people.

It is to be hoped that the people will sanction the proceedings and the deliberations of this convention. I have no doubt that every member here is willing and ready to submit the constitution which we are about to revise, to the people, for their approbation or rejection. *When* once approved by the will and sanction of the people, let it stand there, to be the organic and supreme law of the land. Not a few men, representing private interests, can destroy the liberties of the people again. No, sir, two-thirds is not enough; let it be three-fourths.

Let us go back to the constitution of 1812, and see what was done there. Under that constitution, Mr. President, a majority of all the members elected to each House was necessary.

Now, if we examine the articles on revising the constitution, we perceive under article 140, "Any amendment or amendments to this constitution may be proposed in the Senate or House of Representatives, and if the same shall be agreed to by three-fifths of the members elected to each House, and approved by the governor," such shall be adopted.

Now let us go back to 1852. "Any amendment or amendments to this constitution may be proposed in the Senate or House of Representatives, and if the same shall be agreed to by two-thirds of the members elected to each House, etc," shall be adopted.

Now sir, shall we contend for a principle which is not in accordance with the spirit of our institutions?

I belong with the people, and when this constitution that we are now about to revise, shall be submitted to them—for we must have their approval—for the sake of Louisiana, for the preservation of our liberties now and forever, let it be the organic law of the land, and let it not be amended or changed, until the Legislature is perfectly satisfied that the proposed amendments are required or asked for by the people of Louisiana.

Sir, I have no doubt that the report of the committee, which has been submitted by my friend, Mr. Cutler, has received that due consideration which he gives to all subjects coming under his consideration, and it seems to me, sir, that it is rather a compliment to him, as assistant of that committee, that this is the only change or amendment that we propose to make. The modification, although very slight, means a good deal. It is a trivial modification, but the "three-fourths" vote is an expression of the majesty and will of the people, the other of a minority, and I will, for one, vote against it.

Mr. SHAW—Mr. President, in examining the constitution of 1812, '45 and '52, it is plain to be seen that a perceptible progress has been made by the Conventions of this State in liberality, on the question of the amendment of their work.

The Convention of 1812 did not seem to want their work amended at all. That constitution could not be amended without calling a Convention at an expense of hundreds of thousands of dollars, to change it in the smallest particular—and the people submitted to great annoyance for the space of thirty-two or three years on account of the great difficulty of making an alteration.

The Convention that sat in 1845 made a constitution, in which they provided that three-fifths of the members elected to both Houses might submit an amendment to the people of this State.

In 1852, a Convention which has been accused for the last twelve years of having endeavored to shackle the people of this State, by what they adopted, was still liberal enough to allow the Legislature to call an election of the people, to pass upon an amendment proposed by a vote of two-thirds of the members elected to each House.

Here *we* are, without having adopted any of the leading parts of our constitution; without having adopted anything in relation to the Legislative, Executive or Judiciary Department,—the most important parts of the constitution. Before we know what our constitution is to be, we are so well pleased with our work, that we are about to fasten it upon the people by requiring a three-fourths vote to submit an amendment to the people.

According to the constitution of 1812, no number whatever could submit an amendment to the people.

According to the constitution of 1845, out of ninety-eight members in the lower House, fifty-eight could vote to submit an amendment to the people.

According to the constitution of 1852, sixty-six could vote to submit an amendment to the people; but hereafter, a small and possibly interested portion of the Legislature, amounting to only one-fourth, should they wish, can keep the people of this State by the rule we are about to adopt, from making any change.

Why should our work stand any firmer than that of our predecessors? Is it because we have only ninety-five out of one hundred and fifty members due to this Convention, representatives coming almost exclusively from the city of New Orleans and the parishes on the lower Mississippi; is that any reason why our work should be fastened upon the people hereafter?

I look upon this question as one involving a matter of fairness. If any part of our work should prove wanting, let sixty-six out of ninety-eight members propose an amendment and submit it to the people. If a majority of the people of Louisiana then find any portion of our work to be imperfect, let them amend. Why should we make restrictions greater than any convention has deemed necessary, always excepting the Convention of 1812.

Mr. CUTLER—Mr. President, if there is no further discussion, I desire merely to make a suggestion.

Mr. THORPE—Mr. President, I would like to offer an amendment.

Resolved, That the final vote upon the section providing for the revising or amending the constitution, lie upon the table, until all articles preceding it in order be adopted.

I should like to know, Mr. President, what kind of constitution we are to have, before we provide for its revision and amendment.

Mr. PURSELL, of Jefferson—I move a suspension of the rules, in order that the resolution may be adopted at once.

PRESIDENT—Neither amendment nor suspension of the rules, are necessary. The proper motion would be for the report to lie over on its third reading until the other reports are acted on.

Mr. CUTLER—The proper mode, I consider, would be to end the discussion on the merits now; but I do not desire to argue the question much further. I desire only to trouble the Convention for a moment with a few remarks. I see no objection to the remarks of my friend, Judge Howell, in the mass. The question is merely whether the people are sovereign. He desires that the Convention now, as a matter of policy, shall fix the number at three-fourths of both Houses of the General Assembly, who shall propose and adopt an amendment before it shall be submitted to the people. There is no little inconsistency in this proposition if it is to be understood that the people are the sovereign power of the State. You most certainly abridge their rights by requiring three-fourths of the members of both Houses of the General Assembly to adopt an amendment before it can be submitted to them. If you assume that the sovereignty is in the people, a mere majority would be sufficient to send the amendment to the people themselves.

As for my learned friend from Rapides, with his gushing eloquence and his profound knowledge of constitutions, he has laid down propositions and introduced arguments in which he contradicts himself. He argues that the constitutions of 1812, 1845 and 1852 sustain the views advocated by Judge Howell. Now, gentlemen, just refer for one moment to those constitutions. By the constitutions of 1812 and 1845 you will see that his propositions and arguments do not agree. The constitution of 1812 does not even require two-thirds, a bare majority is all that is necessary:

"When experience shall point out the necessity of amending this constitution, and a majority of all the members elected to each House of the General Assembly shall, within the first twenty days of their stated annual session, concur in passing a law specifying the alterations intended to be made," etc.

Now, let us turn to the constitution of 1845:

"Any amendment or amendments to this constitution may be proposed in the Senate or House of Representatives, and if the same shall be agreed to by *three-fifths* of the members elected to each House."

So it is seen that the gentleman argues from one premiss and all that he quotes is against him.

Let us turn now to the constitution of 1852; that convention which has been accused of attempting to fasten its bantling upon the sovereign people in such a manner that it would be impossible to shake off any portion of it:

"Any amendment or amendments to this constitution may be proposed in the Senate or House of Representatives, and if the same shall be agreed to by two-thirds of the members elected to each House, such proposed amendment or amendments shall be entered on their journals with the yeas and nays taken thereon," etc.

If it is for the purpose of sustaining the sovereign power in the hands of the people that this Convention is assembled, let us show ourselves as liberal as former conventions have done—let us be as liberal as the convention of 1861, save in the act of that convention when they passed an ordinance seceding from the United States of America.

I am not, however, one of those who would look only to former constitutions of the State. Experience, not only in Louisiana, but in other States, has been such as to bear out the report of this committee. If you make it necessary to obtain, before an amendment can go to the people, a three-fourths vote of both Houses of the General Assembly, you abridge the rights of the people. You destroy, to a certain extent, their sovereignty. Let us, then, in adopting this constitution, bear in mind that the sovereign power is in the people, and should never be abridged; that instead of prolonging the time between the adoption of a simple amendment to the constitution by the General Assembly and its submission to the people, we act up to the spirit of the age, and adopt measures that will be consonant with the rights of the people, and at the same time we should do well to remember that we are in an anomolous position; we are not exactly in a state of peace. It is, in my opinion, a state *quasi* civil and *quasi* military. There is only a part of the State within the Federal lines; the city of New Orleans and the several parishes below, on the river, with a few others that are represented here. We are a redeemed people; the sword, the bayonet and the cannon protect us. It may be then that we are not angels, and such being the case, the laws which we promulgate may be expected to be fallible. But let us show that we are men disposed to do justly, honestly and fairly; that we are willing to submit to the will of the people, without abridging their rights.

You will find that the report is in perfect harmony with the spirit of the age and of the times.

It does not propose anything that is inconsistant with the genius and spirit of the people. It is they whose rights are to be preserved by the constitution which we should adopt. Their wishes ought to be observed, and we should remember that our action in this Convention ought to be subservient to the will of the people.

Its provisions are simple, and it provides for speedy and prompt action:

"Any amendment or amendments to this constitution may be proposed in the Senate or House of Representatives, and if the same shall be agreed to by two-thirds of the members elected to each House, such proposed amendment or amendments shall be entered on their journals with the yeas and nays taken thereon. Such proposed amendment or amendments shall be submitted to the people at an election to be ordered by said Legislature, and held within ninety days after the adjournment of the same, and after thirty day's publication according to law; and if a majority of the voters at said election shall approve and ratify such amendment or amendments, the same shall become a part of the constitution.''

Gentlemen, the time will come—God grant that it may come soon—when the country will be at peace; when the circumstances that surround us will have changed, and it may be that the people of Louisiana will then think proper to change some article of the constitution. If it be so, let them have the power to act upon it whenever an amendment shall have been adopted by a two-thirds vote of both Houses of the General Assembly. Let it go forth to the sovereign people of the State, and let it not be said that the Convention has attempted to fasten irrevocably—or with means of amendment which will require two or three years to change it in any particular—its work upon the people of the State. Let such a mode of amendment be adopted as can be effected within a reasonable time. Are not the amendments as provided for in the report of the committee to be submitted to the people? Where, then, lies the danger to republican institutions in their adoption?

"If more than one amendment be submitted at a time, they shall be submitted in such manner and form that the people may vote for or against each amendment separately."

Mr. President, I do not oppose this amendment, because I believe that the report of the committee is perfect and incapable of amendment. I am willing to hear the arguments presented on both sides, and if it can be shown that there is anything improper in it; that this report, in its present form, is not the best that can be devised, and if any improvement can be suggested, then I shall offer no objections; but the tendency of the amendment proposed is to abridge the rights and power of the sovereign people, and therefore I oppose it.

Mr. Abell—Mr. President, I do not rise to make a speech on this question; I think it has been fully discussed. As I have sometimes been governed by a precedent, I shall in this case be governed by precedent in casting my vote. In the constitution of the United States I find this language: "Whenever two-thirds of the members of both Houses shall deem it necessary to propose an amendment to the constitution, or upon the application of two-thirds of the Legislatures"—in both cases requiring the concurrence of the House and Senate and the concurrence of the Legislature, I think is a very good precedent to govern any vote in this matter.

Mr. Howell—I believe, as the mover of the amendment, I have a right to close the debate, not that I desire to take the time of the Convention, but wish to say simply there has been some misrepresentation of my attempted argument. It is not the object of the proposed amendment to restrict the power of the people at all; it is rather to restrict the facility of the Legislature in acting upon this matter. I believe, sir, that too great facility in amending the fundamental law of the country is injurious, and I do not believe, if the amendment proposed is adopted, that the rights of the people will be restricted one iota. The people have a right to call a convention at any time to revise the constitution, notwithstanding; and, as a proof of that, I would ask the gentleman to inform me how many amendments have ever yet been adopted by means of the Legislature? My only motive for presenting this amendment is in consideration of the shortness of the time fixed in the report for making any changes. In 1812 it required an enormous amount of formality before an amendment could be made to the constitution, otherwise than by calling a convention.

In the constitution of 1845, when the Legislature had to propose an amendment, it had in the succeeding general election to be submitted to the people, and then come back to the Legislature, and if adopted by them, submitted a second time to the people. In 1852 the constitution required a vote of two-thirds of the Legislature, and the proposed amendment had to be submitted to the people at the next election, and published in every parish in the State for three months preceding that election. That was a sufficient safeguard. A Legislature assembled in January had to adjourn within sixty days. Their amendments were proposed, and if the general election occurred that fall, the people passed upon them, but they had to be submitted at the next general election, and sometimes we had a term of the Legislature when the general election did not succeed the adjournment, so the people had ample opportunity to deliberate on these matters and consider the importance and necessity of the proposed amendments. Their attention would be directed to them, and by the time the election came on they were prepared to pass definitely upon them; but by the amendment adopted by the committee, it can all be done within ninety days of the time that amendment is proposed. An amendment may be offered by the Legislature within three days of its adjournment and passed on by a two-thirds vote, and it is submitted to the people and made a part of the constitution within ninety days. Now, I ask, if the attention of the people in every part of this State will in all probability be brought to properly consider the importance and bearings of all the amendments that may be proposed with that short space of time? In this Convention, where we have nothing else to do, we will probably require ninety days before we will get through with this matter; and are we to suggest a plan by which politicians, and not the people, may hurry through amendments to the constitution in such rapid facility as to defeat entirely the virtue of fundamental law? I beg the gentlemen to consider these matters before they vote.

Mr. Thorpe—I believe my motion is in order.

[The motion was read.]

Mr. Bell—I move to suspend the rules for its adoption.

President—I will state to the Convention what the chair considers to be the parliamentary rule in this matter. A bill may be adopted and amendments offered at either reading; at the close the question comes up: "Shall it be read again? shall the bill be read a second time?" and on the second reading: "Shall it be read the third time?" although in modern practice it is usual to leave amendments, for facility in business, to the third reading. If, on putting the question, "shall the bill be read the third time?" the Convention decides it shall not, that puts an end to the bill, unless otherwise disposed of. The resolution offered is not an amendment, but it is for the disposition of the bill, and will come up when the question is put: "Shall the bill be read the third time?" The question now is on the amendment of substituting "three-fourths" for "two-thirds."

[The question was put and declared lost.

It was moved and seconded that the report be adopted and lie over.]

Mr. CUTLER—It should not be adopted until the constitution, as a body, is adopted. The mode of revising the constitution ought not to pass as part of the organic law until we know what the law is, and therefore I accept the proposition to lie over.

[The resolution to accept the report was then carried.]

Mr. HARNAN—I move the Convention adjourn.

[The motion was seconded and carried.]

THURSDAY, April 28, 1864.

[At five minutes past 12 o'clock the president called the Convention to order, and the proceedings were opened with prayer by Rev. Mr. Strong.

The secretary called the roll, and only sixty-eight gentlemen answered to their names.

After waiting till twenty minutes past 12, the following gentlemen having answered to their names, viz:

Messrs. Abell, Ariail, Austin, Balch, Bailey, Baum, Beauvais, Bell, Bofill, Bonzano, Bromley, Brott, Burke, Campbell, Cook J. K., Cook T., Crozat, Cutler, Davies, Dufresne, Duane, Dupaty, Durell, Edwards, Ennis, Fish, Flagg, Flood, Foley, Fosdick, Geier, Goldman, Gorlinski, Gruneberg, Gaidry, Healy, Harnan, Hart, Heard, Henderson, Hills, Hire, Howell, Howes, Kavanagh, Knobloch, Kugler, Maas, Maurer, Mendiverri, Millspaugh, Montamat, Montague, Murphy E., Murphy M. W., Newell, Normand, O'Conner, Payne J., Pintado, Poynot, Purcell J., Pursell S., Schroeder, Seymour, Shaw, Smith, Spellicy, Stocker, Stumpf, Stiner, Stauffer, Sullivan, Terry, Thomas, Wells, Duke, Decker—76,

The chair announced a quorum and directed the secretary to read the minutes of the previous day's proceedings.

The substitute of Mr. Pursell to the report of the Committee on Federal Relations was read thus: "The United States are one government. The several States auxiliary thereto, with local powers."]

Mr. S. PURSELL—Mr. Secretary, the substitute is "*is*" one government, not "*are*."

SECRETARY—I read it as it was written, but will make the correction.

[The secretary finished the reading, and the minutes were adopted without further correction.]

PRESIDENT—Are there any petitions?

[None.]

PRESIDENT—Memorials then are in order.

Mr. GOLDMAN—Mr. President, I have a memorial which I wish to read to the Convention. [A voice—"Louder!"] Mr. President, I am speaking as loud as my voice will permit. [Several voices—"Louder! We can't hear."] Mr. President, I wish you would keep order here, and not interrupt a man when he is speaking. Shall I be permitted, Mr. President, to read the memorial?

PRESIDENT—The gentleman will proceed with his memorial.

[Mr. Goldman proceeded to read:]

The present war—which must eventually terminate in the triumph of the nation over the rebellious States—opens a new epoch in our national history. The Federal constitution is not only to be re-established over the entire nation, as the supreme law of the land, but the powers of which it has been stripped, from time to time, by the aggressive spirit embodied in the pernicious doctrine of "State Rights," must be re-asserted, maintained and enforced. Our happiness and safety require that, hereafter, the fundamental law of the nation shall absolutely prevail, "anything in the constitution and laws of any State to the contrary notwithstanding." The constitution gives to the national Congress the exclusive power to coin money and to regulate the value thereof, and to make all laws which shall be necessary and proper for carrying into execution these powers. The constitution says: "No State shall coin money, emit bills of credit, make anything but gold and silver coin a tender in payment of debts."

The obvious meaning of these provisions is, that with the United States alone rests the power of authorizing the bills and notes to circulate as money, and that it is one of the powers which the States are prohibited from exercising. This is the view of the acknowledged authorities on constitutional interpretation. Therefore, the system of State banking is, and has been, a gross and palpable usurpation by the States of a power exclusively granted to the nation.

The State banking system, thus lawlessly maintained, has been fraught with more evil to the moral and material interests of the nation than all other causes together.

Were it possible to compute the loss which the industry of the nation has sustained during the last seventy-five years, by the rates of discount and exchange and the failure of State banks, the sum total would be enough to pay the debt created by the present war. But it is not only the loss of money with which the industry of the nation may justly charge this system. It has inflicted injury on the morals of the nation.

Thus every consideration should bring the people to the determination to put an end to State banking at once and forever. The national government has removed every obstacle in the way of carrying this out. The plea that the wants of commerce imperatively demanded a paper circulation has no longer any force. By the act of Congress entitled "An act to provide a national currency, secured by a pledge of United States stocks and to provide for the circulation and redemption thereof," approved February 25th, 1863, a system of banking is established which will meet all the wants of trade and commerce in every portion of our country, by an issue of paper money based on the national debt—a system that will free us from the evils of discounts, exchanges and failures, and put an end to the favoritism and partial dealings of the State bank system, which it is designed to supercede.

The banks now in this State have no legal existence. By the provisions of the constitution of 1852 and the laws of the State, under which these banks were created, they have all forfeited their charters. By the pre-eminent part they all took in promoting the rebellion, there can be no doubt that all their property is confiscable to the United States. Those managing and chiefly interested in them, were, and still are, the most influential and inveterate of rebels. The constitution and laws of the State made their refusal at any time, to redeem their notes in gold or silver, *ipso facto* a forfeiture of their charters. Although those interested may say that the legal formalities have not been carried out to give judicial effect to the forfeiture, we can, and I trust will, pronounce the merited sentence of death upon these faithless banks.

The pretext urged at the time of their suspension of specie payments, of having been coerced into this act of dishonesty, has been long since disproved. They themselves, no doubt, suggested the scheme to the rebel government, and by its adoption, gave that government what it could not else have had—*a currency*. By this course they made for the time inordinate profits, but with corresponding losses to the suffering people, who conferred on them their privileges and who trusted them. These institutions, acting thus in bad faith, conferred on the rebel government a power which alone enabled them to protract the war to the present day.

Considering then—1st. That as the Federal government, and not any State government, has the power to establish banks or to create banking corporations with authority to issue bills of credit; 2d. That the Federal government, in the exercise of its rights, has created a banking system free from all the objections inherent in the State bank system; 3d. That the banks of this State, having by their infidelity to the people and the nation, their dishonest and treasonable action, forfeited all claims, moral or legal, on our consideration;

Be it Resolved, That banking corporations, under the authority of the State, are prohibited, and that those banks which are doing banking business at present, or have done so hitherto, are hereby forbidden to continue such business.

EDMUND GOLDMAN.

Mr. BALCH—Mr. President, I could not hear a word that the gentleman has said. I shall move his expulsion on the ground that he cannot speak the English language.

Mr. DAVIES—I move that the memorial be read by the secretary.

PRESIDENT—I would ask the gentleman if this is a memorial signed by himself.

Mr. GOLDMAN—It is.

PRESIDENT—A petition or memorial cannot be signed by a member.

Mr. GOLDMAN—It is a memorial and a resolution.

PRESIDENT—Mr. Secretary, pass it back to the gentleman.

Mr. HENDERSON—Mr. President, I have an amendment to the report of the Committee on the Judiciary, which I wish to offer.

PRESIDENT—I cannot hear what the gentleman says.

Mr. HENDERSON—I wish to offer an amendment to the report of the Committee on the Judiciary Department at the proper time, but do not know whether this is the proper time or not.

PRESIDENT—It cannot be offered until after resolutions have been called for.

PRESIDENT—Resolutions?

Mr. HENDERSON—I offer my amendment as a resolution.

Mr. GOLDMAN—Mr. President, I call for the reading of my resolution. I sent it up to the secretary.

PRESIDENT—(To Mr. Goldman.) You are not in order. A gentleman has the floor.

[Mr. Henderson read:]

An amendment to the report of the Committee on the Judiciary Department:

Art. 21. The Supreme Court, except in cases hereafter provided, shall have appellate jurisdiction only, both as to law and fact with such exceptions and under such regulations as the Legislature shall make, which jurisdiction shall extend to all cases when the matter in dispute shall exceed three hundred dollars, exclusive of interests; to all cases in which the constitutionality or legality of any tax, toll or impost whatsoever, or of any fine, forfeiture or penalty imposed by a municipal corporation, shall be in contestation, and to all criminal cases.

Mr. GOLDMAN—I call now for the reading of my preamble and resolution; it contained a resolution, and the memorial was merely a preamble.

Mr. BALCH—I move that it be laid on the table.

Mr. DAVIES—Mr. President, I move that it be read by the secretary.

PRESIDENT—The secretary informs me that he is unable to read the gentleman's hand writing.

Mr. GOLDMAN—I will read it myself.

[Re-read the resolution constituting the latter portion of his memorial.]

Mr. MONTAMAT—Mr. President, I move to lay the resolution on the table.

PRESIDENT—It lies over.

Mr. GRUNEBERG—Mr. President, I desire to offer a resolution:

Whereas, The constitutional Convention of the State of Louisiana has been called principally to decide on the abolition of slavery in this State; *whereas*, the adoption of this measure, in whatever manner or form, will necessarily require great modifications in all parts of the organic law of the State; *whereas*, for these reasons this Convention cannot or ought not to come to a final decision on the reports of any of the standing committees on constitutional amendments, before voting on emancipation; *and, whereas*, the question of emancipation being the most important of all, requires the longest and most mature deliberation of this assembly;

Be it therefore Resolved, That this Convention will take in consideration, first, the reports of all the standing committees on constitutional amendments, with substitutes and amendments thereto, except the report of the Committee on Emancipation, but they shall not pass further than a second reading, that then the report of the Committee on Emancipation shall be taken up, and be then regularly passed to a final vote; and that afterwards the reports of all the other standing committees shall pass to their third reading and to a final vote thereon;

And moreover, Resolved, That this Convention shall only adjourn from day to day until the reports of all the standing committees on constitutional amendments, except that of emancipation, shall have passed a second reading.

PRESIDENT—If there are no further resolutions, I will call for reports of standing committees. Committee on Legislative Department.

Mr. FOSDICK—Will be prepared to report to-morrow.

PRESIDENT—Executive Department.

Mr. FISH—No report.

PRESIDENT—Internal Improvement.

Mr. GORLINSKI—Not ready to report.

PRESIDENT—Schedule.

Mr. GRUNEBERG—No report.

PRESIDENT—Ordinance.

Mr. SHAW—Progress.

PRESIDENT—Enrollment.

Mr. MILLSPAUGH—On behalf of Colonel Thorpe, chairman of the Committee on Enrollment, I report the following acts enrolled and ready for the president's signature, viz.:

A resolution reqesting the governor to issue his proclamation for an election of a delegate from the Tenth Representative District of the Parish of New Orleans.

A resolution relative to Powers's statue of Washington.

A resolution requesting State auditor to furnish the Convention with a statement showing the receipts and expenditures, etc., under the administration of Governor Shepley.

Mr. BELL—I move that the report be received and the acts signed by the president.

Mr. BALCH—What is the nature of the

proclamation? Read the resolution—I want to know what the proclamation is?

PRESIDENT—If the gentleman had kept up with the proceedings of the House, he would have known the nature of the proclamation.

Mr. STOCKER—The call for the reading of the resolution at this moment is not in order. These resolutions have been duly passed and are now presented merely for the signature of the president, and no member, under these circumstances, has a right to demand their reading; I therefore move that the reading of the resolution be dispensed with.

PRESIDENT—The call for the reading of the resolution is unprecedented, but the chair will do anything to accommodate the gentleman. I shall put the question. The question is, shall the reading of the resolution be dispensed with.

[The vote was taken and the motion to dispense with the reading was carried.]

PRESIDENT—Committee on Printing.

[No report.]

PRESIDENT—Expenses.

PURSELL, of Jefferson—No report.

PRESIDENT—Statue of Washington.

Mr. SULLIVAN—Mr. President, the committee is ready to report.

[Read.]

To the honorable the president and members composing the Constitutional Convention of the State of Louisiana:

GENTLEMEN—We, the undersigned delegates, appointed to correspond with and request of the authorities at Washington, the return of Powers's grand statue of Washington, taken as a trophy from Baton Rouge, and now placed in the Patent Office in Washington,

Beg leave most respectfully to report to this Convention that according to the resolution passed we have addressed a communication to the Hon. E. M. Stanton, secretary of war, asking and requesting that the statue be restored to the State of Louisiana.

JOHN SULLIVAN, Chairman.
JAMES ENNIS,
YOUNG BURKE,
J. H. STINER.

Mr. BELL—I move that the report be received.

[The motion was put and carried.]

PRESIDENT—Unfinished business.

Mr. BROTT—Mr. President, you have not called upon the Committee on Finance.

Mr. M. W. MURPHY (at the same time)—Mr. President, I have a report:

To the president and members of the Convention for the Revision and Amendment of the Constitution of Louisiana:

The Committee on Compensation of officers and employés of this Convention beg leave to report that, in their opinion, the chief enrolling clerk should receive ten dollars per day, and the two translating clerks each eight dollars per day.

Mr. FOLEY—Mr. President, I move that the report be received and adopted.

[The question was put and the motion adopted.]

Mr. BROTT—On behalf of the Finance Committee, Mr. President, I wish to make a partial report. We have presented to us, from day to day, numerous bills that have been before the Convention, on contingent expenses, and upon examination we find that there is no appropriation, except the appropriation of one hundred thousand dollars, which appears to have been appropriated for a specific purpose—for paying the mileage and per diem of the members, officers and employés of the Convention. I therefore, in order to obviate this difficulty, desire to submit a motion that the Committee on Expenses be instructed to make an estimate of the amount of funds they are likely to require, and prepare a bill for an appropriation to meet it.

Mr. BALCH—I wish to submit a motion that will solve all these difficulties. It is parliamentary, notwithstanding the objections of the gentleman from New York. When a matter has been once decided by a Convention that it cannot be brought up again during the session. We have already adopted a resolution making an appropriation for the payment of the mileage and per diem of the members and officers of this Convention, and have no right to adopt it again.

Mr. STOCKER—Mr. President, my recollection is that the appropriation was for the payment of contingent expenses as well as for the payment of the mileage and per diem of the members.

Mr. MONTAMAT—The resolution has been enrolled. I presented it myself; it was for a special purpose—the payment of the members and officers of this Convention. I ask the secretary to read the resolution.

[The resolution was read by the secretary.]

Mr. BROTT—I move that the Committee on Contingent Expenses be instructed to make an estimate of the probable amount they will require, and prepare a bill to cover contingent expenses.

Mr. PURSELL, of Jefferson—Mr. President, I wish to explain.

PRESIDENT—There is no motion before the House.

Mr. PURSELL—Whether there is or not, I think an explanation is certainly due to the House from the Committee on Expenses.

PRESIDENT—Debate is out of order unless there is a motion before the House.

Mr. PURSELL—I desire only to say further, that the Committee on Expenses have simply approved bills, leaving it to the gentlemen of the Finance Committee to order them paid out of the appropriation, or not, as they saw proper.

PRESIDENT—The special order of the day is next in order.

Mr. BROTT—My motion is in order, Mr. President.

PRESIDENT—It was not seconded.

Mr. BEAUVAIS—I seconded it, Mr. President.

Mr. STOCKER—I seconded it.

PRESIDENT—Very well; it lies over one day under the rules. The next business is the order of the day—the report of the Committee on General Provisions. Read it, Mr. Secretary.

[The secretary read the following :]

REPORT OF THE COMMITTEE ON GENERAL PROVISIONS.

Article 1. Members of the General Assembly, and all officers, before they enter upon the duties of their offices, shall take the following oath or affirmation:

"I (A B) do solemnly swear (or affirm) that I will support the constitution and laws of the United States and of this State, and that I will faithfully and impartially discharge and perform all the duties incumbent on me as ———, according to the best of my abilities and understanding, so help me, God."

Art. 2. Treason against the State shall consist only in levying war against it, or in adhering to its enemies, giving them aid and comfort. No person shall be convicted of treason, unless on the testimony of two witnesses to the same overt act, or his own confession in open court.

Art. 3. The Legislature shall have power to declare the punishment of treason; but no attainder of treason shall work corruption of blood or forfeiture, except during the life of the person attainted.

Art. 4. Every person shall be disqualified from holding any office of trust or profit, in this State, and shall be excluded from the right of suffrage, who shall have been convicted of treason, perjury, forgery, bribery, or other crimes or misdemeanors.

Art. 5. All penalties shall be proportioned to the nature of the offence.

Art. 6. The privilege of free suffrage shall be supported by laws regulating elections, and prohibiting, under adequate penalties, all undue influence thereon from power, bribery, tumult, or other improper practice.

Art. 7. No money shall be drawn from the treasury but in pursuance of specific appropriation made by law, nor shall any appropriation of money be made for a longer term than two years. A regular statement and account of the receipts and expenditures of all public moneys shall be published annually, in such manner as shall be prescribed by law.

Art. 8. It shall be the duty of the General Assembly to pass such laws as may be proper and necessary to decide differences of arbitration.

Art. 9. All civil officers for the State at large shall reside within the State, and all district or parish officers within their districts or parishes, and shall keep their offices at such places therein as may be required by law.

Art. 10. All civil officers, except the governor, and judges of the Supreme and Inferior Courts, shall be removable by an address of two-thirds of the members of both Houses, except those the removal of whom has been otherwise provided for by this constitution.

Art. 11. In all elections by the people, the vote shall be taken by ballot, and in all elections by the Senate and House of Representatives, jointly or separately, the vote shall be given *viva voce*.

Art. 12. No member of Congress, nor person holding or exercising any office of trust or profit under the United States, or either of them, or any foreign power, shall be eligible as a member of the General Assembly, or hold or exercise any office of trust or profit under the State.

Art. 13. None but citizens of the United States shall be appointed to any office of trust or profit or be employed on the *public works* in this State, providing the same be paid from the public funds, except the compensation be less than nine hundred dollars ($900) per annum.

Art. 14. The laws, public records, and the judicial and legislative written proceedings of the State, shall be promulgated, preserved, and conducted in the language in which the constitution of the United States is written.

Art. 15. That no power of suspending the laws shall be exercised, unless by authority of the Legislature.

Art. 16. Prosecutions shall be by indictment or information. The accused shall have a speedy public trial by an impartial jury of the parish in which the offence shall have been committed. He shall not be compelled to give evidence against himself; he shall have the right of being heard by himself or counsel; he shall have the right of meeting the witnesses face to face, and shall have compulsory process for obtaining witnesses in his favor; he shall not be twice put in jeopardy for the same offence.

Art. 17. All persons shall be bailable by sufficient sureties, unless for capital offences, where the proof is evident or the presumption great, and the privilege of the writ of *habeas corpus* shall not be suspended, unless when in cases of rebellion or invasion the public safety may require it.

Art. 18. Excessive bail shall not be required; excessive fines shall not be imposed, nor cruel and unusual punishments inflicted.

Art. 19. The right of the people to be secure in their persons, houses, papers and effects, against unreasonable searches and seizures, shall not be violated, and no warrant shall issue but upon probable cause, supported by oath or affirmation, and particularly describing the place to be searched and the persons or things to be seized.

Art. 20. No ex-post facto law, nor any law impairing the obligations of contracts, shall be passed, nor vested rights be divested, unless for purposes of public utility, and for adequate compensation previously made.

Art. 21. That all courts shall be open, and any person, for any injury done him, in his lands, goods, person or reputation, shall have remedy by due course of law, and right and justice administered without denial or unreasonable delay.

Art. 22. The press shall be free; every citizen may freely speak, write and publish his sentiments on all subjects; being responsible for an abuse of this liberty.

Art. 23. The Legislature shall have power to grant aid to companies or associations of individuals, formed for the exclusive purpose of making works of internal improvement, wholly or partially within the State, to the extent only of one-fifth of the capital of such companies, by subscription of stock or loan in money or public bonds; but any aid thus granted shall be paid to the company only in the same proportions as the remainder of the capital shall be actually paid in by the stockholders of the company; and, in case of loan, such adequate security shall be required as to the Legislature may seem proper. No corporation or individual association, receiving the aid of the State as herein provided, shall possess banking or discounting privileges.

Art. 24. No liability shall be contracted by the State as above mentioned, unless the same be authorized by some law for some single object or work, to be distinctly specified therein, which shall be passed by a majority of the members elected to both Houses of the General Assembly, and the aggregate amount of debts and liabilities incurred under this and the preceding article shall never, at any one time, exceed eight millions of dollars.

Art. 25. Whenever the Legislature shall contract a debt exceeding in amount the sum of one hundred thousand dollars, unless in case of war to repel invasion or suppress insurrection, they shall, in the law creating the debt, provide adequate ways and means for the payment of the current interest and of the principal when the same shall become due. And the said law shall be irrepealable until principal and interest are fully paid and discharged, or unless the repealing law contains some other adequate provision for the payment of the principal and interest of the debt.

Art. 26. The Legislature shall provide by law for all change of venue in civil and criminal cases.

Art. 27. No lottery shall be authorized by this State, and the buying and selling of lottery tickets within the State is prohibited.

Art. 28. No divorce shall be granted by the Legislature.

Art. 29. Every law enacted by the Legislature shall embrace but one object, and that shall be expressed in the title.

Art. 30. No law shall be revived or amended by reference to its title; but in such case the act revived or section amended, shall be re-enacted and published at length.

Art. 31. The Legislature shall never adopt any system or code of laws by general reference to such system or code of laws, but in all cases shall specify the several provisions of the laws it may enact.

Art. 32. Corporations with discounting privileges, may be either created by special acts or framed under general laws. But no corporation or individual shall have the privilege of issuing notes or bills except those which are already chartered.

Art. 33. In case of the insolvency of any

bank or banking association, the bill holders thereof shall be entitled to preference in payment over all other creditors of such bank or association.

Art. 34. No person shall hold or exercise at the same time, more than one civil office of trust or profit, except that of justice of the peace.

Art. 35. Taxation shall be equal and uniform throughout the State. All property on which taxes may be levied in this State, shall be taxed in proportion to its value, to be ascertained as directed by law. No one species of property shall be taxed higher than another species of property of equal value, on which taxes shall be levied; the Legislature shall have power to levy an income tax, and to tax all persons pursuing any occupation, trade or profession.

Art. 36. The citizens of the city of New Orleans shall have the right of appointing the several public officers necessary for the administration of the police of the said city, pursuant to the mode of election which shall be prescribed by the Legislature; *Provided*, That the mayor and recorder shall be ineligible to a seat in the General Assembly, and the mayor and recorders shall be commissioned by the governor as justices of the peace, and the Legislature may vest in them such criminal jurisdiction as may be necessary for the punishment of minor crimes and offences.

Art. 37. The Legislature may provide by law in what case officers shall continue to perform the duties of their offices until their successors shall have been inducted into office.

Art. 38. The Legislature shall have power to extend this constitution and the jurisdiction of this State over any territory acquired by compact with any State, or with the United States, the same being done by consent of the United States.

Art. 39. None of the lands granted by Congress to the State of Louisiana for building or constructing the necessary levees and drains, to reclaim the swamp and overflowed lands in the State, shall be diverted from the purposes for which they were granted.

Art. 40. The Legislature shall pass no law excluding citizens of this State from office for not being conversant with any language except that in which the constitution of the United States is written.

Respectfully submitted,

W. D. Mann, Chairman.
Ernest Wenck,
John Foley,
J. K. Cook,
John Buckley, Jr.,
Geo. Geier,
H. Maas.

Mr. Pursell, of Jefferson—Mr. President, is an amendment to that report in order now?

President—No, sir; not on the first reading. The question is shall it be read a second time?

Mr. Harnan—I move that it be read a second time.

Mr. Cutler—Mr. President, I would move that it be postponed and taken up in its order, as was the report of the Committee on the Mode of Revising the Constitution.

President—There has been no proposition to read a second time.

Mr. Cutler—I move that the second and third reading be postponed to come up in its regular order, after the reports preceding it have been adopted.

[The motion was put and carried.]

President—It goes over to a day unsettled.

[Secretary read the report of the Committee on Federal Relations, viz:]

The constitution and laws of the United States are the supreme law of the land, anything in the constitution and laws of this State, notwithstanding.

Mr. Montague—Mr. President—

Mr. Brott—Mr. President—

President—The gentlemen are out of order.

Mr. Montague—Mr. President, I merely wish to correct what appears to be an error of the printer—the report should read anything in the laws of this State to the contrary notwithstanding. It will be perceived that the words "to the contrary," have been left out by the printer.

President—How is that, Mr. Secretary?

Assistant Secretary Murphy—[To the president]—There is no error. The printed report is an exact copy of the written one.

Mr. Brott—Is it in order now for me to offer my minority report?

President—No.

Mr. Brott—Will the president state why?

President—Because the report is not before the House. The gentleman will have due notice when it is in order. There is no error in the report. The question will be upon its adoption; this is the third reading.

Mr. Foley—I move that it be adopted.

President—It is open to debate. [To

Mr. Brott]—Now you are in order with your minority report.

[Mr. Brott read :]

Whereas, The constitution of the United States, framed by the heroes of the revolution, who were greatly distinguished for their wisdom and patriotism, has been the Magna Charta for more than eighty years of the American nation, under which the United States have grown in wealth, intelligence and power, until they have reached the first rank among the nations of the world; and

Whereas, The territory now composing the State of Louisiana was purchased and paid for out of the treasury of the United States; that this State, under the Federal constitution and laws, has, at all times, at home and abroad, been amply protected, both in her honor and interest; that at no time and in no act has the Federal government infringed or in any way imperilled the political or religious rights of this State, that we deem that public faith of the State and sound policy require that she should continue loyal to the general government; and

Whereas, The Convention which assembled at Baton Rouge on the 20th of January, 1861, did, without sanction of law, and in violation of the Federal constitution, adopt and pass the following ordinance of secession:

"An ordinance to dissolve the union between the State of Louisiana and other States united with her, under the compact entitled the 'Constitution of the United States of America.'

"We, the people of the State of Louisiana, in Convention assembled, do declare and ordain, and it is hereby declared and ordained, that the ordinance passed by us in Convention on the 22d of November, A. D. 1811, whereby the constitution of the United States of America, and the amendments of said constitution, were adopted, and all laws and ordinances by which the State of Louisiana became a member of the Federal Union, be, and the same are hereby repealed and abrogated, and that the union now subsisting between Louisiana and other States, under the name of 'the United States of America,' is hereby dissolved.

"We do further declare and ordain, that the State of Louisiana hereby resumes all rights and powers heretofore delegated to the government of the United States of America; that her citizens are absolved from allegiance to said government, and she that is in full possession and exercise of all those rights of sovereignty which appertain to a free and independent State.

"We do further declare and ordain, that all rights acquired and vested under the constitution of the United States, or any act of Congress, or treaty, or under any law of this State, and not incompatible with this ordinance shall remain in force, and have the same effect as if this ordinance had not been passed."

Therefore, Resolved, That we, the representatives of the people of this State in Convention assembled, do hereby expunge from the records said ordinance of secession. We repudiate the asserted right of that convention to pass any ordinance to imperil the jurisdiction of the general government in rights not reserved to the State, as a political heresy, directly instigating and promoting treason, civil war, and the end of all stable government.

Resolved, That the alleged reasons of the political leaders of this State in justification for this act of treason and rebellion, among which were the imperfect execution of the fugitive slave law, the personal liberty laws passed by several of the non-slaveholding States, and the election by the people of a president not their choice, we declare these alleged wrongs as imaginary, not founded in fact; and further, that every administration of the Federal government has watched with a zealous care the rights of each State, and have on all occasions shown its fidelity to the constitution of the country.

Resolved, That we recognize the constitution of the United States as the supreme law of the land, that all powers delegated by the constitution to the general government belong to the nation and cannot be resumed again at pleasure.

Resolved, That we declare that the rebellion now existing against the government of the United States is unjustifiable, without a parallel in the history of nations. Unlike our fathers of the Revolution, they make no declaration of their alleged wrongs, but like Macbeth, while enjoying the emoluments of office, entrusted with power, they stab their friends; but, unlike him, they ask "to be let alone," that they may accomplish this most wicked tragedy.

Resolved, That we hail as friends to the loyal people of this State the Federal army and navy, who have imperilled their lives to restore to us our political rights and our free constitution, and when their arms are triumphant, our State will again march on in a degree of prosperity never before reached in her history.

GEO. F. BROTT.

[The secretary read the minority report, omitting the secession ordinance.

The roll was then called on the question of laying on the table, and the motion was lost by the following vote :]

AYES—Messrs. Abell, Balch, Davis, Henderson—5.

NAYS—Messrs. Ariail, Austin, Bailey,

Barrett, Beauvais, Bell, Bofill, Bonzano, Brott, Bromley, Burke, Campbell, Cook T., Cook J. K., Crozat, Cutler, Collins, Dufresne, Duane, Dupaty, Decker, Ennis, Fish, Flagg, Flood, Foley, Fosdick, Gastinel, Geier, Goldman, Gorlinski, Gaidry, Healy, Harnan, Hart, Heard, Hills, Hire, Kavanagh, Knobloch, Kugler, Maas, Maurer, Mendiverri, Millspaugh, Montague, Murphy E., Murphy M. W., Newell, Normand, O'Conner, Payne J., Pintado, Poynot, Purcell J., Pursell S., Schroeder, Shaw, Smith, Spellicy, Seymour, Stumpf, Stiner, Stauffer, Sullivan, Terry, Thorpe, Thomas, Wells, Wilson—70.

Mr. Wilson—I move the substitute be received, and be made the order of the day for Monday next.

Mr. Balch—This question has been already voted down, and we should not, by taking it up again, stultify ourselves. I most certainly enter my protest against such a course of proceeding, and at the same time present for your solution this question: Whether, when a question has been put and acted upon emphatically, any other resolution of a similar character can be introduced during the same session? Now, sir, for the purpose of facilitating business, I beg gentlemen not to do this thing and thus postpone our business from day to day. If they do, I will thwart them, and do everything in my power to hinder the progress of the Convention. If, on the other hand, I see honesty of purpose and straightforwardness of intention to do what is right, I will further their plans to the utmost to expedite matters. But this introducing resolution after resolution of the same tenor, throwing the Convention into difficulties and outside contempt, is a shame.

Mr. Austin—If in order, I offer the following amendment:

That the third reading of the report of the Committee on Federal Relations be made the order of the day for Tuesday, May the 3d, and that the minority report be printed for use of the Convention.

Mr. Balch—I move we adjourn *sine die.*

Mr. Campbell—I second the motion.

[Motion lost.]

Mr. Stauffer—I rise to a question of privilege and offer the following:

I move that the sergeant-at-arms be instructed to remove the member from Iberville, and a vote of censure be passed upon him for his conduct in this Convention.

Mr. Stocker—I move to lay on the table.

[Motion lost.

[Yeas and nays were demanded, and the secretary called the roll, when the motion was declared lost—yeas 25, nays 48.

As it was asserted that no quorum was present, the roll was called to ascertain, when seventy-six gentlemen responded.

[Yeas and nays were called for on the adoption of the resolution, with the following result:

The resolution was adopted.]

Mr. Henderson—The language of that resolution is such—consequent probably upon its having not been drawn up in the best temper—that I voted against it.

The resolution tends not only to censure the gentleman for impropriety on his part, but to deprive him of his membership. If it is proposed to censure the gentleman, a charge should be made against him setting forth the reason for which he is censured, then he could be brought before the house in a proper manner and action could be taken on it in such a manner that the people of the State would know for what he was censured.

I say that I, for one, have heard, upon this floor, propositions more absurd than the one just made—to adjourn *sine die*—made with no other purpose than to delay the business of this body, and that gentleman may have intended the motion as a censure upon the House for wasting time If the gentleman puts himself in a way to make himself obnoxious to the Convention by opposing this, that and the other question, we can, at a proper time, vote to censure him; but when a motion is made to adjourn *sine die*, and a motion follows that the gentleman making the first motion be taken out of the Convention, I say and think that the last motion is more out of order and more censurable than the action of the gentleman. This is a proposition tending to deprive him of the right to represent the sovereign people merely because he moved to adjourn. I am astonished that a deliberative body like this—as cool-headed as I know it to be—should for a moment entertain the proposition. He might as well rise to move to displace the president of this Convention on any ground whatever. It might be unbecoming, and he might be censurable, but that would be no reason why some gentleman should move that he be expelled. I think the resolution is exceedingly unbecoming, and hope it will be lost.

Mr. HILLS—It seems to me this matter has gone for enough. While I voted against laying the resolution on the table, I shall certainly vote against the resolution itself. I think the vote already taken is sufficient censure, and I therefore move that the member have permission to withdraw that resolution.

Mr. STAUFFER—I withdraw it. My reason for offering it was to preserve the order of this body, and I wish to see members come into it in a fit condition to do business. I did not offer the resolution because the gentleman moved to adjourn *sine die.*

Mr. STOCKER—I object to the withdrawal of the resolution.

Mr. BALCH—The gentleman's insinuation is a mistake, and he is unfortunate in making the allusion. When I made the motion to adjourn, I did it in good faith. Why? You represent about six thousand votes in the State of Louisiana, and I am confident, you do not represent the city of New Orleans nor the State of Louisiana. You can expel me at once; I am willing to go home. I prefer to stay in my garden and work there among my negroes, to remaining here if you are going to set up houses one day and knock them down the next. A resolution is offered and acted upon, and that resolution should not be introduced again, but it is done every day. We stand now where we stood yesterday and where shall we be next? I desire to go away; expel me.

PRESIDENT—The questions is on the permission to withdraw the resolution.

[The question was put and carried by a rising vote of 50 to 24.]

Mr. STOCKER—I ask the privilege of explaining my reasons for voting as I did. In the first place I voted to lay that resolution on the table, because I believe when a gentleman wishes to censure another, he should not make the charge without giving good reasons for it. For that reason I voted now against his withdrawing it.

[Mr. Stauffer then withdrew his motion.]

PRESIDENT—The question is on the amendment offered to print the amendment to the report of the Committee on Federal Relations.

Mr. THOMAS—I understand that to be a minority report.

Mr. BROTT—It is.

Mr. THOMAS—I move that it be printed and laid over for action next Tuesday.

[The motion was seconded and carried.]

PRESIDENT—The question now is on the substitute of Mr. S. Pursell.

Mr. HILLS—I move that action on the substitute be postponed until after the minority report is acted upon.

[Seconded and carried.]

Mr. HILLS—If it is in order, I would like to submitt a brief report on the subject referred to in the memorial of yesterday.

[There being no objection, the report was read:]

To the president and members of the Convention for the Revision and Amendment of the Constitution of Louisiana:

The undersigned, members of the Committee on Public Education, to whom was referred the very able and interesting memorial of A. Vallas, respectfully submit the following report:

That while the memorial in question reflects great credit upon its author, they are unable to concur in its recommendations, especially in the proposition to merge the State Seminary into the University. It seems proper to the committee that the vast stretch of territory in Western Louisiana should have an institution of learning in which her youth may be liberally educated, and in which those wishing to enter the University may receive a preparatory course.

In the judgment of the committee, such an institution will become a great public necessity, nor can the undersigned perceive that the fact cited by Mr. Vallas, that traitors attempted to turn the Academy into a rebel military school, renders its existence less desirable or necessary. It is to be hoped that under the benignant influence of freedom and the new civilization that is rising from the ruin of our former institutions, the delusion which sought to sunder the bonds of the Union will become extinct. Your committee therefore recommend the adoption of the following resolution:

Resolved, That the thanks of this body

are due to A. Vallas, late superintendent, etc., for the able and patriotic memorial he has presented on the subject of public education.

Respectfully submitted.

ALFRED C. HILLS, Chairman.
M. W. MURPHY,
X. MAURER,
J. RANDALL TERRY,
H. C. EDWARDS,
T. M. WELLS,
EDWARD HART,
JO. R. BALCH,
YOUNG BURKE.

Mr. WILLSON—I move it be accepted and printed, and made the order of the day when the regular reading comes up.

[The motion was carried.

A motion to adjourn till the usual time to-morrow was then made and carried.]

FRIDAY, April 29, 1864.

[At 12 o'clock the House was called to order, and after prayer by the Rev. Mr. Gilbert, the roll was called and the following gentlemen responded:

Messrs. Abell, Ariail, Austin, Balch, Bailey, Barrett, Baum, Beauvais, Bell, Bofill, Bonzano, Bromley, Buckley, Burke, Cazabat, Cook J. K., Cook T., Crozat, Collin, Davies, Dufresne, Decker, Dupaty, Edwards, Ennis, Fish, Flagg, Flood, Fosdick, Fuller, Geier, Goldman, Gorlinski, Gruneberg, Gaidry, Healy, Harnan, Hart, Heard, Henderson, Hills, Howell, Kavanagh, Knobloch, Kugler, Maas, Maurer, Mendiverri, Millspaugh, Montamat, Montague, Morris, Murphy E., Murphy M. W., Newell, Normand, O'Conner, Ong, Payne J., Pintado, Poynot, Purcell J., Pursell S., Schroeder, Schnurr, Seymour, Shaw, Smith, Spellicy, Stocker, Stumpf, Stiner, Stauffer, Sullivan, Terry, Thorpe, Thomas, Waters, Wenck, Wells and Wilson 81.

[The minutes of yesterday were read and approved.]

Mr. BELL—Mr. President, I have a petition which I desire to offer.

To the president and members of the constitutional Convention:

GENTLMEN—Having been engaged for six days prior to the election of M. DeCoursy, Esq., as sergeant-at-arms, in fitting up hall, &c., I respectfully solicit such compensation as you may be willing to grant.

HY. COPELAND.

MR. WILSON—I move it be referred to the Committee on Compensation.

[The resolution was carried without objection.]

Mr. HARNAN—I offer the following resotion:

Whereas, There are several members absent from their seats in this Convention, and drawing their per diem, and as there was a resolution adopted by this Convention declaring their seats vacant after an absence of three days; therefore, be it

Resolved, That all members who are absent beyond the time specified in the said resolution, that their seats be declared vacant, and that the secretary be directed to stop their per diem for every day that said members are absent, until otherwise ordered by this Convention.

Mr. MONTAMAT—I move the rules be suspended and the resolution taken up.

[The motion to suspend the rules was carried.]

Mr. MONTAMAT—I move the resolution be carried.

[The motion was carried, by a rising vote of yeas 37, nays 26.]

PRESIDENT—Reports of standing committees are in order.

Mr. GORLINSKI—The Committee on Internal Improvement report progress.

Mr. GRUNEBERG—The Committee on Schedule report progress.

Mr. SHAW—The Committee on Ordnance report progress.

Mr. PURSELL—The Committee on Expenses are ready to report. We report as follows:

To the honorable the president and members of the Free State Convention of Louisiana:

Your committee have the honor to report their approval of bills amounting to three thousand six hundred and sixty-five 55-100th dollars, ($3665 55) for which vouchers were furnished by the sergeant-at-arms.

There being no funds provided for the payment of contingent expenses, your Committee respectfully recommend an appropriation of twenty-five thousand dollars for that purpose, and offer the following resolution:

Resolved, That the sum of twenty-five thousand dollars be and the same is hereby appropriated out of the general funds of the State, for the purpose of paying the contingent expenses of the Convention.

Respectfully submitted,

S. PURSELL, Chairman.
JAMES DUANE,
JOHN A. NEWELL,
R. B. BELL,
JOHN PAYNE.

Mr. S. PURSELL—I move a suspension of the rules for the purpose of acting on it.

Mr. SULLIVAN—Before it is adopted I wish the items read. I move the committee be obliged to hand in their report with the items allowed.

PRESIDENT—The question is on the reception of the report.

[The report was received without objection.

The motion to suspend the rules was then put and carried.]

Mr. DUANE—The committee have seen all the items, and they are very numerous. The amounts are from one dollar and upwards, and the reading of them would detain this Convention for a long time.

Mr. STAUFFER—I hope the gentleman will withdraw his motion, as the chairman has stated that vouchers have been furnished, and I presume they can be examined by any member.

Mr. SULLIVAN—It seems to have got abroad that expenses are incurred that are not necessary, and I wish to know what they are.

Mr. BELL—As a member of that committee I will state that the bills have been duly examined and vouchers presented, and all has been found correct.

PRESIDENT—The question has not been seconded. It is an unusual motion, as the bills are open for the examination of any gentleman.

[The resolution to adopt the report was then carried.]

PRESIDENT—Reports of Special Committees are in order.

Mr. WILSON—The Committee on Assault of Members will be ready to report next Thursday, Mr. President.

[The secretary read a communication from the secretary of state transmitting returns of the election of Mr. Orr and a protest of Mr. McGuire, contesting the election.]

Mr. BELL—I move that it be received and adopted.

Mr. WILSON—I amend by referring it to the Committee on Credentials.

[The motion was carried.]

PRESIDENT—Unfinished business is now in order. Committees will call up their resolutions.

Mr. BELL—I call up the resolution of Mr. Brott, offered yesterday.

[The secretary read the following :]

Resolved, That the Committee on Expenses be and are hereby requested to make an estimate of the contingent expenses required by said committee.

Mr. STAUFFER—We have already passed a resolution that will cover that.

Mr. GOLDMAN—I call for the reading of my resolution.

[The secretary read :]

Be it resolved, That banking corporations, under the authority of the State, are prohibited, and that those banks which are doing banking business at present, or have done so hitherto, are hereby forbidden to continue such business.

EDMUND GOLDMAN.

Mr. WILSON—I move to lay it on the table.

[The motion was seconded.]

Mr. STAUFFER—I call for the yeas and nays.

[The call was sustained and the roll called with the following result :]

YEAS—Messrs. Abell, Austin, Bailey, Barrett, Baum, Beauvais, Bell, Bofill, Bromley, Buckley, Burke, Cook T., Crozat, Dufresne, Edwards, Fish, Flagg, Flood, Fuller, Geier, Healy, Harnan, Henderson, Hire, Kavanagh, Maas, Mendiverri, Montamat, Murphy E., Murphy M. W., Howell, Poynot, Shaw, Stocker, Spellicy, Stumpf, Terry, Wilson—38.

NAYS—Messrs. Ariail, Bonzano, Cazabat, Cook J. K., Collin, Davies, Duane, Decker, Ennis, Foley, Fosdick, Goldman, Gorlinski, Gruneberg, Gaidry, Hart, Heard, Hills, Howell, Knobloch, Kugler, Maurer, Millspaugh, Montague, Morris, O'Conner, Ong, Payne J., Pintado, Purcell J., Pursell S., Schroeder, Seymour, Smith, Stiner, Stauffer, Sullivan, Thorpe, Thomas, Waters, Wenck, Wells—42.

[The motion was lost.]

Mr. THOMAS—I move the resolution be referred to the Committee on General Provisions.

Mr. STAUFFER—I move to amend by referring it to a special committee of five, on banking, appointed by the president.

Mr. MONTAGUE—I move to amend by referring it to the Judiciary Committee.

Mr. HILLS—I move to lay all the amendments on the table.

[The motion was carried.]

Mr. CAMPBELL—I rise to explain the object I had in voting not to lay it on the table. This is a matter of very grave importance to the Convention, and should not be acted on in a hasty manner. I wish to hear a debate on this question, and hope the Convention will take time to consider it well; therefore I move that a day be fixed when there is no other business and the question can be considered.

Mr. STOCKER—I move the matter be postponed until the first day of January next.

Mr. DAVIES—I move to lay it on the table. If the Convention has the power,—

Mr. STOCKER—I rise to a point of order. The gentleman moved to lay it on the table, and that motion cannot be discussed.

[The motion to table was apparently carried, when a division was called for and a rising vote taken with the following result—yeas 55, nays 10.]

PRESIDENT—The question now is upon the adoption of the resolution.

Mr. HENDERSON—The gentlemen will perpetually insist upon our legislating. They bring a question before this body that in no wise concerns it.

I do not think there is much to censure in a gentleman who endeavors to postpone all such matters. If the gentleman wishes a resolution of the nature of a provision of some portion of our constitution, let him prepare it and have it inserted; but suppose the Convention should cast a majority vote in favor of it, will it stop the bank? Our constitution must act prospectively, and when it goes into effect it becomes the law of the land. I cannot consider why we fritter away so much time in useless propositions. It is time some common sense was used. The resolution, if passed, is but an expression of opinion, and when the Convention dies it is a dead letter, for this is entirely a matter for the Legislature.

Mr. HILLS—I was opposed to laying this resolution on the table, at the same time I agree in the main with the remarks of the last gentleman, and for that very reason I am in favor of referring it to the Committee on General Provisions. It is a subject for legislation, and we have no power to legislate. It may be necessary to have some clause in the constitution bearing on this subject; therefore I move to lay all the amendments to the motion referring it to the committee on the table.

Mr. THOMAS—Before the vote is taken, I wish to say a few words. I notice in the constitution of 1852, article 118 provides for the creating of corporations with banking and discounting privileges:

"Corporations with banking or discounting privileges, may be either created by special acts, or formed under general laws," etc.

In the report of the Committee on General Provisions, article 32, they have reported: "Corporations with discounting privileges," leaving out "banking." My reason for referring this matter to the committee was, I believe it naturally belongs to that part of the constitution. Certainly, sir, it should be a part of the constitution of this State to prohibit *some* kinds of banking privileges. There are men here, undoubtedly, who will oppose, and with much reason, any banking privileges. There are men here who have lost, since this war began, enough to discourage them, and destroy their faith in any bank. To-day we see under the present system these banks doing business under their charters requiring them to redeem their bills in specie, and yet the bills of one bank bear a premium of ten per cent., and another at a discount of forty per cent. I agree with the gentleman who first spoke, that this is a question of great importance, and deserves the consideration of the Committee on General Provisions, and the full expression of this body.

Mr. GOLDMAN—My object in bringing that resolution up was simply to assist our national treasury. A declaration in favor of a national currency will be a great progressive step, and do as much to assist the government as the addition of one hundred thousand men to our armies. I am for a national currency and a national language. I intended to have the resolution if passed inserted in the report of the Committee on General Provisions. I wished to move to strike out article 32, and I believe I am justified in doing this, because by referring to the constitution of 1845, which was adopted by the people of undoubted integrity and talent, it will be seen that it is expressly stated in article 123, that "corporations shall not be created in this State by special laws, except for political or municipal purposes, but the Legislature shall provide by general laws for the organization of all other corporations except corporations with banking or discounting privileges, the creation of which is prohibited."

What injury can arise fron a national currency instead of a thousand banks? I think we owe it to the people of the State to protect them from "wild cat" banks. The injury already inflicted is serious enough. I am not bent upon passing this resolution to-day, but hope to see it considered thoroughly, and made a special business.

Mr. WILSON—Though I voted to lay on the table, I am strongly in favor of sustaining our own banks. They have done remarkably well, in my opinion, through this terrible revolution. They have always stood at the head of American banking institutions. If it were possible to become legislators, in place of framers of organic law—and we should pass a resolution to shut up these banks—we should see here to-day, after our adjournment, a great panic, which would affect the poorer classes — a useless panic. I am in favor of doing all that is possible for the national armies and the national banking institutions of the country, but this system has not been tried in this country before this time, probably never under the same circumstances, and many of the wisest men of the nation were opposed to its adoption.

Mr. BELL—I move that the matter be put in the hands of the Committee on General Provisions, and when that reports it will be open to debate.

Mr. FOLEY—As chairman of the Committee on General Provisions, I move that Judge Howell be appointed upon that committee.

[The motion was seconded.]

PRESIDENT—It lies over for to-day.

Mr. GRUNEBERG—I call for my resolution.

[The secretary read the following:]

Whereas, The Constitutional Convention of the State of Louisiana has been called principally to decide on the abolition of slavery in the State; whereas, the adoption of this measure, in whatever manner or form, will necessarily require great modifications in all parts of the organic law of the State; whereas, for these reasons this Convention cannot or ought not to come to a final decision on the reports of any of the standing committees on constitutional amendments, before voting on emancipation; and, whereas, the question of emancipation being the most important of all, requires the longest and most matured deliberation of this assembly; be it therefore

Resolved, That this Convention will take into consideration, first, the reports of all the standing committees on constitutional amendments, with substitutes and amendments thereto, except the report of the Committee on Emancipation, but they shall not pass further than a second reading; that then the report of the Committee on Emancipation shall be taken up and be then regularly passed to a final vote; and that afterwards the reports of all the other standing committees shall pass to their third reading and to a final vote thereon.

And, moreover, Resolved, That this Convention shall only adjourn from day to day until the reports of all the standing committees on constitutional amendments, except that of emancipation, shall have passed a second reading.

CHAS. H. L. GRUNEBERG.

Mr. WILSON—I move that it be printed and copies furnished to every member.

Mr. THOMAS—I amend, and move that it be made the order of the day for Monday next.

[The amendment was accepted and the motion as amended carried.]

Mr. CAMPBELL—I rise to a question of privilege. It is to explain to this Convention the object I had yesterday in seconding the motion to adjourn *sine die*. Mr. President, if any of us will read the proceedings in Congress now going on, we will find that there has been a bill passed by the House of Representatives (ten voices only dissenting) in favor of amending the constitution in regard to slavery. We also find that the Senate has passed the bill, and that it now only awaits the signature of the president.

I seconded the motion to adjourn, because I thought that any action we might take here, referring to that matter, would be neither in time nor place, as it might conflict with the disposition made of the matter by the national Congress, and therefore considered this action of ours premature, thinking we should take none before seeing the result of the deliberations at Washington. That is one reason.

Another is, that there is now a bill pending before the national Congress, the object of which is to provide for the reconstruction of rebellious States. How do we know what the result of this may be? I therefore contend that anything we do here may amount to nothing, and, *therefore*, think it was proper and honest in me to have seconded that motion. If I have made myself understood, I have nothing further to say.

Mr. CAZABAT—I move we adjourn.

[The motion was lost.]

PRESIDENT—We come to the special order of the day: Report of Committee on Judiciary Department and the second reading. Amendments have been submitted by Messrs. Sullivan and Henderson. The question is, whether they shall be committed or read a second time?

Mr. STAUFFER—I offer the following substitutes for articles eleven and twelve of the original report and Mr. Sullivan's amendment.

ART. 11. The Judges, both of the Supreme and Inferior Courts, shall be appointed by the governor, by and with the advice and consent of this Senate, for the term of eight years. And it shall be the duty of the governor at the end of each term to submit to the Senate the names of the occupants, to be continued in office or rejected.

Art. 12. The clerks of the inferior courts shall be elected by the people, and they shall hold their offices during six years, subject to removal by the judges respectively, with the right of appeal in all such cases to the Supreme Court.

Mr. GOLDMAN—I second.

Mr. STAUFFER—I move that the substitute be printed.

[The motion was carried.]

Mr. MOMTAMAT—I wish to offer the following amendment to article 11:

The Judges of the Supreme Court shall be elected by joint vote of the General Assembly, and for a term of ten years. They shall have power to appoint their own clerks.

The Judges of the inferior courts shall be elected by the qualified voters of the district in which they reside, and shall hold their courts at such time and place as the General Assembly may direct. They shall hold their office for a term of six years, and until their successors are elected and qualified.

Clerks of the inferior courts in this State shall be elected for the term of four years, and should a vacancy occur subsequent to an election, it shall be filled by the judge of the court in which such vacancy exists, and the person so appointed shall hold his office until the next general election.

Mr. STAUFFER—I ask if the gentleman offers that as an amendment to my substitute?

Mr. MONTAMAT—Yes, sir.

Mr. HARNAN—I move it be printed.

[The motion was carried.]

Mr. FOLEY—I move that the third reading be this day week.

[The motion was carried.]

Mr. CUTLER—I desire to submit to the consideration of this Convention, the propriety of acting upon the reports of different committees in regular order. The order for one o'clock to-day was the judiciary report. Several amendments have been proposed and one or two substitutes offered. This is a question of very serious and vital importance, and hence in my humble opinion there is a necessity for grave examination.

I would, therefore, move, for the purpose of disposing of all those questions, and for the purpose of our acting in harmony, that we go on in regular order, and be governed in our actions by the rules adopted by the convention of 1852, and that the second reading of the Committee on Judiciary be postponed, together with all the substitutes and amendments, so far as any future action is concerned, until the reports of all the previous committees be received and adopted.

PRESIDENT—The motion lies over for one day.

Mr. FOLEY—I move a reconsideration of the motion, making the report of the Judiciary Committee, the amendments and substitutes thereto, the order of the day for this day week.

[The motion was carried.]

Mr. HENDERSON—When the report of this committee comes up, will it be on the second reading?

PRESIDENT—When it comes up again it will be on the third reading.

Mr. HENDERSON—When the report of a committee is once read, it cannot be read again on that day. When a bill comes up on its second reading—I refer to Jefferson's Manual, page 60—discussions take place and amendments are proposed. When the amendments come up those opposed should make the first attack, not wait until the third reading and then put it to vote. When that reading does come, we make a law.

Now we do not know but that some gentleman may move an adjournment before the third reading, and then we are in a bad fix. I am willing to listen with attention to the arguments of any other gentleman, and he may have the honor of converting me, or I of converting him to my opinion, but we must open the attack somewhere.

Mr. CUTLER—One word of explanation. My learned friend has been firing his large battery at an imaginary enemy—a mere shadow. All parliamentary bodies well know that a motion may be made to postpone, and when made and seconded the orginal motion may or may not be open to debate.

My motion was not for the purpose of cutting short the debate, on the contrary, to invite it; and after having invited it, to make known what the object of some members of this committee was—that is, to postpone the final action until all the other committees report. My motion was a very simple one, Mr. President, and as a matter of course, left the qustion of the judiciary report, the substitute and amendment, open to debate.

Mr. HEARD—I wish to plant myself upon Jefferson's Manual, and rules and orders of the Senate and House of Representatives of the State of Louisiana. When I asked the question whether this report of the Judiciary Committee would come up on its second reading on the day fixed, the president said, "No, on the third." Now, sir, I contend that neither the amendment, nor any substitute, nor any report of the committee has been adopted on its second reading, and, according to parliamentary usage, it must be before it can be engrossed for a third reading. I refer to Jefferson's Manual, article 98, to sustain my position. I contend that when this report, with the substitute and amendment, come up at the day fixed, it will come up on its second reading, and then is the time to discuss the question, approve or reject, and then engross and pass it to its third reading.

[Upon motion, the rules were suspended in order to adopt the resolution of the gentleman from Orleans—Mr. Cutler.]

Mr. HILLS—I would like to know if the report and amendments are open to debate.

PRESIDENT—If this resolution is not carried they will be.

[In order to allow debate the resolution was withdrawn, for that purpose only.]

Mr. HILLS—Mr. President, this question is one of the most important that will come before this Convention, and the gentlemen who have presented it, with the amendments and substitutes to it, it seems to me, ought to be ready at present to discuss them at this time. If they are, and we take up the question at once, it will be seen that we have commenced to work. I am anxious to hear the gentlemen on this matter without further delay.

Mr. STOCKER—Mr. President, I wish to know what the question is—whether report on the amendments or the substitutes are before the House, and which of them.

Mr. PURSELL, of Jefferson—Mr. President, in order to get a question before the House, I move that the amendment of Mr. Sullivan be adopted.

PRESIDENT—That is not in order.

Mr. SHAW—I move that we take up the report, section by section, and in connection with each section the substitutes and amendments that apply to it.

Mr. WILSON—Mr. President, as some of these amendments have not been printed, and are really not before the House, I think that there ought to be a little delay in order to give the printer time to have them printed for the use of the Convention.

I therefore move that it be adjourned until Monday, so as to give the printer time to put them before the House.

Mr. THORPE—I move to lay that motion on the table.

Mr. HILLS—I second the motion.

[The question was put; ayes, on a rising vote, 25, nays 47.]

Mr. HILLS—Mr. President, I suppose the question is now open to debate. I am opposed to the motion to lie over till Monday. It seems to me that the gentlemen who have offered amendments are ready to discuss them now, and now is the time that they should be heard. I can see no necessity for any longer delay.

Mr. Balch—A motion to adjourn is in order. I renew my motion to adjourn; the motion is not debatable.

Mr. Stocker—The question, to use the language of my distinguished friend on my right, is one of the most important that will come before us. We have a number of amendments thrust upon us to-day. The proposition that the gentlemen who have offered the amendments are ready to debate them may be very true as far as it goes. I confess, however, that so many of them have been brought up this morning that I am hardly prepared to express my own views. and there are no doubt many of us here who may desire to express our views on the question who have not offered amendments, and I believe that a little time to allow us to inform ourselves more fully of the nature of the amendments would not be time thrown away.

Mr. Henderson — I expected just this course would be pursued by this House to-day. When there is anything to be done you adjourn; when there is nothing to do you stay. There are now but two subjects before this House. The gentlemen say they are not prepared for argument. If they are not prepared to argue the question, we are prepared to show them how to argue it, and to show them, too, that we are prepared to argue it now.

One of these two questions is, whether the judiciary shall be elective or appointive, and the other whether the Supreme Court shall in its appellate jurisdiction decide, in criminal as well as civil cases, points of fact as well as of law. These questions can be discussed to-day. We can discuss the question of an elective or appointive judiciary to-day as well as next week or next January. There is nothing to hinder it. Your amendments can be put off till another day; you can put them upon it until the third reading, and then you can put a rider upon *that* if you choose, which will kill the whole bill.

We have amendments here that are already printed, and besides, if we delay, and lay the report over every time an amendment is presented, we shall never get through with our work. We don't know how many amendments may be proposed if we wait for them. We cannot prevent every member from coming in with his amendment by debating the question now and on the third reading; if a rider comes up which may kill the whole bill, we can't postpone that,—you can't postpone a rider. But this is not the question now. We do not propose to adopt amendments at this time. Nothing can be adopted on the second reading. You cannot adopt either the report or the amendments now; but I think it would be a waste of time to postpone discussion. I can see no objection to making the main points now. We can do it as well to-day as on Monday.

Mr. Abell—Mr. President, I came here to-day in the belief that this was the first reading of the report. It seems though that I was wrong. But I have an amendment that I do not wish to have cut off.

President—It is not in order.

Mr. Cutler—Before you put the question, Mr. President, I will remark that I am inclined to the opinion that there has been an error committed. My motion to postpone was before the House. I did not withdraw it for any other purpose than that of permitting debate on account of the desire of some gentlemen to discuss the report now upon its second reading. I received it for the purpose of allowing discussion on this question. Had any gentleman proposed any other motion, mine would not have been waived. This being the case, the chair should have entertained nothing else. Had anything else been presented, the chair, instead of entertaining a variety of other matters, should have called upon me either to withdraw my resolution or have asked for its presentation.

President—There has been no misunderstanding. The question is on the adjournment of debate, and a motion is made to table the motion to postpone.

[The question was put and a rising vote decided in the negative; yeas 32, nays 51.]

President—The motion now is that it be

taken up article by article, with the amendments and substitutes relating to each article.

[Question put and carried without objection.]

PRESIDENT—Now the motion to postpone comes up.

[The question was put and the resolution carried.]

PRESIDENT—That resolution does not cut off debate on this second reading.

Mr. SHAW—I move that article I. be read.

[The secretary read the article.]

Mr. HILLS—Mr. President I move that that be passed to a third reading.

Mr. HENDERSON—That is out of order. You cannot move to pass to a third reading.

Mr. CAZABAT—Mr. President, I have an amendment to article IV.

PRESIDENT—We shall come to that bye-and-bye.

Mr. STAUFFER—Mr. President, I move that article I. be adopted.

[Several voices.] "That is out of order."

PRESIDENT—Mr. Secretary, if there is no objection, read article I. with the amendments.

[The secretary read article I.]

Mr. ABELL—Mr. President, if I am in order, I move an amendment to that article. I wish to know if I am in order?

[The secretary read the amendment of Mr. Henderson.]

MR. ABELL—Mr. President, is my amendment in order?

PRESIDENT—Read the amendment of Mr. Sullivan, Mr. Secretary. [To Mr. Abell.] Yours will come next and will be taken up first.

SECRETARY — Mr. Sullivan's amendments do not apply to to this article.

PRESIDENT—Very well. [To Mr. Abell.] The gentleman will read his amendment.

[Mr. Abell read his amendment. After which it was re-read by the secretary.]

Mr. HENDERSON—The question now comes up on the qualification. The only question I make is that the Supreme Court shall have appellate jurisdiction.

PRESIDENT—The question comes up on the last amendment.

Mr. ABELL—Mr. President, this amendment proposes an important matter, more important, perhaps, than would be thought at first sight. I, therefore, move that this amendment be printed and lie over to some other day.

Mr. CUTLER—The motion of the gentleman should not prevail, because the resolu-that has been adopted by the Convention within the last fifteen minutes was to the effect that not only the third reading, but all the substitutes and amendments should be postponed until after all the reports of the other committees which, according to the classification of 1852, precede it in order, have been finally acted on. Hence, if the gentleman's motion be to postpone, it must be to postpone until all these other reports have been adopted.

PRESIDENT—That depends upon the time that the debate is continued on this second reading.

Mr. ABELL—Mr. President, I am willing for it to lie over until next Tuesday.

PRESIDENT—You take your chances. If the debate continues until that time, you can offer it then. Mr. Secretary, read Mr. Henderson's amendment.

[The secretary read the amendment.]

Mr. HENDERSON—Under the present constitution the Supreme Court has appellate jurisdiction in *a civil case*, when the demand in controversy exceeds three hundred dollars, to all cases in which the constutionality or legality of any tax, toll or impost whatsoever, or of any fine, forfeiture or penalty imposed by a municipal corporation shall be in contestation, and to all criminal cases.

The Supreme Court has jurisdiction in a criminal case, and upon law only, where the party is convicted of a capital crime; when the party, on conviction, may be punished with hard labor; and, lastly, where the *price actually imposed* exceeds three hundred dollars. In no other class of cases has the Supreme Court appellate jurisdiction under the constitution of 1852.

The amendment proposed enlarges the appellate power of the Supreme Court, and especially confers upon it the right to review questions of fact as well as law in a criminal as well as a civil suit, under such exceptions and under such regulations as the Legislature in its wisdom may provide, from time to time. The manifest defect in the present constitution is that it fixes the nature and amount of controversies to be had in the Supreme Court, without leaving any discretion in the Legislature. I am fully aware that my plan is objectionable in some of its features, when compared to a better system. For my part, I would give unlimited power to the Legislature to prescribe the nature and terms of an appeal from one judicial tribunal to another, for if it errs the redress is within their own hands, and they can readily modify or repeal the law, and thus remedy the evil. But not so if the defect exist in a fundamental law—the constitution—for it is not so easily altered.

In some of the States of the Union, the court of last resort is one empowered to examine *law only*. But where this system prevails there exists one or more intermediate courts between the court of original jurisdiction and the court of last resort; and by means of such intermediate courts, the *facts* become thoroughly sifted and clearly ascertained, so that the court of final resort has substantially nothing else to do but to apply the law to the facts found.

In other States the highest court examines *fact* as well as *law*, in both *criminal* and *civil* cases, irrespective of the amount in controversy. In Louisiana the Supreme Court has a mixed but limited jurisdiction of *fact* and *law*. In civil suits it is limited to an amount in controversy over $300, but can examine *law* and *fact* in such a case. In a criminal suit it is limited to *crimes* where the punishment is *capital* or *hard labor*, and it is further limited in these two classes of cases to an examination of *law only*. In a criminal suit where a fine actually imposed exceeds three hundred dollars—the Supreme Court has appellate jurisdiction, but is confined to an inquiry of *law alone* in such a case. Such a restricted constitution is evidently unjust to the people; and more innocent suffer by it than guilty. Under the system I propose, the appellate jurisdiction of the Supreme Court is enlarged or restricted according to the discretion of the Legislature—which is qualified in a very limited degree by the constitution itself. My amendment is taken from the constitution of the United States, Art. III. This enumerates the class of cases to which the jurisdiction of the Supreme Court shall extend under exceptions and restrictions imposed by Congress. It confers a vast discretion on Congress. A like discretion I wish the constitution of the State of Louisiana to confer on the Legislature under it. When the constitutionality of any act of a Legislature, or the legality of an ordinance of a corporation is controverted, the Supreme Court should be invested with the power to revise such law or ordinance on the points so controverted, irrespective of the amount in suit under such act or ordinance. The celebrated *cent* case that went up from the Supreme Court of New York to the Supreme Court of the United States, is a strong illustration of this principle. There a lady sued a post-master to recover back one cent, paid by her under protest for a newspaper. She succeeded in the Supreme Court of the United States, but lost in the State courts. The costs of this cent suit were enormous, yet she recovered the entire amount. In small suits and petty offences the Legislature will confine their original and appellate jurisdiction to inferior courts. In criminal cases the Legislature has the power, by the constitution, to define in what cases the Supreme Court shall have appellate jurisdiction. It also has the right to say in what criminal cases the Supreme Court shall investigate the *law and facts together*, and in what cases it shall have the power to investigate the *law only*.

If the Legislature in its experience ascertains it is the best policy to have the *facts and law* reviewed by the Supreme Court in criminal as well as civil cases, it can maintain this policy. On the other hand, if it should be of the opinion that the *law only* should be so reviewed in such cases, then let this policy be pursued. Again, if they deem it best to have the *law* only examined by the Supreme Court in a civil or criminal case, or in *both*, they then can adopt this plan. Again, if the Legislature choose to discriminate, by determining in what class of cases—criminal, or civil or both—the facts as well as the law shall be reviewed by the appellate tribunal, then be it so. Other instances of legislation might be given, but I forbear. It is for you, gentlemen of the Convention, to determine whether the amendment I propose, or the provision contained in the constitution of 1852, is the better. I thank you, gentlemen of the Convention, for your attention during my remarks.

Mr. SULLIVAN—I move to adjourn.

[The motion was carried.]

SATURDAY, April 30, 1864.

[The Convention was called to order by the president at the usual hour, and the proceedings opened with prayer by Rev. T. W. Gilbert—after which the secretary called the roll, and the following gentlemen answered to their names, viz:

Messrs. Abell, Austin, Barrett, Baum, Bell, Beauvais, Bofill, Brott, Buckley, Burke, Cazabat, Collin, Cook J. K., Cook T., Crozat, Davies, Decker, Dufresne, Edwards, Ennis, Fish, Flagg, Flood, Foley, Gaidry, Geier, Goldman, Gorlinski, Gruneberg, Harnan, Hart, Healy, Heard, Henderson, Hills, Hire, Kavanagh, Knobloch, Kugler, Maas, Mann, Maurer, Mendiverri, Millspaugh, Montamat, Montague, Murphy E., Murphy M. W., Newell, Normand, O'Conner, Pintado, Poynot, Purcell J., Schroeder, Schnurr, Seymour, Shaw, Smith, Stumpf, Stiner, Stauffer, Sullivan, Terry, Thomas, Waters, Wells, Wilson—69.

There being no quorum present, the sergeant-at-arms was directed to procure the attendance of absent members.

Soon after, Messrs. Bromley, Campbell, Cutler, Duane, Howell and Wenck having entered the hall, the president announced that a quorum was present.

The minutes of the previous day's session were read and adopted.]

Mr. THOMAS—Mr. President, I have a preamble and resolution to offer, as follows:

Whereas, The State of Louisiana, under the census of 1860, is entitled to seven electors for president and vice-president of the United States, instead of six, as under the former census;

And whereas, There is no probability that the Legislature will be convened prior to the approaching presidential election, and that the State cannot, therefore, be divided into electoral districts by that body within said time;

Be it Resolved, That a committee of five be appointed to report as to the manner in which seven electors for president and vice-president of the United States shall be chosen in this State for the coming presidential election.

Mr. WELLS—Mr. President, I move a suspension of the rules, in order to take immediate action on that resolution.

[The motion was carried.]

Mr. BELL—I move to adopt the motion.

Mr. SULLIVAN—I second the motion.

[The motion was carried.]

PRESIDENT—By whom shall the committee be appointed?

Mr. THOMAS—The rules provide that the president shall appoint all committees, unless otherwise specially appointed.

Mr. DAVIES—I wish to offer Mr. Goldman's resolution of yesterday, with the preamble.

PRESIDENT—There is no preamble.

Mr. GOLDMAN—Since a memorial should be signed by a person not a member, I wish mine to be considered a preamble and resolution.

PRESIDENT—I did not hear anything about a preamble.

Mr. STOCKER—I have no objection to the gentleman offering another preamble, but do object to his offering what purported to be a memorial the other day.

Mr. GOLDMAN—I called it a memorial, because I was not aware that a memorial must be signed by a person not a member, as I was sorry to find out; but as I am made aware of it, I call it a preamble and resolution now, as I should have done before.

Mr. DAVIES—I move to print the resolution and add the preamble.

PRESIDENT—The proper motion will be for the gentleman to move to append his preamble to the resolution of Mr. Goldman and read the preamble.

Mr. DAVIES—But it is not my preamble, it is Mr. Goldman's.

PRESIDENT—If Mr. Goldman desires to offer a preamble he is present and can offer it himself.

Mr. CAMPBELL—I have an amendment to the constitution which I desire to offer:

ART. —. No tax, State or municipal, shall be imposed by the General Assembly upon the actual capital engaged in the following industrial arts, viz: All manufactories of cloth, leather, yarn and cotton bagging—and those engaged in shoe manufacturing, provided twenty hands, at least, are employed. The General Assembly may, however, exempt such others as they deem advisable; this exemption to be allowed for the term of ten years, from and after the date of its establishment.

PRESIDENT—It lies over one day under the rules.

Mr. STAUFFER—I move it be referred to the Committee on General Provisions.

PRESIDENT—It lies over one day, unless you suspend the rules.

Mr. STINER—Mr. President, I have a resolution to offer:

Resolved, That no license be granted to gambling houses in this State.

Mr. CAZABAT—I did not hear the last resolution read.

Mr. HEALY—I move to suspend the rules for its adoption.

Mr. HILLS—If I am not mistaken, the motion of referring a resolution to a committee is in order. I think it is the rule that it can be referred to a committee without lying over one day. Therefore, I move that the resolutions of Messrs. Stiner and Campbell be referred to the Committee on General Provisions.

PRESIDENT—I think the motion is out of order. Under the rules all resolutions are required to lie over one day. When it comes up you can move to refer it to a committee. The question now is on the suspension of the rules.

Mr. HILLS—I rise to a point of order. I do not wish to put myself in opposition to the chair, but ask for information, for this is something we ought to understand. I call for the reading of the rule.

PRESIDENT — Mr. Secretary, read the rule.

[The secretary read rule XXXI.]

PRESIDENT—That is the rule, but under a resolution that you have made it must lie over one day.

Mr. STOCKER—As I had the honor of introducing that resolution, I will explain it. The resolution reads thus:

"All resolutions or ordinances, unless referred to a committee, shall lie over one day before being acted upon by the Convention."

PRESIDENT—If that is the reading of the resolution, the gentleman is correct.

Mr. HILLS—I renew my motion to refer the two resolutions to the Committee on General Provisions.

Mr. MANN—I think we should not include both in the same vote.

Mr. STOCKER—I move we take them up separately.

Mr. HILLS—I accept the amendment.

[The resolutions were referred to the Committee on General Provisions.]

Mr. DAVIES—Would it be in order to read the preamble offered by Mr. Goldman.

PRESIDENT—It must be offered by yourself; Mr. Goldman is present.

Mr. HENDERSON—That is no preamble.

Mr. GOLDMAN—I offer the following preamble:

The present war—which must eventually terminate in the triumph of the nation over the rebellious States—opens a new epoch in our national history. The Federal constitution is not only to be re-established over the entire nation, as the supreme law of the land, but the powers of which it has been stripped, from time to time, by the aggressive spirit embodied in the pernicious doctrine of "State Rights," must be re-asserted, maintained and enforced. Our happiness and safety require that, hereafter, the fundamental law of the nation shall absolutely prevail, "anything in the constitution and laws of any State to the contrary notwithstanding." The constitution gives to the national Congress the exclusive power to coin money and to regulate the value thereof, and to make all laws which shall be necessary and proper for carrying into execution these powers. The constitution says: "No State shall coin money, emit bills of credit, make anything but gold and silver coin a tender in payment of debts."

The obvious meaning of these provisions is, that with the United States alone rests the power of authorizing the bills and notes to circulate as money, and that it is one of the powers which the States are prohibited from exercising. This is the view of the acknowledged authorities on constitutional interpretation. Therefore, the system of State banking is, and has been, a gross and palpable usurpation by the States of a power exclusively granted to the nation.

The State banking system, thus lawlessly maintained, has been fraught with more evil to the moral and material interests of the nation than all other causes together.

Were it possible to compute the loss which the industry of the nation has sustained during the last seventy-five years, by the rates of discount and exchange and the failure of State banks, the sum total would be enough to pay the debt created by the present war. But it is not only the loss of money with which the industry of the nation may justly charge this system. It has inflicted injury on the morals of the nation.

Thus every consideration should bring the people to the determination to put an end to State banking at once and forever. The national government has removed every obstacle in the way of carrying this out. The plea that the wants of commerce imperatively demanded a paper circulation has no longer any force. By the act of Congress entitled "An act to provide a national currency, secured by a pledge of United States stocks and to provide for the circulation and redemption thereof," approved February 25th, 1863, a system of banking is established which will meet all the wants of trade and commerce in every portion of our country, by an issue of paper money based on the national debt—a system that will free us from the evils of discounts, exchanges and failures, and put an end to the favoritism and partial dealings of the State bank system, which it is designed to supercede.

The banks now in this State have no legal existence. By the provisions of the constitution of 1852 and the laws of the State, under which these banks were created, they have all forfeited their charters. By the pre-eminent part they all took in promoting the rebellion, there can be no doubt that all their property is confiscable to the United States. Those managing and chiefly interested in them, were, and still are, the must influential and inveterate of rebels. The constitution and laws of the State made their refusal at any time to redeem their notes in gold or silver, *ipso facto* a forfeiture of their charters. Altough those interested may say that the legal formalities have not been carried out to give judicial effect to the forfeiture, we can, and I trust will, pronounce the merited sentence of death upon these faithless banks.

The pretext urged at the time of their suspension of specie payments, of having been coerced into this act of dishonesty, has been long since disproved. They themselves, no doubt, suggested the scheme to the rebel government, and by its adoption, gave that government what it could not else have had—*a currency*. By this course they made for the time inordinate profits, but with corresponding losses to the suffering people, who conferred on them their privileges and who trusted them. These institutions, acting thus in bad faith, conferred on the rebel government a power which alone enabled them to protract the war to the present day.

Considering then—1st, that as the Federal government, and not any State government, has the power to stablish banks or to create banking corporations with authority to issue bills of credit; 2d, that the Federal government, in the exercise of its rights, has created a banking system free from all the objections inherent in the State bank system; 3d, that the banks of this State, having by their infidelity to the people and the nation, their dishonest and treasonable action, forfeited all claims, moral or legal, on our consideration;

Be it Resolved, That banking corporations, under the authority of the State, are prohibited, and that those banks which are doing banking business at present, or have done so hitherto, are hereby forbidden to continue such business.

EDMUND GOLDMAN.

Mr. STOCKER—I believe under our rules whenever a member asks a gentleman to reduce his resolution or preamble to writing it shall be so ordered. I now ask that Mr. Goldman be required to reduce his preamble to writing.

PRESIDENT—The gentleman will offer his preamble in writing. Reports of standing committees are now in order.

Mr. GORLINSKI—The Committee on Internal Improvement will report Monday.

Mr. MILLSPAUGH—In the absence of the chairman of the Committee on Enrollment, I report as correctly enrolled the resolution appropriating $25,000 for contingent expenses of the Convention.

Mr. BELL—I move that the report be received and the resolution signed by the president.

[The motion was carried without objection.]

Mr. PURCELL—Mr. President, as chairman of the Committee on Printing, I beg leave to read the following report:

To the president and members of the Louisiana State Convention:

Your Committee on Printing, after mature deliberation, beg leave to submit the following rates of compensation to the Official Printer of this Convention:

1. For two hundred copies of the Journal of the Debates of the Convention, in book form, in English and French, printed in brevier, and composed with the matter published in the Journal, the pages to be

seventy-one lines in length, including the title, the blank line under the title, and the foot line, and forty ems in width—the book to be stitched and bound in the same manner as law books—five dollars will be allowed for each page, and for every two hundred copies after the first two hundred, four dollars per page.

2. For all documents, reports or other matter printed in book or pamphlet form, in English or French, composed in bourgeois, the pages to be of the same length and breadth as the Journal—five dollars per page for the first two hundred copies, and for every additional two hundred copies, four dollars per page.

3. For resolutions, memorials or reports of committees, printed on foolscap, or similar sized paper, in English or French, composed in bourgeois type, thirty-six ems wide and ninety-five lines in length, for the first two hundred copies, eight dollars per page, and for each additional hundred copies, four dollars per page.

4. For all matter marked "official," and published in the official journal, one dollar per square for the first insertion, and fifty cents for each subsequent insertion. The square being considered in size equal to ten lines in agate type.

Your committee would respectfully state, in conclusion, that they have based their report, and fixed the prices as above stated, upon the increased high prices of paper, labor and printing material.

All of which is respectfully submitted.

JOHN PURCELL, Chairman.
JOHN T. BARRETT,
JAMES FULLER.

Mr. MONTAMAT—I move it be adopted.

Mr. GASTINEL—I amend that it be accepted, printed and made the order of the day on Friday next.

The question on the adoption of the amendment was put and a rising vote taken—ayes 32, nays 29.

The ayes and nays were called, with the following result:

YEAS — Messrs. Ariail, Austin, Bailey, Barrett, Beauvais, Bonzano, Bromley, Burke, Campbell, Cook T., Cutler, Davies, Dufresne, Edwards, Ennis, Flagg, Foley, Fosdick, Gastinel, Geier, Goldman, Gorlinski, Gruneberg, Gaidry, Harnan, Hart, Heard, Henderson, Hills, Hire, Howell, Knobloch, Kugler, Maas, Mann, Maurer, Millspaugh, Montague, Morris, Murphy E., Murphy M. W., Newell, Normand, O'Conner, Ong, Pintado, Purcell J., Pursell S., Schnurr, Seymour, Smith, Stumpf, Stiner, Stauffer, Sullivan, Terry, Thorpe, Waters, Wenck—60.

NAYS—Messrs. Abell, Baum, Bell, Bofill, Buckley, Collin, Cook J. K., Crozat, Decker, Duane, Flood, Montamat, Poynot, Stocker, Thomas, Wilson—16.

The motion was carried.

Mr. MONTAMAT—The Committee on Credentials will have a report on Monday.

Mr. WILSON—The Committee on Absent Members will report on next Thursday.

PRESIDENT—Unfinished business is in order. Gentlemen will call up their resolutions.

Mr. FOLEY—I call up my resolution of yesterday.

Resolved, That Mr. Howell be added to the Committee on General Provisions, in consequence of the illness of the chairman of that committee.

Mr. GOLDMAN—I move its adoption.

[The motion was carried.]

Mr. BURKE—I call for the resolution of Mr. Wells, on adjournment.

PRESIDENT—I am told by the secretary that it has been three or four days uncalled for. Resolutions must be taken up on the following day. The next business is the adjourned discussion on the judiciary report.

Mr. ABELL—The order of the day, if I remember aright, is the report on public education.

PRESIDENT—We do not arrive at the order of the day until we get through with unfinished business. The debate on the judiciary report now comes up.

Mr. ABELL—Mr. President, upon that I rise.

Mr. AUSTIN—We cannot hear.

PRESIDENT—So much the worse for the gentleman.

Mr. ABELL—I think, Mr. President, that nothing can be sound and reliable unless based upon logic. However illogically anything may be stated or proposed, it must, to be solid, be based upon a logical proposition.

We are now discussing the judiciary department.

The constitution that we are now called upon to amend is the work not merely of those who framed it, but it is the logical work of ages. It is the logical work of the best minds, perhaps, that the world has ever known, and, sir, I contend that in framing the judiciary department and the requisites connected with it, it is impossible for any gentleman upon this floor to properly cast his vote to legislate upon that subject until the first parts of this constitution shall have been framed. I ask whether any gentleman in this House who has a mind to think would vote for a Supreme Court precisely with the same understanding? would we vote for the numbers, for the salary, for the mode of appointment, for the tenure of office, with the same understanding that we could, if we knew what powers were granted to the Legislature?

Could we vote understandingly on these great and important questions that concern the judiciary, which is the corner-stone upon which all that we do is to rest, until we know what kind of an executive we are to have, and yet, according to the logic of making constitutions, both of these departments stand anterior to the one under discussion. I do not rise for the purpose of discussing the question of the judiciary; nor do I desire to do so, nor shall I ever do so, until I know what kind of an executive is to have the appointments. I say all that must be settled before I can, and before, I think, any gentleman here can, vote understandingly upon the judiciary of the State. If we should adopt an election of an executive by the legislative body—which is the case in several of the States—in one of them at least—certainly, sir, I should have more reliance in the chance of the intelligence of that man, that governor, than one elected by the people.

I would have more confidence in a governor who was elected for six or eight years than one elected for one year, because, sir, it takes time for the most ordinary things to mature, and it requires time for an executive to fully understand the importance, and suit himself to the great and important duties of the office to which he is called. I, for one, never would intrust power to an executive who was appointed for a single year, or who was elected by the people for two years. We have seen enough of the freaks of the people, and I trust this Convention will take no further steps with regard to the judiciary until we know the logic of that which precedes it. Then each one will be able to vote understandingly on the subject. But I contend that not a man here can discharge his duty to the people of Louisiana in respect to the judiciary department until he first and foremost knows in what manner the executive is to be appointed.

Therefore, I move that all discussion upon the subject of the judiciary be postponed, to be taken up at such time as it shall be logically reached.

Mr. HENDERSON—Mr. President, I move to lay that motion on the table.

Mr. ABELL—It cannot be done.

PRESIDENT—This motion lies over one day, under the rules which have been adopted by the Convention.

Mr. FOLEY—I move a suspension of the rule for the purpose of taking up the motion.

[The motion was carried, and Mr. Abell's motion was adopted.]

PRESIDENT—Is there any other order for to-day, Mr. Secretary?

SECRETARY—The report of the Committee on Public Education.

Mr. HENDERSON—Mr. President, since postponement is the order of the day, I will make a similar motion with respect to this subject. I will move that all subjects be postponed until they come up in their order. The judiciary report was logically in order and before the Convention to-day, but was summarily postponed. There is no use in this mode of proceeding. We might as well not discuss questions as to commence the discussion and then let them lie over.

PRESIDENT—Mr. Secretary, read the report of the Committee on Public Education.

[The Secretary read the report.]

Mr. SULLIVAN—Mr. President, am I in order with an amendment?

PRESIDENT—This is the second reading of the report of the Committee on Education, with amendments and substitutes. The question will be, Shall the report be read a third time? Now you are in order with your amendment.

Mr. STOCKER—Mr. President, does the substitute come up first, or the report, or the amendments, and which?

PRESIDENT—The report, with the substitutes and amendments, all come up together.

Mr. STAUFFER—Mr. President.

Mr. WELLS—Mr. President, I move that Mr. Henderson's motion be laid on the table.

PRESIDENT [to Mr. Wells]—A gentleman has the floor.

Mr. STAUFFER—Mr. President, I move to strike out the third article.

Mr. DAVIES—I wish to offer an amendment to the first article, so as to make it two years instead of four years, and to strike out everything in the fourth line after the word "direct."

Mr. GRUNEBERG—Mr. President, I move as an amendment that the word "only" be struck out of the article, so that it shall read "the English language shall be taught in the common schools."

Mr. BONZANO—Mr. President, I wish to offer an amendment. It is to strike out "four" and insert "three" faculties; in the 7th article to strike out "arts and sciences," and insert "collegiate."

Mr. HEARD—Mr. President, I rise to a point of order. Now, sir, according to all parliamentary rules, the report has to be taken up section by section, and then the amendments can be made to each section as it is taken up. I see no occasion for giving notice of amendments. Why, sir, it puts a blush upon all parliamentary rules. I move, therefore, that we proceed according to parliamentary rules, and take up the report section by section.

Mr. MONTAMAT—I believe the gentleman is right.

Mr. HARNAN—I move to lay all the amendments on the table.

PRESIDENT—The motions lie over one day.

[A motion to suspend the rules in order to take up the motion of Mr. Heard was carried, and the resolution was adopted.]

PRESIDENT—Mr. Secretary, read the first article.

Mr. DAVIES—Am I in order now with my amendment?

PRESIDENT—No, sir, not till the article is read.

[The secretary read the article.]

Mr. HARNAN—I move its adoption.

Mr. DAVIES—I wish to offer an amendment.

[Renewed his amendment.]

Mr. MONTAMAT—I move to lay the amendment on the table. At the adoption of the constitution of 1852, the office of superintendent of public schools was certainly necessary. Now, if it is necessary at all, it will be necessary to continue it. At the time of the adoption of that constitution there was great objection to a system of public schools. It was only through the instrumentality of a few earnest men that they were established in New Orleans. I think that if it is intended to establish a system of public schools throughout the State, it will be necessary to provide for the permanent retention of the office.

Mr. THOMAS—Mr. President, I have a few remarks to submit to this body before this substitute is passed upon. I consider the subject of public education one of the highest importance to the people of this State. If it is necessary that public education should be fostered, it is necessary to have a superintendent of public education. It is the universal rule of all the free States of this Union to have such an officer.

The constitution of 1845, Art. 133, provides that: "There shall be appointed a superintendent of public education, who shall hold his office for two years. His duties shall be prescribed by law. He shall receive such compensation as the Legislature may direct."

That in substance is exactly the same thing as the substitute of the gentleman from Jefferson, except that his substitute provides that he shall be *elected* every four years. Inasmuch as he is an officer of the State at large, I see no reason why we should fix his term for two years while the other State officers, the governor, the treasurer, and the auditor, are fixed at four. I am in favor of fixing this one the same as the others, at four years, and I would strike out that portion of the constitution of 1852, which says that the "General Assembly shall have the power to abolish the said office whenever in their opinion it shall be no longer necessary." When will it be no longer necessary to have a superintendent of public instruction in Louisiana? If it is necessary to-day it will always be necessary; as much so as any officer in the State and more so. It may, or can never become unnecessary in this State; and if we desire to see the children now growing up educated; if we desire to see them inspired with the spirit of progress and advancement, let us foster in every manner the means of education. Let us by all means have a superintendent of public education; and let us make it an office that cannot be abolished by the whim or caprice of any Legislature that hereafter may be convened.

For these reasons, Mr. President, I shall vote for the substitute offered by the gentleman from the parish of Jefferson.

Mr. Hills—Mr. President, I have not much to say on this subject. The committee were unanimous, so far as its members were present. We agreed that the Constitution of 1852 could not be improved on that point. The gentleman seems to found his objections to the term we have reported, upon the assumption that the terms of the other State officers have already been fixed at four years. I would call his attention to the fact that we have not yet fixed the terms of any of the State officers. We have not fixed the term of the governor at four years. I, for one, am in favor of short terms. I have not that distrust of the sovereign people that some gentlemen profess. I believe that in those States where the governor is elected every two years, he is, and the State officers elected with him are, as free from the objection of corruption as where they are elected for longer terms. In the State of New York, for instance, they are elected for two years, and American history does not furnish a more illustrious list of names than of the governors of New York.

I shall not refer particularly to other States, but I believe the same rule will be found to apply.

I am in favor of electing the superintendent of public education, and I am not certain that I shall not advocate the election of all State officers every two years. Then if we get a good governor, and good State officers, we can keep them four years, but if we should get a bad set, for God's sake, give the people a chance to change them every two years.

For the same reason I should give the people, through their representatives, the right to abolish the office of superintendent of public education, whenever in their opinion it became no longer necessary

Mr. Cutler—Mr. President, I rise not for the purpose of making a speech, but for the purpose of submitting to the Convention the propriety of acting upon the reports of all the committees in that order and according to that classification which they have said they will act upon in the mode of revising the constitution and in the judiciary report. It strikes my mind that we should calmly, coolly and dispassionately consider all the reports of the standing committees, that we should act upon them in their order, according to the classification of 1852. This Convention has already very wisely decided that before they pass their final vote upon the report of the committee on the mode of revising the constitution, that all the reports preceding it in order shall be adopted. They have to-day, in my opinion, adopted another wise provision in regard to the judiciary committee. They have decided that all the reports which precede that in order shall be discussed and disposed of before final action on that, and that it shall be taken up in its regular order under the classification of the constitution of 1852.

Now, Mr. President and gentlemen, I deem it a matter of considerable importance that we should take up the business in the order which has been proposed. Then, instead of being engaged in thus summarily disposing of the important subject of education in Louisiana, we should pass upon it, knowing something of the other branch of the constitution. I think, Mr. President, that we are taking up this matter prematurely.

I am not quite certain that it would not be an important step for the members of this Convention to take up the subject of emancipation first. Such a course would certainly be gratifying to their constituents. As to the preamble to the constitution, it would be time enough for us to have a preamble after we know what the constitution is; but it is certainly important that the distribution of powers should be fixed before we proceed to take up the subject of public education.

It is equally important that the report of the Committee on the Judiciary should be acted upon and discussed before minor questions come up. If there is any one thing of more serious importance than another it is the judiciary. It is they who have the life, property and liberty of men in their power. Internal improvements is not so important; it is next in order; and the next is public education. After the maturer minds are provided for will be the time to look out for the education of the rising generation. When that question comes up, Mr. President, I propose to give this Convention some of my views. If it is forced upon me, I will take occasion to do so to-day; but I think there are substitutes and amendments that demand the attention of the members of the Convention, and that the further discussion of the question should lie over until all the preceding reports shall have been adopted. With these remarks I move that all further debate on the report, and that all action of this Convention thereon be postponed, to come up in its regular order.

Mr. HILLS—Mr. President, I second the motion.

Mr. HENDERSON—Mr. President, I should like to know if we dispose of every question that comes before us in this summary manner, how we are to do any business. [A voice: "Put a rider on."] For my own part, I am tired of it, and if this is the way we are to proceed, I shall insist on the observance of the rules which the Convention has adopted. [Reads rule.] The other time we could postpone the order of the day to take up a question out of order, and now it is moved to postpone that to take up something else. Now I wish to call for the reading of the 16th rule.

Mr. HOWELL—Mr. President, I agree with the views of the gentleman on my right. If we should not, by adopting his motion, find ourselves out of business for some days, I would inquire if we have anything further for to-day, or for Monday, or Tuesday. I know we have for Wednesday.

SECRETARY—Monday, report of the Committee on the Executive Department; special report of the Committee on Education on the memorial of Professor Vallas.

Mr. HOWELL—That is connected with this matter.

PRESIDENT—It is a separate matter.

Mr. HOWELL—We should not get ourselves out of business and virtually adjourn over from day to day by postponing the question.

PRESIDENT—The proper motion is to suspend the rules to take action on the motion. I shall put no motion unless a motion is first made to suspend the rules. The question is upon the adoption of Mr. Pursell's substitute.

Mr. GASTINEL—I move—

Mr. HOWELL—Mr. President, I agree with all the gentlemen who have expressed their views, and with every other person, in the importance of the subject of public education. I think it becoming to this Convention to act upon this, as well as every other subject that comes before it; that it prove itself to be a deliberative body.

In 1845 the constitution contained a provision upon the same matter, if not in the same words as the substitute now under consideration. Many of the members will recollect that it was at that time the subject of public education as a State institution was first attempted. As it progressed in the machinery of State, considerable difficulty was felt in establishing the system so as to be beneficial throughout the whole State, instead of in New Orleans alone. Here it has become a fixed, established system, working admirably in its effects and results. I am aware that the majority of the Convention now sitting is composed at present of members residing in the city of New Orleans, and who know very little of the practical operation of the public school system in the country parishes, and it is highly important that these gentlemen should inform themselves, if not already familiar with the subject.

It will occur to their minds, upon a little reflection, that a system that will work well in the city of New Orleans may not work as well in the country parishes where the population is sparse and scattered, and we should do well to regulate our educational operations in reference to that fact. One of the first things suggested is the appointment of a superintendent of public education. It will be remarked that this Convention does not attempt to designate the duties of the superintendent. It simply provides that one shall be elected, and leaves the fixing of his duties to the General Assembly. It was contended, when the adoption of the system of 1845 was discussed, that after the system was once adopted and put in operation, that the necessity for a superintendent would cease. It was warmly urged, prior to the adoption of the constitution of 1852, that after the organization of the system the necessity for a superintendent would cease, and that Convention ended the controversy, very wisely, in my opinion, and left the question to the Legislature to dispense with the office when it should be found no longer necessary, in the same manner as they fixed his duties. Now, if we find that we shall have such an officer and leave it to the General Assembly to fix his duties, why may we not leave it to the General Assembly to dispense with the office if they shall find it unnecessary.

Indeed, I hear it said that the State treasurer may perform all the duties with the assistance of parish superintendents, and I believe the system is practicable. I believe that with a superintendent in each parish that the treasurer or some other officer of the State department would be able to perform all the duties which would be imposed upon the State superintendent. But, sir, I admit the necessity now for a State officer, because I believe that the system will be materially modified. I believe the new element introduced into this subject will make it necessary to have the constant attention of a superintendent to whom that particular business should be referred. After the system is regulated, when it is brought into working order so as to make it uniform throughout the State, I do not think it would be good policy for this Convention to say that there should always be such an officer, because I believe that it will not always be absolutely necessary, and if the Legislature should at any time find it unnecessary, I would give them power to abolish it. It is not such a question as I believe would be dangerous to leave to further legislation. It is different in its character from some others, without which we cannot have a republican government. In our system of government there are three departments necessary to its existence, the *Legislative*, *Executive* and the *Judicial*, and I think it unsafe to leave the distribution of either of these powers to one of the others. But when you come to other matters, that are not essential to the existence of the government, I do not think it dangerous to leave them to the legislators to dispense with these officers, and place their duties upon other officers, if they shall think the public welfare will be benefited by so doing; and I think that no gentleman on this floor should desire this Convention to adopt a policy which may prevent the people, through their representatives in the General Assembly, from making a change of that kind, if they think necessary, without the necessity of calling a convention to change the constitution. The office was fixed in the constitution of 1845, but in 1852 a different policy was adopted, and it was changed, leaving it for the Legislature to abolish it, when, in their opinion, it became no longer necessary. These are my views on this question. I may be wrong, but I am willing to learn from anybody and from everybody. If they can show me a better plan, I shall gladly advocate it. I think, however, that we should adhere as much as possible to the work of the constitution of 1852, and only depart from it when it fails to come up to the spirit of the age and the advancement of civilization; and I think this is one of the cases where a departure from the plan of 1852 is not required.

Mr. HARNAN—In regard to fixing the time of office at four years, without any restriction upon him, I certainly second the remarks of my friend Judge Howell.

Mr. STOCKER—Mr. President, it seems to me that this is taking a longitude altogether unjustifiable by the tenor of the substitute; but as that contains a provision that the duration of the office shall be fixed by the Legislature in the same manner as its duties are fixed, I shall vote for the substitute.

Mr. MONTAMAT—I call for the yeas and nays on the adoption.

Mr. CAZABAT—Mr. President, I move that the substiute be laid on the table.

Mr. SULLIVAN—The secretary will please read the substitute.

The yeas and nays were called, when it was found that there was not a quorum present.

Mr. DAVIES—I move that we adjourn till Monday next.

Mr. MONTAMAT—I move to lay that motion on the table.

The motion to lay on the table was lost. The motion to adjourn was then put and carried.

MONDAY, May 2, 1864.

[The Convention met at 12 o'clock M., and the roll being called, the following gentlemen answered to their names:

Messrs. Abell, Ariail, Austin, Barrett, Bell, Bofill, Bonzano, Bromley, Brott, Burke, Campbell, Cook J. K., Crozat, Davies, Dufresne, Duane, Duke, Edwards, Ennis, Fish, Flagg, Flood, Foley, Fosdick, Gastinel, Geier, Gorlinski, Gaidry, Healy, Harnan, Hart, Heard, Henderson, Hills, Hire, Kavanagh, Kugler, Maas, Mann, Millspaugh, Montamat, Montague, Murphy M. W., Normand, O'Conner, Ong, Payne J., Pintado, Poynot, Purcell J., Pursell S., Schroeder, Schnurr, Seymour, Smith, Spellicy, Stumpf, Stiner, Stauffer, Sullivan, Terry, Thomas, Waters, Wells, and Wilson—66 members.

There being no quorum, the sergeant-at-arms was directed to bring in absent members.

Messrs. Cutler, Baum, Mendiverri, Buckley, Collin, Cook T., Thorpe, Beauvais, Wenck and Cazabat, having taken their seats, the president announced that a quorum was present.

The minutes of Saturday were read and adopted.]

Mr. TERRY—I have a resolution which I desire to offer.

Whereas, Several persons are holding offices, State and municipal, who are not citizens of the State, or qualified, as per order of the President, December 8, 1863; therefore, be it

Resolved, That all persons holding State or municipal offices not qualified voters of the State, or who have not complied with the oath of the President's proclamation of December 8, 1863, that it is the sense of this Convention they should be promptly removed by the governor of the State and mayor of the city, who are respectfully requested to enforce this resolution.

Mr. FOLEY—I move the rules be suspended for its adoption.

Mr. DAVIES—I move the gentlemen offering the resolution furnishes the names of those holding offices who have not complied with the order.

[A motion to lay the resolution on the table was lost.]

Mr. HEARD—This is the second edition of the resolution introduced by the same gentleman on the second day of the Convenion. I wish to understand if this Convention is going to form itself into an inquisition. If so, let us know it, and elect a grand inquisitor, and have our racks of torture. I would like to know what we have to do with the officers of the city of New Orleans—what right have we to dictate to the governor and mayor whom to retain in office and whom to turn out. If I understand the reason why I am sent here it is to revise and amend the constitution; the appointment of officers has nothing to do with it. The primary object that has brought us together, as I understand it, is to wipe out slavery, and let us go to work and grapple with the question. I see no use in consuming the valuable time of this Convention in acting on frivolous resolutions, and I call this so, with all due respect to the gentleman. We have been here four weeks, and so far have done nothing. Our time has been spent in debating resolutions and motions to lay on the table, and if we go on in this way we shall stay here the balance of the year, and the Convention will become a laughing stock. I feel the responsibility of the posision I occupy, and wish to discharge the duties I am entrusted with. I intend to offer a motion which, I think, will simplify our proceedings and enable us to go on with business. My motion is this:

Resolved, That all reports of the different committees, all amendments and all substitutes which have been offered, be laid on the table, subject to call, and that we take up the constitution of 1852, beginning with the preamble, and taking it up, article by article, and section by section, and act upon them.

By doing this we will get through within thirty days.

Mr. Cazabat—I second the motion.

Mr. Henderson—Another similar resolution was brought before this Convention, but under different circumstances. It was then suggested that the offices of all the various office-holders of the city and State, who had not taken the iron-clad oath, should be forthwith declared vacant. On that occasion I voted against it, as I thought it interfered with the province of the governor and mayor; but upon this occasion I find a motion that meets my full approbation, and particularly at this time, as I have good reasons to believe that there are numerous persons holding offices in the city who are defying us, and wish for the defeat of Gen. Banks. I would have all such expelled, and therefore I hope it will be the sense of this Convention that they should be removed forthwith, whether they hold State or municipal offices. [Applause.]

When it comes to instructing the governor, we do it in the way of recommendation. I ask if we do not stand here to-day elected on the governor's ticket, and did not our opponents unite on the radical and copperhead tickets? Therefore we stand with the administration and with Gen. Banks, and last, though not least, with Michael Hahn, because he is in the midst of a struggle sustaining the President and the commander of our forces. When we find men are holding office through the clemency of the executive of the State and the mayor of the city, and defying us, it is time they were removed, and I would not have them remain one day. Rather than copperheads, opposed to the administration, give me an out and out Jeff. Davis man, who openly advocates the dissolution of the Union, but the copperhead is one day a Davis man and the next a Lincoln man. A man in the Confederacy is bound to be a Jeff. Davis man, or hang; but we permit men here to spit upon and revile us, and say they are good Union men at the same time that they are carrying out measures against the administration. I am for the Union, right or wrong. [Applause.]

There are many here who, sympathizing with the party adverse to us, would rather see Zach. Taylor's son here to-day than Gen. Banks, and I wish they were destroyed politically, because they are the worm that is eating the body politic, and by degrees may destroy it. I do not wish to ostracise men for their opinions. On ordinary occasions I am a Democrat, but now, there is but one question, and that is: "Are you in favor of your country?" If Gen. Grant or Gen. Banks opposed the administration, I would advocate their annihilation as soon as that of these men holding offices. I vote for and sustain this proposition on the ground that it is right in principle. I have a slight knowledge of the mayor and of the governor, and have good reason to believe they stand on the right ground in regard to this question; therefore, I am in favor of having the opinion of this Convention, and want no minority vote. I want more than two-thirds of those who are elected here to say if any man who sympathizes with those against us holds an office, he shall be removed.

Mr. Montamat—I am not here to censure the appointments of the governor and mayor. I have no doubt if the gentleman, or any member of this Convention, will go to these officers and state that such persons are not citizens, they will be at once removed. I shall vote against the resolution, for the reason that I do not wish to censure the governor and mayor. They may not know that these persons are not qualified; and if any member knows of any such, let him report them.

[The resolution was again read by the secretary; and on the yeas and nays being demanded, the roll was called, with the following result:]

Yeas—Messrs. Bailey, Bell, Bofill, Bonzano, Bromley, Campbell, Cazabat, Cook J. K., Cook T., Crozat, Collins, Duke, Davies, Duane, Dufresne, Ennis, Fish, Flagg, Flood, Foley, Geier, Gorlinski, Gaidry, Healy, Harnan, Hart, Henderson, Hills, Hire, Kavanagh, Maas, Millspaugh, Murphy E., Newell, Normand, O'Conner, Payne John, Poynot, Purcell J., Pursell Samuel, Schroeder,

Seymour, Shaw, Smith, Spellicy, Stocker, Stumpf, Stiner, Stauffer, Sullivan, Terry, Thorpe, Waters, Wenck, Wells and Wilson—56.

NAYS—Messrs. Abell, Austin, Barrett, Baum, Beauvais, Brott, Buckley, Burke, Cutler, Fuller, Gastinel, Heard, Kugler, Mann, Mendiverri, Montamat, Montague, Murphy M. W., Ong, Schnurr and Thomas—21.

[The resolution was adopted.]

Mr. HENDERSON—I believe I voted on this question under misapprehension, and spoke accordingly. I opposed the other resolution on the ground that no names were mentioned. [Cries of "out of order."] I wish to reconsider the question, and if any gentleman knows the names of such State or city officers to be removed, to specify them, so that our application will not be abstract. Therefore, I move a reconsideration.

Mr. HEALY—I move to lay the motion on the table.

[The motion was carried.]

Mr. BROMLEY—I offer the following resolution:

Resolved, That the future sessions of this Convention shall not be of less than four hours' duration, and that the pay per diem of the members of this Convention shall cease on and after the fortieth day from its organization.

Mr. MONTAMAT—I move to suspend the rules for its adoption.

[Carried.]

Mr. HEALY—I move to lay the resolution on the table.

[The motion was carried.]

PRESIDENT—Reports of committees are in order.

Mr. FOSDICK—The Committee on Legislative Department will report to-morrow.

Mr. SHAW—The Committee on Ordinance reports "progress."

Mr. MONTAMAT—As chairman of the Committee on Credentials, I beg leave to report that Mr. McGuire, who sent a protest against the election of Mr. Orr, desires permission to withdraw it.

Mr. SULLIVAN—I move he be allowed to withdraw it.

[The motion was carried.]

[Mr. Montamat then read the report of the Committee on Credentials:]

To the president and members of the State Constitutional Convention:

GENTLEMEN—Your Committee on Credentials, after due examination of all witnesses produced before us by Mr. T. F. McGuire, contesting the election of Mr. B. H. Orr, the delegate from the Tenth Representative District, beg leave to report that Mr. B. H. Orr has been duly elected as a delegate to this Convention, to represent the Tenth Representative District of the city of New Orleans; that he is duly qualified and is entitled to a seat in this Convention.

All of which is respectfully submitted.

JOHN P. MONTAMAT, *Chairman.*

Mr. SULLIVAN—I move that the report be received.

[The motion was carried.]

Mr. HENDERSON—One of our members, Mr. Montague, desires leave of absence on account of illness in his family. I move it be granted.

[The request was granted.]

Mr. AUSTIN—I call the attention of the Convention to the fact that Mr. Howes, from the ward I have the honor to represent, has only been in the Convention four days. It is not on account of sickness, and he has drawn his pay. I now ask what is our duty in regard to it.

Mr. TERRY—I move it be referred to the Committee on Absent Members.

[The motion was carried.]

[A communication from the Secretary of State was read by the secretary, enclosing the returns of the election of a delegate to the Convention in the parish of Jefferson, to fill the place of Christian Roselius, resigned.]

[Referred to the Committee on Credentials.]

PRESIDENT—Unfinished business is now in order.

Mr. WILSON—I call for the reading of Mr. Gruneberg's resolution.

Mr. HILLS—I rise to a point of order. I believe the first unfinished business is the vote on the resolution of Mr. Purcell, for the first article of the report of the Committee on Public Education, which was declared lost, when it was found there was not a quorum present.

PRESIDENT—The first business is on the resolution.

[Mr. Gruneberg's resolution was then read by the secretary.]

MR. GRUNEBERG'S PREAMBLE AND RESOLUTION.

Whereas, The Constitutional Convention of the State of Louisiana has been called principally to decide on the abolition of slavery in this State; whereas, the adoption of this measure, in whatever manner or form, will necessarily require great modifications in all parts of the organic law of the State; whereas, for these reasons this Convention cannot, or ought not to, come to a final decision on the reports of any of the standing committees on constitutional amendments, before voting on emancipation; and whereas, the question of emancipation being the most important of all, requires the longest and most mature deliberation of this Assembly; be it therefore

Resolved, That this Convention will take in consideration: First, the reports of all the standing committees on constitutional amendments, with substitutes and amendments thereto, except the report of the Committee on Emancipation; but that they shall not pass further than a second reading; that then the report of the Committee on Emancipation shall be taken up, and be then regularly passed to a final vote; and that afterwards the reports of all the other standing committees shall pass to their third reading, and to a final vote thereon; and, moreover.

Resolved, That this convention shall only adjourn from day to day until the reports of all the standing committees on constitutional amendments, except that of Emancipation, shall have passed a second reading.

C. H. L. GRUNEBERG

Mr. WILSON--I move that the resolution be adopted.

[The motion was carrried.]

PRESIDENT—The order of the day now comes.

Mr. HILLS—If I understand the rule in regard to unfinished business it is this: the first article of the report of the Committee on Public Education was under consideration. Mr. S. Pursell offered a substitute which was voted upon and declared to be carried. The yeas and nays were called for, when it was found there was not a quorum present. A motion to adjourn was then made and carried. If I understand it, the business before the house is the vote on that substitute.

PRESIDENT—The motion to adopt must be renewed.

Mr. S. PURSELL—If necessary, I renew my motion to adopt that substitute.

[The article and substitute were read.]

ART. —. There shall be elected a superintendent of public education, who shall hold his office for the term of four years. His duties shall be prescribed, and compensation fixed, by the general assembly.

Mr. CAMPBELL—I move to amend by striking out "four" and inserting "two" for the term of the superintendent's office.

Mr. FOLEY—I move to divide the article.

[The motion was lost.]

The question of adopting the resolution was put and declared lost. The yeas and nays were called for, and the result was as follows:

YEAS—Messrs. Abell, Bailey, Barrett, Beauvais, Bell, Bennie, Bonzano, Bromley, Brott, Buckley, Burke, Campbell, Collin, Crozat, Cutler, Davies, Duane, Dufresne, Duke, Ennis, Fish, Flagg, Flood, Foley, Fuller, Gastinel, Geier, Gruneberg, Gaidry, Heard, Hire, Kugler, Maas, Mann, Mendiverri, Millspaugh, Montague, Murphy E., Normand, Ong, Orr, Paine J., Pintado, Purcell J., Pursell S., Schroeder, Seymour, Shaw, Stocker, Stumpf, Stiner, Stauffer, Terry, Thomas and Wenck—55.

YEAS—Messrs. Ariail, Austin, Cazabat, Cook J. K., Cook T., Edwards, Gorlinski, Healy, Harnan, Hart, Hills, Murphy M. W., Newell, O'Conner, Poynot, Schnurr, Spellicy, Sullivan, Thorpe, Waters, Wells and Wilson—22.

[The substitute was therefore adopted.]

The second section of the report was read with Mr. Sullivan's substitute.

Substitute:

The general assembly shall establish free public schools throughout the State, for all free white children, by general taxation or otherwise, and all moneys shall be distributed to each parish, in proportion to the number of white children, between such ages as shall be fixed by the general assembly.

Mr. FOLEY—I move to lay the substitute on the table.

[Lost, by a vote of 47 to 23.]

Mr. STAUFFER—I voted against the amendment for the reason that it is almost word for word the same as the substitute of Mr. S. Pursell; therefore I move that all substitutes brought up hereafter, that are identical, be laid on the table.

Mr. STOCKER—I think the motion of the

gentleman an extraordinary one. For instance, I take up a resolution, and, by erasing or changing a word, alter the whole sense. It strikes me there is a vast difference between the two amendments referred to. Mr. Pursell's says the money raised shall be distributed in proportion to the number of children; the other in proportion to the number of white children. That, I think, is a very wide difference.

Mr. SULLIVAN—My substitute is to the second article of the original report. It strikes out colored children altogether, because I think white people have enough to do to attend to their own affairs, without attending to the education of negro children.

Mr. THORPE—I believe that in all deliberative bodies, where special committees are appointed to bring in reports, that those reports shall have some consideration, and I believe that a few remarks are perfectly correct.

The whole gist of this discussion, if narrowed down, is, whether black children of the State shall be educated or not. I think we cannot pass hastily upon so important a matter as this proposition; and I think, too, it is a very singular proceeding upon the part of members upon this floor, who hold their offices under the call of Gen. Banks, to come here and presume to elect who the children shall be, who shall be educated, when his orders imperatively provide for the education of these very children, and levy a tax for that purpose. [Applause.] It would take me a full half hour, if limited to it, to give my ideas upon the importance of this question. It is one of very serious and tremendous importance, and I do not understand how it is that a resolution containing such a matter, of so great import, so materially affecting the interest of the State, so materially affecting the interests of the gentlemen who are members of this Convention, in all future time, should be brought up here with so little importance.

Now, gentlemen, if I may be permitted to make some criticism, I would say that we have been here nearly a month, and with some experience I can say, I never saw such an illustration of the manner of piling one amendment upon another as here, and that motions to adjourn and lay upon the table never prevailed so extensively as here.

We are here for a most solemn and serious purpose, not that of making a new constitution for the State of Louisiana, but to amend and correct the one already existing. This is one of the most solemn and in one respect the most glorious things to be entertained; but while we have some thirty State constitutions before us, and three or four already in this very State, we have, so far as work is concerned, if done honestly, very little to do. I believe all we have to do in this convention is to pass some regulations with regard to the education of the colored children, which will meet the changes to be made, I suppose, by the Emancipation Committee.

It is also proposed to make some changes in regard to the judiciary. If these are the only things, all these discussions and piling amendments on amendments are out of place, and, in my opinion, unnecessary. I do not know, Mr. President, how to get this Convention clear from all this noise and contention. It seems to me we are here to discuss rules and not amendments, and I say to gentlemen again that we come here to work and treat these subjects with *some* solemnity. *I* do not believe we come here with the right spirit and sense of duty. We are not engaged in any ordinary transaction, nor as a legislative body, nor in making any laws; but in amending and revising a constitution already in existence. We have power to strike out all objectionable features, to select what we please. I hold that the constitution of 1852 was passed by as good a deliberative body as was ever assembled in this or any other State. What is the reason we cannot take it up and follow it *verbatim*, except where changes must be made. Do that and nothing else. Is not that enough? We propose alterations in regard to the judiciary; to engraft upon it also the principle of emancipation, and this last we must do or perjure ourselves. We propose further to arrange this school system.

I wish to put on record, in regard to myself, that I stand here prepared to attend to business only, and hope any gentleman will call me to order if I move to table or adjourn if there *is* any business before this body. We have a liberal compensation, which I voted for and would again. For that compensation I am willing to do a fair day's work, and then we *deserve* our pay, but if we trifle as we have done, we are open to criticism, and the finger of censure must be justly pointed against us. [Hear, hear.] We *can* do our work here in sixty days, and make a good Constitution. We are legislating not only for Louisiana, but all the States; and I wish you to understand this fact: that the president of the United States, and Gen. Banks, and certain parties who sympathize with the rebellious States, have towards us a kindly feeling, and have been mainly instrumental in getting up and ordering this Convention, which is to bring back Louisiana under civil instead of military power. If we fail to come up to their expectations, and the expectation of the North, what will be the result? I tell you this is the last time the protection of the United States will be held out to any rebellious State in this nation. [Hear, hear.] If we fail, nothing hereafter will settle our status but the sword, and if we do not do our work well, we do not deserve anything else.

What are the facts? Every single day that we meet here, and hesitate to frame a free State Constitution, is so much against us. No matter what may be said to the contrary, this war is rapidly assuming an aspect conflicting with every christian principle. Our soldiers are murdered in cold blood; the scenes being enacted cry to Heaven and will fill the civilized world with horror. I ask you to look at those men who fell at Fort Pillow, who were not only mrdered in cold blood, but burned, buried alive; and see what a war is being fastened upon us. I ask if ever in the annals of christendom or the history of mankind, there is any precedent; in a State like Louisiana, fairly and honestly taken possession of by a hostile army, for citizens, without authority of the law, arming themselves in band and under the name of guerrillas and jay-hawkers, going through the country, murdering and butchering?

I tell you a strong feeling is rapidly growing up at the North in opposition to this. Look at the files of Northern papers which came to us yesterday; they are one shriek of agony at the horrors of this civil war, and I say that if you do not now make a constitution equal to the occasion, worthy of Louisiana, the opportunity is past, and you lose a most glorious opportunity of glorifying yourselves and preserving the country.

Mr. Abell—Mr. President, it does strike me with a good deal of force that all our work here is a good deal on the principle of putting the cart before the horse. There are some nations I believe who manage to do work in that way, and they succeed to some extent. But, sir, I should like to know, and therefore ask for information, what right we have here to presume so far upon future legislation as to attempt to assume such a state of facts as is contemplated by the remarks of the gentleman who has just spoken, with respect to a matter upon which there has been no action in this Convention. How do we know that the master would permit the slave to go to the schools if we establish them. We are sent here to amend a constitution, but we might as well adjourn *sine die* as to attempt to persist in doing business in the manner in which this Convention seems determined to proceed. Here we are quibbling over the education of slave children. I know the gentleman has told us that no such persons exist, but I would as soon trust to the Constitution and laws of the United States, and to the proclamation of Abraham Lincoln, as to the statement of the gentleman. And the proclamation of Abraham Lincoln of January, 1863, declares that this very district shall be exempted from its effects. What, then, are we legislating for? Is it to educate the slaves in that part of this State still in the Confederacy.

I ask upon what authority—I ask upon what principles, or by what right you can legislate for the education of slave children before you have taken any action to change their status. How can you presume, before such action is taken, that it will be done?

What logic, or in plainer words, what sense is there in such a mode of proceeding with the work which you have laid out? I confess I can see in it neither logic nor sense, and Mr. President, I think I shall make a motion before I sit down, and if I do not think of it I hope some other gentleman will, to postpone this matter until we shall know exactly where and how we stand.

I say, that notwithstanding Gen. Banks has issued his proclamation, declaring so much of the constitution of 1852, and the laws relating to slavery, null, because there is no class of persons to whom they apply—notwithstanding these laws and the adjudications thereon are of the highest and most undoubted authority, he has laid them prostrate. I do not question the authority of Gen. Banks in the premises, or inquire into his reasons for adopting such a measure. It is a military measure, made necessary perhaps by the existence of war, but the existence of the military power will at some time be at an end here; and when such time shall arrive, when the force that has laid them postrate is removed, they will be revived. When the State has resumed her sovereignty as one of the States of this Union, as resume it she will as soon as her people have the power and privilege to speak, these laws will again be in force.

One of the gentlemen from the Second District (Mr. Thorpe), to my astonishment, has threatened us with Gen. Banks and the North. If the North has a constitution to submit for the government of this people, I have no objection. But, sir, that this Convention, called together by the sovereign people of the State to represent their interests, that they should stand here to make a constitution to please the people of the North, or Gen. Banks, is preposterous. And, sir, Gen. Banks does not expect it; as far as he is concerned, I know he does not. If he had intended to make a constitution for this people, instead of a convention at a cost of fifty thousand dollars a month, he could have employed a clerk to make it at a much less sum. He expected us to act as freemen. He expected us to make it as honest men, and to be free hereafter. He meant no such thing as has been intimated by the gentleman, and if I had the papers here I could demonstrate it, I believe. He has never threatened us. But, sir, we are told that everything is to be turned upside down if we do not make such a constitution as will please certain men. Now, sir, if we make any constitution we should make such a one as will suit and please the people of Louisiana; we should not go beyond their wishes and their rights. We have no right to make constitutions for the North nor for the Confederacy. We must consult the wants and the rights of the people of Louisiana, whom we represent, and we are bound to represent them faithfully. Look for yourselves at the surrounding circumstances, and say whether your fellow-citizens will approve the steps you may take in this matter.

But, sir, this is not a new question. The great men who framed the constitution of the United States, the great charter of your liberties, had this whole matter before them. That body, comprising such great names as those of Washington, Franklin and Madison, the wisdom of the nation, did not see fit, in their wisdom, to take such action as we assume is already taken by this body.

Mr. President, I have never before heard such language on such an occasion, as that used by the member from the Second District; but, sir, such language will not frighten men of the South; no man will be frightened by it. If we believe that it will be to the interest of the people to free the negroes, we should do it; but not under any other consideration should this Convention alter in any respect their constitution. I know it is said by some that this is a Free State already. But, sir, I know that the President excepted this part of the State in his emancipation proclamation. We are therefore standing upon the same ground we stood on before this proclamation was issued, except so far as the proclamation of Gen. Banks goes; and whether that proclamation was intended to humiliate the people or as a permanent war measure, I am not here to inquire. He has taken the matter under his own control for the present, and during the war, perhaps. But for the future—he has called us together in order that we may say what is to the interest of Louisiana, not to-day, but hereafter.

I know that there are some gentlemen here who differ with me in opinion. I know that there are some who entertain opinions diametrically opposed to the opinions that I entertain; but, sir, I stand here as one who never believed in slavery as a principle. I never believed in the Bank of the United States; I never really believed in any banks; I believe them to be overreaching institutions. But, sir, slavery has come down to us through legitimate channels, having taken root in the old world even before the discovery of America. Yes, sir, in the most ancient times slavery existed, not only in the nations of the earth, properly so speaking, but it existed during the time of the theocracy. The divine government of God over his chosen people. Abraham had servants that he bought with his money—servants that he bought of strangers. (Gen., verses 26 to 27.) Egypt, where we find the earliest traces of civilization, had its slaves and was the hot-bed of slavery, is in the sacred scriptures termed "the house of bondage."

Greece, the great nursery of the arts and sciences, had her slaves. At one time in Attica, one of the States, there were 400,000 slaves and but 21,000 resident burghers and 10,000 foreigners. Egina, as we learn from Aristotle, had 470,000, and Corinth, according to Timaceus, 460,000 slaves, a greater proportion of slaves than was ever known to exist in any portion of this land. Cicero tells us that in Rome at one time no less than ten to twenty thousand slaves were owned by a single planter. But, Mr. President, this is a part of the system which, as a stream, has run down to the present—unbroken as time itself. Even at the advent of our Savior into this world, Roman slavery, in its most horrid and terrible form, existed. Theirs was a system most cruel and barbarous, when compared with ours; but notwithstanding all this, Mr. President, the blessed Savior, although he rebuked idolatry, crimes, and hypocrisy in every form; no one can find one denunciation by him against slavery, because it existed as a part of the order of society and as

"Order is nation's first law, and this confest,
Some are and must be greater than the rest."

Let us trace it rapidly down the stream of time to the present, and what do we find? Why, sir, we find that until about the nine hundredth year of the Christian era, none but the white and Asiatic races were enslaved. But, sir, when the sleek, fat, and well-kept negro is called a slave, then goes up a howl that reaches the heavens—a howl of unmitigated wretchedness, on account of the suffering of the well-fed, well-kept, well cared for, sleek, fat, and happy negro.

I defy any gentleman here, sir, to look at the facts as they exist, and say to this assembly that the system is a cruel one. Why, sir, it is a patriarchal institution. The master is a kind of patriarch to the negroes, and they are guarded as the apple of his eye, and woe to the man that attempts to invade one of the plantations, and ventures to lay a hand upon a single negro—both blacks and whites, sir, will fall upon him without mercy. This you all know as well as I do, or can tell you.

The negro, under our present system of slavery, is well fed, well taken care of, and well provided for; and, Mr. President, I consider slavery one of the best evils that exists upon the earth—one of the best, because the negro is benefited by it, because it keeps them out of houses of prostitution, out of our jails and workhouses, and prevents them from being burdens upon society. But gentlemen here say that they wish to protect the negro; their sympathies are so strongly aroused and the injuries to the negro so strenuously urged that one would suppose that these were the wretched part of mankind, the only wretched, distressed and down-trodden of our age. How came it so? Have they visited the cellars of New York, or the dens of infamy in this city? Have they seen the poor widow toiling incessantly for a virtuous and insufficient support, until forced to a life of crime to support herself? Have we no protection to offer these?

Mr. Austin—I rise to a point of order; the gentleman is getting away from the point under discussion.

President [to Mr. Austin]—The gentleman will sit down. The gentleman has the floor, and is in order.

Mr. ABELL—I think I understand the question perfectly, Mr. President. The question is upon the education of the black children, and, sir, here is one who will never vote for it. Never will I vote for a measure that will imbrue the hands of the people in blood. The question is upon Mr. Sullivan's substitute if I am not mistaken, and if I am, I call upon the chair to correct me. That substitute does honor to the gentleman who moved it. It does honor to the State and nation. To those who have acquired a little property and have invested it in negroes, he says it is a shame that your property shall be torn from you and then that you shall be taxed to educate negro children. I say the proposition is an honor to the State and not a disgrace. I say that the levying of taxes upon us to pay for the education of a race that we expect to be torn from us, is an indignity. Why are we called upon to educate these negroes? They have been acquired and held heretofore under the laws of the land; acquired by purchase, earned by the sweat of honest industry. Is it to be said that this Convention, representing the people of this State, instead of affording protection to the property of the people, shall tear away millions of that property, and then levy a tax upon them to educate it? Shall we tear away the slave from his master and then force the master to educate him?

What right, they ask, have we to such property? Why, sir, the same right that any man has to any property; the triple right of purchase, custom and guarantee, by the constitution and laws of the United States. All the States have legislated upon it and admitted it to be property, and this is the first time in the history of our country that a convention has ever been called upon to tear away at one fell stroke, from widows and orphans, $150,000,000 of property; and in addition to this, to tear from loyal owners in this State property to the amount of at least nine or ten hundred millions. Let us return, Mr. President, to the great charter of our nation's rights, in which slavery has been acknowledged no less than three times. Once in the declaration that certain persons may be imported until a certain time. It provides, also, that fugitives owing service or labor, &c., shall be returned; and once in making up a representative basis.

It has been legislated upon for three quarters of a century past, and repeated, and uniform judicial decisions have recognized it and declared it to be property. It has not only been recognized and held as property by the various State courts, under the laws of the land, but some of the wisest and ablest judges that have ever graced the bench of any nation, such as Chief Justice Marshall, and a host of others, have all given decisions with a uniformity almost unparalleled, recognizing it, calling it slavery, and treating it in every respect as property. Now let me ask you if we are a wiser body of men than those who have decided this species of property to be guaranteed by the great charter—the Constitution. If we are, we are the wisest body of men that has ever yet assembled.

The Constitution and laws of the United States are with me; justice and every consideration of manhood is with me; therefore I shall never, never sign an enactment to take one solitary dollar from the worst much less from the best of men without a fair and just remuneration for his property.

As it is, we are about at one fell stroke to tear $150,000,000 of property from its legitimote owners. You will have to look them in the face. You are bound to look them in the face and to answer when they ask you the question: Why did you tear from me my property?

Mr. AUSTIN—I rise to a point of order—the gentleman has occupied more than half an hour.

PRESIDENT—He has not occupied half an hour. I am keeping the time.

Mr. AUSTIN—But, Mr. President—

PRESIDENT—The gentleman will sit down and not interrupt a member while speaking.

Mr. ABELL—All should know, Mr. President, that I am strictly and emphatically a law abiding man. As I contended three years ago, when these streets were red with blood flowing from the veins of naturalized foreigners, that they had an inalienable right to protection, under the constitution and laws of the United States, so I contend now, that we hold our property by the most indefeasible and inalienable title in the land. Then I stood as I stand now. I felt that from a principle of manliness, from a principle of honor, I was bound to stand up to sustain them in their rights. I am not in favor of slavery—I am opposed to it; but, sir, when my countrymen have acquired property, honestly, and under the sanction of the laws of the State and of the nation, I will defend it while God blesses me with health and strength to do so, by my vote at least.

PRESIDENT—The half hour is up.

Mr. THORPE—Mr. President, I move that the gentleman be permitted to proceed with his remarks.

Mr. AUSTIN—I move to adjourn.

[The motion was lost.]

Mr. MONTAMAT—I move that the rules be suspended, in order to allow the gentleman to proceed with his argument.

[Mr. Montamat's motion was made and carried.]

Mr. ABELL—Mr. President, it is said that one good turn deserves another. I am not well, and the gentlemen have doubtless perceived that my voice is failing. The gentlemen have been very kind in giving me permission to go on; but I would be extremely obliged if they would adjourn till to-morrow, and give me a little time, say fifteen or twenty minutes, in the morning.

Mr. MONTAMAT—I move to adjourn till 11 o'clock to-morrow morning.

PRESIDENT—That is out of order, unless a motion is first made to suspend the rules.

[A motion was then made to adjourn, and on being put to the House was carried.]

TUESDAY, May 3, 1864.

[The Convention was called to order by the president at 12 o'clock M., and after prayer by the Rev. Mr. Horton, the roll was called and the following gentlemen answered to their names:

Messrs. Abell, Barrett, Bennie, Bofill, Bonzanó, Bromley, Buckley, Burke, Collin, Cook J. K., Crozat, Davies, Decker, Duane, Dufresne, Duke, Edwards, Ennis, Fosdick, Foley, Fuller, Geier, Goldman, Henderson, Healy, Heard, Hills, Howes, Kavanagh, Maas, Mann, Millspaugh, Murphy M. W., Newell, Normand, O'Conner, Paine J. T., Payne J., Pintado, Poynot, Pursell S., Schroeder, Schnurr, Stumpf, Terry, Thomas, Wells, Wilson and Mr. President—50.

There not being a quorum present, the sergeant-at-arms was directed to procure the attendance of absent members.

Messrs. Ariail, Balch, Baum, Beauvais, Bell, Campbell, Cook T., Dupaty, Fish, Flagg, Gastinel, Gaidry, Harnan, Hart, Hire, Kugler, Mendiverri, Montamat, Murphy E., Ong, Orr, Smith, Stiner, Stauffer, Sullivan, Thorpe and Waters having taken their seats, the president declared a quorum present.

The minutes of yesterday were read and adopted.]

Mr. SULLIVAN—Mr. President, I have a resolution I desire to offer, to lie over under the rules:

Resolved, That the clerks, officers and employés of this Convention be and are hereby exempt from serving, during the sesison of this Convention, as jurors in the several District Courts of this parish.

Mr. MONTAMAT—Mr. President, I desire to offer a resolution:

Resolved, That the resolution adopted by this House fixing the hour of 12 o'clock M. for the meeting of this Convention, be and the same is hereby repealed.

Resolved, further, That this House will hereafter meet at 11 o'clock A. M.

Mr. FOSDICK—I move to suspend the rules for the purpose of taking up the resolution of Mr. Montamat.

[The motion was lost.]

Mr. FOSDICK—Mr. President, I desire to submit the report of the Committee on the Legislative Department:

REPORT OF THE COMMITTEE ON LEGISLATIVE DEPARTMENT.

To the president and members of the Convention for the Revision and Amendment of the Constitution of the State of Louisiana:

The undersigned, members of the Committee on Legislative Department, have the honor to submit the following report:

Art. —. The legislative power of the State shall be vested in two distinct branches, the one to be styled the House of Representatives, the other the Senate, and both the General Assembly of the State of Louisiana.

Art. —. The members of the House of Representatives shall continue in service for the term of two years from the day of the closing of the general elections.

Art. —. Representatives shall be chosen on the first Monday in November every two years, and the election shall be completed in one day. The General Assembly shall meet annually on the first Monday in January, unless a different day be appointed by law, and their sessions shall be held at the seat of government.

Art. —. Every duly qualified elector under this constitution shall be eligible to a seat in the General Assembly; provided, that no person shall be a representative or senator unless he be, at the time of his election, a duly qualified voter of the representative or senatorial district from which he is elected.

Art. —. Elections for the members of the General Assembly shall be held at the several election precincts established by law.

Art. —. Representation in the House of Representatives shall be equal and uniform, and shall be regulated and ascertained by the number of qualified electors. Each parish shall have at least one Representative. No new parish shall be created with a territory less than six hundred and twenty-five square miles, nor with a number of electors less than the full number entitling it to a Representative; nor when the creation of such new parish would leave any other parish without the said extent of territory and number of electors. The first enumeration by the State authorities, under this constitution, shall be made in the year one thousand eight hundred and sixty-six, the second in the year one thousand eight hundred and seventy, the third in the year one thousand eight hundred and seventy-six; after which time the General Assembly shall direct in what manner the census shall be taken, so that it be made at least once in every period of ten years for the purpose of ascertaining the total population, and the number of qualified electors in each parish and election district; and in case of informality in the census returns from any district, the Legislature shall order a new census taken in such parish or election district.

At the first session of the Legislature after the making of each enumeration, the Legislature shall apportion the representation amongst the several parishes and election districts on the basis of qualified electors as aforesaid. A representative number shall be fixed, and each parish and election district shall have as many Representatives as the aggregate number of its electors will entitle it to, and an additional Representative for any fraction exceeding one-half the representative number. The number of Representatives shall not be more than one hundred and twenty, not less than ninety, until an apportionment shall be made, and elections held under the same, in accordance with the first enumeration to be made, as directed in this article.

The representation in the Senate and House of Representatives shall be as follows:

For the parish of Orleans, forty-four Representatives, to be elected as follows:

First District		5
Second do.		8
Third do.		6
Fourth do.		3
Fifth do.		3
Sixth do.		3
Seventh do.		3
Eighth do.		2
Ninth do.		2
Tenth do.		7
Right Bank, Algiers		2
The Parish of	Livingston	1
do.	St. Tammany	1
do.	Point Coupée	2
do.	St. Martin	2
do.	Concordia	1
do.	Madison	1
do.	Franklin	1
do.	St. Mary	1
do.	Jefferson	3
do.	Plaquemines	1
do.	St. Bernard	1
do.	St. Charles	1
do.	St. John the Baptist	1
do.	St. James	1
do.	Ascension	1
do.	Assumption	2
do.	Lafourche	2
do.	Terrebonne	2
do.	Iberville	1
do.	West Baton Rouge	1
do.	East Baton Rouge	2
do.	West Feliciana	1
do.	East Feliciana	1
do.	St. Helena	1
do.	Washington	1
do.	Vermillion	1
do.	Lafayette	2
do.	St. Landry	3
do.	Calcasieu	2
do.	Avoyelles	2
do.	Rapides	3
do.	Natchitoches	2
do.	Sabine	2
do.	Caddo	2
do.	DeSoto	2
do.	Ouachita	1
do.	Union	2
do.	Morehouse	1
do.	Jackson	2
do.	Caldwell	1
do.	Catahoula	2
do.	Claiborne	3
do.	Bossier	1
do.	Bienville	2
do.	Carroll	2
do.	Tensas	1
do.	Winn	2
Total		118

And the State shall be divided into the following senatorial districts: All that portion of the parish of Orleans lying on the

19

left bank of the Mississippi river shall be divided into two senatorial districts; the First and Fourth Districts of the city of New Orleans shall compose one district and shall elect four senators, and the Second and Third Districts of said city shall compose the other district and shall elect three senators.

The parishes of Plaquemines, St. Bernard and all that part of the parish of Orleans on the right bank of the Mississippi river shall form one district, and shall elect one senator.

The parish of Jefferson shall form one district, and shall elect one senator.

The parishes of St. Charles and Lafourche shall form one district, and shall elect one senator.

The parishes of St. John the Baptist and St. James shall form one district, and shall elect one senator.

The parishes of Ascension, Assumption and Terrebonne shall form one district, and shall elect two senators.

The parish of Iberville shall form one district, and shall elect one senator.

The parish of East Baton Rouge shall form one district, and shall elect one senator.

The parishes of West Baton Rouge, Point Coupée and West Feliciana shall form one district, and shall elect two senators.

The parish of East Feliciana shall form one district, and shall elect one senator.

The parishes of Washington, St. Tammany, St. Helena and Livingston shall form one district, and shall elect one senator.

The parishes of Concordia and Tensas shall form one district, and shall elect one senator.

The parishes of Madison and Carroll shall form one district, and shall elect one senator.

The parishes of Morehouse, Ouachita, Union and Jackson shall form one district, and shall elect two senators.

The parishes of Catahoula, Caldwell and Franklin shall form one district, and shall elect one senator.

The parishes of Bossier, Bienville, Claiborne and Winn shall form one district, and shall elect two senators.

The parishes of Natchitoches, Sabine, De Soto and Caddo shall form one district, and shall elect two senators.

The parishes of St. Landry, Lafayette and Calcasieu shall form one district, and shall elect two senators.

The parishes of St. Martin and Vermillion shall form one district, and shall elect one senator.

The parish of St. Mary shall form one district, and shall elect one senator.

The parishes of Rapides and Avoyelles shall form one district, and shall elect two senators.

The House of Representatives shall choose its speaker and other officers.

Every white male who has attained the age of twenty-one years, and who has been a resident of the State twelve months next preceding the election, and the last six months thereof in the parish in which he offers to vote, and who shall be a citizen of the United States and able to read and write, shall have the right of voting.

The Legislature shall have power to pass laws extending suffrage to such other persons, citizens of the United States, as by military service, by taxation to support the Government, or by intellectual fitness, may be deemed entitled thereto.

No voter, on removing from one parish to another within the State, shall lose the right of voting in the former until he shall have acquired it in the latter. Electors shall in all cases, except treason, felony or breach of the peace, be privileged from arrest during their attendance at, going to, or returning from elections.

Art. —. The Legislature shall provide by law that the names and residences of all qualified electors shale be registered in order to entitle them to vote; but the registry shall be free of cost to the elector.

Art. —. No pauper, no person under interdiction, nor under conviction of any crime punishable with hard labor, shall be entitled to vote at any election in this State.

Art. —. No person shall be entitled to vote at any election held in this State except in the parish of his residence, and in cities and towns divided into election precincts in the election precinct in which he resides.

Art. —. The members of the Senate shall be chosen for the term of four years. The Senate, when assembled, shall have the power to choose its own officers.

Art. —. The Legislature, in every year in which they shall apportion representation in the House of Representatives, shall divide the State into senatorial districts.

Art. —. No parish shall be divided in the formation of a senatorial district, the parish of Orleans excepted. And whenever a new parish shall be created, it shall be attached to the senatorial district from which most of its territory was taken, or to another contiguous district, at the discretion of the the Legislature; but shall not be attached to more than one district. The number of senators shall be thirty-four, and they shall be apportioned among the senatorial districts according to the electoral population contained in the several districts: *Provided*, that no parish be entitled to more than seven senators.

Art. —. In all apportionments of the Senate, the electoral population of the whole State shall be divided by the number thirty-four, and the result produced by this division shall be the senatorial ratio entitling a senatorial district to a senator. Single or contiguous parishes shall be formed into districts, having a population the nearest possible to the number entitling a district to a senator; and if in the apportionment to make a parish or district fall short of or exceed the ratio, then a district may be formed having not more than two senators, but not otherwise. No new apportionment shall have the effect of abridging the term of service of any senator already elected at the time of making the apportionment. After an enumeration has been made as directed in —th article, the Legislature shall not pass any law until an apportionment of representation in both Houses of the General Assembly be made.

Art. —. At the first session of the General Assembly, after this constitution takes effect, the senators shall be equally divided by lot, into two classes: the seats of the senators of the first class shall be vacated at the expiration of the second year; of the second class at the expiration of the fourth year; so that one-half shall be chosen every two years, and a rotation thereby kept up perpetually. In case any district shall have elected two or more senators, said senators shall vacate their seats respectively at the end of two and four years, and lots shall be drawn between them.

Art. —. The first election for senators shall be general throughout the State, and at the same time that the general election for representatives is held, and thereafter there shall be biennial elections to fill the places of those whose term of service may have expired.

Art. —. Not less than a majority of the members of each House of the General Assembly shall form a quorum to do business; but a smaller number may adjourn from day to day, and shall be authorized by law to compel the attendance of absent members.

Art. —. Each House of General Assembly shall judge of the qualifications, election and returns of its members; but a contested election shall be determined in such manner as shall be directed by law.

Art. —. Each House of the General Assembly may determine the rules of its proceedings, punish a member for disorderly behavior, and, with a concurrence of two-thirds, expel a member, but not a second time for the same offence.

Art. —. Each House of the General Assembly shall keep and publish weekly a journal of its proceedings, and the yeas and nays of the members on any question shall, at the desire of any two of them, be entered on the journal.

Art. —. Each House may punish, by imprisonment, any person not a member, for disrespectful and disorderly behavior in its presence, or for obstructing any of its proceedings. Such imprisonment shall not exceed ten days for any one offence.

Art. —. Neither House, during the sessions of the General Assembly, shall, without the consent of the other, adjourn for more than three days, nor to any other place than that in which they may be sitting.

Art. —. The members of the General Assembly shall receive from the Public Treasury a compensation for their services which shall be eight dollars per day, during their attendance, going to and returning from the sessions of their respective Houses. The compensation may be increased, or diminished, by law, but no alteration shall take effect during the period of service of the members of the House of Representatives by whom such alteration shall have been made. No session shall extend to a period beyond sixty days, to date from its commencement, and any legislative action had after the expiration of the said sixty days shall be null and void. This provision shall not apply to the first Legislature which is to convene after the adoption of this constitution.

Art. — The members of the General Assembly shall in all cases, except treason, felony, breach of the peace, be privileged from arrest during their attendance at the sessions of their respective Houses, and going to or returning from the same, and for any speech or debate in either House shall not be questioned in any other place.

Art. —. No senator or representative shall, during the term for which he was elected, nor for one year thereafter, be appointed or elected to any civil office of profit under this State, which shall have been created, or the emoluments of which shall have been increased during the time such senator or representative was in office, except to such offices or appointments as may be filled by the elections of the people.

Art. —. No person, who at any time may have been a collector of taxes, whether State, parish or municipal, or who may have been otherwise entrusted with public money, shall be eligible to the General Assembly, or to any office of profit or trust, under the State government, until he shall have obtained a discharge for the amount of such collections, and for all public moneys with which he may have been entrusted.

Art. —. No person, while he continues to exercise the functions of a clergyman of any religious denomination whatever, shall be eligible to the General Assembly.

Art. —. No bill shall have the force of a law, until, on three several days, it be read over in each House of the General Assembly, and free discussion allowed thereon, unless in case of urgency; four-fifths of the

House, where the bill shall be pending, may deem it expedient to dispense with this rule.

Art. —. All bills for raising revenue shall originate in the House of Representatives, but the Senate may propose amendments, as in other bills; provided they shall not introduce any new matter, under the color of an amendment, which does not relate to raising revenue.

Art. —. The General Assembly shall regulate, by law, by whom and in what manner writs of election shall be issued to fill the vacancies which may happen in either branch thereof.

Art. —. The Senate shall vote on the confirmation or rejection of officers, to be appointed by the governor, with the advice and consent of the Senate, by yeas and nays, and the names of the senators voting for and against the appointments, respectively, shall be entered on a journal to be kept for that purpose, and made public at the end of each session or before.

Art. —. Returns of all elections for members of the General Assembly shall be made to the secretary of State.

Art. —. In the year in which a regular election for a senator of the United States is to take place, the members of the General Assembly shall meet in the hall of the House of Representatives on the second Monday following the meeting of the Legislature, and proceed to the said election.

GEO. A. FOSDICK, Chairman.
C. W. STAUFFER,
A. CAZABAT,
T. M. WELLS,
E. H. KNOBLOCH,
WM. H. HIRE,
MARTIN SCHNURR,
T. B. THORPE signs with the understanding he can object to the clause relating to what shall constitute an elector.

Mr. HILLS--I move that the report be accepted and made the order of the day for this day week.

Mr. STAUFFER—I amend so as to let the report lie over until it comes up in its regular order.

Mr. HILLS—I accept the amendment.

The motion was carried.

PRESIDENT—The unfinished business of yesterday, the second reading of the report of the Committee on Public Education, is now in order.

Mr. ABELL—Mr. President, I rise before this Convention for the purpose of submitting some additional observations upon the subject before the Convention. I submit, Mr. President, that the question before the House is upon the substitute to the second article of the report of the Committee on Public Education presented by Mr. Sullivan, and that this substitute has for its object the limitation of the school fund to the white children of the State of Louisiana. The article for which the substitute is offered has in its terms no application to any particular children, but to the children of the State of Louisiana, and the direct limitation of the honorable member who presented the substitute is to limit the application of the fund specially to the white children. Before I proceed to make any observations on the question before this body, I desire to make some explanation as to my general views with regard to the objects of this Convention. I have first and last, from the beginning to the end—or, at least, to the present time—believe that a military government should have prevailed in this department, and I most sincerely believe that a military government would furnish a better government, a more secure government, and what is more, Mr. President, but one government. Any subsidiary government that we can frame, or that could be made by the wisdom of men, would be rather a detriment to the interests of the people than otherwise. A military government in this department is an absolute necessity. It cannot be dispensed with in this department; and, Mr. President, New Orleans being the centre or base of it, I believe that with a military governor, with the advice of the commanding general, the right and interests of the people would be far better subserved, and greater security afforded to them than could possibly be done by any auxiliary government that could be made for the purpose at present. It is these views that I have expressed first and last, up to the present time at least.

Two gentlemen here, both I believe from the North, urged upon the Convention in the debate yesterday—with a degree of zeal that at least astonished me—that we were called together by Gen. Banks for the purpose of performing certain duties, and that those duties he would like to have performed with extraordinary promptness. I said yesterday and I repeat to-day that Gen.

Banks meant no such thing. I then said that if I had the documents here I could prove it. I then said that he meant for us to meet here for the purpose and for the sole purpose of legislating for the people of Louisiana. Some efforts have been made to show that I have prejudices against Gen. Banks, which account for my course towards him. Sir, as far as my position towards Gen. Banks is concerned, I look upon him as the man who ought to control the whole matter here at present. I look upon Gen. Banks as one who knows and can see the results and workings of his own plans as well as any man. In that respect I regard him as of equal capacity with Abraham Lincoln himself.

I therefore think that no gentleman here can stand upon this floor and say that I have any desire to throw any obstacle in the way of Gen. Banks. But I will show this Convention that Gen. Banks made his own decree in reference to this matter, and registered it himself, without calling a convention to do it, at an expense of $50,000 a month. I say, sir, that only one week before the election of delegates to this body took place, the commanding general issued his decree in reference to the subject we have now under consideration, and this question cannot be contested by any gentleman on the floor, for here is the decree as signed by order of Gen. Banks and Richard B. Irvin, assistant adjutant general. If we are called here simply to register his will, why did he not call upon us by express words to do so. No, sir; he has done no such thing. We have no right to say that he has called upon us to register his will. No, sir, he has manifested his own will by his military orders. I have nothing to do with them. I have not studied them. I know only that when they are issued it is my duty to obey them, and if I do not choose to do that he will make me obey them:

HEADQUARTERS DEPARTMENT OF THE GULF,
New Orleans, March 22, 1864.

General Orders No. 38.

In pursuance of the provisions of General Orders No. 23, current series, for the rudimental instruction of the freedmen of this department, placing within their reach the elements of knowledge which give intelligence and greater value to labor, and reducing the provisions necessary therefor to an economical and efficient school system,

It is ordered that a Board of Education, consisting of three persons, be hereby constituted, with the following duties and powers:

1st. To establish one or more common schools in each and every school district that has been or may be defined by the parish provost marshals under orders of the provost marshal general:

2d. To acquire by purchase, or otherwise, tracts of land, which shall be judged by the board necessary and suitable for school sites, in plantation districts, to be not less than one half acre in extent; to hold the same in trust to themselves until such schools shall have been established, when they shall transfer all the right and title thereto that may have vested in them to the superintendent of public education, or other competent State authority:

3d. To erect upon said plots of land such school-houses as they may judge necessary and proportioned to the wants of the population of the district, where there are no buildings available and proper for school purposes. And in this, as in all other duties, they shall exercise the strictest economy:

4th. To select and employ proper teachers for said schools, as far as practicable from the loyal inhabitants of Louisiana, with power to require their attendance for the purpose of instruction in their duties one week at least at a normal school, to be conducted by the board.

5th. To purchase and provide the necessary books, stationery and apparatus for the use of such schools, and in addition thereto to purchase and furnish an outfit of a well-selected library, &c., for each freed person in the several school districts who is above the age of attending school duty, at a cost to each, including a case for the same, not exceeding two and a half dollars, which sum shall be included in the general tax hereinafter provided, but shall be deducted from the laborer's wages by his employer, when such books are furnished.

6th. To regulate the course of study, discipline and hours of instruction for children on week days, and adults on Sundays; to require such conformity to their regulations and such returns and reports from their teachers as they may deem necessary to secure uniformity, thoroughness and efficiency in said schools.

Gentlemen, that is about half the will of Gen. Banks upon the subject. That is about half the order; the rest of it is in the same strain, and I will not detain the Convention any longer by reading more of it. Sufficient is it for us to know that the General's will has gone forth upon the subject—that his order has been issued and directed to a class of men here who are bound by every principle of duty to Gen. Banks to carry out his orders or to take the consequences — the military consequences of not doing so.

When the learned gentleman who first addressed the Convention was on the floor, he told us a great many things about the North; he told us of a great excitement that existed there—that there had been a large number of negroes killed at Fort Pillow, and that the North was greatly excited on the subject. Well, I presume such is the case; but I should like to know, Mr. President, what the North expects to do with us loyal citizens here if we do not please them. The gentleman urged that this matter must be attended to immediately. Aye, sir, it must be done quickly, and I must confess, Mr. President, that I do not know what the great people of the North are going to do with us if we do not do something in the matter, or what we have to do with it. Gen. Banks having, by his own order, decided what was to be done, and how it was to be carried out, called upon the people of Louisiana for the purpose of assembling a convention to legislate for themselves. He assumed that the olive tree of peace has already been planted and extends its branches sufficiently to justify him in adopting this measure and in calling upon them to elect a convention to legislate for them.

In this order he has embodied all that is requisite in order to enable him to carry out a matured mental purpose, and, right or wrong, I have nothing to say upon this question; but I admire the determination he has shown in carrying it out.

In the early session of this Convention I took occasion to spread my views before the people and this Convention, on this subject. I then stated that I did not believe that any power had the right to proceed in such a manner to levy taxes. That stands as a part of the record, and my opinions on the subject are not in the least changed. I deny that the President, the Congress of the United States, or Gen. Banks, has the power to levy a single cent as a tax upon the people of this State, for such a purpose, without their consent. It was a simple question of the taxation of tea in 1774 that had a great influence in bringing on the revolution, and the principle is not changed now. That, gentlemen, was my opinion, and it is not changed; and if I should tell you it was changed in the slightest degree, I should tell you a falsehood.

We are the representatives of the people, and as such have the sole power to limit or extend the powers that belong to them.

Mr. President, I fear I have already detained the Convention too long upon this point; but before leaving it I will say that the sentiments I have uttered I entertain and believe as profoundly and sincerely as though they were sent from the throne of high heaven; and I feel that I should be condemned were I to retract one iota of what I have said on this important question under discussion. Yesterday, while I was discussing the question, I was interrupted first by a false alarm as to time, and shortly afterwards the true mace came down, admonishing me that my half hour was up. I was discussing the rights of the slave: in my remarks upon the substitute of the gentleman, I said that if any persons were to be provided for, it was the whites and not the negroes. That was the proposition that came from the gentleman, and was the subject under debate. I was endeavoring to show the Convention that it had not power, even if it had the will, to legislate for the education of the negroes, against the laws of the land—at least until they were freemen. I said that they had no power to say that the slave should be educated, because that is not a part of the law of the land. They have no power to say that this gentleman's slaves or that gentleman's slaves shall be educated. He has a right to educate them, if he chooses, and we have no power to interfere with him, for they are his property—his through the foundation on which property in slaves rests. And, Mr. President, I went on to some extent to show that the power and the right of the owner was one that was founded in the heighth and depth, the length and breadth, of the constitution and the laws of the land. I proceeded thus far, and then I desired to say that it was found in the great charter in words not my own, but that proceeded from such men as—I presume, if they were assembled here, they would throw us into the shade, in point of experience, at any rate—the framers of the great charter of American freedom. I quote the constitution of the United States:

ART. 1, SEC. 3. Representatives and direct taxes shall be apportioned among the several States which may be included in this Union according to their respective numbers, which shall be determined by adding to the whole number of free persons, including those bound to service for a term of years and excluding Indians not taxed, three-fifths of all other persons, &c.

Remember, gentlemen, that this is the work of great intellects. Washington owned slaves, Jefferson owned slaves, and so did most of the others. "What did they mean?" says one, "they did not say slaves." I say it is unworthy the mind of any man in this Convention to introduce such a quibble, for it is a mere quibble to say it does not mean slaves. I would say to my Northern friend that this is a quibble, too, that is unworthy the question under debate, and this Convention. It is a subject vast and all-important, one that in the early legislation of the country occupied the attention of a Washington, a Franklin, a Jefferson, a galaxy of such men as the world has never before seen gathered together in one deliberative body.

I will now read of the constitution of the United States, where it says:

ART. 4, SEC. 3. No person held to service or labor in one State, under the laws thereof, escaping into another, shall in consequence of any law or regulation therein be discharged from such service or labor, but shall be delivered up on claim of the party to whom such service or labor may be due.

Who can say that they did not know what was meant by this legislation? They knew it meant slavery. It was known all over the country. Nobody misunderstood it. Every one in the great republic knew what they were doing; knew that they were deliberating upon the question of slavery, and knew that this legislation referred to slavery. About five pages in large type comprise the whole of this great charter—the constitution framed by this body of great lights. We find the question raised in such a manner that no uncertainty can arise respecting it. There can be no mistaking the signification of it by any man of intelligence.

I read from the constitution of the United States:

ART. 5. Provided, that no amendment which may be made prior to the year 1808 shall in any manner affect the first and fourth classes in the 9th section of article 1st; and that no State, without its consent, shall be deprived of its equal suffrage in the Senate.

Now, gentlemen, what say you to the great and powerful safeguard that this instrument throws around this species of property? Here, Mr. President, is a ratification of the repeated declarations in the other portions of the constitution; but, Mr. President, this matter is not a subject on which there can be any misapprehension. I do not undertake to say, however, that if this institution had not been known and had not existed at the time—if it was not a known fact that slavery existed—that there is anything in the constitution which would have made its existence known positively—and some ambiguity might have existed. But at that time slavery was universal throughout the land; every New England State at that time was a slaveholding State, and had not such been the case, there might have been some misunderstanding of the instrument. But, sir, you must make some allowance for the powerful intellects that framed that constitution. They fully grappled everything they saw around them. They knew well that slavery was universal throughout the land, and that the object and intent of that instrument could not be misunderstood.

I wish to call attention to a decision of the Supreme Court of the United States on this question. This decision is not the only one in reference to the subject. It has been legislated upon in nearly all the States, and there are numerous decisions upon it in the State courts, and in the district and circuit courts of the United States, in the Supreme Court; and the decisions all run like a smooth, uniform, unbroken current, that reaches down to 1852, when we find the Supreme Court penning the following: "No one can pretend to misunderstand it; if he does, there is not only one, but four or five thousand cases, all tending in the same direction, all recognizing the institution, and slaves as property."—(Dred Scott *vs.* Sandford, 19th Howard.)

This, some gentleman tell us, is a prejudiced case; but, sir, it is the decision of the Supreme Court of the United States, and you may as well undertake to shake the foundation of a mountain as to attempt to shake it, because the substratum upon which it acts stands like the base of a mountain. You may pick from it the grass and shrubs that cover it; you may remove piles of rubbish and dirt from it; but, sir, the great base remains still. So with this decision; and it will stand firm as the rock, for it is founded upon a substratum that cannot be undermined. I quote from the opinion of Justice Taney, 19 Howard Rep., 451, in the case of Dred Scott *vs.* Sandford: "Now, as we have already said in an earlier part of this opinion upon a different point, the right of property in a slave is distinctly and expressly affirmed by the constitution. The right to traffic in it, like an ordinary article of merchandise and property, was guaranteed to the citizens of the United States in every State that might desire it for twenty years. And the government, in express terms, is pledged to protect it in all future time, if the slave escapes from his owner. This is done in plain words—too plain to be misunderstood—and no word can be found that gives Congress a greater power over slave property, or which entitles property of that kind to less protection, than property of any other description," etc.

Here is the substratum, and here is the structure built upon it—the right of property in slaves.

I have said that if the owner of this property could be compensated fairly—I do not say in full—but if I could see a fair compensation provided—if Congress would step forth and say that the loyal owner should be fairly compensated, there is no man in this Convention that would more gladly support the movement. If you could show me that it would not endanger the integrity and safety of the State, there is no man that would more gladly subscribe an ordinance article which would sweep slavery out of existence. As I said yesterday, respecting the case of the foreigners, I say to-day, I stood by them and I would again. I then thought, and now think, that every consideration of manliness demands that every man should defend them in their rights which they had acquired under the laws of this country. It was then argued that no other country had given such privileges to foreigners; but no such argument satisfied me. To me, every consideration of manliness and justice demanded that, as they had acquired rights, they were in justice entitled to those rights as fully and as just as we are entitled to the rights guaranteed to us by the constitution of the United States in slaves.

Mr. President, God knows I do not own a slave upon the earth. There is no one that can say that I am a slave owner. I have owned some of them in past times, but, God knows, I was not a cruel master. In my case and in my experience the slave generally had the advantage.

But, sir, I do not like to see the property of others torn from them in the summary manner proposed by the gentlemen who have spoken on this question. I can see nothing that will justify us in legislating it away from them. No, sir! I would not legislate away the old hats of this Convention without you could show me that I had a right to do it.

Lastly, I come to the proclamation of the president, and let us see if that stands. It says:

Now, therefore, I, Abraham Lincoln, president of the United States, by virtue of the power in me vested, as commander-in-chief of the army and navy of the United States, in time of actual armed rebellion against the authority and government of the United States, and as a fit and necessary war measure for suppressing said rebellion, do, on this first day of January, in the year of our Lord 1863, and in accordance with my purpose so to do, publicly proclaim for the full period of one hundred days, from the first day above mentioned, order and designate as the States, and parts of States, wherein the people respectively are this day in rebellion against the United States, the following, to-wit: Arkansas, Texas, Louisiana, (except the parishes of St. Bernard, Plaquemines, Jefferson, St. John, St. Charles, St. James, Ascension, Assumption, Terrebonne, Lafourche, St. Mary, St. Martin, and Orleans, including the city of New Orleans,) &c., and which excepted parts are, for the present, left precisely as if this proclamation were not issued.

Here, gentlemen, we have the last proclamation of the president on this subject—the first and the last that has ever said that men should be deprived absolutely of slave property. Now I appeal to the Convention, and ask what has been the result of that proclamation. We are excepted from its effects on account of our loyalty to the Government. And why is it, I call upon you to-day to say, why is it that the very parishes excepted are the parishes in which the negroes are to-day free? and in the parts that are not excepted slavery in all its horrors exists as it did before the proclamation was issued. Why is this, I ask? Why is it that this Convention is disposed to-day to deprive loyal owners of their slaves in the excepted parishes, while the disloyal men in the parishes not excepted riot and grow rich upon the labor of their slaves? Why is this Convention disposed to make this discrimination against loyal men who are specially excepted by the President? Let us, in God's name, let us pause before we are guilty of placing the loyal men of Louisiana—men who have been loyal under the most trying circumstances—in a worse position than the rebels who are enriching themselves upon slave labor to-day. No, Mr. President, I am not prepared to believe it; not until I see an ordinance of emancipation drawn up and signed, will I believe that the subject of negro education will be further discussed in this Convention.

This is a kind of legislation that is unprecedented. Slave property has never been torn away from the owners in the Northern States, where it once existed, but does not exist now. We might do well to take a lesson on this subject from old Pennsylvania, where it was abolished, as in the other States where it once existed, by providing that all slaves born after a certain period should be free at a certain age. In Pennsylvania it was fixed at twenty-eight years. The legislators of old Pennsylvania saw and appreciated the difficulties and the injustice of tearing away from legitimate owners hundreds of millions of property, and did not deem it right or politic to adopt such a measure as I fear will be adopted by this Convention. They adopted a measure which I think could be adopted by this State with justice to the master and with honor and dignity to the State.

I quote from Stroud's Pennsylvania Digest, page 789, act of March 1, 1780, section 3, where it says:

All persons, as well negroes and mulattoes as others, who shall be born within this State, shall not be deemed and considered as servants for life or slaves; and all servitudes for life or slavery of children in consequence of the slavery of their mothers, in the case of all children born within this State, from and after the passage of this act as aforesaid, shall be, and hereby is, utterly taken away and forever abolished.

Sec. 4. Provided, always, that every negro and mulatto child born within this State after the passage of this act as aforesaid (who would, in case this act had not been made, have been born a servant for years or life, or a slave,) shall be deemed to be, and shall be by virtue of this act, the servant of such person, or his or her assigns, who would in such case have been entitled to the service of such child until such child shall attain unto the age of twenty-eight years, in the manner and condition whereon servants bound by indenture are holden, &c.

Here, Mr. President, is an act worthy an enlightened, intelligent people, which, if we should adopt, would enable the people to adapt themselves to the circumstances which the change would bring about, and the slaves to adapt themselves to their change of condition. The children, before arriving at the age of twenty-eight, could be of great service to their owners, and the old slaves that are full of vice would pass off with the progress of time, as in the case of the Israelites, who wandered in the wilderness, living upon bugs, birds, and the gum from trees, half starved, half naked and eaten up with lice for forty years. Such an act would do justice to the slave-owner, and in the meantime the slave would be better prepared to enjoy and appreciate his freedom.

I shall at some future time, Mr. President, have something to say upon this floor upon the main question, which is not properly before the House, if I am permitted, either in defence of my minority report, or in approximating to the majority report.

The report, sir, to which we are discussing a substitute, requires us to provide for the education of 75,000 negro children. What is to be the expense of this? You must mark it well up in the millions. Suppose we adopt this report. Suppose we agree to educate these negro children, and their number will be increased to 100,000. Suppose we free the negroes and attempt to educate 100,000 of them. Where are the several millions necessary for education to come from? Great God! gentlemen, pause before you take this step, and think what you are doing. Pause before you tear from the widow, the orphan and the loyal men their slave property, and then take their money to pay for its education.

The gentleman tells us that three hundred of that poor, down-trodden and oppressed race have been massacred at Fort Pillow; and from the accounts that reach us, I believe that more than four hundred of our race have been slain on Red River. The widows and orphans that have been brought to grief by the desolating effects of this war are not to be counted by hundreds of thousands, but by millions; and why is it that gentlemen's sympathies are with the negroes instead of with these? Will they tell us why their sympathies are enlisted for the well-fed, contented and happy negro, instead of for the unfortunate of their own race? But, sir, I am willing for the sympathies of these gentlemen to flow out in such direction as their own tastes may suggest; but for my part, if there is a tear to fall from my eye, it must be for the down-trodden and the oppressed, the widows and orphans of my own race and color.

Did they ever know a negro to be obliged to go to market without money. I hardly think such a case ever occurred. They are a class that always have money to go to market.

Sir, the condition of the slave is only pitiable when he has a cruel master. I grant that there are cruel masters, and that slaves sometimes suffer at their hands. But, sir, some wives are choked or beat to death by cruel husbands; but would you forego the pleasures of the domestic relation because some wives are choked or beat to death by cruel husbands?

I do not think that the proportion of cruel masters is greater than that of cruel husbands. Frequent our docks for one month, and you will see evidences of cruelty in the mashed up faces of maltreated wives whose husbands are wretches unworthy the name.

There are bad men in all conditions and classes of society. Government has its share of them, preying and fattening upon it like sharks in the wake of a ship. The sacred desk has its hypocrites, donning the sacred robes for greed or gain; and is it strange that under a system of slavery there should be bad masters?

Mr. President, I have already detained the Convention too long, and with one or two more remarks I shall have done.

What are we to do, Mr. President, with the 312,000 negroes that are to be turned loose upon us? To keep a standing army to keep them down would involve an enormous expense that would make us hewers of wood and drawers of water. Are you going to make them all free? Then they will all be found squatting down on the margins of our lakes and bayous, hunting and fishing for a mere subsistence.

Why, sir, if you want to see the free negro, look at him in the Northern States where he is free; you will find that there his condition is worse, far worse, than it is in the slave States where he is taken care of. Go anywhere where they are free and you will find the same state of facts. Travel through Mexico, where they stand on a political equality with their lighter skinned neighbors, and you will find them a worthless, shiftless, lazy, degraded set. God has set his mark upon them, and it is not within the bounds of human power to remove it.

But, sir, if you make them free, they will come in competition with white labor. You cannot make laws to restrain them, because laws must be general. If you make any discrimination you only remove one system of slavery by introducing another. What do the gentlemen propose to do with them when they make them free? The two races cannot live and flourish together in a state of freedom; and, gentlemen, mark well my words, they will dispose of us or we shall dispose of them. They cannot, gentlemen, be permitted to come into competition with the white race.

The American race, Mr. President, is superior to all others, because of its admixture with the blood of every nation under heaven. Homely as is the proverb "blood will tell" it is no less true of the human race than of animals. And in the American race we see the effects of it. We have here the admixture of the Celt with the Teuton, the sturdy Saxon with the more sprightly southern races of Europe. In short an endless, untraceable admixture, which can only be seen in its results. Its results are apparent and noticeable. Whenever we have come in contact with the armies of any other nation, those armies have always had to take the heel.

In the first war with England her armies overran our country, but were eventually driven back. Again, in the war of 1812, she laid waste our capital, but was again driven out. This present war is not a war of races. Here, brother is fighting against brother. It is the American race that is fighting on both sides. It is not Americans fighting another great power. And when intellect is substituted for brute force then will this great struggle pass from over this great and mighty land. Sir, there is no use in talking of the respective valor and courage of the parties; they will fight on like the Kilkenny cats until there is nothing left of either—until both are pretty much used up. But I say again, sir, that the race cannot come in contact with the negro. You will have not only to contend with the three hundred thousand already in the State, but three millions more that will pour in from every part of the South. You tell me that the white race is coming, too. Well, suppose it is. Tell me what chance the negro stands in New York, where there is only one to several hundred whites. There they are driven into houses, and the houses assaulted and perhaps burned, to prevent them from competing with white laborers. Yet here they will pour in like the locusts of Egypt, and the white men will be driven out—not by the superior force of the negroes, but because they cannot come here and put themselves in competition with the negro. White men will never work for as low wages as the negro. Look at the admirable system of Gen. Banks—it was an admirable system under the circumstances. When they were flocking here, deluging the city, he ordered them into the country, fixing the wages of first-class hands at eight dollars per month, second at six dollars and the third class at four dollars a month. Where is the white man that could support himself and his children on such wages? Where is the white man that would be willing to go and dig and have his wages so cut down? And yet if I wanted to hire to make money, and I suppose that in that respect I am much like other men, I should hire the black man much quicker than the white.

Instead of the glory and dignity of the State that you expect will necessarily and inevitably follow the system you propose, you would find that the white men would go away, and sir, the bone and sinew of the country would be driven out, and but very few would remain upon the soil to defend it.

The negroes, when they are in slavery, have homes where they are cared for and protected; make them free, and they will be driven out upon the world, a most miserable, outcast, homeless set—the most wretched people on the face of the earth. At home in slavery they are—with the exception of those under cruel masters, and God knows I detest a cruel master from the bottom of my heart—a happy, contented people. They pour by their labor the products of the earth into the lap of commerce. The North receives the cotton and the West the sugar, the products of their hands, and they receive a rich return for their labor under a well organized system of slave labor. This is as it should be, and except in cases of cruelty, I say that of all systems of labor, slavery is the most perfect, humane and satisfactory that has ever been devised; and a slave under a good master is the most happy being in the world.

Now, if we disturb this system, Mr. President, we drive out the white laborer, for it is impossible for him to compete with the free negro. Look at the free negro in his native jungles, and, sir, what do you find? a mere bug-eater; a fruit-eater; a mere naked, destitute wretch, as incapable of social enjoyment as a brute.

If we disturb this system we drive out the white laborer, for he can never be brought into competition with this class of laborers. He will never stand it. A few may demand him for some time, but the result will be the gradual removal of the few enterprising men we have here to the North. There is an incompatibility between systems of white and free negro labor that will cease only when driven out. They will never exist together except in some such State as Mexico.

The report of the committee assumes that the Convention has forever freed the negroes of this State. That, I hope, this Convention will never do. I hope, on the contrary, that it will adopt such a system as that adopted by Pennsylvania.

Gentlemen, I thank you kindly for the great indulgence you have shown me. And if, in what I have said, I have given offence to any man, I have only to say that if it was the last moment of my life, before God I would say that from the bottom of my heart I believe it, and intended no unkindness to any gentleman. Again I thank you, gentlemen, for your kindness, courtesy and attention.

Mr. Thorpe—I do not rise to answer the logical arguments of the gentleman from the Fifth District, but he has taken occasion to allude to some remarks in a manner that justifies some explanation. I have never spoken on this subject, and do not intend to do it now. I referred yesterday to the fact that we were called together for a certain purpose, and should endeavor to perform our duties as expeditiously as possible. I admire the honesty of the gentleman who has just taken his seat, but I think his view is totally unfitted for this people, and inconsistent with the iron-clad oath taken on the second day of the Convention, or previously. [Applause.] I am not surprised that the gentleman spoke so glibly on that occasion of his willingness to take oaths. I must confess that what I have heard to-day and yesterday satisfies me that my friend has either a very poor idea of the sacredness of an oath, or else for the last two or three years he has been living in some obscure region where the mighty progress of revolution that is sweeping before it the old landmarks failed to make an impression on his mind with regard to coming here to register the orders of Gen. Banks. I think the allusion is unkind and uncalled for. As to Gen. Banks threatening this Convention if they did not do their work quickly and promptly, I deny it in toto. I think the wide range this debate was taking, and the fact that we sat quietly to hear the gentleman through for nearly two days, shows a want of dsposition to come up to the work of our high calling. We do not come into this Convention with that solemn feeling and stern resolve that, with my consciousness of the magnitude of our duties, I would like to see. I may be mistaken, and I hope I am, but I call upon this Convention to make a solemn resolve—to vow before God and in their own consciences that they will endeavor to find out what is their duty, and do nothing else. I say if this Convention fails to do its duty, and that is to make a free State constitution for Louisiana, and provide for the education of those suddenly thrown on the world, we fail to do what we are called upon and what we swore before Almighty God we would do when we came into this Convention. We are not here to legislate exclusively for Louisiana, but for all the rebel States. The Federal government has, with a feeling such as has never been shown to a rebellious people before, enabled us to assemble here to represent the people—I will not say in their sovereign capacity, it was ridiculous before the rebellion and is now too late for States to talk about sovereignty—

but to pass upon a constitution and amend it in a certain way was obligatory on the part of the Convention. Now, I say if we fail in doing this, we will not again have the olive branch of peace offered on the part of the Federal government and loyal States.

I referred to the massacre of some 400 or 500 of our soldiers in cold blood at Fort Pillow, and I am sorry to hear that the same dreadful tragedy has been repeated on Red River. Look at the items accumulating from all parts of the country that is desolated, and you will find terrible instances of cruelty already enacted, or being enacted, and the perpetrators, like young tigers, are beginning to taste human blood. God only knows where it will end, in a few months, unless stopped. If we make a constitution equal to the times and the demand made upon us, we set an example to the rebellious States that will have great effect in inducing them to follow, and do more to solve the question of this great revolution than can be performed by our noble armies in the field. The gentleman said so much about slavery, and used the word so often, that I was on the point of calling the sergeant-at-arms to turn on the gas—the atmosphere seemed black with the horrid word, and with his unhappy and unholy argument. He asks one practical question at least. What are you going to do with the 300,000 slaves to be turned loose? One of the most extraordinary fallacies of the arguments brought up is, that the moment they are made free they cease to be of any value. If you should free those men and carry them out of the country, you would strike Louisiana down, because you would deprive her of her industrial labor, and send away more than one-half of her capital and power to produce wealth. I ask the gentleman who is such an admirer of this institution, whether 300 slaves on plantations toiling under the lash, will produce more for the avaricious man than the same number working on the same plantation at reasonable wages? You do not destroy all labor of such property, but merely change a certain conventional relation, and give to every man thus regenerated some human hope and a position where it can brought into exercise. But the gentleman has done more than that. He has absolutely, but perhaps unconsciously, stated that the arrival of the flag here and the restoration of a portion of this State to the Union, under command of Gen. Bauks, has placed us in a worse condition than we had occupied under the flag of Jeff. Davis, in the midst of the rebellious government; for here we are deprived of the sources of the involuntary service of the negroes, but in the Confederacy all such privileges are still enjoyed. I will not spend one moment defending this institution. I do not think it is necessary, and do not believe we are called here for that purpose. This discussion has taken such a wide range that it is not within the province of this Convention. I hold we have no right to discuss whether emancipation is right or wrong. We agreed, when we came here, to accept the proclamation of the president, and I did not dream that any person would say a word in favor of the institution, whatever their early predilection might have been. It is no place, and we should not again listen to such things.

I am in favor of carrying out fully the bond I made with my constituents when I came here; and having done that work in the shortest possible time, of putting wings to the instrument and sending it forth to the world. If you make that constitution according to the expectations of the people—if you disappoint the slanderers of our motives—if you do your work justly and nobly, and decide who should have been our friends, and yet who raise the arm to strike us down, you will place them in the dust and beneath contempt, and record your names on an instrument second only to the Declaration of Independence; that will go forth to the world for all time as an example of men who love their race to follow.

Mr. Cazabat—I have listened with some surprise to the remarks made upon the report of the Committee on Education. I must confess, Mr. President, that the remarks of the gentleman from the Fifth, [Mr. Abell,] if not inappropriate, were at least uncalled for upon the discussion of the subject presented to the Convention; for it is not the question of emancipation of slavery which is now before us, but simply whether education should be granted by the people of Louisiana to that unfortunate, despised race which we intend to make free, or rather, which is free already, and has been so ever since the first day we attempted to destroy the most perfect and liberal government devised by the wit of man. Sir, the work we are called upon to perform is to complete what the spirit of rebellion has produced. I have not the least doubt in my mind, Mr. President, that the gentleman is sincere, conscientious and honest in the expression of his feelings and views on this subject. I admire his boldness as I do his honesty; but I do not rise here to discuss the merits or demerits of the institution of slavery, as to whether it is right or wrong, a good or an evil, a curse or a blessing, a divine or human institution. Suffice it to say that it is a question of the past, dead and gone forever, beyond the power of human redemption or resurrection.

The finger of God is upon it—the wise decree of Providence has banished it forever from the American continent; not only in Louisiana, but all through the sunny South, not only for the good of the African, but for the true benefit of the poor white man. The gentleman has, with great ability, perhaps, eulogized an institution which exists no longer *de jure* or *de facto*—an institution which has caused more bloodshed, more misery, more tears, than any other question which ever agitated the human mind. Look at it, gentlemen of the Convention, and Mr. President—look at the precious blood that has been shed for the last three years; look at the misery, yes, the distressing misery of thousands of helpless orphans and unprotected widows. You contend that the institution exists *de facto;* I deny it. You stand upon false premises, and your conclusions are wrong. If slavery really does exist, as you pretend, for God's sake go to the various battle-fields along the Mississippi valley—go under the breast-works of Port Hudson—go to Fort Pillow, where the villified African soldier has been murdered and massacred in cold blood to protect and defend the flag of human freedom. Go to those places and bring your slaves back if you can, or if you dare. But will you refuse this race that education which is necessary to freemen, to enable them to distinguish between right and wrong, in order that they may be a blessing instead of a curse to the white race, and become useful members of society in their humble sphere?

Sir, I am in favor of the article proposed by the committee in regard to public education. I do not see how any man within the sound of my voice, whether in favor of slavery or not, if he is a true man, if he is true to his conscience, can consider himself otherwise than bound to maintain this people, until, at least, we can devise better means of disposition by legislative provisions.

The hue and cry of negro equality, the declaration of future danger, manifests a spirit of cowardice. Are you afraid that the despised African shall become your equal or superior? No conflict, no result of the kind is to be apprehended; the negro will keep his proper place, and will find his level, provided you give him education, and make him a useful and responsible being, which is neither more nor less than his due.

Mr. President, I feel strong in my views, because among the gentlemen who signed the report is the name of a young friend of mine, T. M. Wells, son of our worthy Lieutenant Governor, who was born and raised in Louisiana, in the midst of slavery, and who has as much at stake, perhaps, as any man inside or outside of this Convention. I say, God bless him! Although a slaveholder, identified with slavery, he is willing to give to the African that which some of us, I am sorry to say, would refuse him.

Mr. Cutler—Mr. President and gentlemen, I rise to give my views upon the important question.

It has been said, Mr. President, that in a multitude of counsel there is wisdom, and I sincerely hope that the saying strictly applies to the members of this Convention. The opening remarks of yesterday, by the same learned gentleman who opened the ball of discussion to-day, induced me to believe that an impression prevailed that there was a portion of the members of this Convention not disposed to come up quickly and promptly to their work. I, for one, sir, entertain the opinion that there is not a man here who does not sincerely and honestly act from the pure motives within his own breast. We may differ in opinion, but the great State of Louisiana is pretty well represented. We have members from nearly every parish, and a large majority, at any rate, of delegates of the State are assembled in this Convention. The will and wish of the entire people can, it seems to me, be properly expressed by the sentiments of this Convention.

It was suggested, in the heat of argument on yesterday, Mr. President, that the substitute then and now under discussion might have a certain tendency disgraceful to the members of this Convention. My view is this: that we are here for the purpose of reasoning together on the revising and amending a constitution in which, in the wisdom of the sovereign people, needs amending and revising; and it strikes me that we should reason on that subject in a spirit of friendship, respect and truth. Argument does not consist in mere denunciation; high-sounding words, but is founded in reason. Now, if any gentleman desires to reason upon the question, it is for the purpose of enlightening the general mind and this Convention, and if it is for any other purpose, it is not for an improper one.

Mr. President, I am, perhaps, the most feeble and unlearned of the members of this Convention. I have not come here to make speeches, but to represent my constituents and to do my duty to the best of my humble ability. My opinion is that this Convention has it in its power to accomplish more for the State of Louisiana and the general government than three or four, yea, a half dozen, well-fought battles, provided it acts with that deliberation, coolness and determination of purpose which should actuate every public, political and statesmanlike mind. I have seen but little amiss in our general conduct, and that existed in the body as a whole; which was the beginning at the foot of the ladder or, rather the tail end of the fish, rather than the head, and thus commencing with the wrong end of the question. The order of emancipation, which has been discussed both yesterday and to-day, should have been passed ere this. [Applause.] Two-thirds of that discussion was foreign to the question presented by the resolution before the House, but the ball has been put in motion, the wheel is rolling upon its plane, and it is proper now, after what has passed, that we should proceed with this discussion, because with it ends all trouble in regard to emancipation and the education of the free colored children of the State.

I think, Mr. President, that two-thirds of the argument of my learned and worthy friend, Mr. Abell, was upon a question not then debatable before this house. [Applause.] Mr. President, I told you on Saturday, it was my desire that all questions should come up in their regular order; I told you that the question in regard to public education should come up after the settlement of that of emancipation; but you did not hear my motion on yesterday, nor did you hear me ask for the resolution I presented, which I had offered for the postponement. I am aware of Mr. Gruneberg's resolution, and it is a very proper, clear and concise one, which should have been adopted on the very day we met, instead of on to-day or yesterday. When we come to the serious and important question I have before spoken of, I have promised to then give you my views, freely, frankly, and only ask sufficient time.

[Granted.]

Mr. President, I am in favor of immediate emancipation. [Applause.] Mr. President, I go farther—I am in favor of providing ways and means to educate the emancipated; [applause]—but, mark you, I may differ with you in detail. These questions, presented by my learned friend (Mr. Abell) under the constitution and laws of the United States, as well as of this State, are, in my opinion, foreign to the issue. My views go farther back, not because I am wise, but because I look upon things as they are now. The condition of our country makes the enforcement of our constitution and laws different from what it would be in a state of profound peace. I say that the gentleman does not argue correctly.

I say, Mr. President, that the gentleman considers us as living in a state of profound peace, and all his arguments invoking the aid of the constitution of the United States, its laws, and the arguments of our great statesmen, proceed upon this assumption. Are there not such times that the liberties of a people demand quick, prompt and particular action, which is not anticipated by any constitution or laws? Why is this? Because constitutions are framed slowly; because laws are the result of constitutions and subsequent legislation. It is impossible in time of perfect peace, when constitutions and laws are made, to provide for all those circumstances which may arise during a state of war. I would ask these gentlemen if, in case their lives were imperilled, they would not make use of the laws of nature quickly, in such a manner as to repel all possible personal danger? The government of the United States is made up of individuals and individual States. The sovereign power of that government is the people, and the people have the right to say what is necessary at any and all times. Mr. President, how is it possible, even with the argument of our adversaries—those who honorably entertain these scrupulous notions of things so out of keeping with the progress of the age—with their personal knowledge and that common sense which every man of even ordinary understanding possesses—how can they resist the impression that now the constitution and laws of times of peace can prevail to the same extent as in such times as these? How can their minds be so bewildered, so lost to the condition of things as to entertain such an opinion? Why, Mr. President, this war is the cause of the assembling of this Convention; of the emancipation of the negro; of the great changes and the apparent bendings of the constitution of the United States and the laws thereof. Who would have dreamed at this moment of any of these things, had not this great rebellion occurred?

Are we to be told, then, that the powers vested in the president of the United States, by the letter and spirit of the constitution --or that the laws under the constitution are sufficient? Have we not seen the practical result thereof? They are sufficient for the purpose of suppressing a temporary insurrection, repelling invasion or the enforcement of some laws; but, sir, has it not been acknowledged by the sovereign, loyal people of this country, that this is a rebellion beyond that position of things?

Then, if I am correct, sir, we are in a state of civil war, which makes even the constitution and laws bend for the public good. Such has been the case because neither the constitution, laws of the United States, nor that of Louisiana, has any provision made for the meeting of this Convention, the coming of Federal troops into Louisiana, nor for the President of the United States to do many acts he has done. When the nation is in danger are we to stop for legislation, or to act promptly, and forcibly for the best interests of the people?

Mr. President, these are my views in regard to the foundation principle of the question discussed and attempted to be discussed, both on yesterday and to-day. If my propositions are true, why argue that the question of slavery is subservient to the constitution and laws of either the United States or the State of Louisiana? It is the result of military necessity coupled with national pride, and, I may add, humanity. These are the principles, and not those advocated, upon which I for one will vote for the emancipation of slavery in Louisiana. I am not in favor of emancipating them because their condition is at this moment better off in Dixie; nor of keeping them in bondage because they are better off as slaves, but because of the fact that we have a great rebellion in our midst, and it is necessary, in the opinion of the Government and people, to do so in order to put down this rebellion. That, sir, is to my mind the strongest reason, for I am not one of those abolitionists who desire the emancipation simply because it is a great good to humanity, nor am I here to discuss whether a state of slavery or a state of freedom is most beneficial to the negro. I leave that to some other time, as the question does not necessarily arise now; but I do say that the slaves in every State of this rebellions country should be set at liberty, for the purpose of crushing out this odious rebellion. [Applause.] When they are liberated, free men, then, in my opinion, will be time enough for us to consider the secondary question presented in this report.

I do not agree with the gentleman that there are now slaves in Louisiana. No, sir, not one is there. But, sir, it is in such a state that it becomes necessary for the people of Louisiana, in convention assembled, to declare in the most solemn manner whether it shall any longer exist within our territorial jurisdiction. For one, I am of opinion that all the secessionists in our State, all the registered enemies added thereto, with all the loyal traitors and powers of hell combined, cannot resurrect slavery among us. [Applause.]. This is my opinion; but I am not a negro worshipper, notwithstanding.

Let us now come to the grave consideration of the respective rights of our loyal people in regard to the education of the freedmen.

The report of my learned friend, the chairman of the committee, Mr. Hills, is, no doubt, the sincere conclusions of that body, and I shall speak upon it with perfect candor, without intending any disrespect. I find the following in that report:

Art. —. The General Assembly *shall* establish free public schools throughout the State for all children, and shall provide for their support.

It is my intention, Mr. President, to offer a substitute to this clause of but one word; that is to strike out "*shall*" and insert "*may*." Now, I will give you my reasons, for in my opinion any man who states a proposition, and cannot give any reason for it, ought to abandon it.

First of all, Mr. President, I am in favor of providing ways and means for the education of freedmen, but not in favor of doing so hastily. I am also in favor of giving life and spirit to the organic law of Louisiana, and of abolishing all its odious provisions, but not in favor of positively imposing upon any Legislature the unqualified and imperative duty of educating any but the superior race of man—the white race. We are scarcely now in a condition to educate those of our own color, letting alone those who have by the power of the white race been emancipated from their state of bondage. While we have the highest respect for that people, and a desire to promote their interest in every way, our pecuniary condition does not now allow us to do it; but hereafter, by the help of the United States Government, we *may* be able to do so. Let me ask, first of all, what are our resources for educating the white children? Taxes were formerly levied upon real estate, slaves and some species of personal property. Now, Mr. President, there were not less than about three hundred thousand slaves, not less than one half of the entire taxable property belonging to the loyal people of Louisiana, which is totally taken from them by virtue of the passage of the emancipation ordinance. Then, if you have taken one-half of the property upon which taxes is levied, or from which you derive taxes, I would ask, in carrying out this principle, if you do not increase the number to be educated to at least double? Weigh these facts well. You also decrease the amount of revenue by the emancipation of the slaves. Then it is a matter of easy calculation to show if the per cent was one, it would now be four or five; because the taxes are limited to the property remaining as such. Then the rates of taxation are increased fourfold, and now, sir, upon whom does it operate? Does it operate upon the secessionist and disloyal man? No, because his property is already in the possession of the officers of the Government and under their control, and if confiscated it is purchased by loyal men. If this Convention attempts to impose absolutely a tax upon the loyal men—and it would be imposing it upon no other—by directing or giving power to the Legislature to establish free public schools to educate colored children, it will be imposing an obligation on the loyal people impossible for them to bear. It is all they can do to get the necessaries of life and educate the white race at present. I hope this state of things will not continue long. I am in favor of educating all persons, of whatever nation, who are disposed to reside in the State. This state of things certainly cannot exist long, but it will exist for a time. Leave it, then, to the Legislature. Who will compose that body? Will it not be Louisianians? Then if you find by a change of circumstances and the progress of time it is necessary to establish these schools, do so, otherwise not. But it is not proper for us, under these circumstances, to say the Legislature shall do so. When is the first Legislature to convene? We are to fix the time, and it may be in November, it may be earlier—certainly it cannot be later than January. If this rebellion is crushed—and I hope to God it will be soon—then it will be time enough for this Convention, by its ordinances or organic law, to attempt to enforce upon the Legislature the absolute and imperative right and duty to create public schools for that class of persons who are not now able to earn their own living. Let them earn their own support as far as may be, and live with us as freemen, but let them earn it by the sweat of the brow; do not educate them at the expense of the loyal citizens until then. I say, we ought not to educate these classes alone, for it is as much the pride of the general government as it is of Louisiana, to free the slaves. I speak not of the North, South, East or West, but of a great united nation of enlightened people, whose leader and father was the immortal Washington. I want to know how it is that Louisianians are to be burdened with the entire tax and the entire education and promotion of the welfare of that people which it is the nation's pride to emancipate? Make it general, and do not impose it alone on the Louisianians. Would not my friend from the North feel proud in contributing to the general welfare of that people who, having possessed slaves, now give them up for the good of the common country? I believe too much in the sincerity and honesty of the North, to think that they would fail to act in this matter for the good of our common country. If this matter is justly represented to Congress, will they say that Louisiana, or any of the seceding rebel States, shall be compelled to bear alone the burden of emancipation and the education of the emancipated? No, never. When you, in this Convention, frame ordinances to that effect, and ask of the general government, of which we claim to be a member, to extend its aid and support, they will frankly and freely contribute to the education of this people. Then, am I not right in saying that the question of education should not be made now, but continued for a short time — postponed until the Legislature meets? I was astonished to hear a gentleman argue to this body that Gen. Banks ever intended that his order in relation to the education of the freed people would extend beyond the time when the action of this Convention would go into operation. It is an element in the estimation of the wise major general of this department for crushing out of this State, at least, the rebellion he had come to conquer, and not to infringe on the rights of the sovereign people.

Consequently, the commanding general of this department, in obedience to orders from the president and cabinet of the United States, issued his proclamation, holding out the olive branch to the loyal people of Louisiana, in order that the power might again be vested in them, through this Convention, to form a State government in accordance with the spirit of progress and advancement of the age. Why, the gentleman himself is sent here by the sovereign people. That is the best argument against the position he assumes that this Convention is controlled by military power. It is the military power that makes existing constitutions bend to necessity. But we are not called here to make a military constitution. This Convention is called upon to make a constitution in accordance with the spirit of the age, untrammeled by Gen. Banks. When he issued his proclamation, he withdrew all military interference. He said, go up and make a constitution that will be acceptable to the people. Where is the military influence or the military interference with this Convention? There is none whatever. We are free as the air we breathe; we fear no interference. We do as we please, and ac in accordance with our own convictions.

I am somewhat hoarse, and would ask to be excused from any further remarks at present.

A motion to adjourn was made and carried.

WEDNESDAY, May 4, 1864.

[The Convention was called to order at 12 M., and the proceedings were opened with prayer by the Rev. Mr. Andrews. The roll was called, and the following gentlemen answered to their names:

Messrs. Abell, Ariail, Austin, Balch, Barrett, Bell, Bennie, Bofill, Bonzano, Bromley, Buckley, Burke, Campbell, Collin, Cook T., Cook J. K., Crozat, Davies, Decker, Duane, Dufresne, Duke, Dupaty, Edwards, Ennis, Flood, Fosdick, Gaidry, Geier, Goldman, Gorlinski, Gruneberg, Hart, Healy, Heard, Henderson, Hills, Hire, Howes, Knobloch, Kugler, Maas, Mann, Maurer, Mayer, Millspaugh, Montamat, Murphy M. W., Newell, Normand, Ong, Orr, Payne J., Pintado, Poynot, Purcell J., Pursell S., Schroeder, Schnurr, Seymour, Shaw, Smith, Spellicy, Stumpf, Stiner, Stauffer, Sullivan, Terry, Thorpe, Waters, Wells, Wilson—72.

Messrs. Fish, Flagg, Foley, Montamat and Murphy E. having taken their seats, the president declared a quorum present.

The minutes of yesterday were then read and adopted.]

Mr. STAUFFER—Mr. President, I have a resolution to offer, as follows:

Resolved, That the following be printed and added as articles amending the report of the Committee on General Provisions:

Art. —. No person who now holds, or may hereafter hold any office, civil or military, under the so-called Confederate States, or under any authority adverse to the government of the United States, shall be eligible to any office of honor, trust or profit in this State.

Art. —. No debt created by or under the so-called Confederate States, or under the sanction of any usurping power, shall be recognized and paid.

PRESIDENT—The resolution must lie over one day, under the rules.

Mr. SHAW—The Committee on Ordinance reports progress.

Mr. WILSON—Mr. President, the Committee on Assault of Members will be ready to report to-morrow.

Mr. SULLIVAN—I call up my resolution of yesterday, exempting members of the Convention from serving as jurors during the session, and move its adoption.

[The resolution was carried.]

Mr. THORPE—I offer the following, and move a suspension of the rules for its adoption:

Resolved, That this Convention, setting aside unfinished business and the order of the day, do now proceed to take up the report of the Committee on Emancipation, and do proceed to consider the same until it be finally disposed of.

[The rules were suspended.

The yeas and nays were called on the adoption of the report, with the following result:]

YEAS—Messrs. Austin, Bell, Bennie, Bonzano, Bromley, Brott, Buckley, Burke, Cook J. K., Cook T., Collin, Davies, Duane, Duke, Edwards, Ennis, Fish, Flagg, Flood, Foley, Fosdick, Gastinel, Gaidry, Geier, Goldman, Gorlinski, Hart, Healy, Henderson, Hills, Hire, Howes, Kugler, Maas, Mann, Millspaugh, Murphy E., Newell, Normand, Pintado, Poynot, Purcell J., Pursell S., Schroeder, Schnurr, Shaw, Smith, Spellicy, Stiner, Stauffer, Terry, Thorpe, Thomas, Wilson—54.

NAYS—Messrs. Abell, Balch, Bailey, Barrett, Bofill, Campbell, Crozat, Decker, Dufresne, Dupaty, Gruneberg, Heard, Knobloch, Maurer, Mayer, Mendiverri, Montamat, Murphy M. W., O'Conner, Ong, Orr, Stumpf, Seymour, Sullivan, Waters, Wells—26.

[The resolution was adopted.]

Mr. ABELL—I move, Mr. President, that it be made the order of the day for Monday next. I understand that it is the order of the day for that day; but this Convention, in its usual desultory mode of doing business, may change it. I think it would be unfair and unjust to the opposition, to those who are in favor of the minority report, to press the question upon us now. I would have liked to have had some preparation. I would have been glad to have had an opportunity to consult some authorities, in order the more successfully to defend the minority report, and I trust the Convention will not insist on this mode of taking us by surprise.

Mr. HENDERSON—Mr. President, I move to lay that motion on the table.

[The motion was carried.]

Mr. HILLS—Mr. President, I move to amend that resolution by adding the words, "and that no other report shall be taken up by the Convention until that has been disposed of."

Mr. MONTAMAT—I move to lay that motion on the table.

[The motion was lost.]

Mr. GRUNEBERG — Mr. President, is that open to debate?

[The question was put and the amendment adopted.

A motion was made to take up the minority report first, and it was carried without objection.

Mr. Abell read the minority report. See page 97.]

Mr. FOLEY—I move to lay the minority report on the table. It is not a report at all, but an argument in favor of slavery.

Mr. HILLS—I second the motion.

[The motion was lost.]

Mr. HENDERSON—I voted against laying the report on the table for the reason that I desire that this Convention should, on all occasions on questions relating to the constitution, give every gentleman an opportunity to be heard; and for the purpose of opening discussion upon it, I voted against laying it upon the table. Now, in order to a free discussion upon it, a motion must be made either for its adoption or rejection. I therefore move that the minority report be rejected.

Mr. CAZABAT—Mr. President, permit me to say one word.

PRESIDENT—After the question is put.

[The chair put the question.]

Mr. CAZABAT—Mr. President, as a matter of propriety, courtesy and politeness, I voted against laying the report on the table, although I differ entirely from the minority report from beginning to end, from the first to the last, but still I desire to give a chance to the gentleman who presented it to explain himself freely. Let him advocate his own cause, and if he can succeed in convincing this Convention that he is right, I, for one, if convinced, have no hesitation in saying that I will go with him. With this explanation, and for these reasons, I voted No.

Mr. ABELL—Mr. President and gentlemen of the Convention, I must confess that the action of the Convention upon the present occasion has put me to a very unexpected task. I have rested since Monday last perfectly satisfied that this question was to lie over. I wish every member of the Convention to understand that I expected that this Convention would let this report lie over until every other report had been taken up and passed to its third reading in pursuance of a resolution adopted on Monday, and if there was any consistency in the action of this Convention, I had every right to expect that it would lie over until that time. This Convention decided that all the reports of standing committees would be taken up and passed to a third reading before this question was again raised, and now, contrary to expectation, they have taken it up. The gentlemen seeing clearly that they were flanked—the vote for the proposition of yesterday could never have been swallowed by this Convention—they tack—I am not very familiar with military terms. I have been a civilian all my life. They found that they would be utterly routed by the question under discussion yesterday, and they press up the question of emancipation.

I feel very thankful for the great liberality of the Convention in voting against laying the minority report on the table, because I know there are many gentlemen here who have voted against it upon the express ground that justice and fairness required that an opportunity should be left open that all who might wish could express themselves upon it.

Mr. BONZANO—Mr. President, as the gentleman states that he is unprepared, I move to adjourn the discussion of this question until next Monday.

Mr. THORPE—The question comes up regularly to-day, in its order.

PRESIDENT—The gentlemen will proceed, the motion is not properly seconded.

Mr. GASTINEL AND Mr. MONTAMAT—I seconded the motion.

PRESIDENT—It requires two-thirds.

Mr. GASTINEL—Do I understand that it requires two-thirds of the members to second a motion to postpone debate?

PRESIDENT—According to your own rules it requires two-thirds to suspend the rules, and this motion cannot be acted upon unless the rules are first suspended.

Mr. STOCKER—I move to suspend the rules

in order to take action on the motion to postpone the debate.

[The ayes and nays were called with the following result:

YEAS—Messrs. Abell, Austin, Balch, Bailey, Barrett, Bell, Bofill, Bonzano, Buckley, Campbell, Cook T., Crozat, Decker, Dufresne, Duke, Edwards, Fosdick, Gastinel, Healy, Heard, Maurer, Mendiverri, Millspaugh, Montamat, Murphy M. W., Murphy E., Normand, O'Conner, Ong, Orr, Poynot, Schroeder, Seymour, Spellicy, Smith, Stocker, Stumpf, Stiner, Sullivan, Waters, Wenck —41.

NAYS—Messrs. Ariail, Beauvais, Bennie, Bromley, Brott, Burke, Collin, Cazabat, Cook J. K., Cutler, Davies, Duane, Ennis, Fish, Flagg, Flood, Foley, Geier, Goldman, Gorlinski, Gaidry, Hart, Henderson, Hills, Hire, Howes, Kavanagh, Knobloch, Kugler, Maas, Mann, Mayer, Morris, Newell, Pintado, Purcell J., Pursell S., Schnurr, Shaw, Stauffer, Terry, Thorpe, Wells, Wilson—44.

The motion to suspend was lost.]

PRESIDENT—The gentleman will proceed with his argument.

Mr. ABELL—Mr. President, the Convention has already extended to me so many favors that I must confess I have no right in the world to complain of its action, but it would have afforded me a great deal of pleasure to have had a little more time to prepare; but now I have merely to say that first or last, prepared or unprepared, when it comes to tearing away from the people of Louisiana ten or twelve hundred millions of property without making any adequate compensation therefor, I will fight the question in every aspect in which it may come up before this Convention. I repeat, that for one, that never while this hand is attached to this body, will it sign an ordinance to tear from the citizens of the State their property, as men expect to do by the action of this Convention.

Before I proceed I will notice the conclusions to which I have arrived.

[Read his minority report.]

To the president and members of the Convention for the Revision and Amendment of the Constitution of Louisiana:

The undersigned having failed to arrive at the same conclusion with the majority of your committee, begs leave to submit the following minority report:

Your committee would gladly acquiesce in any proposition for the emancipation of slaves in this State, that would be consistent with the honor, the integrity and safety of the State, the rights of the master, and the future welfare, safety and happiness of the slave, and their final removal from the State.

He could not view as just to the master, honorable to the State, or advantageous to the slave, any proposition which has for its object the immediate emancipation of the slave without the consent of the master, or a fair compensation for his property.

The master having acquired a vested right in his property, by virtue of the customs of the country, guaranteed by the constitutions of this and the United States, the various acts of the Legislature of the several States and the Congress of the United States, confirmed by numerous decisions of the highest courts in the land, and assented to and acted upon by the wisest statesmen, perhaps, of the world, your committee does not believe that this Convention could divest the master of his property without doing a flagrant injustice.

Were he to consider the interest of the slave, without reference to the right of the master, or advantage or detriment to the State, it would not be their interest to be immediately emancipated. Their tendency to idleness, their general ignorance and want of skill to provide for themselves, would leave them the prey of their vices and dissipation, and of disease and deatn; and any law that would force them to a different system of labor than is required of the white race, would be a violation of their rights as free men, and only a change from the present system of servitude or slavery to that of another.

Tne money-making speculator would be substituted for the kind and interested owner. The object of the sharper would be to make money; the kind master's interest to preserve and improve his property.

But, above all considerations, your committee believe that the State has the deepest interest in preserving its safety and forwarding the interests of the white race. With the lights now before the Convention, emanating from our sister States, New York, Pennsylvania, Ohio, and the Western States generally, with free white labor this State would rise in population, wealth and grandeur; but in competition with 312,000 negroes with a natural increase unparalleled in the history of any people, surrounded by millions who would make Louisiana their asylum, the Convention cannot be blind to the fact that a system of peonage or slavery would be established, all inducement for white labor over-ridden, and the safety of the State menaced.

I say, Mr. President, that the conclusions I have arrived at are not based on any predilections in my own mind in favor of slavery, for I have often repeated on this floor that I never saw a day or a moment in my life when I was in favor of slavery as an abstract principle. But, sir, wiser men than we are have attempted to grapple with this same subject; but the wisest men have shrunk back when they met the monstrous proposition that is before you to-day to tear from the people millions of property, though it were slaves. What does the Convention propose to do with the majority report? That report proposes at one single swoop to dispossess owners of their property, not one nor ten, but to sweep from thousands of upright and honest people all they possess on this earth. I desire each member of this Convention to ask himself the question, is this right, is it fair, is it honest? Is it acting upon the great principle that requires you to do to others as you would that they should do to you? I ask you to-day if you had any species of property, let it be one negro or twenty, which you had earned fairly and honestly under the guarantees of the constitution, would you look upon it as right for this Convention to sweep it away from you? I do not think you would. If you would get up here and swear it, I would not believe it. Then act upon the great principle of doing as you would be done by. You can do it and justify yourselves before your constituents when you go home. I ask you, when you retire at night to sleep, if you can say you have been just before God, when you have swept from the widow and orphan their property without compensating them? That is the question you have to meet. This is what I propose to suspend until there are means to do it. I talk to you as men imbued with the highest principle of honor. Without compensation we are called upon to strike down the rights of these people. Does this minority report propose to do anything of the kind? Oh! no!

It appears, according to the preaching of the gospel, when God either had to be a liar, or else there had to be a mediator, Christ stepped in and reconciled the whole matter. If you take up this minority report, you cancel the freedom of the negro consistently with the great fundamental principles of right and reason. It is done in this way, and I believe when you come to reflect upon it, a large majority will say it must be adopted. By such action justice can be done, and the negro freed. Can this great nation of more than thirty millions of people pay for these negroes? We are all brethren, and a small but general contribution will enable justice to be done, and when you go home to your constituents you can look them in the face and hear them say, "well done, good and faithful servant." If you adopt the other report, and free these people, you will have to look them in the face, and their posterity, because there is no right or justice in it. I have spoken on this subject on two days, and now I want to do a little talking. I am in earnest, and you will be in earnest some day or other. Be just, and then you can face all mankind fearlessly; but tear from these people hundreds of millions of property, which they have honestly acquired, and how will you meet them? The best way will be to go north or west, or go somewhere else, for you cannot, as an upright man, meet them. You cannot stand and say to them: "I have torn from you your property and left you and your posterity beggars." You have just this question to meet. It is not merely a stroke of the pen, that is easily done.

You must meet these questions upon this floor.

You may be able to sign your name to a document which recites that "we hereby transfer from you(the people) and your heirs, a hundred and fifty millions"; that would be a nice little day's work, easily done—but that is not all; for this matter must go before the world.

Gentlemen, the minority report before you does not contemplate any such thing; but is plain and simple, though perhaps not so feeling as the other. It will meet the great ends of justice, and satisfy the people of Louisiana. You cannot, you have too much sense in your heads, too much manliness, I hope, to sweep away property, as has been proposed. Adopt, then, my report, and give all an opportunity in helping in the great work. I am perfectly willing that all here should sign the majority report, but I did not come here to represent myself—but on the contrary, the people of Louisiana, their interests and wishes. Am I told that that report embodies these ? How do we learn that ? Ten thousand voters are represented here, but of these, six thousand are inhabitants of New Orleans, where there are but few negroes ; yet we are here for the purpose of divesting the other part of their wealth in this property, of their substance. Are you willing and ready to do this ? If you are, I cannot help you. All that I can do is to lay before you the proposition to let Congress and the Legislature of the State devise ways by which this population may be liberated, so that justice may be done without oppresing anybody. If you do not heed this, you commit a most grievous oppression against one part of this State without giving the other an opportunity to aid. If this is a good and holy work, ought not everybody to aid it ? If it is a work of infamy and wrong, or illegitimate, are you to be instrumental in carrying it out, and thus expose yourselves to the scorn of the world ?

Reason upon it, and see what is the character of this undertaking to liberate three hundred and twenty thousand negroes! What are you going to do with them ? There will only be a change from one species of master to another, and they will not only be oppressed—not only for the sake of money making—but when their capacity is exhausted, then good bye to them—no mistake about that !

These very negroes who are now so well cared for, except under bad masters will, in future, when frail, sickly and old, be turned loose to die, unprotected and uncared for; while their masters are engaged in the sweets of speculation. Those who have muscle will pour it forth to enrich the capitalists, while the rest, numbered by thousands and tens of thousands will die from hunger and thirst. Why should they not when none have any farther interest in caring for them ?

The best men will hardly ever do anything of this kind unless through *some great* interest ; assuredly, then, the speculator will not do it at all, and these will grow rich, while the others, turned loose, will be the most miserable of wretches ! The large majority will want bone and muscle ; therefore they will be driven like dogs from their kennel, kicked and cursed hither and thither until they bring up in houses of prostitution or in prison. Yet we think we are doing great things in freeing them. No, sir, you are not freeing them, but only changing the mode of servitude, and they will ever be the most dependent creatures on earth.

How are they in the North and West, as compared with those who have an idea of depending upon their own exertions ? They are eventually driven into dens of infamy. Now when the white race comes into contact with them here, will it be more willing to bow down to the great negro and coalesce with him ? No, sir ! The same war must go on here, and I say that if left at liberty, they will, led by faction, by desperate men, imbrue their hands in the blood of the white race.

Trained as they now are to arms, that faction *will* rise. You must have a gospel minister at the corner of every street and on ever plantation, and then you cannot keep them straight.

Mr. TERRY—Like the last gentleman, I dit not come here prepared to debate this report, but when I listen to such language on this floor, knowing that the majority of these members were elected under the banner of a Free State, pledged to immediate and instantaneous emancipation, what am I to think when I hear such arguments in such a loud, boisterous voice ? I am astonished that there is a man upon this floor who does not place his fingers in his ears and come at once to the conclusion that the gentleman is twenty years behind the age. It arouses the inner humanity within me, and brings a desire to look above the earth and appeal to the invisible world for a suitable reply to such an argument. The gentleman has been talking about slavery. Does it exist ? Was not the public mind prepared during the last campaign to vote in favor of the Free State nominations, when in the inaugural address of the governor he said he was in favor of immediate emancipation? What gentleman here who came from that canvass—who was elected under the Free State nominations, can stand upon this floor and advocate otherwise, or vote differently, when the question is put?

Mr. President, look abroad around the country; look at this man—the downtrodden African. What is he doing to-day for each and all of you? Why are we sitting here arrayed in broad-cloth and fine linen, living on the fat of the land? Go to Fort Pillow and see him bleeding and dying for you all. (Applause.) See him fighting there to uphold the folds of the glorious banner of the Union; and yet the cry is, "enslave him." It is the most despicable and outrageous calumny that could be expressed against one who is fighting our battles.

Mr. President, as time progressed, the question arose with the learned and intelligent minds who guard the welfare of the State. From the moment our forefathers formed the constitution of the United States, there was found to exist in these united colonies two spirits—the spirit of war and the spirit of the slavery. As we have gone on in growth, these have shown their hydra heads, and have at last come in contact, and open rebellion and civil war now reigns. In all this, Mr. President, the finger of Providence has pointed to the delivery of the injured people, as to the Children of Israel of old, and they have at last found their Abraham. What was necessary for the preservation of this Union? It became necessary that slavery should cease to exist, and therefore that wise man issued the decree of immediate emancipation.

To show how far the South is behind in various ways, I will read the following:

[Read from address of Dr. Dostie, "Freedom *vs.* Slavery."]

"Soon after the adoption of the Constitution, all the Northern States abolished and repudiated, slavery, as a violation of human rights. The blighting influence of this curse caused the great flow of immigration to settle in the Northern States; hence followed the preponderance of population, wealth and power, and the vast advantages in all the avenues of happiness the now enjoy. Listen to facts to prove 'the earth is made to shrink in barrenness' from the malign influence of slavery.

"See the poverty, ignorance and desolation of the slave lands in contrast to great Freedom's onward and upward course. In 1790, the population of Virginia was double that of the State of New York. In 1850, that of New York was twice as great as that of Virginia. In 1791, the exports of New York amounted to about equal those of Virginia. Sixty years after, New York surpasses Virginia in her exports more than eighty millions. In 1790, the imports of New York and Virginia were about equal. Sixty years after, New York surpasses Virginia more than one hundred million dollars. In 1850, the products, manufactures, mechanics and arts in New York amounted to more than *one billion* dollars moreṭhan those of Virginia. In the same year, the value of real property in Virginia (including the negroes) is nearly one billion dollars less than that of New York. In 1856, the real and personal estate assessed in the city of New York was worth more than the whole State of Virginia. The value of the farms, farming utensils, mechanical and agricultural products in New York exceed those in Virginia in the same ratio. In 1850 the hay crop in the free States amounted to more than four times the value of the cotton, tobacco and the sugar crop of the fifteen slave States. The total value of the property of the free States is more than three times that of the slave States. The bushel products, the pound measure products, the gallon and the mining products of the Northern States are similary ahead of the same products of the South, notwithstanding the superior advantages of the South in soil, climate, rivers, harbors, minerals, forests, and 245,000 more squares miles of territory. In 1850 there were only eighteen hundred adult persons in Massachusetts who could not read and write. In the same year eighty thousand of the white adult inhabitants of North Carolina could neither read nor write. The comparative intelligence is presented to illustrate the ignorance, poverty and imbecility pervading the land of slavery in contrast with the land of freedom, were intelligence, wealth, prosperity, progress and happiness are everywhere visible."

I ask you, do you expect any sympathy from slaveholders, who were the last class to come forward as a majority and show their allegiance to their country. I stood in the hall a clerk under Col. French, in the days of Gen. Butler, and handled the records, and knew the status of every man, and found the poor laboring men—the mechanics—were almost the only men who proved their loyalty to their country. (Applause.) As an advocate of these men, but not a lawyer, do I stand here and debate this question to-day. But I repeat, what does any gentleman expect from those in rebellion? Some have talked of the tears of widows and orphans appealing to Heaven. I ask, gentlemen, where are the tears and cries of the widows and orphans of the hundreds of thousands who have been slain in the war fighting under the old flag to maintain its supremacy? Talk not to me of the tears of slaveholders. Who were the husbands of these widows? Who are to be robbed, as the gentleman calls it, of their slaves? Mr. President, there is every reason to believe the greater portion of them fell on the field of battle in deep-dyed, bloody rebellion. There are always two sides to a question, and this may be the popular one or not. These are my sentiments. I give way for some other gentleman of more talent to argue this question.

MR. HENDERSON—In examining the report of the minority, two points are unfolded, the first, slavery, whether it exists in point of law or fact; second, supposing it does, will this Convention provide ways and means to indemnify the owner of the slave in case of emancipation? I will meet the last question first, and think that if my remarks are understood, the learned gentleman will be one of the first to shudder at the enormous responsibility devolved upon him by his minority report. He says that according to the language of the State constitution, there is a vested right in a slave, and the law of the land demands before that right is taken away, an indemnity.

Now is there any action of the courts which intimates that masters are to be paid *before* emancipation is carried into effect? Has the gentleman any foundation of right to say that twelve hundred millions of dollars should be paid in advance? On the other hand is he so ignoble as to declare that this sum should be assessed on unborn generations? Our ancestors issued continental money which has never been redeemed, although we obtained our independence through the blood of the country. Should we again create a national debt, only to wipe it out? If we adopt the gentleman's proposition the whole amount will be repudiated, I believe, as our government did on that former occasion.

Did not the South owe the North millions of money? Yet who howled for money? Why, the South? So does the bankrupt. What became of these moneys? All were wiped out by the signature of the Southern President. Suppose the position of the gentleman is true, that all should be paid for in advance, will you vote to draw the money out of the Treasury forthwith? There is no slavery *de facto* or *de jure* inside of the Confederate lines, and if you tell me that a thing exists when it does not, the fact is not changed. Can any man now sue for a slave or hire out one? Even under the old system, some of the courts would not decree any compensation at all.

We are told that we are legislating prospectively. I deny the fact! Slavery is so dead, politically and morally, that it can never be resurrected. I ask what old England did during the Colonial Government, after bringing over slaves? Scarcely had that been done, when she sent emancipation to all in Canada. Now, Mr. Presisident, how did Massachusetts get rid of *her* slaves?

Massachusetts had the constitutional clause, "all men are born free and equal." But under the Constitution slavery existed *de facto*. A case was brought. A negro held as a slave sued for his freedom, and the court decided that although slavery existed *de facto*, it did not exist, and could not, under the constitutional provision, exist *de jure*, and the negro was set free.

The Supreme Court of Massachusetts decided, affirming the decision of the court below, that slavery *de facto* was contrary to the fundamental law of the land, and therefore in violation of the constitution. That is an authentic case, and if the gentleman will produce the volume of Reports, I will show him the very case from the decision of which every slave in Massachusetts was emancipated, and thus slavery was abolished in Massachussetts by judicial decisions and not by legislative act, as was the case in other States. Well, why were the owners not paid? We are told that these beautiful Yankees took their fine negroes, run them off to Virginia, and sold them for tobacco! Was there anything strange in this? The very man who introduced the first emancipation resolution, was John C. Calhoun, the head and trunk of this rebellion! In South Carolina some slave traders were brought before Judge Campbell, and a grand jury who were sworn to support the laws. There was a statute prohibiting the African slave trade, but not a man was in favor of finding a bill against them, but they violated their oath in order to carry out their caprice. South Carolina and Georgia, by the way, required the abolition of the slave trade to be postponed until 1806. The slave Confederacy at this day forbids the African slave trade, and yet at at the same time it is warring on this very question of slavery, and nothing else.

Slavery is both contrary to the law of nations and natural law, and at most but a qualified property in man has and does exist, according to all writers. If you carry a negro into England or Ireland, his shackles fall off; but yet if he chooses to go back to the land of his birth, they may be rivetted on him again. Beautiful consistency! That is English philosophy! While England brought slaves to Massachusetts, she turned right around on Canada, and introducing there the common law, put an end to the system. I was willing some four years ago to abolish slavery gradually, and would have voted to do so; but I wake as from a dream, and find this great republican master spirit of the world demands the abolition of it now, in order to save the Union. So I say down with it! (Applause.) I say that there are but two issues before the American people, the Union with or without slavery. This is not a rebellion, because that can be put down by a *posse comitatus;* but it is a civil war, only to be ended through the might of armies and navies. The Southern States are out of the Union, and must come back under such terms as may be prescribed by the conqueror. If the gentleman wishes an illustration of my doctrine, let him look to Rhode Island and North Carolina who refused at first to enter into the compact with our original eleven States. Thus they were isolated, liable to fall into the clutches of old mother England; and when Congress placed a tax upon all their imports and exports, they applied for admission and were received. Louisiana is out of the Union, for the majority of the people are inside the Confederate lines fighting for that cause, and when they return they must come under the same government that now rules over ten Federal parishes—a government antagonistic to that they are now supporting.

We have in the old territory of Louisiana, two governments, Federal and Confederate, the one representing patriotism, the other treason; and the latter can only be brought back to its allegiance by physical force. That is my position, and when I am asked if I am in favor of rebellion and slavery, I say no! I am in favor of immediate emancipation. I contend that slavery does exist, and that we must incorporate into our constitution the clause "involuntary servitude, except as a punishment for crime, shall not exist in the State of Louisiana."

Mr. Hills—Mr. President: In the National Convention of 1794, a proposition was made to abolish slavery in the American colonies belonging to France. A member of that body arose and proceeded to defend the principles of universal liberty, whereupon he was interrupted by another member, who exclaimed: "President! do not suffer the Convention to dishonor itself by a protracted discussion!" It seems to me that for three days we have been witnesses of a most extraordinary spectacle. A body of men assembled on the avowed principles of universal freedom—elected on a platform of immediate emancipation, accepting seats on this floor under the proclamation which declared the slave laws in Louisiana inoperative and void, because they did not apply to any class of persons in this State—I say, a body so elected under that proclamation and upon that platform, is compelled to listen for three days, to one of its members standing up here and defending the accursed system of American slavery as it existed before this war. I said in my previous remarks, we could not do anything to perpetuate slavery without committing perjury before God and man. For that remark I have been arraigned here as attempting to menace this Convention by some authority of the commanding general. I repel all such insinuations as false and groundless, but I repeat, that in my opinion, gentlemen, members of this Convention cannot stand up here and argue in favor of slavery in any form, without committing moral perjury. That is what I said, and to that I shall adhere. [Applause.]

Mr. President, the gentleman from the Fifth District [Mr. Abell] has seen fit to make a long argument to overthrow my assertion that slavery does not exist in the State of Louisiana. I say that assertion is literally true, that there is not a slave in the State of Louisiana to-day. There is no slavery, and can be none without the presence of physical power to enforce the obedience of the slave to his master. That is an indispensable element of slavery, without which it cannot exist. I ask the gentleman, where is the force to-day to compel the labor of the slave in this State? Where is the auction-block? where is the lash? where is the power of the master to whip his slave and to enforce his will? The auction-block has disappeared in the light of the new civilization that has dawned upon us; the slave marts, where human beings were crowded together like cattle, thank God! is no more among us; and the lash has been abolished—first by the great law of necessity, and secondly by the proclamation of military power.

If the gentleman thinks slavery still exists, let him attempt to sell a slave within the Federal lines. Suppose he advertises a slave for sale at auction to-morrow. On the way the slave says, "I wish to cross the street." He goes, and the gentleman from the Fifth follows and attempts to seize him by the collar and drag him to the auction; what is the result? The gentleman from the Fifth is arrested for a breach of the peace, committed for assault and battery (laughter) and brought into the court, and under the present laws of the State the man he has attempted by force to take to the auction-block stands his equal, as he does in the sight of that almighty law of justice which has overthrown slavery in this State forevermore. (Applause.) There is no slavery here and never can be. If all the thunder bolts of Jove could be gathered together and discharged at once, they could not shake the earth enough to awaken from its eternal sleep the carcass of this miserable institution. The gentleman has attempted to justify slavery from the example of the Egyptians. I admire him for it. It is most fitting and proper that the man who stands up in this day and age to justify such a system, should go back to the Egyptians, whose religious altars smoked with human sacrifices, and whose idols were the most gross and obscene of all the Pagan nations of which we have any historical record. I intend no disrespect to the gentleman. He is much my senior in age, and my superior in learning; but I say if the gentleman were to die, I should expect to see him embalmed in an Egyptian sarcophagus, with a hieroglyphical inscription upon his tomb, which, if I were permitted to suggest, would consist of two words: "Old Fogy." (Laughter.) Let him go back to the Egyptians—that is where slavery belongs. Let him go back to the Romans and Greeks—that is where it belongs. It belongs to the rude ages of mankind, before the light of Christianity and civilization had fallen upon the human family. Has he forgotten that these very men whom he holds up as models for us to follow and copy, had gladiatorial shows, and that under their institutions men were thrown into the arena to be devoured by wild beasts? He can justify that as well as slavery. He can justify polygamy by the example of the ancient nations, and every other species of voice and crime. But I supposed we had grown up beyond the Greeks, Romans and Egyptians. I thought that we were free-born and enlightened Americans—living in a time of revolution, to be sure, but still adhering to those great landmarks of freedom that were so dear to our fathers, and which, I believe, are dear to the majority of this Convention.

Not satisfied with attempting to justify slavery by the Egyptians, Greeks and Romans, he has attempted to bring to its side the divine Scriptures and the sublime teachings of Christianity. Now, Mr. President, if you go back in the ecclesiastical history of the world, you will find every infamy that has been perpetrated has been done in the name of some religion. It is not the first time that men have stolen the livery of heaven to serve the devil in. How many wars and massacres have been committed in the name of Christianity? Does that prove that Christianity countenances massacre, butchery, robbery and crime? Not at all; it only proves they were done hypocritically in its name. If the gentleman wishes to go into an argument in favor of fraud, he might distort some parts of the Scripture to prove it was right. He might take the case of Jacob and Esau, where the former clearly swindled the latter out of his birthright, to prove that swindling is a proper and divine institution, and ought to be incorporated into the constitution of Louisiana, which we are here to frame to-day. I am ashamed that any man in the latter half of the nineteenth century, with so much learning and ability, should spend time in attempting to make us believe that slavery is in accordance with the precepts of religion. Sir, that divine Being, who came down to teach us the right path, gave us one commandment, one precept, which blasts forever the institution of slavery, and human wrong and injustice of every kind: "All things whatsoever ye would that men should do unto you, do ye even so unto them." I say that in this precept he blasted forever this institution of slavery, which is essentially unjust in itself, and founded in piracy and robbery—a system of violence and usurpation from beginning to end.

Not satisfied with the Egyptians, Greeks and Romans and religion, the gentleman has brought to his aid the illustrious names of American history—those men who founded our institutions. He has told us they were slaveholders, but very judiciously has he refrained from telling us what they thought of slavery itself. He has referred to Washington, but forgot to tell us what was the dearest wish of his heart. Washington said: "This is among the first wishes of my heart, to see some plan adopted by which slavery in this country may be abolished by law." Henry Laurens, of South Carolina, wrote to his son in 1776: "I abhor slavery." Jefferson has been quoted here. In speaking of the slaves he says: "We must wait with patience the workings of an overruling Providence, brethren." "Brethren" is the word which Thomas Jefferson applied to these men. "When the measure of their tears is full—when their groans shall have enfolded heaven itself in darkness, the God of Justice will awaken to their distresses, and by diffusing light and liberality among their oppressers, or at least by His exterminating thunder, may manifest to the world that they are not left to the guidance of blind fatuity."

Mr. President, the exterminating thunder has come! The accumulated wrongs which this people have heaped upon an unfortunate race, brought it down from high Heaven, and it has obliterated this system in Louisiana, as it has throughout the whole land. (Applause.)

Now, I propose to let Mr. Abell answer Mr. Abell, by referring to different portions of his speeches. I will put the gentleman from the Fifth District against the gentleman from the Fifth District; and I think it is better so than to answer him myself.

He tells us with a great deal of flourish that the nature of the negro is idleness, that he will not work unless compelled to under the lash of the driver. In the next breath he tells us he believes if these same lazy, idle, good-for-nothing vagabond negroes are set free, they will come in competition with the white laborers, who will stand no chance at all. There is Mr. Abell against Mr. Abell. (Laughter and applause.)

In the same strain he boasted that the American people, being a mixture of all the blood of the world, was the greatest, the most powerful, civilized, and altogether the smartest race ever existing on the face of the earth. He boasted we had whipped England two or three times, and that we could thrash France, and were never whipped ourselves and never could be, in the nature of things. The next moment he says if the slaves are freed in Louisiana they will rise up and imbue their hands in the blood of his posterity. Though not at all afraid of England, France or any other white nation, he is much afraid of the negroes!

Another instance of the gentleman answering himself is where he says the white never would labor for so small pay as negroes. Then he asks what we are going to do with the negroes if we set them free. I think he gave a good answer to his own question when he said they would work for less wages than the white man.

He says again the negroes are perfectly miserable—are in a most degraded condition—entirely incapable of taking care of themselves. Then he states that slavery is a civilizing and elevating institution. Now I want to know how many centuries it takes to elevate a race so that it is capable of taking care of itself? This institution, which the gentleman would have us believe is so benignant and elevating to the blacks, has been in existence in Louisiana from the earliest period of her history down to the moment of rebellion, and yet, according to the same gentleman, to-day this race has become so degraded that it is utterly unable to take care of itself!

Another instance of this logic. He says the bone and sinew of the country would be driven out of the State by the emancipation of the slaves. In the next breath almost, he tells us that negroes, organized under slavery, will work a great deal better than if they are free. Now, then, if the negroes are going to work more in slavery than when they are free, I wish to know how freeing them is to drive the white laboring man out of Louisiana? If the negro will work better as a slave, I think the white man has less chance of employment under a system of slavery!

The gentleman, in the course of his remarks, has seen fit to speak of the people of Louisiana under the presidential and military authority as an "oppressed" people. If the people of Louisiana are oppressed, as the gentleman would have us believe, I wish him to tell us by whom we are oppressed? He seems to forget that three years ago the rebellion was forced upon the country by the slaveholding oligarchy; that Louisiana was in the full enjoyment of commercial and agricultural prosperity, and that under the protecting ægis of the Union her slaveholders were in secure possession of their slaves; that it was the rebellion that interrupted this prosperity, destroyed slavery and plunged the State into the condition in which we now find her. I would like to have him point out in what manner the military authorities have ever oppressed the people of Louisiana—to point out to us how this Convention would have been called together but for these very authorities.

Mr. President, I could but feel as I have listened to this discussion, that we see here at least some of the fruits of the efforts of our noble soldiers who have fallen in the battle-field for their country. Let me ask the gentleman, if I had stood upon this floor, or any other in Louisiana, three years ago, and said what I have said to-day, what course would have been pursued by this slaveholding oligarchy he stands up here to defend? The halter, sir, was the penalty for free speech in Louisiana then. Does not the gentleman know that intellectual bondage is inseparably connected with slavery everywhere? Does he not know that as the most gross and loathsome productions of nature flourish only in her darkest recesses, so the loathsome and hideous institution of slavery can grow only where the light of civilization and free speech are carefully excluded? He knows that before the Federal flag came up the river on the flagship of that gallant old tar, Farragut, to stand up in this hall, and speak as I have spoken and as others have spoken, would have been met with the penalty of instant death. Talk to us of oppression! Let him go back and read the annals of slavery, and see how many murders have been committed in its behalf and under its shield. There is no crime against free speech, free conscience, free opinion, that has not been perpetrated in behalf of this system; and yet the gentleman stands up and calls the people of Louisiana oppressed! How many rights would he enjoy if the Federal flag were not here?

He has told us he thought civil government in Louisiana would be detrimental to the people. I ask the gentleman why then he is here? If the interests of the people are opposed to this Convention, why does he consent to occupy a seat in this hall? If the Federal flag were to be displaced by that bastard banner, the flag of the Confederacy, the gentleman might escape the halter for having so faithfully defended the rebellion here, but even that might not be sufficient to save his neck,—

Mr. ABELL—I call the gentleman to order. I have not advocated the rebellion on this floor.

THE CHAIR—The gentleman from the Second District (Mr. Hills) is in order.

Mr. HILLS—I assert that for three days the gentleman from the Fifth (Mr Abell) has defended the rebellion on this floor.

Mr. ABELL—I call the gentleman to order again, sir. I deny that I have advocated the rebellion.

THE CHAIR—The gentleman is in order.

Mr. ABELL—Then, sir, I respectfully appeal from the decision of the chair.

[The question was then put: Shall the chair be sustained?]

[The question was carried.]

Mr. HILLS—I trust the interruption will not be deducted from my half hour. I asserted, with a full knowledge of the meaning of my words, that for three days the gentleman has defended the rebellion on this floor. I will now explain what I meant. I say that any man who stands up and defends slavery defends the rebellion, for they are synonymous terms at this moment. [Applause.] The gentleman has taken, I suppose, the "iron-clad" oath of the president. If so, he has sworn allegiance and obedience to the proclamation of the president, and to all the laws of Congress framed on this subject. The rebellion is the legitimate child of slavery. Slavery was sure to bring on rebellion in this country, and the wisest men in the land foresaw it years ago. The prophetic words of Jefferson, which I repeated, foreshadowed it. The framers of our constitution did not believe that it would long remain in existence in the United States, and carefully avoided all direct allusion to it in the constitution, because they regarded it as a disgrace and a system that ought to be and would be abolished.

If the gentleman will take the trouble to examine the debates on the adoption of the constitution, he will find that such is the fact. All the wise men who helped to frame that constitution believed that slavery was an evil, and would speedily die out.

He has mentioned some illustrious names. Let me ask him if he knows the opinion of Benjamin Franklin on the subject? I beg to remind him he was the president of the first abolition society ever organized in the United States. Does he know the opinion of Judge Jay? Can he bring forward, in the annals of our country, the name of one great man of the revolutionary period who said a single word in defence of slavery?

PRESIDENT—The time is up.

Mr. TERRY—I move that the gentleman have leave to conclude his remarks.

[The motion was carried.]

Mr. HILLS—Gentlemen, I am much obliged to you, but do not desire to proceed farther to-night.

Mr. TERRY—I move that we adjourn, and that Mr. Hills have the floor to-morrow morning, with leave to conclude his remarks.

[The motion was carried.]

THURSDAY, May 5, 1864.

[At 12 o'clock M. the president called the Convention to order. The roll was called, and the following gentlemen answered to their names:

Messrs. Abell, Ariail, Austin, Bailey, Barrett, Baum, Beauvais, Bell, Bofill, Bonzano, Buckley, Burke, Campbell, Cook T., Cook J. K., Crozat, Davies, Decker, Duane, Duke, Dufresne, Edwards, Ennis, Fish, Flagg, Fosdick, Flood, Foley, Gastinel, Gaidry, Geier, Goldman, Gorlinski, Gruneberg, Hart, Healy, Heard, Hills, Howes, Kavanagh, Kugler, Knobloch, Maas, Mann, Maurer, Mayer, Mendiverri, Millspaugh, Montamat, Murphy M. W., Newell, Normand, O'Conner, Orr, Payne J., Pintado, Poynot, Purcell J., Pursell S., Schroeder, Schnurr, Seymour, Shaw, Smith, Spellicy, Stumpf, Stiner, Stocker, Stauffer, Sullivan, Terry, Thorpe, Waters, Wells, Wilson—77.

The minutes of yesterday were read by the secretary and approved.]

Mr. TERRY—Mr. President, I have a preamble and resolution to offer, which I desire to have read and laid over for one day.

Whereas, Large sums of money have, during the past year, been remitted to this State for the purpose of aiding in the formation of a free State government in Louisiana, and it is now a fitting time that the said moneys should be applied to the patriotic purpose of the donors; and this Convention is informed that said moneys are in the hands of the so-called "Free State General Committee," of which Thomas J. Durant is president, James Graham, secretary, and Edward Heath, treasurer;

Resolved, That the auditor and treasurer of the State be requested to report to this body whether said funds have been paid into the treasury of the State, for the purpose of being properly devoted to the objects of the contributors; and if not, that the said auditor and treasurer be empowered to demand of the said Thomas J. Durant, James Graham and Edward Heath, and officers of said committee, the delivery of said funds, or an account of the uses to which they may have been applied; and that the said auditor and treasurer be instructed to make such further inquiries and investigations as may be necessary, and report the result thereof to this Convention.

Mr. BELL---I desire to offer the following resolution:

Resolved, That the thanks of this Convention be and are hereby tendered Captain Stephen Hoyt, U. S. army, and acting mayor of the city, and G. W. R. Bayley, city surveyor, for the able and efficient manner in which they have, by their untiring energy and attention, fitted up this hall for the Louisiana State Constitutional Convention.

Mr. STAUFFER—I call up my resolution of yesterday.

Mr. HILLS—I move it be referred to the Committee on General Provisions.

[The motion was carried.]

Mr. ABELL—Mr. President, I have a resolution to offer. I have noticed that for several days Judge Howell has been absent from his seat. Now, this is a question of great importance, and every member ought to be present during its consideration. No member should be allowed to dodge his responsibility to his constituents on the issues involved in this question. Therefore,

Resolved, That the sergeant-at-arms be and is hereby directed to ascertain the cause of the non-attendance at the Convention of the Hon. R. K. Howell, of the Seventh Representative District.

Mr. HILLS—I agree with the gentleman perfectly as to the importance of the issues involved and the necessity of having every member present, and I therefore move to amend his resolution so as to include all the members of the Convention absent from this body now in the city, and move a suspension of the rules in order to take immediate action on the resolution.

[The rules were suspended, the amendment carried, and the resolution as amended adopted.]

Mr. CAMPBELL---I offer a resolution:

Resolved, That no vote on emancipation be taken by this Convention until every member of this Convention be present.

PRESIDENT---The resolution lies over one day under the rules. The unfinished business, the order of the day, now comes up.

Mr. BROTT---Mr. President, I move to substitute for the minority report the following, which I wish to have added to the majority report as one more section, to follow sec. 5:

Sec. 6. The governor of this State, on or before the 1st of June next, shall appoint three commissioners, who shall hold their office till the 1st of January, 1865. The commissioners, so appointed, shall be loyal to the government of the United States, and qualified voters in this State at the last gubernatorial election. They shall have their office in the city of New Orleans, and hold their sessions six hours each day, (Sundays excepted.) The sum of three thousand dollars shall be paid each of them, as salary, during their term of office. It shall be the duty of said commissioners, on application of any citizen of this State, for compensation for any slave or slaves, to determine as follows: First, the loyalty of the claimant; second, the ownership or title of the claimant to his slaves; third, the relative value of the slaves so claimed. They shall classify the slaves and determine their value as follows, to-wit:

First class	$300 00
Second class	200 00
Third class	100 00

The said commissioners shall report to the Legislature, during its session in 1865, the names of claimants under this provision, with their conclusions as to who are entitled to payment and what sum they should be allowed. It shall be the duty of the Legislature, if they approve the whole or any part of said report made by the commissioners to pass an act authorizing the bonds of the State to be issued, payable twenty years from date, bearing interest at four per cent. per annum, interest payable annually, which bonds shall be delivered to such claimants in such sums as the Legislature shall determine, being in compensation in full for the slaves hereby emancipated. No claim for compensation shall be considered or allowed after the first day of January, 1865.

PRESIDENT—It must lie over under the rules.

Mr. HILLS—Mr. President, at the conclusion of my half hour, yesterday, the Convention very kindly voted that I should have leave to continue my remarks. I declined to do so at that time, but understood that I was to have the floor this morning. If any gentleman objects to me proceeding against the rules, I will yield the floor; but if there is no objection, I should like to make some further observations on this most grave and interesting subject. [Cries of "no objection," and "go on!"]

Mr. HILLS continued—I intend to speak of principles and not of men. For the gentleman from the Fifth District [Mr. Abell] I have personal respect and esteem, but his principles, as set forth on this floor, I hold in utter detestation. At the same time it may be useful to have a representative of these heathenish sentiments in the Free State Convention. We have all heard of the temperance lecturer who found it useful to take his drunken brother along as a horrible example of intoxication, and as a contrast to the results of total abstinence. And so it may serve to set forth our noble work of emancipation in more glowing colors, if we have constantly with us a champion and defender of the faith delivered unto the Copperheads. I said yesterday that the gentleman from the Fifth District had for three days advocated rebellion on this floor; but the gentleman's interruption and the stroke of the president's hammer prevented me explaining this remark so fully as I desired to explain it. I endeavored to show that the framers of the constitution of this republic were opposed to slavery as a principle, and only tolerated it because it existed, and because they thought that in a very few years it would be abolished by the progress of freedom and civilization. I also stated that in the constitution which they framed they did not mention the word "slave" or "slavery." While certain provisions of that wise document have evident reference to the subject of slavery, and recognize it as an existing institution, I deny emphatically that slavery finds any support in the constitution or laws of the National Legislature. Slavery, sir, is a local institution, founded upon State laws and not upon any national law. The slaveholder of Louisiana, before the war, did not rely on the constitution of the United States for the right to sell his slaves on the auction-block; he did not rely upon any of the laws of Congress for his authority to wield the lash on his plantation, but he derived his power from the Black Code of Louisiana, and the acts of the Legislature of this State. But we find, sir, that notwithstanding all the framers of the constitution were opposed to slavery as a principle—believing it to be wrong, cruel, unjust, and opposed to the interests of the country, the new doctrine was promulgated by the slaveholding oligarchy and seemingly gained growth year after year, that slavery was a divine institution and sanctioned and sanctified by the laws of God and humanity, and that it found secure shelter and perpetual support in the constitution and laws of the land. Year after year the slave power came on apace with its aggressions, and demanded this and that surrender on the part of these States. Surrender after surrender was made, until the people of the free States finally arose in their majesty and said to the slave power, "thus far shalt thou come and no farther—the territories of the country, the national domain in which all have an equal interest, shall hereafter be free!" That is what they said when they elected Abraham Lincoln, our worthy chief magistrate. They did not propose to strike down the right of slaveholders in Louisiana—they did not propose to interfere with slavery in any of the States.

I know the falsehood was insidiously circulated by the pro-slavery press, both North and South, that the Republican party was an ablition party. But as one of its members, who had, I believe, pretty good knowledge of its principles, I tell you that party had no intention of interfering with the institution of slavery in the States where it existed by law. The issue upon which we went to the country was the extension or the non-extension of slavery into the national territories, which we believe were free by the great laws of nature, and ought to remain free forever. But after the election—when the sovereign people had decided that the doctrine of non-extension should prevail, what was the course of the slaveholding oligarchy, for whose rights the gentleman from the Fifth is so solicitous? Why, sir, they said the will of the people should not be obeyed—that the constitution and the laws should be set at defiance; that Abraham Lincoln, although rightfully and legally elected, should not be president of the slaveholding States. They revolted, and what was the cause of it? Slavery, sir.

The slave power was balked in its purpose to draw to its embrace the free territories of the nation. The champions and instigators of the rebellion told us they seceded in order to protect their divine institution of human bondage. It was slavery first, last and always; slavery in the beginning,the middle and the end! The vice-president of the so-called Confederacy told us that slavery was the corner stone of that extraordinary fabric. Every slaveholder and every candid pro-slavery newspaper that has spoken on this subject since the outbreak of the war, has told us it was all in the interest of slavery; and every one who studies the subject candidly and impartially cannot fail to come to the conclusion that slavery is the great and the sole cause of the rebellion. Therefore it is, I said, the gentleman has for three days advocated rebellion on this floor; and I assert, without the fear of logical contradiction, that no man can defend slavery without also defending the rebellion.

Mr. President, we have all heard of men who upset their own kettle of fish, and it strikes me the gentleman from the Fifth has given us a luminous example of this catastrophe. He labored for two long days, all through Monday and Tuesday, to show that slavery was justifiable, not only by the example of the Greeks, Romans and Egyptians, and by the Scriptures, but he would make us believe it was justifiable in itself—right in the abstract, and every way; that it was beneficent to the slave and the white man. After laboring two days, to build up, establish and defend the divine right, origin and historical sanctity of this institution, what did he tell us yesterday? In the very beginning of his speech he says, "I have repeated, and again say, that I never saw the day, and never expect to see it, when I was in favor of slavery!" So that after spending two days to convince us that it is right, he states on the third day he does not believe in it himself. I ask why he does not believe in it, if it is divine, and sanctioned, and sanctified by the Scriptures and by Almighty God? If it is the best thing that can possibly happen to the African and the master, I ask him why in God s name he is not in favor of it? I should be the last man, if I believed in his argument, to say I was not in favor of it.

The gentleman in his remarks of yesterday tried to convince us that liberating the slaves of this State by constitutional enactment would be a species of wholesale robbery on the part of this Convention, and told us, in substance, Mr. President, that the government of the United States had stolen all the property of the disloyal people, and that the Convention now proposes to steal all that is left in the hands of the loyal. Now, Mr. President, if there is no slavery in this State to-day, I want to know who is responsible for it? If there has been any robbery of slaves in Louisiana, I wish him to explain who are the robbers? I will tell you who they are. They are the people of Louisiana themselves, who of their own accord, by pass ng the act of secession, and by inaugurating the rebellion, ruined and destroyed their slave property forever. If there is any robber, it is the secessionist, not the Union army, who came down to uphold the honor and integrity of the country. This people inaugurated the civil war against the United States, and in its progress, as wise men foresaw from its beginning, it became a military necessity to emancipate their slaves. Emancipation came not as an act of robbery, not as an act of violence against the people, but, as I have said, as an act of military necessity, and to uphold the integrity and honor of the flag. When a country is at war, its government can tax its resources to the utmost for its defence. When the national life is at stake, will any body say that the Government has not a right to free slaves, or take any species of property in any

State or any part of the country, to maintain its own existence? The gentleman might as well say that the Government has no right to demand his time of the soldier. There are thousands and hundreds of thousands of men in the army to-day, who were making more money at home than they possibly can in their present situation. The gentleman might, I say, consider this a species of robbery, thus to make these men devote their time and leave their business to join the ranks, and the argument would be as good in one case as in the other. It became necessary to liberate the slaves of rebels, because the Southerners were using them against us---upon the plantations to raise products while the rebels were fighting us. More than this, they were in the rebel service, employed as teamsters, and in some instances, as there is pretty good reason for believing, even as soldiers. To strike down slavery was then to strike down the strong arm of the rebellion.

The gentleman has told us that certain parishes are excepted in the President's proclamation. I wish to look at that for one moment. If any one entertains the idea that because Mr. Lincoln exempted certain parishes in his proclamation of emancipation, he therefore secured or guaranteed slavery in them, he his very much mistaken. He did not, in that document, guarantee any rights whatever to slaveholders, but merely said that while the institution was abolished in certain parishes, it was in the others left to take care of itself.

Mr. President, slavery *has not been able to take care of itself* in the parish of Orleans or in any of the other excepted ones, because, as I have said, it is the creature of local law, depending upon State legislation for its existence, and by the act of rebellion the State laws were suspended if not abolished, and there are now no operative laws under which slavery can be supported or upheld in this State. The element of physical brute force, to compel the obedience of the slave to his master, is wanting, since it does not exist in this parish nor any within our lines.

Mr. Lincoln, by his proclamation, as I admit, leaves the claim of the slaveholders in the excepted parishes to be adjudicated hereafter. They can bring their claims against Louisiana or the national government for their property, as they call it, when perhaps they will get compensation and perhaps they will not. Slavery does not exist in any parish for the reason I have already stated, and for another and perhaps a better reason, which is that a large portion of those who formerly were slaves are now soldiers in the ranks of the Union army. (Applause.) Will the gentleman tell us that the men who have imperilled their lives in the defence of the flag of their country, the men who wear the uniform and carry the bayonet of the Union, are ever to be made slaves again? Mr. President, the ensanguined fields of Port Hudson bear witness to the valor of those men, who, in three successive charges in the very mouth of the enemy's guns, proved the fact that the negro would die for the Union. (Great applause.) Does he tell us that such men, their relatives, wives or children, shall ever wear the shackles of slavery again? It would be a shame, a disgrace, a stain upon the nation, which the blood of all our soldiers could never wash out. Mr. President, the earth cannot receive in the same instant the footprint of a soldier and a slave! (Applause.)

The gentleman from the Fifth has flaunted in our faces, during a three days' speech, the phantom (for it is a phantom) of negro equality. Now, if you go to the free States, you find there is no negro equality there. Is the gentleman afraid that the white race is so much upon a level with the negro that negro equality will prevail, unless we forever subject the blacks to the most foul injustice and keep them perpetually under our feet? I suppose he is one of those who are afraid of amalgamation, or, as it is politely termed in these modern days, miscegenation! I suppose he fears if the slaves are liberated, that all the fair daughters of the land will be seized with a desire to marry negroes, and that the young men will also wish to marry negresses! Now, Mr. President, according to my belief, that is a matter of taste. [Laughter.] I have no taste for that sort of equality myself, and accordingly have no fear of it. If gentlemen fear any such thing, I cannot undertake to explain their reasons for it. So far as the matter of equality and amalgamation is concerned, I do not see that the Northern or free States have given so luminous an exemple of it as the slave States. for I have observed, during some four years spent in Maryland, Virginia and Louisiana, that there are a great many so-called negroes, with very white faces, and I believe that they were born in a State of slavery! There must be some practical explanation of this. I have seen more mulattoes, quadroons, and all that sort of persons, in one day in Louisiana, than I ever saw in all my life in any free State! I am not afraid of negro equality, because I believe that the white race is the dominant race in this country, and always will be. I believe it is superior in intelligence and skill, and that the Anglo-Saxon race is destined in the providence of God, to rule this country forever. The mean fear of this phantom of negro equality never has kept me awake for a single moment, and I do not believe it ever will.

The gentleman tells us that if the slaves are free, we shall have to place a gospel minister upon every street corner and plantation, and that with all that trouble we cannot keep them straight. Well, Mr. President, I agree with the gentleman perfectly, if these gospel ministers are to preach the same kind of gospel that the gentleman has preached on this floor; I think that that kind of gospel never would succeed in keeping negroes or anybody else straight, particularly when we consider that gentleman's exposition of the divine precept, "All things whatsoever ye would that men should do unto you, do ye even so unto them." It struck me in listening to the gentleman's exposition, that he had a very singular method of applying that commandment, and that it should, according to him, read like this: "All things whatsoever the slaveholder would that slaveholders should do unto him, do ye even so!" He leaves out the slave entirely. Here, let us suppose, is a man with two hundred slaves, and the gentleman says, I will do unto this man as I would have him do unto me, if I were a slaveholder, but of the two hundred men he says nothing. That is *his* gospel, but *I* believe that the divine command of Christ applies to the African as well, and that we should do unto him as we would that he should do unto us. (Applause.) I prefer to take my theology, not from the lips of the gentleman from the Fifth District, but from the lips of the Divine Teacher, who said, "Inasmuch as ye have done it unto the least of these my little ones, ye have done it unto me." The lowest and most degraded being has claims upon us, equal to those of the highest and greatest; and this divine gospel, which is so distorted to apply to the slaveholder, but not to the slave, I say applies as much to the one as to the other. If the gentleman from the Fifth prefers to seek the emblems of his gospel among negro whipping-posts and negro auction-blocks, the lash and insignia of despotic power; if he wants the instruments of the slaveholder's tortures—the thumb-screw and the heavy irons—to represent his gospel, he is welcome to them; but these do not represent my gospel. (Applause.) I prefer to take mine from Paul, who tells us that God "hath made of one blood all the nations of men to dwell upon all the face of the earth." I prefer the sublime words of Isaiah, who said: "Is not this the fast that I have chosen, to loose the bands of wickedness, to undo the heavy burdens and let the oppressed go free?" I don't believe the negro whipping-post is the best emblem of Christianity and civilization; if the gentleman does, he is welcome to his views.

The gentleman from the Fifth District, among the other illustrious names quoted, to show that slavery is legal and right, has cited that of Judge Taney, of the Supreme Court of the United States, and his decision in the famous Dred Scott case, in which, with disregard for all natural law, and, as I think, for all constitutional law, that judge tells us that the negro has no rights which the white man is bound to respect. Mr. President, I am not much of a lawyer, although I did read Blackstone, Kent and a few such books, when several years younger, but it strikes me there ought to be the principle of justice and common sense in all law. But it would seem, from the gentleman's argument, that he was trying to convince this Convention that the law is utterly devoid of both. I believe there are statutes and codes higher than constitutions, written in the hearts and affections of men no legislation can obliterate. There are moral obligations resting upon every man which no statute can change. I think we have a good illustration of the instability of Judge Taney's law in the course of events since that decision was promulgated. The slaveholding oligarchy boasted that, by this famous decision, slavery was fixed forever more—nothing could disturb it in this country. But I think we have found by this time that even Judge Taney's decision was not sufficient to blot out from the human heart those laws, written there by the finger of God, and that the divine laws are stronger than the decisions of any judge. Since that decision was promulgated, slavery, in spite of it, has been swept away by the course of events, and Judge Taney's decree, and all other laws ever made, or attempted to be made, to uphold it, have proved impotent to circumvent the decrees of Heaven. (Applause.)

As one of the results of this system of slavery, which the gentleman has so ardently advocated, we have heard a great deal of slaveholding chivalry ; we have been told that the sons of slaveholders were particularly noted for heroic and chivalric qualities. If I understand chivalry from some reading of it, as it was practiced in the earlier ages, it is that principle that leads the strong to defend the weak ; wherever innocence, virtue and helplessness presented itself and was in peril, there the true knight was bound to draw his sword and go to its defence. It seems to me this slaveholding chivalry, which has been illustrated at Fort Pillow, is a very different article. I understand upon Red river it has been illustrated in a similar manner, that soldiers—native-born white citizens of Louisiana, who have volunteered for the defence of their country and this State against its armed enemies, have been most brutally murdered in cold blood by these sons of chivalry. This is a poor time of day to stand up here and defend this system of slavery, that so brutalizes those who wield its power. One of my colleagues from the Second District [Col. Thorpe] has already told us what an excitement prevails in consequence of the massacre at Fort Pillow. It seems as though the enemies of this country were determined this should become a war of extermination —were determined to do everything that may be done to provoke the United States government to a bloody retaliation. These crimes are all committed in behalf of slavery, and still in a Free State Convention, elected on the platform of immediate emancipation, called into existence under a proclamation declaring slavery abolished, we have for three days listened to a gentleman advocating it as sanctified by ancient example, and approved by Christianity itself.

Mr. President : It was my fortune, on Monday, to stand on the consecrated field of Chalmette, now green with the verdure of spring, and eternally green in the memory of patriots as the scene of Jackson's fame—a spot sanctified by the blood of those noble heroes of the second war, who fought and bled for the honor and integrity of their country. The occasion was the dedication of the ground as a cemetery for Union soldiers, and I was pleased to see on that historic field a great number of the delegates of this Convention, and I could not but feel as I walked over that hallowed spot, that the struggle which made it forever historic was not so important as this which is now going on. The men of that generation periled their lives and fought for the integrity of their country, but the soldiers of this conflict are fighting under the impulses of a new civilization ; there is a new epoch in our history more glorious for liberty, and it seems to me any man whose feet pressed that soil, must have come away feeling it is a solemn and momentous duty we have to perform here—to uphold that same flag, that same honor, that same liberty, for the martyrs of which that burial ground has been set apart. (Great applause.)

Mr. BROMLEY—I wish to ask the members of this Convention if we are legislating for the past or the present; whether we are called upon to listen to arguments in favor of slavery, such as we have heard for the last three days from the gentleman from the Fifth District? He has seen fit to unearth the skeleton of slavery. He has unwrapped the bandages that envelope the mummy, with a patience and zeal that would do credit to Layard, or any other antiquary seeking for fossils and relics of the buried past. If the gentleman will continue his work of resurrection, he may find its history inscribed in these words: "*Mene, Tekel, Upharsin,*" which, according to the interpretation of these latter days, reads: "*Mene;*" God numbered thy kingdom and finished it. "*Tekel;*" thou art weighed in the balances and found wanting. "*Upharsin;*" thy kingdom is divided among the Yankees and Abolitionists!

He has seen fit to refer to the widow and orphan, who, by immediate emancipation, will lose $150,000,000 in slaves. Allow me to ask the gentleman from the Fifth District to enlighten us as to the meaning of the terms widow and orphan? Are these undesirable conditions of life confined entirely to the slaveholding white race? Look over the items going to swell that $150,000,000. There you will find widows indeed, who were made so by the mild laws which regulate that heaven-born institution. We believe the emancipation and education of the colored race will prove to be an element of wealth and prosperity to these slave States that will be unparalleled in the history of nations. We claim that the immediate emancipation of this people, with an enlightened system of common school education, will develop higher moral and mental qualities, making that race an element of success and advancement in this State, where old laws, old forms and old customs are fast passing away, to make room for a better state of things. Mr. President, this institution is as much a thing of the past in the history of the United States, as is the feudal system a thing of the past in the history of Europe. Slavery is dead, and we have spent time enough at the tomb; let us cast our eyes towards the resurrection of the free, and the dawn of that better existence.

I trust that it will not be said that this State, after emancipating the negro, made no provision for the education of negro children. I hope that the members of this Convention, instead of raking up the past, will let it rest in its grave. We have spent some thirty days in attempting to revise the constitution of this State, and what has been done? We have been wasting our time on resolutions and legislating upon subjects that do not properly come before this Convention, and now we are employing it in the attempt to resuscitate the Pagan and barbarian institution of slavery.

Mr. STOCKER—I shall vote in favor of the motion now before the House, which is, I believe, to reject the minority report. After stating that fact, I desire to state also to this Convention, that it is not from any sentimental feelings or conscientious feelings I have against slavery that I vote for its rejection and support the majority report, but because I believe our country demands it of us. Although I was born and reared in a slave State, I have never met with the horrors that have been pictured to this Convention. The gentleman from Orleans, Mr. Terry, has spoken of the "down-trodden African." I have never seen him. I have no sympathy with the African; my sympathies are with the white man and not with the negro. My hand is against the African, and I am for pushing him off the soil of this country.

The gentleman has referred to the massacre at Fort Pillow. We have no official information that these acts have been committed, although I believe it as much as any other gentleman, but until it is officially reported, we have no right to say such things have occurred.

I say that until we pass the ordinance of emancipation slavery *does* exist, because we have the proclamation of the president saying that it does exist in the parish of Orleans and other parishes. I am in favor of the Convention saying by its action that slavery does not exist; but as long as the law stands let us support the law, yet the sooner we arrive at the conclusion the president is wrong in saying that slavery does exist in Orleans, the better it will be for us in my opinion. As I suffered with the minority in the Convention of 1861, I desire to raise my voice in favor of the minority of the Convention of 1864. In that Convention I was one of the minority, and we could not introduce a resolution, ordinance or motion but that some opposing member would move to lay it on the table. For this reason I voted to give the gentleman from the Fifth District a chance to express his opinions, and, if possible, to represent his constituents; but when the majority report comes up you will find me going to the full extent of that report, because I believe it is the duty of every man, in order to bring about the end of this war.

Mr. Wilson—Mr. President: Slavery is a word which has become particularly obnoxious to a civilized and a christian community. It has taken nearly a century to erase it from our political vocabulary, but it will be erased; and future generations will look back with pride on those men who were first to raise their voices in favor of *immediate emancipation.* I hold, Mr. President, that the gentlemen composing the Free State Convention of Louisiana will be among the first to immediately strike the shackles off the slaves.

It is true, that from 1774 to 1830 several of our Northern brethren, in their halls of legislation, passed a prospective law for the emancipation of the negro. They declared that the offspring should be free from birth. But how did that declaration or law operate? It forced the owner to sell the mother and her unborn child to some slave speculator going South; and thus, though it removed the evil from the Northern States, it did not eradicate it. It brought in its train separation of families, and had no feature of humanity to commend it to any philanthropist who was opposed on principle to owning property in man.

History informs us that slavery was introduced into this country in the year 1620, on account of the scarcity of white labor. According to the census of 1790 there were in New Hampshire 158 Africans in involuntary servitude, and 17 in Vermont; and, even as late as 1830, there were slaves in every New England State but Vermont. The sin of its introduction does not rest on the American people; but England had rid herself of its last vestige long before we seriously contemplated carrying out the spirit as well as the letter of the constitution, which proclaims that "all men are born free and equal!"

The sages who framed that almost divine instrument, the constitution of the United States, did not admit the word "slavery" into any of its salutary provisions. They probably, in the plenitude of their wisdom, with prophetic vision, looked far into the future, and saw that the "institution" would become a power; that negro bondsmen would be counted by millions in place of thousands; and that what then appeared a necessity would eventually become a curse! All honor to such men. They

"———Write their names
On Time as on a rock, and in immortalness
Stand on it as upon a pedestal."

It has been asserted that these men—the founders of our republic—were opposed to slavery. Granted. But there is no record that points out, in any instance, where they tried to wrest from a loyal people their slave property without giving them compensation.

The question naturally arises, what position will these 4,000,000 of freed slaves occupy in the body politic? Will they enjoy the rights of citizenship, or remain irresponsible?

I do not believe, Mr. President, that the African is the EQUAL of the white man, either socially or politically. I am no admirer of the new-fangled doctrine of miscegenation, or amalgamation with a race whom, on the authority of M. Du Chaillu, an American of French descent—recently commissioned by the Academy of Philadelphia, to visit the equatorial regions of Western Africa, and who has given his experience to the world in a book of surpassing interest—expose human flesh for sale in their public markets, whose domiciles are surrounded by piles of human bones and skulls, fragments of the ordinary meals, who sell each other to foreign traders, and make sheaths for their knives from human skin.

We have also the authority of Drs. Barth and Livingstone to show that the native Africans have clung to barbarism with a tenacity which makes me believe it to be inherent in their nature.

Look at the West India Islands; look at the free negro here! Has not the most bitter, the most vindictive, the most cruel master that ever owned a slave, been always found in the free colored population of Louisiana? Consult the past and you will there find that the negro slave-owner has been the hardest taskmaster!

Mr. President, I am in favor of saying to the negro "you are free;" but I would leave him there. If, hereafter, he evinced a desire to earn his bread by the sweat of his brow, I would encourage such a spirit. But if, when free, he is to drift about society, we, who claim to be intelligent, should, in justice to him, and in justice to ourselves, see to it that he become not a vagabond and an outcast, a burden upon the community.

I appreciate the efforts made by the commander of this department, Major General Banks, to solve the problem of the African's future by an order to put him on the plantation to work. That is the proper place for him. But it is apparent to every gentleman within the hearing of my voice that this labor is compulsory; that the negro is not a free agent; and, I think, if he were, he would prefer a life of indolence, with its concomitant rags, to one of honorable industry.

The Legislature of Louisiana will have to settle this point. And we simply do our duty in instructing them to to act. I am in favor of immediate emancipation; but I would not, in casting my vote therefor, despoil any loyal citizen of his just due, as guaranteed to him by laws which date at least two generations back. I believe in justice too strongly to think that, as a member of this Convention, I can abrogate the right of any loyal man, who conscientiously believes himself entitled to compensation for property which our act may place beyond his control. All who wish compensation, and who can prove a clear record, shall, as far as my vote goes, have their claim. I know that many men, abler than myself, members of this Convention, who have been hunted down by rebels, will oppose my views; but I give my views honestly and fearlessly, conscious that in doing so, I am doing my duty; and I ask all such to bear in mind that there are men—slaveholders if you will—who would sacrifice everything—aye, even life itself—to see our starry flag float again over the length and breadth of the land, and be borne in triumph over every sea.

I have done. I will vote in favor of the rejection of the minority report, reserving to myself the right to propose an amendment to the first section of the report of the majority, which will favor compensation.

Mr. Smith—I wish to speak on this subject—on this subject of compensation—for it is a bone of contention here. Whom do you wish to compensate? Those who have participated in this rebellion? Is it the loyal slaveholders? Take a list of names and see if you can point out any such. No, sir! Instead of seeking to regulate the welfare and happiness of the country, they endeavored to elect a man for the purpose of rearing up a great slave oligarchy, to trample under foot the flag of freedom, the only one on the earth. Can these men compensate the country for the evils they have inflicted upon it? Can they bring back the lives lost upon the battle fields? No, sir, they cannot do it, but still they now claim compensation. I say, sir, and repeat it, that there is no loyalty in the slave-holding community; there may be a few exceptions, but they are very few.

The gentleman has said that the institution has descended from sire to son, from generation to generation, until it has become a precious legacy to us, and that we must cherish and sustain it for that reason. He has told us that all ancient history acknowledges the right; gave us Abraham and the children of Israel, who had their slaves. So they did, but they had also the year of jubilee, and the seven years when the bondmen went free, besides which they were commanded to provide for them and their offspring.

Lastly, he has come to the classical and poetical—to Greece, the mother of the fine arts and the model of civilization. He tells us that Athens and Corinth had slaves, but not a word about another—Sparta.

Go into our streets and Sunday Schools, and ask, if you can, in whose veins flows the best blood of the chivalry. The gentleman's sympathies extend to the free negro, but not to the other class, held in bondage in our midst. Is it not time that this should be done away with?

He tells us we cannot tear from these loyal citizens their property. Who was it tore from the government all our forts, and proclaimed that fifteen hundred millions of property should not be paid—debts contracted, too, in good faith?

He says we have to look in the face poor widows and orphans, whom we have despoiled of their property. Not a word has he for those who periled everything for the Union, who have been hunted down with dogs like beasts, their families being left to starve by these loyal slaveholders—not a word of all this!

He has taken up those ruthless laws that tore away brothers and sons, and armed them against their own kindred. Were these made by slaveholders or by the loyal class? If this is loyalty and they ask compensation, they have, it seems to me, a very singular way of showing their loyalty! (Applause.)

Mr. Thorpe—Mr. President: It is very evident that the gentlemen who are in favor of this proposition have not taken the last official report of property in this State, as pubished in 1860, as the basis of their estimates, when they propose compensation to slave owners. In the parish of Tensas there were 1262 white people to be taxed. In the Fifth District, New Orleans, which the gentleman represents, the white population is set down at 894,404, and by a singular coincidence, the property of the two localities is precisely the same. Now I ask if they suppose for one moment that when we abolish slavery in this State that the hard-working men of New Orleans are going to be over-burdened with taxes for the payment of compensation to slave owners, who are only one class of losers by the rebellion? If we undertake to pay for losses, let me ask him are those to be paid who have suffered from the destruction of their fences, the scores of notes due, which can never be collected, and the burning down of their houses? We shall find if we undertake this compensation, that it involves us in a mass of injustice, an inextricable confusion that we shall never see the end of. For my part, I look upon the destruction of property as second only to the destruction of life, the most formidable that the rebellion presents. I know that the loyal slave owner has to suffer great inconvenience, but he is not alone in his losses, and I can see no justice in refusing to compensate him for his losses, unless we at the same time provide for the payment of the losses of all loyal men by the war, not only of slaves but of houses burned and property destroyed and of notes owed by Southern men to Northern firms.

If we attempt this thing, the laboring men who have sent us here will hold us responsible for such an attempt to impose upon them taxes which are unnecessary and unjust, and while they had no hand in originating the original losses, which are invoked as a reason for these objectionable and unjust taxes.

While I look around this Convention, I see many gentlemen here who were born and bred large slaveholders. Their willingness to sit here in this deliberative body, elected on a platform of immediate emancipation, presents a most sublime spectacle. I regard them as showing a spirit of justice and fairness consistent with the spirit of the times that are upon us, and the work we are called upon to do; and, gentlemen, I am willing to go to them, to learn whether I am to vote on the question for or against compensation to slaveowners.

Mr. Abell—As no other gentleman has seen proper, Mr. President, to address the Convention upon the important question before it, I will now, on behalf of the minority report, submit the concluding observations that I have to make upon the subject. There has been considerable effort made upon the part of gentlemen here to show that my observations come in conflict with the military authorities. On the contrary, I will state that not in the slightest degree, not in a single sentence, have I uttered that which could legitimately lead any one to such a conclusion; and I again state, that I believe it would have been better for the people of Louisiana, had they remained under the military government until there was no longer a necessity for it, because any auxiliary government that we may make, will only create a swarm of new officers.

New Orleans is the soul and center of the military department of the gulf, and a military governor, aided by the advice of the commanding general, and the recommendation of the loyal citizens, would have been able to appoint for us more efficient officers than it would have been possible for us to elect; and I am willing at any time to cast my vote for this Convention to adjourn *sine die*, and I think this is the best thing we can do, because we can only create a swarm of officers who will have very little control over the affairs of state. One of the gentlemen (Mr. Henderson) remarked the other day that it was well known that a *de facto* government, controlled by another military power, existed over nine-tenths of the territory of the State. I believe his estimate is rather large, but the very fact that a *de facto* government exists over a large portion of the territory of the State is an argument against any legislation in this body for the State. I believe it to be the duty of this Convention, under all the circumstances, not to proceed any further. But if we do go on legislating let us make the best laws we can.

Since my remarks on Monday, several gentlemen who have stood upon this floor, instead of discussing the great questions that are before this Convention and before the country, have leveled their entire artillery at a single individual, and he one of the most humble in this community. Sir, the learned gentleman from the Second District took the greatest possible occasion to place me in the attitude of supporting the rebellion. But I did not utter a sentence nor a syllable that would warrant him in drawing such a conclusion. He undertook to make it appear that I said the negro was superior to the white man, and would bring him into subjection. I said no such thing. I did say that the white man was greatly the superior of the negro; that he would not compete as a laborer with the free negroes, and that the preponderance of the latter would cause him to go North. I did not say, as he represented, that we had fought all nations. I said I did not believe any nation could come in contact with us successfully; that England had tried it twice, and failed. I did not say either that we had ever fought the French. They have established a monarchy right under our nose and we have not fought them, and will not, in my opinion, until the old democracy wakes up, and then they will find that they have made a very warm nest for themselves. I feel rather complimented by the epitaph the gentleman proposes for me. I am willing to be called an old fogy in these days, when progress means theft and acquisition by all possible means; when the men of progress would make one clean sweep with one hand upon the government, and the other upon the rebels, gathering for their own benefit all within their reach, who, when they find a good fat Union man in their reach, will sweep him as clean as they will a rebel. These, gentlemen, are the progressive principles of to-day which you would have us adopt.

But what shall I say to the school-boy arguments of the gentleman? He spun it out yesterday, sir, just to the half hour, and when the mace came down, admonishing him that the time was up, I saw the end of the tale come out of his mouth. And when the Convention voted to let him go on he had nothing more to say till he could go and learn another lesson. And this morning he comes and repeats it. I admire the industry of the gentleman, and if you would give him till to-morrow morning, I have no doubt he would come with another lesson equally well conned. But, sir, he did not touch the question as to the right to tear from the people of Louisiana their property. I do not see that the gentleman is more in favor of the freedom of the slaves than I am, or of the freedom of everybody. Why, sir, I would, if it was in my power, make everybody free, rich and happy. But in thinking of the slave, I do not forget the master and the rights of which it is proposed to divest him.

The gentleman seems to labor in perpetual dread of a halter. Three times he informed the Convention that the halter would await us were it not for the presence of the military. But what has this to do with the great question before the Convention? We are to decide this question for the future, and yet it has been urged with all the fulminations that could be thundered forth, that we are indebted to the military authorities to keep from our necks the halter, the fear of which the gentleman has constantly before his mind. He dwelt upon this topic so much that I fear that if he should see one of those great steamer loads of rope, such as used to come down the Mississippi, he would get frightened and run North.

He thought that we could not remain here two hours if it were not for the military force to keep our necks out of the halter. Well, I will amend it to two hours and a quarter. But, sir, if we could not stay here without being supported by the military authorities, what right, I ask, have we here at all? Who are we representing if we could not? I call upon the Convention to answer.

We shall have the question to answer some day. I agree with the gentleman, that if the military were removed the halter might be shaken over our heads. I do not deny it. But, sir, what business has the halter in this Convention. I think that this is no place for gentlemen to drag it into. But perhaps the gentleman wants to know something of the history of the halter. I can enlighten him some on that point. I used to live in Kentucky. There was a class of men that used to be called abolitionists—much like a certain class of progressive men we have now-a-days--that used to come over and steal a negro occasionally, and march him off. When they got over into Indiana, it frequently happened that some good, honest Indianian would get hold of them, and march back both abolitionist and slave. Well, sir, when they were thus marched back, the abolitionist would get a short piece of rope without charge; but I trust the gentleman who has been shaking it over our heads does not think himself entitled to the same gratuity.

I come here, Mr. President, for the purpose of representing fairly and boldly what was for the interest of the people, and I shall not be dissuaded from my purpose.

There is one gentleman who claims a slight advantage over me in this discussion, but I shall not yield on that point, though he only claims advantage in lungs. I will contest it with him. He quoted from an old abolition tract, issued perhaps half a century ago. Well, sir, what would you expect from an abolitionist? They are covered with whitewash, while the inside is unfurnished. No one will say that I said the negro was equal to the white man. Will any gentleman say that I said so? No, sir. The gentleman who said it is an honest, upright man, but he is misled on this subject. He scorns my principles. I scorn, with equal hate, his; I scorn the idea of tearing from a nobleman, an honest man, or a thief even, if you please, one iota of his property; and I denounce our attempt to tear the property from the people of Louisiana, while the enemy all around us is in the enjoyment of his, of the same species, as a cowardly act unworthy this assembly.

If I forage upon anybody it will be upon my enemies, and not upon my friends; and yet you tell me you despise my principles. I despise yours, and before this question is put to vote, Mr. President, I propose that this body form themselves into a Committee of the Whole and go out and see that the ragged rebels give up their slaves before we call upon loyal men to give up theirs. I would have all over fifty years of age excluded from that committee. That suits you, Mr. President, don't it? I am glad we agree for the first time, and will be excused from fighting the ragged rebels; we belong to modern antiquity, sir, and will be excused from the grand committee. I want my Northern friend there to form part of this committee.

I want the gentleman from the Second District to be made president of it, and when he informs this body that all the rebels' slaves have been got out, I will sign an ordinance of emancipation. My distinguished friend Terry I should expect to go along, and before they started I should want to give them some special instructions. I should instruct my friend Terry not to get too near those ragged rebels for fear that they should play the cannibal on him, as he is so fat and sleek those hungry fellows might be tempted to eat him.

The gentleman from the Second District I would instruct not to go where there is too much rope, lest the sight of it should awaken fears that would prevent him from farther prosecuting the business of the committee. Let them go and despoil the enemy, and then it will be time enough to talk about despoiling their friends. Thus much for the instruction. It will be an admirable arrangement for our Northern friends. I do not know though but we shall have to excuse my friend Brott from acting on it, on account of the admirable plan which he has brought in providing for payment. Three hundred dollars, it is true, is rather a low estimate, but it is better than nothing. When my friend sells goods he wants pay for them, and when he takes the property from other men by legislation he is willing for them to be paid for it. No other course would be just to loyal men. If we take their property from them—property that they have acquired under the guarantees of the laws of the land—we can in justice do no less than pay them for it.

The gentlemen tell you that I am in favor of slavery. They are wrong. I am not in favor of it. I apologize for it just as the old Democratic party apologized for a bank. We were always opposed to it from the time I was a boy, and that was not very recently. But if you had overthrown the banks, say three or four years ago, before these times were upon us, the result would have been a complete breaking up of business of all kinds. They were a necessary evil. Property vested in them under the guarantee of law must be respected, and their destruction would have carried ruin and destruction all over the country.

I advocate slavery upon the same principles that I advocated the rights of foreigners in this country five or ten years ago. They had acquired vested rights under the laws of the land, and we were bound to protect them in the enjoyment of those rights. This is as far as I have advocated slavery. I have said that slavery was the best evil that I ever saw, and that I never in my life saw a moment when I approved it. Vast minds have grappled with the subject, but no one has ever yet devised a plan to destroy it, and do justice to all the parties interested in it.

President—The time is up.

Mr. Montamat—I move that Mr. Abell be allowed to proceed.

[The motion was carried.]

Mr. Abell — I thank you, gentlemen. You have placed me under additional obligations by your courtesy. I will endeavor not to abuse it. You will see, gentlemen, by the last clause of my report, that this Convention can provide for the final extinction of slavery, and act justly to all concerned. If you adopt this report you virtually continue this Convention for an indefinite period of time. If you adopt this the next Legislature can devise means for the payment of the master. You can do justice in this way, and if the Legislature finds that they can do justice by adopting a scheme like that of my friend Brott, let them adopt it. I think the amount he fixes is low, but we cannot now make provision for compensation. The matter must be left to the Legislature. It is probable that the next Legislature and a magnanimous Congress will be able to make provision for adequate means from which the slave owner can be paid a fair and reasonable compensation. If we do this we can justify ourselves before our constituents. You will find that you cannot stand before the people and justify yourselves if you tear away from them their property. You cannot justify yourselves before the world. If you do this you not only tear away the property from American citizens but from foreigners, who have acquired vested rights under our laws—from the Frenchman, the Spaniard, the Italian and the German—and your action will not end with the passage of the ordinance.

I propose, sir, to leave this Convention open for forty years, if necessary. Better that it should adjourn and reassemble than to adopt the majority report, and this is how it is to be done.

Now, Mr. President, I beg of the gentlemen to look at that paragraph. If you adopt the minority report, the first Legislature has the power to, conjointly with the Congress of the United States, take the proper measures to emancipate the slaves and compensate slave owners, and thereby you reconcile the principles of justice with the great end proposed here without incurring the evils of immediate emancipation. That cannot be done with safety to the community and justice to the people now. But you tell us that slavery is already dead; a military order has decreed it, and it does not exist. You are right, so far as the present is concerned, but, sir, every lawyer knows that a title may be in abeyance, and that it may be revived when certain contingencies occur. That, sir, is the case with this property, where titles are in abeyance, and will be revived when the war shall be at an end. But, sir, under the constitution, in the amendment that I propose, the result could be reached, as it has been in Pennsylvania and the other Northern States. If the Legislature should deem it to be for the interest of the State to adopt such a mode, the matter will remain open to them. They may abolish it at any moment; then why not adopt the minority report? Why, sir, the war can hardly be ended in one year. It is almost impossible. During that time the military power would be here, and the institution would remain in *statu quo*.

I will not impugn the motives of gentlemen who oppose my views.

Mr. President, I am informed that Mr. Cazabat desires to make some remarks on this question. If the gentleman desires it, I will willingly give way to give him an opportunity to speak on it.

Mr. HILLS—Mr. President, I move that Mr. Abell be permitted to give way for Mr. Cazabat to speak, and to resume his remarks thereafter.

[The motion was carried.]

[A motion to adjourn was lost.]

Mr. CAZABAT—Mr. President, under the rules adopted by this Convention, the gentleman who presented the minority report is entitled to close the argument, and unless permitted to speak now, I should be precluded from participating in this debate, on account of my absence yesterday. I therefore thank the gentleman from the Fifth District of Orleans (Mr. Abell) for his courtesy, however I may be opposed to his principles.

I do not rise here as a politician or lawyer, but as an humble member of this Convention, as a citizen of Louisiana, to express my convictions according to the dictates of my conscience, to say what I deem right and true, to sustain, if possible, the majority report in favor of *immediate and unconditional* emancipation.

But why should not the gentleman be allowed to give us his full views upon this important subject? Let him raise his voice —let not the wrongful impression go abroad, that this is a *party* convention—let the whole country know that the deliberations of this body are not, in the least, under the control or influence of military rule, that as the representatives of the loyal people of Louisiana we meet and act here as freemen, entirely independent of arbitrary power—let us show to the world that we are in favor of maintaining the freedom of speech, and the freedom of the press—let our measures be criticised by our opponents. Are we afraid of the ultimate result of this discussion? No—a thousand times, no—for our principles are based upon eternal truth and justice.

If so, let the gentleman advocate and apologize the "*immaculate institution*" until doomsday, if he desires, dares, or concludes to do so, for the special benefit of its sympathizing friends and supporters.

That doctrine belongs to the past, and is of no avail at present. It is the war cry of the privileged few against the oppressed many—it is the dying voice of slavery, ignorance and darkness, opposed to light, instruction and freedom—it is the last struggle between right and wrong, between treason and loyalty.

Unfortunately, however, for the gentleman, he has failed not only to convince this Convention, but also the masses of the people of Louisiana.

His extreme fear of doing wrong prevents him from doing right, and in his attempt to prove too much he has utterly failed to prove anything, for his premises are without foundation and his conclusions erroneous.

Talk about the vested and acquired rights of slaveholders! In the first place, sir, the population of this State is not, and never was entirely composed of that class.

On the contrary, the majority of the people owned very few slaves. The humble and honest farmer, the poor mechanic, the hard-working classes, the bone and sinew of the land, have suffered by this cruel and unfortunate war, in loss and destruction of property, as much in proportion, if not more, than the wealthy planter; therefore, if you grant compensation to one class, the other will be also entitled to compensation, and thereby you will ruin forever the people and the State already impoverished and reduced to the most distressed condition produced by the bloody struggle of the last three years.

Talk about the vested and pretended rights of slave owners! They have none, morally and legally speaking, and even, if conceded for argument's sake, they have forfeited them when violating not only the constitution of Louisiana, but the national constitution, the supreme law of the land, by raising their hands and their voices against the most merciful government on the face of the earth. I go further. I contend that slavery is not recognized, either expressly or by implication, by the constitution.

I challenge the gentleman who quotes so loudly about the constitutional guarantees of slavery, to point to any clause or article of the constitution wherein the word *slave* or *slavery* can be found.

I am not inclined, Mr. President, to find fault with, and descant against, slavery, because it is dead and gone. I admit that the planters of Louisiana, as a general rule, were humane, kind and intelligent masters; the slave himself, when well treated, seemed contented with his condition. Never was a country blessed with so much prosperity and real happiness as Louisiana, before the year 1861; more sugar and cotton were exported from the city of New Orleans than from any other port in the world; but the insane spirit of rebellion has done its work, and both the guilty and the innocent are now to suffer the consequences. Slavery must disappear now and forever, because it is the original cause of all our national troubles.

Its immediate and utter destruction, without condition, is a matter of necessity. Such is the deep-seated and immovable conviction that fills the mind of every true and loyal citizen, whose patriotism is not kindled by prejudice, or warped by self-interest.

But, Mr. President, in my desire to do what is right, I am not prepared to do wrong.

If there are men in Louisiana—and I know there are some, though few and far between—men who have been truly loyal in their unfaltering devotion to the government, in the name of justice and equity, gentlemen of the Convention, do not let such men lose one dollar or one cent, on account of having been deprived of their property. So help me God, if I can rely upon the honest intentions of my co-workers in this Convention, I believe there is no one here, willing, either by his voice or vote, to do injustice to his fellow-man.

As soon as the act of immediate and unconditional emancipation is passed, I hold in my hand a resolution which I intend to offer to this Convention, and which in my humble opinion is calculated to obtain justice for these loyal men—[applause]—for I rely with confidence upon the liberality and magnanimity of the federal government.

But, strange to say, Mr. President, the faithful, loyal citizens are almost all opposed to compensation: they claim no indemnity for the loss of their slaves. They regard this project of compensation as a ruse to prolong, if possible, the existence of the institution, and they know perfectly well that if adopted by the State, the rebels would be the principal ones to profit by it. As far as the loyal men are concerned, they are willing and ready to offer up their losses in slave labor, as a cheerful sacrifice, to secure the restoration of peace and harmony in the national and State government. I will now ask the gentleman directly (Mr. Abell) if he goes so far as to claim compensation for disloyal men, and specially the guilty leaders who deluded the honest masses and attempted, either directly or indirectly, our national destruction?

Mr. ABELL—No, never.

Mr. CAZABAT—He answers, no! I am glad to hear it. Sir, I do not wish to hurt any man's feelings. God knows that this question, involving the welfare of the country, requires kind and deliberate consideration. It is only thus that we can arrive at such a conclusion as shall be beneficial, not only to a certain class of the community, not only to a certain interested portion, but to every class and interest; not only to the black race, but to the white; for permit me to remark, the emancipation of the African is nothing more nor less than that of the white. Yes, sir, it will prove to be, in the course of time, the true liberation and emancipation of the poor white laboring classes of the South, heretofore "the hewers of wood and drawers of water"; for it cannot be denied that all over the South the political and ruling power was in the hands of the very few at the expense of the very many. The legislation of Louisiana, for the last sixty years, was made by slaveholders for the sole and exclusive benefit of slaveholders. It is to be hoped that the people will hereafter remember that "vigilance is the price of liberty."

I have no fears that the negroes will ever imbrue their hands in the white man's blood. Give them education, make them useful and good, and both classes will cooperate in the great work of civilization and progress now before the American nation. [Applause.] As I have already stated, a suggestion of that character is, in my mind, an exhibition of a spirit of cowardice. Are you, sir, afraid lest the so greatly despised African, your proclaimed "*inferior*," shall become your equal or superior? I do not believe there is a man within the sound of my voice who apprehends such result. If I am wrong, let that voice answer. Not one responds, sir!

I am in favor of freedom, no matter what may be the system of slavery, for, in my opinion, it must always be incompatible with the rights of one race and the interests of the other. I wish to call the gentleman's attention to the declaration, upon his dying bed, of Washington, the Father of his country, most entitled to our respect, and who in the most exquisite terms, instructed, as his last wish upon earth, that those who had been held as slaves during his life time should be emancipated.

Again, the great savant of the eighteenth century, admired by both Europe and America as a statesman and philosopher—the immortal Franklin—was opposed to slavery; was the first man who presented to the Congress of the United States a petition on behalf of the African's rights.

Douglas—the lamented Douglas—fought manfully as long as he could, at the head of the democratic party, for the maintenance and preservation of slavery, but against its extension; and I, as one of his most humble but ardent and devoted followers and admirers, was willing to fight for it, so long as it was not opposed to the existence of our government.

But the public mind has been wonderfully modified by the great events which have taken place during the last three years, and what I considered in 1860 as a matter of safety, I am in 1864 convinced is tending to the destruction of the nation.

Let me ask you, Mr. President, and members of the Convention, what has produced and caused this bloody civil war?

Slavery! Yes, slavery is the root of our present national woes. The preservation of the republic now demands its utter destruction. The progressive spirit of the age and christian civilization requires this cheerful sacrifice. Then, and then only, shall the American republic be truly the home of freedom, disenthralled, regenerated and perpetuated.

Mr. President and members of the Convention, the federal army may meet with sad reverses, but the ultimate result of this conflict is written above. Look in the heavens and you can almost see blazing with dazzling lustre the words, "Success to America! success to the cause of human freedom and human rights!" (Great applause.)

A motion was made and carried to adjourn.

FRIDAY, May 6, 1864.

[At 12 o'clock M. the president called the Convention to order, and the proceedings were opened with prayer by the Rev. Mr. Strong, after which the roll was called and the following members answered to their names:

Messrs. Abell, Balch, Bailey, Barrett, Beauvais, Bofill, Bromley, Burke, Campbell, Collin, Cook J. K., Cook T., Crozat, Decker, Dufresne, Duke, Dupaty, Edwards, Ennis, Fish, Flagg, Flood, Gaidry, Geier, Goldman, Gorlinski, Gruneberg, Hart, Healy, Heard, Henderson, Hills, Hire, Howes, Kavanagh, Kugler, Maas, Mann, Maurer, Mayer, Millspaugh, Montamat, Normand, Orr, Pintado, Poynot, Schroeder, Schnurr, Seymour, Shaw, Smith, Spellicy, Stumpf, Stiner, Stauffer, Sullivan, Taliaferro, Terry, Thorpe, Waters, Wells, Wilson, and Mr. President—63.

There being no quorum present, the sergeant-at-arms was directed to bring in absent members.

Messrs. Austin, Bell, Bonzano, Davies, Foley, Fosdick, Fuller, Harnan, Knobloch, Morris, Payne J., Paine J. T., Purcell J., Pursell S., and Stocker having taken their seats, the president announced a quorum.

The secretary read the minutes of the previous day's proceedings, and they were adopted.]

PRESIDENT—If there are no petitions or memorials, resolutions are in order.

Mr. CAMPBELL—Mr. President, I call up my resolution offered yesterday.

PRESIDENT—It has not been reached; when we come to it you can call it up. If there are no new resolutions, reports of standing committees are in order.

Mr. SHAW—The Committee on Ordinance reports "progress."

Mr. THORPE—Mr. President, as chairman of the Committee on Enrollment, I offer a resolution in order to be instructed by the Convention as to the number of copies it is desired to have printed for the use of the Convention of the journals and debates:

Resolved, That the printer of this Convention be instructed to print ——— copies of the journal, one-half of said number to be in the French language and one-half of said number to be in the English language.

Mr. WILSON—I move to fill the blank with the number one thousand.

Mr. MONTAMAT—I amend to three thousand.

[The amendment was lost, and the motion of Mr. Wilson was adopted.]

Mr. WILSON—Mr. President, on the appointment of Col. Thorpe upon the Committee on Assault of Members, the whole evidence was submitted to him, and through a misunderstanding of the motion of Mr. Henderson to postpone other business until the question of emancipation was disposed of, the committee will not be ready to report until this question is disposed of.

[The secretary read:]

NEW ORLEANS, May 6, 1864.

To the president and members of the Convention for the Revision and Amendment of the Constitution of the State of Louisiana:

GENTLEMEN—I hereby resign my seat as a member of the Convention from the Seventh Representative District of Orleans.

R. K. HOWELL.

Mr. HENDERSON—I move that the resignation be accepted.

Mr. WILSON—I move that it be accepted, and that the usual notice be given to the governor to order a new election to fill the vacancy.

Mr. BELL—I move, as a substitute, that it be laid on the table.

[The motion to table was lost, and the motion of Mr. Henderson carried, on a rising vote, 55 ayes to 22 noes.]

Mr. CAMPBELL—I call up my resolution.

[The secretary read:]

Resolved, That no vote on emancipation be taken by this Convention until every member of this Convention be present.

Mr. FOLEY—I move to lay the resolution on the table.

Mr. HARNAN—That ought to be amended by putting some penalty, or we never will get them all here.

[The resolution was tabled on a rising vote, ayes 45, noes 23.]

Mr. BELL—Mr. President, I call up my resolution.

Mr. HILLS—I rise, Mr. President, to a question of privilege in connection with the resignation of Judge Howell. He has resigned without assigning a reason; but I understand that he feels aggrieved at the action of this Convention in sending the sergeant-at-arms yesterday to bring him in.

The circumstances were these: Mr. Abell moved, or made a suggestion, that Judge Howell was absent and ought to be in his seat. I moved to amend, and that the sergeant-at-arms be dispatched to bring in all absent members in the city. I think it highly important that every member should be found in his place to vote on the emancipation question, and it was with this view that I made the motion. Personally, I have the highest regard for Judge Howell; and sincerely regret it if any action of mine has had anything to do with bringing about his resignation.

Mr. ABELL—Mr. President, I desire to make some apology myself. The seat of Judge Howell was the only one I had noticed vacant, and it had been vacant for some days. I made the motion respecting Judge Howell because he was the only member whose absence I had observed. I should have made the same motion respecting any other member, and if any other gentleman attempts to shirk the. responsibility of recording his vote on this question I shall make a similar motion respecting him; and if I catch any man shearing wool from the sheep's back, as the phrase goes, so that it may drop off on either side, I shall not hesitate to expose him. I want everything to appear on the *postea* when it goes before the people.

Mr. TERRY—I move that the apologies of the gentlemen be reduced to writing and sent to Judge Howell.

Mr. FOLEY—I move that the acceptance of the resignation be reconsidered.

[The motion was tabled.]

PRESIDENT—The next business in order is the unfinished debate. The question is on the rejection of the minority report of the Committee on Emancipation.

Mr. HEARD—Mr. President, the amendment to that report offered by Mr. Brott yesterday, does not that come up this morning?

PRESIDENT—It was not called up in its order, and consequently must be regarded as withdrawn.

Mr. HILLS—I rise for information. Yesterday Mr. Abell gave way for Mr. Cazabat.

Mr. ABELL—I desire to know before proceeding whether Mr. Cazabat has the floor.

Mr. CAZABAT—I have no desire to make any further remarks on the question at the present time.

Mr. ABELL—*Mr. President and gentlemen of the Convention:* The question under debate is the rejection of the minority report of the Committee on Emancipation. That report proposes to leave this whole matter as though the Convention was sitting for one or forty years. The matter can be taken up at any time, discussed and acted upon as it was in the State of Pennsylvania, whenever the Congress of the United States and this State may by joint action be able to emancipate the slaves and do justice to the owners. You may adopt the minority report, and it leaves the question open so that your friends and those owning slave property may be paid for their property; it leaves the matter open so that the honest loyal man may receive a fair and just compensation for his slaves. If you should hereafter be a member of the State Legislature, the same question, according to the minority report, is open, and whenever the Congress of the United States shall say it will pay three hundred dollars for each and every slave belonging to the loyal men, and the State says it will pay one hundred dollars—which will make four hundred dollars—and if that be a fair and just amount, the Legislature has not only the power, but it becomes its duty to do so, and then the owner is honestly paid. Are you in favor of that fair, honest proposition that keeps the question open? If we were now to say that we would pay three hundred, or even one hundred dollars for each slave, are we prepared to meet such an appropriation? No, sir. The State is already pressed down. I have stated, and state again, that the circumstances of war have placed it out of the power of the people of the State of Louisiana to compensate the slaveholders. They can scarcely make a living now. I beg to say to the gentleman of "The Era," that while that paper, the great medium of the government here, may have made its $200,000, his poor neighbors cannot support themselves. By freeing the negroes without compensation at this time, you take from these people the means of a living. Every rational man knows full well that it is out of our power to do this at this time. The gentleman from the Second District said I had issued the second and third edition of my speech. Sir, Blackstone has gone through twenty-seven editions, but is a good work yet. I have other works that have passed through several editions, but because of the truth they contain they are read by all. Falsehood ought not to have but one edition, and I think the remarks of some of the gentlemen on this floor ought never to undergo a second edition.

How are you to compensate these masters? Some of them are French, Spanish, German, Irish, but all your neighbors; how are you going to meet their just demands? You cannot do it; you are perfectly prostrate yourselves, and if you make your own living you may be very thankful; but suppose the Congress of the United States should step in next year and offer to pay three hundred dollars for each slave, as it has already been intimated, you would see the resources of this State once more invigorated and in a prosperous condition. All wars must add to the distresses of men, and cause the desolation of many a fair field. Many loyal families have been prostrated in this part of our country, and yet these people must now lose what little prospect they have ahead, and be left in a state of utter destitution.

From a resolution offered by the gentleman from the Third District, we learn that a large amount of money has been appropriated. He says that Mr. Graham and Mr. Durant have *large sums of money* which were appropriated for the purpose of making this a free State. In that resolution he asks that these large sums of money shall go into the treasury of the State of Louisiana. Where is that free State government? I know of no free State government. I ask the mover, if he expects to buy up a free State government? There is no free state here. What is to be done with it? Is it to purchase this Convention? How much will the gentleman himself take? It appears there are *large* sums of money for the purpose of erecting a free State.

I believe the gentleman from the Third is loyal to the core. I believe he can and has beat any man in singing the "Bonnie Blue Flag." I am told that he had even the whole structure of the battle of Manassas here. I do not say he had it here, for I did not see it; but I have understood he made a most beautiful representation of the scene. Does the gentleman wish some of this money? Let him go to Messrs. Durant and Graham, for I am sure the Convention will not contaminate its hands with it.

The gentleman from the Second District says we would not be permitted to stay here two hours but for the presence of the armies of the United States. Does he mean that it would take but two hours to get rope enough for us all? If not, what does he mean? Does he mean we stand here representing people who do not want us? I believe it, if that is what is meant. I never believed that we represented the people of Louisiana. I have told you so from the start. We are representing a faction. I look at over 50,000 voters represented by 5000 or 7000. I do not understand it. The gentleman has not touched on the real question—on the great question of spoliation or no spoliation.

Fifty-two summers have rolled over my head, but never have I witnessed one instance of that cruelty of which we hear so much. Unlike my opponents, I am ready to show the very page, verse and section of the law, and can show ten cases where husbands have imbrued their hands in their wives' blood, where they can show one of cruelty to a slave. Slaves must of course be corrected, though I have always opposed punishment by the lash.

Mr. President, this is the last attempt to argue this question before this Convention, and I feel that it is too great a one for a brain like mine. It affects hundreds of thousands of men, and I would say to you, gentlemen, let this be settled when the State resumes its sovereignty. This spoliation is carried on in reference to millions of property, recognized by the noble of the world, by our constitution and laws, and considered in the laws of Congress and State Legislatures. At any rate, I would like to have the matter rest for the present. In the last clause of my report, this Convention is authorized to extend all its power to the Legislature, and then whenever Mr. Terry's moneys are expended, a mode is provided in which justice may be done, upon fitting deliberation.

Oh! the beauty of liberty! Without it for a foundation, a government is like chaff blown before the wind.

But you must be just before you are generous. It is a beautiful thing to bestow liberality, but without charity, all that you do is a sounding brass and a tinkling cymbal. Mr. President, what is the proposition of our abolition friends, who array themselves not against my principles, but against me, personally? Well, sir, for the last twenty-five years the abolition party has been arrayed against this country, while the people have slept, and while it has been repeatedly said in Congress on every occasion, that the people of the slave States were entitled to their slave property as much as to any other. The sovereign people have said that the negroes should remain where they are, until by the will of God they should be liberated.

[The president's hammer came down.]

PRESIDENT—The time is up.

Mr. HILLS—I rise to a question of order. I think Mr. Abell is entitled to the floor, as, according to the vote of yesterday, he is to have sufficient time in which to conclude his remarks.

PRESIDENT—That was not the disposition of yesterday. The gentleman gave notice that he would close the debate, but before filling out his time he gave way to Mr. Cazabat. That was not counted against him, but now he has spoken for half an hour under the rules.

Mr. HILLS—I appeal from the decision of the chair.

[The yeas and nays were called, when the House negatived the president's decision; yeas 29, nays 47.]

Mr. ABELL—Mr. President, I never saw in any part of the country one worthy of the names of a man and a Mason, but that I loved him. I shall always remember with the kindest feelings the gentleman from the Second District, and for the indulgence granted to me by you, Mr. President, and the Convention, I most sincerely thank you. The magnanimity of the gentleman from the Second will speak for him in all future time, because I must acknowledge that I have been somewhat severe in personal remarks referring to him.

I will now proceed with regard to the great cause of the war.

The negro, sir, has been the cause of the war. Now, I have no doubts of the honesty of those who have peculiar ideas in regard to slavery, though I have often heard it said that those who believed in its direct abolition were dishonest.

Predilections, teachings, etc., exercise a great influence upon a man's mind. I am honest in my opinions, and the only difference between the gentleman (Mr. Hills) and myself is, as to the rights that grow out of the possession of this property, considering the manner of its acquirement. Since my youth, and that was not yesterday, since my mind received its earliest impressions to the present, I have been opposed to slavery in the abstract, in principle; but, sir, much slave property has been acquired in this State, and it is the proposition of the power and right of this Convention to tear it away, though honestly acquired, that startles me. I would with the greatest pleasure vote for emancipation were any fair provision made for compensation. I admit, though, that I do not believe in the assumption by the State of all the debt. Make this a free State in the manner proposed, and you make it an asylum for all outcasts. The people of the State will be driven out and the safety of the State endangered.

The great stress laid upon the slave status is not true, and I would read from the True Delta one single remark, to show that others suffer as well as the negroes. It is in regard to the sewing woman: "A brisk woman can furnish four pairs of drawers, containing 1800 stitches each, by constant labor, from 7 A. M. to 9 P. M., and for each pair she receives 4 cents, or 16 cents per day." Here are fourteen hours' hard labor for a compensation of sixteen cents, and yet not a tear have I seen yet in the eyes of any gentleman. I am told that our abolition friends, many of them, cheat them out of half of that. I don't believe they cheat them out of *half*. I put it at about one-third. Here is the negro, fat, sleek and well fed, but all the tears are to be poured forth for them, and it is said that slavery must be abolished. Why, gentlemen, if I was going to cry, I would begin to get ready now.

I was going on to say, in regard to the horrors of slavery pictured here, I have never seen any of them, although I have been raised among slaves. The reason is apparent, for who is going to abuse a man who is valuable to him? I have never seen a negro whipped in cruelty, and only two or three for the purpose of correction, in fifty-two years. I am speaking of what I have seen. When I hear gentlemen reading long tracts, I ask, where is their authority?

Do you hear, Mr. President? You seldom hear what I say; but you must this about the poor sewing woman. My distinguished friend from the Second District, will sixteen cents get you a breakfast, or half of it, or even a quarter? Oh, no; but perhaps a whole family is supported upon that amount. My tears shall be for the white, and not for the colored race.

Who are the loyal citizens to be paid? I suppose that, according to my friend from the Second District, there is not one here. Some might say, the gentleman who sung the "Bonnie Blue Flag" so beautifully is the only loyal one among us, that is loyal. Others might say, that no one is loyal who has not stolen three negroes, at least; but I do not know that anybody here goes as far as that. Now, I come to Mr. Cazabat, because he pressed the question, and I feel bound, when a question is asked, to throw it back, and ask him who is a loyal citizen? Is he one who has ever borne arms against the Yankees?

Mr. CAZABAT—I leave that for the Federal government to decide.

Mr. ABELL—The constitution of the United States makes full provision for those who are not loyal, in article III, section 3, and in article IV, section 2, clause 2, and in amendments IV and VI.

You see I come here with the documents in my hand to sustain my exact position. By these provisions the status of every man can be determined according to the laws of the land.

Some of these very nice men here, who are continually harping on loyalty, would, if the English, French, Spanish or Confederate flag were raised here to-day, be the first to harp in its favor.

Mr. THORPE—I call the gentleman to order. I think this is all wrong.

Mr. ABELL—Since this is so hard to take—but must be taken—I will give it to you in small doses. I will give the gentleman his share. He ought not to be passed here. I shall not do it. I have passed him because I have found him one of the most honest, candid men on this floor. He told you on the second or third day, and was the only gentleman who told you, that we were assembled here for a certain purpose, and that purpose ought to be accomplished quickly. I would say to him, and all who believe as he does, as did Paul when speaking on the subject of slavery—in his bold and powerful language he said, "Servants, obey your masters." I came here for no other purpose than to forward the interests of the people of Louisiana. I came here as their servant, and intend to obey them as long as I stand upon this floor. I advise the gentleman to pursue the same course and obey his master.

If, Mr. President, we have a great, noble and grand government, can it not overlook the sins of those who have erred? How can it know but that its subjects have been forced to err? One thing is certain; when a people have rebelled—and governments all over the world have had rebellions—and that people have been dismantled of their power, those governments have overlooked their sins, as do fathers those of their children when they have been misled, and come back penitent and ready to submit to them. The government casts the shadow of its wings over them, and from that moment all goes on as before. The people of Louisiana return to their allegiance—I do not care who they are, or what you say about them, the government, in its greatness and majesty, should act towards them the father's part. I say that every man who comes back under the flag of the United States stands to-day upon the same footing as before, and, like a returned prodigal, is entitled to his right. Therefore, let their property stand as before, and in time they will aid us.

Most of them have subscribed to the iron-clad oath, and I believe, sir, that such men are as good as I, or any other man, and that the country should extend its arms to receive and welcome them back. The government should never divest them of their property, for forfeitures have never taken place in such cases. That is my theory; and no man can have his property taken from him unless by a conviction before a tribunal of his country. I have demonstrated upon this floor, by the constitution of the United States, by the decisions of the Supreme Court, and the proclamation of President Lincoln, that this parish is excepted; and I say now, once for all, that slavery exists here as much as it ever did. The subject is almost beyond the mind of man, and I must tear myself from it after reading the minority report.

[Mr. Abell read the minority report.]

Mr. President, you have now heard every word of my minority report. It opens up the way for the slave to be free in due time, for the master to be compensated for his property, and for this Convention to do honor to itself.

I speak not for myself, but for the people and honor of the State of Louisiana. I speak not for the abolitionists, but all others. The people do not want the master despoiled of his property—they want the integrity of the nation and the honor of the State preserved.

I again thank you, gentlemen of this Convention, and you, Mr. President, for your forbearance.

Mr. HILLS—I ask to suspend the rules in order to regulate the vote on this question of emancipation. I offer the following:

Resolved, That every vote on the subject of emancipation shall be taken by yeas and nays, and members not present shall be sent for by the sergeant-at-arms and required to record their votes.

Mr. FOLEY—I move the rules be suspended to act on that resolution.

PRESIDENT—Mr. Secretary, call the roll; I do not think there is a quorum present.

[The roll was called and only seventy-five members answered to their names. The sergeant-at-arms brought in a member.]

Mr. HILLS—I now move a suspension of the rules to act on my resolution.

[The motion was carried by a rising vote, ayes 61, nays 2.]

Mr. HENDERSON—I shall demand a strict adherence to rule XLI, which requires a two-thirds vote to suspend the rules.

Mr. HENDERSON—A short time since another gentleman introduced a motion here that upon any important question every member shall be required to vote, and if not present we were to suspend the proceedings until the absent member was sent for. Now we have another similar absurd motion that we shall wait from day to day until every member votes on the question of emancipation. If this is done, a large portion of the time will be consumed in waiting for absent members, and is tantamount to asking the Convention to adjourn *sine die*.

Mr. HILLS—The gentleman is fighting a man of straw. My proposition is not to suspend the business of this Convention until every member is sent for, but that every vote shall be taken on the question with the ayes and noes, and if members are absent they shall be sent for, and when they come shall be made to record their votes.

[The resolution was then adopted by a rising vote, ayes 66, noes 1.]

[The motion to reject the minority report on emancipation then came up.]

Mr. HENDERSON—Does it include the amendment of Mr. Brott?

PRESIDENT—Mr. Brott's amendment was not seconded, nor called up in time, and must be considered as withdrawn.

[The roll was then called on the motion to reject the minority report on emancipation, with the following result:

YEAS—Messrs. Ariail, Austin, Bailey, Barrett, Baum, Beauvais, Bell, Bonzano, Brott, Bromley, Burke, Cazabat, Collin, Cook J. K., Cook T., Crozat, Cutler, Davies, Duane, Dupaty, Edwards, Ennis, Fish, Flagg, Flood, Foley, Fosdick, Fuller, Gaidry, Geier, Gorlinski, Goldman, Harnan, Hart, Healy, Henderson, Heard, Hills, Hire, Howes, Kavanagh, Knobloch, Kugler, Maas, Mann, Millspaugh, Morris, Murphy E., Newell, Normand, Orr, Payne J., Paine J. T., Pintado, Poynot, Purcell J., Pursell S., Schroeder, Seymour, Shaw, Smith, Spellicy,

Stocker, Stiner, Stauffer, Taliaferro, Terry, Thorpe, Thomas, Wells, Wilson—71.

NAYS—Messrs. Abell, Balch, Bofill, Buckley, Campbell, Decker, Dufresne, Duke, Gastinel, Gruneberg, Maurer, Mayer, Mendiverri, Montamat, Murphy M. W., O'Conner, Stumpf, Sullivan, Waters—19.

The motion to reject the minority report was carried.

A motion to adjourn was then made and carried.]

SATURDAY, May 7, 1864.

[At 12 o'clock the Convention was called to order, and the roll called, when the following gentlemen answered to their names, viz:

Messrs Abell, Ariail, Austin, Balch, Bailey, Barrett, Baum, Beauvais, Bell, Bofill, Bonzano, Bromley, Brott, Buckley, Burke, Campbell, Cook J. K., Cook T., Crozat, Davies, Decker, Dufresne, Duane, Dupaty, Edwards, Ennis, Fish, Flagg, Flood, Foley, Fosdick, Fuller, Gastinel, Geier, Goldman, Gorlinski, Gruneberg, Healy, Harnan, Hart, Heard, Henderson, Hills, Hire, Howes, Kavanagh, Knobloch, Kugler, Maas, Mann, Maurer, Mayer, Mendiverri, Millspaugh, Murphy E., Newell, Normand, O'Conner, Ong, Payne J., Paine J. T., Pintado, Poynot, Purcell J., Pursell S., Schroeder, Schnurr, Seymour, Shaw, Smith, Spellicy, Stumpf, Stiner, Stauffer, Sullivan, Taliaferro, Terry, Thomas, Waters, Wenck, Wells, Wilson—79.

The minutes of the previous meeting were read by the secretary.]

Mr. ABELL—Mr. President, before the minutes are adopted I wish to amend them by recording *nunc pro tunc* the votes on the rejection of my minority report of the members absent then, but present now.

[The president stated the question and directed the secretary to call the names of members absent when the vote was taken.]

Mr. CAMPBELL—I desire to know by what rule members are required to vote on a question after the vote has already been announced, unless the subject is under reconsideration.

Mr. GRUNEBERG—I desire to explain my vote. Being unwell yesterday, I was forced to be absent when the vote was taken on Mr. Abell's report. Permit me, Mr. President, to make a few remarks to explain the manner in which I shall vote.

I want it to be well understood that I don't grudge liberty to any human being; also that I came here without any distinct pledge to vote for immediate, unconditional emancipation. Before the election I have explained to a good many of the voters of Lafourche, fairly and squarely, my views on this subject, namely: that I was in favor of the immediate emancipation of the negroes, if thereby peace could be restored to the country; that the loyal owner should receive a fair compensation for his loss; that the negro, as much as possible, should be forced to return to plantation work; that by judicious laws his moral and social condition should be improved; that by laying a reasonable per centage on the cash wages of the negroes, in a few years a sufficient sum could be raised to indemnifv the owners; that by continuing this system, in case experience would show that the two races, both free, cannot live together, the State would soon be able to colonize the negroes somewhere else.

Mr. STAUFFER—Mr. President, I rise to a point of order. The question is not open to debate. The gentleman is making a speech.

Mr. SEYMOUR—I hope the gentleman will be allowed to proceed. He represents a parish owning ten thousand slaves, and has had no other opportunity to be heard on this question.

PRESIDENT—The gentleman has a right to explain his reasons for casting his vote. This is an exceptional case, and the rule does not apply.

Mr. GRUNEBERG—The vote of the 28th of March last, in the parish of Lafourche, demonstrates already that the foregoing propositions were, by the people there, considered as judicious, and I say it with pride, that on that day I did not lose a single vote cast in my parish.

Now, Mr. President, a few days ago I had a chance to see some of my constituents of Lafourche, and I have found that there is now in my parish an aversion to the immediate, unconditional emancipation of the negroes. This is the result partly of the daily increasing insolence and laziness of the negroes themselves, and also of the fear that the orders of the commanding general, which provide for the education of the colored before the white ones, might be followed up by laws from this assembly which would destroy the birth-right of the white man.

I mean, Mr. President, to represent my constituents on this floor honestly and fearlessly, at every hazard, with so much more assurance, as my change of ideas in the last six weeks has kept pace with theirs.

Threats have been insinuated to me, Mr. President, that in case this assembly—nay, that even if the United States government did not grant the full measure of their supposed rights to the blacks, that then "our colored brethren" would rise in their majesty and power, and conquer from the white race, by force, what might be withheld from them by constitutional enactments.

In that case, Mr. President, even the philanthropic editor of the Era will not find grace before them; and we, every one of us, unless we concede to the native-born negro the full privilege to fill, one of these days, the chair of Governor Hahn or of President Lincoln, shall be in danger of having the halter placed round our neck by the "outraged sons of Africa."

In the sacred name of religion, so-called infidels have been burned at the stake, and I fear, Mr. President, that the few on this floor who entertain different opinions from the majority will be ostracised for the sake of their opinions. For my own self, I shall protest against such a proceeding, because I know in my own heart and conscience that the sole object of my coming here was the desire to secure the welfare of the now enfranchised portion of Louisiana. My motto is not *fiat justitia et pereat mundus*, but rather *pereat* the loyal Southern man. No, sir, I shall endeavor to do justice to the loyal men, both North and South.

My choice in this matter would be that the State of Louisiana should go back into the Union on the propositions of President Lincoln himself, of 1862—that is, with emancipation in 1900.

PRESIDENT—The gentlemen is out of order. He has no right to debate the question. The debate was closed yesterday. He may give his reasons for his vote. But I shall decide anything further out of order.

Mr. GRUNEBERG—I shall vote no.

[The result of the vote was as follows:

YEAS—Messrs. Baum, Brott, Collin, Dupaty, Gorlinski, Harnan, Murphy E., Paine J. T.—8

NAYS—Messrs. Balch, Bofill, Campbell, Dufresne, Gruneberg, Mendiverri—6.

The minutes of the previous day, corrected by adding the votes just taken to the vote as previously recorded, were adopted.]

Mr. HENDERSON—Mr. President, I rise to call the attention of the chair, for one moment to the fact, that there was some misapprehension of facts on the part of Judge Howell, that caused him to tender his resignation, and as I moved that the resignation be received, I now move a reconsideration, in order to move that he be requested to withdraw it.

PRESIDENT—Are we to understand that Judge Howell desires to withdraw his resignation.

Mr. HENDERSON—I certainly had such an intimation, or I should not have made the motion.

Mr. SULLIVAN—A motion to reconsider is out of order. It has been acted on once and lost.

PRESIDENT—It cannot be made again the same day.

Mr. HENDERSON—I move that the Convention rescind its action accepting the resignation of Judge Howell, and move a suspension of the rules in order to take up the question at once.

Mr. DAVIES—I move to lay that motion on the table.

Mr. HILLS—I move to amend by reconsidering the vote on Mr. Howell's resignation.

[Mr. Henderson's motion to suspend the rules was put. The yeas and nays were called with the following result:

AYES—Messrs. Ariail, Bailey, Barrett, Baum, Bell, Bonzano, Bromley, Brott, Burke, Collin, Cook J. K., Cook T., Crozat, Duane, Duke, Dupaty, Ennis, Flagg, Flood, Foley, Fosdick, Gastinel, Geier, Goldman, Gorlinski, Heard, Henderson, Hills, Hire, Howes, Kavanagh, Maas, Mayer, Mendiverri, Millspaugh, Murphy E., Orr, Poynot, Seymour, Shaw, Smith, Spellicy, Stocker,

Stumpf, Stiner, Stauffer, Taliaferro, Terry and Wilson—49.

NAYS—Messrs. Abell, Balch, Bofill, Buckley, Campbell, Davies, Decker, Dufresne, Gruneberg, Healy, Harnan, Hart, Knobloch, Mann, Maurer, Montamat, Murphy M. W., Normand, O'Conner, Payne J., Paine J. T., Pintado, Purcell J., Pursell S., Sullivan and Waters—26.

The motion to suspend was lost for want of a two-third vote.]

Mr. BROMLEY—I have a resolution to offer:

Whereas, The citizens of this State, residing in the country parishes, are in a continual state of alarm, bordering on a panic, which threatens an interruption of all labor, by a simultaneous abandonment of all unprotected parishes in the country, in consequence of raids from the guerrillas: Therefore be it

Resolved, That a committe of five be appointed to confer with the governor and the adjutant general of this State to devise ways and means to organize the militia, whereby we may be properly protected in life, liberty and the pursuit of happiness.

Mr. PURSELL (of Jefferson)—Mr. President, I have an amendment to offer to the report of the Committee on General Provisions, viz:

ART. —. All civil officers for the State at large shall be voters of and reside within the State, and all district or parish officers shall be voters of and reside within their respective parish or district, and shall keep their offices at such places therein as may be required by law.

ART. —. The seat of government shall be at the city of New Orleans. The General Assembly shall have power to dispose of the present capitol property in Baton Rouge and provide, by purchase or otherwise, suitable lands and buildings for a State capitol in New Orleans.

ART. —. Taxation shall be equal and uniform throughout the State. All property shall be taxed in proportion to its value, to be ascertained as directed by law. The General Assembly shall have power to exempt from taxation property actually used for church, school or charitable purposes. The General Assembly shall levy an income tax upon all persons pursuing any profession, occupation, trade or calling, and all such persons shall obtain a license, as provided by law. All tax in income shall be pro rata on the amount of income or business done.

Art. —. No profession, occupation, business or calling, requiring a license from any authority within this State, shall be carried on, exercised or followed by any other than citizens of the United States, or those having made legal declaration of becoming citizens.

ART. —. The General Assembly shall provide by law for the establishment of a poor-house in each parish of the State, for the care of the destitute within their respective limits. and to be conducted as shall be provided by law.

Mr. HARNAN—I move that it be made the order of the day for some day.

PRESIDENT—It lies over.

Mr. BROTT—Mr. President, I have a resolution to offer:

Resolved, That this Convention do adjourn on the 25th inst., at 2 o'clock P. M.

PRESIDENT—The resolution must lie over under the rules.

Mr. HIRE—I have a resolution to offer:

Resolved, That after next Monday this Convention hold an evening session, to commence at 6 o'clock P. M., to afford an opportunity for all members to address the Convention, without prolonging our session to an unnecessary length.

PRESIDENT—Reports of committees are in order.

Mr. GORLINSKI—As chairman of the Committee on Internal Improvement, I would state that the committee will be ready to report on Monday.

Mr. SHAW—The Committee on Ordinance reports "progress."

Mr. WILSON—The Special Committee on Assault of Members reports "progress."

Mr. CAMPBELL—I move that that committee be discharged.

PRESIDENT—The motion lies over. The order of the day, the majority report of the Committee on Emancipation, is next in order.

Mr. ABELL—Mr. President. this is Saturday, and the work before us is one of considerable magnitude. I move that we now adjourn, in order to take up the question on Monday, with the beginning of the week.

[The motion was carried.]

MONDAY, May 9, 1864.

[Convention met pursuant to adjournment and the secretary called the roll, the following gentlemen responding:

Messrs. Abell, Ariail, Bell, Bonzano, Buckley, Burke, Cook J. K., Crozat, Dufresne, Duke, Edwards, Ennis, Fish, Flagg,

Geier, Goldman, Gruneberg, Healy, Hart, Heard, Henderson, Hills, Howes, Maas, Mann, Mayer, Millspaugh, Murphy M. W., Newell, Normand, O'Conner, Ong, Pintado, Pursell S., Schroeder, Schnurr, Seymour, Shaw, Spellicy, Stocker, Stumpf, Stiner, Terrry, Thorpe, Waters, Wenck, Wells, Wilson and Mr. President—49 members present.

There being no quorum, the sergeant-at-arms was directed to bring in absent members.]

Mr. MONTAMAT—I move we adjourn, as there is a primary election, in which many of the members are engaged.

Mr. HILLS—I object. Since the gentleman has stated his reasons, the motion is debatable. We have nothing to do with primary elections—are not sent here as politicians to attend elections of *any* kind. We are here to serve the people, and I think it would be disgraceful to record upon the minutes an adjournment for any such reason.

[The motion to adjourn was lost on a a rising vote—ayes 32, nays 36.]

[After some delay, the roll was called to ascertain if a quorum was present, when the following members having taken their seats, viz: Messrs. Austin, Bailey, Barrett, Bofill, Brott, Campbell, Collin, Cook T., Davies, Dupaty, Flood, Foley, Fosdick, Fuller, Gastinel, Gorlinski, Harnan, Hire, Maurer, Mendiverri, Montamat, Murphy E., Payne J., Purcell J., Smith, Stauffer, Taliaferro and Thomas—28 members,

The president announced that a quorum was present.

The minutes of the previous day's pro ceedings were read and adopted.]

Mr. HILLS—I now move the secretary be instructed to call the names of all the absentees who have not voted on the question of emancipation.

SECRETARY—In consequence of the absence of the assistant secretary, I shall have to call the roll, as the previous vote is in his possession.

Mr. STAUFFER—I would like to know what right the assistant secretary has to carry away any documents of the Convention.

PRESIDENT—I think the Convention ought to know why the assistant secretary is absent.

Mr. HARNAN—He is on a big drunk. I move that an assistant secretary be appointed, and the matter of voting laid over till to-morrow.

Mr. STAUFFER—If we are to proceed to the election of an assistant secretary, I should like to have the office vacated first.

Mr. HILLS—I call for a division of the question.

[The first division of the question was put and lost, and the question to defer the calling of the names carried.]

PRESIDENT—Resolutions are in order.

Mr. STUMPF—I offer the following:

Whereas, The object of this war on the part of the United States against the so-called Confederate States is, first, to maintain the Union, to enforce the laws and uphold the constitution of these United States, and all acts of Congress made in pursuance thereto; and in doing this we must not be unmindful of those truly loyal citizens whose interest and whose only wealth consisted in that species of property which the war has destroyed, or rendered useless as property; be it, therefore,

Resolved, by this Convention, That all truly loyal citizens of Louisiana, who have taken the President's amnesty oath of Dec. 8. 1863, up to this date, be paid by the United States government a reasonable indemnity for each and every slave assessed in their name as property for the year 1861.

Mr. PURCELL—I offer the following preamble and resolution:

Whereas, In the fitting up of Liberty Hall for the use of this Convention, provision was made for the accommodation of an audience, and a portion of the same was specially appropriated for ladies, but which fact was not publicly made known; therefore, be it

Resolved, That the ladies be and are hereby invited to attend the sessions of this Convention.

Mr. STOCKER—I move to suspend the rules for its adoption.

[The motion was carried, yeas 71, noes 0.]

Mr. MILLSPAUGH—I move to lay the resolution on the table.

[The motion was lost and the resolution adopted.]

Mr. S. PURSELL—I offer the following:

Whereas, The notes issued by the city of New Orleans being the only currency now in circulation in this State fully entitled to the confidence of the people (the currency of the United States excepted); and whereas, designing and bad men, traitors to their country and false to every obligation due to that generous magnanimity that permits them to remain under the protection of a good government, are using every means to depreciate the said notes of the city of New Orleans ; therefore, be it

Resolved, That any institution or person refusing to receive the said city issue, either on deposit or in payment, is unworthy the confidence of the people, and deserves the attention of the authorities competent to rectify such matters.

Resolved, That this Convention urgently recommend and desire that all heads of departments, either civil or military, having power in the premises, do suppress any and all banks that may be in operation by sufferance, and failing in their duty in accordance with the exigency of the times.

Mr. STOCKER—As I consider that important, I move that one hundred copies be printed and laid on the desks of the members.

[The motion was carried.]

PRESIDENT—Reports of committees are in order.

Mr. THORPE—Mr. President, as chairman of the Committee on Assault of Members, I beg leave to submit the following report:

REPORT OF THE COMMITTEE ON ASSAULT.

Following the election of members of this Convention, but before they had officially assumed their duties, the chief active conservator of the peace of this city, under most aggravated circumstances, especially as far as the proprieties of place were concerned, assaulted a member elect of this Convention.

A careful examination of the facts, however, make it evident that the assault had not the slightest necessary connection with the rights, privileges or dignities of this body.

The effect, however, of this gross breach of the peace by an officer solemnly sworn to conserve the peace ; and the time and place selected for this gross violation of good order, naturally, in these troublous times, create more than ordinary excitement ; and when the report went abroad that an assault had been made upon another member of the Convention, and under circumstances which appeared to justify the belief that a gross violation of privilege had been committed, many members of the Convention desired that some official notice should be taken of the matter, and the honorable member from the Second District, parish of Orleans, called the attention of the Convention to the subject, and a committee was promptly appointed to inquire into the history of the assault—thus the circumstances came officially before the Convention. The report of the committee stated the facts of the assault clearly enough, yet concluded without any expression of opinion, and a matter that was insignificant as a record of a violation of law and good citizenship, became, nevertheless, of momentous importance, if the Convention treated the principle involved, viz: That a breach of privilege was unworthy of an especial notice, and thereby, possibly, establishing a precedent which might for all time be deeply injurious to the best interests of the law-abiding citizens of this State, and especially to the local populations of New Orleans.

The power of the Convention to protect itself in the persons of its members is undoubted. This is not a power derived from constitutions or precedents, "*it is an original power*," and to destroy it would be an absurdity, for it would at once strike down all order and all law ; for if one man can assault a member of a deliberative body with impunity, then an overwhelming force of conspirators could with equal propriety drive us from our seats and break up the Convention.

It is fortunate for the history of civilization that a breach of privilege is of rare occurrence. Many generations have passed away since a thing of the kind has occurred in England. In France, since the establishment of its deliberative bodies, at the close of the reign of Louis XVI, in the highest excitement of the conventions which were assembled in the "reign of terror," there never occurred a breach of privilege. In the British Parliament and in our national Congress and State Legislatures, contempts growing out of witnesses refusing to answer, or attempts to bribe members, are not uncommon. All the deliberative bodies referred to have asserted the right to protect themselves by punishing the contumacious witness and the dishonest citizen ; but the punishment of the breach of privilege, viz: the assault of a member of a deliberative body for his official acts is rare indeed, because in all Christian countries, when the people have elected their representatives to deliberate for the good of the State or nation, a profound respect is enteraine d by the people for their own sacred rights, for the time being, centered and personated in their chosen representatives.

In the year 1832 the nation was profoundly agitated by a breach of privilege committed upon a member of Congress, the facts of which regarding the assault are stated in the following note:

"*To the Hon. A. Stevenson, Speaker of the House of Representatives:*

"*Sir*—I was waylaid in the street near to my boarding-house last night about 8 o'clock, attacked and knocked down by a bludgeon, and severely bruised and wounded by Samuel Houston, late of Tennessee, for words spoken in my place in the House of Representatives, by reason of which I am confined to my bed and unable to discharge my duties in the House, and attend to the interest of my constituents. I communicate this information to you, and request that you will lay it before the House. Very respectfully, yours,

"William Stansberry,

"Member of the H. R. from Ohio.

"April 14th, 1832."

After the reading of the communication, Mr. Vance, of Ohio, offered the following resolution:

"*Resolved*, That the speaker do issue his warrant, directed to the sergeant-at-arms attending to the House, commanding him to take in custody, wherever to be found, the body of Samuel Houston, and the same in his custody to keep, subject further to the order and decision of the House."

His resolution called forth an exciting debate, and the able men then in Congress expressed their views with the ability and freedom that characterized our national representatives of that era.

Mr. Jenifer, of Maryland, observed to those who moved to lay the subject on the table, that he did not suppose it were possible that a single voice could have been raised in that House or nation against the exercise of a power which must be dictated by common sense. The constitution imperatively called upon them as representatives of the people, to protect themselves in the exercise of their duty. He then read the article of the constitution, conferring the power, and maintained it to be the duty of the House to protect itself from assassins. Mr. Jenifer concluded by demanding the yeas and nays upon the resolution.

Mr. Speight, of North Carolina, moved to amend the resolution by striking out all after the word resolved and inserting the following:

"That a select committee be appointed to whom shall be referred the communication of the Hon. W. Stansberry, a member of the House of the State of Ohio, in relation to an assault committed on him by Samuel Houston, with power to take such steps as will insure a thorough investigation of the transaction."

Mr. Coulter, of Pennsylvania, said that if the House were to adopt the course proposed by Mr. Speight, they would apply the torch and the torpedo to the sanitary power of the House vested in it by the constitution. The House must necessarily possess in itself (without the interference of a committee) the power of protecting its own deliberations. He said if a member whose person had been assailed in the public streets for words uttered in debate was to be thrown off to a distance, till reports of committees were proposed and debated, they might as well leave Mr. Stansberry to bring his complaint before a justice of the peace, and thus subject the privilege of that House, privileges of the people of the United States, to the determination and award of the court which sat in the neighboring building.

Mr. Conneter, of Pennsylvania, in the face of the power of the House to punish hierarchy privileges, said that if it were otherwise the members of the House had better remain within their own State, where patriotism might speak without the fear of the bravo. They would retire from the ten miles square, and abandon it to the contest of bullies and blackguards.

The debate was concluded by Mr. Everett of Massachusetts, who ended his remarks by saying what was done by an individual might be done by armed mobs. Suppose, then, that an armed mob, instead of insulting an individual, should waylay twenty or thirty of the members, would the insulted members ever turn to the courts of the district to seek redress for assault and battery. The case need but be stated to insure its consideration. Why was the place of assembly removed from Philadelphia? Was it because an insult had been offered to one of their body? No personal violence was offered; no one was kept at home; no encroachments upon the privileges and interruption of the balance took place; but an insult was offered. They were told at the time that the State would protect them; that its courts were open to them, and that it would extend the shield of its whole authority over them, but Congress said no; we will go where we can establish a jurisdiction, where we can protect ourselves without needing the aid of constables or sheriffs. It was for this reason that the government fixed its seat on the Potomac, where it now stands, and if ever the time should come when an assault committed on a member for words spoken in debate is to be turned on the courts, the constitution would be no longer worth living under; they had better at once break up and go home or return to a state of nature. Mr. Wickliffe called for the yeas and nays, and the motion of Mr. Vance was carried by 145 yeas against 25 nays. Not a member of Congress from Louisiana voted against the resolution, and for representatives at the time were the Hon. E. D. White, of Lafourche, and that eminent patriot, Gen. Philemon Thomas, of Baton Rouge.

In accordance with the preceedings noted and the subsequent action, Samuel Houston was brought to the bar of the House, was allowed counsel, and all the forms of a legal trial were gone through with, and the prisoner found guilty of the charges brought against him.

There then arose in Congress a warm debate as to the punishment that should be inflicted; it was finally accepted that the House had no power to imprison beyond its sitting, and that it was in their power to choose between imprisonment and a reprimand from the speaker.

The resolution was finally adopted, that Samuel Houston be brought to the bar of the House on Monday next, at 12 o'clock, that he be reprimanded by the speaker for the contempt and violations of the privileges of the House, of which he has been guilty, and that he be then discharged from the custody of the sergeant-at-arms.

In the fulfilling of the important trust imposed upon the speaker, among other things, in reprimanding the prisoner, he said: "If, in fulfilling the order of the House, if I were called upon as its presiding officer to reprimand an individual uneducated or uninformed, it might be expected that I should endeavor, as far as I was able, to impress upon him the importance and propriety of sedulously guarding from violation the rights and privileges secured to the members of the House by our valuable constitution, but when addressing a citizen of your character and intelligence as one who has himself been honored by the people with a seat in this House, it cannot be necessary that I should add to the duty enjoined upon me by dwelling upon the character and consequences of the offence of which you have been charged and found guilty." Whatever has a tendency to impair the freedom of debate in this House—a freedom no less sacred than the authority of the constitution itself, or to detract from the independence of the representatives of the people in the rightful discharge of these high privileges, you are no doubt sensible, must in the same proportion mar and degrade, not only the Legislature itself, but the character of our free institutions.

There was nothing physically atrocious in the attack made upon the honorable member of this Convention, but the sentiment intended by the offender was evidently that the assaulted party might be disgraced, and through him bring contempt upon this body. Under any circumstances, the Convention would be indifferent to its honor if a case of this kind, however superficially unimportant, were passed over without some notice. New Orleans, the metropolitan city of the South, will show, by examination of her judicial and criminal records, that the large mass of her citizens have always been law-abiding; yet her public character for peace and order has been, more or less, always misrepresented abroad by acts of a certain class in the community who seem to have presumed, in their especial cases, upon their power to over-ride justice and escape punishment—an evil in society, and especially in a city like New Orleans, made up of a hetereogenous population—though originally small in itself, like a revolving ball of snow, naturally enlarges by its onward progress; and the liberty of a few to take in their own hands the law of redressing their real or imaginary wrongs, from what would be scarcely noticeable at first, in time becomes a fearful evil and a reign of terror, results under the influence of which the liberty of speech and liberty of political action become nullities. There has been a time in New Orleans when peaceful citizens were publicly struck down at the polls and assaulted in the highways, by a combination of men whose influence and acts, however baneful and reprehensible, generally escaped punishment; and these things, so disgraceful to modern civilization, were falsely glossed over in the crystalization of a narrow-minded and false political principle, and made especially offensive to that class of citizens who, from the oppressed countries of Europe, have fled here for an asylum of peace and a quiet home.

This honorable body has no power o¶ give vitality to good laws left inoperative by the supineness of its ministers, nor is it in the power of this Convention to produce a direct reform in the evils of which all good men and well-wishers of the prospect of this city have complained; nor is it just and proper that we should not use all charity with regard to the character of the House, knowing full well that not only in times of civil war, but in the years that precede such a sad catastrophe, the moral sense of the people suffer, and bad men take advantage of the disintegration that constantly goes on.

In conclusion, we would recommend, that if the members of this Convention are satisfied with the evidence, as it now stands before them, that a breach of privilege has been committed, that the accused be arrested and brought within the bar of this House and receive a reprimand therefor from the president of this Convention, and then be discharged, to the effect that they may place upon the records of this Convention our detestation of the principle of individuals taking the law of personal redress, for supposed or real wrongs, into their own hands.

(Signed) T. B. THORPE,
J. H. WILSON,
ALFRED SHAW.

Mr. THOMAS—I move it be received, and made the order of the day for Wednesday.

[A motion to lay it on the table was lost.]

Mr. DUANE—I move the rules be suspended to adopt the report.

[Lost, 37 only voting in the affirmative. The motion of Mr. Thomas was carried.]

PRESIDENT—Unfinished business is next in order.

Mr. HENDERSON—I call for the resolution rescinding the action of this Convention in relation to the resignation of Judge Howell.

[The resolution was read.]

Mr. HENDERSON—I believe that each and every gentleman who has been elected by his constituents and has the qualifications required by law should remain a member of this body until we have completed our business. I do not speak particularly with reference to Judge Howell, but because when the question came up first I acted in reference to Mr. Roselius. I admire the scholarship and experience of that gentleman, but when he could not take the prescribed oath and voluntarily withdrew, I could do no differently than move that his resignation be accepted. I know that every one of us feel high respect for the gentleman in question and will be glad if he withdraws his resignation, and he is permitted to act as before; and I hope that this body will show the proper kindness of disposition and charity of feeling and permit the resignation to be withdrawn. Therefore, I move now that the action of this body in relation to the acceptance of Judge Howell's resignation be rescinded.

Mr. STAUFFER—I agree with the gentleman in regard to the respect this body has for Judge Howell, but I wish to know the reason for which he sent in his resignation. Certainly he considered the subject before sending it in, and the circumstances that brought us here are such that every patriotic man in the State of Louisiana and throughout the United States would be willing to come forward and accept a seat here, and, after having done so, to hold it. I cannot conceive why any member of this Convention, after having remained here for twenty-five days, should withdraw from it when we have come to the most important business. I voted for his resignation and to suspend the rules and adopt the resolution. If he is willing to come forward and cast his vote on this question, I will vote to rescind the resolution passed here; but if it is for any other reason, I will vote against it. I came here to perform my duty faithfully, to the best of my ability, and do what I could for the benefit of my constituents, and I shall stand by this Convention even if I am the last man. I am not afraid of the circumstances that surround us; I am not afraid to stand anywhere and everywhere and raise my voice in defence of my country. Therefore I say, when a man resigns his seat in this Convention, he should state his reasons. If it is his desire to come back into the Convention, I want to make a proviso that he shall apologize to this Convention when he comes in; otherwise I shall vote against receiving him back again.

Mr. ABELL—I believe the ostensible cause of his resigning is that he was called in person to give some account why he remained out four or five days. That was on my motion; but every member in this House knows that I have no animosity against him, because, first and last, I sustained him for the president of this body. I state this to show that I was not actuated by any kind of ill feelings towards him; I have the highest esteem for him, as well as for Mr. Roselius; but on both occasions I have stood firm for the acceptance of their resignations. I occasionally play with children, but when it comes to men, I remain firm with them. We are elected here to represent the people, and I contend gentlemen have no right to be absent from this House, and if absent myself an unreasonable time, I should thank a gentleman to take occasion to call me by name, if he sees proper, and have me brought into this House to show why I was neglecting the business of the people. I shall oppose any rescinding of the orders of this House in regard to Judge Howell or any other gentleman on this floor, whatever may be his pretensions or name. If he sees proper to disregard the duty he owes to his constituents and the Convention, let him go, in the name of peace.

[The yeas and nays were called for on the motion of Mr. Henderson, and the roll was called with the following result:

YEAS—Messrs. Ariail, Bailey, Barrett, Bonzano, Brott, Campbell, Cazabat, Cook J. K., Cook T., Cutler, Davies, Duane, Dufresne, Duke, Ennis, Fosdick, Fuller, Gastinel, Goldman, Gorlinski, Harnan, Heard, Henderson, Hills, Hire, Howes, Knobloch, Maas, Mann, Mendiverri, Millspaugh, Murphy E., Normand, Ong, Payne J., Seymour, Spellicy, Stocker, Stumpf, Stiner, Taliaferro, Thorpe, Waters, Wells, Wilson—45.

NAYS—Messrs. Abell, Bell, Bofill, Buckley, Burke, Collin, Crozat, Dupaty, Edwards, Flagg, Flood, Geier, Gruneberg, Healy, Hart, Maurer, Montamat, Murphy M. W., Mayer, Newell, O'Conner, Pintado, Purcell J., Pursell S., Schroeder, Schnurr, Stauffer, Sullivan, Terry—29.

The resolution was carried.]

Mr. MONTAMAT—I move to adjourn.

Mr. HILLS—I call for the yeas and nays.

[The call was not sustained and a rising vote taken; yeas 34, nays 38. The motion was lost.

It was stated there was no quorum present, and the calling of the roll demanded. The roll was called and seventy-six members responded.]

Mr. MONTAMAT—I move to adjourn.

Mr. HILLS—I demand the yeas and nays on the motion.

[The demand was sustained and the roll called, with the following result:

YEAS—Messrs. Abell, Ariail, Bailey, Bofill, Brott, Buckley, Burke, Collin, Cook J. K., Dufresne, Duke, Dupaty, Flagg, Fuller, Gastinel, Geier, Gruneberg, Harnan, Hart, Heard, Henderson, Howes, Knobloch, Maas, Maurer, Mayer, Mendiverri, Montamat, Murphy M. W., O'Conner, Purcell J., Schnurr, Seymour, Spellicy, Sullivan, Waters—36.

NAYS—Messrs. Barrett, Bell, Bonzano, Cazabat, Cook T., Crozat, Cutler, Davies, Duane, Edwards, Ennis, Flood, Fosdick, Goldman, Gorlinski, Healy, Hills, Hire, Mann, Millspaugh, Murphy E., Newell, Normand, Ong, Payne J., Pintado, Pursell S., Schroeder, Shaw, Smith, Stocker, Stumpf, Stiner, Stauffer, Taliaferro, Terry, Thorpe, Wells, Wilson—39.

The motion was lost.

The majority report of the Committee on Emancipation, being the order of the day, was read by the secretary.

AN ORDINANCE TO ABOLISH SLAVERY AND INVOLUNTARY SERVITUDE.

We, the people of the State of Louisiana in Convention assembled, do hereby declare and ordain as follows:

Section 1. Slavery and involuntary servitude, except as a punishment for crime, whereof the party shall have been duly convicted, are hereby forever abolished and prohibited throughout the State.

Sec. 2. The Legislature shall make no law recognizing the right of property in man.

Sec. 3. The code of laws known as the Black Code, and legislation on the subject of slavery, are hereby declared annulled and abolished.

Sec. 4. No penal laws shall be made against persons of African descent, different from those enacted against white persons.

Sec. 5. The Legislature shall, at its first session under this constitution, enact laws providing for the indenture of persons of African descent as apprentices to citizens of the State, on the same terms and conditions as those prescribed, or which may hereafter be prescribed, for the apprenticing of white persons.

Adopted in Convention this — day of ——, in the year of our Lord one thousand eight hundred and sixty-four, and of the Independence of the United States eighty-eight.

M. F. BONZANO, Chairman,
A. CAZABAT,
H. C. EDWARDS,
EDMUND GOLDMAN,
E. MURPHY,
T. B. SCHROEDER,
W. T. STOCKER,
R. K. HOWELL.

Mr. WILSON—I amend the first section by adding the words "and that loyal owners be compensated."

Mr. CAZABAT—I move to lay the amendment on the table.

Mr. HILLS—I call for the reading of the section as amended.

[The section was read.

The yeas and nays were demanded on Mr. Cazabat's motion and the roll called, with the following result:

YEAS—Messrs. Ariail, Austin, Bailey, Bonzano, Burke, Collin, Cazabat, Cook J. K., Cutler, Davies, Duane, Dupaty, Edwards, Ennis, Fish, Flagg, Flood, Foley, Fosdick, Goldman, Gorlinski, Healy, Harnan, Hills, Hire, Howes, Maas, Mann, Millspaugh, Murphy E., Newell, Normand, Payne J., Pintado, Pursell S., Schroeder, Schnurr, Shaw, Smith, Spellicy, Stauffer, Taliaferro, Terry, Thorpe, Wells—45.

NAYS—Messrs. Abell, Barrett, Bell, Bofill, Brott, Buckley, Cook T., Crozat, Dufresne, Duke, Fuller, Gruneberg, Hart, Heard, Henderson, Knobloch, Maurer, Mayer, Mendiverri, Montamat, Murphy M. W., O'Conner, Ong, Seymour, Stocker, Stumpf, Stiner, Sullivan, Waters, Wilson—30.

Cries of "no quorum."]

Mr. MONTAMAT—I move we adjourn.

[The yeas and nays were called.

YEAS—Messrs. Abell, Bofill, Buckley, Burke, Collin, Cook J. K., Crozat, Duane, Dufresne, Duke, Dupaty, Fuller, Heard, Henderson, Knobloch, Maas, Maurer, Mayer, Mendiverri, Montamat, Murphy M. W., O'Conner, Ong, Schnurr, Seymour, Stocker, Stumpf, Sullivan, Waters—29.

NAYS—Messrs. Ariail, Austin, Bailey, Barrett, Bell, Bonzano, Brott, Cazabat, Cook T., Cutler, Davies, Ennis, Flagg, Flood, Foley, Fosdick, Goldman, Gorlinski, Healy, Harnan, Hart, Hills, Hire, Howes, Mann, Millspaugh, Murphy E., Newell, Normand, Payne J., Pintado, Pursell S., Schroeder, Shaw, Smith, Spellicy, Stiner, Stauffer, Taliaferro, Terry, Thorpe, Wells and Wilson—43.

The motion was lost.

The section was then adopted by a *viva voce* vote.]

Mr. MONTAMAT — There is no quorum voting. I protest against the action of the House.

PRESIDENT—The gentleman is out of order.

[Section second was read.]

Mr. HILLS—I move its adoption.

Mr. ABELL—Mr. President, is this question going to be thus thrust down the throats of the people? I know it can be thrust down the throats of the Convention without any deliberation. But when you attempt to thrust it down the throats of the people, it is a different affair. And I tell you that if you persist in doing business in this manner, if you refuse a call of the House when it is called for—when from repeated votes it is evident that there is not a quorum present—I can only say the people, the honest people, of the State of Louisiana will not recognize your action. It cannot be expected that they will recognize it. What, sir, is this second proposition? [A voice—"A very good one."] Yes, a very good one, I grant, but it may involve us in a world of trouble; but, sir, Mr. Montamat has twice demanded a call of the House, and shall we proceed in this hasty and unceremonious manner, to use the power of this Convention to cram this thing down the throats of the people of Louisiana when we have no quorum. Let us hear what it is we are forcing upon them read.

[The secretary read—"The Legislature shall make no law recognizing the right of property in man."]

Mr. ABELL—Is this the great question that is to be crowded through this Convention in this unceremonious manner, and crammed down the throats of the people of one of the greatest and noblest of communities that has ever graced the union of States?

I have fought this question in another form. I have fought it to the best of my power and abilities. I have no personal property interest in the question to fight for. I own very little property—none that would be affected by it—and I only fight it on account of the injustice that would inevitably result from it.

It is only the other day that my friend from the Second District (Mr. Hills) accused me, very unjustly as I believe you are all satisfied, with having aided the rebellion. Why, sir, when you adopt this report you aid the rebels more than you would by marching ten thousand armed men to their support. You sow seeds of bitterness, ruin and desolation that will never be rooted up. You say to the rebels we are sure to tear away from loyal men hundreds of millions of property.

Mr. CAZABAT—Mr. President, I move that members be prohibited from going out. We have no quorum.

Mr. ABELL—I move a call of the House.

PRESIDENT—The gentleman must proceed with his argument according to parliamentary rules. No gentleman has a right to demand a call of the House repeatedly for the purpose of impeding business. The doorkeeper will close the door and permit no member to pass out.

[The roll was called and a quorum answered to their names, after the sergeant-at-arms had brought in a number of absentees.]

Mr. STAUFFER—Mr. President, I move the previous question.

[The question was put.]

Mr. CAMPBELL—I do not understand this. I cannot vote. I cannot vote unless I understand on what I am voting.

PRESIDENT—If the gentleman had been in his seat he would have known. The question is upon the adoption of the second section of the majority report of the Committee on Emancipation. The previous question has been moved, which cuts off all debate.

Mr. CAMPBELL—I would ask if this is on its second or third reading.

PRESIDENT—The second.

Mr. CAMPBELL—All right. I have a proviso which I wish to move as an amendment to the first.

PRESIDENT—You are too late, it is already adopted.

Mr. CAMPBELL—That is what I protest against, in the name of my constituents. I will read it.

PRESIDENT—You are out of order. You will sit down.

Mr. HILLS — Mr. President, as we have already adopted a resolution which requires every vote on the question of emancipation to be taken by yeas and nays, the first section not having been so voted on, is not adopted. I move that we take the vote over.

[Mr. Campbell proceeded to read his proviso.]

Mr. HENDERSON—I call the gentleman to order.

PRESIDENT — The sergeant-at-arms will take the gentleman in custody and keep him in custody. We must have order.

[Mr. Campbell continued to read his proviso—many members rising to their feet, crying "order," "put him out," etc., causing a scene of confusion, amid which many remarks were lost by the reporters. The sergeant-at-arms, with one of his assistants, approached Mr. Campbell and made a feeble attempt to pacify him, but he shook them off without paying them the slightest attention, until he had read his proviso to the end, and then he resumed his seat, and they gave up the attempt to arrest him.

The secretary proceeded to call the roll.]

Mr. BUCKLEY—Are we to be pressed in this way?

Mr. SULLIVAN—Do I understand this to be the first or second reading?

Mr. STAUFFER—I move that Mr. Abell be required to vote on this question, or that he be expelled from this Convention.

Mr. MONTAMAT—Amendments are in order.

Mr. SULLIVAN—It seems there is a party here oppressing us.

Mr. ABELL—Mr. President, I have a right to explain my vote.

PRESIDENT — Yes, but not to make an argument.

Mr. STAUFFER—Under the rules, the gentleman has no right to explain his vote. I came here to vote on this question, and I intend to do it, if we stay here till doomsday.

Mr. HILLS—I move a suspension of the rules, in order to allow the gentleman to explain his vote.

PRESIDENT—Do gentlemen wish to disgrace themselves, this Convention and the people that sent them here, by such proceedings. Cannot you keep order? I think that there is no intention on the part of the majority to oppress the minority; but I do think there is evidently an intention on the part of the minority to prevent the majority from doing business. You must abide by the rules of your own making; it is the only way to do business in this the highest legislative body known in our land.

I want every officer of this Convention to obey the president when he gives an order. I want the officer to have nerve enough and physical force enough to enforce the rules which govern this Convention, and when a member shows himself in such a condition of mind that he is willing not only to disgrace himself before the people, but to throw contempt upon this Convention, I want the officer of this Convention whose duty it is to obey the president to do his duty, which has not been done this morning. Now let us go on. The gentleman has a right to explain his vote, but if he proceeds to make an argument I shall bring down the speaker's hammer, and I hope that it will be obeyed.

Mr. ABELL—I desire to say that I am not prepared to act on this question until the amendment of Mr. Campbell has been acted on. As he has offered an amendment, it is due to the citizens of Louisiana, whom we are here to represent, it is due to justice, to common naked justice, that this amendment should go before the Convention, before I, as a representative of the people, am called on to cast my vote.

Mr. HENDERSON—I have not heard the

gentleman vote. Every member must vote on this question.

Mr. ABELL—I vote no.

[Mr. Campbell, when his name was called, declined to answer.]

Mr. HENDERSON—I give notice that I shall prefer charges against the gentleman for refusing to attend to the business before the Convention. He is evidently paying no attention; while this vote is being taken, he is reading a newspaper.

Mr. CAMPBELL—Mr. President, I do not know what I am voting for. I offered a proviso to this, and you have not put the proviso.

PRESIDENT—Take your seat.

[Mr. Collin's name was called by the secretary.]

Mr. COLLIN—I should like to know what I am voting for. Mr. Campbell has offered an amendment. I should like to vote on the amendment.

PRESIDENT—You will sit down and vote.

[The secretary proceeded to the end of the roll without further interruption.]

Mr. HENDERSON—Before taking up the next section, it is but right that the gentlemen who have refused to vote on this should be called upon to vote, or state their reasons for refusing.

Mr. COLLIN—I vote "no."

Mr. CAMPBELL—Upon section 1st, as read here, I vote "no."

Mr. MONTAMAT—I move we adjourn.

Mr. HILLS—I call for the ayes and noes.

[The call was sustained and the result was as follows:

YEAS—Messrs. Abell, Ariail, Bailey, Bofill, Brott, Buckley, Burke, Collin, Cook J. K., Dufresne, Duke, Dupaty, Flagg, Fuller, Gastinel, Geier, Gruneberg, Harnan, Hart, Heard, Henderson, Howes, Knobloch, Maas, Maurer, Mayer, Mendiverri, Montamat, Murphy M. W., O'Conner, Purcell J., Schnurr, Seymour, Spellicy, Sullivan and Waters—36.

NAYS—Messrs. Barrett, Bell, Bonzano, Cazabat, Cook T., Crozat, Cutler, Davies, Duane, Edwards, Ennis, Flood, Fosdick, Goldman, Gorlinski, Healy, Hills, Hire, Mann, Millspaugh, Murphy E., Newell, Normand, Ong, Payne J., Pintado, Pursell S., Schroeder, Shaw, Smith, Stocker, Stumpf, Stiner, Stauffer, Taliaferro, Terry, Thorpe, Wells and Wilson—39.

Mr. ABELL—On this question I have the floor. Do I understand that after I have opened the debate on a question—

Mr. HILLS—I understood that the previous question was moved on the second section.

PRESIDENT—It was. The secretary will call the roll.

Mr. HEARD—Mr. President, I rise to a point of order.

PRESIDENT—In rising to a point of order when the ayes and noes are being called the gentleman is out of order.

Mr. ABELL—It must go down. Let us take it.

[The secretary proceeded to call the roll.]

Mr. MONTAMAT—I desire to explain my vote. I am in favor of the section, but as there is an attempt to oppress the minority, I vote no.

Mr. FOLEY—I move to adjourn.

Mr. TERRY—I call the ayes and noes.

[The call was sustained and the motion follows:

YEAS—Messrs. Ariail, Austin, Bailey, Barrett, Bell, Bonzano, Brott, Burke, Collin, Cazabat, Cook J. K., Cook T., Crozat, Cutler, Davies, Duane, Dupaty, Edwards, Ennis, Fish, Flagg, Flood, Foley, Fosdick, Fuller, Goldman, Gorlinski, Healy, Harnan, Hart, Henderson, Hills, Hire, Howes, Maas. Mann, Millspaugh, Murphy E., Murphy M. W., Newell, Normand, O'Conner, Ong, Payne J., Pintado, Purcell J., Pursell S., Schroeder, Schnurr, Shaw, Smith, Spellicy, Stocker, Stumpf, Stiner, Stauffer, Taliaferro, Terry, Thorpe, Thomas, Wells, Wilson—62.

NAYS—Messrs. Abell, Bofill, Buckley, Campbell, Dufresne, Duke, Gastinel, Heard, Knobloch, Maurer, Mayer, Mendiverri, Montamat, Seymour, Sullivan, Waters—16.

And the Convention adjourned.]

TWENTY-SEVENTH DAY.

TUESDAY, May 10, 1864.

[At 12 o'clock M., the president called the Convention to order, and the proceedings were opened with prayer by Rev. Mr. Strong.

Upon calling the roll the following gentlemen answered to their names:

Messrs. Abell, Ariail, Austin, Barrett, Baum, Beauvais, Bell, Bennie, Bofill, Bonzano, Burke, Collin, Cazabat, Cook J. K., Crozat, Decker, Duane, Dufresne, Duke, Edwards, Ennis, Fish, Flagg, Flood, Fosdick,

Gastinel, Geier, Goldman, Gorlinski, Healy, Harnan, Hart, Heard, Hills, Hire, Kavanagh, Knobloch, Maas, Mann, Mayer, Mendiverri, Millspaugh, Murphy M. W., Newell, Normand, O'Conner, Ong, Orr, Payne J., Poynot, Pursell S., Schroeder, Stauffer, Schnurr, Seymour, Spellicy, Stumpf, Stiner, Sullivan, Taliaferro, Terry, Thomas, Wells and Wilson—64.

There being no quorum, the sergeant-at-arms was instructed to bring in absent members.

The following gentlemen having entered the hall, viz: Messrs. Bailey, Beauvais, Buckley, Cook T., Davies, Dupaty, Foley, Henderson, Morris, Murphy E., Montamat, Maurer, Purcell J., Stocker and Thorpe, constituting a quorum,

The minutes of the previous day's proceedings were read and adopted.

The names of members who had not previously voted on the motion to reject Mr. Abell's minority report of the Committee on Emancipation was then called up, with the following result:

YEAS—Mr. Ong.

NAYS—Mr. Schnurr.]

Mr. ABELL—Mr. President, I trust that the motion made by Mr. Hills the other day will be enforced. I notice Mr. Wenck has not yet voted on that question. He was here yesterday, and when the subject was brought up left very suddenly. I hope he will be brought in.

Mr. DUANE—I would mention that Mr. Wenck is very sick. I met him on the way home.

Mr. ABELL—He is not too sick to be in the streets.

Mr. BUCKLEY—I saw him in his office this morning. He did not appear to be sick.

Mr. HILLS—I trust that the sergeant-at-arms will be instructed to bring in all members in the city to vote on the questions discussed yesterday.

Mr. WELLS—I move that the doors be closed for one hour.

Mr. ABELL—I move that the members not in the city be excused from voting.

PRESIDENT—Mr. Secretary, call the names of those who have not voted.

The names were called.

Mr. ABELL—Mr. President, I desire the secretary to call the name of Mr. Balch. He is a very independent man, and will vote yes or no.

Mr. BALCH—I vote no.

Mr. ORR—I desire to make a few remarks.

PRESIDENT—You can explain your vote, but you have no right to make an argument.

Mr. MANN—I desire to call the attention of the president to rule XVII.

Mr. ORR—If I am not permitted to say now what I desire to say, I shall take another occasion to say it. I vote yes.

Mr. CAMPBELL—Mr. President, I should like to see the rule that requires a man to vote to-day on a question that was disposed of yesterday.

Mr. FOLEY—I hope Mr. Wenck will be sent for.

PRESIDENT—I understand that he is sick.

Mr. THOMAS—I left him in court an hour ago.

Mr. ABELL—I have seen him perambulating the streets this morning, looking as well as anybody.

Mr. HILLS—I hope the sergeant-at-arms will either bring him or a surgeon's certificate that he is not able to come.

Mr. HEARD—Mr. President, I wish to explain the absence of my colleague, Mr. Kugler. He received a dispatch from Baton Rouge Saturday, and important business called him home for a short time. When he returns he will record his vote.

Mr. ABELL—Mr. Gruneberg is a very good kind of man, and has not, I believe, voted on the first two sections of the majority report. I move that he be brought in.

[Mr. Wenck was brought in, and the result of the vote was as follows:

YEAS—Messrs. Baum, Beauvais, Geier, Kavanagh, Morris, Orr and Poynot.

NAYS—Mr. Balch.]

Mr. GORLINSKI—Mr. President, the Committee on Internal Improvement is ready to report.

Mr. CAMPBELL—I have a minority report.

Mr. HILLS—Mr. President, I move that these reports be received, printed and taken up in their order.

[The motion was carried.]

Mr. STOCKER—Mr. President, the Committee on Absent Members, on account of the difficulty of getting information from the country, are not prepared to report, and ask further time.

Mr. STUMPF—Mr. President, I call up my resolution offered yesterday.

[Secretary read the resolution.]

Mr. HIRE—I move that it be referred to the Committee on Emancipation.

Mr. CAZABAT—I offer this resolution as a substitute:

Resolved, That a committee of five be appointed by the president of this Convention, to draw appropriate resolutions expressing and recommending to the president and Congress of the United States the justice and equity of making such appropriations as may be deemed proper and right for a fair compensation to loyal citizens of Louisiana for the loss of their property, upon such terms, conditions and proof as may be required.

Mr. ABELL—I move to amend by adding the words, "this shall be done before any slave is freed."

[The chair put the question and declared it carried.]

Mr. ABELL—Mr. President, was that carried with my amendment?

PRESIDENT—No, sir. Your amendment was not seconded.

Mr. ABELL—I think it was seconded by at least six.

PRESIDENT—Gentlemen must speak so as to be heard by the chair.

Mr. BELL—I call up my resolution, tendering the thanks of this body to Capt. Hoyt for fitting up this hall.

[Secretary read.]

Mr. STOCKER—I should like to inquire when that was offered.

SECRETARY—Last Thursday.

PRESIDENT—It is withdrawn, then. It should have been called up the next day.

Mr. BELL—Do I understand that when a member is prevented from calling up a resolution the next day after it is offered, that it cannot be called up subsequently.

PRESIDENT—Yes; such is the rule adopted by the Convention. Gentlemen must take care of their own offspring.

Mr. PURSELL, of Jefferson—I call up my resolution.

Mr. STAUFFER—I move that it be referred to a special committee of five, to be appointed by the president.

Mr. THORPE—I brought a resolution before the House the other day for information as to how many copies of the journals and debates should be printed. There was an error in the resolution, which I desire to have corrected. The word "debates" was omitted. I desire to amend the resolution by inserting the words "and debates" after the word "journal," and move that the rules be suspended in order to take up the question now.

[The motion was put: ayes, 44. Less than two-thirds the members present having voted for suspension of the rules, the motion was lost.

Messrs. Wenck and Decker having been brought in by the sergeant-at-arms, were called upon to vote on the question of the previous day.

Mr. Wenck voted "aye" on the motion to reject Mr. Abell's minority report, and on the motions to adopt the first two articles of the majority report.

Mr. Decker, on the same questions, voted "no."]

Mr. ABELL—Mr. President, I wish to give notice that I shall offer amendments to several articles of the majority report as they come up. I shall offer an amendment to the third section, to the fourth section, to the first clause of the fifth section, and to the second clause of the fifth section.

[Secretary read Art. 3.]

Mr. GOLDMAN—I move its adoption.

Mr. ABELL—I move to amend by adding the words: "Provided, always, that the Legislature shall never pass any act authorizing free negroes to vote, or to immigrate into this State, under any pretence whatever."

Mr. MONTAMAT—I second that.

Mr. GORLINSKI—I move to amend by adding the word "forever" to the end of the section.

Mr. BONZANO—I move to lay the amendment on the table.

Mr. FOLEY—I call for a division of the amendment.

Mr. HENDERSON—I moved to lay the amendment on the table. A motion for a division of the question having been made, I withdraw my motion. I wish to vote for the first clause of the amendment, but not for the second.

[The ayes and noes were called, and a call of the roll ordered.]

Mr. DAVIES—I move to lay it on the table.

Mr. ABELL—Mr. President—

PRESIDENT—Do not interrupt the calling of the roll.

Mr. ABELL—I ask that the president state the question fairly and in parliamentary form.

PRESIDENT—I have stated it fully and fairly. This incessant interruption is intended to interrupt and embarrass the proceedings.

Mr. ABELL—[emphatically]—I DENY IT.

PRESIDENT—I will state it again. The question is on the laying on the table the first part of the amendment of Mr. Abell, to the first article of the report of the Committee on Emancipation. "Notwithstanding the Legislature shall never pass any act to permit free negroes to vote." Those who vote aye, vote to lay the amendment on the table. Those who vote no, vote against laying the amendment on the table.

[The secretary proceeded to call the roll.]

Mr. STAUFFER—If there is no objection, I desire to explain my vote.

Mr. STOCKER—The gentleman was right to explain his vote.

[Consent was given by the Convention.]

Mr. STAUFFER—I vote to lay the amendment on the table, because it is a question that belongs to the legislative department, and not to that of emancipation.

Mr. BONZANO—I shall vote to lay it on the table, because it would be out of place as a part of the article.

Mr. DAVIES—I moved to lay it on the table, because it was out of place.

Mr. HILLS—I vote to lay it on the table, because the subject belongs to the legislative department and not that of emancipation.

Mr. STOCKER—I vote against laying it on the table, because a negro shall never vote in this State with my consent.

Mr. GOLDMAN—I think the gentleman, being a member of the Committee on Emancipation, had no right to move an amendment, but should have made his recommehdations in his minority report.

PRESIDENT—Are you explaining your vote?

Mr. GOLDMAN—No, sir.

PRESIDENT—You are out of order.

Mr. SHAW—I rise, Mr. President, to a question of order. It is this: An amendment ought to be germain to the subject of the original proposition which it proposes to amend; and I think you should rule this amendment out of order on the ground that it has nothing to do with the subject of the proposition it proposes to amend.

Mr. THORPE—I vote to lay the amendment on the table, because I agree with the gentleman who has just spoken, that it is not germain to the subject of the section proposed to be amended.

Mr. SHAW—I would like for the chair to decide that question.

PRESIDENT—The chair decides that it is germain to the subject and in order.

Mr. GOLDMAN—I believe that the gentleman who offered it, being a member of the Committee on Emancipation, had no right to move an amendment to that report, and therefore I ask to be excused from voting.

[The Convention refused to excuse Mr. Goldman from voting, and the following was the result of the vote:

YEAS—Messrs. Ariail, Austin, Bennie, Bonzano, Collin, Cazabat, Cook J. K., Davies, Dupaty, Ennis, Flagg, Flood, Fosdick, Goldman, Gorlinski, Hills, Hire, Maas, Newell, Pintado, Schroeder, Shaw, Stauffer, Taliaferro, Thorpe, Wells—26.

NAYS—Messrs. Abell, Bailey, Barrett, Baum, Beauvais, Bell, Bofill, Buckley, Burke, Cook T., Crozat, Decker, Duane, Dufresne, Duke, Edwards, Fish, Foley, Gastinel, Geier, Gruneberg, Healy, Harnan, Hart, Heard, Henderson, Kavanagh, Knobloch, Mann, Maurer, Mayer, Mendiverri, Millspaugh, Montamat, Morris, Murphy E., Murphy M. W., Normand, O'Conner, Ong, Orr, Payne J., Poynot, Purcell J., Pursell S., Schnurr, Seymour, Spellicy, Stocker, Stumpf, Stiner, Sullivan, Terry, Thomas, Wenck, Wilson—55.

The motion was lost.

The question recurring upon the adoption of the first part of the motion, it was adopted by the following vote:

YEAS—Messrs. Abell, Ariail, Bailey, Barrett, Baum, Bennie, Beauvais, Bell, Bofill, Bonzano, Brott, Buckley, Burke, Cutler, Campbell, Cook J. K., Cook T., Crozat, Davies, Decker, Duane, Dufresne, Duke,

Edwards, Ennis, Fish, Flood, Foley, Fuller, Gastinel, Geier, Gruneberg, Healy, Harnan, Hart, Heard, Henderson, Kugler, Kavanagh, Knobloch, Maas, Mann, Maurer, Mayer, Mendiverri, Millspaugh, Montamat, Morris, Murphy E., Murphy M. W., Newell, Normand, O'Conner, Ong, Orr, Payne J., Poynot, Purcell J., Pursell S., Schroeder, Schnurr, Seymour, Spellicy, Stocker, Stumpf, Stiner, Stauffer, Sullivan, Taliaferro, Terry, Thomas, Wenck, Waters, Wells, Wilson—68.

NAYS — Messrs. Austin, Bennie, Collin, Cazabat, Dupaty, Flagg, Fosdick, Goldman, Gorlinski, Hills, Hire, Pintado, Shaw, Smith, Thorpe—15.]

Mr. FOLEY—I move to lay the last part of the amendment on the table.

Mr. DAVIES—I second the motion.

[The ayes and nays were called with the following result:

YEAS—Messrs. Ariail, Bailey, Bennie, Bonzano, Brott, Burke, Collin, Cazabat, Davies, Duane, Dupaty, Edwards, Ennis, Fish, Flagg, Flood, Fosdick, Geier, Goldman, Gorlinski, Hart, Henderson, Hills, Hire, Maas, Mann, Morris, Murphy E., Normand, Payne J., Pintado, Poynot, Pursell S., Shaw, Smith, Spellicy, Stiner, Stauffer, Terry, Thorpe—40.

NAYS—Messrs. Abell, Austin, Baum, Barrett, Beauvais, Bell, Bofill, Buckley, Cook J. K., Cook T., Crozat, Decker, Dufresne, Duke, Foley, Gastinel, Harnan, Healy, Heard, Kavanagh, Knobloch, Maurer, Mayer, Mendiverri, Millspaugh, Montamat, Murphy M. W., O'Conner, Ong, Orr, Purcell J., Schnurr, Seymour, Stocker, Stumpf, Sullivan, Thomas, Waters, Wenck, Wilson—40.]

Mr. DAVIES—I move that the president vote.

PRESIDENT—The chair would vote, as a matter of course, without a motion. I think the proper parliamentary practice is not to keep up this continual voting to lay on the table, but to come to a direct vote. I shall therefore vote "no," though on a direct vote I should most certainly vote against the amendment.

[The motion to lay on the table was lost.]

Mr. HENDERSON—Mr. President and gentlemen, in 1847 the Wilmot proviso was issued and inserted into both the free and slave States, actually forbidding negro emigration into the States, from which it is easy to see that the Yankee does not love the negro any more than does a Southerner.

I wish gentlemen to understand that I draw a distinction between political franchise and unanimity. I believe that a negro should possess his wife, his house and his horse, but that a negro shall have the same elective franchise as a white man, is impossible. Has the North granted this right to the Indian? No State but Mississippi has done so, and that was on account of Harrison's election. I am in favor of ameliorating their condition. The first subject is emancipation, and without it we are their masters in every respect and must control them.

Why do we not allow women to vote? New Jersey did so for many years, and many a woman in her bloomers, voted for Jackson or whom she pleased. Do not women vote as stockholders in a bank? Yet I am not willing to see them go into the halls of Congress, but prefer to have them mcve in their respective provinces. I want to see man rule.

We have three hundred thousand negroes, and the best way to get rid of them is to let them go into Yankeedom and die there—that is their business. But do not let us keep them among us because they are free. I am in favor of their going from the State, as is provided in the constitution of Missouri; then they can neither get in or out. This is the reason that Indiana has passed the law now in force there. Now women and girls can do some work, but when you come to a plantation, can you hire four or five hundred whites to take the negro's place? No, sir, because it is impossible to control them.

Give to this class permission to go to and fro, acquire property, be qualified citizens, as in case of a woman or a minor, but as to voting—that is another question. As strange as it may seem, Indiana only ceased, in 1852, being a slave State by thirteen votes; yet in this very State a negro can hardly exist. I hope that the day will come when the doctrine of property in a human being will be unknown upon this earth, for I do not believe it is right.

In the days of the Greeks and Romans, about which so many gentlemen are harping, when white men were slaves, compensation was never made. In Massachusetts, this doctrine has been also advocated and sustained in, and by the courts, though *de facto* slavery at that time existed there.

I am in favor of allowing the free negro to go from Massachusetts to California, and anywhere else within the States or territories acquired or hereafter to be acquired by the United States. They are now fighting under yonder flag, and we come here not as worshippers of the Southern cause, but, under a kind Providence, to change our laws and customs so that we may do rightly in the future.

If you adopt this amendment, it will be manifestly against public policy. I must vote against it, and hope that my friends in this Convention will think as I do, and vote that the Legislature shall have no power on the subject. For all these reasons I am in favor of the first and opposed to the second division of the amendment.

Mr. Hills—I repeat I hope that the amendment will not be adopted by this Convention. In the first place, sir, both amendments offered are out of place; they do not belong to this report at all. I shall vote against this amendment for the same reason that I voted against the other—that the subject does not belong here. It belongs to another portion of the constitution. It seems to me it would be very disastrous to the commercial and agricultural interests of this State to prohibit emigration and free egress into this State. We have been told, time after time, that the plantations of Louisiana can only be worked successfully by negro labor, and that the white man is not fitted by nature to till the plantations of this State; and if we are to limit the negro population of the State to those already here and may hereafter be born here, it seems to me we shall put a very serious obstruction in the path of our agricultural interests. The time may come, and very soon, when it may be a public necessity to have negroes brought here for the very purpose of cultivating our plantations; but under this clause of the constitution it is proposed to prevent any such emigration.

Another reason is: I do not believe it is right or just that this Convention should take any such action. I do not believe we have any right or justice to prohibit any class of persons that may choose to do so. I have failed to see any force in the objection of the gentleman who has addressed the House on this question. I fail to see that by allowing the negroes to immigrate here we are to give the State over to them. I do not believe anything of the kind. I believe, as I said before, the Anglo-Saxon is the dominant race in Louisiana and this country, and we need have no fear that the negroes will come to rule us; it is impossible, in the nature of things. For that reason, I do not believe in inserting any such clase in the constitution as has already been adopted—that the Legislature shall never pass any laws authorizing the free negroes to vote. I do not think the Legislature would wish to pass any such laws. I believe it is our business to fix the qualifications, and leave the future Legislatures to take care of themselves. This generation is not in favor of negro equality in any shape.

This proposition to prevent emigration is one that never can be carried. You cannot prevent it, if you try. Under this provision you would prevent negro soldiers from being brought here by the government. How are you going to prevent it? Suppose in times of war negro soldiers are ordered here. Do you suppose this provision of the constitution is going to stop them from coming into the State? Not by any means. You cannot do it; nor can you, with so large a negro population as we have here, and will have for many generations to come, make any law to prevent this emigration. For these reasons I shall vote against the amendment, and hope that it will be voted down by the Convention; for I believe it would be unjust and cruel in itself and opposed to the best interests of the State.

Mr. Stocker—It seems my misfortune to differ very frequently with my friend from the Second District. I hope this proposition will prevail, and a great many of the reasons urged by the gentleman have forced me to that conclusion. My mind was not entirely made up before the gentleman made his remarks; but now I am well satisfied that this amendment should prevail. I am not only in favor of preventing emigration of the negroes, but am also in favor of pushing those out who are already here, [applause] and sending them to Massachusetts, or some other place, where our great philanthropists come from. [Applause.] I am not one of them. I have no friendship for the negro. I am against him and will be against him, and wherever my voice can be raised to put down a negro I will do it, either in the shape of emigration, education, or any other —*tion*.

Mr. STAUFFER—The gentleman is very anxious to send all the negroes out of the State to Massachusetts, or some other State. I ask whether the negroes are not now protecting him and us? [Applause.] Whether they are not garrisoning our forts? Let him go to Carrollton and other places throughout the State, and see what they are doing for us to-day. I am opposed to this resolution for one particular reason, and that is that there is not a clause in the constitution of the United States that forbids any one from coming into the country, and I believe this question belongs to the Legislature and not to this body. We are not here to legislate, but to form a basis for legislation, under peculiar circumstances. I am not willing to say what is going to follow in this State, or any other, when this war is over. It may be—though I trust it will not—that the very men whom the gentlemen wish to expel from the State will be glad to call upon them to defend the homes and families of the gentlemen. [Applause.] The colored population of this State is as willing to fight for our country and to maintain our rights as any member of this Convention. [Applause.]

I, for one, will raise my voice against excluding them from the State. No law that we might make would prevent the military authorities from bringing negroes here when they are required. We are here to form a foundation whereon the Legislature shall act, and not here to legislate specifically. Therefore I am opposed to any decisive action on the matter on the ground taken by the gentleman from the Fifth, (Mr. Abell,) that we represent only a certain portion of this State, but hereafter when this war is over—when the flag of the Union floats over every acre of territory that belongs to the United States—then I will ask you to legislate on this question and not before. [Cheers.] When the proper time comes, let the gentleman, if he is running for the Legislature, advocate the expulsion of the negro, and if I do not agree with him I will oppose him and let the people decide; but I am most emphatically opposed to the question being decided before this House. I believe it is brought up here for no other purpose than to prevent the balance of the resolution being acted upon. I believe the gentleman knows that it does not properly belong here.

Mr. SULLIVAN—I would like to inquire of the gentleman who says the negro soldiers are protecting us, what they did some months ago at Fort Jackson? It seems there are several kinds of abolitionists on the floor. I consider myself a good Union man, but I am not in favor of giving the negro the same right as I possess. There are those who are not really in favor of freeing the negroes without compensation, but of miscegenation, the intermarrying of the whites and blacks. I say there are some here who think the race would be bettered by such a stock. I am in favor of emancipation, and of paying every man for his slave.

Mr. WELLS—Since coming into this Convention, I have been a silent but close observer of the ground taken by the members. I was sent here by the loyal slaveholders of the parish of Rapides to represent them in this Convention, to revise and amend the constitution of the State of Louisiana, of which I am proud to be a native. I am sorry to find that many members of this Convention think there is no place in the State outside of the city of New Orleans. I am very sorry to say that they mistake this hall for the House of Representatives, and I am still sorrier to see them biassed by private opinions. As for myself, I am called upon to define my opinions, and am going to give them plainly and emphatically to everybody.

I am for immediate and unconditional emancipation. [Applause.] I am for the education of the negro, [great applause,] for the simple reason that I believe he will be better to himself and more useful to the country and the white race. [Cheers.] I am for compensating the loyal owners, provided the Federal authorities confiscate the property of disloyal owners—[renewed applause, and cries of "out of order"]—provided the Federal authorities confiscate the property of disloyal owners to meet these payments. Furthermore, I am in favor of prosecuting this war under the present occupant of the White House. This is where I stand. [Great applause.]

Mr. DUANE—I think it is inconsistent with reason and common sense to pass that portion of the amendment which is before the House, for we have to-day 10,000 black men in arms in defence of the United States who are to return to their homes and families, but by such action would be excluded.

Mr. THORPE—Mr. President, though unprepared to speak on the subject matter, I am not willing that a vote should be taken upon this important amendment without at least spreading my protest against it upon the records of this Convention. I think, myself, that it was brought in to embarrass the action of this Convention upon the original clause, though the fact is denied. I cannot understand this provision as legally and properly belonging to this section of the constitution, for it is a matter purely legislative, and should have been left to be dealt with when the section relating to the legislative department is before the Convention.

I came into this Convention with the determination to do my best towards having this constitution passed in as few words and sentences as possible. I am in favor of leaving everything we possibly can to the Legislature, and believe most emphatically it is not a matter for us to assume legislative powers.

One gentleman upon my right, (Mr. Stocker,) says, in the most glib and pleasant manner imaginable: "I am against the negro—in favor of driving him out of the State," etc. Let me say one word to that gentleman. The negro slave population of this State, four years ago, was officially announced as being worth a hundred and seventy millions seven hundred and thirty-three thousand dollars. Let us suppose it possible to carry out the gentleman's proposition—to drive out of Louisiana that amount of productive industry; the consequence would be that all your industrial interests would be at one fell swoop struck to the earth, and you would become so poor that you would hardly have clothing for your backs or food to put into your mouths. But more than that, this is a matter of humanity. I am opposed to any equality of diverse races. The allusions to miscegenation, made by some gentleman upon this floor, I consider out of place, and an insult to any gentleman to whom such language is addressed in this hall. I believe, before God and man, that the violation of the constitution of the United States, and the inhumanity of the proposed amendment, makes the proposition too monstrous to be entertained. I believe the subject involved should be left to the wisdom of the Legislature, to the operation of circumstances, and the experiences of time.

I was sorry to notice that this inhuman proposition was seconded and advocated by a gentleman whose antecedents would lead me to suppose that he would sympathize with the down-trodden and oppressed everywhere. It grates harshly upon my ear to hear this honored son of the Emerald Isle, (Mr. Sullivan,) who was in his youth deprived of all civil, political and religious rights, now that he is enfranchised under our republican institutions, lending his influence to enforce on others a fundamental law of this State, the effect of which would permit abuses and persecutions that should have no place except in the bottomless pit. In the name of Him who preached peace and good will toward all men, cannot this subject of slavery be treated calmly and dispassionately? Is there any necessity of this undue excitement, or of putting anything in the constitution which is legally or conventionally wrong, or opposed to the plainest principles of political economy, justice and humanity? Let us pass the emancipation clause of the section; say, if you please, the negro shall not vote; but, for God's sake, gentlemen, let it stop there.

Go into the country parishes and examine into the intricate and delicate relations that generations of slavery have created there, to say nothing of the social life of this city—you who talk so glibly, or amuse yourselves in the treatment of this solemn question—and see how deep and wide would strike the operations of your proposed constitutional provision. I am not ignorant of the important character of this act of emancipation, and I am disposed to treat it accordingly. Let us therefore come up nobly, but considerately, to the work, and humanely, dispassionately, and in a Christian manner, provide for the important interests of the future.

There are among the populations of Louisiana many of mixed blood, who are good citizens and who were once large proprietors. I am told the colored people of New Orleans alone are taxed on thirteen millions of dollars worth of property. I know myself of one neighborhood, where for miles along the Mississippi coast are nothing but rich sugar plantations, owned by this mixed race, colored, or negroes, if you please. In that section of country, Rapides, which is represented on this floor with so much honor by Mr. Wells, there are rich neighborhoods of negro plantation owners; and these men have been permitted, even under the black code, as all other Louisiana laws, to enjoy the happiest privileges of citizenship, that of being slaveholders, as owning large landed estates worked by slaves, as some one or two of these negro slaveholders at least have been by the Legislature of the State, made voters at the polls. But now, gentlemen, these men, these late slaveholders, who have been good citizens, or have any possible claim upon the State and the people, are struck down by the proposed amendment and placed in an infinitely worse position than they were under any of the antecedent pro-slavery constitutions of this State.

I do not ask for negro equality, or to have any intercourse with the race beyond the necessary contact of neighborhood residence or the relation of business. I have lived in Louisiana nearly thirty years, and no one must throw in my face anything of a sectional character, or taunt me about the North, Massachusetts, or any other particular part of the country. I claim to be a man of the entire country, and as such I never desire to call myself a New Yorker, a Louisianian, or a Massachusetts man; I am a citizen of the Union, and if I am capable of sitting in my chair and doing justice to Louisiana, I must legislate for the nation.

There are other things that gentlemen talk about, with what seems to me to be a singular levity. Are we to pass this amendment, or have the old laws re-enacted relating to free colored seamen coming to this harbor in foreign ships? What kind of a free State constitution is this that you would pass, when you blacken it by a provision most disgraceful to Christianity as well as to all just and equitable laws? When a ship comes here from New York, Boston, or from an English port, these colored seamen on board are free men; are they to be taken, as in old times, and be thrust into prison, without any reason, until the craft is prepared to leave the port—these poor men, who have committed no crime in the sight of God or man—are such men, under a free State constitution, to be treated as villains? I ask you, gentlemen, who hold in your hands the real solution of this difficulty, what are you going to do with the deck hands or waiters, from sister States, who come to New Orleans on the floating palaces of the Mississippi, which magnificent vessels, I hope, with returning peace, would crowd our levee miles in extent? What is to be the fate of these useful river men? Are they, under your free State constitution, to be imprisoned, or held in *durance vile*, until the steamer on which they are employed is ready to leave our midst? Certainly, such legitimate deductions would seem to say that we understand but little of the fundamental principle of liberty or just law.

Drive the negro population from the State, and you would desolate your State, and remove from it the labor-power that made Louisiana before the rebellion in the eyes of the world a State of planters and merchant princes. No, gentlemen; let us act wisely, humanely, and again I repeat, leave all the details of this exciting subject where it belongs, to the Legislature.

I believe that we here to-day represent the whole, entire State of Louisiana, and I have no sympathy with the sentiment or with the legal exception, that because one member represents but comparatively few parishes we do not represent the State. We were in rebellion against the United States, and had forfeited not only our property but our lives, being entitled to no consideration, though I believe that when an election was held in this State on secession, there was a majority of the people who voted for the Union. But the State was impelled into ruin by bad men, who have induced our citizens by thousands to shoulder their muskets, and who are to-day in our borders, in arms against the State. But Louisiana, Georgia or Mississippi, or where exists the darkest spot of this rebellion, I contend that if there is one true and loyal man in such a spot, he represents, under the Federal flag, the State in which he resides, and he is the official bond that connects his State with the Union. So we here assembled to-day, fortunately for our cause, a body representing under any circumstances a majority of the population of the State, do wholly, literally and legally represent the entire State. But more than this: with a liberality that will eternally redound to our honor, we have solemnly declared and enacted, that what would have been a majority if all the parishes were represented, should alone constitute a majority in our official action, and therefore as merely a matter of majority we represent Louisiana. This is the way I look upon the subject of our right here to represent the State, and view the grave question of our undisputed responsibility and power to speak for the State.

I cannot sit down without paying a tribute of my admiration to the gentleman from Rapides (Mr. Wells.) Before he was well out of his boy-clothes I had the honor of knowing his family. Through the troublous times, when the State was closed against loyal intercourse, I used to speculate, while in the North, who among all my old acquaintances in Louisiana were true to the Union, and foremost among the noble group I placed the Wellses, of Rapides. I believe that subsequent experience has shown me that I never, in a single instance, made a mistake in my speculations. I am glad to hear the scion of such a noble house, a representative of one of the largest slave properties in the State, declare himself in favor of immediate emancipation and all corresponding measures, consistent with such an act and harmonious with humanity. In this declaration he does honor to himself and adds dignity to this Convention—other gentlemen on this floor, who are, like him, representing country parishes, and large slaveholders, are among the most earnest friends of the Union, and for all measures that will make Louisiana a free State—I cannot honor these gentlemen enough.

Mr. Orr—Since I have been here I have done nothing but vote on the various questions that came up. I am perhaps differently situated from any member of this Convention. I was sent here pledged to support no particular measures. I was sent by the people of the Tenth Representative District who had confidence enough in me to leave me free and untrammeled. Before coming into this Convention I have been denounced as a secesh, as a copperhead, and through some of the newspapers as a man belonging to a party that was endeavoring to retard the progress and efforts to restore Louisiana again to the galaxy of the Union. I am willing to let my actions speak for me. I voted to free the negroes. I voted for immediate emancipation. I voted for it because I considered slavery to be morally wrong. I considered the Declaration of Independence where it says, "*all men* are born free and equal," not all white men, a stigma on the country claiming to be the most enlightened nation on the globe, and holding at the same time four millions of human beings in bondage. In regard to educating the negro, I am in favor of giving him the elements of an English education, provided the whole expense is not saddled on the people of Louisiana. It is a measure that concerns the whole United States as much as Louisiana. It is only in accordance with the principles of humanity that the negro shall receive a liberal share of education. We cannot expect the majority will acquire anything more than the rudiments, but whatever they have the capacity to learn, in God's name let them learn it. Still I am not willing that the people of Louisiana shall bear the whole burden. I am willing to allow the slaveholder compensation, provided others, equally deserving, are allowed it.

There are thousands of poor laboring men throughout the State who toil from morn till night to support their families, who have been prevented from following their avocations by the proclamation of Gov. Moore, made to force them, through starvation, to shoulder the musket and go into Confederate ranks.

I voted against giving the negro the right of suffrage; I shall vote against it on all occasions. I do not think he is entitled to it. Some of the gentlemen have said he was defending us, and may be called again to defend us from the attack of the rebel army. If the white men are not willing to defend themselves, I do not think they ought to be defended. I shall never ask for such defence for the protection of myself and family. I think the white man can do anything the negro can, on a plantation or any where else. I have seen white men laboring under the sun day after day, in the mud and water of the canals, where a negro could not have stood it for twelve hours. In regard to the colored sailors, etc., who come here, I think they are a violent, reckless set, and should be excluded forever. I steamboated for twenty years and know the character of the free negro. It was never necessary to send them to prison; the captain had to give bonds to take them away. I am in favor of the amendment prohibiting slavery, and there is not one man in fifty in Louisiana but who will vote for it. If allowed, the free negroes will swarm wild this State and make it a colony of negroes.

Mr. TALIAFERRO—As many of the gentlemen have defined their position, I will say, I was born in the State of Louisiana, and never was in a free State in my life; but, in regard to the freeing of the negroes, I unqualifiedly endorse the doctrine of Mr. Wells. I have two brothers fighting under the flag of the Union, and I intend to fight under it myself before long. [Applause.]

A motion to adjourn was made and carried—yeas 48, nays 28.

WEDNESDAY, May 11, 1864.

[At the usual hour the Convention was called to order, aud the proceedings were opened with prayer by the Rev. Mr. Andrews.

The secretary called the roll, and the following gentlemen answered to their names, viz:

Messrs. Abell, Ariail, Austin, Beauvais, Bell, Bennie, Bofill, Bonzano, Bromley, Buckley, Burke, Campbell, Collin, Cook T., Cook J.K., Davies, Decker, Duane, Dufresne, Duke, Edwards, Flagg, Flood, Fosdick, Gastinel, Goldman, Geier, Gorlinski, Gruneberg, Hart, Healy, Heard, Henderson, Hills, Hire, Howes, Kavanagh, Kugler, Maas, Mann, Maurer, Mayer, Millspaugh, Murphy M. W., Newell, Normand, O'Conner, Payne J., Pintado, Pursell S., Schnurr, Seymour, Shaw, Smith, Spellicy, Stumpf, Stauffer, Stiner, Taliaferro, Terry, Waters and Wenck —62.

There not being a quorum present, the sergeant-at-arms was directed to procure the attendance of absent members.

Messrs. Barrett, Baum, Fish, Foley, Fuller, Mendiverri, Montamat, Orr, Poynot, Purcell J., Schroeder, Stocker, Sullivan, Thorpe, Thomas and Wells—16, having taken their seats, the president announced that a quorum was present.

The secretary read the minutes of the previous day's proceedings.]

Mr. CAMPBELL—Mr. President, I desire to record my vote on the amendment of Mr. Abell to Art. 3 of the report of the Committee on Emancipation.

Mr. FOLEY—Mr. President, I believe that amendment has nothing to do with emancipation, but is directly opposed to it.

Mr. HILLS—I move that the gentleman be permitted to vote.

[The motion was carried.]

Mr. CAMPBELL—I vote yes.

Mr. GRUNEBERG—Mr. President, I also desire permission to vote on that amendment.

[Permission was given.]

Mr. GRUNEBERG--I vote yes.

Mr. FOLEY—I move that Mr. Kugler be allowed to vote on the first and second articles of the report of the Committee on Emancipation.

Mr. KUGLER--On the first section I vote yes. On the second section I vote yes.

Mr. MANN—Mr. Kugler desires to record his vote on the amendment providing that the Legislature shall never pass any law allowing free negroes to vote, &c.

Mr. KUGLER—On that amendment, I vote yes.

Mr. WATERS—I vote yes on that amendment.

Mr. CUTLER—I vote aye on the amendment.

Mr. BENNIE—I vote aye on the amendment.

Mr. FULLER—On the amendment I vote yes.

Mr. GORLINSKI—Mr. President, I wish to explain why I voted ———.

PRESIDENT—You are not in order.

Mr. GORLINSKI—Then I shall take another opportunity to explain.

[The minutes were adopted.]

Mr. HEARD—Mr. President, I rise to a question of privilege. In the Era of this morning I find the following: "Another most noticeable fact is that those who have opposed emancipation in the Convention, and have done all in their power to revive the wicked proscriptive laws that were in force before the war, are, most of them, office-holders under the civil government recently organized here—some but just appointed, and others who have fed upon the public crib nearly ever since the Federal occupation of New Orleans. We hold that on matters of such importance, there is something unbecoming, to say the least, in having a free State government represented by the bitterest supporters of slavery. If our government be in fact a free State government, as all the world has been taught to believe, we do not see what propriety there can be in its agents and pensioners voting against a free State on every occasion, and even going to the extent of a violent disregard of parliamentary rules to confuse and embarrass its friends. The sole issue before the people, when Mr. Hahn was a candidate for the gubernatorial chair, was that of a free State. This was avowed over and over again, in every possible form, and was reiterated by Mr. Hahn, in his inaugural address. The gentlemen who have accepted office under him could not possibly have been ignorant of the fact; and yet some of them are scarcely seated in positions of honor and profit under this very free State government before they turn around, and in a most violent and offensive manner do everything they can do to preserve slavery from the certain overthrow to which it has been doomed. We cannot believe the real sentiments of these men were known when they were appointed to office. But now they have shown their hand, and, in our judgment, they do no credit to the government whose agents and representatives they are. We have not spoken thus freely without great reluctance; but it is a duty we owe to ourself and to the public, and we shall not shrink from its performance. We say, then, frankly, that the power by which these men were appointed will be and already is held responsible before the world for their conduct in the Convention. At the same time, we believe the course it will pursue in view of existing facts, will be such as to vindicate its own dignity and honor; and so believing, we dismiss the subject for the present."

From the tenor of this article it would seem that every member of this Convention is expected to obey implicitly whatever that paper enunciates, for it has constituted itself the conscience-keeper of members. Now I enter a plea to the jurisdiction. I spurn the idea that I have to bow to the dictates of any man or set of men in matters of conscience. It is true, sir, I have been appointed by Gov. Hahn to an important and dignified office. But, sir, I can and do say here that I did not seek the office, but it sought me. Before Gov. Hahn had even been nominated as candidate for governor, I had been recommended by a large number of the loyal citizens of Baton Rouge to Gov. Shepley for the very place to which I have been appointed, and before the inauguration of our present governor, I had been recommended by the Union Association of Baton Rouge, consisting of some one hundred and fifty members, without any solicitation on my part, for the position to which I have been appointed. In accepting the appointment, I reserved to myself the right of discharging the duties appertaining to that office according to law, justice and the dictates of my conscience. As well might the Era assume the right of dictating what I should do on the bench, as to read me a lecture on the manner in which I should vote in this body The Era says it was expected that every member elected to this Convention would vote for emancipation. I was prepared to do so if the proviso for compensating loyal slaveholders had been incorporated in the ordinance of emancipation.

Mr. FOLEY—Mr. President, the gentleman is out of order.

PRESIDENT—He is not out of order, and will proceed.

Mr. HEARD—I had a proviso to offer to that effect, but was choked off by that terrible engine of legislation, the previous question. I understood the issue before the people at the gubernatorial election, and voted for Gov. Hahn, and under the circumstances would do so again; but I could not in conscience vote for a measure unconditionally which would tear from loyal people the small remnant of what they have left, without at least making an effort to compensate them—

PRESIDENT—The gentleman is out of order. No member has a right, on a question of privilege, to go into a general debate.

On the resolution of Mr. Cazabat, relative to compensation of loyal citizens, I appoint Messrs. Cazabat, Wells, Fosdick, Abell and Taliaferro. Unfinished business is now in order.

Mr. THORPE—I call up my resolution of yesterday, which I desire to amend by adding the words "and debates," which were accidentally omitted in drafting the resolution as it passed.

Mr. FOLEY—I move that the gentleman be permitted to amend the resolution as he proposes.

Mr. ABELL—I move that instead of one thousand,—— I am pleased with the suggestion. I think that our action is for the benefit of the people, and that there should be a larger number printed than has been ordered. I move that five thousand be printed.

Mr. MONTAMAT—I second the motion.

Mr. EDWARDS—I move to lay the amendment on the table.

[The motion was lost.

The amendment was carried, and the resolution, as amended, adopted.]

PRESIDENT—The unfinished business, the report of the Committee on Emancipation, now comes up.

Mr. WENCK—I really think we are assuming too much power, with which we have not been invested by our constituents. We are assuming power that belongs only to the Legislature. I cannot see how it is that the gentlemen take more time to pass an act to repeal the black code. We have already provided that slavery shall not exist, and if slavery is abolished, the black code falls of itself. We have already done away with that code by abolishing slavery, and there is no necessity of formally passing upon a separate article to repeal it. The existence of slavery is necessary to the vitality of that code. We have reached the point arrived at in the article, by doing away with slavery, and further action on it would be useless and meaningless. I have voted for the first article, and for the second, and for the amendment, but I shall say plainly, that the third article does not belong here. If it belongs anywhere, it is a matter for legislative action, and not for the action of this body. And let me tell you, furthermore, that there is no clause in our constitution of 1852, or any other constitution, that provides that free negroes shall not come into the State; but such provisions have been made by special legislation. If it was not done in the constitution of 1852, why do it now? Why not leave the matter for the Legislature, as was done in that constitution? Why not go to work at once and perform the duties for which we have been elected? We have an ample number of precedents before us, in the constitutions of other States, from which to make a constitution.

And in closing, let me repeat, we have already abolished slavery; all that we would add by way of amendment necessarily follows, and is something that has nothing to do with us, and that we have nothing to do with. It is a matter of legislation, and by acting on it we are assuming legislative power, which does not belong to us.

Mr. Fosdick—I have a very few words to say on this subject—simply to say that I shall oppose the amendment of Mr. Abell. As I have said before, this body was called here for a distinct purpose. We are called here to make a constitution, and no authority to legislate in any manner whatever has been delegated to us. We have been here five weeks, and what have we done? We have listened to debates upon every subject but that which we are called upon to perform. The proposition that I voted against yesterday had no business there. I considered it as an insult offered to the committee of which I am chairman, (on Legislative Department.) This body has no power to legislate upon that subject; it belongs to the Legislature alone. The constitution of the United States does not make any distinction between its free citizens; and, sir, I deny the right of this Convention to close the door against men in this State who are citizens of the United States, and who, the gentleman himself knows, are by industry, by wealth, and by intelligence, entitled to a voice in the administration of the affairs of the State. I repeat, sir, that we are sent here to do an important duty as free State men. I, for one, shall do it freely and fearlessly, and there is not power enough in the United States to make me say no when I mean yes. If the gentleman who offered the amendment will refer to the constitution of the United States, he will find, art. IV, sec. 2, that "The citizens of each State shall be entitled to all privileges and immunities of citizens in the several States." Under this provision, the free citizens of the United States have a right to the same privileges in all the States—this State as well as others. Let the gentleman show me a right to shut out a free citizen of any other State from coming to Louisiana, if it is in his power to do it.

The charge has been made on this floor that the negro crews of vessels are the worst men who visit this port. I deny it, sir, and I aver that the negro sailor is equal to the white, and that so far as obedience to the master is concerned, he is superior, and I call upon masters of vessels to prove my assertion.

I regret, Mr. President, exceedingly to see gentlemen elected as free State men now hesitate to cast their votes as free State men, yet such is the case, and to such an extent, that I begin to think that Louisiana is not a free but a pro-slavery State.

Mr. Gorlinski—Mr. President, I voted no on the first amendment of Mr. Abell, and will vote no on this, for this reason: we have abolished slavery in the first section, and in this amendment he says "provided always that the Legislature shall pass no laws allowing negroes to vote," etc.

It is evident to my mind that the gentleman introduced this amendment for the purpose of overshadowing the acts of this Convention in regard to the emancipation of slaves. The next reason is, that I believe it to be entirely inconsistent with the section it proposes to amend. If the matter belongs anywhere, it belongs to the legislative department. The same gentleman who introduced it (Mr. Abell) has been advocating slavery on this floor for two weeks. I do not come here to advocate slavery or to justify myself before the advocates of slavery; but to oppose them to the end, here, as our noble soldiers are doing on the battle-field. I shall vote "no" on the amendment.

Mr. Stauffer—I call for the previous question, and move to strike out entirely the third clause from the report, with all the amendments thereto.

Mr. Thomas—I amend by adding sections IV and V.

Mr. Hills—I second the motion.

Mr. Stauffer—I accept the amendment.

Mr. Stocker—I rise to a question of order. I believe that the only question before the House is on the second division of the amendment, and the motion to lay that upon the table has been decided in the negative.

Mr. Henderson—The motion was properly put, is in order and cuts off all debate.

Mr. Abell—That is exactly in keeping with the course affairs have taken in this Convention. I would like to hear the gentleman express himself on the question, but he is as afraid of truth as the devil is of holy water.

Mr. HILLS—I seconded the motion to strike out the second, third, fourth and fifth sections, with the amendments.

Mr. ABELL—I move to lay that resolution on the table.

[The ayes and noes were called with the following result:

YEAS—Messrs. Abell, Barrett, Bofill, Buckley, Campbell, Crozat, Decker, Dufresne, Duke, Edwards, Gastinel, Gruneberg, Heard, Kugler, Mann, Maurer, Mayer, Mendiverri, Montamat, Murphy M. W., Normand, Payne J., Stocker, Stumpf, Sullivan—25.

NAYS—Messrs. Ariail, Austin, Bailey, Beauvais, Bell, Bennie, Bonzano, Bromley, Burke, Collin, Cook J. K., Cook T., Cutler, Davies, Duane, Dupaty, Flood, Foley, Fosdick, Fuller, Geier, Goldman, Gorlinski, Healy, Harnan, Hart, Henderson, Hills, Hire, Howes, Maas, Millspaugh, Murphy E., Newell, O'Conner, Orr, Paine J. T., Pintado, Poynot, Purcell J., Pursell S., Schroeder, Schnurr, Shaw, Smith, Spellicy, Stiner, Stauffer, Taliaferro, Terry, Thorpe, Thomas, Wenck, Wells, Wilson—55.]

Mr. DUANE—I move the previous question, the motion to strike out.

Mr. HILLS—I second the motion.

Mr. ABELL—Is it not debatable?

PRESIDENT—No.

[The motion was adopted—ayes 56. The main question was then put, the secretary began to call the roll, and Mr. Stocker started towards the door.]

Mr. DUANE—I protest against any gentleman's leaving the floor.

Mr. STOCKER—I wish the members of this Convention to understand that I am opposed to this choking process.

PRESIDENT — [To the sergeant-at-arms.] Let no member leave the floor. [To Mr. Stocker.] Take your seat, sir, and keep order.

Mr. CAMPBELL—Would a motion be in order, Mr. President?

PRESIDENT—No.

Mr. STOCKER—I would like to explain my vote. [No objection.] I am in favor of striking out the third and fourth sections, and of passing the others; but as I am compelled to vote on the whole, I rose to ask for a division, but as I did not catch the president's eye, I vote "yes."

Mr. WENCK—I wish to explain my vote. [No objection.] I shall vote "yes," but should like to have had the matter taken up section by section.

Mr. MORRIS—I don't exactly understand it. I beg to be excused from voting.

PRESIDENT—Under the rules you have adopted every member must vote, unless excused by the Convention.

Mr. MORRIS—I vote "no," then.

[The following is the result of the vote:

YEAS—Messrs. Ariail, Austin, Bailey, Beauvais, Bell, Bennie, Bonzano, Bromley, Burke, Collin, Cook J. K., Cook T., Cutler, Davies, Duane, Dupaty, Fish, Flood, Foley, Fosdick, Fuller, Geier, Goldman, Gorlinski, Healy, Harnan, Hart, Henderson, Hills, Hire, Howes, Maas, Mann, Millspaugh, Morris, Murphy E., Newell, O'Conner, Orr, Payne J., Paine J. T., Pintado, Poynot, Purcell J., Schroeder, Schnurr, Shaw, Smith, Spellicy, Stocker, Stumpf, Stiner, Stauffer, Taliaferro, Terry, Thorpe, Thomas, Wenck, Wells, Wilson—60.

NAYS—Messrs. Abell, Barrett, Bofill, Buckley, Crozat, Decker, Dufresne, Duke, Edwards. Flagg, Gastinel, Gruneberg, Heard, Kugler, Maurer, Mayer, Mendiverri, Montamat, Morris, Murphy M. W., Normand, Ong, Pursell S., Sullivan—24.]

Mr. THOMAS—I move that the rules be suspended for the purpose of reading the two first sections a third time.

PRESIDENT—The report has passed its second reading. The next business in order is the—

Mr. PURSELL—Mr. President, I desire to explain the vote that I have just given.

PRESIDENT—You are too late. You may explain through the newspapers; that is the proper mode now.

Mr. PURSELL—I know I can, but it will cost.

Mr. THORPE—I would like for the report of the Committee on Assault of Members to lie over for a few days, and move that it lie over till Monday.

[The motion was carried.]

Mr. HENDERSON—There was a motion to postpone the order of the day; such a motion is always in order; and I move now that the first two sections of this report be taken up and made the order of the day, and move a suspension of the rules in order to take them up now.

Mr. STOCKER—I move to lay that motion on the table.

[The motion to table was lost.]

Mr. CAMPBELL—Mr. President, will a motion be in order now?

PRESIDENT—What is it about?

Mr. CAMPBELL—It is about the matter under consideration.

PRESIDENT—Send it up to the secretary.

Mr. CAMPBELL—I wish to move to commit the whole matter of emancipation to a special committee of five, to be appointed by the whole House.

PRESIDENT—It is out of order.

Mr. CAMPBELL—Such a motion is in order at any time.

PRESIDENT—You must wait till the third reading.

Mr. CAMPBELL—Mr. President, I have the documents here to prove that it is in order at any time.

Mr. FOLEY—I move a call of the House.

[The roll was called and 85 members answered to their names.]

Mr. THOMAS—I call for the yeas and nays on the question of suspending the rules.

[The call was sustained.]

Mr. PURSELL—I would like to explain my vote. The reason why I voted—

PRESIDENT—You cannot explain a previous vote.

Mr. PURSELL—I cannot explain this without explaining the other. I am about to vote yes on this question. The reason why I voted no on the—

PRESIDENT—If you cannot explain your vote without explaining a prior vote, you are out of order and will take your seat.

Mr. FOLEY—Mr. President, I protest against members going out.

[The following is the result of the vote:

YEAS—Messrs. Ariail, Austin, Bailey, Barrett, Beauvais, Bell, Bennie, Bofill, Bonzano, Bromley, Burke, Collin, Cook J. K., Cook T., Crozat, Cutler, Davies, Duane, Dupaty, Edwards, Fish, Flagg, Flood, Foley, Fosdick, Fuller, Gastinel, Geier, Goldman, Gorlinski, Harnan, Hart, Healy, Henderson, Hills, Hire, Howes, Kugler, Maas, Mann, Mayer, Millspaugh, Montamat, Morris, Murphy E., Murphy M. W., Newell, Normand, O'Conner, Orr, Payne J., Paine J. T., Pintado, Poynot, Purcell J., Pursell S., Schnurr, Schroeder, Shaw, Smith, Spellicy, Stocker, Stumpf, Stiner, Stauffer, Taliaferro, Terry, Thorpe, Thomas, Wenck, Wells, Wilson—72.

NAYS—Messrs. Abell, Buckley, Campbell, Decker, Dufresne, Duke, Gruneberg, Heard, Maurer, Mendiverri, Ong, Sullivan—12.]

PRESIDENT—The resolution to suspend the rulés is carried. Mr. Secretary, read the first two sections of the report.

[The secretary read:

Sec. 1. Slavery and involuntary servitude, except as a punishment for crime, whereof the party shall have been duly convicted, are hereby forever abolished and prohibited throughout the State.]

Mr. HILLS—Mr. President—

Mr. BONZANO—I move the previous question.

PRESIDENT—Mr. Secretary, read the second section.

Mr. HILLS—Mr. President, I have the floor, but yield to Mr. Bonzano, for a motion which I understand he proposes to make.

PRESIDENT—It is not time to make a motion. Read the second section, Mr. Secretary.

[The secretary read:

Sec. 2. The Legislature shall make no law recognizing the right of property in man.]

Mr. ABELL—Mr. President, I have an amendment—

PRESIDENT—Amendments are not in order on the third reading.

Mr. BONZANO—I move the previous question.

[The motion was carried on a rising vote —ayes 61, noes 24.]

The main question was put, and the secretary proceeded to call the roll.

Mr. ABELL—I consider this disgraceful.

Mr. CAMPBELL—You decided my amendment out of order, and now that I should bring it up on the third reading—

PRESIDENT—I will do justice to both minority and majority, but I shall hold you strictly to the rules of the House.

Mr. CAMPBELL—I do not wish to make any difficulty, but when I presented my document you would not hear to it, and told me to bring it up—

PRESIDENT—My dear sir, you do not understand the rules of the House.

PRESIDENT—The question is, Shall the report be adopted?

Mr. MANN—Mr. President—

PRESIDENT—Sit down, sir, you are are not in order.

[The ayes and noes were called.

The secretary commenced calling the roll.]

Mr. ABELL—Mr. President, I wish to explain my vote. I say, in the name of the people of Louisiana, that this is the most disgraceful, tyrannical, [" order, order,"] unheard of, [cries of " order," " put him down,"] unprincipled—[put down by the sergeant-at-arms.] I vote no.

Mr. CAMPBELL—I vote no, NO, NO, in the name of the people.

Mr. FOLEY—In the name of Jeff. Davis, rather.

Mr. EDWARDS—In the name of the people, yes.

Mr. ABELL—In the name of your master.

Mr. FOLEY—For the good of the Union, I vote yes.

Mr. HENDERSON—I wish it to be understood that I vote for emancipation for no other reason than the preservation of this Union.

Mr. HEARD—I am in favor of emancipation with compensation, but as the Convention has decided to emancipate without compensation, I vote no.

Mr. MONTAMAT—I am of that opinion, and have done everything to have compensation included in the report, but as the majority are not in favor of it, vote yes.

Mr. MORRIS—I have nothing against compensation, but as no value was attached to the negro in Louisiana, I vote yes. [Renewed applause.]

Mr. ORR—In accordance with the principles of universal freedom throughout the globe, Mr. President, I vote yes.

Mr. STUMPF—For the preservation of the Union, I vote yes.

Mr. SULLIVAN—I would vote for the report on emancipation if compensation was included, but as it is not, I vote no.

Mr. THOMAS—I have ever been in favor of immediate emancipation of the slaves in Louisiana, personally, and I went before my constituents and told them so. They elected me by a large majority, and in order that I may not prove untrue to myself and constituency, I vote according to my conduct in this Convention, yes.

Mr. WENCK—I have been against slavery for long years. I vote yes.

Mr. WELLS—For the good of the white and the black race, and in honor of the flag of the Union, I vote yes.

Mr. CROZAT—I change my vote from no to yes.

Mr. HILLS—I move to suspend the rules and allow the president to vote as a member of the Convention.

[The motion was carried.]

PRESIDENT—I vote "yes," gentlemen, with my whole soul. [Prolonged applause.]

[The following was the result of the vote:

YEAS—Messrs. Ariail, Austin, Barrett, Beauvais, Bofill, Bell, Bennie, Bonzano, Bromley, Burke, Collin, Cook J. K., Cook T., Crozat, Cutler, Davies, Duane, Dupaty, Edwards, Fish, Flagg, Flood, Foley, Fosdick, Fuller, Geier, Goldman, Gorlinski, Healy, Harnan, Hart, Henderson, Hills, Hire, Howes, Kugler, Maas, Mann, Millspaugh, Montamat, Morris, Murphy E., Murphy M. W., Newell, Normand, O'Conner, Ong, Orr, Payne J., Paine J. T., Pintado, Poynot, Purcell J., Pursell S., Schroeder, Schnurr, Sullivan, Shaw, Smith, Spellicy, Stocker, Stumpf, Stiner, Stauffer, Taliaferro, Terry, Thorpe, Thomas, Wenck, Wells, Wilson, and Mr. President—72.

NAYS—Messrs. Abell, Buckley, Campbell, Decker, Dufresne, Duke, Gastinel, Gruneberg, Heard, Maurer, Mayer, Mendiverri, Waters—13.]

PRESIDENT—The first and second sections of the majority report of the Committee on Emancipation have passed their third reading and are now a part and parcel of the law of the State of Louisiana. [Enthusiastic cheers.]

Mr. THOMAS—I move that we adjourn.

[The motion was carried.]

THURSDAY, May 12, 1864.

[At 12 o'clock, the Convention was called to order by the chair, and the proceedings were opened with prayer by the Rev. Mr. Andrews. The roll was called and the following members answered to their names:

Messrs. Ariail, Bennie, Bonzano, Bofill, Burke, Collin, Crozat, Decker, Dufresne, Duke, Edwards, Ennis, Gorlinski, Heard, Howes, Kugler, Millspaugh, Murphy M. W., Newell, Normand, O'Conner, Pintado, Pursell S., Shaw, Spellicy, Stumpf, Stiner, Sullivan, Taliaferro, Thorpe, Thomas Wells and Wilson—33.

There being no quorum, the president dispatched the sergeant-at-arms to bring in absent members. After which the following gentlemen answered to their names, viz:

Messrs. Abell, Austin, Bailey, Barrett, Bell, Bromley, Beauvais, Buckley, Campbell, Cazabat, Cook J. K., Cook T., Cutler, Fish, Flagg, Flood, Foley, Fosdick, Gastinel, Geier, Goldman, Gruneberg, Healy, Harnan, Hart, Hills, Hire, Maas, Mann, Maurer, Mayer, Mendiverri, Montamat, Morris, Murphy E., Poynot, Purcell J., Schroeder, Schnurr, Smith, Stauffer, Waters and Wenck—43.

The secretary read the minutes of the previous day's proceedings.]

Mr. BOFILL—Before the minutes are adopted, Mr. President, I wish to change my vote on the report of the Committee on Emancipation. I voted *no*, but should not have done so had I been aware that the resolution of Mr. Cazabat had been adopted, but having learned that fact, I desire to change my vote to *yes*.

[Permission was given by the Convention without objection.]

Mr. HILLS—I hope the roll will be called, and those who have not voted on the question will be brought in to vote.

Mr. SULLIVAN—I wish to change my vote from no to yes, for the same reason as set forth by Mr. Bofill.

[No objection was made, and the vote was changed.]

Mr. CAMPBELL—I wish to explain my vote of yesterday. I voted no on both sections as a whole, but if the two had been separated, after the first had been adopted by so decided a majority, I should have voted aye on the second.

Mr. BENNIE—I vote *aye* on the motion to reject the minority report of the Committee on Emancipation.

Mr. CAZABAT—Mr. President, we have witnessed in this very hall, and upon this very floor, the dying struggles and the agonizing convulsions of slavery; but, thank God! the minority report, the offspring of narrow-mindedness and prejudice, has been voted down, and the sacred cause of eternal truth and justice and human freedom has prevailed. Louisiana stands now forever *free and redeemed* by the voice of her people—by the voice of her noble and worthy sons, such as young Wells of Rapides, Taliaferro of Catahoula, and Edwards of Avoyelles. Immortal trio! Heaven bless them! Mr. President, my views in regard to the provisos and amendments offered by the opposition have been duly and fully expressed by my friend, Mr. Fosdick, of New Orleans. I stand, Mr. President, and members of this Convention, upon the platform of immediate and unconditional abolition of slavery. And now, in performance of my duty to my God, to my country and to my fellow-man, I cast and record my vote—"yes!"

Mr. ABELL—That is the most illiberal act that has ever been permitted in this House. It is a disgrace to the House to permit such remarks on this floor——

[Mr. Abell was called to order and took his seat.]

Mr. ENNIS—I vote *aye* on the adoption of the two first sections of the majority report of the Committee on Emancipation.

[The minutes as amended, were then adopted.]

Mr. WILSON—I move to adjourn till Monday.

Mr. HILLS—I demand the ayes and nays on that question.

[The call for the ayes and nays was not sustained, and the resolution was lost.]

Mr. ABELL—Mr. President, I rise for the purpose of asking to be excused from serving on the select committee appointed by the chair on yesterday, to correspond with Congress relative to compensation for emancipated slaves, and I desire, sir, to offer my reasons for doing so.

Yesterday this Convention passed an ordinance in most indecent haste, without permitting any argument for or against it, by which we have attempted to give away more than one hundred and fifty millions of property belonging to other people; an act which, sir, will at least entitle us to the reputation of being the most liberal givers of other men's property on record, and that, too, sir, without their consent.

I think, sir, that to ask Congress to pay for property of loyal owners after this Convention has so freely wrested it from them, will be a great condescension of this body, and subject it to the contempt of Congress, and would amount at best to a mere blind in order to disappoint, mislead and deceive the people that they have ruined, by holding out to them false hopes which every one knows will never be realized.

Sir, if we intend to act in good faith and deal justly and fairly with the people of the State of Louisiana, let us make a clause in the constitution by which the emancipation act shall take effect so soon as provisions can be made by State and Congress for compensation, and then the committee would be in a position to demand compensation and the slaveholders to expect it, before they are despoiled of their property.

Mr. President, under all circumstances in life I have endeavored to deal candidly with all men, and under no circumstances would I now participate in any act that I think would have a tendency to tantalize, mislead or deceive the great people of Louisiana, whom I am sent here to represent; and such, sir, I believe would be the effect of any action the committee could take under the circumstances. I think, sir, it would be adding the grossest insult to the greatest injury.

For these, sir, and many other reasons, which I will not detain the Convention to enumerate, I ask to be excused from the committee.

Mr. Bonzano—I move that the gentleman's request be granted.

[The motion was carried.]

President—The chair appoints in his place Mr. Ariail.

Mr. Heard—Your Committee on Preamble, to whom was referred the substitute of Mr. Cazabat, upon examination of the minutes, find that the original report has already been adopted, and consequently that the matter has passed beyond the control of this committee, and beg leave to report back Mr. Cazabat's substitute.

Mr. Cazabat—With your permission, Mr. President, I withdraw the substitute.

President—If there is no objection, it can be withdrawn.

Mr. Stocker—I object.

President—It is not withdrawn, then.

Mr. Thorpe—As chairman of the Committee on Enrollment, I would report as correctly enrolled the following bill:

AN ORDINANCE TO ABOLISH SLAVERY AND INVOLUNTARY SERVITUDE.

We, the people of the State of Louisiana, in convention assembled, do hereby declare and ordain as follows:

Section 1. Slavery and involuntary servitude, except as a punishment for crime whereof the party shall have been duly convicted, are hereby forever abolished and prohibited throughout the State.

Sec. 2. The Legislature shall make no law recognizing the right of property in man.

Adopted in Convention, at the City of New Orleans, on this eleventh day of May, in the year one thousand eight hundred and sixty-four, and the eighty-eighth of the Independence of the United States of America.

Mr. Thomas—I would call attention to the fact that the words "of our Lord" are left out of the latter part of the bill, as it was adopted, and I therefore move that it be referred back, and that the committee be instructed to enroll it exactly as it was adopted.

Mr. Shaw—We certainly adopted no formula, and none is necessary.

Mr. Thomas—It may not be necessary, but we adopted it. If it had not been in the report I should not have moved to refer it back.

Mr. Hills—I seconded the motion to refer back, because I believed that in a matter of such grave moment the utmost solemnity should be used.

Mr. Thorpe—Mr. President, I am willing to have the bill re-enrolled, but it seems to me that the gentleman is certainly mistaken about our having adopted any particular formula, but, sir, more than this, a motion was carried to strike out everything after the second section.

Mr. Stocker—I agree entirely with the gentleman on my right. I rose to attempt to call the attention of the Convention to that fact some time ago. There is no question about it; we voted to strike out all after the second article; that of course included the formula which it is claimed was not correctly enrolled, and which is in reality a part of the fifth article.

Mr. Wilson—I disagree with the gentleman. I think that it is entire in itself, and distinct from any of the articles, and I coincide with Mr. Thomas in desiring to have it exactly in the language of the original report.

[The motion to refer back was then put and carried.]

Mr. BELL—I move that the other resolution be received and signed by the president.

PRESIDENT—On the committee respecting the circulation of city money, the chair appoints Messrs. Purcell, Fosdick, Stauffer, Bonzano and Brott.

[The secretary read the following communication from the auditor of public accounts:

STATE AUDITOR'S REPORT.

STATE OF LOUISIANA, AUDITOR'S OFFICE, New Orleans, May 11, 1864.

To the president and members of the State Constitutional Convention:

In compliance with the resolution of your honorable body, "relative to the auditor of public accounts," adopted on the 18th of April, 1864, I have the honor to submit the following report, showing as fully and minutely in detail as the books and papers in possession of this office enable me to do, the receipts and disbursements of public moneys during the administration of Brigadier General George F. Shepley, late military governor of the State of Louisiana.

Your resolution was not received at this office until the 4th instant, which is the reason of my not complying with it sooner.

On entering upon the duties of auditor, on the 4th of March, 1864, the former auditor, Mr. S. H. Torry, refused to transfer the books, vouchers, documents, &c., of the office to my possession, representing to me that he was acting under orders of the ex-military governor, Gen. Shepley; but possession was subsequently taken without the general's consent. Mr. Torry's books exhibit the accounts of the State up to March 9th; consequently this report presents the financial condition of the State on that date.

Amount received by T. C. A. Dexter, late State treasurer, from his predecessor in office, said amount being deposited in the Louisiana State Bank, in "Confederate" notes	$462,752 13
There being no information in this office as to what several funds this amount belongs, I have placed it to the account of "General Fund." (See Statement A.)	
Total amount of receipts by the State during the term of office of S. H. Torry, former auditor, as shown by his books	$702,645 53
Total amount of disbursements during the same period	330,052 70
Leaving on March 9, 1864, a surplus in the treasury, of current funds, of	372,592 83
And of "Confederate" notes of	462,752 13
Making the total amount	$835,344 96

STATEMENT A.

Showing the various sources of revenue, and the funds to which the receipts were credited.

GENERAL FUND.

Confederate notes received from former treasurer	$462,752 13
Received as auction duties	57,516 31
Received as State tax proper	246,038 03
Received as licenses on trades, etc	198,298 50
Received for redemption of lands	387 32
Received from other sources	3,810 14
Total	$968,802 43

The $3810 14 mentioned above was received as follows, viz: From Capt. Norcross, for mess-plates furnished by the State to the Louisiana volunteers, and afterwards turned over to the United States government, $169 14.

From U. D. Terrebonne, sealer of weights and measures for the Second and Third Districts of New Orleans, for fines collected, $39.

From Joseph Hernandez, former State tax collector of the Second District of New Orleans, amount refunded to the State for expenses of reorganizing the office of State tax collector of the Second District of New Orleans, in consequence of the destruction of the records of the office, $454.

From Moses Bates, financial agent, State Penitentiary, a draft endorsed by Gen. B. F. Butler and Gen. Shepley, in favor of T. C. A. Dexter, treasurer, $3148.

SCHOOL FUND.

Received as mill tax	$147,609 89
Received as poll tax	11,995 00
Total	$159,604 89

INTERNAL IMPROVEMENT FUND.

Received as internal improvement tax	$36,990 34

STATEMENT B.

Showing the disbursements from the treasury during the term of office of S. H. Torry, former auditor, as exhibited by his books and vouchers:

FROM THE GENERAL FUND.

As salaries in executive department	$6,816 66
As contingent expenses of executive department	7,500 00
As office expenses	2,478 55
As general contingent expenses	3,699 29
As salaries in auditor's office	8,811 66
As salaries in treasurer's office	6,501 27
As salaries of judges	43,127 73
As salaries of state attorneys	3,063 94
As salaries of clerks of courts	964 90
As expenses of State library	1,985 00
As commissions to tax collectors	39,171 47
As compensation of assessors	19,677 86
As expenses of State Penitentiary	14,249 29
For different charitable institutions	24,539 98
For Louisiana volunteers	1,069 88
For printing and advertising	6,358 40
For registry of voters	2,724 00
For expenses of elections	3,176 50
For State coupons	48,510 00
To Capt. Hawes, A.Q.M., U.S.A.	2,693 80
Total disbursements from general fund	$247,120 18

FROM THE SCHOOL FUND.

To city of New Orleans for the public schools	$78,870 57
To city of New Orleans for the schools of free colored children, by order of Gov. Shepley	1,000 00
To the parish of Jefferson	3,061 95
Total disbursements from school fund	$82,932 52

FROM THE INTERNAL IMPROVEMENT FUND.

(There have been no disbursements.)

It may be proper for me to observe that in regard to certain payments out of the State treasury during the administration of the late military governor, much irregularity seems to have existed. Warrants have been drawn on the treasury, and public moneys paid on account of salaries and services never actually earned or performed.

As an instance of this kind, I would call attention to the fact that three warrants, numbered 75, 167 and 271, were drawn by the late auditor on the treasurer, each of such warrants purporting on its face to have been drawn for the salary of one William B. Lowe, as clerk in the office of the said auditor from October 1st, 1862, to March 9th, 1864, amounting in all to the sum of $2883 33, and which sum was paid out of the State treasury. I am informed, by testimony that I deem reliable, that said William B. Lowe was not at any time employed as clerk in the office of the auditor, therefore the charge for such services as above mentioned is unjust and illegal.

It appears also by warrant No. 4, that the Hon. R. K. Howell was allowed to draw salary from the State treasury, as Judge of the Sixth District Court, from the first of April, 1862, which was twenty-six days before the arrival of the United States forces, and seventy-one days before the promulgation by Gen. Butler, commanding the department, of general orders No. 41, by which the Judge could have restored his status as a *loyal citizen.* So much of his salary as was paid for services rendered prior to that order was paid to a public judicial officer of a government in rebellion to the United States.

A similar instance to this is the payment to the Hon. A. M. Buchanan of the sum of $3750 for salary as Associate Justice of the Supreme Court, from July 1st, 1862, to March 31st, 1863. Judge Buchanan was a member of the Supreme Court of Louisiana previous to the secession of the State.

In my opinion, rebellion had terminated the existence of that court, and it had to be reorganized under appointments made by loyal military power, or by an election by the loyal people, before it could again exist.

Judge Buchanan did not draw his salary accruing previous to July 1st, 1862. If he was legally entitled to draw salary subsequent to that date, he was also entitled to his arrears of salary prior to that date.

The Hon. Charles A. Peabody was appointed by Gen. Shepley, late military governor, to the office of chief justice of the Supreme Court. At the time of, and ever since the appointment, Judge Peabody was holding an office (that of provisional judge of the United States District Court) under the Federal government, and so, according to the provision of the constitution of Louisiana (article 99,) he was ineligible to the appointment in question. Other persons were appointed by the late military governor as associate justices, who declined to accept, so that no Supreme Court was organized, and no judicial services were or could have been rendered by Judge Peabody as a State judge. Notwithstanding these facts, he was permitted by the late auditor to draw from the State treasury, on account of salary, and for which the State had received no equivalent, the sum of $3541 66.

It appears also from warrants on file in this office, that the sum of $2500 was drawn three several times, making $7500, in favor of the late military governor, purporting to be for "contingent expenses of the Executive Department," for which there are no vouchers of the details, or items of that expenditure, as required by law; but vouchers are on file for bills of contingent expenses of the governor's office, which bills are charged to the account of "office expenses," which account appears to contain the legitimate contingent expenses of the several departments of State.

Several thousand dollars were also drawn during the same period, as salaries of several gentlemen as officers of the State, who were at the same time commissioned officers of the United States army, and receiving pay in both capacities.

The account of $2698 80 paid to Capt. Hawes, A. Q. M., U. S. A., was in reimbursement of money collected by the former auditor, of George E. Tyler, as auction duty on certain sales made by him of United States property, which property, by the law of this State, was exempt from duty.

The money was returned to the United States government by order of Governor Shepley.

The returns made to this office by J. M. Serpas, sheriff and tax collector for the parish of St. Bernard, show that he has still in his hands the sum of $2421 24 in Confederate notes, received by him in payment of taxes for the year 1861, previous to the occupation of the State by the Federal authorities.

I await the direction of competent authority to decide what disposition shall be made of these notes, and whether or not Mr. Serpas, having received them in payment of taxes when the State was in rebellion, and they were by the rebel laws legal tender, shall be relieved of so much of his liability to the State.

Respectfully submitted,

A. P. Dostie, Auditor.

Mr. Hills, during the reading of the report, moved that the reading of the items of the report be dispensed with.]

Mr. Stocker—Mr. President, I shall certainly object. I believe the items are the most important part of the report.

Mr. Austin—I move to refer the report to a special committee of five.

Mr. Mendiverri—I move that one thousand copies be printed.

[The motion of Mr. Mendiverri was carried.]

President—A committee of five,—how to be appointed?

Mr. Austin—By the president.

[The motion was carried.]

President—We come now to the order of the day.

Mr. Hills—I should like to inquire now, whether the report of the Committee on Preamble and that on the Distribution of Powers were finally adopted. They were passed on their first reading; but the point I wish decided is, whether they came under the rule, and subsequently passed, that nothing should be finally adopted until it had been read three several times on separate days.

Mr. Abell—I shall move that these reports be read a second and third time in the same manner as the other reports.

President—The report of the Committee on Preamble and that on Distribution of Powers, passed their third reading long ago.

Mr. Heard—As chairman of that committee, I would state that we reported the preamble on the tenth day of the session.

[The secretary read the minutes relative thereto, showing that these reports were adopted on their first reading.]

Mr. Hills—It appears from the minutes that the report of the Committee on Preamble was read and adopted on its presentation, and so, also, that of the Committee on Distribution of Powers. What I wish to know is, whether, under the present rules of the Convention, these were, or were not, finally passed upon.

Mr. Cutler—I rise for the purpose of suggesting that the language of the constitution of 1852 be followed exactly in the preamble, leaving out the words "and recommend its adoption."

Mr. Heard—These words were not intended to be incorporated in the constitution, but are merely an expression of the committee recommending the adoption of the preamble which we report.

[The report was adopted.]

Mr. Hills—Mr. President, I would now call for the second reading of the report of the Committee on Distribution of Powers.

President—That cannot be taken up under the rules we have adopted until the other is disposed of.

Mr. Stocker—I rise to inquire whether either of these reports has been adopted as a part of the constitution?

President—They have not.

Mr. Abell—I move to amend—

President—You are out of order.

Mr. Mann—Mr. President, I would like to know if it can be put upon its third reading without a suspension of the rules. If not,

I move to suspend the rules, in order to take up the report and pass it to its third reading.

[The motion was carried, and the rules suspended, sixty members voting in the affirmative.

The report was read.]

Mr. MANN—I move its adoption.

Mr. HENDERSON—As this is the third reading, I move the previous question.

[The motion was carried by a vote of 64.

The main question was then put, with the following result:

YEAS—Messrs. Abell, Ariail, Austin, Barrett, Bailey, Beauvais, Bell, Bennie, Bofill, Bonzano, Bromley, Buckley, Burke, Campbell, Cazabat, Collin, Cook J. K., Cook T., Crozat, Cutler, Decker, Dufresne, Dupaty, Duke, Edwards, Ennis, Fish, Flagg, Flood, Foley, Fosdick, Gastinel, Geier, Goldman, Gorlinski, Gruneberg, Harnan, Hart, Healy, Heard, Henderson, Hills, Hire, Howes, Kugler, Maas, Mann, Maurer, Mayer, Mendiverri, Millspaugh, Montamat, Morris, Murphy E., Murphy M. W., Newell, Normand, O'Conner, Pintado, Poynot, Purcell J., Pursell S., Schroeder, Schnurr, Shaw, Smith, Spellicy, Stocker, Stumpf, Stiner, Stauffer, Sullivan, Taliaferro, Thorpe, Thomas, Waters, Wells, Wenck, Wilson—79.

NAYS—None.

The report was adopted.]

PRESIDENT—I appoint Messrs. Beauvais, Austin, Thomas, Fish and Wells as committee on communication from the auditor.

Mr. HILLS—I call for the second reading of the report on Distribution of Powers.

[The report was read.]

Mr. HENDERSON—I move to suspend the rules and pass it to its third reading.

[The motion was carried and the secretary read the report.]

Mr. HILLS—I move it be adopted and enrolled as title first, articles 1 and 2 of the constitution.

[The secretary proceeded to call the yeas and nays.]

Mr. STOCKER—I want to know whether I am voting to place the report on Distribution of Powers before the preamble.

PRESIDENT—The preamble is never numbered.

Mr. STOCKER—Then I vote "yes."

[The result was as follows:

YEAS—Messrs. Abell, Ariail, Austin, Barrett, Beauvais, Bell, Bennie, Bofill, Bonzano, Bromley, Buckley, Burke, Campbell, Collin, Cazabat, Cook J. K., Cook T., Crozat, Cutler, Decker, Dufresne, Duke, Dupaty, Edwards, Ennis, Flagg, Flood, Foley, Fosdick, Gastinel, Geier, Goldman, Gorlinski, Gruneberg, Harnan, Hart, Heard, Henderson, Hills, Hire, Howes, Kugler, Maas, Mann, Maurer, Mayer, Mendiverri, Millspaugh, Montamat, Morris, Murphy E., Murphy M. W., Newell, Normand, O'Conner, Pintado, Poynot, Purcell J., Pursell S., Schroeder, Schnurr, Shaw, Smith, Spellicy, Stocker, Stumpf, Stiner, Stauffer, Sullivan, Taliaferro, Thorpe, Thomas, Waters, Wenck, Wells, and Wilson—76.]

Mr. PURSELL—I move that the report of the Committee on Emancipation be placed as title II, articles 3 and 4.

Mr. BONZANO—I move that it be placed at the head of the constitution as an ordinance without numbering.

Mr. ABELL—I move that that report be made the order of day for next Wednesday

Mr. PURSELL—I withdraw my motion.

PRESIDENT—Do you not think it would be more judicious to leave the arrangement of the parts until you decide on the whole?

Mr. HILLS—I move that the further arrangement of articles be postponed until all is decided upon.

[The motion was carried.]

Mr. ABELL—I move that the second reading of the report of the Committee on Legislative Department be postponed until Tuesday next, at 1 o'clock.

[The motion was carried.

[A motion to adjourn till 12 M., Tuesday, May 17th, was then carried.]

TUESDAY, May 17, 1864.

[At the usual hour the Convention was called to order by the chair, and upon calling the roll the following members were found to be present:

Messrs. Abell, Ariail, Balch, Barrett, Beauvais, Bell, Bennie, Bofill, Bonzano, Burke, Cook T., Crozat, Davies, Duane, Dufresne, Edwards, Ennis, Fish, Flagg, Flood, Fosdick, Geier, Goldman, Gorlinski, Hart, Henderson, Hills, Howes, Kugler, Maas, Mann, Mayer, Millspaugh, Montague, Murphy M. W., Newell, Normand, Pintado, Purcell J., Pursell S., Schroeder, Seymour, Shaw, Smith, Spellicy, Stumpf, Stiner, Taliaferro, Terry, Thorpe, Wenck, Wells, Wilson, and Mr. President—54.

There being no quorum, the sergeant-at-arms was dispatched to bring in members, and after some delay, the following members having taken their seats, viz:

Messrs. Austin, Bailey, Baum, Bromley, Buckley, Campbell, Cazabat, Cook J. K., Cutler, Dupaty, Fuller, Healy, Howell, Maurer, Mendiverri, Montamat, Morris, O'Conner, Ong, Orr, Poynot, Stocker, Stauffer, Sullivan and Thomas—25,

The secretary proceeded to read the minutes of the previous day's session.]

Mr. MONTAGUE—I have been absent, Mr. President, unavoidably, for some days, and desire to record my vote on the emancipation question. On the motion to reject the minority report of the Emancipation Committee, I vote yes. On the adoption of the first and second sections of the majority report, I vote yes.

Mr. HOWELL—Mr. President, I have been absent several days. My signature to the report is, I presume, a sufficient vindication of my opinions, but I desire to record my vote, and if allowed, would like to vote on each proposition separately.

Mr. HILLS—I move that he be permitted.

Mr. HOWELL—On the motion to reject the minority report, I vote yes. On the adoption of the first and second sections of the majority report, I vote yes.

Mr. SEYMOUR—I was sick with chills and fever when the vote was taken on the adoption of the first two sections of the majority report. I vote yes.

Mr. STAUFFER—I think the gentleman was here, or some one answered for him.

Mr. STOCKER—I recollect distinctly having heard some answer when the gentleman's name was called.

Mr. SEYMOUR—I was sick and was not in the Convention.

Mr. BALCH—I vote upon both sections without any explanations, except that I vote conscientiously. I vote "no."

SECRETARY—Mr. Balch has already voted.

Mr. BALCH—It is a mistake. I was not present when the vote was taken.

SECRETARY—You are recorded as having voted "no."

Mr. HENDERSON—Mr. President, I have a resolution to offer. I desire that it may be read and lie over under the rules:

Whereas, It has been the invariable custom of every Legislature of the State to make liberal appropriations from the general fund for the support and relief of all incorporated charitable institutions, and in respect to which she is second to no State in the Union, whether numbers, variety or extent of the field of charitable labor is considered; *and whereas*, the Legislature of 1860 did make appropriations as follows under that head, to-wit:

For the Orphans' Home, in New Orleans	$1500
For the St. Mary's Catholic Orphan Boys' Asylum in New Orleans,	4000
For the Female Orphan Asylum, Camp Street,	4000
For the House of the Good Shepherd,	250
For the Jewish Widows' and Orphans' Asylum,	500
For the St. Joseph Catholic Orphan Asylum,	1500
For the St. Elizabeth House of Industry,	1000
For the Society for the relief of the Orphan Boys, Fourth District,	1000
For the Institution for Indigent Colored Boys, Third District,	1000
For the Ladies of Providence, Third District,	750
For St. Anna's Asylum for Destitute Widows and Children,	1500
For the Children's Home of the Protestant Episcopal Church,	500
For the Catholic Institute of Destitute Orphans,	750
For the Catholic Benevolent Association, Baton Rouge,	250
For the Female Orphan Asylum, Baton Rouge,	500
For the St. Vincent Orphan Asylum, Donaldsonville,	500
For the Milne Asylum, New Orleans,	500
Total,	$20,000

And, whereas, In consequence of the calamities, growing out of the rebellious war now prevailing, which has not only dried up to a great extent the sources of private benevolence and diminished their revenues to almost nothing, but has been the means of greatly increasing their burdens by the addition it has made to the list of orphans, indigent widows, and the destitute of all classes who stand in the need of charity, so that the worthy, patient and self-sacrificing sisters and managers of these heavenly-endowed institutions are reduced to the greatest distress to provide food and raiment for the thousands of helpless beings under their charge; and were it not for the bounty of the Federal government, through its officers of this department, in donating them daily army rations for their support, many of them would be compelled to close their doors; be it therefore

Resolved, That the sum of $20,000 be

and is hereby appropriated from the general fund for the support and relief of the charitable institutions as named in the foregoing schedule, to be divided according to the amounts therein stated, and to be paid in the usual manner, by warrants from the auditor on the treasurer, in favor of the managers and authorized agents of said institutions.

Laid over until to-morrow.

Mr. M. W. MURPHY—I second the resolution.

Mr. FOLEY—I have a resolution to offer:

Whereas, Several members of the Louisiana Constitutional Convention have been elected as delegates to Baltimore: *and*. *whereas*, it is vitally important to the interests of Louisiana that the Convention should complete its work without adjournment; therefore,

Be it Resolved, That the members of this Convention, who are elected to the Baltimore Convention, and who choose to go three, shall resign their seats in this Convention immediately, and the governor be requested to issue his proclamation for an election to fill the vacancies in the different parishes and representative districts so vacated.

Mr. MONTAMAT—I do not believe any gentleman has a right to say that members shall resign. We may *request* members to resign, but we have no right to direct it. I move a suspension of the rules in order to act upon the resolution immediately.

[The motion was lost.]

Mr. PURSELL—I move that the report of the Committee on Printing, presented some time ago, be taken up. The compensation of all the officers, except the public printer, has been fixed, and I think it is time for us to take that up now.

Mr. HENDERSON—I think myself that it is right and proper that we suspend the rules to take up that report at once, and I move a suspension of the rules in order to take it up.

PRESIDENT—There is no occasion to suspend the rules; it is part of the regular business.

[Secretary read the report.]

To the president and members of the Louisiana State Convention:

Your Committee on Printing, after mature deliberation, beg leave to submit the following rates of compensation to the official printer of this Convention:

1. For two hundred copies of the journal of the debates of the Convention, in book form, in English and French, printed in brevier, and composed with the matter published in the journal, the pages to be seventy-one lines in length, including the title, the blank line under the title, and the foot line, and forty ems in width—the books to be stitched and bound in the same manner as law books—five dollars will be allowed for each page, and for every two hundred copies after the first two hundred, four dollars per page.

2. For all documents, reports or other matter printed in book or pamphlet form, in English or French, composed in bourgeois, the pages to be of the same length and breadth as the journal—five dollars per page for the first two hundred copies, and for every additional two hundred copies four dollars per page.

3. For resolutions, memorials or reports of committees, printed on foolscap, or similar sized paper, in English or French, composed in bourgeois type, thirty-six ems wide and ninety-five lines in length, for the first two hundred copies, eight dollars per page, and for each additional hundred copies four dollars per page.

4. For all matter marked "official," and published in the official journal, one dollar per square for the first insertion, and fifty cents for each subsequent insertion. The square being considered in size equal to ten lines in agate type.

Your committee would respectfully state, in conclusion, that they have based their report, and fixed the prices as above stated, upon the increased high prices of paper, labor and printing material.

All of which is respectfully submitted.

JOHN PURCELL, Chairman.
JOHN T. BARRETT,
JAMES FULLER.

Mr. THOMAS—I move the adoption of the report.

Mr. CAMPBELL—I rise for information. It strikes me that this report provides for the payment of five dollars per page for the books; that would make, if the books should contain six hundred pages, three thousand dollars a copy, not five dollars a copy. I take it as it reads: I don't know what it means; but we should be careful before we vote away two or three millions for printing a few books, and find out what we are doing.

Mr. HILLS—Mr. President, I am not a member of the Committee on Printing, but having graduated as a printer's devil some years ago, claim to have some knowledge of these matters. The report is very plain and simple. It simply means that for the first two hundred copies five dollars per page shall be paid: that is, that if the book shall contain two hundred pages, the first two hundred copies will cost one thousand dollars—

Mr. CAMPBELL—It does not say so.

Mr. HILLS—And the next two hundred copies will cost eight hundred dollars. And I wish to say, Mr. President, that I do not regard these rates as in any manner exorbitant, and I for one will vote for the report, for I know that the present exorbitant rates of printers' wages and increased cost of material fully justify the rates proposed. I think it just and right, and shall vote for it.

Mr. AUSTIN—I move the previous question.

Mr. CAMPBELL—I cannot take a man's meaning unless I take what he says. I therefore move to refer the report back to the committee. I don't object that the price is too great, but I want the report to be made intelligible.

Mr. BUCKLEY—Five dollars per page is five dollars for a page of type, not for each printed page.

[The previous question was carried.

The main question was put, and the report adopted.]

Mr. PURSELL—I now offer a resolution:

Resolved, That all bills of the official printer of this Convention be audited and approved by the Committee on Printing, the Committee on Finance, and the Committee on Expenses, in accordance with the rates fixed by the Convention, before payment, and that all bills so audited and approved be paid upon the warrant of the president upon the treasurer of the State, out of any moneys not otherwise appropriated.

[On motion, the rules were suspended and the resolution adopted.]

Mr. MONTAMAT—I have a report to make rom the Committee on Finance.

REPORT OF THE FINANCE COMMITTEE OF THE CONSTITUTIONAL CONVENTION OF THE FUNDS APPROPRIATED FOR THE PAYMENT OF PER DIEM OF MEMBERS AND SALARIES OF OFFICERS.

1864.	
May 9—Paid warrant No. 27...	$2,930 00
May 9—Paid warrant No. 28...	405 00
May 10—Pain warrant No. 29...	696 00
May 10—Paid warrant No. 30...	3,500 00
May 14—Paid warrant No. 31...	2,520 00
May 14—Paid warrant No. 32...	1,275 00
May 15—Paid warrant No. 34...	1,420 00
	$12,764 00
May 17—Balance on hand this day	$55,485 40
	$68,231 40

REPORT ON THE FUNDS FOR CONTINGENT EXPENSES.

May 15—Paid warrant No. 33 to Mr. DeCoursey, as per voucher No. 4...........	$1,747 37
May 17—Balance on hand to date	9,585 48
	$11,332 85

[The report was adopted without objection.

The report of the Committee on the Legislative Department being the order of the day, was then taken up.]

Mr. SULLIVAN—Mr. President, I have an amendment to offer to the 33d line.

Mr. STAUFFER—The gentleman is out of order. We have not yet reached that section.

[The secretary read the first article:

Art. 1. The legislative power of the State shall be vested in two distinct branches, the one to be styled the "House of Representatives," the other the "Senate," and both the General Assembly of the State of Louisiana.]

Mr. BELL—I move its adoption.

[The ayes and nays were called and the article carried by the following vote:

YEAS—Messrs. Abell, Ariail, Austin, Bailey, Barrett, Beauvais, Bell, Bennie, Bofill, Bonzano, Bromley, Buckley, Burke, Campbell, Cazabat, Cook J. K., Cook T., Crozat, Cutler, Davies, Decker, Duane, Dufresne, Edwards, Ennis, Fish, Flood, Foley, Fosdick, Fuller, Gastinel, Geier, Goldman, Healy, Hart, Henderson, Hills, Hire, Howell, Howes, Kugler, Maas, Maurer, Mayer, Mendiverri, Millspaugh, Montamat, Montague, Morris, Murphy M. W., Newell, Normand, O'Conner, Ong, Orr, Payne J., Paine J. T., Pintado, Poynot, Purcell J., Pursell S., Schroeder, Seymour, Shaw, Smith, Spellicy, Stocker, Stumpf, Stiner, Stauffer, Sullivan, Taliaferro, Terry, Thorpe, Thomas, Wenck, Wells, Wilson—78.

NAYS—None.

The secretary read:

Art. —. The members of the House of Representatives shall continue in service for the term of two years from the day of the closing of the general elections.]

Mr. Howell—I move its adoption, and I now move that in all articles when there is no opposition, the calling of the ayes and noes be dispensed with, and I move a suspension of the rules to act on the motion, if there is, as I have been informed, a rule requiring the vote to be so taken.

[The motion to suspend the rules was lost.

Section second was adopted by the following vote:

Yeas — Messrs. Abell, Ariail, Austin, Balch, Bailey, Barrett, Beauvais, Bell, Bennie, Bofill, Bonzano, Bromley, Buckley, Burke, Campbell, Cazabat, Cook J. K., Cook T., Cutler, Davies, Decker, Duane, Dufresne, Edwards, Ennis, Fish, Flagg, Flood, Foley, Fosdick, Fuller, Gastinel, Geier, Goldman, Healy, Hart, Hills, Hire, Howell, Howes, Kugler, Maas, Mann, Maurer, Mayer, Mendiverri, Millspaugh, Montamat, Montague, Morris, Newell, Normand, O'Conner, Ong, Orr, Payne J., Pintado, Poynot, Purcell J., Pursell S., Schroeder, Seymour, Shaw, Smith, Spellicy, Stocker, Stumpf, Stiner, Stauffer, Taliaferro, Terry, Thorpe, Thomas, Wenck, Wells, Wilson—76.

Nays—None.

The secretary read the third article:

Art. —. Representatives shall be chosen on the first Monday in November every two years; and the election shall be completed in one day. The General Assembly shall meet annually on the first Monday in January, unless a different day be appointed by law; and their sessions shall be held at the seat of government.]

Mr. Montague—I move to strike out the first Monday in January, and insert first Monday in December.

Mr. Montamat—I move to strike out first Monday in January, and insert third Monday in January. The first Monday may come on the first day of the year.

[The amendments were lost.]

Mr. Abell—I move to strike out first Monday, and insert second Monday.

Mr. Gastinel—I second the motion. The first Monday is blue Monday.

Mr. Stocker—I move to strike out the words "unless a different day be appointed by law."

[The motion was tabled.]

Mr. Pursell — I move to insert the words "after the first Tuesday," so that it will read "the first Monday after the first Tuesday."

[The motion was tabled, and the article adopted, without amendment, by the following vote:

Yeas—Messrs. Ariail, Austin, Bailey, Bell, Bennie, Bofill, Bonzano, Bromley, Buckley, Burke, Campbell, Cazabat, Cook J. K., Cook T., Crozat, Cutler, Davies, Decker, Duane, Dufresne, Edwards, Ennis, Fish, Flagg, Flood, Foley, Fosdick, Gastinel, Geier, Gorlinski, Goldman, Hart, Healy, Henderson, Hills, Hire, Howell, Howes, Kugler, Maas, Mann, Mayer, Mendiverri, Millspaugh, Montague, Morris, Murphy M. W., Newell, Normand, O'Conner, Ong, Orr, Payne J., Paine J. T., Pintado, Poynot, Schroeder, Seymour, Shaw, Smith, Spellicy, Stocker, Stumpf, Stiner, Stauffer, Taliaferro, Terry, Thorpe, Thomas, Wenck, Wells, Wilson—72.

Nays—Messrs. Abell, Barrett, Maurer, Montamat, Purcell J., Pursell S.—6.

Secretary read article 4:

Art. 4. Every duly qualified elector under this constitution shall be eligible to a seat in the General Assembly: *Provided*, that no person shall be a representative or senator unless he be, at the time of his election, a duly qualified voter of the representative or senatorial district from which he is elected.]

Mr. Abell—I have an amendment to offer. Amend so as to read:

Every qualified elector who shall have attained twenty-four years of age shall be eligible to a seat as representative in the General Assembly, and every qualified elector who shall have attained twenty-eight years of age shall be eligible to a seat in the Senate: *Provided*, that no person shall be a representative or senator unless he be, at the time of his election, a duly qualified voter of the representative or senatorial district from which he is elected.

Mr. Montamat—I offer an amendment: "Unless he is a qualified voter and a resident."

Mr. Mann—I move to lay both amendments on the table.

Mr. Montamat—Mr. President, I object to laying two amendments on the table by one vote.

[Mr. Montamat's amendment was then tabled: ayes 46, noes 24.

Mr. Abell's amendment was then tabled: ayes 73, noes 6.]

Mr. Cazabat—I rise, Mr. President, for information. According to our rules no less than one-fifth of the members can call for the ayes and noes. I am not aware that any resolution has been passed requiring the ayes and noes to be called without such a call except on the emancipation question.

Mr. HILLS--My resolution referred only to the question of emancipation; if there is any other resolution requiring the ayes and noes to be called, I am not aware of it.

Mr. MONTAMAT--It was a resolution offered by Mr. Abell.

Mr. HENDERSON--It is?

[The vote was taken with the following result:

YEAS--Messrs. Ariail, Austin, Bailey, Barrett, Bell, Bennie, Bofill, Bonzano, Bromley, Buckley, Burke, Cazabat, Cook J. K., Cook T., Crozat, Cutler, Davies, Decker, Duane, Dufresne, Dupaty, Edwards, Ennis, Fish, Flagg, Flood, Foley, Fosdick, Geier, Goldman, Gorlinski, Hart, Healy, Henderson, Hills, Hire, Howell, Howes, Knobloch, Kugler, Maas, Mann, Maurer, Mayer, Mendiverri, Millspaugh, Montague, Morris, Newell, Normand, Ong, Orr, Payne J., Pintado, Poynot, Purcell J., Pursell S., Schroeder, Seymour, Shaw, Smith, Spellicy, Stiner, Stocker, Stumpf, Stauffer, Taliaferro, Terry, Thorpe, Thomas, Wenck, Wells, Wilson--72.

NAYS--Messrs. Abell, Campbell, Gastinel, Montamat, Murphy M. W., O'Conner, Sullivan--7.

The 4th article was adopted.]

[The secretary read the 5th article.]

Art. 5. Elections for the members of the General Assembly shall be held at the several election precincts established by law.

Mr. FOLEY--I move its adoption.

[The article was adopted by the following vote:

YEAS--Messrs. Abell, Ariail, Austin, Bailey, Barrett, Beauvais, Bell, Bennie, Bofill, Bonzano, Bromley, Buckley, Burke, Campbell, Cazabat, Cook J. K., Cook T., Crozat, Cutler, Davies, Decker, Duane, Dufresne, Dupaty, Edwards, Ennis, Fish, Flagg, Flood, Foley, Fosdick, Fuller, Gastinel, Geier, Gorlinski, Goldman, Gruneberg, Hart, Henderson, Hills, Howell, Howes, Knobloch, Kugler, Maas, Mann, Maurer, Mayer, Mendiverri, Millspaugh, Montamat, Montague, Morris, Murphy M. W., Newell, Normand, O'Conner, Ong, Orr, Payne J., Pintado, Poynot, Purcell J., Pursell S., Schroeder, Seymour, Shaw, Smith, Spellicy, Stocker, Stumpf, Stiner, Stauffer, Sullivan, Taliaferro, Terry, Thorpe, Thomas, Wells, Wilson--80.

NAYS--None.]

Mr. ABELL--Mr. President, before proceeding further, I wish to observe that the resolution offered by me required the reports to be taken up section by section, and that they should not be adopted until they had been read on three separate days. It did not require the vote to be taken by ayes and noes.

[The secretary read the sixth article.]

Art. 6. Representation in the House of Representatives shall be equal and uniform, and shall be regulated and ascertained by the number of qualified electors. Each parish shall have at least one representative. No new parish shall be created with a territory less than six hundred and twenty-five square miles, nor with a number of electors less than the full number entitling it to a representative; nor when the creation of such new parish would leave any other parish without the said extent of territory and number of electors. The first enumeration by the State authorities, under this constitution, shall be made in the year one thousand eight hundred and sixty-six; the second in the year one thousand eight hundred and seventy; the third in the year one thousand eight hundred and seventy-six, after which time the General Assembly shall direct in what manner the census shall be taken, so that it be made at least once in every period of ten years for the purpose of ascertaining the total population, and the number of qualified electors in each parish and election district; and in case of informality in the census returns from any district, the Legislature shall order a new census taken in such parish or election district.

At the first session of the Legislature after the making of each enumeration, the Legislature shall apportion the representation amongst the several parishes and election districts on the basis of qualified electors as aforesaid. A representative number shall be fixed, and each parish and election district shall have as many representatives as the aggregate number of its electors will entitle it to, and an additional representative for any fraction exceeding one-half the representative number. The number of representatives shall not be more than one hundred and twenty, nor less than ninety, until an apportionment shall be made, and elections held under the same, in accordance with the first enumeration to be made, as directed in this article.

The representation in the Senate and House of Representatives shall be as follows:

For the parish of Orleans, forty-four representatives, to be elected as follows:

First District		5
Second do.		8
Third do.		6
Fourth do.		3
Fifth do.		3
Sixth do.		3
Seventh do.		3
Eighth do.		2
Ninth do.		2
Tenth do.		7
Right bank, Algiers		2
The Parish of	Livingston	1
do.	St. Tammany	1
do.	Pointe Coupée	2
do.	St. Martin	2
do.	Concordia	1
do.	Madison	1
do.	Franklin	1
do.	St. Mary	1
do.	Jefferson	3
do.	Plaquemines	1
do.	St. Bernard	1
do.	St. Charles	1
do.	St. John the Baptist	1
do.	St. James	1
do.	Ascension	1
do.	Assumption	2
do.	Lafourche	2
do.	Terrebonne	2
do.	Iberville	1
do.	West Baton Rouge	1
do.	East do. do.	2
do.	West Feliciana	1
do.	East do.	1
do.	St. Helena	1
do.	Washington	1
do.	Vermillion	1
do.	Lafayette	2
do.	St. Landry	3
do.	Calcassieu	2
do.	Avoyelles	2
do.	Rapides	3
do.	Natchitoches	2
do.	Sabine	2
do.	Caddo	2
do.	De Soto	2
do.	Ouachita	1
do.	Union	2
do.	Morehouse	1
do.	Jackson	2
do.	Caldwell	1
do.	Catahoula	2
do.	Claiborne	3
do.	Bossier	1
do.	Bienville	2
do.	Carroll	2
do.	Tensas	1
do.	Winn	2
Total		118

And the State shall be divided into the following senatorial districts: All that portion of the parish of Orleans lying on the left bank of the Mississippi river shall be divided into two senatorial districts; the First and Fourth Districts of the city of New Orleans shall compose one district and shall elect four senators, and the Second and Third Districts of said city shall compose the other district and shall elect three senators.

The parishes of Plaquemines, St. Bernard and all that part of the parish of Orleans on the right bank of the Mississippi river shall form one district, and shall elect one senator.

The parish of Jefferson shall form one district, and shall elect one senator.

The parishes of St. Charles and Lafourche shall form one district, and shall elect one senator.

The parishes of St. John the Baptist and St. James shall form one district, and shall elect one senator.

The parishes of Ascension, Assumption and Terrebonne shall form one district, and shall elect two senators.

The parish of Iberville shall form one district, and shall elect one senator.

The parish of East Baton Rouge shall form one district, and shall elect one senator.

The parishes of West Baton Rouge, Pointe Coupée and West Feliciana shall form one district, and shall elect two senators.

The parish of East Feliciana shall form one district, and shall elect one senator.

The parishes of Washington, St. Tammany, St. Helena and Livingston shall form one district, and shall elect one senator.

The parishes of Concordia and Tensas shall form one district, and shall elect one senator.

The parishes of Madison and Carroll shall form one district, and shall elect one senator.

The parishes of Morehouse, Ouachita, Union and Jackson shall form one district, and shall elect two senators.

The parishes of Catahoula, Caldwell and Franklin shall form one district, and shall elect one senator.

The parishes of Bossier, Bienville, Claiborne and Winn shall form one district, and shall elect two senators.

The parishes of Natchitoches, Sabine, De Soto and Caddo shall form one district, and shall elect two senators.

The parishes of St. Landry, Lafayette and Calcasieu shall form one district, and shall elect two senators.

The parishes of St. Martin and Vermillion shall form one district, and shall elect one senator.

The parish of St. Mary shall form one district, and shall elect one senator.

The parishes of Rapides and Avoyelles shall form one district, and shall elect two senators.

The House of Representatives shall choose its speaker and other officers.

Every white male who has attained the age of twenty-one years, and who has been a resident of the State twelve months next preceding the election, and the last six months thereof in the parish in which he offers to vote, and who shall be a citizen of the United States, and able to read and write, shall have the right of voting.

The Legislature shall have power to pass laws extending suffrage to such other persons, citizens of the United States, as by military service, by taxation to support the government, or by intellectual fitness, may be deemed entitled thereto.

No voter, on removing from one parish to another within the State, shall lose the right of voting in the former until he shall have acquired it in the latter. Electors shall in all cases, except treason, felony or breach of the peace, be privileged from arrest during their attendance at, going to, or returning from elections.

Mr. ABELL—I move to amend by striking out the words "number of electors," in the fifth line, and inserting the words "white population," and the same in the eighth line, and whenever the words "number of electors" occurs in the article.

It strikes me that the number of electors in the several parishes is not just. The language of the constitution of 1852 is "the total population," and therefore I propose this amendment.

[The motion was seconded.]

Mr. GOLDMAN—I move to lay it on the table.

[The motion was carried.]

Mr. ABELL—I offer to amend by striking out all after the word "district," in the sixteenth line, to the end of the eighteenth line, as superfluous.

Mr. HILLS—I move to lay it on the table.

[The motion was carried.]

Mr. ABELL—I move to strike out, in the twenty-first line, "qualified electors" and insert "total population."

Mr. GOLDMAN—I move to lay it on the table.

[The motion was carried.]

Mr. ABELL—I move to strike out "the," in the twenty-third line, and insert "its."

Mr. HILLS—As I have a respect for the English language, I move to lay that amendment on the table.

[The motion was carried.]

Mr. ABELL—I move to strike out, in the twenty-first line, "the number of electors," and insert "population."

[The motion was laid on the table.]

Mr. ABELL—I move to strike out "three," in the apportionment of the Fifth Representative District, and insert "five," as we cast about 600 votes, nearly as many as in any other district.

Mr. FOSDICK—I would like to say a few words in regard to changing the basis of representation. We provided only for the first election, and in doing so thought it was right to adopt that basis fixed by the authorities calling this Convention, and reduce proportionately the number of electors in both city and country. If gentlemen will look at the matter, they will find a deduction in exact proportion.

Mr. MONTAMAT—The Fifth District is one of the largest in the city of New Orleans. We cast 600 votes in the last election, and are entitled to more than the apportioned number of electors.

Mr. ABELL—The gentlemen opposed to me have voted nine times to reject my amendments, and consider the number of electors rather than the number of the population. I have no objection; and, in fact, call upon the Convention to say that the poor negro shall be represented, and have endeavored, with all the power I possess, to induce them to allow it. I am looking to the future—and not thinking of to-day only, but for the next generation—and if this Convention has power to free the negro, it is right for it to provide for their representation, though they have nine times voted not to do so. What do they mean by it? Do they mean to say that the representation should be governed by the electors? In the Fifth Representative District—the centre and government of New Orleans—we have 600 electors, and yet gentlemen wish to say that district shall only have three representatives. I want the Convention to take some position and stand by it, for, otherwise, we shall become a laughing-stock. I claim it as a right that we should have the representatives of the Fifth District increased to five, at least.

Mr. SHAW—I agree with the last gentleman in some of his remarks. It is hard, at this time, to fix upon a perfectly correct basis of representation, and that difficulty arose in calling this Convention, for there was no basis to calculate upon except the census of 1860, and even that was not given to us in detail, so that we were only able to arrive at the aggregate population of each parish. The sub-divisions of the parish of Orleans could not be ascertained; and, as far as I know—unless some one is able to find the original census records of 1860—we are unable to determine the population of the different wards and representative districts. At the time of calling this Convention, I myself took some pains to find out but failed; though if any one can obtain this information we can perhaps make a perfect apportionment. In default, however, of this knowledge, I think the gentleman's objection well taken—that we should not fix the representation of the Fifth, or any other district, by even the presidential election of 1860, for great changes have happened since then, and the numbers of electors have been in each district changed. If we adopt the basis upon which this Convention was called, we must adopt an imperfect one. I have not an amendment at hand at this moment which would strike out a better path for accomplishing a correct result; but at the proper time I shall offer one, providing that the electors throughout this State within the Federal lines shall be registered, and that the representation of the parishes and representative districts proceed upon that basis. That will be just, and the Fifth and every other ward will then have its due.

Mr. Hills—In regard to the question that the gentleman from the Fifth has raised, I shall be very glad to do justice, so far as the information we have will enable us. It will afford me great pleasure to agree with that gentleman—for whom I have great personal respect—from the fact that we almost always differ. It seems to me, that in fixing the representation we should be governed to a great extent by the elections of February 22d and March 28th, for it would certainly be wrong to fix upon any arbitrary rule with such guiding facts before us. The Third District casts over 900 votes. I see that the Tenth District has seven representatives apportioned to it, and I should like to have some gentleman from the Tenth tell us what was the vote of that District in the election of February 22d.

Mr. Orr—It was 1008.

Mr. Hills—That is less than 100 over those cast in the Third District, to which is given six representatives, while the Second District, which casts 675 votes, sends eight representatives. Now, Mr. President, I think that the just basis to be adopted in fixing the relative representation of the districts and wards of the State will be found by consulting the returns of our most recent State elections; and I believe that every member here is perfectly willing to do justice in this matter to the fifth, second, and every other ward. I differ with my friend from the fifth in respect to the right of making the number of electors the basis, and think that having it we should adhere to it. As this is a question of much importance, I move that the secretary of this Convention be instructed to bring in, at the next session, the election returns of this parish for February 22d and March 28th, and read them for the information of this body.

Mr. Mann—I amend and offer to include the returns of all the parishes.

[The amendment was accepted and the motion carried.

On motion the Convention then adjourned till 12 M. to-morrow.]

Wednesday, May 18, 1864.

[At the usual hour the Convention was called to order by the chair, and upon calling the roll the following members answered to their names:

Messrs. Abell, Ariail, Balch, Barrett, Baum, Bell, Bennie, Bofill, Bonzano, Burke, Campbell, Duane, Dufresne, Dupaty, Edwards, Ennis, Fish, Flood, Foley, Fosdick, Geier, Goldman, Gruneberg, Gaidry, Henderson, Howell, Howes, Kavanagh, Maas, Mann, Mayer, Montague, Murphy M. W., Newell, Normand, O'Conner, Pintado, Pursell S., Schroeder, Schnurr, Shaw, Smith, Spellicy, Stumpf, Stiner, Stauffer, Taliaferro, Terry, Waters, Wells, Wilson and Mr. President—52.

No quorum being present, the sergeant-at-arms was dispatched to bring in absent members.

The following members having taken their seats, viz: Messrs. Austin, Bromley, Buckley, Cook J. K., Crozat, Decker, Flagg, Fuller, Gastinel, Healy, Hart, Hills, Hire, Knobloch, Kugler, Mendiverri, Millspaugh, Montamat, Morris, Orr, Paine J. T., Poynot, Purcell J., Stocker, Sullivan, Thorpe, Thomas—27, the minutes of the previous day's proceedings were read and adopted.]

Mr. HILLS—Before offering this resolution, if the Convention will pardon me, I will state that I have just received news from Gen. Grant's army to the — instant. Gen. Grant was steadily driving the rebels towards Richmond, and four thousand prisoners had already arrived at Washington. I now offer a resolution:

Whereas, The absence of a few members of this Convention at the first roll-call seriously interrupts and retards its business, frequently delaying the commencement of the session for a whole hour after the time fixed for meeting; therefore,

Resolved, That any member who is absent without leave or satisfactory excuse at the 12 o'clock roll-call shall forfeit his per diem allowance for every day of such absence.

Mr. FOLEY—I move a suspension of the rules in order that it may be acted upon immediately.

[The motion to suspend the rules was lost.]

Mr. WILSON—I have a resolution to offer:

Whereas, The Convention has now performed the heaviest part of the labor for which it was called together; therefore, be it

Resolved, That it do adjourn *sine die* on the first day of June; and that evening sessions be held daily (Sundays excepted) to the date of adjournment.

Mr. PURSELL—Mr. President, I have a resolution to offer:

Resolved, That the hour of meeting of this Convention in future be 10 o'clock A. M. instead of 12 o'clock.

Mr. BONZANO—I have a resolution to offer

Whereas, The public interest requires that this Convention should not be interrupted in its business without sufficient cause:

Resolved, That no motion for an adjournment for a longer time than twenty-four hours shall be put to question unless it be seconded by a majority of the members present, and if so seconded the yeas and nays shall be called.

Mr. HOWELL—I have a resolution:

Resolved, That the secretary be instructed to collect and collate all motions and resolutions heretofore adopted, as bearing upon the mode of conducting business, or amending the rules and regulations of this Convention, and report to-morrow.

Mr. CAZABAT—I move a suspension of the rules for its adoption.

[The motion to suspend was lost.]

Mr. HENDERSON—I call up my resolution of yesterday, making an appropriation for benevolent objects.

Mr. STINER—I move the adoption of the resolution.

Mr. CAMPBELL—I have an amendment to offer:

Provided, A like sum of $20,000 be and is hereby appropriated for the relief of the destitute widows and orphans of the soldiers in the First and Second Louisiana Infantry, First and Second Louisiana Cavalry, and First and Second New Orleans Volunteers.

Mr. HENDERSON—I move to lay the amendment on the table.

Mr. MONTAMAT—I move to lay the resolution and the amendment on the table.

[The ayes and noes were called.]

Mr. MONTAMAT—I vote yes, because I believe that this body has no right to make such an appropriation. It is a matter that belongs entirely to the Legislature.

Mr. POYNOT—I vote no, because I believe that necessity knows no law.

Mr. STAUFFER—I vote yes, because I think we have no right to make appropriations of this kind.

Mr. WELLS—I am a low-abiding citizen. I believe that we have no legal right to make such an appropriation. I, therefore, vote yes.

[The result of the vote was as follows:

YEAS—Messrs. Abell, Austin, Baum, Beauvais, Bennie, Bromley, Brott, Burke, Campbell, Cazabat, Decker, Dupaty, Edwards, Ennis, Flagg, Gruneberg, Gaidry, Hills, Hire, Howell, Knobloch, Kugler, Maas, Mann, Mayer, Mendiverri, Millspaugh, Montamat, Montague, Morris, Newell, Normand, Paine J. T., Pintado, Pursell S., Seymour, Stauffer, Thomas—38.

NAYS—Messrs. Balch, Barrett, Bell, Bofill, Bonzano, Buckley, Cook J. K., Cook T., Crozat, Duane, Dufresne, Fish, Flood, Foley, Fosdick, Fuller, Gastinel, Geier, Goldman,

Gorlinski, Healy, Harnan, Hart, Henderson, Howes, Kavanagh, Murphy E., Murphy M. W., O'Conner, Orr, Poynot, Purcell J., Schroeder, Schnurr, Shaw, Smith, Spellicy, Stocker, Stumpf, Stiner, Stauffer, Sullivan, Taliaferro, Terry, Thorpe, Waters, Wilson—47.

The motion was postponed.]

Mr. HOWELL—Mr. President, the fact that we are revising and amending the constitution, it seems to me implies the existence of that constitution. I merely desire to call the attention of gentlemen to the first article of that constitution which we are now revising. It reads as follows:

"Art. 1. The powers of the government of the State of Louisiana shall be divided into three distinct departments, and each of them be confided to a separate body of magistracy, to-wit: those which are legislative to one, those which are executive to another, and those which are judicial to another."

And then to article 94 of the same constitution. It reads as follows:

"Art. 94. No money shall be drawn from the treasury but in pursuance of specific appropriation made by law, nor shall any appropriation be made for a longer term than two years. A regular statement and account of the receipts and expenditures of all public moneys shall be published annually in such manner as shall be prescribed by law."

This is the only argument I have to offer against the adoption of this resolution.

Mr. HENDERSON—I am astonished to see gentlemen here that call themselves human beings, undertake, in this body, by very equivocal legislation, to oppose a measure that calls for support for starving women and children. Sir, suppose the Legislature should pass an act to prohibit me from giving water to a man dying, I would take the ground that the law was unconstitutional and as against humanity, and would not obey it.

Shall we let the poor women and children sent to these institutions for protection starve or be turned out in misery and destitution? Such an act would be against humanity.

I might answer my friend, Judge Howell's objection to the legality of such action on the part of this body, by referring to our action in fixing the basis of representation, that is assuming legislative power, and we have the same right to assume legislative power in the one instance that we have in the other.

Shall we wait till January, 1865, before we relieve the wants of these starving women and children in fifteen or twenty institutions in this city? It is against the dictates of justice and humanity. It is one of those cases of necessity which demands prompt and immediate action, and will any man refuse to vote the necessary money for these widows and orphans?

The argument that this body has no power to legislate is not good; we have all power. When the constitution is framed and adopted the legislative power will be properly confined to the Legislature, but until then that power is in this body. We are the sovereign people in Convention assembled. We make constitutions, and our right to make this appropriation is unquestionable. We have a precedent in the convention of Missouri. They submitted nothing to the people, because they knew that the people were at least a majority of them "secesh," and they proceeded to appoint all the officers and carried on the government for near three years, the present governor being an appointee of the convention.

Mr. HILLS—Mr. President, it may be that I am not a human being—the gentleman claims that all who oppose his resolution are not human beings. But human being or not, I will say that that gentleman will never intimidate me from voting exactly as I believe to be right.

The gentleman who has just taken his seat is one who has told us from time to time that this was not a legislative body; that we are not a legislature, and consequently are not invested with legislative powers. I recollect very well that this was the position he assumed when the gentleman from St. Mary's (Mr. Smith) introduced his resolution to compel the capitalists o his section to redeem their bastard currency that they had forced into the hands of the laboring men and mechanics. At the same time I agreed with my friend that the hard-working holders of the stuff ought to have recourse upon the makers to make them redeem it. I was of opinion, as I am now, that we have no right to legislate upon the subject.

Having made these remarks, I desire to offer a substitute for the gentleman's resolution:

Resolved, That the *per diem* allowance of the members of this Convention be reduced to four dollars per day, and that a sum equal to the difference between that amount and the present allowance, viz., six dollars per day, be appropriated to the use of the various charitable institutions of this city.

Mr. HENDERSON---I move to lay the substitute on the table.

Mr. MONTAMAT---I do not think this body has power to appropriate money, except to defray its necessary expenses.

Mr. ABELL---The objects embraced in the resolution offered by Mr. Henderson are among the most worthy and deserving, and had this Convention the right to make appropriations, except such as are necessary to carry out the object for which it was called, I would willingly vote the appropriation, but believing, as I do, that it is beyond the legitimate sphere of our duties, I shall be compelled to vote against it.

Mr. STOCKER---I am somewhat surprised at the positions assumed by some of the gentlemen. I had supposed that we were the people of Louisiana, in convention asembled; that we had the power to make appropriations or to do anything else we saw fit to do.

We are the people, and it seems strange to me that gentlemen learned in the law come up here and tell us we have no power. One gentleman gets up here and refers to the distribution of power in the constitution of '52. I would ask the gentleman where is the Legislature to exercise this power? Why, sir, if necessary, we should stretch our powers a little to meet such a case as this. For one, I am perfectly satisfied that we have the power, and I am willing to take upon myself the reponsibility of voting for the resolution as it now stands.

Mr. BONZANO---I move that Marais Street Institution (fifty-four children) be added to the resolution, with an additional appropriation of five hundred dollars.

Mr. THORPE---I would add the St. Vincent for a like amount.

Mr. MONTAMAT---I move that the Firemen's Charitable Association be added to the list, and that the sum of five thousand dollars additional be appropriated for them.

Mr. HOWELL---I would ask if the substitute of the gentleman from the Second District is to be put to the House?

PRESIDENT---No.

Mr. HOWELL---I would ask why? I, sir, would go as far as any gentleman, in my views of charity; but I think that charity consists in doing that which we have a right to do. Now I, as an individual, am willing to the extent of my ability; but I am not willing to take the money which does not belong to me or to this Convention, and make a charitable distribution of it. If the money belonged to the members, I would vote for the resolution. If this substitute was to go before the House I would vote for it, and I will say that if I am entitled to any per diem, I am willing to give half of it.

Mr. HILLS---I would ask, Mr. President, why the substitute is not to be put to this House?

PRESIDENT---The resolution contemplates the appropriation of money belonging to the State. The substitute proposes a private charity, for the per diem has been appropriated to the members and belongs to them. The appropriation of money belonging to the members has nothing to do with the appropriation of money belonging to the State. Therefore the substitute, being foreign to the matter and substance of the resolution, is out of place, and cannot be put to the House.

Mr. SULLIVAN---I would ask if the Firemen's Charitable Association is included?

Mr. ORR---It is a well-admitted fact that these asylums are the most noble institutions that we have in our country. All the aid that has been afforded them by the United States, the State of Louisiana, and by private citizens, has been as bread thrown upon the waters, and will return fourfold. A gentleman (Judge Howell) has stated that he cannot vote for this resolution, because he is conscientiously opposed to it---because it proposes to appropriate the money of the State. I will go to scripture to show that it should be passed. "Charity covers a multitude of sins." Now, I believe that if we pass this resolution, we shall make charity cover a multitude of the sins of this Convention.

Mr. HILLS—I rise to appeal from the decision of the chair, in deciding that my substitute was not in order.

PRESIDENT—A member must appeal at the time the decision is made, before he permits another member to take the floor. You are too late.

Mr. CAMPBELL—I desire to offer my amendment:

Provided, The destitute widows and orphans of the soldiers who have lost their lives in battle be included.

Mr. FOLEY—I should like to know what soldiers he means.

Mr. HENDERSON—I move to lay the amendment on the table.

Mr. CAMPBELL—I desire to explain.

PRESIDENT—A motion to lay on the table is not debatable.

[The amendment was tabled.

Mr. Thorpe's amendment was then put to vote and adopted.

Mr. Bonzano's amendment was then adopted.

Mr. Montamat's amendment was then put to vote.

The ayes and nays were called.]

Mr. BELL—I vote for it because I think they are as deserving of it as any other association, and more.

Mr. CAMPBELL—I ask to be excused from voting. I was not allowed to explain my amendment, and wish to know if I am obliged to vote on the question.

PRESIDENT—Such is the rule of the Convention.

Mr. CAMPBELL—I am the last man that would offer any obstacle to the proceedings of this Convention. I only asked that I might explain why I offered it, and I was denied the privilege, and I certainly do not think any gentleman would ask me to vote on the question.

Mr. MONTAGUE—I move that the gentleman be excused; he was denied the privilege of explaining.

[The Convention refused to excuse him.]

Mr. CAMPBELL—I vote "no."

Mr. FOSDICK—As one of the oldest firemen in New Orleans, I claim a right to explain my reason for voting against the amendment. We have no information that they are in need of any such assistance. They have never asked it, and I am assured that they have funds and take care of their own widows and orphans; and, therefore, I vote "no."

Mr. HILLS—I deny the right of this Convention to appropriate anything outside of its own expenses; and, therefore, I shall vote "no;" and I wish my vote, with the reason, to be recorded.

Mr. HOWES—I vote "no," for the same reason.

Mr. MONTAGUE—I look upon these objects as being worthy, but I hold that we have no right to appropriate money for any such purpose. I shall therefore vote for the amendment as a rider to kill the original bill. I vote "yes."

Mr. SULLIVAN—I vote "yes" because I think they are a more worthy association than any other in New Orleans.

Mr. THORPE—I vote "no" for the reason that the sum proposed for the Firemen's Association is comparatively large, and they have not asked for anything.

Mr. THOMAS—I vote "yes" for the same reason as Mr. Montague.

Mr. WELLS—I don't care about whipping the devil round the stump. I vote "no."

Mr. T. COOK—I desire to change my vote from "no" to "yes."

Mr. HILLS—Mr. President, I desire my vote to stand as it is.

[The following is the result of the vote:

YEAS—Messrs. Abell, Austin, Balch, Baum, Beauvais, Bell, Bofill, Bromley, Brott, Buckley, Campbell, Cook T., Crozat, Ennis, Fish, Flagg, Foley, Fuller, Geier, Goldman, Gruneberg, Knobloch, Mayer, Mendiverri, Montamat, Montague, Morris, Murphy M. W., O'Conner, Orr, Purcell J., Seymour, Shaw, Spellicy, Stocker, Stumpf, Stauffer, Sullivan, Taliaferro, Terry, Thomas, Waters, Wilson—43.

NAYS—Messrs. Ariail, Barrett, Bennie, Bonzano, Burke, Cook J. K., Cutler, Decker, Duane, Dufresne, Edwards, Flood, Fosdick, Gastinel, Gorlinski, Gaidry, Healy, Harnan, Hart, Henderson, Hills, Hire, Howell, Howes, Kavanagh, Kugler, Maas,

Mann, Millspaugh, Murphy E., Newell, Normand, Paine J. T., Pintado, Poynot, Pursell S., Schroeder, Schnurr, Smith, Stiner, Thorpe, Wells—42.

The amendment was carried.]

[The yeas and nays were then called on the original resolution, as amended.]

Mr. BROMLEY—I vote no. Not because I object to these charities, but because I think this is not the time nor place.

Mr. CAZABAT—I vote no, because we have nothing to do with that question.

Mr. DUANE—I vote no, because I am opposed to the amendment.

Mr. GORLINSKI—I vote no, because it ought to have been referred to a committee to report thereon.

Mr. ORR—In the name of the widows and orphans, I vote yes.

Mr. SMITH—I am in favor of the resolution, believing the Convention has a right to appropriate money. But I am opposed to the amendment, and therefore vote no.

Mr. STOCKER—I am in favor of the resolution, and believe the Convention has a right to appropriate money, and am in favor of the amendment. Therefore, I vote yes.

Mr. STAUFFER—I shall vote no, on the resolution and amendment, because I don't think the people have called us together for the purpose of legislating, or for any other purpose than to revise and amend the constitution.

Mr. TERRY—Believing that the members of this Convention stand greatly in need of the prayers and heart-felt congratulations of the poor and destitute, and agreeing with Mr. Orr that the donations of these charities will cover the sins and transgressions of this Convention, and also believing that we can donate to others as well as ourselves, I vote yes.

[The result of the vote was as follows:

YEAS—Messrs. Barrett, Bell, Bofill, Bonzano, Buckley, Cook T., Crozat, Fish, Flagg, Flood, Foley, Fosdick, Fuller, Geier, Gruneberg, Healy, Harnan, Hart, Henderson, Kavanagh, Montamat, Murphy M. W., O'Conner, Orr, Purcell J., Schroeder, Schnurr, Shaw, Spellicy, Stocker, Stumpf, Stiner, Sullivan, Taliaferro, Terry, Thorpe, Waters, Wilson—38.

NAYS—Messrs. Abell, Ariail, Austin, Baum, Beauvais, Bennie, Bromley, Burke, Cazabat, Campbell, Cook J. K., Cutler, Decker, Duane, Dufresne, Dupaty, Edwards, Ennis, Flagg, Fosdick, Fuller, Gastinel, Goldman, Gorlinski, Gaidry, Hills, Hire, Howell, Howes, Knobloch, Kugler, Maas, Mann, Mayer, Mendiverri, Millspaugh, Montague, Morris, Murphy E., Newell, Normand, Orr, Paine J. T., Pintado, Poynot, Pursell S., Smith, Seymour, Stauffer, Thomas, Wells—51.

The resolution was lost.]

Mr. HILLS—If I am in order, I would like to offer as an original resolution the resolution which I offered as a substitute.

PRESIDENT—It is not in order.

[Resolutions of yesterday were then called up.]

Mr. FOLEY—I call up my resolution:

Whereas, Several members of the Louisiana Constitutional Convention have been elected as delegates to Baltimore; *and whereas*, it is vitally important to the interests of Louisiana that the Convention should complete its work without adjournment; therefore,

Be it Resolved, That the members of this Convention, who are elected and chosen to go to Baltimore, shall resign their seats in this Convention immediately, and the governor be requested to issue his proclamation for an election to fill the vacancies in the different parishes and representative districts so vacated.

Mr. THOMAS—I move to lay it on the table.

[The motion was carried by a rising vote of 50 to 16.]

Mr. STINER—The yeas and nays were called for before the vote was taken, and many members were counted as voting who supposed the secretary was calling the yeas and nays.

PRESIDENT—The call was not heard by the chair. In order to call the yeas and nays, it will be necessary to move a reconsideration.

Mr. STINER—I move a reconsideration.

[The motion was carried.

The roll was called, and the motion to table carried, by the following vote:]

YEAS—Messrs. Austin, Barrett, Baum, Beauvais, Bennie, Bofill, Bromley, Burke, Cook J. K., Cutler, Decker, Duane, Dupaty, Dufresne, Edwards, Ennis, Fish, Flagg, Fuller, Gastinel, Gaidry, Geier, Goldman, Hart, Hire, Howell, Kavanagh, Kugler, Maas, Mann, Mendiverri, Millspaugh, Montamat, Montague, Morris, Newell, Ong, Orr, Paine J. T., Pintado, Purcell J., Pursell S., Seymour, Shaw, Spellicy, Stauffer, Sullivan, Taliaferro, Terry, Thomas, Waters, Wells, Wilson—53.

NAYS—Messrs. Abell, Ariail, Bell, Bromley, Buckley, Campbell, Cazabat, Cook T., Flood, Foley, Fosdick, Gorlinski, Gruneberg, Harnan, Healy, Hills, Howes, Knobloch, Mayer, Murphy E., Murphy M. W., Normand, O'Conner, Schroeder, Schnurr, Smith, Stocker, Stumpf, Stiner, Thorpe—30.

[The order of the day was then taken up, and the sixth article of the report on Legislative Department read.]

Mr. S. PURSELL—I move to strike out the words "and able to read and write" from the following sentence :

"Every white male who has attained the age of twenty-one years, and who has been a resident of the State twelve months next preceding the election, and the last six months thereof in the parish in which he offers to vote, and who shall be a citizen of the United States, and able to read and write, shall have the right of voting."

PRESIDENT—The chair would state to the Convention that, in its ruling of yesterday in regard to the ayes and nays, it was in error ; that the resolution introduced by Mr. Hills requiring the yeas and nays to be called on every section, was confined entirely to the report on emancipation. The resolution of Mr. Abell, requiring each section to be taken up separately, says nothing in regard to calling the yeas and nays. Therefore, unless the Convention determine otherwise, the yeas and nays will not be called.

Mr. S. PURSELL—I object to the report as rendered, because it disfranchises a large number of the citizens—the oldest inhabitants of the State of Louisiana.

Mr. ABELL—When the Convention adjourned yesterday, it had not acted on the amendment to substitute "five" for "three" as the number of electors in the Fifth District.

PRESIDENT — The amendment must be offered again.

Mr. ABELL—I renew the amendment.

PRESIDENT—It is not in order.

Mr. STUMPF—There are many good citizens in this State who can read and write other languages, but are ignorant of the English. Are they rejected as the report stands?

Mr. FOSDICK—It seems to me the language of the report is plain: it is simply that they shall read and write some language. In regard to the proposition, I think that any man who cannot read the constitution submitted by this Convention is unworthy. If the population is not prepared to learn the first principles of education, it is utterly impossible for them to vote knowingly on the questions submitted to their consideration. I am aware that there is a large number in this State who heretofore could not read nor write, and they have exercised the elective franchise on the words of politicians who have misled them. If they had been capable of reading what had happened, we would have been saved all this trouble.

Mr. ABELL—I shall oppose this report as it stands. I have seen some men who understood mathematics and the various sciences, but had scarcely sense enough to walk the street when it was unencumbered ; and I have seen ignorant men fight their way to high positions in the world. If this report is adopted, it may exclude a great many worthy and talented citizens ; and I shall sustain the amendment to strike out the words in question.

Mr. HILLS—I wish to say a few words in behalf of the "old inhabitants" of Louisiana. The gentleman from Carrollton, it seems to me, has placed upon the records of this Convention a gross libel on the old inhabitants of the State. As one of those old inhabitants—one of the oldest of recent importation—I protest against giving out to the world that any very large proportion of the old inhabitants of this State are not capable of reading or writing their names. I do not think that ignorance prevails to such an alarming extent as would be naturally inferred from the gentleman's remark. I wish to place myself upon the records on this question in favor of the report as submitted to the Convention by the committee. I am in favor of the reading and writing qualification as a rule, though there may be exceptions. Men who are incapable of reading and writing with all the advantages of free schools that have been enjoyed by the white population, should not, in my opinion, be permitted to exercise the elective franchise.

Mr. SULLIVAN—I would ask the chairman

of that committee if he would not disfranchise one-fifth of his own constituents.

Mr. FOSDICK—I trust that most of my constituents know how to read and write.

Mr. SULLIVAN—I will tell the gentleman that those who cannot read nor write would go to defend the flag of the country as soon as he would. Twenty years ago there were few public schools in this State, and there are many men fifty years of age who cannot read and write. The question is preposterous.

Mr. SMITH—I am in favor of rejecting that part of the report which disfranchises the people of Louisiana from the simple fact that they cannot read and write, on the same principle that the gentleman has just stated. I am in favor of educating the free children of Louisiana, so that for the future this will not happen. I know there is a large portion of my constituents who cannot read and write, but who are intelligent men, and I feel it would be doing an injustice to deprive them of this right.

Mr. STOCKER—I shall vote in favor of the amendment. In 1861, I was a candidate for assistant alderman in the district represented by the gentleman who makes this report. A gentleman came up to vote for me, and because he could not write his name his vote was rejected, and I stood up for him, and for that reason there was an assault committed upon me, though with the assistance of a friend I succeeded in defending myself; therefore, having fought for a man at the polls who could not read, I certainly shall fight for him here.

Mr. WELLS—With the consent of the Convention and that of the honorable president, I would like to make a few remarks.

We have no way of judging of the future but by the past, and judging thus, it is evident that the work of to-day will be a repetition of the labors of yesterday. I see, sir, and I believe many other members have seen, that there is an under-current in this body intended to retard the progress of this Convention. I, being the junior delegate of this body, feel a delicacy in throwing myself in this turbid stream to obstruct its onward course; but, sir, when I see the rights of my people, of my State, and my constituents trampled under foot, I am in duty bound to raise my humble voice in their behalf. I consider the time of this Convention as belonging to the people. Much of it has been unnecessarily consumed by members introducing resolution after resolution, with little or no alteration, for the sole purpose of evading the questions before the House. Much time has been consumed by discussions on the slavery question—a question that has been attracting the attention of the ablest men of the nation for the last century—a question that is buried in the pit dug for it by the leaders of secession. In connection with this subject, allow me to state that I was once a slave; slave! yes, a slave from the oppression and tyranny of that bastard government, led by that demon of the nineteenth century. I have been, sir, a penniless refugee, driven from my home by the satellites of John Slidell, and have recorded an oath in high heaven against giving aid or countenance towards any man or means that will tend to promote the interests of his followers. And now, sir, when I see the hydra-headed monster of rebellion attempting to diffuse his venom in this body, or when I see the dying embers of secession gasping for one atom of oxygen from the pure air of the Union, or that which is still worse, when I see gentlemen on this floor attempting to resurrect the dead carcass of slavery, I shudder for the frailty and weakness of man. Forbearance sometimes ceases to be a virtue, and therefore I oppose the proposition.

Mr. THOMAS—I call for the previous question.

[The motion was lost, 37 only voting in the affirmative.

Mr. Abell endeavored to take the floor, but was ruled out of order, and some confusion resulted.

The roll was then called on the adoption of the report as amended, with the following result:]

YEAS—Messrs. Abell, Ariail, Austin, Barrett, Balch, Beauvais, Bell, Bennie, Bofill, Bonzano, Bromley, Burke, Cazabat, Cook J. K., Cook T., Crozat, Cutler, Decker, Dufresne, Duane, Dupaty, Edwards, Ennis, Fish, Flood, Foley, Fuller, Gastinel, Gaidry, Geier, Gorlinski, Gruneberg, Harnan,

Hart, Healy, Henderson, Howell, Howes, Knobloch, Kugler, Maas, Mann, Mayer, Millspaugh, Montamat, Montague, Morris, Murphy E., Murphy M. W., Newell, Normand, O'Conner, Ong, Orr, Pintado, Purcell J., Pursell S., Schroeder, Schnurr, Smith, Spellicy, Stocker, Stumpf, Stiner, Stauffer, Sullivan, Taliaferro, Terry, Thomas, Waters, Wilson—71.

NAYS—Messrs. Flagg, Fosdick, Goldman, Hills, Hire, Seymour, Shaw, Thorpe, Wells—9.

[The section was adopted.]

Mr. MONTAMAT—I move to adjourn.

[The ayes and noes were called, with the following result :]

YEAS—Messrs. Abell, Balch, Burke, Cook J. K., Dufresne, Dupaty, Gruneberg, Knobloch, Montamat, Murphy M. W., O'Conner, Stumpf, Sullivan, Waters—14.

NAYS—Messrs. Ariail, Austin, Barrett, Beauvais, Bell, Bennie, Bofill, Bonzano, Bromley, Cazabat, Cook T., Crozat, Cutler, Decker, Duane, Edwards, Ennis, Fish, Flagg, Flood, Foley, Fosdick, Fuller, Gaidry, Gastinel, Geier, Goldman, Gorlinski, Harnan, Hart, Healy, Henderson, Hills, Mire, Howell, Howes, Kugler, Maas, Mann, Maurer, Mayer, Montague, Morris, Murphy E., Newell, Normand, Ong, Orr, Pintado, Purcell J., Pursell S., Schroeder, Schnurr, Seymour, Shaw, Smith, Spellicy, Stocker, Stiner, Stauffer, Taliaferro, Terry, Thorpe, Thomas, Wells, Wilson—66.

Mr. THOMAS—I offer the following amendment:

First District—Strike out five and insert three.

Second District—Strike out eight and insert five.

Third District—Strike out six and insert seven.

Fifth District—Strike out three and insert four.

Sixth District—Strike out three and insert two.

Eighth District—Strike out two and insert three.

Tenth District—Strike out seven and insert eight.

Mr. THOMAS—I have a right to open the debate. The representation of New Orleans, as made in this report, is entirely erroneous, whether you take the entire white and colored population, or the vote of 1860, in the presidential election, or the last gubernatorial election. The vote cast in the First Representative District in the election of 1860 was 1100. The Second Representative District cast 1200, and the Third 2100—nearly as many as the other two. In this Convention the Second District has 11 representatives and the Third 9. According to this apportionment to the Legislature, the Second is entitled to 8 and the Third to 6. The population of the Second in 1860, according to the census, was over 16,000, and of the Third over 24,000. We find similar results in the last election. The Second polled 600 votes and the Third 600 ; yet the Third has six representatives and the Second eight. On this report all I desire is what is right and fair.

Mr. SHAW—I rise to a point of order. I understand the committee intend to accept the amendment, and therefore the discussion is unnecessary.

Mr. FOSDICK—I did not wish to interrupt the gentleman, or should have stated that the amendments were accepted. As I stated yesterday, we fixed the basis of representation the same as that adopted in convening this Convention. The city of New Orleans we gave 44 members, and divided them up on the plan previously adopted. Since then, on obtaining the returns of the last election, I find injustice has been done to some of the districts. I therefore accept the gentleman's amendment.

Mr. HENDERSON—That amendment is merely a portion of what has already been proposed by the committee. It is assumed that the basis ought to be an electoral basis. I am not in favor of that. I am in favor of the one assumed by Gen. Banks, and that is the *white* population. It does not follow that because you are in favor of emancipation, you also include negro equality. We cannot fix the basis of any of the wards until we settle on the basis of representation. Shall it be white men, the electoral vote? The gentleman from the Seventh (Mr. Howell) said he could show that in a majority or a great number of the States representation was based upon the voters. I call upon him for his proof. If it can be shown that a negro has been elected to Congress, I will yield the question ; though I grant that certain privileges are given to the colored man. The two parties that framed the constitution of the United States declared that representation and taxation should go together; in other words, every man taxed is to be represented, and every man who is represented is to be taxed. My question is, as to whether the voters or the white people shall constitute the basis of that representation. I defy any gentleman to show me any State in this nation which does not make the white population that basis on the principle that the negro and Indian should be subordinate. According to the opposite doctrine, if there are 10,000 voters in the parish you are to send 10,000 electors—a doctrine which I say contains neither common sense nor justice. In regard to the third line of the sixth article, I hope, at the proper time, a motion will be made to strike out "qualified electors" and insert "total white population;" and to do the same wherever any such expression occurs, thus narrowing down the question to this: Are you in favor of electors being the basis, or the white population?

Gen. Banks has been charged here with not knowing what he was about. Before issuing that order, he consulted every available means of information, and took as his basis the white population alone—not including the negroes, whether slave or free.

We have a greater white population in the Second than in any other district of like dimensions, but as to the relative number of voters no conclusion can be arrived at, as it is difficult to determine whether a large portion of the population is white or black.

Mr. MONTAMAT—You shall not insult the native-born population. [Confusion—"that is so," etc.]

Mr. HENDERSON—We have here a large colored population of perhaps 400,000, and by virtue of the constitution are a free people, and they occupy the soil of Louisiana, and must have the protection of the government.

Mr. THOMAS—I rise to a point of order. The matter should have been discussed yesterday. The gentleman is not in order.

PRESIDENT—The gentleman is in order.

Mr. THOMAS—I appeal from the decision of the chair.

[The chair was sustained—yeas 64, nays 0. On motion, the Convention then adjourned till to-morrow.]

THURSDAY, May 19, 1864.

[The Convention was called to order at 12 o'clock, and the proceedings were opened with prayer by the Rev. Mr. Stone.

A call of the roll showed that the following members were present, viz:]

Messrs. Abell, Ariail, Austin, Balch, Bailey, Baum, Bell, Bofill, Bonzano, Bromley, Burke, Campbell, Crozat, Davies, Decker, Duane, Dufresne, Edwards, Ennis, Fish, Flood, Foley, Fosdick, Geier, Gruneberg, Gaidry, Healy, Hart, Henderson, Hire, Howell, Howes, Kavanagh, Knobloch, Maas, Mann, Maurer, Mayer, Millspaugh, Montague, Murphy M. W., Newell, Normand, O'Conner, Orr, Payne J., Pintado, Poynot, Purcell J., Pursell S., Shroeder, Schnurr, Smith, Stumpf, Stiner, Stauffer, Taliaferro, Terry, Waters, Wells, Wilson and Mr. President—62.

[There being no quorum, the sergeant-at-arms was dispatched to bring in absentees. After some delay, the following gentlemen, viz: Cook J. K., Cook T., Cutler, Dupaty, Flagg, Gastinel, Gorlinski, Harnan, Hills, Mendiverri, Seymour, Shaw, Thorpe and Thomas—14—having taken their seats, the Convention proceeded to business.]

Mr. HENDERSON—I move a reconsideration of the resolution which I offered yesterday, and which was lost.

PRESIDENT—Did you vote with the majority?

Mr. HENDERSON—I voted with the minority.

PRESIDENT—Then you cannot move a reconsideration.

Mr. GORLINSKI—I voted with the majority, and I move a reconsideration.

Mr. HILLS—I move to lay that motion on the table.

[A rising vote showed ayes 28, noes 40. The motion was lost. The question was then put on the motion to reconsider, and a rising vote showed 40 ayes, 29 nays. The motion was adopted.]

Mr. CUTLER—I move that the matter be referred to a committee of five, to be appointed by the chair.

Mr. AUSTIN—Mr. President, I have a resolution to offer:

Resolved, That two-thirds of all the members of this Convention, as ascertained from the roll of those elected and qualified, shall hereafter constitute a quorum of this body.

Mr. Campbell—I have a resolution to offer, which I would ask to have referred to the same committee as the resolution of Mr. Henderson:

Whereas, The misfortunes of war has thrown in upon us many Union refugees, from different parts of our State and the neighboring States, who are now in a destitute condition and want and require immediate relief; and whereas, this Convention does sympathize with those who have had to leave their homes on account of their Union sentiments; therefore,

Resolved, That the sum of ——— dollars be and is hereby authorized to be placed at the disposal of the governor to relieve the distressed refugees in our city.

Mr. Goldman—I move a suspension of the rules to take it up immediately.

Mr. Hills—I move that the resolution be referred to the same committee.

[The motion was adopted on a rising vote: ayes, 45, noes 8.

Mr. Austin, chairman of the committee to whom was referred the auditor's report, reported "progress."]

Mr. Hills—I call up my resolution of yesterday, cutting off *per diem* of absent members.

Mr. Bell—I move its adoption.

[A motion was made to lay it on the table.

The ayes and noes were called, with the following result:]

Yeas — Messrs. Abell, Austin, Bailey, Buckley, Campbell, Cutler, Dufresne, Dupaty, Flagg, Gruneberg, Gaidry, Henderson, Hire, Kavanagh, Knobloch, Maurer, Mendiverri, Montamat, Paine J. T., Pursell S., Schnurr, Waters—22.

Nays—Messrs. Balch, Baum, Bell, Bofill, Bonzano, Bromley, Burke, Cook J. K., Cook T., Crozat, Davies, Decker, Duane, Edwards, Ennis, Flood, Foley, Fosdick, Gastinel, Geier, Goldman, Gorlinski, Healy, Harnan, Hart, Hills, Howell, Howes, Maas, Mann, Mayer, Millspaugh, Morris, Murphy M. W., Newell, Normand, O'Conner, Orr, Payne J., Pintado, Poynot, Purcell J., Schroeder, Seymour, Shaw, Smith, Stumpf, Stiner, Stauffer, Sullivan, Taliaferro, Terry, Thorpe, Thomas, Wells, Wilson—56.

Mr. Hills—On that resolution I move the previous question.

[The motion was lost.]

Mr. Montamat—I move to insert the word "not" between the words "shall" and "forfeit," so that it will read "shall not forfeit his *per diem.*"

[The motion was lost.]

Mr. Thomas—I desire to explain the reason why I shall vote against the resolution. I never did believe that the quorum was fixed on a correct basis. One hundred and fifty was the number fixed as the whole number of delegates to represent the whole State, but we have never had a hundred, and I do not believe that seventy-six out of one hundred members is a fair quorum. A resolution has been offered to-day, fixing a quorum at two-thirds of the members elected and qualified. I shall vote against this resolution, for the purpose of voting for that.

Mr. Henderson—I think there is no one here more anxious for the success of this Convention than myself. I think, however, we are going on a singular principle. Look for instance at Congress, where the members get thirty dollars per day, and have been wrangling for six months without passing a bill. Why, sir, we have done more than they have, and they have not resorted to any such plan as this resolution proposes, to cut off the *per diem* of a member who may be a few minutes late. I shall vote against the resolution, because I think it unjust, unfair and unparliamentary, and such a one as has never been adopted by any deliberative body on the face of the earth.

Mr. Pursell, of Jefferson—I think I can conscientiously vote against the resolution. I think that the record will show that I have been punctually in my place every day from the commencement of the session. And if all these gentlemen who are so anxious to get through such a resolution as this were found in their seats as punctually as I have been, instead of leaving without voting when an important question is to be voted on, we should always have a quorum.

Mr. Thorpe—I shall oppose anything that proposes to fine members pecuniarily for absence from roll-call. It looks undignified and childish in a body like this. We have been here a long time, and have done but little business, and I wish it put on record by the reporters, that I have never made a motion to adjourn, to lay on the table, or moved the previous question. I agree with the gentleman from the Third District (Mr. Thomas) with respect to our quorum, and I would here remark, for the benefit of the gentleman, that a resolution has recently been adopted by the Senate of the United States fixing a quorum at a majority of all the members elected and returned to that body from the States not in rebellion. The rebellious States are reduced to the condition of territories of the United States, and are no longer States.

We are in precisely the same condition, and to load this Convention down with such an enormous majority for a quorum, is simply to burden ourselves with parishes in the country that we do not recognize and know nothing about.

Mr. Abell—It is my misfortune to differ with the gentleman from the Third District on almost every occasion. He is ashamed that we have been here so long and done so little. But I think we have done a great deal—a great deal too much. We have passed one act that ought to have taken at least ten years. I shall vote against the proposition. It is our duty as gentlemen, as representatives of the people, to be here at the hour of 12 o'clock, and I think that obligation is sufficient, without any attempts to impose fines in so ignominious a manner.

Mr. Hills—Mr. President, the insinuation of the gentleman from Jefferson, that I have not been here regularly and punctually, and have left without voting, I repel. The record will show that I have been regular, and have not moved or voted for adjournments. If I cannot come here promptly, I am willing to lose my per diem. My time is valuable to me outside. It is at a considerable sacrifice that I am able to come here at all.

We have fixed our hour of meeting at 12 o'clock. Then let us meet at that hour. If we cannot meet sooner than 1, let us fix that hour; but while 12 is the hour, let us be punctual.

[The yeas and nays were called.]

Mr. Austin—I voted to lay the resolution on the table, because I did not understand it fully. I thought it was without any qualification, but I find it applies only to those who are absent without leave, without a reasonable excuse. I, therefore, vote yes.

[The following is the result of the vote by which the resolution was adopted :]

Yeas—Messrs. Austin, Balch, Barrett, Bofill, Bonzano, Burke, Crozat, Davies, Duane, Ennis, Flood, Foley, Fosdick, Geier, Goldman, Gorlinski, Harnan, Hart, Hills, Howell, Kavanagh, Knobloch, Maas, Mann, Millspaugh, Montague, Newell, Normand, O'Conner, Orr, Payne J., Pintado, Purcell J., Schroeder, Shaw, Smith, Stumpf, Stiner, Stauffer, Taliaferro, Terry, Wells, Wilson—43.

Nays—Messrs. Abell, Bailey, Baum, Bell, Bromley, Buckley, Campbell, Cook J. K., Cook T., Cutler, Decker, Dufresne, Dupaty, Edwards, Flagg, Gastinel, Gruneberg, Gaidry, Henderson, Hire, Howes, Maurer, Mayer, Mendiverri, Montamat, Murphy M. W., Ong, Paine J., T., Poynot, Pursell S., Schnurr, Seymour, Sullivan, Thorpe, Thomas, Waters—36.

Mr. Henderson—The resolution was not carried; it requires two-thirds to change a rule of this body.

Mr. Wilson called up his resolution.

[The secretary read the resolution fixing the time of adjournment on the first of June.]

Mr. Sullivan—I move to lay it on the table.

[The motion was carried.]

Mr. Pursell, of Jefferson—I call up my resolution.

[The secretary read the resolution fixing the time of meeting at 10 o'clock A. M.]

Mr. Montamat—I move to lay that resolution on the table.

[Mr. Bonzano—I call up my resolution.

The secretary read the resolution, providing that no motion for an adjournment for a longer time than twenty-four hours shall be entertained unless seconded by a majority of the House, and that then the vote shall be taken by yeas and nays.]

Mr. Sullivan—I move to lay it on the table.

[The motion to table was lost, and the resolution adopted on a rising vote—ayes 38, noes 29.]

President—The report of the Committee on the Legislative Department is the order of the day, and is now in order.

Mr. Pursell—I move to strike out these

words, constituting the 88th to the 91st lines inclusive, viz: "The Legislature shall have power to pass laws extending suffrage to such other persons, citizens of the United States, as by military service, by taxation to support the government, or by intellectual fitness may be deemed entitled thereto."

Mr. STAUFFER—I move to lay the motion to strike out on the table.

Mr. GOLDMAN—I second that motion.

[The yeas and nays were called on the motion to strike out.]

Mr. FOLEY—I rise for information. I desire to know if this refers to white men in the military service of the United States.

PRESIDENT—The language is very plain; every gentleman must construe it for himself.

Mr. HARNAN—I vote "yes," because it would let negroes who have property qualifications vote.

Mr. SMITH—I vote "yes," because I believe the constitution should fix the qualifications and not leave it to the Legislature.

Mr. FOLEY—I desire to change my vote from "no" to "yes," because I find the paragraph refers to negroes.

Mr. BARRETT—I desire to change my vote from "no" to "yes." I did not know what I was voting for.

Mr. HILLS—I wish my vote to stand. I also desire that all the members of this Convention who have not voted on this question be required to record their votes.

[The following is the result of the vote:]

YEAS—Messrs. Abell, Balch, Bailey, Barrett, Baum, Bell, Bofill, Buckley, Burke, Campbell, Cook J. K., Cook T., Crozat, Cutler, Decker, Duane, Dufresne, Edwards, Flagg, Flood, Foley, Gastinel, Geier, Gruneberg, Healy, Harnan, Hart. Kavanagh, Knobloch, Mann, Maurer, Mayer, Mendiverri, Millspaugh, Montamat, Murphy M. W., Newell, O'Conner, Ong, Orr, Payne J., Purcell J., Pursell S., Schroeder, Seymour, Smith, Stumpf, Sullivan, Taliaferro, Terry, Thomas, Waters, Wilson—53.

NAYS—Messrs. Austin, Bonzano, Bromley, Davies, Dupaty, Ennis, Fosdick, Goldman, Henderson, Hills, Hire, Howell, Maas, Montague, Normand, Paine J. T., Pintado, Schnurr, Shaw, Stiner, Stauffer, Thorpe, Wells—23.

[The motion to strike out was carried.]

Mr. SMITH—I move to strike out the figure "one" and insert "two," so as to entitle the parish of St. Mary to two representatives instead of one. There has been injustice done to that parish in making the apportionment. More than four hundred votes were polled there at the gubernatorial election, and previously we have always had two representatives and one senator.

Mr. SHAW—The parish of St. Mary, in 1860, had 3500 white inhabitants. Now, if you divide the number of white inhabitants in the State by 118—the number of representatives—you will find that St. Mary, instead of being entitled to two, is only entitled to one.

This report is based on the census of 1860. There are no dates by which a perfectly accurate basis can now be obtained, but I believe that to be as correct a basis as can be fixed at this time.

Mr. SMITH—There is certainly a mistake; we have generally 900 or 1000 voters, and in the last election cast nearly 500. I notice one parish with only 200 more voters than we have with two representatives. I ask it simply as a matter of justice to the parish; we are legally entitled to it.

Mr. HOWELL—As was remarked by the gentleman from the Fourth District, [Mr. Shaw,] members will do well to bear in mind that this portion of the report now under consideration is intended only as a temporary provision until the first legislature can be organized and set to work. It would have been better had this portion of the report been omitted and referred to the Committee on Schedule, and taken up with that report after the Judiciary report has been disposed of. We should then have been relieved of the difficulty of making arithmetical calculations, which cannot well be made by the body of a Convention. That was the course pursued by the Convention of 1852.

Gentlemen should consider where these efforts at amending in this mode will lead the Convention, if carried out. The apportionment is made by an arithmetical calculation, and if you change arbitrarily the number of members in any one parish, you necessarily change the proportion not only of the one parish, but of all the parishes in the State. The report fixes the number of representatives to compose the first legislature at 118. The committee, then, take some fixed number, as the total population or the total number of electors, and divide that number by 118 to ascertain the number of inhabitants or of electors, as the case may be, who are entitled to one representative, thus fixing upon a ratio or divisor to ascertain the number of representatives to which each parish is entitled. Now, gentlemen will see that if you change the proportion in one parish, you change the whole proportion and render it necessary to make another divisor. I think that it would be better to take the report as it stands than for this Convention to go into an arithmetical calculation to change it.

I do not object to the amendment of the gentleman from the Third, (Mr. Thomas,) because it does not change the entire number, (44,) but was only an apportionment of that number to the different representative districts. But if you attempt to go into a different apportionment of the several parishes, you must necessarily make a different calculation for the whole; and I am satisfied, from having given some attention to this question in arriving at the basis of representation for calling this Convention, that the committee have arrived at as correct an estimate as is possible, from the information and data within our reach. I am also satisfied that there is no data which will enable us to arrive at a perfect apportionment, and that the only mode by which we can in future do so is that pointed out in this report. Whether we have an electoral or white population basis, the result will be obtained by the census required.

Gentlemen will recollect that there are always some electors who do not vote, but are entitled to be represented, and it is unjust to limit any parish according to the number of votes actually cast.

In regard to the population, it is, we must admit, very different from that of 1860, when the last census was taken. It will be necessary to arrive at accuracy, whether we adopt the electoral or white population basis.

Upon these considerations, I suggest the propriety of taking the report as it stands, though one or two parishes may be injured, since it is better to do that than to deal unjustly with more.

It is impossible for us to tell what is the electoral vote in parishes not sending delegates to this Convention. So if you take the last gubernatorial election, if you determine for the parish of St. Mary by that, how will you provide for Catahoula, or any other parish, in which no election was held?

[The amendment was lost.]

Mr. Balch—I move to amend by striking out opposite Iberville "1" and inserting "2," as a matter of justice. We have 5743 voters according to the census of 1860. I am extremely astonished at some members who seem disposed to claim all their own rights, but grant none to others. We throw ourselves upon the generosity of New Orleans, and hope gentlemen will sustain the amendment.

Mr. Abell—I do not understand about this matter. I moved on yesterday to strike out "qualified electors," &c., and substitute total population, but each amendment was tabled. I wish to see some degree of consistency in the House.

Mr. Shaw—The Convention has agreed to make the representation from the parishes upon the basis of qualified electors. The first census to ascertain their number is to be taken in 1866, but until that time we must adopt a temporary basis of representation, which, if I understand this report rightly, is to be that of the total white population as it stood in 1860.

In regard to Iberville, it had in 1860 a population of 3793 whites, according to the compendium of the United States census.

I will not argue upon the correctness of this certified copy, but, if it is wrong, will be the first to rectify it. At present, I am in favor of sustaining the report of the committee. In the whole State of Louisiana there are 357,623 whites, and thus there will be one representative to every 3030 of the population.

Mr. Morris—I move to recommit between lines 33 and 80.

[The motion was lost.

Mr. Balch's amendment was lost.]

Mr. Shaw—I move that after "informal," in the 16th line, the word "error" be inserted, because the grossest error may be covered in the most formal manner.

Mr. Fosdick—I accept the amendment.

Mr. Mann—I move to strike out "seventy" in the eleventh line and insert "seventy-five," and to strike out after that to the words "after which." In 1870, if we are a part of the United States, the census then taken will save us the trouble, and then, as many of the other States do, we can take ours at the end of the first five intervening years. This is done in New York, Wisconsin, Michigan, and was in Louisiana under the constitution of 1845.

Mr. Shaw—A census of the inhabitants of the State is not proposed, but merely an enumeration of the qualified electors, which does not cost as much or require as much pains as the taking of a census.

[The amendment was lost.]

Mr. Terry—In place of lines 88, 89, 90 and 91, already stricken out, I offer the following: "The Legislature shall have power to pass laws, extending the right of suffrage to such other white persons, citizens of the United States, as by military services, or rendering other important services, may be deserving of that privilege.

[Laid on the table.]

Mr. Henderson—I propose to insert in the third line "total white population," instead of qualified electors, and to make the same substitution wherever, through the section, the like words occur.

Mr. Goldman—I move to lay on the table.

[Motion lost.]

Mr. Shaw—The Convention should consider well what it is doing before voting on this question. It is settled by our action to-day that the qualified electors will form the basis of representation; therefore this question of the colored population does not enter into the subject at all. The question is: Shall it be the whole white population or the white voters? If you adopt the former, and the House of Representatives be composed of 130 members, the city of New Orleans would have about 63; but if the basis of qualified electors be adopted, New Orleans would have 44. Any gentleman entering into the calculation to be approximately correct, based on the returns of the census, will find this to be the case. The total white population of Louisiana is 357,629, of which New Orleans has 149,068, very nearly half of the whole representation. It may be difficult to account for it; but we have a large proportion of non-voters and subjects of foreign powers here, which are not found in the country parishes, and the difference is so great as to give this State, on the basis of the white population, a representation that is disproportioned. I am in favor of acting fairly by the country, and taking the middle ground and making the qualified electors the basis. Every voter is equal to every other voter, and should have the same representation; but if you take the total white population as a basis, you will give the parish of Orleans a representation it is not entitled to.

Mr. Henderson—We are speculating about fixing the number of members of the Legislature, when we have not fixed upon the basis of representation. I shall sustain the original bill, without any amendment, in regard to the apportionment, but merely for temporary purposes, until the next Legislature meets and we have a census.

In regard to the fundamental portion of the bill, whether the basis shall be the electors or the white population, I am in favor of striking out the words "electors" and "qualified electors" wherever they occur, and inserting "total white population."

[The amendment was lost.]

Mr. Flagg—In the table of representatives for the several districts and parishes, I move to substitute the words "right bank, Orleans," for "right bank, Algiers."

[The amendment was adopted.]

Mr. Thomas—I now move the previous question on article 6.

[The motion was lost, 32 voting in the affirmative.]

Mr. Bromley—I move, in the apportionment of the parishes of Lafourche and Claiborne, to strike out "two" and insert "three."

[The amendment was lost.]

Mr. Bell—I move in the First District to strike out "three" and insert "four" for the number of representatives.

[The amendment was lost.]

Mr. MONTAMAT—I move the previous question.

[The motion was carried by a vote of 61 in the affirmative, and the sixth article adopted on its second reading.

The secretary read article 7 :]

Art. 7. The Legislature shall provide by law that the names and rasidences of all qualified electors shall be registered in order to entitle them to vote ; but the registry shall be free of cost to the elector.

Mr. TERRY—I move its adoption.

[The motion was adopted.

The secretary read article 8 :]

Art. 8. No pauper, no person under interdiction, nor under conviction of any crime punishable with hard labor, shall be entitled to vote at any election in this State.

Mr. FOLEY—I move its adoption.

[The motion was carried.

The secretary read :]

Art. 9. No person shall be entitled to vote at any election held in this State except in the parish of his residence, and in cities and towns divided into election precincts in the election precinct in which he resides.

Mr. BELL—I move its adoption.

[The motion was carried.

The secretary read :]

Art. 10. The members of the Senate shall be chosen for the term of four years. The Senate, when assembled, shall have the power to choose its own officers.

Mr. STAUFFER—I move its adoption.

[The motion was carried.

The secretary read :]

Art. 11. The Legislature, in every year in which they shall apportion representation in the House of Representatives, shall divide the State into senatorial districts.

Mr. BELL—I move its adoption.

[The motion was carried.

The secretary read :]

Art. 12. No parish shall be divided in the formation of a senatorial district—the parish of Orleans excepted. And whenever a new parish shall be created, it shall be attached to the senatorial district from which most of its territory was taken, or to another contiguous district, at the discretion of the Legislature ; but shall not be attached to more than one district. The number of senators shall be thirty-four, and they shall be apportioned among the senatorial districts according to the electoral population contained in the several districts : *Provided*, that no parish be entitled to more than seven senators.

Mr. STOCKER—I move to amend by striking out the words "at the discretion of the Legislature," in the 5th line.

[The amendment was lost.]

Mr. MONTAMAT—I move to strike out "thirty-four," leaving the number of senators blank.

[The amendment was lost and the article adopted as read.

The secretary read :]

Art. 13. In all apportionments of the Senate, the electoral population of the whole State shall be divided by the number thirty-four, and the result produced by this division shall be the senatorial ratio entitling a senatorial district to a senator. Single or contiguous parishes shall be formed into districts, having a population the nearest possible to the number entitling a district to a senator ; and if in the apportionment a parish or district fall short of or exceed the ratio, then a district may be formed having not more than two senators, but not otherwise. No new apportionment shall have the effect of abridging the term of service of any senator already elected at the time of making the apportionment. After an enumeration has been made as directed in the — article, the Legislature shall not pass any law until an apportionment of representation in both Houses of the General Assembly be made.

Mr. FOLEY—I move its adoption.

[The motion was carried.

The secretary read :]

Art. 14. At the first session of the General Assembly, after this constitution takes effect, the senators shall be equally divided by lot into two classes ; the seats of the senators of the first class shall be vacated at the expiration of the second year ; of the second class at the expiration of the fourth year ; so that one-half shall be chosen every two years, and a rotation thereby kept up perpetually. In case any district shall have elected two or more senators, said senators shall vacate their seats respectively at the end of two and four years, and lots shall be drawn between them.

Mr. MONTAMAT—I move its adoption.

[The motion was carried.

The secretary read :]

Art. 15. The first election for senators shall be general throughout the State, and at the same time that the general election for representatives is held ; and thereafter there shall be biennial elections to fill the places of those whose term of service may have expired.

Mr. STUMPF—I move its adoption.

[The motion was carried.

The secretary read :]

Art. 16. Not less than a majority of the members of each House of the General Assembly shall form a quorum to do business; but a smaller number may adjourn from day to day, and shall be authorized by law to compel the attendance of absent members.

Mr. Austin—I move its adoption.

[The motion was carried.

The secretary read :]

Art. 17. Each House of the General Assembly shall judge of the qualifications, election and returns of its members; but a contested election case shall be determined in such manner as shall be directed by law.

Mr. Montamat—I move to strike out all after the word "members," in the second line.

Mr. Harnan—I move that it be adopted.

[The motion to adopt was carried, Mr. Montamat's motion not having been seconded.

The secretary read :]

Art. 18. Each House of the General Assembly may determine the rules of its proceedings, punish a member for disorderly behavior, and, with the concurrence of two-thirds, expel a member, but not a second time for the same offence.

Mr. Stocker—I move to amend the third line by striking out the words "but not a second time for the same offence."

Mr. Healy—I move its adoption.

[The resolution to adopt was carried, Mr. Stocker's motion not having been seconded.

The secretary read :]

Art. 19. Each House of the General Assembly shall keep and publish weekly a journal of its proceedings, and the yeas and nays of the members on any question shall, at the desire of any two of them, be entered on the journal.

Mr. Gorlinski—I move its adoption.

[The motion was carried.

The secretary read :]

Art. 20. Each House may punish, by imprisonment, any person not a member, for disrespectful and disorderly behavior in its presence, or for obstructing any of its proceedings. Such imprisonment shall not exceed ten days for any offence.

Mr. Montamat—I move to strike out "ten days" in the fourth line, and insert "forty-eight hours."

Mr. Foley—I move to lay that motion on the table.

[The motion was carried, and the article adopted as read.

The secretary read :]

Art. 21. Neither House, during the session of the General Assembly, shall, without the consent of the other, adjourn for more than three days, nor to any other place than that in which they may be sitting.

Mr. Gastinel—I move its adoption.

[The motion was carried.

The secretary read :]

Art. 22. The members of the General Assembly shall receive from the public treasury a compensation for their services which shall be eight dollars per day, during their attendance, going to and returning from the sessions of their respective Houses. The compensation may be increased, or diminished by law, but no alteration shall take effect during the period of service of the members of the House of Representatives by whom such alteration shall have been made. No session shall extend to a period beyond sixty days, to date from its commencement, and any legislative action had after the expiration of the said sixty days shall be null and void. This provision shall not apply to the first Legislature which is to convene after the adoption of this Constitution.

Mr. Foley—I move to amend by striking out "eight dollars," and insert "ten dollars" in the third line.

[The amendment was tabled.]

Mr Wilson—I move to strike out the words "and any legislative action had after the expiration of the said sixty days shall be null and void."

Mr. Abell—I move to strike out all after the words "respective Houses."

[The amendements were lost, and the article adopted as read.

The secretary read :]

Art. 23. The members of the General Assembly shall in all cases, except treason, felony, breach of the peace, be privileged from arrest during their attendance at the sessions of their respective Houses, or going to or returning from the same, and for any speech or debate in either House they shall not be questioned in any other place.

Mr. Thomas—I think there is an error here. The word "and" should be inserted between "felony" and "breach of the peace."

Secretary—It is a typographical error in the printed copy.

Mr. Beauvias—I move its adoption.

[The motion was carried.

The secretary read :]

Art. 24. No senator or representative shall, during the term for which he was elected, nor one year thereafter, be appointed or elected to any civil office of profit under this State, which shall have been created, or the emoluments of which shall have been increased during the time such senator or representative was in office, except to such offices or appointments as may be filled by the elections of the people.

Mr. ONG—I move its adoption.

[The motion was carried.

The secretary read :]

Art. 25. No person who may have at any time been collector of taxes, whether State, parish or municipal, or who may have been otherwise interested with public money, shall be eligible to the General Assembly, or to any office of profit or trust, under the State government, until he shall have obtained a discharge for the amount of such collections, and for all public moneys with which he may have been entrusted.

Mr. BELL—I move its adoption.

Mr. CAMPBELL—I move to strike out the word "interested" and to insert "entrusted," in the third line.

PRESIDENT—That is evidently a typographical error.

[The motion to adopt the article was carried.

The secretary read :]

Art. 26. No person while he continues to exercise the functions of a clergyman, of any religious denomination whatever, shall be eligible to the General Assembly.

Mr. STOCKER—I move to strike out that section. It is an insult to the clergy of the State.

Mr. SULLIVAN—I move to lay that motion on the table. The preachers have been the ruin of the country.

[The motion to table was carried by a rising vote of 48 yeas to 18 nays, and the article adopted as read.

The secretary read :]

Art. 27. No bill shall have the force of a law until, on three several days, it be read over in each House of the General Assembly, and free discussion allowed thereon, unless, in case of urgency four-fifths of the House, where the bill shall be pending, may deem it expedient to dispense with this rule.

Mr BELL—I move its adoption.

Mr. STOCKER—There is something here which strikes me as rather singular. I should like to have it explained by the chairman of the committee. I would like to ask him what he considers a "case of urgency?"

Mr. FOSDICK—There was a case of urgency reported here yesterday—a case in which women and children were starving to death. In such a case the Legislature would have power to act at once.

Mr. STOCKER—I agree with the gentleman perfectly, and shall vote for this article.

[The motion to adopt was carried.

The secretary read :]

Art. 28. All bills for raising revenue shall originate in the House of Representatives, but the Senate may propose amendments, as in other bills; provided, they shall not introduce any new matter, under color of an amendment, which does not relate to raising revenue.

Mr. BEAUVAIS—I move its adoption.

[The motion was carried.

The secretary read :]

Art. 29. The General Assembly shall regulate, by law, by whom, and in what manner, writs of election shall be issued to fill the vacancies which may happen in either branch thereof.

Mr. BELL—I move its adoption.

[The motion was carried.

The secretary read :]

Art. 30. The Senate shall vote on the confirmation or rejection of officers to be appointed by the governor, with the advice and consent of the Senate, by yeas and nays, and the names of the senators voting for and against the appointments, respectively, shall be entered on a journal to be kept for that purpose, and made public at the end of each session, or before.

Mr. TERRY—I move its adoption.

[The motion was carried.

The secretary read :]

Art. 31. Returns of all elections for members of the General Assembly shall be made to the secretary of State.

Mr. BOFILL—I move its adoption.

[The motion was carried.

The secretary read :]

Art. 32. In the year in which a regular election for a senator of the United States is to take place, the members of the General Assembly shall meet in the Hall of the House of Representatives on the second Monday following the meeting of the Legislature, and proceed to the said election.

Mr. PURSELL—I move its adoption.

[The motion was carried.]

Mr. PURSELL—I move a suspension of the rules in order to put this upon its third reading and adopting it as a whole.

Mr. SULLIVAN—I move to adjourn.

Mr. HILLS—I call for the ayes and noes.

[The call for the ayes and noes was not sustained, and the motion to adjourn was carried.]

FRIDAY, May 20, 1864.

[At the usual hour the Convention was called to order, and the proceedings were opened with prayer by the Rev. Mr. Gregg.

The following gentlemen answered to their names upon the first roll-call :]

Messrs. Abell, Ariail, Austin, Balch, Bailey, Barrett, Baum, Beauvais, Bell, Bofill, Bonzano, Bromley, Buckley, Burke, Campbell, Collin, Cook J. K., Cook T., Crozat, Cutler, Davies, Duane, Dufresne, Dupaty, Edwards, Ennis, Fish, Flagg, Flood, Foley, Fosdick, Fuller, Gastinel, Geier, Goldman, Gorlinski, Gruneberg, Gaidry, Healy, Hart, Henderson, Hills, Howell, Howes, Kavanagh, Knobloch, Kugler, Maas, Mann, Maurer, Mayer, Mendiverri, Millspaugh, Montamat, Montague, Morris, Murphy E., Murphy M. W., Newell, Normand, O'Conner, Ong, Orr, Payne J., Paine J. T., Pintado, Poynot, Purcell J., Pursell S., Schroeder, Schnurr, Seymour, Shaw, Smith, Spellicy, Stocker, Stumpf, Stiner, Stauffer, Sullivan, Taliaferro, Terry, Thomas, Waters, Wenck, Wells, Wilson and Mr. President—88.

[The minutes of the previous day's proceedings were read.]

Mr. ABELL—Mr. Duke sends word that he is necessarily absent on account of sickness in his family. Mr. Collin is sick.

Mr. WILSON—I desire to call the attention of the secretary to the fact that the — article was not read as amended. I moved to strike out the parenthetical conclusion of the article as unnecessary, and my motion was carried.

Mr. S. PURSELL—It seems by the minutes that my resolution fixing the hour of meeting at 10 o'clock is connected with evening sessions. My motion had nothing to do with evening sessions.

Mr. FLAGG—My motion was to amend by striking out the word "Algiers," in the expression "right bank Algiers," and insert "Orleans." Algiers is not the name of the parish, but of a village in the parish of Orleans.

[The minutes, as corrected, were adopted.]

Mr. BOFILL—Having voted with the majority yesterday on the resolution of the gentleman from the Second District, (Mr. Hills,) fixing a penalty of loss of *per diem* to absentees from the roll-call, I move to reconsider the action of the Convention in adopting that resolution.

Mr. STAUFFER—I move to lay the motion on the table.

Mr. FOLEY—I second the motion.

[The ayes and noes were called, with the following result :]

YEAS—Messrs. Ariail, Bonzano, Bromley, Duane, Edwards, Ennis, Foley, Fosdick, Fuller, Goldman, Gorlinski, Harnan, Hart, Hills, Howell, Kugler, Maas, Mann, Millspaugh, Montague, Morris, Murphy M. W., Newell, Normand, O'Conner, Orr, Payne J., Paine J. T., Pintado, Poynot, Schroeder, Schnurr, Shaw, Spellicy, Stiner, Stauffer, Taliaferro, Terry, Wells—39.

NAYS—Messrs. Abell, Austin, Balch, Bailey, Barrett, Baum, Beauvais, Bell, Bofill, Buckley, Burke, Campbell, Collin, Cook J. K., Cook T., Crozat, Cutler, Davies, Decker, Dufresne, Dupaty, Fish, Flagg, Flood, Gastinel, Geier, Gruneberg, Gaidry, Healy, Henderson, Hire, Howes, Kavanagh, Knobloch, Maurer, Mayer, Mendiverri, Montamat, Murphy E., Ong, Purcell J., Pursell S., Seymour, Smith, Stocker, Stumpf, Sullivan, Thomas, Waters, Wenck, Wilson—51.

[The motion was lost.]

Mr. STOCKER—Mr. President, I rise for information. I see one or two gentlemen who have voted on this question who, under the rule we have adopted, are not here. We have just fined them to the amount of their *per diem* for absence. We cannot expect men to perform services here unless they are paid for it; and having taken from these gentlemen their *per diem* for absence, they cannot be considered as being present.

PRESIDENT—That inasmuch as the gentleman states that he sees the gentlemen here, it is evident that they are present and not absent.

[The motion to reconsider was put and carried.]

Mr. MONTAMAT—I now move that the resolution of Mr. Hills be laid on the table.

Mr. SULLIVAN—I second the motion.

[The motion was carried.]

Mr. AUSTIN—I call up my resolution offered yesterday.

[The secretary read the resolution changing the quorum from 76 to two-thirds of the members elected to the Convention.]

Mr. BELL—I move its adoption.

Mr. STAUFFER—I move to lay that motion on the table.

[The motion to table was adopted.]

PRESIDENT—The majority report of the Committee on the Legislative Department is the order of the day, and now comes up on its third reading.

[The report was adopted.]

Mr. HOWELL—I move that we take up the report of the Committee on the Executive Department.

Mr. THOMAS—I second the motion.

[The motion was carried.

The secretary read the first article :]

Art. 1. The supreme executive power of the State shall be vested in a chief magistrate, who shall be styled the governor of the State of Louisiana. He shall hold his office during the term of four years, and, together with the lieutenant-governor, chosen for the same term, be elected as follows : The qualified electors for representatives shall vote for governor and lieutenant-governor at the time and place of voting for representatives ; the returns of every election shall be sealed up and transmitted by the proper returning officer to the secretary of State, who shall deliver them to the speaker of the House of Representatives on the second day of the session of the General Assembly then to be holden. The members of the General Assembly shall meet in the House of Representatives to examine and count the votes. The person having the greatest number of votes for governor shall be declared duly elected, but if two or more persons shall be equal and highest in the number of votes polled for governor, one of them shall immediately be chosen governor by joint vote of the members of the General Assembly. The person having the greatest number of votes polled for lieutenant-governor shall be lieutenant-governor ; but if two or more persons shall be equal and highest in the number of votes polled for lieutenant-governor, one of them shall be immediately chosen lieutenant-governor by joint vote of the members of the General Assembly.

Mr. AUSTIN—I move the adoption of the first article.

[The motion was carried.

The secretary read the second article :]

Art. 2. No person shall be eligible to the office of governor or lieutenant-governor who shall not have attained the age of twenty-eight years, and been a citizen and resident within the State for the space of four years next preceding his election.

Mr. SULLIVAN—I offer as an amendment, that no man shall be eligible to the office of governor who is not thirty years of age or upward, and who has not been a resident of the State for fifteen years.

Mr. FOLEY—I move to lay the amendment on the table.

[The motion was lost.]

Mr. ABELL—I desire to know what is the amendment, before I vote on it. I might vote for the years and not for fifteen.

Mr. SULLIVAN—I wish to withdraw my amendment, and to make it ten years, instead of fifteen.

Mr. FOLEY—I shall move as an amendment, that no Irishman be eligible to the office of governor.

[The yeas and nays were called.]

Mr. BOFILL—I should like to know, Mr. President, whether I am called upon to vote on Mr. Foley's amendment?

PRESIDENT—The vote is on tabling Mr. Sullivan's amendment.

[The motion to table was lost, by the following vote :]

YEAS—Messrs. Ariail, Bonzano, Bromley, Cazabat, Collin, Duane, Dupaty, Ennis, Fish, Flood, Foley, Fosdick, Gaidry, Geier, Goldman, Gorlinski, Hills, Hire, Maas, Morris, Murphy E., Payne J., Paine J. T., Pintado, Purcell J., Pursell S., Schroeder, Schnurr, Shaw, Smith, Stiner, Stauffer, Wenck—33.

NAYS—Messrs. Abell, Austin, Balch, Barrett, Bailey, Baum, Beauvais, Bell, Bofill, Buckley, Burke, Campbell, Cook T., Cook J. K., Crozat, Cutler, Decker, Dufresne, Edwards, Flagg, Fuller, Gastinel, Gruneberg, Harnan, Hart, Howell, Howes, Kavanagh, Knobloch, Kugler, Mann, Maurer, Mayer, Millspaugh, Montamat, Montague, Murphy M. W., Newell, Normand, O'Conner, Ong, Orr, Poynot, Seymour, Spellicy, Stocker, Stumpf, Sullivan, Taliaferro, Thomas, Wells, Waters, Wilson—53.

Mr. MILLSPAUGH—I move the adoption of the amendment.

[The yeas and nays were called.]

Mr. GORLINSKI—I wish to explain my vote. In 1852 the Convention which revised the constitution fixed the residence at four years. This Convention (a Free State

Convention) proposes to fix it at ten. I think this is going backward, and not forward. Therefore, I shall vote no.

[The amendment was adopted by the following vote :]

YEAS—Messrs. Abell, Ariail, Austin, Bailey, Balch, Barrett, Baum, Bofill, Buckley, Burke, Campbell, Cazabat, Cook T., Crozat, Cutler, Decker, Dufresne, Edwards, Flagg, Fuller, Gastinel, Gaidry, Geier, Gruneberg, Harnan, Hart, Howes, Kavanagh, Knobloch, Kugler, Mann, Maurer, Mayer, Millspaugh, Montamat, Montague, Murphy M. W., Newell, Normand, O'Conner, Ong, Orr, Seymour, Spellicy, Stocker, Stumpf, Stauffer, Sullivan, Taliaferro, Waters, Wells, Wilson—52.

NAYS—Messrs. Beauvais, Bell, Bonzano, Bromley, Collin, Duane, Dupaty, Ennis, Fish, Flood, Foley, Fosdick, Goldman, Gorlinski, Hills, Hire, Howell, Maas, Morris, Payne J., Paine, J. T., Pintado, Poynot, Purcell J., Pursell, S., Schroeder, Schnurr, Shaw, Smith, Stiner, Thomas, Wenck—32.

[The article as amended was adopted.

The secretary read :]

Art. 3. The governor shall enter on the discharge of his duties on the fourth Monday of January next ensuing his election, and shall continue in office until the Monday next succeeding the day that his successor shall be declared duly elected, and shall have taken the oath or affirmation required by the constitution.

Mr. MANN—We have said in our report that the meeting of the Legislature should be fixed for the first Monday in January. I think it would be well to amend this to correspond.

Mr. PURSELL—I move to strike out the word "fourth" and insert "second"—that will remedy the difficulty.

[The motion was carried, and the article as amended adopted.

The secretary read :]

Art. 4. The governor shall be ineligible for the succeeding four years after the expiration of the time for which he shall have been elected.

Mr. BOFILL—I move to strike out that article from the report.

[The motion was carried.

The secretary read :]

Art. 5. No member of Congress or person holding any office under the United States shall be eligible to the office of governor or lieutenant-governor.

Mr. WELLS—I move to amend by inserting in the second line, after the words "United States," or "minister of any religious society."

Mr. STAUFFER—We have already provided that no minister of any religious denomination shall hold any office in the State of Louisiana, and, if that includes this, I can see no reason for inserting such a clause here.

[A motion to lay the amendment on the table was lost.

The amendment was adopted, and the article as amended adopted.]

Mr. ABELL—I voted to strike out the fourth article. I think it was improperly done, and shall move a reconsideration. When a governor has been in office four years his patronage becomes too powerful. He should not be re-elected.

[The motion to reconsider was laid on the table, on a rising vote, by 43 ayes to 29 nays.]

Mr. ABELL—Mr. President, this is a very important question, and it is very evident that there is no quorum voting. I trust that the rules will be enforced—every member required to vote. I ask for a call of the House.

PRESIDENT—Mr. Secretary read article 6.

Mr. ABELL—I wish to know if any member has not a right to ask for a call of the House at any time he pleases when it is manifest from the vote that there is no quorum present. He certainly has no right to do it captiously, but I did not do it in that manner, and as it is manifest from the vote that there is no quorum, I shall claim the right.

PRESIDENT—I do not think a member has such a right, especially when it is manifest that there is a quorum present; but if two members call for it, I will order the roll called.

Mr. GASTINEL—I move a call of the House.

[The roll was called and eighty-seven members answered to their names.

The vote on tabling the motion was taken by yeas and nays, resulting as follows :]

YEAS—Messrs. Austin, Bailey, Beauvais, Bofill, Burke, Cazabat, Collin, Cook T., Crozat, Cutler, Davies, Duane, Dupaty, Edwards, Ennis, Fish, Flagg, Fuller, Gaidry,

Geier, Henderson, Hire, Howes, Kugler, Montamat, Morris, Ong, Payne J., Pursell S., Schroeder, Seymour, Smith, Stocker, Stauffer, Sullivan, Terry, Thomas, Waters, Wenck, Wells—40.

NAYS—Messrs. Abell, Ariail, Baum, Barrett, Bell, Buckley, Campbell, Cook J. K., Decker, Dufresne, Flood, Foley, Fosdick, Gastinel, Goldman, Gorlinski, Gruneberg, Harnan, Hart, Healy, Hills, Howell, Kavanagh, Knobloch, Maas, Mann, Maurer, Mayer, Montague, Murphy M. W., Newell, Normand, O'Conner, Orr, Paine J. T., Pintado, Poynot, Purcell J., Schnurr, Shaw, Spellicy, Stumpf, Stiner, Taliaferro, Wilson—45.

[The motion to lay on the table was lost.

The motion to reconsider was put and lost--ayes 30, noes 52.

The secretary read article 6 :]

Art. 6. In case of impeachment of the governor, his removal from office, death, refusal or inability to qualify, resignation or absence from the State, the powers and duties of the office shall devolve upon the lieutenant governor for the residue of the term, or until the governor, absent or impeached, shall return or be acquitted. The Legislature may provide by law for the case of removal, impeachment, death, resignation, disability or refusal to qualify, of both the governor and lieutenant governor, declaring what officer shall act as governor, and such officer shall act accordingly, until the disability be removed, or for the residue of the term.

Mr. THOMAS—I move its adoption.

[The motion was carried.

The secretary read :]

Art. 7. The lieutenant governor or officer discharging the duties of governor, shall, during his administration, receive the same compensation to which the governor would have been entitled had he continued in office.

Mr. BELL—I move its adoption.

[The motion was carried.

The secretary read :]

Art. 8. The lieutenant governor shall, by virtue of his office, be president of the Senate, but shall have only a casting vote therein. Whenever he shall administer the government, or shall be unable to attend as president of the Senate, the senators shall elect one of their own members as president of the Senate for the time being.

Mr. FOLEY—I move its adoption.

[The motion was carried.

The secretary read :]

Art. 9. While he acts as president of the senate, the lieutenant governor shall receive for his service the same compensation which shall for the same period be allowed to the speaker of the House of Representatives, and no more.

Mr. BEAUVAIS—I offer the following substitute for article 9 :

While he acts as president of the senate, the lieutenant governor shall receive for his services a compensation of $5000 per annum, payable quarterly, on his own warrant.

Mr. J. PURCELL—I second the motion.

[The substitute was tabled and the article adopted as read.

The secretary read :]

Art. 10. The governor shall have power to grant reprieves for all offences against the State, and except in cases of impeachment, shall, with the consent of the senate, have power to grant pardons and remit fines and forfeitures, after conviction. In cases of treason, he may grant reprieves until the end of the next session of the General Assembly, in which the power of pardoning shall be vested.

Mr. TERRY—I move its adoption.

[The motion was carried.

The secretary read :]

Art. 11. The governor shall, at stated times, receive for his services a compensation, which shall be neither increased nor diminished during the term for which he shall have been elected.

Mr. THOMAS—I offer the following as a substitute :

The governor shall receive for his services a compensation of ten thousand dollars per year, payable quarterly, on his own warrant.

Mr. SMITH—I move to amend by making it eight thousand dollars.

Mr. MORRIS—I move to amend by making it seven thousand dollars.

[The last amendment was lost.

The amendment of Mr. Smith was adopted, by a rising vote—yeas 42, nays 36.

The substitute as amended was adopted.

The secretary read :]

Art. 12. He shall be commander-in-chief of the army and navy of this State, and of the militia thereof, except when they shall be called into the service of the United States.

Mr. STAUFFER—I move to strike out the words "army and navy of this State and the militia thereof," and to insert instead, "militia of this State." Under the old articles of confederation, a State had a right in certain contingencies to keep vessels of war, but the constitution declares that no State shall keep troops or ships of war in time of peace without the consent of Congress, etc. I think it will be arrogating to ourselves a little too much authority to say that Louisiana shall have an army and navy.

Mr. CUTLER—I move to lay the amendment on the table.

[The motion to table was lost, the amendment adopted, and the article was adopted as amended.

The secretary read :]

Art. 13. He shall nominate, and by and with the advice and consent of the Senate, appoint all officers whose offices are established by the constitution, and whose appointments are not herein otherwise provided for: Provided, however, that the Legislature shall have a right to prescribe the mode of appointment to all other offices established by law.

Mr. FOLEY—I move its adoption.

[The motion was carried.

The secretary read :]

Art. 14. The governor shall have power to fill vacancies that may happen during the recess of the Senate, by granting commissions which shall expire at the end of the next session, unless otherwise provided for in this constitution; but no person who has been nominated for office and rejected by the Senate shall be appointed to the same office during the recess of the Senate.

Mr. BELL—I move to adopt.

[The motion was carried.

The secretary read :]

Art. 15. He may require information, in writing, from the officers in the Executive Department upon any subject relating to the duties of their respective offices.

Mr. BUCKLEY—I move its adoption.

[The motion was carried.

The secretary read :]

Art. 16. He shall, from time to time, give to the General Assembly information respecting the situation of the State, and recommend to their consideration such measures as he may deem expedient.

Mr. DAVIES—I move we adopt it.

[The motion was carried.

The secretary read :]

Art. 17. He may, on extraordinary occasions, convene the General Assembly at the seat of goverenement, or at a different place if that shall have become dangerous from an enemy or from epidemic, and, in case of disagreement between the two Houses as to the time of adjournment, he may adjourn them to such time as he may think proper, not exceeding four months.

Mr. DUANE—I move its adoption.

[The motion was carried.

The secretary read :]

Art. 18. He shall take care that the laws are faithfully executed.

Mr. BELL—I move its adoption.

[The motion was carried.

The secretary read :]

Art. 19. Every bill which shall have passed both Houses, shall be presented to the governor; if he approve, he shall sign it; if not, he shall return it with his objections to the House in which it originated, which shall enter the objections at large upon its journal, and proceed to consider it. If, after such consideration, two-thirds of all the members elected to that House shall agree to pass the bill, it shall be sent, with the objections, to the other House, by which it shall be likewise reconsidered, and if approved by two-thirds of all the members elected to that House, it shall be a law; but in such cases the vote of both Houses shall be determined by yeas and nays, and the names of the members voting for or against the bill shall be entered on the journal of each House respectively. If any bill shall not be returned by the governor within ten days (Sundays excepted) after it shall have been presented to him, it shall be a law in like manner as if he had signed it, unless the General Assembly, by adjournment, prevent its return, in which case it shall be a law unless sent back within three days after their next session.

Mr. FOLEY—I move its adoption.

Mr. SMITH—I move, as an amendment, to strike out "two-thirds of all the members elected," and insert "two-thirds of the members present."

[The amendment was not seconded, and the article was adopted as read.

The secretary read :]

Art. 20. Every order, resolution or vote, to which the concurrence of both Houses may be necessary, except on a question of adjournment, shall be presented to the governor, and before it shall take effect, be approved by him, or, being disapproved, shall be repassed by two-thirds of the members elected to each House of the General Assembly.

Mr. GORLINSKI—I move to adopt the article.

[The motion was carried.

The secretary read :]

Art. 21. There shall be a secretary of State, who shall hold his office during the term for which the governor shall have been elected. The records of the State shall be kept and preserved in the office of the secretary ; he shall keep a fair register of the official acts and proceedings of the governor, and when necessary shall attest them ; he shall, when required, lay the said register, and all papers, minutes and vouchers relative to his office, before either House of the General Assembly, and shall perform such other duties as may be enjoined on him by law.

Mr. DAVIES—I move we adopt it.

[The motion was carried.

The secretary read :]

Art. 22. There shall be a treasurer of the State, who shall hold his office during the term of two years.

Mr. CAZABAT — I move to strike out "two" and insert "four."

[The amendment was seconded and carried by a vote of 42 to 20, and the section as amended then adopted.

The secretary read :]

Art. 23. The secretary of State and treasurer of State shall be elected by the qualified electors of the State. And in case of any vacancy caused by the death, resignation or absence of the secretary or treasurer of State, the governor shall order an election to fill said vacancy.

Mr. BELL—I move its adoption.

[The motion was carried.

The secretary read :]

Art. 24. All commissions shall be in the name and by the authority of the State of Louisiana, and shall be sealed with the State seal and signed by the governor.

Mr. BUCKLEY—I move its adoption.

[The motion was carried.

The secretary read :]

Art. 25. The free white men of the State shall be armed and disciplined for its defence ; but those who belong to religious societies whose tenets forbid them to carry arms, shall not be compelled so to do, but shall pay an equivalent for personal services.

Mr. STAUFFER—I offer the following substitute :

All able-bodied citizens of the State shall be immediately armed and disciplined for the defence of the State, and those refusing so to do shall be immediately sent across the United States lines into the so-called Confederacy.

Mr. ABELL—I move that all over fifty years of age be exempt.

Mr. SULLIVAN—I move to lay that substitute on the table.

[The question was put and the chair declared the motion lost, but on division called for a rising vote was taken and the substitute tabled—ayes 49, noes 20.]

Mr. THOMAS—I move to amend by striking out the word "free" in the first line, so that it shall read "all white men shall be armed," etc.

Mr. STAUFFER—I move to lay the amendment on the table.

Mr. ORR—I have an amendment to the amendment. I move that the article be altered so as to read, "all free white males between the ages of 18 and 45 be armed and disciplined," etc., striking out all that portion relative to religious societies. Unless we strike that out everybody will be claiming to be Quakers, and we shall have nobody left to defend the country.

Mr. MANN— The gentleman moves to strike out the word "free." I would like to know for what reason he desires to place arms in the hands of criminals and convicts.

Mr. STAUFFER—I accept the gentleman's amendments, except as to the word "free." I think every man ought to be willing to take up arms in defence of the country.

Mr. SULLIVAN—Mr. President, I move to lay the amendments on the table.

[The question was put and carried by a rising vote—ayes 33, nays 30.]

Mr. STAUFFER—Mr. President, I ask for a call of the roll. I do not think there is a quorum present.

[The ayes and noes were called on the motion to lay on the table.]

Mr. CAMPBELL—I would have preferred that the amendment should read "all men," instead of all between 18 and 45. I vote no.

Mr. BALCH—I do not understand the question.

PRESIDENT—It is on laying on the table Mr. Orr's amendment to strike out that portion of the article exempting members of religious societies.

Mr. BALCH—I vote to lay all religious societies on the table.

Mr. Duane—I vote yes for the reason that all free men should be enrolled for the defence of the country. I contend that there are no slaves here now.

Mr. Montague—I am in favor of the principle that all men should be required to defend the State. I am not in favor of incorporating in the fundamental law of the State a provision which will prohibit calling upon those not between eighteen and forty-five, for I believe all men should be required to defend the State when it becomes necessary. I therefore vote yes.

Mr. Stauffer—I shall vote to lay the amendment on the table, as I have another to offer.

Mr. Wenck—I shall vote yes on the ground that all are excluded above the age of forty-five. I think there are many men above that age capable of doing duty in the defence of a State, and they ought not to be excluded.

[The result of the vote was as follows:]

Yeas—Messrs, Abell, Ariail, Balch, Barrett, Beauvais, Bofill, Buckley, Burke, Cazabat, Crozat, Decker, Duane, Dufresne, Edwards, Ennis, Flagg, Foley, Fosdick, Fuller, Gorlinski, Gruneberg, Harnan, Hart, Hire, Howell, Howes, Kavanagh, Knobloch, Mann, Maurer, Montamat, Murphy M. W., Newell, Normand, O'Conner, Poynot, Schnurr, Seymour, Shaw, Smith, Spellicy, Stocker, Stauffer, Sullivan, Taliaferro, Terry, Waters, Wenck, Wells, Wilson—59.

Nays — Messrs. Baum, Bell, Bonzano, Campbell, Cook J. K., Cook T., Cutler, Davies, Fish, Flood, Goldman, Gaidry, Healy, Henderson, Hills, Kugler, Maas, Mayer, Morris, Ong, Orr, Payne J., Pintado, Pursell S., Schroeder, Stumpf, Stiner, Thomas —28.

[The motion to lay the amendment on the table was carried.]

Mr. Stauffer—As my amendment was laid on the table, I desire to offer another. I desire to strike out and insert, so that the article shall read—"all able-bodied men between the ages of eighteen and fifty-five shall be armed and disciplined for the defence of the State."

Mr. Smith—I move to amend by striking out the word "white," so that the article will read, "all the free men of the State," &c.

Mr. M. W. Murphy—I move to lay that amendment on the table.

[The question was put and declared carried; but upon a rising vote it was lost—ayes 40, noes 30.

The amendment was adopted.]

Mr. Duane—I move to adjourn.

[The question was put and declared carried. The yeas and nays were demanded, with the following result:]

Yeas—Messrs. Abell, Austin, Balch, Bailey, Barrett, Baum, Bofill, Buckley, Campbell, Cook J. K., Cook T., Crozat, Dufresne, Duane, Dupaty, Flagg, Flood, Foley, Gorlinski, Gruneberg, Gaidry, Healy, Hart, Hills, Howes, Kavanagh, Kugler, Maurer, Mayer, Murphy E., O'Conner, Orr, Poynot, Pursell S., Schnurr, Smith, Spellicy, Stocker, Sullivan, Terry—39.

Nays—Messrs. Ariail, Beauvais, Bell, Bonzano, Buckley, Cazabat, Cutler, Davies, Decker, Edwards, Ennis, Goldman, Harnan, Henderson, Hire, Howell, Kugler, Maas, Mann, Montague, Morris, Murphy M. W., Newell, Normand, Orr, Payne J., Paine J. T., Pintado, Pursell S., Schroeder, Seymour, Stocker, Stumpf, Stiner, Stauffer, Taliaferro, Thomas, Waters, Wenck, Wells, Wilson—41.

[The motion to adjourn was lost.]

Mr. Stauffer—I desire that all after the word disciplined shall be stricken out. Every man, whatever sect he may belong to, has a right to bear arms in defence of his country, and I desire to see none excluded. This idea that a man belonging to any particular denomination or persuasion should have a horror of bearing arms and should be excluded, is a novel one to be urged at a time like this. What that religious denomination is whose members are to be excluded I have not the faintest idea. As for myself, I am ready and willing to bear arms, and I desire that every man in the State shall be willing to bear arms in defence of the State, and that there shall be nothing to hinder him from so doing, let him belong to what religious denomination he may. It is a great and glorious privilege to bear arms in the defence of our country. It is a privilege that I would deny to none who are worthy of it. I would not by a constitutional enactment prohibit any from exercising it except foreigners—those who have borne arms against the United States, and there are many of them among us, living under the protection of foreign papers, I should not be so willing to excuse under their plea of foreign citizenship or their "religious" scruples; but foreigners who are such in good faith, and have remained neutral, I would not have enrolled.

I am always willing to defend the flag—aye, to defend it with my life, if necessary, as thousands and tens of thousands have done, in maintaining the integrity, the glory and the unity of our country, and the perpetuity of free institutions. They have sacrificed their lives on the altar of their country. I consider my own life as of no more value than theirs. I know no reason why I should be excluded from sacrificing my life on the same altar, made glorious by the blood of heroes. I stand ready and willing to do so; why should I be excluded? Why should any man be excluded? It is a glorious thing to die for one's country; and for such a glorious country! a country whose emblem, the stars and stripes, is known, recognized and respected in every land and clime as the emblem of a free government, a government of the people.

I do not say this for buncombe, Mr. President, but what I say I mean. I am opposed to excluding the members of any persuasion. No man, as a member of any religious society, as a Christian, has a right to ask to be excused from defending the country which guarantees to him the possession of his life, his property, with all the inestimable blessings of a free government, not the least of which is the right to worship God according to the dictates of his own conscience.

Mr. Foley—I move to adjourn.

[The motion was lost.

The question on the adoption of the article as amended was put and the article was lost.]

Mr. Wilson—I move the adoption of the article as it stands.

[The motion was carried.

The secretary read:]

Art. 26. The militia of the State shall be organized in such a manner as may be hereafter deemed most expedient by the Legislature.

Mr. Terry—I move its adoption.

[The motion was carried.]

Mr. Bell—I move to suspend the rules for the third reading of the report.

[The motion was lost, 39 only voting in the affirmative.]

Mr. Foley—I move to adjourn.

[The motion was carried.]

Saturday, May 21, 1864.

[The Convention was called to order at the usual hour.

The following members answered to their names on the first roll-call:]

Messrs. Abell, Ariail, Austin, Barrett, Baum, Bell, Bonzano, Bromley, Burke, Collin, Cook J. K., Cook T., Crozat, Cutler, Davies, Decker, Dufresne, Dupaty, Edwards, Ennis, Fish, Flagg, Flood, Foley, Fosdick, Gastinel, Gaidry, Geier, Gorlinski, Gruneberg, Harnan, Hart, Henderson, Hills, Howell, Howes, Knobloch, Kugler, Maas, Mann, Maurer, Mendiverri, Millspaugh, Montague, Murphy M. W., Normand, O'Conner, Orr, Paine J. T., Pintado, Poynot, Purcell J., Pursell S., Schroeder, Schnurr, Seymour, Spellicy, Stumpf, Stiner, Stauffer, Taliaferro, Terry, Wilson and Mr. President—64.

[There being no quorum, the sergeant-at-arms was dispatched as usual to bring in absent members.

After the following members had entered, viz: Messrs. Barrett, Beauvais, Duane, Smith, Waters, Murphy E., Bofill, Buckley, Healy, Fosdick, Goldman, Montamat—12, the minutes of the previous day's proceedings were read and adopted.]

Mr. Fish—Before the report of the Committee on the Executive Department is put on its third reading, I wish to move a suspension of the rules, in order to add another article providing for the election of an auditor.

[The secretary read the report as adopted the previous day.]

Mr. Stauffer—I wish to have article 25 read again.

[It was read by the secretary.]

Mr. Stauffer—I think the word "white" was stricken out, and that all after the word "defence," in the second line, was also stricken out, so that it read, "The free men of the State shall be armed and disciplined for its defence."

President—You are in error; it was finally adopted as reported.

Mr. Cutler—I move as a rider to the report amendments to articles 9, 22 and 23, as follows: In article 9 strike out all before the word "the," in the first line, and after the word "services," in the second line, strike out to the end of the article, and substitute the words: "A salary of five thousand dollars per annum, payable quarterly, on his own warrant," so that the article will read: "The lieutenant governor shall receive for his services a salary of five thousand dollars per annum, payable quarterly, on his own warrant."

In article 22 strike out the word "two," in the second line, and insert "four," and after the words "treasurer of state," in the first line, insert "and auditor of public accounts;" and strike out "his office," in the first and second lines, and insert "their offices."

In article 23, after the words "treasurer of state," insert the words "and auditor of public accounts."

Mr. President, I think the omission of mention of auditor in yesterday's action was merely a mistake, and only needs to be suggested to be corrected.

I would also suggest the propriety of fixing the salaries of these officers. You have increased the salary of the governor to eight thousand dollars. The secretary of state and the treasurer receive each $2000, and the auditor of public accounts $4000. It strikes me that that is altogether too low, and therefore ought to make them at least $5000.

Mr. Howell—I wish to say simply that it has been the invariable custom in this State for the Legislature to fix the salaries. The representatives in the Legislature are generally direct from the people, and are presumed to know the condition of the country and their constituents. I think it would be as well to let the matter alone; I have no doubt the Legislature will do ample justice to these officers—as much so as this Convention. It may be the Legislature will give them higher salaries, but my only objection is that I think it is a matter that should be left to the Legislature.

Mr. Henderson—The difficulty in regard to the question of compensation is this: we have no Legislature, and probably it will be some five or six months before we do have one. As this body has fixed the basis of representation in order that the people shall be immediately represented, I am in favor of stating the salary of the various State officers until the Legislature shall otherwise provide for them. I have no objection to the Legislature increasing the salaries, as the times and position may require; but I object to their being cut down, for it only tends to political strife, and shall vote for this rider.

Mr. Abell—I wish every step of this Convention to be taken with as much certainty as possible. I do not think the amount of the salaries of these officers is exorbitant, and if any change was made in the amendment, it should be inserted that the salaries should not be diminished but might be increased, if the Legislature thought proper. I vote for large salaries and faithful services.

[Mr. Cutler's rider was adopted.]

Mr. Stauffer—Mr. President, I wish to offer a rider to article 25.

President—That is already adopted and is a part and parcel of the constitution of the State. The next business in order is the order of the day—the report of the Committee on the Judiciary, on its second reading.

Mr. Abell—This is one of the most important questions that has been before this body, and as we have been so successful in commencing on the first of the week, I move that it be made the special order of the day for Monday.

Mr. Hills—I rise to a question of order. The rider of Mr. Cutler was adopted, but not the report.

President—The adoption of the rider is the adoption of the report.

Mr. Henderson—I move to lay the motion on the table.

[The motion was carried, on a rising vote—yeas 36, nays 33.

The report was then read by the secretary.]

Mr. Montamat—I move to adjourn.

Mr. Terry—I call for the yeas and nays.

[The roll was called, with the following result:]

Yeas—Messrs. Abell, Bell, Burke, Collin,

Cook T., Decker, Dufresne, Dupaty, Flagg, Foley, Fosdick, Gastinel, Gaidry, Gruneberg, Hart, Healy, Henderson, Knobloch, Mayer, Montamat, Purcell J., Schroeder, Seymour, Smith, Stocker, Stiner, Sullivan, Waters—29.

NAYS—Messrs. Ariail, Austin, Bailey, Barrett, Baum, Beauvais, Bofill, Bonzano, Bromley, Collin, Cook J. K., Crozat, Cutler, Davies, Duane, Ennis, Fish, Flood, Fuller, Geier, Harnan, Hills, Howell, Kugler, Maas, Mann, Mendiverri, Millspaugh, Montague, Morris, Murphy E., Murphy M. W., Newell, Normand, Orr, Paine J. T., Pintado, Poynot, Pursell S., Schnurr, Spellicy, Stauffer, Taliaferro, Terry, Thorpe, Thomas, Wenck, Wilson—49.

[The motion was lost.

The secretary read :]

Art. 1. The judiciary power shall be vested in a Supreme Court, in such inferior courts as the Legislature may, from time to time, order and establish, and in justices of the peace.

Mr. BELL—I move its adoption.

[The motion was carried.

The secretary read :]

Art. 2. The Supreme Court, except in cases hereafter provided, shall have appelate jurisdiction only; which jurisdiction shall extend to all cases when the matter in dispute shall exceed three hundred dollars; to all cases in which the constitutionality or legality of any tax, toll or impost whatsoever, or of any fine, forfeiture or penalty imposed by a municipal corporation, shall be in contestation; and to all criminal cases on questions of law alone whenever the offence charged is punishable with death or imprisonment at hard labor, or when a fine exceeding three hundred dollars is actually imposed.

Mr. BELL—I move its adoption.

[The motion was carried.

The secretary read :]

Art. 3. The Supreme Court shall be composed of one chief justice and four associate justices, a majority of whom shall constitute a quorum. The chief justice shall receive a salary of ten thousand dollars, and each of the associate justices a salary of nine thousand dollars, annually, until otherwise provided by law. The court shall appoint its own clerks.

Mr. SULLIVAN—I move to amend by striking out the word "ten," in the third line, and inserting "eight;" and by striking out, in the fourth line, the word "nine" and inserting "seven," and by adding to the fifth line the words: "The judges shall be elected by the people for the term of ten years."

Mr. ABELL—Mr. President, I think, sir, we are going over this matter altogether too hastily. To the second article I had an amendment which is on the secretary's table, and should have been disposed of before the article was put on its passage. There are several other amendments in the same condition. I contend, sir, that these amendments were in order and should have been put and that the chair has no right to attempt to rush matters through in this summary manner, regardless of parliamentary rules. I shall not, however, move a reconsideration now, but I think the Convention should adjourn and take up properly and orderly this subject. I do not wish to delay the progress of this Convention, but wish to push business as fast as justice and prudence will allow. I wish to state that several leading members gave me their word they would adjourn this report until Monday. Now, sir, I shall move an adjournment until Monday, and then I shall move a reconsideration.

Mr. FOLEY—I move we adjourn.

Mr. SCHROEDER—I am always opposed to adjournment, but under present circumstances I think it is necessary to do justice to gentlemen who have amendments, and shall vote yes.

Mr. STAUFFER—I do not want to remain in this Convention unless I can do my duty. It is now only half-past 1 o'clock—a quorum was not present until half-past 12. We receive ten dollars each per day for our labors, and I am opposed to adjournment before we have done a good day's work I vote no.

[The motion to adjourn was carried.]

MONDAY, May 23, 1864.

[The Convention was called to order at the usual hour. The assistant secretary being sick, the president appointed Messrs. Winfree and Reuss, and called Mr. Hills to the chair.

The secretary called the roll, and the following gentlemen answered to their names :]

Messrs. Ariail, Austin, Balch, Bailey, Barrett, Baum, Beauvais, Bell, Bromley, Buckley, Burke, Campbell, Collin, Crozat, Davies, Duane, Duke, Edwards, Ennis, Flood, Gaidry, Geier, Goldman, Healy, Henderson, Hills, Howell, Kavanagh, Kugler, Maas, Mendiverri, Morris, Murphy M. W., Newell, Normand, Payne J., Pintado, Purcell J., Pursell S., Schroeder, Schnurr, Seymour, Shaw, Smith, Spellicy, Stumpf, Stiner, Stauffer, Taliaferro, Terry, Thomas, Waters, Wenck and Mr. President—54.

[The sergeant-at-arms was dispatched, as usual, to bring in absent members to make a quorum; after which the following gentleman entered and answered to their names:]

Messrs. Abell, Bofill, Cazabat, Dufresne, Fish, Flagg, Foley, Fuller, Gastinel, Gruneberg, Hart, Howes, Knobloch, Maurer, Mayer, O'Conner, Ong, Poynot, Stocker, Orr, Thorpe and Wilson—22.

[The minutes of the previous day's proceedings were then read and adopted.]

Mr. Shaw—The Committee on Ordinance reports progress.

Mr. Henderson—The Committee on Charity reports as follows. They recommend an appropriation of $21,000, to be distributed as follows:

For the Orphans' Home, in New Orleans......................	$1500
For the St. Mary's Catholic Orphan Boys' Asylum in New Orleans,...	4000
For the Female Orphan Asylum, Camp Street,..................	4000
For the House of the Good Shepherd,......................	250
For the Jewish Widows' and Orphans' Asylum,................	500
For the St. Joseph Catholic Orphan Asylum,.....................	1500
For the St. Elizabeth House of Industry,.....................	1000
For the Society for the relief of the Orphan Boys, Fourth District,....	1000
For the Institution for Indigent Colored Boys, Third District,.......	1000
For the Ladies of Providence, Third District,.....................	750
For St. Anna's Asylum for Destitute Widows and Children,..........	1500
For the Children's Home of the Protestant Episcopal Church,....	500
For the Catholic Institute of Destitute Orphans,..................	750
For the Catholic Benevolent Association, Baton Rouge,...........	250
For the Female Orphan Asylum, Baton Rouge,.................	500
For the St. Vincent Orphan Asylum, Donaldsonville,..............	500
For the Milne Asylum, New Orleans,	500
For the St. Vincent Orphan Asylum,	500
For the Moreau Street Orphan Asylum..........................	500
Total,................	$21,000

John Henderson, Jr., Chairman.

Mr. Sullivan—I move to amend by adding the Firemen's Charitable Association for $5000.

Mr. Davies—I move to lay the amendment on the table.

[The ayes and noes were called on the motion to lay on the table.]

Mr. Pursell—I rise to a point of order. Before any action can be taken on that report, it is necessary to receive it. It has not been received yet.

President—The chair would state that the mere action on the report is a reception of it; that while it is not improper to make a motion to receive it, such a motion is not necessary; the action on it is a reception of the report.

[The result of the vote was as follows:]

Yeas—Messrs. Burke, Campbell, Collin, Cazabat, Davies, Duane, Dupaty, Edwards, Ennis, Flagg, Flood, Foley, Fuller, Gaidry, Goldman, Gruneberg, Harnan, Hart, Henderson, Hills, Howell, Knobloch, Kugler, Maas, Mann, Murphy E., Murphy M. W., Newell, Normand, Ong, Pintado, Poynot, Schroeder, Schnurr, Smith, Stauffer, Thorpe, Wells—38.

Nays—Messrs. Abell, Ariail, Austin, Barrett, Balch, Bailey, Bell, Bofill, Bromley, Buckley, Cook J. K., Crozat, Decker, Duke, Dufresne, Gastinel, Geier, Healy, Howes, Maurer, Mayer, Mendiverri, Morris, Montamat, Orr, Payne J., Purcell J., Pursell S., Seymour, Shaw, Spellicy, Stumpf, Stiner, Sullivan, Terry, Waters, Wenck, Wilson—38.

[There being a tie vote, the motion was lost.]

Mr. Henderson—I now move to lay the report and amendments all on the table. I don't want men to come up here—

Mr. Terry—I amend "subject to call."

Mr. Henderson—I meant no subject to call. I want to see this body disgraced, as they have shown a disposition to treat this matter in this manner.

[The ayes and noes were called.]

Mr. Abell—I desire to explain my vote. I voted to lay the report on the table on the ground simply that we are not sent here as a legislative body. If I was a member of the Legislature, and such a resolution should be brought up, I would vote for it with all my heart; but I believe this body has no power to pass such a bill.

[Mr. Shaw was called to the chair by Mr. Hills.]

Mr. BUCKLEY—I wish to explain my vote. As I see there is a majority here who wish to keep money away from the widows and orphans of the firemen of New Orleans, I vote no, because I am in favor of all charitable institutions.

Mr. GOLDMAN—I wish to explain my vote. When I want to do an act of charity, I do it out of my own private means, not out of funds that belong to the public. I vote yes.

Mr. HARNAN—Gentlemen stand here and argue about the want of power to make this appropriation. I know these institutions to be in a state of starvation, and therefore I shall vote to lay the amendments on the table, "hocus pocus."

Mr. MANN—Before I vote I want to be satisfied that this Convention has a right to make this appropriation. I should vote no, if I was satisfied that we had such a right; but as I am not satisfied of it, I vote yes.

Mr. MORRIS—I vote yes, because I believe we are not a legislative body, and have no power to make any such appropriation.

Mr. ORR—I wish to explain my vote. I stand before this Convention as the advocate of public charity, and shall endeavor to carry out my views as far as possible. I consider the Firemen's Charitable Association as an institution worthy of our consideration, and I can see no grounds for excluding it. I have not voted on the amendment, but when the bill comes up I shall vote for it, as I shall vote for every bill that has for its object the maintenance of charitable associations for the benefit of the widow and the orphan. I vote no.

[The result of the vote was as follows:]

YEAS—Messrs. Abell, Ariail, Austin, Balch, Bromley, Burke, Collin, Cook T., Crozat, Cutler, Davies, Decker, Edwards, Ennis, Flagg, Flood, Fuller, Goldman, Hart, Harnan, Henderson, Hills, Howell, Knobloch, Kugler, Maas, Mann, Mendiverri, Morris, Newell, Normand, Ong, Pintado, Poynot, Pursell S., Schroeder, Schnurr, Seymour, Smith, Stauffer, Wenck—41.

NAYS—Messrs. Barrett, Beauvais, Bell, Bofill, Buckley, Campbell, Cook J. K., Dufresne, Duane, Dupaty, Duke, Foley, Gastinel, Geier, Gorlinski, Gruneberg, Healy, Howes, Maurer, Mayer, Montamat, Murphy E., Murphy M. W., O'Conner, Orr, Payne J., Purcell J., Shaw, Spellicy, Stocker, Stumpf, Stiner, Sullivan, Terry, Thorpe, Waters, Wilson—37.

[The motion was carried.]

Mr. MONTAMAT—Mr. President, I beg leave to present a report from the Committee on Finance:

REPORT OF THE FINANCE COMMITTEE.

May 17—Balance on hand as per report No. 5		$55,485 40
May 17—Paid warrant No. 35	$1,040 00	
May 18—Paid warrant No. 36	644 00	
May 19—Paid warrant No. 38	520 00	
May 21—Paid warrant No. 39	1,240 00	
May 21—Paid warrant No 40	1.130 00	
May 21—Paid warrant No. 41	860 00	
May 21—Paid warrant No. 42	411 00	
May 21—Paid warrant No. 43	108 00	
May 21—Paid warrant No. 44	470 00	
May 21—Paid warrant No. 46	1,876 00	8,299 00
		$47,186 40

May 23—Balance on hand to date of the funds appropriated for the payment of per diem of members and salaries of officers, forty-seven thousand one hundred and eighty-six dollars and forty cents.

REPORT OF THE FINANCE COMMITTEE OF THE FUNDS APPROPRIATED FOR CONTINGENT EXPENSES.

May 17—Balance on hand as per report No. 5	$9,585 48
May 20—Paid M. De Coursey, warrant No. 45	826 00
	$8,759 48

May 23—Balance on hand this day, eight thousand seven hundred and fifty-nine dollars and forty-eight cents.

May 18—The sum of fifteen thousand dollars was paid to W. R. Fish, for printing and advertising, on warrant No. 37, out of the funds not otherwise appropriated by the Convention, as appears per voucher No. 5, on file.

JOHN P. MONTAMAT,
Chairman pro tem.

Mr. HOWELL—It seems that there was some misunderstanding yesterday about amendments to the first and second sections of the report of the Committee on the Judiciary. I therefore, in order to give a fair opportunity to discuss the amendments, move a reconsideration of our action in adopting them.

[The motion was carried.]

PRESIDENT—The next business in order is the order of the day, the report of the Committee on the Judiciary.

[The secretary read :]

Article 1. The judiciary power shall be vested in a Supreme Court, in such inferior courts as the Legislature may, from time to time, order and establish, and in justices of the peace.

Mr. FOLEY—I move its adoption.

[The motion was carried.

The secretary read :]

Art. 2. The Supreme Court, except in cases hereinafter provided, shall have appellate jurisdiction only ; which jurisdiction shall extend to all cases when the matter in dispute shall exceed three hundred dollars ; to all cases in which the constitutionality or legality of any tax, toll or impost whatsoever, or of any fine, forfeiture or penalty imposed by a municipal corporation, shall be in contestation ; and to all criminal cases on questions of law alone whenever the offence charged is punishable with death or imprisonment at hard labor, or when a fine exceeding three hundred dollars is actually imposed.

[Also, Mr. Abell's amendment :]

It shall have a general superintending control over all inferior and other courts of law ; shall have power to issue writs of errors and supersedeas, certiorari, habeas corpus and quo warranto and other remedial writs, and to hear and determine the same.

Mr. CUTLER—I think the amendment is calculated to destroy the results of the action of many wise men on this subject. It gives to the supreme court a supervisory power. The power given to the supreme court by the constitutions of 1845 and 1852 is fully expressed in the report of the committee. The code of practice has fixed the law under these provisions. If there is to be any amendment to the second article, I would suggest as a practical lawyer of the State—one who has had occasion to try all these questions—that the only proper amendment is that of Mr. Henderson. The question of giving the supreme court appellate jurisdiction, both of law and fact, is one that has been commented upon by the entire legal ability of this State for many years, not only in regard to civil cases, but also criminal cases. It is for the Convention to say whether in the amended constitution it is proper that the supreme court should be invested with the power to examine and determine upon the facts of a criminal case as well as the law. It may be that some judges may be wrong in their views, but we must adopt general principles and look to the good of the people at large. If we make this great inroad upon the constitution, we shall do that which will take much time and labor to accomplish. We should confer upon the supreme court duties which would occupy two-thirds of its time. It would be entirely beyond all precedent and reason to place the supreme court in a position to hear the testimony of the witnesses for and against the accused. It seems to me that twelve honest men with the judge is sufficient ; they are the persons who see every nerve and muscle move on the face of the witness. If the verdict of the jury is erroneous in law, let the supreme court judge of that error. There is probably not one of you who has not been on a jury, and no one here will say that twelve men with the judge are not better qualified to decide upon the evidence in any case than would be a court, who never saw the witnesses or perhaps not even the accused. What do you want other than the report of this committee ? It is in strict conformity with those provisions which have been decided upon by such minds as those of Grimes, our own esteemed Roselius and Durant, and in fact of all the able men who have practiced at the Louisiana bar for years, and were in the convention when a similar section was adopted. Why should we undertake to make this inroad at this particular time? In coming back to the question we are to vote upon—whether the amendment of Mr. Abell shall be made a part of the constitution of 1864, or not, let me tell you that that power is already in the supreme court, which should never lose its dignity. If I have made myself understood, I am satisfied.

Mr. HOWELL—As chairman of the committee which reported on the subject before us, I conceive it is my duty to present its views in adopting that section as taken from the constitution of 1852. My remarks apply only to the substitute under consideration. If you take it as a substitute, and I confess I can look at it in no other light, it almost destroys the usefulness and power of the Supreme Court. If gentlemen will look at the second article of the report they will see the powers of the Supreme Court there defined.

This proposition is presented as a substitute, and it simply says the Supreme Court "shall have a superintending control over all inferior and other courts of law." It does not say it shall have appellate jurisdiction over any other court, and that any party against whom a judgment shall be rendered in any other court shall have a right to appeal to the Supreme Court for relief. It may be contended that the Legislature, under this, will provide a remedy of that kind, but that is a very indirect mode of arriving at what the report has already established. Taken as an amendment, it is altogether unnecessary and useless, because the article it proposes to amend has given appellate jurisdiction only. I then contend and respectfully submit to this Convention, that this proposition, either as an amendment or substitute, is entirely useless, and for that reason I shall vote against it.

Mr. Abell—I rise for the purpose of answering, to some extent, arguments which seem to me illogical. The gentlemen have not understood the object and nature of the amendment offered by myself.

The gentleman from the Fourth (Mr. Cutler) has begged the question, and has brought up a matter not before the Convention. The amendment of the gentleman from the Second (Mr. Henderson) rather adds, not subtracts, anything from the report of the committee. Under that gentleman's proposition, a partial or corrupt judge may, where the amount in dispute is less than $300, oppress a man who is entirely remediless. Suppose a judge is my enemy, and on my being brought before him for having committed an assault and battery, almost in self-defence, he intends to injure me. Now, when the jury bring in a verdict of guilty and recommends me to the mercy of the court, he unjustly sentences me to nearly two years' imprisonment, or fines me $299 99, and I am remediless. I say I want a bill of exceptions; I cannot have it under the circumstances, and there is no appeal.

Mr. Cutler—I wish to correct the gentleman. The only question is, shall the Supreme Court become one of inferior character, or shall it maintain its dignity? The gentleman is wrong when he says that it is only in case of a fine of three hundred dollars that an appeal lies. There is no such thing stated in the original report or in the constitution of 1852. The imprisonment is at hard labor, or a fine of three hundred dollars. The bill of exceptions goes to the Supreme Court in every one of the cases supposed by the gentleman (Mr. Abell.)

The only question, then, is whether we shall adopt what seems to me to be this anomaly, this extraordinary proposition, to make a mere machine of the great court of Louisiana. My friend from the Seventh (Judge Howell) is correct when he says that if you adopt this, either as a substitute or an amendment, you disturb the great power and fundamental principles of the Supreme Court of the State.

Mr. Abell—I am very much astonished at the gentleman's readiness to dodge this question. I ask him, as a lawyer, whether there can be an appeal from a charge of assault and battery.

Mr. Cutler—The gentleman does not understand that—

Mr. Abell—I do, and you cannot blind me. I ask the judge of the Fifth District Court, now before me, whether I can appeal from a judgment against me of $299 99. Judge Hanlon—"No, sir."

Mr. Abell—That is right, sir. You do not dodge the question. My amendment will remedy this, and therefore I claim that it shall be put.

[The question was put; a *viva voce* vote was undecisive, and the roll was called, resulting as follows:]

Yeas—Messrs. Abell, Balch, Bailey, Bell, Bofill, Buckley, Burke, Campbell, Collin,

Cook T., Decker, Duane, Dufresne, Dupaty, Duke, Ennis, Flood, Gaidry, Gruneberg, Knobloch, Maurer, Mayer, Mendiverri, Montamat, Murphy E., Murphy M. W., Normand, Ong, Orr, Schroeder, Schnurr, Smith, Stiner, Stocker, Stumpf, Terry and Waters—37.

NAYS—Messrs. Ariail, Austin, Barrett, Beauvais, Bromley, Cook J. K., Crozat, Cutler, Edwards, Fuller, Gastinel, Geier, Goldman, Harnan, Hart, Henderson, Hire, Howell, Kugler, Maas, Mann, Morris, Newell, Payne J., Poynot, Purcell J., Pursell S., Seymour, Shaw, Spellicy, Stauffer, Sullivan and Wilson—33.

[Cries of "no quorum, and move we adjourn."

The ayes and nays were taken upon the question of adjournment, with the following result:]

YEAS—Messrs. Abell, Austin, Balch, Bailey, Bofill, Buckley, Burke, Campbell, Cook J. K., Cook T., Crozat, Cutler, Decker, Duke, Duane, Dufresne, Edwards, Flood, Fuller, Gastinel, Goldman, Gruneberg, Hart, Knobloch, Maas, Maurer, Mayer, Mendiverri, Montamat, Murphy E., Murphy M. W., O'Conner, Ong, Orr, Poynot, Schnurr, Seymour, Smith, Spellicy, Stocker, Stumpf, Sullivan, Waters—43.

NAYS—Messrs. Ariail, Barrett, Beauvais, Bell, Bromley, Collin, Dupaty, Ennis, Geier, Gaidry, Henderson, Hire, Howell, Kugler, Mann, Morris, Newell, Normand, Payne J., Purcell J., Pursell S., Schroeder, Stauffer, Stiner, Terry, Thorpe, Thomas, Wenck, Wells, Wilson—30.

[The Convention adjourned.]

TUESDAY, May 24, 1864.

[At the usual hour the Convention was called to order, and the following members answered to their names:]

Messrs. Abell, Ariail, Austin, Bailey, Barrett, Beauvais, Bell, Bofill, Bromley, Burke, Campbell, Cazabat, Collin, Cook T., Cook J. K., Davies, Decker, Dufresne, Duke, Edwards, Ennis, Fish, Flagg, Flood, Foley, Fosdick, Geier, Goldman, Gorlinski, Gruneberg, Healy, Heard, Henderson, Hills, Hire, Howell, Knobloch, Maas, Mann, Montamat, Morris, Murphy M. W., Newell, Normand, O'Conner, Payne J., Pintado, Poynot, Pursell S., Shaw, Smith, Spellicy, Stumpf, Stiner, Terry, Wenck, Wells, and Mr. President—58.

[There being no quorum, the sergeant-at-arms was dispatched to bring in absentees.

The following getlemen having taken their seats, viz:

Messrs. Baum, Cutler, Duane, Dupaty, Fuller, Gastinel, Gaidry, Harnan, Hart, Howes, Kugler, Mayer, Mendiverri, Murphy E., Schroeder, Stocker, Stauffer, Sullivan, Thorpe, Waters, Wilson—21,

The minutes of the previous day's proceedings were read.]

Mr. ABELL—I want the words "no quorum," in reference to the vote on my amendment, stricken out. My amendment was carried, and I wish it so stated in the minutes. Thirty-seven is a majority of the votes, and under the repeated ruling of this House a quorum must be presumed to be present.

Mr. STAUFFER—The chair did not decide the motion carried. I called on him for his decision when the motion to adjourn was made.

Mr. HENDERSON—Both gentlemen are correct. A gentleman rose to a question that there was no quorum. A motion to adjourn was made and carried, without the announcement of any decision on that question by the chair.

Mr. S. PURSELL—That statement is correct.

Mr. ABELL—I now move that the president declare that vote carried, if Mr. Shaw had not the nerve to do it. I want the president to decide it, and then, if gentlemen want to move a reconsideration, I have no objection.

Mr. CUTLER—I do not think it is a question of nerve. There was no quorum voting.

Mr. ABELL—It was carried. No gentleman has a right to go upon the presumption that there was not a quorum present.

PRESIDENT—As gentlemen very well know, the chair has always decided that when a vote was taken, whether the compound sum of the ayes and noes was sufficient to constitute a quorum or not, the question was always carried by the majority vote, without regard to the number of votes cast. It makes no difference if the majority were not more than ten or even five, the question is carried unless a call of the House is asked for, and it is ascertained, and a quorum found, on calling the roll, not to be present. Any gentleman has a right to move a call of the House to ascertain whether a quorum is present, but until that is done, it must be presumed to be present. But this is a question on the adoption of the minutes, and it is not the province of the chair to decide whether they are correct or not; that can only be decided by the House.

[The question was put and the minutes were adopted as read, on a rising vote—ayes 43, noes 18.]

Mr. MONTAMAT—I have a resolution to offer, and move a suspension of the rules for its adoption:

Resolved, That Maj. Gen. N. P. Banks and staff be respectfully invited to visit this Convention, and that a committee of five members be appointed by the chair to wait on Gen. Banks and communicate this resolution to him.

[The resolution to suspend the rules was carried and the resolution adopted.]

Mr. HILLS—I have a resolution which I desire to offer:

Whereas, The absence of a few members at the 12 o'clock roll-call results in a great delay of business; therefore,

Resolved, That the members of the Convention who do not answer to their names within fifteen minutes after 12 o'clock M., shall forfeit their per diem allowance for every day of such absence.

Mr. MONTAMAT—I have another resolution, Mr. President:

Resolved, That the office of assistant secretary, occupied by Mr. T. H. Murphy, be declared vacant.

Resolved further, That the secretary be authorized to appoint a suitable person to fill said vacancy during the balance of the session.

In offering this resolution, I will remark, that I am the one that nominated Mr. Murphy for assistant secretary. I worked for him and got him a good many votes which he would not otherwise have received, but he has acted very badly. I am sorry he has done so, and now I can see nothing better that can be done than to declare the position vacant.

Mr. CUTLER—I hold in my hands a letter sent to me this morning by Mr. Murphy, setting forth that he is sick and unable to be present, and asking for a leave of absence. I beg leave to present it for the consideration of the Convention. I do not know what may be the cause for the gentleman's not appearing, but if he is really sick, it seems to me that it would be unfair to take this action against him.

Mr. ABELL—Let us forgive him this time, and if he does not come up within a day or two, I would be in favor of adopting such a resolution.

Mr. MONTAMAT—If it was the first time, I would forgive him; but it is eight or ten times.

Mr. HILLS—No action can be taken on the resolution to-day.

Mr. HENDERSON—I wish to call attention to the fact that the other assistant secretary, to whose faithfulness you can all bear testimony, is sick. I have in my hand a letter requesting a leave of absence for him for a few days.

[The request was granted without objection.]

PRESIDENT—On the committee to wait on Gen. Banks and invite him to visit this Convention, I name Mr. Montamat, Mr. Shaw, Mr. Cutler, Mr. Howell and Mr. Heard.

Mr. TERRY—Mr. President, I have a resolution to offer:

Resolved, That the sum of one hundred dollars is hereby allowed out of any funds in the State treasury, not otherwise appropriated, to defray the expenses necessary for the enrollment on parchment, framing, etc., of the act of emancipation, in English and French, adopted by this Convention on the 11th day of May, 1864.

Mr. STOCKER—I have a resolution to offer:

Resolved, That the sum of twenty-two thousand five hundred dollars be, and the same is hereby, appropriated out of any money now in the treasury, not otherwise appropriated, for charitable purposes.

Be it further Resolved, That a committee of five be appointed by the chair to carry the above resolution into effect.

Mr. THORPE—I have a resolution to offer:

Resolved, That the official printer be requested to publish every morning, in the True Delta, as full a report of the previous day's proceedings of the Convention as possible, including the votes on the call for yeas and nays, and so much of the debates as will give to members of the House a clear idea of each day's proceedings.

Mr. HARNAN—I move a suspension of the rules for its adoption.

[The motion was lost.]

Mr. HENDERSON—On the report on charitable institutions, I voted to lay the report on the table. I now move a resolution that we reconsider the vote on tabling that report.

Mr. HILLS—I was appointed one of the Committee on Charitable Institutions, and the first that I knew of the action of that committee was the report which came in signed, "on behalf of the committee, John Henderson, Jr.," which report I never saw nor heard of until it was laid before the Convention. I have said, however, that if the matter could rest until the very last of the session, that I would be in favor of voting for the appropriation. But I think it injudicious to press the matter now, because I think it would be opening a dangerous door to appropriations, and check our progress in the work we have been sent here to do. I therefore believe that it will be better for the matter to rest until the rest of the business is done, and move to lay the resolution to reconsider on the table.

[The motion was carried.]

Mr. CAMPBELL—I wish to ask, for information, why the special committee (on charity) to whom was referred my amendment, have reported without making any mention of my amendment? They have made their report, but have not reported on my amendment. I ask that they be instructed to report on it.

PRESIDENT—The committee have made their report. Silence is sometimes a report that speaks in very loud tones.

Mr. AUSTIN—Two members of the Committee on the Auditor's Report are absent, and I would ask the appointment of two others in their places.

PRESIDENT—I appoint Mr. Cutler and Mr. Heard.

[The secretary read a communication from the secretary of state, enclosing one from the state librarian:]

STATE OF LOUISIANA,
OFFICE OF SECRETARY OF STATE,
New Orleans, May 23, 1864.

To the honorable president and members of the Constitutional Convention of Louisiana:

GENTLEMEN—Herewith I enclose to you a report, addressed to me by the State librarian, relative to a portion of the State library, which was saved just previous to the destruction of the capitol, in December, 1862. These books are a part of some 80,000 volumes of works published by the State of Louisiana and by the United States, which could not be removed when the Union forces evacuated Baton Rouge, in the previous August. About 4500 volumes were conveyed by the librarian to a place of security, and can be removed to this city at a comparatively small expense.

Now, there is no fund for the expenses of the library, and as these works are necessary for the use of the State officers, I would respectfully suggest that an appropriation of ——— dollars be made for the object herein mentioned and for the general expenses of the State library.

I have the honor to be, gentlemen, very respectfully, your obedient servant,

S. WROTNOWSKI,
Secretary of State.

STATE LIBRARY,
New Orleans, May 23, 1864.

Hon. S. Wrotnowski, Secretary of State:

SIR—In the month of December, 1862, under the apprehension that the State House might be destroyed by shells from the fleet, or by incendiaries on shore, I removed about 4500 volumes of State law works to a secure place, some twelve miles southeast of the capitol, in a Masonic lodge, where they remained in safety.

These works, consisting of reports of the Supreme Court, late acts of the Legislature and revised statutes, are necessary to the several State officers, and could be brought down here at a comparatively small expense.

But, as there has been no appropriation made to this department during the last two or three years, I do not know to whom to apply for relief.

Yours, respectfully,
I. N. CARRIGAN,
State Librarian.

Mr. HILLS—I move the matter be referred to a special committee of three.

[The motion was carried.]

PRESIDENT—I appoint Messrs. Hills, Howell and Campbell.

Mr. FLOOD—Am I in order to offer an amendment to the fourteenth article of the report of the Committee on the Judiciary Department?

PRESIDENT—Not in order.

Mr. ABELL—I now ask the President to declare my amendment carried on the vote of yesterday.

PRESIDENT—The Convention has declared the minutes correct.

Mr. ABELL—Then what will you do with the amendment; is it again open for discussion?

PRESIDENT—The business of the day commences with the second section of the report of the Committee on the Judiciary. Mr. Secretary, read the article, with Mr. Abell's amendment and Mr. Henderson's amendment.

[The secretary read art. 2 of the judiciary report, with the following amendments:]

AN AMENDMENT TO THE REPORT OF THE COMMITTEE ON THE JUDICIARY DEPARTMENT.

Art. 2. The Supreme Court, except in cases hereafter provided, shall have appellate jurisdiction only, both as to law and fact, with such excceptions and with such regulations as the Legislature shall make, which jurisdiction shall extend to all cases when the matter in dispute shall exceed three hundred dollars, exclusive of interest; to all cases in which the constitutionality or legality of any tax, toll or impost whatsoever, or of any fine, forfeiture or penalty imposed by a municipal corporation shall be in contestation, and to all criminal cases.

JOHN HENDERSON, JR.

SUBSTITUTE TO ARTICLE TWO OF REPORT OF JUDICIARY COMMITTEE.

Art. 2. It shall have a general superintending control over all inferior and other courts of law; shall have power to issue writs of errors and supersedeas, certiorari, habeas corpus and quo warranto and other remedial writs, and to hear and determine the same.

EDMUND ABELL.

PRESIDENT—The question is on the amendment of Mr. Henderson—that was the last.

Mr. ABELL—Mine was the last offered.

Mr. SHAW—The gentleman is correct; his amendment was the last offered, and was under discussion when the Convention adjourned yesterday.

Mr. HENDERSON—My amendment was prior to that of Mr. Abell.

PRESIDENT—The amendment of Mr. Abell is then before the House.

Mr. SHAW—Is not the retaking of the vote on that question now in order?

Mr. ABELL—It was the duty of the chair to decide that question yesterday. It must be decided or this Convention will present an anomaly.

PRESIDENT—That question arose upon reading the minutes. The chair decided nothing on that question, and the Convention decided that the minutes were correct. The minutes show that the question was not decided. Now the question is upon the adoption of the amendment of Mr. Abell.

Mr. PURSELL—I move the previous question.

Mr. SHAW—I second the motion.

Mr. ABELL—I hope the gentleman will withdraw his motion.

[The motion was withdrawn.]

Mr. ABELL—I want to know if the question comes up *de novo*.

PRESIDENT—It does.

Mr. ABELL—Mr. President—

Mr. PURSELL—I rise to a point of order. The gentleman has spoken on it already.

PRESIDENT—He has not spoken on it today. The question comes up anew.

Mr. ABELL—It has been long the case when a man goes to the supreme court, however grievous his complaint of the wrong and injustice of the court below, if his claim was less than three hundred dollars, he could get no redress. The court says we cannot hear the case because it is not within the purview of the appellate jurisdiction of this court. I could bring thirty decisions in proof. I ask for jurisdiction to be given to that court, as proposed in my amendment, because it is important to the people of the State for the protection of their rights. I never have any suits of my own and have no personal interest in the matter; but, sir, I ask you whether or not, when you go to the supreme court and present a fair showing that a wrong has been done and demand a remedy, you will get it? The court will tell you at once, if the amount is less than three hundred dollars, that they cannot hear the case, because it is not within the appellate jurisdiction vested in that court. They are without power, and therefore you are without remedy. I say that if you go to the supreme court when the sum is under three hundred dollars, or even over three hundred dollars, when the facts are in controversy, the court will tell you that however evident your rights may be, you have no remedy. What remedy does the gentleman propose when the amount is less than three hundred dollars? None in the world.

They tell you you are among the unfortunate and you have to stand it, for the supreme court has no power to give you relief. There is no remedy in the world, directly or indirectly, for the man aggrieved in the lower court, if his claim is less than three hundred dollars, unless the constitutionality of a law is called in question. A man may be fined two hundred and ninety-nine dollars—the court may go to the extent of the law—and he has no remedy unless he is sentenced to imprisonment at hard labor and fined three hundred dollars. I repeat to-day that I desire to hold the lash over those judges who may wrong my clients or your constituents, and my substitute does it. If you will adopt it, when you are wronged you will have a remedy. The inferior courts will be under the control of the supreme court; and knowing that that court has power to compel them to do right, there will be little need for the exercise of that power.

I do not blame the representatives of the judiciary, in this Convention, for not voting with me, because my substitute proposes to hold the lash over them. Perhaps they may have an enemy they want to punish, or a friend they want to favor. I want the lash held over them, so that they shall not be able to do it; and if my substitute is adopted, they will not attempt it. This will prove a remedy that will be effectual.

In this report there is no remedy for the class of cases I have alluded to, and for which I want to see a remedy provided. If a judge puts his hand into your pocket and takes out a sum under three hundred dollars, you have no remedy. There have been rascals on the bench, and may be again, who will take advantage of their position to punish an enemy, bring the judiciary into contempt, and wronging the individual. I wish to prevent a recurrence of the like dangers in the future. There are some men who would be utterly ruined by the loss of three hundred dollars, and yet the district judges have the power and the final jurisdiction, where they make the fine less than that sum.

It is in the criminal branch of our jurisprudence that the great error is found. In the case of murder, treason, felony, or any other offence, where the penalty is imprisonment in the penitentiary, there is an appeal; but in that class of cases known as misdemeanors, where the penalty does not require imprisonment in the penitentiary, you are without appeal, unless the fine, which is in the discretion of the judge, is over three hundred dollars. This may work a most serious injury, in many cases. Suppose, for instance, in that very common case, simple assault and battery, many cases of which are deserving of but slight notice, so prone are men under various circumstances to indulge the belligerent propensities with which nature has endowed them; suppose, for instance, I should strike my friend from the Second District, (Mr. Hills,) I am brought before the criminal court. The law says no words will justify an assault and battery. Now, sir, the judge of the First District Court has the right, as well as power, to say, "You shall go to the parish prison for two years, and I will fine you, in addition, two hundred and ninety-nine dollars. I will take good care that you do not appeal. You are no friend of mine." This he has the power to do, in the simplest case of assault; and, sir, however unjust or cruel the decision, there is no appeal from it. Any judge of the criminal court can mulct you in a sum less than three hundred dollars, and, in addition, incarcerate you in the parish prison for two years, and you have no remedy.

Suppose he refuses you a subpœna for a witness, upon whom your defence depended, you have no remedy. There have been such cases as this. There are hundreds of men who will inflict any judgment if they have the power. Suppose I was to ask for a continuance on proper grounds and it was to be refused, where is the power that would aid me? There is none, though the decision should be of the most arbitrary and unjust character.

The impeachment of the judge, after you have suffered to the extent of his ability to punish you, does not reach the case. It does not right your wrong. True, such cases may occur, but rarely, but we may again have a Jeffries on the bench, and we should be prepared against such a contingency. Every principle of manliness tells us that we are not bound to submit to any wrong. We are bound to submit to no wrong whatever, unless that wrong is a great evil fastened upon us by the laws of our country, and then we should only submit to it until we could so change those laws as to provide for it a remedy. This is our duty now. It is required by the great principle that a government is bound to extend its protection to every man. This is a position that cannot be controverted. I defy the judges on this floor, some four or five of them, to stand up here and controvert the principles I have enunciated here.

There is a large class of cases for which no remedv is provided in the report of the committee. My substitute provides the remedy. It is no new and untried remedy. It has been adopted in other States, and has been found to work well, and no one here can reasonably object to giving the supreme court the power, if district judges attempt to abuse the power with which they have been intrusted, to compel them to do right or punish them.

The appeal in this case is confined properly to the report of the committee. That report says who and in what cases the right of appeal shall be granted. I do not propose to alter that. My amendment has a different object:

It shall have a general superintending control over all inferior and other courts of law; shall have power to issue writs of error and supersedeas, certiorari, habeas corpus and quo warranto, and other remedial writs, and to hear and determine the same.

Now, sir, this is not an appeal. It has no reference to an appeal. It provides remedial writs. It can be done at once—in five minutes. It provides, when district judges throw obstacles in the way of justice, writs to remove them, and compel the judges to perform their duty.

Mr. HENDERSON — Mr. President, my learned friend has seen fit to propose that the Supreme Court shall issue writs of error, etc. His proposition applies as well to justices of the peace and recorders as to the district courts. Now, in ordinary cases, I should appeal from a justice of the peace to the Third District Court, but the gentleman's amendment provides for an appeal direct from the justice of the peace or recorder's court to the Supreme Court, which can only be done when the constitutionality of a law is called in question.

Mr. ABELL — My amendment provides that the Supreme Court shall exercise a supervisory control over all inferior courts to compel them to do their duty, over justices of the peace and recorders, as well as over district courts. Now, if they decide wrong against you, you have no remedy, except the pardoning power of the governor.

With an honest bench you may have justice administered, I care not how small the calibre of the men. With a dishonest bench justice is very uncertain, I care not how talented the men. I do not think that courts are, as a rule, unjust and arbitrary, but they are liable to be, and the liability is greater in the district and inferior courts, each composed of a single man, than in the Supreme Court, composed of five, a majority of whom is necessary to constitute a quorum, and of two evils I believe it is always best to choose the lesser.

The amendment which I propose is not original with me; I borrowed it from that glorious document which no man can gainsay, on account of the wisdom of the men who framed it, the constitution of the United States. It is not, therefore, original with me, but is a part of that constitution.

As I have no desire to speak again on this subject, I wish merely now to call attention to the other amendment proposed, as if that is adopted mine will of course be rejected. That amendment appears to me to be a mass of incongruities and absurdities. It is an absurdity to say that the supreme court should have jurisdiction in all civil suits of three hundred dollars and upwards, and in all criminal where it is five dollars. It is not the amount in criminal cases that should govern; it is the injury done for which we want a remedy, not the amount of the fine. My amendment provides a speedy and certain redress in criminal cases, and I am willing that the judgment of the district courts shall be conclusive in civil cases when the amount is over three hundred dollars, and we have given power to the Legislature to make such inferior courts as they may see proper.

Mr. HENDERSON—The question has been under the old constitution decided in different ways. I put it three hundred dollars exclusive of interest, to settle the question. There is no necessity for touching the question of interest; that is a mere question of computation for clerks. I am, therefore, in favor of excluding it, and giving the Supreme Court appellate jurisdiction in all civil cases of three hundred dollars and over, exclusive of interest: and of giving the Legislature power to regulate the appellate jurisdiction in all other cases. Now, if the court refuses a continuance, you have no redress, but must stand it. This, in a criminal case, should be remedied. In a civil suit, when the amount is under three hundred dollars, I am willing for the judgment to be final, for no great harm can result from it; but in criminal cases, when not only a man's property but his liberty is in jeopardy, he should have some redress besides the very uncertain one of the proceeding of impeaching the judge or the exercise of the pardoning power of the governor.

Mr. ABELL—Mr. President, I agree with the gentleman in part, but—

PRESIDENT—The gentleman has already spoken on the question, and cannot have the floor again while any other member desires to speak. Mr. Howell has the floor.

Mr. HOWELL—Louisiana has been a State for something more than fifty years. In 1812 the first constitution of the State was adopted, and in 1845 it was amended, and again in 1852. Now, in 1864, we are still progressing in amendments. It would seem we are far beyond such men as Judge Porter, Bernard Marigny, and a host of others, who formed the first constitution of this State; far ahead of such men as Bradford, Benjamin, Hunt, and others, who formed and amended the constitution of 1852; far, far ahead of the galaxy of intellects that formed the constitution of 1845. These men failed to see the errors and oppressions of which the gentleman has been speaking. It was found beyond the ken of their intellect to present a remedy for the outrages perpetrated by the judicial officers of the State, and it rests with the Convention of 1864 alone to find these remedies. Now, what is the remedy proposed? "It shall have a general superintending control." What is the meaning the word *it?* To what does it refer? for by its own terms it is nothing but a substitute. I will refer to the article, however, as an amendment.

I learn from the whole burden of the gentleman's argument or speech what his sole objection to the article of the report of the committee is, that it deprives litigants, whose claims are under $300, of any remedy, when the judge decides against them. I admit frankly, if it requires an admission, that the article in the report has that effect, so far as it goes. It limits the appellate jurisdiction of the Supreme Court to claims which exceed $300. I ask the gentleman if his article remedies this? I ask every gentleman of this Convention to scan that article and see if it will have the effect the gentleman proposes to attain. Adopt this amendment, and the Legislature is the only power which can put it into operation. It does not say the Legislature shall limit the right of appeal; it does not say that in all cases there shall be an appeal to the Supreme Court. When this constitution is adopted by the people, with this amendment, what will be necessary in order to put it into operation, on the supposition that it can be, which I deny? The Legislature will have to pass laws regulating the business of the Supreme Court, the district courts and all the other courts which may be established under this constitution. In doing so we may presume fairly that the Legislature will respect the wishes of the people of Louisiana, and that the Legislature will have regard for the mode and object of conducting the business in the Supreme Court; that the Legislature will not overload the Supreme Court to such an extent as will amount virtually to a denial of justice; because, if you give the right of universal appeal to the Supreme Court, every man who loses a case will take an appeal, upon the certainty that his case will not be reached in five, or perhaps ten years. Let every case be carried to the Supreme Court, and there will be a perfect stop to judicial business. How is it now? One court alone, since the 1st of November, 1862, has granted over four hundred appeals to the Supreme Court, besides those which have gone up from other courts, and the hundreds already pending under the old *regimé*. There are now pending no less than 1500 or 2000 cases. Adopt this universal right of appeal, and you put a stop to all legal business so far as the rights of the people are concerned. The oldest cases have the preference, and no Legislature can deprive them of that right. These cases must be disposed of before new appeals are taken up, and those coming up under this constitution will be postponed for years and years.

I think there are seven justices of the peace in this city, and ordinarily four recorders. Every justice has from 500 to 1500 cases every year, and sometime ago the number was far beyond that, as high as 3000. Every district court has brought before it during the judicial year from 700 to 1300 cases, and there are five of them. Now give every party the right of appeal and what do you do? You must necessarily make fifty supreme courts. No supreme court that has been made or will be made can dispose of one-twentieth of the cases that would be carried up. It is already complained that business accumuletes too rapidly. There are cases which have been pending for at least five years, and I think there are some that have been there ten years. This change, then, is inoperative. Instead of benefiting the poor, it will be an irremediable injury to them. The gentleman is a proud representative of the poor people of Louisiana. Let him have a client—a poor man who has worked ten days for some conscienceless rich man and earned $15, which is all the money he has; he brings a suit before a justice of the peace and gets a judgment; the rich man takes an appeal, and there is an end of the gentleman's client; his $15 are gone. That is an incident that would be multiplied by thousands. It may be there are cases of hardship in judicial proceedings, as there are in all human proceedings. Every one is liable to abuse and imperfection, but it is the part of every man to select that course which will be free from the greatest number of defects, and that is all we are called upon to do in this matter.

The object of the Supreme Court is not so much to decide whether you owe me or I owe you, but to settle the jurisprudence. Poor men have not suffered in Louisiana from the judiciary. I deny emphatically that they have been oppressed here or in any other State, or that judges are by habit corrupt and willing to oppress the poor and aid the rich.

The common instincts of the human heart repel any such accusation. That there are such instances, no one attempts to deny, but shall that direct our action with reference to the matter? Such is not the consideration for men who are acting for the great interests of the country.

Another part of the gentleman's argument was in regard to the criminal jurisprudence. It is the burden of his song, that a man who commits an assault and battery may be punished unjustly by the judge because of his personal feeling against him. I admit that it is a possibility, but is it a probability? I say no, it is not, from the intelligence of the judge, from his knowledge of human nature and of the consequences of such an act upon himself; besides, there are restrictions and restraints imposed by the law, which prevent it. The criminal judge is forbidden by law to make any remarks on the facts of the case; he is simply to judge of the law, and the peers of the criminal are to judge of the facts. If the judge had ever so much disposition to influence the jury on the question of fact, he has not the power. If the judge inflicts the maximum of punishment, is he to be condemned? The people made the law, and he must enforce it. For what purpose are criminal laws enacted? Was it the intention to make laws to protect the criminal? I trow not. They are enacted for the punishment of criminals and the prevention of crime. If a man suffers the maximum of punishment, the effect on society is good. I say the chances are but few where a man will be dealt with unjustly in a criminal trial, and it is probably better for the sake of society that there should be a possibility of some man receiving the maximum of the punishment awarded by law than that you should make such a provision as will increase crime. Make the Supreme Court judge of the facts in all cases of whatever character, and the criminal will know readily he can commit his crime with partial impunity. He will escape the clutches of the law because of its very constitution, as every man, excepting in one or two instances, has the right to appeal. I ask gentlemen to look at the consequences of this amendment, and to give some weight to the experience and investigations of those who made the three previous constitutions. The gentleman claims to be a native of Kentucky. I have the constitution of that State in my hand. It says: "The Court of Appeals, except in cases otherwise directed by this constitution, shall have appellate jurisdiction only." It leaves the Legislature the right to limit that jurisdiction. The committee debated and considered this question. They took counsel from the past, without pretending to be wiser than those who went before them, and they were satisfied that the system that has worked so well for over fifty years will work well for a few years to come.

Mr. ABELL—So far as the argument of the gentleman from the Seventh (Judge Howell) is concerned, I must say that it never touched the case. I ask him where he has shown any mode of redress in the instances I have previously suggested.

The gentleman cannot understand my amendment; cannot understand the word "it." "It" refers to the Supreme Court. He also objects to the carrying of my proposition for the reason that every case can then be appealed. I pronounce that a most unreasonable construction, for this does not contemplate any such thing. I wish the lash to be held over inferior courts—to make them do their duty. Is that proposing anything in regard to appeals? It is not, and no man of logical mind or ordinary sense will say so.

Such a proviso as I propose can be found in the constitution of Arkansas and many other States, brought hither from England. No good judge will object to it, only the rascals.

Mr. HILLS—I would ask if the gentleman intends his proposition to stand as article 22, or to add it to that article as an amendment?

Mr. ABELL—To be added simply. To return: In the second volume of Blackstone, page 35, we find the following: "It"—referring to the Court of King's Bench, which corresponds to our Supreme Court—"keeps the inferior courts within bounds of their authority—may command them to remove their proceedings to be determined or prohibit their progress in the courts below. It superintends all the courts in the kingdom, and commands all to do what their duty calls upon them to do." That is exactly the power I wish our Supreme Court to have. There is no appeal, but a command is simply sent to a judge to do his duty. In the name of right and justice, I ask that my amendment shall be adopted.

Mr. FOLEY—I move the adoption of the amendment.

Mr. CAZABAT—I move to strike out of the amendment proposed by the gentleman from the Fifth the words "and errors."

Mr. CUTLER—I move to lay on the table both the amendments of the gentleman from the Fifth and that of the gentleman from Rapides (Mr. Cazabat.)

[The secretary called the roll:]

YEAS—Messrs. Arial, Bailey, Barrett, Beauvais, Bromley, Campbell, Cazabat, Cook J. K., Crozat, Edwards, Fuller, Gaidry, Hart, Harnan, Heard, Howell, Howes, Knobloch, Kugler, Mann, Mayer, Morris, Newell, Normand, Payne J., Pintado, Poynot, Pursell S., Shaw, Stumpf, Terry, Thorpe, Wells—33.

NAYS—Messrs. Abell, Austin, Bell, Bofill, Burke, Collin, Cook T., Cutler, Davies, Decker, Duane, Duke, Dupaty, Ennis, Fish, Flagg, Flood, Foley, Fosdick, Gastinel, Geier, Goldman, Gorlinski, Gruneberg, Henderson, Healy, Hills, Maas, Montamat, Murphy E., Murphy M. W., O'Conner, Ong, Purcell J., Schroeder, Stocker, Stauffer, Stiner, Sullivan, Wenck, Wilson—41.

Mr. CAMPBELL—I change my vote from "yes" to "no."

[The following amendment proposed by Mr. Henderson was then read:]

Art. 2. The Supreme Court, except in cases hereafter provided, shall have appellate jurisdiction only, both as to law and fact, with such exceptions and under such regulations as the Legislature shall make, which jurisdiction shall extend to all cases when the matter in dispute shall exceed three hundred dollars, exclusive of interest; to all cases in which the constitutionality or legality of any tax, toll or impost whatsoever, or of any fine, forfeiture or penalty imposed by a municipal corporation shall be in contestation, and to all criminal cases.

Mr. PURCELL—I move to lay that on the table. I think time enough has been spent in discussing this thing.

[The motion was put and lost:]

YEAS—Messrs. Ariail, Austin, Bailey, Barrett, Beauvais, Burke, Cazabat, Cook J. K., Crozat, Cutler, Davies, Edwards, Fish, Fuller, Geir, Goldman, Hart, Henderson, Heard, Howell, Howes, Kugler, Maas, Mann, Morris, Newell, Normand, Ong, Orr, Payne J., Pintado, Poynot, Purcell J., Pursell S., Schroeder, Shaw, Stumpf, Stauffer, Thorpe, Wenck, Wells—41.

NAYS—Messrs. Abell, Bell, Bofill, Bromley, Campbell, Collin, Cook T., Decker, Dufresne, Duane, Duke, Dupaty, Ennis, Flood, Foley, Fosdick, Gastinel, Gaidry, Gorlinski, Gruneberg, Harnan, Healy, Hills, Knobloch, Mayer, Montamat, Murphy E., Murphy M. W., O'Conner, Smith, Stocker, Stiner, Sullivan, Terry, Waters, Wilson—36.

[Mr. Burke changed his vote from "yes" to "no."]

Mr. CAZABAT—I ask a call of the House.

[The roll was called and it was found that there was not a quorum present.]

Mr. SULLIVAN—I move we adjourn.

[The motion was carried.]

WEDNESDAY, May 25, 1864.

[At the usual hour the Convention was called to order and the roll called, the following gentlemen answering to their names:]

Messrs. Abell, Ariail, Barrett, Beauvais, Bell, Bofill, Bromley, Buckley, Burke, Cazabat, Campbell, Collin, Cook J. K., Cook T., Crozat, Davies, Decker, Duane, Dufresne, Dupaty, Duke, Edwards, Ennis, Fish, Flagg, Flood, Foley, Fosdick, Fuller, Gastinel, Gaidry, Geier, Goldman, Gorlinski, Gruneberg, Harnan, Heard, Henderson, Hills, Hire, Howell, Knobloch, Kugler, Maas, Mann, Maurer, Mayer, Mendiverri, Montamat, Morris, Murphy M. W., Newell, Normand, O'Conner, Payne J., Pintado, Poynot, Pursell S., Shaw, Schnurr, Smith, Spellicy, Stumpf, Stiner, Stauffer, Sullivan, Terry, Thorpe, Wenck, Wells, Wilson and Mr. President—72.

[There being no quorum, the sergeant-at-arms was directed to bring in absent members.

Messrs. Baum, Hart, Healy, Kavanagh, Murphy E., Purcell J.—6, having entered, the secretary read the previous day's proceedings, and they were adopted.

The secretary read a bill of the city of New Orleans, to the amount of $6139, for expenses of fitting up the hall for the use of the Convention.]

Mr. PURSELL—I move to refer to the Committee on Contingent Expenses.

[The motion was carried.]

Mr. HILLS—I call up my resolution offered yesterday:

Whereas, The absence of a few members at the 12 o'clock roll-call results in a great delay of business, therefore

Resolved, That members of the Convention who do not answer to their names within fifteen minutes after 12 o'clock M., shall forfeit their per diem allowance for every day of such absence.

Mr. BELL—I move its adoption.

Mr. FULLER—I move to lay it on the table.

[The motion to lay on the table was lost.]

Mr. STOCKER—I move to amend by inserting the words "without a good excuse." As the resolution stands, every member who fails to be on hand at the moment loses his per diem, whether he has an excuse or not.

Mr. HILLS—I accept the amendment.

Mr. KAVANAGH—I move to lay the resolution, as amended, on the table.

PRESIDENT—The motion is out of order.

Mr. ABELL—I would be glad if I could, as I almost universally differ with my friend, (Mr. Hills,) agree with him once, but I find it impossible this time. It is the duty of every member to be present; and the experience of the last two days has shown that they will do it without resorting to such measures. The proper mode is to have a member who is contumacious brought before the president and punished.

[The ayes and noes were called with the following result:]

YEAS—Messrs. Ariail, Austin, Barrett, Bell, Bromley, Burke, Cazabat, Collin, Cook T., Davies, Duane, Dufresne, Ennis, Fish, Flood, Foley, Fosdick, Geier, Goldman, Gorlinski, Harnan, Healy, Hills, Howell, Kugler, Maas, Mann, Mayer, Montamat, Morris, Newell, Normand, Pintado, Purcell J., Schroeder, Shaw, Smith, Stocker, Stumpf, Stiner, Stauffer, Terry, Thorpe, Wells and Wilson—45.

NAYS—Messrs. Abell, Bailey, Beauvais, Bofill, Buckley, Campbell, Cook J. K., Crozat, Decker, Dupaty, Edwards, Flagg, Fuller, Gastinel, Gaidry, Gruneberg, Hart, Heard, Henderson, Hire, Howes, Kavanagh, Knobloch, Maurer, Mendiverri, Murphy E., Murphy M. W., O'Conner, Ong, Orr, Payne J., Poynot, Pursell S., Schnurr, Seymour, Spellicy, Sullivan and Waters—39.

[The resolution was adopted.]

Mr. TERRY—I call up my resolution offered yesterday.

Resolved, That the sum of one hundred dollars is hereby allowed out of any funds in the State treasury, not otherwise appropriated, to defray the expenses necessary for the enrollment on parchment, and framing, &c., of the act of emancipation, in English and French, adopted by this Convention on the 11th day of May, 1864.

Mr. WELLS—I move to lay it on the table.

[The motion was lost.]

Mr. WILSON—I move to refer it to the Committee on Contingent Expenses.

[The motion was carried.]

Mr. STOCKER—I call up my resolution appropriating the sum of $22,500 for charitable purposes.

Mr. SMITH—I move to lay the motion on the table.

[Before putting the question, the chair decided the motion carried.]

A division was called for, and a rising vote showed 47 ayes and 27 noes.

Mr. STOCKER—I move a call of the House.

[The roll was called, and eighty-four members found to be present.]

Mr. STOCKER—I now ask that the roll be called and every member required to vote.

[The ayes and noes were taken.]

Mr. HENDERSON—I desire to explain my vote. I presented a resolution making appropriations to certain charitable institutions. The resolution was referred to a committee, the committee made a report on it, and seeing that the Convention was not disposed to act immediately on it, I, myself, moved to lay it on the table, intending to call it up at a future time, late in the session, and with that determination I call a vote to lay this resolution on the table.

Mr. ORR—I wish to explain my vote. I consider the resolution as too indefinite to be considered by the Convention, and therefore vote to lay it on the table.

Mr. SHAW—I voted a few days ago for a resolution which made a special appropriation for certain specific purposes, which I believed the Convention had the power to make; but I believe this is beyond the power of the Convention, and shall vote to lay it on the table.

Mr. SULLIVAN—I am in favor of all charitable appropriations, and shall vote against laying the resolution on the table.

[The following is the result of the vote:]

YEAS—Messrs. Abell, Ariail, Austin, Bailey, Baum, Beauvais, Bofill, Bromley, Burke, Cazabat, Collin, Crozat, Davies, Decker, Dupaty, Duane, Duke, Edwards, Ennis, Flagg, Fosdick, Fuller, Goldman, Henderson, Hills, Hire, Howell, Howes, Knobloch, Kugler, Maas, Maurer, Mayer, Mendiverri, Morris, Montamat, Murphy M. W., Newell, Normand, Ong, Orr, Payne J., Pintado, Poynot, Seymour, Shaw, Smith, Spellicy, Stauffer, Sullivan, Waters, Wenck, Wells—53.

NAYS—Messrs. Barrett, Bell, Buckley, Campbell, Cook J. K., Cook T., Dufresne, Fish, Flood, Foley, Gastinel, Gaidry, Geier, Gorlinski, Gruneberg, Harnan, Hart, Healy, Heard, Kavanagh, Mann, Murphy E., O'Conner, Purcell J., Pursell S., Schnurr, Schroeder, Stocker, Stump, Stiner, Terry, Thorpe, Wilson—33.

[The chair declared the resolution laid on the table, upon which a few members applauded.]

Mr. STOCKER—I move that the names of the gentlemen who applauded be taken down, and published in the minutes.

[The motion received no second.

The order of the day—article 2 of the report of the Committee on the Judiciary—was then taken up.]

Mr. HENDERSON—I have a substitute for the article and all the amendments, which I desire to offer, and in offering this substitute I desire to withdraw my amendment.

PRESIDENT—It can only be withdrawn by the consent of the party who seconded it.

Mr. HILLS—I seconded the amendment. I consent to its withdrawal.

Mr. HENDERSON—The substitute is as follows:

The Supreme Court shall have appellate jurisdiction upon law and fact in civil and criminal cases, as may be prescribed by the Legislature, and shall have supervisory control over all inferior courts.

[Mr. S. Pursell moved to lay the substitute on the table, and on a rising vote the motion was lost—ayes 32, noes 44.

The ayes and noes were called on the adoption of the substitute :]

YEAS—Messrs. Abell, Bailey, Buckley, Collin, Cook T., Decker, Duane, Dufresne, Dupaty, Duke, Ennis, Fish, Flagg, Flood, Foley, Fosdick, Gaidry, Gorlinski, Gruneberg, Henderson, Hills, Kavanagh, Maurer, Maas, Mendiverri, Murphy M. W., Murphy E., O'Conner, Orr, Schroeder, Seymour, Smith, Stumpf, Stiner, Stauffer, Sullivan, Terry, Thorpe, Waters—39.

NAYS—Messrs. Ariail, Austin, Baum, Barrett, Beauvais, Bell, Bofill, Bromley, Burke, Campbell, Cazabat, Cook J. K., Crozat, Davies, Edwards, Fuller, Gastinel, Geier, Goldman, Harnan, Hart, Healy, Heard, Hire, Howell, Howes, Knobloch, Kugler, Mann, Mayer, Montamat, Morris, Newell, Normand, Ong, Payne J., Pintado, Poynot, Purcell J., Pursell S., Schnurr, Shaw, Spellicy, Stocker, Wenck, Wells, Wilson—47.

[The motion was lost.

The question on the adoption of the article as reported was then put to the House, and the article was adopted.

The secretary read :]

Art. 3. The Supreme Court shall be composed of one chief justice and four associate justices, a majority ot whom shall constitute a quorum. The chief justice shall receive a salary of ten thousand dollars, and each of the associate justices a salary of nine thousand dollars, annually, until otherwise provided by law. The court shall appoint its own clerks.

Mr. TERRY—Mr. President, in this clause arises the great question whether we shall have a judiciary that shall be appointive or elective. The battle, if I understand it, is to commence here. When I look over this report, Mr. President, it does not strike me with astonishment. It has not deceived me. I anticipated the result of their labors would be in favor of an appointive judiciary. Reigns there a king in the State? Is a monarchical form of government to supercede the last, or are we, republicans and prophets, to expound the doctrines of a true democracy? Shame be to the man who would change the fundamental law of the State, and introduce the tyranny of monarchical despotism. [Applause.] Let us look at this question rationally. An appointive judiciary—appointed for ten years, for life, or on ground of good behavior. What arguments are in its favor? One says we have too many elections for our country's good—too much internal and intestine strife. Place in the hands of the executive the appointing power and this does cease. Another, a friend, tells me thus: Suppose, imagine a poor man is brought before a judge, three months prior to the judge's re-election before the people ; this poor man can influence not a vote, whereas his prosecutor can influence a hundred. Will not that judge consign that poor man to prison on scarcely any evidence whatever, in order to be able to control the hundred votes of his opponent? I answer yes, if he be a villain, and will perjure himself in sight of God and man. Human nature is weak but not infallible.

Mr. President, to drown at once all arguments in favor of an appointive judiciary, is it not the stepping-stone to despotism and institutionalisms? Is not an appointive judiciary an institutior, an establishment appointed, prescribed and founded by authority? One of those great bug-bears of humanity; a curse to constitutional freedom and true democracy? [Applause.] Like the great Chinese wall, a stupendous and systematic effort to keep the individual permanently within or without. The individual never suffered to grow and expand save to the circumference of the appointive judiciary circle. As an institutionalism, its powers over the liberties and tertiary characteristics of individuals is tremendous; few can withstand the popularity of its despotism. He who, unfortunately, has been nursed by the handmaid of institutions; rocked in the cradle of popularity; fed gruel with the silver-spoon of aristocracy, and sung to sleep in the lap of opulence, is not the man for the people! No! the people's man, on the contrary, is always born in a manger. He hath the blood of the people in him. He declares that institutions were made for men, not man for institutions. Governments and religions are less than man, for from his mind they emanated. Therefore, all laws are really subject to the will of the people.

Mr. President, the conservative may cry aloud for the safety and sancticity of institutions, and pile them up Olympus high in another form, and shaped in all the beautiful rhetoric and eloquent language of an appointive judiciary, but heed him not. His voice cometh not from the open field, nor from the mountain's top—far from it: on the contrary, his cries proceed from the wilderness of crime and marshes of despotism, which are ten-fold more dangerous than the miasmas arising from the swamps of Louisiana.

Change the scene from America—cross the Atlantic and let your gaze be extended to poor down-trodden Ireland. Is it not the home of despotism, tyranny and persecution? "Has she not given the world more than her share of genius and greatness? Her noble, brave and generous sons have fought successfully in all battles but its own. In wit and humor it has no equal, while its harp, like its history, moves to tears by its sweet and melancholy pathos." What has seized this nation in its strangling grasp? With what does it wrestle day after day with a grim and unrelenting enemy, snapping its very heart-strings, beggering and famishing her people, driving them forth houseless and homeless, separating husband from wife, father from son, mother from daughter, until their feet turn westward and they leave the honors of an appointive judiciary behind, and seek a new home in free and enlightened America. Who, here, Mr. President, within the sound of my voice, in reading the dying speech of Robert Emmett, his noble vindication from calumny, has not felt the throes, the remorse, the anguish, which animated that inspired hero when he exclaimed: "My country was my idol, to it I sacrificed every selfish, every endearing sentiment, and for it I now offer up my life. No, my Lord, I acted as an Irishman, determined on delivering my country from the yoke of a foreign and unrelenting tyranny and from the more galling yoke of a domestic faction, which is a joint partner and perpetrator in the parricide. For the ignominy of existing with an exterior splendor and of conscious depravity. It was the only wish of my heart to *extricate my country from its double riveted despotism.*" What despotism did he allude to, more than the very despotism and institution which was trying him for his life; the justice to whom he appealed was *senseless stone!* He knew no pity, no compassion, save that which had been previously expressed by the executive or appointing power.

Mr. President, return from Ireland and turn your gaze on the executive of state. Methinks I see them now, thronging the halls of the executive chamber, applicants for positions under an appointive judiciary, each bearing in his hand a letter setting forth his merits, signed by an hundred members of the bar whose signatures are only reversed upon the supplications of the others. What talented judges has an appointive judiciary given? Look at the Federal judiciary, most of them antiquated "*old fogies,*" not up to the present emergencies of the age, have forgotten that young America has been growing while they have fallen into the "sear and yellow leaf." Look at their decisions. The Dred Scott case was a good one to hand down to posterity. Hear ye that infamous decision: "*The black man has no rights which the white man is bound to respect.*" A decision which has shocked the humanity and justice of the world, with the exception of the vulgar, slave-holding oligarchy of the South, who, in the words of Emmett, "have lorded it over man as over the beasts of the fields."

Mr. President, I could dwell for hours upon the wonderful decisions, emanations of an appointive judiciary, that damned the system to eternal infamy not many days ago.

One of our talented appointive judges, in a communication to the press, over his own signature, stated that the people were as fit to elect a judge as a blacksmith is to repair the works of a watch. Then, if the people are not sufficiently qualified to elect a judge, how much less qualified are they to elect an executive, who, in accordance with this system, has the appointment of all judges.

Which is the most ennobling to the intellectual man, to be placed in the judicial chair by the voice and sufferage of the people, or to beg, fawn, smile or couch to the executive and ask of him to give them what the people gave unto him—*a position.* [Applause.] Then, Mr. President, who are fit for judges? In my humble opinion, and as an American citizen of the 19th century, believing myself entitled to an opinion and can freely express it, I would elect none to office only such as would act and legislate according to *nature and reason*, and work for *equal justice* and *universal liberty*. Why let their merits be canvassed, let them come before the people for suffrage and if there is any wrong in them, it will see the light of day in honest competition. They are greater than the executive of the State. They cause more happiness or woe; they are greater than kings; they sit upon a higher throne; a trust from the people. Then who will stand on the floor of this Convention and advocate the robing of the people of these rights, the people who sent each and all of us here by their suffrage to legislate for each and all of them to the best of our abilities. Can any here say their constituents charged them to advocate an appointive judiciary, to pilfer, steal, and rob them of an elective franchise and right? No, Mr. President, I cannot believe there is one from the great body of the people who will sell his birth-right of liberty. "That liberty, as a radical law of mind, has struggled and labored on the tide of ages, like a ship with waves and storms, amid the consolidations of monarchy, amid rocks and sandbars thrown up in the sea of human experience, by the nocturnal workers of modern days." That liberty which has spoken from the fountain centres of the universe to the heart of universal man. That liberty in true souls has kindled a fire of boundless love. That liberty our forefathers have borne sublime witness to thy divine majesty!

Shade of Washington, Jefferson, and Franklin, where are thy great lights which once guarded the Temple of American Liberty? Their lights departed from earth lie buried within the tomb, not even by the present generation properly revered.

Shrines of patriot souls speak from your invisible receptacles of thought, spread abroad thy wings of love, harmony and good fellowship, bequeathing to thy friends on earth refulgent light of reason and wisdom, open and expand the preception of man and instruct him the bounteous goodness of Heaven.

Rob—ROB—not those who sent us here, THE PEOPLE! [Applause.]

Mr. WENCK—I am surprised that the gentleman, after three mohths' preparation, should have made so poor an argument. The gentleman was entirely mistaken in his views. The appointment does not depend on a single individual, but on the concurrence of the Senate elected, as well as the governor, by the people. The Senate, after the nomination of an individual, are to pass upon his qualifications and say whether he is fit, worthy, honest and able to perform the duties of the position. The gentleman has been unfortunate in his allusions to history; his arguments are drawn from the judiciary of the seventeenth century; he dare not quote anything later in support of his position. We need not go so far back to find the workings of the appointive system. Under the laws of our own State the judiciary, previous to the adoption of the constitution of 1852, was always appointive, and our own experience has shown this to be the wiser system.

The president of the Convention is a judge distinguished for his learning in the law, and I appeal to him to say if any lawyer of ability would leave a lucrative practice to run before the people for a position on the bench. It would be throwing thousands of dollars into the streets; but when it came to a permanent appointment, the case was very different. If judges were sure to remain during good behavior, talent could be commanded. Men who understood their profession would consent to sit upon the bench. I have discussed the matter before my constituents and they are in favor of an appointive judiciary, and I believe that if the gentleman would consult his own constituents, he would find himself in error in asserting that the people are in favor of an elective judiciary. An appointive judiciary is for the benefit and the interest of the poor man. It will prevent those who have money without ability from buying elections, as has been done heretofore in New Orleans; and the corruption that has controlled the judiciary elections for so considerable a portion of the time during the last twelve years will be at an end if we adopt the appointive system.

Mr. Bell—Mr. President, I think the question of the gentleman (Mr. Wenck) has been well put to the president, asking if he would run before the people for a position on the bench, and in turn I would ask if he would not. Why he went before the people as a candidate for membership in this Convention. I think that the very fact that gentlemen are here is evidence of itself that they are willing to go before the people. I agree with the gentleman that previous to 1852 the judiciary was appointive; but we should not go back to the constitutions of 1812 and 1845 for precedents to guide our action in 1864. We are entering a higher state of progress and advancement by making the judiciary elective and not appointive. We advanced one step in the constitution of 1852, in making that change, and ought not to go backward. And for one, I, in the name of the people of the First District, shall protest against taking away from the sovereign people of this country one iota of the power of making their own judges, which power legitimately belongs to them and to them only.

Mr. Sullivan—I am in favor of an elective judiciary, and I believe that the people of the State are in favor of it. The judiciary was appointive until 1852; but before that time it was found out that the judges appointed under the constitutions of 1812 and 1845 were corrupt, and the members of the Convention of 1852 found it expedient to abolish that system for the elective, and since that time Louisiana has had as talented a bench as any State in the Union. John C. Larue was elected, and he was an oracle of wisdom and legal learning—a terror to evil-doers—and yet he was a very popular gentleman.

But the report does not stop with the judges. It takes away from the people the right of electing their own sheriffs, clerks, and even justices of the peace. The framers of the report wanted to make an emperor or a czar of the governor, but I believe the people are capable of making their own selections to fill all these positions, and I shall go in for making the judiciary elective.

Mr. Wilson—The Committee on Judiciary embraces the names of gentlemen whose experience on the bench and at the bar guarantees a thorough knowledge of the subject on which they have reported. These gentlemen ignore the election of judges, and suggest their appointment by the governor, by and with the advice and consent of the Senate. Though not myself a lawyer, I have nevertheless closely scrutinized the operation of the elective judiciary system in this city for the past eleven years, and as the result of this scrutiny, I cheerfully endorse the suggestions of the framers of the report.

It has been contended that the appointment of judges is a retrogade republican movement, and much sophistry has been used to show that the people will be mulcted out of their dearest right—the right of elective franchise—by this mode of procedure. But I leave it to you, Mr. President; I leave it to this Convention, can there be a more degrading spectacle than that presented by a judge courting popular applause in the bar-rooms of a great city; arguing politics, and soliciting pledges, in many instances from men of notoriously bad repute? Does it not detract from the dignity of the judge, stain the judicial ermine, and make Justice herself weep? It cannot truthfully be denied that the system of electing judges is open to this abuse. It were useless to cite instances which have come under my personal observation. For I do not believe that argument is ever strengthened by personalities, or truth made more potent by personal invective. Appoint the judges, pay them liberal salaries, and all chance of witnessing such degrading scenes will be removed.

It is unnecessary to tell you, Mr. President, that law is a science. That it is the essence of human reason, based on the ten commandments, and brought down to the present generation as rules of action. In ancient times the judge wielded immense power, and error and crime were punished with much more severity than they are now. Joquet, in his "Origin of Laws," tells us that perjury was punishable by death, forgery and counterfeiting by cutting off the hands of the offenders, treachery by cutting out the tongue, and adultery by burning to death. I will not waste the valuable time of the Convention by entering into a detail of the punishments inflicted upon criminals by the Mosaic law, but just state, in passing, that rape, incest, adultery, homicide and Sabbath breaking were sure to entail upon the offender either stoning or burning to death. My object is briefly to point out the sacredness of the judiciary, and to show that a man may be a good citizen, yet be totally incapable of passing upon the qualifications necessary in a judge. As well might a citizen vote upon the merits of a candidate for the chair of mathematics in a college as for the judge of the supreme or district court. I would even go so far as to have justices of the peace appointed; and in every instance I would wish to see lawyers occupy such seats. There is more injustice, more ignorance, more wrong perpetrated in these petty courts in one day than would make angels veil their faces for shame.

Mr. President, I do not wish to be misunderstood; I would not check the corrective influence of the ballot-box. I would not diminish one iota the rights of the people. But I feel convinced that political judges are just as bad as political preachers, and I think the masses will sustain me when I assert that both should be excluded from all participation in the excitements arising from political canvass.

I will conclude, by one or two allusions to Mr. Terry's remarks ou "Ireland" and Judge Taney. I think it is a far-fetched argument which the gentleman has introduced about Ireland. Emmett and his brother martyrs knew that their judges had no power. It was the jurors, packed by a monarchical government, who were the tyrants.

When Mr. Terry alludes to Judge Taney, of the Supreme Court of the United States —a man whose name should be held in reverence, who has grown gray in the study of law, and accuses him of violating his oath, and sacrificing his high and well-earned position by rendering an unjust decision, I think he has overstepped his ability to judge, and I must state that I disagree with him, and I will even go the length of stating that Judge Taney's decision in the red Scott case was perfectly constitutional. I will vote against Mr. Sullivan's amendment.

Mr. Campbell—I merely rise to say I shall support unhesitatingly an elective judiciary. I am an old resident of Mississippi and have seen the working of the appointive system. I particularly remember one judge of a district court, and must say he was a perfect stick, of which we could not get rid. We changed the constitution, and what was the result? We elected, among others, a judge who was a very unpopular man, who so well carried out the duties of his office that he was afterwards unanimously elected against four or five other candidates. Political notions did not govern either. Irish was a whig and so was Sharkey, yet both were elected judges, and the latter held his office up to the breaking out of the rebellion. So much for Mississippi, and now let us look at Louisiana for the last five years. When I first came here there was an appointive judiciary, even in the city courts. I was a member of a company of Louisiana volunteers, and services were demanded of me in two different places. I was cited to appear before the city court, and produced my papers substantiating the above facts; but the judge said: "It made no difference —I make my judgment and will not change." The judgment was against me, notwithstanding the evidence in my favor. Accordingly, I am in favor of an elective judiciary, and believe judges should never be so far removed from the people as to hold their offices during their life-time. Never, so long as I have a vote in this Convention or elsewhere, will I cast it in favor of an appointive judiciary.

Mr. Smith—I believe this right belongs to the people, and that it is the surest safeguard of Americans. Take from them this right and you destroy what is inherent in every republican government. (Applause.) I shall certainly vote for an elective judiciary and for *election* to every other office. (Applause.)

Mr. Abell—Mr. President and gentlemen of the Convention, I rise to speak on what is, in my opinion, the emancipation act excepted, the most important question that has arisen, or will arise here. I must confess that I differ from gentlemen who have preceded me. I believe, and I am sure I want nothing but will give us a highly respectable bench, and mark what I tell you, you cannot command the best talent without paying therefor a large compensation. You cannot tell me that gentlemen like Mr. Roselius, and a dozen others whom I could name, would leave a lucrative practice of perhaps $20,000 a year for a judge's salary of $6000. Let us compromise this matter, and, by giving a salary of $12,000, strike a medium between the low salaries heretofore given here and the extremely liberal ones allowed in England. Honor is a very good thing; but a man cannot go to market with it, and it is the ultimate advantage of the people that we must consider.

I think there is no justice unless administered according to the laws of the land, and not merely according to the dictates of any man's reason, but in that which, in the language of Coke, is the "refinement of reason and experience of ages," and not only that, but the law of the land. I contend that no man *can administer* the law *without* a long experience. If you wanted a watch that would give you the time correctly, you would go to some experienced mechanic—the best watchmaker in the country. I say, you would be prompted by a sense of interest to go to the best establishment, where the most excellent workmanship of that character was produced. How are you to know what is the best? Can you depend upon yourself simply? Suppose you should examine the machinery, could you tell whether or not it was of the proper character? If this is so in the ordinary transactions of life, how much more would it be the case in regard to the experience necessary in this most complicated department of government? I wish to state, in the commencement, that while I believe it is for the interest of the whole country that we should have an appointive judiciary throughout, I am equally frank to confess myself satisfied that such is not the sense of this Convention or the people. Therefore, I, as a true democrat, am ready and willing to compromise the matter, by having the judges of the Supreme Court appointed by the governor, with the advice of the Senate, and the judges of the distrtict courts elected by the people—and I make this concession only as a compromise. An additional reason for my taking this course is, that I do not believe that this Convention, or the people of the State, are prepared for an entirely appointive judiciary. The appointing power in England has been vested in the crown time out of mind, but was seldom exercised without great consideration and consultation, in order to select only the most experienced and pure of the members of the bar to be judge.

It is not unlikely that the king himself sat in judgment as late as the time of Edward I, (1272,) but for nearly 600 years the judges have been appointed by the crown; and from the time of Edward I to III William and Mary, about 400 years, the judges held their appointment at the pleasure of the king, and were removable at his option, which was not unfrequently exercised by displacing the most upright judges and substituting some craven wretch, who was ever ready to obey his master and to do any unprincipled act that might be assigned him. Such were Tresghan, Saunders, Jeffries, and others; and such judges would as readily subserve the interest and purposes of a mob, that would keep them in power, as they would their master, the king.

But, Mr. President, these examples only show the danger of these uncertain tenures; but it would be invidious and unjust not to mention the exceptions, for, during this period, we find many reverend judges and sages of the law—Hale, Coke, and others—who have left imperishable monuments of learning and judicial purity, and they, Mr. President, were sometimes removed to give place to the most corrupt and vicious.

My constituents wish to place the Supreme Court on a permanent basis, and also to awe judges from any abuse of power—to drive them into the path of rectitude. During the time that this appointive power in England was vested in the crown, which has been nearly six hundred years, dating from Edward I, (1272,) the judiciary held their offices solely at the king's pleasure.

During that time some of the most atrocious judges that ever lived on earth or disgraced humanity carried out his wishes, or suffered immediate removal, to give place to others who would better subserve the interests of the king. In 1688 this was so far altered as to enable a judge to hold his position during the king's life-time. That was considered a great point gained, because then and from that time the king could make no removal. This continued for nearly one hundred years, when, in 1760, upon the accession of George III, an act of Parliament was passed, at his instance, by which judges held their offices during good behavior. Let us incorporate the same provision into our constitution, for otherwise the best judges and truest men are liable to be swept from the bench after a short term of four years, as they have been to my certain knowledge from the Second, Third and Fifth District Courts, for no other reason, that I was ever able to discover, unless on account of their being pure and upright judges. Tell me why such men as Hunt, Morgan, Kennedy and Eggleston were removed? Only because they were not prepared to submit to those who were combined to make judges to suit themselves. Under the appointive power of the king some of the most wicked judges that ever lived were placed upon the bench. Such as Jeffries, Saunders, and a thousand others who held their positions as long their master said they should, or they subserved his purposes. That is the danger to be feared by the people, who are undoubtedly virtuous in intent, but all know the danger of their usurpation under such a system. Gentlemen will remember the words of Ulysses, where he says: "The worst of tyrants is an usurping crowd."

And thus the people will drive the best magistrates from their places, and fill them with demagogues, who will aspire to the vacancies and serve their master's meanest purposes.

That is my opinion on the subject of the elective judiciary, for the people will certainly oppose or support a judge accordingly, as they do or do not like him, or according as to whether or no he will serve their purposes, and thus our judges will become a reproach and a disgrace.

[The president's hammer fell at the expiration of the half hour.]

Mr. Terry—I move the gentleman be allowed to proceed.

[No objection was made.]

Mr. Abell—Since the change of 1688, the decisions of England have been the most uniform, regular and consistent that the world has ever known, excepting, perhaps, the Supreme Court of the United States. How is it with this court, of which our esteemed president is an honorable member? The judges and associate judges have, from the beginning to the present time, been appointed during good behavior. Look into the voluminous reports and see, as the result of this, the most noble, uniform and consistent line of decisions. Why is this? Because the bench of the United States is dependent on nobody, for not even the president and Congress have power to remove them. I ask you, Mr. President and gentlemen, whether the State of Louisiana will not adopt this glorious system at once--that the Supreme Court shall not only be nominated by the governor, and that nomination be submitted to the Senate for approval. Then, without going any farther, I will compromise at that stage and elect the district judges.

I am in favor of giving the judges high salaries, that they may stand independent. In England, the lord chancellor receives no less than £10,000, or more than $50,000, the chief justice of the Queen's Bench £8000, associate justice £5000, chief justice Common Pleas £7000, associate justice £5000, chief justice exchequer £7000, and the associate justices £5000. As a contrast, chief justice of the United States gets $6500, associate justices $6000. If we have an appointive judiciary to guard against each extreme, I favor a salary of $12,000 for our chief justice, $10,000 for each associate, and $8000 for each of the district judges. I withdraw, for the present, as I wish to have a general expression of opinion on this important subject.

Mr. Cutler—I am disposed to give my opinion to the Convention on this, one of the most important questions that could engage its attention; but it is too late to do so to-day. I wish to speak during the twenty remaining minutes of the session, and if you will do me the favor of allowing me to occupy the floor for a short time to-morrow, I shall be under many and lasting obligations.

[Permission granted.]

I feel that I am not gifted, as many are, by the Almighty, with the power to convince men. I have not that quality, through a frailty and imperfection of my nature, and perhaps, because I am a lawyer, in the estimation of some, even of men who pretend to be lawyers and to know something of this judiciary question. If, however, I fail to show the members of this Convention that I know something about it, then take for naught what I may say. I am not a dramatist, phrenologist, psychologist, spiritualist, Macduff, Macbeth, minister of the gospel or priest. I am an humble citizen of Louisiana, and in behalf of its people I am disposed to illustrate this question—not by written speeches, studied for months; not by impromptu eloquence and spirit, emanating from some gentlemen, merely through personal prejudice; but to try to argue to this Convention on principles founded on justice and long experience. Because, if we are to be governed by personal prejudice, I think that the Supreme Ruler of man should at once withdraw his spirit and presence from this body. If we are to be governed by principle, precedent, intelligence and humanity, let us use and listen to reason, and in so listening do not pretend to listen to me alone, [hear, hear,] but to those arguments which may be presented *pro* and *con* on this great question which now engages the attention of this Convention. It is the judiciary which holds your lives, liberty and prosperity in their hands. Scorn it; treat it with contempt; to God you must then appeal and no longer to man!

It might be considered improper in me to make these remarks, but I have heard men speak and use such harsh words here, and that, too, with such characteristics of manner, as calls forth what I am now saying.

Lawyers! law! There are pettifoggers that bear the name of lawyers; but a lawyer, in the proper sense, is one learned in the laws of God and man. What governs us? what causes us to assemble here? The power of the law! Everything about us, from the dust that we tread under our feet to the heavenly bodies above us, rolling in illimitable space, are governed by law! Show me a principle that is not based upon law; a country or anything else that is not based upon or governed by law. Yet a lawyer is spoken against here because he bears that name, and because lawyers constitute this committee. Some of you scoff at them and their report. Why? Look at your origin, at the very blood in your veins, at your systematic structure, at the world and all its features and contents, they are all based upon and governed by law. Man's law is founded upon the law of God. Will you ridicule, then, the law and the lawyer who expounds it? It is a shame and a disgrace for men to raise their voices here against that which Almighty God has established pre-eminently above all other things—the law! the law of God and of man!

I hope, gentlemen, that I offer no insult. I want you to understand that the speaker (myself) is no aspirant for office—wants no judgeship. He, as a lawyer, thank God, makes his living honestly by the practice of the law. I am not here, as a lawyer of that committee, to advocate an appointed judiciary upon any other grounds but that of principle, justice and the best interests of the people. It is principle and justice that actuated me. Do not mistake me; do not suppose for a moment that I shall be governed by prejudice, pecuniary interest, or any other petty motive, which seems so apparent with some of you. Then, if you will listen to me and believe me, I ask you to listen to me to-morrow, while I shall attempt to argue these principles, illustrate these facts, and apply them to the appointed instead of the elected judiciary.

[On motion, the Convention then adjourned.]

THURSDAY, May 26, 1864.

[The president called the Convention to order at 12 o'clock M.

Prayer was offered by the Rev. Mr. Gilbert.

The roll being called, the following members answered to their names :]

Messrs. Abell, Ariail, Austin, Bailey, Barrett, Baum, Beauvais, Bell, Bennie, Bofill, Bromley, Buckley, Burke, Campbell, Collin, Cook J. K., Cook T., Crozat, Cutler, Davies, Duane, Dufresne, Duke, Dupaty, Edwards, Ennis, Fish, Flagg, Flood, Foley, Fosdick, Fuller, Gaidry, Geier, Goldman, Gorlinski, Gruneberg, Harnan, Hart, Healy, Heard, Henderson, Hills, Hire, Howell, Howes, Kavanagh, Knobloch, Kugler, Maas, Mann, Maurer, Mayer, Mendiverri, Montamat, Murphy E., Murphy M. W., Newell, Normand, O'Conner, Ong, Orr, Payne J., Paine J. T., Pintado, Poynot, Purcell J., Pursell S., Schroeder, Schnurr, Seymour, Shaw, Smith, Spellicy, Stocker, Stumpf, Stiner, Stauffer, Sullivan, Terry, Thorpe, Waters, Wenck, Wells, Wilson and Mr. President—86.

[A quorum being present, the journal of yesterday was read and approved.

Mr. Thorpe presented the following resolution, which lays over under the rules :]

Resolved, That the pen used by the president of this Convention in signing the ordinance of emancipation, be presented, along with proper endorsements of its genuineness, to Major Gen. N. P. Banks, commanding the Department of the Gulf.

Mr. MONTAMAT—I move to reconsider the vote on the resolution of Mr. Hills, in regard to the forfeiture of the per diem of members.

Mr. HILLS—I move to lay that motion on the table.

[The yeas and nays were demanded, and the motion lost by the following vote :]

YEAS—Messrs. Ariail, Barrett, Beauvais, Bell, Bromley, Burke, Collin, Cook T., Dufresne, Duane, Edwards, Ennis, Flood, Fosdick, Foley, Geier, Goldman, Gorlinski, Harnan, Hills, Howell, Kugler, Mann, Newell, Normand, Payne J., Purcell J., Pursell S., Schroeder, Shaw, Smith, Stiner, Stauffer, Terry, Thorpe, Wells, Wilson—36.

NAYS—Messrs. Abell, Bailey, Baum, Bennie, Beauvais, Bofill, Buckley, Campbell, Cook J. K., Crozat, Cutler, Davies, Decker, Duke, Dupaty, Fish, Flagg, Fuller, Gaidry, Gruneberg, Hart, Healy, Heard, Henderson, Hire, Howes, Kavanagh, Knobloch, Maas, Maurer, Mayer, Mendiverri, Montamat, Murphy E., Murphy M. W., O'Conner, Ong, Orr, Paine J. T., Pintado, Poynot, Schnurr, Seymour, Spellicy, Stocker, Stumpf, Sullivan, Waters, Wenck—49.

[The motion was therefore lost.

On the motion to reconsider the yeas and nays were demanded, and being taken, resulted as follows :]

YEAS—Messrs. Abell, Balch, Bailey, Baum, Beauvais, Bennie, Bofill, Buckley, Campbell, Cook J. K., Crozat, Cutler, Davies, Decker, Duke, Dupaty, Fish, Flagg, Fuller, Gaidry, Gruneberg, Hart, Healy, Heard, Henderson, Hire, Howes, Kavanagh, Knobloch, Maas, Maurer, Mayer, Mendiverri, Montamat, Murphy E., Murphy M. W., Ong, O'Conner, Orr, Paine J. T., Pintado, Poynot, Schnurr, Seymour, Spellicy, Stocker, Sullivan, Waters, Wenck—49.

NAYS—Messrs. Ariail, Barrett, Bell, Bromley, Burke, Collin, Cook T., Duane, Dufresne, Edwards, Ennis, Flood, Foley, Fosdick, Geier, Goldman, Gorlinski, Harnan, Hills, Howell, Kugler, Mann, Newell, Normand, Payne J., Purcell J., Pursell S., Schroeder, Shaw, Smith, Stumpf, Stiner, Stauffer, Terry, Thorpe, Wells, Wilson—37.

Mr. BOFILL—I move to lay the resolution on the table.

[The resolution was read and Mr. Stauffer protested against the vote being taken, on the ground that the resolution was not correctly read. He was ordered to take his seat as the question was being put, and the motion to lay on the table was carried.

The second reading of the report on judiciary, article 2, and Mr. Sullivan's amendment, was then taken up.]

Mr. CUTLER—For the kindness of the Convention yesterday in allowing me to conclude my remarks to-day on the great subject before the Convention—the report of the Judiciary Committee—I am under lasting obligations to this body. As I stated yesterday, it is one of the most important questions that has engaged the attention of this Convention; hence the importance of our understanding the matter well before voting, because whatever action we take it will continue to exist and form a part of the constitution until another convention may be assembled. The ordinance of emancipation was one of great importance, but as yet it forms no part of the constitution. It is a mere ordinance. I hope when the time comes, and under the head of general provisions, it will be engrafted there as a part of the constitution. Then, sir, in making the organic law of Louisiana, allow me to say once more that the question of appointed or elected judiciary is one of the greatest and most vital now. I submit to you that the amendment is premature; not that I wish to dodge the question. I desire now to present my entire views on the subject, be they weak, good, bad or indifferent. According to parliamentary law, the chair and the Convention can only act upon the subject matter presented to its consideration. What is it, then? It is upon the third article of the Judiciary Committee. That article reads thus:

Art. 3. The Supreme Court shall be composed of one chief justice and four associate justices, a majority of whom shall constitute a quorum. The chief justice shall receive a salary of ten thousand dollars, and each of the associate justices a salary of nine thousand dollars, annually, until otherwise provided by law. The court shall appoint its own clerks.

The amendment does not come in the proper place. It reads:

Art. 3. The Supreme Court shall be composed of one chief justice and four associate justices, a majority of whom shall constitute a quorum. The chief justice shall receive a salary of eight thousand dollars, and the four associate justices each seven thousand dollars, annually, until otherwise provided by law. The court shall appoint its own clerks. The judges shall be elected for the term of ten years.

But Mr. Sullivan, who offered this in perfect candor, I am willing to admit, has mistaken the report of the committee, and has added thereto an amendment which does not belong there; that is, that judges shall be elected for a term of ten years. Now, gentlemen, turn to article 11 of the report: "The judges, both of the supreme and inferior courts, shall be appointed by the governor, by and with the advice and consent of the Senate, and they shall hold their offices during good behavior." Then, Mr. President, according to parliamentary law, the amendment in regard to the elected or appointed judiciary does not apply to this article of the report at all. It is necessary, in order to proper legislation, not only to act in harmony, but in accordance with parliamentary law, as well as in that spirit of justice which is demanded at our hands, and we should make amendments at the proper time and in proper places. But, inasmuch as the question of appointed or elected judiciary has been thoroughly and ably discussed by several gentlemen, it is not necessary, nor perhaps would it be proper, to cut short the final argument; therefore I will proceed, in order to bring the debate to a final termination. Whatever I say shall be said without prejudice or personal motive, and without a view to office.

The gentlemen who are opposed to me are men of honor, intelligence and respect, and I shall not lose my respect for them if they continue to persist in their notions in regard to the elected judiciary. As a man and citizen, and no politician—one who despises politics, and wants nothing to do with them, I shall speak on this question. Some of the learned gentlemen of this Convention have said that the appointed judiciary is anti-democratic; that it is anti-republican; in other words, it is stealing from the people—robbing the people of their just prerogative. I want to meet you upon principle. You have laid down principles on this floor that it is robbing or depriving the people of their just rights. In other words, the people are to be heard in all elections—are to have their voice in the election of all officers, be they executive, legislative or judicial. Is not that a fair statement of the proposition? Now, let us look at our country—and I mean the country of Washington, Madison, Jefferson—the United States of America. You speak of an appointed judiciary as being anti-democratic, and against the people. Do you believe to-day that great as we may be we are superior to our forefathers, who fought, bled and endured greater hardships than we to achieve independence we now enjoy? We may be, but it is not my opinion. What did they do? They have engrafted on the constitution of the United States this high, heaven-born principle, that the judges of the Supreme Court of the United States and of the district courts of the different States, and the commissioners which answers to the word justices of the peace, shall be appointed by the president and confirmed by the Senate. Are you tired of that system? Look back at the organic law that gave your liberty birth. There is the foundation to build upon, and a sufficient reason for the appointed judiciary in a State. The governments of the different States are modeled after the general government, and the nearer we come to the original model the more perfect our new structure.

We have the supreme court, district courts and justices of the peace in the different States, precisely on the same plan and principle as that of the general government. Look at your constitution. You are all Americans, are you not? If you happen to be an Irishman or German by birth, that does not make a distinction, if you are an American in principle. Now, as Americans, under an American constitution and American democratic laws, am I wrong when I say that our forefathers in their wisdom thought it proper to place and that they were right in placing in the constitution of the United States that sacred article that the Supreme Court of the United States, and also the district courts and justices of the peace, should be appointed by the president, with the sanction of the Senate? If not, then, in God's name, what becomes of your argument and of your principle? Never say again that it is anti-republican and contrary to American institutions! It is democratic, it is republican, it is American, that you shall appoint judges of the Supreme Court, district courts and justices of the peace; that done, and you have a judiciary in this State modeled after the judiciary of the United States, and will have sanctioned a principle founded in wisdom and justice.

I ask no better authority than the blood of our forefathers to sustain my argument. Where is your argument? You have promised to meet me upon principle. Where is your answer to that argument? Look at the constitution of the United States, and you will see I am speaking the truth. The State is merely an integral part of the great country in which we live, and should model after its superior.

Mr. President, let me call your attention to the constitution of 1845. Let us leave Washington, Jefferson, Madison, Adams, and the host of men who brought us into the liberty we now enjoy, and come down to our own State. What says the constitution of 1845? Where were we then? Was there then a great war? Who lived then? A Livingston, a Grimes, a Martin, a Roselius, yea, and many others—practicing lawyers—no, not all of them, but all were honest men, whose history it does me good to refer to. What do they say? If you are to be governed by reason and principle, now thwart the principle I introduce, based upon experience of great and good men and able and worthy jurists; do it, if you can, but do it fairly and honestly, not by abuse and high-sounding words. "The Supreme Court shall be composed of one chief justice and three associate justices, a majority of whom shall constitute a quorum. The chief justice shall receive a salary of $5500. The court shall appoint its own clerks. The judges shall be appointed for a term of eight years." I read from the constitution of 1845. Turn back to 1812, and you find the same system and principle, and it prevailed and governed in the State of Louisiana until 1852. Now, turn to the constitution of 1852, and what do you find there? Do you not see that *such men* as the arch traitors Slidell, Benjamin, and others—workers in the crime and slime of treason—are the authors, directly or indirectly, of the elective judiciary feature of that constitution? The very men who, in Louisiana and Mississippi and Washington City, plotted treason against our common country, are the authors, directly or indirectly, of that which my opponents wish to vote for to-day.

In 1812 the constitution of this State was modeled after the example of our forefathers, in respect to the appointed judiciary. Look back and see what you can complain of under the appointed judiciary. Look at the decision of the courts; look at our judges, and I ask if there is one of you who can say they were not in perfect accordance with the laws of justice and humanity? By the most diabolical thuggery, and through the instrumentality of the infamous Benjamin and others—not democrats, and they never were, or they would have been honest—they over-rode and out-generaled such noble and true statesmen as Roselius and many others. The question for to-day is, whether we will sanction the same principle? That is what I want to know. Do you want to say, by the power held by this Convention, that there shall be an elected judiciary in Louisiana, in conformity to the will and wishes of the thugs and fraudulent scoundrels and traitors? If you want it, after this, I have nothing to say. The history of Louisiana tells you that I am right. One of my opponents says he is in favor of an elected judiciary, and is willing to give us the appointment of the supreme court, but is not willing to include the district courts and justices of the peace. Let us come to the strongest principle. I want you, my friend of the Eleventh Ward (Campbell,) particularly to listen to this. By what principle is it argued in favor of the appointment of the supreme court and not the district courts and justices of the peace? You give us no reason at all. Let me give you a few reasons why it is more important to appoint the district judges than the supreme judges.

We are all practical men, and have some business which we pursue. Let us reason upon principle. Where do you institute your suit? Do you institute it in the district court or the supreme court? Here is a poor man who has a debt due him and is desirous of enforcing payment. Where does he bring that suit? The supreme court never has had original jurisdiction in ordinary cases, and I do not believe this Convention will so far forget itself as to give it original jurisdiction. On the contrary, it has already decided that the supreme court shall have appellate jurisdiction. Now, in conformity with that principle, let me ask you if it is not the district court instead of the supreme court that takes cognizance of your cause? It is the district court that tries the case, if the amount is over one hundred dollars; if the sum exceeds three hundred dollars, there exists the right of appeal to the supreme court. If there is such a thing as prejudice in a judge, let me ask you where it begins? It is where you bring the suit and receive the testimony—in the district court where it begins. It is there that you hear witnesses. When the testimony is reduced to writing the party has a right to appeal to the supreme court. It goes up to the supreme court in writing, but there is no such thing as that court hearing witnesses. The testimony only is read as written down by a clerk under the dictation and in the presence of the district judge. This is the system everywhere. It is engrafted in the federal constitution, and is carried out by the judges of the federal courts, and is the system we now propose. Then, how can there be any prejudice in the supreme court, that only reads the cold documents, sees no witnesses, hears no party, and does not know the parties except by name? If the supreme court of the State of Louisiana is exempt from the position of prejudice, I would like to have the gentleman answer me, how it is important that they should be elected or appointed? It matters not how it is done, so far as this matter is concerned; but in the court of the justice of the peace, where you bring your small claim to the threshold of either justice or injustice. In the district court, when you bring a suit exceeding $100, you desire to have your testimony heard; then it is that this prejudice is printed indeliby to go up to the supreme court. How will you get over this—what is the remedy? I have shown you that the supreme court has no opportunity to become prejudiced, but it is not so with the justice of the peace. He sees every movement of the witness' face and knows whether to believe or disbelieve. If he is a dishonest man, he may give preference to dishonesty; and it may be carried out with perfect innocence by the supreme court. You are to manufacture judges either by the public voice at the ballot-box, or through the mouth of the executive and Senate. John Smith, Bob Johnson and Red Bill are candidates for judge. You cannot have forgotten the scenes of 1853, '54 and '55; if you have, I remember them, associated with the sword and revolver. Do you want men to sit on the judicial bench who go into beer saloons, five-cent coffee-houses and groggeries and electioneer for the purpose of becoming judges? Is that your appreciation of American institutions and of liberty, right and justice? The executive department is a trivial thing in comparison with the judiciary. Then, do you want a man who electioneers in the grogshops to secure his election? If he would stop there I would have no objection, but it does not stop there. Here is a man who has $300,000, and the thug, assassin and scoundrel is aided by the rich man. You can elect Red Bill to-morrow under these principles. (Applause.) Every man who has electioneered for the last six weeks for this principle of elected judiciary—I mean the gentleman on my right, the auditor of public accounts—knows it. It is strange that a man of reason, sense, honor and integrity should condescend, in this State, to sanction thuggery and the election of grogshop electioneerers to the dignified position of judge. I mean no insult to any man, but what I have told you is based upon principle. If I deviate from that, call me to order. I wish to know if in the Constitutional Convention of 1864 you want again to perpetrate these outrages, which have been so often perpetrated in New Orleans and elsewhere.

"Convince a man against his will,
And he is of the same opinion still."

I had rather say nothing than undertake to talk to a man who is entirely impervious. If he is on his dying bed and you tell him there is a God, he will refuse to believe it. Such men are unworthy of any argument. I know I have no powers to convince, but while I remain a member of this Convention I do not wish to be recreant to my duty, and shall say something on these important questions. I am going to test your loyalty, to see whether you are in favor of rebel or Union men.

Look at New York. Now, let the gentleman (Mr. Hills) from the Empire State—may Almighty God preserve her thus, for she is a great and deserving one—go to his city. In 1822, if I remember rightly, (and if I do not, correct me, for I want nothing but the truth,) you had an appointed judiciary. You had, dating a short time after the Declaration of Independence, say from 1784, men of principle and honesty upon the bench, and no one can dispute it. Nor did this stop there, but went down to 1846, and it was not until your tomb-shyster Russell became judge of the city court, under the elective system, that you became involved in thuggery and desperation in the shape of riots. Is it not true? Did you ever have such a riot until you had Russell upon the bench? Why was it? Because those bullies, organized thugs, anti-repub licans, anti-democrats, cowards and scoundrels collected under him, and with the dollars in their pockets, placed him in the high position of city judge.

Do not, for God's sake—looking at the history of your country, to the old States, to reason—do not vote here for such a system of thuggery again. Let us save ourselves from it. There is an instance in the Empire State that ought to make a man blush for the institutions of his country, and no man knows it better than my friend from the "Second," (Mr. Hills.) A mere machine, a mere scoundrel, a man without principle and much less without law knowledge, promoted after the adoption of the elective system to the judgeship of the city court. As for this scoundrelism, the men who voted for him were bullies, thugs, knownothings, and when they committed an offence could go at large upon "straw" bail, while an honest citizen of New York, (as it was here in New Orleans years ago,) who happened to be arrested, would have to give double bonds to the city or town authorities.

Pass from an elected judiciary. Let a governor of New York, Massachusetts or Rhode Island appoint a man, and he never selects a thug or assassin. Tell me, if you can, when that was ever done? No, sir, it never was. The dignity of the executive and Senate require greater support than to allow them to promote thugs and assassins to office. Gentlemen, save Louisiana, save Louisiana, in God's name!

I will tell you another thing just before I get through. Let me ask you a question. Is every man in Louisiana a loyal man? Do you say "yes?" [Cries of "no," "no." Of *course* "no." [Voice—"some mixed."] Yes, they are *considerably* mixed; a *little too much* mixed, ("You are right, sir") to risk the experiment of an elective judiciary, especially in the country. *Here* are men from the country, who are truly loyal, and I will stand by them to the very death. I do not doubt the gentleman from the Tenth, (Mr. Campbell,) or any other man here, but I say, gentlemen, that you are laboring under a great mistake when you pretend that you can submit to the people of Louisiana the election of that power which holds your life, liberty and property at stake. You *cannot* do it *now*. It is not the governor of Louisiana that has any power over you in comparison with a judge. The same is true of the Legislature, but the judiciary can even say that your property is not yours. Go to any parish, as St. Mary's, (I mean no disrespect,) in which you are summoned before a jury who have taken the oath of allegiance—oh, yes! but your vote in this Convention consigns you to the penitentiary or to prison, whether you are in the right or wrong. Are the people loyal enough to vote for judges who may pass upon your life, liberty and property? [Cries of "no."] I said I intended to test the loyalty of this Convention. *I* do not brag of too much loyalty. I *think* I am a loyal man. I try my best for my country, but do not wish to brag of anything. I think you will say that my argument is not composed of harsh epithets and abuse, but of principles.

If you vote for an elective judiciary, do you not inculcate an unholy principle in giving a chance to disloyal men to place upon the bench a disloyal traitor? [Applause, and cries of "yes," "yes."] I would rather vote against emancipation if it was to come up again, but I feel certain it is a fixed fact, as God knows, I *hope* it never will—against *anything* else, than against the appointive judiciary—at least, until the war is over. You put a governor in office now, I care not *who* he is, he will select a loyal man and will not have upon the bench of Louisiana a disloyal man.

Is all I have said worthy of any consideration here? Are you still determined to vote for an elective judiciary and let the proclamation of the governor go forth to call the people to an election for judges and *invite* men who you know did not come up to vote at the last gubernatorial election, but who are ready to vote *now* to defeat propositions that may emanate from this Convention? [Applause.]

I want, in perfect candor—meaning no abuse at all to the gentleman from the Third, (Mr. Terry,) whom I respect as an honorable member of this Convention—to ask him what he means by what he said on yesterday? Does he *know* what he means? Can he get up here to-day, leave his papers, and say anything against the principles I have enunciated? If he can, I would like to have him do it. I care not whether you write it out or speak impromptu, as I do, dictated by reason and principle, but only wish to know what you mean by what you read from your manuscript, the fruits of your six weeks' labor? [Laughter and applause.] Do you intend to thwart the great principles that move us? If you do, you can make a laughing-stock of me, or the majority of this Convention. *This* is no place to make fun and laugh and sneer, or treat anybody with disrespect. It is a place for us to *work*—for great God knows, there never was a Convention that ever met before under such extraordinary circumstances as this. Your abuse should not be thrown forth here! There is no argument in such stuff, for argument is based upon principle, philosophy and fact, with a view to good and noble purposes. *That is argument!* I wish to God the gentleman had never read from those papers what he did, for A. J. Davis, of New York, destroyed all his fictions in about two minutes! Give us something new — something that suits the present day and action — that is connected with what we are here concerned with.

Are we now in the midst of a great rebellion, or a time of peace? I wish it was the latter, but it is not, and therefore it is necessary that we should be exceedingly careful. Do not be too hasty. Do not suppose that, because you had an idea that might prevail in proper time, that you are to force it now upon this Convention! That is the only reason why I seriously blame my esteemed friend (the auditor of accounts) for attempting to use his influence upon this Convention, for the purpose of thwarting one of the noblest projects within its power. We have done him the honor to elect him to the noble position he holds. He should never have set his foot upon the floor of this Convention for that purpose; but now that he has, how many of you are influenced by him?

No matter how high may be the position

of any man, however much he may try to influence your vote, be governed by noble aims, by principle and justice. I fear, upon this question, no man's vote, who is not already trammeled, if he takes occasion to go into a private caucus, gets his constituents to come forward and instruct him how to vote upon a certain question, that is wrong. Each one, after election, should come here as a man, like Chas. O'Connor, free from every prejudice and partiality—devoted to principle.

You may say I have made allusions to somebody. I may have, to certain men, I call not their names, but am assured that such is the fact, and I ask you, without anybody else knowing who you are, to discard such petty prejudices and vote like men, though all the secessionists and scoundrels in the country favor an elective judiciary. On this subject I am done. I have spoken sincerely.

Now, gentlemen who pretend to have an adverse opinion, do not act like stubborn men and vote anyhow, but rise in your seats, exhibit your views and tell us why you do as you do, and I will vote with you, if you show me how our forefathers devised a wrong. Show me how badly this great system has worked from their time down to the present. Show me an instance anywhere where an appointed judiciary is worse, or any system is as bad, as the elective—give me an instance, if you please.

There is some great mistake about this. Some members are of opinion that the governor has an almighty power, and that whoever he selects is the man. Gentlemen, the report of the committee reads in no such way. It says that the governor shall nominate, and submit the nominee to the Senate for its approval. If there is an error in the judgment of the executive, the Senate, to be composed of many of you men—I shall not be there, for I do not want and will have no more office—will correct that error, which will prevent us from having the property of loyal men taken unjustly from them while they are smitten to the dust by the election of disloyal judges, who might be elected, not only in the country, but I fear also in New Orleans.

With these remarks, I thank you, as I yesterday said I would, and take my leave of the subject. [Applause.]

Mr. Thorpe—The elective judiciary had been a failure in all the States where it had ever been tried, not because the people were not competent to elect the judiciary, but because the people did not find time to attend properly to the election, and hence the machinery of an elective judiciary naturally fell into the hands of political gamblers or speculators; and an elective judiciary, as a consequence, was characteristic of the source from whence it originated. Having already incorporated in the constitution the ordinance of emancipation, which was to be submitted to the people, it was doubly necessary that the judiciary that was to decide all the important relations under that ordinance should be independent, over and as far as possible removed from all improper and especially from all political influences. Suppose in submitting this ordinance to the popular vote, the responsibilities of the iron-clad oath be removed, who in this Convention believes it would be ratified by the inhabitants of the State. So, too, if we make the judges elective: just as soon as the franchise is extended so as to permit the loyal, semi-loyal and the obstinate disloyal people to vote they would elect judges who would make the emancipation ordinance a nullity; and the members of this Convention, who have honestly voted for the ordinance and sustained the federal government would find these elective judges none other than Jeffries, so terribly would be the example of an abused judiciary.

The gentleman from the Fifth District (Mr. Abell) has given a succinct history of the use of British jurisprudence, and I do not propose to go into the history of the supreme and inferior courts of the country, as my friend Mr. Cutler has just done in so able a manner; and were it not for my horror of an elective judiciary, and my desire to be placed on the record in favor of an appointed judiciary, I might not have made any remarks on this subject. I cannot approve of the compromise which the gentleman from the Fifth District (Mr. Abell) proposed to offer—to appoint the supreme court and elect the district judges and justices of the peace. On the contrary, I believe the most tyrannical portion of our system was an elective justice of the peace. This was the court whose arbitrary decisions bore directly on the great mass of poor people. One of the greatest blessings enjoyed by the citizens of New Orleans, while Gen. Butler was in the city, was the entire cessation of the functions of justices of the peace. The people, for the time being at least, were free from their corrupt and arbitrary influences. When they were elected they soon grew to be a terrible scourge to the community, and the scenes of destitution and misery brought to light by their action, in turning helpless women and children into the streets, were enough to wring the hearts of all well disposed persons with sorrow. This evil, after Gen. Butler departed from the city, was carried to such an extent that several gentlemen, among them myself, called on Gov. Shepley and induced him to issue an order calculated to put a stop to such proceedings; and if it had been carried out and not allowed to become a dead letter soon after its promulgation, much of the present suffering of the poor people of the city would have been obviated.

If he wanted to give protection to the poor man in the inferior courts, he would make the judges of those courts appointive. The poor man should place no dependence in those who meet him in the grog-shop and ask him for his vote to elect him as a justice of the peace, promising favors as a consideration for the vote. He would ask gentlemen where elective judges were made in New Orleans? He would ask them if it would be inappropriate to post up over the door of every five cent grog-shop in the city a sign emblazoned with the device, "Justices of the Peace made here!" Justices of the peace and judges were nominated in back-rooms, and elected by grog-shop politicians! Men of standing in the community, as a general thing, had very little to do with the judiciary elections.

The elective system was particularly ill adapted to the sparsely settled portions of Louisiana, on account of the fact that frequently whole communities were relatives. Twenty years ago it was a common remark, "that if a man could get Ed. White as a lawyer, and a Lafourche jury, he could carry any thing;" and in many of the country parishes there were persons who, by their personal influence with their numerous relatives and their great wealth, boasted that they feared nothing from the courts; and they had nothing to fear, for they had the power to do anything they pleased. I was in New York in December last, when the election for city judges took place. The issue was distinctly made between McCunn's friends and the honest people of New York.

The New York bullies, junk shopkeepers, petty thieves and swindlers, told the people that they wished to, and were determined, to force McCunn down their throats, and they succeeded in doing it. This matter had been carried so far that Jas. T. Brady, that noble and patriotic son of Ireland, and most eminent jurist of the Empire State, had been heard to say, "That when a client presented himself to him for advice, that he first learned enough of the case to ascertain before what court it must be brought, and if it was before a judge whom he had opposed in politics, he felt bound to decline to undertake the suit."

I would repeat that when the elective judiciary system had been tried, the law-abiding citizens living under its influence felt that it was a miserable failure. It was an absurd fallacy to say that to make it appointive would be an infringement upon the rights of the people. Such an assertion was as unjust as ridiculous. The mass of the people have not time to select their servants, especially their judges, as those to whom they delegate their powers are just as much the representatives of the people as are individual ballots the representatives of the people. The governor of the State of Louisiana, by virtue of his election and office, represents the voice of the entire people of the State; and if the people should agree to leave the judicial appointments to him, they placed a great responsibility on him to ascertain who were qualified to fill the positions, and relieved themselves of it; and it was sheer nonsense for demagogues to call this an invasion of the people's rights.

It is but a few days since I heard a man in the St. Charles hotel denouncing in no measured terms one of the United States judges appointed, occupying the bench in this city. After exhausting his stock of vile epithets, he concluded with : "If that judge were to come before the people for election, I would spend fifty thousand dollars but what I would defeat him." This is but an instance of the influence brought to bear in judicial elections, and of the influences which generally control them.

The death of Robert Emmett, which has been alluded to in such glowing terms by my friend (Mr. Terry) yesterday, was not owing to the fact that the judge who tried him was appointed by the English crown; his death, if unjust, was the direst result of the English spy system, which still existed in England to a considerable extent ; a system by which the English government was enabled to bring any number of its employés to swear falsely in its interest ; and any judge with the same testimony before him, whether elected by the people or appointed by the crown, if he acted in accordance with his oath, to decide according to law and the testimony given, would have been obliged to give the same decision, and condemn Emmett to death.

In the great excitement which reigned throughoat the country at the time of the trial of Aaron Burr for treason, we can now form but a slight idea. The nation was convulsed, and the most intense political rancor prevailed. Patriotism and freedom went hand in hand to blind the popular mind and keep the mass of the people free from a judicious and correct opinion. How refreshing it was amid the storm to witness the dignified and dispassionate conduct of Chief Justice Marshall. He sat unmoved amid the storm, listened in a dispassionate manner to the witnesses and to the argument of counsel, and when the case was closed he took home the record and deliberated upon his conduct. Public opinion and its representative, the press, had already condemned Burr. Men of all classes, civil and religious, looked upon him with horror and clamored for his condemnation. Fortunately, Marshall was not dependent on an election for his position. He could act coolly and independently amid all this excitement. At the proper time he released Burr, and for the moment literally received the denunciations of what appeared the indignation and sneers of a great people. But time has vindicated the Chief Justice ; and Burr's crime, of what was at the time termed treason, now looks little else than a fillibustering spirit developed in advance of a sympathetic public opinion.

The Dred Scott decision I was always opposed to ; every feeling of my heart is abhorrent to such a decision. I believe it is one of the most blackening and damning records that has ever blotted the page of American jurisprudence. Yet I cannot but admire the independence of Chief Justice Taney. When the popular excitement ran so high, when the abolitionists on the one side and the Southerners on the other were boiling over with excitement, Roger B. Taney sat fearlessly and immovable as a rock upon the bench. He knew that he had not to go back to the people for a re-election, and gave his decision regardless of the popular clamor. It is impossible not to admire the man and action ; and though we believe the decision to be against the teachings of humanity and against the laws of God, still it was in accordance with the law as it existed, and bad as the law was Judge Taney could do no less than sustain the law. Then a better public sentiment and a great rebellion changed the law, and made Judge Taney's decision a relict of barbarism, having no quality to admire about it, except as it illustrated the noble character and independence of an appointed judiciary.

The gentleman who preceded me (Mr. Cutler) made a strong and patriotic appeal to the people of Louisiana, and I will ask the question, "Are you prepared to place a man on the judicial bench to try me for my vote on the question of emancipation ?" I believe that such would be the effect of allowing the election of judges to be made by a popular vote. If the military should be removed or the obligation of the iron-clad removed from voters, thousands who did not vote at the election will vote if the franchise should be extended to them, and they will defeat every loyal man.

We are not framing a constitution in ordinary times—half the State is in rebellion, and a large number of those who are within the lines are far from being cured of their rebellious sympathies. It is only a few days since I saw five hundred of these fanatics, who had been for nearly three years enjoying the protection of our government, well dressed gentlemen, most of them, and numbers of them have made large sums of money under the protecting influence of the national armies during the last two years; yet when the news (bogus) had been received that Grant had been defeated, and the national cause was in danger, these five hundred fanatics rushed into the Picayune office, evidently frantic with joy at the receipt of such intelligence. If you see this in these fanatics, who for two years had hoarded and accumulated wealth under the protecting folds of that flag, (pointing to the banner over the speaker's desk) who for two years have heard the tramp of the soldiers—nature's noblemen of the North and West—in this city, and whose homes have not been disturbed nor their property destroyed—who had seen a Butler, like an Eastern despot, dispensing justice everywhere—who had seen Gen. Banks, no less true to the country and to humanity, endeavoring by kindness and a mild rule to win this people back—what may be expected in the country parishes and in those not yet reclaimed? Are we ready to risk an elective judiciary now?

The commissary department has kept for nearly three years two-thirds of the people from starvation. When Lovell and his craven set went off on the Jackson railroad, they left here a vast heritage of abandoned wives and daughters—they have been protected and cared for. Their homes have not been invaded by national troops; though many of them were left destitute, they have not been allowed to suffer. Numbers of children were left here whose cheeks were blanched by starvation. Now they wear the rugged bloom of health and show that they command plenty. And yet all this mercy has not softened the hearts of any one of these men who were gloating over the false news that Gen. Grant had been defeated, and that the Union cause had been again stricken in the dust.

At the late election of the governor there were about ten thousand votes cast, and the consciences of these voters were held in check by the iron-clad oath. Remove that check and where would we be now? We do not represent a majority of the people of the State, but we represent the entire loyalty of the State. There are many who have taken the iron-clad who are restless in harness; I don't know but there are one or two in this body. They don't like it, and will kick out of the traces and throw off the harness entirely if ever they have an opportunity. I would not object to an election of the judiciary if assured that no man would be allowed to vote but those who voted at the election of members for this Convention; but he was satisfied, that if the military power was removed from the State, and the elective system was applied to the judiciary, no loyal man, for many years to come, could be elected to a judgeship. While he respected the views of those who favored that system, because he believed they were sincere, he would warn them to be careful how they suffered the scepter to depart from Judah, and how they allowed disloyalty to again assert supremacy at the polls.

[At the close of Mr. Abell's speech, Mr Henderson obtained the floor, but a motion to adjourn prevailed, and the Convention adjourned.]

FRIDAY, May 27, 1864.

[The president called the Convention to order at 12 o'clock M.

The roll was called, and the following members answered to their names:]

Messrs. Abell, Ariail, Austin, Balch, Bailey, Barrett, Baum, Beauvais, Bell, Bennie, Bofill, Bromley, Brott, Buckley, Burke, Cazabat, Collin, Cook J. K., Cook T., Crozat, Davies, Decker, Duane, Dufresne, Dupaty, Duke, Edwards, Ennis, Fish, Flagg, Flood, Foley, Fuller, Gastinel, Gaidry, Geier, Goldman, Gruneberg, Hart, Healy, Heard, Henderson, Howell, Howes, Knobloch, Maurer, Maas, Mann, Mayer, Mendiverri, Montamat, Morris, Murphy M. W., Newell, Normand, O'Conner, Orr, Payne J., Pintado, Poynot, Purcell J., Pursell S., Schroeder, Schnurr, Seymour, Shaw, Smith, Spellicy, Stocker, Stumpf, Stiner, Sullivan, Terry, Thorpe,

Waters, Wells, Wilson, and Mr. President —78.

[The journal of yesterday was read and approved.

The following resolutions were presented and laid over under the rules :]

By Mr. Bell :

Resolved, That the following be adopted as a standing rule of this Convention :

When a question has been once decided by the Convention, it shall not again be brought up for consideration, except by a motion to reconsider, which motion must be made on the same or succeeding day, or by a vote of two-thirds of the members present.

By Mr. Waters :

Be it Resolved, That from and after this date, the police force of the city of New Orleans shall receive from the city treasury the annual pay of one thousand dollars, payable monthly, and shall furnish bond in the sum of one thousand dollars for the faithful performance of their duties while acting in the capactity of policemen.

Mr. HOWES—I move a suspension of the rules to act on it at once.

Mr. WELLS—I move to lay it on the table.

Mr. FOLEY—I move a suspension of the rules to act on it at once.

Mr. SMITH—I move to lay it on the table.

Mr. BELL—I second Mr. Foley's motion.

[The motion to lay the motion to suspend the rules on the table was carried.]

Mr. MONTAMAT—The committee appointed to wait on Gen. Banks and invite him to visit this Convention, with his staff, beg leave to report that they waited on the general, and he promised to meet the committee in the parlor of the mayor at 1 o'clock to-day.

Mr. THORPE—I call up my resolution of yesterday, to present the pen with which the ordinance of emancipation was signed to Gen. Banks.

[The resolution was adopted.]

Mr. HENDERSON—I did not conclude my remarks yesterday, but will give way now and conclude at some future stage of the debate.

Mr. ABELL—The judiciary department is one of the highest importance, exceeded only by the emancipation order. Its temples should in purity stand only second to the sanctuaries of God.

A pure, enlightened and firm judiciary is the pride and anchor of state and the bulwark of liberty. It strikes down injustice and oppression, gives stability and honor to the State, and confidence and protection to the people.

As legislators, then, it becomes our duty to devise the best means of securing the best talent and purest men of the State to be judges.

My veneration for a pure judiciary might lead me to adopt any mode that could be pointed out that would best promote and secure its establishment upon the most independent and permanent basis.

Feeling a veneration for precedents, and relying upon the lights of the past, I shall beg the indulgence of the Convention while I briefly review the history of the English Bench for the last six centuries, and the American for the past hundred years.

Were we to penetrate further into the past, we might find much instruction and lights to guide us in our duty from the august courts of ancient nations, which during the days of their purity stood as eternal monuments of justice, and honor to their State ; but unfortunately the most of them yielded to the influence of the Crown, or became corrupted by luxury and avarice ; but, while confined to their legitimate sphere, have always proved the bulwark of liberty to the people, and the glory of the State.

The duty of this Convention, in my humble judgment, is to provide the strongest safe-guards againts undue influence upon the judges, by securing them on the one hand by ample salaries from pecuniary apprehensions, and on the other from being captiously removed from office.

This independence and leisure would enable the judges to devote their entire minds and energies to their duties.

The theory of all monarchial governments is that all power is derived from the crown, and republics from the people, and that the judges are the ministers of the government or people, and the only security for the entire independence of the court is to keep the judges as far removed from the influence of the appointing power as possible.

This, Mr. President, can be done only by appointing the judiciary by the governor, or by joint ballot of the House of Representatives, and not by election. A judge having received his appointment by the governor, and confirmation by the Senate or by joint ballot, is at once and forever as free from the influence of the appointing power, as from that of the humblest individual in the State; left to his own will, uninfluenced, and impelled by the highest considerations of honor, none but the naturally corrupt would swerve from his duty.

Mr. HILLS—I rise to move that, in view of the great importance of this question and the interest it has assumed, the time of debate be unlimited, and so the number of times of speaking. For that purpose I move to suspend the rules.

[Motion to suspend carried.]

Mr. HARNAN—Twice is enough for any man to speak on the same subject.

Mr. HILLS—I withdraw the latter portion.

[Motion adopted.]

Mr. ABELL—The tenure of "life and good behavior" is the only one that will insure the best talents and greatest experience. No eminent lawyer would yield up a lucrative practice for an uncertain office, from which he might be removed at the end of a short term, or be compelled to become a whining politician in order to retain his position.

Examples are not wanting in this city to show that our most eminent judges have been thus treated. The 1st, 2d, 3d and 5th courts have had judges thrown out, without fault, thereby losing the advantage of experience to the State, introducing irregularities and hindrance to public business. Nor should the exposition of an upright judge to the shame of being thus treated without cause be without weight.

But, Mr. President, any mode of appointment for a term short of good behavior would open the door to intrigues in order to retain office; which, I contend, is highly inconsistent with the required purity and elevation of the bench and interest of the public.

We are a captious people, and old Ulysses said: "The worst of tyrants is a usurping crowd."

Mr. President, I am not captious as to the mode of appointment, but I stand firm for a life tenure, and for the independence of the judge of the appointing power; leaving him nothing to fear but his own mal or misfeasance. If elected by the people, for short terms or even long terms, the influence of party organizations and personal claims will be pressed to an extent to be resisted only by superhuman virtue and manly firmness; and the only reward for these virtues would be defeat at the end of his term. This, sir, is the language of experience.

DOORKEEPER—Maj. Gen. Banks and staff!

The distinguished guests advanced to the rostrum and were seated on either hand of the president. After the applause had somewhat subsided, President Durell welcomed the general in the following words:

General—This Convention, the representatives of the loyal people of Louisiana, and the result of your wisdom and of your statesmanship, embraces you with its whole heart. Its love for you, its confidence in you, grows with each growing day; and as each day wanes, its love, its confidence, and its hopes, increase for the morrow.

General, this Convention has performed the largest portion of its labors, and has completed the work for the performance of which it was mainly called into existence. It has adopted an ordinance giving liberty to more than three hundred thousand of the inhabitants of the State of Louisiana, [applause,] and men and women and children, who but yesterday were held as cattle in the market, to-day stand up as free as any man in this assembly. [Great applause.] In completing this work, general, upon you has devolved the solution of the problem growing out of the substitution of free for forced labor, and you are solving the problem with a wisdom which has compelled the admiration of the broadest and deepest thinkers in Europe.

General, as the organ of this Convention, I again extend to you the welcome which is due to a citizen, who, both as a citizen and as a soldier, deserves well of his country.

Gen. Banks addressed the Convention as follows:

Mr. President—No convocation of such intelligence and character as that in the presence of which I now stand could do otherwise than impress me with feelings of respect and awe, devoted as you are—as I know and as I have been told by your president—to the development of measures for the restoration and preservation of our government. There is scarcely a higher duty with which gentlemen can be charged than that of providing for the legislation of the future. The legislation of the day is enough to tax the energies and wisdom of almost any class of men; but to him, or to them, to whom it is committed by the organization of constitutional government, to shape the destinies of half a century, is charged with a duty of which he or they may be proud, and, if well and wisely performed, will win honors which can rarely fall to any other class of men. They give, as Bacon said of the law-givers of England, "to God that which to him pertaineth, to Cæsar that which is Cæsar's, to the subject that which belongs to the subject." [Applause.]

Sir, I always feel a deep interest in assemblies of this character. The most anxious, the most interesting, and let me say the most satisfactory part of my life was passed as a member of an assembly of this kind. When I look over the broad fields of legislation of this country, and see what has been accomplished by these constitutional assemblies, what States have been created, what cities and towns have grown up as it were in a night, what power, prosperity and peace have been sown broadcast over this continent, I feel it is indeed one of the greatest privileges that could be conferred upon men to participate in such labors. But in a time of revolution it is perhaps of higher import than in any other, while in every other part of this country men are ranked against men in arms, seeking amid the doubtful strife of war for supremacy, you sit in peaceful assembly to reconstruct the government which has been rent asunder by revolution and treason. If you accomplish this work, the people of this country must hold you forever in grateful remembrance.

I know, sir, I have no right to trespass on your attention, or interrupt your deliberations. I may say, however, that the progress of this Convention has given me the greatest satisfaction. I know that the problems submitted to your decision are not to be solved in a moment. I know perfectly well that not only deliberation but patience and the lapse of time are necessary to the completion of your work; and if it be done well, I say to you with the utmost satisfaction, that I shall accord to you the highest honor. The act of emancipation contains words as fitting and proper to that great subject as can be found in the whole circle of English literature. [Great applause.]

The closing article of that act, which declares that "The Legislature shall hereafter pass no laws recognizing property in man," exemplifies the wisdom of man, and carries into effect the law of God. He gave to man supremacy over the beast and the bird and the brute creation, but the title of lord over man He retained to Himself alone, and never created in His image, of whom it may be said, or to whom it should be said, that he was lord over the creatures of God. That, sir, is enough, but you will do more. In taking this position, the Convention is compelled to follow, and the legislators that will succeed will also be compelled to follow, in completion of the work so honorably begun.

Sometimes when I am riding along the Mississippi, the majestic stream that passes you, and which in the end will be found to have bound this continent together against all the machinations of men to destroy the union of States, I feel as if prosperity and power were limited to the country through which it passes. When its rolling flood leaps from its bed, and breaks in upon the prosperous and beautiful plantations that line its banks, you seek to restrain the torrent and re-establish your control over its waters. But you cannot again re-establish the levee where it stood. You must build it upon new ground, bring to it new supports, and make it cover new elements of power. So it is with the great currents of time. Revolutions swell their turbid waters; they deluge and desolate the country; and when you come to repair the damage that has been done, you find you cannot re-establish the ancient boundaries again. It is immaterial what may be the opinions of men; you must take new ground; gather new elements of power, and bring to your support elements of strength that may have been disregarded as unnecessary.

This, sir, is a lesson which it is but just for us to consider. In the restoration of the constitutional forms of your government, you are compelled to go beyond the lines which were occupied by you before. You must take in new elements of strength, and give to the institutions that you are to establish a broader basis than your State has known before. Of this you have given evidence yourselves. The act of emancipation is a great and parent act of wisdom. The education of the people, and the extension of franchise hereafter, will be objects that will attract the attention of the country, and you will have the proud satisfaction of knowing that while you have done what is necessary for you to do in this generation, those that succeed to your work and follow your example will alse be compelled to carry out your ideas in the future.

We have witnessed the vindication of the freedom of the Mississippi; we have participated in the creation of a free State, and we now must proclaim the measures necessary to maintain the prosperity and happiness of a free people. That is glory enough for any State, and honor enough for any representative of the people. [Great enthusiasm.]

Mr. Stocker—I desire to call the attention of the chair to the resolution which was unanimously adopted this morning:

Resolved, That the pen used by the President of this Convention, in signing the ordinance of emancipation, be presented, along with the evidence of its genuineness, to Major Gen. N. P. Banks, commanding this Department.

I think this is a very proper occasion for this to take place, and move to do so.

Mr. President—I would state to the Convention that it is impossible for that resolution to be carried into effect at this time, but it will be at the earliest possible moment.

Mr. Abell—I am perhaps one of the most awkward men in the world, but it seems to me it would be appropriate if we should give a vote of thanks to Major Gen. Banks, the warrior and the statesman, and his staff, for the consideration they have paid us by visiting us upon this day, and in doing this, if not entirely inappropriate, that Mrs. Banks should be included.

[Motion carried.]

Mr. Stocker—I move for a recess of twenty minutes.

[Motion carried.]

Mr. Abell—Mr. President, the idea of a judge seeking public favor to retain office, is, to my mind, one of the greatest prostitutions of judicial purity and dignity that could be imagined; and yet, sir, on the elective principle, he must do so, or he will perhaps have to give his position, at the end of his term, to some aspiring demagogue, by which government is injured and disgraced and public justice laid prostrate. I repeat, that the elective judiciary is dangerous to the public weal, and must, in the end, bring the wonted dignity and purity of the bench into contempt.

The appointing power in England has been vested in the crown time out of mind, but was seldom exercised without great consideration and consultation, in order to select *only* the most experienced and pure of the members of the bar to be judges.

It is not unlikely that the king himself sat in judgment as late as the time of Edward I, A. D. 1272; but for nearly 600 years the judges have been appointed by the crown, and from the time of Edward I to 3d William and Mary, about 400 years, the judges held their appointment at the pleasure of the king and removable at his option, which was not unfrequently exercised by displacing the most upright judges and substituting some craven wretch who was ready to obey his master and to do any unprincipled work that might be assigned him. Such were Tresylian, Saunders, Jeffries, Wright, and others, and such judges would as readily subserve the purposes of a mob, that would keep them in power, as they would their master, the king.

But, Mr. President, these examples only show the danger of these uncertain tenures, and it would be invidious and unjust not to mention the exceptions, for during this period we find many reverend judges and sages of the law—a Hale, a Coke, and others, who have left imperishable monuments of learning and judicial purity; but they, Mr. President, were sometimes removed to give place to the most corrupt and vicious.

But, happy for the advancement of civilization and judicial certainty, in the third year of William and Mary (1691) the appointment was no longer at the option of the king, but expired at his death, which was considered at that time a great point. But the crowning act of judicial certainty was reserved for George III, A. D. 1760, who, in the very first year of his reign, extended the tenure of the office to the life of the judge or during good behavior, since which time the English bench has been ornamented by the most learned and eminent judges, whose decisions challenge the admiration of the world for their learning, impartiality and uniformity.

The United States of America admitted the safety of the rule of a life tenure, and adopted it in its organic law in the following language: "The judges both of supreme and inferior courts shall hold office during good behavior, and shall, at stated times, receive for their services a compensation which shall not be diminished during their continuance in office." (See constitution, art. 3, sec. 1, clause 2.)

The supreme and auxiliary courts of the United States, organized upon the principle of a life tenure, has presented a series of decisions for wisdom, learning and uniformity unsurpassed by the English or any other courts upon the globe. Being independent of the government, the court has stood prominent for its impartiality and wisdom.

Many of the United States adopted the same tenure, and in every instance has proved the wisdom and policy of the appointive judiciary.

Mr. President and gentlemen of the Convention, I ask, will you be governed by reason and those high examples, or will you leave this branch of government, which requires so much certainty, to the fluctuations of elections? Reason and experience answer, No! no!

The salaries of judges is a question that should not be left out of mind. When a judge has received his appointment and entered upon the duties of office, he should not be trammeled by pecuniary considerations, but should feel that he has a freehold estate in office, such as would meet all present and future wants; in order to enable him to devote all his energies, skill and talent to the service of the State and promotion of justice.

The great end and object, I repeat, is to secure the best talent, skill and learning; this can be done only by making the tenure "for life," and with ample salary.

What amounts to a sufficient salary is a question on which men would be likely to differ, but we might draw a just conclusion in a medium between the princely salaries of the English judges, and the shamefully low salaries of the judges of the courts of the United States:

The chief justice U. S. gets......	$6.500
The associate justices U. S., each,	6.000

As a contrast:

The lord chancellor of England gets.......	£10.000
The vice chancellors, each,.......	5.000
The chief justice queen's bench,	8.000
Four associate justices, each,....	5.000
The chief justice common pleas,	7.000
Four associate justices do., each,	5.000
The chief justice exchequer,....	7.000
Four associate justices do., each,	5.000

This contrast is great, but not uninstructive. Guarding against each extreme, I favor a salary of $12,000 for our chief justice, $10,000 each for the associate justices, and $8,000 each for the district judges.

In fixing the salaries above mentioned, I assume that the judges are to be appointed for a life tenure, or during good behavior; for if the judiciary remains elective, subject to party intrigue or popular whims and clamor, then I am opposed to any salary whatever, but for paying the judges the ordinary wages of day laborers—$2 50 a day for district and $3 for the supreme judges, and docking them every day they are not in actual service.

Sir, instead of studying the nicer balances of justice, and applying the great principles of the law, they are compelled to calculate the chances of re-election. They look to this and that combination of political tricksters, and are certain to want to know what are the chances for the Dutch and Irish vote. No sooner has this dream vanished, than the chances of nomination press upon their feverish brain. Such, Mr. President, has been the experience of this city for the past twelve years, and such I predict will be the case as long as an elective judiciary is tolerated.

Sir, I pronounce an elective judiciary a failure, and a reproach and disgrace to the age.

Mr. HENDERSON—Mr. President, I believe that no question has been presented to this body that has elicited so much favorable debate, and without passion, and with discrimination, as that whether the judiciary shall be appointive or elective, and, Mr. President, there is no question of more vital political importance to the citizen that can come up for discussion before this body, than the one now under consideration. It affects all classes, from the highest to the lowest, and from the lowest to the highest. It is the department which to a greater extent than any other exercises a controlling influence over the lives, the liberties and the property of mankind.

We find that in every age in which man has lived money has been the measure of labor, and talent the measure by which men through their industry have acquired various positions. And the pay should be proportioned to the services to be performed, and to the availability of the man. A judge can have no one to represent him. All the labor required of him he must perform himself. He cannot employ a clerk to do it for him. It can only be done by one fit to hold that position. We live in an age of progress; and while I am a native-born American citizen, and claim that we stand one of the best and proudest nations of earth, I am proud to look to old England for an example of the best judiciary system on earth. Her House of Lords and Court of King's Bench are proud monuments to show what a judiciary ought to be. Though our institutions differ politically, theirs being monarchical and ours republican, when it comes to the judiciary, they are similar and should be alike. There is no fear that an appointed judge will be a political judge. Politicians, when placed on the bench for long terms, cease to be politicians and become jurists. Such was the case with Taney, who S. S. Prentice declared was the political demagogue that removed the deposits, yet after he came upon the bench said of him that "he is a god in human flesh." John Marshall was a Federalist, of the old school of politics, and was in favor of the appointment by the Senate of all ministerial and judiciary officers—and George Washington subscribed the doctrine—yet after he went upon the bench he became one of the most celebrated men as a jurist of modern times.

No nation ever set out to make a republican government except the United States. Mankind had no faith in the mass of the people. They had no faith in themselves. The Jews once had a republican government, if the Scriptural accounts are true; but they were not satisfied with it, and called on God to give them a king, and hence the doctrine that the king could do no wrong. That doctrine is, however, exploded in this country, and I say to-day that I feel fully satisfied that two of the three branches of the government, the executive and the legislative, are elected directly by the people, and believe that the ends of justice would be promoted by making the third, the judicial, purely appointive.

In an elective judiciary it makes little difference in the result whether we have a man of great mind and a high order of talent or not, if he runs against the political party which happens to be in power, no matter what the character of his competitor, he will be defeated. It is so everywhere. Political parties will, if they elect a judiciary, have their political candidates for the bench, and the party in power will elect a party man. This is a matter that party politics should not enter into. There are no party questions, no great political principles involved in the issues, and party politics ought to be rigidly excluded from the judiciary. There is no danger that the governor will appoint a mere politician, because the Senate will act as a check upon him. If he nominates a man in whom they have no confidence. they can refuse to confirm him, as was done by the Senate of the United States when John Tyler was president.

Tyler was elected vice president as a whig, but when he, by the death of Harrison, came to be president, he proved to be anything but a whig, or a democrat either, and neither party had any confidence in him. He sent the name of Judge Spencer, then secretary of war, a man of great learning and ability, to be confirmed as associate judge of the Supreme Court, but between the whigs and the democrats in the Senate they rejected him, and Tyler was obliged to substitute another.

When the Senate, in the State of New York, was the Court of Errors, it was composed of the highest talent of the country, and administered justice a great deal better than the Supreme Court of that State, which is elective, does now.

One gentleman has attempted to stand here and place ignorance before intelligence on this question. Which do you prefer to have on the bench, ignorance or intelligence? Why, sir, the constitution of 1845 contained a provision that none but a lawyer should be appointed to a judicial position, and yet gentlemen stand up here and in terms of sneering sarcasm tell us that the members of that high and honorable profession, a profession that stands higher than any other except that of the military chief [turning towards Gen. Banks] who commands the department.

We are told, sometimes, that the civil power is first. In the governments of South America, whether monorchical or republican, where the Roman Catholics predominate, you will find that they are governed by the Queen of Spain in fact, if not nominally, because they believe in the supremacy of the spiritual over the temporal government—the subordination of the State to the papal power.

In the United States you will find it different. You will find all the Catholics are republicans. This is our theory of government—ours is a progressive government, while those are not. Roger B. Taney belongs to the Roman Catholic Church, and when he was once called upon to give an opinion as to whether a man could be made responsible for an act on account of his religious belief, replied that the constitution of the United States prohibited the establishment of any religion. Jefferson himself was once desired to make the Baptist religion the law of the land. He replied: "I, myself, will use my political influence to have an amendment made to the constitution, declaring that Congress never shall make a law establishing a religion or preventing the free exercise thereof."

Writers on international law tell us that religions are part of the local laws. If you go to China, you must observe their laws respecting the worship of the sun. If you go to Egypt, you must observe their religious regulations respecting the animals they worship.

How does man know that God inspired Moses, and chose the Jews from among the surrounding nations for his own people, and decreed that the others should be hewers of wood and drawers of water for them? And yet you must believe it, if the Bible is true.

Before the flood, white men were made slaves, and the slavery of the negro was never heard of till modern times.

When our constitution was formed it existed, and a great effort was made to crush it; such men as Jefferson, and Washington, and Livingston, and St. Thomas Jenifer, and Butler, of South Carolina, wanted to destroy it. The deputies from eleven States wanted to destroy it, but Ben Franklin, the founder of the first abolition society in America, in order to preserve harmony and please the other two, was willing, for the sake of peace and harmony, to admit that the Declaration of Independence was not right, and that men were not born with certain inalienable rights; and from that period is dated the denial of the right of the national government to make laws regulating slavery.

The appointment of judges at this time, and the necessity of having good men under a tenure that cannot be endangered by the caprice of the popular mind, is particularly important. Suppose, for instance, the question respecting the constitutionality of the emancipation of slaves, or the making of greenbacks a legal tender, should arise? Such a question has lately been tried in New York, and I say the judge who has decided in favor of the constitutionality of greenbacks is worthy of all honor for sustaining the national treasury. But we all know that, aside from military necessity, the president has no right, Congress has no right, Gen. Banks, the military commader of the department and exponent of Abe Lincoln, has no right to emancipate a single slave in any State. I appeal to you, Gen. Banks, to say if you did not, when you held a distinguished position in the House of representatives, as a republican, deny the right of Congress to interfere with slavery in the States. He says yes. The republican party denied the right of Congress to legislate for the States on that subject, with the approbation of the president; and it is only through the war power the right is derived. The constitution declares that Congress has the right to declare war. But says some Southern gentlemen, Congress did not declare war--it was Abe Lincoln. Who declared war in 1846? It was Polk. He told Taylor where to go with his troops. The territory was in dispute, both parties claiming it; and Taylor said the war was just and holy. He was defending a position that he had been ordered to occupy, and to which we had just as good a right, to say the least, as any body. But when the question of making him president arose, he became the candidate of the whigs, who condemned the war as unjust and unholy, in much stronger terms than he had justified it before.

The question in this case arises, whether we should give up our position among the nations of the earth, whether we should lose our power in the political world forever? Says Abe Lincoln: "I am in favor of the government"——

Mr. Austin—Mr. President, I call the gentleman to order. He is not speaking to the question.

President—The gentleman is in order, and will proceed with his argument.

Mr. Henderson—I never yet have asked a gentleman because he differed with me to take his seat. We are representing a minority of the people to make a constitution for the State of Louisiana. We have as good a right to our position as one of the States of the Union as Virginia has. She has but a small part of her territory free from rebel rule, and yet she has her two senators in Congress. And where would she be to-day if her people had the power to elect either branch of her government? Where would Missouri and Tennessee be, if the voice of their people was to be followed? If a majority vote was to control these States, they would be back in the rebellion to-day. And what is the recent action of the House, which declared that a State shall give a majority vote before it shall be permitted to come back?

Mr. President, we have a great many things at stake here on this question, but I now defer to speak longer without the approbation of this meeting, and therefore yield the floor, and ask that the question of adjournment be put to this House.

[The motion to adjourn was put and carried.]

Saturday, May 28, 1864.

[The president called the Convention to order at 12 o'clock, and the roll being called, the following members answered to their names:]

Messrs. Abell, Ariail, Balch, Bailey, Barrett, Bell, Bofill, Bromley, Buckley, Burke, Campbell, Cazabat, Cook J. K., Crozat, Decker, Duane, Dufresne, Duke, Dupaty, Edwards, Ennis, Flood, Foley, Geier, Goldman, Gorlinski, Harnan, Hart, Healy, Henderson, Heard, Howes, Kavanagh, Maurer, Maas, Mann, Mayer, Montamat, Morris, Murphy M. W., Newell, Normand, O'Conner, Orr, Pintado, Poynot, Pursell S., Schroeder, Schnurr, Shaw, Smith, Spellicy, Stauffer, Stiner, Stumpf, Sullivan, Terry, Waters, Wells, Wilson and Mr. President—61.

[There being no quorum, the sergeant-at arms was directed to bring in absent members.

After some delay the following members appeared and took their seats:]

Messrs. Baum, Collin, Fish, Mendiverri, Fosdick, Kugler, Cook T., Seymour, Fuller, Austin, Davies, Howell, Hire, Beauvais, Stocker, Thorpe—16.

[A quorum being announced, the journal of yesterday was read and approved.

Mr. Cazabat presented a resolution to the effect that this Convention will adjourn *sine die* on the 6th day of June.]

Mr. MONTAMAT—I move to suspend the rules for its adoption.

[The motion was lost, and the resolution laid over.

Reports of standing committees being in order,

Mr. Pursell, on behalf of the Committee on Contingent Expenses, reported favorably on the bill of the city of New Orleans for fitting up Liberty Hall for the use of the Convention, and accompanied the report with a resolution providing for the payment of said bill.

The same member, on behalf of the same committee, reported unfavorably on the resolution of Mr. Terry, to appropriate one hundred dollars for enrolling on parchment and framing, etc., of the ordinance of emancipation.]

Mr. MONTAMAT—I move the report be adopted.

[Carried.

Unfinished business was taken up, and Mr. Bell's resolution of yesterday read :]

Resolved, That the following be adopted as a standing rule of this Convention :

When a question has been once decided by the Convention, it shall not again be brought up for consideration, except by a motion to reconsider, which motion must be made on the same or succeeding day, or by a vote of two-thirds of the members present.

Mr. BOFILL—I move to lay it on the table.

[Carried.

Mr. Waters's resolution was read :]

Be it Resolved, That from and after this date, the police force of the city of New Orleans shall receive from the city treasury the annual pay of one thousand dollars, payable monthly, and shall furnish bond in the sum of one thousand dollars for the faithful performance of their duties while acting in the capacity of policemen.

[A motion was made to lay it on the table, and on it appearing to be carried, the yeas and nays were called for, with the following result :]

YEAS—Messrs. Ariail, Balch, Bailey, Beauvais, Collin, Cazabat, Crozat, Davies, Duke, Dufresne, Dupaty, Edwards, Ennis, Fosdick, Heard, Hills, Hire, Howell, Howes, Kugler, Mann, Mayer, Morris, Orr, Pintado, Pursell S., Shaw, Stauffer, Thorpe, Wells—30.

NAYS—Messrs. Abell, Barrett, Bell, Bofill, Buckley, Burke, Campbell, Cook T., Cook J. K., Duane, Fish, Flood, Foley, Fuller, Geier, Goldman, Gorlinski, Harnan, Hart, Healy, Henderson, Howes, Maas, Maurer, Mendiverri, Montamat, Murphy M. W., Normand, O'Conner, Poynot, Purcell J., Schroeder, Schnurr, Seymour, Smith, Spellicy, Stocker, Stumpf, Stiner, Sullivan, Terry, Waters, Wenck, Wilson—44.

[Mr. Sullivan offered a substitute for Mr. Waters's resolution. The substitute was accepted.

Mr. Cazabat moved to table the substitute, upon which motion the yeas and nays were demanded, and being taken resulted as follows :]

YEAS—Messrs. Ariail, Austin, Balch, Bailey, Beauvais, Bromley, Burke, Campbell, Collin, Cazabat, Cutler, Davies, Dufresne, Duke, Dupaty, Edwards, Ennis, Fosdick, Gorlinski, Heard, Hills, Hire, Howell, Kugler, Mann, Mayer, Morris, Orr, Payne J., Paine J. T., Pintado, Pursell S., Shaw, Stumpf, Thorpe, Wells, Wilson—37.

NAYS—Messrs. Abell, Barrett, Bell, Bofill, Buckley, Cook J. K., Cook T., Duane, Fish, Flood, Foley, Fuller, Geir, Goldman, Harnan, Hart, Healy, Henderson, Howes, Maas, Maurer, Mendiverri, Montamat, Murphy M. W., Normand, O'Conner, Poynot, Purcell J., Schroeder, Schnurr, Seymour, Smith, Spellicy, Stocker, Stiner, Stauffer, Sullivan, Terry, Waters, Wenck—40.

Mr. DAVIES—I move the whole subject be referred to the next Legislature.

Mr. ABELL—I desire to call the attention of the Convention to a clause in a hand-bill which I presented to my constituents, and I believe it was read pretty generally in the parish of Orleans. It is this:

I will advocate strenuously a permanent police organization for this metropolis, to consist of permanent citizens of good character, to hold office during good behavior, with salaries never to be less than eighty dollars per month, and removable only by charges preferred before a committee to be appointed by the executive for the purpose, subject to an appeal to the Board of Aldermen; when discharged, never again to be eligible; and with suitable provisions for those who may be disabled in the faithful discharge of their duties. The safety and credit of this city, and justice to a faithful officer, demand greater certainty than now exist.

So far as the power of this Convention is concerned to pass upon this matter, we have as much power to engraft it on the constitution as any branch of the judiciary. We have a right to have something permanent here. For the last fifteen years the police has been a mere hook for politicians to draw themselves into office, and many a young man, to whom was held out hopes of office, has been almost ruined in consequence. While we are making a permanent, solid judiciary, let us not forget the solidity of the city of New Orleans, and take this dangerous power out of the hands of politicians.

I desire to move that this amendment be made the order of the day for Monday week, and be printed.

Mr. Cazabat—I cannot perceive the object of this amendment, and this matter is incompatible with the duties we are called upon to perform. We are here, not to make regulations for the police of New Orleans, but to revise the constitution of the State. I move that the whole subject be laid on the table.

[The chair decided, that as a motion had been made and lost to lay the resolution on the table, the present motion only embraced the amendment and the motion to make it the order of the day.

The yeas and nays were called for and the motion lost—yeas 37, nays 40.

The motion of Mr. Abell was then carried.

Mr. Bofill moved a call of the House, when the roll was called, and 77 members answered to their names.

A motion to adjourn, by Mr. Bofill, was lost.]

Mr. Henderson—I can understand how it is that I see many men here of learning and experience sent here to make a constitution. Why didn't the people make a constitution themselves instead of sending us here to make it? Why did not they get together in a body and enact a constitution themselves, without calling for the intervention of this body? The parties might have made a party test and have made the constitution themselves, that would have been democratic. The old parties were whig and republican. There was no such thing as a democratic party until Jefferson's election; when the name was given in derison by the federalists. Mr. Jefferson accepted the name, and always afterwards required his party to be called the democratic party. The people did not, simply because it was not policy; because it was a better policy for us to come here and call the ayes and noes than for them to come and vote *viva voce.* And why is it that men here when they are called on to vote *viva voce* vote one way, and when the ayes and noes are called vote the other? It is because they know they are responsible to their constituents, and are afraid for the record to go before them.

So far as politics is concerned, I don't care which way the question goes. I am for the people as much as anybody, and if we do anything, want to do what they will like; for if they don't like our acts they will not sustain our work, but will reject the constitution which we may make, and leave the constitution of 1852 in full operation. But when I come to offer an amendment I am responsible to the people when I again go before them for my action. They have elected me because they thought I had some discrimination. We are responsible to our constituents, and they will hold us responsible.

Mr. Stauffer—Mr. President, I am sorry to say that I perceive that the members in favor of an appointive judiciary are attempting to crush out the members in favor of an elective judiciary, and in all candor I must say that those members have shown very little courtesy to the members in favor of the elective system.

Much has been said upon the question of an appointive or elective judiciary, though I fear as yet, with all the talent that has combined against the elective judiciary, they have so far been unable to convince any member of the justice of the principles involved in this subject.

We are here to frame an oganic law for the State; that law must be based on the principles of the general government. We must be guided by the principles that guided our fathers when they framed the constitution of the United States: and I ask you, has any man a right to reject those principles, founded as they are in the justice and wisdom of a past generation? One great principle lies at the foundation of our government and distinguishes it from the other nations of the earth. I will tell you what that principle is, and if I am wrong correct me. The great fundamental principle is that all power is inherent in the people, and based upon that authority and instituted for their peace, prosperity and happiness. Upon these great principles enunciated and acted upon by our fathers in framing our national government, this Convention must build the fabric they are enacting. We should not for a moment lose sight of it, for it is the only safe foundation upon which they can rely.

In attempting to establish an appointive judiciary we are departing from these principles ; and yet, sir, no one who argues the policy of that system dare to come forward and say that these are not the great and true principles of a republican government; and hence all their arguments must fall to the ground, because they do not rest on the proper foundations, and are opposed to the great principles which form the chief corner-stone of our great and glorious government.

One of the gentlemen, Mr. Abell, has stated on this floor that power in the hands of the people is dangerous, and that he is afraid to trust them on this question. If he is afraid to trust them on the judiciary, why trust them on any question ? Are they not as capable of judging for themselves on this question as on any other ? Are they not as capable of choosing their own judges as they are of choosing the governor and senators whom you propose to give the power to appoint your judiciary ? Is it true that any man in this day has so little confidence in the principles of our fathers, which have been tested in our American system of government, as to declare in 1864 that he has no faith in the people ; that he does not believe the people are capable of governing themselves ? Sir, the people are capable of governing themselves now, and always will be. If there was ever a time when they were capable of judging of their rights, it is now ; and when I speak of the people, I refer to the loyal people of Louisiana.

Mr. President, the people are jealous of their rights. I am jealous of my rights. I will not yield to any man my rights, however much confidence I may have in him. If I vote for a judge who is incompetent to do me justice, I am to blame, and I am responsible for my action. It is the people who elect judges who are the sufferers, and if they elect men who are incompetent they must suffer for it. It is their right to elect their own judges. I have stated that all power is inherent in them, and they are responsible for the proper use of it. It was for these rights that our forefathers fought the war of independence, and it is our duty to guard them with jealous care. Washington, the Father of our country, who stands before me—look at him, [referring to a painting of Washington, facing the entrance to the hall and in the rear of the speaker's chair] — cautioned the people against the danger of allowing the exercise of these great principles to be usurped, and to guard them with jealous care. He chose to trust the people rather than any one man, though that one man was himself, for such was the confidence of the people in him, that he had it in his power to retain a power without limit, and to transmit it to a successor for all time, but he chose to abandon this power to the people, who would have made him a king had he desired it. He was afraid to take this power, because it was the principle for which he had fought. The principle for which the war between England and the Colonies was waged, was the maintenance, on the part of the Colonies, of the principle that all power is inherent in the people. And now, in 1864, after another war on a most gigantic scale is being fought for the maintenance of the same principle, is it not strange that we find one man who dares to stand on this floor and tell us that "the people are not to be trusted." What, I ask, are we to think of that system, built upon such a foundation—a system with such a corner-stone ? Is it reasonable to suppose that such a system could meet the approbation or gain the confidence of the people ? Is it not most certain that the distrust would be mutual, and that a judiciary, appointed on the principle that the people were not to be trusted, would not be trusted nor respected by the people ?

But, sir, there are other grounds which have been urged against the elective judiciary. The country parishes, it is argued, will suffer greatly if this elective judiciary pervails; that we cannot reach the object which an appointed judiciary will give us, namely, *talent*.

Sir, I am in favor of securing the best talent the State can produce. And will these gentlemen tell me that I cannot choose for myself competent men? Will they admit that the people, in 1864, have so degenerated as to be unable to judge for themselves? If so, gentlemen, our government has failed, and we had better have an emperor or a king to govern us.

The Supreme Court of the United States has been referred to as an example for our guidance in this matter. Let us compare it with the Supreme Court of this State. [See constitution of Louisiana, article 62.] There is nothing that comes before the Supreme Court of the State that has any relation to the United States. And, although the Supreme Court of the United States is an appointive court, it has nothing to do with the people of the States. The State courts settle all matters between citizens of their respective States. If I should commit an assault upon a member of this Convention, I should be held answerable before the State courts, and not before the courts of the United States. I should be brought before a judge who has been elected by the people of this State or appointed, and should have no appeal to the United States courts.

My friend from the Fourth District, (Mr. Cutler,) for whom I have the greatest respect, said that he contended for principles derived from Almighty God. Those are the principles *I* contend for, but I do not think he has exactly expressed them. Doing away with evil is one of the great principles of Almighty God. The gentleman must, then, want to do away with all evil—the grogshops and everything bad; but I dare say, that the gentleman, according to his own showing, would be willing to continue them, and therefore could not maintain his ground.

A judiciary cannot be established on the principles of our government that will be independent of party, because the executive *must* be *elected*, and he will almost always give precedence according to his party feeling. I will illustrate my statement. Suppose, Mr. President, we were to elect a governor under a constitution containing the appointive power; then he has all the judiciary to appoint. Suppose I am a candidate for the governorship. I go to all the men who want a judgeship and say if you will use all your influence in my favor, I, upon my election, will appoint you to the desired position. On the other hand, my opponent says the same, so that in the end party has as much to do with the matter as if it came directly before the people, for one faction is arrayed against the other. Can you avoid this argument? I will say that I believe our present executive will appoint only the best men, but this constitutional question had no bearing upon his election, of which it was entirely irrespective. But what is to come hereafter? The governors hereafter must be elected under this very constitution, if it lasts, when, if this article is adopted, as reported, and if any judgeships happen to be vacant, he can wield a vast power, through promising them to influential parties who will use their influence in his favor.

Another argument is that the judges are independent of the executive after they are appointed. I admit that. Now, I ask you, are they not independent after they are elected? If the first is the case, the latter is also. The people for six or eight years, whatever may be the official term, have no more power than the governor, because the judge is under no greater or different obligations to one than to the other.

The great argument which it has been the aim of my opponents to impress upon this Convention, is, that an elective judiciary is and naturally must be corrupt, simply because elected. If any judge after taking a solemn oath before God Almighty that he will decide only according to the right, and then does decide in favor of any man or party on political grounds, I say he is unfit to take his seat, and that he will favor the appointive or elective power which procured him his office. If the people are so corrupt as to be unable to elect a man who will discharge his duty faithfully, I say we cannot by any means secure an honest judiciary. The point has been emphatically argued that the people are corrupt. Who are the people? Are we not a convention of the people? [Applause.] According to the position which has been taken, that there is not an honest man in the State, our judiciary must be corrupt! Are not some of the members of this Convention making an attempt to use up the rights of the people. I say that they are endeavoring to go beyond the powers conferred upon them, when they seek to make the judiciary appointive. We are not here by the appointive but by the elective power. [Applause.]

It is easier to bribe one man than an entire community, and I might show that bribery and corruption has existed even in legislative bodies and conventions. I know of an instance, in the legislative body of Minnesota, where an attempt was made to do an injustice to the people. For the sake of one man's vote I have known the members of that body to sit in their seats, sleeping and eating there, for nine days and nights—though plotting against the liberties of the people. They sent six hundred miles for one member, and, finally, when he came he cast his vote in favor of the people! [Applause.]

Members maintain that if we, at this time, allow the people to elect the district court judges, the secessionists will elect their own judges, and that therefore the loyal citizens will not have any chance of a fair trial under them. Now, sir, I ask if we are not making laws for the secessionists? Are we afraid of them? [Cries of "Yes," "No."] If we are to make a constitution that will last simply during the war, then I say give me an appointive judiciary in the country parishes; [applause,] but if we are to make a constitution to last for future generations—and it will be very little honor to make one which will endure for only two or three days—I am willing to compromise this question, as you will see, by the amendments I have offered to articles 11 and 12 of the judiciary report. I will go farther. If we cannot get a judiciary directly from the people, let us get one from the most intelligent body in the State. My amendments are as follows:

The judges of the supreme court shall be elected by joint vote of the General Assembly, and for a term of ten years. They shall have power to appoint their own clerks.

The judges of the inferior courts shall be elected by the qualified voters of the district in which they reside, and shall hold their courts at such time and place as the General Assembly may direct; they shall hold their office for a term of six years, and until their successors are elected and qualified.

Clerks of the inferior courts in this State shall be elected for the term of four years, and should a vacancy occur subsequent to an election it shall be filled by the judge of the court in which such vacancy exists, and the person so appointed shall hold his office until the next general election.

My reasons for offering the foregoing I will explain. If we cannot reach, through the people directly, the talent we wish, it must certainly be admitted that the General Assembly contains the selected intelligence of the community, composing the representatives of all classes and parties. *They* will know who are the talented men in their several parishes.

Suppose we make the judiciary appointive, and I am then sent as a judge into the country parishes where no body knows me. How soon will there be a howl—though I decide rightly—that I, so totally unacquainted, have no business there? Are you willing, (I ask the country members) to have the executive send a man from this city into your country parishes, there to officiate as judge? [Cries of "no," "no."] Will you admit that you are incompetent to determine who are fit to hold your offices, or that your representatives are not fit to decide for you? If you will, I will yield all. I only say that if the people are directly or indirectly incapable of judging for themselves in this instance, they are incompetent to elect any officer from president to the lowest.

What, I ask, is more ennobling to me than to have the people place me in a situation where I can fulfill my duty towards them by doing justice between them? The scheme of an appointive judiciary is repugnant to the principles upon which our government has been reared, and especially to its chief one, that all authority is inherent in the people. Why, sir, when the representatives met to frame a constitution they were even afraid to trust the different States by electing their members to Congress for them, because of this antagonism!

Talk about England—about the talent of her bench! That is all very well! If our fathers had not fought against that government, I might consider action right, but as it is, let us not forget the principles upon which we act to-day. We must support those principles of the grand charter of our liberty and independence, or if not prepared to do that, may as well bring our labors to an end.

[A motion to adjourn was put and carried.]

MONDAY, May 30, 1864.

[The Convention met pursuant to adjournment, and after prayer by the Rev. Mr. Horton, the roll was called and the following members answered to their names:]

Messrs. Abell, Ariail, Balch, Bailey, Beauvais, Bofill, Bromley, Buckley, Burke, Campbell, Collin, Crozat, Davies, Dufresne, Duke, Edwards, Ennis, Fish, Flagg, Flood, Foley, Fosdick, Gastinel, Geier, Harnan, Hart, Healy, Heard, Hills, Howell, Howes, Kavanagh, Kugler, Maas, Mann, Maurer, Mayer, Montamat, Murphy E., Murphy M. W., Newell, Normand, O'Conner, Ong, Orr, Paine J. T., Pintado, Poynot, Purcell J., Pursell S., Schnurr, Seymour, Shaw, Smith, Spellicy, Stumpf, Stiner, Stauffer, Sullivan, Terry, Thorpe, Waters, Wenck, Wells, Wilson and Mr. President—66.

[There being no quorum, the sergeant-at-arms was directed to procure the attendance of absent members.

The following members having entered and taken their seats, viz: Messrs. Barrett, Cazabat, Cook T., Cutler, Duane, Fuller, Henderson, Hire, Morris, Schroeder and Stocker, (11) the president announced that there was a quorum present.

The minutes were read and adopted.]

Mr. HILLS—I offer the following resolution:

Resolved, That members of this Convention who have not leave of absence, and who shall fail to answer to the roll-call within twenty minutes after 12 M., shall forfeit their per diem allowance for every day of such absence, unless able to give a satisfactory excuse to the Convention.

Mr. STOCKER—I move to suspend the rules for its adoption.

[Two-thirds not voting in the affirmative, the motion was lost and the resolution laid over.]

Mr. MONTAMAT—I offer the following:

Resolved, That a copy of the resolution adopted by this Convention, tendering thanks to Major General N. P. Banks, be sent to him, (the same to be written on parchment.)

I move a suspension of the rules to adopt it.

[The motion was lost—yeas 36.]

Mr. ORR—I offer the following:

Resolved, That it shall be the duty of the Legislature, at its first session, to fix, by legislative enactments, the compensation to be paid to foremen, mechanics, cartmen and laborers employed on the public works under the government of the State of Louisiana and the city of New Orleans, at not less than the following rates:

Foremen of mechanics....	$4 00	per day,
Foremen of carts.........	3 00	" "
Foremen of laborers......	3 00	" "
Mechanics................	3 00	" "
Laborers.................	2 00	" "

[The motion was laid over.

Reports of committees being in order, Mr. Wells, in the absence of the chairman of the Committee on Correspondence Relative to Compensation of Loyal Owners, submitted the following report:]

REPORT OF THE COMMITTEE ON THE COMPENSATION OF LOYAL OWNERS FOR SLAVES EMANCIPATED.

To the honorable the president and members of the constitutional Convention:

Your committee—appointed in obedience to the following resolution, adopted May 10th—

"*Resolved*, That a committee of five be appointed by the president of this Convention to draw appropriate resolutions, expressing and recommending to the president and Congress of the United States the justice and equity of making such appropriations as may be deemed proper and right, for a fair compensation to loyal citizens of Louisiana for the loss of their property upon such terms, conditions and proof as may be required"—respectfully submit the accompanying memorial and resolutions for your adoption.

A. CAZABAT, Chairman,
M. R. ARIAIL,
T. M. WELLS,
GEO. A. FOSDICK,
R. W. TALIAFERRO.

This memorial of the constitutional Convention of the State of Louisiana respectfully showeth:

That this Convention was convened at Liberty Hall, in the city of New Orleans, in obedience to the proclamation of the Hon. Michael Hahn, governor of the State of Louisiana, and to the order No. 35, issued by Major Gen. N. P. Banks, commanding the department of the gulf, to revise and amend the constitution of the State of Louisiana; being impelled by a due regard for the public welfare, and an earnest desire not only to suppress existing rebellious combinations against the laws, honor and dignity of the United States, but to forever remove whatever may tend to mar the future peace and general welfare of the whole country, have passed an ordinance which is the fundamental and supreme law of the State, abolishing forever involuntary servitude, except as a punishment for crime, and forbidding future Legislatures from passing any act recognizing property in man.

Your memorialists further represent, that in the year 1860, according to the census then taken, there were within the State of Louisiana 331,726 slaves, valued at 150,000,000 dollars, and that a number of the owners thereof ever have been, and still remain loyal citizens of the United States, and that in consequence of this their loyalty and unfaltering devotion to the cause of Union and freedom, their property has been sacrificed and destroyed by the enemy, and themselves driven into an exile of poverty and destitution. In thus giving up what in many cases is their last earthly possession, they are actuated by no other motive nor have they any other wish than to re-establish and maintain the constitution and institutions of the United States. But they respectfully submit that in justice and equity they are entitled to such relief from the Federal government as may in some measure compensate loyal slave-owners for the great sacrifice they have made for the general welfare; and that the whole burden ought not to fall on the loyal people of Louisiana, impoverished as they already are by the destruction and devastation which always prevail on the theatre of war.

That other States in which the emancipation of slaves has been effected without assistance from the Federal government have done so in times of peace and prosperity, and by a gradual process which enabled the owners to provide for the change in the labor system and reimburse themselves for the expense of raising the infant slave. But as any such plan of emancipation, under present existing circumstances here, is impracticable, they have declared the immediate and unconditional emancipation of every slave within the State, having a full and confident reliance on the magnanimity of the people of the United States and of their representatives in Congress assembled for such compensation as may be just and equitable.

Your memorialists further represent, that Great Britain pursued this course with signal success in emancipating the slaves of her West India colonies, the system of apprenticeship which was then introduced and continued for about four years compensated the former owners for the support of that class of aged and infirm persons which must here become paupers to be supported at public expense.

The State must also expend large sums of money in the education and moral culture of these emancipated slaves, that they may be fitted for their new position and increased privileges as freemen.

Your memorialists freely acknowledge that the institution for which they ask compensation was a wrong *per se*, but of that wrong they were not the exclusive perpetrators—the whole nation participating in the guilt of its introduction—and many of the slaves now emancipated are the lineal descendants of those who were brought from more northern States when slavery ceased to be profitable and emancipation there became inevitable.

The loyal citizens of Louisiana are in the same position that was occupied by, and have the same claims for compensation that were urged in favor of the citizens of the District of Columbia. Nay, their claim is even stronger, for theirs is a voluntary sacrifice made for the public weal, while the other was a compulsory order made and executed by Congress.

Without attempting to fix the amount of compensation or to suggest the manner in which it ought to be made, your memorialists submit this, their petition, with a full reliance in the justice and equity of their claim, and that the liberality and honor of the nation will recognize its rightfulness.

Resolved, That the committee on the compensation of loyal citizens for slaves emancipated be directed to cause the accompanying memorial to be engrossed in duplicate, signed by themselves and attested by the president and secretary of this convention, and that they also transmit one copy of the same to the senate and the other to the House of Representatives of the United States.

Resolved, That the committee be instructed to correspond upon the subject of compensating loyal slave-owners with such members of the Congress of the United States as they may think proper.

Mr. ABELL—I offer the following amendment:

Provided, That the payment be made to

the loyal citizens before the final adoption of this constitution.

Mr. Cazabat—I move to lay the amendment on the table.

[The motion was carried by a *viva voce* vote.

The report was then accepted—yeas 42 nays 7.

Mr. Abell appealed from the decision of the chair in regard to laying the amendment on the table. The chair was sustained and the yeas and nays called for, but not a sufficient number arose to support the demand.]

Mr. Montamat—I move that 300 copies of the report be printed.

Mr. Wenck—I amend to 200.

[Amendment was accepted and the motion carried.]

Mr. Abell—I move that the same number of copies of the amendment be printed.

[A motion to lay the last motion on the table was lost.]

Mr. Hills—I voted to lay the amendment on the table, but I like to see justice done, and I understand that Mr. Abell called for a division on the laying of his amendment on the table, therefore I move to reconsider the vote by which that amendment was tabled.

[The chair decided that it was too late, as the report had been adopted.

The motion to print the amendment was then carried.

Mr. Montamat, of the Committee on Expenses, submitted the following reports :]

May 23—Balance on hand as per report No. 6.....		$47,186 40
May 24—Paid warrant No. 47.	$1349 00	
May 24—Paid warrant No. 48.	416 00	
May 25—Paid warrant No. 49.	1730 00	
May 28—Paid warrant No. 50.	1630 00	
May 28—Paid warrant No. 51.	2330 00	
May 28—Paid warrant No. 52.	1828 00	
May 28—Paid warrant No. 54.	860 00—	$10,143 00
May 30—Balance on hand this day		$37,043 40

Thirty-seven thousand and forty-three dollars and forty cents.

JOHN P. MONTAMAT,
Chairman *pro tem.* Finance Committee.
New Orleans, May 30, 1864.

May 23—Balance on hand as per report No. 6.....	$8759 48
May 27—Paid M. DeCoursey for contingent expenses, as per voucher on file, warrant No. 53.......	1830 85
May 30—Balance on hand this day,	$6928 63

Six thousand nine hundred and twenty-eight dollars and sixty-three cents.

JOHN P. MONTAMAT,
Chairman *pro tem.* Finance Committee.
New Orleans, May 20, 1864.

[Mr. Cazabat's resolution of Saturday, relative to a final adjournment on the 6th of June, was laid on the table.

The order of the day was then taken up, and the discussion of the judiciary report resumed.]

Mr. Smith—I wish to say a few words to explain my vote. I wish to ask if the people are interested in this branch of the government, and if this is the only department that is not subject to improvement? It has been asked if we are wiser than those who have gone before — than Washington, Adams, Franklin, and such great men of the olden time. If Robert Fulton could be put on board of one of the floating palaces that traverse our rivers, he would not even know how to let on the steam or shut it off, although he is the inventor of the steamboat. It would be strange if this subject has not been subject to progress. If the people are interested in the judiciary, they alone have the right to say whether it shall be elected or not. Franklin said he believed that such would be the progress of the next century, that the mails would be carried between Boston and Philadelphia in five days, but now it is done in a few hours. In arguing this question, a gentleman has tauntingly asked if the people were competent to decide. Will he go home to his constituents and use the same argument—that they can be swayed by prejudice and their votes bought? I supported the amendment of Mr. Abell, that the Supreme Court should have a supervisory control over the other courts. As the gentlemen are afraid the judiciary will be contaminated by the touch of the people, I have a substitute I wish to offer, and that is that the judges be elected on the same principle as our United States senators. Let us keep the executive hand out of it, for fear there might be some little prejudice.

[The chair decided that it would not be in order till the present amendment was disposed of.]

Mr. SMITH—I wish to refer to one State in which the people have less liberty than in any other State. An appointed judge in Charleston, after the result of the last presidential election was received, said "every right of the people had been swept away by the ballot-box." I say this belongs to the people, and I shall always sustain their rights in this matter.

Mr. TERRY—Mr. President and gentlemen, this is Liberty Hall, do as you please. "The evil that men do live after them; the good is oft interred with their bones." Thus exclaims the great Bard of Avon—who held the mirror up to nature and drew the characters of men. But Brutus was an orator—I am none. Not like the drowning man catching at straws, but as a free and loyal citizen, native to the soil and manner born, of this great American republic, do I stand here and grapple with ye. You have seized in your great and mighty arguments the *people* as the *common herd*. Like the Indians of the far West driving before them the buffalo herd onward to the edge of a steep and yawning abyss, when beholding their danger they turn and trample their drivers beneath their feet. I hear you all exclaim this is not argument. I will give you argument; not a six weeks' speech, but one prepared in six hours. Not influenced, not prejudiced, but alone and unaided—and all I ask is your patient hearing—beseeching you if my principles are to die here, you will give me respectful burial, and do me the honor to say to my constituents I flinched not, neither did I waver from the great fundamental principles of American liberty!

Give me an extemporaneous speech says one—my style of extemporaneous speaking might be too severe; therefore I will be lenient, and express what I have to say on paper, in order to keep the thread of your mighty arguments.

Mr. President, in throwing down the gauntlet I anticipated the great opposition in argument which has been displayed on this floor, and will endeavor to answer to the best of my humble abilities.

Mr. Wilson stated: "That an appointive judiciary worked so well that there never was a complaint against it from 1812 to 1852." If this be true, how came it, the elective to be instituted, then, if an appointive judiciary worked so harmoniously? It was overthrown in '52, and an elective substituted. He might say this was the work of thugs and know nothings, who did this to benefit by it. Then if this be so, their day has come and gone, and to-day the honest, hard-working laborer and loyalist are the voters, and there is no fear of one of these noted thugs, Red Bill and Bob Johnson included, being elected to office. He says it is not retrograding—"an appointive judiciary not retrograding." It is surely not a step to advance civilization, but rather one to retard it, losing all confidence in the people, sapping at the very foundations of that greatest of all bulwarks, *American liberty*. What is this great battle? Who are the opponents? Is it not the lawyers against the people, and the people against the lawyers? Do not the people know who are talented lawyers, and who are mere walking-sticks? If two talented men are pitted against each other in a campaign, if they have committed any errors, will it not see the light of day in honest competition? Mr. Wilson also says: "If the judge is appointed he is independent." I cannot see it in that light. The same power that appoints him makes him dependent thereto and holds a great influence over him, and he has only to please one instead of the populace.

Permit me to state how independent they are at the present day, and what one of the honorable judges thinks of the honorable members of this Convention. A learned and honorable judge, when asked the question, "If he was a member of this honorable body?" he replied, "Thank God, he had not reached that depth of degradation yet."

Mr. Abell says: "All know the people's

usurpations." The people will hurl a good judge from office and place a demagogue in his place." In the history of this State I have failed to find it. But I have known that within the last two years demagogues have been appointed, and a petition signed by a thousand loyal citizens has failed to remove them, simply because it found its way in the paper basket of a military governor. My learned and honorable friend——

R. *King* Cutler says—"He is no dramatist, no phrenologist, no psychologist, nor a Macbeth, or a Macduff." Now, I shall certainly exclaim with Macbeth, on the argument, "Damn'd be he who first cries hold! enough!" But Macbeth belongs not to my side of the question, but, as a *King*ly character, holds to the appointive. Therefore, when the gentleman mentioned the two opposites in such close proximity, he took upon himself the *King*ly crown, and has only become *terrified* at the close proximity of Macduff and the great "Burnim wood which has come to Dunsinane" against him—*the people*. Now, then, let me state here I am "no lawyer" but a tack driver, and will endeavor with my humble ability to nail his argument. He says that "law controls the universe and our very being;" such is the fact, but they are the unerring laws of nature and justice, conceived and given by the Almighty, and controlled by Him. These are Divine laws, not lawyers' laws. The laws of the Medes and Persians, bad and unchangable, were laws. The Draconian laws were laws of blood. The Lycurgian, which ruled the Spartans in glory and renown five hundred and sixty-nine years, were laws of equal and humane rights. The Solon laws of Greece were aristocratic, and unequal for good. The thousand and one laws of inhumanity and wickedness might be enumerated. The laws of the Cannibals, Chinese and Juggernaut of India, and the damnable black code of Louisiana, these are laws, but not the infallible laws of universal justice. Now, then, does the gentleman show there is any harmony existing between nature's laws, which control the universe and our own being, and the laws of the Medes and Persians, the Draconian, the Chinese, the Juggernaut of India, and the damnable black code of Louisiana—I fail to see it. But I am no lawyer, only a tack driver.

The gentleman from the Fourth, the Hon. R. King Cutler, with very questionable taste, takes members to task who oppose an appointive system, because they are not lawyers, and tells us we are meddling with a subject which we do not understand. Now, notwithstanding my high estimate of Mr. Cutler as a man of learning, I do not and shall not admit that all the honesty and wisdom of the world is centered either in that gentleman or the legal profession of which he is so bright a member.

The worthy son of Æsculapius, the merchant, the planter, the farmer, the editor, the mechanic and even the humble disciple of the immortal Bard of Avon, possess some degree of common sense and honesty. They, at least know that the people have rights, which it is our duty to guard and protect, among which is the right sacred to every American heart—the right of *electing their own rulers*—a right which they will never give up, and for which I shall contend as long as I breathe the breath of life.

Mr. Cutler, it appears to me, was most unfortunate in his allusion to John Slidell and Judah P. Benjamin, in connection with the judiciary, and after his earnest appeal to decide this question with reason, and his modest insinuation that all the learning and wisdom were on his side, the greatest portion of which was centered in *himself*. He was particularly unfortunate in his assertion that John Slidell was a member of the convention of 1852, and that it was to Slidell and Benjamin the people are indebted for an elective judiciary, and displays a want of candor or of information at which I am astonished.

In the first place, John Slidell was not a member of that convention; in the second place, although he was nominally a democrat, he was at heart an aristocrat, and opposed to an elective judiciary, and in favor of the very principle contended for by Mr. Cutler.

Mr. Benjamin was in the convention of 1852, and by reference to the proceedings of that convention it will be seen that he used precisely the same argument in favor of an appointive system, and in opposition to an elective one, as Mr. Cutler does. In fact, if Mr. Cutler does not borrow his speech from J. P. Benjamin, he furnishes an apt illustration of the popular refrain, "*great minds think alike.*"

The gentleman says: "A judge who is running before the people has to cater for votes in beer saloons and grogshops." The honorable members of this Convention occasionally do frequent these very grogshops, and the honorable gentleman was free to admit—"*He liked good whiskey.*" Now suppose a judiciary election was at hand, would he, the honorable gentleman, or any of the other honorable members of the Convention, if applied to by an aspirant for judicial honors, consent to support him because *per se, he too liked good whiskey*, or would you be men, citizens entertaining a proper appreciation and solemn obligation to your duties, and answer no! and nominate and vote for the man or men to these honorable positions for their virtues and high worth in the community?

The gentleman says, "I am influenced and prejudiced by others." *I deny the assertion*, unless a man's fixed principles be prejudice. All the learned rhetoric and arguments that have been displayed on this floor have failed to convince me that *wrong was right!*

He says I was six weeks preparing my argument; on the contrary, I was but twenty-four hours, but I waited six weeks to deliver it.

The gentleman says, "Save Louisiana;" are we not saving her, in saving her free, liberal and loyal institutions by upholding the people in their elective franchise and rights? In a republic *all laws proceed from the people!*

The gentleman says, "Ten thousand votes were cast in the last election." Was one vote cast on the question of appointive judiciary? Was the judiciary question at all involved in either of the elections? No, and the gentleman knows it well. He knows well if the friends of loyalty and freedom had been consulted on this question, the honorable gentleman had not now the honor of a seat, especially if the people had known his sentiments; and let him and all who think with him beware how they misrepresent the people on this vitally important question. The free State party to-day are in favor of an elective judiciary, because they have conceived the idea that we are verging into a monarchial government. I wish to save the constitution. I hope and wish it may be ratified; but I tremble for the consequences *if* the gentleman's principles prevail. Mr. President, I was astounded at the admission of the gentleman that he preferred the success of the appointive judiciary to the immortal ordinance of emancipation. The appointive judiciary and aristocratical institution—the few ruling the many—rather than the enfranchisement and the liberation of man from *hell-bound bondage*. What a comparison! Have we ears and do we hear? I stand amazed and ask, shall this white slavery be inaugurated?

The honorable gentleman also says I used unbecoming language. I wish the printer had published my remarks, it would have aided the gentleman to have pointed it out. What were his remarks in behalf of our worthy auditor? Was his language becoming or not? making a personal attack on one who was unarmed—who had not the power to reply to him. I wish to God we had a thousand men like him to-day, and we would have proper men in office. He is not to be pandered to by dinners and emoluments, but as a fearless and just servant of the people serves them faithfully, and makes no distinction between the learned judge of the bench and the ignorant though honest hod-carrier. I do not believe that State officer ever used his office to convince men, but as A. P. Dostie, the friend of union and liberty, claimed that right as well as the talented judges that I see visit here to advocate their views in regard to the appointive.

Mr. Thorpe argued as if the constitution is to continue only so long as the war lasts. But I hope and believe that our work will stand for ages.

While the war lasts military law is paramount—above this Convention and above its work. The military law is not only amply able to take care of the well dressed 500 men who so frantically rushed to the Picayune office for the bogus proclamation, and disturbed the nerves of Mr. Thorpe, but it will see to it that the Red Bills and Thugs about whom he has said so much shall not control the judicial election, any more than any other election.

If there be so much danger of the rebels electing our judges, as Mr. Thorpe and others seem to think, is there not the same danger of their electing the governor and senate, the first of whom it is proposed shall nominate our judges and the second confirm them for life.

But I deny that there is any danger of the rebels electing either, and only allude to that portion of the ad captandum appeal of the friends of the appointive system, in order to show, that, like a two-edged sword, it cuts both ways. If it is an argument against an elective judiciary, it is an argument which applies with equal, if not greater force, against any election by the people, especially against the election of a governor, who this Convention has already decided shall be elected by the people.

Col. Thorpe touches on the death of Robert Emmett, that noble and inspired martyr of liberty. But he perverts history. Look at his dying speech; it is short—with your permission I will read one or two quotations from it, that all may judge.

[Reads quotations.]

Ten years hence the same scene may be enacted in America by an appointive judiciary, the power behind the throne, for we are liable to drift in the direction of tyranny when we deprive the people of their right to govern.

Some say the affairs of this State are so complicated that it is not consistent with the times nor safe to elect judges for the present. Some offer a compromise. Listen to the compromise that I and my constituents are willing to accept. Under the title of ordinace of the constitution, I am willing for the insertion of this article—that no election for judges, justices of the peace, sheriffs, coroners, tax collectors, assessors, district attorneys, &c., shall be held until two years after peace. Then the remedy rests in your own hands. Let the judges be elected two years after peace, give them a proper salary, and let the election be made the great campaign of the State. THE *people* are greater than the executive—greater than conventions—greater than aristocracy, oligarchies and monarchies—say next to God himself.

Mr. WENCK—The gentleman's speech has certainly not convinced me, nor do I believe it could any other man who takes an interest in the subject. As a specimen of the platform which the people approve, I will read the following, from a circular addressed to his constituents by a member of this Convention:

FELLOW-CITIZENS: I am a candidate for your suffrages.

Having at all times opposed the frauds and violence perpetrated upon a large portion of our citizens and the ballot box, I would now prefer a defeat to success by fraud and violence.

If elected, I would favor a judiciary appointed by the executive, by and with the advice and consent of the Senate, to hold office during good behavior, with ample salaries, and removable by impeachment only.

As an example of the interest which the people have in this question of elective judiciary, let us refer to the last election held here in 1860, for district judge. At that time four votes were cast in the name of a man who had been buried for the last two or three years. The gentleman says that now thuggery had ceased and will rule no more; but even if this be so, we shall have parties none the less. Suppose a copperhead, a secessionist and a Union man should run for the same office, would the gentleman cast his vote for the former? No, he would not; but party consideration would dictate his vote. In a case of an elective judiciary, the candidate pledges himself to men who will support him in his efforts to obtain the office to which he aspires, and consequently he cannot be impartial. Is it not against conscience to raise up such judges? I ask you, in God's name, if you can show me any satisfactory law made by an elective judiciary? I say you cannot, and that the decisions which have been of the most authority have for the last hundred years been given by an appointive judiciary. Do you believe if Judge Martin was living that he would, for the four or six years office, run around among the people? Certainly not; and from men who will resort to these means to obtain a judgeship you can never form a court of talent or obtain that impartiality which otherwise will exist. Go among the laboring classes and bring a candidate before them; very many will cast their votes without knowing what they are doing. Let us then have an appointive judiciary, who will hold their offices during good behavior; then the people, both rich and poor, will be benefitted thereby, but otherwise it will be dollars and cents that will carry the election.

Mr. HOWELL—Mr. President, I certainly should not desire to proceed when it is evident that a considerable portion of this Convention is already tired of hearing speeches, did I not deem it an imperative duty for this Convention to dispatch their business, and not waste their own and the time of the people in considering foolish resolutions.

I feel that it is particularly unfortunate that the closing of this argument devolves upon me. Unfortunate, because I am myself a member of the department to which the question relates. Unfortunate, because I feel to-day less prepared to argue the question than I was the first day of the discussion. Unfortunate, because I have been preceded by gentlemen who have so successfully carried with them the popular sentiment, against which it will be difficult for a man in my position to contend. Nevertheless, as a matter of duty, I shall not shrink from the task that devolves upon me, and in doing so, I shall endeavor to divest my remarks of appeals to passion and to prejudice. I shall endeavor to refrain from that character of declamation which is suited to the rostrum rather than to a deliberative body. I shall direct my remarks to the reason and common sense of this body, and shall ask a patient hearing.

In the first place we must ascertain the points before the Convention. They are raised under article 3 of the report of the Committee on the Judiciary Department. That article refers to the Supreme Court, shows how it shall be composed, fixes the majority necessary to do business and the salaries of the judges, and provides that the court shall appoint its own clerks, etc. To that an amendment has been offered, upon which this debate has originated. That amendment, submitted by the gentleman from the Third District, (Mr. Sullivan,) gentlemen, by observing, will perceive is in reality a substitute for the article 3 of the report, and differs from it in only two points. It varies the salaries of the proposed judges of the Supreme Court, and following, almost literally, the words upon the same subject in the constitution of 1852, declares that the judges of the Supreme Court shall be elected for the term of ten years. With this exception, and the change in the salaries, the amendment does not differ from the report. Now, the point is, whether the judges shall be elected or not. The debate has taken a wide range, and it would be well for members to bring their thoughts to this one point before they decide either upon the adoption of the report or the substitute which has been offered, and upon which they are called upon to vote. This substitute provides that the judges shall be elected. The report says, in another part, they shall be appointed. It is not my part, Mr. President, to arraign either one of these modes before this Convention. It is not necessary, sir, for us to come to a radically correct conclusion that one of the modes is wholly bad, or that the other is wholly good, for all systems of human invention are imperfect, and it is the duty of wise men, in organizing a system for the good of the country, to carefully select that system which has the fewest defects. And in coming to this conclusion it will be my purpose to show that the appointive is the one which has the fewest defects. Not that there no good points in the other; that the elective is wholly wrong, and that all judges who have been elected have been partial and unjust; nor that the judiciary under the elective system has been a failure. But, sir, my purpose and object are to show that under our former system of government the interests of the people are best secured under judges appointed by the governor, with the advice and consent of the Senate.

All the arguments we have heard against this system divide themselves into two distinctive characters:

First, That it is a denial of the right and the capacity of the people to elect judges.

Second, That it is placing too much power in the hands of the governor.

To these propositions I propose to direct attention for a few minutes. Why is it a denial of the rights of the people, in what particular is it a denial of the capacity of the people to select their judges? If that question were necessary to solve the point, I would answer readily that the people have the capacity and the right to select all their officers. But I do not think that question is necessarily involved in this subject. It is not necessary to deny their capacity, it is not necessary to deny their right, but it is a question of policy, of expediency, to determine which it is necessary to look at the object for which the judiciary is established in our form of government, and the character of that department.

Our government consists of three departments, each separate and distinct in its functions from the other, the executive, the legislative and the judiciary. You all know the duties devolving upon the legislative. It is to make laws for the people. They are the representatives of the people in declaring the sovereign will, which is law. The executive is the arm of the people, to execute that law. And the judiciary is to interpret and maintain the law. Mark well the distinction—to interpret, enforce and maintain the law. If you enact a bad law, the judge must, under his oath, execute it, whatever may be his convictions of its want of correctness and injustice. However his conscientiousness may be opposed to it he must enforce it. The remedy is in the law-making power, but the judiciary is best calculated to show the defects of the law, and this is left to the judiciary department.

Is it necessary that a judge, when he is chosen to pass upon the constitutionality or the force of a law, should be chosen by a popular vote to represent the popular sentiment of any particular party or locality? Must a judge, in order to enable him to decide the constitutionality of a law, represent the popular sentiment of any particular class of citizens? The judiciary are governed only by the principles of law, and it is the interest of the people that everything like political character should be excluded from it—that there should be no temptation for the judge, to let political considerations enter his mind while forming his judgments. That interest is badly promoted by putting the judge before the people as the candidate of a political party. It is to their interest that the judge should be as far removed from all political commotion and public excitement as it is possible for men to be removed. To effect this what is the best mode? I take the position that the appointive is the best that the intellect of men has presented, and for these reasons and many others. The governor is elected by the whole people of the State. True, he is elected by some political party being in the majority, but when once elected he represents the whole people of the State, and in making his selections for judges of the Supreme Court, he is not responsible to the people of any particular locality, and the judge appointed by him has no inducement to look to the political sentiments of any particular locality. He knows that he is appointed by the power which represents the whole State.

But, sir, there is a stronger argument than this. The great danger is not that the judge will be influenced by political considerations, but that the people will suspect him of it. However pure and unbiased a decision may be, there are those who will attribute the maintenance of legal principles, which led to certain conclusions, to political motives. A mere accusation of that kind tends more to degrade the judiciary and make the law ineffective in accomplishing its great mission. It is an effect that, more than any other, renders it necessary that an appointing power should select the judges of the Supreme Court.

I am aware of the power of the appeal which is made upon this floor, that the rights of the people are infringed in the effort to remove the judiciary from popular commotions. Gentlemen forget, in their appeal, the real interest of the people which they desire to advocate. It is not true, sir, that the advocates of the appointive system desire for one moment to infringe upon the rights of the people of Louisiana. But they do not hold, sir, that the only right a people has is to vote—to vote often, early and to vote all the time, and to vote for every thing. Will the gentlemen look for a moment at the statistical record of the elective judiciary in Louisiana. The first election of judges took place in 1853; what was the popular vote on that occasion? I have not the statistics, but my recollection is that about 40 per cent. of the voting population alone took part in that vote. I know that in New Orleans in 1857 the popular vote for judges was about 3700 or 3800, something under 4000. In 1861 the popular vote was still less than in '57. What does this argue? Gentlemen will bear in mind that the popular vote cast at the election immediately preceding them were some 10,000. What does this vote argue? If the people feel that this is an abridgement of their rights—if the election of the judiciary by popular vote be so essential to the enjoyment of their political rights—how do gentlemen account for the small number of votes cast at these elections?

Mr. Smith—How was it in the country parishes?

Mr. Howell—I am aware how gentlemen will attempt to evade the question by reference to the country parishes, but I will not confine myself to New Orleans; I will take you to the country. In one of the parishes when the succesor of Tho. Slidell was before the people as a candidate, no polls were opened. In the parish of Concordia, in one small precinct, the polls were opened and four votes were cast for Merrick. The whole voting statistics show a beggarly want of numbers in every judicial election since 1853, and is a tremendous commentary upon the elective system, and the result is necessarily this: that the election of judges falls into the hands of political characters and professional voters—men who hold themselves in the market to cast their votes for the party or the candidate who will take the most trouble and bear the expense of securing their votes. I do not say, that this has always been done, but I say that this is the tendency of the system. If everybody who was entitled to a vote would turn out and cast his vote without prejudice and without influence, the system would be less objectionable. And every man here will sustain me in the assertion that the elective system has been a magnificent failure in regard to the appreciation of the voters. That good men have been selected under it, it does not become me to deny; that bad men have been selected under it, is not necessary for me to assert. But I do say, most unhesitatingly, that to continue the election of judges tends to place the selection of the judiciary in the hands of those who have no time to do anything but to vote—in the hands of political tricksters.

Mr. President, I will yield the floor for a motion to adjourn, and, with the consent of the Convention, will conclude my remarks to-morrow morning.

[A motion to adjourn was made and carried.]

Tuesday, May 31, 1864.

[The Convention met pursuant to adjournment, and was called to order by the president.

The proceedings were opened with prayer by the Rev. Mr. Strong.

The roll was called, and the following members answered to their names:]

Messrs. Abell, Balch, Bailey, Barrett, Bofill, Bromley, Buckley, Burke, Campbell, Collin, Cook J. K., Crozat, Decker, Duke, Dufresne, Edwards, Ennis, Fish, Flagg, Flood. Foley, Gorlinski, Harnan, Healy, Heard. Hills, Howell, Howes, Kavanagh, Maas, Mann, Mayer, Mendiverri, Montamat, Morris, Murphy M. W., Newell, Normand, O'Conner, Ong, Orr, Payne J., Paine J. T., Pintado, Poynot, Purcell J., Pursell S., Schroeder, Schnurr, Seymour, Shaw, Spellicy, Stumpf, Stiner, Stauffer, Sullivan, Terry, Waters, Wells, and Mr. President—60.

[There being no quorum present, the sergeant-at-arms was directed to procure the attendance of absent members.

After some delay, Messrs. Beauvais, Bell, Fosdick, Gastinel, Geier, Goldman, Hart, Henderson, Hire, Maurer, Murphy E., Smith,

Stocker, Thorpe, Wenck, and Wilson entered, took their seats and answered to their names.

The minutes were read and adopted.

No resolutions being offered, unfinished business was declared in order, when Mr. Stocker moved a suspension of the rules to allow Mr. Thorpe to offer a resolution, he not having submitted it in order.

The rules were suspended by a vote of 54 in the affirmative.]

Mr. THORPE—I propose the following resolution, which I should be much pleased to see adopted:

Resoved, That after this date (May 31st, 1864,) the order of the day shall be taken up immediately after the minutes shall have been read by the clerk and accepted by the Convention, and that Saturday of each week shall be appropriated to miscellaneous business.

[On motion, the rules were suspended for its adoption—yeas 55.]

Mr. MONTAMAT—I move the resolution be laid on the table.

[Lost—yeas 21, nays 51.

The resolution was then adopted by a vote of 54 to 18.

It was stated there was no quorum, and a call of the House was demanded by Mr. Sullivan.

The roll was called, when 76 members answered to their names.

Mr. Hills's resolution of yesterday was read.]

Mr. MONTAMAT—I offer the following amendment:

That the honorable member of the Second Representative District (Mr. Hills) shall forfeit his per diem for every day he shall fail to answer to his name within fifteen minutes after 12 o'clock M.

[On motion, the resolution and amendment were laid on the table.

Mr. Orr's resolution of yesterday was read.]

Mr. SMITH—I move to lay it on the table.

[The yeas and nays were demanded, but the call not being sustained, the resolution was laid on the table by a rising vote of 40 to 35.

Mr. Montamat's resolution of yesterday was read and adopted.

The order of the day was then taken up, the second reading of the report on judiciary, and the discussion resumed.]

Mr. HOWELL—Mr. President, in my remarks yesterday I endeavored to show that it was not necessary in this debate to deny the right or the capacity of the people in order to arrive at a rational conclusion in this matter. The people have a right to make laws in their own name and in their own assembly, but in a large community it is impracticable, and they must necessarily elect their representatives—their agents for making laws for the community. If every voter becomes perfectly familiar with the qualifications and the fitness of every candidate for the judiciary, he will have the capacity to make a proper selection; but in order to ascertain the qualifications and the fitness of the judge, the majority of the people must necessarily depend upon information derived from others. An attorney or counsellor-at-law has the reputation of being a prominent lawyer. His peculiar qualities as a lawyer are known to those who come in contact with him; but his general reputation and particular fitness for any department or branch of the law is known to a few, and circulated only by those who know them. So, however fit a man may be for the judgeship, I contend, and appeal to the experience of every man within the hearing of my voice, that every voter in the district or city in which he may be a candidate is not familiar with his peculiar fitness for that judgeship. I argue from this that the people, in order to make a judicious selection, must necessarily depend upon the advice and information of a few; and in applying this argument I say that the governor has the same facility—the same means for obtaining that knowledge—which the mass of the people have. I say the governor, if he be such a governor as the intelligent people of this State should select, has a better opportunity for making the most appropriate selection, because the whole people have not the opportunity to investigate the merits and reliability of the information communicated to them on that point; while the action of one man, directed to one particular purpose, all will admit must be more effective than those diffuse and diversified efforts of the most of the people. I will ask of the members of this Convention, how many of them personally knew the candidates for whom they voted for the Supreme Bench of this State, and how they got their information?

As to the qualifications of the various candidates, the answer is readily to the minds of every one. Upon the point, then, as to the capacity of the people, I contend, that the people, when properly informed, have the capacity; I contend furthermore, that the appointing power, aided by the Senate of the State, have equal capacity and greater opportunities. The governor directs his examination with reference to the applicants before him. He sets on foot investigation and inquiry. If he be an honest man—and I trust Louisiana will never elect any other as governor—he will direct his investigation with respect to the peculiar fitness of the man to the position. He will have the aid and advice of the representatives from the particular locality where each of the candidates reside; and when he has come to his conclusion, and made his selection, it is then again investigated and passed upon by the conservative part of the representative government of the State. All the means, all the facilities within the reach of man are afforded for coming to an accurate and correct determination; while it very frequently happens that in elections the votes are controlled more by party organization and the dictates of party leaders, than by a just knowledge of the qualifications of the candidates.

I attempted, also, to show yesterday that the small vote which was uniformly cast in Louisiana for the judiciary, is an argument that the people do not place so high an appreciation upon their right to select their judges as the advocates of that system contend for. If each voter in the State of Louisiana felt the interest in this subject which he should feel, and which the advocates of the elective system contend he does feel, every one would turn out and cast his vote for the judgeship; but late experience informs us such is not the case. I contend from that fact that the people do not desire that this right shall be exercised by them. I contend from that fact that the people prefer to constitute a certain agency for this purpose, and I claim that that agency which is best suited for the purpose is the governor, with the assistance and advice of the Senate, for the reasons which I have attempted to explain.

I also attempted to show, Mr. President, that the character of and the duties which devolve on the judiciary department demand that the selection of the judges shall be as far removed from popular commotion as possible. It is not necessary now to repeat what I attempted then to elucidate. I leave it to the intelligence of each man on this floor to carry out this subject, and determine what are the duties of the judiciary, and the rights involved. I leave it for the gentlemen here, who can come to as accurate conclusion upon these points as I can myself. I do not distrust the intelligence of this Convention; I do not distrust the intelligence of the people; I only ask the gentlemen to reflect, to canvass this subject calmly and deliberately; I ask them to divest themselves of that feeling which seems to influence some in regard to popular rights, and not let their zeal be greater than their knowledge. I contend that the interests of the people are better guarded by a judiciary which is removed from the political arena—which is removed from political excitements—than that judiciary which must necessarily be more or less affected by these causes. The State of Mississippi has been referred to as presenting an admirable system of the elective judiciary. I would not object to taking the example of the State of Mississippi on this point if I were familiar with the history of that State, but I will say that, ordinarily, I would as soon go to any other State in the Union, except, perhaps, South Carolina, as to Mississippi for instruction. The system may work admirably there for aught I know, but I prefer to confine my considerations to the State in which the question before us is most intimately concerned. It is with the judiciary of Louisiana that we are now concerned.

I refer this Convention to the history of the elective judiciary in this State. I refer them to the history of the judiciary system since this State has been organized. Let me premise by referring particularly to the reading of a clause in the constitution of

1812 on this subject: "The Supreme Court shall consist of no less than three judges, nor more than five, a majority of whom shall form a quorum," etc. Here, it may be remarked, that the constitution did not fix the specific number composing the court, but provided only the maximum and minimum numbers. It left open a door which, in my opinion, should have been kept closed. I refer to the door left open for legislative action. The judiciary, under that constitution, was organized in the beginning of 1813.

From 1813 to 1846, (thirty-three years) with a life tenure and bench of three judges; to 1831, (eighteen years,) of four judges (for seven years,) to '38, and of five judges to '46, (eight years,) there were thirteen judges—average, one judge to over two and a half years.

From 1846 to 1853, (eight years,) a tenure of eight years and a bench of four judges, there were six judges—one judge to one and a half years.

From 1853 to 1862, (nine years,) with a tenure of ten years, subject to removal every two years, and a bench of five judges, there were twelve judges in nine years—one to every nine months.

I direct attention to the relative instability of the two systems. From 1846 to 1853, a period of seven years, with a bench of four judges, there were six judges who occupied the bench. This gives one year and a halt to each one. As the system begun to be tampered with and changed, changes in the judiciary began to increase. From 1853, when the elective judiciary went into operation, to 1862, when it was partially suspended, a period of nine years, with a tenure of ten years, and a bench of five judges, there were twelve judges—one to every nine months. That gives an idea of the practical working of the two systems. In the first period of our judicial history, we had five judges, in eighteen years, under the appointive system, before the Legislature began to tamper with the system. In the last nine years, under the elective system, we had twelve judges following each other in a succesion of every nine months. What is the necessary result, effect of this upon the jurisprudence of the State? There are no two minds which look at the same state of facts in the same light. You form a bench. They direct their attention to the principles of law which are to be applied by them to the cases brought before them. They soon establish and fix a regular system of jurisprudence. They establish principles which the public come to understand, and they can rely upon. When parties have differences to settle, they have some principles upon which they can rely, for they know that the jurisprudence of the State is based upon settled principles. Let that bench be changed by only one man, and you change the system of jurisprudence which was then existing, and thereby create an uncertainty which is instilled into the minds of the people and weaken the confidence of the people in the judiciary. They begin to look upon it as a matter of lottery, and not in the light in which the highest judicial tribunal of any State should be viewed. All parties who have their rights to be passed upon and determined, should have some confidence in the stability of the principles involved in the settlement of those rights. Your elective system will necessitate these changes, for it provides for a change every two years, in addition to the changes which the hand of nature may cause. Why is it these changes every two years are proposed? It is only because of the uncertainty as to the mutations of the principles which the people desire to prevent. It is because of the disposition of the representatives of the people to prevent stability. It is because of the popular dread which sometimes is presented of men holding office too long. That is an unsafe doctrine in the judiciary. It may apply well in the other departments of the government, but when you act upon the principle that the judiciary should not be permanent, you recognize the doctrine that the rights of the people are changeable—a doctrine which I contend is inconsistent with the truth, with the principles upon which human governments are based. I contend, Mr. President, that the great principles of right, the great principles upon which all laws should be based, are unchangeable. There may be progress in the mode of applying these principles, but that there should be progress in the principles themselves, I contend is unnatural and contrary to reason. I adopt the doctrine enunciated by the gentleman from the Fourth District, that all laws are derived originally from a great divine source, and that the laws of man, though changeable, are necessarily based upon the principles which pervade a divine law. When you depart from that, you destroy the very basis of human rights and human liberty. I will not here attempt to carry this point further, but will now endeavor to direct my attention for a few moments particularly to some of the arguments against the appointed judiciary.

It has been asserted—and I do not deny the truth of the assertion in the abstract—that all power is inherent with the people in a republican form of government. This is an axiom, and upon this axiom is based the fabric of our great government. It was an axiom, as stated by the gentleman from the Fourth District, our forefathers recognized and enforced; but I think he was peculiarly unfortunate in referring to that doctrine and its application by our forefathers themselves. What was the application which they made of that doctrine on the subject of the judiciary? Did they say that the power was inherent in the people themselves to select the Federal judges—to select their president directly? Did they say the power was inherent in the people to select their senators to the Congress of the United States? Where, in any one instance, was the practical application of that doctrine made consonant with the application the gentleman has attempted to make of it? In but one that I call to mind now, the election of members to the House of Representatives. So, while our forefathers recognized that doctrine and made it the basis of the mighty structure which they erected, the application they made of it coincided perfectly with the views which the committee have embodied in this report—that while the people may have the right, and are the source of all political power, it is not always expedient or best that they shall exercise that power directly.

I go to the next. It is asserted that the appointive judiciary is a species of monarchical despotism, and that it places too much power in the hands of one man. Mr. President, I have a hallowed respect for the memory, the intelligence and the patriotism of our forefathers. I believe, sir, they were statesmen. I believe they appreciated the principles of a republican form of government. It is from that source that I have derived my views and knowledge of the principles of a republican form of government. I wish to go to no other source; but shall it be said that they perpetuated a species of monarchical despotism upon the people of this country? Gentlemen mistake; instead of being a species of monarchical despotism, it is, in my opinion, the palladium of the rights of the people. Say what you can about the writ of habeas corpus, the trial by jury, and of the constitution, but without an independent, intelligent and elevated judiciary, these rights are but light, and the constitution is but frail indeed. The judiciary stands as a conservative principle in this and all other governments. In a monarchical form of government, the conservative principle is exercised in behalf of the people against the crown; in a republican form of government this principle stands between popular prejudice and individual rights. Instead of being a despotism, it is the protector of the people's rights, because the people feel secure if they can approach an independent, intelligent judiciary with perfect confidence that their rights will be maintained. They will feel that their rights are not dependent upon the caprices of the age or political changes. They have confidence in a judiciary thus established, and there can be no taint, no shadow of the charge of monarchical despotism in an appointive judiciary. The governor is of the people, the senate is of the people, and they represent them in making their selection. It is committed to them because it is the most easy and feasible mode of making a proper selection. This includes the other charge that it is a curse to constitutional governments.

That it places too much power in the hands of the governor can be refuted upon a moment's reflection, because upon a judiciary appointed during good behavior, but one governor—at the time of the adoption and upon the inauguration of that system—has the power and opportunity of filling the whole bench. When he shall have filled the judiciary with its incumbents the bench is complete, and the next governor may not have to make a single judicial appointment. Where, then, is the dangerous power committed by this report to the executive of the State? He has, I admit, a most onerous and responsible duty resting upon him, but the people are not distrustful, as a general thing, of their officers. The governor will be elected with reference to this very subject. The people will know that it *may be* that the governor they are to vote for will have to appoint the judges, that their rights are to be determined by those judges, and they will have the greatest inducement to make a judicious selection, to elect a discreet governor, if they remember this. They have, besides, a guarantee that their senators will have a voice in this matter. For my part, sir, I cannot see the application of remarks about "placing too much power in the hands of one man." It has failed yet to strike my mind with any terror or apprehension, perhaps owing to my bluntness or my partiality for the appointive system, and let me inform gentlemen that I recollect the time when this subject was first agitated in the State of Louisiana. I have noticed well and carefully its origin, progress and results. I was as strong an advocate for the elective system, at first, as any gentleman upon this floor; and let me here say, that possibly I may be able to correct a doubt or error as to the position of some prominent men, whose names were mentioned here yesterday. Those men were at *one* time, sir, advocates for an elective system, but those very men, after this system was tried, changed their views. It was an experiment, upon the trial of which they altered their sentiments, and I never condemn a man for honestly changing his opinion, however much I may differ from him.

My first observations were directed to the manner of conducting elections for judges of the district and supreme courts. I there witnessed the contentions, the excitement between the parties on the part of the candidates; for I must confess that the candidates did not withdraw themselves from the arena—did not withhold themselves from the polls, but mixed with the people, using the various means for securing their election. Will it be contended that this is consistent? *I* admit that it *is* wrong, and I contend that it is *inconsistent* with the dignity of the bench. I say that any system which presents such temptations to men is wrong. It is an *abuse*, I admit, but it is one which is too frequently resorted to and made use of. That men *should not do so*, we all say, but that men *have done so*, we must all admit.

It might be said, and I believe has been asserted here, that there will be fawning and cringing to the governor. If the governor be worthy of his position, when that is seen, such applicants will be hurled with contempt from his presence. Let us not suspect all men! Let us not too easily suspect our own agents, but us let so guide our own actions as to avoid all the temptations and evils to which these various systems are subject.

It is asked, "Have the people no interest in this question?" "Are they to relinquish all right to it?" "Are they to take no part in it?" I answer that they have an interest in the selection of judges—the highest interest—and for the protection of those interests I would remove the selection of judges as far from popular commotions as possible, for I have already said and believe that according to reason, the great interests of society are best subserved by such a course. I think it requires only a little reflection for any one to come to the same conclusion. It is not for the people's interest to be always running to the polls to cast their votes. Many men prefer to leave the election of certain officers to deputies and authorized agents, selected in a proper way, while they devote their attention to their private business. Whatever may be the motive, the truth is, sir, that men, generally, do not desire to exercise so constantly and so universally the right of suffrage.

Reference has been made to the debates in the convention of 1787, in which was formed that model of human genius and wisdom, the constitution of the United States; and the opinions expressed in that convention have been presented here in advocacy of the elective system. The best answer, without argument, is that those opinions failed to convince the convention. However wise the men who uttered these sentiments, they failed to convince the members of that convention, and we have as the result of their labors a judiciary system which leaves the appointment of the judges to the president of the United States, with the advice and consent of the Senate; and I hope, for the sake of the people of Louisiana, that however worthy, however intelligent and however wise the gentlemen who advocate the elective system, that they will fail to convince this Convention that their system should be adopted. I hope this because I feel an interest in the people. I claim to be one of the people, and I am, as an individual, possessed of as much regard for the rights of the people as any other man; because, if I deny the rights of the people I deny my own rights. But, I am free to confess, that I do not believe their rights to be endangered by an appointive judiciary, but that in such a system rests the surest guarantee of their safety and perpetuity.

I beg gentlemen of this Convention that they will free their minds from the prejudice which attaches to the charge, that the advocates of the appointive system denounce the common people as the common herd. They do themselves, as well as us and the people, great injustice by such a mode of argument.

It is not necessary to a rational, elevated discussion upon this question to refer to these exclamations of detraction and abuse. Let us look at the subject as men. Let us reason upon it as men of intelligence; and, for myself, I heartily repel the accusation that we denounce the people as the common herd.

It has been suggested that there might be a compromise upon this subject, and that we might leave the selection of judges to the General Assembly. I hope gentlemen will reflect well upon the operation of this compromise. The General Assembly is composed of representatives of the different parishes of the State. Now, sir, what right have the representatives from the parish of Morehouse, for instance, to appoint the judges for the parish of Orleans? The executive represents and is voted for by the whole people of the State. The Legislature is composed of men who represent different localities, and a majority of whom, consequently, have no direct interest in the selections they are called upon to make, except in the selection of a chief justice. The law directs that the State shall be divided into four districts, from each of which one of the associate judges shall be selected. Now, if the selection is left to the General Assembly the associate from one-fourth of the State is chosen by three-fourths outside of that particular district. While the representatives of only one-fourth are directly interested in the selection of that judge, the right to make the selection is controlled by the other three-fourths, who have not such direct interest in the matter. In that view, the appointment by the governor presents many advantages over the other system. The governor is elected by the people every four years, and is supposed to and does represent the whole people. In the selection of the judges for the inferior courts, he would be guided by the representation of the parishes which were interested in the appointment. The governor could not be expected to know personally the people of all the parishes, nor who was best qualified to fill the benches of the district courts, and hence he would necessarily be governed by the representatives of those districts, and instead of having the judges for the country parishes selected by the representatives of New Orleans, they would be selected by the representatives of the parishes directly interested in their selection.

Another compromise is suggested, that is, that we shall adopt the elective system now and say to the people in the next breath you are not competent to elect now. We will adopt a constitution providing for an elective system, but the operation of that clause will be postponed to some indefinite period, to which we shall arrive two years after the restoration of peace.

Mr. Campbell — All the compromise I have understood was, that I was willing to have appointive judges for the Supreme Court only for the term of ten years.

Mr. HOWELL—Will any gentleman inform me when that will be; whether speedily or only after years of war?

I trust it will come speedily; but it is certainly a time indefinite and possibly remote. And we shall present the strange incongruity of adopting a constitution with an elective system in it and at the same time denying the right of the people to execute it. These are war times, and it is impracticable and dangerous to leave this matter to the people; but I say, Mr. President, let us have a system that is practicable now; a system that shall go into immediate operation, and let the people be immediately supplied with a permanent system. This attempt to blend the two systems and to adopt the one, and provide that it shall not go into operation, are strange productions whose results have never been observed; while the appointive system supplies us with a permanent system which has long been tested—a system than which the ablest minds have never yet suggested a superior. And, sir, I contend that this is practicable now, and that it is right now, to have the judiciary permanently established.

Another element of discussion has been introduced which I regret exceedingly. It is the effort to array the people—to create a prejudice between the people and the legal profession. It is asserted that this is a contest between the people and the lawyers. There can be no difference of interest between the lawyers and the people on this question. Are not the lawyers dependent on the people for their business and employment? And I should not be surprised to learn, that the very gentlemen themselves who are attempting to excite this prejudice, were the very first when they get into trouble to go to the lawyers for assistance. Will they not commit to these very lawyers all their rights of property and reputation? Such arguments are unworthy a deliberative body.

Mr. President, let us be men, conscious of our own dignity and the true nature and magnitude of the work before us. Let us appreciate the progress and logic of events. Let us realize the momentous fact, that in the full glow of civilization, with the accumulated experience of ages, with all the wealth of the past, we, foremost in the files of time, have been called to the exalted business of nation-making. Let us bear in mind that in the work so boldly and wisely entered upon by the great and grand men of the past century and continued by their illustrious successors, some unsound materials were admitted into the structure, and that, as master-builders, engaged with others, it is our task, in this apartment of the common edifice, to remove whatever is tainted with unsoundness and add that which is solid and enduring.

Yes, sir, a nation is in process of completion, and all its parts must be fitly joined together, and the symmetry of the whole perfected. In one of the epochs of that process, the sword and the bayonet became necessary to clear away some obstructions, and the work here is now committed to our hands, and we owe it to the people, to humanity, to see that it is well done, and that from this Hall shall go forth the proclamation to the world that Louisiana, reconstructed, is an inseparable integral portion of this mighty nation, and the sure abiding place of the eternal principles of freedom and justice.

Mr. ORR—Mr. President—

PRESIDENT—The debate is closed. It was the understanding that Mr. Howell was to close the debate.

Mr. ORR—I had no such understanding, Mr. President, or I might have submitted a few remarks sooner.

PRESIDENT—I believe it was the understanding yesterday, that Mr. Howell was to have the close of the debate.

Mr. ABELL—There was no such understanding. The only understanding was that—

Mr. SULLIVAN—As the mover of the amendment, I had the right to close the debate. I delegate that right to Mr. Orr.

Mr. TERRY—That is right. Mr. Sullivan offered the amendment under debate, and has the right to close.

Mr. SULLIVAN—I do not delegate my right to close to Mr. Orr, but will reserve it.

Mr. ORR—Mr. President, after the many

able remarks that have been made upon the important question—that of the organization of the judiciary of this State—now before this Convention, it may be presumptuous on my part to say aught; but deeming it to be the duty of every member of this body to define his position upon questions of importance that may come before it, I shall not hesitate to perform what I consider to be my duty in the matter. In regard to this question of the judiciary lengthy arguments, containing strong and positive points, may and can be adduced on either side. Those who support the appointive side of the question will contend that an appointive judiciary will be more pure, honest and capable than the other. Now I would ask the advocates of this if the persons to whom may be delegated the appointive power are proof against corrupt influences? If a governor or a legislature, elected possibly by corrupt partisan influences, will seek out for appointment men of pure principles? or is it not more reasonable to suppose that the watchword of party, "to the victors belong the spoils," will be adopted, and the qualifications required will be the number of votes that have been cast in favor of the elected by the aspirant's friends? In regard to the possibility of rebels, copperheads, and thugs of that nature voting for judges, I would ask if it is not possible, aye even probable, that this same class of people would vote for governor or for the legislature? Mr. President, in my humble opinion, the people of this State are fully as competent to elect judges as they are to elect a governor or any other office of the government. Now, sir, if it is admitted that the people are competent to choose by ballot the law-making power, why not competent to choose the persons to administer these laws? Supposing, sir, that the appointive system is adopted, and for the position of supreme judge there comes before the executive the claims of two candidates for the position, one of them a man of limited legal knowledge and of principle of a questionable character, but possessing a political influence that has been successfully used in securing the election of the executive; the other aspirant a man of undoubted character, of superior legal attainment, of profound judgment—in fact, possessing all the ennobling virtues of manhood, but possessing no political influence, or who, perhaps, opposed the election of the executive—which is the most likely to receive the appointment? There can be but one answer: the politician would be appointed.

Mr. Howell tells us that he hopes that Louisiana will never elect any but an honest governor. I will ask the honorable gentleman if Thomas Overton Moore was an honest governor? If he was not elected by the people—thugs, know-nothings and *United Americans* included? If, in the past, a dishonest governor has been elected, what surety have we that such again will not be the case?

And what kind of a judiciary might we have expected if their appointment had been left to Thomas Overton Moore, though Moore himself was not such a bad man, but he was not the governor? The government was really in the hands of Moise and two or three others.

And John Slidell, with his immense wealth, it is well known, was in the habit, in days past, of corrupting our legislatures. Well, all the John Slidells are not dead yet. We have others in the State yet—we have other Moores, we have other Moises, too, and what guarantee have we that these men will not some day fill the same position and be called upon to make these appointments of judges? Now, I contend that we have no right to take away from the people the right to elect their own judges. They have the right to elect every officer from the governor down to the very lowest. And it is the height of injustice to take from them this right and place it in hands where it is liable to be abused.

The honorable member (Mr. Wenck) read Mr. Abell's tract, showing wherein he (Mr. Abell) stated to his constituents that he would advocate an appointive judiciary. If he (the gentleman) had read the concluding clause of that tract, he would have informed the honorable members of this Convention that Mr. Abell also promised to advocate to increase the pay of policemen. Now, which class of his constituents elected him, the advocates of an appointive judiciary, or the police force, the advocates of increased pay?

I will now touch up my friend, Mr. Howell, a little.

He asks: "How many of the members of this Convention personally knew the candidates for supreme judge for whom they have voted?" I answer the question by asking another. How many personally knew the man they voted for for governor? and how many will personally know hereafter the men they vote for for governor or for the legislature?

The same gentleman says that the interests of the people are no better subserved by an appointive than by an elective judiciary. I contend that their interests are better subserved by an elective than by an appointive system.

He tells us that a governor elected for a term of four years may not have the appointment of a single judge, while, according to the gentleman's own figures, the next may appoint a half dozen. He refers to instances where the candidates were at the polls mixing with the people. Is there any harm in that? Is it such a sin for the candidates for the supreme bench to mix with the people, whose servants they are, and whose interests they are elected to subserve? And for this cause, because candidates, if the office is elective and not appointive, will mix with the people, he would remove their selection for the position as far as possible from the people.

There has been a good deal said about judges and candidates for judgeships who would, if the position was elective, visit all kinds of grogshops and resorts of loafers and vagabonds for the sake of securing votes. Admit, for the sake of argument, that this is true, that they will do it, and I shall hold that the matter is not mended by appointing the judges. For instance, my friend, Smith, is a candidate for governor; his friend, Jones, in order to secure his (Smith's) election, is in the habit of going around to these miserable hells, groceries, beershops, and burning his inwards with bad whiskey to make votes for Smith. Smith is elected. Jones, as a reward for his self-sacrifice, demands a judgeship. Now which, let me ask, is the worst, for a man to visit these places on his own account, or for another man? I say "let every tub stand on its own bottom," whether it is a whiskey tub or a tub of another kind. If it is necessary for men to make whiskey barrels of themselves in order to secure elections, let every man do his own portion of the work for himself and not saddle it upon another, and give him the power to reward by a fat office for a life-time with a large salary as a compensation for his self-sacrifice.

We have a good illustration of the efficacy, uprightness and loyalty to the interests of the people, in the judiciary of South Carolina—that State that first trampled upon the flag of our fathers, the glorious emblem of that liberty which they bequeathed to us. There, in South Carolina, they have ever regarded the people as incompetent to elect their own judges.

Gentlemen, do you wish to place the people of this State in the humiliating position that is contemplated by this appointive system? Shall the people of Louisiana go before the governor and the General Assembly, and on bended knees say to those gentlemen, "pray, dear sirs, hear our petitions, give ear, now, to our supplications, and appoint a judge to rule over us, for we are incompetent in and of ourselves to choose one from among us to fill with becoming dignity that honorable and important position?" Would you place the people of Louisiana in so humiliating a position before the civilized world?

We consider ourselves capable, we consider ourselves competent, to elect our governor, our General Assembly, and our national Congress. We are capable, we are competent to elect our own judges.

If we are not, we are not competent to elect the appointing power.

Some gentlemen have argued that the qualifications required of a judge are almost superhuman; that a man must be endowed with powers almost godlike in order to be able to comprehend and expound the law. My answer to this is, that if the laws are so intricate and abstruse that it requires a superhuman intellect to unravel them, for

God's sake, and for the sake of the people who are legally bound to understand them or take the legal consequences, repeal them, and the sooner it is done the better, and let us adopt laws so plain that the wayfaring man, though a fool, need not err therein, and that he who runs may read them.

Mr. MORRIS—Mr. President, I have not consumed the time of this honorable body, in any instance as yet, but, sir, the subject of the judiciary as reported by the able committee, and amendments offered, is of the present and succeeding, and as I conceive of articles of grave importance, and should be well considered before we say to the people, in the organic law, that we shall submit to them that are not competent to elect their judicial officers; and with all due deference to the wisdom, talent, learning and experience of the committee, I most respectfully differ as to the mode of choosing our judicial officers.

Therefore, Mr. President, I desire to make some brief statements why I am in favor of an elective judiciary, and opposed to an appointing power. We are a people occupying a portion of the earth, wish a government of our own choosing, in which the people is the source of all power.

It is a government which springs directly from the people, republican in its nature, in which the interest, rights, opinions and commands of the people should not only constitute the guiding but the original power, and no man who is a member of this social compact, be his position ever so humble, should be deprived of the high privilege of participating in the selection of the officers that are to adjudge and decree upon his rights and destinies in our municipal corporations as States.

Mr. President, all the States that have framed or revised constitutions since the year 1840, within my knowledge, have provided for an elective judiciary.

Municipal ideas having become more generally diffused throughout the more civilized portions of the world, the people, the mass are beginning to feel their might and to claim their right. Now, Mr. Presi-dent, will this Convention conceive to itself more wisdom on the judiciary department than all the conventions of the sister States of the twenty-four years past? I think not. Or, are we, as a people inhabiting the State that encircles the mouth of the great river Mississippi, so steeped in degradation that we are not qualified to step up to the ballot box, the very palladium of liberty under all circumstances, and there cast our voice?

If so, may the All-wise Creator of the Universe bring about a renovation, and may we be enabled to shake off this lethargy of degeneration, and come forth as becomes citizens of a free, independent and republican government, honest in our intentions, upright in our purposes. We have a republican government by name, let us have one in essence.

Mr. President, in this enlightened age—in this, the latter part of the nineteenth century, while the discoveries and sciences are developing and progressing—must we acknowledge and believe that man is retrograding—that we are unqualified to perform the duties to-day that we have heretofore performed? Sir, I cannot come to such conclusions.

Mr. President, the right upon which we stand is the right of opinion. God gives to us the power to form opinions. and the organic or constitutional law of our State should secure to us the right to act upon those opinions; and the constitution of the State should be so formed as to confer upon every citizen their independent and intelligent action upon all matters appertaining to their interest. And for such rights, Mr. President, I shall ever contend while I have the honor to represent my constituents. Therefore I shall not vote for any provisions, clause or clauses in a constitution that deprives us of such high prerogatives as the selection of the officers in a judicial or any other capacity that are to preside over us. I am opposed to the creature being above its creator.

Mr. President, with all the lights of the present day before us, I, for one, fear not to trust the people. If they are true to themselves, they will elect good and intelligent officers to preside over their interest, rights and destinies; if they do not, he burden is upon their own shoulders, and they will remedy the evil when the opportunity comes.

Our government being a democracy, we should have the right left to the voice of the people to elect all the officers, in the judicial or any other department, so far as pertains to our State institutions.

Mr. President, should this Convention hand over to the people a constitution for adoption, with a retrogade step in it, abridging their rights in the elective franchise, sir, it will be rejected by them ; and we, as a deliberative body, held up to public gaze as men behind the age in which we live, who had given birth to an illegitimate issue, that a republican people would not recognize.

Mr. President, we should recollect, the constitution framed by the wisdom of this honorable body has to run the race over the track of adoption and rejection, and if we encumber it with too much dead weight, with the numerous riders that we have already mounted in the legislative department, rejection will come out first, and, sir, we will be where we commenced, with the public purse minus from $100,000 to $200,000.

Mr. President, with all due respect to this honorable body, it appears to me, that one among the first things we did was to attend to our own interest. Secondly, that we intend attending to the interest of the office-holders. Well, Mr. President, the people will have the consolation of increased taxation. If that satisfies them, it will all be right.

Mr. President. we should, as a people, acknowledge no original source of inequality and primary element of power, or inequality of sagacity.

With the vast majority of persons the sentiment of self-comparison is sufficiently satisfied by being allowed an equal right with others.

Every good citizen, whether good by nature or good by education, like all benevolent men, is content with acknowledged and admitted equality politically, and he does not ask any exclusive right of speaking and deciding for the rest of his fellow-beings, but relies on his own personal possession of some of the original elements of power.

Though undoubtedly there are always to be found, in democratic and republican government as in the social circle, a certain class to whom the condition of equality is irksome—men in whom the desire of superiority is strong while the sentiment of benevolence is weak—however they may be possessed with an over-weaning idea of their own wisdom and virtue and their opinions of others probably not so favorable. But a great many men of superior capacity, when they chance to live under a popular form of government, are very generally the greatest admirers and warmest supporters of those popular forms, for the obvious reason that those forms, and those forms alone, open a high road to merit and talent.

At the present time we have a bright example in the chief executive of the United States.

It is not such men who are filled with fears lest the people should fall under the exclusive control of mere flattering demagogues.

Though they may never have investigated the subject scientifically, and may therefore be unable clearly to state how they know it, yet they know well that admiration is the true basis of political influence, and they know, too, that in order to excite admiration there must be an actual or apparent superiority of some sort or other, the place of which all the demagogues in the world can never supply.

It is the fundamental idea of Rousseau's famous essay on the social contract that there exists in the numerical majority of the people an exclusive right to control the community, so much so that they regard the democratic form alone legitimate and all other governments as mere usurpations.

The majority have the right to appoint and select their agents that they desire to carry on the government.

Mr. Foley—Mr. President, I move to adjourn.

[The motion was lost by a rising vote—ayes 21, noes 33.]

Mr. Cazabat—Mr. President, as there seems to be no quorum, I move a call of the House.

[The roll was called and only 73 members answered to their names.]

PRESIDENT — The sergeant-at-arms will bring in absent members.

Mr. FOLEY—Mr. President, I move to adjourn.

Mr. TERRY—I call the ayes and noes.

[The call was sustained, and the roll called with the following result—ayes 30, noes 33.

The motion was lost.

After half an hour's delay a sufficient number of members to constitute a quorum was brought in by the sergeant-at-arms.

The question on the adoption of the substitute of Mr. Sullivan for the third article of the report of the Committee on the Judiciary was put and lost.]

PRESIDENT — The question now recurs upon the third article of the report.

Mr. MONTAMAT—Mr. President, I have an amendment to offer.

PRESIDENT—You are too late. Amendments are not in order.

Mr. MONTAMAT—I merely wish to amend—

PRESIDENT—You are out of order. The question is on the adoption of article 3 of the report of the Committee on the Judiciary.

Mr. ABELL—Mr. President, I do not see how it is that amendments are not in order now——

[The yeas and nays were called and the secretary proceeded to call the roll.]

Mr. PURSELL—I rise to explain my vote. I considered that Mr. Montamat's amendment was in order until the last moment. I vote no.

Mr. BELL—I am in favor of the first two lines, but not of the salary, consequently I shall vote no.

Mr. FLOOD—I don't vote for the ten thousand dollars, but I vote for all the balance.

Mr. FOLEY—I am opposed to paying any judge a higher salary than the governor receives. I vote no.

Mr. HILLS—Mr. President, I am in favor of the article as reported, but as I believe that gentlemen have a right to offer amendments to it, I vote no.

Mr. MONTAMAT—I am in favor of an appointive judiciary, but as I wanted to offer an amendment, and was choked off by the chair, I vote no.

PRESIDENT—I wish to state to those whose votes have been influenced by the action of the chair, that parliamentary rules must be enforced, or there will be no end to amendments. There have been three amendments and one substitute, all acted on in their regular order, and voted down, until now we come back to the original report. If gentlemen fail in their duty in this respect, and keep back their amendments until it is too late to offer them, they cannot expect the chair to fail in his duties because they have in theirs.

Mr. ORR—I am opposed to an aristocratic judiciary; judges—[cries of out of order! Vote! vote!]—with aristocratic salaries of ten thousand dollars a year. I vote no.

Mr. SMITH—I am in favor of the salary, but not of the appointive system. I vote no.

Mr. STOCKER—I am opposed to the whole article. I want the people to have the power of making the judges. I therefore vote no.

Mr. SULLIVAN—As I am opposed to the monarchical principle of the bill, I vote no.

Mr. WENCK—As I am in favor of an independent judiciary, with good salaries, I vote yes.

[The following is the result of the vote—ayes 30, noes 46.]

Mr. FOLEY—I move to adjourn.

[The motion was carried.]

WEDNESDAY, June 1, 1864.

[The Convention met pursuant to adjournment. The roll was called by the secretary, and the following members answered to their names:]

Messrs. Ariail, Austin, Balch, Baum, Barrett, Buckley, Burke, Campbell, Cook J. K., Collin, Decker, Dufresne, Duke, Edwards, Flagg, Flood, Fuller, Geier, Goldman, Gorlinski, Gruneberg, Healy, Heard, Hills, Howell, Howes, Mann, Montamat, Newell, Normand, O'Conner, Pintado, Poynot, Pursell S., Schroeder, Schnurr, Shaw, Spellicy, Stumpf, Stiner, Stauffer, Sullivan, Wells and Mr. President—44.

[There being no quorum present, the sergeant-at-arms was directed to procure the attendance of absent members.

After some delay the following gentlemen entered and took their seats: Messrs. Abell, Bailey, Beauvais, Bell, Bofill, Brott, Bromley, Crozat, Cutler, Duane, Fish, Foley, Fosdick, Gastinel, Hart, Henderson, Hire, Kavanagh, Maas, Mayer, Mendiverri, Morris, Murphy M. W., Ong, Orr, Purcell J., Smith, Stocker, Terry, Thorpe, Waters, Wenck, Wilson—33.

The president announced that a quorum was present.

The minutes were read and after some slight corrections adopted.

Under the resolution of yesterday, the order of the day was taken up and article 4 of the judiciary report read.

Mr. Stocker moved to reconsider the vote of yesterday rejecting article 3; but he having voted in the minority it was ruled not in order.]

Mr. MONTAMAT—I move to reconsider that vote. I voted in the majority.

[The motion was carried.]

Mr. MONTAMAT—I wish to offer the following amendment to article 3:

"Seven thousand five hundred dollars," instead of "ten thousand dollars," as the salary of the chief justice, and "seven thousand dollars," instead of "nine thousand dollars," as the salary per annum of the associate justices.

Mr. ABELL—I move to amend by striking out $7500 and inserting $10,000.

Mr. STINER—I move to amend by striking out $7500 and substituting $8000.

[On motion, the last amendment was laid on the table.

Mr. Abell withdrew his amendment.]

Mr. THORPE—I offer as an amendment: "The salaries of all the judges shall be fixed by the Legislature."

Mr. MONTAMAT—I move to lay it on the table.

[Carried—yeas 33, nays 31.

The original amendment was then read.]

Mr. HILLS—I move to lay it on the table.

[The roll was called and the motion lost.]

YEAS—Messrs. Abell, Balch, Baum, Bailey, Bromley, Brott, Collin, Cook J. K., Davies, Decker, Duane, Dufresne, Duke, Edwards, Flood, Foley, Fosdick, Gorlinski, Healy, Hills, Hire, Howell, Howes, Murphy M. W., Normand, O'Conner, Orr, Poynot, Schroeder, Smith, Spellicy, Stocker, Terry, Thorpe, Wenck, Wilson—36.

NAYS—Messrs. Ariail, Austin, Barrett, Beauvais, Bofill, Buckley, Burke, Campbell, Cazabat, Crozat, Cutler, Fish, Flagg, Fuller, Gastinel, Geier, Goldman, Gruneberg, Hart, Heard, Maas, Mann, Meyer, Montamat, Morris, Newell, Ong, Pintado, Purcell J., Pursell S., Schnurr, Seymour, Shaw, Stumpf, Stiner, Stauffer, Sullivan, Waters, Wells—39.

[It was stated there was no quorum voting, and a call of the House demanded, upon which the roll was called and seventy-seven gentlemen responded.

Mr. PURSELL—I offer an amendment, inserting after the word "be," in the second line, the words "increased or."

[Accepted.

The article as amended was then adopted.

The following articles were separately read, and adopted as reported:]

Art. 4. The Supreme Court shall hold its sessions in New Orleans from the first Monday of the month of November to the end of the month of June, inclusive. The Legislature shall have power to fix the sessions elsewhere during the rest of the year; until otherwise provided, the sessions shall be held as heretofore.

Art. 5. The Supreme Court and each of the judges thereof shall have power to issue writs of *habeas corpus*, at the instance of all persons in actual custody under process, in all cases in which they may have appellate jurisdiction.

Art. 6. No judgment shall be rendered by the Supreme Court without the concurrence of a majority of the judges comprising the court. Whenever the majority cannot agree, in consequence of the recusation of any member or members of the court, the judges not recused shall have power to call upon any judge or judges of the inferior courts, whose duty it shall be, when so called upon, to sit in the place of the judge or judges recused, and to aid in determining the case.

Art. 7. All judges, by virtue of their office, shall be conservators of the peace throughout the State. The style of all process shall be "the State of Louisiana." All prosecutions shall be carried on in the name and by the authority of the State of Louisiana, and conclude against the peace and dignity of the same.

Art. 8. The judges of all courts within the State shall, as often as it may be possible so to do, in every definitive judgment refer to the particular law in virtue of which such judgment may be rendered, and in all cases adduce the reasons on which their judgment is founded.

[Article 9 was read:]

Art. 9. The judges of all courts shall be

liable to impeachment; but for any reasonable cause, which shall not be sufficient ground for impeachment, the governor shall remove any of them, on the address of three-fourths of the members present in each House of the General Assembly. In every such case the cause or causes for which such removal may be required shall be stated at length in the address, and inserted in the journal of each House.

Mr. CAMPBELL—I move to strike out "two-thirds" and insert "a majority."

Mr. CAZABAT—I move to lay it on the table.

[Lost, and the amendment adopted.]

Mr. STOCKER—I move to amend by striking out the words "present in" and inserting "elected to."

[The amendment was carried and the article adopted as amended.

Article 10 was read:]

Art. 10. The judges both of the supreme and inferior courts shall, at stated times, receive a salary which shall not be diminished during their continuance in office; and they are prohibited from receiving any fees of office or other compensation than their salaries for any civil duties performed by them.

Mr. S. PURSELL—I wish to amend by making the second line read, "which shall not be increased nor diminished," etc.

[A motion to lay the amendment on the table was lost—yeas 18, nays 46.]

Mr. ABELL—I know of no precedent that absolutely fixes in the constitution the salary of the judges; but it has generally been incorporated that it shall not be diminished during the term of office. I trust the Convention will leave this matter to the discretion of the Legislature, so far as increasing the salaries is concerned. It is manifest that the judges should receive an ample salary, though as to the exact amount, there is a diversity of opinion; but, surely, all will agree that there should be an ample salary given to the judges. If we should leave this entirely to the caprice of the Legislature, they might reduce it in order to drive the judges from the bench. The currency of the country is becoming depreciated, and it may go so low as to render it impossible to get judges on the bench if the amendment is adopted. It seems to me that it would be improper in us to say that the salaries of the judges shall not be increased. The judges of the Supreme Court of the United States stand precisely on the ground taken by the report, that the salaries shall not be diminished. If the matter is left as reported, the judges cannot get more unless by the action of the Legislature. The men composing that body come directly from the people, and, certainly, never will increase the salaries af the judges unless it was necessary. If there be a necessity for it, I think we should leave the door open to allow them to comply with the necessity. For these reasons I hope the amendment will be rejected.

Mr. HENDERSON—The report says the salaries of the judges shall not be diminished, and the amendment of Mr. Pursell provides that they shall neither be increased nor diminished during the time they hold their offices. I think the subject should be left to the Legislature. Therefore, the report of the committee that the salaries shall not be diminished, is the proper way. The constitution of the United States is a good precedent. The chief justice and the associate justices of the Supreme Court of the United States have had their salaries increased within a few years, because the sum they had previously received was not sufficient under a different state of things. The duties of the judiciary are very important, and provision should be made for their adequate compensation under all circumstances.

Mr. HOWELL—I wish to state to the gentleman who moved the amendment, that it may operate unjustly to the public. Suppose the Legislature should find it necessary to lessen the number of justices, and increase the extent of their territory, as has been done. Their labors are increased, and consequently their salaries should be increased. It was done within the last five years—in 1861, I think. The report contemplates that the Legislature shall fix the salaries of the district judges throughout the State. If, at any time, the interests of the country should demand that the number of judicial districts be lessened, and the labor of the judges increased, it would be just in such a contingency to increase their salaries, and for that reason I think the report is correct, and that the amendment may operate to the prejudice of the people of the State.

[The amendment was then put and lost.]

Mr. MONTAMAT—I offer as an amendment, that the judges of the inferior courts shall receive a salary of $5000 per annum.

Mr. STOCKER—I consider the amendment entirely out of order. In rejecting the last amendment we have virtually said that the salaries may be increased. If we adopt the amendment of the gentleman, we go back to the question just put.

PRESIDENT—Will the gentleman permit me to make a remark. The constitution provides for the existence of the supreme court. The Legislature may see fit not to have district courts, and may call for other courts; therefore the amendment is not necessary.

Mr. MONTAMAT—If that is the case I withdraw my amendment.

[Article 10 was then adopted.

Article 11 was read, and the substitute and amendment:]

Art. 11. The judges, both of the supreme and inferior courts, shall be appointed by the governor, by and with the advice and consent of the Senate, and they shall hold their offices during good behavior.

[Mr. Stauffer's substitute:]

The judges of the supreme court shall be elected by joint vote of the General Assembly, and for a term of ten years. They shall have power to appoint their own clerks.

[Mr. Montamat's amendment:]

Art. 11. The judges, both of the supreme and inferior courts, shall be appointed by the governor, by and with the advice and consent of the Senate, for the term of eight years. And it shall be the duty of the governor, at the end of each term, to submit to the Senate the names of the occupants to be continued in office or rejected.

Mr. CAZABAT—I move to lay the substitute and amendment on the table.

[The roll was called, and the motion lost:]

YEAS — Messrs. Ariail, Bailey, Baum, Beauvais, Bofill, Burke, Cazabat, Crozat, Cutler, Duane, Fish, Flagg, Fuller, Geier, Heard, Hire, Howell, Mayer, Newell, Normand, Ong, Poynot, Purcell J., Schnurr, Seymour, Stumpf, Thorpe, Waters, Wenck, Wells, Wilson—31.

NAYS—Messrs. Abell, Austin, Balch, Bell, Bromley, Brott, Buckley, Campbell, Collin, Cook J. K., Cook T., Decker, Dufresne, Duke, Edwards, Flood, Foley, Fosdick, Gastinel, Goldman, Gorlinski, Gruneberg, Hart, Henderson, Healy, Hills, Howes, Maas, Mann, Mendiverri, Montamat, Morris, Murphy M. W., O'Conner, Orr, Pintado, Pursell S., Shaw, Smith, Spellicy, Stocker, Stauffer, Stiner, Sullivan, Terry—45.

[Mr. Montamat withdrew his amendment, with the consent of the member seconding it.]

Mr. GRUNEBERG—I move to amend the substitute by striking out "They shall have power to appoint their own clerks."

[The amendment was accepted.

On the motion to adopt the substitute, the roll was called, and the substitute rejected by the following vote:]

YEAS—Messrs. Bell, Buckley, Campbell, Cook T., Decker, Dufresne, Duke, Flagg, Gastinel, Geier, Goldman, Gruneberg, Howes, Mayer, Morris, O'Conner, Orr, Poynot, Sullivan, Schnurr, Smith, Stocker, Stauffer, Terry—24.

NAYS—Messrs. Abell, Ariail, Austin, Barrett, Balch, Bailey, Baum, Beauvais, Bofill, Bromley, Brott, Burke, Cazabat, Cook J. K., Collin, Crozat, Cutler, Duane, Edwards, Fish, Flood, Foley, Fosdick, Fuller, Gorlinski, Hart, Healy, Heard, Hills, Howell, Henderson, Hire, Howell, Maas, Mendiverri, Mann, Montamat, Murphy M. W., Newell, Normand, Ong, Pintado, Purcell J., Pursell S., Shaw, Seymour, Spellicy, Stumpf, Stiner, Thorpe, Waters, Wells, Wenck, Wilson—53.

[Mr. Sullivan's amendment was then taken up, and the yeas and nays being ordered thereon, resulted as follows:]

YEAS—Messrs. Bell, Buckley, Campbell, Collin, Cook J. K., Cook T., Decker, Duke, Flagg, Flood, Geier, Goldman, Gorlinski, Gruneberg, Howes, Maas, O'Conner, Orr, Poynot, Pursell S., Smith, Spellicy, Stocker, Stauffer, Sullivan, Terry—26.

NAYS—Messrs. Abell, Ariail, Austin, Balch, Barrett, Bailey, Baum, Beauvais, Bromley, Bofill, Brott, Burke, Cazabat, Crozat, Cutler, Duane, Dufresne, Edwards, Fish, Fosdick, Foley, Fuller, Gastinel, Hart, Healy, Hills, Heard, Henderson, Hire, Howell, Maas, Mann, Mendiverri, Montamat, Morris, Murphy M. W., Newell, Normand, Ong, Pintado, Purcell J., Schnurr, Shaw, Stiner, Seymour, Stumpf, Thorpe, Waters, Wenck, Wells, Wilson—51.

[Consequently the amendment was rejected.]

Mr. SHAW—I have an amendment which I wish to offer; striking out all after the word "Senate" and inserting, "The judges of the Supreme Court shall hold their offices during a term of six years, and those of the district courts during a term of four years."

Mr. HILLS—I rise to say a word in favor of the amendment. I have not taken any part in the discussion of this important question thus far, because I preferred to leave it to those who had a better understanding of it than I felt I possessed. From the first I have been in favor of the system of appointment, for I have seen what seems to me to be very great and serious evils arise from the system of elected judges. At the same time I believe there should be a limit to the term for which the judges are appointed. One gentleman has remarked in his very able argument on this subject, that all we can do is to provide, as far as possible, against the evils which will necessarily arise from all human institutions, which are imperfect in their very nature. While I believe that the appointive system is far superior to the elective, at the same time the system of appointment is also subject to imperfections, and under it we are liable to have bad and incompetent men placed on the bench, and I believe in having a remedy by which they can be removed. I think the proposition of the gentleman provides for such a contingency. If we have a bad judge, we do not want him saddled on the people for life, nor to go through the tedious process of impeachment, which frequently fails; when, if justice was done, the judge would be impeached. Therefore, I say, fix a limit to his term of office. I would agree and preferred to have made it eight years, and had prepared an amendment, but I am ready, nevertheless, to support the proposition, and limit the term of the judges of the Supreme Court to six years, and of the inferior courts to four years, and hope it will prevail.

Mr. SHAW—I wish to say the amendment has nothing to do with the manner of choosing the judges; but only limits the term of their office.

Mr. ABELL—Is this debatable? [Question, question.] Gentlemen, you have been skirmishing in this matter for some time, but this is where the battle comes in. This is the main battle; now mark what I tell you—[cries of question, question—don't debate it.] I hope gentlemen will not pass upon this question without considering it well. A little time spent here would be better spent perhaps than anywhere else. It involves more than everything else that is to follow it, except, perhaps, the public school system, and I will, with the consent of the Convention, make a few more arguments against the proposition of the gentleman from the Fourth District, (Mr. Shaw,) and that of the gentleman from the Second, (Mr. Hills,) because these propositions, if adopted, will at once strike down all that stability and all that certainty which has ever been the boast and will ever be the boast of countries that have a permanent and independent judiciary.

We have reduced the matter to a very narrow point. The question now is upon the length of time that judges shall hold their offices, for if the action of this body yesterday is any criterion of its future action, the judges are to be appointed, for we yesterday twice so decided.

Mr. STOCKER—I call the gentleman to order. That question has not been decided.

PRESIDENT—He is in order.

Mr. ABELL—That question, as I said, has twice been decided by the vote on Sullivan's amendments, and another vote equally important taken yesterday. That question being decided, forces the issue, as we say in the common law, by bringing the question down to a single point: What shall be the tenure by which our judges are to hold their offices? I say that this Convention decided yesterday, by an overwhelming vote, that the elective system is laid upon the table. It is therefore settled that we are to have an appointive judiciary, and the only question is simply that of the tenure of the office appointive, as we have decided to make it. And both these amendments are designed to make the tenure short; the one is better than the other only as it makes the tenure longer.

Mr. STOCKER—The question is simply upon the term, not the tenure.

PRESIDENT—The gentleman is in order and must not be interrupted.

Mr. STOCKER—I appeal from the decision of the chair.

Mr. ABELL—The term I have understood to be the tenure, and that I understand now upon these amendments to be the question involved. One gives a little longer tenure than the other, but otherwise there is no difference between that of the gentleman from the Fourth District, [Mr. Shaw,] and that of my friend from the Second, [Mr. Hills.] It is simply a question of policy, whether you adopt one or the other. You will find, gentlemen, that the article as presented by the majority of the committee, the judges, both Supreme and inferior courts, shall be appointed by the governor, by and with the advice and consent of the Senate, and shall hold their offices during good behavior. This is the tenure proposed by the original article, as reported by the committee. That is the tenure that I have contended for, from the commencement of this discussion. And, sir, as I will show to gentlemen on this floor, it is the tenure that I contended for long before the assembling of this Convention. I wish to show you, gentlemen, that it is not only during the sessions of this Convention that I have publicly advocated this tenure, but that before that time I advocated those principles before the people, and that they were ratified in my election by the largest vote, perhaps, of any individual in the parish of Orleans. I was elected, sir, by a larger majority than the gentlemen on the same ticket with me, and my views upon the judiciary thereby fully ratified; and when I read from the card I circulated among the voters of the Fifth District before the election, you will say whether this is with me a new-fangled idea or not:

If elected, I would favor a judiciary appointed by the executive, by and with the advice and consent of the Senate, to hold office during good behavior, with ample salaries, and removable by impeachment only.

Mr. TERRY—Will the gentleman permit me to ask him a question?

Mr. ABELL—Certainly.

Mr. TERRY—Will he read a little further on his "circular?"

Mr. ABELL—Certainly, I will; but it has nothing to do with the question. [Reads:]

I will advocate strenuously a permanent police organization for this metropolis, to consist of permanent citizens, of good character, to hold office during good behavior, with salaries never to be less than eighty dollars per month, and removable only by charges preferred before a committee, to be appointed by the executive for the purpose, subject to an appeal to the Board of Aldermen; when discharged never again to be eligible, and with suitable provisions for those who may be disabled in the faithful discharge of their duties. The safety and credit of this city and justice to a faithful officer demand greater certainty than now exist.

Mr. TERRY—That is not the portion to which I referred. I had reference to that portion relating to making the term of office of the governor six years, and the election of the present incumbent by the Convention. I did not refer to the police.

Mr. FOLEY—He's right on that.

Mr. ABELL—I have no objection to that portion of the circular, but it has nothing to do with the question. The gentleman need not be alarmed; I'll give him a touch in a minute. I presented these views to the people; they knew that these were my principles, and they ratified them by an overwhelming vote.

I was not a member of this Judiciary Committee. I had nothing to do with it; was not consulted by the committee who presented it, but it meets my views of the subject perfectly and to the fullest extent.

It is certainly most desirable, on account of the grand future before our State, that the utmost certainty should be attached to our judiciary system. Our position is such that we must eventually become one of the greatest and grandest States of this Union, and our judiciary should be in keeping with our progress. But what will be the effect of these amendments? We have from time to time discussed the great misfortune of the election of the judges. I think that the experience of the State has been that an elective judiciary has proved a failure and a disgrace to the State from the time of its inauguration up to the present day. Search the records and you will find the proofs of what I say, that it has proved a disgrace to the State. You will find that they never made any decisions of great principles, they never evinced any signs of progress forward, or gave any evidence of that improvement attainable by experience. Why is this? What reason can you assign for it? Sir, the reason is manifest. They had no certainty of remaining in office more than a single term. They had not that incentive to make themselves thorough and superior in their positions, and the time for which they were elected was not sufficient for it had they all the incentive that could be placed before the mind of men anxious to become celebrated in their position.

Show me an instance where a judge, within the last twenty years—since the elective system was adopted in Louisiana—that has made his mark. Not a solitary instance can you point out. No solitary judge has left that mark that is attainable, and will be attainable, and will present itself so soon as you shall have established the judiciary upon correct principles. To reach this result the judiciary must not only be established on the appointive system, but the tenure must not be uncertain. No sooner than a man is appointed a judge with a life tenure than all the power of the governor over him is expended and he stands, with regard to the judge, as one of the most humble persons. His power is expended in making the appointment. He cannot remove, and the judge having nothing to fear from the authority of the appointing power, or the caprice of the people, stands independent in his sphere, with nothing in the way of his advancement to the highest pinnacle of glory which is attainable by application during a long, uninterrupted and independent career.

After he is once appointed by the governor he is not necessarily looking forward to the end of his term of four years and devising ways and means to secure an appointment for another term. He is in fact as far removed from the governor as from the humblest individual in the State. He meets none of those hindrances to progress and advancement that beset the path of the judge elected or appointed for a short term.

Gentlemen, I ask you to look at this matter for your own good, and for the good of your constituents, and say whether it is not better to avoid the evils of an elective system and of short term appointments, and to secure an independent judiciary by appointing your judges for life?

The first year or two perhaps these judges, so appointed, may not evince any striking evidences of superiority; but in a few years they will have marched forward, and will stand in the foremost ranks of advancement in legal science, though they may not, at the date of their appointment, have been particularly distinguished either as lawyers or jurists. Though they may never have shown any extraordinary degree of ability, they will overcome every obstacle, and, if they be only good, respectable men, they will become great, because their minds will be free from everything else, and they will look only to the glory and honor of the people.

It is argued that men holding for life terms will become corrupt. The argument is bad. True, there may be corrupt men on the bench, but the position is not one that has a tendency to corrupt men; on the contrary, all its influences are elevating. The very fact of investigating and defining the great principles on which society is based and which governs the relations of man with his fellow man, is one of the most ennobling and elevating that the human mind can conceive. The mind of the judge is elevated and he becomes great in spite of himself. These are some of the effects of appointments for life terms, and they are effects which have a most powerful influence, not merely in that single though most important branch of the government, the judiciary, but which, by its influence upon the other departments of the government and upon the interests of society in general, tend greatly more than almost anything else to the honor, dignity and stability of a free government.

What is the history, Mr. President? I must be indulged, for now we have the battle to fight, and upon it depends the fate, the honor, the dignity and the prosperity of one of the greatest of States. Sir, if legislation be favorable to Louisiana, her future will be great and grand, beyond comparison. Placed as she is, near the mouth of one of the largest rivers in the world, where the commerce of the whole South and West will pour untold wealth into her lap, with facilities for communicating by means of numerous rivers and bayous with an immense and incomparably fertile territory, her commerce will be the wonder of the world, and her prosperity, populousness and advancement will place her chief city in a position second to but one city in the nation.

Now, Mr. President, in view of these important facts, I ask: Have we a right to trifle for a single moment with this great subject? Shall we stand here and say that we will take up this amendment, that amendment, merely to trifle with the subject? I look not merely at what any man is to do or what is to be said concerning our action, but in the action I take I look to the great future of Louisiana. And as I was going on to say, nothing but corrupt and bad legislation can prevent Louisiana attaining a great, glorious and grand position in this government.

If we review the history of the judiciary during several past centuries, we find that where there has been a permanent judiciary there has been a series of the most illustrious decisions. From the time of Edward I, of Great Britain, for about four centuries, though there are hundreds of instances of the most illustrious decisions, yet from the fact that the judges were removable at the pleasure of the king, that stability and greatness which appeared at a later day was wanting. Why is this, unless it is because the position of the judge was not fixed. He could be removed at the pleasure of a capricious sovereign, and the position was not worth having.

Sir, during the time of the arbitrary reign of the Stuarts, excepting during the existence of the Commonwealth, there was a new chief justice appointed every two years—eleven chief justices in twenty-two years. But, sir, since the time of William and Mary, there has been a current of judicial decisions, unsurpassed for the learning and the justice with which they expound the laws. Why is this? It is plainly because the tenure of the office enables the judges to dig to the very depths of legal science and learning, and to acquire that eminence, and clear, ready comprehension that is only to be acquired by a long experience on the bench. It requires years of experience to fit a judge for his position, and yet if we adopt either of the amendments proposed we shall not give him half the chances for improvement that we give a common clergyman.

These decisions of which I have just spoken were not given by judges of three, four, or ten years standing. They held their positions during the life of the king, and this was a mighty step in advance of the earlier custom to make them removable at the king's pleasure. It was not, however, customary to remove them under this system at the death of the king. They were generally recommissioned, though this was not always done; and it was not until the time of George III that the appointments were made during good behavior, and from this time instead of having a new judge every two or three years we find some illustrious instances of long terms.

Mansfield remained in the office thirty-two years; Kenyon fourteen; and the result of this system is seen in an unbroken current of great and impartial decisions that have come down to us—a series of judicial decisions unsurpassed in the world's history for their clearness and their impartial justice.

Look for a moment, gentlemen, at the Supreme Court of the United States. Is that court composed of judges elected or appointed for terms of two, four, six or ten years? You all know that the judges hold their offices during good behavior; and I assert that our worthy president, as one of the members of the federal bench, is as independent in his position as the president of the United States. The president has no right to remove him. He can only be removed on account of his own *laches*. A great many of your neighbors are mechanics, gentlemen. Did you never notice how proud they are of their advancement in their position? How they seek to attain eminence in their respective callings. It is so with a judge. Actuated by the same sentiments of a common humanity, he seeks to place his own name high on the roll of eminent jurists, and this is in my opinion the most eminent position attainable.

I look upon the position of kings and monarchs as insignificant when compared with that of the judge. I cannot compare a George III with such a man as Coke.

Since the appointive system for a lifetime has been adopted, there has not been one judge in a thousand that has disgraced his office or been disgraced in office. And why is this? When you look back for one hundred and four years into English history, and for nearly one century in the United States, and see the glories of that judiciary system, who is there to say that there is danger that these men will become corrupt? What inducement has a judge to become corrupt? Suppose he does, he has the bar and all honorable men against him at once. Sir, he may as well be in prison as when corrupt and on the bench. He becomes at once the contempt of all honorable men. Every consideration tends to prevent the judge for good behavior from corruption. What must be an appointive judiciary when judges may become eminent and great in learning and usefulness? Can these requisites be expected of men appointed for two, four or six years?

My whole soul is wrapt up in this subject; not for to-day nor to-morrow, but for the people of Louisiana of to-day and of the future.

The States at an early day had the system for which I am contending—every one of them, with, perhaps, a single exception; and some of them have handed down some most illustrious decisions, while their reports, since they have adopted the elective system, have become a disgrace to the jurisprudence of the country. In the reports of criminal cases you will find decisions that will cover the worst rascals in New Orleans, because they have been given by judges who knew that unless they favored rascals they never could be re-elected.

By the amendment of the gentleman from the Second District (Mr. Hills) I am not much astonished, as he is not a lawyer; but that the gentleman from the Fourth District (Mr. Shaw,) a gentleman in whose legal abilities, quick perception and sound judgment I have the highest confidence, should introduce such a resolution, surprises me.

There is no partiality in the action of a judge. I care not, friend or foe, they are bound to decide in the same way, if they decide according to law. I believe that questions of national politics, which concern the people, should be discussed before them thoroughly, so that they may be well aware of the questions at issue, and so be able to vote understandingly. But in regard to the judiciary there is no distinction. Every judge is bound to decide in the same manner and according to the law of the case.

The term of four years which the gentleman proposes is so brief a term that few wise men could accept it. There are few that could afford it. A lawyer whose practice is three or four times as valuable as the salary proposed would hardly break up his practice to accept such a position for so short a time. This short-term principle we have been fighting for three weeks in the elective system; but no sooner had we, as I thought, finally disposed of it, than here it comes again in another shape. Suppose we adopt this system? The result is that the governor, at the end of every four years, has to re-appoint a supreme court. Now this proposition, I take it, if we adopt it, will only be a fresh bid for corruption. Why, sir, let us suppose now that the governor appoints judges for four years, I ask if the judiciary cannot make a contract with the then present executive, or with another candidate, to re-appoint them, provided they will cast their influence for his election or re-election? This will be easy of accomplishment; the judiciary will become a matter of bargain and sale, and will be a tremendous and dangerous engine of political corruption.

Could this be done, would not it be done? [Voice "Yes, that's so."] I am talking for the future of Louisiana, and just as certain as there are dishonest men among politicians this office will become, if this amendment is adopted, a matter of bargain and sale. The "outs" will always find the "ins" corrupt, and will remove them on the ground that they are rascals; they will swear it, because they want to go in. The same principles apply to the amendment of Mr. Hills, but they will not occur quite as often. You will have a parcel of barnacles in office that will be unworthy of appointment. If our governor should now appoint for life, he would have no power to make a bargain with the appointees afterwards, nor would his successor be in a better condition in that respect.

I am unconditionally for the report as it stands. I wish, sir—I would not care if every word was written in letters of gold and seen by every man in Louisiana. I, however, desire no office—God knows I have no aspirations in that direction. I believe that office is like the Indian's gun, it costs more than it comes to.

I voted against tabling the amendment because I wanted to test that by a vote; but I shall vote against both of them, and against every other amendment in every shape that is not exactly consistent with my views as the report is.

Again, I thank you, Mr. President and gentlemen, for your indulgence; and I trust that, before choosing by your votes between the amendments and the report, you will look at the danger to our institutions on the one hand, and to the glorious future of Louisiana on the other.

Mr. HENDERSON—There are two objections to the amendment of the gentleman from the Fourth (Mr. Shaw.)

The first is, that we are trying to fix the salaries for judges who have no existence. As we do not know as we shall have any district court, it is proper for the Legislature to fix the proper amount, when they decide what inferior courts shall be established, if any.

If gentlemen are striving to fix the term of an appointive judge at four years, I will go for an elective judiciary. I believe that judges should hold their offices during good behavior. If the amendment is to prevail, we might as well have new judges once a week. Why not? On the score of policy, and because judges should have experience, as it is well known that it is not the best lawyer who makes the best judge, for the business of the former is to look at and present only one side of a case as strongly as possible, whereas the latter must look impartially upon both sides.

As to the statement that a nomination is the same as an appointment, did you ever hear of a whig being proposed as a judge during the time when we had a democratic governor and Senate? Mississippi shows a noble exception; and though she is on the wrong side to-day, I am proud to say that judges are not there appointed in accordance with political views, because they know that they have more power than the whole Senate and governor together. Read your Bibles and you will there find that the judges were most important and powerful—called, in fact, "the wise men." In Mississippi appointment papers have been refused by the secretary of state to a judge on the ground that he was no lawyer, though elected a judge. A judge may, under our State laws, be appointed a judge who knows nothing of law, and you may swing on that account solely, and you ought to be hung for putting such a man on the bench.

According to your votes of yesterday, you decide both ways on this question, and I would like to know where you are. I would like to have you show me any other question where so much log-rolling has been practiced as in regard to this. For that very reason I am *willing* to take an elective judiciary. [Applause.] I am in *favor* of an appointive judiciary, but on the very instant you elect judges for ten or fifteen years or appoint judges for from one day to six years, I say there is no difference between the official corruption that will ensue under the appointive or elective, because you can operate directly upon them. Why is it that the constitution provides for election of judges on a different day from that of any other officers? Because, it was thought best that the judges should not come before the people in that way—at the time of popular excitement—and in order to avoid mixing that election with one dependent upon political issues.

The reason why the people do not turn out more largely on occasion of a judicial election, has been asked by my friend from the Seventh, (Judge Howell.) I say it is because there is no money or political favors to be given out by the man who is to come into power.

If I was the executive and two men were presented to me as candidates for nominees to the bench—one being a secesh and the other a unionist—I could gratify whatever proclivities I might have.

I say, that if I see a disposition among part of this House to make a mockery of this Convention, I am responsible to my constituents and will vote for the sovereign action of the people. [Applause.] I want to know where we stand. Judges for four or six years will make a mere laughing stock of the judiciary, and the whole matter will become purely one of political speculation. But when a governor nominates a man and the Senate confirms the nomination, placing him upon the bench for lifetime or good behavior, it becomes a solemn and serious affair, and they will endeavor to consider well beforehand. Good behavior is the best test, and you can provide for cases of insanity or other disabling cause.

Mr. SULLIVAN—I move to adjourn until Thursday, at 12 M.

[The motion was carried by a rising vote of 54 yeas to 23 nays.]

THURSDAY, June 2, 1864.

[The Convention met pursuant to adjournment. The roll was called and the following members answered to their names :]

Messrs. Ariail, Austin, Balch, Baum, Barrett, Bell, Burke, Campbell, Cazabat, Collin, Cook J. K., Crozat, Decker, Duane, Duke, Dufresne, Edwards, Flagg, Flood, Foley, Gastinel, Gaidry, Geier, Goldman, Gruneberg, Harnan, Healy, Heard, Henderson, Hills, Howell, Knobloch, Maas, Mann, Maurer, Mayer, Montamat, Morris, Mewell, Normand, O'Conner, Payne J., Pintado, Pursell S., Schnurr, Seymour, Shaw, Spellicy, Stauffer, Stumpf, Sullivan, Terry, Wells, Wilson, and Mr. President—55.

[There being no quorum present, the sergeant-at-arms was directed to bring in absent members.

After some delay the following members entered the hall and answered to their names :]

Messrs. Abell, Bailey, Beauvais, Bofill, Bromley, Fish, Fosdick, Fuller, Gorlinski, Hart, Hire, Howes, Mendiverri, Murphy M. W., Ong, Orr, Paine J. T., Purcell J., Smith, Stocker, Stiner, Waters—22.

[The president announced a quorum present.

The minutes of yesterday's proceedings were read and adopted.]

Mr. MONTAMAT—I move for a suspension of the rules in order to offer a resolution.

[52 members rose ; rules suspended.]

[Mr. Montamat then offered the following :]

Resolved, That the office of assistant secretary, now filled by Mr. T. H. Murphy, be and is hereby declared vacant.

Resolved, further, That the secretary be authorized to employ a proper person to fill said vacancy during the balance of the session.

Mr. ABELL—Mr. President, the scriptures command us tc forgive seventy times seven, and I hope you will allow Mr. Murphy to remain with us. I pledge myself to say nothing more upon the matter, if he, at a future time, is not competent to attend to business.

Mr. MONTAMAT—It is not the first time this thing has occurred. I am informed that on three times he has neglected his duty very much and has been absent from this Convention. I nominated him on the representation of one of my friends from the Third Ward—knowing nothing about him. Seeing that he was not doing his duty, I requested him to resign, but he would not.

Mr. CAZABAT—I move the resolution be laid on the table.

[Seconded.]

Mr. STOCKER—I move Mr. Murphy be allowed to explain.

[Seconded.]

PRESIDENT—If the gentleman is to remain here, I should direct the sergeant-at-arms to remove him, as he is even now incapable of performing his duty.

Mr. STOCKER—The gentleman is here and I claim that he should be heard. Our ideas will be advanced by allowing him to explain.

Mr. MONTAMAT—According to a vote we can declare any office vacant without giving any reasons.

[Resolution carried and office declared vacant.

The secretary thereupon appointed Mr. Philip Winfree to fill the vacancy occasioned by the adoption of said resolution.]

Mr. HILLS—I rise to make a motion which I believe to be in order, and it is to offer an amendment to the amendment of Mr. Shaw, proposed on yesterday. In doing so, I beg leave to offer a single word in regard to what I said on yesterday. I approve of short terms of office for the judiciary, but not of terms so short as those proposed by Mr. Shaw, which fixes the appointment of judges with every change of administration. Therefore, as an amendment to that amendment, I move that the terms be fixed at ten years for judges of the Supreme Court, and those of judges of inferior courts at eight years.

Mr. FOLEY—I second that.

Mr. SMITH—I move to lay the amendment on the table.

[Seconded—Yeas 33, nays 48.
Motion to table lost.]

Mr. HOWELL—If any gentleman on the floor wishes to advocate the affirmative, I would like to hear him before I proceed. As chairman of the committee, I claim the right to close the argument on the part of the opposition to the amendment.

Mr. ORR—I think Mr. Abell has been peculiarly unfortunate in his argument. He has submitted that the appointive system is totally defective unless the appointments are for life, and that a system of bribery and corruption will be successfully pursued on the part of applicants to the offices of the judiciary. He has made use of the same argument which I presented day before yesterday, in favor of the elective system. He has dragged before the Convention the British system of judiciary and laws, which has nothing to do with this country. We are the United States of America—not the Kingdom of Great Britain. He had advocated the aristocratic system of appointment, and I only wonder he has not gone further in urging the aristocratic salaries of that country.

I wish to call the attention of the gentleman from the Second to the importance of possessing a good memory, and of remembering to-day what he may have said yesterday. I will read a portion of one of his speeches, made on the nineteenth day, when the subject of education was before the Convention. He says:

I have not much to say on this subject, The committee were unanimous, so far as its members were present. We agreed that the constitution of 1852 could not be improved on that point. The gentleman seems to found his objections to the term we have reported, upon the assumption that the terms of the other State officers have already been fixed at four years. I would call his attention to the fact that we have not yet fixed the terms of any of the State officers. We have not fixed the term of the governor at four years. I, for one, am in favor of short terms. I have not that distrust of the sovereign people that some gentlemen profess. I believe that in those States where the governor is elected every two years, he is, and the State officers elected with him are, as free from the objection of corruption as where they are elected for longer terms. In the State of New York, for instance, they are elected for two years, and American history does not furnish a more illustrious list of names than of the governors of New York.

I shall not refer particularly to other States, but I believe the same rule will be found to apply.

I am in favor of electing the superintendent of public education, and I am not certain that I shall not advocate the election of all State officers every two years. Then if we get a good governor, and good State officers, we can keep them four years, but if we should get a bad set, for God's sake give the people a chance to change them every two years.

That is what I say. [Applause.]

Mr. THORPE—Mr. Abell, in dwelling on the corruption that would take place in the supreme judges, under limited terms of office, has acted very much like the cow that gives a good pail of milk and then kicks it over. I cannot understand how it is when a judge is appointed for ten years, if he wishes to be re-appointed, must be necessarily corrupt, and bring corrupt influences to accomplish his wishes. I do not believe there are so many corrupt influences brought to bear on the executive. I am in favor of the appointive system, but I have seen the evils of life appointments under the Federal government, to which I will not allude, and in the State of Louisiana. If the gentleman will refer to the circumstances that called the convention of 1845, he will see that the chief reason was to get clear of certain dead wood connected with the judicial bench. A great deal has been said about Judge Martin, whom I consider would be a judicial light in any State of the Union; he is only second to such a man as Marshall. States are faster than the Federal government—are more progressive and rapid in their movements, and require, consequently, a different system; and I think that ten years is quite enough to trust any judge on the bench.

Go back four years, for instance, and what was the state of public opinion in Louisiana then? What a monstrous proposition it would have been to have told the people of Louisiana that in four years this Convention would be assembled in this State, and pass, with hardly any opposition, the ordinance of emancipation. If we have a judiciary for ten years, it is all we should ask, because some revolution in public sentiment may occur again in that time, and I would rather have a bench that can be removed every ten years. I have nothing more to say with reference to the appointment of the judiciary. I agree with Mr. Abell, but should like to have the compromise of Mr. Hills accepted, but between the life appointment and the elective judiciary, I shall vote for the elective.

Mr. STOCKER—I am one of those who, throughout my life, have taken that which came the nearest my own preferences, and Mr. Shaw's amendment approaches nearer than that of Mr. Hills, therefore I shall support it. The main ground upon which I opposed the appointive judiciary was on the clause of "during good behavior." A man may behave well and at the same time be incompetent for the position he occupies, through physical infirmities, and many other causes. One of my reasons for supporting the elective judiciary was the rotation in office, for the oftener changes are made the better it will be for the people. If a man is found to be good, the people will again elect him, but if bad he cannot be re-elected. For these reasons I am in favor of the amendment, making the term four and six years.

Mr. SMITH—We are told by the gentleman from the Fifth, (Mr. Abell,) that the judge has no incentive to rise, simply from the fact that the people can displace him at their pleasure. I am in favor of the elective judiciary, because I believe it is clearly a right belonging to the people, and to no other. I think the gentleman's going to Great Britain for great decisions is in bad taste. How many of the masses of the people of England have had an interest in them from the days of Edward I down to the days of Queen Victoria? They are not for the mass of the people, but it is different in our republican government, and the people are interested in these matters. How many here ever heard of Lieut. Gen. Grant six years ago, but who has not heard of the name of Gen. Scott, the pampered favorite of the government and the citizens? Take the history of the military commanders to-day, and who are fighting our battles? Every man has sprung from the people alone and raised to the different ranks they hold, and yet we are all told the people have no right to the elective judiciary.

Mr. HILLS—I would inquire whether I have a right to close this debate. I have not yet spoken on the question.

PRESIDENT—You have the right to close the debate.

Mr. STAUFFER—I desire to give my reasons for voting to lay the last amendment offered on the table. Under the existing circumstances the people are not prepared for these changes. This question has not been agitated before the people when the members to this Convention were elected, and I do not wish to take the resposibility of voting against the wish of the people. At the time the only question I raised was that of emancipation, but I believe in voting for the elective judiciary, I am voting for the people.

Mr. HARNAN—Mr. President, though I am not gifted in that loquacious delivery of eloquence as my predecessor, in rising to say a few words, I claim a few moments of their attention.

I am opposed to the appointing power in one man, and I am in favor of putting every thing in the hands of the people. Yes, we may be told that the governor will select suitable persons for the office of judges.

One will say that the governor has good intentions and means well; it is an old saying that hell is paved with good intentions; and if you give the power to one man you will find that you will have hell's paving stones hurled at you every day by the way of appoinments, and some of them very remote.

Look at appointment of bureaus of the city of New Orleans; they do not publish any of their acts for the public good. Some people outside inform me that there never was any of the proceedings of the bureaus published, only the one about the woodpile.

Mr. HOWELL—In andition to the intimations which members on the floor exhibit in regard to taking the question, I am still more embarrassed by the seeming confidence of the advocates of these amendments in their success; because even with an experienced speaker it is a disadvantage to attempt to argue against that which he feels is already decided against him, and much greater is it to one who has so little experience in public speaking as I have. It is a sense of duty that still impels me to raise my voice upon the question before us, in which the highest interests of the people of Louisiana are involved. It is my appreciation of the prerogative and character of the judiciary which influences my action, and I am willing to admit that every other gentleman is actuated by similar motives, and that he desires only the highest interests of the State. In that feeling do I approach this subject, and I shall oppose both amendments, because I believe the best good is attainable in the mode pointed out by the report itself. I believe the great object of the Convention should be—and I am willing to say it is—to adopt the system of judiciary which will secure the best good to the people, and be most acceptable to them. It is important and necessary to look at the character and prerogative of this department ot the government. I agree with the gentleman that it is right and necessary that the people shall retain the control, but contend that, in our form of government, owing to inherent principles already maintained, that there must be a conservative principle in the government, or the popular form of government necessarily tends to anarchy and the power of the mob. I contend that the safest check, the only check in our form of government to that tendency, is in an independent judiciary. To attain the independence of the judiciary, is to remove it as far as possible from all political concerns. The appointive system for good behavior is only made to effect that. It does not astonish me to find the advocates of the elective system in favor of this amendment; but to find those who advocated the appointive judiciary from principle favoring it, is a matter inexplicable. I do not contend for the appointive power simple to take it away from the people—simply to place it in the hands of the governor—but on the ground that it is the only mode by which, if properly carried out, the independence and the stability of the judiciary can be attained. Is it true that the independence of the judiciary is attained by a limited term, either elective or appointive?

There is no system which is permanent, because man's existence is uncertain; but the system we propose to establish attains this as near as it is possible under the institutions of man. I say, then, it astonishes me to find men advocating the appointive system and asserting that they prefer an election of the judges to the appointment, during good behavior. It is just as inconsistent as it is to say, that if I cannot get what I want I will have nothing at all. The judiciary established by the appointing power, during a good behavior, secures the independence and stability of that system as far as it is possible to be obtained, for these reasons among others: that when the bench is once formed it cannot be tampered with or changed, except as the laws of nature or the will of the invidual judge affords occasion. The judge appointed during good behavior, the people know he is there during his own will, up to the day of his death. He has the certainty that the duties of his office are entrusted to him and that he is responsible to his God for the manner in which he discharges those duties. I believe in the doctrine of the statesman who said that the judiciary should be responsible alone to God; not, mind you, as a man, but as an officer who sits between man and man—who sits between men and their God. It is essential that you should have some authority when the disputes between men are to be determined, and hence it is important that the principle upon which these rights and disputes are to be determined should be stable and uniform. But when the judiciary is constantly subject to change, you destroy the possibility of that uniformity. I refer the members of this Convention to the comparison of the jurisprudence of Louisiana under the two systems. Those familiar with the Supreme Court of this State, refer with pride and confidence to the application of the great principles of the law as made under the appointive judiciary for good behavior, when, at the same time, they refer with distrust and uncertainty to those decisions reported since that time. So common has become that feeling, that it has been asserted in law courts by eminent counsel upon applying for appeal from a decision against them, to admit to the inferior judge that his decision is correct but that the party wished to succeed and might do so by appealing, there being so much uncertainty in the Supreme Court. It has become so because of the changes of the judges. There is no other cause. This is a degradation to the judiciary of the State, and had it been in the power of the district judges to have done so, it would have been proper to have punished it as contempt, but the law did not permit. Let me say, as I have already alluded to lawyers, that if the bar of this State were actuated by their individual and personal interests, they would advocate the shortest terms possible, because the frequent changes in the judiciary increases litigation. It renders uncertain and unsettled the jurisprudence of the State, and what may be decided as a true principle of law to-day, may be decided to be incorrect next year. Where a contract has been made to-day with reference to certain enunciated principles of law, of the Supreme Court, and that bench is changed, there may be another enunciation of the same principle. Before leaving this portion of my argument, I will take the liberty of saying, that so far as my knowledge of the legal profession extends, and so far as they have expressed their opinions, they are opposed, not only to the elective judiciary, but to any limit of the term. I take this as a guarantee of the honesty of the profession, which needs no defence from me, and is a proof that the principles I advocate are true, because when all men advocate that principle that tends to lessen their profits, I am satisfied of two things, that they are honest in their conclusions and that their conclusions are most apt to be right.

I shall oppose this amendment on the further ground that for the sake of the governor himself, as well as for the sake of the judge and the people, this amendment should not be adopted. There is no more powerful or appropriate expression of prayer, in all the history of human language, than that contained in the few words, "Lead us not into temptation." By the action of this Convention the governor has a right to be continued in office during life, if he can secure his repeated re-election. If it be contended that bad men may be appointed judges, it is not a very rash assertion to say that a bad man may be elected governor; and if that be possible, is it not possible for him to use the appliances of his office to secure his re-election? There are at present fourteen judicial districts outside of New Orleans, with fourteen judges, and there are six district judges in this city, making twenty in all, who under the amendment have to be re-appointed every eight years or four years. The first governor elected under this constitution, or holding office under it, will fill the first bench. He serves out one term without reference to the appointing of the judges, if they are appointed for eight years. If he be continued, before the election comes on the batch of judges have to be re-appointed. Is it contrary to nature to say that these twenty judges, having a jurisdiction throughout the whole State, will not feel peculiarly interested in the election for governor? Will it be impossible that the candidate for governor should feel a disposition to obtain the influence of those judges? The appointment for life, or good behavior, removes that temptation; the judges themselves are removed from that temptation. But it is urged that bad judges may be on the bench. A great many things may happen, and have happened; there may be a bad governor, and he may place a bad judge on the bench, but is it necessarily true that he would do so? That he would desire to do so is admitted; but that he is tempted not to do so, or may be, cannot be denied. I would not oppose the limited term, for the sake of the judge himself, nor for the sake of the people only, but because it is better to bear with a bad judge than to establish a system which will necessarily produce far greater evils. The minds of the Convention have been directed to one or two instances of bad judges—instances so rare that it is a compliment to the judiciary of the civilized world. The most prominent example is that of the ignominious Jeffries, of the English bench. The instance of Judge Taney is presented. Have the gentlemen read the Dred Scott decision, and will they inform me what it was? I admit there were sentiments enunciated in the opinions in that case to which I do not give my assent; but I say that that decision itself was right. It only decides on the facts in that particular case—that the man, Dred Scott, had not the right to stand in judgment as a citizen. The objectionable part of that case can be designated in legal parlance as *obiter dictu.* While referring to that tribunal, let me pay a feeble tribute of praise to the correctness of the principles upon which it is established. While the whole country has been going wild on State rights, franchise, and those questions which have stirred up the masses in this country, that bench has been firm and unshaken, and but one solitary man has withdrawn from it in consequence of the troubles, and he was an Alabamian who had been there but a short time. Others were there from the South, but they did not resign. Allusion has been made to Chief Justice Martin, and he has been held up as bringing about the change in the judiciary system. Gentlemen before making that assertion ought to know a little of the history of the State, and particularly the jurisprudence. I admit that it was asserted occasionally that he had become imbecile and should be taken from the supreme bench; but those who made that assertion either did not know what they were talking about, or had personal and sinister motives; and I refer the people to the very last decision rendered by that eminent judge. He evinced the perfect soundness of his judgment in his last official act. It was not the supreme bench that brought the judiciary into disregard. It was the parish judges, a system where there was a little monarch in every parish of the State; and to get rid of them was one of the principal reasons for calling the Convention of 1845. The main question was that of universal suffrage, and the Convention should bear in mind that this discussion upon the question of slavery has been growing and growing throughout the history of this government. I believe that the elective judiciary has contributed as much as any other cause in this country to bring about the troubles now upon us. It is my earnest desire that, now we have an opportunity of starting anew, we should avoid every cause which contributed to bring us into our present troubles. And I most earnestly contend that the independence and permanency of the judiciary is the very best means of protecting the people against these commotions, periodical changes and excitements that run over all countries. It is the great sheet-anchor of republican institutions in this country. While all parts of the Union were shaken by popular excitements, the independent judiciary stands unmoved and unshaken. The serene atmosphere which pervades its precincts was untroubled by popular commotions. Admit them once, and you impair the security of our form of government.

I fear I am becoming tiresome, but I would like to direct the attention of the Convention, for a moment, to the practical application of the amendments now before us. We have decided that the judges—without passing on the last branch of the question—that the supreme judges shall not be elected for ten years. We decided that in taking a vote on Mr. Sullivan's amendment to the third article of this report, and in rejecting it. Upon another amendment, that of Mr. Stauffer, we decided that the district court judges shall not be appointed for six years, or the judges of the inferior courts. But now, when we have concluded, virtually, that the judiciary shall be appointed, we have a proposition presented to appoint for eight and ten years, and this, if adopted, takes the place of the original amendment, which its mover explained had no reference to the mode of appointing. Suppose we adopt this amendment to the amendment, what will be the effect in the article as amended? There can be no other mode of arriving at the appointment of the judges than by the governor, with the advice and consent of the Senate. If we reject it, what will be the condition of affairs? We will either be left with a court without judges, or we must go back and undo what we have already done.

Gentlemen should not, in my opinion, be so fearful of the judiciary. What man in this Convention, or what man of their constituents, will say that he has suffered by the judiciary because they were judges? It is necessary to have judges, and it is the part of this Convention to determine the mode of selecting the best ones; and when they have been selected, let them remain. If an occasional man is appointed who is unworthy of his place, it is better to bear with the evils of which you know, than to take upon you those which may be of far greater weight. You suspect not only the people and the judges, but the governor in this matter. You are unjust to both, because you say that when a bad judge is put upon the bench there is no mode of getting rid of him, but by the appointing power what was the action of the Convention yesterday? You then struck a serious blow to the permanency of the judiciary in this State, in deciding that a mere majority of the General Assembly shall remove a judge. If you want the people to be guarded against a bad judge, you have in that as full a guaratee as you can have by leaving it to the governor to change him at the end of the term, because it is unfortunately true, that in the politics of this country certain influences can be brought to bear which will retain even objectionable men in office. I contend, from this, that if there be a bad judge, who is totally unfit for his position, it is as easy for the people to get rid of him through the action of the Legislature as through that of the governor. All will readily understand my position, if they do not agree with me.

It is not the ordinary signification of the words "good behavior" only which is involved in the constitution. It refers to a judge's official behavior, and includes that just as much as his social and moral behavior. The man who makes himself so oppressive to the people as to become a Jeffries, is not a man who continues in good official behavior, and I contend, sir, that the laws of nature and the various interests that operate upon human motives, will produce and bring about all the changes which the people require. Judges *do* resign, gentlemen, and *do* die, and thus as many changes occur as it is well to effect. Judges Porter and Bullard resigned, as did Judge Martin, at one time, but was reinstated. Judge Matthews died, and so did Judge Martin, a short time after he left his office. But how many resignations were there under the eight-year term, under the constitution of 1845? More, in proportion, than there were under the appointive system for life. Judge Preston was killed, and his place was supplied by Judge Campbell, who resigned. I cannot now call to mind the names of many others. Judge Ogden was another instance, though he was an elective judge. There was a judge to every year and a half, through that term of eight years, to which the judiciary was limited. In the nine years succeeding it, under the elective system, there were twelve judges. In the eighteen years—the first after the organization of the State—there were, I think, five different judges; one of them was advanced to the United States District Court, and his place was filled by appointment; another resigned, and another died—both places being filled by appointment; so that you see this talk about continuing men in office for life and saddling them upon the people, loses its force with regard to the judiciary. It is better even that the judiciary should be permanent than that the jurisprudence should be unsettled.

Mr. AUSTIN—I move we adjourn.

[The motion was seconded.]

Mr. HILLS—I believe it is conceded by the chair, that I have a right to close this debate. I do not propose to take more than ten minutes, and if other gentlemen wish to speak, I will, as I do not wish to cut them off, give way for a motion to adjourn.

Mr. AUSTIN—If gentlemen wish to speak, I will withdraw my motion.

Mr. SULLIVAN—I renew it.

[The yeas and nays were demanded and the motion lost.]

YEAS—Messrs. Abell, Austin, Baum, Bailey, Buckley, Campbell, Cook J. K., Crozat, Decker, Dufresne, Duke, Flagg, Flood, Foley, Gaidry, Goldman, Gruneberg, Hart, Maurer, Mendiverri, Murphy M. W., Newell, Normand, O'Conner, Ong, Orr, Poynot, Purcell J., Schroeder, Spellicy, Stocker, Stumpf, Sullivan, Waters—34.

NAYS—Messrs Ariail, Barrett, Beauvais, Bell, Bofill, Bromley, Burke, Cazabat, Collin, Cook T., Cutler, Duane, Edwards, Fish, Fosdick, Fuller, Gastinel, Geier, Gorlinski, Harnan, Healy, Heard, Henderson, Hills, Hire, Howell, Howes, Knobloch, Maas, Mann, Mayer, Montamat, Morris, Payne J., Paine J. T., Pintado, Pursell S., Schnurr, Seymour, Shaw, Smith, Stiner, Stauffer, Terry, Thorpe, Wenck, Wells, Wilson—48.

Mr. CAMPBELL—I am very sorry to detain this Convention longer than it desires to be detained, and will endeavor to make my remarks so brief as not to detain you long. A great many gentlemen have addressed this Convention on the opposite side of the question, and I must say most of their guns have been badly shotted and have scattered badly. Mr. Abell, it seems, sir, has gone back, away back to antediluvian times when the world was a wild, as well as others. I want to show that I can go back to the ancient times, too, to prove my side of the question. Now, sir, I am going back beyond the time to which the gentleman referred—to our first parents in the garden of Eden. Our old mother Eve, sir, betrayed her lord and master Adam, and, sir, she was appointed for him. Had he been allowed to elect a companion she would not have betrayed the trust. So much for antediluvian times. My friend went back to the time of the ancient Egyptians, who thought the world was a dead plain and that the sun went around it every day, as a specimen of opposition times.

Now, sir, I am not done with the gentleman from the Fifth District, (Mr. Abell) yet. He says that all the old puritan States adopted the appointive system. They appointed the judges, Mr. President, and what did those judges do? Why, sir, they tied people to stakes and burnt them for witches. That, sir, was in puritan times, under appointive judges. But, sir, they do not still hold to the system—they have seen the error of their ways and have returned to the people their right to elect their own judges, and the elective judiciary has done away with the burning of witches.

The gentleman from the Fifth tells us that the judges are bound to decide, or like to decide, any given case, according to law. Now, sir, that is just exactly my position. And the question I shall ask, respecting a judge who was to decide a case to which I was a party, would be: "*Is he honest?*" If he is, sir, and my case comes before him, whatever the case may be, there are nine cases out of ten when his decision will be right, and if taken to the Supreme Court will be sustained.

My friend says that he has no ambition; he wants no office—not he. The gentleman is very modest, very modest indeed. I admire his modesty. It is refreshing in these times to meet a modest man sometimes. We sometimes read of them in the records of the times to which the gentleman has referred. Richard III was one of them. He was a modest man—very. He did not want a crown. He would n't be a king. He would n't wear a crown under any consideration. Yet he managed to get the better of his scruples.

Mr. STOCKER—I claim the floor.

PRESIDENT—I think you have spoken twice.

Mr. STOCKER—Only once, Mr. President. My friend from the Seventh, (Mr. Howell,) a gentleman whom I respect highly, has made some assertions here which I desire to answer. He has spoken at least five times of the independent judiciary. He says the independent judiciary has been unshaken before the country, and wishes to know if any one has suffered from the judiciary, etc. I want to know what he means by the independent judiciary; whether he means a judiciary independent of the people? [Applause.] I do not know of anybody who has suffered from an elective judiciary, but I do know of some who have suffered from an appointive judiciary, and without going back to Jeffries and Taney, I will refer to Judge Garland, of this State. Mr. President, I see that I am not treated with respect by the members of this Convention, and therefore decline to say anything further on this subject.

Mr. FLOOD—I hear a good deal said about the constitution of 1812. Under it a man could not vote unless he owned and paid taxes upon a certain amount of property; nor be a member of the Legislature, or Senate, unless under the same restrictions. Under the constitution of 1812, Judge Elliott was impeached and convicted of naturalizing whole shiploads of Irish before the law would have allowed him to.

There was Judge Garland, who forged a note for a large sum, and was imprisoned, but through intercessions was set at large, and is living in Texas at this very day.

These are some of the specimens of appointive judges. Show me any judges elected in 1852 that are equal in rascality to these two!

As for my part, I go in for electing the judiciary, and every other office-holder in Louisiana. [Applause.]

Mr. HILLS—Mr. President and gentlemen of the Convention: If you will give me your attention, I will let you up lightly; but if you interrupt me, I shall put it to you for a whole hour.

I regret very much, Mr. President, that the defence of this proposition, which I have had the honor to submit, should devolve upon myself, as most of the gentlemen preceding me have opposed it.

Before entering upon the discussion of the main question, I wish to say a word to my friend from the Tenth District, (Mr. Orr,) who saw fit to entertain this audience by reading a portion of one of my printed speeches, delivered upon the subject of education, in which I spoke in favor of short terms for elective officers. The applause which followed the reading, seemed to me sufficient evidence that it was regarded as the best part of that gentleman's remarks. [Laughter.] There was no inconsistency, however, between what I said then and do say now. I *am* in favor of short terms for officers elected by the people, but am not in favor of the election of judges by the people at all. [Applause.]

I do not propose to argue the merits of the elective or appointed judiciary. I regard that question as settled already very clearly, since we have, on two or three different occasions, voted against an elective judiciary. The gentleman from the Fifth (Mr. Abell) very properly said that the issue was narrowed down to the single point of the length of the term of the judges' offices. It is whether they shall be appointed during good behavior, or whether a limit shall be placed to that tenure—making it for a certain number of years.

The argument of the gentleman from the Fifth District, in favor of life tenure, is based wholly upon the supposition that the people are very corrupt; that all elections are carried by fraud and corruption. If his argument does not mean that, it does not mean anything. He says, in speaking of the corruption which would be resorted to in order to elect a governor, with the understanding that he was to appoint a judiciary, that corruption is the "prevailing rule." Now, sir, I do not so far distrust the people; but while I do not believe that it is safe to entrust the people with the election of judges, I *do so far trust them* as to believe that at stated periods, not too frequent, they should have the privilege of expressing their approval or disapproval of judicial officers. Under both systems, it seems to me, we are liable to corruption on the bench.

The gentleman asks: "What motive an appointed judge will have to act against justice, if appointed for life?" *I* ask if the history of the world does not show that men, whose interest it was to go right, have frequently gone wrong? How was it with Lord Bacon, one of the most philosophical men the world ever produced? Why, sir, he was bribed, upon the bench. There is no such thing as human perfection. Appointed judges may be corrupt and so may elected judges; but in my opinion the latter will go wrong nine times where the former will once. [Applause.] Now, then, I say we must get as near to perfection as we can. I believe in the power of the people in their rights, but not in the right to elect their judges directly. I propose by this measure to steer as nearly as I believe it possible, between the evils of both systems, to take that middle course which has generally been found to be the safest, be tween extreme conservatism upon the one side and radicalism upon the other.

My friend from the Fifth is very much given to figures of speech. He frequently takes illustrations from whips, harnesses, and that sort of thing. I propose to borrow one of his figures. We see that there are two principles involved in construction of the harness—the go-ahead principle—the propelling power, and the hold back strap. I call the first the progressive and the latter the conservative. Sometimes the conservative power is lodged with the government and the courts, and sometimes with the people. If we read the constitutional history of England, which has been so frequently referred to by the gentleman, we find that for centuries there was a struggle between the people and the king. For what? To preserve those rights and liberties, against the king and his judiciary, to which every nation and people are entitled.

The people are not always corrupt. The people may be trusted, but on this question they must not be trusted too far. If the bench is made liable to the fluctuations of public sentiment every three or four years, time is not given to establish the dignity, character, and impartiality of the judges who are to dispense justice, who *should* do right. Therefore, it is that I propose to take the middle course, and by placing the duration of the terms at ten years, to give the people at the lapse of every ten years a chance to express their approval or disapproval of their judicial officers. If the judges or the government become corrupt, then the people become the conservative power, and I propose to place in their hands the conservative principle, by which they may, on occasion necessary, sustain their rights and liberties. Ten years, as a rule, make a term long enough for any man to hold office, in my humble opinion.

The gentleman from the Seventh, (Judge Howell,) for whom I have a very high respect as a lawyer and a gentleman, has told us that judges often resign and frequently die. Now, Mr. President, my observation is, that appointed judges never resign and seldom die. [Laughter.] There may have been exceptions, but this, I believe, is the rule, and if I were in the life insurance business, I would issue a policy to an appointed judge with a good salary without asking him the state of his health! [Great applause.]

That gentleman has, with what seems to me perfect consistency, stood up here to defend the decision in the celebrated case of Dred Scott. He tells us that that decision was right. I stand up here to declare, that of all the decisions ever recorded in the history of the bench, there is none so infamous as that same decision of Judge Taney's. [Great applause.]

Mr. MANN—What did the court decide?

Mr. HILLS—It decided that a negro was not a citizen of the United States, and in deciding that it told us that a black man had no rights which a white man was bound to respect. Was that decision right? [Loud cries of "no."] Limiting ourselves to the first statement, I say that if that is right then Attorney General Bates is wrong; for the reason, that in an elaborate and able opinion delivered a short time ago, he decided directly against Judge Taney on that very point, and decided farther that negroes are citizens. That judgment was no credit to the chief justice, and it is a pity, in my opinion, that he did not resign before he gave a decision so infamous. But we have him saddled upon us and how can we get rid of him? He will not resign, and there is not, as I have heard, any prospect of his dying! [Applause.] There are some men in this world whom it would seem the devil does not wish to take to himself, (I do not wish to apply this to Judge Taney); some, on whom he has a mortgage upon, but does not wish to foreclose it, because it will be against his interest. I do not wish to be understood as making any personal application, but such men have been known on the English bench under an appointed system, and certainly such may have been in our Supreme Court, I will not say in regard to it.

My friend from the Fifth was not surprised at my amendment, knowing that I am not a lawyer. If to be a lawyer is to approve such a decision as that—if to be a lawyer is to go against all justice and common sense, reason and humanity, then I must thank God I am not a lawyer. [Applause.]

But, Mr. President, I do not desire to detain the Convention, and will merely repeat that, in my opinion, this proposition avoids, in the first place, all the evils of the elective system, and in the second, by limiting appointments to ten years, leaves in the hands of the people a remedy against a corrupt bench. It seems to me that a fairer proposition could not be made regarding either the elective or appointed judiciary to remedy the expensive evils of both. I believe it to be founded in justice, reason and common sense, and shall therefore vote for it.

[The amendment of Mr. Hills to the amendment of Mr. Shaw was then put to vote, and upon roll call lost:]

YEAS—Messrs. Bromley, Cazabat, Duane, Fish, Foley, Fosdick, Fuller, Goldman, Gorlinski, Harnan, Healy, Henderson, Hills, Hire, Mayer, Normand, Paine J. T., Pintado, Stumpf, Stiner, Thorpe, Waters—22.

NAYS—Messrs. Abell, Ariail, Austin, Bailey, Barrett, Baum, Beauvais, Bell, Bofill, Buckley, Burke, Campbell, Collin, Cook T., Cook J. K., Crozat, Cutler, Decker, Duke, Dufresne, Edwards, Flagg, Flood, Gastinel, Gaidry, Geier, Gruneberg, Hart, Heard, Howell, Howes, Knobloch, Maas, Maurer, Mann, Mendiverri, Morris, Murphy M. W., Newell, O'Conner, Ong, Orr, Payne J., Poynot, Purcell J., Pursell S., Schroeder, Seymour, Schnurr, Shaw, Smith, Spellicy, Stauffer, Stocker, Sullivan, Terry, Wenck, Wells, Wilson—59.

Mr. SHAW—I desire to make a merely verbal correction of my amendment, and instead of saying, "judges of the district courts," to insert in place thereof "judges of inferior courts, except justices of the peace," etc.

[On the roll call the amendment of Mr. Shaw was adopted:]

YEAS—Messrs. Barrett, Baum, Bell, Buckley, Campbell, Cook J. K., Cook T., Decker, Duane, Dufresne, Duke, Fish, Flagg, Flood, Fosdick, Gastinel, Gaidry, Geier, Goldman, Gorlinski, Gruneberg, Harnan, Hart, Hire, Howes, Knobloch, Maas, Maurer, Mayer, Mendiverri, Morris, Murphy M. W., Normand, O'Conner, Ong, Orr, Payne J., Paine J. T., Poynot, Purcell J., Pursell S., Shaw, Schroeder, Schnurr, Seymour, Smith, Stiner, Spellicy, Stocker, Stumpf, Stauffer, Sullivan, Terry—53.

NAYS—Messrs. Abell, Ariail, Austin, Bailey, Beauvais, Bofill, Bromley, Burke, Cazabat, Collin, Crozat, Cutler, Edwards, Foley, Fuller, Healy, Heard, Henderson, Hills, Howell, Mann, Newell, Pintado, Thorpe, Waters, Wenck, Wells, Wilson—28.

[Loud applause.]

Mr. TERRY—I have a substitute for the article as amended.

[Several motions to adjourn were made, and upon the question being put, the Convention separated until 12 M. of Friday, June 3d.]

FRIDAY, June 3, 1864.

[The Convention met at 12 o'clock M. and was called to order by the president. The roll was called and the following members answered to their names:]

Messrs. Abell, Ariail, Austin, Barrett, Baum, Bell, Bromley, Burke, Campbell, Collin, Cook T., Crozat, Davies, Decker, Dufresne, Dupaty, Flagg, Flood, Foley, Gaidry, Gastinel, Geier, Gorlinski, Harnan, Healy, Heard, Henderson, Hills, Howell, Kavanagh, Knobloch, Maas, Mann, Mayer, Maurer, Montamat, Morris, Murphy E., Newell, O'Conner, Ong, Payne J., Pintado, Poynot, Purcell J., Pursell S., Schroeder, Schnurr, Shaw, Smith, Spellicy, Stiner, Stauffer, Sullivan, Terry, Waters, Wells, Wilson and Mr. President—59.

[There being no quorum, the sergeant-at-arms was directed to bring in absent members, and after some delay the following members took their seats and answered to their names, viz:]

Messrs. Bailey, Bofill, Cazabat, Cook J. K., Duane, Duke, Edwards. Fish, Fosdick, Hart, Hire, Howes, Murphy M. W., Normand, Seymour, Stocker, Stumpf—17.

[The president announced a quorum present.

The minutes were read and adopted.

The order of the day was taken up, article 11, of the report on the judiciary as amended.]

Mr. BAUM—I voted in the majority and I move to reconsider the vote of yesterday on Mr. Shaw's amendment.

Mr. FOLEY—I move to lay the motion on the table.

[The yeas and nays were ordered and the motion lost, as follows:]

YEAS—Messrs. Barrett, Bell, Buckley, Campbell, Cook J. K., Cook T., Davies, Dufresne, Dupaty, Flood, Gastinel, Gaidry, Geier, Gorlinski, Harnan, Howes, Henderson, Knobloch, Maurer, Montamat, Morris,

Murphy M. W., Normand, O'Conner, Orr, Payne J., Poynot, Pursell S., Schnurr, Spellicy, Smith, Stocker, Stauffer, Sullivan, Terry, Waters---36.

NAYS---Messrs. Abell, Ariail, Austin, Bailey, Baum, Beauvais, Bofill, Bromley, Burke, Collin, Cazabat, Crozat, Cutler, Decker, Duane, Edwards, Fish, Flagg, Foley, Fosdick, Hart, Healy, Heard, Hills, Hire, Howell, Kavanagh, Maas, Mann, Mayer, Murphy E., Newell, Ong, Pintado, Schroeder, Seymour, Shaw, Stumpf, Stiner, Wells, Wilson---41.

[The motion to reconsider was then carried :]

YEAS---Messrs. Ariail, Austin, Baum, Bailey, Beauvais, Bofill, Bromley, Burke, Cazabat, Collin, Crozat, Cutler, Duane, Dupaty, Edwards, Fish, Flagg, Foley, Fosdick, Gaidry, Hart, Heard, Henderson, Hills, Hire, Howell, Kavanagh, Knobloch, Maas, Mann, Mayer, Murphy M. W., Newell, Ong, Pintado, Seymour, Shaw, Stumpf, Waters. Wenck, Wells, Wilson---42.

NAYS—Messrs. Abell, Barrett, Bell, Buckley, Campbell, Cook J. K., Cook T., Davies, Decker, Dufresne, Flood, Gastinel, Geier, Gorlinski, Harnan, Healy, Howes, Maurer, Montamat, Morris, Murphy E., Normand, O'Conner, Orr, Payne J., Poynot, Pursell S., Schroeder, Schnurr, Smith, Spellicy, Stiner, Stocker, Stauffer, Sullivan, Terry---36.

[During the call Messrs. Abell and Terry explained their votes.]

Mr. ABELL---It is well known on this floor that I have advocated, with my whole soul, the appointment of the judges during good behavior. If we cannot have an appointment of that character, I care not what kind of an appointment we have, and therefore vote no.

Mr. TERRY---I have a substitute to offer for the article and amendment, and shall vote no.

[The motion was declared carried.]

Mr. FOLEY---I move that the rmendment be rejected.

Mr. HILLS---I second the motion.

Mr. FOLEY---I understand the gentleman has a substitute to offer, and with the consent of my second I withdraw my motion.

Mr. MANN---I renew the motion.

[The yeas and nays were ordered and the motion to reject carried.]

YEAS—Messrs. Abell, Ariail, Austin, Bailey, Baum, Beauvais, Bell, Bofill, Bromley, Burke, Cazabat, Crozat, Cutler, Davies, Dupaty, Duane, Edwards, Fish, Flagg, Flood, Foley, Fosdick, Fuller, Gaidry, Gorlinski, Hart, Healy, Heard, Henderson, Hills, Hire, Howell, Kavanagh, Knobloch, Maas, Mann, Mayer, Murphy E., Murphy M. W., Newell, Ong, Pintado, Seymour, Stumpf, Stiner, Thorpe, Waters, Wenck, Wells, Wilson—50.

NAYS—Messrs. Barrett, Buckley, Campbell, Collin, Cook J. K., Cook T.. Decker, Dufresne, Gastinel, Geier, Harnan, Howes, Maurer, Montamat, Morris, Normand, Orr, O'Conner, Payne J., Poynot, Pursell S., Schroeder, Schnurr, Shaw, Smith, Spellicy, Stocker, Stauffer, Sullivan, Terry—30.

Mr. TERRY—I offer the following substitute for article 11 :

The judges, both of the supreme and inferior courts, and justices of the peace, shall be elected by the qualified voters of the State ; provided, that until two years after the present rebellious war is ended in this State, the proof of which shall be a proclamation from the President of the United States to that effect, the said judges and justices of the peace shall be appointed by the governor, by and with the advice and consent of the Senate, and the term of office as herein expressed and for which they shall have been so appointed, shall be stipulated in the commissions of the said judges and justices of the peace.

After that period, the governor shall issue his proclamation ordering an election for judges of the Supreme Court, inferior courts and justices of the peace, by the legal voters of the State, in accordance with the enactment contained in this article.

Mr. AUSTIN—I move to lay it on the table.

[The yeas and nays were demanded and the roll called :]

YEAS—Messrs. Abell, Ariail, Austin, Bailey, Baum, Beauvais, Bofill, Bromley, Burke, Cazabat, Collin, Cook J. K., Cook T., Crozat, Cutler, Davies, Decker, Duane, Dupaty, Dufresne, Edwards, Fish, Foley, Fosdick, Fuller, Gastinel, Gorlinski, Harnan, Hart, Healy, Heard. Henderson, Hills, Hire, Howell, Kavanagh, Maas, Mann, Maurer, Mayer, Murphy E., Murphy M. W., Newell, Normand, Ong, Pintado, Poynot, Schroeder, Schnurr, Shaw, Spellicy, Stiner, Stauffer, Thorpe, Waters, Wenck, Wells, Wilson—58.

NAYS—Messrs. Barrett, Bell, Buckley, Campbell, Flagg, Flood, Gaidry, Geier, Howes, Knobloch, Morris, O'Conner, Orr, Payne J., Pursell S., Seymour, Smith, Stocker, Stumpf, Sullivan, Terry—21.

[The substitute was accordingly laid on the table.]

Mr. GASTINEL—I move the Convention take a recess of fifteen minutes.

Mr. HILLS—I have the floor and wish to offer a substitute, but if it is the wish of the Convention to take a recess, I will yield the floor.

[The motion to take a recess was lost.]

Mr. HILLS—I offer the following substitute for article 11:

The judges, both of the Supreme and inferior courts, shall be appointed by the governor, by and with the advice and consent of the Senate. The judges of the Supreme Court shall hold their offices for the term of twelve years, and the judges of the inferior courts (except justices of the peace) shall hold their offices during the term of ten years; but all appointments of judges, made by the present governor, shall expire with his term of office.

Mr. TERRY—I move to lay it on the table.

[The motion was carried:]

YEAS—Messrs. Abell, Ariail, Barrett, Baum, Beauvais, Bell, Bofill, Bromley, Buckley, Burke, Collin, Cook J. K., Cook T., Crozat, Cutler, Davies, Decker, Duane, Dufresne, Dupaty, Flagg, Flood, Foley, Fuller, Gastinel, Geier, Goldman, Gaidry, Healy, Hart, Heard, Hire, Howell, Howes, Knobloch, Maas, Maurer, Montamat, Morris, Murphy M. W., Mayer, Normand, O'Conner, Orr, Payne J., Pintado, Poynot, Pursell S., Seymour, Smith, Spellicy, Stiner, Stauffer, Sullivan, Terry, Wenck, Wilson—57.

NAYS—Messrs. Austin, Bailey, Campbell, Cazabat, Edwards, Fish, Fosdick, Gorlinski, Harnan, Henderson, Hills, Kavanagh, Murphy E., Newell, Ong, Schroeder, Schnurr, Shaw, Stocker, Stumpf, Thorpe, Waters, Wells—23.

Mr. STINER—I offer the following substitute:

The judges of the Supreme Court shall be appointed for the term of ——— years, and the judges of the inferior courts shall be appointed for the term of ——— years.

When the first appointments are made under this constitution, the chief justice shall be commissioned for ——— years, one of the associate justices for ——— years, one for ——— years, one for ——— years and one for ——— years.

The inferior judges shall be divided by lot into four classes, as nearly equal as can be, and the judges of the first class shall be commissioned for ——— years, those of the second for ——— years, and those of the third for ——— years, and those of the fourth for ——— years.

Mr. MONTAMAT—I offer the following amendment:

The judges, both of the supreme and inferior courts, except justices of the peace, shall be appointed by the governor, with the consent of the Senate and House of Representatives in joint session. The judges of the Supreme Court shall hold their offices for a term of eight years, and those of the inferior courts, except justices of the peace, for a term of six years.

[On motion, both substitute and amendment were tabled by a *viva voce* vote.]

Mr. SMITH—I offer the following substitute:

The judges of the supreme and inferior courts shall be appointed by the governor during the existence of the present war, and for two years thereafter; at the expiration of that time the judges of the Supreme Court shall be elected by the lower branch of the General Assembly, the judges of the inferior courts to be elected by the qualified voters of their respective districts, their term of office to be fixed by the Legislature.

Mr. STOCKER—Before the vote is announced, I would ask the secretary if he has checked Mr. Mendiverri's, as although he is not present, some one answered to his name.

SECRETARY—No, sir, I did not. I am aware of the fact.

YEAS—Messrs. Abell, Ariail, Austin, Bailey, Baum, Beauvais, Bofill, Bromley, Burke, Collin, Crozat, Cutler, Davies, Dupaty, Edwards, Fosdick, Fuller, Heard, Hills, Hire, Howell, Kavanagh, Newell, Normand, Ong, Shaw, Thorpe, Waters, Wenck, Wells, Wilson—31.

NAYS—Messrs. Barrett, Bell, Buckley, Campbell, Cazabat, Cook J. K., Cook T., Decker, Duane, Dufresne, Fish, Flagg, Flood, Foley, Gastinel, Geier, Goldman, Gorlinski, Gruneberg, Gaidry, Healy, Harnan, Hart, Henderson, Howes, Knobloch, Maas, Mann, Maurer, Montamat, Morris, Murphy E., Murphy M. W., Mayer, O'Conner, Orr, Payne J., Pintado, Poynot, Purcell J., Pursell S., Schroeder, Schnurr, Seymour, Smith, Spellicy, Stocker, Stumpf, Stiner, Stauffer, Sullivan, Terry—52.

[The motion to lay on the table was therefore lost.]

Mr. GOLDMAN—I move the previous question on the substitute.

[Motion seconded.]

Mr. BAUM—I offer the following amendment to the subsitute.

PRESIDENT—The previous question cuts off all amendments and substitutes.

Mr. GOLDMAN—With the consent of my second, I withdraw it.

Mr. BAUM—I offer the following:

The judges both of the supreme and inferior courts shall be appointed by the governor by and with the advice and consent of the Senate. The judges of the Supreme Court shall hold their offices during a term of ten years, and those of the inferior courts during a term of seven years. Their terms shall commence with the date of their commission.

Provided, That appointments made during the existence of the present rebellion shall not be construed as within the meaning of this article.

The first appointments and confirmations under this article shall be made during the first session of the Legislature that may be held after the restoration of peace.

Mr. BELL—I move to lay on the table.

YEAS — Messrs. Abell, Ariail, Barrett, Bell, Buckley, Campbell, Cook J. K., Cook T., Decker, Duane, Dufresne, Dupaty, Fish, Flagg, Flood, Gastinel, Geier, Goldman, Gorlinski, Gruneberg, Gaidry, Harnan, Howes, Knobloch, Maurer, Montamat, Morris, Murphy M. W., Mayer, Normand, O'Conner, Orr, Payne J., Poynot, Purcell J., Pursell S., Seymour, Smith, Stiner, Stauffer, Sullivan, Terry, Waters, Wells and Wilson—45.

NAYS—Austin, Bailey, Baum, Beauvais, Bofill, Bromley, Burke, Collin, Cazabat, Crozat, Cutler, Davies, Edwards, Foley, Fosdick, Fuller, Healy, Hart, Heard, Hills, Hire, Howell, Kavanagh, Maas, Mann, Murphy E., Newell, Ong, Pintado, Schroeder, Schnurr, Shaw, Spellicy, Stocker, Stumpf, Thorpe and Wenck—37.

[Amendment tabled.]

Mr. BAUM—I move to strike out of Mr. Smith's substitute all after "appointed by the governor."

[Laid on the table by *viva voce* vote.]

Mr. BAUM—I move to adjourn.

[Motion lost—ayes 36, nays 44.]

Mr. TERRY—I move the adoption of the substitute.

[Substitute adopted.]

YEAS—Messrs. Barrett, Baum, Bell, Buckley, Campbell, Cook J. K., Cook T., Decker, Duane, Dufresne, Duke, Fish, Flagg, Flood, Foley, Gastinel, Geier, Goldman, Gorlinski, Gruneberg, Gaidry, Healy, Harnan, Hart, Howes, Knobloch, Maas, Maurer, Montamat, Morris, Murphy M. W., Mayer, O'Conner, Orr, Payne J., Poynot, Purcell J.. Pursell S., Schnurr, Seymour, Smith, Spellicy, Stocker, Stiner, Stauffer, Sullivan, Terry—47.

NAYS—Messrs. Abell, Ariail, Austin, Bailey, Beauvais, Bofill, Bromley, Burke, Collin, Cazabat, Crozat, Cutler, Davies, Dupaty, Edwards, Fosdick, Fuller, Heard, Henderson, Hills, Hire, Howell, Kavanagh, Mann, Murphy E., Newell, Normand, Ong, Pintado, Shaw, Stumpf, Thorpe, Waters, Wenck, Wells, Wilson—36.

Mr. HILLS—I move we adjourn.

[The Convention then adjourned until 12 M. of Saturday, June 4.]

SATURDAY, June 4, 1864.

[The Convention met pursuant to adjournment. The roll was called and the following members answered to their names:]

Messrs. Abell, Ariail, Austin, Balch, Barrett, Baum, Bell, Bofill, Bromley, Buckley, Burke, Campbell, Cook J.K., Crozat, Davies, Decker, Duane, Dufresne, Edwards, Flood, Foley, Geier, Goldman, Gorlinski, Gruneberg, Healy, Hart, Heard, Knobloch, Maas, Mann, Maurer, Mendiverri, Montamat, Murphy E., Murphy M. W., Normand, O'Conner, Orr, Pintado, Poynot, Purcell Jno., Pursell S., Schroeder, Smith, Stumpf, Stiner, Stauffer, Sullivan, Terry, Wenck, Wilson and Mr. President—53.

[There being no quorum, the sergeant-at-arms was directed to bring in absent members.

Messrs. Cook T., Dupaty, Flagg, Hills, Hire, Morris, Ong, Schnurr, Seymour, Shaw, Spellicy, Stocker and Waters entered and took their seats.

The president having temporarily vacated the chair, on motion of Mr. Waters, the secretary was called to the chair, and on motion of Mr. Gorlinski, Mr. Hills was chosen to preside as president *pro tem.*

The convention then adjourned until Monday next at 12 M.]

MONDAY, June 6, 1864.

[The Convention met and was called to order, pursuant to adjournment, Hon. E. H. Durell, president, in the chair, and the following members present, viz:]

Messrs. Abell, Ariail, Balch, Baum, Bell, Bromley, Brott, Burke, Campbell, Cook T., Cook J. K., Crozat, Davies, Edwards, Ennis, Flagg, Foley, Fuller, Geier, Goldman, Gorlinski, Gruneberg, Gaidry, Hart, Heard, Henderson, Howell, Kavanagh, Knobloch, Maas, Maurer, Murphy E., Murphy M. W., Mayer, Newell, Normand, O'Conner, Pintado, Poynot, Pursell S., Schroeder, Schnurr, Smith, Spellicy, Stumpf, Stiner, Stauffer, Waters, Wilson—50

[There being no quorum, the sergeant-at-arms was directed to bring in absent members.

After some delay, the following members appeared and took their seats: Messrs. Austin, Bailey, Barrett, Bofill, Dufresne,

Dupaty, Fish, Flood, Fosdick, Gastinel, Harnan, Hills, Hire, Howes, Kugler, Mann, Montamat, Morris, Orr, Paine J. T., Purcell J., Seymour, Shaw, Stocker, Sullivan, Terry and Thorpe—27.

The president announced a quorum present.

[The minutes of the previous day were read.]

Mr. HILLS—The secretary is in error in stating there that I took the chair. A motion was first made by Mr. Sullivan, and seconded by Mr. Orr, that the secretary take the chair.

Mr. SULLIVAN—The gentleman is mistaken, I never made such a motion.

Mr. ORR—I seconded the motion, and am willing to have it spread upon the minutes.

Mr. HILLS—I beg the gentleman's pardon, it was Mr. Waters who made the motion.

[The minutes, corrected as suggested, were adopted.]

PRESIDENT—The unfinished business now in order is the report of the Committee on the Judiciary.

Mr. ABELL—I believe the police resolution was made the order of the day.

Mr. GOLDMAN—I desire to call attention to the rule, Mr. President, that unfinished business comes up first.

Mr. SMITH—Is it necessary to require a suspension of the rules to take up that resolution?

PRESIDENT—I am well aware that that resolution was made the order of the day, but the Convention subsequently passed a resolution that this question should be disposed of before anything else was taken up.

Mr. THORPE—I introduced a resolution, which was passed, under which, I think, this must lie over till next Saturday.

PRESIDENT — Mr. Secretary, read Mr. Thorpe's resolution.

[The secretary read:]

Mr. ABELL—The police bill was fixed for 1 o'clock to-day, and previous to this——

PRESIDENT—I know this very well; but this resolution covers this case.

Mr. STAUFFER—Rule XXXI provides that this question cannot come up until unfinished business is disposed of.

Mr. ABELL—I only desire to make one more——

Mr. STAUFFER—I call the gentleman to order.

Mr. ABELL—I desire to remark that under Mr. Thorpe's resolution this is unfinished business. Saturday being set apart for miscellaneous business, this matter is left over, and is, consequently, the unfinished business of Saturday, and must come up now.

Mr. HENDERSON—The rules are that unfinished business must be taken up first. On Friday, unfinished business, the judiciary report. On Saturday there was no special business. One day having intervened on which there was no business upon which action was had, this resolution cannot be unfinished business.

PRESIDENT—The order of the day is article 12 of the judiciary report.

Mr. SULLIVAN—I would like to know, then, when my resolution is going to come up. We have legislated long enough for rich men, and now I want to legislate some for poor men.

Mr. ABELL—Mr. President, I think this question should come up; I believe it is in order and I—

PRESIDENT—Very well, take your appeal.

Mr. ABELL—I most respectfully appeal from the decision of the chair.

[The ayes and noes were called.]

Mr. HENDERSON—Mr. President, I believe there is no quorum, and ask a call of the House before the vote is declared.

[The secretary called the roll. Mr. Cutler entered during the roll-call, when it was ascertained that there were 76 members present. Mr. Cutler, by permission of the Convention, cast his vote, and the House refused to sustain the chair.

PRESIDENT—The order of the day is Mr. Sullivan's resolution relative to the police.

[The secretary read the resolution.]

Mr. FOLEY—I wish to amend line seven by striking out "$275" as salary of chief of police and inserting "$200" instead.

Mr. ORR—Mr. President, I wish to amend as follows:

Provided, That the compensation of all foremen, mechanics, cartmen and laborers employed on public works under the governments of the State of Louisiana, city of New Orleans, and Police Juries of the various loyal parishes of the State, shall also be increased to not less than the following rates, viz:

All foremen not less than $3 50 per day.
All mechanics not less than $3 00 per day.
All cartmen not less than $3 00 per day.
All laborers not less than $2 00 per day.

Mr. THORPE—I second Mr. Orr's amendment.

Mr. PURSELL—I move to lay the whole matter on the table.

Mr. SULLIVAN—This motion is out of order. It has already been decided. The motion was made the other day and voted down.

Mr. ABELL—I wish to state that when this resolution was offered there was a motion made to lay it on the table and it was lost. Now, sir, they cannot lay the resolution on the table. They can lay the amendment to the amendment on the table, and the amendment itself, but a motion cannot be entertained to lay the resolution.

Mr. HEARD—Mr. President, I move that the resolution and the amendments be rejected.

PRESIDENT—It had passed out of my mind that the motion to lay Mr. Sullivan's resolution on the table was made and lost. Now the motion is to lay the amendment of the amendment on the table.

[The ayes and noes were called, and the secretary proceeded to call the roll.]

Mr. BURKE—Before the vote is announced, I desire to change my vote from *yes* to *no*.

Mr. WATERS—I change my vote from *yes* to *no*.

Mr. HENDERSON—I change my vote from *yes* to *no*.

Mr. BARRETT—I change my vote from *yes* to *no*.

[The result of the vote was as follows—yeas 9, nays 66.]

Mr. POYNOT—I move the adoption of the amendment.

Mr. ABELL—I wish to know if that is open to debate, and if so, I desire to say a word or two. [Voices: "Louder."] I am slow of speech, and it sometimes takes me some time to get my voice up so as to be heard by the House. I regret very much that the gentleman has offered his amendment to this bill, and my reason is that I fear it will have some effect upon the main question before the House. Now, sir, this bill that has been offered—or we might call it an article, to be placed in the constitution at such place as may be proper—is one in which I feel that there is no trifling interest involved. The interests involved are really greater than can be presented to this Convention at this time. It will be contended that this Convention has no such power. I think we have the power. I think we have power to make and to destroy corporations, to control them and to direct them; and unless we do it I think our work here will be very ineffectually done. I contend, sir, that the corporation of New Orleans has wholly failed in every respect to furnish any protection to one hundred and fifty thousand permanent residents, and perhaps three times as many transient persons. We have been beaten down, and thugged, and oppressed in every way. The city has totally failed to perform its functions, and even now the little protection we have is due to the Federal arms and police. We have had no protection previously for twelve years. Now, sir, I ask, when a corporation has wholly failed to perform its functions; to secure to the people their rights, their safety, their personal property; I ask, whether it is not the duty of the Convention to prepare a proper safeguard against a recurrence of the occurrences that have taken place. I am not joking about this, sir; it is no matter of joke, and I intend to fortify, I intend to instruct. If necessary I will repose, and renew the attack from time to time, until we secure protection. And I know of no way to insure to the people that protection which is their right, except by the very mode attempted here. Talk about our want of power. Admit that this Convention has no power to afford protection to one hundred and fifty thousand citizens—and in four or five years it will be four or five hundred thousand. It is simply absurd. If we have not this power, we have no power whatever.

Without remarking upon the objects contemplated by the amendment of the gentleman, (Mr. Orr,) I regret exceedingly that he offered it, because I believe the design was to kill the bill. Notwithstanding all this, I hope that this Convention will at once vote upon the bill. They voted against laying it on the table by a very large majority. I hope that when they come to the amendment they will vote it down.

Men engaged on the public works are differently situated from policemen. They can go where they please, and demand such remuneration as their services are worth; their wages are not fixed by law, and they can take as much as their employers will agree to pay. But the salary of the policeman is fixed. He cannot take more than the law allows him. Let him be caught taking more, and he is at once censured or discharged. When he is discharged there is not another corporation to employ him. The workman commands his own hire, and can put it where it will be of most value to him. Such are the facts, and I trust the Convention will look at the matter in its true light, and vote down this amendment, and let the article of the report stand upon its merits.

Mr. CAZABAT—I have not occupied the attention or time of the Convention for several days. I have not participated in the discussions of the questions that have come up, because I felt a reluctance to do so. At the beginning of the Convention I offered a resolution prohibiting the introduction of any resolution which was not directly connected with the amendment of the constitution, but it was voted down by a large majority. If it had been adopted, we would not have been where we are now, in respect to the accomplishment of our business.

Mr. MONTAMAT—I rise to a point of order. The gentleman is not discussing the police bill at all.

Mr. CAZABAT—I have never interrupted any gentleman on the floor; but when members were speaking I begged the Convention to allow them to continue, and speak till doomsday if they chose, and I have uniformly exhibited to the Convention the courtesy that was due. It is said I am not touching the question under discussion. There is no power inside or outside of this Convention that can make me deviate from the path I deem true and right—no power to make me adopt a resolution which is contrary, or in opposition to the object we have in view. The minutes of our proceedings will show that I have advocated the revision and amendment of the constitution, and that alone. I wish the poor man to be paid for his labor; I am a poor man, and sympathize with that class. I know what it is to be cast on the world friendless, homeless and penniless. I wish the police officers to be well paid also. [A voice "vote for it."] I shall do no such thing; because we have no right to bring such a proposition before this body. If the resolution had recommended to the mayor or proper authorities such a course, I would have supported it cheerfully.

But since you seem determined to legislate, contrary to your right and duty, upon any and every outside matter not connected with the amendment and revision of the constitution, let me warn you now. Beware, beware, I say, how you trifle with the majesty of an outraged people. In these days of political and social revolution, the day may come when you will be sorry for your arbitrary acts in this Convention.

Mr. THORPE—Since I have been here I have endeavored twice to get a resolution before this body that would facilitate the business of the Convention. The first I introduced some five weeks ago, but by the decision of the chair I found I had failed in accomplishing my object. On the 31st of May, I introduced a resolution that the order of the day should be immediately taken up after the minutes were read and accepted. The president decided this morning—and properly, I believe—that the police bill had no place here.

Now, gentlemen of the Convention, I have a few plain words to offer on this question. We have not assembled here for this miscellaneous business, and I say it is unjust to gentlemen who have come here with the sincere purpose of regenerating Louisiana and amending the constitution. These outrageous interruptions and irrelevant business are an insult to good order, good taste and the transaction of business. [Applause.] I say that any man that goes into the streets of New Orleans and tells the people I am opposed to the firemen, states what is absolutely false; and yet this has been done many times in the city. In regard to this proposition to give the poor laborer a fixed pay, I say any man who has any logical mind, any person coming from abroad, who listens to the proceedings of this Convention, would say we are all a set of lunatics, in reference to the character of our debates and business. What have we to do with what the State shall pay the laborers on the public works? What have we to do in regard to fixing the police regulations? This constitution has got to be passed upon by the whole State, and there are fifty or sixty parishes. Is every man to come up and sit in judgment on this police bill? It is a most extraordinary absurdity.

With regard to the laboring men: when the fleet came up the river, and the Federal forces took possession of this city, Gen. Butler did me the honor to put in my possession the laboring men and the poor people of this city, and I know something of them. I have not shown my sympathy with that class by getting up and making buncombe speeches, or presenting buncombe resolutions. When I came here I went about quietly, honestly and earnestly to help these poor men. Gen. Butler was forced to admit, and it is certainly fearfully true, with most honorable exceptions, that it was only the poor men who were constantly and undisguisedly loyal. It is the poor laboring men who have worked on the canals and streets, and added millions of dollars to the wealth of the city, and they deserve the consideration of the Convention. What gentleman here dare get up and say that the firemen, as a class, have ever shown their loyalty? I have never seen it since I have been here. I have seen but one engine company, and that was composed of Germans, who had the courage and honesty to bear the stars and stripes.

Gentlemen come in here, I believe, with political purposes, or else to break up this Convention and make it ridiculous in the eyes of the world. In regard to the police bill I believe in its object. It is true, as the gentleman stated, that disorder has always reigned here and thuggery has been predominant, and the police have been no better since the Federal fleet came up here than they were before. To-day the mass of the policemen are disloyal in their hearts, and lose no opportunity to strike down a Federal soldier. I despise and hate this police, and have done all I could to put it down, though there are are some noble exceptions, but you cannot put it down. You cannot introduce the proposition of its reform into this Convention, and cannot have anything to do with it legitimately and honorably, therefore I wish to leave it out. There is but one subject outside of the legitimate duty of the Convention that can be legitimately attended to, and that is the cause of humanity—the cause of God. In voting on the resolution appropriating sums for charitable purposes, although the same rule applies, but the necessity was so great as to warrant in overstepping it. The day is nearly past, and if the president had been sustained in his decision, it would not have been lost, and several thousand dollars would not have been added to the debt of the State and the credit of the Convention. We have so great a responsibility resting upon us, and when the eyes of the nation are turned towards us, when the solution of all these questions depends upon our action, I hope the fact will impress itself upon our minds, and not allow the time to be absorbed by considering the policemen and firemen and such matters, but let us come to the great subject and form a constitution which will solve this difficulty and restore these rebellious States. Let us show to the loyal States that the Louisianians have come together to seriously and earnestly perform their work. I as well as others have got something to do besides come into this Convention—[a voice, "resign then."] I will not resign. I came here to do my work, and I ask again if it is not possible to come in here from day to day and attend to our legitimate business and get through with it and go home?

Mr. Kavanagh—As I am one of the nine members who voted to lay Mr. Orr's amendment on the table, I will say that I did so because I thought we had nothing to do with the subject under consideration. I do not see what the salaries of laborers have to do with those of police officers. We might as well introduce into the bill a resolution fixing the salary of the governor. I am not opposed to increasing the pay of laborers, but am in favor of compensating them well for their services. Mr. Thorpe has stated that the laboring men were the only true loyal men. I would ask him who were the men who went on the police force—went against their friends, whom they had known for years, and supported the Federal government? I would ask him if the police force is composed of rich or poor men, and whether they or the rich men supported the Federal government when the forces came here?

Mr. ORR—Some gentlemen have made arguments here without point; but the gentlemen from the Second and Fifth (Messrs. Henderson and Abell) have talked about everything that has come before this Convention, and been uniformly unfortunate in their arguments. The former is so dull of comprehension that he cannot understand the amendment I offered, but has resorted to a legal quibble and made it say what it does not. He says it refers to the workmen under the United States, etc. I say it does not. Nor does the language of the amendment admit of being construed in any such manner. It says nothing about United States works, but simply reads as follows:

Provided, That the compensation of all foremen, mechanics, cartmen and laborers employed on public works under the governments of the State of Louisiana, city of New Orleans, and Police Juries of the various loyal parishes of the State, shall also be increased to not less than the following rates, viz:

All foremen not less than $3 50 per day.
All mechanics not less than $3 00 per day.
All cartmen not less than $3 00 per day.
All laborers not less than $2 00 per day.

It does not pretend to control or fix the compensation of laborers employed by the United States government.

The latter gentleman has made some admissions which are very unfortunate for him, and the class which he represents. He has asserted that unless you give the officers of the police force and its humble members the salaries set forth in this resolution, they will be incompetent and unworthy policemen—will not do their duty, &c. I say gentlemen that any police officer or any other officer of the city of New Orleans or State, who is unwilling to discharge his duties in a faithful manner because he receives a small salary, would not discharge them any better, any more faithfully, if you give him all the money in the treasury. [Applause.]

Gentlemen have accused me of insincerity in offering this amendment. I hurl back the accusation in their very teeth! I stand here sincere in regard to all I offer. Although I did not make any pledges to the laboring men and mechanics, that if they would vote for me I would vote to increase their pay, and then opposed it, as has been the case of some members here, who advocate the other side, but I consider it the right and due of these men that their pay should be increased. I have no objection to increasing the pay of the police force, and think it deserves it, but at the same time think we have as much right to and should legislate for the mechanic and day laborer. [Applause.] Their pay is not more than sufficient to keep their souls and bodies together, and is not sufficient to clothe their families in the manner in which they should be clothed.

Gentlemen, these men have *rights*. They have to their sorrow and misfortune been led away time and again by political leaders, who, previous to elections, take them by the hand *and* ask, "How do you do?" "Am so glad to see you." "How is your little wife and children." "Come and take a drink." Finally get them drunk, endeavor to buy their votes, in which they too often succeed, and then after they have been elected, say *to them*, "I never knew you." Sir, I have seen this and know it to be the case, and defy any one to contradict it.

Now, gentlemen, I say if we have a right to legislate for all State officers, governor, secretary of state, treasurer, &c., not excepting the judges, and to fix large salaries from ten thousand dollars per annum down, I say that we have the same right to give to the deserving laborer the small pittance that he earns by the sweat of his brow. [Applause.]

I am in favor of giving to the poor man, who labors with his hands in the midday sun on the canals, streets, etc., a sufficient amount to support himself and family in a decent manner at least. Mr. Abell has said it was not necessary that any legislation should be had in regard to poor laboring men, and that if they did not want to work in New Orleans for $1 50 per day, they could quit and go somewhere else. I think that will apply as well to the police as to the laboring man, and that if he is not willing to work for $50 or $60 a month he might quit. Gentlemen, I want all justice done here, and don't want to see one class of men benefited at the expense of another—the rich man at the expense of the poor man. Supposing the increased pay of the police should be given, and the same in regard to the laboring man and the mechanic; I ask you, who will pay for it? The very men; the poor men pay. That is the principle established by Cobden, of England, in regard to imports; that the importer does not pay the duty, but the consumer; and so it is with regard to the laboring men and mechanics of New Orleans. Increase their pay and they will appropriate a larger share of it to satisfy their higher rents; for the landlord does not pay the taxes, but merely advances the money. Gentlemen have taken exception to this resolution, because I have brought it up in the form of an amendment to the police bill. I have a right to offer an amendment to any bill, and would as soon have offered it to any other as to this, as I feel disposed to vote for it—the police bill—especially if you will incorporate my amendment therein. I do not say anything about laborers employed by private individuals, but only speak of those in the employ of the city and State, on the public works. I do not attempt to fix the price that any individual shall pay or receive, and do not contend that we have a right to do any such thing, but that if we have a right to fix the compensation of one class in public service we have a right to fix that of all classes so employed.

Now, gentlemen the laboring classes have been very badly treated. The gentleman from the Second District (Mr. Thorpe) said that they were under his charge. protection, etc. I know he had a good deal to do with these matters—giving them employment, etc., but he did not state to this Convention that at one time, although he may have had nothing to do with it, if so I would exonerate him, while these men were working in the employ of the city of New Orleans, the very men who pretended to be their friends cut down their pay, from the paltry pittance of one dollar to fifty cents a day; and even went so far as to declare that too much, and that the laboring man should live on two bits a day as well as they could on four. I told the foremen, when this was done, to give their men full time if they only worked one day in the week. [Applause.]

Now, gentlemen, I want, if possible, to fix the compensation to be paid these laboring men by the city and State governments, so that they may not be forced hereafter to work for fifty cents a day, or starve or steal; but that they shall always be entitled to receive not less than a fair compensation for their labor. I do not ask you to make these men rich, but to give them enough to eat, drink and wear; and God knows that, for men who are willing to work, is as little as can be given them.

[Cries of "Question, question."

The yeas and nays were then called on the adoption of the amendment of Mr. Orr, with the following result:]

YEAS — Messrs. Abell, Ariail, Austin, Balch, Barrett, Baum, Beauvais, Bell, Bennie, Bromley, Buckley, Burke, Campbell, Cook J. K., Cook T., Crozat, Cutler, Davies, Dufresne, Dupaty, Edwards, Ennis, Fish, Flagg, Flood, Foley, Fosdick, Fuller, Gastinel, Goldman, Gorlinski, Gaidry, Healy, Harnan, Hart, Henderson, Hills, Hire, Howes, Knobloch, Kugler, Maas, Mann, Maurer, Montamat, Morris, Murphy M. W., Mayer, Normand, O'Conner, Orr, Poynot, Purcell J., Pursell S., Schroeder, Schnurr, Seymour, Shaw, Smith, Spellicy, Stocker, Stumpf, Stiner, Sullivan, Terry, Thorpe, Waters—67.

NAYS — Messrs. Bailey, Bofill, Cazabat, Gruneberg, Heard, Howell, Kavanagh, Newell, Paine J. T., Pintado—10.

[Before the result was announced, Mr. Abell changed his vote from "no" to "yes."

The amendment was accordingly adopted.

The amendment as amended was then adopted by a *viva voce* vote.

The motion to adopt the resolution of

Mr. Sullivan, as amended, was then put and carried by the following vote :]

YEAS—Messrs. Abell, Barrett, Baum, Beauvais, Bell, Bofill, Buckley, Cook J. K., Cook T., Cutler, Dufresne, Fish, Flood, Foley, Fuller, Gastinel, Gorlinskl, Gruneberg, Healy, Harnan, Hart, Henderson, Hire, Howes. Kavanagh, Kugler, Maas, Maurer, Montamat, Murphy M. W., Normand, O'Conner, Orr, Poynot, Purcell J., Pursell S., Schroeder, Schnurr, Smith, Spellicy, Stocker, Stumpf, Stiner, Sullivan, Terry, Waters—46.

NAYS—Messrs. Ariail, Austin, Balch, Bailey, Bennie, Bromley, Burke, Campbell, Cazabat, Crozat, Davies, Dupaty, Edwards, Ennis, Flagg, Fosdick, Goldman, Gaidry, Heard, Hills, Howell, Knobloch, Mann, Morris, Mayer, Newell, Paine J. T., Pintado, Seymour, Shaw, Thorpe—31.

[On motion of Mr. Smith, the Convention then adjourned till 12 M. June 7th.]

TUESDAY, June 7, 1864.

[Pursuant to adjournment the Convention met, and was called to order at 12 o'clock M. The roll was called, and the following members answered to their names :]

Messrs. Abell, Bell, Bennie, Burke, Buckley, Cook J. K., Cook T., Crozat, Edwards, Ennis, Fish, Flagg, Foley, Geier, Gorlinski, Healy, Heard, Henderson, Knobloch, Mann, Mayer, Montamat, Morris, Normand, O'Conner, Pintado, Poynot, Pursell S., Spellicy, Shaw, Stumpf, Stiner, Stauffer, Sullivan and Mr. President—35.

[After some delay the following members answered to their names :]

Messrs. Austin, Bailey, Barrett, Baum, Beauvais, Bofill, Bromley, Campbell, Collin, Cutler, Davies, Flood, Fosdick, Fuller, Gastinel, Gaidry, Gruneberg, Harnan, Hart, Hills, Hire, Howell, Howes, Kugler, Maas, Maurer, Mendiverri, Murphy M. W., Murphy E., Newell, Ong, Orr, Purcell J., Schroeder, Seymour, Smith, Stocker, Terry, Thorpe, Waters, Wenck, Wilson—42.

[After some delay a quorum was announced as being present.

The minutes of yesterday's proceedings were read and adopted.]

Mr. PURSELL—Mr. President, I move a reconsideration of the vote on Mr. Sullivan's resolution, and the amendment thereto, fixing the wages of the police and of laborers on the public works.

Mr. BOFILL—I move to lay that resolution on the table.

[The ayes and noes were called at the same time that the question was put, and the question was declared.]

Mr. HILLS—I rise to a point of order. Many gentlemen rose for the ayes and noes who did not intend to vote and were counted by the secretary as voting.

PRESIDENT—When the ayes and noes were called a sufficient number did not rise.

Mr. PURSELL—There was certainly a misunderstanding. I would not have voted to table my own motion.

[The ayes and noes were called.]

Mr. GEIER—I change my vote from *no* to *yes*.

Mr. BURKE—I change mine from *yes* to *no*.

[The result of the vote was as follows :]

YEAS—Messrs. Abell, Bailey, Baum, Bell, Beauvais, Bofill, Buckley, Cook J. K., Cook T., Cutler, Fish, Flagg, Flood, Foley, Gastinel, Geier, Gorlinski, Gruneberg, Harnan, Hart, Healy, Henderson, Howes, Maurer, Maas, Mendiverri, Montamat, Murphy M. W., Murphy E., O'Conner, Orr, Poynot, Smith, Schroeder, Seymour, Spellicy, Stocker, Stiner, Stumpf, Sullivan, Terry, Waters—42.

NAYS—Messrs. Austin, Balch, Bennie, Bromley, Burke, Campbell, Collin, Crozat, Davies, Ennis, Fosdick, Gaidry, Heard, Hire, Hills, Howell, Knobloch, Kugler, Mayer, Mann, Morris, Newell, Normand, Ong, Pintado, Pursell S., Shaw, Stauffer, Thorpe, Wenck, Wilson—31.

[The motion to reconsider was tabled.]

Mr. DAVIES—Am I in order, Mr. President, to offer a resolution.

Mr. HEALY—I move a call of the House.

PRESIDENT—The order of the day is the second reading of the report of the Committee on the Judiciary.

Mr. BAUM—Mr. President, I move to reconsider the vote of last Friday.

Mr. HILLS—I second the motion.

Mr. SMITH—I protest against this action. We cannot reconsider at this time, after two days has passed.

PRESIDENT—This is the first time the order of the day has come up.

Mr. HENDERSON—Saturday was not a day known to this Convention.

Mr. SMITH—We met and adjourned, and I protest against this action now.

PRESIDENT—It is too late to reconsider, under article 36 of our rules and regulations. It might have been moved yesterday before the order of the day was taken up. Saturday I do not consider a day of business, under the resolution of Mr. Thorpe. If it had been offered yesterday it might have been taken up.

Mr. CUTLER—I wish merely to explain, that Saturday, there being no quorum, it could not have been taken up, and Monday was specially set apart for consideration of bills and resolutions, consequently it could not be taken up then, and this is the first day, and more, it must be in time, and that this is the first day under the rules; and believing this to be the proper day, I shall, with all due respect to the decision of the president, appeal from the decision.

Mr. ABELL—I think the president will perceive at once the error into which he has fallen, and will retract it. On motion of Mr. Thorpe, it was decided that after the reading of the minutes the order of the day should be taken up. By this resolution it is especially declared that the order of the day shall be taken up immediately after the reading of the minutes. This precludes other business, and puts it out of the power of the House to take action on anything else. Yesterday, by special order, the police bill, being the order of the day, came within the exact purview of Thorpe's resolution.

Mr. PURSELL—Mr. President, is white black, or is black white? The question resolves itself to this: not whether this or that was the order of the day, but whether yesterday was a sitting day. The question has once been decided that it was a regular sitting day.

Mr. MONTAMAT—Mr. President, I understand that the gentleman informed the House last Friday that the next time that the bill came up he should move a reconsideration.

PRESIDENT—The best way to decide the question is to take an appeal from the decision of the chair.

Mr. CUTLER—An appeal has been taken, Mr. President.

Mr. HENDERSON—I desire to make a statement in order that all present may be right in voting. If the decision is right to-day the decision yesterday was wrong; but you voted against the decision yesterday, and the same gentlemen who voted against it yesterday are bound to sustain it to-day if they wish to be consistent.

Mr. PURSELL—Mr. President, I call attention to rule XXXV to show that an appeal from the decision of the chair is not debatable.

PRESIDENT—The rule has no application to this case.

Mr. STOCKER—The gentleman has entered into some special pleading, and objects because the judiciary question was not the order of the day yesterday. The rules do not say that the judiciary question shall be the order of the day. It was decided that the order of the day was Mr. Sullivan's resolution, and the rules say that a motion to reconsider must be made before the order of the day is taken up, whatever it may be. Rule 26 is as follows:

When a motion has been once made and carried in the affirmative or negative, it shall be in order for any member of the majority to move for a reconsideration thereof: *Provided*, it is made on the same day or the next sitting day, before the order of the day is taken up. And a motion for immediate reconsideration shall supercede a notice that a reconsideration will be moved.

The Convention decided that the order of the day was the resolution of Mr. Sullivan, and this motion to reconsider should have been made before that was taken up.

PRESIDENT—The question is on the appeal from the decision of the chair. The chair decides that it is too late to entertain a motion to reconsider the action of the Convention Friday, in regard article 11.

[The question was put and the chair sustained—yeas 37, nays 35.]

Mr. HOWELL—I move a call of the House, as a quorum has not voted.

[The roll was called and seventy-six members responded to the call.

Article 12 of the report on judiciary department was read:]

Art. 12. The clerks of the inferior courts shall be appointed by the judges thereof, and they shall hold their offices during good behavior, subject to removal by the judges respectively, with the right of appeal, in all such cases, to the Supreme Court.

[Mr. Stauffer's amendment was read:]

Clerks of the inferior courts in this State shall be elected for the term of four years, and should a vacancy occur subsequent to an election it shall be filled by the judge of the court in which such vacancy exists, and the person so appointed shall hold his office until the next general election.

[Mr. Sullivan's amendment was read :]

The clerks of the inferior courts in this State shall be elected for the term of four years, and should a vacancy occur subsequent to an election, it shall be filled by the judge of the court in which the vacancy exists, and the person so appointed shall hold his office until the next general election. The judges of the several inferior courts shall have the power to remove the clerks thereof for breach of good behavior, subject, in all cases, to an appeal to the Supreme Court.

Mr. MONTAMAT--I offer the following amendment to it :

Art. 12. The clerks of the inferior courts shall be appointed by the governor during the existing war, and two years thereafter; then, to be elected by the qualified voters for a term of four years.

Mr. SULLIVAN--I accept the amendment.

Mr. HENDERSON--I have a few words to say on Mr. Montamat's amendment. It provides that during the existence of the war the appointment shall be made by the governor, and that he shall hold his office for a certain period of time, until the war is over, and thereafter. The clerk shall be elected by the people. I favor it all the way through, and hope it will meet the approbation of this body.

Mr. ORR--I move to lay it on the table.

[The yeas and nays were taken, and the motion lost.]

YEAS—Messrs. Baum, Beauvais, Burke, Campbell, Collin, Foley, Fosdick, Gastinel, Gorlinski, Gruneberg, Hart, Hills, Howell, Howes, Knobloch, Kugler, Mann, Maurer, Morris, Normand, Orr, Pintado, Poynot, Pursell S., Schroeder, Stauffer, Waters, Wenck, Wilson—29.

NAYS—Messrs. Abell, Austin, Balch, Barrett, Bailey, Bell, Bennie, Bofill, Bromley, Buckley, Cook J. K., Cook T., Crozat, Cutler, Davies, Edwards, Ennis, Fish, Flagg, Flood, Gaidry, Geier, Harnan, Healy, Heard, Henderson, Hire, Maas, Mayer, Mendiverri, Montamat, Murphy E., Murphy M. W., Newell, O'Conner, Ong, Seymour, Shaw, Smith, Spellicy, Stocker, Stumpf, Stiner, Sullivan, Terry, Thorpe—46.

Mr. HENDERSON—I move the adoption of the amendment.

[The roll was called and the motion lost by the following vote :]

YEAS—Messrs. Abell, Balch, Barrett, Bell, Bennie, Bofill, Buckley, Burke, Cook T., Crozat, Edwards, Ennis, Fish, Flagg, Flood, Geier, Gaidry, Healy, Harnan, Henderson, Maas, Mendiverri, Montamat, Murphy E., Murphy M. W., Normand, O'Conner, Seymour, Shaw, Smith, Stocker, Stumpf, Stiner, Stauffer, Sullivan, Terry, Thorpe—37.

NAYS—Messrs. Austin, Bailey, Beauvais, Baum, Bromley, Campbell, Collin, Cook J. K., Cutler, Davies, Foley, Fosdick, Gastinel, Gorlinski, Gruneberg, Hart, Heard, Hills, Hire, Howell, Howes, Knobloch, Kugler, Mann, Maurer, Morris, Mayer, Newell, Ong, Orr, Pintado, Poynot, Pursell S., Schroeder, Spellicy, Waters, Wenck, Wilson—38.

[The amendment of Mr. Stauffer was then taken up.]

Mr. TERRY—I move to amend by striking out "two" and inserting "four."

Mr. SULLIVAN—I move to lay the motion on the table.

[Carried.

The yeas and nays were called for on the adoption of Mr. Stauffer's amendment and the motion carried, as follows :]

YEAS—Messrs. Abell, Balch, Bailey, Barrett, Baum, Bell, Bofill, Buckley, Campbell, Collin, Cook J. K., Cook T., Davies, Ennis, Fish, Flagg, Flood, Gastinel, Geier, Gorlinski, Gruneberg, Healy, Harnan, Hart, Henderson, Howes, Knobloch, Maas, Maurer, Mendiverri, Montamat, Morris, Murphy E., Mayer, Orr, Poynot, Pursell S., Shaw, Smith, Spellicy, Stocker, Stiner, Stauffer, Sullivan, Terry, Thorpe, Waters—47.

NAYS—Messrs. Austin, Beauvais, Bennie, Bromley, Burke, Crozat, Cutler, Edwards, Foley, Fosdick, Gaidry, Heard, Hills, Hire, Howell, Kugler, Mann, Murphy M. W., Newell, Normand, Ong, Pintado, Schroeder, Seymour, Stumpf, Wenck, Wilson—27.

[Article 13 was adopted as read :]

Art. 13. The Legislature shall have power to vest in clerks of courts authority to grant such orders and do such acts as may be deemed necessary for the furtherance of the administration of justice, and in all cases the powers thus granted shall be specified and determined.

[Article 14 was read :]

Art. 14. The jurisdiction of justices of the peace shall not exceed, in civil cases, the sum of one hundred dollars, exclusive of interest, subject to appeal in such cases as shall be provided for by law. They shall be appointed by the governor, with the advice and consent of the Senate, and shall hold their offices during good behavior. They shall have such criminal jurisdiction as shall be provided by law.

[Mr. Sullivan's amendment :]

The jurisdiction of justices of the peace shall be limited in civil cases to cases where the matter in dispute does not exceed two hundred dollars, exclusive of interest, subject to appeal in such cases as shall be provided for by law. They shall be elected by the qualified electors of each parish, district or ward, for the term of two years, in such manner, and shall have such criminal jurisdiction as shall be provided by law.

Mr. FLOOD—I offer the following amendment:

All differences and disputes under $25 shall be finally settled by arbitration.

Mr. MONTAMAT—I move to lay on the table.

[Carried.

Mr. Stiner offered an amendment to Mr. Sullivan's substitute, making the office of justice of the peace appointive until two years after the present war, which amendment was laid on the table.

Mr. Flagg offered an amendment, providing that justices of the peace shall be appointed by the governor, and shall hold their offices until two years after the proclamation of peace, after which time they shall be elected by the people, and further providing that their jurisdiction shall not exceed one hundred dollars.

Laid on the table by a rising vote of 45 yeas to 17 nays.]

Mr. MONTAMAT—I move the adoption of the original.

Mr. S. PURSELL—I move to strike out "two," in the fifth line of Mr. Sullivan's amendment, and insert "four."

Mr. MONTAMAT—I move to lay that on the table.

[The motion was lost—yeas 26, nays 67.

The amendment was then adopted.

PRESIDENT—The question now is on the adoption of Mr. Sullivan's amendment as amended.

[The amendment as amended was adopted by a *viva voce* vote.

Article 15 was read :]

Art. 15. There shall be an attorney general for the State, and as many district attorneys as may be hereafter found necessary. They shall be appointed by the governor, with the advice and consent of the Senate, and shall hold their offices during the term for which the governor shall have been elected. Their duties shall be determined by law.

[Mr. Sullivan offered the following substitute:

There shall be an attorney general, who shall be elected by the qualified voters of the State, and the district attorneys by the qualified voters of each district, on the day of the election for governor of the State. They shall hold their offices for a term of four years.

Mr. TERRY—I wish to amend by inserting after the word "State," in the amendment, "who shall receive a salary of $5000 per annum."

Mr. SULLIVAN—I accept the amendment.

[The motion to adopt the amendment was declared lost, when a division was called, with the following result—yeas 32, nays 40.]

Mr. MONTAMAT—I move to reconsider the last vote. I was voting only on the amendment of Mr. Terry, and did not understand that it had been accepted.

[The motion to reconsider was carried.]

Mr. MONTAMAT—I move to strike out "five" and insert "four."

[Motion to table was lost, and the amendment to the amendment lost on division called—ayes 30, nays 39.]

Mr. STAUFFER—The amendment will destroy the sense of the whole article.

Mr. TERRY—No, sir, it will not.

[The amendment was then adopted by a rising vote of 42 ayes to 31 nays, and the article was adopted as amended.

The following was read :]

Art. 16. A sheriff and a coroner shall be appointed in each parish, by the governor, with the advice and consent of the Senate, and they shall hold their offices for the term for which the governor shall have been elected, unless sooner removed. The Legislature shall have power to increase the number of sheriffs in any parish.

Mr. SULLIVAN—I offer the following substitute for article 16 :

A sheriff and a coroner shall be elected in each parish by the qualified voters thereof, who shall hold their office for the term of two years, unless removed. The Legislature shall have the power to increase the number of sheriffs in any parish. Should a vacancy occur in either of these offices subsequent to an election, it shall be filled by the governor ; and the person so appointed shall continue in office until his successor shall be elected and qualified.

The Legislature may determine the mode of filling the vacancies in the offices of the inferior judges, attorney general, district attorneys, and all other offices not otherwise provided for in this constitution.

Mr. HENDERSON—I move to strike out "two" before years, and insert "four."

Mr. MONTAMAT—As an amendment to the amendment, I move to strike out "four" and insert "one."

[Both were tabled.

Mr. Sullivan's amendment was adopted, as was the report as a whole.

The Convention adjourned until 12 M. of Wednesday, the 8th inst.]

WEDNESDAY, June 8, 1864.

[The Convention met and was called to order pursuant to adjournment, Hon. E. H. Durell, president, in the chair. Fifty members answered to their names at first roll call.

After some delay, twenty-eight other members appeared and answered to their names, when a quorum was announced. Absent—the following members :]

Messrs. Balch, Baum, Bonzano, Brott, Cazabat, Decker, Duane, Duke, Flagg, Fuller, Goldman, Kavanagh, Lobdell, Millspaugh, Montague, Payne J., Paine J. T., Taliaferro, Thomas—19.

[The journal of yesterday was read and approved.]

Mr. HEARD—Mr. President, I wish to move a suspension of the rules in order to offer a resolution.

Mr. MONTAMAT—Let us hear the resolution.

PRESIDENT—Mr. Secretary, read the resolution.

[The secretary read :]

Resolved, That from and after to-day, every member who fails to answer to his name at roll-call, or within fifteen minutes thereafter, shall forfeit his per diem, unless he be absent by leave, or can furnish some legitimate excuse for his absence.

Mr. FOLEY—I move a suspension of the rules in order to adopt it.

[The motion to suspend the rules was lost.]

Mr. ABELL—Mr. President, I rise to a point of order. Under the resolution of Mr. Thorpe adopted by the Convention, all such business must come up on Saturday.

PRESIDENT—The order of the day, the report of the Committee on the Judiciary, is now in order.

Mr. CAMPBELL—I move to reconsider that part of the report which gives jurisdiction to justices of the peace for two hundred dollars, and move to amend it to one hundred dollars.

Mr. BOFILL—I move to reconsider the whole report.

[Mr. Smith moved to lay the motion to reconsider on the table, upon which motion the yeas and nays were demanded, and being taken, resulted as follows :]

YEAS—Messrs. Austin, Buckley, Burke, Cook J. K., Flood, Harnan, Henderson, Howes, Maurer, Morris, Murphy M. W., Orr, Poynot, Purcell J., Pursell S., Schroeder, Schnurr, Smith, Spellicy, Stocker, Sullivan, Stauffer, Terry, Waters—24.

NAYS—Messrs. Abell, Ariail, Bailey, Barrett, Beauvais, Bell, Bennie, Bofill, Bromley, Campbell, Collin, Cook T., Crozat, Cutler, Davies, Dufresne, Dupaty, Edwards, Ennis, Fish, Foley, Fosdick, Gastinel, Geier, Gorlinski, Gruneberg, Gaidry, Healy, Hart, Heard, Hills, Hire, Howell, Knobloch, Kugler, Maas, Mann, Montamat, Mendiverri, Murphy E., Mayer, Newell, Normand, Ong, O'Conner, Pintado, Seymour, Shaw, Stumpf, Stiner, Thorpe, Wenck, Wells, Wilson—54.

[Consequently the motion was lost.

The question recurring on the motion to reconsider, the yeas and nays were demanded, and being taken, resulted as follows :]

YEAS—Messrs. Abell, Ariail, Bailey, Barrett, Beauvais, Bennie, Bofill, Bromley, Burke, Campbell, Collin, Cook T., Crozat, Cutler, Davies, Dufresne, Dupaty, Edwards, Ennis, Fish, Foley, Fosdick, Gastinel, Gorlinski, Gaidry, Hart, Heard, Hills, Hire, Howell, Knobloch, Kugler, Maas, Mann, Mendiverri, Murphy E., Mayer, Newell, Normand, O'Conner, Ong, Pintado, Schroeder, Seymour, Shaw, Stumpf, Stiner, Thorpe, Waters, Wenck, Wells, Wilson—52.

NAYS—Messrs. Austin, Bell, Buckley, Cook J. K., Flood, Geier, Gruneberg, Healy, Harnan, Henderson, Howes, Maurer, Montamat, Morris, Murphy M. W., Orr, Poynot, Purcell J., Pursell S., Schnurr, Smith, Spellicy, Stauffer, Stocker, Sullivan, Terry—26.

Mr. BOFILL—I move that the original report of the judiciary, with the substitutes and amendments thereto, be recommitted.

[Motion seconded.]

Mr. WILSON—I move, as an amendment, that it be referred to a special committee of nine, to be appointed by the chair, to report as early as practicable.

[Amendment accepted and motion carried as amended.]

PRESIDENT—I shall appoint this committee to-morrow, and as there has been a majority in favor of an elective judiciary, I shall appoint five on that side of the question and four on the other.

Mr. STINER—I move to reconsider Mr. Bonzano's resolution relative to adjournment.

PRESIDENT—That is all out of order. The next question before the Convention is the report of the Committee on Impeachment.

[The secretary read the report.]

Mr. ABELL—I rise to a question of order. I say we cannot proceed, until there is a rescision of the rules, to take up this. There is an order that declares we shall proceed categorically and logically, and that until the judiciary question is disposed of, we shall consider nothing else. I contend that without a suspension of the rules we cannot proceed with anything.

PRESIDENT—You are wrong, sir. When a matter is recommitted, the next one in order comes up.

Mr. FOLEY—I move we adjourn until Monday next, at 12 o'clock.

[Motion carried, and the Convention separated until 12 M. of Monday, the 13th inst.]

MONDAY, June 13, 1864.

[The Convention met and was called t order pursuant to adjournment, Hon. E. H. Durell, president, in the chair, and the following members present:]

Messrs. Abell, Austin, Barrett, Bofill, Campbell, Collin, Cook J. K., Crozat, Dufresne, Edwards, Ennis, Fish, Flood, Foley, Fosdick, Fuller, Gastinel, Geier, Gorlinski, Healy, Heard, Henderson, Hire, Howell, Howes, Maas, Maurer, Mayer, Mendiverri, Montamat, Morris, Newell, Normand, O'Conner, Payne J., Pintado, Poynot, Seymour, Smith, Spellicy, Stocker, Stumpf, Stiner, Stauffer, Sullivan, Terry, Wells and Wilson—48.

[After some delay the following members appeared and answered to their names, when a quorum was announced as being present:]

Messrs. Bailey, Baum, Bell, Bromley, Buckley, Cook T., Cutler, Davies, Duane, Dupaty, Flagg, Harnan, Hart, Hills, Kavanagh, Kugler, Mann, Murphy M. W., Paine, J. T., Purcell J., Pursell S., Schroeder, Schnurr, Shaw, Thorpe, Waters and Wenck —27.

[The journal of the last session was read and approved.]

Mr. THORPE—I wish to present a resolution.

Mr. MONTAMAT—I move a suspension of the rules in order that the gentleman may do as he wishes, as we had no meeting on Saturday, our regular day for resolutions.

Mr. STAUFFER—Let us know what the resolution is about.

[The secretary read the following:]

Resolved, That in future a quorum shall consist of two-thirds of the members elected to the Convention.

[Seconded.]

Mr. ABELL—I propose as an amendment that the number be fixed at sixty-one.

[Seconded.

Rules not suspended — only forty-three members rising.]

Mr. ABELL—The object of the gentleman from the Second was to keep up our regular order of business, for order is nature's first law. Therefore I move, in consideration of this, that we do nothing else until this is disposed of, and adjourn until to-morrow at 12 M.

PRESIDENT—When one bill goes over, another takes its place. This is very easily understood, and the Convention should do its work. The order of the day is the report of the Committee on Impeachment.

Mr. ABELL—I would like to see the rule.

PRESIDENT—If you will read treatises on parliamentary law you will find that stated at length. Is the Convention ready to take up the order of day?

[Cries of "Yes!"]

Mr. FLAGG—I ask for a call of the House.

[Mr. Secretary read the following:]

REPORT OF THE SPECIAL JUDICIARY COMMITTEE.

The Special Judiciary Committee respectfully submit the following report:

Article 1. The judiciary power shall be vested in a Supreme Court, in such inferior

courts as the Legislature may, from time to time, order and establish, and in justices of the peace.

Art. 2. The jurisdiction of the Supreme Court shall extend to all cases where the matter in dispute exceeds three hundred dollars, exclusive of interest; to all cases in which the constitutionality or legality of any tax, toll or impost whatsoever, or of any fine, forfeiture or penalty imposed by a municipal corporation shall be in contestation; and to all criminal cases on questions of law alone, whenever the offence charged is punishable with death, or imprisonment at hard labor, or when a fine exceeding three hundred dollars is actually imposed. It shall also exercise a general superintending control over all inferior and other courts of law, and shall have the power to issue the writs necessary for that purpose. The Legislature shall have power to restrict the jurisdiction of the Supreme Court in civil cases to questions of law alone.

Art. 3. The Supreme Court shall be composed of one chief justice and four associate justices, a majority of whom shall constitute a quorum. The chief justice shall receive a salary of $7500, and each of the associate justices a salary of $7000 annually, until otherwise provided by law. The court shall appoint its own clerks.

Art. 4. The Supreme Court shall hold its sessions in New Orleans from the first Monday in the month of November to the end of June inclusive. The Legislature shall have power to fix the sessions elsewhere during the rest of the year; until otherwise provided, the sessions shall be held as heretofore.

Art, 5. The Supreme Court, and each of the judges thereof, shall have power to issue writs of *habeas corpus* at the instance of all persons in actual custody under process, in which they may have appellate jurisdiction.

Art. 6. No judgment shall be rendered by the Supreme Court without the concurrence ot a majority of the judges comprising the court. Whenever the majority cannot agree in consequence of the recusation of any member or members of the court, the judges not recused shall have power to call upon any judge or judges of the inferior courts, whose duty it shall be, when so called upon, to sit in the place of the judge or judges so recused and to aid in determining the case.

Art. 7. All judges, by virtue of their office, shall be conservators of the peace throughout the State. The style of all process shall be, "the State of Louisiana." All prosecutions shall be carried on in the name and by the authority of the "State of Louisiana," and conclude against the peace and dignity of the same.

Art. 8. The judges of all courts within the State shall, as often as it may be possible so to do, in every definitive judgment, refer to the particular law in virtue of which such judgment may be rendered, and in all cases adduce the reasons on which their judgment is founded.

Art. 9. The judges of all courts shall be liable to impeachment; but for any reasonable cause, which shall not be sufficient ground for impeachment, the governor shall remove any of them on the address of a majority of the members elected to each House of the General Assembly. In every such case the cause or causes for which such removal may be required shall be stated in full in the address and inserted in the journal of each House.

Art. 10. The salaries of the judges of the supreme and inferior courts shall not be changed during their term of office.

Art. 11. The judges, both of the supreme and inferior courts, and justices of the peace, shall be appointed by the governor, by and with the advice and consent of the Senate. The judges of the Supreme Court to hold office for the term of six years, the judges of the inferior courts for four, justice of the peace for two---after which term the judges of the supreme, inferior and justices courts shall be elected by the legally qualified voters. Appointments in every instance to date from the ratification of this constitution by the people. The Legislature to fix the day for election.

Art. 12. The clerks of the inferior courts shall be appointed by the governor, for the same term as the judges, but, on the commission of any crime, may be removed, with the power of an appeal to the Supreme Court. After the service of this term they shall be elected by the legally qualified voters for the same term as the judges.

Art. 13. The Legislature shall have power to vest in clerks of courts authority to grant such orders and do such acts as may be deemed necessary for the administration of justice; but in all such cases the powers thus granted shall be specified and determined.

Art. 14. Justices of the peace shall have jurisdiction in civil cases, the sum not to exceed one hundred dollars, exclusive of interest. They shall receive a salary of $2500 in the city, and the Legislature shall fix the salaries in the country parishes. Returns shall be made by them quarterly to the auditor of public accounts, under oath; and all fees received over the above salary must be faithfully returned to said auditor.

Art. 15. There shall be an attorney general for the State. He shall be appointed by the governor, by and with the advice and consent of the Senate, and shall hold his office for the term of four years, after which term he shall be elected by the legal voters. He shall receive a salary of $5000.

Art. 16. There shall be as many district attorneys appointed by the governor, by and with the advice and consent of the Senate, as may hereafter be found necessary, their term of office to be two years from the date of the ratification of this constitution. The Legislature to fix their salaries, and declare the office elective after first term.

Art. 17. A coroner shall be appointed by the governor, by and with the advice and consent of the Senate, for two years. After which term he shall be elected. The General Assembly to fix his salary at its first session.

Art. 18. The governor shall appoint, by and with the advice and consent of the Senate, sheriffs for the several parishes of the State. They shall hold office for two years. The Legislature shall have the power to increase the number of the sheriffs in any of the parishes whenever it may be deemed necessary. They shall be all elected after the first term, which dates, as in every other case, in this report, from the ratification of this constitution by the legally qualified voters of this State.

Art. 19. Grand and petit jurors shall be paid the sum of three dollars and a half per day for each day of service during term.

(Signed) J. H. WILSON, Chairman.
CHARLES SMITH,
JNO. PURCELL,
O. H. POYNOT,
M. W. MURPHY,
JOHN BUCKLEY, JR.

Mr. BELL—I move its adoption.

Mr. SULLIVAN—I ask for a call of the House.

PRESIDENT—This is the second reading. Mr. Secretary read article 1.

[Article was read.]

Mr. SULLIVAN—I would like to know if there is a quorum present.

PRESIDENT—Call the House.

[Only sixty-seven answered to their names.]

PRESIDENT—This is the doorkeeper's fault.

Mr. GASTINEL—No, sir, he had no orders regarding the egress of members.

Mr. ABELL—I am glad of this result. I move we adjourn until 12 o'clock to-morrow.

[Ayes and noes were called for, but not a sufficient number rose in response, whereupon the Convention adjourned until 12 M., Tuesday, the 14th inst.]

TUESDAY, June 14, 1864.

[The Convention met and was called to order pursuant to adjournment, Hon. E. H. Durell, president, in the chair, and the following members present:]

Messrs. Abell, Austin, Balch, Bell, Bromley, Buckley, Burke, Campbell, Collin, Cazabat, Cook J. K., Cook T., Crozat, Davies, Decker, Dufresne, Duke, Ennis, Fish, Flagg, Flood, Foley, Fosdick, Geier, Gorlinski, Harnan, Howes, Maas, Mann, Mayer, Maurer, Murphy E., Murphy M.W., Newell, Normand, Payne J., Purcell J., Pursell S., Schroeder, Smith, Stocker, Stumpf, Stiner, Stauffer, Terry, Waters, Wilson—48.

[After considerable delay, the following members appeared and answered to their names:]

Messrs. Bailey, Barrett, Beauvais, Bennie, Cutler, Dupaty, Fuller, Gastinel, Gaidry, Healy, Hart, Hills, Hire, Howell, Kugler, Mendiverri, Montamat, O'Conner, Ong, Orr, Paine J. T., Pintado, Seymour, Shaw, Sullivan, Thorpe, Wenck, Wells—28.

[Absent—Messrs. Ariail, Baum, Bonzano, Brott, Duane, Edwards, Goldman, Gruneberg, Heard, Henderson, Kavanagh, Knobloch, Lobdell, Millspaugh, Montague, Morris, Poynot, Schnurr, Spellicy, Taliaferro, Thomas—22.]

Mr. MONTAMAT—I move the reading of the minutes be dispensed with.

[No objection made.]

Mr. TERRY—I move a suspension of the rules, for the adoption of the following resolution:

Resolved, That from and after the 14th day of June, all members absent fifteen minutes after the first roll-call, without a good and sufficient excuse, shall forfeit their per diem.

[The motion was carried—yeas 61.]

Mr. DAVIES—I move to amend by striking out "without excuse."

[Accepted.]

Mr. MANN—I offer the following amendment:

Whereas, Members of this Convention, elected by the people for the purpose of amending and revising the constitution of the State of Louisiana, have absented themselves without permission, or giving any reason therefor; therefore, be it

Resolved, That from and after this date, each and every member of this body, who shall not have been granted leave of absence for cause that is satisfactory to this Convention, who are not present to answer to his or their name, at 12 o'clock roll-call, they shall not be allowed their per diem, for each and every day that they are delinquent; and the secretary is hereby required to furnish to the chairman of the Finance Committee the names of delinquents, that the deductions from their per diem may be made, for each and every day of such delinquency.

[The amendment was accepted.]

Mr. STOCKER--While I should have supported the resolution in its original form, I feel constrained to oppose it as amended. A man may get his leg broke and yet if absent it would be no excuse. There are a dozen things that may justify the absence of a member. Of course, unless it is satisfactory to the Convention, it ought not to be accepted.

[The resolution as amended, was then adopted.]

Mr. ABELL—Judge Heard is compelled to attend the district court at Baton Rouge to-morrow, and I move a leave of absence be granted to him for a short time.

[Cries of "I object."]

Mr. SMITH—I would like to inquire how long.

Mr. HILLS—I object to any member leaving the Convention at this stage of the session; if any gentleman wishes to leave, he ought to resign.

Mr. ABELL—I withdraw my motion for the present, as I understand there is a motion before the Convention to reduce the quorum.

PRESIDENT—There is no such motion before the House.

Mr. ABELL—I then renew my motion to excuse Judge Heard.

[The motion on being put was lost.

The order of the day was then taken up. The second reading of the report of the Special Committee on the Judiciary Department.

President called Mr. Abell to the chair.

The report was read by the secretary.]

REPORT OF THE SPECIAL JUDICIARY COMMITTEE.

The Special Judiciary Committee respectfully submit the following report:

Article 1. The judiciary power shall be vested in a Supreme Court, in such inferior courts as the Legislature may, from time to time, order and establish, and in justices of the peace.

Art. 2. The jurisdiction of the Supreme Court shall extend to all cases where the matter in dispute exceeds three hundred dollars, exclusive of interest; to all cases in which the constitutionality or legality of any tax, toll or impost whatsoever. or of any fine, forfeiture, or penalty imposed by a municipal corporation shall be in contestation; and to all criminal cases on questions of law alone, whenever the offence charged is punishable with death, or imprisonment at hard labor, or when a fine exceeding three hundred dollars is actually imposed. It shall also exercise a general superintending control over all inferior and other courts of law, and shall have the power to issue the writs necessary for that purpose. The Legislature shall have power to restrict the jurisdiction of the Supreme Court in civil cases to questions of law alone.

Art. 3. The Supreme Court shall be composed of one chief justice and four associate justices, a majority of whom shall constitute a quorum. The chief justice shall receive a salary of $7500 and each of the associate justices a salary of $7000 annually, until otherwise provided by law. The court shall appoint its own clerks.

Art. 4. The Supreme Court shall hold its sessions in New Orleans from the first Monday in the month of November to the end of June inclusive. The Legislature shall have power to fix the sessions elsewhere during the rest of the year; until otherwise provided, the sessions shall be held as heretofore.

Art. 5. The Supreme Court, and each of the judges thereof, shall have power to issue writes of *habeas corpus* at the instance of all persons in actual custody under process, in which they may have appellate jurisdiction.

Art. 6. No judgment shall be rendered by the Supreme Court without the concurrence of a majority of the judges comprising the court. Whenever the majority cannot agree, in consequence of the recusation of any member or members of the court, the judges not recused shall have power to call upon any judge or judges of the inferior courts, whose duty it shall be, when so called upon, to sit in the place of the judge or judges so recused and to aid in determining the case.

Art. 7. All judges, by virtue of their office, shall be conservators of the peace throughout the State. The style of all process shall be, "the State of Louisiana." All prosecutions shall be carried on in the name and by the authority of the "State of Louisiana," and conclude against the peace and dignity of the same.

Art. 8. The judges of all courts within the State shall, as often as it may be possible so to do, in every definite judgment, refer to the particular law in virtue of which such judgment may be rendered, and in all cases adduce the reasons on which their judgment is founded.

Art. 9. The judges of all courts shall be liable to impeachment; but for any reasonable cause, which shall not be sufficient ground for impeachment, the governor shall remove any of them on the address of a majority of the members elected to each House of the General Assembly. In every such case the cause or causes for which such removal may be required shall be stated in full in the address and inserted in the journal of each House.

Art. 10. The salaries of the judges of the supreme and inferior courts shall not be changed during their term of office.

Art. 11. The judges both of the supreme and inferior courts and justices of the peace shall be appointed by the governor, by and with the advice and consent of the Senate. The judges of the Supreme Court to hold office for the term of six years, the judges of the inferior courts for four, justice of the peace for two—after which term the judges of the supreme, inferior and justices courts shall be elected by the legally qualified voters. Appointments in every instance to date from the ratification of this constitution by the people. The Legislature to fix the day for election.

Art. 12. The clerks of the inferior courts shall be appointed by the governor, for the same term as the judges, but, on the commission of any crime, may be removed, with the power of an appeal to the Supreme Court. After the service of this term they shall be elected by the legally qualified voters for the same term as the judges.

Art. 13. The Legislature shall have power to vest in clerks of courts authority to grant such orders and do such acts as may be deemed necessary for the administration of justice; but in all such cases the powers thus granted shall be specified and determined.

Art. 14. Justices of the peace shall have jurisdiction in civil cases, the sum not to exceed one hundred dollars, exclusive of interest. They shall receive a salary of $2500 in the city, and the Legislature shall fix the salaries in the country parishes. Returns shall be made by them quarterly to the auditor of public accounts under oath, and all fees received over the above salary must be faithfully returned to said auditor.

Art. 15. There shall be an attorney general for the State. He shall be appointed by the governor, by and with the advice and consent of the senate, and shall hold his office for the term of four years, after which term he shall be elected by the legal voters. He shall receive a salary of $5000.

Art. 16. There shall be as many district attorneys appointed by the governor, by and with the advice and consent of the Senate, as may be hereafter found necessary, their term of office to be two years from the date of the ratification of this constitution. The Legislature to fix their salaries, and declare office elective after first term.

Art. 17. A coroner shall be appointed by the governor, by and with the advice and consent of the Senate, for two years. After which term he shall be elected. The General Assembly to fix his salary at its first session.

Art. 18. The governor shall appoint, by and with the advice and consent of the Senate, sheriffs for the several parishes of the State. They shall hold office for two years. The Legislature shall have the power to increase the number of the sheriffs in any of the parishes whenever it may be deemed necessary. They shall be all elected after the first term, which dates, as in every other case, in this report, from the ratification of this constitution by the legally qualified voters of this State.

Art. 19. Grand and petit jurors shall be paid the sum of three dollars and a half per day for each day of service during term.

(Signed) J. H. WILSON, Chairman.
CHARLES SMITH,
JNO. PURCELL,
O. H. POYNOT,
M. W. MURPHY,
JOHN BUCKLEY, JR.

Mr. STOCKER—I offer the following substitute for the whole bill:

MR. STOCKER'S SUBSTITUTE TO THE REPORT OF THE COMMITTEE ON THE JUDICIARY DEPARTMENT.

To the president and members of the Convention for the Revision and Amendment of the Constitution of Louisiana:

The Committee on Judiciary Department beg leave to report the following articles, and recommend their adoption as the portion of the constitution of this State on the subject of the judiciary, to-wit:

Article 1. The judiciary power shall be vested in a Supreme Court, in such inferior courts as the Legislature may, from time to time, order and establish, and in justices of the peace.

Art. 2. The Supreme Court, except in cases hereafter provided, shall have appellate jurisdiction only, which jurisdiction shall extend to all cases when the matter in dispute shall exceed three hundred dollars; to all cases in which the constitutionality or legality of any tax, toll or impost whatsoever, or of any fine, forfeiture or penalty imposed by a municipal corporation, shall be in contestation; and to all criminal cases on questions of law alone whenever the offence charged is punishable with death or imprisonment at hard labor, or when a fine exceeding three hundred dollars is actually imposed.

Art. 3. The Supreme Court shall be composed of one chief justice and four associate justices, a majority of whom shall constitute a quorum. The court shall appoint its own clerks.

Art. 4. The Supreme Court shall hold its sessions in New Orleans from the first Monday of the month of November to the end of the month of June inclusive. The Legislature shall have power to fix the sessions elsewhere during the rest of the year; until otherwise provided, the sessions shall be held as heretofore.

Art. 5. The Supreme Court and each of the judges thereof shall have power to issue writs of *habeas corpus*, at the instance of all persons in actual custody under process, in all cases in which they may have appellate jurisdiction.

Art. 6. No judgment shall be rendered by the Supreme Court without the concurrence of a majority of the judges comprising the court. Whenever the majority cannot agree, in consequence of the recusation of any member or members of the court, the judges not recused shall have power to call upon any judge or judges of the inferior courts, whose duty it shall be, when so called upon, to sit in the place of the judge or judges recused, and to aid in determining the case.

Art. 7. All judges, by virtue of their office, shall be conservators of the peace throughout the State. The style of all process shall be "the State of Louisiana." All prosecutions shall be carried on in the name and by the authority of the State of Louisiana, and conclude against the peace and dignity of the same.

Art. 8. The judges of all courts within the State shall, as often as it may be possible so to do, in every definitive judgment refer to the particular law in virtue of which such judgment may be rendered, and in all cases adduce the reasons on which their judgment is founded.

Art. 9. The judges of all courts shall be liable to impeachment; but for any reasonable cause, which shall not be sufficient ground for impeachment, the governor shall remove any of them, on the address of a majority of the members elected to each House of the General Assembly. In every such case the cause or causes for which such removal may be required shall be stated at length in the address, and inserted in the journal of each House.

Art. 10. The judges both of the supreme and inferior courts shall, at stated times, receive a salary which shall be fixed by the Legislature; and they are prohibited from receiving any fees of office or other compensation than their salaries for any civil duties performed by them.

Art. 11. The chief justice of the Supreme Court shall be elected by the qualified voters of the State, and the associate judges of the Supreme Court, together with the judges of the inferior courts, shall be elected by the qualified voters of their several districts, as determined by the Legislature, and they shall hold their several offices during such term or terms as shall be fixed by the Legislature.

Art. 12. The clerks of the inferior courts shall be elected by the qualified voters of their several districts, and shall hold their offices during such term or terms as shall be fixed by the Legislature, subject to removal by the judges respectively, with the right of appeal in all such cases to the Supreme Court.

Art. 13. The Legislature shall have power to vest in clerks of courts authority to grant such orders and do such acts as may be deemed necessary for the furtherance of the administration of justice, and in all cases the powers thus granted shall be specified and determined.

Art. 14. The jurisdiction of justices of the peace shall not exceed, in civil cases, the sum of one hundred dollars, exclusive of interest, subject to appeal in such cases as shall be provided for by law. They shall be elected by the qualified voters of their several districts, and shall hold their offices during such term or terms as shall be fixed by the Legislature. They shall have such criminal jurisdiction as shall be provided by law.

Art. 15. There shall be an attorney general for the State, and as many district attorneys as may hereafter be found necessary. The attorney general shall be elected by the qualified voters of the State; the district attorneys shall be elected by the qualified voters of their several districts. The attorney general and district attorneys shall severally hold their offices during such term or terms, and shall severally receive such salaries as shall be determined by the Legislature.

Art. 16. A sheriff and coroner shall be elected for each parish by the qualified voters of the same; and they shall severally hold their offices for such term or terms, and shall receive such remuneration for their services as the Legislature may determine.

Mr. Smith—I move the substitute be rejected.

Mr. Balch—I second the motion.

Mr. Foley—I ask that it be read by the secretary.

[It was read.]

Mr. SULLIVAN—I move that the report be taken up section by section.

Mr. SMITH—I move that the substitute be rejected.

[It was seconded.]

Mr. SMITH—I withdraw my motion to reject.

Mr. HOWELL—What is the position of the question before the House now?

PRESIDENT—There is a report from a special committee before the House; to that report a substitute has been offered by Mr. Stocker, and the question is whether the substitute shall be received or rejected.

Mr. HILLS—The motion to reject has been withdrawn, therefore, I call for the reading of the first section of the substitute.

Mr. CUTLER—I rise to a point of order. The subject is debatable, and I have something to say on this question in reply to our worthy president.

PRESIDENT—The gentleman from the Seventh (Mr. Howell) has the floor, and until he resigns, he is entitled to it.

Mr. HOWELL—I contend that the mover of that motion has no right to withdraw it at this point of the proceedings. There was a motion made to reject the substitute, and after a speech had been made against the motion the mover proposes to withdraw it in order to cut off debate.

PRESIDENT—I think the gentleman had a right to withdraw it at any time with the consent of the second.

Mr. HOWELL—I refer to the rules the Convention has adopted, where it will be found that without the consent of the Convention, no motion that has been seconded can be withdrawn. Am I right, sir? and can I proceed with my remarks?

PRESIDENT—The gentleman is right.

Mr. HOWELL—Then, Mr. President, following the remarks of the worthy gentleman who has just taken his seat, I will take the liberty to say, that my position in this Convention and in this community upon the question now under consideration is fully known, and I have not yet witnessed one single event or heard a single objection or argument sufficient to change my views upon that question and the course which I consider it my duty to my constituents and the people of this State to pursue. I disagree with the gentleman in the opinion that the majority of this Convention is in favor of an elective judiciary. [Applause.] On the contrary, sir, but for the inopportune offering of an amendment to article 11, fixing very short terms, I feel convinced that the report of the original committee would have been adopted, so far as it related to the judiciary of the State of Louisiana, and I believe as to the other officers contained in that report, there would have been radical changes made, and changes which I should not have strenuously opposed.

But let us come to the question now before the House. The substitute which is proposed here is subject to some serious objections, and among these I will state as the first and highest in importance, the insecurity and instability which that substitute gives to the judiciary of this State. It is of the utmost importance, as I have had occasion to say previously, that each of the main, distinctive departments of government should be as independent of each other as possible. By this substitute, what, sir, is the judiciary of the State of Louisiana but a creature of the Legislature? Every man will know readily, that if the Legislature has the power to fix the term and the salaries of the judges, it has the right also to change the term and the salaries, because what the Legislature may do one session it may change or undo at the next session, and if you leave it to the Legislature to fix the term of office of any of the judges, you put it in the power of the Legislature—the political department of the government—to change the judiciary to suit the political necessities of the times. The Legislature may fix, under this substitute, the term of the Supreme Court for twenty years, if you please. There is nothing in the substitute proposed which will prevent the next Legislature from changing that term. The Legislature may fix the salaries of the judges to be ten thousand dollars, if you please; there is nothing in the substitute which prevents the next Legislature from changing or reducing them to such a sum as to compel the judges to resign, and thereby effect a change in the judiciary. If it is possible for such an event to occur, it is more objectionable than the report we adopted a few days ago. That it is more objectionable than the report of the special committee, I cannot say, because that report, I will say, with due respect to the members of the committee, is inconsistent in itself; but it is not under consideration at present. The motion now is to reject the substitute, and I think that so far as it changes the judiciary system under consideration it should be rejected.

I am aware, Mr. President, of the great weight of authority against which I am now contending. I am aware, sir, that the influence of the presiding officer of a deliberative body is almost irresistible in that body when brought to bear upon the floor. But, sir, such is my interest in the question now under consideration that I am willing to breast any influence brought to bear on this question which I think injurious to the people, and the one consideration which I have already presented, is, in my opinion, sufficient of itself to defeat this substitute, but there are other objections, sir. The adoption of the system contained in the substitute will deprive the citizens of Louisiana of a Supreme Court at least for six months after the adoption or ratification of this constitution by the people, and any one familiar with the judicial interests of the State of Louisiana at the present time, must be aware of the importance of having that tribunal organized as soon as possible. If the substitute, sir, is adopted, the constitution which we shall submit to the people will have to be acted upon by the people and elections will have to take place under this constitution for the various officers, and among the rest, will have to be an election for the Legislature. That Legislature will have to assemble and hold its deliberations, and it may be that the deliberations will be protracted as ours have been and will be. The Legislature will have to order an election for the supreme judges, the various district judges and the various officers at a future period. The election must necessarily require some time to be advertised and all the necessary preliminary formalities observed, which will throw the election of the judges far into the middle of the next year, 1865. It will be almost impossible in the natural course of events, in times of peace, for a supreme court to be organized under the provisions of the substitute prior to the month of April or May, 1865. Already, as I have before said, there is now pending in the Supreme Court of Louisiana sufficient business to occupy that tribunal for eighteen months. If we postpone organizing the Supreme Court by the action of this Convention until next April, or even next January, you will prolong the time for the increase of business which will be ready for them when they enter upon their duties; but by forming a court under appointment of the governor for a short time, if you will, gentlemen, you can, within twenty days after the ratification of this constitution, have a Supreme Court in this State which will at once enter upon its duties and relieve suffering creditors, for it is not always true that the defendant or appellee is in the right. District courts may commit errors, just as other tribunals and individuals do, and it is frequently the case that the appellant is more injured and oppressed by delay, than the defendant or appellee would be by the execution of the judgment. It will work more injuriously upon the litigants and people of this State to procrastinate the business of the court, than delay will benefit any of them. There are now in the Supreme Court of Louisiana cases involving thousands and thousands of dollars which are held thus, simply for delay, which are first debts due to the parties who have their judgments. The defendants or debtors in these cases are paying only five per cent. interest for the use of the money which they thus unjustly withhold, and for which they get from eight to twenty-five per cent. Let this Convention fasten upon the people of this State such a system, and it will place in the power of these parties to continue their unjust advantage and oppression.

I ask the members of this Convention not to act from partiality, nor with reference to their individual views alone, but be just to all the people of the State. It is possible that the war, so far as it is confined to Louisiana, may be closed or ended by the fall;

but I think, Mr. President, that the events now transpiring within the knowledge of this body rather negative such a result—rather forbid this body to entertain such a hope. When we entered upon our duties, we had the brightest prospect that before the conclusion of our labors Louisiana would be within the folds of the Union, and the whole State represented in this body. What is it now? We have actually less territory under the control of the Federal authority in Louisiana now than on the sixth day of April, when we assembled here. Instead of approaching near to the period when the Legislature of Louisiana can be elected and convened, and this judiciary system put into operation, we are further from it than we were at the beginning of our work; and it is unreasonable for this Convention to base its action on the hypothesis that a Legislature can be elected and convened within a suitable time for putting our judiciary system into operation. I very much fear, from present appearances, that we will be unable to have a Legislature for six or eight months. I very much fear, however much I may hope and wish to the contrary, that we will be unable to have a Legislature in time to give Louisiana a judiciary system under this substitute before the middle of next summer. We should direct our deliberations and actions with reference to the contingencies which we are justified in considering. I shall not strenuously contend for a life appointment, although I believe it to be the best system, but shall contend for the appointive system, because it makes the judiciary more independent than any other, and because it will give a judiciary system for the loyal portion of the State, whether they have a Legislature or not.

Mr. President, we are already sufficiently obnoxious to the charge of unnecessary delay in our work, in completing our labors. So much are we subject to that charge at the present time, that I believe it to be the more imperative on the members of this Convention to shape their labors in such a way, to bring about such a result as will benefit the people in the shortest possible time. To-day, sir, if I calculate not incorrectly, is the seventieth day since we first assembled here, and although we have done a mighty work in adopting the ordinance of emancipation, independent of that great act we have really done nothing that is beneficial to the people of the State of Louisiana. We have, it is true, adopted some departments of the constitution, but we have adopted them in such a form as not strictly to be as beneficial as the same portions of the constitution of 1852 were, and we should now *begin* at least to do something which *will* result in *immediate* benefit to the people, and instead of debating such measures as will *postpone* the benefits of our labors, we should be studious to adopt that course and those measures from which the people themselves can immediately be benefited. As it is now, sir, it is impossible for the State of Louisiana to have a Supreme Court. Under the constitution of 1852, the governor may fill a vacancy in the district judgeships, but it is impossible for the governor to organize a Supreme Court under that constitution. And when this Convention finds that they can adopt a system consistent with the good of the people and not inconsistent with their own views, I think, sir, and declare it the imperative duty upon every member of this House, to adopt that course. The greatest objections that I have to the substitute proposed are those which I have named and which I think are insurmountable. Other gentlemen upon this floor may be able to urge other and still greater objections, but with me, sir, these are sufficient—that it makes the judiciary dependent upon the will of the Legislature; that it makes the judiciary of Louisiana unstable; that it puts it in the power of the Legislature at any time, not only to change the judges of the State, but to change the system itself, and it also puts it in the power of the Legislature, Mr. President, to deprive the State of Louisiana of any judiciary. I do not contend that the Legislature will ever do so, but it is a possibility which *may* occur.

And why, Mr. President, shall the Legisluture be better qualified to fix the terms of office than this body? Upon what principle in political economy or in the system of republican governments are the members of the Legislature better qualified to fix the terms of office and salaries of the judiciary, of one department of the government than that body which forms the fundamental law under which the Legislature derives its existence? How is it possible that the Legislature is more directly from the people than this Convention? My understanding and appreciation of constitutional conventions, sir, are, that a constitutional convention is the representative of the people in their sovereign capacity. The Legislature is but the representative of the people for law-making under the constitution.

Will this Convention admit to their constituents that it is incapable of fixing the term of office for the judiciary, when it has already determined the terms and salaries of most of the other offices, and have also gone so far as to fix the terms of office for the police of the city of New Orleans? Will this Convention say to the people of Louisiana, that the police of New Orleans is of more importance to them and of a higher grade of office than the judiciary? That the police of New Orleans can hold their offices during good behavior, but that we cannot fix the term of office for the judiciary? That we can fix the wages of the police of New Orleans but cannot fix the salary of the judiciary? And is it true, Mr. President, that the police of New Orleans is higher in the grade of governmental rights and duties than the judiciary of the State? I trust the members of this Convention will pause and consider before they adopt a measure which will even admit of such a suspicion against them.

I contend, sir, that it is far more important that the judiciary shall hold their offices during good behavior than that the police of New Orleans shall hold *theirs* during good behavior. I think that the interests of the people of Louisiana, the sovereign people of Louisiana, would be far better protected by a judiciary appointed during good behavior, than the citizens of New Orleans will be protected by a police appointed during good behavior.

[Hammer fell.]

Mr. Hills—I believe I have the floor.

President — The gentleman from the Fourth [Mr. Cutler] has the preference.

Mr. Cutler—Mr. President, I believe, sir, that you and all the members of this Convention will do me the justice to bear testimony that it has been some time since I have troubled this Convention with anything like an argument or speech, and now, sir, it is not my intention to dwell upon this subject for any great length of time. On the contrary, I intend to be very brief; but, sir, the hour is getting late and I may not get through with my remarks to-day. I should not rise again to speak upon this subject were it not for the extraordinary remarks of the presiding officer of this Convention, and were it not for the extraordinary position in which this Convention, through the action of its presiding officer, had placed itself. I hoped that the discussion on this question had been entirely ended; that the subject had been exhausted; and that it only remained for us to cast our votes. But there is scarcely a day but what there is some person in this Convention that gives a new character or introduces a new feature into the discussion.

To look at the proceedings here since this question has been taken up one might well doubt that we were here for the purpose for which we were called together, by the order of Gen. Banks, that of revising and amending the constitution of Louisiana. There is no definition that can with justice be applied to some of the remarks made on this floor. They may as well be undefined, unless our work results in a constitution that will be acceptable to the masses; for, unless our work is established on fundamental principles that prove acceptable to the people, it might as well not be done at all.

Now, Mr. President, I am extremely sorry to say that the maiden speech of the presiding officer of this Convention, upon the floor of this hall, has proved an abortion, as I think every one who heard it will admit. But I am not less astonished at the reasons assigned than at the position assumed by the learned gentleman. The ground which he sets forth as an apology for assuming the novel position in which he places himself are not borne out by the facts, as is evident to any intelligent observer of the phases this question has assumed in this hall during the time it has been under discussion. There has evidently been a mistake in the declarations of the learned gentleman respecting the wishes of this body, to correct which it is only necessary to travel back over the record of the question. And after examining that carefully, and observing the votes cast, no man will dare to stand here and say that this body have shown that they desire an elective judiciary, instead of one appointed by the governor, by and with the advice and consent of the Senate. No, sir, the action of this body has shown that the majority of this body is in favor of an appointive judiciary, and not an elective one. Such has been the vote all the time, sir, and no man can gainsay it now, after it has been repeatedly manifested during this week's debate. Now, how is it possible, sir, after this debate, after this protracted discussion, after these arguments, which go to show that, and after presiding over this body for so long a time, and listening as attentively as I know he has done; how is it possible, I ask, after all this, that a man of his superior learning and ability should come to the conclusion that a majority of this body was in favor of an elective judiciary? Why, sir, on the contrary, it is the very reverse. Now, sir, what are the facts in regard to this matter? Has it not been evident from the first, that a majority of this body was in favor of an appointive judiciary? I know that they have, that they have always and are now in favor of the appointive system, and not of the elective. It is true that I am one of the committee that signed the first judiciary report. I signed that report, but I signed it, sir, with a full knowledge and understanding that I for one did not believe that this Convention would ever swallow entire the recommendations of that report, to appoint all the officers of the State, from the judges of the Supreme Court to constables. My object as a member of that committee was to preserve harmony. I believe that the judiciary should be appointed, and none other; and when I signed the report I did it with a fair understanding that I was opposed to the appointment of any other officers than the judiciary. I signed it for the purpose of conciliation, for the purpose of promoting harmony in this Convention, and because I didn't wish to show a disagreement or a want of conciliation by bringing in a minority report. I thought I would rather sanction the report temporarily, and have the Convention to decide which was right and which was wrong, than to exhibit a disposition to disturbance, contrary to their peace and unity of action, which should always characterize the action of this body. But, sir, the report was brought in and has been acted upon, and I believe I run no risk in stating that which is untrue when I say that so far as the judiciary is concerned, there is a large majority in favor of its appointment. Then, sir, I was not the only man of the original committee who was willing to accept a compromise for the report of that committee. Mr. Stiner, I think it was, who proposed to substitute a term of years for "good behavior." I thought it best for the purpose of conciliation to adopt that proposition, and thus the article passed and we proceeded harmoniously; and with this amendment, and an amendment striking out "fixing the salaries of the judges of the Supreme Court" the report passed its first and second reading—except article 16—by a large majority. And this, sir, has been the action of this body on the question from which my learned and superior friend is convinced that this Convention is in favor of an elective judiciary. How is it, I ask, that this gentleman, for whose talents, legal learning, and his superior knowledge for the arts and sciences I have the highest respect, has made this discovery after these repeated and unmistakable acts on the part of this body? How can it be possible that he has so far forgotten the votes as to entertain the idea that this Convention is in favor of an elective judiciary?

When the report came up at its third reading it was referred back. A special committee of nine was called for by the Convention to take the subject under consideration and report. Then he remarked that he was satisfied that a majority of the Convention was in favor of an elective judiciary, and consequently he should appoint on the committee four in favor of the appointment of the judiciary and five in favor of making it elective. That, sir, was an act of great injustice to this Convention. It is a greater injustice that it should be reiterated to-day. Now, sir, what I am saying is with due deference to the scholarship and talents of the gentleman, but he has fallen into error, and that error may destroy the judiciary of Louisiana because he is the presiding officer of this body, and when he descends from the chair to discuss a question before the House, his influence, owing to the respect in which the presiding officer is held, is presumed to be incalculable. His maiden speech was made to-day, and I well know the effect of opinions when they flew from such high sources, and I only ask in replying to him, a careful examination of the past, and I will leave you to decide whether I am correct in this matter or whether the matter is with the learned gentleman. I am willing to admit, sir, that there is a considerable number that have from the first and all the time advocated an elective judiciary. I admire them for their perseverance and consistency, for I believe it comes up from their hearts. Men differ in principles. They differ in sentiment. The best men differ. The great constitutional convention of the United States contained some of the best men that ever lived in America. They did not all agree on all points. They differed on this very question but their deliberations resulted in the establishment of a judiciary appointed by the president, by and with the advice and consent of the Senate; and such was the result of the deliberations of this body. I want no better proof than the report of the special committee, sir. They have adopted the report of the original committee, sir, with very slight modifications. When the debate had ended; when arguments had been exhausted; when men's minds were made up on the subject, the original report was ignored and a special committee of nine was composed to take the subject under consideration and report upon it. That committee was composed of nine men, five of them originally in favor of an elective judiciary and four in favor of appointing judges, and one of the latter number did not serve on the committee; and now, sir, we have their report. It is very clear and concise in its terms, and it goes beyond my expectations. We, as a body, have become tired of this matter. The question is an irksome one. We have become tired of this everlasting, eternal debate. These gentlemen, nine in number, eight serving under all these circumstances, and after all that had been done by this Convention, went calmly and deliberately to work, the Convention having adjourned to give them plenty of time to grapple with and consider all the positions of members on this floor, and to look at the result of the deliberations of this body, and in view of all the facts, they bring in their report declaring that every officer in the State shall be appointed; they declare that not only the judiciary but the sheriffs, coroners and various State officers shall be appointed.

Mr. Balch—That's right, by heavens!

Mr. Cutler—Then, sir, what is the object of this substitute? Is it introduced for the purpose of ridiculing this Convention? Is it intended to hold us up to ridicule? In God's name, tell us what it is for. It seems to me that when you have appointed a committee to take the subject under consideration, and have agreed that no lawyer should serve on that committee, when they have in their report sanctioned the principles of the report of the original committee, that that ought to be considered the last toll of the bell. It seems to me that if we intend to do our duty, and take any action in this matter, that that report is the last toll of the bell, and that there should be some action taken on it at once. It seems to me that when this Convention is held up to ridicule, it is time to act. I, for one, am willing to accept the report of the committee. I am willing that justices of the peace should be appointed for two years, judges of District Courts for four, and of the Supreme Court for six. I am willing to accept this as a compromise, for the sake of reconciliation and harmony in this Convention; but the report does not reflect my sentiments. I believe the time should be longer; but if this is the result of the cool deliberation of this body, I am willing to accept it. It is a compromise, and I believe it is such a compromise as this Convention ought to accept.

But, sir, before closing my remarks, in which I designed merely to correct the errors into which the learned gentleman has fallen, I assure you, Mr. President, that in my opinion, after the argument and the votes that have been had on this question, you have no right as president of this Convention to entertain that substitute. The opinions of the Convention have been so clearly expressed by numerous votes that I believe you would be perfectly justifiable in refusing to entertain it. The only change made in this report, from the substitute of Mr. Sullivan, is that this report proposes to leave the duty of fixing the judiciary, which legitimately belongs to this Convention—a duty which we have been sent here to discharge and which we are expected to perform—to the Legislature. If we do this, the Legislature may rise up some day and fix God knows what for a judiciary. We should not do this. It is our duty to decide upon a judiciary, and let us not shrink from its performance. The object of this substitute is to postpone this work, and therefore to wipe from this Convention every act that we have done in the premises—everything that we have done towards making an independent judiciary. A judiciary that should be appointed for terms of remarkable length would be worthy of this Convention. But, sir, if this body passes a vote now to lay aside the report of this committee and adopt this substitute, there is no telling what the judiciary will be. If you adopt this substitute you not only give the Legislature the power to make the judges elective, but to fix their terms and their salaries. By leaving these to the Legislature you destroy the independence, the power and the dignity of the judiciary of this State.

Whatever arguments may be urged in favor of an elective judiciary, I take ground that it is not a proper time to adopt it. I took occasion, in my former remarks, to refer to the condition of the country. If you refer the election of the judges to the people now, you refer the matter to a people not qualified to elect those who are to decide upon your property, your life or your liberties? It cannot be done at this time, as we all admit. I think I have heard this admission from the lips of the strongest advocates of the elective system. We are all agreed that we ought not to elect a judiciary now. The people of the country parishes, particularly, are not in a proper state of mind to select their judges, either of the Supreme Court or of the inferior courts, or even their justices of the peace, and they all agree that we can only appoint at this time, and until the end of this unholy war. I believe the strongest advocate of an elective judiciary on this floor admits that the only practicable system is for the governor to appoint until the end of this war.

Now, we do not know how long this war may last. It is making hot progress now. God grant it may come to a speedy close. But, sir, if we adopt this substitute, we place before the people now the election of these judges of the supreme and inferior courts and justices of the peace. I say now, because this Convention has it in its power to order the election of a Legislature—and in my opinion we should order it—to commence next January. I believe it will be done, because I believe that we not only have the power, but that it is our duty to do so.

But, sir, this substitute not only leaves the election of judges to the Legislature, but it provides that the salaries and the districts of the district courts shall be fixed by the same body. Now, in conclusion, let me ask if the custom of the past has not sufficiently demonstrated the folly and danger of leaving this power in the hands of a legislative body? The proposition is too monstrous to be entertained. It does not need even a short trial to show that it is not suited to the wants of this people, for I trust it will be voted down here.

Mr. HILLS—Mr. President, I——

Mr. BALCH—I move we adjourn.

[The motion was lost.]

Mr. HILLS—Mr. President, it seems to me that we have had argument enough on this question. Members of this Convention should remember that there is a limit to human endurance. I believe every one's mind is made up on it, and that we are ready to vote. The question has been fully and fairly discussed, and if the ghost of Cicero were to present itself in the lobby and ask to be admitted to debate this question, I would not hear him. And now, sir, in view of these facts, I move the previous question.

Mr. HENDERSON—I move to lay that motion on the table.

[The motion to table was lost.]

PRESIDENT—The question is on the adoption of the substitute.

Mr. STAUFFER—I call attention to rule XXIII.

Mr. WILSON—I rise to a question of order. Mr. Smith moved that the substitute be rejected.

Mr. STAUFFER—Order!

Mr. BALCH—I move to adjourn.

Mr. SEYMOUR—I move that the sergeant-at-arms take charge of the gentleman from Iberville.

Mr. STAUFFER—Order! I call the gentleman to order!

Mr. DURELL—Mr. President, the question is on Mr. Terry's motion to take up the report, section by section.

Mr. SULLIVAN, (in the chair)—The question is on the rejection of the whole substitute, and the previous question has been carried. The question, as I understand it, is on taking up the substitute, article by article, instead of the original report.

Mr. WILSON—I desire to call the attention of the chair to the fact that when Mr. Howell got up to debate the question, Mr. Smith made a motion to reject the substitute, and that the chair, instead of putting the question, allowed Mr. Howell to go on.

Mr. HILLS—I rise a point of order. The gentleman is not speaking to any question befor the House.

Mr. BALCH—I move to adjourn.

PRESIDENT, (SULLIVAN)—The question is on the adoption of the substitute.

Mr. MONTAMAT—I move that the substitute be printed.

Mr. ORR—I second the motion.

Mr. S. PURSELL—I move the whole substitute be rejected.

Mr. BALCH—Mr. President, we must adjourn, there is no order here.

[The president (Durell) took the chair.]

PRESIDENT—The question is on the adoption of the substitute. Mr. Secretary, read the first article.

[The secretary read:]

Art. 1. The judiciary power shall be vested in a Supreme Court, in such inferior courts as the Legislature may, from time to time, order and establish, and in justices of the peace.

Mr. FOLEY—I move its adoption.

[The motion was carried.

The secretary read:]

Art. 2. The Supreme Court, except in cases hereafter provided, shall have appellate jurisdiction only; which jurisdiction shall extend to all cases when the matter in dispute shall exceed three hundred dollars; to all cases in which the constitutionality or legality of any tax, toll or impost whatsoever; or of any fine, forfeiture or penalty imposed by a municipal corporation, shall be in contestation; and to all criminal cases on questions of law alone whenever the offence charged is punishable with death or imprisonment at hard labor, or when a fine exceeding three hundred dollars is actually imposed.

Mr. HILLS—I move its adoption.

[The motion was carried.]

Mr. FOLEY—I rise to a point of order. I believe it has been decided that the votes should be taken by ayes and noes.

PRESIDENT—Sit down, sir, there is no such decision.

[The secretary read:]

Art. 3. The Supreme Court shall be composed of one chief justice and four associate justices, a majority of whom shall constitute a quorum. The court shall appoint its own clerks.

Mr. TERRY—I move its adoption.

[The motion was carried.

The secretary read:]

Art. 4. The Supreme Court shall hold its sessions in New Orleans from the first Monday of the month of November to the end of the month of June inclusive. The Legislature shall have power to fix the sessions elsewhere during the rest of the year; until otherwise provided, the sessions shall be held as heretofore.

Mr. HARNAN—I move its adoption.

Mr. HOWELL—I have an amendment.

Mr. MONTAMAT—I move to adjourn.

Mr. ORR—I second the motion.

[The motion was lost on a rising vote—ayes 27, noes 45.]

Mr. WILSON—I ask a call of the House, there is no quorum voting.

[The roll was called; 76 members answered to their names.]

Mr. MONTAMAT—I move to adjourn.

[The ayes and noes were called, with the following result:]

YEAS — Messrs. Balch, Bailey, Barrett, Beauvais, Burke, Cook J. K., Cook T., Crozat, Decker, Duke, Gruneberg, Gaidry, Healy, Harnan, Knobloch, Maas, Mendiverri, Montamat, Murphy E., Murphy M. W., Orr, O'Conner, Ong, Payne J., Schroeder, Seymour, Sullivan, Waters—28.

NAYS—Messrs. Abell, Austin, Bell, Bofill, Bromley, Campbell, Collin, Cazabat, Cutler, Davies, Dufresne, Dupaty, Ennis, Fish, Flagg, Flood, Foley, Fosdick, Fuller, Gastinel, Geier, Gorlinski, Hart, Henderson, Hills, Hire, Howell, Howes, Kugler, Mann, Maurer, Mayer, Newell, Normand, Paine J., T., Pintado, Purcell J., Pursell S., Shaw, Smith, Stocker, Stumpf, Stiner, Stauffer, Terry, Thorpe, Wells, Wilson—48.

Mr. TERRY—I move the previous question.

Mr. HILLS—I second the motion.

Mr. MANN—We have already carried the previous question.

[The previous question was lost.]

Mr. HOWELL—I desire to offer an amendment. After the word "governor," I desire to insert, "the chief justice shall receive a salary of $7500, and the associate justices each $7000 per annum, until otherwise provided by law."

Mr. BALCH—I move to adjourn.

[The motion was carried.]

WEDNESDAY, June 15, 1864.

[The Convention met and was called to order pursuant to adjournment.

Present, Hon. E. H. Durell, president, in the chair, and the following members:]

Messrs. Abell, Austin, Bailey, Barrett, Baum, Beauvais, Bell, Bofill, Bromley, Buckley, Burke, Campbell, Collin, Cazabat, Cook J. K., Cook T., Crozat, Cutler, Davies, Decker, Duane, Dufresne, Duke, Ennis, Fish, Flagg, Flood, Foley, Fosdick, Fuller, Gastinel, Geier, Gorlinski, Gruneberg, Gaidry, Healy, Harnan, Hart, Henderson, Hills, Hire, Howell, Howes, Kavanagh, Knobloch, Kugler, Maas, Mann, Maurer, Mayer, Mendiverri, Montamat, Morris, Murphy E., Murphy M. W., Newell, Normand, O'Conner, Ong, Orr, Payne J., Paine J. T., Pintado, Purcell J., Pursell S., Schroeder, Schnurr, Seymour, Shaw, Smith, Spellicy, Stocker, Stumpf, Stiner, Stauffer, Sullivan, Terry, Thorpe, Waters, Wenck, Wells, Wilson—83.

Absent: Messrs. Ariail, Balch, Bennie, Bonzano, Brott, Edwards, Goldman, Heard, Lobdell, Millspaugh, Montague, Poynot, Taliaferro, Thomas—15.

Mr. MONTAMAT—I move that Mr. Poynot be excused. He is sick in bed.

Mr. STOCKER—I hope the rule will be enforced. Yesterday, when it was offered, I endeavored to have provision made for cases of this kind, and you refused my proposition. Now I ask for the enforcement of the rule.

Mr. SPELLICY—I move Mr. Poynot be excused; he is very sick.

Mr. ABELL—I second the motion.

Mr. MONTAMAT—I move a suspension of the rules, in order to act in this case.

Mr. CAZABAT—I move to dispense with the reading of the minutes.

[The resolution was lost.

The secretary read the minutes.]

Mr. SMITH—Before the minutes are adopted I wish to know if my amendment was not adopted, providing that after a member had been absent for three successive days, his seat should be declared vacant?

PRESIDENT—It was not adopted.

[The minutes were adopted.]

Mr. SPELLICY—I move a suspension of the rules to excuse Mr. Poynot, on account of sickness, and to take up Mr. Goldman's resignation.

[The question on excusing Mr. Poynot was put and carried.]

PRESIDENT—The secratary will read Mr. Goldman's resignation. It was laid on my table some days ago, placed in the drawer with other papers and forgotten.

[The secretary read:]

NEW ORLEANS, June 7, 1864.

To the president and members of the Constitutional Convention:

GENTLEMEN—The undersigned hereby tenders his resignation as a member of the "Louisiana State Convention." Having come into that honorable body with the intention to assist in accomplishing the work of statesmen, and not that of municipal politicians, I consider this course consistent and even incumbent upon me after yesterday's action in passing the police bill.

I have the honor to remain respectfully yours, etc.,

EDMUND GOLDMAN.

Mr. MONTAMAT—I move it be accepted.

Mr. HILLS—I move that it be accepted, to date from the date of the letter.

Mr. STOCKER—Is this debatable.

PRESIDENT—Certainly.

Mr. STOCKER—I am opposed to its acceptance for the reason that he states that he resigned, because this Convention did not pursue a certain course to please him. Now, sir, if every member who finds himself in a minority pursues such a course, we should soon all resign. I think the resignation shows a want of respect for this body, and therefore shall vote against accepting it, as it would be setting a dangerous precedent to let every man resign who came here expecting to carry everything his own way and failed.

Mr. SEYMOUR—I move that it be laid on the table.

Mr. MONTAMAT—I believe that it is an insult to this Convention, and I shall move that the sergeant-at-arms be dispatched to bring him here before the bar of the House, and that a vote of censure be passed upon him.

Mr. STOCKER—The best thing is to act on his resignation.

Mr. ABELL—I wish to state, that with regard to Mr. Goldman, he has placed his resignation on the ground that he, as a statesman, is so far above the members of this Convention, that he feels that he is condescending too much to remain with us. I believe it is best to let all such men go, and shall therefore vote for accepting his resignation.

[The ayes and noes were called, with the following result—yeas 40, nays 35.

Mr. Gruneberg presented the following, which was ordered to lay over under the rules :]

Resolved, That the sergeant-at-arms, or his assistants, be sent instanter to summon before this Convention all the members absent, whether residing inside or outside of New Orleans, and compel their attendance.

And resolved, That the traveling or other expenses incurred by the sergeant-at-arms, or his assistants, for the purposes aforesaid, shall be collected from the members so in default.

Mr. O'CONNER—I move to lay it on the table.

PRESIDENT—It is out of order to-day. Order of the day, Mr. Stocker's substitute to the report on the judiciary.

Mr. HILLS—I rise to a point of order. Judge Howell's amendment was put to vote on a *viva voce* vote. It was doubtful whether it was adopted. A division was called, and before the vote was announced the Convention adjourned.

PRESIDENT—He can offer it again.

Mr. HOWELL—I wish to amend the third line by inserting the "chief justice shall receive $7500 and the associates $7000 each per annum, until otherwise provided by law."

[The amendment was carried.]

Mr. CAMPBELL—Is it too late to offer an amendment to the amendment.

PRESIDENT—No, sir.

Mr. CAMPBELL—I move then to strike out "until otherwise provided by law."

[The motion was carried by a rising vote —ayes 54, noes 12.

The article as amended was adopted.

The secretary read :]

Art. 4. The Supreme Court shall hold its sessions in New Orleans from the first Monday of the month of November to the end of the month of June inclusive. The Legislature shall have power to fix the sessions elsewhere during the rest of the year: until otherwise provided, the sessions shall be held as heretofore.

Mr. CAZABAT—I move its adoption.

[The motion was carried.

The secretary read :]

Art. 5. The Supreme Court and each of the judges thereof shall have power to issue writs of *habeas corpus*, at the instance of all persons in actual custody under process, in all cases in which they may have appellate jurisdiction.

Mr. HARNAN—I move its adoption.

[The motion was carried.

The secretary read :]

Art. 6. No judgment shall be rendered by the Supreme Court without the concurrence of a majority of the judges comprising the court. Whenever the majority cannot agree, in consequence of the recusation of any member or members of the court, the judges not recused shall have power to call upon any judge or judges of the inferior courts, whose duty it shall be, when so called upon, to sit in the place of the judge or judges recused, and to aid in determining the case.

Mr. HILLS—I move its adoption.

[The resolution was carried.

The secretary read :]

Art. 7. All judges, by virtue of their office, shall be conservators of the peace throughout the State. The style of all process shall be "the State of Louisiana." All prosecutions shall be carried on in the name and by the authority of the State of Louisiana, and conclude against the peace and dignity of the same.

Mr. BELL—I move its adoption.

[The motion was carried.

The secretary read :]

Art. 8. The judges of all courts within the State shall, as often as it may be possible so to do, in every definitive judgment refer to the particular law in virtue of which such judgment may be rendered, and in all cases adduce the reasons on which their judgment is founded.

Mr. TERRY—I move its adoption.

[The motion was carried.

The secretary read :]

Art. 9. The judges of all courts shall be liable to impeachment ; but for any reasonable cause, which shall not be sufficient ground for impeachment, the governor shall remove any of them, on the address of a majority of the members elected to each House of the General Assembly. In every such case the cause or causes for which such removal may be required shall be stated at length in the address, and inserted in the journal of each House.

Mr. HARNAN—I move its adoption.

[The motion was carried.

The secretary read :]

Art. 10. The judges, both of the Supreme and inferior courts, shall, at stated times, receive a salary which shall be fixed by the Legislature ; and they are prohibited from receiving any fees of office or other compensation than their salaries for any civil duties performed by them.

Mr. HOWELL—I move to amend by striking out, after the word shall, the words "be fixed by the Legislature," and inserting instead the words "not be diminished during their continuance in office."

Mr. STOCKER—I shall oppose the amendment offered by Judge Howell. The question of salary ought in my opinion to be left to the Legislature, for the salary should depend on the condition of the currency. The salaries, at present rates of specie, would only be worth about $3500 for the chief justice, and less for the associates. Now it is apparent to every one that when we return to a specie basis these salaries will be entirely insufficient, and therefore the matter should be left to the Legislature. A gentleman suggests that I am wrong. I am—I stand corrected ; but I hold that the Legislature, coming fresh from the people from time to time, will be better qualified to fix the salaries than we can be now. The question was not raised in this contest, and in electing legislators it might be, and the Legislature could act on it, knowing the will of their constituents. For these reasons I shall oppose the amendment.

[The amendment was adopted, and article 10 adopted as amended.

Article 11 was read :]

Art. 11. The chief justice of the Supreme Court shall be elected by the qualified voters of the State, and the associate judges of the Supreme Court, together with the judges of the inferior courts, shall be elected by the qualified voters of their several districts, as determined by the Legislature ; and they shall hold their several offices during such term or terms as shall be fixed by the Legislature.

Mr. BOFILL—I offer the following substitute :

The judges of the Supreme Court shall be appointed by the governor, by and with the advice and consent of the Senate, for a term of eight years. The judges of the inferior courts for a term of six years.

Mr. HILLS—I move its adoption.

Mr. STAUFFER—I move to lay the substitute on the table.

[The yeas and nays were demanded, and the secretary proceeded to call the roll.]

Mr. HENDERSON—I vote against laying it on the table, but shall vote against the proposition when it comes up.

[The motion was lost, as follows :]

YEAS—Messrs. Bell, Buckley, Campbell, Collin, Cook J. K., Cook T., Decker, Duke, Dupaty, Flagg, Flood, Geier, Gorlinski, Gruneberg, Gaidry, Harnan, Howes, Knobloch, Maas, Mayer, Morris, O'Conner, Orr, Purcell J., Pursell S., Schnurr, Smith, Spellicy, Stocker, Stiner, Stauffer, Sullivan, Terry—33.

NAYS—Messrs. Abell, Austin, Bailey, Barrett, Baum, Beauvais, Bofill, Bromley, Burke, Cazabat, Crozat, Cutler, Davies, Dufresne, Duane, Ennis, Fish, Foley, Fosdick, Fuller, Gastinel, Healy, Hart, Henderson, Hills, Hire, Howell, Kavanagh, Kugler, Mann, Maurer, Mendiverri, Montamat, Murphy E., Murphy M. W., Newell, Normand, Ong, Payne J., Paine J. T., Pintado, Schroeder, Seymour, Shaw, Stumpf, Thorpe, Waters, Wenck, Wells, Wilson—50.

Mr. ONG—I move to amend by inserting "seven" instead of "six," and "nine" instead of "eight."

[Laid on the table.]

Mr. SMITH—I offer the following amendment:

Art. 11. The judges, both of the Supreme and inferior courts, shall be appointed by the governor. The judges of the Supreme Court to hold office for the term of six years; the judges of the inferior courts for four years; after which term the judges of the Supreme and inferior courts shall be elected by the legally qualified voters. Appointments in every instance to date from the ratification of the constitution by the people.

Mr. FOLEY—I move to lay it on the table.

[Carried, by a rising vote of 47 yeas to 31 nays.

The roll was called on the adoption of the substitute.]

Mr. ABELL—Being the first to cast my vote, I wish to explain. I am opposed to anything less than a life appointment, but I vote "yes" because I think it the best I can do.

[The substitute was adopted by the following vote:

YEAS—Messrs. Abell, Austin, Beauvais, Bailey, Baum, Bofill, Bromley, Burke, Cazabat, Crozat, Cutler, Davies, Duane, Dufresne, Ennis, Fish, Foley, Fosdick, Fuller, Gastinel, Healy, Hart, Henderson, Hills, Hire, Howell, Kavanagh, Kugler, Maurer, Mann, Mendiverri, Montamat, Murphy E., Murphy M. W., Newell, Normand, Ong Payne J., Paine J. T., Pintado, Schroeder Seymour, Shaw, Spellicy, Stumpf, Thorpe Waters, Wenck, Wells, Wilson—50.

NAYS—Messrs. Barrett, Bell, Buckley, Campbell, Collin, Cook J. K., Cook T., Decker, Duke, Dupaty, Flagg, Flood, Geier, Gorlinski, Gruneberg, Gaidry, Harnan, Howes, Knobloch, Maas, Mayer, Morris, O'Conner, Orr, Purcell J., Pursell S., Schnurr, Smith, Stocker, Stiner, Stauffer, Sullivan, Terry—33.

[Article 12 was read:]

Art. 12. The clerks of the inferior courts shall be elected by the qualified voters of their several districts, and shall hold their offices during such term or term as shall be fixed by the Legislature; subject to removal by the judges respectively, with the right of appeal in all such cases to the Supreme Court.

[Mr. Montamat offered an amendment, which was laid on the table.

Mr. Smith moved to strike out of Mr. Stocker's substitute for article 12 the words "and shall hold their offices during such term or terms as shall be fixed by the Legislature."

Laid on the table.]

Mr. DAVIES—I move the adoption of the original article.

Mr. HOWELL—I do not wish to detain the Convention, but inasmuch as we have fixed the terms of the judges, and as we may have judges appointed before the Legislature may assemble, I move to amend in the third line by striking out "such term or terms as shall be fixed by the Legislature," and inserting "a term of six years."

Mr. MONTAMAT—I amend by making it four years.

Mr. HOWELL—I accept the amendment.

[The amendment was lost by the following vote—yeas 29, nays 38.

The question to adopt article 12 recurring, a rising vote was taken—yeas 29, nays 5.

Article 12 was accordingly declared rejected.]

Mr. HILLS—I would ask if it is in order to offer an article in its place?

PRESIDENT—It is not.

[Article 13 was read:]

Art. 13. The Legislature shall have power to vest in clerks of courts authority to grant such orders and do such acts as may be deemed necessary for the furtherance of the administration of justice, and in all cases the powers thus granted shall be specified and determined.

Mr. STOCKER—We have just decided by a large majority that the courts shall not have any clerks; therefore this article is perfectly superfluous, and I move to strike it out.

[A motion was made and carried to reconsider the vote on article 12.]

Mr. HILLS—The objection to article 12 is, I believe, that the clerks are subject to removal by the judges. ["That's it."] I move to strike out "judges respectively" and insert "Legislature."

Mr. S. PURSELL—I move to amend by

striking out all of the last sentence, "subject to removal, etc."

Mr. HILLS—I accept the amendment.

[The amendment was adopted.]

Mr. HILLS—I now move to strike out "such term or terms as shall be fixed by the Legislature," and insert "a term of four years."

[The amendment was adopted, and the article as amended.

Article 13 was then adopted.

Article 14 was read.]

Art. 14. The jurisdiction of justices of the peace shall not exceed, in civil cases, the sum of one hundred dollars, exclusive of interest, subject to appeal in such cases as shall be provided for by law. They shall be elected by the qualified voters of their several districts, and shall hold their offices during such term or terms as shall be fixed by the Legislature. They shall have such criminal jurisdiction as shall be provided by law.

Mr. SULLIVAN—I move to amend by striking out "one hundred" and inserting "two hundred."

Mr. SMITH—I move to insert "seventy-five" instead.

[Both amendments were laid on the table.]

Mr. THORPE—I offer the following substitute:

The jurisdiction of justices of the peace shall not exceed, in civil cases, the sum of one hundred dollars, exclusive of interest, subject to appeal in such cases as shall be provided for by law. They shall hold their offices during such term or terms as shall be fixed by the Legislature. They shall have such criminal jurisdiction as shall be provided by law. Returns shall be made by them, under oath, quarterly, to the auditor of public accounts; and all fees received over the fixed salary must be faithfully returned to said auditor. A failure to make such returns as herein provided shall be cause of removal. They shall be appointed by the governor, by and with the advice and consent of the Senate.

Mr. HILLS—I move its adoption.

Mr. SULLIVAN—I move to lay it on the table.

[The motion was carried—yeas 43, nays 32.]

Mr. HILLS—I move to amend by striking out "elected by the qualified voters of their several districts," and insert "appointed by the governor, by and with the advice and consent of the Senate."

[Laid on the table.]

Mr. TERRY—I call for the previous question.

[The motion was lost, 35 voting in the affirmative.]

Mr. S. PURSELL—I move to strike out during "such term or terms as shall be fixed by the Legislature," and insert "a term of four years."

Mr. MONTAMAT—I amend to two years.

[The amendment was adopted—yeas 41, nays 32.

The article, as amended, was then adopted.

Article 15 was read:]

Art. 15. There shall be an attorney general for the State and as many district attorneys as may be hereafter found necessary. The attorney general shall be elected by the qualified voters of the State; the district attorneys shall be elected by the qualified voters of their several districts. The attorney general and district attorneys shall severally hold their offices during such term or terms, and shall severally receive such salaries as shall be determined by the Legislature.

Mr. BELL—I offer the following substitute:

There shall be an attorney general for the State, and as many district atterneys as shall hereafter be found necessary.

The attorney general shall be elected every four years, by the qualified voters of the State. He shall receive a salary of $5000 per annum, payable on his own warrant quarterly.

The district attorneys shall be elected by the qualified voters of their respective districts, for a term of four years. They shall receive such salaries as shall be provided by the Legislature.

[A motion to lay on the table was lost—yeas 19, nays 41.

The substitute was then adopted—yeas 48, nays 22.

Article 16 was read:]

Art. 16. A sheriff and coroner shall be elected for each parish by the qualified voters of the same; and they shall severally hold their offices for such term or terms, and shall receive such remuneration for their services, as the Legislature may determine.

Mr. SULLIVAN—I offer the following amendment:

A sheriff and a coroner shall be elected

in each parish by the qualified voters thereof, who shall hold their offices for the term of two years, unless sooner removed.

The Legislature shall have the power to increase the number of sheriffs in any parish. Should a vacancy occur in either of these offices subsequent to an election, it shall be filled by the governor, and the person so appointed shall continue in office until his successor shall be elected and qualified.

Mr. WENCK—I move to lay it on the table.

[Lost.]

Mr. STOCKER—I desire to amend by striking out "unless sooner removed."

PRESIDENT—That means by death.

Mr. STOCKER—If he will insert "by death," I will accept it.

[The amendment was adopted.]

Mr. S. PURSELL—I offer the following additional article:

Art. 17. The governor shall fill, by appointment, all offices whose election are provided for in this title, who shall hold their various positions for the same terms as if elected, dating from the time of the ratification of this constitution, except in the parish of Orleans, in which elections shall be ordered by the first Legislature held under this constitution.

Mr. MONTAMAT—I move to lay it on the table.

[Carried.

The roll was then called on the adoption of the substitute, as a whole, on its second reading.]

Mr. ABELL—I desire to explain my vote. I am opposed to this substitute, but I believe it is the best we can do, and I vote "yes."

Mr. ORR—I am opposed to the appointive system, and therefore vote "no."

Mr. STOCKER—Being constitutionally and conscientiously opposed to the appointive system, and believing this Convention is acting against the wishes of their constituents, I vote "no."

Mr. SULLIVAN—I believe the people are in favor of an elective judiciary for all officers, I vote no.

Mr. TERRY—Being a young politician and not having turned my coat, I do not intend to turn it at this late stage of the proceedings, and vote no.

[The substitute was adopted by the following vote:]

YEAS—Messrs. Abell, Austin, Bailey, Baum, Beauvais, Bofill, Bromley, Burke, Cazabat, Cook J. K., Crozat, Cutler, Davies, Decker, Duane, Duffesne, Ennis, Fish, Flagg, Foley, Fosdick, Fuller, Gastinel, Gorlinski, Gruneberg, Gaidry, Healy, Harnan, Hart, Henderson, Hills, Hire, Howell, Kavanagh, Kugler, Maas, Mann, Maurer, Mendiverri, Montamat, Morris, Murphy E., Murphy M. W., Newell, O'Conner, Ong, Payne J., Paine J. T., Pintado, Purcell J., Schroeder, Schnurr, Shaw, Spellicy, Stumpf, Stiner, Thorpe, Waters, Wenck, Wells—60.

NAYS—Messrs. Barrett, Bell, Buckley, Campbell, Collin, Cook T., Duke, Dupaty, Flood, Geier, Howes, Knobloch, Mayer, Normand, Orr, Pursell S., Seymour, Smith, Stocker, Stauffer, Sullivan, Terry, and Wilson—23.

Mr. MONTAMAT—I move to suspend the rules, to put the substitute on its third reading.

[The motion was carried by a vote of 69 in the affirmative.

The substitute as amended was read by the secretary.]

PRESIDENT—This is the third reading of the substitute as amended. The question now is, shall it pass its third reading?

Mr. HENDERSON—It must be taken up article by article.

PRESIDENT—Not on its third reading.

Mr. HENDERSON—I desire to offer the following rider to article 2:

Art. 2. The Supreme Court, except in cases otherwise provided in this constitution, shall have appellate jurisdiction only, which jurisdiction shall extend to all cases when the matter in dispute shall exceed three hundred dollars, exclusive of interest; to all cases in which the constitutionality or legality of any tax, toll or impost whatsoever, or of any fine, forfeiture or penalty imposed by a municipal corporation shall be in contestation, and to all criminal cases, both as to law and fact, with such exceptions and under such regulations as the Legislature shall make.

Mr. MONTAMAT—I move to lay it on the table.

[Carried.]

Mr. STOCKER—I ask for information as to the effect of the vote on the rider. Does the vote laying it on the table carry the second section with it?

PRESIDENT—No, sir.

[The roll was called on the adoption of the substitute on its third reading, when the following gentlemen explained their votes:]

Mr. ABELL—Having to lead off, I wish to explain again. I am opposed to the substitute, but I believe it is the best we can do, and therefore I vote yes.

Mr. DECKER—My constituents are in favor of an elective judiciary. I therefore vote no.

Mr. HOWELL—The bill, as it is adopted, is far from according with my feelings and views. I am, and I have always been, in favor of an appointive judiciary, and the appointment of all the officers belonging to that department, but find I am unable to obtain the adoption of my views, and I take this as the next best.

Mr. ORR—I intend to move a reconsideration, and vote yes.

Mr. SMITH—I have been in favor of the elective all the time, but I deem it unsafe to elect at present; and as some of the officers have been made elective and some appointive, I shall vote against the whole bill.

Mr. STOCKER—Being opposed, as I stated before, to appointments, and not having, like my friend Mr. Howell, gained *something* in this bill—but, on the contrary, I think I have lost everything—I shall still maintain my position, and vote no, because it does make some of the officers appointive.

Mr. SULLIVAN—As I do not want to see any of the rights of the people taken away from them, I vote "no."

Mr. ORR—I desire to change my vote from "yes" to "no."

Mr. BURKE—I desire to change my vote from "no" to "yes."

[The substitute was adopted by the following vote :]

YEAS—Messrs. Abell, Austin, Baum, Bailey, Beauvais, Bofill, Bromley, Burke, Cazabat, Cook J. K., Crozat, Cutler, Davies, Dufresne, Duane, Ennis, Fish, Flagg, Foley, Fosdick, Fuller, Gastinel, Gaidry, Gorlinski, Gruneberg, Healy, Harnan, Hart, Hills, Hire, Howell, Kavanagh, Kugler, Maurer, Maas, Mann, Mendiverri, Montamat, Morris, Murphy E., Murphy M. W., Newell, Normand, O'Conner, Ong, Payne J., Paine J. T., Pintado, Purcell J., Schroeder, Schnurr, Shaw, Stumpf, Stiner, Thorpe, Waters, Wells, Wenck—58.

NAYS—Messrs. Barrett, Bell, Buckley, Campbell, Collin, Cook T., Decker, Duke, Dupaty, Flood, Geier, Henderson, Howes, Knobloch, Mayer, Orr, Pursell S., Seymour, Smith, Spellicy, Stocker, Stauffer, Sullivan, Terry, Wilson—25.

Mr. BOFILL—I move a reconsideration of the vote adopting the substitute.

Mr. CAZABAT—I move to lay the motion on the table.

[Carried.]

Mr. SULLIVAN—I move we adjourn.

[The motion was carried and the Convention adjourned till 12 M. Thursday.]

THURSDAY, June 16, 1864.

[The Convention was called to order pursuant to adjournment. Present, Hon. E. H. Durell, president, in the chair, and the following members :]

Messrs. Abell, Austin, Balch, Bailey, Barrett, Baum, Beauvais, Bell, Bofill, Bromley, Buckley, Burke, Campbell, Collin, Cazabat, Cook J. K., Cook T., Crozat, Cutler, Davies, Decker, Duane, Dufresne, Dupaty, Ennis, Fish, Flagg, Flood, Foley, Fosdick, Fuller, Gastinel, Geier, Gorlinski, Gruneberg, Gaidry, Healy, Harnan, Hart, Henderson, Hills, Howell, Howes, Kavanagh, Knobloch, Kugler, Maas, Mann, Maurer, Mayer, Mendiverri, Montamat, Morris, Murphy E., Murphy M. W., Normand, O'Conner, Ong, Orr, Payne J., Paine J. T., Pintado, Purcell J., Pursell S., Schroeder, Schnurr, Seymour, Shaw, Smith, Spellicy, Stocker, Stumpf, Stiner, Stauffer, Sullivan, Terry, Thorpe, Waters, Wenck, Wells, Wilson—83.

Absent—Messrs. Ariail, Bennie, Bonzano, Brott, Duke, (excused,) Edwards, (excused,) Heard, Goldman, Lobdell, Millspaugh, Montague, Newell, Poynot, (excused,) Taliaferro and Thomas—14.

[On motion of Mr. Smith, Mr. Balch was excused for his absence on yesterday.]

Mr. KNOBLOCH—I ask for Mr. Duke to be excused. He is sick in bed.

Mr. WELLS—I present a certificate of a physician that Mr. Edwards is sick, and move that he be excused from attendance today.

[The motion was carried.]

Mr. HENDERSON—I wish to change my vote on the judiciary bill. I voted no. I wish to change my vote to aye.

Mr. STAUFFER—I object.

Mr HILLS—I move that the gentleman's request be granted.

[The motion was carried.]

PRESIDENT—I would observe that gentlemen coming in during the reading of the minutes, must necessarily be considered in time, because they cannot interrupt the secretary while he is reading the minutes.

Mr. SMITH—I move that Mr. Balch be excused for non-attendance yesterday. He was sick, as his appearance bears evidence to-day.

PRESIDENT—He is here, and can speak for himself.

Mr. BALCH—I desire to be excused. I was sick yesterday; not able to attend.

[The motion was carried.]

PRESIDENT—The next business is the order of the day. The report of the Committee on Impeachment, on its second reading.

[The secretary read the report.]

Mr. SMITH—I move the report be adopted as a whole.

[The secretary read:]

Art. 1. The power of impeachment shall be vested in the House of Representatives.

Mr. THORPE—I move its adoption.

[The motion was carried.

The secretary read:]

Art. 2. Impeachments of the governor, lieutenant governor, attorney general, secretary of state, state treasurer, and of the judges of the inferior courts, justices of the peace excepted, shall be tried by the Senate; the chief justice of the Supreme Court, or the senior judge thereof, shall preside during the trial of such impeachment. Impeachments of the judges of the Supreme Court shall be tried by the Senate. When sitting as a court of impeachment, the senators shall be upon oath or affirmation, and no person shall be convicted without the concurrence of two-thirds of the senators present.

Mr. HILLS—I move to amend the second line by inserting after the word "treasurer" "auditor of public accounts."

Mr. TERRY—I second the motion.

[The motion was carried.]

Mr. FOLEY—I move to amend the second line by striking out the words "two-thirds," and inserting "a majority."

Mr. BOFILL—I move to lay that amendment on the table.

[The motion to table was lost, the amendment adopted, and the article adopted as amended.

The secretary read:]

Art. 3. Judgments in cases of impeachment shall extend only to removal from office, and disqualification from holding any office of honor, trust or profit under the State; but the convicted parties shall, nevertheless, be subject to indictment, trial and punishment, according to law.

Mr. TERRY—I move to adopt it.

[The motion was carried.

The secretary read:]

Art. 4. All officers against whom articles of impeachment may be preferred, shall be suspended from the exercise of their functions during the pendency of each impeachment; the appointing power may make a provisional appointment to replace any suspended officer until the decision of the impeachment.

Mr. HILLS—I move its adoption.

Mr. WILSON—In line three there appears to be a typographical error. The word "each" should be "such."

Mr. HILLS—I move the secretary be instructed to correct the error.

[The motion was carried and the article adopted.

The secretary read :]

Art. 5. The Legislature shall provide by law for the trial, punishment, and removal from office of all other officers of the State by indictment or otherwise.

Mr. HILLS—I move its adoption.

[The motion was carried.]

Mr. FOLEY—I move the adoption of the report as a whole, on its second reading.

[The motion was carried.]

Mr. HILLS—I move a suspension of the rules in order to put it on its third reading.

[The motion was carried.]

Mr. MONTAMAT—I move that it be adopted as a whole and the yeas and nays taken on it.

[The roll was called with the following result:]

YEAS—Messrs. Abell, Austin, Balch, Bailey, Barrett, Baum, Beauvais, Bell, Bofill, Bromley, Buckley, Burke, Campbell, Collin, Cazabat, Cook J. K., Cook T., Crozat, Cutler, Davies, Decker, Duane, Dufresne, Ennis, Fish, Flagg, Flood, Foley, Fosdick, Fuller, Gastinel, Gaidry, Geier, Gorlinski, Gruneberg, Healy, Harnan, Hart, Hills, Hire, Howell, Howes, Kavanagh, Knobloch, Kugler, Maas, Mann, Maurer, Mayer, Mendiverri, Montamat, Morris, Murphy E., Murphy M. W., Normand, O'Conner, Ong, Orr, Payne J., Paine J. T., Pintado, Pursell S., Schroeder, Schnurr, Seymour, Shaw, Smith, Spellicy, Stocker, Stumpf, Stiner, Stauffer, Sullivan, Terry, Thorpe, Wilson—76.

NAYS—Messrs. Dupaty, Henderson, Waters, Wenck, Wells—5.

[The report was adopted.]

Mr. THORPE—I move to reconsider the whole report.

Mr. BOFILL—I move to lay that motion on the table.

[The motion was carried.]

PRESIDENT—The next business in order is the report of the Committee on General Provisions.

Mr. CUTLER—Before we proceed to take up this report, Mr. President, I desire to submit the propriety of inserting as the first article a subject which is not treated of in the report. It is this: we have passed an ordinance of emancipation. I think it proper that the substance of that ordinance, if not the entire two sections, should be inserted in the constitution. As it now stands it is a mere ordinance, and it is apparent to your mind and to that of every member of this Convention, that it will amount to nothing, unless it is embodied in the constitution. I have, therefore, prepared an article embracing the entire substance and spirit of the article, as follows:

Article 1. Slavery and involuntary servitude are forever abolished and prohibited throughout this State, and the Legislature shall make no laws recognizing the right of property in man.

You will observe that the entire substance of the ordinance is preserved, but it is in one article instead of two.

PRESIDENT—I will observe that the ordinance of emancipation is the report of a committee that has regularly passed its third reading, and as such, is as much a part of the constitution as the report of the committee of the judiciary, or any other report that has passed its third reading regularly, and I certainly must express my astonishment that there should be any doubt on the subject in the mind of any member of this Convention. You will find that the committee on emancipation was the first committee appointed and was composed of some of the ablest members of this Convention, and their report becomes, on being passed, registered, as it was, part and parcel of this constitution.

Mr. ABELL—I desire to know, merely for information, what amendment that is to the constitution. I think it is all wrong from begining to end, but I think the gentleman is right in his position. That certainly means something or it means nothing. If it does mean anything it must be placed somewhere in the constitution, in order to have any force or effect. In regard to the judiciary, the case is different. We have a judiciary in the constitution, and the amendment of that portion is a part and parcel of our duty.

In the constitution there is no such title as emancipation, and consequently, unless we incorporate this specially in that instrument, it is a mere nullity. It is not an amendment, but an addition, and is not part of the constitution until it is made so by the action of this Convention; and I think that when this question comes up this body will permit it to stand as far away from the constitution as possible, that they will not lay it any nearer than it now is, and will permit it to stand as a mere resolution or recommend of this body. If you want to make a recommend, I have no objection. But the negroes are not free now; they are just as much slaves as they ever were.

Mr. WILSON—I think the gentleman is out of order.

Mr. ABELL—I am just as much in order as ever. I am just in order. I say they are not free, and will not be free, until that is made a part of the constitution and ratified by the people of Louisiana. I say they are not free, because Abraham Lincoln, the head of the military power of the United States, has said that these parishes are exempt from the effect of his emancipation proclamation. He is better authority than even my friend from the Second District, (Mr. Hills,) whom I always take as authority on any subject of which he is cognizant. They are no nearer free than they were four years ago.

Mr. FOLEY—What was the meaning of that procession the other day?

Mr. ABELL—It meant either the elevation of the negro or the lowering of the flag of the Union. You may call it which you please.

Mr. HILLS—Will the gentleman allow me to ask him a question?

Mr. ABELL—Certainly.

Mr. HILLS—Was ever such a procession as that got up by slaves?

Mr. ABELL—I will answer the question by asking what it would have been if no white men had been concerned in it? Mr. Lincoln says in his emancipation proclamation that slaves shall be free, and he specially excepted these parishes.

How, then, I ask you as fair and honest men, how can you say, then, that they are free here and still refuse to pay the owners for them? (Hear, hear.) I say I am willing to sign your articles of emancipation if you will first provide for the payment of about four hundred dollars apiece for them, by putting the money into the treasury out of which the payment should be made, and putting a sufficient guard over the treasury to prevent them from stealing it. I would be just before I attempted to be generous.

I have said the negroes were as much slaves as they were thirteen years ago. You did not know that, did you? (No.) I'll show it by authority of the laws of the United States, by the proclamation of the president, by the rights of purchase. He is as much a slave as ever, and will remain so until this Convention has said in its sovereign might that they shall be free, and the people have ratified it as a part of the constitution of Louisiana. Until this great people—they are a great people, oppressed as they may be——

PRESIDENT—Out of order. The chair will decide that any report, after having been read regularly three times and adopted on its third reading, becomes a part and parcel of the constitution which this Convention intends to adopt, and cannot be added to any other report or part of the constitution that has not also passed its third reading, thereby subjecting it to the chance of being rejected. By permitting a report already adopted to be attached to one not finally passed, as is proposed now, it is liable to be constantly reopened, and we should never get through with our work.

Mr. CUTLER—I desire most respectfully to appeal from the decision of the chair, and would like to be heard on the appeal, and will show that you are wrong, and leave it to the Convention to decide.

I am ready to give my explanation, and if I am wrong, the Convention will say so. The preamble of the report, made by the wisdom of this Convention, reads thus:

Provided, That a committee of ——— members be appointed by the president of this Convention, to whom shall be referred the subject of the immediate and the permanent abolition of slavery in the State of Louisiana, with instructions to report, as early as practicable, an ordinance or provisions in relation thereto, to be incorporated in the constitution of this State.

PRESIDENT—We have already incorporated it.

Mr. CUTLER—I know your decision, and you need not cite it twice. You are wrong, sir; this is to be incorporated in the constitution of the State. It has passed its first, second and third readings and has been adopted by this Convention; and I dare say there is not a man here who wants to tear from it a word or letter, but it is necessary that it should be engrafted into the constitution, and why? It was the object of that committee that it should be engrafted in the constitution, and the preamble of the ordinance says so. Now, sir, I recur to the argument of the gentleman from the Fifth, that the calling of this Convention together for the purpose of revising and amending the constitution of 1852, does not embrace the subject of emancipation. It is nowhere to be found and no amendment can be made—no revision made of the constitution of 1852 including these articles of emancipation. The articles of the report of the emancipation committee is an ordinance, and I defy any man of intelligence in this Convention to say it is anything else. It is an ordinance of emancipation, just as much as the ordinance of secession passed by the rebel convention of 1861, and it must be placed somewhere in the constitution so that your constituents and mine, when the constitution is placed before them for ratification or rejection, can see what it is they are voting upon. If you leave it as an ordinance, it can no more come before the people to be ratified or rejected than the ordinance passed by this Convention for the purpose of turning out certain officers who were supposed to be disloyal. It has no more to do with the constitution than this fan has, in its present condition. The revising and amending of the consitiution of 1852 is to be submitted,

I hope, to the people; and when you submit that constitution to them, the ordinance of emancipation reads that it is to be incorporated in the constitution. Where are you to incorporate it? We have passed upon the legislative, executive, judiciary and impeachment reports, and have come to general provisions, and we have not placed it in the constitution yet, and it cannot be placed in it by the arbitrary dictum of the president, nor by a committee. It must be done by the sanction of the Convention. Now, sir, are the resolutions of a convention ever submitted to the people for adoption or rejection? Is it to be engrafted in the constitution? The president has decided that it is already a part of it; if so, in what part does it appear? No where! [Applause.] Where is it now engrafted in the constitution? It is idle to talk thus. You must vote and say it is to be placed *somewhere;* either in the executive, judiciary, general provisions, or somewhere, and it is that which I arose to do. I arose for the purpose of making it the first article under the head of general provisions; and then, when the constitution is printed and goes forth to the people, they will read what they are to adopt, and know, when they cast their votes, whether they are voting for a constitution that has the emancipation clause in it or out of it. Then, sir, I hold, in perfect candor, that no man need be "astonished at the intelligence of the gentleman who presented this resolution." I admit that he may be astonished, but it is in a false principle; it is like the dog looking at the moon and barking fiercely—astonished because he cannot comprehend. I am plain, for the reason that no such reflections should be cast on pure motives, which are for the purpose of engrafting on the constitution of 1864 the great work of this Convention, that of emancipation. Let it be placed in its proper place, and there is no better place than under the head of general provisions.

Mr. Henderson—I partly concur in what the gentleman says and partly concur in what he does not say. I know him to be an astute lawyer, but he forgets that when we commenced we decided that the arrangement and classification of the several departments in the constitution should take place when they were finished; but to say that the emancipation bill has not been passed, is the same as saying that the legislative or judiciary bills have not been passed, because they have all to take their order in the constitution and be numbered. We say "article ——" because we do not know where they will come in; but they will be no more a part of the constitution then, except as a matter of reference. I understand the gentleman wishes to insert it under the head of general provisions, article 9; I don't say that it may not be effected, but that the gentleman is wrong as to the time. When all the parts are revised and amended, then we come to number them, and the gentleman can have it made No. 1 or 50. Therefore, while I agree with the president, I concur with the gentleman that it has yet to be numbered, although that time is when we come to the final arrangement. I hope, gentlemen, the president will be sustained in this matter.

Mr. Cutler—Mr. President——

Mr. Stauffer—I hope the gentleman is not going to speak three times.

Mr. Cutler—I rise to make a motion, not a speech. In order to cut off further debate and delay, I will withdraw my motion and the appeal from the decision of the chair, and will now offer this——

President—You are out of order; you cannot withdraw the motion unless the second assents.

Mr. Bofill—I seconded and consent to its being withdrawn.

Mr. Cutler—Then I will move that the ordinance shall be inserted under the head of general provisions as articles 1 and 2.

President—That will come up when the report passes its third reading, not before. According to my ruling, you cannot, when a bill has passed its third reading, subject it again to the new uncertainty of debate and vote by adding it to a bill on its second reading; otherwise there would be no end to it. When the report has passed its third reading, you can make that motion.

Mr. Stauffer—I wish to call the attention of the Convention to a fact, and if I am wrong the House will correct me. I refer the Convention to the report of the Emancipation Committee——

Mr. HILLS—I rise to a point of order; that question is not before the House.

PRESIDENT—The matter for consideration now is the second reading of the report of the Committee on General Provisions.

[Article 1 was read and adopted.]

Article 1. Members of the General Assembly and all officers, before they enter upon the duties of their offices, shall take the following oath or affirmation:

"I (A B) do solemnly swear (or affirm) that I will support the constitution and laws of the United States, and of this State, and that I will faithfully and impartially discharge and perform all the duties incumbent on me as ——, according to the best of my abilities and understanding, so help me God!"

[Article 2 was read:]

Art. 2. Treason against the State shall consist only in levying war against it, or in adhering to its enemies, giving them aid and comfort. No person shall be convicted of treason, unless on the testimony of two witnesses to the same overt act, or his own confession in open court.

Mr. STAUFFER — I move to amend by striking out "to the same overt act."

Mr. HILLS—I move to lay it on the table.

PRESIDENT—The amendment has not been seconded.

[The article was then adopted as read.

Article 3 was read:]

Art. 3. The Legislature shall have power to declare the punishment of treason; but no attainder of treason shall work corruption of blood or forfeiture, except during the life of the person attainted.

Mr. STAUFFER — I move to amend by striking out all after the first clause, "but no attainder," etc.

Mr. MONTAMAT—I move to lay it on the table.

[Carried.]

Mr. HILLS—I move to amend by striking out "or forfeiture."

Mr. HENDERSON—I move to lay the amendment on the table.

[Carried by a rising vote—yeas 43, nays 25.

The article was then adopted.

Article 4 was read and adopted:]

Art. 4. Every person shall be disqualified from holding any office of trust or profit, in this State, and shall be excluded from the right of suffrage, who shall have been convicted of treason, perjury, forgery, bribery, or other high crimes or misdemeanors.

[Article 5 was read and adopted:]

Art. 5. All penalties shall be proportioned to the nature of the offence.

[The secretary read the following:]

Art. 6. The privilege of free suffrage shall be supported by laws regulating elections, and prohibiting, under adequate penalties, all undue influence thereon from power, bribery, tumult, or other improper practice.

Mr. MONTAMAT—I move to amend by adding, "No negro shall be permitted to vote."

Mr. FOLEY—That has been decided upon in the report of the Committee on the Legislative Department.

Mr. STAUFFER—It is out of order on that account.

PRESIDENT—The chair decides that inasmuch as that question was finally passed upon in connection with the report of the Committee on Legislative Department, it is out of order.

Mr. MONTAMAT—I appeal.

Mr. HENDERSON—Under the report adopted, only free white male citizens can be voters, and that is strong enough.

Mr. MONTAMAT—I appeal. I have a right to.

PRESIDENT—Take your seat. I am about to put your appeal.

A VOICE—Put that man out.

Mr. MONTAMAT—You can't put me out. I am as good as anybody, and perhaps a damned sight better.

PRESIDENT—Take your seat, sir. Sergeant-at-arms, take charge of that man.

Mr. MONTAMAT—I beg to be excused. I thought the chair refused to put my appeal.

PRESIDENT—My dear sir, you should attend to business, and then there would be no necessity of asking to be excused.

There has been an appeal from the decision of the chair against the amendment offered by the gentleman from the Fifth, (Mr. Montamat,) that no negro shall have a right to vote. The chair decided that to be out of order, inasmuch as that point has been determined by the final action of this body on the report of the Committee on the Legislative Department. That having been so determined and passed its third reading, it cannot be brought up again on the second reading of this bill to pass through another ordeal of arguments and votes, otherwise there would be no end to labor. On this question the yeas and nays are demanded. Those of you in favor of sustaining the chair, will answer yes; contrary, no.

YEAS—Messrs. Austin, Bailey, Baum, Beauvais, Bell, Bromley, Burke, Collin, Cazabat, Cook J. K., Cook T., Crozat, Cutler, Davies, Duane, Dupaty, Ennis, Fish, Flagg, Flood, Fosdick, Fuller, Geier, Gorlinski, Gruneberg, Gaidry, Healy, Harnan, Hart, Henderson, Hills, Hire, Howell, Howes, Kavanagh, Knobloch, Kugler, Mann, Mayer, Murphy E., Normand, Ong, Payne J., Paine J. T., Pintado, Purcell J., Pursell S., Schroeder, Schnurr, Seymour, Smith, Spellicy, Stocker, Stumpf, Stiner, Stauffer, Terry, Thorpe, Wenck—60.

NAYS—Messrs. Abell, Balch, Bofill, Buckley, Campbell, Decker, Dufresne, Gastinel, Maas, Maurer, Mendiverri, Montamat, Murphy M. W., Orr, Sullivan, Waters, Wilson—17.

[Chair sustained. Applause.]

PRESIDENT—I would state to the Convention that under the rules adopted by it, a two-thirds vote is required to overrule the decision of the chair. But on account of being willing to give way to a superiority of judgment, I have privately, without saying any thing to any one, adopted the rule of the majority. There have never been two-thirds voting against the chair.

Mr. SULLIVAN—I move the following amendment to art. 6:

No negro shall be allowed to practice law or physic in this State, nor shall they be taught or instructed in the art or mystery of any trade or profession, under such penalties as may be fixed by the Legislature.

Mr. BUCKLEY—I second that.

Mr. HILLS—I understand it to be that no negro shall take physic. [Laughter.]

Mr. SULLIVAN—No, sir.

[Motion to table was carried on rising vote—ayes 48, nays 20.

Art. 6 was then adopted.

The secretary read the following:]

Art. 7. No money shall be drawn from the treasury but in pursuance of specific appropriation made by law, nor shall any appropriation of money be made for a longer term than two years. A regular statement and account of the receipts and expenditures of all public moneys shall be published annually, in such manner as shall be prescribed by law.

Mr. HILLS—I move as an amendment, "no negro shall be permitted to draw money from the treasury." [Laughter]

Mr. SULLIVAN—I second that.

[Motion to table was lost.]

Mr. HILLS—I withdraw my amendment.

Mr. SULLIVAN—Too late!

[Motion to adjourn until 12 M. of Friday, the 17th inst., was carried by a rising vote of 35 ayes to 34 noes.] [Applause.]

FRIDAY, June 17, 1864.

[Pursuant to adjournment, the Convention met at 12 o'clock M., Hon. E. H. Durell, president, in the chair.

The roll was called and the following members found to be present:]

Messrs. Abell, Austin, Balch, Bailey, Barrett, Baum, Beauvais, Bell, Bofill, Bromley, Buckley, Burke, Campbell, Collin, Cazabat, Cook J. K., Cook T., Crozat, Cutler, Davies, Decker, Duane, Dufresne, Duke, Dupaty, Ennis, Fish, Flagg, Flood, Foley, Fosdick, Fuller, Gastinel, Geier, Gorlinski, Gruneberg, Gaidry, Healy, Harnan, Hart, Henderson, Hills, Hire, Howell, Howes, Kavanagh, Knobloch, Kugler, Maas, Mann, Maurer, Mayer, Mendiverri, Montamat, Morris, Murphy E., Murphy M. W., Newell, Normand, O'Conner, Ong, Orr, Payne J., Paine J. T., Pintado, Purcell J., Pursell S., Schroeder, Schnurr, Seymour, Shaw, Smith, Spellicy, Stocker, Stumpf, Stiner, Stauffer, Sullivan, Terry, Thorpe, Waters, Wenck, Wells, Wilson—85.

Absent—Messrs. Ariail, Bennie, Bonzano, Brott, Edwards, (excused,) Heard, Lobdell, Millspaugh, Montamat, Poynot, (excused,) Taliaferro, Thomas—12.

[The minutes of yesterday were read and adopted.]

Mr. SULLIVAN—Mr. President, I rise to a question of privilege. I saw in the proceedings of the Constitutional Convention, as published in the Era, of New Orleans, of this morning's issue, that in its report of the proceedings I am styled an office-holder. Is it, sir, because I happen to be an office-holder, which is published to the people (as if it were a crime to hold office,) by this contemptible scribbler of that paper, that I am compelled to give up my rights as a freeman on the floor of this Convention, and pander to his or any one else's wishes; that I have to give up, for the sake of holding office, the sacred rights of the people who selected me to represent them, and whose wishes I respect and will endeavor to carry out to the extent of the feeble abilities which I possess? If I am an office-holder, I will not allow any man, with impunity, to insult me in this manner without some rebuke from me.

It is true I hold office, and by the wishes of his excellency the governor of this State, Michael Hahn. He thought I was worthy and competent to fill an appointment. He had it tendered to me. I accepted it, with my thanks for it. I voted for him, and the other honorable gentlemen on the same ticket with him for State officers, and would to-morrow cheerfully do so again, thinking him the most suitable man in this State at the present time for that distinguished position. I have known him for a long period of time in this community. I supported him for that position, because I thought him to be patriotic, able, and competent to discharge the functions of that office, and that he was ever faithful to the people and to the Government.

Mr. President, I have lived for a long time in this city, I believe for a period of twenty-six years, and during that long residence there cannot be a single charge of the slightest nature brought against me, derogatory to my character or standing as a man and a citizen. I have held office, and several honorable positions, from the people, during that time; and I believe I discharged the several duties connected with them to the satisfaction of the people.

The first vote I ever cast was given by me to the Hon. Lewis Cass, of Michigan, for president of the United States, in the year 1848. From that time up to the time that this unfortunate rebellion broke out, I supported and advocated the democratic party, never once deviating from its liberal principles. I never during that period of time voted for either a whig or a know-nothing. I ever have been, as every one who knows me can prove, consistent in my political opinions; therefore, every man knows where to place me. I am not of those who deviate or swerve from my principles, which I hold to be as sacred as my religion.

I can also state to this honorable Convention that I was nominated and elected by the almost unanimous voice of the people of the Third Representative District of this city. I did not, gentlemen, have to go out of my own ward, where I reside, to another ward, to buy a candidate from a ticket already nominated, to run before the people, without a nomination, for a position as delegate in this Convention, as the scribbler of the Era did. No, sir, as I stated to this Convention, I was honorably nominated and elected by the people whom I have the honor to represent, and whom I am proud to serve. I may speak, however, without egotism to myself, that I sincerely believe I would be chosen again to represent them, if I came before them for election. I ask the question, would this individual, by his course on the floor of this Convention, merit a re election from the people of the district which he represents?

Look at his conduct towards me as a member of this Convention. At any time, if I should think proper to bring forward for the consideration of this honorable body a bill, for the purpose solely of benefiting the poor white people, to which class I have the honor to belong, this individual at once brands my resolution as a shame and a disgrace, and that I ought to be brought before the bar of the House for a contempt, to be punished for advocating the right of the poor who elected me to faithfully represent them here.

In conclusion, Mr. President and gentlemen, I spurn from me with utter contempt both the writer and his paper that contained the insult. These, gentlemen, are my sentiments.

President—The order of the day is the report of the Committee on General Provisions. Mr. Secretary, read article 7.

[The secretary read General Provisions, article 7.]

Mr. Howell—I move its adoption.

[The motion was carried.

The secretary read article 8.]

Mr. Foley—I move its adoption.

[The motion was carried.

The secretary read article 9.]

Mr. Pursell—I have a substitute: "All State officers shall be residents of the State, and all parish or district officers shall be residents of the parish or district for which they shall be chosen, and shall keep their offices at such places as may be directed by law."

Mr. HILLS—I second the substitute.

[The substitute was adopted.

The secretary read article 10.]

Mr. HILLS—I believe that this is already provided for in the judiciary report. If it is, I move to strike it out entirely.

[The motion was carried.

The secretary read article 11.]

Mr. SMITH—I move to strike out *viva voce* and insert yeas and nays.

Mr. PURSELL—If I am in order, I will ask the gentleman to withdraw his motion a moment, in order to move a reconsideration of the vote rejecting article 10. I voted to reject it, but I have had time to look at it now and wish to reconsider it, for I find that it does not conflict with article 9 of the judiciary report.

[The motion to reconsider was carried.]

Mr. ABELL—I move to refer this article to a special committee of five, to be appointed by the chair, to report in one hour.

Mr. HILLS—I second the motion.

Mr. HOWELL—Mr. President, is this motion debatable?

PRESIDENT—It is.

Mr. HOWELL—If the gentleman will compare article 9 of the judiciary report, he will find no conflict. That article provides that the removal of the judges shall be made by a majority of the Legislature. Now, all that is proposed to do by this article is to provide for the removal of other officers—all except the governor and the judges, whose removal is provided for in their respective titles. The only objection I see to this article is, that it makes it more difficult to remove a clerk or district attorney than it does to remove a judge. But this Convention has seen proper to make the judiciary as unstable as possible. This provides that all other officers shall be removable by two-thirds of the General Assembly. If you strike this out, you will have no provision at all for their removal.

Mr. ABELL—The gentleman's explanations are partly good and partly not good. It certainly would be very inconsistent to say that a judge should be removed by a majority of the Legislature, while you require two-thirds to remove a coroner or a clerk. I think the matter could be remedied by a committee without delaying the business.

Mr. CUTLER—Mr. President, my first impression was that there was an inconsistency, but I respectfully submit that there is none. Article 9 of the judiciary report provides that a majority of the Legislature shall remove the judges. Ample provision is made in that article for the removal of the judges. Now, this article provides that all, except those already provided for, prove there is no conflict whatever. This merely provides for those not otherwise provided for.

Mr. BEAUVAIS—I move to lay the motion to refer to a committee on the table.

[The motion was carried.]

Mr. WILSON—I move to amend the article to read in this way: "All civil officers, except the governor and judges of the supreme and inferior courts, shall be removable by address of a majority of the members of both Houses of the General Assembly, except those the removal of which has been provided for in this constitution."

Mr. ABELL—That is satisfactory. I second it.

[The article as amended was adopted.]

[The secretary read Art. 11.]

Mr. HARNAN—I move to strike out "*viva voce*" and insert "yeas and nays."

[The motion was carried and the article as amended was adopted.

The secretary read Art. 12.]

Mr. BELL—I move its adoption.

[The motion was carried.

The secretary read Art. 13.]

Mr. STAUFFER—I move to amend, in the second line, after the word "provided," insert the words "that none but citizens of the United States shall be appointed to any office of trust or profit in this State."

Mr. THORPE—I move to lay that motion the table.

Mr. WILSON—I second the motion.

Mr. CAZABAT—I second the motion.

Mr. HOWELL—I move to amend that amendment by striking out the whole article.

Mr. MONTAMAT—I move to lay all the amendments on the table.

[The motion to table was lost. Mr. Stauffer's amendment was adopted, and the article as amended was adopted.

The secretary read Art. 14.]

Mr. FOLEY—I move its adoption.

[The motion was carried.

The secretary read Art. 15.]

Mr. BELL—I move its adoption.

Mr. HOWELL—I move to strike out and insert, so that the article shall read as follows:

No power of suspending the laws shall be exercised except by the Legislature or by its authority.

[The amendment was adopted, and the article as amended was adopted.

The secretary read Art. 16.]

Mr. FOLEY—I move its adoption.

[The motion was carried.

The secretary read Art. 17.]

Mr. HOWELL—I desire to offer as a substitute article 104 of the constitution of 1852.

Mr. STAUFFER and Mr. ABELL—I second the amendment.

Mr. MONTAMAT—I move to lay the motion on the table.

Mr. HOWELL—That gentleman is always moving to lay my motions on the table.

[Mr. Montamat's motion was not seconded. The amendment was adopted, and the article adopted as amended.

The secretary read Art. 18.]

Mr. FOLEY—I move its adoption.

[The motion was carried.

The secretary read Art. 19.]

Mr. BELL—I move its adoption.

[The motion was carried.

The secretary read Art 20.]

Mr. CAMPBELL—I move to amend by adding "no attorney shall give evidence in a cause or suit in which he may be employed."

[The amendment was adopted, and the article adopted as amended.

The secretary read Art. 21.]

Mr. HILLS—I move its adoption.

Mr. CUTLER—I shall move to strike out this article as wholly unnecessary, because the matter it proposes is already provided for. That "all courts shall be open" is pure surplusage: it is more, it is contrary to common sense. The very existence of a court to redress wrongs and enforce rights implies that it must be open. If it was not it would be no court; and I am opposed to lumber up the fundamental law of the State with such a useless provision.

Mr. STOCKER—Mr. President, I cannot agree with the gentleman that when courts are organized it necessarily follows that they are always open, or that they always administer justice; and this article proposes that they shall be open, and shall administer justice—and because it contains this provision, that they shall administer justice, I shall object most decidedly to striking it out.

Mr. FOLEY—I move to lay the motion on the table.

[The motion to table was lost, and the article adopted.

The secretary read Art. 22.]

Mr. SULLIVAN—I move to amend by striking out, in the second and third lines, "shall be responsible" and inserting "the writer shall take the consequences of his abuse."

Mr. TERRY—I offer the following amendment to article 23:

No monopoly shall be created by the Legislature, by the grant to joint stock companies or to individuals of exclusive rights to build and operate canals, railroads, plank or other roads in this State or through any portion thereof; neither shall exclusive rights for any kind of manufacture be granted.

Mr. SMITH—I offer the following amendment to the amendment:

The Legislature shall have no power to grant aid to companies or associations of individuals formed for any purpose.

Mr. MONTAMAT—I move to lay it on the table.

[Carried.

Mr. Terry's amendment was also tabled by a rising vote of 42 to 34.]

Mr. HOWELL—I move to amend by inserting after "the Legislature shall" the word "not;" and after "individuals," where it first occurs, the words "except such as are."

Mr. MONTAMAT—I move to lay it on the table.

Mr. HOWELL—The gentleman is always moving to lay my amendments on the table. This amendment, if adopted, will confine the Legislature in giving aid to the particular corporation or gentlemen included in this article.

[The amendment was accepted.]

Mr. STOCKER---If I understand the amendment of the gentleman, it will exclude the Legislature from making appropriations for charitable purposes.

Mr. HOWELL---I think I can satisfy the gentleman. If he will refer to the constitution of 1845, he will find the following article:

The State shall not become subscriber to the stock of any corporation or joint stock company.

The following article—"No corporate body shall be created, renewed or extended with banking or discounting privileges"—is the one contained in article 23 of this report.

The committee, of which I have become a member, said this report was prepared throughout, by this article, to meet the objects contained in the constitution of 1845, and to limit the aid of the Legislature to all companies and associations of individuals, except such as are founded for the exclusive purpose of internal improvements. In all the alterations of this same provision of the constitution of 1845, the Legislature did give aid to charitable institutions, which are not considered as companies or associations of individuals. To incorporated charitable institutions this article will have no reference whatever.

Mr. CAMPBELL---I propose, as an amendment to the amendment of Mr. Howell, to add after the word "are" the words "and shall be."

Mr. CAZABAT---I beg leave to offer a substitute for the whole article, which reads as follows:

The Legislature shall have no power to grant exclusive privileges or monopolies of any kind to individuals, companies or corporations whatsoever, except for charitable purposes.

[The substitute was, by a *viva voce* vote, laid on the table—yeas 44, nays 15.]

[The amendment to the amendment was adopted, and article 23 thereupon adopted, as amended.

The following articles were separately read and adopted, as reported :]

Art. 24. No liability shall be contracted by the State as above mentioned, unless the same be authorized by some law for some single object or work, to be distinctly specified therein, which shall be passed by a majority of the members elected to both Houses of the General Assembly, and the aggregate amount of debts and liabilities incurred under this and the preceding article shall never, at any one time, exceed eight millions of dollars.

Art. 25. Whenever the Legislature shall contract a debt exceeding in amount the sum of one hundred thousand dollars, unless in case of war to repel invasion or suppress insurrection, they shall, in the law creating the debt, provide adequate ways and means for the payment of the current interest and of the principal when the same shall become due. And the said law shall be irrepealable until principal and interest are fully paid and discharged, or unless the repealing law contains some other adequate provision for the payment of the principal and interest of the debt.

Art. 26. The Legislature shall provide by law for all change of venue in civil and criminal cases.

[Article 27 was read.]

Art. 27. No lottery shall be authorized by this State, and the buying and selling of lottery tickets within the State is prohibited.

[And also Mr. Stiner's amendment :]

No licenses shall be granted to gambling houses in this State.

Mr. HOWELL—The committee beg leave to report favorably on Mr. Stiner's amendment and recommend that it be made a part of article 27.

Mr. STINER—I propose this amendment, because I consider it not only a bad but a wicked policy for a State or people to encourage vice and crime of any description; and that gambling is both vicious and criminal, I think no gentleman of this Convention will pretend to deny.

How many unfortunate families have been ruined, through the head of the family resorting to the gaming-house, and sacrificing there the means that should have been devoted to the support of those dependent upon him.

How many merchants have failed in business, in this city, through resorting to these accursed dens of iniquity, while their clerks and employés, following the example set them, have been induced to cheat, wrong and defraud. In the whole catalogue of crimes, none is more utterly demoralizing than the vice of gambling. There is no stronger passion implanted in the human breast than that which impels to the sin of gambling; and when bad men, who pursue it as a profession, having all these paraphernalia, these marked cards, ropers-in and machinery perfected for the purpose of making the robbery of unsuspecting persons certain and sure, and once licensed by the State to do this thing, to commit this crime, I think we had better abolish all laws for the punishment of crime, and license thieves, pickpockets, burglars, and even murderers.

It is no excuse for fixing a license on gambling to say that you cannot prevent these houses being kept, and that therefore the State had better make a virtue of necessity, and turn a criminal traffic to a source of profit. Stealing cannot be prevented; therefore we must license thieves! Other species of vice cannot be prevented; and consequently we must make them a source of revenue! I trust a doctrine so monstrous, so immoral, will never prevail in this State, and that the wisdom of the course pursued by past Legislatures, in refusing to license these dens of fraud, thieves and iniquity, will be fully indorsed by this Convention, and that the amendment which I have offered, forbidding the Legislature from licensing gaming houses, will become a part of the organic law of the State.

Then, if the police force, or the regularly constituted authorities, cannot ferret out these places and prevent these iniquities and bring the swindlers of the unsuspecting or simple-minded in the community to justice, it will not be the fault of the law-makers of the State that crime exists, for it will not have been fostered by law. Trusting the Convention will adopt this amendment as a measure of moral reform, and thanking the gentlemen for their attention, I close my remarks.

Mr. MONTAMAT—I move as an amendment to the amendment that "lotteries and gambling houses shall be licensed by the Legislature."

Mr. SULLIVAN—I second.

Mr. STOCKER—I offer the following as a substitute to the amendment and the amendment to the amendment:

The Legislature may grant licenses to gambling houses in this State, provided the tax shall not be less than ten thousand dollars per annum on each house so licensed.

Mr. ABELL—I regret to differ from my amiable friend from the Second, (Mr. Stiner,) and must confess that I have great doubts as to whether this Convention passes his amendment.

I do not think that the Convention should put any restrictions upon the Legislature. There is first a doubt as to whether it would not be better for both the old and young men to have public gambling houses, protected by law, as they have been for the last thirteen years. It is impossible to restrain men either from drinking or gambling, and I doubt as to whether, if we should pass a law to-day, making it a part of the constitution that no man shall drink liquor, it would make a particle of difference. I cannot, myself, say, as I am not a gambler, and have not paid much attention to the matter, whether it would be *better* to exclude notice of this matter entirely, but my views are these: If, sir, these places are licensed, as bar-rooms are, whenever a man goes into one of them he will know and feel that the eye of the community is upon him; that it will form an opinion of him which will cause him to suffer for the act. When going into such a place, where every one can go, where there is no exclusion, where his friends can all see him, in nine cases out of ten that man would be found by some good friend and be advised for his good, and would be saved from going at all. But, sir, we have, and unless we adopt a different course will have, as we have had for many years—for fifteen, to my certain knowledge—for fifteen or seventeen years—gambling houses in secret places, to which men go through by-ways, so that the eye of the world is not upon them, and where they can hide themselves from the eye of friends. If good men could go into one of those houses as they could into those of San Francisco—as I saw them there in 1852 or '53, when they were open to every one and there were no secret gambling hells—that good man or any friend could warn and dissuade any there in whom an interest might be felt.

I contend, not that a man should go into a gambling house whether licensed or not, but that we should leave the matter as it stands now, giving the Legislature power to license or not as may seem most proper. Under some circumstances it might be well to license. I believe that two to one are ruined in secret gambling to what there would be if gambling was public. Therefore, Mr. President, I shall oppose this amendment, with the hope that the Convention will leave this matter open to the Legislature, and the Legislature, coming fresher from the people, may do as may appear best to their constituents.

I never saw the inside of one of these places, and do not know much about them, but do know that they exist, and that men creep into them secretly. As I said before, if these places were public one friend could go and warn another, whereas, entrapped into the dark, unknown dens, where there is no chance whatever of being reached by a friend, as the decoys themselves know, the result is that a man proceeds step by step, and at length is fleeced in the most infamous manner—such as in a public house not even a professional gambler would dare to undertake. It is in the secret hells that a man is fleeced, as I knew one to be of sixteen thousand dollars in a single night, through practices which it would be impossible to carry out in a public gamiag house of any respectability.

Mr. HOWELL—I do not desire to intrude upon the time of this Convention, but as I am a member of the committee the report of which is under consideration, I wish to state the facts which actuated the committee upon this subject. Individually, sir, I was at first opposed to making any allusion whatever to the subject in the constitution, until it was suggested that under military authority gambling houses had been licensed in this city. It might well be contended that if a Legislature should come into existence and find these gambling houses still existing, it would not interfere with them, but would be induced to derive a revenue from them for the public service; and as I am opposed to deriving any revenue for this State from immoral sources, I was induced to accede to the other members of the committee and insert it here in order to prevent the continuance of any house in existence, (whether or not they do exist I am unable to say,) and to prevent such an event forever happening hereafter.

I can see no principle of ethics which will induce this Convention to prevent the sale of lottery tickets, and at the same time recognize the right to establish a gambling house. If there be anything more immoral in selling lottery tickets than in establishing gambling houses, I have yet to learn a new code of morals. The subject now under consideration has been one of debate in this State ever since my recollection, and there may be some members in this House who lived in New Orleans at the time gambling houses were licensed, who will recollect the great number which existed in this city. I have been told that on Camp street it was at one time a common sight to see, on the lower floor, right at the front door, all kinds of gambling carried on. I am reminded that this was not confined to Camp street, but that the same was the case on other streets.

Now, Mr. President, this excited the indignation of the people of this city and of this State. Through the exertions of one Larry Moore, a senator from the parish of St. Helena, a bill was passed prohibiting the licensing of gambling houses, and the citizens of New Orleans, by subscription, tendered to that individual a silver service, worth some $6000, as a memorial of their gratitude for his services in that cause. Ever since that, session after session, have efforts been made to reinstate the system of licensing gambling houses in Louisiana. They have fortunately failed so far, but I fear that unless we do something at this time to prevent the success of efforts of that nature, the influences which have been brought to bear upon society, overturned as it has been by the troubles growing out of this war, may be crowned with success. I think it will be a shame and disgrace to the moral standing of this Convention to decide to permit the licensing of gambling houses. With these views, the committee came to the conclusion that it was right, proper and necessary to insert the proposed clause in article 27 of the constitution.

Mr. SMITH—The question is: Will the Legislature prohibit gambling in the State? If this Convention passes a law that gambling shall not exist in the State of Louisiana or city of New Orleans, which will be effectual, I will vote for it. But I do not believe it will prevent the evil, for it will still exist in a worse form. Make the establishments pay a heavy license, which will drive out the little hells, while those who do pay will be compelled to do business on an honorable system. Make them pay, I say, such a license as will dry up the smaller hells, and there will be almost no danger of the evils we hear of.

Mr. STOCKER—Having introduced this amendment, which has given rise to such an eloquent debate, I feel myself called upon to say something in its favor.

It is a well known fact, although some of the speakers have stated that they do not know whether these gambling houses exist, and though I have not been in them, I *do* know that they exist in St. Charles street and other streets of this city. The only question is, shall these places pay a license to the State, or surreptitiously to the police? *That* is the *question!* If these dens are not broken up, and they must pay *some one* for the privilege of carrying them on, that is certainly what the whole matter is resolved into. Now, sir, *I* propose that they shall pay this license to the State, and I contend, sir, notwithstanding what has been said on the other side, by giving such a license there is less danger for the young man; and as my friend on my right (Mr. Abell) has said, for the old man also; because if I have a young man in my employment, I can go and see if he frequents such places, and if I find him in these gambling shops, I can dismiss him, fearing that he would spend my money as well as his own. But when these places are closed, and one can only gain admittance by secret knocks and through influences of which only the initiated understand, then, sir, the employés of merchants and others can go unnoticed and spend the funds of their principals, as many do. That is the reason why I offered my substitute.

Now, sir, one gentleman (Mr. Howell) has very uncourteously alluded to the gentlemen who introduced, and by whose great exertions got the bill passed for the prohibition of gambling houses, but forgot to tell you that Moore was himself a gambler, and introduced that bill with the express purpose of fleecing unsuspecting persons. *That* he forgot to tell you, sir; but the fact is within the memory of many men within this hall.

This same gentleman has spoken of the large number of gambling houses we had in 1835. I, sir, lived in New Orleans in '35, but being then very young, my own memory does not go back to that time and is hardly sufficient to bear me out. After applying, however, to others that were older and lived here at the same time, I find my impression confirmed, and that there were just eighteen gambling houses then in the city, which paid licenses to the amount of eighteen thousand five hundred dollars ($18,500) per annum each. The doors were open to any one. One thing which should be considered in favor of such a law in 1864 against the same in 1835, is that the people of New Orleans are now civilized, while at that time you will find, if you examine the records, that they were only semi-civilized. It is not to be supposed, that because a man could not, in 1835, proceed through our back streets without running in danger of losing his life, that the same state of affairs exists in 1864. We who live here now know this, and New Orleans of 1864 is not to be compared with New Orleans of 1835. I believe it will be for the best interests of the State if the substitute offered by myself passes.

Mr. MONTAMAT—I have no objection to the substitute of the gentleman, if he will include the sale of lottery tickets in its provisions.

Mr. STOCKER—I have no objection to doing so.

Mr. THORPE—I may, perhaps, be misunderstood, for I am no gambler or frequenter of gambling houses, but shall nevertheless advocate the substitute offered by the gentleman from the First, (Mr. Stocker.)

No question that has ever been brought before the moralists of the world and good men who take an interest in the welfare of mankind, has been more difficult to manage than this question of gambling. Now I have not been an unobservant spectator during my life, and believe that the effect o licensing will be simply this : It would relieve the secrecy, and consequently one half of the wickedness of gambling; the money which now goes, in a very large degree, into the hands of secret gamblers, would go into the treasury of the State to support the poverty and crime which results from this damnable institution. When I first came to the city of New Orleans, gambling-houses were licensed. I recollect distinctly that there were large signs over their doors, and I, or any other gentleman of this Convention, could go into them as we now do into stores; could look about, watch the progress of the different games, and come out, or, if we were fools enough, take a hand and lose our money. What would now be the result of this system, if the Convention could ask in here to-morrow the big gamblers, and license fifteen of the most infernal scoundrels that ever lived? If those men should pay us a license of ten thousand dollars per annum, which would be very reasonable, besides thus enriching the treasury, those men would be better able to put down the secret gambling houses than all the police of New Orleans together; because if you license for ten thousand dollars a year, you at the same time impose a penalty upon secret gamblers; and the men who pay the large licenses are the best ones in the world to see that their rights are not infringed upon.

As regards the passion for gambling, you cannot get it out of a man's nature, for it is as much a part of it as our wives, and we cannot help it. I am a constitutional exception to this passion, and never lost six cents in my life; but yet I never see a game going on without wishing my fingers in it. A distinguished officer in the British army became in a manner insane in regard to killing out this attribute of our nature, and made it a business to go among the soldiers and punish those whom he found gambling, taking away their cards, dice, etc., even prohibiting their running foot races. Still, they would find some means to gratify their instincts for gaming, and would bet upon what chicken of a crowd in a yard would run through a fence first. So he stopped that; and when at last he satisfied himself, in the vanity of his wishes, that gambling was at an end, when, one day, seeing two soldiers sitting around a little spot of grass, he stole up to see what they were at, and found they had procured a sheet of white paper, across which they had drawn a pencil mark, and were picking vermin from their heads and betting as to which of the vermin would pass over the pencil mark before the other. He came to the conclusion, finally, that gambling was inherent in human nature; that the resources for gambling were universal, and that it was impossible to put it down. He changed, therefore, his tactics, and said that whenever the men indulged in games which brought upon themselves loss and injury, he should punish them severely for the crime, and this put an end to the whole matter. As we cannot put a stop to gambling—as we cannot do what the gentleman from the Fourth (Mr. Howell) desires—to take this passion out of the unregenerate heart of man, let us at least turn it into a source of revenue.

Let us be able, when young men come to New Orleans and live under this constitution—when our friends from the country come here with their pockets full of money, which they desire to waste—when we lose them at night, and suspect that they are in gambling houses—let us be able, I say, by public law, to go from one of the houses to another, find the victims, take them away, and make them behave themselves. Let not wicked men introduce them into the St. Charles hotel, private rooms, or fashionable grog-shops; and let them not be led away into those secret hells, to be ruined in morals and property, but let these things be done in open daylight. Let them not only be licensed, but let there be placed over the doors, in large golden letters, "gambling house," so that when a merchant, or lawyer, or any man, goes into one of them, public opinion can mark him. I am willing, as far as I am individually concerned, to live in a city thus emblazoned, and I doubt very much whether any man will point the finger of scorn at me and say I have been part and parcel of this iniquity.

Go into Wall street to-morrow. What is all this gambling and speculating in gold but one of the most fearful scenes ever witnessed in the world? so corrupting that it makes even patriotic men almost beseech that the armies of the Union may be defeated that gold may go up. Yet this very question has been brought up before the Legislature of New York time and again; and, I believe, that so extraordinary is the state of public opinion in that State, that a legislator who would gravely get up and say what I have to-day in favor of public gambling houses, as a political and State-revenue supporting measure, would not find quiet for six months after. Yet the proprietor of one of the leading hotels of New York city told me, when I was in New York, in February last, that I could probably find in his hotel fifty tables in full operation, that he knew nothing about. So much for secret gambling.

Now, gentlemen, let us throw aside all instinctive feelings and all the public feeling against gambling. Do not let us, confound these with our duties as legislators That is my idea. Do not let us in a moment of haste, say one word in favor of gambling, but oppose it as we should. Let us, as moralists, as good men, as members of society, say and do everything we can against this horrible crime, which, too frequently, consumes in one night the labors of years, and is one of the most damnable of all institutions. But we are here to take a higher position than a mere sentimental one, and are bound to look upon it as philosophers and legislators—bound to remember the views the gentleman from the First (Mr. Stocker) has brought before us; showing, among other things, that Moore, who secured the passage of the bill prohibiting the licensing of gambling houses in New Orleans, was himself a gambler, and by its adoption secured for himself the gambling monopoly he wished.

I therefore, gentlemen, shall vote for this substitute, and trust that it will receive a majority of the votes of this Convention.

Mr. CUTLER—This discussion on article 27 of the report of the Committee on General Provisions is brought up incidentally by a resolution or amendment offered by the gentleman from the Second (Mr. Stiner,) which has been accepted by the members of that committee.

I am not such a theorist and moralist as to be able, perhaps, to illustrate the other side of this great and serious question. There has been many a grave question presented for the consideration of this Convention, but when you come to handle the passions of men, you touch a matter of a very important character. I am one who entertains an opinion that this demands the cool and serious deliberation of this Convention.

One honorable member of this Convention has suggested that the Convention had not perhaps the power of legislating upon this subject. In my humble judgment, Mr. President, it is for this Convention to say whether gambling or any other immoral practice shall be tolerated within the territorial jurisdiction of this State.

Personally, sir, I am not a very great moralist, but I do believe that christianity and morals should have a resting-place in the soul of every man. Now, sir, while I entertain these views, I am one of those who are disposed to the opinion, and entertain it freely, that all men are not theorists or moralists; that there is a difference of opinion among our fellow-men, and, I dare not say, sir, but that the majority is opposed to christianity. Be that, sir, as it may, we are now discussing a subject that entirely invokes the passions of men. The question now presents itself, philosophically, whether of one, two or three evils this Convention, in its wisdom and moral judgment—I may say its wisdom-judgment—shall choose the least, or shall run counter to the passions of men, and thereby inflict a greater punishment than they could possibly inflict otherwise. I entertain the opinion, Mr. President, that it is in perfect concurrence with the current and weight of argument that has been adduced before this Convention to-day—that it is better for the public good, conduces less to evil, and on the whole is the least of the two great evils, to try to control rather than to endeavor to suppress human passions.

Now, sir, it may be possible that all I may say upon this subject will be of a very limited and contracted nature, because I may want knowledge in regard to this particular matter; for, sir, I tell you there never was any gambling-house to my personal knowledge. I never hazarded money on anything, except a horse race or a dog fight—[laughter]—and that was in small sums. Now, sir, as to the statement that the passion for gambling is inherent in the nature of man, I emphatically deny it. I do not believe that Alm ghty God, in the creation of the human mind, ever intended to implant any such principle, and therefore my learned friend from the Second, (Mr. Thorpe,) in his observations is entirely mistaken. It is the result of the habits of men, because every man's mind is dependent upon the surrounding circumstances. If a man is born in South Africa, he will be a Hottentot; if accustomed to either private or public gaming he will be a gambler, notwithstanding the teachings of morality and religion. Then, sir, I am one that is disposed to accept the least of two or three great evils.

Now let me illustrate: There has been a statute upon the statute books of the State of Louisiana, well known to you all, prohibiting the vending of lottery tickets in this State. Previous to this war, when men lived in peace and plenty—when free and public opinion ran like the waters of the Mississippi—when no man was restrained in his conduct--that was a public statute in virtue of our organic law; but not a day rolled around in this great city that there was not one but dozens of persons dealing in lottery tickets. In the windows of all the cigar shops and coffee-houses you could find lottery tickets exposed for sale. I remember when Judge H——— was upon the bench an attempt was made to carry this law into effect, and a number of persons were arrested for vending these lottery tickets. The trial proved an abortion, for the subject of it was running with the great current, following the passions of men. You cannot convict in such cases. Now, sir, illustrative of the arguments made on this floor in regard to gambling, I have to-day the good or bad fortune of being the counsel of two or three men arrested for gambling in violation of this law, and I expect to show on the floor of the First District Court, when the case comes up, permits from the military power allowing them so to do. Then, I ask you, what is the use of a statute--what is the use of a law prohibiting a thing and fixing the penalty, when you cannot enforce that law? Why, it is a blank sheet of paper; it is worse---it is teaching your young men that it is right to violate the law. It is wrong to have a law if you hold it in contempt, ridicule and disgrace, and do not obey. Then, sir, not being able to discuss further the moral principle---not being able to illustrate further for want of knowledge of the internal arrangement of gambling houses---I desire to add only this: According to the arguments adduced to-day—and I have no doubt but those gentlemen understand what they say—that gambling houses cannot be broken up, and that it will be better to have them public than private, then I submit to you, sir, and the Convention, that it is much better, in a choice between the evils, to choose that which will be the most conducive to morality, christianity and the welfare of the public, not only in a moral, but in a pecuniary point of view. Therefore, I offer this substitute for the amendment and the substitute already offered, in lieu of article 27 of the original. It is this:

The Legislature shall have the power to license the selling of lottery tickets and the keeping of gambling houses; said houses in all cases shall be on the first floor and kept with open doors; but in all cases not less than ten thousand dollars per annum shall be levied as a license or tax on each vendor of lottery tickets and on each gambling house, and five hundred dollars on each tombola.

[The amendment was accepted.

Mr. Harnan offered the following, which was laid on the table:]

No lottery shall be authorized by this State, but every tombola shall be allowed by paying to the State, for each and every tombola, the sum of five hundred dollars; the same to be divided *pro rata* to each inmate which is beholden to receive charity in the orphan asylums within this State.

[Mr. Howes moved to amend Mr. Cutler's substitute by adding: "a large sign shall be placed over the door, with the words gambling house painted thereon." The amendment was tabled.]

Mr. Abell.—I think, Mr. President, that no member on this floor will argue that the position taken by my amiable friend, Mr. Stiner, in his amendment, is not a very worthy and moral one in its designs. I would like, on account of the amiability of my young friend, to vote for his amendment and would do so if I thought it would meet the case. But I think it involves a very important subject. It is a question that is not raised for the first time now. It has been under discussion for three or four thousand years at least.

No one will stand upon this floor, Mr. President, and advocate gambling. I am opposed to it, and have always been, and while I have sometimes indulged in small games for amusement, I never entered upon, anything that might be called gambling. I believe it to be immoral. But, sir, it has been demonstrated by the experience of four thousand years, that men, actuated by that wonderful principle of a love of gain and the excitement attendant upon gambling, will do it in spite of legislation. In examining this question we should go back to first principles. We believe gambling to be an evil. The first question to be asked then is, will this amendment stop it? I answer unhesitatingly, *no*. Men would gamble as much as they do now. The only effect it would have would be to make men more secret about it. It would not diminish the evil. If this would not lessen the effect, Mr. President, I ask what are we to do with it? If you cannot stop it, what can you do better than to place it under the public eye, where you can get hold of it and control it.

You must place it where it cannot send out its emissaries to bring in unsophisticated young men with their pockets full of money, by back ways and secret passages, to these dark hells in order to be fleeced.

If you place it where the community can walk in and see their operations, you will, in a great measure, check this evil. You can only do it by giving publicity to their nefarious business, and by so doing society will be better protected from the results of their schemes. If you or I have a clerk who is in the habit of gambling, he would be seen there, and the habit learned probably, before he had gambled away his own money and yours or mine with it. If I should find my clerk in such a place, I should approach him at once, and if satisfied that he had been misled, might overlook it the first time, but for the second offence I should discharge him without ceremony.

Another advantage in having gambling houses open to the public, is that there is not the danger of the unsuspected being cheated out of their money that there will be if licenses are not granted. If anything of that kind is attempted, there will generally be those by who will detect it. Now, when a man is invited to one of these gambling houses that is only open to the initiated, it is just as certain before he enters that he enters to be fleeced as that he goes in at all. This is decided upon before he is invited there.

No man would vote for the amendment more readily than I would, Mr. President, if I thought it would suppress gambling, but I do not believe it would have that effect. I believe that instead of suppressing, it would only increase the evil. A similar question has been presented in Europe with regard to houses of prostitution. England has carried the matter farther, perhaps, than any other nation. She has refused to give them the slightest encouragement or countenance, and the result is, that to-day in London the lowest dens of prostitution in the world are to be found, and yet they have never given it the protection which is necessary. On the continent they have proceeded on more philosophical principles; they have taken nature as they found it and given these places license.

There is one city, however, where prostitution is utterly ignored, and the result is, says a writer, that nearly every private house is a house of prostitution. This we find to be the case, Mr. President, where prostitution is punished with the heaviest penalties the result is that almost every private house becomes a house of prostitution. So with gambling. Men will gamble, I care not how you attempt to suppress it. If you license them, you have them before you. You can see what they are doing. Every man can go into a licensed house You have the power to examine everything that is going on. You will find the bank broke sometimes, by a fair dealer and with fair play. You see it often in San Francisco, sir, when gambling houses were licensed there. Every turn of the wheel is open to view of persons of experience in these matters, and the result is that what losses players meet with are due to the chances of the game and not the knavery of their opponents.

There is another effect that will be the result of this system of licensing gambling houses and that will be to break up these private places. You all know the old maxim, "set a thief to catch a thief." Well, sir, make parties pay ten thousand dollars for a license, and they will be the most effective detectives to ferret out those who carry on these private dens, and they will be broken up. Make it to the interest of the licensed gambler, by requiring of him a high price for a monopoly, and you accomplish more towards breaking up private dens than you could do by any other mode of legislation; and if you go still farther and declare that when a man loses money in one of these private hells the presumption shall be that it was stolen, we shall finish them up completely. The presumption, heretofore, has been that it was lost in play, and the owners of the establishment always have a pack of their own sort at their backs to swear for them, and the man has no redress. Now, sir, if this Convention will, in addition to the licenses proposed to be granted at ten or twenty thousand dollars—I don't care how large you make it—declare that if a man loses money at a private gambling estabment the presumption shall be that the owner or keeper of the establishment stole it, these establishments will be completely broken up.

These public nuisances, Mr. President, must be controlled. They cannot be broken up. Suppose, for instance, you were to-day to pass an ordinance totally prohibiting prostitution. What would be the result? It would be that the insults to decent ladies in this city would be as common as it was for them to walk the streets. When the storms of nature rise in man, sir, it is impossible to keep him within bounds, and if you attempt it by legislation, your wives and daughters will be insulted in the streets.

Leave the matter alone, though let it be known that certain houses are houses of prostitution, and society will not be in any way harmed by them, and your criminal laws will keep them within bounds.

The only thing you can do with gambling is to leave it open to the Legislature, as proposed by Mr. Cutler, to grant licenses upon condition that they pay a tax which will become a part of the revenue of the country. By doing so you will be enabled to control these houses and bring them into proper subjection; and I trust that you will lay upon the table all narrow amendments, and that you will adopt Mr. Cutler's resolution, not only by a large majority, but with hardly a dissenting voice.

Mr. Howes—I move as an amendment that "all such houses shall have a large sign over the door, with the words *Gambling House* printed over the door."

Mr. Terry—I second the amendment.

Mr. Wells—I move to lay it on the table.

Mr. Hills—I move to lay the whole subject matter on the table.

[The motion to table Mr. Howes's amendment was carried. The motion of Mr. Hills was lost, and the yeas and nays were called on the adoption of Mr. Cutler's substitute, with the following result:]

Yeas—Messrs. Abell, Bailey, Barrett, Baum, Beauvais, Bell, Bofill, Buckley, Burke, Cook J. K., Cook T., Crozat, Cutler, Davies, Decker, Dufresne, Duke, Ennis, Fish, Flood, Foley, Gastinel, Geier, Gruneberg, Gaidry, Healy, Harnan, Hart, Henderson, Howes, Knobloch, Kugler, Maas, Maurer, Mayer, Mendiverri, Montamat, Murphy E., Murphy M. W., Newell, O'Conner, Ong, Orr, Purcell J., Pursell S., Schroeder, Schnurr, Seymour, Spellicy, Stocker, Stumpf, Stauffer, Sullivan, Terry, Thorpe, Waters, Wells—57.

Nays—Messrs. Austin, Balch, Bromley, Campbell, Collin, Cazabat, Dupaty, Flagg, Fosdick, Gorlinski, Hills, Hire, Howell, Kavanagh, Mann, Morris, Normand, Payne J., Paine J. T., Pintado, Seymour, Smith, Stiner, Wilson—24.

[The substitute was adopted.]

Mr. FOLEY—I move to adjourn.

[The ayes and noes were called.]

Mr. STOCKER—Some one voted yes for me when my name was called. I vote "no."

Mr. SPELLICY—Before the vote is announced, I wish to change my vote from no to yes.

[The following is the result of the vote:]

YEAS—Messrs. Abell, Austin, Balch, Bailey, Bofill, Buckley, Campbell, Decker, Dufresne, Duke, Ennis, Flagg, Foley, Gastinel, Gruneberg, Gaidry, Healy, Harnan, Hart, Henderson, Kavanagh, Knobloch, Maas, Maurer, Mayer, Mendiverri, Murphy E., Murphy M. W., Newell, Normand, O'Conner, Orr, Pintado, Purcell J.. Schroeder, Schnurr, Seymour, Shaw, Spellicy, Stumpf, Stiner, Sullivan, Waters and Wells—44.

NAYS—Messrs. Barrett, Baum, Beauvais, Bell, Bromley, Burke, Collin, Cazabat, Cook J. K., Cook T., Crozat, Cutler, Davies, Dupaty, Fish, Flood, Fosdick, Geier, Gorlinski, Hills, Hire, Howell, Kugler, Mann, Montamat, Morris, Ong, Payne J., Paine J. T., Pursell S., Smith, Stocker, Stauffer, Terry, Thorpe and Wilson—36.

[The motion to adjourn was carried.]

SATURDAY, June 18, 1864.

[The Convention met and was called to order pursuant to adjournment, Hon. E. H. Durell, president, in the chair, and the following members present:]

Messrs. Abell, Austin, Balch, Bailey, Barrett, Baum, Beauvais, Bell, Bofill, Bromley, Buckley, Burke, Collin, Cazabat, Cook J. K., Cook T., Crozat, Cutler, Davies, Decker, Duane. Dufresne, Duke, Dupaty, Ennis, Fish, Flagg, Flood, Foley, Fosdick, Fuller, Gastinel, Geier, Gorlinski, Gruneberg, Gaidry, Healy, Harnan, Hart, Henderson, Hills, Hire, Howell, Howes, Knobloch, Kugler, Maas, Mann, Maurer, Mayer, Mendiverri, Montamat, Morris, Murphy E., Murphy M. W., Newell, Normand, O'Conner, Orr, Payne J., Paine J. T., Pintado, Poynot, Purcell J., Pursell S., Schroeder, Schnurr, Seymour, Shaw, Smith, Spellicy, Stocker, Stumpf, Stiner, Stauffer, Sullivan, Terry, Thorpe, Waters, Wenck, Wilson—82.

Absent—Messrs. Ariail, Bennie, Bonzano, Brott, Campbell, Edwards (excused,) Heard, Kavanagh, Lobdell, Millspaugh, Montague, Ong, Taliaferro, Thomas and Wells—15.

[The minutes were read.]

Mr. CAZABAT—Before the minutes are adopted I desire to make one correction. I offered a substitute for article 23 of the report on General Provisions, which is not given in the minutes.

Mr. HOWELL—In article 8 there seems to be a typographical error. The article should read "differences by arbitration," instead of "differences of arbitration," as given in the minutes.

[The necessary corrections were made and the minutes adopted.]

Mr. HOWELL—Before the order of the day is taken up, as there seems to be some doubt as to the construction of rule 26, in regard to moving a reconsideration, I move (having voted in the majority) to reconsider the vote on article 23, and defer the matter to Monday next for action, if the Convention is not ready to act upon it now. I desire to amend the article so as to read: "The Legislature shall not have power to grant aid to companies or associations of individuals, except such as are or shall be formed for charitable purposes, or for the exclusive purpose," etc.

PRESIDENT—The question must be taken up at once.

[The motion to reconsider was carried, and the amendment laid over till Monday.]

Mr. THORPE—I offer the following resolution:

Resolved, That a committee of five be appointed to wait on Maj. Gen. Sickles, and learn from him when it would be agreeable to him to receive an official visit from the members of this Convention.

Mr. SULLIVAN—I move to amend by including also Maj. Gen. Canby.

Mr. THORPE—I accept the amendment.

Mr. WENCK—I move to lay the resolution and amendment on the table.

Mr. CUTLER—I move, as an amendment to the amendment, that the name of Maj. Gen. Canby be inserted first.

[The amendment was carried, and the resolution adopted.]

PRESIDENT—The chair appoints on that committee Messrs. Thorpe, Sullivan, Cutler, Terry and Campbell.

Mr. FOSDICK—I desire to offer the following resolution, and before any action is taken I wish to explain my reasons for presenting it:

Whereas, In the opinion of this Convention a large majority of the loyal people of the city of New Orleans are desirous of having the civil government of the city reestablished: be it therefore

Resolved, That his excellency the governor of the State be and he is hereby requested to immediately issue his order of election for mayor, recorders, street commissioner, aldermen and assistant aldermen, in conformity with the city charter.

Resolved, That the secretary of this Convention be and he is hereby instructed to transmit a copy of the foregoing resolution to his excellency the governor.

Mr. SULLIVAN—I amend by including the treasurer and surveyor of this city.

Mr. WENCK—I amend by adding the recorders.

Mr. ABELL—I second it.

Mr. SMITH—I amend by embracing the district attorney and the city attorney also.

Mr. FOLEY—I amend by adding the cororner.

PRESIDENT—I would state that under the law constituting the city charter a certain number of the officers are elected by a joint ballot, by two-thirds of the board of aldermen. This was the case in regard to the city attorney, the assistant city attorney, the treasurer, and, I think, the surveyor.

Mr. MONTAMAT—I move to include all the city officers elected under the city charter.

PRESIDENT—Gentlemen will draw up their amendments in writing.

Mr. SULLIVAN—I withdraw my amendment.

Mr. FOSDICK—Mr. President, in introducing the preamble and resolutions which have just been read, I desire to disclaim any intention to reflect in any way on the gentleman who is now acting mayor of the city, for I esteem him as a man, and appreciate the manner in which he has performed the duties of that office since his appointment; but, sir, I consider it a duty that I owe, not only to my constituents, but to this Convention and myself, to endeavor, if possible, to find some means by which we can be relieved from what I consider the false position in which we are now placed, by having a civil government for the State and a military government for the city. I desire to call the attention of the Convention to the events which preceded our convocation. The commanding general of this department, believing that there were enough loyal voters in this State to entitle them to a civil government, issued his order of election for a governor and the various State officers necessary to put the machinery in motion, and they were elected on the 22d February and inaugurated on the 4th of March. I need not tell you, Mr. President, that policy had my most cordial support, and the wisdom of the measure was fully proved by the votes of the people. At that election there was polled 11,414 votes, of which the parish of Orleans cast 5761. What followed? This Convention was called to revise and amend the constitution of the State, and I find that at that election there were 6355 votes polled, of which 3832 were cast in this parish. I most cordially approve of that measure, as my presence on this floor fully confirms; but, Mr. President, I am at a loss to understand the reason, if reasons there are, why the city of New Orleans is deprived of a civil government, casting one half of the loyal votes of the whole State? Now, sir, I have acted from the beginning of this movement on principle, and I desire to see the executive of the State, who was elected on that principle, carry it out, by giving the people of New Orleans what is so clearly their right—that of electing their own city officers. I have, sir, it is true, for the last day or two, heard it rumored on the streets that Capt. Hoyt has resigned his commission in the army of the United States, and received the appointment from his excellency the governor, of acting mayor; but, sir, I cannot and will not believe, until better proof than mere rumor is presented, that his excellency the governor has so soon forgotten the principles under which he was elected, as to tell the 5761 loyal voters of New Orleans, who cast their suffrages to elevate him to the position he now occupies, that, in his opinion, not one of them was sufficiently competent or trustworthy to fill that position, and that he has, therefore, selected a non-resident for their chief magistrate.

Mr. HENDERSON—We have already had two resolutions of a similar nature before this body, and I have seen their inefficiency and will vote no more such resolutions. We passed a resolution that certain men known to be copperheads and holding office in New Orleans should be summarily disposed of by the executive and mayor, but to my positive knowledge the men whose names were concealed from this body are still holding office, and that the resolution absolutely amounts to nothing. I am not in favor of this proposition. The city of New Orleans is defunct until it is incorporated in the constitution and made a part of the law of the land. In 1845 and 1852 the city was incorporated in the organic law of the State, and cannot be changed except by changing or modifying the constitution itself. Suppose every member of this body should vote for this resolution, what authority has the governor to change the constitutions of 1812, 1845 and 1852, or the constitution of 1864? Therefore, I said when we passed the police bill, by a large majority, it was a mere empty sound, an expression of opinion of the members of this body. If you want to give it efficacy you must incorporate it in the city charter. The proposition is to elect all the elective officers of the city downwards. You may go and give them orders and pass resolutions, but you will become the laughing stock of your own constituency. It reflects on the high office of the governor and the man in that office, notwithstanding the gentleman asserts that it does not. Michael Hahn, a free State governor, has already made suitable appointments, and he is now arraigned before this body because the occupant of the office of mayor is a non-resident. Wherefore is the accusation and whom does it attack if not the governor?

I tell you the very instant this constitution of 1864 is ratified, the military authorities have a right to suspend it at any time they please on military grounds. I am in favor of New Orleans being incorporated, and I am astonished that the charter has not already been incorporated in the constitution of 1864. Unless this is done, the corporation is lost, and the city of New Orleans is reduced to a parish. I speak of this because the country parishes are opposed to the city, and have been so. This proposition as a resolution is valid. We passed a resolution here in regard to securing the statue of Washington, carried from Baton Rouge to Washington City Where is the power to compel the president to order its return? You may pass this resolution, and when presented to the mayor it will be the same as if some private citizen should go to him and say: "Will you please to remove yourself? I will be much obliged to you." The governor is not a civil governor, although he ran as such; but ere he had taken the place, the power before him required that he should be a military as well as a civil governor; and if he did not wish to be a military as well as civil ruler, he could have tendered his resignation. This, however, was not done, and we have a military governor with civil power. Fearing I have taxed your patience too long, I leave the subject.

Mr. Cutler—Mr. President, I have no speech to make on this subject, and gentlemen need not be impatient. Either we are to be governed by law or no law. There is a law or there is no law. The idea of there being no law is to say all men are corrupt. The president of the United States has never ignored the constitution and laws of Louisiana, only so far as military purposes required. The statutes of the State of Louisiana have been executed by our courts, and they are the law of the land as much now as they ever were, save the exceptions made for military purposes. Then, while I do not impugn the motives, while I have the highest respect for the gentleman who has offered this resolution with the intention of having New Orleans governed by a civil power, instead of any wing or branch of the military power, I beg to call his attention and the attention of the Convention to the law as it exists, and as long as it does exist as a law this constitutional Convention has no power to ignore it. It is this:

And the mayor shall cause to be published in the official journal, at least five or six days before the election, a proclamation setting forth the day on which the election is to take place, the precinct of the polls, etc.

Here, then, in the charter of the city of New Orleans, is the law; and will this Convention undertake to arbitrarily over-ride the law? I think not; I believe not. We have no such power, however congenial to the public good it might be. I, for one, am of the opinion that the time has come when the citizens of the State of Louisiana, inside the Federal lines, as well as those of the city of New Orleans, should be governed exclusively by civil power; but this Convention has not the power in law, in equity, nor by military toleration, to ignore the statutes of the State passed in times of peace. Then, if this Convention should vote that the executive of this State shall order an election for the chief magistrate, aldermen, etc., it would be extremely absurd, and in open violation of the written statute of the State. Men are sometimes impatient and think they know all, and that others know but little. It is wrong in any man to place himself suporior to his fellow man; it is wrong for any person, or set of persons, to undertake to say that they are necessarily right and all others are wrong. It is equally wrong not to have patience and forbearance in your nature. In God's name, what right has this Convention to ignore the statutes of this State more than those of any other? It is an abuse, a wrong; it is absurd, and would be a stain upon the records of this Convention. Wait with proper patience, and when we have done our work, look to the powers that be and see that they perform their duty, and censure not until the suitable time arrives.

Mr. THORPE---Mr. President, in rising to make a few remarks on this question, I wish to be distinctly understood as only doing my duty as a member of this Convention. I do not arraign anybody---Gov. Hahn, Mayor Hoyt, Gen. Banks, nor anybody else. I hold it to be true---and I do not believe any member of this Convention will say otherwise---that we all want a civil government as soon as we can have it, and want to be free from all military authority exalted over us, it being in violation of the instincts and feelings of our nature. When Gen. Butler came to New Orleans he told the mayor and common council of the city if they would come forward and take the oath of allegiance they could retain their offices, because, he said, the worst thing that could be done for the city was to deprive it of its civil government, and he did not wish to do so. That was his opinion of civil government. I voted for the chief magistrate, and considered it one of the most important acts; but I declare---and I believe I represent the people of the State in making the assertion---that I consider the election of a city magistrate by the people not less important. I am astonished that this has not taken place even long before---that such an election has not been already ordered. While we have had a civil governor for some two or three thousand people, two-thirds of the loyal population of Louisiana are still under military authority. I do not see any consistency or common sense in this matter, and I must confess that the remarks of the gentleman from the Second (Mr. Henderson) are tainted with most fearful consequences. Gentlemen get up and say we have no authority in this Convention to order or request Gen. Banks to order an election. I deny this. If this Convention should order or ask Gen. Banks to take one soldier out of this city, or remove a gun from Camp Parapet, Gen. Banks would tell us, you are meddling with things that do not concern you; if you meddle with things that do not concern you, I will put you in prison by military authority. But when we come back to our civil status, we have a right to *order* him to do anything reasonable, and he is bound to obey; and when gentlemen learned in the law talk as they have done on the opposite side, I am thunderstruck! Why are we here to-day? I admit a military order sanctioned our coming here. Why are the civil courts in vogue in the city to-day? Because military authority sanctions them, it is true; but when the military power permits us to do a thing, and we have accomplished that thing, the power is passed so far as civil matters are concerned, and we are left to act as we please and independent of military affairs; and when a man gets up here and talks about the military authorities over-riding the civil authority, he does a gross injustice to himself and to civil liberty, for I tell you we should be suspicious and sensitive with regard to anything that relates to military power, and we should grasp every particle that we can from that aristocratic power, and do all we can under a civil government to assert our rights. I think that the military civil government of New Orleans for the last two years—and I was a memberf it for a long time—has been economical; I do not think that, under the circumstances, a more prudent was ever insfituted, as the records of the city will show. I believe the resources of the city have been used with the greatest discretion; I believe every subordinate officer has done his duty; but the time has come when the city of New Orleans should say who should be its officers. When the gentleman tells me that if we pass this resolution unanimously it will be treated with contempt, I do not believe it. I believe our request will be respected, and I no more believe that Mayor Hoyt, Gov. Hahn, or Gen. Banks would so treat such a request, to restore the civil rights of New Orleans, than I believe either is capable of insulting a lady, or doing any mean and contemptible action; for they are men of high principles. Gov. Hahn occupies one of the most exalted and difficult positions that was ever put upon a man, and I believe he will fill that place with honor to himself and those connected with him. It is for you to prepare the road by making this request. Let me amend the resolution of Mr. Fosdick by adding that Gov. Hahn, by virtue of his office and military power, order an election within two weeks. Gen. Banks, by virtue of his office, is supreme; he has the power of life and death in his hands. It is almost incredible to understand the power of the commander of a military department. He has distinguished himself through his whole career in the South, not for his interest in military matters, but for his interest in civil matters, and has devoted more time to the regeneration of the civil rights of Louisiana than to military matters; but I believe when his life is drawing to a close—when this rebellion is ended—whatever may be his power now, as commander of cannon, muskets and soldiery—I believe that Gen. Banks, in the hour of retirement, considers in his heart to-day, if he has done anything that will emblazon his name on the tablets of the future, when the history of this rebellion is written, and the book is unfolded—when history sits down to dispassionately record all his acts in these terrible times—I believe that he feels that what he has done for the civil regeneration of Louisiana will be most likely to place his name where future generations will honor and respect it. Above the chair of the speaker are inscribed the words he used at the inauguration of Gov. Hahn: "Louisiana—the first returning State: her voice is for liberty." [Applause.]

I consider that if I should get up here and say that Mayor Hoyt was governed by other than patriotic motives—that he wanted to stand in the way of a civil election—I should only do an injustice to a man who has often imperiled his life in this war. A man like that would never wish to hold a position for the mere sake of the salary, and would not retain his place if the people desired an election. Let us come up to this work candidly and fearlessly. Let this Convention ask Gov. Hahn to appoint an election, and let it be not very far off, and let me insist on the amendment I have proposed. Gentlemen who do not understand patriotic men and Gov. Hahn's wishes think he will not respond quickly and spontaneously to our appeal; but in a fortnight we will inaugurate a chief magistrate, with as much glory and honor to ourselves as we did on the 4th of March, when we elected that noble man our governor.

Mr. Shaw—The argument has been on the propriety of restoring the civil government of the city of New Orleans, the importance of which no one can question. It is based upon a principle that must prevail. The city of New Orleans ought to have a civil govenrnment, and I have no doubt, Mr. President, it will be the duty of this Convention before its adjournment to make such a provision as will guarantee to New Orleans an early resumption of its civil governmen; but let us not be illogical, not act hastily, by suddenly bringing up a resolution on Saturday morning and partially debating it and then immediately taking action. What is our city government? It is under a charter, and that charter was given by the Legislature. It is a legislative act made in pursuance of a section of the constitution, and that very section will perhaps come up to-day, if the order of the day is taken up. Article 124 of the constitution of 1852 says: "The citizens of the city of New Orleans shall have the right of appointing the several public officers necessary for the administration of the police of the said city, pursuant to the mode of elections which shall be prescribed by the Legislature." The committee has reported an article which may stand, greatly modified, in place of that in the constitution of 1852. That goes so far as not only to guarantee the rights of the people, but indicates, to some extent, who those officers shall be ; that they shall be the mayor, recorder, aldermen, assistant aldermen, etc. When we come to that section we may perhaps, define these things differently, and, perhaps, change this article in essential particulars. If we pass this resolution to-day we prescribe the election of the officers as defined in the constitution of 1852, and legislative acts under it, which we may find occasion to modify or change. I am not certain that this Convention in revising this article may not have something to say about the framework of the city government. We certainly cannot pass a resolution saying that this part of the constitution shall not be altered or modified. By adopting this we make a fixed system of government. The act of 1856 says the city government shall consist of two separate bodies of council; large and complex bodies, requiring an intricate system of elections, and a vast amount of detail in their organization. Perhaps it is expedient to put such a thing into immediate effect, but I have great doubts about it. Military orders have changed these things, and we should define whether our city government is to be the same as that of 1856 or not. Military acts have changed the number of recorders ; the present bureaus of the city government have altered the organization in many important particulars. I believe the organization of the police is different, and many of the departments are changed ; and the passage of this resolution requires many changes to be made. I do not oppose the spirit of this resolution at all ; I only make these remarks for the purpose of cautioning you against a hasty passage of this resolution. Let us first go on through general provisions until we get to article 36, and see how we are going to pass the paragraph affecting the city government — whether we are going to have these exact names, mayor, recorder, aldermen, assistant aldermen, etc., as in the constitution of 1852. When we have seen to that, then this resolution may be properly considered. The only object of my remarks is for the purpose of preventing the adoption of a crude resolution. and for this reason I now move that the future consideration of this resolution shall be postponed until next Saturday morning.

Mr. Cazabat—I second the motion.

Mr. Abell—Mr. President, I talk a good deal, and I wish to talk a little on this question, if the Convention will hear me. I wish to say something respecting the argument of my friend who has just taken his seat (Mr. Cutler,) because I think his argument is nothing but a bundle of inconsistencies. It is nothing else ; and is not a very big bundle at that. Now, sir, the gentleman argues, and I have no doubt he is sincere in it, but his argument seems to me to be wholly inconsistent. He argues that we, as a Convention of the State of Louisiana, are a government all civil. Now, I have on several occasions expressed my convictions to this Convention that we should be better off with a government all military. We should have a single government that would be consistent with itself. We should have a military governor for the State, and a military government, perhaps, for the city. But, sir, on what ground does the gentleman base his argument? He tells us that only about one-third of the electoral vote of the State is outside of the city of New Orleans. Now, upon what does he base his argument that it is right, or just, or proper for the one-third outside of the city to have a civil government of their own choice, while the loyal two-thirds in this city are still under the rule of a military government? Now, I do not attack the purity of our governor; I am willing to admit he is as pure as a man can be—as pure as are angels of light. I will suppose, for the sake of the argument, he is. I do not desire, either. to be understood as speaking disparagingly of Mayor Hoyt. I believe him to be a good man ; granted for the sake of the argument that he is as good as men get to be in this world. But I ask, are you, gentlemen of the Convention, ready to admit to your constituents, when you go home, and face them, that we in this Convention are willing to have a civil government for one-third of the voters of the State, but that at the same time we are willing to accept for the loyal people of Louisiana in the city of New Orleans a military government?

Mr. FOLEY—I protest against members leaving the hall.

Mr. SULLIVAN (in the chair)—Mr. Sergeant-at-Arms, allow no member to pass out.

Mr. HILLS—I move that the sergeant-at-arms be dispatched to bring in the members who have just gone out.

Mr. SULLIVAN (in the chair)—Mr. Sergeant-at-Arms, bring in those members.

Mr. ABELL—I move a call of the House. This is an important question, and I am determined for the members to hear me on it.

Mr. CAZABAT—Mr. President, if the gentleman will give way for a moment, I desire to say a word.

Mr. ABELL—I desire to go on as soon as we can get a call of the House and a quorum. I intend to bring this to an aye and no vote pretty soon, and I want a quorum here.

Mr. CAZABAT—Mr. President, the second gentleman who occupied the floor on this question (Mr. Henderson) has, it seems to me, offered a direct insult, unintentionally perhaps, to the country members, in stating that the country was opposed to the city. On the contrary, sir, the most perfect harmony has existed between the country and the city from the beginning of the session. I hold in my hand, sir, the minutes of our proceedings, which show beyond dispute and beyond a shadow of doubt, that the country parishes are in perfect harmony with the city of New Orleans. Sir, when I hear remarks on this floor which are calculated to circulate abroad a wrong impression respecting the action of the members of this Convention, I feel bound to say it is a falsehood, and I challenge any man to show the contrary in this case. Sir, we have exhausted here hour after hour, day after day, week after week, month after month, upon questions which have no connection whatever with the object for which we were called together: upon resolutions that have nothing to do with revising and amending the constitution of Louisiana; and I for one shall protest against bringing up these resolutions, or any matters foreign to the business legitimately coming before us as a body elected to revise and amend the constitution. It matters not from what source they may come, or how honest and patriotic the motives of the parties who introduce them, I shall do all in my power to vote them down. Sir, are we sent here to legislate solely for the interest of New Orleans? I understand our duty to be to frame a constitution for the State of Louisiana. I deny that we are here for any other purpose. We must frame that constitution for the State, either for weal or woe, and not waste our time in passing resolutions for the exclusive benefit of the city. I know political proscription may be the doom of men who have nerve and spunk enough to raise their voices against resolutions such as the police bill, which are calculated to disgrace this body and bring it into contempt and ridicule. But, sir, if it was the last act of my life, I for one would not give my consent to this mode of proceeding.

I have no doubt that the gentleman who brought in this resolution was actuated by the purest of motives. I know his views well. I have seen him at the head of the Committee on the Legislative Department, and, sir, he stood there among the boldest and most liberal men of this Convention, manfully advocating by his voice and counsel the right and the justice of giving the Legislature the power to extend the right of suffrage—not to colored people, not to *niggers*, if you please—but upon citizens of the United States. That clause was voted down by a majority; unjustly, as I believe. [Order. Hear, hear.] Yes, I know that has nothing to do with the question under discussion. I only mentioned it to show my personal regard for the gentleman who introduced the resolution. I have and will upon principle vote against every resolution or motion not directly connected with the revision and amendment of the constitution.

You talk about civil government and military authorities. I thank God that we have Gen. Banks and Gen. Canby to protect you and to protect me. You wish them to restore civil government *in toto* to your city immediately; the time has not yet come. If they do the streets of this city will run red with blood. You will be the first victims of our enemies. There is no use in concealment. Let the truth be known. Do not be afraid of stubborn facts. If it were not for the protection of Federal bayonets, neither you nor I, nor any one of us, would stand on this floor to-day. What security would you have for your life liberty, or property? No, sir, the majority of the people of New Orleans seem to be in favor of secession, or at least to sympathize with the Confederates. I admit that there are men truly loyal, men who have sacrificed everything for the promotion of the principles of freedom and human liberty; but still I am sorry to acknowledge the fact that the majority of the disloyal people are against our civil and military authorities.

Sir, I hope our worthy governor, Michael Hahn, will remain where he is now, both civil and military governor, for the next four years, or at least until we finally extinguish the life and spirit of secession, that spirit that dawned upon us only to desolate and devastate this glorious country. With these remarks, sir, and on these grounds, I shall cast my vote against the resolution.

Mr. Smith—Mr. President—

Mr. Abell—Mr. President, I have the floor, but will give way for the gentleman for a few minutes.

Mr. Smith—Mr. President, it seems to me that this question has resolved itself to this simply: Is the constitution which we frame to be submitted to the people for their ratification? If so, we have no right to order an election until it is ratified by the people. If the people ratify our work there can be an order issued immediately for the election. Michael Hahn was elected by the people, and exercises the powers, by commission from the president, of military as well as civil governor, and I am surprised that people will throw themselves back upon the constitution of 1852, which was declared null and void by the convention which assembled in this very hall in 1861. Now if the one we shall make is accepted by the people, it will be time enough to commence action under it after it is so accepted. But until that time we have no right to order an election anywhere.

Mr. Foley—I call the previous question.

Mr. Sullivan [in the chair]—Mr Abell has the floor.

Mr. Abell—Mr. President, I was not satisfied that there was a quorum in the House, and when the gentleman from Rapides rose, I had my head down and was not really aware where the explosion came from. It was not very heavy, but just sufficiently so to cause me to raise my head, and upon doing so I spied my little friend Cazabat thundering away with all his artillery.

Now, sir, he evidently got up to make what may be termed a double buncombe speech, not an ordinary buncombe speech, for his guns were doubly shotted. What did he mean when he said that I had arrayed myself against the country?

Mr. Cazabat—I did not allude to the gentleman at all.

Mr. Abell—The gentleman need not be alarmed so easily. I will get to him after awhile.

Mr. Cazabat—I rose to explain that my remarks were not intended for the gentleman; but he can take them as he pleases.

Mr. Abell—I beg the gentleman's pardon. I am glad to find that I misunderstood him. I desire the gentlemen who oppose this resoluion to tell us upon what principle of logic they would argue that it is right and just for the people of the State to hold an election for civil officers to conduct the State government, and at the same time deny the privilege, the right of the citizens of New Orleans to elect their mayor and other civil officers. [Hear, hear.] Yes, some of you ought to hear, and to remember what you are proposing to do upon this very important question. Yes, sir, I am perfectly willing—I feel as large an interest in the people outside as I do in the city of New Orleans; but I contend that the people of New Orleans have an inalienable right to govern themselves, not only under the laws and under the charter, but if the charter has failed, the power has reverted now to this body. But, surely, if the charter has not failed, we have no power here. If it has, and the rights under the incorporation has failed, I ask the Convention, I ask you, Mr. President, whether that power has not reverted to this Convention, and whether it is not our duty to say that the city at large is brought under civil authority—to say that this great and mighty incorporation, which embraces a majority of the voting population of the State, shall, as is its right, be placed under civil authority, under civil officers of its own election. I ask you, gentlemen, if it is not time for us to take this step? This is a question you will have to answer to your constituents.

If we had a military governor, then I would say let your city government be military also; but as, by the election of Michael Hahn, the State government was changed from military to civil, and the corporation having failed to carry out these great principles, I ask you, sir—I ask all of you, gentlemen—whether it is not time for the people, through their representatives here, to say that the people of New Orleans should be governed, not by a military mayor, but by one of their own choice?

The great corporation of London has existed for more than seven hundred years, and during that time there has never been a time that they did not claim and exercise the right which we now ask.

If we are under a military government we must dissolve this Convention; we must dissolve it immediately. If we are under a civil government we have a right to have our own mayor, and why not say so at once? Now, if we are under a military government, I for one am willing to dissolve this Convention to-day, and let the power revert to the military authorities; but if we retain it from the military, let us give it to the people, to whom it belongs, as this resolation requires.

I have been charged here by my distinguished friend, (Mr. Henderson,) with making rebel speeches. I regret that he is not here to hear me now; but that speech which he has just made strikes me as about the best rebel speech that has been made on this floor.

Mr. Austin—Mr. President——

Mr. Abell—That is the best friend I have; he interrupts me oftener than any other man in this Convention. Now, I ask if we are really under a military or a civil government, or is it mixed, half military and half civil? Now, if it is military, and they want the people to be sovereign, or if they want them to be oppressed, will they carry it out? If they want the people to elect, will they order an election? If it is actually a civil government, you must do it yourselves. If it is military, as they contend, and the military authorities desire the election, they have only to order it. These are my views. I advocate the resolution as a right of the people, a large portion of the loyal people of the State, not because I consider the city opposed to the country. I was raised in the country, and there is not a country member here for whom I have not a warm feeling of regard. But this is a question of rights, of the rights of the people. Shall the city, as the State has already done, elect its own officers, or shall they be elected by military authority? That is the question. I say the city has the right and should not be prevented from exercising it, and I hope the Convention will respond to the same effect. If you don't, I want your names recorded in black and white, so that we shall see whether you are in favor of the civil or military government.

Mr. President and gentlemen, with these remarks, and without any reflections upon the governor—for I have no reflections to make upon him; I believe him to be actuated by noble and honoroble principles, and high and pure motives—without any reflections upon Mayor Hoyt—for I have no reflections to make upon him; I believe him to be a high minded, honorable gentleman—and in behalf of New Orleans, repeating that for two long years she has been deprived of the right of selecting her own officers, and that the time has come when she has entrusted this Convention with her interests; when the city and country have concentrated their powers in this body, and with confidence that their rights and interests will be faithfully secured, and that the trust will not be misplaced. And now I respectfully submit that she has the right, and claim that the Convention should pass this resolution almost unanimously.

Mr. Abell—I ask, sir—["Question, question."]

Mr. Pursell—Mr. President, I rise to a point of order. As Mr. Abell has already spoken twice on this question, I think he is not entitled to the floor again at this time.

Mr. Austin—Mr. President, I believe that I have the floor.

President—Mr. Abell has the floor.

Mr. Austin—I appeal from the decision of the chair.

Mr. Purcell—Mr. President, we have a rule that no member shall speak a second time on any question until—

President—The sergeant-at-arms will put that gentleman down.

Mr. Abell—I only desire the floor for a moment, to reply to my friend who has just spoken, and then I will give way. The gentleman appeals with a good deal of force to the constitution of 1852. Now, that is a very good constitution. If the gentleman invokes that as the authority under which we are acting, he should refer to the article which provides for its revision, and then tell us, if that is in force, under what authority we are acting here. I ask if he will attempt to say that we are acting under that provision? And yet, sir, if the gentleman's argument is good as to the election of city officers, it will hold also as to our action here. If that is the correct position, we had better dissolve ourselves at once, for we cannot stand for a moment on that constitution.

Mr. Shaw—I think the gentleman has misunderstood me. I said that we had not yet reached the portion of the constitution relating to that subject, and argued that we should, before acting on this resolution, pass our constitutional article on this subject.

Mr. Abell—The argument is good, but it is an old and homely saying, that "what is sauce for the goose is sauce for the gander."

Mr. Austin—Mr. President, I should like to know how many times the gentleman is going to speak on this question?

President—You are out of order.

Mr. Abell—If that gentleman runs for any office in my district, I'll vote for him. He interrupts me more than any other man on this floor. But, as I was going on to say, the argument of the gentleman, if it is good in one case it is good in the other, if the election of city officers must be governed by the constitution of 1852. If that constitution is in force for one purpose, it is in force for all purposes; and this Convention, not being assembled in accordance with its provisions, is no Convention, and better be dissolved at once.

Now, Mr. President, as it appears to me, this great corporation has for two years been deprived of its rights. Sir, no great corporation in the world ever had its rights suspended so long. I defy any gentleman to show me a solitary case where a great corporation has, for two years, been deprived of its rights. There is no case, in my knowledge, where it has ever been done. Even in the case where Edmund Sandford declared the charter of London forfeited to the crown, it was not half a year until the rights of the election of mayor and other officers were restored. Yet, sir, here is an ancient corporation, with its rights suspended for two years. Sir, the like has never been known before in the history of the civilized world. No corporation on the face of God's earth, that has ever existed in any civilized country, has ever had its rights suspended for such a length of time.

What is this corporation? Corporations are either proscriptive, where they have existed time whereof the memory of man runneth not to the contrary, or they exist by grant of the Legislature, as is the case with this, though it has existed for nearly a century. This charter has been revised, modified and continued under all the constitutions that have existed, and I call upon gentlemen to show where such a corporation, embracing the largest floating population of any city in the world. Why, sir, you can get on a log in Kentucky and float to New Orleans. I never raised any objection to military authority. I won't to-day, if the gentleman can show me that the whole State is under military rule; but if he shows that the State is under a civil governor, I contend that the city also shall be under civil officers of its own choosing. I support the rights of the corporation. You have sovereign rights and should be allowed to exercise them; and the corporation to-day is entitled to a mayor and aldermen of its own choice. You have a governor elected by your votes. You have a president elected by a popular vote, and you have a right to a mayor elected by your own votes. You have a right to elect these officers. It is a right that cannot be alienated. Let us see by your votes on this resolution whether you intend to enforce this right. I call upon you, gentlemen, to register your names in favor of maintaining, by your votes for this resolution, these rights that have descended from God. These rights the people expect to enforce through their representatives. They expect you to enforce them. You are sent here for that purpose. You have no right to tell the people that you have no right to act in this matter. You have the right, and they expect you to exercise it, and to return to them their rights, sacred and inviolable, that they enjoyed uninterruptedly for a century. You have but to pass this resolution and the work is done—pass this resolution and the governor will obey it as the voice of the sovereign people. Yes, sir, he will obey it. And I will say, sir, that if Gen. Banks was directed by this Convention, or if we should request him to order an election for mayor of this city, it would be done. He would not hesitate for one moment to do it. There is no question, sir, of our power, and I hope that every man in this Convention, who is in favor of sustaining the rights of the people, will, when his name is called, vote for the resolution as his duty to the city and to the State requires him to do.

Mr. WILSON—Mr. President, I move we adjourn.

PRESIDENT—Mr. Austin has the floor.

Mr. AUSTIN—Mr. President, am I in order to offer a resolution?

PRESIDENT—If it has anything to do with this question.

Mr. AUSTIN—It is on miscellaneous business, but does not relate to this question.

PRESIDENT—Then it is out of order.

[The yeas and nays were called on the motion to adjourn, with the following result:]

YEAS—Messrs. Beauvais, Buckley, Burke, Crozat, Davies, Duane, Dufresne, Duke, Ennis, Flagg, Foley, Hire, Maas, Maurer, Murphy E., Murphy M. W., O'Conner, Payne J., Schroeder, Stiner, Wilson—21.

NAYS—Messrs. Abell, Austin, Balch, Bailey, Barrett, Baum, Bell, Bromley, Bofill, Collin, Cazabat, Cook T., Cook J. K., Cutler, Dupaty, Fish, Flood, Fosdick, Gastinel, Geier, Gorlinski, Gruneberg, Gaidry, Harnan, Hills, Howes, Knobloch, Kugler, Mann, Mayer, Montamat, Morris, Newell, Normand, Orr, Paine J. T., Pintado, Poynot, Purcell J., Pursell S., Schnurr, Seymour, Shaw, Smith, Spellicy, Stocker, Sullivan, Stumpf, Stauffer, Terry, Thorpe, Waters—52.

Mr. FOLEY—Mr. President, there is no quorum voting. I move a call of the House.

Mr. DAVIES—I have an amendment to offer, as follows:

Resolved, That the governor of the State be requested to order that elections be held in every incorporated city and town within the Union lines for all city and town officers; said elections to be held on the same day as the elections of officers for the city of New Orleans.

Mr. HARNAN—I move to lay the amendment on the table.

Mr. SHAW—My motion was to postpone the further discussion of this question until next Saturday. I believe the motion is properly before the House, and hope the question will be put.

[The motion was carried.]

Mr. WILSON—I move to adjourn.

[The motion was carried.]

MONDAY, June 20, 1864.

[The Convention met pursuant to adjournment.

Present, the Hon. E. H. Durell, president, and the following members:]

Messrs. Abell, Austin, Balch, Bailey, Baum, Beauvais, Bell, Bofill, Bromley, Buckley, Burke, Campbell, Collin, Cazabat, Cook J. K., Cook T., Crozat, Cutler, Davies, Duane, Dufresne, Duke, Dupaty, Ennis, Fish, Flagg, Flood, Foley, Fosdick, Fuller, Gastinel, Geier, Gorlinski, Gruneberg, Gaidry Healy, Harnan, Hart, Henderson, Hills,

Hire, Howell, Howes, Kavanagh, Knobloch, Kugler, Maas, Mann, Maurer, Mayer, Mendiverri, Montamat. Murphy M. W., Murphy E., Newell, Normand, O'Conner, Orr, Payne J., Paine J. T., Poynot, Purcell J., Pursell S., Schroeder, Schnurr, Seymour, Shaw, Smith, Spellicy, Stocker, Stumpf, Stiner, Stauffer, Sullivan, Terry, Thorpe, Waters, Wenck, Wells, Wilson—81.

Absent—Messrs. Ariail, Barrett, Bennie, Bonzano, Brott, Decker, Edwards, (excused,) Heard, Lobdell, Millspaugh, Montague, Morris, Ong, Taliaferro, Thomas, Pintado, (excused.)

[The minutes were read and adopted.]

Mr. TERRY—I rise to a question of privilege. Since this honorable Convention has been in session, petitions by the mechanics and laboring men have been circulated throughout the parish of Orleans and suburbs, appealing to this body and setting forth their grievances and asking for redress. This can now be granted by inserting a few words in the report now under discussion—general provisions. This memorial, Mr. President, is signed by over two thousand loyal men. I move a suspension of the rules to read the memorial.

[The rules were suspended by a vote of 64.

Mr. Terry then read the following memorial:]

To the honorable president and members of the Constitutional Convention of the State of Louisana:

GENTLEMEN—The undersigned, citizens of the State of Louisiana, beg leave to memorialize your honorable body in behalf of our claims, feeling that this being the only liberty-loving constitutional body, composed purely of the laboring class, that has ever convened in the State of Louisiana for the promotion of the interests of mankind in general, their appeal will not be in vain.

Being composed exclusively of mechanics and artizans, comprising, to a great extent, the *bona fide* resources to cause the hum of business to be heard throughout our noble State, we therefore humbly pray your honorable body will carefully examine into the facts which we present for your favorable consideration, and for your petitioners' elevation to a point in which each one can say, "I, too, am a man, and not a slave!"

The past recurs to our vivid memory with something alike to aversion, when the capitalist could demand and exact from us ten to twelve hours a day devoted to toil, (physical or mental, as the case required;) that they frequently reserved for the white that which was detrimental to the black.

Therefore, your petitioners most respectfully ask of you, your incorporation of some act into the organic law of the State in token of our recognition, by which we may be relieved of the burden we have heretofore borne, that of working to suit the convenience of men who acquired wealth and position to the injury and oppression of us.

Any provision in our law that would secure to us a fixed number of hours as a legal day's work—nine hours being the most that can reasonably be expected for such purpose—we would then be able to devote a part of our time to domestic scenes and the cultivation of the mind.

Trusting it may meet your distinguished consideration, we remain your obedient servants,

R. F. Taylor,	Thomas Lynne,
John Blunk,	Charles J. Care,
Isaac Ward,	Robert Bell,
A. Huhn,	James Mooney,
William May,	Henry Linden,
Joseph O'Neil,	William D. White,
M. Catoire,	Jehn S. Coxe,
Davies Droll,	Michel Burthe,
Charles Beck,	James Reynolds,
Ambrose Hauser,	Peter Kramme,
Charles Krahn,	William B. Daly,
H. Millman,	R. L. Nugent,
Edward Willis,	John Howlett,
S. Hough,	John McDonald,
Peter Caufield,	Edward Willis,
Kobert Crain,	John Killalea,
Michael Corcoran,	O. A. Johnson,
Bryan Conroy,	James Buckley,
Charles Prince,	F. M. Caraden,
William Thompson,	G. B. Williams,
William Lamoney,	John Ryan,
Patrick O'Hara,	Thomas Tierney,
John Pryel,	Patrick Tennessy,
John Lippey,	James Long,
T. Neiglau,	Denis Hefferon,
Charles Leister,	Michael Houlihan,
J. Swainson,	P. Ellis,
Edward Barnard,	N. Whright,
W. Brown,	W. W. Hill,
F. Ewart,	J. Woodward,
D. Larench,	D. Manestirs,
B. Mangles,	William Daley,
B. Posponby,	A. Merrill,
L. Linton,	John Millington,
Henry Day,	D. Wright,
A. W. Neff,	H. Robards,
J. French,	A. Taylor,
A. Sullivan,	C. Guthrie,
T. Pynne,	John Millenton,
C. Rule,	T. Shanks,
J. A. Kendall,	G. Wilson,
F. Pryor,	A. Wilbur,
H. Gray,	T. Brown,
T. J. Rowe,	W. Liggett,
A. Royster,	Thomas Haigh,
Daniel Henderson,	F. Hamilton,
James W. Hill,	Gus. Holtry,
G. Thoul,	T. Honby,

Timothy Tracy,
F. Keunhotz,
Bayard Bourke,
Edward Townsley,
Patrick Mooney,
F. McGuire,
O. Shaw,
Samuel Flagg,
J. Cheever,
Thomas Welch,
Edward Griffiths,
S. Schieffelin,
J. Brown,
B. Pray,
Ben Pacoles,
R. Miner,
L. Rice,
Henry Thompson,
J. Booth,
J. Walworth,
H. Gates,
F. Hubbard,
Sam Greggory,
J. Hays,
F. Leavitt,
T. Delenger,
Thomas Gage,
S. Slawson,
P. Crame,
G. Tracy,
F. Wrightson,
H. Child,
F. Bishop,
Wm. Brown,
P. Tobin,
W. Burden,
Thomas Hogan,
Thomas Riley,
Wm. Kennedy,
Pat O'Brien,
Philip Snaffer,
Joseph Donilan,
Martin Wallace,
Morris Young, .
Nathaniel Bewber,
Harry Gumter,
K. C. Snower,
Hugh Tailor,
W. C. Franciscoe,
Pettie Newman,
Isaac Burton,
D. Henderson,
Wm. Somtendenton,
John Bordman,
Peter Gordon,
Sam Wright,
H. Tomithy,
Louis Canberry,
John Patton,
A. Bavis,
John Daton,
Francis O'Rouk,
John Linerman,
Thomas Booth,
George Grant,
Charles Sonderr,
H. Littledale,
William Have,
A. Howe,
William McGregor,
Thomas Sellar,
Jerry Sullivan,
J. Eller,
A. Stous,
B. W. Douglas,
F. Fellows,
J. Holmes,
F. Booth,
C. W. White,
C. Lockwood,
R. Fraldum,
John Herring,
C. Cushing,
F. Marich,
Wm. Carey,
John Gage,
Herman Potter,
H. Rolfe.
J. Hedley,
J. Puhon,
Wm. Maither,
C. Satting,
H. Pruph,
N. Starbuck,
W. Treadwell,
F. Kennedy,
F. Guetano,
L. Gilbert,
T. Weed,
Thomas Gibson,
Michael Handen,
C. Cragen,
James Moran,
Hugh Welch,
Bernard Duffey,
John Foster,
Simon Pinerton,
Thomas Summerfield,
P. B. Owen,
F. J. Crollery,
Arthur Kenadu,
John O'Riley,
F. A. Short,
J. C. Connelly,
James Harrison,
H. Baker,
S. Lawson,
Henry Johnston,
C. Adason,
Luke Linner,
H. Kenton,
Wm. Young,
Kit Adams,
Michael Delaney,
Morris Kelley,
Robert Higgins,
George Lorance,
Francis Nowlan,
Joseph Marriet,
Thomas Hickey,
Wm. C. Brown,
Van Horriswifom,
John Donely,
B. Surthland,
Amos Belknap,
Wm. Hancock,
Silas Wright,
William Stone,
Thos. H. Penn,
Fran. Wittemur,
Ritchard Bareman,
Patrick Welch,
Martin Block,
Alan Foxe,
John Morow,
C. Hall,
A. C. Welden,
Geo. B. Denison,
P. M. Farell,
S. Stevens,
Henry Russell,
W. C. Patrick,
Joseph Hailey,
Pat. Burns,
Fraren Young,
Henry Strooell,
M. Kimball,
John DeWolf,
Henry Grant,
P. Tremaine,
P. J. Johnston,
Wm. Malone,
Henry Keller,
Walter Newell,
Henry Folsom,
Denis Kenedy,
James W. Collins,
Robert Barrett,
Henry Ziegler,
F. Barnes,
Edward Mannian,
Samuel Guthrie,
Eugène Trémant,
J. Barnens,
Daniel Casey,
Ulrig Reis,
Henry Parker,
R. Dixon,
Henry Thaten,
Patrick H. Fox,
P. Frahling,
W. S. Sawyer,
Charles Frost,
J. States,
Uriah Carty,
G. W. Jackson,
S. C. Yeiser,
Frederick Braun,
James Rostry,
Charles Stott,
B, Rice,
B. Casys,
Thomas More,
Francis Rein,
Wm. Martin,
S. G. Stover,
R. Murphy,
Chas. Johnson,
Francis Wedger,
Martin O'Mara,
Philip Sponner,
John Oaks,
Jack Whip,
Hiche Kelley,
W. Ketchum,
L. Snapher,
Sol. Offehy,
J. W. Cohram,
S. DeBont,
B. L. Williams,
Henry Louis,
P. S. Grant,
John Barret,
Mich. Hoyte,
A. G. Green,
John Glenn,
James Eeleford,
Daniel Todd,
G. T. Beard,
B. W. Brown,
Charles Gormon,
James Parks,
William Brown,
John Cashady,
Matthew Mullen,
John Sixsmith,
John F. Potter,
Daniel Spruce,
Alexander Ritchie,
John Fagan,
Daniel Shaffry,
Michel Hennesy,
Thomas Toohey,
John Mulvagh,
Johnson Magruder,
Thomas Townly,
William Walsh,
J. H. Marr,
Theodore Hering,
Patrick Dooly,
John McCormick,
Thomas Shipton,
U. N. Compton,
S. R. Mills,
Thornton Willis,
S. Branold,
Thomas Harwell,
H. Donner,
E. H. Cunningham,
Terence Driscoll,
Bernard Kelly,
H. Riley,
W. W. Hunter,
H. Costello,
Wm. Parker,
Wash. Dixon,
L. Lynch,
John Birmingham,
J. G. Fitzpatrick,
John Conners,
Wm. Higgins,
P. Burke,
C. J. Meighan,
M. Easterly,

Eugene F. Norden,
John Zolly,
Thomas Chase,
S. H. Young,
Deforest Bayle,
Joseph Varet,
Wm. Morgan,
H. Bennitt,
A. Lapaneye,
J. S. Jenkins,
Jacob Dawson,
F. Beeker,
F. Luster,
Barney Morris,
Morris Ganby,
W. J. Laurens,
Richard Brockbank,
Richard Sheridan,
F. Roman,
Francis Fry,
M. Herbert,
Patrick Shaw,
J. Willis,
S. W. Reardon,
John Bishop,
Samuel Cooke,
E. Coldin,
P. Leonard,
J. Myers,
S. L. Keary,
O. W. Pratt,
C. Fox,
Sebatian Mannu,
L. Child,
L. Livingston,
Wm. R. Plant,
G. Kingsland,
James Ferguson,
Daniel McCord,
Henry Beck,
J. Dent,
J. Jones,
J. Sherman,
T. Townley,
George Gay,
Philip Burton,
L. Vickox,
B. Bart,
Thomas Cailin,
J. A. Mattison,
N. Edwards,
Maurice Greenhouse,
Charles Folger,
H. Gates,
James Applegate,
S. Flikenger,
H. Bounsford,
John Ryan,
James Jacobs,
Henry Renshaw,
Morton Strothman,
H. Boszer,
Andrew Walk,
John Haser,
Charles Brown,
John Walker,
H. S. Mead,
Lawless Clinton,
P. J. Galpin,
C. Calabeet,
Harvey Cornell,
H. Victor,
W. B. Small,
J. Curtis,
L. Ridgley,
W. L. Ludlow,
F. S. Foster,
Batise Bennue,
B. Hays,
Filibert Cotoree,
F. Frohock,
B. O'Brien,
John Downy,
Michael Williams,
Wm. Sullivan,
B. Stannard,
John Campbell,
Albert Lemon,
James McGuinn,
Frederick Nichols,
James Arandt,
Geo. Smidt,
F. Bowen,
D. Peabody,
Geo. Palsey,
Joseph Lanier,
Henry Deys,
Daniel Bradley,
B. Reynolds,
J. Kite,
Thomas Wing,
S. Tatum,
Gabriel Bird,
John Harris,
W. W. Waggoner,
Richard Overton,
T. Johnson,
G. Jones,
J. Jennings,
M. Virdin,
B. Baker,
Wm. Stone,
Thomas Bonner,
S. Bouton,
J. Coleman,
George Burmet,
David Landreth,
J. W. Brown,
B. Wood,
Cyrus Davenport,
William Dean,
Robert Lucas,
G. Watt,
F. Webster,
John Bushnell,
John Casey,
William Leet,
H. Treat,
John Saltenstall,
Henry Valcot,
B. Law,
Thomas Fitch,
Christ Sloen,
Timothy Daley,
Michael Danner,
John McLaughlin,
Thomas Tung,
James Griffin,
R. Thomas,
F. Williams,
G. Dusson,
Mat Finegan,
G. Dueker,
Christopher Sloh,
D. H. Anderson,
John Cox,
L. Reynolds,
Henry Devoe,
J. R. Fairchild,
W. Westiook,
Edward Hopkins,
John Haynes,
George Winthrop,
T. Baldwin,
John Webster,
Theodore Estfield,
John Gray,
J. W. Moore,
Wm. McReady,
S. Mott,
Henry Brundage,
F. Prince,
T. Stearns,
D. Merritt,
W. Gray,
H. Cook,
George B. Allen,
S. Fagan,
Arthur Barrett,
L. Goupil,
B. Lawny,
F. Fowler,
J. Hooper,
F. Plant,
Robert Rait,
Ed. Jenkins,
R. Richards,
S. Carter,
J. Horner,
G. Dawson,
J. Dodson,
George Hyer,
A. B. Reynolds,
G. Taylor,
James Alexander,
Charles Roose,
James Shields,
Tim Hoyt,
Lewis Craig,
R. Gresham,
Benjamin Avery,
Robert Anderson,
G. Lengerberger,
H. Smith,
Thomas Bridgford,
D. Wright,
F. Hall,
P. Evens,
William Pitkin,
Val Turnbull,
Matthew Griswold,
J. C. Smith,
Oliver Wallcot,
George Treadwell,
H. Tomlinson,
James S. Peters,
Henry Edwards,
Samuel Foote,
Wm. Ellsworth,
C. Cleveland,
C. Bissell,
William J. Seymour,
Henry Law,
T. Sparkman,
C. W. Smith,
Edward Trustan,
G. Lasset,
Thomas Lighte,
Henry Newman,
Henry Bradbury,
Thomas Vimm,
Robert Alexander,
D. Mitchell,
A. Berryhill,
R. Whitside,
Robert Adams,
L. Rogers,
J. Morgan,
J. Lindsay,
J. Spiles,
William Gormly,
E. Thomas,
James Irvine,
John Little,
J. Estep,
A. Cullum,
J. Grant,
R. Gainsborough,
T. Noble,
J. Crozier,
E. Penn,
James Mason,
Frank Trader,
John McCord,
A. Clark,
M. Harris,
B. Bartletts,
Henry Addison,
Charles Jamison,
James Eddy,
J. Harmans,
J. Betts,
A. Hughes,
J. Sage,
D. Faulds,
John Hews,
B. Gould,
M. Mattison,
C. Baldwin,
W. Amory,
G. Howe,
P. Goodhue,
Edward Page,
F. Smith,

S. Bacon,
J. S. Hall,
P. Dodds,
John Largue,
Henry Turchell,
G. Gray,
J. A. Reed,
A. Hoyt,
C. Pond,
C. Hopkinson,
F. W. Chapin,
P. Buckley,
R. Manghen,
B. Stopleton,
J. Lawson,
F. Pierce,
S. Bartley,
V. Johnson.
R. Bartley,
Wm. Richardson,
H. Hunt,
Thomas Hunt,
G. Atkinson,
J. Thomas,
W. Watkins,
R. Owsley,
P. Mitchell,
R. Pearce,
James Wingate,
Fred Millet,
D. Depont,
C. Thornton,
E. Hawkins,
B. Braverson,
John Gault,
H. Ryan,
D. Holbrook,
G. Meadows,
C. Snead,
B. Avery,
J. Chwoffine,
S. Dunlap,
John Ford,
L. Shreve,
C. Harris,
R. Carhart,
B. Needham,
John Gaddis,
S. B. Martin,
C. T. Franey,
Thomas Handy,
Henry Gray,
Michael Murray,
Michael Cunney,
A. D. Colon,
Alexander Welsh,
Bernard Murphy,
Henry Kish,
William F. Skerrett,
S. Cummings,
M. Bayless,
James Mackie,
John Monelle,
John Chase,
Michael Dunn,
B. L. Bottol,

John Roberts,
Francis Jones,
H. C. Cochran,
Thomas Smith,
J. H. Sockard,
Henry North,
George Kelley,
Henry Pitfield,
Owen Murphy,
L. D. Rounson,
Pat Flood,
Charles Short,
William Langerton,
James Black,
Owen Buttler,
William Crawford,
Peter Goldsmith,
Howe Richards,
John Mullen,
Peter Snapper,
Morris Delaney,
Kenedy Morehouse,
William Sutley,
Isaac Knuts,
Hugh Bradey,
John Sumerfield,
A. Woodworth,
Michael Varmouth,
Chalen Staam,
Canby Douglas,
John Kippen,
John Goletung,
George Gulpen,
Bernard Rollen,
W. Smith,
Pat Casedy,
Witton Calhoun.
S. Wilbour,
H. Moore,
Simon Kuntz,
James Donelly,
Francis Peaborton,
Matthew Tilton,
Isaac West,
Thomas Quinn,
L. Navels,
Bernard Munday,
W. E. Jones,
Joseph Alexander,
James Young,
Samuel Barry,
John Roberts,
Pat Green,
M. Moffat,
Michael Donoghu,
August Hilderbrand,
C. Collins, Jr.,
Wm. Montgomery,
L. Lyons,
Theodore Swift,
James Mahen,
M. Taylor,
B. S. Crawford,
George McCormick,
Mart Young,
S. N. Cotton,

William McCracken,
Edward Linder,
M. J. Hughes,
Barney Murphy,
Bill Patterson,
John Wild,
Dennis Monehan,
Frederick Dunigan,
Batt Eastman,
Joseph Rolans,
William Davis,
Samuel Baker,
John Warner,
Warren Davis,
W. R. Stewart,
F. Brittle,
John Stewart,
Ben. Barton,
L. J. C. Dobbs,
William Hutter,
Pat. Cawfield,
John Wright,
L. R. Hobensack,
Sam Tailor,
B. Straughter,
S. Hodges,
George Diven,
John W. Ray,
Bernard Kilpatrick,
William Dickson,
E. C. Cotton,
John Crocker,
Dick Smiley,
Henry Morgan,
Richard Disberan,
Natbaniel Brettel,
John Phrem,
Lorenzo Bretagne,
Michael Darlon,
Owen Murphy,
S. W. Noyes,
Bernard Bready,
Henry Trainor,
Abott Lawrence,
Thomas Groves,
William Mason,
B. Bristow,
George Curtis,
Henry Root,
J. Leate,
W. F. Hill,
F. D. Dash,
J. Howe, Jr.,
F. Bellee,
Bat. Finagan,
U. F. Beebee,
Thomas Trindle,
A. McKenzie,
John Syms,
C. Scribner,
P. Pillas,
E. G. Dyckink,
Thomas Wheeler,
Th. Davids,
G. Pomeroy,
John Francis,

J. C. Rountree,
John Tetter,
John Manghen,
Patrick Manghen,
Henry Price,
Bernard Lacy,
Bart. Linn,
Robert Wells,
Patrick Burns,
John Clayton,
M. Kallet,
Francis Sprat,
George Lemorton,
Andrew Suter,
James Black,
Moses Varnor,
C. C. Sholes,
J. E. Tounsley,
Patrick Nileloct,
Bernard Buckley,
James McConley,
Peter Mainge,
John Jones,
J. D. Stodds,
James Bnerll,
Tom Wenery,
Louis Richards,
Abraham Edwards,
Sam Lousun,
H. R. Ingham,
George Kendrickton,
Bill Sicks,
Carroll Small,
F. L. Flacher,
C. Taylor,
Cornelius Crasgum,
B. P. Orr,
B. Brecer,
Walter Smith,
John Ottis,
F. Louther,
George Hale,
Barney Duffy,
Edward Carroll,
John Gibbs,
J. Davis,
William Jones,
U. Bridges,
B. Reed,
John Conners,
S. McMurray,
Theodore Ivison.
G. Sheldon,
Henry Phinney,
Thomas Blackman,
James Wild,
A. Woodward,
L. Nicholy,
T. Pickney,
John Clark,
Thomas Noyes,
A. Whitlessey,
James Allen,
L. Ackerman,
Thomas Harris,
J. Berrian,

Henry Loutwell,
John B. Corbett,
John Morey,
Thomas Hand,
C. Haskell,
I. Ballard,
H. Boardman,
S. Gray,
William Shaw,
John Blodgett,
Henry Fisher,
Thomas Hallet,
W. Davis,
J. Chickering,
George W. Webb,
H. S. Oliver,
John Lange,
B. Duncan,
F. Sherman,
Henry Aiken,
Johnson Fiske,
O. Elsworth,
George Cushing,
F. Rutledge,
N. Clifford,
Thomas Randolph,
William Bradford,
John Lee,
Robert Smith,
Cæsar Breckinridge,
John Rodney,
Richard Pinkney,
William Rush,
John Wirt,
William Bauan,
John Taney,
Felix Butler,
Benjamin Grundy,
S. J. Taylor,
Andrew Weber,
Henry Smith,
William Stevenson,
Martin Fish,
Robert Calwell,
Edward Connoy,
Charles Stewart,
Thomas Insley,
P. Drummond,
P. W. Ross,
M. Sonner,
James McCoy,
John Kenna,
J. Pough,
B. W. Noris,
B. Cole,
E. J. Hammond,
J. F. Robinson,
Patrick McKeever,
Timothy Fahy,
August Brandagee,
H. H. Fay,
Owen King,
J. M. Schowell,
P. Schwartz,
A. B. Reeder,
James S. Bradford,
John Holmes,
Sandy Butler,
B. Valentine,
George Hillman,
Thomas Fanning,
H. Wegman,
William Clark,
J. Beck,
H. G. Gilpin,
J. J. Legare,
Hugh Nelson,
B. Critenden,
Nathan Mason,
John Clifford,
Red. Toucy,
Isaac Johnson,
Henry Cushing,
Wm. M. Morrison,
John Ball,
James Black,
Thomas Sherlock,
C. Basham,
John Dwyer,
Alex. McCord,
Henry Good,
Fred. Babbit,
A. Adams,
Moses McClelan,
Theodore Monroe,
S. Seymour,
H. Debesay,
A. Gallop,
Thomas Gaddis,
R. Knobe,
George D. Winchell,
Henry Gahele,
A. Lisson,
F. Band,
N. Burer,
Henry Payen,
John Young,
Allen Logan,
Patrick Murphy,
John Hurley,
James Smith,
J. C. Wattson,
C. J. Dillon,
James O'Malley,
Denis Clency,
W. Konkleman,
Toney Karl,
Michael Leister,
S. Flannigan,
John O. Rourke,
James Wadsworth,
F. L. Woods,
M. O'Harra,
Denis Clohesy,
Edward Mulvah,
Thomas Mulvah,
Joseph Kelly,
Thomas O'Reilly,
J. S. Leppard,
U. Leppard,
Henry Lasman,
Robert Robinson,
Hiram Goldsborough,
George Lusk,
H. V. Dorsey,
J. S. Labonisse,
J. J. Brown,
Henry Wilson,
B. Shaffer,
John Liddings,
Patrick Cassedy,
Charles Woodin,
Frank Butler,
Matthey Riardon,
Zeb. Caldwell,
Thomas Wentworth,
E. P. Walton,
S. Wordsworth,
E. Harris,
Andrew Maxwell,
Louis Benix,
Van Horn,
Geo. Patterson,
Lawrens Mareen,
S. J. Cook,
John Straider,
William F. Minor,
Terence Raymond,
Charles J. Walls,
William Lowby,
John Moore,
H. Lenox,
Francis Keatry,
Simon Morris,
Michael Cleriney,
Luke Buddy,
John Fenigan,
John Speed,
William B. Ferry,
John Dunn,
E. R. Perry,
E. Congan,
Edward Burke,
George Bapsh,
Patrick Kelly,
John Birminghan,
Mike Birmingham,
Dennis Downing,
Patrick Lynch,
Joseph Elliott,
Hugh Kelly,
Frank Ober,
T. Flannigan,
Lawrence Boyle,
Peter Donovan,
O. Branold,
Peter Costello,
Billy Fogarty,
L. Kelly,
Thomas Sullivan,
Daniel Leo,
John L. Smith,
Valentin Brown,
H. Sigel,
E. O. Rielly,
William Cain,
P. S. Fox,
Thomas Turner,
Henry Robinson,
Timothy McCarthy,
Henry Doyle,
Thomas Doyle,
T. Glennon,
F. Hurley,
John Knox,
Fred Cansland,
J. G. Wing,
Varlent M. Hent,
Henry Shuling,
L. S. Wild,
B. Plunkett,
John S. Marting,
B. Winkleman,
John Illy,
David Hart,
Thomas Hart,
Matthew Clarke,
Thomson Barnes,
J. Chapman,
Nelson Uling,
S. Howard,
Allen Jackson,
John Cliney,
L. Fahy,
Thomas Burke,
John O'Nell,
Willis Gilding,
Theodore Onecyne,
H. S. Kunnholtz,
S. Stupt,
Maurice Dillon,
Sebastian Leopold,
George Bassett,
William Lynne,
James Cauffield,
Mar. O'Sillen,
John Stewart,
John O'Rilley,
Patrick Daly,
Michael Conner,
Thomas Gleson,
Bernard Fitspatrick,
Robert Newdashen,
E. Daley,
James Higgins,
M. C. Russell,
William Higgins,
B. S. Shayer,
A. E. Van Loon,
J. G. Gannon,
P. Donner,
M. Wheatley,
J. Dow Clement,
Daniel Hartnett,
James Ward,
Patrick Gray,
Thomas McHugh,
Luke Mallon,
Samuel White,
Charles Smith,
J. H. McCrearey,
C. M. Daley,
Robert Gardner,
Henry Louis,

H. S. Kennedy,
John Reynolds,
Thomas Ford,
Lawrence Finney,
B. S. Theben,
William Smedley,
Horatio Williams,
James Williams,
Eugène J. Jormon,
S. Webb,
H. Keaghoh,
Henry J. Joynt,
Robert Bayz,
Theodore J. Smith,
J. G. McCleland,
Frances Isherwood,
L. Negreponte,
B. Dafonta,
Henry Smith,
Geo. B. Salomon,
John Perkins,
W. B. Bennett,
Thos. Flanders,
Geo. Smyth,
Bernard McGill,
Thomas Coyne,
John Grussy,
Thomas Haley,
Patrick Pavell,
James Dickson,
John Gilding,
James Brown,
William Barclay,
John Tucker,
S. Freeman,
P. H. Weeks,
Thomas Cosgrove,
Edward Johnstone,
E. H. Clayton,
Benjamin Whitlock,
Oliver Haverstick,
Henry Dodge,
Fred. Cammeyer,
Edward Sprague,
John Stetbine,
Patrick Magan,
John Allen,
Robert Davis,
H. Pratt,
H. Hardenbaugh,
R. W. Viedenburgh,
John White,
Robert Stam,
Phillip Sears,
William Partrige,
George H. Eddy,
Thomas Mohawk,
Henry Hudson,
Franklin Mors,
Frederick Slocum,
John P. Smith,
M. Taytor,
William Dixon,
B. Gravel,
M. B. Sanford,
George Carsons,

Z. Chauman,
D. Hubbard,
Thomas Potter,
B. Morrill,
Hugh Roney,
E. Spalding,
John Brady
Isidore Hull,
Pat. Bradley,
J. M. Sanders,
Patrick Murphy,
Horace Fairbans,
G. H. Shaw,
Abel Buver,
John White,
A. Sutherland,
Thomas Maille,
W. J. Davis,
C. W. Cristy,
Louis Patterson,
S. Hildebrand,
John McEntosh,
J. B. Spencer,
Terrence Haly,
Hugh O'Neill,
Thomas Stone,
H. Oliver,
C. Storeme,
G. McRae,
E. Washburn,
Isaac Hinkly,
J. Dickinson,
P. Adams,
O. Bayley,
E. Straw,
John Shaw,
William Shearer,
John Smith,
B. Cole,
John Rogers,
Henry Knight,
D. Way,
L. A. Nightingale,
R. Waterman,
B. Rider,
Charles Parker,
R. Redding,
L. Pailey,
L. Bangs,
Robert Sears,
J. S. Brown,
R. Buckett,
W. Phallyrs,
C. Curtis,
T. Dexter,
M. Tappan,
G. Folger,
Charles Hubbard,
B. Stevens,
J. Harmans,
A. Thaxter,
J. Phillips,
R. Samsson,
H. Prescott,
H. B. Stowe,
N. Hall,

Harvey Hard,
C. B. Menford,
Thomas Bond,
H. Caningstone,
Robert B. Retricke,
John Fuller,
Sylvester Lord,
N. Morgan,
P. Lorrelard,
John Connolly,
James Taylor,
Henry Mitt,
Theodore Pierson.
R. B. Trull,
George Stearns,
Hiram Thornso,
Frank Ondeslyer,
John Marvin,
P. Hark,
Henry Tower,
L. Bradford,
S. T. Crosby,
J. Phepne,
C. Raullett,
F. Badaeus,
John H. Campbell,
Martin Willow,
Basel Pike,
Jacob Bafo,
Francois Peras,
Oscar Sharp,
P. A. Tesson,
Henry Lee,
F. C. Lagennessen,
Henry Sommerfield,
Lewis Maurice,
Cristopher Carson,
Henry Beaumont,
Charles Tuplin,
James Powers,
Ransom Clark,
Owen Roberts,
Thomas Gillpin,
John Parish,
Celis Hudson,
Louis Minart,
N. L. Wallop,
Hiram Powers,
J. P. Dernsha,
Lewis Brow,
Raphael Menard,
John Petit,
John Little,
James Wheeler.
Oscar Percey,
Perry L. Wallace,
H. W. St. Clair,
A. L. Haydon,
V. Merrick,
John McArthur,
W. M. Jowers,
George Jones,
J. H. Abrams,
Maurice Vernor,
C. J. McManus,
Timothy Driscole,

D. Walland,
M. Stitch,
R. Hildette,
J. McCauley,
John Jewett,
H. Gross,
M. Russell,
E. H. Derby,
S. G. Ashton.
Rufus Clark,
J. B. Reed,
S. Cutler,
G. Turnbull,
C. Sweet,
D. D. Franget,
W. Zenney,
Robert Hall,
J. Hovey,
Thomas Cutler,
H. Newell,
R. Doe,
John Haller,
A. W. Lawrence,
Alexis Hyat,
J. F. Abert,
William Gilpin,
R. Dillin,
Isaac Thompson,
John Coffin,
John McAthur,
Matthew Katton,
J. S. Lowe,
Walter Abot,
Lewis Falmouth,
William Kunnuns,
Phillip Treanor,
Oscar Dwight,
J. Ludlow,
H. C. Callolley,
Charles Preeuss,
Theodore Talbot,
Albert Wilkis,
Thomas Fitzpatrick,
R. J. Brenkly,
John Frederic,
Charles Clark,
T. Mellhauser,
Harvey Clayton,
William Dodds,
Henry Neugent,
Oscar Syker,
B. Cradock,
E. A. Smithley,
Frederick Napier,
J. B. Doyle,
George Hodges,
G. A. Murat,
John Jack,
A. H. Commins,
Geo. Lejune,
K. C. Lyons,
C. G. Reed,
B. Machless,
W. L. Woods,
Joseph Brocket,
Lewis Martin,

Paul W. Stagg,
Matthew McAdams,
J. Suggons,
O. Sherron,
Henry Wolf,
Thomas Hays,
Thomas Wiggins,
Charles Moore,
G. S. Wengent,
Charles Rossetter,
J. F. Fleenup,
Jacob Garrett,
Thomas Paxton,
H. F. Brown,
James Peterson,
F. G. Simpson,
F. Pendegrast.
F. S. Orleander,
Francis Gables,
S. J. Barbet,
John Jurney,
George Thomas,
Charles Jurney,
Henry Achworth,
T. H. Farris,
M. Adams,
Frederick Bower,
W. K. Pattison,
James Morpey,
James Gardner,
H. Hardee,
Frank Carter,
John J. Harrison.

Mr. MONTAMAT—I move to refer it to a special committee of five.

Mr. STINER—I amend to seven.

[Carried.]

Mr. FOSDICK—I move a suspension of the rules, for the purpose of taking up the resolution which I had the honor of presenting yesterday.

Mr. DUANE—I move to lay the motion on the table.

[Lost by a rising vote of 21 yeas, 45 nays.

The yeas and nays were called on the motion to suspend the rules, and the motion carried, as follows :]

YEAS—Messrs. Abell, Austin, Balch, Bailey, Baum, Bell, Bofill, Buckley, Campbell, Cook J. K., Cook T., Dufresne, Duke, Flagg, Flood, Fosdick, Gastinel, Geier, Gorlinski, Gruneberg, Harnan, Hart, Hills, Howes, Knobloch, Maas, Maurer, Mayer, Montamat, Murphy E., O'Conner, Orr, Poynot, Purcell J., Smith, Sullivan, Thorpe, Waters, Wilson—39.

NAYS—Messrs. Beauvais, Bromley, Burke, Collin, Crozat, Cutler, Davies, Duane, Dupaty, Ennis, Fish, Foley, Fuller, Gaidry, Healy, Henderson, Hire, Howell, Kugler, Mann, Murphy M. W., Newell, Normand, Payne J., Paine J. T., Pursell S., Schroeder, Schnurr, Seymour, Shaw, Stocker, Stumpf, Stiner, Stauffer, Terry, Wells—36.

Mr. MONTAMAT—I move for a suspension of the rules, for the purpose of reading the report of the Finance Committee, as there was no opportunity to present it on Saturday.

[Carried—yeas 63.]

Mr. MONTAMAT—I offer the following report:

REPORT OF THE FINANCE COMMITTEE, UP TO JUNE 18.

1864.	
June 18—Amount paid out, as per warrants up to date, for *per diem* of members, mileage and salaries of officers......	$94,485 60
June 18—Balance on hand to date......................	5,514 40
	$100,000 00
June 18—Amount paid out for contingent expenses, as per vouchers and warrants....	$18,027 97
June 18—Balance on hand, to date......................	6,972 03
	$25,000 00

June 18—Amount paid out for printing and advertising, as per vouchers and warrants, $48,128 32. This sum was paid out of funds not otherwise appropriated, with the exception of seven thousand dollars, which was paid from the funds appropriated for contingent expenses, and is to be refunded to that account.

June 8—The sum of six thousand one hundred and thirty-nine dollars and thirteen cents, ($6,139 13,) was paid to J. S. Walton, treasurer of the city of New Orleans, for fitting up Liberty Hall.

Your committee respectfully report that it is necessary that an appropiation be made for the payment of members, officers and employés of this Convention for the balance of the term; wherefore, your committee beg leave to recommend the following resolution:

Resolved, That the sum of twenty thousand dollars be and the same is hereby appropriated out of the general funds of the State treasury, not otherwise appropriated, for the payment of *per diem* and salaries of members and officers.

JOHN P. MONTAMAT,
Acting Chairman Finance Committee,
L. P. NORMAND,
JOHN SULLIVAN,
MARTIN SCHNURR.

New Orleans, June 18, 1864.

Mr. WILSON—Mr. President, before acting in the matter, I would make a motion that a detailed statement be made to this Convention of all the moneys paid out, to whom and what for, and that it be printed and laid on the desks of the members.

Mr. MONTAMAT—The books of the Finance Committee are open for examination by every person who wishes to do so.

Mr. HENDERSON—I move to lay the motion on the table.

Mr. Foley---I move that the report be accepted and the resolution adopted.

[Carried.

The motion of Mr. Wilson was laid on the table.]

President—The chair appoints as a committee to whom the memorial presented this morning is to be referred, Messrs. Terry, Geier, Stiner, O'Conner, Balch and Orr.

Mr. Hire --I ask that Mr. Pintado be excused from attendance, on account of sickness in his family.

[No objection was made.

The report of the Committee on General Provisions was then taken up.]

Mr. Howell---Upon a motion offered by myself the action of the Convention adopting article 23 was reconsidered, for the purpose of exempting charitable institutions. At that time I suggested that it might be inserted in the second line, but I think the following part of the article rather inconsistent, and therefore I propose that it be added to the end, in these words: "*Provided*, that this article shall not apply to charitable institutions."

Mr. Cazabat---I move to strike out the remainder of the article, after the words "internal improvement."

[The last amendment was lost, and the amendment of Mr. Howell adopted.

Article 28 of the report was then read :]

Art. 28. No divorce shall be granted by the Legislature.

Mr. Smith---I move to amend by adding, "nor any minor emancipated."

Mr. Wilson---I move to amend by making the article : "Divorces shall be granted by the Legislature."

Mr. Fosdick---I desire to offer this substitute for the whole article :

The Legislature may enact general laws regulating the adoption of children, emancipation of minors, changing of names, and the granting of divorces, but no special laws shall be enacted relating to particular or individual cases.

Mr. Foley---I move to strike out of the substitute the words, "change of names."

[Laid on the table.

The substitute was then adopted.

Article 29 was read :]

Art. 29. Every law enacted by the Legislature shall embrace but one object, and that shall be expressed in the title.

Mr. Henderson—Mr. President, I move to strike out that article. I wish it to be struck out because there has been a great deal of dispute and objection as to what it means—the Supreme Court having passed many times upon the meaning of that article in the constitution of 1852, and its meaning is yet not clearly defined or understood. In a majority of cases that have been taken up on it, the law has been decided unconstitutional. I mean to show you that such men as Thomas Slidell and other distinguished jurists have never been able fully to determine what is the subject matter of any given law in the meaning of the constitution of the State. If you adopt this, you make it necessary for the Legislature to decide what is the subject matter; and if they fail to decide properly and to insert it correctly in the title, the law is unconstitutional. Every single law, gentlemen, shall embrace but one single subject, and the subject matter must be expressed in the title, or it will be unconstitutional. Sir, there is no one man in this room that can do what is required in order to insure the constitutionality of a law under this provision. Previous to the adoption of the ordinance of emancipation, we had free negroes and slaves. Now, suppose a law passed referring to free negroes, slaves and mulattoes. A case brought under this law would be taken to the Supreme Court and decided unconstitutional because it referred to more than one single subject; slaves and free negroes being distinct subjects, it would perhaps be decided to be necessary to have a law for each, or it would be unconstitutional. A law regulating evils in all criminal cases has been decided unconstitutional, because it was held that there should be a separate act for justices of the peace and recorders' courts, etc., because they were each a single subject, and a law applicable to all criminal cases embraced too many subjects.

Why, sir, there is not one legislator in the State that can comply with this article if it is adopted. Why not, then, strike it out entirely and let a law, when it has been properly passed, be a law, if it does not conflict with the other provisions of the constitution? If we adopt it, I can have nine-tenths of the laws that may be passed declared unconstitutional.

Mr. ABELL—I have had two great objects in this Convention: the first was compensation to loyal owners. In this I was defeated. The second was an appointive judiciary for life; and I was defeated in that. Now, sir, I have another great object, and that is to get the members of this Convention to adjourn. They say their time has a charm, and I trust I shall succeed this time. I do not intend to make a lengthy speech, but I wish to say the defects of the former framers of the constitution, in the formation of this article: "Every law enacted by the Legislature shall embrace but one object, and that shall be expressed in the title;" and it has been declared a hundred times by the Snpreme Court was to simplify the law so that every person could understand it, and so that there should not be a half dozen laws embraced under one head. The gentleman says that the Legislature makes this mistake very often, but I believe I can convince the gentleman that it is the reverse of his statement; that it does not happen once in a hundred cases; so that the objection amounts to nothing.

PRESIDENT—I do not think the motion was seconded.

Mr. ABELL—Then, sir, I move the adoption of the article as reported.

[The motion was carried.

Article 30 was read and adopted:]

Art. 30. No law shall be revived or amended by reference to its title; but, in such case, the act revived or section amended shall be re-enacted and published at length.

[Article 31 was read and adopted:]

Art. 31. The Legislature shall never adopt any system or code of laws by general reference to such system or code of laws, but in all cases shall specify the several provisions of the laws it may enact.

Article 32 was read:]

Art. 32. Corporations with discounting privileges may be either created by special acts or formed under general laws. But no corporation or individual shall have the privilege of issuing notes or bills except those which are already chartered.

Mr. HOWELL—I am directed by the committee to offer a substitute for that, growing out of the resolution offered by Mr. Goldman. It is in these words:

Art. 32. Corporations shall not be created in this State by special laws, except for political or municipal purposes, but the Legislature shall provide by general laws for the organization of all other corporations, except corporations with banking or discounting privileges, the creation, renewal or extension of which is hereby prohibited.

Mr. FOLEY—It is accepted by the committee, and I move its adoption.

[Carried.

Article 33 was read.]

Art. 33. In case of the insolvency of any bank or banking association, the bill holders thereof shall be entitled to preference in payment over all other creditors of such bank or association.

Mr. SMITH—I move to insert the word "not" making it read, "shall not be entitled to preference, etc."

Mr. BELL—I move to lay it on the table.

[Carried.

The article was then adopted as read.

Article 34 was read:]

Art. 34. No person shall hold or exercise, at the same time, more than one civil office of trust or profit, except that of justice of the peace.

Mr. CAZABAT—I move to strike out "except that of justice of the peace."

[The amendment was lost and the article adopted as read.

Art. 35 was read.]

Art. 35. Taxation shall be equal and uniform throughout the State. All property on which taxes may be levied in this State, shall be taxed in proportion to its value, to be ascertained as directed by law. No one species of property shall be taxed higher than another species of property of equal value, on which taxes shall be levied; the Legislature shall have power to levy an income tax, and to tax all persons pursuing any occupation, trade or profession.

Mr. PURSELL—I offer the following substitute:

Art. 35. Taxation shall be equal and uniform throughout the State. All property shall be taxed in proportion to its value, to be ascertained as directed by law. The General Assembly shall have power to exempt from taxation property actually used for church, school or charitable purposes. The General Assembly shall levy an income tax upon all persons pursuing any occupation, trade or calling, and all such persons shall obtain a license, as provided by law. All tax on income shall be pro rata on the amount of income or business done.

I propose in this amendment to tax all kinds of property. The original article refers only to such property as may be taxed.

Mr. HOWELL—If there be anything in the substitute proposed by the gentleman which is not contained in article 35, by his construction, it is totally unnecessary, because the article as presented, effects the very object which he proposes to effect by his substitute.

Mr. HARNAN—If you tax a man under the excise laws of the United States, you tax him upon his income, and every one then pays in proportion as he receives.

Mr. CAZABAT—The last clause fixes the tax pro rata on the amount of the income or business done. If I have a stock worth $100,000, I must pay on that, but if I am a poor man, I must pay on the amount invested. It protects the poor man and makes the rich man pay on his capital, and I shall sustain the substitute.

Mr. ABELL—I understand it does not provide for taxing the licenses of lawyers, but taxes every man according to his capital.

Mr. CAZABAT—The party must first obtain his license to follow his occupation, and then pays on his income.

[The substitute was then adopted.

Article 36 was read:]

Art. 36. The citizens of the city of New Orleans shall have the right of appointing the several public officers necessary for the administration of the police of the said city, pursuant to the mode of election which shall be prescribed by the Legislature: *Provided*, That the mayor and recorders shall be ineligible to a seat in the General Assembly, and the mayor and recorders shall be commissioned by the governor as justices of the peace, and the Legislature may vest in them such criminal jurisdiction as may be necessary for the punishment of minor crimes and offences.

Mr. SULLIVAN—I offer the following substitute for article 36:

The citizens of the city of New Orleans shall have the right of appointing the several public officers necessary for the administration of the police of said city, pursuant to the mode of elections which shall be prescribed by the Legislature.

Provided, That the mayor and recorders shall be ineligible to a seat in the General Assembly; and the mayor and recorders shall be commissioned by the governor as justices of the peace, and the Legislature may vest in them such criminal jurisdiction as may be necessary for the punishment of minor offences and as the police and good order of said city may require.

And that the city of New Orleans shall maintain a police force which shall be uniformed with distinction of grade, to consist of permanent citizens of the State of Louisiana, to be selected by the mayor of the city and to hold office during good behavior, and removable only by a police commission, to be appointed by the governor of the State for the term of two years, at a salary of no less than one thousand dollars each per annum, a majority of whom shall remove for delinquencies. Members of the police when removed shall not again be eligible to any position on the police for a term of one year.

Interfering or meddling in elections in any manner will be a sufficient cause for instant dismissal from the police by the Board.

The chief of police shall give a penal bond in the sum of ten thousand dollars; lieutenants of police, five thousand dollars; sergeants and clerks, each, three thousand dollars; corporals, two thousand dollars, and privates one thousand dollars each, with good and solvent security as the law directs, for the faithful performance of their duties. The various officers shall receive a salary of not less than the following, to wit:

	PER MONTH.
The chief of police to receive......	$250
The lieutenants of police to receive..	150
The sergeants of police to receive...	100
The clerks of police to receive......	100
The corporals of police to receive...	90
The privates (both day and night) each	80

And that the compensation of all foremen, mechanics, cartmen and laborers employed in the public works under the government of the State of Louisiana, city of New Orleans, and police juries of the various loyal parishes of the State of Louisiana, also be increased to no less than the following rates:

All foremen...	$3 50
All mechanics....................	3 00
All cartmen...	3 00
All laborers.....................	2 00

Which pay may be increased but not reduced.

Mr. AUSTIN—I move to lay it on the table.

[The yeas and nays were called on the motion.

Before the vote was announced Mr. Harnan changed his vote from "yes" to "no."

The motion was lost.]

YEAS—Messrs. Austin, Bromley, Burke, Campbell, Collin, Cazabat, Cutler, Davies, Duke, Dupaty, Ennis, Flagg, Fosdick, Gorlinski, Gaidry, Henderson, Hire, Howell, Knobloch, Kugler, Mann, Mayer, Newell, Payne J., Paine J. T., Purcell J., Pursell S., Schnurr, Seymour, Stauffer, Thorpe, Wenck, Wells, Wilson—34.

NAYS—Messrs. Abell, Balch, Beauvais, Bailey, Bell, Bofill, Buckley, Cook J. K., Cook T., Crozat, Dufresne, Flood, Foley, Fuller, Gastinel, Geier, Gruneberg, Harnan, Hart, Hills, Howes, Maas, Maurer, Montamat, Murphy E., Murphy M. W., Normand, O'Conner, Orr, Poynot, Schroeder, Smith, Stocker, Stumpf, Stiner, Sullivan, Terry, Waters—38.

[Cries of "no quorum!"]

Mr. HOWELL—I move a call of the House.

[The secretary was directed to call the roll.

[There being no quorum, the sergeant-at-arms was directed to bring in absent members. A quorum was announced after some delay.]

Mr. FOLEY—I move that the substitute be read and the vote retaken.

Mr. HILLS—I move as an amendment, that every member of the Convention be required to record his vote upon all of these questions relating to the police bill, when they shall come in.

PRESIDENT—The secretary will call the roll, to ascertain if there is a quorum present.

[A quorum was present.]

PRESIDENT—The question is on the adoption of Mr. Sullivan's substitute.

Mr. CUTLER—I move that a committee of three be appointed by the chair, to whom the whole subject shall be referred, both the original resolution, the amendments and the substitute, and that they report to-morrow the necessary article to be engrafted into the constitution.

Mr. SULLIVAN—I move to lay it on the table. Lost.

[The motion of Mr. Cutler was then carried.]

PRESIDENT — The chair appoints Messrs. Cutler, Abell and Sullivan on that committee.

[Article 37 was read and adopted :]

Art. 37. The Legislature may provide by law in what case officers shall continue to perform the duties of their offices until their successors shall have been inducted into office.

[Article 38 was read and adopted :]

Art. 38. The Legislature shall have power to extend this constitution and the jurisdiction of this State over any territory acquired by compact, with any State, or with the United States, the same being done by consent of the United States.

[Article 39 was read and adopted :]

Art. 39. None of the lands granted by Congress to the State of Louisiana for aiding in constructing the necessary levees and drains, to reclaim the swamp and overflowed lands in the State, shall be diverted from the purposes for which they were granted.

[Article 40 was read and adopted :]

Art. 40. The Legislature shall pass no law excluding citizens of this State from office for not being conversant with any language except that in which the constitution of the United States is written.

Mr. THORPE—As chairman of the committee appointed to wait upon Gens. Canby and Sickles, I submit the following :

The committee would respectfully report that they waited upon Maj. Gen. Canby and Maj. Gen. Sickles and represented the desire of the Convention to pay them a ceremonious visit.

The distinguished soldiers replied, in substance, that they felt deeply grateful for the compliment paid them by the members of the Louisiana Free State Convention, and instead of receiving a formal visit from the members of the Convention, that they would take an early opportunity of paying their personal respects to the honorable members of this Convention.

[The report was accepted.]

Mr. WILSON—In this connection I offer the following :

Resolved, That the president of this Convention be instructed to invite Maj. Gens. Canby and Sickles to visit this Convention.

Mr. HOWELL—I desire to offer the following additional articles to the report on general provisions :

Art. 41. No liability, either State, parochial or municipal, shall exist for any debts contracted for, or in the interest of the rebellion against the authority of the United States government.

Art. 42. The seat of government shall be and remain at New Orleans, and shall not be removed without the consent of two-thirds of both Houses of the General Assembly.

Art. 43. The Legislature may determine the mode of filling vacancies in all offices for which provision is not made in this constitution.

Mr. ABELL—I move to amend by striking out "three-fourths" and inserting "a majority."

Mr. HOWELL—I accept the amendment.

Mr. STAUFFER—I rise to a question of order. I offered some additional articles several weeks ago, which were adopted and printed, and I think they come first in order.

PRESIDENT—Out of time.

Mr. S. PURSELL—I submit the following substitute for the whole matter:

Art. 42. The seat of government shall be at the city of New Orleans. The General Asssmbly shall have powev to dispose of the present Capitol property in Baton Rouge and provide, by purchase or otherwise, suitable lands and buildings for a State Capitol in New Orleans.

Mr. CAZABAT—I move to amend by striking out "New Orleans" and inserting "parish of Jefferson."

Mr. WATERS—I move to lay the amendment on the table.

[Carried.]

Mr. GRUNEBERG—I move to lay the substitute on the table.

[Carried.]

Mr. STAUFFER—I offer the following as a substitute:

No debt created by or under the so-called Confederate States, or under the sanction of any usurping power, shall be recognized or paid.

Mr. WATERS—I move to lay it on the table.

Mr. SMITH—I wish to ask if the article covers the money issued by the parishes to meet the wants of the people; if so, I shall vote against it.

PRESIDENT—It covers all money issued under Confederate authority.

[The article was then adopted by a rising vote—ayes 44, noes 13.

Article 42, the second offered by Mr. Howell, was then taken up and adopted.

Article 43 was read and adopted.

On motion, the Convention then adjourned till 12 M., Tuesday, June 21st.]

TUESDAY, June 21, 1864.

[The Convention was called to order, pursuant to adjournment.

Present, Hon. E. H. Durell, president, in she chair, and the following members:]

Messrs. Abell, Austin, Bailey, Barrett, Baum, Beauvais, Bell, Bofill, Bromley, Buckley, Burke, Campbell, Cazabat, Collin, Cook J. K., Cook T., Crozat, Cutler, Davies, Decker, Dufresne, Duke, Dupaty, Edwards, Ennis, Fish, Flagg, Flood, Foley, Fosdick, Fuller, Gastinel, Geier, Gorlinski, Gruneberg, Gaidry, Healy, Harnan, Hart, Henderson, Hills, Hire, Howell, Howes, Kavanagh, Knobloch, Kugler, Maas, Mann, Maurer, Mayer, Mendiverri, Montamat, Morris, Murphy E., Murphy M. W., Newell, Normand, O'Conner, Orr, Payne J., Paine J. T., Poynot, Purcell J., Pursell S., Shaw, Schroeder, Schnurr, Seymour, Spellicy, Smith, Stocker, Stumpf, Stiner, Stauffer, Sullivan, Terry, Thorpe, Waters, Wenck, Wells, Wilson—83.

Absent—Messrs. Ariail, Bonzano, Brott, Duane, Heard, Lobdell, Millspaugh, Montague, Ong, (excused,) Pintado, (excused,) Taliaferro and Thomas.

[The minutes of yesterday were read and approved.

On motion of Mr. Cutler, Mr. Ong was excused for his absence on account of sickness.]

Mr. FOSDICK—I move the rules be suspended for the purpose of bringing up the resolution I offered on Saturday last.

Mr. HILLS—I second that motion.

Mr. CAZABAT—I move to lay it upon the table.

[On *viva voce* vote the rules were declared suspended; but on division called, the question was decided in the negative—ayes 14, nays 34.

On suspending the rules:]

YEAS — Messrs. Abell, Balch, Bailey, Baum, Bell, Bofill, Buckley, Campbell, Cook J. K., Cutler, Decker, Dufresne, Duke, Flagg, Flood, Fosdick, Gastinel, Gorlinski, Gruneberg, Healy, Hills, Knobloch, Maas, Maurer, Mendiverri, Murphy E., Newell, O'Conner, Orr, Poynot, Smith, Stauffer, Sullivan, Thorpe, Waters, Wenck, Wells, Wilson—38.

NAYS—Messrs. Beauvais, Bromley, Burke, Collin, Crozat, Davies, Dupaty, Edwards, Ennis, Fish, Foley, Fuller, Geier, Gaidry, Harnan, Hart, Henderson, Hire, Howell Howes, Kavanagh, Kugler, Mann, Mayer

Montamat, Morris, Murphy M.W., Normand, Payne J., Paine J. T., Purcell J., Pursell S., Schroeder, Schnurr, Seymour, Shaw, Spellicy, Stocker, Stumpf, Stiner, Terry—42.

Mr. TERRY—The committee appointed yesterday are ready to report in favor of an article to be inserted in the report of the Committee on General Provisions:

Believing that our mechanics, artizans of every grade, and laboring men are the most afflicted portion of our race; working for the most part under the most depressing circumstances, they live and have their being at a great disadvantage. Unless capricious fortune seems to smile especially upon their efforts, laboring people, in the present social disorder, are most likely to be kept down in the cesspool of poverty, simply by the antagonism between labor and capital. It is unspeakably difficult for a laboring man to earn enough to meet the current expenses of his family and at the same time avoid debt and dishonesty. If he does this in our city, he must forego every species of comforting luxury and all cultivated amusements. His disadvantages are very numerous. If he be a mechanic, there are, probably, certain months in each year when his services are not required. But his house rent and family expenses go on just the same as when his labor is in demand. The wealthy man can pay cash for his dry goods and groceries and can purchase them at wholesale prices, which gives him the advantage. But the poor man must buy in small quantities, must pay high interest for credit, and so lives at a perpetual loss. When he goes to the market he pays the butchers and stall-keepers fifty per cent. more than the original cost of the articles. When he goes to the grocer, he must defray the accumulated and combined profits upon tea, sugar, soap, molasses, etc.; first, of the producer; second, of the wholesale merchant; third, of the retailer. Here is a mass of profits which the consummer must pay, and he must work hard and live very economically to do it. Again, when he wants muslin, cloth, and calico for his family, he must pay sufficient *over* and *above* the actual cost and value of these fabrics originally, to support the manufacturer, the various second-handers and wholesale go-betweens, and lastly the retailer of whom the goods are purchased. Your committee believe this is *all wrong*, and the laboring classes—who produce all the wealth there is in the State—are the constant and only real sufferers under this system. To illustrate the injustice of this system, the manufacturer, the wholesale merchant, and the flourishing retailer, can live in $50,000 houses, environed with all the comforts and privileges thereof, the poor hard-working man and woman, with a large family of children to feed, clothe and edncate, are compelled to occupy uncomfortable rooms for which they pay a high rent and toil perpetually on, ofttimes without the least glimmering of a hope that their circumstances will ever improve. Your committee, knowing full well that all the multitudinous complications of the mercantile world must be supported, desire to show that between the producer and the consumer there now exist in all kinds of industry, numerous intermediates; these produce nothing, they add nothing valuable to the State, they serve as speculative go-betweens. But they must all be fed, clothed and enriched, and the mechanic and laboring classes must do it all. These must support all non-producers; not by direct taxation, but in this way: producers support non-producers by paying higher prices for everything they purchase, and by paying rents to landlords, who, out of it, pay the taxes. This popular speculating, this fashionable subsisting upon the labor of the mechanics and workingmen, is becoming well nigh intolerable. The homage that capital requires of labor is beginning to be insupportable and detestable. Some efficient plan must soon be instituted to relieve the poor man from his manifold oppressive disadvantages; to give him a fair and equal chance to enjoy his existence; to emancipate him from the mountainous interests and antagonisms that now oppress and keep him in bondage to poverty—therefore your committee, after carefully examining into the facts of your honorable petitioners, (though their request being a subject more appropriate for a legislative body) are in favor of granting their humble request, in order to enable your petitioners to devote a part of their time to domestic scenes and the cultivation of the mind, respectfully submit the following article to be inserted in report of general provisions:

Article —. Nine hours shall constitute a day's labor for all mechanics, artisans and laboring men employed on public works of the State and city.

J. RANDALL TERRY, Chairman.
GEORGE GEIER,
BENJAMIN H. ORR,
YOUNG BURKE,
P. K. O'CONNER,
J. A. STINER.

Mr. SCHROEDER—Mr. President, I wish to offer an additional article, and a memorial, upon which I base it.

[The secretary commenced reading the memorial.]

Mr. SULLIVAN—I believe this is out of order.

Mr. WATERS—I move to lay it on the table.

Mr. MONTAMAT—Memorials can only be offered on Saturday.

PRESIDENT—I believe this is out of order; I did not understand what it was or I should not have permitted the reading to be commenced. The secretary will return it to the gentleman.

Mr. SCHROEDER—Mr. President, I did not offer it as a memorial; I offered an additional article, and desired to have this read as showing my reasons for offering the article.

Mr. CUTLER—Mr. President, as chairman of the committee to whom was referred the subject of the police resolution, with Mr. Orr's amendment, I have a report to make; but before presenting it wish to make a few remarks. I am aware that much has been said and done in this Convention and outside in regard to the police bill. My original position was in favor of the police bill and against the amendment of my friend, Mr. Orr, but when that was adopted and the whole came up, I voted for the whole, although it was not in the form I desired to see it. I thought then that there was not too much in the bill for the wants of the present time, and I am of opinion now that no better bill could have been framed, save and except with a few alterations, which we have made, and which I hope will prove acceptable to this body and to the people of the city of New Orleans.

I am not one who is disposed to admit that this is an ordinary State convention, with ordinary powers only, and without powers of legislation. I have said, on this floor, and I repeat, that the powers of this Convention are not civil, in the proper acceptation of the term; but that they are quasi civil and quasi military; that we have powers vested in us never before vested in a constitutional convention of the State of Louisiana. The work of restoring the State to its proper position among the States of this Union devolves upon us. To do this, extraordinary powers were necessary, and it is our right to exercise them. But in the clause which we report I can see nothing repugnant to the constitution of 1852. If you will compare this with article 124 of that constitution you will find that the one is in harmony with the other. It has been objected that the constitution ought not to fix the salaries of the police, but that it should be left to the municipal legislative authorities. Well, we have thought best not to fix the salaries, but we have established the minimum rate of pay, leaving the maximum to be settled upon by the Legislature. I can see no objection to adding two or three clauses, which will redound to the honor and glory of the State, to the work of the Convention of 1852. I admit that it is not best as a rule to attempt to legislate, but there are exceptions; they have been acted on, and will be again, as I believe, for the good of the people. It is under these circumstances and with these views that we have modified somewhat the article on this subject in the constitution of 1852, and have added to it two or three clauses, which I desire to submit to this Convention. [Read:]

REPORT OF SPECIAL COMMITTEE ON ARTICLE NO. 36 OF THE REPORT OF THE COMMITTEE ON GENERAL PROVISIONS.

The citizens of the city of New Orleans shall have the right of appointing the several public officers necessary for the administration of the police of said city, pursuant to the mode of elections which shall be prescribed by the Legislature.

Provided that the mayor and recorders shall be ineligible to a seat in the General Assembly, and the mayor and recorder shall be commissioned by the governor as justices of the peace; and the Legislature may vest in them such criminal jurisdiction as may be necessary for the punishment of minor offences, and as the police and good order of said city may require.

And that the city of New Orleans shall maintain a police force which shall be uniformed with distinction of grade, to consist of permanent citizens of the State of Louisiana, to be selected by the mayor of the city, and to hold office during good behavior. and removable only by a police commission composed of five citizens, viz: one to be selected from each district of the city, and the mayor, who shall be president of the board. The commission to be appointed by the governor of the State for the term of two years, at a salary of not less than one thousand dollars each per annum; a majority of whom shall remove for delinquencies. Members of the police when removed, shall not again be eligible to any position on the the police for a term of one year.

Interfering or meddling in elections in

any manner will be a sufficient cause for instant dismissal from the police by the board.

The chief of police shall give a penal bond in the sum of ten thousand dollars; lieutenants of police, five thousand dollars; sergeants and clerks, each three thousand dollars; corporals, two thousand dollars, and privates one thousand dollars, with good and solvent security, as the law directs, for the faithful performance of their duties.

The various officers shall receive a salary of not less than the following rates:

The chief of police	$250	per month.
" lieutenants of police	150	" "
" sergeants of police	100	" "
" clerks of police	100	" "
" corporals of police	90	" "
" privates (day and night each)	80	" "

The Legislature may establish the price and pay of foremen, mechanics, laborers and others employed on the public works of the State or parochial or city governments.

R. King Cutler, Chairman,
John Sullivan,
E. Abell.

Now, whatever may be the opinion of the learned gentlemen on this floor in regard to any man's position, I want it distinctly understood that so far as I am concerned, that there is no political movement on my part in this. I believe it to be right. I have no other motive in presenting it than that it is right, and just, and necessary. And to convince you that I am not seeking police votes, I tell you that in the course of two weeks I expect to move out of the city of New Orleans to my residence in the parish of Jefferson. My conclusions on this question have only been reached after mature reflection and deliberation, and my only reason, as I have already said, for advocating the article is, that I believe it to be just, right and necessary. [Applause.]

Mr. Orr—I am astonished at this report, but more so by the fact that two such legal gentlemen as Mr. Cutler and Mr. Abell should have introduced such a report into this Convention. I do not think they have exhausted their duty under the resolution under which they were appointed. They were appointed for the sole purpose, as I understood, of placing these resolutions, which have already been adopted, in a more brief and concise form, and there has been no power delegated to them to take away or to add to them, and I contend that they are powerless to do anything of the kind. When the police bill was introduced this amendment of mine fixing the per diem of laborers on the public works was introduced, and the Convention refused, by a large majority, to table it, and it was carried. Afterwards a motion to reconsider it was made, and the Convention refused, by a large majority, to reconsider, and now we cannot reconsider. It is too late. It has already passed, and no part can be done away. I am, under these circumstances, astonished that any gentlemen, and particularly two such legal gentlemen as Mr. Abell and Mr. Cutler, should so far overlook their duties as to throw out one part and report another. They have been very careful in the wording of their report. "The Legislature *may*" do it. It does not say that they *shall*, but leaves it entirely optional with them. If they do not see proper to do it, they need not do it. But, on the contrary, in the police matter they do not leave it for the Legislature to decide upon the per diem. Now, I contend that if we have a right to legislate for the police, we have a right to legislate for the laboring men. Mr. Abell when he gets the floor spends the time and occupies the time of this Convention in advocating legislation for the benefit of the *poor* slaveholders, but is not willing to legislate for the benefit of the laboring men, who have lost a great many days' work on account of the rebellion brought about by these very slaveholders. Why should you legislate for the police and not for the laboring man? On what ground do you base your refusal to legislate for the laboring man? Is it because he is not as well dressed as the policemen? Is it because he wears a hickory shirt, or any other kind of shirt that he can get? You have adopted a judciary bill giving enormous salaries to judges. And the whole course of this Convention seems to show that they partake little of the sentiments of Burns when he wrote the following:

The rank is but the guinea-stamp—
The man's the goud for a' that.

They lay a great deal of stress on the bond which the policemen are bound to give.

Why, sir, that is nothing new; a provision exists already that a man shall give bond in order to get a position in the police; and in regard to the police interfering in elections, that law exists, and has existed, but has always been a dead letter, and I ask gentlemen to point out a single instance where it has ever been executed.

No, gentlemen, I am opposed to your thriving off the laborers; they have as many rights as the police, and as many claims upon this body as any other class. Far be it from me to complain of the increased pay of the police; I have no objections to it; but, gentlemen, I will never vote; I am not willing, for one, for one class to be benefited at the expense of another.

These gentlemen have no right—they have no power to rescind this resolution. They may refuse to incorporate it in this report on General Provisions, but it is a law—notwithstanding it is a resolution—adopted by this body and cannot be altered; and I am surprised that they should attempt to take off one portion of it—by so doing they run a risk of losing the whole. They cannot do away with one part and keep the other. If they keep any part of it they must keep the whole.

I never made any promises to the police, as the gentleman from the Fifth did, by pledging myself if elected to vote for an increase of their pay. I never made any such promises to the laborers. And I am simply acting on my own convictions of right and justice when I take the ground that the working man is as much entitled to legislative protection as the policeman.

If my position is not sustained; if the president of this Convention decides that they have a right to strike out my amendment from their report, I offer it again as an amendment to their report, viz:

Provided, That the compensation to be paid to all foremen, mechanics, cartmen and laborers employed on the public works under the government of the State of Louisiana, city of New Orleans and the police juries of the various parishes of the State, shall not be less than as follows, viz: foremen, $3 50 per day; mechanics, $3 00 per day; cartmen, $3 00 per day; laborers, $2 00.

My position is, that this has already passed and cannot be rescinded; and that this Convention has no power now to take away from it nor add to it, it having been added to and passed as an amendment to the police bill.

PRESIDENT—No police bill has passed this body. It was a mere resolution. The whole matter is now open to debate.

Mr. HENDERSON—Mr. President, the gentleman who has just taken his seat must be a very careless observer of the transactions of this body. He has gone all around the question. He has tacked to every point of the compass but the right one. It is true that this Convention passed a police resolution; but, sir, that is not the question. We have now come to that portion of the constitution which fixes the relations between the State of Louisiana and the city of New Orleans. We do not assume that this particular resolution is already a part and parcel of the constitution. A resolution was passed, and when the question came up here, the whole matter was referred to a special committee. That committee has reported. It has reported the police bill without material alteration, while the portion relating to the per diem of employés on the public works is so modified as to leave it to the discretion of the General Assembly to fix their compensation or not, as they see proper. The gentleman has no right to complain of this. I have as much right to complain as any one, because after fighting for six weeks for the appointment of judges for life-time, I was defeated.

Where, sir, is the necessity of fixing the wages of workmen by constitutional provision? Is it not going far enough to leave the matter open to legislative enactment? What more can gentlemen ask than these things be fixed by law, without engrafting such a provision as this in the organic law? We might as well fix the fees of the priest and the physician as to do this thing that the gentleman proposes. This Convention, it seems to me, has already gone far enough with legislation of a similar character. Why, sir, you have passed a law that no attorney shall be a witness in any case in which he may be employed; you might with equal consistency pass a law that every man who goes to church shall pay ten cents. I do not, however, see any harm, Mr. President, in referring the matter to the Legislature. As soon as that body meets, it can fix the salary, but I have never yet seen such legislation. I have never known the price of labor fixed, except by agreement with the authorities. The price contemplated may be too much by a hundred per cent., or there may be circumstances in which it would not be enough. If there was a great deal of work, and but few laborers, wages would be high. If, on the other hand, there was but little work and a great many laborers, they would be low.

The other day I was in favor of the gentleman's resolution because it was a mere resolution, imperative upon nobody, merely an expression of the opinion of seventy-eight gentlemen in this Convention. But, sir, when you come to make a constitution, and you insert in that instrument either an ordinance or a resolution you come to what properly belongs to this body in one respect and in another does not, because it belongs rather to the Legislature.

Now in regard to the police, if the Convention see fit to fix their salaries there can be no objection to it, for they are public officers. I believe that these matters should be left open for the city to pass her own laws in regard to what shall be the salaries of the officers and employés of the city, but if the Legislature shall see proper to fix them I have no objection. But if you say that they must be fixed by the constitution, I can only tell you that I do not think that the proper way.

The gentleman with his complaint forgets that the gentleman on my right has had a special report adopted on its second reading, and when it came up on its third reading it was rejected and an entirely different one passed by this House. He forgets the manner in which we finally got a judiciary report through. How after a month's debate the original report with amendments and substitutes finally passed on its second reading, and on its third reading was rejected and then referred to a new committee, and how when they reported their report was not taken up at all, but the substitute o another gentleman was adopted in its place.

Mr. SMITH—I want to ask one simple question. Is not a laborer on the public works as much in the employ of the city or the government as a state auditor, a state treasurer, or any other officer, and if he is why have we not the same power and the same right to regulate the price to be paid for the services of the one class as for the other? We have said that judges on the bench shall have seven thousand five hundred dollars per annum, and that the governor shall receive eight thousand dollars a year, for their services in the employ of the government. and we have just as good a right to say what compensation shall be paid to every other class of employés, and there would be just as much injustice in refusing to do it. As far, however, as the police is concerned, I take the ground that we have nothing to do with it, because it belongs under the charter to the city, and not to us nor to the Legislature.

Mr. CAZABAT—Although entirely opposed to this police bill as an article to be embodied in the constitution of the State, because it belongs properly to the Legislature, or rather to the City Council of New Orleans, since the matter is forced upon this Convention, and the majority seem determined to act upon it, I beg to offer the following substitute and amendment, in order to defeat it if possible:

Provided, That laborers employed on public works shall not be required to work more than nine hours per day, and will receive one hundred dollars per month; and provided also, that the salaries of the police will be, one hundred and twenty dollars per month for corporals and clerks, and one hundred dollars per month for night and day privates.

Mr. DAVIES—I offer an amendment: "That no person shall be eligible to serve on the police unless he has been a resident of this city five years, and that preference be given to heads of families."

Mr. ORR—I would call your attention to the enrollment of the resolution. It has been enrolled and bears the signature of the president of this Convention. If it is but a part of the proceedings of this Convention, the president had no right to sign it. It has passed beyond the power of this Convention to alter it.

Mr. HOWELL—I move to amend Mr. Davies' amendment by striking out "five" and inserting "two."

Mr. SULLIVAN—I move to lay Mr. Cazabat's amendment on the table.

[The ayes and nays were called, and the motion to table was carried.]

Mr. ABELL—Mr. President, I consider that the matter now before the Convention is one of the greatest importance, or, at least, of such importance as to deserve the entire consideration of this Convention. I believe that the city members generally know that this matter was mooted and agitated before the election of the delegates to this Convention. I will read you in evidence of that fact an extract from a hand bill, issued by myself, and read widely among the city members before the election, and received with the greatest approbation: "I advocate strenuously a permanent police organization for the metropolis, to consist of prominent citizens, of good character, to hold office during good behavior; the salaries never to be less than eighty dollars per month, and removable only by charges preferred by a committee appointed by the executive." And, Mr. President, I was elected, in a small district, by nearly four hundred votes over my antagonists, and with every man in the district having that in his hands. This doctrine was laid down before the election and was read in every district in the parish. I call upon the country members to hear me, when I tell them that for the last eleven years—since 1853—the great corporation of New Orleans has failed to perform the functions of protecting its citizens—it has failed to furnish protection to one hundred and twenty thousand citizens. The city has suffered from a system of police whose members have beaten down in the streets some of the best citizens. I claim to be but an humble citizen, but I have been attacked by more than one hundred for saying, in my good-humored way, that I believed a good man, though a foreigner, was as good as if native born. I say, then, that it is important to you—to the honor of the State—to the rights of every man within my hearing, that we should have a permanent police, to consist of respectable men. It was objected to by Mr. Orr because it did not include all the poor men. Has the gentleman been engaged in overseeing men, or had anything to do with them? I say, sir, when I hear a man boasting of his christianity, I doubt it; when I see a man stamp on this or any floor and there talk so much for the poor man—for every other word is the "*poor*" man—I doubt his real feeling for that man. When you hear a man talking about his honesty, doubt that honesty.

Mr. ORR—I call the gentleman to order.

PRESIDENT—The gentleman is in order.

Mr. ABELL—The gentleman has seen proper here, on more than one occasion, to state to this body some of the misfortunes of the *poor* man. O, the poor man! He had only fifty cents a day, etc. Now, Mr. Hills, will you read this resolution, as I cannot read very well when excited.

[Mr. Hills read a report of the Finance Committee, showing what was the pay of laborers, and the rations that they received at the same time.]

Mr. ABELL—The gentleman (Mr. Orr) did not see proper to tell us that these men had rations in addition to their pay, which at that time cost a high price. He forgot that in his zeal for the *poor* man. The poor man!

I say there is not a gentleman on this floor—and I appeal to every man here that knows me personally—who is more kindly disposed, to the extent of his ablity, to the poor man, or who is willing to do more for him. But when I hear a man boast of his christianity, I doubt that he has a spark of it; and when I hear a man boasting of being the poor man's friend, I doubt if he would not cheat him to-morrow. [Great applause.] I doubt if he would not cheat the poor man to-morrow. I have spared you, my friend, as long as I could.

We have tendered here by the committee what I term a decent police bill. We might go on *ad infinitum* and fix the payment for all classes of mechanics, workmen, etc., and no one would doubt our power to do so, but sensible men doubt the *policy* of such things. We have made what we consider a protection for the rights of the corporation of the city of New Orleans, and have made a respectable bill.

Speaking of Mr. Orr and his *poor men*, why did he not tell what the *poor* shoemakers shall have? The burden of his song is the *poor*, POOR men! We have now a fair bill, that every man here can submit to his constituents—a bill that, unless it is passed, the action of this Convention will never be ratified. I have no interest in the police—they have been my friends. I have opposed their rascality, and they know it, and I will oppose rascality in anybody.

This is a subject upon which I could speak all day, but I am going to stop, because I believe that this Convention feels it its duty to provide for the protection of this great metropolis, and pass a bill by which the police will be no longer a mere means of traffic for the mayor. I will refer to a fact which I have already used. Just before the election, every policeman had to swear positively to support those in power. Without this pledge the parties would be kicked out before the election. There are between two thousand and three thousand voters, ignorant but honest men, who believe what these office-seekers tell them when they are promised offices in return for their support. I am told that a single office has been promised to as many as fifty voters. Many of these disappointed persons have come to me, after the election, to obtain redress. These were *poor* men, as my friend Mr. Orr says, and they hoped to obtain places to earn bread for themselves and their families, and many of them, thus beguiled and disheartened, were ruined. We have offered you a bill that we say will unquestionably relieve this great evil, and is one that you will not be ashamed of. In my humble opinion, I consider it one that will do credit to this body, credit to the constitution, and do much to ensure its acceptance by the people. There are some things I would have liked to have cut off, and some things abridged even more, but we have submitted it, and I ask you in the name of the people—of their safety—to adopt it. [Applause.]

Mr. WILSON—Mr. President, I have been entirely opposed to the regulating of any salary for the police. We might as well regulate the salaries of all workingmen in the city or fix a tariff for professional services. The compensation of men in the trades and professions depends on individual exertion. A man must depend upon himself and by his own energy qualify himself, to excel in his particular sphere, and there will be no necessity of fixing his compensation by law. He will always command sufficient remuneration for superior services, and it would be unfair to limit him by law to a compensation fixed at a uniform rate for workmen of the same trade, but not equally well skilled.

With regard to the police of New Orleans, I am sorry to say, that since I have been in the city, I have found them to be exponents of the party in power; I have seldom seen one who had any polical views of his own. There are a few—a very few—who take a position on the police, because they cannot get other employment whereby they can support their families. The majority of the policemen are men who are not disposed to work hard, and have obtained their situations for past political services. It may be thought that I observe these things from a narrow point of view, but my experience for the last ten years, I think, warrants the conclusions to which I have come.

Now, if we fix the compensation of the police, we shall find that it will have a tendency to destroy the energy of the poor man. Such is the effect of fixing the salary for any business: men seek for position, and obtaining it, with fixed salaries, there is no incentive for advancement or improvement. If we go to work and say that mechanics shall receive only a certain fixed price, we take from the laborer his right to dictate his own terms. There is another peculiarity about this police and labor bill: it is brought forward and upheld almost entirely by parties holding some position in the state or city government. I cannot name one of its supporters outside of that class of persons. I would like to see some of its advocates who do not hold some such position. Show me the man who is loudest in his laudations of the working-man, and I will convince you that he has the engagement of the carts used by the city. Show me the man who advocates the rights of poor men—who knows none but poor men—and I will show you a man holding a fat position in the city government. A man who, if he had to pay workmen for services out of his own pocket, would sing an entirely different song.

Mr. ORR—My remarks upon laboring men seem to have stirred up a hornet's nest among these gentlemen, some of whom appear to be pretty badly stung. They are smarting under the lash inflicted upon their guilty consciences! I would say to them in the language of scripture, "the laborer is worthy of his hire," [applause] and I intend to apply it in this manner to the gentleman from the Fifth, (Mr. Abell.) He promised policemen that if they would vote for him he would look out for them, although when he used that circular he was upon the citizens' ticket; but finding there was a fair show, by some hocus pocus contrived to get on the free State ticket. [Laughter and applause.] I say the laborer is worthy of his hire, but the gentleman has seen fit to advocate the police bill at the expense of the laboring community.

Gentlemen have seen fit to go into personalities on this floor, who are possibly ignorant of this matter, and as I believe have been egged on by others. They have charged me with accepting bribes, levying black-mail, &c.

Mr. ABELL—*I* never did.

Mr. ORR—I say all these charges are not only false and libelous, but that I defy them to prove those charges. The gentleman from the Fifth has made a great outcry, and at the end of every sentence has referred to me as advocating the cause of the "POOR MAN." He, at the time that the emancipation act was before this House, made a three days' speech, and at the close of every sentence put the "POOR SLAVEHOLDER,"—the very species of man who did more to bring about this horrible rebellion than all the "poor men" in this country, and yet the gentleman said that these *old* and respectable gentlemen, who by this war have been dragged down from an eminent position, as far as regards riches, &c., and are now "POOR SLAVEHOLDERS," and goes in for taxing the people of this State, goes in for taxing the laboring class, goes in for taxing the mechanic and the very men whose cause he pretends to advocate, the policemen, in order that the "POOR SLAVEHOLDER" may be remunerated for his labor. [Enthusiastic applause.] He was opposed to emancipation unless he could get compensation for these "POOR SLAVEHOLDERS." The gentleman opposed also the charity bill—a bill brought in for the purpose of furnishing relief to the starving children who are in the orphan asylum of this State, on the ground that this Convention had no right to legislate upon it, and yet he comes in here and proposes to legislate for the police officers of this State!

The gentleman says that when he sees a person advocate a point strenuously, he is inclined to doubt the sincerity of that person; then I say the gentleman could not have been sincere in all he said on the slavery question. He is a political weathercock, shifting wherever the wind may blow him!

The gentleman said he never expected to hold an office again. I don't expect he will, and think he has damned himself politically while in this Convention, by opposing the destruction of slavery, and seeking to fix upon the people of this State the compensation of slaveholders.

Another gentleman (Mr. Wilson) has declared that the laboring man or mechanic can always find enough to do, and is always independent of any city or State. Under some circumstances such is the case certainly. This amendment of mine is couched in such a form as to apply to none but laborers on the public works, and the intention is not to have it apply to all laborers throughout the State. I contend that if we have a right to legislate for police officers and fix their salaries, we have a right to legislate in relation to and fix the salaries of any employés of this State, as much for the laboring men as for any one else.

The same gentleman has said that the adoption of my proposed measure will detract from the efficiency of laborers on the public works. You fix the salaries of governor, judges, etc., but say nothing about the giving them large salaries as tending to prove injurious to them. It is only when the "poor man" is brought in question that that view of the question is taken. When they take up the "poor man" they view him through two or three concave lenses, and endeavor to reduce him and try to diminish him to the least possible point they can; but when they come to rich men, they put on a convex lens and magnify everything that appertains to them, as was the case with Mr. Abell in regard to the "POOR SLAVEHOLDERS." He has endeavored to magnify them into loyal men, and to make us believe that they deserve the charity of the State and government. I say that if *they* are deserving of charity, the poor men employed on the public works of this city and State are entitled to receive a fair compensation for their work.

The gentleman from the Fifth introduced something in relation to the surveyor being allowed to employ men at fifty cents a day and rations. I am aware of that, and do not blame either the surveyor or government; but the rations that were drawn were not half enough for the employés themselves, let alone their families. [A voice, "That is so."] At the time I spoke of, when the governor had orders to employ those men, no rations were given, and they were paid by the city, out of the city treasury, and the officers even then wished to cut that down, and said that the laborers ought to live on twenty-five cents a day! Dr. Ames was one of those men and S—— was another.

I have tired you, gentlemen, long enough. I am sorry to see any trouble about this matter, to have any personalities introduced, but I consider it my right and duty to vindicate myself. With these additional remarks, I take leave of the Convention, and recommend the gentleman from the Fifth to the consideration of his "LOYAL SLAVEHOLDERS."

Mr. ABELL—Mr. President, I should rather judge from the course of his argument that he is a "backsliding preacher." I do not say he *is*, but should *rather* judge so. I would not have risen to answer him except for one thing, which is, that he drags in here a great question. I never contended that the slaveholder was a "poor man," but stated a great principle of right. I *never* contended for the "poor man;" *never* placed my argument on that ground, as my speeches which are before the country will show, while I *did* contend that no man could legally or constitutionally divest even a slaveholder of his property. *That* is my doctrine. I repel the assertion that I placed my argument on that ground. I am *not* opposed to poor men. I have already stated that it is necessary, in my opinion, for us to have a permanent police in this city. I am not here to advocate myself, and do not care if I am attacked by every member of this Convention. I stand upon what I believe to be principle, and those who know me will bear me out; but I contend that it is necessary for the protection of New Orleans and for the good of the people to fix the police upon a stable foundation.

Mr. President, this bill is not the work of to-day, and I have advocated the principle for the last twelve years. I assert that there is not a man more attached to the real interest of the working men than I am; but, sir, I say that if you adopt our bill you will give a respectable footing to our city force. I am willing, as far as the police are concerned, to do well by them, but I look at the great interest of the people. The police have to stand on their feet all day and watch all night for the protection of the people, but it is for the great corporation of New Orleans that I speak and not merely for the "poor man." It is for the good of the commonwealth that I stand here to-day and beseech you in its behalf that the police should be established on a firm and stable foundation, that your lives and property may be protected, and that order may reign throughout the State.

Mr. STOCKER—Mr. President, I desire to say but a few words. There is one part of the report of the special committee that meets my approbation; and there is another portion that meets my condemnation. I am in favor of that part which fixes the salaries of the police; but in order to gain the vote of this Convention to carry that, they cover up that which refers to the laboring men and refer it to the Legislature. That meets my condemnation. I am in favor of the policemen having sufficient pay, but I am also in favor of the laboring men being sufficiently paid, and I do not like this way of playing fair on one side and dark on the other. It has been said it should be left to the Legislature. If so, why not leave the whole matter to the Legislature? why call upon the Convention to say that policemen occupy a superior position to the laboring men? I am not willing to concede that; for I believe that both occupy the same position with myself and you, Mr. President. If one is recognized then the other must be; and if the case of one is left to the Legislature, the other must be also. Mr. Abell, in speaking of his circular, is mistaken in regard to the First District. He said his address was read and approved everywhere; but so far as the First District is concerned, we never heard of it until he came into this Convention. My colleagues will corroborate me in this statement. Mr. Abell says he never came down to the poor man. If he did not come down to the poor men, the poor men came down to him, or he never would have been here. Sixteen times, as I have counted, and Heaven only knows how many more, he has made use of the word "necessary," and all directed against the laboring man. I have no doubt he owes his election to the police, from the tenor of his remarks. Understand me, I am in favor of the police; but I am opposed to their monopolizing the attention of the Convention and receiving all the benefit of our action in this direction. As I see there is a distinguished gentleman desirous of saying something on this question, I will give way for him.

Mr. Poynot—I will not detain you long, but beg your attention for a few minutes. I am one of the defenders of the police bill, and am willing to make sacrifices to ensure its adoption. It must go through, but at the same time I wish you to understand that the laborers' bill must go through with it. [Applause.] I say the laborers' bill must go through with it, because if we have a right to legislate for the police—which I believe we have—we have a right to legislate for poorer men still. [Applause.] I prefer to defend the poor man—not the rich man—and hope the poor man will prevail.

[A motion was made to adjourn.]

Mr. Poynot—I will yield the floor for a motion to adjourn.

[The motion was not put.]

Mr. Poynot—I give the floor to Mr. Cutler, who has the closing of the debate.

Mr. Wells—I moved to adjourn, and the motion was seconded.

Mr. Cutler—As chairman of the committee, I have a right to close the debate, but if the Convention desire I will give way for a motion to adjourn.

[The motion was lost.]

Mr. Poynot—I claim the floor. I yielded it to Mr. Cutler.

Mr. Smith—I ask the floor for the purpose of disabusing the minds of some members of this Convention of the statement made in the arguments on this question in regard to mechanics, etc. I wish to say that this bill of Mr. Orr's applies only to men employed on *public* works. I wish it distinctly understood, for the idea has gone abroad that it cuts off honorable competition, because the pay is fixed and there is no incentive to energetic action.

Mr. Austin—I rise to a point of order. Mr. Cutler has the floor.

Mr. Poynot—I claim the floor, since it was only yielded to Mr. Cutler.

Mr. Cutler—I gave the floor to Mr. Smith, because as chairman of the committee I have a right to close the debate.

President—Are you ready to close the debate?

Mr. Cutler—I have yielded the floor to Mr. Smith.

Mr. Poynot—I yielded the floor only to Mr. Cutler.

Mr. Smith—I only wished to have it distinctly understood that the bill only refers to men employed by the State, and not to mechanics and laborers generally.

Mr. Poynot—I move we adjourn.

Mr. Cutler—I yield the floor to Mr. Harnan.

Mr. Harnan—I have only a few words to say. We have a right to legislate for a police for the State and fix their salaries, but no more right to legislate for this corporation than for Baton Bouge and other places. If you form a State police, then let there be inspectors to take charge of the whole State.

Mr. Austin—The gentleman who occupied the chair in the temporary absence of the President permitted Mr. Cutler to go on with his remarks, and I now ask that he proceed.

Mr. Cutler—I am on the floor.

Mr. Poynot—I yielded the floor to Mr. Cutler and nobody else.

Mr. Stauffer—I have a right to say something before Mr. Cutler closes the debate, and I insist upon it. Every member has a right to speak on the question.

President—I must express my astonishment with regard to this order of the proceedings of this day. I have called some six persons to the chair to-day, understanding that I was considered somewhat severe, and I have found as I have called them indiscriminately and honestly to preside over you, at the moment I did so, you became disorderly. This matter I do not understand. Gentlemen should have respect for themselves and keep order. As far as I am concerned, there is no member of this Convention who shall not have his rights in debate, but he must have it under the strict parliamentary rules—that is the only way to do business. The reporter of the substitute for article 36 has a right to close the debate, and he has given that right to you, to a large extent, but there is a limit to it. He now claims his right and it belongs to him under all parliamentary rules, and I shall most assuredly give it to him unless I am overruled by a vote of two-thirds of the Convention. Mr. Cutler, you have a right to close the debate.

Mr. Stauffer—I contend, sir, that he has not, until every man has been heard. I appeal from the decision of the chair.

Mr. Henderson—I move a call of the House; there is no quorum.

[The secretary was directed to call the roll.]

Mr. Cutler—Will you allow me one word?

President—No, sir.

[The roll was called.]

President—We have 72 members present. There is no quorum.

Mr. Fosdick—I move we adjourn.

[The motion prevailed, and the Convention adjourned till 12 M. Wednesday, June 22.]

Wednesday, June 22, 1864.

[The Convention met pursuant to adjournment, and was called to order by the president.

The roll was called and the following members answered to their names:]

Messrs. Abell, Austin, Balch, Bailey, Barrett, Baum, Beauvais, Bell, Bofill, Bromley, Buckley, Burke, Campbell, Collin, Cook J. K., Cook T., Crozat, Cutler, Davies, Decker, Duane, Dufresne, Duke, Dupaty, Edwards, Ennis, Fish, Flagg, Flood, Foley, Fosdick, Fuller, Gastinel, Geier, Gorlinski, Gruneberg, Gaidry, Healy, Harnan, Hart, Henderson, Hills, Hire, Howell, Howes, Kavanagh, Knobloch, Kugler, Maas, Mann, Mayer, Maurer, Mendiverri, Montamat, Morris, Murphy E., Murphy M. W., Newell, Normand, O'Conner, Orr, Payne J., Paine J. T., Pintado, Poynot, Purcell J., Pursell S., Scroeder, Schnurr, Seymour, Shaw, Smith, Spellicy, Stocker, Stumpf, Stiner, Stauffer, Sullivan, Terry, Thorpe, Waters, Wenck, Wells, Wilson—85.

Absent—Messrs. Ariail, Bennie, Bonzano, Brott, Cazabat, Heard, Lobdell, Millspaugh, Montague, Ong, (excused,) Taliaferro and Thomas.

[The minutes of yesterday were read and adopted.]

President—The order of the day is the report of the Special Committee on article 36 of the report of the committee on General Provisions, with amendments. The last amendment offered will be taken up first. Mr. Secretary read Mr. Davies' amendment.

[The secretary read:]

"That no person shall be eligible to serve on the police of this city who has not been a resident thereof at least two years previous to his appointment; and that preference shall be given in all cases to heads of families to serve as policemen."

Mr. Waters—I move to lay that on the table.

[The motion was lost.]

Mr. Howes—I move to amend by inserting, "five" years in place of "two."

[The motion was carried.]

A *viva voce* vote on Mr. Davies' amendment left the matter indeterminate, when on a rising vote, it was adopted—ayes 32, nays 18.

[The article reported by the Special Committee was then adopted as amended.]

Mr. ORR—I move a reconsideration.

Mr. CUTLER—What has become of the amendment of the gentleman from the tenth? [Mr. Orr.]

PRESIDENT—I consider that the adoption of the last amendment throws out all before it.

On reconsideration:

YEAS—Messrs. Balch, Barrett, Buckley, Bell, Cook J. K., Cook T., Decker, Duane, Dufresne, Edwards, Ennis, Flagg, Fish, Flood, Foley, Fosdick, Geier, Gorlinski, Gaidry, Healy, Hart, Hills, Hire, Maas, Mann, Maurer, Mayer, Montamat, Morris, Murphy E., Newell, Normand, O'Conner, Orr, Payne J., Poynot, Pursell S., Schroeder, Seymour, Shaw, Smith, Spellicy, Stocker, Stauffer, Terry, Thorpe, Waters, Wenck —48.

NAYS—Messrs. Abell, Austin, Beauvais, Bailey, Baum, Bofill, Bromley, Burke, Collin, Campbell, Crozat, Cutler, Davies, Duke, Dupaty, Gastinel, Gruneberg, Harnan, Henderson, Howell, Howes, Kavanagh. Knobloch, Kugler, Mendiverri, Murphy M. W., Paine J. T., Purcell J., Schnurr, Stumpf, Stiner, Sullivan, Wells, Wilson—34.

Mr. Davies' amendment was accordingly reconsidered.

PRESIDENT—Mr. Davies' amendment is now before the House again.

Mr. FOLEY—I move to amend by inserting, "and that he be a citizen of the United States."

Mr. STAUFFER—He cannot be a citizen of the State, without being a citizen of the United States. The article provides that he shall have been a citizen of the State five years.

Mr. STOCKER—I ask to have the article read. I believe it provides that he shall have been a resident of the State for five years. A man may be a resident, and not a citizen.

Mr. ORR—I ask if this amendment will prevent action on the amendments which precede it, if it is adopted?

PRESIDENT, [Mr. Howell]-It only prevents action on amendments on the same subject.

Mr. SMITH—I wish to ask, for information, if this amendment will, if passed, have the effect of removing from the police men now on it who have not been residents of the city for five years? I know some deserving men now on it—refugees whom I should dislike very much to see removed.

[The motion to lay on the table was lost.]

Mr. HILLS—Mr. President, as I am not a candidate for office on the police, although I may be termed a new-comer, I will say that I look upon that amendment as very unjust. I think that it is a sufficient qualification for a man to be a citizen of the State of Louisiana, and of the United States. I think that is the proper qualification. I therefore move to strike out five years and insert "citizen of Louisiana."

PRESIDENT, [Mr. Howell]—The question is out of order, because there is a motion pending.

Mr. STAUFFER—I wish to show the inconsistency of the amendment proposed by Mr. Foley, that a man should reside five years in the State.

Mr. FOLEY—I beg leave to correct the gentleman. That is not my motion.

Mr. STAUFFER—There is such an amendment before the House. I think that it was offered by Mr. Foley.

Mr. FOLEY—No, it was Mr. Davies. Mine was that they be citizens of the United States.

Mr. STAUFFER—We have passed an article here which says that any citizen of the United States who has been a resident of the State for one year, and of the parish six months, is eligible to the General Assembly. Now you wish to introduce a clause here that men must reside in the State five years before he can go on the police. Suppose one of our soldiers, who had been fighting for us for three years, should be a candidate for a position on the police.

Mr. FOLEY—I call the gentleman to order He is not speaking to my amendment.

Mr. STAUFFER—I think this, as it now stands, is an outrage; but I would be willing to accept it if the words five years were stricken out.

Mr. WELLS—I move to lay the whole subject on the table.

[The motion was lost.]

Mr. THORPE—I have an amendment to offer to the amendment as follows:

"No man shall be appointed on the police who has been mustered into the rebel army."

[The ayes and noes were called on the amendment.]

Mr. FOLEY—I wish to explain my vote. I believe there has been as good Union men mustered into the rebel army as there is in this city. Therefore I shall vote yes.

Mr. HEALY—I think I am as good as any other man, and I shall vote yes.

Mr. CROZAT—I wish to change my vote from no to yes.

Mr. TERRY—Owing to the rainy weather, I wish to change my vote from yes to no.

Mr. MANN—I change my vote from no to yes.

The vote resulted as follows:

YEAS—Messrs. Abell, Austin, Balch, Barrett, Baum, Bell, Bofill, Buckley, Cook T., Cutler, Decker, Duane, Dufresne, Edwards, Fish, Foley, Fosdick, Fuller, Gastinel, Geir, Gruneberg, Healy, Hart, Henderson, Howell, Kavanagh, Knobloch, Kugler, Mann, Mayer, Mendiverri, Montamat, Murphy E., Murphy M. W., Normand, O'Conner, Orr, Poynot, Purcell J., Schroeder, Schnurr, Seymour, Shaw, Spellicy, Stocker, Stumpf, Stiner, Sullivan, Waters, Wilson—50.

NAYS—Messrs. Bailey, Beauvais, Bromley, Burke, Campbell, Collin, Cook J. K., Crozat, Davies, Duke, Dupaty, Ennis, Flagg, Flood, Gorlinski, Gaidry, Harnan, Hills, Howes, Maurer, Morris, Newell, Payne J., Paine J. T., Pursell S. Smith, Stauffer, Terry, Thorpe, Wenck, Wells—31.

[The motion to lay on the table was carried.]

Mr. SPELLICY—I move to lay Mr. Davies' amendment on the table.

[The motion was carried.]

The secretary then read Mr. Cazabat's amendment:]

Provided, That laborers working on public works shall not be required to work more than nine hours per day, and will receive one hundred dollars per month; and provided also, that the salaries of the police will be one hundred and twenty dollars per month for corporals and clerks, and one hundred dollars per month for (night and day) privates.

Mr. SULLIVAN—I move to lay it on the table.

[The motion was carried.

The secretary read Mr. Orr's amendment:]

Provided, That the compensation to be paid to all foremen, mechanics, cartmen and laborers employed on the public works under the government of the State of Louisiana, city of New Orleans, and the police juries of the various parishes of the State, shall not be less than as follows, viz: foremen, $3 50 per day; mechanics, $3 00 per day; cartmen, $3 00 per day; laborers, $2 00 per day.

Mr. HEALY—I move its adoption.

Mr. MONTAMAT—I move to lay it on the table.

[The ayes and noes were called.]

Mr. FOLEY—Mr. President, there are members of this Convention who make it a business to leave whenever a vote is being taken. I protest against members leaving.

Mr. HILLS—I move that members now absent be required to record their votes on these questions in the morning, or whenever they appear.

Mr. SULLIVAN—I move to lay that motion on the table. I want no electioneering outside of this Convention.

[The following is the result of the vote:]

YEAS — Messrs. Abell, Austin, Balch, Bailey, Beauvais, Bofill, Bromley, Burke, Campbell, Crozat, Cutler, Duke, Edwards, Gruneberg, Gaidry, Henderson, Howell, Kavanagh, Mayer, Mendiverri, Murphy M. W., Newell, Shaw, Wenck, Wells, Wilson—26.

NAYS—Messrs. Barrett, Baum, Bell, Buckley, Collin, Cook J. K., Cook T., Davies, Decker, Duane, Dufresne, Dupaty, Ennis, Fish, Flagg, Flood, Foley, Fosdick, Fuller, Gastinel, Geier, Gorlinski, Healy, Harnan, Hart, Hills, Hire, Howes, Knobloch, Kugler, Maas, Mann, Maurer, Montamat, Morris, Murphy E., Normand, O'Conner, Orr, Payne J., Paine J. T., Poynot, Purcell J., Pursell S., Schroeder, Schnurr, Seymour, Smith, Spellicy, Stocker, Stumpf, Stiner, Stauffer, Sullivan, Terry, Waters—56.

[The motion to table was lost.]

Mr. TERRY—I move the adoption of the amendment.

[The ayes and noes were called with the following result:]

YEAS — Messrs. Abell, Balch, Barrett, Baum, Bell, Bromley, Buckley, Collin, Cook J. K., Cook T., Davies, Decker, Duane, Dufresne, Duke, Dupaty, Ennis, Fish, Flagg, Flood, Foley, Fosdick, Fuller, Gastinel, Geier, Gorlinski, Gaidry, Healy, Harnan, Hart, Henderson, Hills, Hire, Howes, Knobloch, Kugler, Maas, Mann, Maurer, Montamat, Morris, Murphy E., Murphy M. W., Normand, O'Conner, Orr, Payne J., Poynot, Purcell J., Pursell S., Schroeder, Schnurr, Seymour, Smith, Spellicy, Stocker, Stumpf, Stiner, Stauffer, Sullivan, Terry, Waters—62.

NAYS—Messrs. Austin, Bailey, Beauvais, Bofill, Burke, Campbell, Crozat, Cutler, Edwards, Gruneberg, Howell, Kavanagh, Mayer, Mendiverri, Newell, Paine J. T., Shaw, Wenck, Wells, Wilson—20.

PRESIDENT—The question now is on the adoption of the report of the Special Committee on Art. 35, as amended.

[The yeas and nays were ordered and the report adopted as follows :]

YEAS—Messrs. Abell, Balch, Barrett, Bell, Baum, Buckley, Cook T., Cook J. K., Crozat, Decker, Duane, Dufresne, Fish, Flood, Foley, Fuller, Gastinel, Geier, Gorlinski, Healy, Harnan, Hart, Henderson, Hills, Hire, Howes, Kavanagh, Kugler, Maurer, Maas, Mendiverri, Montamat, Murphy E., Murphy M. W., Normand, O'Conner, Orr, Poynot, Purcell J., Schroeder, Schnurr, Smith, Spellicy, Stocker, Stumpf, Stiner, Sullivan, Terry, Waters—50.

NAYS—Messrs. Bailey, Beauvais, Burke, Campbell, Collin, Cutler, Davies, Duke, Dupaty, Ennis, Flagg, Fosdick, Gruneberg, Gaidry, Howell, Knobloch, Mann, Mayer, Morris, Newell, Payne J., Paine J. T., Pursell S., Seymour, Shaw, Stauffer, Wenck, Wells, Wilson—31.

PRESIDENT—The question now is on the adoption of the report on General Provisions as a whole as amended.

[The report was adopted by a *viva voce* vote.]

Mr. HILLS—I move to suspend the rules for the purpose of putting the bill on General Provisions on its third reading.

[The motion was lost : yeas, 49.]

Mr. CUTLER—I rise for information in regard to another subject. I wish to know who are the members of the special committee to whom was referred the auditor's report, and what disposition they have made in the matter, in order to have it come up before the Convention in time.

PRESIDENT—The order of the day is the report of the Committee on Internal Improvements—second reading.

[The secretary read the following report:]

REPORT OF THE COMMITTEE ON INTERNAL IMPROVEMENTS.

To the president and members of the Convention for the revision and amendment of the constitution of the State of Louisiana:

The undersigned, members of the Committee on Internal Improvements, have the honor to submit the following :

Art. —. There shall be appointed by the governor a state engineer skilled in theory and practice of his profession, who shall hold his office at the seat of government for the term of four years, and shall have the superintendence and direction of all public works in which the State may be interested, except those made by joint stock companies, or such which may be under the parochial authorities exclusively and not in conflict with the general laws of the State. He shall communicate to the General Assembly, from time to time, his views concerning the same, recommend such measures as in his opinion the public interest of the State may require, and shall perform such other duties as may be prescribed by law. His salary shall be fixed by the General Assembly. He shall appoint a secretary, and all officers engaged on public works, the number and salary of which shall be fixed by law.

Art. —. The General Assembly may create such internal improvement districts, composed of one or more parishes, and may grant the right to the citizens thereof, to tax themselves for their improvements. They shall have right to appoint commissioners and other officers to fix the pay and regulate all matters relative to the improvements of their districts, provided such improvements will not conflict with the general laws of the State.

Art. —. The General Assembly may grant aid to said districts out of the funds arising from the swamp and overflowed lands granted to the State by the United States, for that purpose or otherwise.

Art. —. The General Assembly shall have the right of abolishing the office of state engineer, by a two-thirds vote of all the members elected to each branch, and substitute such other board of public works as the General Assembly may deem it necessary.

Respectfully submitted,

JOS. GORLINSKI, Chairman.
M. R. ARIAIL,
J. J. HEALY,
EDMOND FLOOD.

[The following minority report was then read :]

MINORITY REPORT OF THE COMMITTEE ON INTERNAL IMPROVEMENTS.

To the honorable president and members of the Constitutional Convention:

GENTLEMEN : A minority of your committee, to whom was referred that part o the constitution relative to internal improvements, beg leave respectfully to report: That,

Art. 1. The Legislature shall establish a board of public works, when necessary for the State at large, to represent the interest of the State in all works of public improvements in which the State is concerned, fix the pay of officers, provide for their dismissal for neglect of duty, and require them to report to the General Assembly, from time to time, the condition of all public works in which the State at large is interested, recommend changes, &c.

Art. 2. The Legislature may create other internal improvement districts of one or more parishes, and may grant the right to the citizens thereof to tax themselves for the purpose of their improvements. They shall have the right to appoint commissioners, and other officers, to fix the pay, and regulate all matters relative to the improvements of their districts; provided said improvements will not conflict with the general laws of the State at large.

Sec. I. The Legislature may grant aid to said districts from the fund arising from the swamp or overflowed land granted to the State by the United States for that purpose, or otherwise.

Sec. II. All appropriations made by the State for the benefit of a district internal improvements, shall be paid to the police jury, (the city of New Orleans excepted), or juries of the parish, or parishes comprising a district; and shall be bound in such terms as the Legislature may direct, for the faithful performance of their duties.

Sec. III. The city of New Orleans shall compose one internal improvement district, and all appropriations made for that purpose, shall be paid into the treasury of the city of New Orleans.

B. Campbell.

Mr. Terry—Mr. President, I offer the following as a substitute for both reports:

Art. 1. There shall be appointed by the governor a state engineer, skilled in the theory and practice of his profession, who shall hold his office at the seat of government for the term of four years; he shall have the superintendence and direction of all public works in which the State may be interested, except those made by joint stock companies, or such which may be under the parochial or city authorities exclusively, and not in conflict with the general laws of the State. He shall communicate to the General Assembly through the governor, annually, his views concerning the same, report upon the condition of the public works in progress, recommend such measures as in his opinion the public interest of the State may require, and shall perform such other duties as may be prescribed by law. His salary shall be four thousand dollars per annum. The state engineer and each of his officers to give bonds for the performance of their duties, as may be prescribed by law.

Art. 2. The General Assembly may create internal improvement districts, composed of one or more parishes, and may grant the right to the citizens thereof to tax themselves for their improvements. Said internal improvement districts, when created, shall have the right to elect commissioners, shall have power to appoint officers, fix their pay and regulate all matters relative to the improvements of their districts, provided such improvements will not conflict with the general laws of the State.

Art. 3. The General Assembly may grant aid to said districts out of the funds arising from the swamp and overflowed lands granted to the State by the United States for that purpose or otherwise.

Art. 4. The General Assembly shall have the right of abolishing the office of state engineer, by a majority vote of all the members elected to each branch, and of substituting a board of public works in lieu thereof, should they deem it necessary.

Mr. Gorlinski—As chairman of the committee, I accept the substitute.

President—The chairman cannot accept it.

Mr. Campbell—Do I understand that it is a substitute for the majority report?

President—It is a substitute for the whole matter.

Mr. Campbell—Then I move to strike out all after the first article, and insert the following:

[Commenced to read his own report.]

President—You are reading from your own minority report, which cannot be offered as an amendment.

Mr. Campbell—I have not a copy of the substitute before me, but I wish to amend it so that the state engineer shall be appointed for a term of four years, and at the expiration of that term shall be elected by the people.

Mr. Hills—I move to lay the amendment on the table.

[Carried—yeas 30, nays 27.

Art. 1st of the substitute was read.]

Mr. Wilson—I move to amend by making the term two, instead of four years, and leaving the salary to be fixed by the Legislature the same as the assistants. If it is right for the Legislatvre to fix the salaries of the assistant engineers, then that body is equally competent to fix the salary of the chief engineer.

Mr. FOLEY—I move to lay the amendment on the table.

Mr. HILLS—I second the motion.

[The motion was lost—yeas 22, nays 40.]

Mr. HILLS—I call for a division of the question, and then we can vote on the two amendments separately.

[The question was divided and the first part of the amendment relating to the term of office was lost—yeas 32, nays 39.

The adoption of the other part of the amendment was about being put when the door-keeper announced Maj. Gen. Canby and Maj. Gen. Sickles, who, accompanied by Federal members of their staffs, were shown to the speaker's stand by Mr. Thorpe.

The president welcomed them as follows :]

Generals—This Convention to-day receives with high appreciation two distinguished soldiers of the great and patriotic army which is now doing battle for the right and for the life of our country. Hard is the fate of that people whose history compasses not a century of years; hard is the fate of that people whose story is the story merely of one generation and then is silent forever. It is not strange that our enemies should desire for us such a fate. It is not strange that those who are envious of our great progress in all of physical, in all of mental life, should desire for us such a fate; but when Iphiclus strives to strangle the infant Hercules in his cradle, it is an act most foul, most unnatural.

Generals—Every loyal citizen of the United States in this great contest will act his several part. To you has been given the joy to listen to the roar of cannon. To you has been given the glory to pass through the smoke and fire of battle. To these gentlemen here assembled is given a different but equally important labor. We rebuild where others destroy, and as victory follows victory in this great struggle, and as territory after territory is reclaimed from the grasp of traitors, so similar assemblies will be called in our sister States to restore the rights of the people and to rebuild with still fairer and more magnificent proportions the temple of liberty.

Generals, as the organ of this Convention, I wish you and present to you a welcome—a most hearty welcome. [Applause.]

[Maj. Gen. Canby replied to the president in a few words, but spoke in so low a tone that the reporters were unable to take down his remarks.

Maj. Gen. Sickles being loudly called for, responded as follows :]

Gentlemen of the Convention—I trust I do not fail to appreciate the high honor of this reception.

The civilian and soldier go side by side in redeeming our country from the crime and devastation of this rebellion, and it is most true, as your president has so eloquently said, that your functions are not of less importance in the restoration of order and tranquillity, than are the duties of the soldier in subduing the enemies of the Republic. Let me assure you, gentlemen, that your labors attract the attention not only of the people of Louisiana, but of the whole Union. The President and the Congress of the United States, the loyal people everywhere, look with solicitude upon the great duty you have to perform. Upon its efficient and wise performance depends not only the future of Louisiana, but perhaps in no inconsiderable degree, the great work of reconstruction, which is the problem of our present condition.

Louisiana did not share in the struggles of the revolution, but yet her people were the descendants of our allies. When France ceded Louisiana to the United States, she gave in that act an additional pledge of that alliance and of that friendship which had been so precious to us in the dark time of the revolutionary struggle. On your soil the flag of the Union was maintained by a Jackson against a foreign foe. A Livingston has illustrated in his accomplishment as a civilian, your history. You have erected a statue to a Clay. Let me say to you that Lafayette, Jefferson, Livingston, Jackson and Clay, those whom you have delegated most to honor, were they with you to-day, would rejoice in your noble patriotism and applaud your greatest act—the declaration that henceforth and forever Louisiana is a free State! [Great applause.]

Although this is my first visit to this beautiful city, where I have been delighted to see so many evidences of culture, enterprise and future greatness—remote as is my own home, I do not regard myself a stranger in your midst, for I know enough of the inmost convictions of the American people, to feel sure that under all circumstances, come what will, cost what sacrifices it may, Louisiana must and ever will be a part of the American Union. [Enthusiastic applause.]

Mr. President and gentlemen, I have already trespassed longer than I had intended upon your kind attention. [Cries of "not all." "Go on."] I am accustomed to think, gentlemen, that I can, with more propriety than ever, now adopt the axiom that "short speeches are always the best," especially as I have to address you under some circumstances of personal inconvenience.

Gentlemen, your State has before it a glorious future. It is worth all the sacrifices which the loyal men of Louisiana have made for it. Be assured that although loyalty everywhere is prized, and justly prized, as a jewel, the loyalty of those who have been faithful to the old flag, under all the terrors and tortures of rebel rule, as you have been, commands the heartiest and truest homage.

We have passed through one cycle of our history and progress. Our nation has ever been powerful, and we have been accustomed always to revere it as great. But it certainly contained within itself an element of dissolution, that always occasioned to the early fathers of the republic profound alarm. Whatever of calamity or of suffering this rebellion has brought with it, it at least has done for us this great good. It has restored to our constitution and our polity that symmetry which was necessary to perfection, and has removed from it the only serious element of danger which menaced our security. To recall the past is impossible; to improve the present is our duty, and to look to the future is the part of a statesman. The America of the future—a nation entirely free from ocean to ocean, will be a greater and better country than ever we could boast of before. [Applause.] Let us then, gentlemen, in our respective spheres, do all we can to promote this end. Let us feel impressed with the justice of the cause in which we are engaged, and let us be guiltless of any act of injustice to others. Let us prove that in our system of government we find the resources for every trouble—a shield against every danger. Let us prove to the advocates of monarchy and of despotism that freedom, free institutions and liberty are self-sustaining. Let us prove that no combination of foreign powers, with the wiles and intrigues of their diplomacy; that no internal danger, even though it be in the form of the most stupendous rebellion of modern or ancient times, is powerful enough to overcome that love of free institutions, that intelligence, that patriotism, that indomitable will which are characteristic of the American name. [Prolonged applause.]

Mr. Henderson—I move the Convention take a recess of ten minutes.

[The motion was carried without objection.

At the expiration of the time, after the visitors had received the congratulations of the members of the Convention, the House was called to order by the president, and as the visitors left the hall, three hearty cheeers were given for Maj. Gen. Canby and three cheers for Maj. Gen. Sickles; three cheers for the staff and three cheers for loyal men.

On motion the convention then adjourned.]

Thursday, June 23, 1864.

[The Convention met pursuant to adjournment.

Present—the Hon. E. H. Durell, president, in the chair, and the following members:]

Messrs. Abell, Austin, Balch, Bailey, Barrett, Baum, Beauvais, Bell, Bofill, Bromley, Buckley, Burke, Collin, Cook J. K., Cook T., Crozat, Cutler, Davies, Decker, Duane, Dufresne, Duke, Dupaty, Edwards, Ennis, Fish, Flagg, Flood, Foley, Fosdick, Gastinel, Geier, Gorlinski, Gruneberg, Gaidry, Healy, Harnan, Hart, Henderson, Hills, Hire, Howell, Howes, Kavanagh, Knobloch, Kugler, Maas, Mann, Maurer, Mayer, Mendiverri, Montamat, Morris, Murphy E., Murphy M. W., Newell, Normand, O'Conner, Orr, Payne J., Paine J. T., Pintado, Poynot, Purcell J., Pursell S., Schroeder, Schnurr, Seymour, Shaw, Smith, Spellicy, Stocker, Stumpf, Stiner, Stauffer, Sullivan, Terry, Thorpe, Waters, Wenck, Wells, Wilson—83.

Absent—Messrs. Ariail, Bennie, Bonzano, Brott, Campbell, (excused,) Cazabat, Fuller, Heard, Lobdell, Millspaugh, Montague, Ong, (excused,) Taliaferro and Thomas.

On motion of Mr. Abell, Mr. Campbell was excused for absence.

[The minutes of yesterday were read and adopted.]

Mr. Pursell—I move a reconsideration of the vote of yesterday on General Provisions, as I have some additional articles to offer. They are very important and will not detain the Convention long. I voted with the majority.

Mr. Orr—I move to lay that motion on the table.

[Motion lost.

Yesterday's action was then reconsidered; rising vote—ayes 53, nays none.]

Mr. Pursell—My first article reads as follows:

Art. —. No profession, occupation, business or calling, requiring a license from any authority within this State, shall be carried on, exercised or followed by any other than citizens of the United States, or those having made legal declaration of becoming citizens.

Mr. HARNAN—I move that be laid on the table.

[Motion lost.]

Mr. MONTAMAT—I move its adoption.

[Motion seconded.]

Mr. CUTLER—Mr. President, my object in arising, is not for the purpose of any lengthy debate, but I believe, sir, that this Convention does not understand the full meaning of this article. It strikes my mind as a very singular one—ignoring all those principles well recognized by international law. We are at peace with foreign countries, and are we, in this Convention, to pass this which will prevent a citizen of France, England, Germany or any other country from coming here and engaging in commercial pursuits? It is astounding! I am perfectly willing that they should come, and to exclude them will be a violation of our treaties, to which I hope this Convention will not assent. The gentleman from Jefferson cannot surely wish to exclude all persons of foreign birth, who, according to the laws of nations, have a right to live in our midst and transact business.

Look at our city now. We have hundreds of merchants who are not naturalized citizens of the United States, who, according to our laws, are entitled to a business residence among us. This article excludes citizens of all nations, except our own natives and adopted, and this can only be done in open violation of the constitutional laws of the United States. You will, by your organic law, if this is passed, exclude those persons whom every State has a right to recognize. With these remarks, I say that it strikes me that justice should be done to all classes of men.

Mr. WILSON—Mr. President, I am rather astonished at this resolution. The Baltimore Convention is in favor of emigration, in favor of sustaining capital, whether it comes from the North, South, East or West, by opening the large and uncultivated fields of America to every man who has the energy to frame and build up for himself a home and household.

What does this article mean? Simply that a man cannot do any business in New Orleans unless a citizen; that even an inchoate citizenship amounts to nothing. Why I want to tell you that this country has been made by the energy of these very foreigners who are willing to fight and battle for the old flag. These truths should urge us to the belief that we have nothing to fear from the men who do not come here with their capital to overthrow our national principles. Give a just liberty to every man who can show himself energetic and honest, and allow him also to develop those qualities. Refuse to adopt this article to entertain any such narrow-minded policy and you will prove yourselves Americans; but if you deny to a man who is not a citizen the right of doing business and his lawful liberties, at that instant you deny to him the right of coming here to fight our battles.

Mr. SULLIVAN—On looking into this article I consider it the most damnable know-nothing-proposition that ever emanated from any man in this Convention or any other Legislative body in this country.

Pass this resolution, and you sweep from the State of Louisiana millions of capital owned by foreign capitalists in this State. What will become of the foreign capital owned by them in the several corporations in this city; I ask what will become of it in the Gas Works, Water Works, or the foreign capital in the banking institutions of this State. How many cotton factors, sugar brokers, and in fact all the principal business men of this city are foreigners? Drive them from amongst us by the adoption of this narrow-minded resolution, and you will shortly have grass growing in the principal streets of our city. Business is bad enough now, without making it worse. Gentlemen, I appeal to you to vote down this infamous resolution.

Mr. HENDERSON—I am somewhat astonished, Mr. President, that a man who calls himself an American, and who understands something of our nation, should attempt to insert such an article as this in our constitution, in violation of the international laws and public policy of all nations on the earth. Your American-French, Spanish residents, trading in this city to-day, under heavy licenses, have a right to continue so to do under the law of nations. Are we to do this injustice to those who never contemplated becoming American citizens? The supposition is an outrageous one. There are hundreds of men who have come here to invest their capital, to enrich our city, but who never expected to become citizens of the United States. Such know-nothingism, such suicidal policy will only bring down upon us the condemnation we deserve from every intelligent man on the face of the earth, and therefore I hope, Mr. President and gentlemen, that you will not adopt it. Our alien friends can no longer invest their capital under this article, which is of itself a great reason for your not passing it.

Mr. THORPE—Mr. President, I should like, before this question is put, the privilege of saying a few words to put myself on record. I don't like to sit in a body and have a resolution like this brought before it: it is offensive, and I take occasion to say that the working in this body of the political denomination called the "know-nothings," is one of the most extraordinary things that has taken place here. There is, or will be a provision in our constitution, that a man must live in Louisiana for ten years before he can be governor, and so with regard to mayor. I think that all these things are proscriptive; that no such qualifications should be required for office in this State, except that a candidate should be a citizen of the United States, and a resident of the State. I do not like this way of encumbering, putting politics into such Chinese-shoes that every man's feet are so small as to prevent his walking. To tell me that a man cannot come here and enrich the State by furnishing to it his industry, labor and intelligence, without being a citizen, is one of the most outrageous propositions ever brought into a legislative body. I must allude to the action of the Baltimore Convention, in encouraging emigration, and thus deciding a question which has been much discussed among our politicians.

I am not afraid of any man's coming here and hurting me. When I consider our armies, our million of men in the field, and that, right or wrong, this war must be fought to the bitter end, I must say that I think we are right in opening our arms to the people of every land, and in asking them to come and fill up the places left vacant by this destruction. Why, gentlemen, the leading merchant of London, Peabody, is an American, and I question if he has ever been naturalized? The chancellor of England, who recently died, was a Boston boy, and the mayor of Stratford upon Avon, so famous as associated with Shakspeare's memory, has been for the last twenty years a citizen of the United States.

Since we are assembled to make a constitution for the people, and worthy of the nineteenth century, let us work wisely, and not pass this resolution, which will give to our labors the hue of insincerity and make our act of emancipation a farce instead of one of the noblest acts of our age.

Mr. S. PURSELL—Mr. President, when I offered these additional articles, I proposed to have them go before the Convention without any debate; but, gentlemen who have some pretensions to intelligence, have called me a know-nothing.

I believe that if the record were brought up here that term would apply more aptly to a majority of these very men, than to myself.

I never was a member of the organization, and my life has been in years past endangered through them. These resolutions are called narrow-minded. The mind that construes the language of this article into know-nothingism is narrowed down to so fine a point that it could not be discovered by a very strong magnifying glass.

This article proposes to protect the foreigner who comes here in good faith—not the foreigners here who enlisted and formed a batallion to fight for the Confederate cause, and who otherwise can now come back and form cliques and rendezvous for all the secessionists in the land.

The language of the article is very plain and simple. Does it shut out the foreigner? Not by any means. It guarantees him liberty and the protection of his rights in conducting his business. What do we see now? The houses of those aliens who have lived here unnaturalized for the last twenty years are the regular rendezvous of all the secessionists. They receive dispatches, send them out, hold lengthy meetings and inform the enemy of all that is going on in regard to the army, scoffing at other citizens, foreign or native. No man ever heard me call another Irish, French, Dutch or anything else, for I take a man as I find him, whether he be native-born or naturalized. He who calls me a know-nothing is mistaken in his man, and he who understands this article as leading to know-nothingism, cannot comprehend a common sentence in the English language.

Mr. SCHROEDER—I am entirely opposed to those foreigners who have been here for a long time and now throw in my face such expressions as, "You are a d—d fool to become a citizen; we make a great deal more money than any naturalized foreigner and do as we d—d please." (Applause.)

Mr. SMITH—With regard to know-nothingism, I can simply say that I have never been a know-nothing; but, as to those men who are said to have come here and helped to make our country, I would ask whether they have become citizens or declared their intention to do so. You shall take the foreigners of this city who have never been citizens or declared their intention of becoming citizens, and in nine cases out of ten, their sympathies are with the rebel cause. They have been the men who have smuggled across the lines and given to the enemy aid and comfort; yet, gentlemen will get up here and attempt to arouse prejudice by saying certain others are know-nothings. I have lived in a parish where almost every one was a member of that order, when it was in its palmiest days, and never had anything to do with it.

The doors of this country are opened to all who, under our starry flag can find a home and rest, and as for these monarchists who wish to do away with all this, who would bring their armies upon our soil and interfere with us, to say that requiring them to declare their intention of becoming citizens is narrow-minded policy or anything else, is what I consider injustice. We are told this country was made by men that came from foreign countries. I grant you, sir, there have been some noble men who have thus come, but their determination has been to become citizens of our free government, (applause,) and were not in favor of extending monarchial institutions. I am as much in favor of giving each man his rights and privileges as any gentleman upon this floor, but I consider that we must take some measures to insure the safety of our government.

Mr. STOCKER—I desire to put myself on the record in regard to this matter. I am free to acknowledge, sir, that I did at one time belong to the know-nothing party, but my feelings even then never carried me so far as this resolution seems calculated to carry this House. I hope, sir, for the reputation of Louisiana, that this resolution will not pass. Holding the position I do at this time, being one of the State tax collectors, I know something of the value of these foreign merchants to the commerce of our State. I say that when you cut them off, you cut off a large portion of the taxes that are now being paid into the State treasury, and, besides, we are attempting to meddle with that which does not belong to us, but to the Congress of the United States. The constitution of the United States says: "Congress shall have power to regulate commerce, etc.," and this resolution seeks to do nothing more nor less than to exercise that very power; not according to its exact language, but in effect it amounts to nearly the same thing. If this article should prevail here, I say that it must be a disgrace to this Convention and the State of Louisiana. That, sir, is my solemn opinion.

[The amendment was rejected by the following vote:

YEAS — Messrs. Bofill, Bromley, Burke, Cook J. K., Decker, Ennis, Flagg, Flood, Geier, Gaidry, Kugler, Maas, O'Conner, Paine J. T., Poynot, Pursell S., Schroeder, Smith—18.

NAYS—Messrs. Austin, Balch, Bailey, Barrett, Baum, Beauvais, Bell, Buckley, Collin, Cook T., Crozat, Cutler, Davies, Duane, Dufresne, Duke, Dupaty, Edwards, Fish, Foley, Fosdick, Gastinel, Gorlinski, Gruneberg, Healy, Harnan, Hart, Henderson, Hills, Hire, Howell, Howes, Kavanagh, Knobloch, Mann, Maurer, Mayer, Mendiverri, Montamat, Morris, Murphy E., Murphy M. W., Newell, Normand, Orr, Payne J., Pintado, Purcell J., Schnurr, Seymour,

Shaw, Spellicy, Stocker, Stumpf, Stiner, Stauffer, Sullivan, Terry, Thorpe, Wenck, Wells, Wilson—62.

[The following article was read, being the second of Mr. Pursell's amendments :]

Art. —. The General Assembly shall provide by law for the establishment of a poor-house in each parish of the State, for the care of the destitute within their respective limits, and to be conducted as shall be provided by law.

Mr. HARNAN—I move to lay it on the table.

[Carried.]

Mr. GORLINSKI—I offer the following additional article :

Art. —. The Legislature shall have power to pass laws extending the right of suffrage to such persons, citizens of the United States, as by military service, by taxation to support the government, or by intellectual fitness, may be deemed entitled thereto.

Mr. SULLIVAN—I move to lay it on the table—that's a nigger resolution.

[On a *viva voce* vote the article was declared rejected ; but upon the roll being called, the article was adopted ; Mr. Healy changing his vote from "no" to "yes," before the result was announced.]

YEAS—Messrs. Austin, Barrett, Bromley, Bell, Collin, Cook T., Crozat, Cutler, Davies, Duane, Dupaty, Ennis, Fish, Flagg, Flood, Foley, Fosdick, Geier, Gorlinski, Healy, Harnan, Henderson, Hills, Hire, Howell, Howes, Kavanagh, Kugler, Mann, Murphy E., Newell, Normand, O'Conner, Paine J. T., Pintado, Purcell J., Schroeder, Seymour, Shaw, Smith, Spellicy, Stumpf, Stiner, Stauffer, Terry, Thorpe, Wenck, Wells—48.

NAYS—Messrs. Balch, Bailey, Beauvais, Baum, Bofill, Buckley, Burke, Cook J. K., Decker, Dufresne, Duke, Edwards, Gastinel, Gruneberg, Gaidry, Hart, Knobloch, Maas, Maurer, Mayer, Mendiverri, Montamat, Morris, Murphy M. W., Orr, Payne J., Poynot, Pursell S., Schnurr, Stocker, Sullivan, Wilson—32.

Mr. TERRY—I offer the following additional article :

Nine hours shall constitute a day's labor for all mechanics, artizans and laborers on the public works of the State.

Mr. MONTAMAT—I move to lay it on the table.

[The motion was lost by a rising vote of 33 yeas to 37 nays.]

Mr. TERRY—In explaining why I offer this article, I would simply state, that for the last two months, throughout every workshop in this city, not only those belonging to the government but to private contracts, has this memorial and petition been circulated and signed by hard-working men--by men who by the sweat of their brow earned their bread in this climate under an almost tropical sun. These men—two thousand of them, and I want you to understand that there would have been ten thousand if time had been allowed—ask you for a little thing—only one hour—making nine hours instead of ten. Why do they ask it? They ask it, because of the heat of our sun—because, through the perspiration starting from every pore of each man's body he is oozing forth his very life. They ask this, that they may have one hour longer for domestic scenes, to read your constitution when it comes before them for ratification. That is why they ask it. Give it to them, and they will ratify our work. It is a slight thing, and does not defraud any one. These men, gentlemen, have claims upon us, too. You whose brows have been wet with toil, understand this—know how refreshing it will be to return one hour sooner to their families, and with their little infants fondling around their knees, they will instruct those innocent ones to say, "God bless that Constitutional Convention of 1864!" (Applause.)

That is the instructive lesson, Mr. President, which they will teach their children, that will go abroad. I wish you to accomplish this great, glorious and good work, and give them, at least, this additional hour.

Mr. WENCK—Mr. President and gentlemen of the Convention : I am really astonished at seeing the members of this Convention assuming a power which never has been delegated to them. I ask you, Mr. President, what we have to do with all these matters? What have we to do with regulating the hours of the working classes, who are under the control of men who provide for them out of the public fund? Shall we do this in order to obtain votes for the acceptance of this Constitution? If that is the idea, I say let us vote against it. If we have a right to regulate one, we have a right to regulate each and every trade or business. (Applause.)

Now let us understand one thing. Are we always to remain under the circumstances that now surround us, or is this constitution to be adopted only until the war is over? If this is the case, whenever a new one takes the place of this constitution, the people can make such laws for themselves. We are not here to please one party, but must, I believe, please the people of the whole State. (Applause.) Now, if this article becomes a part of the constitution emigration is stopped, and those who now receive $1 50 per day will want the State to pay them a salary of $2. I speak for my constituents and the people, and say we have no right to make any such matter a part of our constitution; and if any such law is to be passed, let the Legislature do it.

Mr. THORPE—I offer as an amendment that "seven" be inserted in place of "nine."

Mr. TERRY—I move to lay it on the table.

[Carried.]

Mr. TERRY - The gentleman from the Fourth District (Mr. Wenck) has whipped around the stump, but never come to the question. My article refers to the laborers upon the works of the State and to none other. He says this is legislating. Are we not already legislated here? I think we have to our hearts' content, for we have adopted the police bill, fixed salaries for laborers, etc. Now I think it is no more than right that we should fix the hours of labor as well. We are not catering for the good of one man more than another, and we have legislated for both poor and rich men. Under this article, the private contractor can engage a laborer to work twelve hours per day; but I wish a law restricting the hours of labor for workmen on the public works to nine hours. Such a law can be as rightfully inserted in the report of the Committee on General Provisions as can a clause fixing the pay of laborers, and the one is just as necessary as the other. I do not wish to detain the Convention with any further debate, and simply ask for the reading of the article before the roll is called.

[The article was read.]

Mr. WELLS—I beg to be excused from voting.

[Criers of "I object;" "vote!"]

Mr. WELLS—When I came to this Convention I did not come to legislate. I vote "no."

[Messrs. Montamat, Abell and Fish were allowed to vote, though absent when the question was put.

The article was adopted by the following vote:]

YEAS — Messrs. Bailey, Barrett, Baum, Bell, Buckley, Burke, Collin, Cook J. K., Cook T., Crozat, Davies, Duane, Dufresne, Duke, Dupaty, Ennis, Fish, Flood, Foley, Fosdick, Geier, Gorlinski, Gaidry, Harnan, Healy, Henderson, Hills, Hire, Howes, Knobloch, Maas, Maurer, Montamat, Morris, Murphy E., Murphy M. W., Newell, Normand, O'Conner, Orr, Payne J., Pintado, Poynot, Purcell J., Pursell S., Schroeder, Seymour, Shaw, Smith, Stocker, Stiner, Stumpf, Stauffer, Sullivan, Terry, Thorpe—56.

NAYS — Messrs. Abell, Austin, Balch, Beauvais, Bofill, Bromley, Cutler, Decker, Edwards, Flagg, Gastinel, Gruneberg, Hart, Howell, Kavanagh, Kugler, Mann, Mayer, Mendiverri, Paine J. T., Schnurr, Spellicy, Wenck, Wells, Wilson—25.

Mr. FOLEY—I wish to add the following article:

ART. —. The Legislature shall pass no laws requiring property qualification for office.

Mr. WELLS—I move to lay that on the table.

[The motion was lost.

The article was adopted.]

Mr. BROMLEY—I move the following article be added:

ART. —. No member of this Convention shall be eligible to any office under the municipal government of New Orleans during a term of three years from the adoption of the free State consitution.

Mr. SULLIVAN—I move that be laid on the table.

[The motion was carried.]

Mr. SULLIVAN—I move the adoption of the report on its second reading, as amended.

[The motion was declared carried on *viva voce* vote, when a division was called and the report as amended adopted: ayes 47, nays 24.]

Mr. STINER—I move a suspension of the rules that the report may be put upon its third reading.

[The motion was lost.]

PRESIDENT—Order of the day.

Second reading of minority report of Committee on Internal Improvements, Terry's substitute.

[The secretary read :]

ART. 1. There shall be appointed by the governor a State engineer, skilled in the theory and practice of his profession, who shall hold his office at the seat of government for the term of four years ; he shall have the superintendence and direction of all public works in which the State may be interested, except those made by joint stock companies, or such which may be under the parochial or city authorities exclusively, and not in conflict with the general laws of the State. He shall communicate to the General Assembly through the governor annually, his views concerning the same, report upon the condition of the public works in progress, recommend such measures as in his opinion the public interest of the State may require, and shall perform such other duties as may be prescribed by law. His salary shall be four thousand dollars per annum.

Mr. STOCKER—I wish to amend by striking out all after "per annum," down to the word "State."

Mr. HEALY—I move to lay that on the table.

[The motion was lost.

Mr. Stocker's amendment was then adopted by a rising vote : ayes 33, nays 23.]

Mr. GRUNEBERG—I ask for a call of the House.

[House called, when 76 members answered to their names.]

Mr. GASTINEL—I offer an amendment to the amendment, to strike out "six" and insert "four."

[Motion to table was lost, and amendment to the amendment, adopted on a rising vote : ayes, 36, nays, 23.]

Mr. STOCKER—In order to make the article as amended read properly, I offer the following :

The mode of appointment, number and salaries of his assistants, shall be fixed by law.

[The amendment was adopted, and the second division of article 1 adopted as amended.

The secretary read :]

ART. 2. The General Assembly may create internal improvement districts, composed of one or more parishes, and may grant the right to the citizens thereof to tax themselves for their improvements. Said internal improvement districts, when created, shall have the right to elect commissioners, shall have power to appoint officers, fix their pay and regulate all matters relative to the improvements of their districts, provided such improvements will not conflict with general laws of the State.

Mr. SULLIVAN—I wish to amend by inserting on the second line the following :

Art. —. And that the municipal corporation of the city of New Orleans shall be prohibited from adjudicating, selling by sealed proposals, or in any manner contracting for the working or completing of any public works under their supervision and control.

And, Mr. President, I beg leave of the Convention to listen to a few brief remarks, giving my reasons why I offered this amendment to the second article of the report of the Committee on Internal Improvements.

Gentlemen, all the old residents of this city—you who have lived in this community for a long period of time, know as well as I do, that the system of letting out contracts for the completing of public works, so far as this city was concerned in it, as carried out for the last twenty years by the authorities of this city, was a stupendous fraud on the public, a perfect swindle on the taxpayer, and an oppression on the laboring classes of the city.

We all remember well, to our cost, how the contractors completed their contracts. We all know the corrupting influences brought to bear to have their ill-done work passed. Let us see how this contract system was carried out. The contract was sold in the controller's office to the lowest bidder, after its having been advertised for a period of, I believe, ten days ; this contract was generally bid in by a favorite of the surveyor, as there was at all times a perfect understanding between the surveyor and the contractor. None would dare bid unless he was a favorite of the party in power. Let certain contractors take the work ever so low, money must come out of the job. The engineer or surveyor was on hand to make his share of the profits—giving his official signature to the city treasurer that the work was done according to the specification on file in his office ;

when in reality the contractor did not do one-half of the work required of him according to the specification. What cared the surveyor so long as he made half of the spoils plundered from the poor property holders.

I state it boldly here, in this Convention this day, without fear of contradiction, a more corrupt set of swindlers than had control of the contracts in this city for years past, never existed in any other city on this continent; and I will also place in company with them their coadjutors in iniquity the officials who were always willing to be partners in their rascality and villainy.

But, on the arrival of Gen. Butler in this city, their infamous career ceased. He at once annulled all contracts then existing, which was, up to that time, a fraud on the community as every one knows. This order of his, doing away of contracts, I consider one of the best acts of his life. He placed all the public works of the city in the hands of the city authorities. Immediately under their control and supervision over two thousand men were put to work in opening and cleaning of canals. New streets, miles long, were opened and repaired, thereby bringing this city to a state of cleanliness that was never known before when the contract system ruled, although all their improvements were made at a less expense and cost than was pocketed heretofore by these shoddy contractors.

Let us see what has been done here lately within the last few weeks in this city. The bureau of streets and landings, in their wisdom, contrary to all precedents now ex-existing, and contrary to any ordinance that I know of, gives out to one of these favorites, I suppose, of the city surveyor or of the bureau of streets and landings, the contract of cleaning out of a portion of the city canals. When he received this bogus contract he could not get men to do the work, when a plan was immediately concocted by his allies, the surveyor and the bureau of streets and landings, so that he could get men. How was it done? The bureau of streets and landings transmit a letter to Mr. Surveyor, ordering him to suspend forthwith the city works, throwing out of work seven hundred poor laborers, perfectly penniless, without the means of earning a sufficiency to support either themselves or their families. All this misery was created by the bureau of streets and landings falling back on this corrupt system of contracting.

Mr. President, are we to allow this state of things to exist to our knowledge? No, sir. I never will let it be done while I have a voice to raise against it. I will, in conjunction with you, gentlemen, put my utter condemnation on all contracts and contractors, and also the officials who uphold them in their nefarious designs, because I consider them the enemies of the working men and the people at large.

Let us, then, break up this vile system of contracts forever. Let us give work to the men of families who have lately been thrown out of employment by such unfair means. We have plenty of money in the treasury and plenty of improvements to be done to embellish our city. Let us employ them. This is all these men require. They must get it—the laborer is worthy of his hire.

I again urge on every man in this Convention who has his heart in the right place to vote for this amendment—it is an amendment that the working men will feel proud of; it will show at least that we have endeavored to do justice to them; it will redeem the promise we made to them when they honored us so much by voting for us to represent them on the floor of this Convention. It will keep the Legislature or any other body from again reviving this contract system, so pernicious to the working man, so dishonest to the tax-payer and it is also mockery—a delusion and a fraud on the people.

Mr. Harnan—I am no contractor and I am against this contracting. I want to see the citizens of New Orleans employed and to have the corporation take care that their work is properly done. Since the last two years, under the supervision of the city corporation, our streets are properly cleaned and everything is done to perfection.

Mr. Bofill—I move the adoption of Mr. Sullivan's amendment.

[The motion was carried, and article 2 of the substitute was adopted as amended.

The secretary read :]

Art. 3. The General Assembly may grant aid to said districts out of the funds arising from the swamp and overflowed lands granted to the State by the United States for that purpose or otherwise.

[The article was adopted.

The secretary read :]

Art. 4. The General Assembly shall have the right of abolishing the office of State engineer, by a majority vote of all the members elected to each branch, and of substituting a board of public works in lieu thereof, should they deem it necessary.

[The article was adopted.]

Mr. Montamat—I move to amend by substituting "majority" in place of "two-thirds."

[The motion was carried and article 4 adopted as amended, and the substitute was adopted as a whole.]

Mr. Harnan—I move a suspension of the rules for the purpose of taking up, on its third reading, the substitute of Mr. Terry.

[The motion was lost.]

A motion to adjourn was put, and as the *viva voce* vote was indeterminate a rising vote was taken, when the Convention, by a vote of 38 ayes to 33 nays, adjourned until 12 m. of Friday, the 24th inst.

Friday, June 24, 1864.

[The Convention met pursuant to adjournment. Present, the Hon. E. H. Durell, president, and the following members :]

Messrs. Abell, Austin, Balch, Bailey, Barrett, Baum, Beauvais, Bell, Bofill, Bromley, Buckley, Burke, Campbell, Collin, Cazabat, Cook J. K., Cook T., Crozat, Cutler, Davies, Decker, Duane, Dufresne, Duke, Dupaty, Edwards, Ennis, Fish, Flagg, Flood, Foley, Fosdick, Fuller, Gastinel, Geier, Gorlinski, Gruneberg, Gaidry, Healy, Harnan, Hart, Henderson, Hills, Hire, Howell, Howes, Kavanagh, Knobloch, Kugler, Maas, Mann, Maurer, Mayer, Mendiverri, Montamat, Murphy M. W., Newell, Normand, O'Conner, Orr, Payne J., Paine J. T., Pintado, Poynot, Purcell J., Pursell S., Schroeder, Schnurr, Seymour, Shaw, Smith, Spellicy, Stocker, Stumpf, Stiner, Stauffer, Sullivan, Terry, Thorpe, Waters, Wenck, Wells, Wilson—85.

[The minutes of yesterday's proceedings were read and adopted.]

Mr. Terry—I call for a suspension of the rules in order to offer this patriotic resolution :

Resolved, That the sum of one thousand dollars be and is hereby appropriated out of the State funds, not otherwise appropriated, for the celebration of the 4th of July, and that a committee of five be appointed to consult with the city authorities regarding its proper expenditure.

[Motion lost.

ORDER OF THE DAY.

The secretary proceeded to read the following report :]

REPORT OF THE COMMITTEE ON SCHEDULE.

Mr. President—Your Committee on Schedule beg leave to make the following report :

Art. 1. The Constitutional Convention over which you preside derives its authority from no other source than the mandate of the commanding officer of the Department of the Gulf, Maj. Gen. N. P Banks, which he published on the eleventh day of March, 1864. This order defines clearly the extent of powers which the general has thought fit and proper to grant to you. By this order the Constitutional Convention of the State of Louisiana was called together to "revise and amend the constitution of the State of Louisiana," and for no other purposes. Our task was to pass in review every line, article and title of this constitution, and to make therein the necessary changes. The moment that we overstepped these landmarks and presumed to introduce new subject-matter, of which not a vestige can be found in the old constitution, and attempted to legislate thereon, we made ourselves liable to be accused of an unwarranted assumption of powers not granted to us—and the decisions on matters outside of the jurisdiction of this Convention will stand as mere expressions of opinions, but have no binding force as parts of the organic law of the State. This is the case with the attempted emancipation of the negroes in this State. The status of the negroes has been fixed by the proclamation of President Lincoln, of the 1st of January, 1863, which makes the negroes free in one part and suffers them to remain slaves in another part of the State. In this latter part the rights of the master over his slave have been suspended for the time being by the supreme military authority, but they have never been abrogated by any constitutionally appointed power.

All orders issued from the pen of the commanding general are as clear and precise as language can make them, and his utter silence on the grave and important subject of emancipation in the order which convoked this Convention must be of the greatest significance. This order is so plainly worded that the most subtle arts of implication cannot extort therefrom the faint shadow of an authority for this Contion to touch the emancipation question.

Notwithstanding the harangues of stump orators and the clamor of interested persons. your committee are forced to entertain the firm conviction that the commanding general has intended to withhold from us the power to legislate on the question of freedom or slavery of the negroes. And, inasmuch as the closest scrutiny cannot discover any article in the constitution of 1852, which we were called together to revise and amend, which has reference to or names the negro, we had no right to legislate on his status.

Your committee, in consideration of the above explained reasons, do therefore respectfully recommend, that the sections relating to the emancipation of the negroes in this State be expunged from this constitution as having no place therein, and as being the result, on the part of this Convention, of an unjustifiable assumption of authority not granted to it.

Art. 2. The constitution adopted in 1852 is declared to be superseded by this constitution, and in order to carry the same into effect it is hereby declared and ordained as follows:

Art. 3. All rights, actions, prosecutions, claims and contracts, as well of individuals as of bodies corporate, and all laws in force at the time of the adoption of this constitution, and not inconsistent therewith, shall continue as if the same had not been adopted.

Art. 4. And in order that the civil government of the State may be carried on in a proper way until this constitution, whenever it shall have been ratified and adopted by the people, can be put into effect, it is hereby furthermore ordained as follows:

Art. 5. There shall be chosen by ballot by the members of this Convention from among the most worthy loyal citizens of the State, a select permanent committee of nine members, to be styled "the Provisional Executive Committee of the State of Louisiana;" four of the members of this committee shall be taken from the residents of the city of New Orleans and five from the country parishes, provided there be no more than one member from any one of the said country parishes. The Provisional Executive Committee shall co-operate with the executive of the State in all appointments of officers, which have been made appointive under this constitution, and in that case five members of said committee shall constitute a quorum, and said committee shall also have power to remove summarily, on request of the governor of the State, such officers from their office as shall have proved themselves unworthy of the trust reposed in them or incapable to fill their respective offices. Seven members of said committee shall be necessay to form a quorum for the purpose of removal from office of any officer, and five of this number must be in favor of such removal before it can be accepted and acted upon by the governor.

The first session of the Provisional Executive Committee of the State of Louisiana shall commence two weeks after this Convention shall have finished its labors, and it shall thereafter meet in the city of New Orleans on the first Mondays of January and July of each year, until the government under this constitution is organized. It shall each time sit no longer than three weeks, and its members shall receive, during their time of service, the same mileage and per diem as the members of the constitutional Convention are now entitled to.

Any vacancies in said committee, occasioned by death, resignation or otherwise, shall be filled in such a manner as said committee, at its first sitting, may determine upon—however the proportion of city and country members shall always be preserved as above stated. Said committee shall be entitled to appoint a secretary during its sittings, with such salary as the committee may determine upon. A correct report of its proceedings shall be kept, and the same shall be published at the end of each session of said committee in two of the newspapers of the city of New Orleans, to be selected by said committee.

Art. 6. The governor of the State, and the other State officers elected by the people on the 22d day of February last, 1864, as well as all other officers holding commissions from Gen. Shepley, or from the present governor of the State, shall remain in office, unless said offices have been made elective under this constitution, until the organization of the government under this constitution, and the entering into office of the officers to be appointed or elected under said government, and no longer.

Art. 7. The governor shall appoint all the officers whose appointment has been conferred on the executive of the State by this constitution, except to such offices which are already filled, as provided in Art. 6 of this report, by and with the consent and advice of the Provisional Executive Committee of the State of Louisiana, and said officers shall retain their places until the organization of the government under this constitution, and the entering into office of the new officers to be appointed under said government, and no longer, provided that the governor shall not appoint judges, except for districts, where courts can be held in at least two parishes belonging thereto, and then the salary of said judges shall be proportioned to the number of parishes in which they hold court.

Art. 8. The governor shall issue his proclamation for the election of all other officers which have been made elective under this constitution, to be elected in the same ratio as it was done under the constitution of 1852, as well in the city of New Orleans as in all other parishes of the State, where the vote given for State officers on the 22d day of February last was at least one-third of the votes polled in each respective parish in the presidential election of 1860. The writs for said elections shall be issued by the governor as soon as convenient after the final adjournment of this Convention, but not longer than six weeks after such adjournment. And in all the other parishes of the State the governor shall be authorized to appoint all the officers of said parishes, at his discretion, by and with the consent and advice of the Provisional Executive Committee. Such officers, whether elected or appointed, shall hold their office until the organization of this government under the new constitution, and the entering into office of the new officers, to be elected under said government, and no longer.

Art. 9. Whenever the governor shall believe that any officer, either appointed or elected, has proved himself unworthy of the trust confided to him, or to be incapable for the office, for which he has been either appointed or elected, he shall apply to the Provisional Executive Committee for the removal of said officer or officers, and said committee shall act on this request of the governor in the manner provided for in article 5 of this report.

Art. 10. The laws of the State, relative to the duties of the several officers, executive, judicial or military, shall remain in full force, though the same be contrary to this constitution, and the several duties shall be performed by the respective officers of the State, according to the existing laws, until the organization of the government under this constitution, and the entering into office of the new officers to be appointed or elected under said government, and no longer.

Art. 11. Appointments to office by the executive under this constitution shall be made by the governor, to be elected under its authority.

Art. 12. The Legislature shall provide for the removal of all cases now pending in the Supreme or other courts of the State to courts created by or under this constitution.

Art. 13. The first Legislature sitting under the authority of this constitution, shall determine when the time of service of all officers chosen by the people at the first election under this constitution shall terminate, and also upon the rotation of the seats of senators and the seats of the judges of the Supreme and Inferior Courts, and of all other officers which the executive of the State shall appoint according to the provisions of this constitution.

Respectfully submitted,

CHAS. H. GRUNEBERG, Chairman.
P. L. DUFRESNE.

PRESIDENT—I find that this report is signed by only two members of a committee of seven. How does this happen?

Mr. GRUNEBERG—Five of the committee did not understand English, sir.

PRESIDENT—Why, then, did you report this in such a manner? The third reading of the substitute for the report of the Committee on Internal Improvements is now in order.

Mr. GORLINSKI—I offer the following rider to art. 1, line 12:

Strike out the word "four" in the twelfth line and insert "five," so as to make the salary of the chief engineer five thousand dollars; and also to strike out all of the second article after the word "State" in the seventh line.

Mr. HILLS—I would ask for information whether a rider can be laid on the table without also laying on the table the whole report?

PRESIDENT—It cannot. The proper motion is to reject.

Mr. HILLS—If the rider is rejected, is the whole report also rejected?

PRESIDENT—No, sir; it comes back on its third reading.

[The rider was rejected, and the substitute passed its third reading.]

PRESIDENT—Third reading of report of Committee on General Provisions.

Mr. FOLEY—I move a recess of fifteen minutes.

[The motion was carried.

The secretary read the report.]

Mr. PURSELL—As a rider to art. 3, I move to strike out everything after "blood."

Mr. FOLEY—I move its adoption.

[Motion lost.]

Mr. FOLEY—As a rider to art. 4, I move to add: "or who shall have registered himself an enemy of the United States."

[Rider lost on division. Called: ayes 12, nays 57, on question of adoption.]

Mr. CAZABAT—I offer the following rider to art. 20:

Insert the words, "or retroactive," after the words "*ex post facto*," in article 20, and to strike out all after the word "made," in the fourth line of the same article.

[Adopted.]

The Supreme Court of the United States has already decided that there is a distinction between "*ex post facto*" and "retroactive," and unless we include the latter the meaning of the article will not be sufficiently explicit.

Again, if I have a civil suit before a court of Louisiana, and my only witness happens to be a counsel, the opposing party will secure that counsel and thereby deprive you of important testimony. I therefore move the adoption of the rider.

Mr. HENDERSON—I desire to say a word: In Washington, a large business is done in cashing land claims, procuring pensions and cashing them, etc.; now, if a law should be passed, depriving men of the testimony of counsel, how many poor men and women would be deprived of their all. Business men place their most valuable transactions in the hands of their counsel, who are witnesses to the same, and where, if they cannot be allowed to testify, nothing on earth can restore the property to the hands of the rightful owner.

Our courts have determined that the word "attorney" has a double signification—meaning "attorney in fact, and in law, also." Would a merchant call his clerk as a witness? He is an attorney in fact, and cannot testify. In cases involving testimony of relatives, etc., the fact of some existing ties or interest between the parties, goes merely to the credibility, and not to the competency of the witness, and this should be the case as regards attorneys.

Mr. CUTLER—I sincerely hope there will be no objection on the part of any member of this body to the adoption of the rider. Although I belong to that class of men, and may be considered by some of my friends as advocating a principle personal to myself; yet, I wish to say a few words and will be as brief as possible. I sincerely hope the rider will be adopted. In the first place the words *ex post facto* do not embrace as much as they should, and hence the word "retroactive," it is important to place there. I wish to illustrate in regard to preventing an attorney-at-law testifying in a case in which he is a counsel. I presume there is no man on this floor who is not to a greater or less extent a practical business man, pursuing some business, profession or occupation and however much we may be disposed not to litigate, to keep aloof from courts of practice, yet in the course of business it is as natural as for water to seek its level. It is unfortunate for the classes generally and those who litigate ordinarily are the poorer classes, for the rich man very often will refuse the payment of a debt to a poor man simply because he is a rich man, and is to do so. Let us look at this matter practically. There are certain conservative orders which courts of justice may grant and in the parishes clerks have the power to grant such orders; for instance, one is a writ of attachment, another is sequestration, another provisional seizure, etc. If you prohibit the attorney from testifying in any case in which he is counsel, let me say to you, that you deprive yourself of these conservative orders on many occasions. You have a store, for example, or are in any kind of business, but are about to depart for the time being. A certain man named Day owes you a sum of money and is about to leave the State permanently. You have your regularly employed counsel, which has become a habit with the people of Louisiana, the same as to have a regular family physician. It comes to the knowledge of your attorney that this man is about to leave the State permanently and take with him all his effects, and he owes you this just and honest debt which you have earned by the sweat of your brow; you are absent and cannot make an affidavit, you cannot swear he is about to leave and you cannot obtain a writ without, and if your attorney is prevented from making this affidavit, your debt is entirely lost. But the law as it now stands—and I am proud that it stands thus—was made by wiser men than myself, long ago, in a time so far distant that it has been the best of experience. Then your counsel may go forth and make the necessary affidavit and cause you to secure your debt. Again here is a poor man—and much has been said of the poor men—who labors for one hundred dollars, and has earned it working by the month or job, and the amount is due him from a rich man. It is only necessary in order to obtain payment to go into the justice's court — the sum being within the jurisdiction of that court; but such is the law of Louisiana, that unless that poor man, who desires to enforce his claim, makes an *amicable demand*, the rich man may go into court and plead *want of demand*; and when he makes out that plea in law, it throws the costs of that suit on the poor man, unless he proves an amicable demand. Here is one of the most striking cases of the operation of this law, and should induce you to vote freely and frankly for the rider offered by Mr. Cazabat. It is the poor man who is unable to lose a dollar, who is working nine hours a day, and who comes forth honestly to ask his dues. The rich man refuses and goes into the court. Then, would you wish to exclude the testimony of the lawyer, because he acts for the poor man, and goes to the rich man and says, "I have a claim against you for $100, and demand the money." He says, "I will not pay it," and the suit is brought, and he pleads the want of an amicable demand. The lawyer steps up and says, "I presented that bill, and he refused to pay it," and there is an end to that plea, and the poor man gets judgment, and the rich man pays the cost.

We should do justice to all classes of men, and while I advocate the testimony of the lawyer being admitted, I say there are many men, who practice at the bar, who doubtless would abuse this power; but they are the exceptions to the general rule. The members of the bar, particularly of New Orleans, have refrained from testifying. The district judges do not approve of it, but there are cases where such evidence is important and desirable. For these reasons it is certainly important the clauses should be stricken from the constitution and that the rider should prevail.

Mr. ABELL—Mr. President, I wish to submit only a few words: I wish gentlemen of the Convention to know I am as much opposed to lawyers testifying in their own cases as any man on this floor. I appeal to the president, who is one of the United States judges, and to the gentlemen on this floor, to state whether they ever saw me testify in a case of my own? I believe I was once called on to say whether I thought a man's character was good or not. I think this is the only case in which I have ever been called upon to testify within the last ten or fifteen years. Where a lawyer comes forward, and testifies for his client, I generally feel some prejudice against him. In considering this clause, I beg you will remember what great injustice you would do the people generally. It represents that the greatest prejudice exists against the lawyers, which I know is not the case with the masses generally. There may be some narrow-minded lawyers, but as a class, there is not a more honorable fraternity upon earth. If you give to any member of the bar a note for $150 to be collected, it becomes necessary for him to employ an agent to make the demand, since he cannot make it himself and testify to the facts, and this must all be done at your expense. Therefore, I consider it a duty you owe to yourselves as well as your constituents to adopt this rider; for it is not the lawyer that is injured, but yourselves, by refusing to admit his testimony. It is no disadvantage; he gets nothing for his services, but does it as a part of his duty, and if you exclude him from that duty, you must have some other agent to perform it, and he would charge in proportion to the time he had to use in doing so. I therefore consider that this intelligent body of men assembled here, representing intelligent people, will not dare to say, and I say it with all due respect, that lawyers shall not be permitted to prove a simple fact in court.

Mr. SMITH—I believe the lawyers to be an honorable and high-minded class of men; but I do not believe that all the virtues nor all the disinterested motives are centered in them. I hold it to be true and believe it to be just, that no man interested in any case has a right to testify. We know very well that there is a class of lawyers who are employed in small cases, for no poor man can afford to employ those of first-class talent in small cases; and they may be much influenced by reason of their fees depending upon the result of the case, and thus the lawyer will come upon the stand and swear as an interested party. I have seen these things and I am the last one to vote for a lawyer to testify in a case in which he is interested. If he knows anything about it, I do not believe he has a right to be in the case.

PRESIDENT—Will you permit your president to make one remark?

[Cries of "go on!"]

PRESIDENT—A lawyer draws up a will; is his testimony to be excluded? If so, estates may go differently from what you intended.

[The rider was then adopted by a *viva voce* vote.]

Mr. CAZABAT—I offer the following rider to article 5:

But capital punishment is forever abolished and prohibited in this State.

Mr. FOLEY—I move its rejection.

Mr. CAZABAT—I have no intention of discussing the subject, and I only present it through motives of humanity. We ought to be very careful when we are engaged in framing the supreme law of the State of Louisiana; how we place in the hands of a judge, or in the hands of twelve citizens, the right to take the life of a fellow being. Soon pleasant peace may smile upon us again, and the day is not perhaps far off when men who have been engaged in destroying our government will come one after another, and participate in the blessings of the free State government of Louisiana.

I contend that a man or a body of men has no right to take the life of a fellow being; that which is given by the Creator must only be taken by Him. (Applause.) Men often suffer the penalty of death when they are entirely innocent, as our reports amply show. In 1848, in the midst of the French revolution, the great advocate of human rights and human freedom, Victor Hugo, advocated the introduction of a clause into the French law prohibiting capital punishment.

This article is perhaps a little premature, and may require some discussion before its adoption. I thought on the subject at the beginning of the session, and of the necessity of engrafting it in the constitution after the adoption of the emancipation act. There is one thing that is dearer than liberty, and that is life itself; and we have no right to take that which we cannot restore by any human power.

Mr. TERRY—If I understand the rider rightly, it prohibits capital punishment. Gentlemen, this is a very dangerous matter to touch upon, and if this rider was incorporated so as to become the law of the State, all the safety we now enjoy would be destroyed—for murder, if not punished by death, would be committed every day. I believe that my life is safe to-day by this law of capital punishment existing; but for that I would not give a feather for my life, because it has been threatened in this very hall. For murder, I would hang a man as high as rope would stretch him. I remember being once a foreman of the jury in a murder trial here in this very city, when, according to the law and evidence, the man was guilty of the crime. I talked to that jury two hours to convince them, and they finally brought in a verdict and hung the man. We want no man to flinch in the face of law and evidence, and I believe it to be the duty of one who sits in so exalted a position, were his own father or brother accused of the crime of murder and found guilty according to the law and evidence, it should be his duty and he should not flinch in saying that the culprit should be hung. I hope I shall never change in these principles. If I ever so far forget myself as to commit this great crime, I should say it would be a blessing to hang me at once, for I believe that it is an easier punishment than any imprisonment. We see every day floating in this Convention petitions and resolutions for minor offences. They have only to get into a higher range of society and petition for the release of the criminal who has committed murder. As long as there is life there is hope, and the criminal feels it even when the rope is descending upon his neck. I do not think it is necessary to debate this question; I believe every sensible man knows he should vote against, and I hope the rider will be rejected.

Mr. HENDERSON—I would direct the attention of this body to the fact that Louisiana is probably the only State in this Union that has gone almost to the extent proposed in this rider. It may seem strange, but it is nevertheless a fact, that the punishment of any crime may be reduced to a life imprisonment in the Penitentiary. There is no State in the Union that punishes crime under the common law. If a man strike a blow in the heat of passion and the person dies from its effects, in most of the States it is manslaughter. Murder requires premeditation, and for this crime the most of the States have prescribed hanging; yet the Convention of Louisiana has gone one step further and borrowed her theory of Livingston, who made a code of criminal law and did away with capital punishment. I believe that when you put a man in the Penitentiary for life, you inflicted the greatest punishment upon him. The government may reprieve him, and under the common law of the land in any case a jury has a right to reduce the punishment for murder down to a term in the Penitentiary.

I move to amend the rider by giving the jury power to reduce the punishment for murder to imprisonment.

Mr. CAZABAT—I accept the amendment.

Mr. HENDERSON—It may be necessary to find a verdict of guilty unqualifiedly and thereby the criminal suffers the sentence of death. There are extreme cases, and I am in favor of a constitutional provision that the jury shall have power to punish according to their own discretion.

Mr. CAZABAT—I withdraw my rider with the consent of the Convention.

PRESIDENT—The amendment offered to the rider is that all penalties shall be proportioned to the nature of the offence, and capital punishment is forever prohibited unless the jury trying the case shall determine otherwise.

Mr. FOLEY—I move its rejection.

Mr. ABELL—Mr. Cazabat having withdrawn his rider, I do not think it is necessary to say any more. Perhaps there is no man who is more tender in feeling than I am. I once killed two animals, one a squirrel and the other a bullock, and I always regretted it. There are cases where a man may commit murder when he had no intention of doing so, and then I think the jury should have discretionary power. At one time in England there were three hundred different crimes punishable by death; but most of them are now punished by transportation, imprisonment, etc.; but so far as murder is concerned, I have no hesitation in saying that it is the interest of the republic and the duty of the jury when it is a clear case of malice aforethought, to put it out of the power of the individual to commit murder again.

[The rider was lost by a rising vote of 20 yeas to 50 nays.]

Mr. S. PURSELL—I offer the following rider to art. 44:

Provided the conditions herein contained shall only apply to white persons.

[On the motion to adopt, the yeas and nays were demanded, but before the question was put, a call of the House was taken to see if a quorum was present, when seventy-nine members responded.

On motion of Mr. Fosdick the Convention then adjourned till 12 M., Saturday, June 25.]

SATURDAY, June 25, 1864.

[The Convention met pursuant to adjournment. The roll was called and the following members answered to their names:]

Messrs. Abell, Austin, Balch, Bailey, Barrett, Beauvais, Bell, Bofill, Bromley, Buckley, Burke, Campbell, Cazabat, Collin, Cook J. K., Cook T., Crozat, Cutler, Davies, Decker, Duane, Dufresne, Duke, Dupaty, Edwards, Ennis, Fish, Flagg, Flood, Foley, Fosdick, Fuller, Gastinel, Geier, Gorlinski, Gruneberg, Gaidry, Healy, Harnan, Hart, Henderson, Hills, Hire, Howell, Howes, Kavanagh, Knobloch, Kugler, Maas, Mann, Maurer, Mayer, Mendiverri, Montamat, Morris, Murphy E., Murphy M. W., Newell, Normand, O'Conner, Orr, Payne J., Pintado, Poynot, Purcell J., Pursell S., Shaw, Schroeder, Schnurr, Seymour, Spellicy, Smith, Stocker, Stumpf, Stiner, Sullivan, Terry, Thorpe, Waters, Wenck, Wells, Wilson—83.

[On motion, Mr. Stauffer was excused for non-attendance.

The minutes of yesterday were read and adopted.]

Mr. SULLIVAN—Mr. President, this being

near the close of the session, I hold in my hand a resolution which was offered in the early part of the session by Mr. Henderson. I am informed, sir, that some of the institutions for which relief is here proposed are in a very destitute condition and unable to furnish meat and vegetables to the children, and many of them are in danger of suffering from scurvy. The resolution is as follows, viz:

Resolved, that the sum of twenty-four thousand two hundred and fifty dollars be, and is hereby, appropriated out of the State treasury, to be distributed to the following charitable institutions of the city and State, as follows:

For the Orphans' Home, New Orleans	$1,500
For the St. Mary's Catholic Asylum	4,000
For the Female Asylum, Camp street	4,000
For the House of the Good Shepherd	500
For the Jewish Widows' and Orphans' Home	500
For the St. Joseph Catholic Orphan Asylum	1,500
For the Firemen's Charitable Association, benefit of its widows and orphans	3,000
For the Elizabeth House of Industry	1,000
For the Society for the Relief of Orphan Boys, Fourth District	1,000
For the Institution for Indigent Colored Boys, Third District	1,000
For the Ladies of Providence, Third District	750
For the St. Ann's Asylum for Destitute Widows and Children	1,500
For the Childrens' Home of the Protestant Episcopal Church	500
For the Catholic Institute for Destitute Orphans	750
For the Catholic Benevolent Association of Baton Rouge	250
For the Female Orphan Asylum, Baton Rouge	500
For the Milné Asylum, New Orleans	500
For the St. Vincent's Orphan Asylum	500
For the Moreau Street Orphan Asylum	500
For the St. Vincent Orphan Asylum, Donaldsonville	500
	$24,250

Mr. HILLS—I wish to ask if the Sisters of Charity are included in that resolution?

Mr. CUTLER—I would inquire if the lawyers are included? Many of them would like to go north this summer.

Mr. FOLEY—I move to strike out the Firemen's Charitable Association, because I don't believe they are worthy of it.

Mr. THORPE—I move to lay the whole matter on the table.

[The ayes and nays were called.]

Mr. MAYER—I wish to change my vote from yes to no.

[The following is the result of the vote:]

YEAS—Messrs. Abell, Balch, Campbell, Collin, Cutler, Davies, Decker, Dufresne, Dupaty, Edwards, Ennis, Flagg, Gruneberg, Gaidry, Howell, Kugler, Mann, Maurer, Mendiverri, Newell, Normand, Pintado, Seymour, Wenck, Wells—25.

NAYS—Messrs. Austin, Bailey, Barrett, Beauvais, Bell, Bofill, Bromley, Buckley, Burke, Cazabat, Cook J. K., Cook T., Crozat, Duane, Duke, Fish, Flood, Foley, Fosdick, Fuller, Gastinel, Geier, Gorlinski, Hart, Henderson, Hills, Hire, Howes, Knobloch, Maas, Mayer, Montamat, Morris, Murphy E., Murphy M. W., O'Conner, Payne J., Poynot, Purcell J., Pursell S., Schroeder, Schnurr, Shaw, Smith, Spellicy, Stocker, Stumpf, Stiner, Sullivan, Terry, Thorpe, Waters, Wilson—53.

Mr. FOLEY—I move to strike out the Firemen's Charitable Association.

Mr. BELL—I move to lay that amendment on the table.

[The ayes and noes were called.]

Mr. BEAUVAIS—Mr. Secretary, change my vote from no to yes.

Mr. MORRIS—Mr. Secretary, I desire to change my vote from no to yes.

Mr. CUTLER—Mr. Secretary, change my vote from no to yes.

Mr. J. PAYNE—I desire to change my vote from no to yes.

Mr. STOCKER—I wish my vote to be changed from no to yes.

Mr. HOWELL—I voted through a misapprehension of the question, and wish to change my vote from yes to no.

[The following is the result of the vote:]

YEAS—Messrs. Abell, Barrett, Beauvais, Bell, Bofill, Buckley, Burke, Collin, Cook J. K., Cook T., Crozat, Cutler, Decker, Duane, Dufresne, Dupaty, Fish, Fuller, Gastinel, Geier, Gruneberg, Gaidry, Henderson, Hire, Howes, Kugler, Maas, Maurer, Mayer, Mendiverri, Montamat, O'Conner, Payne J., Pintado, Poynot, Purcell J., Pursell S., Schroeder, Schnurr, Seymour, Shaw, Spellicy, Stocker, Stumpf, Stiner, Sullivan, Terry, Waters, Wenck, Wilson—50.

NAYS—Messrs. Austin, Balch, Bailey, Bromley, Campbell, Cazabat, Davies, Duke, Edwards, Ennis, Flagg, Flood, Foley, Fosdick, Gorlinski, Harnan, Hart, Hills, Howell, Knobloch, Mann, Morris, Murphy E., Murphy M. W., Newell, Normand, Smith, Thorpe, Wells—29.

[The motion to lay on the table was carried.]

Mr. GORLINSKI—Mr. President, I have a substitute to offer:

Resolved, That the sum of twenty-five thousand dollars be and is hereby appropriated out of the general fund for different charitable institutions and other purposes, to be expended under direction of a board of almoners, consisting of five citizens, to be appointed by the governor.

Mr. BEAUVAIS—I move to lay it on the table.

Mr. DAVIES—I wish to amend by inserting twenty-five hundred dollars for the relief of the widows and orphans of this State, whose husbands and fathers have lost their lives in fighting to uphold the government of the United States.

Mr. SULLIVAN—I move to lay that motion on the table.

[The motion to lay on the table was carried.]

Mr. BEAUVAIS—I wish to amend by inserting, "and that the sum of five hundred dollars be appropriated to the Convent of the Sacred Heart in the parish of St. James."

Mr. SULLIVAN—I accept the amendment.

Mr. SMITH—I wish to amend so as to include all the country within the Federal lines. This appropriating the money exclusively to the city, I am not in favor of.

Mr. PURSELL—I wish to amend by appropriating one thousand dollars to the Female Asylum in the city of Carrollton in the parish of Jefferson.

Mr. DECKER — I offer an amendment: "Whereas many widows and orphans are now in a starving condition in the parish of St. John the Baptist; provided that the sum of two thousand dollars be appropriated to their relief."

Mr. HARNAN— I want to know if they are the widows of rebels. I move to lay it on the table.

Mr. SULLIVAN—I desire to know if there is an asylum there. If there is, I will accept the amendment.

Mr. CAZABAT—I have an amendment to offer:

Provided, That all of said appropriations for charitable purposes be paid from the last amount of twenty thousand dollars already appropriated for the per diem pay of the members of this Convention.

And, provided also, That the following be included, to-wit:

For the relief of destitute Union refugees from Louisiana........	$3,000
Orphan's Asylum in Jefferson parish........................	2,000
Pioneer Fire Co. No. 1, city of Jefferson......................	1,000
St. Vincent's Asylum, Donaldsonville........................	1,000
Orphans and widows of Union soldiers from Louisiana, who lost their lives in the United States service......................	1,000

Mr. HOWES—I move to lay that on the table.

[The motion was carried.]

PRESIDENT—The question now was upon the original resolution as amended.

Mr. HOWELL—I move that the further consideration of the matter be postponed until next Saturday.

[The ayes and nays were called.]

Mr. CAMPBELL—Inasmuch, as I see a disposition here to exclude the widows and orphans of our soldiers who have fallen in defence of the Union, I vote no.

Mr. ORR—I do not understand the question, but vote yes.

Mr. POYNOT—I understand the question, and vote yes.

Mr. SMITH—I want it distinctly understood that I am not opposed to these appropriations, but they have refused to include my parish, and I vote no.

Mr. CUTLER—Mr. Secretary, I wish my vote to be recorded no.

SECRETARY—Do you wish it changed?

Mr. CUTLER—I do.

[The vote resulted as follows:]

YEAS—Messrs. Austin, Barrett, Beauvais, Bell, Bofill, Buckley, Burke, Cook T., Crozat, Duane, Fish, Flood, Fuller, Gastinel, Geier, Gorlinski, Harnan, Hart, Henderson, Hills, Hire, Howes, Murphy E., Murphy M. W., O'Conner, Orr, Purcell J., Pursell S., Schroeder, Shaw, Stocker, Stiner, Sullivan, Terry, Waters, Wilson—36.

NAYS — Messrs. Abell, Balch, Bailey, Bromley, Campbell, Collin, Cazabat, Cook J. K., Cutler, Davies, Decker, Dufresne, Duke, Dupaty, Edwards, Ennis, Flagg, Foley, Fosdick, Gruneberg, Gaidry, Howell,

Knobloch, Kugler. Maas, Mann, Maurer, Mayer, Mendiverri, Montamat, Morris, Newell, Normand, Payne J., Pintado, Poynot, Schnurr, Seymour, Smith, Spellicy, Stumpf, Thorpe, Wenck, Wells—44.

[The resolution was lost.]

Mr. TERRY—I have a resolution to offer:

Resolved, That the sum of one thousand dollars be and is hereby appropriated out of the State funds, not otherwise appropriated, for the celebration of the 4th of July, and that a committee of five be appointed to consult with the city authorities regarding its proper expenditure.

Mr. SULLIVAN—I move to lay it on the table.

[The motion was carried.]

Mr. ABELL—Mr. President, I have a resolution to offer:

Resolved, That the sum of one hundred dollars be allowed to each of the reverend clergymen who have officiated in this Convention.

Mr. SULLIVAN—I move to lay that on the table.

[The motion was carried.]

Mr. AUSTIN—As chairman of the committee to whom was referred the auditor's report, I have a report to make:

To the president and members of the State Constitutional Convention of Louisiana:

Your committee, to whom was referred the report of the auditor of public accounts, beg leave to make the following report, to-wit:

Under all the surrounding circumstances, we find no serious objection to the manner and form in which the State auditor has seen proper to present his report. As to the Confederate notes, we look upon them as *trash*, and lost to the State.

Your committee are of opinion that we should not interfere with the military powers, and therefore, are unanimous in saying that, inasmuch, as the late auditor of public accounts, the Hon. S. H. Torry, has issued warrants only by authority of the military governor, Gen. Shepley, he is not only excusable, but justifiable. As to the Hon. R. K. Howell and the Hon. A. M. Buchanan, your committee are of opinion that they have drawn their salary according to the constitution and the laws of the State of Louisiana, and that the opinion of our auditor, the Hon. A. P. Dostie, "That rebellion had terminated the existence of the Supreme Court," is unfounded and contrary to the prevailing opinion of all loyal citizens of Louisiana, "*that the State has never been out of the Union.*"

As to the Hon. Charles A. Peabody, your committee are of opinion that he never was chief justice of the State of Louisiana, for the irresistible reasons that neither the military authorities, nor the civil powers in this State, ever created a Supreme Court since the arrival of the honorable gentleman in this State, nor was he eligible to a seat on the bench of the one created previous to his arrival, because he was not, and is not, a citizen of the State of Louisiana. And, further, because he was, and is a judge created by the president of the United States, to preside over a court created by the same authority, "the United States Provisional Court for the State of Louisiana." That as judge of said court, he has been receiving a salary from the United States government; and therefore, he has received the sum of $3,541 66 from the treasury of the State of Louisiana, as salary, under the pretence of being chief justice of the State, without any authority, and in open violation of the constitution and laws of the State of Louisiana.

Under these circumstances, your committee recommend that in consequence of these illegal acts of the said Charles A. Peabody, in obtaining said sum from the State as aforesaid, that the attorney general of the State be requested to institute such legal proceedings as may be necessary to recover said sum, with interest, damages and costs. Your committee further recommend, that inasmuch as the necessity for said U. S. Provisional Court has long since ceased to exist, and that the same is but a stumbling block in the way of the administration of justice, and to the loyalty of the good people of Louisiana, that the commanding general of this department, Maj. Gen. N. P. Banks, and his excellency, M. Hahn, governor of the State of Louisiana, be requested to petition the president of the United States to withdraw the commission from, and recall the said Charles A. Peabody, and thereby put an end to the further existence of said court.

As to Mr. Serpas, sheriff of the parish of St. Bernard, your committee are of opinion that as the Confederate notes in his possession were received for taxes collected by him during Confederate rule, he should be exonorated from all blame and released from all responsibility on handing over the same to the treasurer of the State.

O. W. AUSTIN, Chairman.
W. R. FISH,
R. BEAUVAIS,
R. KING CUTLER.

Mr. TERRY—I move that the report be printed and made the order of the day for Saturday next.

[The motion was carried.]

Mr. SCHROEDER—Mr. President, I have a memorial and a resolution here which I have been waiting three weeks to offer.

To the Constitutional Convention of Louisiana.

The memorial of the undersigned respectfully begs leave to call your honorable body's attention to the defects in the law relative to births and deaths, and the necessity of amending the same, as the law as it now stands is defective. By the acts of 1855, page 41, relative to births and deaths, it will be seen that in case of a birth or death, the declaration of the party declaring the same, in the parish of Orleans, (persons residing in the country parishes are not required to record either,) is not supported by an affidavit, thus leaving the door open to fraud; as, for example: suppose a man is married to a woman who possesses in her own right property, both real and personal, and that their marriage is barren of issue; and suppose the wife has relations in the ascending or collateral line, who are non-residents of the State, and who are ignorant of her circumstances, and, may be, of her existence, and, for argument's sake, say the latter; and suppose, too, this man, unknown to his wife, to go, under the provision of the law referred to, and declare before the recorder that a child had been born to him by his wife; and suppose his wife to die intestate, and in total ignorance of such a declaration, what would be the consequence? The husband would, with the assistance and connivance of others, proceed in his right as the natural tutor of his minor (fictitious) child, to get the administration and possession of his deceased wife's estate, and by fictitious claims swallow up the movable property, together, probably, that of the realty, thus defrauding the legal heirs. This, however, is but one way of committing a fraud to the prejudice of the wife's legal heirs, for the wife herself could connive at the proceedings of her husband, for the purpose of cutting off her ascending heirs, if she so desired. What may be said of births may be said of deaths; for instance: a person of the next of kin to an heir of an estate in Europe, residing in this country, to whom such inheritance is unknown, may declare here, before the recorder of births and deaths, the death of the heir, and get a certificate from him to that effect, and have the same certified to by the proper consul, go to Europe, and by the production of such proof obtain, as next of kin, the property bequeathed to or inherited by the heir represented as dead.

These are a few of the defects of the law of 1855. There are others: It will be seen that in the parish of Orleans only is it compulsory for persons to record births and deaths. It is not so in the country. Why is this? If fraud can be practiced in this parish, what a greater latitude there is for its practice in the country parishes.

We, your memorialists, therefore, pray that your honorable body will give this matter your consideration, and devise such means as will prevent the abuses to which, by the villainy of man, the law of 1855 is subject.

CHARLES F. WARNEY.
JOHN SMITH,
and others.

Resolved, That the Legislature shall, at its first session after the adoption of this constitution, provide in each parish an officer for the registration of births, marriages and deaths throughout the State, whose duty shall be to keep for the purpose suitable books, and cause to be entered therein a registry of each birth, marriage and death, giving the name of each parent and the sex of every child born within their parish as above provided; and they shall further enact a law providing for punishment, by suitable fine, all parents of children, born as above stated, who do not report within a reasonable time, to the register above named, the birth and sex of each child so borne; and, also, it shall be the duty of each register above named to keep a registry of the death and marriage of all persons, giving their sex, age and name, with sufficient proof of the same.

[The memorial was, on motion, received.]

Mr. HILLS—I move that a committee of five be appointed by the chair to report next Saturday what appropriations are necessary for the various charitable associations of the State.

Mr. HARNAN—I amend by striking out "five" and inserting "one from each parish and twelve from the city of New Orleans."

Mr. HILLS—I am sure the gentleman did not understand my motion, or he would not have offered his.

Mr. HARNAN—I want all the parishes represented.

[Mr. Hills' motion was put and carried.]

PRESIDENT—The chair appoints Messrs. Hills, Howell, Sullivan, Stocker and Smith.

Mr. SHAW—I have seen a letter, Mr. President, from Mr. Stauffer, stating that he is very sick. I move that he be excused for non-attendance during his illness.

[The motion was carried without objection.]

Mr. WELLS—I wish to offer a resolution and I desire to have the ayes and noes called on it, and I hope the secretary and reporters, and particularly the Times' reporter, will not make any mistakes in recording them.

Whereas, There are many truly loyal ladies teaching the youth of our country, and filling the various positions in our public schools with honor to themselves and the community generally, and who are dependent upon their daily labor for the support of themselves and their families :

Therefore be it resolved, That the proper authorities be notified to raise their salaries twenty-five per cent. on the original sum

Mr. BEAUVAIS—I move its adoptiou.

Mr. BELL—I move to lay it on the table.

Mr. SMITH—I believe that they have salary enough ; I vote yes.

[The vote resulted as follows :]

YEAS—Messrs. Bell, Duke, Edwards, Hills, Howell, Knobloch, Mayer, Murphy M. W., Normand, Payne J., Schnurr, Smith, Sullivan, Wenck—14.

NAYS—Messrs. Abell, Austin, Barrett, Beauvais, Bofill, Bromley, Buckley, Burke, Campbell, Collin, Cazabat, Cook J. K., Cook T., Crozat, Cutler, Davies, Duane, Dufresne, Dupaty, Ennis, Fish, Flagg, Flood, Foley, Fosdick, Fuller, Gastinel, Geier, Gorlinski, Gruneberg, Gaidry, Harnan, Hart, Henderson, Hire, Howes, Maas, Mann, Maurer, Mendiverri, Montamat, Morris, Murphy E., Newell, O'Conner, Orr, Pintado, Poynot, Purcell J., Pursell S., Schroeder, Seymour, Shaw, Spellicy, Stocker, Stumpf, Stiner, Terry, Wells, Wilson—60.

[The motion to lay on the table was lost.]

Mr. HOWES—I have an amendment, Mr. President. I move to add the words "if compatable with the public interest."

Mr. BELL—I second that motion.

[The motion was lost, and the resolution adopted.]

Mr. BEAUVAIS—I move that this Convention do adjourn sine die on Saturday, the 2d day of July, at 3 o'clock P. M.

[The motion was tabled.]

PRESIDENT—The next business in order is Mr. Fosdick's resolution. Read it Mr. Secretary, with the amendment of Mr. Davies.

[The secretary read :]

Whereas, In the opinion of this Convention a large majority of the loyal people of the city of New Orleans are desirous of having the civil government of the city reestablished ;

Be it therefore resolved, That his excellency, the governor of the State, be and he is hereby requested to immediately issue his order of election for mayor, recorders, street commissioner, aldermen, and assistant aldermen, in conformity with the city charter.

Resolved, That the secretary of this Convention be and he is hereby instructed to transmit a copy of the foregoing resolution to his excellency the governor.

Resolved, That the governor of the State be requested to order that elections be held in every incorporated city and town within the Union lines, for all city and town officers, said elections to be held on the same day as the elections of officers for the city of New Orleans.

Mr. DUANE—I move to lay the amendment on the table.

[The motion was carried.]

Mr. FOSDICK—Mr. President, if any other---

Mr. BOFILL—I move to lay the whole subject on the table.

PRESIDENT—The question is to lay the whole matter on the table.

Mr. HILLS—I rise to a point of order.

PRESIDENT—You had better sit to a point of order.

Mr. HILLS—I have a right to rise to a point of order. It is this : that before the motion to lay on the table was made, Mr. Fosdick had the floor and was recognized by the chair ; consequently, the motion to lay on the table at that time was out of order.

Mr. BOFILL—This being the case, I will, with the consent of my seconder, withdraw my motion. I certainly should not have made it had I observed that a gentleman had the floor.

Mr. WENCK—I seconded the motion, and I consent to its withdrawal.

Mr. FOSDICK—Having introduced the resolution, I believe I have a right to close the debate on it. If any gentleman wishes to speak on it, I quit the floor as I have no desire to speak until I close the debate.

Mr. HENDERSON—When the question was up last week, I heard it said by some of my best friends, and those, whom I supposed to be informed, in the matter that if this body did pass a certain resolution it would be carried into effect either by Gen. Banks or Governor Hahn, it was immaterial which. Since that time I have taken some pains to ascertain, and I am satisfied that neither of them will do it. Now, what is the use in our making a request for a city election when it appears by our action that we have so amended the city charter that the officers would have to be changed as soon as the constitution is adopted. The officers, if elected under this resolution would scarcely be inaugurated before a new election would be ordered under the new constitution. It can only at farthest make but one or two months' difference, and the money that would be spent in the election might well be spared for other purposes. I do not differ with the gentleman in regard to the right of the people of this city. The late elections have showed over ten thousand votes in this State, more than half which were in this city, and there is no question of the right of five thousand loyal voters in the city of New Orleans. The only question is one of expediency.

Mr. MONTAMAT—I have no objection to electing the city officers, but I think before it is done the city charter should be revised. That will probably be done by the Legislature which we elect next November.

Mr. STOCKER--I desire to make a motion, but before doing so, I desire to call the attention of the chair to rule XXII; and having done so, I now move to postpone indefinitely——

PRESIDENT—Out of order.

Mr. CUTLER—My object in rising is to carry out the principles that I enunciated on this question one week ago. I am willing to uphold the people in their rights to the election of their own officers of this corporation, but I do not think such an election would be practicable, right or just under the existing state of things. I do not believe it would be right or just to organize a municipal government under the charter as it exists--under the constitution of 1852. That charter requires revision and amendment in order to adapt it to the existing state of things. It is highly important that it should be changed to adapt it to the regulations made by this body. There are many changes required which the next Legislature will undoubtedly make. One of which will be to inaugurate the police system which has been fixed by this Convention by a large majority and incorporated in the constitution. The Legislature will probably think it necessary, too, to make a change in the number of aldermen and assistant aldermen. They may also think it necessary to make other changes in regard to various other offices. Now, we shall have an election after our adjournment on the adoption or rejection of this constitution, and another in November for a Legislature, and then after the adjournment of the Legislature there will necessarily be an election for city officers under the amended charter. It appears to me that we are getting about as many elections as it would be expedient to hold within so short a time, and that there is really no necessity for more; the expense will be enormous to the city treasury, to say nothing of other considerations. One city election is, in my opinion, sufficient, and that one should be held after the charter is amended. But, sir, if it is the determination of my learned and worthy friend to have a city election now, and to force upon this Convention the consideration of the propriety or consistency of requesting Gen. Banks, or the governor, or some other person, to order such an election, let me tell him that first of all I hope he professes to be a law-abiding man. Let me tell him, that this Convention, in their wisdom, have not yet ignored law, and I hope they will not. Then, sir, you are to take the charter as it exists, and when you force upon the people an election in this city, you must do it in some manner consistent with the law. I contend that if you adopt this resolution you ignore the law. You ignore that provision of the charter of 1852 which is so plain that he who runs may read. That charter makes it incumbent on the mayor to order the election for city officers.

Now it may be that some gentlemen of this Convention desire to be officers. It may be that some gentlemen wants to be city treasurer, aldermen, councilmen, or something else; and that may be the reason that some gentlemen have for attempting to force upon this Convention a subject which does not belong to it. I do not pretend that such is the case with Mr. Fosdick; but I do say that it is a matter with which this Convention has nothing to do, and I ask the gentleman to lay his finger on the authority which gives the governor the power which in the resolution he has offered he assumes to be in the governor. There is no such power granted to him by the constitution. There is no such power given him by the law: the law makes it the duty of the mayor to issue his proclamation for the election of city officers, and such will be the case while the charter remains as it does at present. Now, sir, I will not vote for this resolution; but, if it was in proper shape and in accordance with the law, it would be a very different question.

Who was it that took from the proper law the civil power—the power of electing their own officers? Was it the governor? I answer no. It was the military authority —the commanding general. Then, sir, that power, which wrested from the people that government should restore it. The governor has no such power. There is no law authorizing him to issue his proclamation for an election of city officers. The commanding general had the power to wrest the civil government from the people, and he alone has power to restore it. He may be requested to do it, and he may issue his proclamation, and there is no other form in which it could be logically or consistently done. If this Convention should pass a resolution ordering such an election, it would be mere words. We have no power to order a municipal election, much less to order a person, not known to the law, to order one. The whole thing is premature. It is absurd, not because the people are not loyal enough—I believe they are—but because we have made amendments to the constitution which require the action of the Legislature in regard to the charter of the city of New Orleans, and, until that is done, the order for a municipal election in New Orleans is premature.

President Durell—Mr. President and gentlemen, I rise under a feeling of great delicacy to speak upon this question. Down to this time I have been part and parcel of the military government of this city. I took my position in it on the first day of July, 1862, as chairman of the Bureau of Finance, and have remained there much against my will from that moment up to the present time. Three times have I tendered my resignation; three times that resignation has been refused. I tendered it to Gen. Butler, afterwards to his successor, the military governor, Gen. Shepley, and lastly to Major Gen. Banks.

On this subject gentlemen know perfectly well my opinion. Early in 1863 I advised the then military governor to bring about an election by the people for the government of the city in order to bring it back to its normal state and rescue it from its anomalous position. I advised it, not only because I thought that the people were ready and willing to resume the government of themselves, but I considered it as a great and most important political question, which would have its effect both at home and abroad. The city of New Orleans represents, not itself, not the State of Louisiana only, but it represents the whole Valley of the Mississippi. England, France, Austria, Prussia and Russia know nothing of Louisiana or the Mississippi—know nothing of Kansas or the other States bordering this great river and its tributaries, with thirty-five thousand miles of navigation ending at our levee—they only know New Orleans, and therefore I said to that General, "bring back the city of New Orleans—restore it to its normal state, and let Europe see the people of this city casting their votes according to our free institutions for their rulers, and it will tell more for our cause than a great battle won upon a bloody field." There is no doubt of this, and I do think that after two years of this military rule—if there are Union men enough in New Orleans, as I believe there are, to fill the places—they should be filled. As we are at this time framing a new constitution, and claim now to be in the Union, I do think that this great city should also come in under a new dispensation.

Gentlemen have spoken about the present charter. A new one can be made at any time. There are faults about that charter, no doubt, but there are merits in it also. Our constitution has nothing to do with it. When the first Legislature meets under this constitution, if it sees fit to give New Orleans a different charter, it can do so, but this is no reason why we should longer remain in our present anomalous postion. It is no reason why one of our own citizens, of strong common sense and good business habits, should not sit in the mayor's chair. [Applause.] A foreigner to this soil knows nothing about our people, and knows nothing about their wants or resources. I say that a soldier should not be placed in that chair to rule over us. I said eighteen months ago to the military governor of this State, "Sir, put a civilian in that chair," and he promised to do so, but never did.

With regard to this resolution, it simply requests a certain thing, and if Gen. Banks chooses not to comply with it, he will signify that in a proper manner. But if this convention *does* make this request, he certainly will do what you ask, for he desires it as much as any man in this city. It will be the crowning glory of his administration to bring back this great city to its normal state. I hope that gentlemen will not vote improvidently, without consideration, for this is a very important matter and deserves your careful reflection.

Mr. WELLS—I shall vote for the gentleman's bill for several reasons which I, within my own mind, deem good and proper. First—I desire to meet the wants and demands of the people, if possible, by my actions in this Convention. Second—I desire to meet, if not in conflict with the rights of loyal citizens of my native State, the wishes of the president of the United States, in restoring Louisiana to the Union, and place her once more under civil law. By an order from the president we have gone on and elected all of her State officers, and step by step let us proceed without fear or favor in this work of restoration—teach the governor by this Convention, even should it be somewhat out of place or order, and compel him to do his duty whilst we do ours; let the people of this city elect their officers, and the governor be ordered to call an election for that purpose, and that within ten days after the adjournment of this honorable body. This will be but right, and but another step towards the restoration and the operation of civil law in Louisiana. Go on then from parish to parish as we get them under the stars and stripes, and organize them. This city contains over one-half of the population of the State, and to deny them the right of the election of their municipal officers would be but a mockery of what you pretend to be aiming at—the restoration of the Union. You will have acted with duplicity if you dare deny it them, for you urged it upon them—the election of State officers—with the promise that step by step civil law would be restored and they would assume all the functions of citizens. Now, when justice demands it of you—when all that is due loyal citizens requires it, will you deny and refuse to aid them in the restoration of civil law—preclude them from aiding in the administration of civil law in the State?

All power emanates from the people, and to ascertain their loyalty, place them in that situation where their sincerity can earliest be tested. The fundamental law of the State, as we are all aware, by the proclamation of the commander of the Gulf, is martial law. Then we can do no wrong by placing the city under the full control of our citizens, for this check will preclude the possibility of improper city legislation, as her councils can, at a word, be broken up by the sword—that fundamental law.

Then, gentlemen, why deny all that is due civil liberty, or rather a loyal community, asking the right to each and every one of them to administer civil law? Can any one of you face the people of this city—ask them for their suffrage, after telling them that they are incapable of self-government? I think not, unless a self-exalted opinion deludes you to the act.

Mr. SMITH—Before Mr. Fosdick, who closes the debate, takes the floor, I wish to explain my vote. In every single instance have I advocated the right of the people to elect their officers, so far as my vote and my voice would do it; but I maintain that if this Convention orders an election, it may be legal, but, I ask, is it safe? I ask you, Mr. President and gentlemen, how has the reputation of this city gone abroad in Europe? Has it gone abroad as a loyal city? Have the foreigners of this city written home and declared that New Orleans was loyal? Take, for example, a paragraph written by Mitchell, when he says that the Mississippi is as much in the possession of the rebels as the Federals, and that three-fourths of the people of the States bordering the Mississippi, and of

New Orleans, to-day, are bitter rebels. And yet, sir, we are told, at this time, that New Orleans is so loyal that she can elect her own officers at once. We must not trust our present executive; we must not wait until the Legislature is elected, according to the provisions of the constitution we are about to give to the people; no, we must have it forthwith; not trusting those men who have administered the government since it was wrested from the hands of the rebel authorities. Two months is too long a time to divide the loaves and the fishes among the anxious expectants for office. I assert, that to-morrow, if you submit an election of city officers and let men come up and give their votes under the oath they will be required to take, that not a member of this Convention could be elected to any office. On my way home last night, in the upper part of the city, I heard a little knot of men discussing politics. I did not know them and I am certain they did not me. One said the Convention was squandering the money of the State and was a curse to the community. Another said, if an election was ordered in the city of New Orleans, he would swallow the oath for the purpose of voting against every one that had supported the Federal authorities. I assert, if this election is ordered at the present time, that true, loyal Union men will stand no chance at all, for such people will take the oath for the purpose of beating you. Let the Legislature decide this thing. We have nothing to do with the charter; it was abrogated by the act of rebellion in this hall. The city was eminently disloyal and has no rights or claims to its former charter, and our business here is to revise and amend, or create, if necessary, a new constitution.

Mr. Poynot—I am astonished at the course of some of my most intimate friends. I know there are men in this Convention from the country parishes who were never there when the votes were taken; but I have no more to say about it.

I admit the enthusiasm of my country friends. I know myself that a great many of the parishes from where my friends have come they cannot have an election. From the disturbance here in the Convention I think I must come to a conclusion—that I cannot proceed any further. ["Go on."]

Mr. President, I stand to-day where I stood the first day I entered this Convention. I came here an elective man and have continued so, and have always objected to allowing the governor or Gen. Shepley to appoint men even for a single day, but necessity and political movements have compelled me to yield. I also yielded on the judiciary question, although at the time the amendment limiting the term was brought up I was sick at home. I think if the people of New Orleans are competent, as they have proven themselves to be, to elect a Free State governor they can elect a Free State mayor, Free State recorder and Free State everything else in the parish; therefore I say I shall support the elective system all through.

Mr. Stocker—I rise to a point of order. I have refrained from saying anything during this wild discussion. Gentlemen have not been speaking for the last hour on the question before the House; my motion was to postpone indefinitely this matter, and they have been speaking on every question but that. Out of courtesy I have refrained from calling them to order, but I now demand if there is any more discussion on this matter it shall be to the point before the House.

President—When a motion to postpone indefinitely is before the House it is subject to debate, and it is right to discuss the merits of the question. I trust gentlemen will preserve order on the floor while members are speaking. If any correction or remark is to be made the chair should be addressed and not the speaker directly.

Mr. Cazabat—Mr. President, I do not wish to violate any of the rules we have adopted, but the remarks of the gentleman (Mr. Poynot) in regard to the country parishes are untrue, unjust and offensive to every country member on this floor. The loyalty of some of your city gentlemen is beyond question, but you must remember that the *registered enemies* are not from the country. We have no fear to trust the people, for we are of them, with them and for them. It is true that many of us are not able to go back to our respective homes, but is it our fault? I went from New Orleans to Red river during the last campaign, and the scenes of suffering and distress I witnessed there were sufficient to excite the sympathy of any Union man.

I have no interest whatever in the city government. If the loyal people of New Orleans desire a local election, let them have it; I will not oppose that measure in due time; but as a matter of principle, I voted against all kind of resolutions brought improperly before us, and I shall vote against this, because we have nothing to do with municipal elections. (Applause.)

Mr. ABELL—After the aspersions cast against the loyal people of New Orleans, I feel impelled, as a matter of duty and as one of this body, to enter my solemn protest against the sentiments that have been uttered. I say that the people of New Orleans are as much entitled and as capable of conducting themselves and their business as any other loyal people within the United States of America. (Applause.) From the first to the last up to the present time, as you well know, I have been opposed to the civil government; but if we are to have a civil government, which is the decree that has gone forth from those in authority, then I say the loyal people of Louisiana have a right to govern and control, not only the offices, but all the finances of the city of New Orleans. I have no objection to any public functionary that has officiated in this city under the military rule. The military government of this city has been of such a character that I do not know where you would be able to point to a single individual of importance who has not discharged his functions with fidelity. I believe that the military government, the late mayor and present mayor, and the present commanding general, have done everything that was consistent with the interests of the people, and they have done to my perfect satisfaction; but if we are to have a civil government at all, the people of Louisiana are capable of electing such a government. If the people of the State are capable of electing a Legislature, I ask, would the people electing that Legislature be more loyal than those electing a mayor and other city officers? It has been said that the authorities would not regard our wishes in this matter. I think that is an insult to the authorities—even an intimation that such would be the case. It is the people who speak through us. To say that the people of New Orleans, who pay a tax of over two millions of dollars, shall not have the power to appropriate it in accordance with the wants and advancement of the city, is the most astounding proposition that could possibly be made. You may search through all the musty books of every library in the city, and you will not find a precedent recorded where a single corporation has ever been two years deprived of its corporative rights. Here we have a great intelligent people, and if there is any loyalty in this State, it is here.

Mr. FOSDICK—Mr. President—

Mr. CUTLER—I rise to a question of order. It has been the decision of the chair that the chairman of a committee, or the mover of a resolution, has the right to close the debate; therefore, I think that Mr. Fosdick, before taking the floor, should ask if there is any member who is desirous of speaking.

Mr. FOSDICK—I have no objection to gentlemen speaking.

Mr. BELL—I wish to know if I am in order to offer an amendment?

PRESIDENT—You are not: the question is on the postponement.

Mr. BELL—I wish to say that the charter of the city is one of the most infamous I have ever seen, and an election under it would deprive the loyal people of what they are justly entitled to, and I shall vote against it.

Mr. CUTLER—I have very little to say in addition to what I have already said: I have acted sincerely, and I am not a candidate for office; that makes the difference. I know there is a motion before the House to postpone the matter indefinitely; but as the chair, has correctly decided, it involves the question presented by the original resolution. I hold in my hand a remedy for this. I do not desire to make a speech on the subject, but to say simply that something is due to both sides of this question, and justice demands that cool, quiet and proper deliberation should be had upon this subject. For that reason, and without adding a word more, I will read what I desire to present: "That the subject of calling a city election be referred to a committee to be appointed by the chair with instructions to examine where any practical difficulties exist in the way of again putting in force the provisions of the charter of the city, and what provisions, if any, may be required to be passed on the subject by this Convention."

Mr. Fosdick—*Mr. President and gentlemen of the Convention*—I had no idea when I submitted the resolutions to the consideration of the House, on Saturday last, that the mere enunciation of the principle under which this Convention was called into existence, coupled with a request to his excellency the governor to issue his order of election for municipal officers, (not an order or instructions as gentlemen have so strenuously and unjustly endeavored to impress on the minds of members, for I do not claim that power,) that I would provoke such a lengthy, and, I must say, uncalled for debate; nor did I expect that any gentleman on this floor would attempt to choke off action for a whole week. But, in this, sir, I was disappointed; for the opposition have on two occasions, Monday and Tuesday, refused to suspend the rules to take up the resolutions and dispose of them. I shall only occupy the time and attention of the Convention but a very short time in replying briefly to the gentlemen who have arrayed themselves in opposition. I have attentively listened to the arguments of the gentlemen, and have not heard one word that changes or destroys the correctness of the position that I assume; but, sir, I believe they all admit that I stand upon high ground so far as principles are involved, but seek to defeat the resolutions by mere legal quibbles and by what I consider unfair means. My friend and colleague, Mr. Henderson, in a labored though eloquent speech, endeavored in the first place to convince this Convention that I sought to cast censure on the honorable gentleman who is now acting mayor of the city, and that in the face of my assertion to the contrary. Now, sir, I want that gentleman and this Convention to understand that I never do an act covertly that I shrink from doing openly; for if I have one fault more than another, if fault it can be called, it is in a fearless expression of my sentiments, regardless of consequences or personal interests; and in proof of this assertion I appeal to my friends who have known me for the past twenty-seven years for their testimony. He also informed us that it was a mere expression of opinion, to which not the slightest attention would be paid or notice taken. Sir, I must express my surprise and astonishment to hear any gentleman on this floor make such an assertion. What, sir, an expression of opinion from the representatives of the people, and after full discussion and due deliberation, promulgated by them, will meet with no respect or attention from the executive of the State. I, at least, will do him no such injustice, nor will I permit any gentleman on this floor to charge him with such a wanton disregard of the rights of his constituents. He also says that the military power is supreme. Now, sir, no one that I am aware of disputes that proposition. I, at least, certainly do not, for I am well aware that in time of war the civil law is necessarily subordinate to the military power; but do I understand the gentleman to mean that there are not loyal men enough in the city of New Orleans to form a civil government that would harmonize with, and, in fact, from their personal knowledge of the people, render material service and aid to the military? If he does, it is an injustice to his own constituents, and with such views, he should never have accepted a seat in this Convention. I desire to ask the gentleman if, during the disgraceful riots in the city of New York last summer, which have left a foul stain on the escutcheon of the Empire City which can never be obliterated, whether the military power superceded the civil authority? He knows perfectly well that it harmonized with, and acted in concert with, the United States troops—the mayor, during that fearful time, retaining and maintaining his position as chief magistrate of the city.

The gentleman from the Fourth Representative District, Mr. Cutler, for whom I entertain the highest respect, entered into a lengthy legal argument to show that the power was not vested in the governor, but that the mayor was the only officer that could issue an order of election. Now, sir, while I make no pretensions to the wisdom that the gentleman intimated men were prone to assume, I do make pretensions to some little common sense, and therefore contend that the civil government of both State and city were, in consequence of the rebellion, and of the acts of those in authority, in abeyance, and could only again be revived and resumed by permission of the parent government, on such terms and under such prohibitions as might be prescribed.

The distinguished representative of the general government, the commanding general of this department, with a liberality and foresight that entitle him to the gratitude of every Louisianian, solved the question, and by the powers vested in him reconstructed our State government as far as it was then practicable, and immediately thereafter convened this Convention to revise the constitution of the State to suit our changed condition. Now, Mr. President, I take it that the governor elected under his authority, has some power, which I believe he has exercised by the appointment of a number of officers to fill vacancies until an election could be held according to law, and as the city of New Orleans has no civil mayor authorized to act under the laws of the State, we must necessarily apply to him for relief. I am aware that it is contended that the governor has made no appointment of mayor, but only continued Mr. Hoyt in the office. But, sir, I know of no difference between a continuance and an appointment. Now, sir, from whence does he claim his authority? As civil governor he certainly has none, and would only be justified on the grounds of necessity, from our unusual position, and only then until an election could be held. If he claims to be military governor, the people have no knowledge of the fact, for I hold that a civilian can only hold that position by appointment from the president, and confirmation by the Senate of the United States; and in that case can only appoint an officer of the army to the office of mayor. My friend, Mr. Shaw, with his usual frankness, admitted that the principle was right, but urged in opposition article 124 of the constitution of 1852, and the possibility that this Convention might change in some way its reading, and we should therefore wait with patience and act with caution. Now, sir, that gentleman knew full well that the article, and the action of this Convention thereon, had nothing to do with the point at issue. I call the attention of members to the article which passed under the head of General Provisions, on its second reading, a day or two since, and I think without the slightest change. It simply confers the right on the citizens of New Orleans to elect their own municipal officers. The gentleman admitted that the city had a charter from the Legislature, but he neglected to inform you that it was in force to-day only so far as inapplicable to the changed state of the negro population, just as much as the constitution of the State is, under which the governor is now acting, and which he swore to support, except so far as it relates to slavery and the legislation thereon. I ask the gentleman, now, if such is not the case? Then why stave off action on the resolutions? The gentleman counsels patience. Did the advocates of an immediate election for State officers have any patience when they were urged to postpone the election until after a convention was held to revise and amend the constitution of the State? No, sir, they did not, and I am frank enough to admit, that I sustained the policy of an immediate organization of a free State government, by the election of our State officers, as the wisest course, and I believe that most, if not all the gentlemen on this floor, were the advocates of that policy. Now, sir, a few more words of personal explanation and I am done. Mr. President, I have learned that the charge has been circulated, both in and out of this Convention, that disappointment at not receiving the appointment, for which it has been stated I was an applicant, was the reason that induced me to bring the matter up before this Convention. Now, sir, I pronounce the slander false as the hearts of those who invented it, for I defy any man to say that I have applied for any office under general, State, or municipal government; for it is well known to several of my colleagues and others, that I was elected to the seat I hold in this Convention, contrary to my desire, frequently expressed. As I stated in my remarks on Saturday last, I have acted from the beginning of this movement on principle, and whether I have been consistent in my course on this floor, I leave my acts and votes as recorded on the official journal of the Convention to speak for me; but, Mr. President, I consider we have occupied a most ridiculous attitude before the whole country, with a civil government for the State, a Convention now in session revising and amending the constitution of the State, and a military government for the city. If there are reasons for this, to me anomalous state of affairs, I, as a representative of the people, want to know them, and consider I have the right to demand them. I did not come here, sir, for the purpose of representing any one man, or any one particular interest, but solely for the good I might be able to accomplish for the State of Louisiana, and in furtherance of that great principle of a free State government—universal freedom. Exceptions have been taken to my closing remarks of Saturday last, as arraigning the governor of the State. Now, sir, what I then said could not be construed into the slightest censure, unless the rumor I referred to was true. And, Mr. President, as I have since learned, to my astonishment, that it is, I desire to say that I consider it an uncalled for insult offered to the loyal people of this great city, which I, as one of their representatives, am unwilling to pass by unrebuked, and were he my own brother I would arraign him at the bar of public opinion.

In conclusion, Mr. President, I wish it understood, that I am satisfied to have either a military or civil government—one or the other. If the former, ignore the election of State officers and dissolve this Convention; but if the latter, give the city of New Orleans, who cast over half the entire vote of the State at the several elections held, what is clearly her right—the immediate choice of her own municipal officers.

[The motion of Mr. Cutler, to refer the matter to a committee, was then adopted by the following vote:]

YEAS—Messrs. Austin, Barrett, Bell, Bofill, Bromley, Burke, Campbell, Collin, Cazabat, Crozat, Cutler, Davies, Duane, Dupaty, Edwards, Ennis, Flagg, Flood, Foley, Fuller, Geier, Gruneberg, Gaidry, Healy, Harnan, Hart, Henderson, Hire, Howes, Mann, Mayer, Mendiverri, Montamat, Morris, Murphy M. W., Newell, Normand, Payne J., Pintado, Purcell J., Schroeder, Schnurr, Seymour, Shaw, Smith, Spellicy, Stocker, Stumpf, Stiner, Sullivan, Terry, Wenck, Wilson—53.

NAYS — Messrs. Abell, Balch, Bailey, Buckley, Cook J. K., Cook T., Dufresne, Duke, Fish, Fosdick, Gastinel, Gorlinski, Hills, Knobloch, O'Conner, Orr, Poynot, Pursell S., Thorpe, Waters, Wells, Durell —22.

On motion, the Convention then adjourned till 12 M., Monday, June 27th.

MONDAY, June 27, 1864.

[The Convention met pursuant to adjournment. Present, the Hon. E. H. Durell, president, and the following members:]

Messrs. Abell, Austin, Balch, Bailey, Barrett, Baum, Beauvais, Bell, Bofill, Bromley, Buckley, Burke, Campbell, Collin, Cazabat, Cook J. K., Cook T., Crozat, Cutler, Davies, Duane, Dufresne, Duke, Dupaty, Edwards, Fish, Flagg, Flood, Foley, Fosdick, Fuller, Gastinel, Gaidry, Geier, Gorlinski, Gruneberg, Healy, Harnan, Hart, Henderson, Hills, Hire, Howell, Howes, Maas, Mann, Maurer, Mayer, Mendiverri, Montamat, Morris, Murphy E., Murphy M. W., Newell, Normand, O'Conner, Ong, Orr, Payne J., Paine J. T., Pintado, Poynot, Purcell J., Schroeder, Schnurr, Seymour, Shaw, Smith, Spellicy, Stocker, Stumpf, Stiner, Sullivan, Taliaferro, Terry, Thorpe, Waters, Wells, Wilson—80.

[On motion, the following gentlemen were excused for non-attendance, viz: Messrs. Knobloch, Baum, Kugler, Ennis, S. Pursell and Orr.

The minutes of Saturday's proceedings were read and adopted.]

PRESIDENT—The chair appoints, under a resolution adopted Saturday, respecting a city election, Messrs. Cutler, Fosdick, Hills, Orr and Henderson.

Mr. HILLS—Mr. President, the question being on the adoption of the report on

General Provisions, on its third reading, I move the previous question.

[The previous question being carried, the main question was put, and the report on General Provisions adopted on its third reading.]

PRESIDENT—The next business in order is the report of the Committee on Public Education. Mr. Secretary read the report with the amendments.

[The secretary read :]

REPORT OF THE COMMITTEE ON PUBLIC EDUCATION.

To the president and members of the Convention for the revision and amendment of the Constitution of Louisiana :

The undersigned members of the Committee on Public Education have the honor to submit the following report:

Article —. There shall be elected a superintendent of Public Education, who shall hold his office for the term of two years. His duties shall be prescribed by law, and he shall receive such compensation as the Legislature may direct, provided that the General Assembly shall have power, by a vote of the majority of the members elected to both Houses, to abolish the said office of superintendent of Public Education whenever in their opinion said office shall be no longer necessary.

Art. —. The General Assembly shall establish free public schools throughout the State for all children, and shall provide for their support by general taxation on property or otherwise, and all moneys so raised or provided shall be distributed to each parish in proportion to the number o- children between such ages as shall be fixed by the General Assembly, but all schools for colored children shall be separate and distinct from schools for white children.

Art. —. In order to promote the more extensive diffusion of knowledge, the General Assembly shall make annual appropriation for the encouragement of private schools throughout the State, but the General Assembly shall not be required to make such appropriation for private schools in the parish of Orleans that do not number two hundred pupils, and in other parishes the General Assembly shall determine what private schools are sufficiently large to deserve such appropriations.

Art. —. The English language only shall be taught in the common schools in this State.

Art. —. An university shall be established in the city of New Orleans. It shall be composed of four faculties, to-wit: one of law, one of medicine, one of the natural sciences and one of letters. The Legislature shall provide by law for its organization, but shall be under no obligation to contribute to the establishment or support of said university by appropriation.

Art. —. The proceeds of lands heretofore granted by the United States to this State for the use or support of schools, and of all lands which may hereafter be granted or bequeathed to the State, and not expressly granted or bequeathed for any other purpose, which hereafter may be disposed of by the State, and the proceeds of the estates of deceased persons to which the State may become entitled by law, shall be held by the State as a loan, and shall be and remain a perpetual fund on which the State shall pay an annual interest of six per cent., which interest, together with the interest of the trust funds, deposited with this State by the United States, under the act of Congress approved June 23, 1836, and all the rents, of the unsold lands shall be appropriated to the support of such schools, and this appropriation shall remain inviolable.

Art. —. All moneys arising from the sales which have been or may hereafter be made of any lands heretofore granted by the United States to this State for the use of a seminary of learning, and from any kind of donation that may hereafter be made for that purpose, shall be and remain a perpetual fund, the interest of which, at six per cent. per annum, shall be appropriated to the support of a seminary of learning for the promotion of literature, and the arts and sciences, and no law shall ever be made diverting said fund to any other use than to the establishment and improvement of said seminary of learning in such manner as it may deem proper.

ALFRED C. HILLS, Chairman.
M. W. MURPHY,
X. MAURER,
J. RANDALL TERRY,
J. M. WELLS,
GEORGE HOWES.

Edward Hart signs the above, intending to offer an amendment to the third clause.

H. C. Edwards signs, dissenting entirely from the third clause in said report.

Young Burke coincides with Mr. Edwards.

MR. BONZANO'S AMENDMENTS TO THE REPORT ON PUBLIC EDUCATION.

Art. 3. To be entirely stricken out.

Art. 5. An university shall be established in the city of New Orleans. It shall be composed of three departments, to-wit: one of law, one of medicine and one of natural science and letters.

Art. 7. All moneys arising from the sales which have been or may hereafter be made, of any lands, heretofore granted by the United States to this State for the use of a seminary of learning, and from any kind of donation that may hereafter be made for that purpose, shall be and remain a perpetual fund, the interest of which, at six per cent. per annum, shall be appropriated to the support of a collegiate department of the university, and no law shall ever be made diverting said fund to any other use than to the establishment and improvement of said collegiate department, and the General Assembly shall have power to raise funds for the organization and support of said department in such manner as it may deem proper.

MR. DAVIES' AMENDMENT.

Art. 1. There shall be elected a superintendent of Public Education, who shall hold his office for the term of four years. His duties shall be prescribed by law, and he shall receive such compensation as the Legislature may direct.

AMENDMENT TO ARTICLE THREE OF THE REPORT OF COMMITTEE ON EDUCATION.

In order to promote the more extensive diffusion of knowledge, it shall be the duty of the General Assembly to make annual appropriations for the encouragement of all private schools throughout the State, which are, or may hereafter be, incorporated by legislative enactments.

EDWARD HART.

MR. S. PURSELL'S SUBSTITUTES.

Art. —. There shall be elected a superintendent of Public Education, who shall hold his office for the term of four years. His duties shall be prescribed and compensation fixed by the General Assembly.

Art. —. The General Assembly shall establish free public schools throughout the State for white children, and shall provide for their support by general taxation on property or otherwise, and all moneys so raised or provided shall be distributed to each parish or incorporated city, in proportion to the number of children of such ages as shall be fixed by the General Assembly.

Art. —. The General Assembly shall establish free public schools for colored children between the ages of six and sixteen, who shall be taught the primary branches of an English education, the means of support and the distribution shall be the same as provided for other public schools.

Art. —. The English language only shall be taught in the primary departments of the public schools of this State.

Art. —. The General Assembly shall establish an university in New Orleans, and shall have power to pass such laws as may be necessary for its regulation and the promotion of law, medicine, literature and science.

S. PURCELL.

Mr. SHAW—I move we take up Mr. Pursell's substitute for the whole, section by section.

Mr. ABELL—I move to lay it on the table.

[The motion was carried.]

PRESIDENT—The next is Mr. Bonzano's amendment to strike out art. 3.

Mr. BELL—I move to lay that on the table.

[The motion was carried.]

PRESIDENT—Mr. Bonzano's amendment to article 5.

[The secretary read Mr. Bonzano's amendment to article 5.]

Mr. FOLEY—I move to lay it on the table.

[The motion was carried.]

Mr. HOWELL—I wish to inquire for information if the vote now will preclude any one from offering them as amendments when the articles to which they apply come up in the original report.

Mr. HILLS—I rise to a point of order: It is this, that the report should come up at once, section by section, with all the amendments, and I move that it be so taken up.

PRESIDENT—It is not necessary to make such a motion. Mr. Secretary read article 1.

[The secretary read article 1 of Pursell's substitute.]

Mr. SEYMOUR—I move to strike out "two" and insert four.

Mr. CUTLER—I think the secretary will find, by examination of the minutes, that that amendment has been made and the article adopted. If it is to come up again, though, I second the motion.

[The motion was carried, and the article, as amended, adopted.

The secretary read article 2.]

Mr. BELL—I move its adoption.

Mr. SULLIVAN—I have a substitute to offer for that article.

[The secretary read:]

The General Assembly shall establish free public schools throughout the State, for all white children, by general taxation or otherwise, and all moneys shall be distributed to each parish in proportion to the number of white children between such ages as shall be fixed by the General Assembly.

Mr. SMITH—I move to lay it on the table.

[The ayes and noes were called.]

Mr. THORPE—I shall vote no in order to get a direct vote on the question.

[The following is the result of the vote :]

YEAS—Messrs. Abell, Austin, Bell, Bromley, Burke, Collin, Cazabat, Cook J. K., Cook T., Davies, Duane, Dupaty, Fish, Flagg, Flood, Foley, Fosdick, Gorlinski, Gaidry, Healy, Henderson, Hills, Hire, Howell, Mann, Maurer, Murphy E., Newell, Normand, O'Conner, Paine J. T., Pintado, Poynot, Purcell J. Schnurr, Seymour, Shaw, Smith, Spellicy, Stumpf, Stiner, Taliaferro, Wells, Wilson—44.

NAYS—Messrs. Balch, Baily, Barrett, Baum, Beauvais, Bofill, Buckley, Campbell, Crozat, Cutler, Dufresne, Duke, Edwards, Fuller, Gastinel, Geier, Gruneberg, Hart, Howes, Maas, Mayer, Mendiverri, Montamat, Morris, Murphy M. W., Ong, Orr, Payne J., Stocker, Sullivan, Terry, Thorpe, Waters—33.

[The motion to table the substitute was carried.]

PRESIDENT—The question now recurs upon the adoption of the article.

Mr. CUTLER—My amendment is in order if the other is laid upon the table. My amendment is to strike out the sixth and seventh lines of the article and to insert the word "white," in the second line between "all" and children, and to strike out the word "shall" in the second line and insert in its place the word "may."

PRESIDENT—That is precisely the same thing as the amendment just tabled.

[The ayes and noes were called on the adoption of the article.]

Mr. ABELL—Mr. President, I wish the world to know that I vote no.

Mr. SULLIVAN—I will never tax white men to educate negro children. I vote no.

[The vote resulted as follows :]

YEAS—Messrs. Austin, Barrett, Bromley, Bell, Burke, Collin, Cazabat, Cook T., Davies, Duane, Dupaty, Fish, Flagg, Flood, Foley, Fosdick, Gorlinski, Gaidry, Healy, Harnan, Henderson, Hills, Hire, Howell, Howes, Mann, Maurer, Murphy E., Murphy M. W., Newell, Normand, O'Conner, Ong, Payne J., Paine J. T., Pintado, Poynot, Purcell J., Seymour, Shaw, Smith, Spellicy, Stumpf, Stiner, Taliaferro, Terry, Thorpe, Wells, Wilson—49.

NAYS—Messrs. Abell, Balch, Bailey, Baum, Beauvais, Bofill, Buckley, Campbell, Cook J. K., Crozat, Cutler, Dufresne, Duke, Edwards, Fuller, Gastinel, Geier, Gruneberg, Hart, Maas, Mayer, Mendiverri, Montomat, Morris, Orr, Schnurr, Stocker, Sullivan, Waters—29.

[The secretary read article 3.]

Mr. MONTAMAT—I move to lay it on the table.

Mr. SMITH—I second the motion to lay it on the table. Let private institutions take care of themselves.

[The ayes and noes were called.]

Mr. ABELL—I change my vote from yes to no.

Mr. FLOOD—I change my vote from yes to no.

[The vote resulted as follows :]

YEAS—Messrs. Baum, Beauvais, Bofill, Bromley, Cazabat, Cutler, Davies, Duke, Dupaty, Edwards, Fish, Gaidry, Hire, Howell, Mann, Mayer, Montamat, Newell, Normand, Ong, Payne J., Paine J. T., Pintado, Shaw, Smith, Stumpf, Taliaferro—27.

NAYS—Messrs. Abell, Austin, Balch, Bailey, Barrett, Bell, Buckley, Burke, Campbell, Collin, Cook J. K., Cook T., Crozat, Duane, Dufresne, Flagg, Flood, Foley, Fosdick, Fuller, Gastinel, Geier, Gorlinski, Gruneberg, Healy, Harnan, Hart, Henderson, Hills, Howes, Maas, Maurer, Mendiverri, Morris, Murphy E., Murphy M. W., O'Conner, Orr, Poynot, Purcell J., Schnurr, Seymour, Spellicy, Stocker, Stiner, Sullivan, Terry, Thorpe, Waters, Wells, Wilson—51.

[The motion to table was lost.]

Mr. FOLEY—In line 27, I move that it be so amended as to read, "all schools that are loyal."

Mr. THORPE—I have an amendment to offer :

That the schools of the parish of Orleans under the immediate charge of the Roman Catholics, receive from the State treasury such sums of money for the support of education as will be fairly equal to the appropriation made for the public school system adopted by the State.

[A motion was made to lay it on the table.

The yeas and nays were ordered.

Before the vote was announced, Messrs. M. W. Murphy, Harnan, Schnurr and Healy changed their votes from "yes" to "no," and Mr. Burke from "no" to "yes."

The motion was carried by the following vote :]

YEAS—Messrs. Bailey, Baum, Bofill, Bromley, Burke, Campbell, Collin, Cazabat, Cook J. K., Cutler, Duke, Dupaty, Edwards, Fish,

Flagg, Foley, Gastinel, Geier, Gaidry, Hart, Hire, Howell, Maas, Mann, Maurer, Mayer, Montamat, Morris, Newell, Normand, Ong, Payne J., Paine J. T., Pintado, Poynot, Purcell J., Seymour, Shaw, Smith, Spellicy, Stumpf, Taliaferro, Wells---43.

NAYS---Messrs. Abell, Austin, Balch, Barrett, Beauvais, Bell, Buckley, Cook T., Crozat, Davies, Duane, Dufresne, Flood, Fosdick, Fuller, Gorlinski, Gruneberg, Healy, Harnan, Henderson, Hills, Howes, Mendiverri, Murphy E., Murphy M. W., O'Conner, Orr, Schnurr, Stocker, Stiner, Sullivan, Terry, Thorpe, Waters, Wilson---35.

Mr. HENDERSON---I demand a recall of the roll; I think the motion was not carried.

Mr. SULLIVAN---I second it; the result has not been given correctly. ["Call the roll again."]

Mr. DAVIES---I feel astonished, Mr. President. I feel at a loss to understand how a number of gentlemen assembled here—— ["Out of order."]

Mr. SULLIVAN---The gentleman is out of order.

PRESIDENT---The gentleman is not in order; there is no question before the House.

Mr. CAZABAT---I offer the following substitute:

No appropriation whatever shall be made by the General Assembly for the support of private schools, but encouragement may be granted to public schools throughout the State.

Mr. SULLIVAN---I insist upon a recall of the roll on the last question. ["Call the roll."]

PRESIDENT --- Sergeant-at-arms ask that gentleman to take his seat, and see that he does it.

[Mr. Cazabat read his amendment again.]

Mr. HEALY---I move to lay it on the table.

[The motion was declared carried by a *viva voce* vote, when a division was called for.]

Mr. SULLIVAN---I demand the vote on Mr. Thorpe's amendment be recounted. I appeal from the decision of the chair.

[The rising vote on the tabling of Mr. Cazabat's amendment was as follows: yeas 28, nays 32.]

PRESIDENT---Now, before going any farther, inasmuch as there appears to be a misunderstanding and a great desire for disorder, I will count over the returns of the ballot of yeas and nays on the amendment of Mr. Thorpe, as given by the secretary, and as I call out the name and the way the member voted, if there is any mistake he will correct it.

[The president then read over the yeas and nays, and they were found to be correct.

The yeas and nays were then ordered on the motion to lay Mr. Cazabat's substitute on the table, the result being as follows:]

YEAS---Messrs. Abell, Austin, Balch, Barrett, Bell, Buckley, Burke, Cook T., Cutler, Duane, Dufresne, Flagg, Flood, Foley, Fosdick, Fuller, Gorlinski, Gruneberg, Healy, Harnan, Henderson, Hills, Howes, Maurer, Mayer, Mendiverri, Murphy E., Murphy M. W., O'Conner, Orr, Purcell J., Schnurr, Spellicy, Stiner, Sullivan, Terry, Waters, Wells, Wilson---39.

NAYS---Messrs. Bailey, Baum, Beauvais, Bofill, Bromley, Campbell, Collin, Cazabat, Cook J. K., Crozat, Davies, Duke, Dupaty, Edwards, Fish, Gastinel, Geier, Gaidry, Hart, Hire, Howell, Maas, Mann, Montomat, Morris, Newell, Normand, Ong, Paine J. T., Payne J., Pintado, Poynot, Seymour, Shaw, Smith, Stocker, Stumpf, Taliaferro, Thorpe, ---39.

[There being a tie, the president voted no, and the motion was lost.]

Mr. HILLS---I wish to call attention to the fact that the proposition is but a repetition of article 2. That article provides for the support of the public schools, and he proposes to repeat it in substance in the second article. If we are going to reject article 3, it should be rejected upon its merits, but it seems absurd to repeat.

Mr. DAVIES---If the third article is carried it will be the means of breaking up the public schools altogether.

Mr. SULLIVAN---We may as well break them up as they are conducted now.

Mr. CAZABAT---My object in offering this substitute was to prevent the Legislature hereafter from making appropriations for the support and encouragement of private schools of all denominations. In order to make it satisfactory to all parties I will withdraw the last portion of the substitute, making it read "no appropriation whatever shall be made by the General Assembly for the support of private schools." I now call for the yeas and nays on its adoption.

Mr. HEALY---I move to lay it on the table.

The motion was carried by a rising vote. Yeas 39, nays 32.

Mr. MONTAMAT—I move to stirike out the whole article.

Mr. HILLS—I move to lay that motion on the table.

Mr. FOLEY—We have already voted on that in considering Mr. Bronzano's amendment.

PRESIDENT—That is true; the question now is on the adoption of the article as reported.

[The ayes and noes were called.]

Mr. FOLEY—I change my vote from "yes" to "no."

YEAS—Messrs. Abell, Austin, Balch, Barrett, Bell, Buckley, Cook T., Duane, Dufresne, Flagg, Flood, Fosdick, Gorlinski, Gruneberg, Healy, Harnan, Henderson, Hills, Howes, Maurer, Mayer, Morris, Murphy E., Murphy M. W., O'Conner, Orr, Purcell, J., Stocker, Stiner, Sullivan, Terry, Thorpe, Waters, and Wilson—34.

NAYS—Messrs. Bailey, Baum, Beauvais, Bofill, Bromley, Burke, Campbell, Collin, Cazabat, Cook J. K., Crozat, Cutler, Davies, Duke, Dupaty, Edwards, Fish, Foley, Fuller, Gastinel, Geier, Gaidry, Hart, Hire, Howell, Maas, Mann, Mendiverri, Montamat, Newell, Normand, Ong, Payne J., Paine J. T., Pintado, Poynot, Schnurr, Seymour, Shaw, Smith, Spellicy, Stumpf, Taliaferro, and Wells—44.

The article was rejected.

Mr. FOLEY—Having voted in the affirmative, I now move for a reconsideration of the vote.

Mr. MONTAMAT—I move to lay the motion on the table.

[Lost. The motion to reconsider was then put and lost.]

Mr. DUANE—I move to adjourn.

[The motion was lost.

The secretary read :]

Art. 4. The English language only shall be taught in the common schools of this State.

Mr. HILLS—I have a substitute for that article, which perhaps all of the Committee on Education will accept, but I had no chance of conferring with them. With the permission of the chair I wish to make a single remark in regard to this article. The object of the committee was not to prohibit the study of the French language in the schools, but evidently such would be the effect as the report stands now. The object of the committee was this: To put in such a clause as would require every school to teach the English language, because we have schools in the State now in which no language except French is taught, and the result is the children grow up unable to speak English, and we wish to provide against this evil. Therefore I offer the following as a substitute for article 4:

"The general exercises in the common schools shall be conducted in the English language."

[A motion to lay it on the table was lost.]

Mr. MONTAMAT—I have an amendment to the substitute: "The English language shall be taught in the public schools in this State.

Mr. HEALY—I move to lay it on the table.

[The motion was lost.

The amendment to the substitute was then adopted.

On the adoption of article 4, as amended, a division was called for and the motion lost—yeas 31, nays 36.

The substitute of Mr. Hills was then adopted.

The Secretary read :]

Art. 5. An university shall be established in the city of New Orleans. It shall be composed of four faculties, to-wit: one of medicine, one of natural science and one of letters. The Legislature shall provide by law for its organization, but shall be under no obligation to contribute to the establishment or support of said university by appropriation.

Mr. GORLINSKI—I move to strike out all after organization.

[The amendment was laid on the table.

Mr. HOWELL—I move to substitute for this article, article 139 of the constitution of 1852: "The University of Louisiana, in New Orleans, as now established, shall be maintained.

[The motion was lost.]

Mr. SMITH—I wish to amend by saying, "The university shall be established at such place as shall be determined by the Legislature of the State." I do not believe in giving everything to New Orleans.

[The motion was tabled.]

Mr. BAUM—I move to strike out the whole article.

Mr. HILLS—I move to lay that on the table.

[The motion was carried.]

On *viva voce* vote article 6 was announced as carried, which was confirmed on division called—ayes 43, nays 23.

A roll of the House was called—78 members found present.

[The secretary read article 6 of the original report.

Mr. CAZABAT—I move to insert "public" before "schools."

Mr. HILLS—I accept the amendment.

[The article was adopted as amended.

The secretary read article 7 of the report.]

Mr. HARNAN—I move to lay the whole article on the table.

Mr. SULLIVAN—I second the motion.

[The motion was lost and article 7 adopted as reported.

On the motion to adopt the report as a whole on its second reading the ayes and noes were called.

YEAS—Messrs. Austin, Barrett, Bell, Bromley, Burke, Cazabat, Collin, Cook J. K., Davies, Fish, Flagg, Flood, Fosdick, Fuller, Geir, Gorlinski, Gaidry, Hills, Hire, Howell, Mann, Morris, Murphy E., Normand, Payne J., Paine J. T., Pintado, Poynot, Seymour, Shaw, Smith, Spellicy, Stumpf, Thorpe. Wells, Wilson—36.

NAYS—Messrs. Abell, Balch, Baum, Balley, Beauvais, Bofill, Buckley, Campbell, Cook T., Crozat, Cutler, Duane, Dufresne, Duke, Edwards, Foley, Gastinel, Gruneberg, Aealy, Harnan, Hart, Henderson, Howes, Maas, Maurer, Mayer, Mendiverri, Montamat, Murphy M. W., Newell, O'Conner, Ong, Orr, Purcell J., Schnurr, Stocker, Stiner, Sullivan, Taliaferro, Terry, Waters—41.

[The report was rejected.]

Mr. SULLIVAN—I move we adjourn.

[The motion was carried, and the Convention adjourned until 12 M. of Tuesday, the 28th inst.]

TUESDAY, June 28, 1864.

[The Convention met pursuant to adjournment. Present, the Hon. E. H. Durell, president, and the following members :]

Messrs. Abell, Austin, Balch, Bailey, Barrett, Baum, Beauvais, Bell, Bofill, Bromley, Buckley, Burke, Campbell, Collin, Cazabat, Cook J. K., Cook T., Crozat, Davies, Decker, Duane, Dufresne, Duke, Dupaty, Edwards, Fish, Flagg, Flood, Foley, Fosdick, Fuller, Gastinel, Geier, Gorlinski, Gruneberg, Gaidry, Healy, Harnan, Hart, Henderson, Hills, Hire, Howell, Howes, Maas, Mann, Maurer, Mayer, Mendiverri, Mor tamat, Morris, Murphy E., Murphy M. W., Newell, Normand, O'Conner, Ong, Payne J., Paine J. T., Pintado, Poynot, Purcell J., Pursell S., Schroeder, Schnurr, Seymour, Shaw, Smith, Spellicy, Stocker, Stumpf, Stiner, Sullivan, Taliaferro, Terry, Thorpe, Waters, Wenck, Wells, Wilson—81.

On motion of Mr. Campbell, Mr. Stauffer was excused for non-attendance, on account of sickness.

[The secretary read the minutes.]

Mr. FOLEY—Mr. President, the secretary read that my motion "provided the schools be loyal," was lost. The question was never put to the House. I wish the minutes to be corrected on that point.

[The minutes were corrected as suggested and adopted.]

Mr. CAZABAT—Before proceeding, I wish to move a suspension of the rules to act immediately on a resolution which I wish to offer, viz :

Resolved, That this Convention do adjourn *sine die* on Monday, the 4th day of July next.

[The motion to suspend the rules was lost.]

Mr. BEAUVAIS—Before proceeding further I move a reconsideration of the vote on the report of the Committee on Public Education.

Mr. FOLEY—I move to lay that on the table.

[The motion to table was lost, and the motion to reconsider carried on a rising vote—ayes 56, noes 16.]

Mr. BEAUVAIS—I now move to refer the whole matter to a special committee of five, to be appointed by the chair, to report tomorrow morning.

Mr. SMITH—I move to lay the whole subject on the table.

Mr. FOLEY—I second the motion.

Mr. BALCH—I second the motion.

[The motion to table was lost and Mr. Beauvais' motion carried.]

PRESIDENT—The next business in order is the report of the Committee on the Mode of Revising the Constitution.

Mr. BEAUVAIS—Before we proceed I wish to say I believe the report of the Committee on the Mode of Revising the Constitution passed its final reading and was adopted. I think if the secretary will refer to the minutes he will find it is so.

The secretary was directed to ascertain.

PRESIDENT—On the special committee to whom the whole subject of education is referred to make a report to-morrow, the chair appoints Messrs. Beauvais, Hills, Howell, Wells and Campbell.

Mr. HILLS—I desire to be excused from serving on the committee. I have already made a report satisfactory to myself.

Mr. MONTAMAT—I move then none of the old committee be appointed on the special committee.

PRESIDENT—I will appoint Mr. Shaw instead of Mr. Hills.

Mr. SHAW—As I am already on two committees, requiring all my time, I ask to be excused.

PRESIDENT—I will appoint Mr. Sullivan in place of Mr. Shaw.

Mr. BEAUVAIS—I move that Mr. Thorpe be appointed also on the committee.

Mr. HEALY—We ought to have none of the members of the first committee. Mr. Wells was on that committee.

PRESIDENT—The Convention leaves the appointment to the chair, and the chair will do its duty. [Applause.] If the Convention desires to appoint the committee, it may do so.

Mr. MONTAMAT—I move the Convention appoint the committee.

[The motion was lost.]

PRESIDENT—The committee will stand as appointed—the secretary informs the chair that the report on mode of revising the constitution was adopted on its second reading, but that it was not taken up section by section.

Mr. BEAUVAIS—There is but one section in the report.

PRESIDENT—Then it is on its third reading.

[The secretary read the report :]

REPORT OF THE COMMITTEE ON MODE OF REVISING THE CONSTITUTION.

To the president and members of the State Constitutional Convention.

Your committee, to whom was referred the "mode of revising the constitution," beg leave to submit the following report, and recommend the adoption of the following instead of article 141 of the constitution of 1852 :

Art. —. Any amendment or amendments to this constitution may be proposed in the Lenate or House of Representatives, and if the same shall be agreed to by two-thirds of the members elected to each house, such proposed amendment or amendments shall be entered on their journals, with the yeas and nays taken thereon. Such proposed amendment or amendments shall be submitted to the people, at an election to be ordered by said Legislature, and held within ninety days after the adjournment of the same, and after thirty days' publication according to law ; and, if a majority of the votes at said election shall approve and ratify such amendment or amendments, the same shall become a part of the constitution. If more than one amendment be submitted at a time, they shall be submitted in such manner and form that the people may vote for or against each amendment separately.

Respectfully submitted,

R. KING CUTLER, Chairman.
JOSEPH G. BAUM,
J. H. STINER,
PATRICK HARNAN,
E. A. KNOBLOCH.

Mr. MONTAMAT—I offer as a rider article 141 of the constitution of 1852 :

Any amendment or amendments to this constitution may be proposed in the Senate or House of Representatives, and if the same shall be agreed to by two-thirds of the members elected to each House, such proposed amendment or amendments shall be entered on the journals with the yeas and nays taken thereon ; and the secretary of state shall cause the same to be published three months before the next general election for representatives of the State Legislature in at least one newspaper in French and English, in every parish in the State in which a newspaper shall be published ; and such proposed amendment or amendments shall be submitted to the people at said election, and if a majority of the votes at said election shall approve and ratify such amendment or amendments, the same shall become a part of the constitution. If more than one amendment be submitted at a time, they shall be submitted in such manner and form that the people may vote for or against each amendment separately.

Mr. BEAUVAIS—I move its rejection.

[The motion carried—yeas 66, nays 18.]

Mr. SMITH—I move as a rider to strike out of the third line "two-thirds" and insert "a majority." The other portions of the constitution we have changed to a majority, and this alone stands two-thirds.

[The rider was rejected by a rising vote —yeas 33, nays 31, and the repo.t was then adopted as presented.]

PRESIDENT—The next report in order is schedule.

Mr. TERRY—I move a new committee be appointed on schedule.

Mr. FLAGG—The report is nearly ready and should be sent here from the printer this afternoon.

Mr. SHAW—I move the Convention take a recess of thirty minutes.

PRESIDENT—The chairman of the Committee on Ordinance, and also a member of the Committee on Schedule state that the reports are now in the hands of the printer, and it is moved that the Convention take a recess of thirty minutes.

[The motion was carried.

When the House was called to order the roll was called and sixty-seven members answered to their names.

There being no quorum, the sergeant-at-arms was directed to bring in absent members.

A motion was made to adjourn.]

PRESIDENT—Permit me to say to the gentlemen who wish to adjourn, that these two bills are mere matters of form, and when the Convention has a quorum, they will pass rapidly through the third reading, so that this Convention can close its business this week. I think the gentleman who is unwilling to remain here, until we can, under the rules of the Assembly, get a quorum, wishes to prolong the Convention. We are rapidly drawing to a close, and I will say in this connection, that I feel that this Convention has done its duty honorably and honestly, and have made a constitution superior to any which has been made by any previous Convention on this continent. [Applause.]

[Upon the motion to adjourn, the yeas and nays were called with the following result:]

YEAS—Messrs. Abell, Balch, Bailey, Bofill, Buckley, Burke, Campbell, Cook J. K., Crozat, Decker, Dufresne, Duke, Fosdick, Fuller, Gastinel, Gruneberg, Harnan, Hart, Hills, Hire, Maas, Maurer, Mayer, Montamat, Murphy M. W., O'Conner, Payne J., Pintado, Poynot, Schroeder, Schnurr, Seymour, Shaw, Spellicy, Stumpf, Stiner, Sullivan, Waters—38.

NAYS—Messrs. Austin, Barrett, Beauvais, Bell, Bromley, Cazabat, Cook T., Davies, Edwards, Fish, Flagg, Flood, Foley, Geier, Gorlinski, Gaidry, Henderson, Howes, Howell, Mann, Morris, Murphy E., Newell, Normand, Ong, Purcell J., Pursell S., Smith, Stocker, Taliaferro, Terry, Thorpe, Wenck, Wells, Wilson—35.

[The Convention accordingly adjourned until 12 M. of Wednesday, June 29.

WEDNESDAY, June 29, 1864.

[The Convention met and was called to order, pursuant to adjournment.

Present, Hon. E. H. Durell, president, in the chair, and the following members:]

Messrs. Austin, Balch, Barrett, Baum, Bell, Beauvais, Bofill, Buckley, Burke, Campbell, Cazabat, Collin, Cook J. K., Cook T., Crozat, Davies, Decker, Duane, Dufresne, Dupaty, Duke, Edwards, Fish, Flagg, Flood, Foley, Fosdick, Fuller, Gastinel, Geier, Gorlinski, Gruneberg, Gaidry, Healy, Harnan, Hart, Henderson, Hills, Hire, Howell, Howes, Kavanagh, Maas, Mann, Maurer, Mayer, Mendiverri, Montamat, Morris, Murphy E., Murphy M. W., Newell, Normand, O'Conner, Orr, Payne J., Paine J. T., Pintado, Poynot, Purcell J., Pursell S., Schroeder, Schnurr, Shaw, Smith, Stocker, Stumpf, Stiner, Sullivan, Taliaferro, Terry, Thorpe, Waters, Wells, Wilson—76.

Absent, the following members:

Messrs. Abell, (excused,) Ariail, Bennie, Bonzano, Bromley, Brott, Cutler, Ennis, (excused,) Heard, Knobloch, (excused,) Kugler, (excused,) Lobdell, Millspaugh, Montague, Ong, Seymour, (excused,) Stauffer, (excused,) Thomas and Wenck.

[The journal of yesterday was read and approved.]

Mr. MONTAMAT—Mr. President, I move that Mr. Abell be excused for non-attendance this morning as he is very sick and unable to be here.

Mr. BUCKLEY—I have a letter from Mr. Abell stating that he is sick and unable to be present to-day, and I move he be excused.

Mr. POYNOT—I move that Mr. Spellicy be also excused on account of sickness.

Mr. FLAGG—I move that Mr. Seymour be excused.

Mr. WATERS—I move that Mr. Fuller be excused.

Mr. FOLEY—I object to having Mr. Abell excused.

Mr. GRUNEBERG—I wish to state for Mr. Bromley, that he is absent on government business, and I shall therefore ask for him to be excused.

PRESIDENT—The gentleman will be excused unless there are objections.

Mr. FOSDICK—I wish to move a suspension of the rules in order to take up my resolution in regard to the report of the Committee on the Legislative Department. The committee find that there has been a mistake on their part or a misprint, by which injustice has been done to some of the parishes, and they desire to correct the error.

[The motion to suspend the rules was lost, only thirty-five members voting for it.]

Mr. HOWELL—Mr. President, the majority of the Special Committee on Education beg leave to present a report:

REPORT OF THE COMMITTEE ON EDUCATION.

To the president and members of the Convention:

The undersigned beg leave to submit the following as their report on Public Education:

Article 1. The Legislature shall establish free public schools throughout this State and provide for their support, by taxation on property or otherwise; and all moneys so raised shall be distributed to each parish in proportion to the number of children between certain fixed ages.

Art. 2. Instruction in the English language only shall be required in the common schools of this State.

Art. 3. A university, composed of a law department, a medical department and a collegiate department, combining therewith the state seminary of learning, shall be established and maintained.

Art. 4. All moneys arising from grants, donations or other sources for educational purposes, shall be and remain a perpetual fund, the interest of which, at six per cent., shall be appropriated exclusively to said purpose.

R. K. HOWELL,
T. M. WELLS,
B. CAMPBELL,
A majority of the Special Committee.

Mr. DAVIES—I move the adoption of the report.

Mr. BEAUVAIS—I happened to be chairman of that committee, and as we were unable to come to a unanimous conclusion, I beg leave to present a minority report:

MINORITY REPORT OF THE COMMITTEE ON EDUCATION.

To the president and members of the State Constitutional Convention:

Your committee, to whom was referred the report of the Committee on Education, being unable to agree upon any report, the chairman of said committee respectfully begs leave to submit the following:

Art. —. The Legislature shall provide for the education of the children of the State by the maintenance of free public schools.

Art. —. A university, composed of a law school, a medical school, and a collegiate school, combining therewith the State seminary of learning, shall be established and maintained.

Art. —. All moneys arising from grants, donations, or other sources, for educational purposes, shall be and remain a perpetual fund, the interest of which, at seven per cent. per annum, shall be appropriated exclusively to said purposes.

R. BEAUVAIS, Chairman.

Mr. SULLIVAN—Mr. President, I have another minority report which I wish to offer:

MINORITY REPORT OF THE COMMITTEE ON PUBLIC EDUCATION.

Article 1. There shall be elected a superintendent of public education, who shall hold his office for the term of two years. His duties shall be prescribed by law, and he shall receive such compensation as the Legislature may direct, provided that the General Assembly shall have power, by a vote of the majority of the members elected to both Houses, to abolish the said office of superintendent of public education, whenever, in their opinion, said office shall be no longer necessary.

Art. 2. The General Assembly shall establish free public schools throughout the State for all children, and shall provide for their support by general taxation on property or otherwise, and all moneys so raised or provided, shall be distributed in proportion to the number of children between such ages as shall be fixed by the General Assembly; but no money shall be appropriated, under any circumstances, except upon satisfactory evidence that there are scholars regularly educated, in established schools, to receive the benefit of the money appropriated. All associations, combining the mixed character of charity, asylums for orphans, and primary educational schools, containing over two hundred scholars, shall be considered public schools of the State.

Art. 3. The general exercises in the common schools shall be conducted in the English language.

Art. 4. An university shall be established in the city of New Orleans. It shall be composed of four faculties, to-wit: one of law, one of medicine, one of the natural sciences, and one of letters. The Legislature shall provide by law for its organization, but shall be under no obligation to contribute to the establishment or support of said university by appropriation.

Art. 5. The proceeds of all lands heretofore granted by the United States to this State for the use or support of schools, and of all lands which may hereafter be granted or bequeathed to the State, and not expressly granted or bequeathed for any other purpose, which hereafter may be disposed of by the State, and the proceeds of the estates of deceased persons to which the State may become entitled by law, shall be held by the State as a loan, and shall be and remain a perpetual fund, on which the State shall pay an annual interest of six per cent., which interest, together with the interest of the trust funds, deposited with the State by the United States, under the act of Congress approved June 23, 1836, and all the rents of the unsold lands, shall be appropriated to the support of such schools, and the appropriation shall remain inviolable.

Art. 6. All moneys arising from the sales which have been or may hereafter be made of any lands heretofore granted by the United States to this State for the use of a seminary of learning, and from any kind of a donation that may hereafter be made for that purpose, shall be and remain a perpetual fund, the interest of which, at six per cent. per annum, shall be appropriated to the support of a seminary of learning for the promotion of literature, and the arts and sciences; and no law shall ever be made diverting such funds to any other use than the establishment and improvement of said seminary of learning; and the General Assembly shall have power to raise funds for the organization and support of said seminary of learning, in such manner as it may deem proper.

(Signed,) JOHN SULLIVAN.

Mr. BELL—I second Mr. Sullivan's report.

Mr. WILSON—I move to lay it on the table.

Mr. FLAGG—Mr. President, the Committee on Schedule report as follows:

REPORT OF THE COMMITTEE ON SCHEDULE.

The Committee on Schedule begs leave to report as follows:

Art. 1. The constitution adopted in 1852 is declared to be superceded by this constitution, and in order to carry the same into effect it is hereby declared and ordained as follows:

Art. 2. All rights, actions, prosecutions, claims and contracts, as well of individuals as of bodies corporate, and all laws in force at the time of the adoption of this constitution, and not inconsistent therewith, shall continue as if the same had not been adopted.

Art. 3. In order that no inconvenience may result to the public service from the taking effect of this constitution, no officer shall be superceded thereby; but the laws of this State relative to the duties of the several officers—executive, judicial and military, excepting those made void by military authority, and by the ordinance of emancipation—shall remain in full force, though the same be contrary to this constitution, and the several duties shall be performed by the respective officers of the State, according to the existing laws, until the organization of the government under this constitution, and the entering into office of the new officers to be appointed under said government, and no longer.

Art. 4. The Legislature shall provide for the removal of all causes now pending in the Supreme Court or other courts of the State, under the constitution of 1852, to courts created by or under this constitution.

G. H. FLAGG,
A. GAIDRY,
ALFRED SHAW,
J. DUPATY.

[Also, the following minority report of Messrs. Gruneberg and Dufresne on Schedule:]

REPORT OF THE COMMITTEE ON SCHEDULE.

Mr. President—Your Committee on Schedule beg leave to make the following report:

Art. 1. The Constitutional Convention over which you preside derives its authority from no other source than the mandate of the commanding officer of the Department of the Gulf, Maj. Gen. N. P. Banks, which he published on the eleventh day of March, 1864. This order defines clearly the extent of powers which the general has thought fit and proper to grant to you. By this order the Constitutional Convention of the State of Louisiana was called together to "revise and amend the constitution of the State of Louisiana," and for no other purposes. Our task was to pass in review every line, article and title of this constitution, and to make therein the necessary changes. The moment that we overstepped these landmarks and presumed to introduce new subject-matter, of which not a vestige can be found in the old constitution, and attempted to legislate thereon, we made ourselves liable to be accused of an unwarranted assumption of powers not granted to us—and the decisions on matters outside of the jurisdiction of this Convention will stand as mere expressions of opinions, but have no binding force as parts of the organic law of the State. This is the case with the attempted emancipation of the negroes in this State. The status of the negroes has been fixed by the proclamation of President Lincoln, of the 1st of January, 1863, which makes the negroes free in one part and suffers them to remain slaves in another part of the State. In this latter part the rights of the master over his slave have been suspended for the time being by the supreme military authority, but they have never been abrogated by any constitutionally appointed power.

All orders issued from the pen of the commanding general are as clear and precise as language can make them, and his utter silence on the grave and important subject of emancipation in the order which convoked this Convention must be of the greatest significance. This order is so plainly worded that the most subtle arts of implication cannot extort therefrom the faint shadow of an authority for this Convention to touch the emancipation question.

Notwithstanding the harangues of stump orators and the clamor of interested persons, your committee are forced to entertain the firm conviction that the commanding general has intended to withhold from us the power to legislate on the question of freedom or slavery of the negroes. And, inasmuch as the closest scrutiny cannot discover any article in the constitution of 1852, which we were called together to revise and amend, which has reference to or names the negro, we had no right to legislate on his status.

Your committee, in consideration of the above explained reasons, do therefore respectfully recommend, that the sections relating to the emancipation of the negroes in this State be expunged from this constitution as having no place therein, and as being the result, on the part of this Convention, of an unjustifiable assumption of authority not granted to it.

Art. 2. The constitution adopted in 1852 is declared to be superceded by this constitution, and in order to carry the same into effect, it is hereby declared and ordained as follows:

Art. 3. All rights, actions, prosecutions, claims and contracts, as well of individuals as of bodies corporate, and all laws in force at the time of the adoption of this constitution, and not inconsistent therewith, shall continue as if the same had not been adopted.

Art. 4. And in order that the civil government of the State may be carried on in a proper way until this constitution, whenever it shall have been ratified and adopted by the people, can be put into effect, it is hereby furthermore ordained as follows:

Art. 5. There shall be chosen by ballot by the members of this Convention from among the most worthy loyal citizens of the State, a select permanent committee of nine members, to be styled "the Provisional Executive Committee of the State of Louisiana;" four of the members of this committee shall be taken from the residents of the city of New Orleans and five from the country parishes, provided there be no more than one member from any one of the said country parishes. The Provisional Executive Committee shall co-operate with the executive of the State in all appointments of officers, which have been made appointive under this constitution, and in that case five members of said committee shall constitute a quorum, and said committee shall also have power to remove summarily, on request of the governor of the State, such officers from their office as shall have proved themselves unworthy of the trust reposed in them or incapable to fill their respective offices. Seven members of said committee shall be necessary to form a quorum for the purpose of removal from office of any officer, and five of this number must be in favor of such removal before it can be accepted and acted upon by the governor.

The first session of the Provisional Executive Committee of the State of Louisiana shall commence two weeks after this Convention shall have finished its labors, and it shall thereafter meet in the city of New Orleans on the first Mondays of January and July of each year, until the government under this constitution is organized. It shall each time sit no longer than three weeks, and its members shall receive, during their time of service, the same mileage and per diem as the members of the Constitutional Convention are now entitled to.

Any vacancies in said committee, occasioned by death, resignation or otherwise, shall be filled in such a manner as said committee, at its first sitting, may determine upon—however the proportion of city and country members shall always be preserved as above stated. Said committee shall be entitled to appoint a secretary during its sittings, with such salary as the committee may determine upon. A correct report of its proceedings shall be kept, and the same shall be published at the end of each session of said committee in two of the newspapers of the city of New Orleans, to be selected by said committee.

Art. 6. The governor of the State, and the other State officers elected by the people on the 22d day of February last, 1864, as well as all other officers holding commissions from Gen. Shepley, or from the present governor of the State, shall remain in office, unless said offices have been made elective under this constitution, until the organization of the government under this constitution, and the entering into office of the officers to be appointed or elected under said government, and no longer.

Art. 7. The governor shall appoint all the officers whose appointment has been conferred on the executive of the State by this constitution, except to such offices which are already filled, as provided in article 6 of this report, by and with the consent and advice of the Provisional Executive Committee of the State of Louisiana, and said officers shall retain their places until the organization of the government under this constitution, and the entering into office of the new officers to be appointed under said government, and no longer, provided that the governor shall not appoint judges, except for districts, where courts can be held in at least two parishes belonging thereto, and then the salary of said judges shall be proportioned to the number of parishes in which they hold court.

Art. 8. The governor shall issue his proclamation for the election of all other officers which have been made elective under this constitution, to be elected in the same ratio as it was done under the constitution of 1852, as well in the city of New Orleans as in all other parishes of the State, where the vote given for State officers on the 22d day of February last was at least one-third of the votes polled in each respective parish in the presidential election of 1860. The writs for said selection shall be issued by the governor as soon as convenient after the final adjournment of this Convention, but not longer than six weeks after such adjournment. And in all the other parishes of the State the governor shall be authorzed to appoint all the officers of said parishes, at his discretion, by and with the consent and advice of the Provisional Executive Committee. Such officers, whether elected or appointed, shall hold their office until the organization of this government under the new constitution, and the entering into office of the new officers to be elected under said government, and no longer.

Art. 9. Whenever the governor shall believe that any officer, either appointed or elected, has proved himself unworthy of the trust confided to him, or to be incapable for the office for which he has been either appointed or elected, he shall apply to the Provisional Executive Committee for the removal of said officer or officers, and said committee shall act on this request of the governor in the manner provided for in article five of this report.

Art. 10. The laws of the State, relative to the duties of the several officers, executive, judicial, or military, shall remain in full force, though the same be contrary to this constitution, and the several duties shall be performed by the respective officers of the State, according to the existing laws, until the organization of the government under this constitution, and the entering into office of the new officers to be appointed or elected under said government, and no longer.

Art. 11. Appointments to office by the executive under this constitution shall be made by the governor, to be elected under its authority.

Art. 12. The Legislature shall provide for the removal of all cases now pending in the Supreme or other courts of the State to courts created by or under this Constitution.

Art. 13. The first Legislature sitting under the authority of this constitution shall determine when the time of service of all officers chosen by the people at the first election under this constitution shall terminate, and also upon the rotation of the seats of senators and the seats of the judges of the Supreme and inferior courts, and of all other officers which the executive of the State shall appoint according to the provisions of this constitution.

Respectfully submitted,
CHAS. H. GRUNEBERG, Chairman.
P. L. DUFRESNE.

Mr. TERRY—I move to lay the minority report on the table.

PRESIDENT—Out of order.

MR. SHAW—Mr. President, the Committee on Ordinance are now ready to report ; the report is in the hands of the Secretary ; I ask that he read it :

[The secretary read :]

REPORT OF THE COMMITTEE ON ORDINANCE.

To the honorable the president and members of the Constitutional Convention :

The undersigned, Committee on Ordinance, respectfully report as follows :

Article 1. Immediately after the adjournment of the Convention, the governor shall issue his proclamation directing the several officers of this State, authorized by law to hold elections, or in default thereto such officers as he shall designate, to open and hold polls in the several parishes of the State, at the places designated by law, on the third Monday in July, 1864, for the purpose of taking the sense of the good people of this State in regard to the adoption or rejection of this constitution ; and it shall be the duty of the said officers to secure the suffrage of all qualified voters. Each voter shall express his opinion by depositing in the ballot-box a ticket whereon shall be written "the constitution accepted," or, "the constitution rejected." At the conclusion of the said election the officers and commissioners appointed to preside over the same shall carefully examine and count each ballot as deposited, and shall forthwith make due return thereof to the secretary of state in conformity to the provisions of law and usages in regard to elections.

Art. 2. Upon the receipt of said returns, or on the first Monday of August, if the returns be not sooner received, it shall be the duty of the governor, the secretary of state, the attorney general and the state treasurer, in the presence of all such persons as may choose to attend, to compare the votes at said election for the ratification or rejection of this constitution, and if it shall appear at the close that a majority of all the votes given is for ratifying this constitution, then it shall be the duty of the governor to make proclamation of the fact, and thenceforth this constitution shall be ordained and established as the constitution of the State of Louisiana. But whether this constitution be accepted or rejected, it shall be the duty of the governor to cause to be published the result of the polls, showing the number of votes cast in each parish for and against the said constitution.

Art. 3. As soon as a general election can be held under this constitution in every parish of the State, without hostile molestation or interference, the governor shall, by proclamation, or in case of his failure to act, the Legislature shall, by resolution, declare the fact, and order an election, to be at a day fixed in said proclamation or resolution, and within sixty days of the date thereof, for officers of the State. The officers so chosen shall, on the fourth Monday after their election, be installed into office. The terms of office of the State officers elected on the 22nd day of February, 1864, shall expire on the installation of their successors as herein provided for; but under no state of circumstances shall their term of office be construed as extending beyond the length of the terms fixed for said officers in this constitution. The officers elected under this article shall hold their offices for the terms prescribed in this constitution, counting from the second Monday of January next preceding their entering into office.

Art. 4. This constitution shall be published in English and French in the official journal of the convention, from the period of its adjournment until the election for ratification or rejection on the third Monday of July, 1864.

ALFRED SHAW,
M. D. KAVANAGH,
A. MENDIVERRI,
O. H. POYNOT.

Mr. SHAW—I wish to ask the Convention to suspend the rules, and I hope it will be granted in this matter. There is a necessity for an early session of the Legislature of this State, and unless an amendment is made to the report of the Committee on the Legislative Department, it cannot be had. The objects to be gained by it are that it will enable us to participate in the presidential election and entitle us to a representation in Congress at its next session. I think the objects to be gained by it are sufficient to warrant us in suspending the rules to act on the matter, and I trust the suspension will be carried.

Mr. HOWELL—Mr. President, if that was the only mode in which the object sought could be reached, I consider that there would be no objection to it, but I consider it now out of place, because that matter can be provided for as it was in the constitution of 1852, in the very report now under consideration which has just been reported by the Committee on Schedule and I am now preparing an amendment to that report which will meet the case.

Mr. SHAW—Mr. President, I will answer that it is not the province of the Committee on Ordinance to report anything except provisions for putting the constitution into operation, and it would be uncourteous to the Committee on Legislation to report a provision contrary to a provision of their report already adopted. The Legislative report provides that the session of the General Assembly shall take place in January, and it is for the purpose of giving this provision the same effect as though it had been a part of that report that I made the motion.

Mr. HOWELL—I do not wish to offer to this Convention any statement of facts which is not sustained by proof. If the members of this Convention will refer to article 152 of the constitution of 1852, they can see there in an ordinance it is provided, and on the fourth Monday in December following the adoption of that constitution, an election was ordered to be held for governor, lieutenant governor, members of the General Assembly, secretary of state, treasurer, and superintendent of public education. By adopting a similar provision in the ordinance report presented to-day, we will procure the election of all officers at one time and save the necessity of two or three elections.

[The motion to suspend the rules was carried—ayes 60.]

Mr. STOCKER—In order to meet the views of the gentleman who made the motion to suspend the rules, I will offer this as an amendment to article 3 of the Legislative report:

There shall also be a session of the General Assembly in the city of New Orleans on the first Monday in October, 1864; and it shall be the duty of the governor, as soon as practicable, after the acceptance of this constitution, to cause a special election to be held for members of the General Assembly in all the parishes where the same may be held with safety to the electors, and in other parishes or districts he shall cause elections to be held as soon as it may become practicable, to fill the vacancies for such parishes or districts in the General Assembly.

The term of office of the first General Assembly, shall expire as though its members had been elected on the first Monday of November, 1863.

Mr. HOWELL—It seems to me, sir, if we act upon this plan of proceeding, now, with this Convention at the very moment of adjournment, to suspend the rules and amend any part of this constitution, we may annul the ordinance of emancipation or any act we have already done. I trust this Convention will not, after having adopted a department of the constitution, re-open the question and make amendments to that part of the constitution. It is entirely irregular—it is unparliamentary, and opens the door to the destruction of our whole work, and if this is done, I shall certainly make an effort to do away with all objectionable features in the constitution, particularly the police bill, gambling-house bill, and everything else I consider objectionable in that constitution. For these reasons, I trust the Convention will not go back to amend the Legislative report.

Mr. STOCKER—I hope the Convention will not be led away by what has been said by my distinguished friend who has just taken his seat. If the gentleman's assertions were carried out by the facts, his position would be correct. There were two attempts made to suspend the rules for the purpose of offering this amendment, and certainly this Convention never consented to suspend the rules until they knew what it is for. As to the assertion that we might go back and undo everything we have done, it is paying a very poor compliment to the common sense of the Convention. I do not believe the gentleman could get a suspension of the rules for the purpose of doing what he wishes. For instance the gambling bill has passed, and I do not believe he could get the rules suspended to amend that bill. I am sure there would be far more difficulty in overruling the ordinance of emancipation.

Mr. WENCK—I agree with the opinions expressed by Judge Howell. If we go back and reconsider everything we have adopted, we shall never get through our business and perform our duty. It is entirely out of order, and we have no right according to the rules we have adopted to offer an amendment to a bill after it has passed its third reading. If there is any reconsideration, the change proposed must come in as a rider. No amendment can be offered whatever and I shall oppose this motion.

Mr. SHAW—The gentlemen have not even discussed the question. It is strange if there is a grave omission in the constitution we cannot rectify it.

PRESIDENT—The gentleman has already spoken twice.

Mr. HENDERSON—We are assembled here as a body for the purpose of making a constitution, and the rules and regulations we have—to-wit: Jefferson's manual—govern us so far as they are applicable and no farther. I admit that when a bill has gone through the third reading, according to the rules laid down, that bill is at an end, and nothing further can be added to or taken from it; but gentlemen forget that though we have passed every provision in this constitution, it has not even been ratified by us. We do not know that a majority of this House will sign the constitution; and if a majority fail to sign it, there is no constitution to submit to the people. Any time before we take our vote, we have a right to correct any portion from the commencement to the end. But when we do so, if we open the issue upon one point, we open it upon another, and it may be better to submit to some evils we have, than to seek those we know nothing of. We have a right to say from what time the term of the officers shall date, but this cannot be done in the shape of an amendment, except by a suspension of the rules. Then comes the reconsideration of so much of the bill as is referred to in the amendment and there is no other portion before this body to be acted upon. The only question now is, shall we change the the time of the election? I shall vote for it.

Mr. Terry—I see no harm in going back to retrieve any errors made, and only wish to consider one point. You can adopt this article, and when the time comes to number the articles you can place it where you please.

President—Before putting the question I beg leave to say that it was with great reluctance I put the question to suspend the rules, for I had great doubts whether it was in order. It was certainly very unparliamentary. The proper place for inserting the proposed amendment is in ordinance, but if the Convention sees fit to undo its work, I suppose it has the power. It is certainly a very strange and dangerous action on the part of the Convention, and I must express my surprise that the gentleman who made this motion, who is acquainted with parliamentary matters and possesses much ability, should have introduced it.

[The motion was carried on rising vote—ayes 46, nays 20. [Applause.]

Mr. Hills—I would ask the unanimous consent to present a letter from Mr. Bailey, resigning his seat.

To the president and members of the Constitutional Convention:

Gentlemen—My objections to the —— article of the report on General Provisions relative to the extension of the elective franchise to all persons, without distinction of race or color, under certain specified conditions, being such that I could not conscientiously sign the constitution of which that article was made a part by the vote taken on yesterday, I hereby most respectfully tender my resignation as a member of your honorable body.

Respectfully, A. Bailey.
New Orleans, June 29th.

I move that it be accepted.

[After a *viva voce* vote, a division was called and the resignation accepted—ayes 54, nays 14.]

Mr. Howell—I move a suspension of the rules in order to take up on its second reading the minority and majority reports of Committee on Public Education.

Mr. Foley—I move they both be printed and made the order of the day for tomorrow.

[Mr. Howell's motion lost on rising vote, and the last motion carried by *viva voce* vote.]

Motion to suspend the rules and take up on its second reading the reports of Committee on Schedule, was lost, as was the same motion in regard to report of Committee on Ordinance.

Motion to adjourn lost on rising vote—ayes 29, nays 42.]

Mr. Beauvais—I move a reconsideration of the vote refusing to suspend the rules in order to take up the report of Committee on Education.

[The motion lost.]

Mr. Thorpe—I ask for information, whether this House did not adjourn on yesterday, to take up the educational question again to-day?

President—No, sir.

Mr. Healy—I move we adjourn until 12 M., of Thursday, the 30th.

[The motion was carried.]

Thursday, June 30, 1864.

[The Convention met pursuant to adjournment. Present, the Hon. E. H. Durell, president, and the following members:]

Messrs. Abell, Austin, Balch, Barrett, Baum, Beauvais, Bell, Bennie, Bofill, Burke, Buckley, Campbell, Collin, Cazabat, Cook J. K., Cook T., Crozat, Cutler, Davies, Duke, Decker, Duane, Dufresne, Dupaty, Edwards, Ennis, Fish, Flagg, Flood, Foley, Fosdick, Fuller, Gastinel, Geier, Gorlinski, Gaidry, Gruneberg, Healy, Harnan, Hart, Heard, Henderson, Hills, Howell, Howes, Knobloch, Kavanagh, Maas, Mann, Mendiverri, Maurer, Mayer, Montamat, Morris, Murphy E., Murphy M. W., Normand, O'Conner, Ong, Orr, Payne J., Paine J. T., Pintado, Poynot, Purcell J., Pursell S., Schroedor, Schnurr, Seymour, Shaw, Smith, Spellicy, Stocker, Stumpf, Stiner, Stauffer, Sullivan,

Taliaferro, Terry, Thorpe, Waters, Wenck, Wells, Wilson—86.

Absent—Messrs. Ariail, Bonzano, Brott, Lobdell, Millspaugh, Montague and Thomas.

[Mr. Kugler was excused.

The minutes of yesterday's proceedings were read and approved.]

Mr. MONTAMAT—I move that Mr. Heard be excused for his absence for several days past.

[The motion was carried.]

Mr. HEARD—Mr. President, since the 14th of June I have been absent attending to the business of my court in Baton Rouge. On that day I came here to ask a leave of absence and waited until 2 o'clock—reported that since no quorum was present I could wait no longer, but was obliged to absent myself in order to hold court. I thought that under the circumstances I should be treated with the courtesy to which a member of this Convention was entitled from his fellow-members; but, sir, it seems that I have been singled out as an object for personal indignity. I came here, sir, on the 5th of April, and have attended regularly and punctually until I was obliged to leave in the manner I have already indicated. The sergeant-at-arms was never under the necessity of bringing me into this hall, and the quorum was never broken by my absence, and when I left on the 14th of June I left a written request in the hands of my friend, Mr. Abell, asking a leave of absence, and I did not know what action had been taken on it until I saw in the papers that it had been refused. I do not intend, Mr. President, to arraign the action of this Convention. They have a right, if they choose to exercise it, to censure me and to censure any other member of this body; but, sir, I have never permitted any man nor any set of men to put upon me a public indignity. I have always been and am always willing to extend whatever is demanded by courtesy to members, and I am now willing to make my bow to this Convention and go home and attend to my official duties. I was obliged to adjourn my court to return, and am perfectly willing to go back at once.

MR. DAVIES—I considered that the gentleman had been a member of this body for some time, and that it was but due that he should ask a leave of absence before leaving at such a time. I had heard him say, several times before, that at such a time he was going to leave.

Mr. SULLIVAN—I move that he be excused.

PRESIDENT—He has already been excused.

Mr. WELLS—I ask that Mr. Harnan be excused for non-attendance to-day. He has been sent for by the provost marshal.

PRESIDENT—I am inclined to think there is some mistake here. No gentleman has attended more punctually or been more faithful in the dischaige of his duties, and this Convention would not knowingly offer an insult to any one, more especially to one of its own members.

PRESIDENT—The order of the day, Mr. Sullivan's amendment to the report on education.

[The secretary read article 1st:]

Art. 1. There shall be elected a superintendent of public education, who shall hold his office for the term of two years. His duties shall be prescribed by law, and he shall receive such compensation as the Legislature may direct, provided that the General Assembly shall have power, by a vote of the majority of the members elected to both Houses, to abolish the said office of superintendent of public education whenever in their opinion said office shall be no longer necessary.

Mr. HOWELL—I wish to offer an amendment in the first article—change "two" to "four."

Mr. TERRY—I wish to amend by striking out the words, "he shall receive such compensation as shall be provided by law," and inserting instead, "he shall receive a compensation of four thousand dollars per annum.

Mr. MONTAMAT — I move to lay that amendment on the table.

Mr. THORPE—I second the motion.

[The motion to table was lost, and Mr. Terry's amendment adopted, and Howell's amendment was adopted.]

Mr. PURSELL—Mr. President, is a substitute to the whole matter in order?

PRESIDENT—Yes, sir.

Mr. PURSELL—Then I wish to offer a substitute for the whole matter. It has passed its second reading once already:

Art. —. There shall be elected a superintendent of public education, who shall hold his office for the term of four years. His duties shall be prescribed and compensation fixed by the General Assembly.

Mr. MONTAMAT—I move to lay it on the table.

[The motion to table was carried, and the article as amended adopted.

The secretary read:]

Art. 2. The General Assembly shall establish free public schools throughout the State for all children, and shall provide for their support by general taxation on property or otherwise, and all moneys so raised or provided shall be distributed in proportion to the number of children between such ages as shall be fixed by the General Assembly; but no money shall be appropriated, under any circumstances, except upon satisfactory evidence that there are scholars regularly educated, in established schools, to receive the benefit of the money appropriated. All associations combining the mixed character of charity, asylums for orphans, and primary educational schools, containing over two hundred scholars, shall be considered public schools of the State.

Mr. HILLS—I move its adoption.

Mr. DAVIES—I move to reject the article.

Mr. HENDERSON—I move to lay the motion to reject on the table.

[The motion to table was lost.]

Mr. THORPE—Mr. President, I desire, before this question is disposed of, to make a few remarks, not so much with the idea of shedding any new light on the discussion as to leave it impressed upon the journals of the Convention, as an act of justice to myself, what are my views on this always exciting subject. There has no question ever been brought before a deliberative body in this country that has occasioned the same amount of acrimonious and bitter feeling, and every just-thinking statesman and patriot takes alarm at the idea of dividing up the common school fund, and thus possibly imperiling a system of education which seems most eminently adapted to our republican institutions. But I deny any desire either to favor sectarianism by appropriations from the State treasury, or to build up private schools from the same source. I look upon private schools the same as I do upon any other personal enterprize. If a lady or gentleman desires to go into the business, they have the same right that the merchant has to open a store, or a seamstress a dress-making establishment. If the parties interested, by literary accomplishments, or business tact, succeed, well and good; if not, in either case the public have little to do with it. In asking for money to be appropriated for educational purposes, where the recipients are connected with public institutions possessing the mixed character of a home for orphans and a rudimentary school, I deny, emphatically, that there is any desire to sustain private schools or favor sectarianism. I look above the narrow views of bigotry and make an appeal in behalf of humanity itself.

New Orleans, from its peculiar geographical position, must ever be the centre of misfortune. It is here that the poor and friendless of the great Valley of the Mississippi naturally gather, while for the outside world the broken down and dispirited foreigner seeks the hospitable shores of our city in hopes of finding that abundant reward for industry for which it has always been famous. As a result, as death does its work among the mature, it leaves a crowd of orphans, doubly strangers in a strange land to be not only looked after, so far as the mental training is concerned, but also to be morally trained, for being destitute of home and home influences, if they get not much discipline at school, they will receive it no where, and grow up wholly destitute of any knowledge of the relation that exists between themselves and their Maker. In one asylum in the Third District there are four hundred full orphan boys, who are not only taught the primary branches of a practical education, but they are, in addition, by the earnest and self-sacrificing spirit of the Sisters, fed and clothed. Nay, more, the duties of these angels of mercy stop not here, for these unfortunates are lodged also, and thus wholly taken care of within the walls of the asylum. Now, I would ask the gentlemen here, who claim to be not only possessed of humane sentiments, but also our legislators, what amount is saved to the city and State treasury by the fact that these four hundred orphan boys are preparing to be useful men in their day and generation, instead of being so many outcasts upon society, which would be the case, but for the benevolent institution alluded to. It is true that institute referred to is under the charge of the Roman Catholic church, but the proposed provision of the constitution does not say that any sect shall be supplied with funds from the State. The idea is to afford succor to all institutions of whatever creed, which combine the moral character of charity and educational institutions, and possessing two hundred permanent beneficiaries, shall receive from the State the amount of money due the same number of pupils in the public schools. Now, I ask again, how much is the State directly benefitted by these institutions. Suppose they were all to be suddenly closed—from want of means they should be shut up—or their hundreds of now passive and innocent inmates be turned into the streets, how much do you think would be the addition to the immorality and crime of the city, and how much through criminal expenditures would be the additional tax on the State. The moral degredation is appalling, and the money tax would be a hundred fold more than I ask to be given these institutions as public schools. Now, while I think it is our duty to discountenance, in any possible way, anything that leads to sectarianism, it is also our duty to look beyond the fact that these schools are under the support of religion denominations. It requires the spirit of religious enthusiasm to keep them organized and supported; this is a necessity founded in the deepest and in the best feelings of our hearts; we will accept the fact, and then only legislate in behalf of the general good these institutions do in training up our unfortunate orphans of both sexes, which in its vast sweeping ameliorations is as universal as humanity, and as free from sectarianism as is the law of God.

We all admire and take pride in our public schools, and we have great respect for these official representations. The delegation of lady teachers, who recently visited this hall, by their bright eyes, intelligent faces and womanly appearance, inspired us with delight. How gorgeously they were arrayed in all the panoply of rich dresses, in artificial flowers that would deceive the industrious bee; in the panoply and mystery of crinoline, it is safe to say, that Solomon, in all his glory, was not arrayed like one of these well paid and justly honored teachers of a public school, and I am not surprised that by an almost unanimous vote the Convention recommended that the proper authorities make addition to their salaries. In fact I cannot admire enough my gallant young friend, from the parish of Rapides, for the enthusiasm with which he supported the resolution. Graver and older heads, indeed, than his were for a moment turned by the unexpected display of taste and beauty. But suppose I should go into the religious retirement of these orphan asylums, to which I have alluded, and could, by a temporary suspension of the severe rules of the church, bring forth a number of these devoted sisters who have abandoned all the vanities of the world in their devotion to the cause of education and religion. If these sisters were to come into this hall and take their places among the "seats appropriated to the ladies," you would find no apparel glowing like the trembling colors of the rain-bow. Handsome, sorrow-stricken, and resigned faces you would see—faces that bear the transcendant beauty of a peace that passeth understanding—but they would be arrayed in the habiliments of sackcloth, and upon their heads in figurative language would be found ashes. They have made the greatest sacrifices to their conceived duty that human beings can make. They have not only foresworn marriage, but they have made possibly a greater sacrifice still, the renunciation of the charms of dress. Night and day do these holy sisters watch over their charge, orphans, who have no mother to cheer them, no father to bless them. In the morning orison these sisters pray for God to bless these orphans. They there feed them from the bounty their own industry has gathered. Then comes the hours of school, when those sisters labor in teaching reading, arithmetic, and other primary school studies until eve, and then, when the darkness of night sets in, those sisters walk sentinel over their sacred charge, so that no harm shall come to those dear unfortunates—and is it sectarian to give to those orphans, thus cared for, the pittance you would allow the same number of scholars in any other public schools? Go to our public schools, of which we are so proud, and see the scholars; most of them have been sent there under the manipulation of a mother's care and a father's support. Many of those children have not only fathers and mothers, and dear relatives, but have wealth to protect them, and yet those children, thus blessed in worldly things, receive the support of the public treasury for their education; and can you withhold from the poor orphans whom God has left on our hands, the little pittance of the school fund for their education!

As legislators, as public men, or as patriots, as members of this Convention, ask yourselves again, and again, what would be the expense to the State, in crime and immorality, if these sisters had not gathered up these orphans; and ask yourselves seriously and conscientiously, if it is not only justice but the wisest political economy to liberally provide for the education of these orphans. Money devoted to their intellectual culture cannot be misappropriated, and no Christian of whatever creed should object to the principle involved in the appropriation.

Mr. HENDERSON—I believe that no man present desires to forward the interests of education through the public schools more than I do. I am, however, opposed to everything like sectarianism in schools I want the branches of an education taught there, and not religious instruction. A public school is not the place to impart religious instruction. That should be a place where the children of parents of every denomination can meet together for the purpose of being taught in the arts and sciences, and where parents, be they of what denomination they may, can feel confident that doctrines that they believe to be heretical or unsound are not being instilled into the minds of their children.

I like the doctrine of Stephen Girard, who left an immense fortune to found a school for orphans, and provided that no person should be empowered as a teacher who was a teacher of any sectarian doctrine.

I don't care if a school is opened even with prayer, there will be those who have no confidence in it. The Episcopalians, if it is not Episcopalian; the Methodists, if it is not Methodist, and so on through the whole catalogue of religious denominations; and so the better way by far is to exclude everything that sounds of sectarianism entirely from the public schools. If parents want religious doctrines taught to their children, let them send them to places provided for that special purpose and supported by their own religious denominations, but let our public schools be kept clear of it.

Jefferson was once solicited to make the Baptist the established religion of the land, and the consequence was he caused an amendment to be made to the constitution of the United States, providing that there should be no established religion.

Having gone thus far, I have only to say that I would have no objection to making appropriation for private schools, but in all cases I should do so under a proviso that no religious or sectarian doctrine should be taught therein. If you will insert such a proviso I will vote for extending the benefit of the public funds to private schools numbering over two hundred pupils, but if not I shall vote against it in every shape in which it can be brought up.

Mr. SMITH Mr. President, I think we have got institutions enough. I am for rendering unto God that which is God's, and unto Cæsar that which is Cæsar's. We have mixed rebels and mixed Union men, and a good many other things that are decidedly mixed. I would therefore move to strike out the words of "a mixed character." I am in favor of public schools, but am not in favor of supporting as public schools institutions of a "mixed" character.

Mr. AUSTIN—Mr. President, am I in order with an amendment to article 2?

PRESIDENT—No, sir, not until the motion to reject is disposed of.

Mr. ABELL—Mr. President and gentlemen of the Convention, I have been very sick, and am afraid my voice will not be as loud as may be necessary. I cannot see the objections urged so strenuously by the gentlemen from the Second to this report. It simply and plainly grants to each and every association we have, or may have, numbering two hundred pupils, the appropriations received by the public schools. It is well known that the schools contemplated in this article are those peculiarly for objects of charity. Some parents may be able to pay in part, some of them may be able to pay entirely, and wish to send to a particular school for the advantage they may derive from it. I contend that it has nothing, directly or indirectly, to do with sectarianism. I have been informed that Catholics have taught in several of the public schools without regard to religion, and I believe it matters not of what denomination the institution is, but whenever the Legislature look at an institution of this kind, and find that it would advance the welfare of the people, it is the duty of that Legislature, but not of the Constitutional Convention, to adopt such means of aid as may be required. I care not what the institution is, so long as its object is to advance the human race.

I shall oppose the article. You are astonished, are you not? I shall oppose it because I find it in bad company. I told you at one time that, whether prepared or unprepared, that I would fight every proposition that looks to the mingling of the colored with the white race.

This proposition at once looks to it, and to-day, prepared or unprepared, and though sick and feeble, I speak for Louisiana, and in her name—not for the abolitionists—I speak for the people of Louisiana who have sent me to this place to represent them. I shall fight the principle, because if you attempt to put it in practice, you will only cause those persons to come in contact with you, and the consequence is that one or the other must go down. Mark what I tell you. The contact with a race which God has marked differently from the white race, is sure to cause the downfall of one or the other. History furnishes numerons examples of this, and there are but few exceptions. Perhaps a few degraded parts of South America might furnish examples of the races continuing to intermingle, but this is not the rule. The moment you bring them in contact one or the other must yield, as sure as one race is white and the other black. Our public schools are all over the land, and what is the result? For three long years the blood of our citizens has been pouring forth; for three long years, and with no prospect at present of a check. If you educate the negro well, perhaps he would be able to pour a good deal out; if he was not so well educated he would not be able to pour out so much. I stand here for no abolition cause, and am no abolitionist, and I do not believe the country demands or wants to see the negro elevated with the white race. If so, why have not the people of the North coalesced with them before now, instead of driving them into their houses and burning the houses over their heads? The races are antagonistic to each other. When I look at this proposed system of public schools, I admire it in almost every respect, but when it comes to these two classes, the report makes no distinction between the negro and the white man. All stand upon a level, and according to this report, the white children may be compelled to attend the same school as the negro children. Already we see the unfortunate results of this course. In old Kentucky, my native State, for one hundred years, they were without public schools, and the country produced many of the noblest men in the land. They had no public schools worth anything till 1845. Now the negro must be educated in the public schools at our expense. We find six or seven negro schools in one parish, and not one solitary school for the white race. Does the proud nation of America wish it? I call from this place to-day—not on the people of New Orleans and the State merely, but on this vast nation, to say if they want six or seven schools in a parish for negroes and not a single one for the whites? I say if the negro race is so grand and superior that they are to be thus set up, what will become of us? We shall hardly be allowed a seat before our firesides.

Liberty is a beautiful thing, and I love it, but the foundation of heaven itself rests not upon liberty but upon justice. This question could have been settled by allowing the negro to remain in *statu quo* until we had done justice to the master by paying for his slave when we were prepared. I do not want to oppress the negro, and there is a mode of arranging this matter of education without oppressing him. My proposition is this : they have in the city of New Orleans $13,000,000 or $14,000,000, and perhaps three times as much property in the State ; now, the Legislature, if it sees proper to create public schools, can form a school fund arising from this property, either by a poll tax or a tax on the labor, or otherwise, and thus do both the negro and the white man justice. But, in the manner proposed, you cannot do the white man the justice he is entitled to. You leave it in the hands of men, like one I might mention, occupying an official position, who say that a negro born here is better than the foreigner who comes into the State. This I have heard, with feelings of shame, on this floor. The door is open for profound justice, and nothing short of that will ever meet the ends of the nation ; and what we are doing will never receive any endorsement from the State or nation. I dare you to put such a work before the people.

I have told you that the same desired justice will flow out of our work if you will tax the property of the negro to provide a school fund, and if 300,000 are not sufficient for the purpose, then say they are not entitled to any. Then you give to Cæsar the things which are Cæsars. I would amend this subject if I could, but will attempt it. I shall not sign the constitution you make, and therefore I shall not put in any amendment. I will help you through with it, but this hand will never sign it.

Mr. Hills—I shall not occupy the attention of the Convention but a few moments. I had very much hoped this question of education would not elicit further discussion, and particularly the portion of the subject touched upon by my friend from the Fifth District, who has just taken his seat. I approve most heartily of the second article of the report of Mr. Sullivan now under consideration. I approve of it from the first word to the last, and I shall stand by it, and vote for it throughout. (Applause.)

I must acknowledge, Mr. President, that I have been surprised that a gentleman in this Convention, and at this time, should stand up here and disclaim against public education—education not alone for the negro, but, unless I greatly misunderstand the gentleman, he is opposed to public education of any description. He seems to think—if his words mean anything—that public education was the cause of this rebellion ; that if we had no public schools, we should have had no war. I certainly so understood him. If he will go back a little in the history of the world, he will find that barbarians and savages can fight about as well as educated men. I believe that in the ancient times, when a tribe or people wanted to select a king, they used to gather the whole tribe together on a plain and make them all stand up and then took for their ruler the tallest man—the one who had the most muscle, bone and sinew ; but, in more modern and civilized times, intellect is supposed to control mere muscle. I do not believe myself that public schools have at all been the cause of this rebellion ; on the contrary, I believe the want of public schools has been one of the chief causes of this whole trouble. (Applause.)

I tell you, sir, if the South had had a system of free general education the same as the North, this rebellion would have never occurred. It was because the mass of the people—not the blacks, but the whites—the "poor white trash," as they were called, were kept down in a state of ignorance by the slaveocracy that ruled and oppressed them. In the north where there is a general system of free public education, where it is a disgrace for a man to be unable to write his own name, or read a newspaper, it took years to get them into a war, even for their own preservation. A people never went to war so reluctantly as the people of the North entered upon this contest. They could not believe men of the same blood and race were really in earnest in this rebellion, and thought they would not carry it out to such an extreme. That was my opinon for many months and that was the opinion of the great mass of northern people. It was because of the general diffusion of intelligence, and if you had had free schools in Louisiana and the rest of the southern States, by which all—the children of the poor as well as the rich—were educated; if you had had free speech and a free press, I tell you that the South never would have undertaken this monstrous insurrection. I say, sir, I am astonished that a man should attempt to trace the cause of this war to the diffusion of knowledge. It seems like going back to the barbarous ages. I am not afraid of the negroes. The gentleman has told us of negro equality—that these men, if they are educated as well as ourselves, perhaps will shed their blood as freely as the white race is now shedding it. I tell you the way to prevent them is to educate them. (Applause.) He says he believes in the law of justice; he does not believe in it any more reverently than I do, but when he tells us what justice is, it reminds me of the celebrated words of Madame Rolland: "O liberty! what crimes are committed in thy name," and under his definition of justice, I would say "O justice! what crimes are committed in thy name!" The oppression of a race and shutting the gates of knowledge in the name of justice, is a definition of justice I fail to comprehend. I said before on the discussion of this question that in my opinion it was our duty, as a matter of self-preservation, to educate this race. It is a matter of preservation for all of us to do them justice, because a race that has for ages and generations suffered injustice, may at last revolt against it. There is a point beyond which the meanest man or class of men will cease to endure oppression, and then it is there is danger of their rising up and imbuing their hands, as the gentleman has expressed it, in the blood of his posterity. Do the negro justice and you place between you and insurrection an impenetrable shield. Do them justice and they will never imbue their hands in your blood, even if they should become stronger, which they never will and never can. The negro is inferior in strength, in skill, and in intellect certainly at the present time, and throughout the world I have no fears that he ever will rise, if we do him justice, and imbrue his hands in our blood. I fear not his competition; I am not envious of his good fortune, if good fortune he can achieve by his own merits. The doctrine of equality, as I understand it, is this: not that a bad man is equal to a good man, not that an inferior man is equal to a superior man, but that in the sight of the Almighty and the law of justice, every human being, however poor and humble he may be, has a natural right to do the best for himself that he can honestly. That is my doctrine of equality. If the gentleman calls it negro equality I am not frightened at the appellation, and I still say every human being has a natural right to do the best he can for himself with such powers and means as the Almighty has placed at his disposal. That is what I believe to be justice, and what I call equality.

It was not my purpose to discuss this question at any length, but I believe this article as it stands is just, right and proper. I believe it is an improvement on the two articles which I reported as chairman of that committee, although in substance the same, and I shall vote for it from one end to the other without change or modification in any manner. [Applause.]

Mr. HOWELL.—It is not my intention to make what is ordinarily termed a speech. I think there has been already too much speaking in this body; but most of what we have heard this morning is not applicable to the question, though it might be appropriate in a Legislative Assembly or Board of School Directors. I wish, sir, simply to direct the attention of the gentlemen of this Convention to the practical operation of the section now under consideration. It involves two principles, which in my opinion are inconsistent with each other. The first is contained in the first six lines. That contemplates that there shall be a system of public schools supported by the State, the means of their support to be raised and distributed in a certain manner. The first portion of this article provides that the schools shall be established and maintained, and that the money raised for that purpose shall be distributed in proportion to the number of children between certain ages, to be fixed by the Legislature. All the money that is raised by taxation for school purposes shall be distributed according to the number of children to be educated in the State. When you have fixed upon the ages between which the children are to be educated, you fix on the number of children who are entitled to that education in every portion of the State. If, for instance, there are one hundred children between the fixed ages in any one school district, those hundred children are entitled to their pro rata of the public school fund, and they will be counted in making the distribution. The appropriation will be made, and they will be entitled to receive it. That is the general principle upon which the system is practically conducted.

Now, sir, the latter portion of this article contains a principle which is destructive of the other, because it pretends to designate certain schools or associations which shall receive that fund.

I will endeavor to make myself understood by an example.

We will take the city of New Orleans, in which the number of children between certain fixed ages is ascertained. The Legislature will set apart, in the parish of Orleans, the amount due to it according to that number of children. But the latter portion of the article says that, although the children in these asylums have been counted and considered in making the distribution, they must besides have appropriated to them, out of the school fund, as a public school. It will result, necessarily, that the fund which has been appropriated to New Orleans must be divided, and a portion of it will go to associations and asylums with 200 scholars, or those schools must be supported in addition to the appropriation which has already been made to the parish. It recognizes the right to divide the school fund—and that is the question to which we must come. That is the only principle upon which the latter part of this article can be maintained, and if you once recognize the right or principle that the school fund shall be divided without reference to the numbers, irrespective of every other consideration, you then recognize the right of any class, corporation or association of any character, to demand an appropriation from the school fund for their pro rata. When you once recognize that you destroy the system of free public schools. [Applause.] You simply raise a tax from the people, giving them a right to take it back again. You permit the taxpayer to give the tax collector a certain sum of money, with the right to demand that it be returned to him again, less the costs of collection. Gentlemen, it is only upon that principle alone that the last clause of this article can be maintained, and it is unjust to adopt a principle and confine it to certain specified cases. You adopt the principle that the school fund can be divided, but you limit the associations to which that division shall apply. You fix it to associations combining charity asylums for orphans and primary educational schools. By what principle can you confine this division of the fund to that class of schools? It can only be recognized upon a sectarian principle, because no such schools and asylums are successfully maintained except by sectarian associations. You open the door to one sect or another; you confine it to sects of religion. It may be that every religious denomination may be able to establish asylums containing one hundred children, and that each one of these religious denominations will get the benefit of this provision, but still you cannot escape the principle upon which that assistance is rendered.

I contend, again, it is still more objectionable upon this ground: that you limit the assistance to those associations which need it less than any others, because when an association, by its own efforts, grows until it can sustain itself with two hundred children, it is then less in need of assistance than one which is just beginning and has to struggle for its existence.

You are partial not only to denominational views, but you confine your partiality to those who are the least needful of it.

Then, sir, to be less prolix, my views are simply these: that public education by the State is a public necessity, and all the children in the State should be educated out of the common fund raised from the property of the State. That that fund should go equally and justly to every child in the

State, within the specified ages. The only mode to fix that is to determine that the fund shall be distributed and apportioned to the children who are to be educated, and not open the door to political interest or religious prejudices. The moment you depart from that general fixed principle, you certainly will open the door either to political designs or religious fanaticism and religious distinctions; and it should be the object of all men engaged in laying down general and fundamental principles upon which a government should be established, always to avoid such results.

Mr. AUSTIN—I offer the following amendment to article 2:

Provided that no special appropriations shall be made by the Legislature for the support of such associations after their recognition as public schools.

Mr. FOLEY—The gentleman is out of order; that is not the question before the House.

Mr. THORPE—I very reluctantly rise to again speak on this subject. In the few remarks of yesterday I endeavored to be brief and clear, and I thought I was so. But from what has been said by the gentlemen who have followed me, I think I must have been either misunderstood or they have taken up some collateral issues which have nothing to do with the subject under discussion.

I would have preferred that the honorable gentlemen who are opposed to granting appropriations to the charitable asylums should have given their reasons for so doing, and not gone off on mere appeals to the prejudices and passions of the members of this Convention, or what is to me of all things most offensive, indulged in long tirades about the "nigger." I read once in a book on natural history, that a gentleman wore a pair of spectacles, one of the glasses of which had a scratch in it so long, that when he took off the spectacles the scratch remained on the retina of the eye, so he constantly saw the scratch, spectacles or no spectacles; the gentleman (Mr. Abell) has worn the negro so long across his vision that he has the almighty darkee impressed upon his brain in such a manner, that it does not make the least difference as to what subject comes before this Convention, we are bound to have a long, and, I am bound to say, not always logical or eloquent harangue about the negro. The article now before the Convention makes no allusion to the negro, but simply says:

The General Assembly shall establish free Public Schools throughout the State for all children, and shall provide for their support by general taxation on property or otherwise, and all moneys so raised or provided shall be distributed in proportion to the number of children between such ages as shall be fixed by the General Assembly; but no money shall be appropriated, under any circumstances, except upon satisfactory evidence that there are secholars regularly educated, in established schools, to receive the benefit of the money appropriated. All associations, combining the mixed character of charity, asylums for orphans and primary educational schools, containing over two hundred scholars, shall be considered Public Schools of the State.

I say, gentlemen, without fear of contradiction, and without fear of being called anything fanatical in the way of an abolitionist, or anything else, that any member of this Convention who deliberately says that he will not trust the Legislature to legislate on the school system, is giving to the people of Louisiana the character of not being capable to elect their representatives. If the General Assembly, fresh from the people, are not competent, under this provision, when it is adopted and becomes a part of the constitution, to establish a public school system suited to Louisiana, then the people of Louisiana had better sell themselves out to some one who can govern them and take care of them. [Applause.]

But that is not the point I wish to get at. The idea seems to have been entertained, by some members of this Convention, that this is an indirect way of appropriating money to private schools. Well, gentlemen, such is not the case, and while I do not ask you to support this proposition, I do not wish you to vote under a misapprehension. All institutions for the education of orphans, must, from their nature, be necessarily public institutions. They must be chartered by the State or be under the direction of a number of publlic spirited individuals; because, an institution that takes care of two hundred orphans, providing for them, clothing, feeding and educating them, needs considerable pecuniary aid to sustain its responsibilities. I limited the number to two hundred, for this reason: it is a number large enough to satisfy the public mind that the institution is an established, important fact, while the number at the same time shuts out any possible speculation on the school fund.

Now, my colleague from the Second, (Mr. Henderson,) who made such an eloquent, and in some particulars, such an extraordinary address, with regard to the education of sectarianism, rather surprised me. I am no sectarian gentlemen, and I am frank to confess that I am no Roman Catholic, though I trust I am catholic in my religious sentiments, and possess humanitarian feelings. I am prepared to give credit to every sect and every religion, as far as I can judge, for exactly what it is worth, in my estimation; and if I were a conscientious Catholic—if I were a member of that church—if I were a child of that ancient and long-established religion, with the natural veneration I have in my character, a natural fondness for what is old and reverend, with that spirit which pervades my whole being, to respect what is venerable in the eyes of mankind and what is great and glorious and good,—with all of these sentiments so largely developed, I should look out upon the past with feelings of peculiar inspiration, the Catholic church, of all other human or divine institutions, if you please, rises up in my mind, magnificent for its age, earnestness and transcendant grandeur, and I am surprised that any gentlemen of this Convention, who are children of the Church, have not sprung to their feet and come to the rescue on this question. I say that that Church, from the earliest records of time to the present, has been peculiarly charitable, above all other charitable associations, and I say to my friend, (Mr. Abell) with his peculir ideas of charity, that that Church has never justified such sentiments as he has uttered on the floor to-day. Go on Sunday to the cathedral opposite Jackson square and see the humble and poor that meet there at early dawn to give their prayers to their God, and I ask him if there is any man standing at the door, saying to blacks and whites respectively that they shall not go in at the same door and worship in the same temple. Go inside and what will you see? You will find that the Catholic Church never made any distinction in their rituals and ceremonies, but through the world, people of every nation and land, of every hue and color, have kneeled down upon the sacred pavements of the Catholic church, side by side (Applause,) and there acknowledged their dependence on the living God. It is in the Protestant churches, in the narrow and bigoted sectarianism of Protestantism, that the distinctions I allude to have been made, and this very city, New Orleans, with its Palmers, its Laycocks and Goodriches, has been desolated by their teachings. It is they who have thrown amongst the people the apple of discord, to stir up this people to rebellion. I ask you, in this connection, if you ever heard of one Catholic priest who has openly and in his sacred character as a priest openly urged on this fratricidal war or sanctioned the cutting, by brothers, of each other's throats. [Cries of "Yes," and "No."] I believe that if I should go among the Catholic churches, I might not find one in ten who is thorougly loyal at heart, and yet I demand, if ever the Church has allowed its priests to fix the politics of the members. I say this, moreover, that if there is any gentleman here, who, when I get through speaking, can get up and name a Catholic priest who has interfered in politics, I wish he would do so. I know of no one who has. While, on the contrary, the sectarian ministers throughout the whole country, have led the way to blood—and instead of being ministers of peace have become ministers of discord—servants of the devil.

But, gentlemen, I do not wish you to treat this subject as a sectarian matter: it is not sectarian, and to call it so is a wilful misrepresentation.

If there be established under this constitution a public institution in which the orphan is taken care of, clothed, reared, and, if as a result our prisons are free from convicts, if our houses of questionable reputation are less intruded upon by the kindlier sex, if all this great good is done, because these sisters, and the good people of any Protestant sect choose to gather together, and feed and care for these poor children and bring them together to teach them to read and write and to be useful in their day and generation : if these men and women, Catholics, Presbyterian, Episcopaleans, Methodists or what you please, choose to do this, and if it is necessary in order to make such an institutions useful, to provide for their support, and if it is necessary to give character, continuity and oneness, to introduce a religious element,—do not, for God's sake, get up here and make tirades against religion, for tell me if a single inspired breath of morality is calculated to make a bad man or a bad woman? I thank God I am open to the good influences of any church, that I have a heart wide enough, an education broad enough, and sentiments liberal enough to secure from all of these what is good, and according to my judgment, to eradicate what is bad. I claim that as the true feeling of a citizen of Louisiana, and of the liberal mind of a citizen of the United States. I am astonished at this narrow-mindedness, — this idea of coming forward and advocating principles which would seem to make out that our minds had been trained, like the women's feet of China,—in wooden shoes of the smallest possible dimensions.

Let us take the broadest possible ground ; let us be as irreligious as my friend from the Second [Mr. Henderson] would wish us to be ; let us be as free from sectarianism as a stone ; let us acknowledge no Superior Being, but stand up in our profanity as a mighty intellect, defying, like Ajax, the thunder of the Gods. But when we get to that point of insanity, let us at least have humanity, and if we sit in this Convention as statesman, if you sit here as legislators, if we sit here to make a Constitution for the future of Louisiana, let us remember this—that every cent of money appropriated for education is elevating this State, and is better than an appropriation for a house of correction or a prison for convicts. Let us remember that every orphan boy taken up and educated, and every orphan child who is brought within these asylums, is not only restored to the State a useful man or woman, but is also lessening our criminal calendar and the number of the inmates of our prisons, the expense of our courts, and decreasing immorality and crime. All of this cannot be done without elevating the morality of our city—without making it morally healthy, wholesome, and a fit habitation for an intelligent being of this century. I hope there is spirit enough to call for the yeas and nays. If you choose to vote it down, I hope that every man here, who has heard this discussion, be it good or bad, has pondered well and has already made up his mind. While I respect the opinions of all, and most especially respect the opinions of my friend from the Seventh, [Judge Howell,] I still think he is wrong, and believe that if he records his vote against this proposition, in a cooler and calmer hour, he, with every other man who follows his example, will regret it, and think that if he could do that work over again, he would give the orphans the pittance appropriated to public schools.

On the motion to reject the article the yeas and nays were called.

Mr. Buckley—I am opposed to educating the negro, and therefore vote "yes."

[The following is the result of the vote :]

Yeas—Messrs. Abell, Austin, Balch, Barrett, Baum, Beauvais, Bell, Bennie, Buckley, Cazabat, Collin, Cook J. K., Cook T., Crozat, Cutler, Davies, Decker, Dufresne, Duane, Edwards, Ennis, Fish, Flagg, Flood, Foley, Fuller, Geier, Gorlinski, Gaidry, Healy, Harnan, Hart, Heard, Henderson, Hire, Howes, Maas, Maurer, Mendiverri, Montamat, Murphy E., Murphy M. W., Newell, Normand, O'Conner, Payne J., Pintado, Poynot, Purcell J., Pursell S., Schroeder, Schnurr, Seymour, Shaw, Smith, Spellicy, Stocker, Stumpf, Stiner, Stauffer, Sullivan, Taliaferro, Terry, Thorpe, Wenck, Wells----66.

Nays—Messrs. Burke, Campbell, Duke, Dupaty, Fosdick, Gastinel, Gruneberg, Hills, Howell, Knobloch, Mann, Mayer, Morris, Paine J. T., Waters—15.

[The following was read :]

Art. 3. In order that no inconvenience may result to the public service from the taking effect of this constitution, no officer shall be superceded thereby ; but the laws of this State relative to the duties of the several officers—executive, judicial and military, excepting those made void by military authority, and by the ordinance of emancipation—shall remain in full force, though the same be contrary to this constitution, and the several duties shall be performed by the respective officers of the State, according to the existing laws, until the organization of the government under this constitution, and the entering into office of the new officers to be appointed under said government, and no longer.

[Article rejected.]

Mr. Bofill—I move to amend by inserting after the word "English," the word French.

[Laid on the table.

Article adopted. (Applause.)

The secretary read the following :]

Art. 4. An university shall be established in the city of New Orleans. It shall be composed of four faculties, to-wit : one of law, one of medicine, one of the natural sciences and one of letters. The Legislature shall provide by law for its organization, but shall be under no obligation to contribute to the establishment or support of said university by appropriation.

Mr. Smith—As an amendment, I move to strike out "New Orleans," and insert "located by the Legislature."

Mr. Stauffer—I offer the following substitute :

A university, composed of a law department, a medical department, and a collegiate department, comprising therewith the State seminary of learning, shall be established and maintained.

Mr. Sullivan—I move to lay it on the table.

[A *viva voce* vote was indeterminate, and on division called, the result was, ayes 37, nays 37 ; whereupon the president voted in the affirmative, thereby tabling the motion.]

Mr. Gorlinski—I move the striking out of all after "organization."

Mr. Sullivan—I move to lay that on the table.

[As the *viva voce* vote did not satisfactorily determine the question, a division was called, when the motion to table was lost—ayes 32, nays 33.]

Mr. Cutler—I offer an amendment to the amendment ; to add two words—"and maintenance."

Mr. Gorlinski—I accept the amendment.

[Amendments adopted, and the article thereupon adopted as amended.]

[The secretary read the following :]

Art. 5. The proceeds of all lands heretofore granted by the United States to this State, for the use or support of schools, and of all lands which may hereafter be granted or bequeathed to the State, and not expressly granted or bequeathed for any other purpose, which hereafter may be disposed of by the State, and the proceeds of the estates of deceased persons to which the State may become entitled by law, shall be held by the State as a loan, and shall be and remain a perpetual fund, on which the State shall pay an annual interest of six per cent., which interest, together with the interest of the trust funds, deposited with the State by the United States, under the act of Congress approved June 23, 1863, and all the rents of the unsold lands shall be appropriated to the support of such schools, and the appropriation shall remain inviolable.

[The article was adopted.]

[The secretary read :]

Art. 6. All moneys arising from the sales which have been or may hereafter be made of any lands heretofore granted by the United States to this State for the use of a seminary of learning, and from any kind of a donation that may hereafter be made for that purpose, shall be and remain a perpetual fund, the interest of which, at six per cent. per annum, shall be appropriated to the support of a seminary of learning for the promotion of literature, and the arts and sciences ; and no law shall ever be made diverting such funds to any other use than the establishment and improvement of said seminary of learning : and the General Assembly shall have power to raise funds for the organization and support of said seminary of learning, in such manner as it may deem proper.

Mr. Waters—I move we adjourn until 12 m. of Friday the first of July.

[On division called the motion was carried—ayes 43, nays 33.

Friday, July 1, 1864.

[The president called the Convention to order at 12 o'clock m. The secretary called the roll and the following members answered to their names :]

Messrs. Abell, Austin, Balch, Barrett, Baum, Beauvais, Bell, Bennie, Buckley, Burke, Campbell, Collin, Cazabat, Cook J. K., Cook T., Crozat, Cutler, Davies, Decker, Duane, Dufresne, Duke, Dupaty, Edwards, Ennis, Fish, Flagg, Flood, Foley, Fosdick. Fuller, Gastinel, Geier, Gorlinski, Gruneberg, Gaidry, Hart, Heard, Healy, Harnan, Henderson, Hills, Hire, Howell, Howes, Kavanagh, Knobloch, Maas, Mann, Maurer, Mayer, Mendiverri, Montamat, Morris, Murphy E., Murphy M. W.,

Newell, Normand, O'Conner, Ong. Orr, Payne J., Paine J. T., Pintado, Poynot, Purcell J., Pursell S., Schroeder, Schnurr, Shaw, Seymour, Smith, Spellicy, Stocker, Stumpf, Stiner, Stauffer, Sullivan, Taliaferro, Terry, Thorpe, Waters, Wenck, Wells, Wilson—86.

[Absent, ten members.

The minutes of yesterday were read and adopted.]

Mr. CROZAT—I move that Mr. Bofill be excused for non-attendance to-day.

[The motion was carried without objection.]

PRESIDENT—The order of this day is the second reading of the report of the Special Committee on Education—article 2 pending.

[The secretary read article 2 of the report of the Special Committee on Education.]

Mr. HOWELL—I move its rejection.

Mr. SULLIVAN—I have an amendment to offer, as follows:

All white children, and private schools of every denomination, who number over two hundred scholars, shall be considered public schools.

Mr. HILLS—Mr. President, I don't understand it; it makes white children public schools.

PRESIDENT—If it does not make sense, your proper course is to vote it down.

Mr. SMITH—Is an amendment in order?

PRESIDENT—It is.

Mr. SMITH—Then I move to strike out the word "white."

Mr. MONTAMAT—I move to lay that amendment on the table.

Mr. BEAUVAIS—Is it in order for me to offer a substitute, Mr. President?

PRESIDENT—No; the question now is on tabling the amendment offered by Mr. Smith.

[The ayes and noes were called.]

Mr. DAVIES—I voted aye through misapprehension. I wish to change my vote from yes to no.

Mr. CAMPBELL—I wish to change my vote from no to yes.

Mr. AUSTIN—I wish to change my vote from yes to no.

Mr. BURKE—It seems that I have voted on this question through a mistake. I am in favor of having education extended to all children. I change my vote from no to yes. It is the first time I have been mistaken in this Convention.

Mr. BEAUVAIS—I change my vote from yes to no.

Mr. WELLS—I change my vote from yes to no.

[The vote resulted as follows:]

YEAS—Messrs. Abell, Balch, Baum Barrett, Buckley, Campbell, Collin, Cook J. K., Crozat, Decker, Dufresne, Duke, Edwards, Gastinel, Geier, Gruneberg, Hart, Heard, Kavanagh, Knobloch, Maas, Maurer, Mayer, Mendiverri, Montamat, Morris, Murphy M. W., O'Conner, Poynot, Purcell J., Pursell S., Stocker, Sullivan, Waters, Wenck—35.

NAYS—Messrs. Austin, Beauvais, Bennie, Bell, Burke, Cazabat, Cook T., Davies, Duane, Dupaty, Ennis, Fish, Flagg, Flood, Foley, Fosdick, Gaidry, Gorlinski, Healy, Harnan, Henderson, Hills, Hire, Howell, Howes, Mann, Murphy E., Newell, Normand, Payne J., Paine J. T., Pintado, Schroeder, Schnurr, Seymour, Shaw, Smith, Spellicy, Stumpf, Stiner, Stauffer, Taliaferro, Terry, Wells, Wilson—45.

[The motion to table was lost.]

PRESIDENT—The motion now is upon the adoption of Mr. Sullivan's amendment. Before putting the question the Convention will permit me to ask the question how it is possible that "all white children shall be considered public schools?"

Mr. HILLS—I move to strike out the words "white children and."

Mr. SULLIVAN—I beg leave, Mr. President, to state to this Convention, why I inserted in my amendment the words "white children."

I am utterly and bitterly opposed to negro children being educated, at the present time, by taxation on white property holders.

Let us view what you have done in regard to the negroes of this State. You have passed an ordinance of immediate emancipation, without making the least provision for the compensation of loyal owners. After taking this species of property from them by force—which I consider nothing less than by force—you propose to heap the agony on by taxing the owners for the education of their former slaves.

I never will be so dishonest as to cast my vote in such a manner that I will tax a white man for the education of a negro. No, sir; I never will disgrace myself by such a vote.

Mr. SMITH—The gentleman brought in a report yesterday without the words white children. I should like to enquire what has caused him to change his mind so suddenly.

PRESIDENT—The gentleman's amendment reads that all white children shall be considered public schools.

Mr. SULLIVAN—I did not intend for it to read that way.

PRESIDENT—Then why was it so written?

Mr. SULLIVAN—I intended for the secretary to put the word white between "all" and "children."

PRESIDENT—The question is on striking out the words "white children."

[The ayes and nays were called.]

Mr. DAVIES—I am laboring under another mistake. Mr. Secretary please change my vote from "no" to "yes."

[The following is the result of the vote:]

YEAS — Messrs. Austin, Bell, Bennie, Burke, Collin, Cazabat, Cook T., Davies, Duane, Dupaty, Ennis, Flagg, Flood, Foley, Fosdick, Gorlinski, Henderson, Hills, Hire, Howell, Howes, Mann, Murphy E., Newell, Normand, Payne J., Paine J. T., Pintado, Schroeder, Shaw, Smith, Stumpf, Stiner, Stauffer, Taliaferro, Terry, Wenck, Wells, Wilson—39.

NAYS — Messrs. Abell, Balch, Barrett, Baum, Beauvais, Buckley, Campbell, Cook J. K., Crozat, Cutler, Decker, Dufresne, Duke, Edwards, Fish, Gastinel, Geier, Gruneberg, Gaidry, Healy, Harnan, Hart, Heard, Kavanagh, Knobloch, Maas, Maurer, Mayer, Mendiverri, Montamat, Morris, Murphy M. W., O'Conner, Poynot, Purcell J., Pursell S., Schnurr, Seymour, Stocker, Sullivan, Waters—41.

Mr. HENDERSON—I have an amendment to offer to the amendment:

Provided, That no religious tenet shall be taught in said schools.

Mr. SULLIVAN—I move to lay that on the table.

Mr. STOCKER—Is not that provided for already?

Mr. MONTAMAT—The gentleman should remember—

Mr. SULLIVAN—I have an amendment to the amendment.

PRESIDENT—Too late. The motion is to lay on the table. Mr. Secretary call the roll.

[Confusion.]

Mr. BELL—Mr. President, there seems to be a contrariety of opinion here. Some understood it one way and some another.

[Vote, vote.]

PRESIDENT—Mr. Sergeant-at-Arms, keep order on this floor; the disorder is growing worse and worse.

Mr. ABELL—As this is the fight for Louisiana, I shall vote no.

The vote resulted as follows:

YEAS—Messrs. Austin, Bell, Bennie, Burke, Collin, Cazabat, Cook T., Duane, Dupaty, Ennis, Fish, Flagg, Flood, Foley, Fosdick, Gorlinski, Gaidry, Healy, Harnan, Henderson, Hills, Hire, Howell, Howes, Mann, Murphy E., Newell, Normand, Payne J., Paine J T., Pintado, Poynot, Schroeder, Shaw, Smith, Spellicy, Stumpf, Stiner, Taliaferro, Terry, Wenck, Wells, Wilson—43.

NAYS—Messrs. Abell, Balch, Barrett, Baum, Beauvais, Buckley, Campbell, Cook J. K., Crozat, Cutler, Davies, Decker, Dufresne, Duke, Edwards, Gastinel, Geier, Gruneberg, Hart, Heard, Kavanagh, Knobloch, Maas, Maurer, Mayer, Mendiverri, Montamat, Morris, Murphy M. W., O'Conner, Purcell J., Pursell S., Schnurr, Seymour, Stocker, Stuauffer, Sullivan, Waters—38.

[The substitute was tabled.]

Mr. TERRY—Mr. President, I wish to offer a new article, as follows:

Art. 1. The Legislature shall establish free public schools throughout this State, and provide for their support by taxation on property or otherwise, of white persons, and all moneys so raised shall be distributed to each parish in proportion to the number of white children between certain fixed ages.

Public schools shall also be organized throughout the State for colored children, and all colored persons shall be taxed for their support.

Mr. BUCKLEY—I move to lay it on the table.

[The motion was not seconded.]

Mr. MONTAMAT—I move to strike out "colored children."

[The motion was lost and the article adopted.]

Mr. HENDERSON—I now call up my amendment.

PRESIDENT—You are too late; the article is adopted. The second reading of the report of the Committee on Schedule is now in order.

Mr. HENDERSON—Mr. President, if you don't call up my amendment I won't vote for the constitution.

[The secretary read the minority report of Messrs. Gruneberg and Dufresne on Schedule.]

Mr. HILLS—I move to lay the report on the table.

Mr. HARNAN—I move to lay the two gentlemen who reported it, on the table.

[The motion of Mr. Hills was carried.

The secretary read :]

REPORT OF THE COMMITTEE ON SCHEDULE.

The Committee on Schedule begs leave to report as follows :

Art. 1. The constitution adopted in 1852 is declared to be superceded by this constitution, and in order to carry the same into effect it is hereby declared and ordained as follows :

Art. 2. All rights, actions, prosecutions, claims and contracts, as well of individuals as of bodies corporate, and all laws in force at the time of the adoption of this constitution, and not inconsistent therewith, shall continue as if the same had not been adopted.

Art. 3. In order that no inconvenience may result to the public service from the taking effect of this constitution, no officer shall be superceded thereby ; but the laws of this State relative to the duties of the several officers—executive, judicial and military, excepting those made void by military authority, and by the ordinance of emancipation—shall remain in full force, though the same be contrary to this constitution, and the several duties shall be performed by the respective officers of the State, according to the existing laws, until the organization of the government under this constitution, and the entering into office of the new officers to be appointed under said government, and no longer.

Art. 4. The Legislature shall provide for the removal of all causes now pending in the Supreme Court or other courts of the State, under the constitution of 1852, to courts created by or under this constitution.

G. H. FLAGG,
A. GAIDRY,
ALFRED SHAW,
J. DUPATY.

Mr. GRUNEBERG—I move to lay on the table.

Mr. ABELL—I second the motion.

[The motion was lost and the article adopted.]

The secretary read the following :

Article 1. The constitution adopted in 1852 is declared to be superceded by this constitution ; and in order to carry the same into effect it is hereby declared and ordained as follows :

[Adopted.

The following was read :]

Art. 2. All rights, actions, prosecutions, claims and contracts, of individuals as well as of bodies corporate, and all laws in force at the time of the adoption of this constitution, and not inconsistent therewith, shall continue as if the same had not been adopted.

Mr. HENDERSON—I offer an amendment :

Provided, That all persons now on a charge of criminal offence, or hereafter to be on such charge, any time before the adoption of this constitution by the people, shall be bailable by sufficient securities, before and after conviction, as soon as this Convention, by the signature of its members, shall prepare said constitution for adoption as aforesaid.

Provided, That no bail shall be allowed in capital cases, where the proof is evident, or presumption great.

Mr. HOWELL—That seems to be a mere resolution which would have no binding effect, because it contemplates the previous adoption of the constitution.

[The amendment was tabled and article 2 adopted thereupon.

The secretary read :]

Art. 3. In order that no inconvenience may result to the public service from the taking effect of this constitution, no officer shall be superceded thereby ; but the laws of this State relative to the duties of the several officers — executive, judicial and military, excepting those made void by military authority, and by the ordinance of emancipation—shall remain in full force, though the same be contrary to this constitution, and the several duties shall be performed by the respective officers of the State, according to the existing laws, until the organization of the government under this constitution, and the entering into office of the new officers to be appointed under said government, and no longer.

Mr. SHAW—I wish to call the attention of the Convention to a typographical error in this article. We intended to copy the constitution of 1852 in this matter, and it should read, "no office shall be," &c., instead of "no officer," &c.

[The article was adopted.]

[The Secretary read :]

Art. 4. The Legislature shall provide for the removal of all causes now pending in the Supreme Court or other courts of the State under the constitution of 1852 to courts created by or under this constitution.

Adopted.

Mr. HOWELL—I beg leave to offer some additional articles.

Art. 5. Appointments to office by the executive, under this constitution, shall be made by the governor to be elected under its authority.

Art. 6. The term of service of all officers chosen by the people, at the first election under this constitution, shall terminate as though the election had been holden on the first Monday of November, 1863, and they had entered on the discharge of their duties at the time designated therein. The first class of senators, designated in article —, shall hold their seats until the day of the closing of the general elections in Nov ber, 1865, and the second class until general elections in November, 1867.

Mr. FOLEY—I move that article 5 be laid on the table.

[The motion was carried.]

Mr. SMITH—I move that article 6 be tabled.

[The motion was carried, and on motion the report was then adopted on its second reading.

The report of Committee on Ordinance was taken up.

The secretary read :]

Art. 1. Immediately after the adjournment of the Convention, the governor shall issue his proclamation directing the several officers of this State, authorized by law to hold elections, or in default thereof such officers as he shall designate, to open and hold polls in the several parishes of the State, at the places designated by law, on the third Monday of July, 1864, for the purpose of taking the sense of the good people of this State in regard to the adoption or rejection of this constitution ; and it shall be the duty of the said officers to secure the suffrage of all qualified voters. Each voter shall express his opinion by depositing in the ballot box a ticket whereon shall be written "the constitution accepted," or "the constitution rejected." At the conclusion of the said election, the officers and commissioners appointed to preside over the same shall carefully examine and count each ballot as deposited, and shall forthwith make due return thereof to the secretary of state in conformity to the provisions of law and usages in regard to elections.

Mr. HARNAN—I move its adoption.

[The motion was carried.

The secretary read :]

Art. 2. Upon the receipt of said returns, or on the first Monday of August, if the returns be not sooner received, it shall be the duty of the governor, the secretary of state, the attorney general, and the state treasurer, in the presence of all such persons as may choose to attend, to compare the votes at the said election for the ratification or rejection of this constitution, and if it shall appear at the close that a majority of all the votes given is for ratifying this constitution, then it shall be the duty of the governor to make proclamation of the fact, and thenceforth this constitution shall be ordained and established as the constitution of the State of Louisiana. But whether this constitution be accepted or rejected, it shall be the duty of the governor to cause to be published the result of the polls, showing the number of votes cast in each parish for and against the said constitution.

[The article was adopted without debate.

The secretary read :]

Art. 3. As soon as a general election can be held under this constitution in every parish of the State, without hostile molestation or interference, the governor shall, by proclamation, or in case of his failure to act, the Legislature shall, by resolution, declare the fact and order an election to be at a day fixed in said proclamation or resolution, and within sixty days of the date thereof, for officers of the State. The officers so chosen shall, on the fourth Monday after their election, be installed into office. The terms of office of the State officers elected on the 22d day of February, 1864, shall expire on the installation of their successors as herein provided for ; but under no state of circumstances shall their term of office be construed as extending beyond the length of the terms fixed for said offices in this constitution. The officers elected under this article shall hold their offices for the terms prescribed in this constitution, counting from the second Monday of January next preceding their entering into office.

Mr. THORPE—I offer the following substitute :

The officers of the State elected on the 22d of February, 1864, shall hold their offices until the 2d Monday of January, 1866, and the election of their successors shall take place on the first Monday in November, 1865, unless otherwise provided by law.

Mr. FOLEY—I move to lay it on the table.

[Carried.]

Mr. BAUM—I offer the following:

The officers of the State elected on the 22d of February, 1864, shall hold their offices for the respective terms assigned to said officers in this constitution; but the said terms shall expire as though their installation into office had taken place on the second Monday in January, 1864.

[Laid on the table.]

Mr. FOSDICK—I have a substitute for the whole article.

Mr. MONTAMAT—I call for the previous question.

[The motion was lost—33 voting in the affirmative.]

Mr. FOSDICK—I offer the following substitute:

ORDINANCE.

Should this constitution be accepted by the people, it shall also be the duty of the governor forthwith to issue his proclamation directing the several officers of the State authorized by law to hold elections, or, in default thereof, such officers as he shall designate, to hold an election at the places designated by law, on the same days on which the election for members of the General Assembly is ordered by article 3 of the report of the Committee on Legislative Department, for governor, lieutenant governor, secretary of state, attorney general, treasurer, auditor, and all officers elected by the people under this constitution; said election to be conducted and the returns thereof made as provided in the second preceding article.

The governor and lieutenant governor shall be installed in office during the first week of the session of the General Assembly, as ordered in the Legislative Department of this constitution, and all other officers so elected shall be immediately commissioned by said governor, and hold their offices as provided for in this constitution.

Mr. FOLEY—I move to lay it on the table.

[The motion to table was carried.]

Mr. TERRY—I move the adoption of the article.

Mr. SHAW—I think there has been some misunderstanding in the Convention, supposing that this article would have the effect of continuing the parish officers in power beyond the term prescribed by the Legislature. It was not the intention of the committee to interfere with the laws of the State with regard to these officers, and therefore I move as an amendment to strike out "officers of the State," and insert "governor, lieutenant governor, secretary of state, auditor, attorney general, treasurer, and superintendent of public education."

[The amendment was adopted.]

Mr. THORPE—Mr. President, I have only one remark to make, and if the Convention will please to listen while I read the first three or four lines of the article, I will explain: "As soon as a general election can be held under this constitution, in every parish of the State, without hostile molestation or interference." I think it will be impossible to get to such a point of time as that for twenty whole years, and it is a premium on the part of officers to encourage petty raids in the parish for all time to come.

Mr. HOWELL—I wish to say a few words in addition to what has already been said. It may be contended that the subsequent clause will rectify that, "but under no state of circumstances shall their term of office be construed as extending beyond the length of the terms fixed for said offices in this Constitution." Now, suppose, Mr. President, that about the expiration of the offices fixed by this Constitution we should have some hostile disturbance in each of the parishes of the State; there could be no election and the State would be without officers. There could be no election ordered, because of hostile interference, and yet the officers are forbidden to continue in office after that period. It seems to me the committee were very infelicitous, to say the least, in the formation of this article. To my mind it presents the appearance of being for the interest of the present State officers, although I do not like to impute such motives to any one, and I shall vote against it.

Mr. STOCKER—I would ask what is the question before the House?

PRESIDENT—The question is on the adoption of article 3, as amended. I must say, sitting in my chair, that I should like to hear the chairman explain these first three lines of the article.

Mr. SHAW—I will endeavor, Mr. President, to make this paragraph clear, and will be glad if the last gentleman, after I have explained it, will correct, and make an amendment to the infelicity he may find in the section. With regard to the point he raises, that these officers will go out of office and there will be no successors, it is distinctly stated that the term of office shall continue until the installation of their successors. The present officers of the State were elected on the 22d February, 1864. I shall not discuss the question here of the validity of that election as binding over the whole State of Louisiana. There are many persons who take the position that that election was binding upon the whole State, and that this Convention has a right to recognize those officers as having been elected for a constitutional term. which was the same in the constitution of 1852 as it is in that we have thus far passed. I say that in consulting upon this question we found that a great part, and perhaps the bulk of opinion, ran in favor of the validity of the election, as binding on the whole State for the whole term of their election. But the committee took a wider basis and assumed a fairer ground. Whether we might make it binding or not, it would be better to act in a spirit of fairness to the whole State. This Convention consists of delegates from only a portion of the parishes of the State. It is true we have a majority of the population; it is true that in the portions directly represented here a large majority of the population is contained. The committee, therefore, have assumed that, under all circumstances, that election was valid, although we have but a portion of the State represented within the lines of the army. In other words, if things were to remain in their present condition in those parishes now beyond the lines, which we cannot reach or govern until the end of the fourth year, then this election would be binding upon us for the next four years. Our condition is unchanged since that election, and the position of affairs has not materially changed in the State since that election was held. We represent about the same number of parishes we then did. The idea, and the leading idea contained in this third article, is that if the whole State of Louisiana should be brought within the lines, so that the citizens of every parish can assemble peacefully and without molestation, proceed to choose their officers, then it is nothing more than fair and right that they should call another election. But it was impossible for the committee to say when that time would come. Some gentlemen wanted it defined; if any member can say when that time will be, let him move an amendment and fix it. We therefore made it a duty, when that time comes, for the governor to issue his writ for the election of his successor and the successors of the other officers of the State. If he fails to perform that duty, we have a check upon him—we have a body authorized to remind him of it, or by its own resolution to call that election. I do not know that any further explanation is necessary.

Mr. MONTAMAT—I move the adoption of the article.

[The yeas and nays were ordered, and the article adopted by the following vote:]

YEAS—Messrs. Abell, Austin, Balch, Barrett, Baum, Beauvais, Bell, Bennie, Buckley, Cazabat, Collin, Cook J. K., Cook T., Crozat, Cutler, Davies, Decker, Dufresne, Duane, Edwards, Ennis, Fish, Flagg, Flood, Foley, Fuller, Geier, Gorlinski, Gaidry, Healy, Harnan, Hart, Heard, Henderson, Hire, Howes, Maas, Maurer, Mendiverri, Montamat, Murphy E., Murphy M. W., Newell, Normand, O'Conner, Payne J., Pintado, Poynot, Purcell J., Pursell S., Schroeder, Seymour, Schnurr, Shaw, Smith, Spellicy, Stocker, Stumpf, Stiner, Stauffer, Sullivan, Taliaferro, Terry, Thorpe, Wenck, Wells—66.

NAYS—Messrs. Burke, Campbell, Duke, Dupaty, Fosdick, Gastinel, Gruneberg, Hills, Howell, Knobloch, Mann, Mayer, Morris, Paine J. T., Waters—15.

[The secretary read the following:]

Art. 4. This constitution shall be published in English and French, in two newspapers to be selected by the president of the Convention, from the period of its adjournment until the election for ratification or rejection on the third Monday of July, 1864.

Mr. CAMPBELL—I move to amend by striking out the word "and" between English and French, and insert "and German."

Mr. SHAW—I offer an amendment to the last. "This constitution shall be published in English and French in two newspapers, and in German in one newspaper published in the German language; the papers to be selected by the president of the Convention."

Mr. HEALY—I move to strike out the word French.

[Motion tabled.]

Mr. AUSTIN—This is the first time I have risen to move an adjournment, but I now make that motion and call for the yeas and nays.

YEAS—Messrs. Austin, Balch, Burke, Collin, Duke, Dupaty, Edwards, Fosdick, Gorlinski, Healy, Harnan, Kavanagh, Normand, Purcell J., Terry, Waters, Wells—17.

NAYS—Messrs. Abell, Barrett, Beauvais, Baum, Bell, Bennie, Buckley, Campbell, Cazabat, Cook J. K., Cook T., Crozat, Cutler, Davies, Decker, Duane, Dufresne, Ennis, Fish, Flagg, Flood, Foley, Gastinel, Geier, Gruneberg, Gaidry, Hart, Heard, Henderson, Hills, Hire, Howell, Howes, Knobloch, Maas, Mann, Maurer, Mayer, Mendiverri, Montamat, Morris, Murphy E., Murphy M. W., Newell, O'Conner, Ong, Payne J., Paine J. T., Pintado, Poynot, Pursell S., Schroeder, Schnurr, Seymour, Shaw, Smith, Spellicy, Stocker, Stumpf, Stiner, Stauffer, Sullivan, Taliaferro, Thorpe, Wenck and Wilson—66.

[The motion was lost.]

Mr. MONTAMAT—I offer the following as a substitute to the whole:

This constitution shall be published in English in the Era, and the official paper of this Convention, and in French in the New Orleans Bee.

Mr. WATERS—I move it be laid on the table.

[The motion was carried on a rising vote; yeas, 42; nays, 27.

Mr. Shaw's amendment was carried, and the article was adopted as amended.]

Mr. HOWELL—I beg leave to present an additional article. I wish, sir, the earnest attention of every member of this Convention, because I feel it to be a very important matter. I have been reflecting upon this a long time, and upon consulting some of my friends have concluded to offer it. It reads, Mr. President and gentlemen, as follows:

Art. 5. At the election for the adoption or rejection of this constitution there shall be had at each poll an additional ballot-box, in which shall be deposited the vote of each qualified voter, on which shall be written: "The ordinance of emancipation accepted," or "The ordinance of emancipation rejected;" and if said ordinance be adopted, it shall be a part of the constitution of the State, and be inserted as the first and second articles of the General Provisions.

Mr. FOLEY—I move that be laid on the table. It is an insult to the Convention.

Mr. AUSTIN—I ask for the yeas and nays, as I wish every man's vote to be recorded.

YEAS—Messrs. Abell, Barrett, Bennie, Bell, Burke, Collin, Cazabat, Cook J. K., Cook T., Davies, Decker, Duane, Edwards, Ennis, Flagg, Flood, Foley, Geier, Gaidry, Gorlinski, Healy, Harnan, Henderson, Hire, Hills, Howes, Maas, Maurer, Morris, Murphy E., Murphy M. W., Newell, Normand, O'Conner, Paine J. T., Payne J., Pintado, Poynot, Purcell J., Pursell S., Schroeder, Schnurr, Shaw, Smith, Spellicy, Stocker, Stumpf, Stiner, Stauffer, Taliaferro, Terry, Thorpe, Wells—53.

NAYS—Messrs. Austin, Balch, Beauvais, Baum, Buckley, Campbell, Crozat, Cutler. Dufresne, Duke, Fish, Fosdick, Gastinel, Gruneberg, Hart, Heard, Howell, Kavanagh, Knobloch, Mann, Mayer, Mendiverri, Montamat, Ong, Seymour, Sullivan, Wilson, Waters, Wenck—29.

[The article was lost, and the announcement of the vote was greeted with loud applause.

On motion, the Convention then adjourned until 12 M. of Saturday, the 2d inst.]

SATURDAY, July 2, 1864.

[The Convention met pursuant to adjournment. Present, the Hon. E. H. Durell, president, and the following members:]

Messrs. Abell, Austin, Balch, Barrett, Baum, Beauvais, Bell, Bennie, Bofill, Buckley, Burke, Campbell, Collin, Cazabat, Cook J. K., Cook T., Crozat, Cutler, Davies, Decker, Duane, Dufresne, Duke, Dupaty, Edwards, Ennis, Fish. Flagg, Flood, Foley, Fosdick, Gastinel, Geier, Gorlinski, Gruneberg, Gaidry, Healy, Harnan, Hart, Heard, Henderson, Hills, Hire, Howell, Howes, Kavanagh, Knobloch, Maas, Mann, Maurer, Mayer, Mendiverri, Montamat, Morris, Murphy E., Murphy M. W., Newell, Normand, O'Conner, Ong, Orr, Payne J., Paine J. T., Pintado, Poynot, Purcell J., Pursell S., Schroeder, Schnurr, Seymour, Shaw, Smith, Spellicy, Stocker, Stumpf, Stiner, Stauffer, Sullivan, Taliaferro, Terry, Thorpe, Waters, Wenck, Wells, Wilson—86.

[The minutes of yesterday were read and adopted.

On motion of Mr. Wells, Mr. Gaidry was excused.

Mr. Orr was excused for his absence on yesterday.]

Mr. Abell—I move to reconsider the vote laying Mr. Howell's additional article to the report on Ordinance on the table. I voted in the affirmative on the question.

President—The matter cannot come up to-day. It has already been decided that this day is set apart for miscellaneous business, and Tuesday next will be the day to reconsider.

Mr. Montamat—I submit the following memorial from the property holders of the Second District:

To the honorable president and members of the Constitutional Convention:

Gentlemen—The undersigned, residents of the suburb Trémé, in the Second District of the city of New Orleans, most respectfully petition your honorable body to pass an ordinance making it the duty of the city authorities to cause to be constructed, as soon as possible, on Galvez street, across Canal Carondelet, a bridge exactly similar to the one built across said Canal Carondelet, on Broad street. The advantages to result by its construction will be immense to the large number of persons residing in that part of the city, enabling them to supply their families at the Trémé Market, the improvement asked by your petitioners shortening the present distance almost one mile, and opening also a direct communication with the First and Third Districts.

The whole is most respectfully submitted to your honorable body, and your petitioners will ever pray.

New Orleans, June 28, 1864.

John Murphy, John P. Montamat,
John Fisher, George Merz,
John Siegenthaler, George Eikz,
Antonie Ramusat, Michael Schally,
Nicholaris Frietsch, Adam Kurtmann,
Karl Steitz, B. Camet,
J. Neuhauser, T. Kiphaut,
F. Aufenkolk, Joseph Gros,
Peter Leind, M. Bourlett,
S. Joseph, M. Fritz,
Ph. Schindler, L. Latto,
E. Hacker, Klofot,
Peter Freibert, Pour,
George Woerney, George P. Lombard,
P. Kerwann, D. Laborde,
S. Kaller, K. Burkert,
Fr. Robert, John Schonhardt,
O. Noack, P. W. Sheridan,
Adam Spies, C. Murphy,
Mme E. H. Behan, J. Rolling,
Cassimer Glade, H. Rolling,
J. W. Bailey, Ch. Rolling,
John Henneberg, S. Oswald,
Henry Leebis, Thomas Killea,
Hte. Demoreulle, P. Grant,
Ernest Demoreulle, Morris Hiccey,
J. Demoruelle, F. A. Siener,
D. Barker, Joney Poley,
Pat. Killea, Mike Byrne,
Larins McDonell, Dan. Byrne,
Felix M. Jacobs, James Dunn,
Joseph Fisher, P. Mofit,
William Rourke, John Cavanagh,
Garret Kirwan, Jary Murphy,
Francis Cullen, J. Warner,
James Cullen, Laurence Rinney,
P. Deverges, S. Roman,
James Lilly, A. Garrer,
Chas. Lawson, Conrad Brand,
Ph. Hoffman, D. Constantine,
F. Graeser, A. Herbee,
John McVittie, W. Graff,
Ruston Newlove, Wolf Shreber,
Henry Gallew, Conrad Graff,
Joseph Upulte, S. Lacost,
Heinriez Scheulte, Murtz Coners,
Pinna Clemant, Barney Kelley,
Hugh Doherty, John Coner,
Thaddeus Oberyefell, James Butler,
A. Beaise, Mrs. Filsgerlid,
J. Baldwin, Ed. Blust,
Valentine Rothany, A. Schamber,
S. Shmizer, G. Doll,
Jos. Muller, Patrick Burke,
Burgard Torer, Raynal Auguste,
Daniel Sheply, Edward Moran,
Chas. J. Lester, L. C. Preston,
Wm. Graham, James Fallon,
Frank Goulemus, Alexander Lea,
Wm. C. Harrison, John T. Ives,
John Koepfer, John Fisher,
James Woulfe, John Buckley, Jr.,
Freedolin Hesty, Jas. A. Mourton,
John Foley, Vor. Hébert, Jr.,
Jeremiah Ryan, M. O'Donnell,
William Myhar, Louis Brevier,
Henry Steward, Conrad Murlsnur,
C. Winketsmann, Ge Hilher-Barb,
Paul, B. Lanaberi,
John Funk, Jacob Eichhorn,
Peter Funk, J. B. Henry,
M. Christoffel, Abrusir Storck,
M. Halbritter, John Orth,
J. Relin, Joseph Henry,
M. Conway, Louis Koch,
Henry Jollissaint, T. F. Kavanagh,
N. Chenal, Ernest J. Wenck,
Dennis Murphy, Henry Boeylin.

Mr. Montamat—Having presented the memorial, I offer the following resolution:

Resolved, That the Legislature shall, at its first session, pass an act making it the duty of the city authorities of the city of New Orleans, to build, as soon as possible, on Galvez street, across Canal Carondelet, a bridge exactly similar to the one built across said Canal Carondelet on Broad street.

Mr. Cazabat—With all due deference to

the gentleman who offers this resolution, and to his constituents, I ask of you, Mr. President and members of the Convention, if this is a legislative body? If it is not, then the proper place to bring such a resolution is before the next Legislature. I have no doubt the gentleman will be entitled to such relief, but this is not the proper place nor the proper time; wait, and in two months you will get your request granted.

Mr. SMITH—I rise for information from the honorable president and members of this Convention. I wish to know if they think that I, a member from the Parish of St. Mary, have any thing to do with bridge-building in the city of New Orleans. (Applause and laughter.)

Mr. MONTAMAT—I only offered the resolution directing the Legislature to pass an ordinance to that effect.

Mr. CAZABAT—I move to lay it on the table.

The motion was carried. Yeas, 46; nays, 23.

Mr. HILLS—As chairman of the committee appointed last Saturday to report on the subject of public charity, I have to state the report is ready. In offering this report, Mr. President, I beg leave to say that I have received communications within the last few days from some of the public charitable institutions of this city representing that they are in a state of destitution, and that unless they receive some relief from this Convention, they are unable to see how they will maintain their various institutions any longer.

To the president and members of the Constitutional Convention of Louisiana:

GENTLEMEN—The undersigned members of your Committee on Public Charities respectfully report:

That in view of the wide-spread destitution and suffering in this community, and the inadequacy of means in the hands of our various charitable institutions, they are of opinion that relief should be afforded by this body, and they therefore recommend the adoption of the following:

Resolved, That the sum of thirty-five thousand dollars be, and the same is hereby, appropriated from the State treasury for purposes of charity, the same to be distributed by a board of almoners to be appointed by the governor, and to consist of five citizens, three of whom shall constitute a quorum for business. The governor of the State shall be ex-officio president of the board, and the money shall be drawn on his warrant, countersigned by the secretary of the board.

All of which is respectfully submitted.

ALFRED C. HILLS, Chairman.
JOHN SULLIVAN,
W. T. STOCKER,
CHARLES SMITH.

Mr. BEAUVAIS—I move to lay it on the table.

[The yeas and nays were ordered on the motion, and the roll called.]

Mr. CAZABAT—I vote "yes" because it does not include widows and orphans of soldiers, who have lost their lives in fighting to sustain the national flag and to sustain the integrity of our national Union. Include them and you have my vote.

Mr. WELLS—If they will include the Union refugees and soldier's wives—

[Cries of "out of order;" "vote."]

I am opposed to anything like legislation and vote "yes."

[The motion was lost by the following vote:]

YEAS—Messrs. Burke, Collin, Cazabat, Davies, Decker, Duke, Dupaty, Ennis, Flagg, Howell, Knobloch, Normand, Paine J. T., Wenck, Wells—15.

NAYS—Messrs. Abell, Austin, Barrett, Baum, Beauvais, Bell, Bennie, Bofill, Buckley, Cook J. K., Cook T., Cutler, Duane, Dufresne, Edwards, Fish, Flood, Foley, Fosdick, Gastinel, Geier, Gorlinski, Gruneberg, Healy, Harnan, Hart, Heard, Henderson, Hills, Hire, Howes, Kavanagh, Maas, Mann, Maurer, Mayer, Mendiverri, Montamat, Morris, Murphy E., Murphy M. W., Newell, O'Conner, Orr, Payne J., Poynot, Purcell, J., Pursell S., Schroeder, Schnurr, Shaw, Smith, Spellicy, Stumpf, Stiner, Stauffer, Sullivan, Taliaferro, Terry, Thorpe, Waters, Wilson—62.

Mr. SMITH—I move its adoption.

Mr. HOWELL—I desire, sir, simply to give my reasons for not signing that report, as I was a member of the committee. To assure this body that I am in favor of charity, I deem to be unnecessary; but, sir, I have endeavored since I have been in this Convention to act upon principle, and be guided in all my votes by my judgment as to principle. I feel satisfied, sir, considering the objects for which this Convention was assembled, that we are going beyond our province when we take up matters of this kind and pass upon them ; and, in addition to that principle, I beg leave to present to the Convention a few facts before they vote upon this resolution.

When this Convention assembled, there was about $385,000 in current funds in the treasury; $32,000 of that sum were in Bank of New Orleans notes; the balance, some $353,000, were in what are denominated current funds of the city and State. Taxes have been brought in by the collectors, and yesterday, at 4 o'clock, there were in current funds in the treasury, $194,-000 44.

Mr. SMITH—Is this a report of the state treasurer, or the charity bill?

Mr. HOWELL—The gentleman need not be alarmed by a statement of facts. I am giving my reasons for not voting for this resolution, and if he will not interrupt me, I will be much shorter than otherwise.

Out of that $194,000 must be taken the school fund, of $68,000, and the internal improvement fund of $41,000, making a sum of $109,000 to be taken from the current fund, which we cannot touch, leaving a balance of only $85,000 in the treasury, yesterday, at 4, P. M. Now, sir, the appropriations of this Convention are not all yet met, because, by the action of this Convention the printer is paid out of the general fund in the treasury, and not out of the fund which we have appropriated and drawn from the treasury ; and I was informed by the treasurer that over $60,000 have been paid on the printing bill, and from his knowledge of the business it will take that much more to pay the printers' bill. Take, then, $60,000 from $85,000, and we have but $25,000 in the treasury; and here we are passing a resolution to appropriate $35,000. The taxes are coming in very slowly, less and less from week to week, and during the summer it is not possible that a sufficient amount in taxes will be collected to pay the actual expenses of the State government. Now, gentlemen, with this statement of facts before me, and the principle that I think should govern this body, that we have no right to go beyond our legitimate business, I shall oppose this resolution.

Mr. ABELL—Mr. President, on this point, from the commencement of the Convention, I have stood on the very ground occupied by the gentleman. I have stated, and I now repeat, that at the close of the formation of the constitution, I should go with all my heart for this measure on the ground of necessity. We stand here as the representatives of the people, and we find that in all times such as surround us, necessity frequently creates or causes a deviation from even the great charter of the country. It is admitted by all parties, that it is necessary that the constitution of the United States should not be strictly followed, in order that the good of the country may be subserved. Under the depleted state of the finances in this part of the country, it has reduced, beyond all question, those institutions now existing, to a most pitiful state, and unless we take upon ourselves, as the representatives of the people, to give them some assistance, they must cease to exist. I think, if the people were consulted, there would be but few who would not sanction our efforts entirely, and they themselves would be benefitted by it. I do not think, as this appropriation is for a most pressing need, that any of us should hesitate to step a little beyond the line which would otherwise confine us. I only support it on the ground of necessity, not on the ground of legitimacy, because it is out of the sphere of this Convention ; but although out of our sphere, it is certainly within our power, and I shall heartily cast my vote for it. I would say, for the encouragement of the gentleman, in regard to the treasury, that as I was coming up here, I met one of the collectors, and he told me he had then, I think, $13,000 to turn into the treasury. That is encouraging. I could have something to say as to the manner of appropriation, but I have every confidence that the governor, as proposed in the resolution, will make the distribution in accordance with the wishes of the Convention.

Mr. CUTLER—Mr. President, I shall vote for the report of the committee simply because I believe it to be just. I am in favor, first, of the poor whites, secondly of the middle classes, and lastly of the rich. We have been bountifully paid, and although there is not a large sum in the treasury, there certainly will be, and I shall heartily vote for the report.

Mr. HILLS—Mr. President, I only wish to make a single remark. I concur fully in the remarks on this subject of the gentleman from the Fifth (Mr. Abell). I also agree with the gentleman from the Seventh, (Mr. Howell,) that this appropriation is without the sphere of our legitimate action as a Constitutional Convention, and for that reason, when the subject was proposed here some weeks ago, I opposed the appropriation, but I told the gentleman who offered that proposition, that at the close of the session of the Convention I would favor the appropriation. I opposed it then because I thought it opened the door for other applications which we could not consistently grant, and therefore was in favor of putting it off to the closesof the session. It seems to me extraordinary circumstances exist in this State that justify the Convention in stepping thus far beyond the legitimate bounds of its jurisdiction, and it was with such view I opposed that report as chairman of the committee, and my associates all agreed with me, except the gentleman who has stated his objections.

As to the condition of the State treasury, I think that inasmuch as this money is not to be paid all at once, but is to be drawn gradually in such sums as the commissioner may decide to be needed; if the treasury is not sufficiently full now, it will be before the whole sum is required, and I think that objection falls to the ground. As I stated before, some of the institutions of charity in this city will absolutely be compelled to close their doors unless this appropriation is made. I will instance the Sisters of Charity, from whom I read a communication in which they stated that unless they received relief from this body they could not possibly continue in their charitable work. I think that it would be one of the greatest calamities the community could suffer to have that institution closed against the helpless orphans who are cared for and protected within its walls, and inasmuch as I have offered this and believe it to be right, I shall vote for it cheerfully and heartily.

Mr. CAZABAT—I offer the following amendment:

Provided, This appropriation for charitable purposes will apply to the relief of destitute Union refugees from Louisiana, and the widows and orphans of Union soldiers who have lost their lives in the service of the United States army.

Mr. MONTAMAT—I move to lay it on the table.

[The motion was carried.

The yeas and nays were ordered on the adoption of the report and resolution.]

Mr. DAVIES—I would vote "yes" provided the amendment of Mr. Cazabat was included; but as it is not I vote " no."

Mr. WELLS—I refuse to vote on the bill.

[Cries of " vote, vote."]

PRESIDENT—Does the Convention excuse Mr. Wells?

Mr. WELLS—If the Legislature—

PRESIDENT—There can be no speech made. How does the gentleman vote?

Mr. WELLS—I refuse to vote on the question and offer my resignation.

Mr. HILLS—I move the gentleman be permitted to explain his vote.

PRESIDENT—He can explain his vote, but not make a speech.

Mr. WELLS—I came here to do justice to the country and State. The resolution before the House is for the sole purpose of benefitting the charitable institutions of the city of New Orleans. (Cries of " no, no.") If you will accept the amendment offered by my colleague from the parish of Rapides, I will vote with my whole soul on the question. If not, I refuse to vote.

Mr. WATERS—The gentleman must vote one way or the other.

Mr. CAZABAT—I move he be excused from voting.

[The motion was lost.]

PRESIDENT—You must vote, sir, under the rules.

Mr. WELLS—I vote " no."

Mr. SMITH—Before the vote is announced I wish to make one remark for the benefit of Mr. Wells.

PRESIDENT—Out of order.

[The report and resolution were adopted by the following vote:]

YEAS — Messrs. Abell, Austin, Barrett, Baum, Beauvais, Bell, Bennie, Bofill, Buckley, Cook J. K., Cook T., Crozat, Cutler, Decker, Duane, Dufresne, Edwards, Fish, Flood, Foley, Fosdick, Gastinel, Geier, Gorlinski, Gruneberg, Healy, Harnan, Hart, Heard, Henderson, Hills, Hire, Howes, Kavanagh, Maas, Mann, Maurer, Mayer, Montamat, Morris, Murphy E., Murphy M. W., O'Conner, Orr, Payne J., Poynot, Purcell J., Pursell S., Schroeder, Schnurr, Seymour, Shaw, Smith, Spellicy, Stocker, Stumpf, Stiner, Stauffer, Sullivan, Terry, Thorpe, Waters, Wilson—63.

NAYS—Messrs. Burke, Collin, Cazabat, Davies, Duke, Dupaty, Ennis, Flagg, Howell, Knobloch, Newell, Normand, Paine J. T., Pintado, Taliaferro, Wells—16.

Mr. AUSTIN—I ask for the reading of the report of the Special Committee on the Auditor's Report.

[The secretary was directed to read it.]

Mr. HILLS—I move the reading be dispensed with, and the whole subject indefinitely postponed.

[The motion was lost.

The secretary read:]

REPORT OF THE SPECIAL COMMITTEE ON SPECIAL REPORT OF AUDITOR.

To the president and members of the State Constitutional Convention of Louisiana:

Your committee, to whom was referred the report of the auditor of public accounts, beg leave to make the following report, to-wit:

Under all the surrounding circumstances we find no serious objection to the manner and form in which the state auditor has seen proper to present his report. As to the Confederate notes, we look upon them as *trash* and lost to the State.

Your committee are of opinion that we should not interfere with the military powers, and therefore are unanimous in saying that inasmuch as the late auditor of public accounts, the Hon. S. H. Torrey, has issued warrants only by authority of the military governor, Gen. Shepley, he is not only excusable but justifiable.

As to the Hon. R. K. Howell and the Hon. A. M. Buchanan, your committee are of opinion that they have drawn their salary according to the constitution and laws of the State of Louisiana, and that the opinion of our worthy auditor, the Hon. A. P. Dostie, "that rebellion had terminated the existence of the Supreme Court," is unfounded and contrary to the prevailing opinion of all loyal citizens of Louisiana—"*That the State has never been out of the Union.*"

As to the Hon. Charles A. Peabody, your committee are of opinion that he never was chief justice of the State of Louisiana, for the irresistible reasons that neither the military authorities nor the civil powers in this State ever created a Supreme Court since the arrival of the honorable gentleman in this State, nor was he eligible to a seat on the bench of the one created previous to his arrival, because he was not, and is not, a citizen of the State of Louisiana; and, further, because he was and is a judge created by the president of the United States to preside over a court created by the same authority, "the United States Provisional Court for the State of Louisiana." That as judge of said court he has been receiving a salary from the United States government—and therefore he has received the sum of $3541 66 from the treasury of the State of Louisiana as salary, under the pretence of being chief justice of the State, without any authority and in open violation of the constitution and laws of the State of Louisiana.

Under these circumstances your committee recommend that in consequence of these illegal acts of the said Charles A. Peabody, in obtaining said sum from the State as aforesaid, that the attorney general of the State be requested to institute such legal proceedings as may be necessary to recover said sum, with interest, damages and costs. Your committee further recommend that, inasmuch as the necessity for said United States Provisional Court has long since ceased to exist, and that the same is but a stumbling-block in the way of the administration of justice, and to the loyalty of the good people of the State of Louisiana, that the commanding general of this department, Maj. Gen. N. P. Banks, and his excellency, M. Hahn, governor of the State of Louisiana, be requested to petition the president of the United States to withdraw the commission from and recall the said Charles A. Peabody, and thereby put an end to the further existence of said court.

As to Mr. Serpas, sheriff of the parish of St. Bernard, your committee are of opinion that as the Confederate notes in his possession were received for taxes collected by him during Confederate rule, he should be exonerated from all blame and released from all responsibility on handing over the same to the treasurer of the State.

Mr. HARNAN—Mr. President, there is one portion of the report of the committee I am constrained to oppose. I refer to that part where they declare that Judge Howell drew his salary according to the constitution and laws of Louisiana. What are the facts? It is charged by the auditor, (and not denied,) that Judge Howell drew his salary for seventy-one days, during which time he was not a citizen of Louisiana or of the United States, by reason of his having taken an oath of allegiance to the rebel government, and of which he had not purged himself. Twenty-six days of the period, it is alleged, Judge Howell was serving as a udge under the rebel government.

Now, sir, if these allegations are true, and the committee do not deny them, I for one can never endorse the opinion of the committee, that Judge Howell had a legal right to his salary before he restored his status as a loyal citizen. I further maintain that for twenty-six days he was acting as a judge under the rebel government—not even the restoration of his status as a loyal citizen entitled him to draw his salary.

I contend, under no circumstances, has an officer under the rebel government a legal claim on the loyal State of Louisiana, for services rendered while he was so employed. With all due respect for the legal talents and private character of Judge Howell, I cannot express my astonishmant at his presenting such a claim.

I am equally surprised that a committee from this body, composed of five gentlemen of well known loyalty, and one, a distinguished lawyer, should attempt to force on this Convention the endorsement of such a dangerous principle. Their report entirely ignores Gen. Butler's order, No. 41, which declares all citizens of Louisiana are disloyal, and that an oath of allegiance to the Federal Government is requisite to restore their rights. It sets aside the president's proclamation on the same subject. It is equivalent to saying in so many words, that an individual who took an oath to support the rebel government did not forfeit his status as a loyal citizen; though I am not learned in the law, sir, and it may be the fault of my ignerance, I can never give my assent to such doctrine. I shall, therefore, not only vote against the report of the committee, but I make a motion that the whole report be laid on the table and the committee discharged.

Mr. SULLIVAN—I second the motion.

[The motion was lost by a rising vote—yeas 15; nays 45.]

Mr. HENDERSON—Mr. President, if I wanted a cudgel to break this committee's head, I should take no better one than the report itself. It is strange that they can see out of one eye and wink out of the other at the same time. It is strange that they can't see that the auditor has done his duty wholly and faithfully as an auditor should do it, and at the same time find that all the disbursements is confined to Judge Peabody. Pray, why do they excuse the auditor? Simply because he was appointed by Governor Shepley, and acted under his orders. I don't see how that can make any difference in his favor. So far as that is concerned, I believe they all stand on precisely the same footing. Governor Shepley was appointed by the president and so was Judge Peabody. They are but minions of the president of the United States. The auditor is further removed, because he was appointed by Governor Shepley under authority delegated to him by the president.

The president, as commander-in-chief of the army and navy, makes appointments for the States recovered from the rebel rule, without consulting the Senate, under the war power. On this point I have no other authority than Judge Heistand himself. This same man Peabody was brought before him, and it was contended by the great champion of the bar, that the president had no right to make such an appointment. That it was in violation of the constitution of the United States. Hear what Judge Heistand says in his decision:

"I consider that it is not within the province of this court, which owes its own existence to the organizations effected by the military governor of this State, who, in turn, holds his position from the president of the United States, in an exercise of his powers as commander-in-chief of the army and navy, to declare null and void the proceedings of a tribunal created by the same high authority, in the exercise of the military power vested in him."

In case of Jacob Barker vs. Chesney.

What has been the authority of Judge Atocha? Who ever heard of a military judge administering civil laws? I call the gentlemen's attention to the fact, that the commission of Judge Peabody states that the court shall be created, and that he shall continue in office until the restoration of the State of Louisiana as one of the States of this Union. That is the kind of court to which he is appointed by the president, and he or his successors are to hold the position until the State is restored. All the judges hold under the same authority, except, that instead of having been exercised directly by the president, it was delegated to the military governor. Judge Howell, Judge Handlin and Judge Hiestand, all hold, under the appointment of the military governor, offices which under the constitution of 1852 were elective, and which the constitution of 1864 makes it the duty of the governor, by and with the advice and consent of the Senate, to fill, by appointments, for a term of years.

I am not discussing the question as to whether the auditor was right or wrong. I have told him, at different times, that he was entirely wrong in the whole matter. I believe that the entire action referred to in this report was military, and as such that it was beyond our control and jurisdiction, and that as the money was paid it was between the United States and Louisiana. But, sir, why do they select one man as a military judge and make him the object of all their animadversion? Why do they aim all their artillery at Charles A. Peabody? I have seen him on the bench. I know him to be a courteous man. No man that I am aware of has ever complained that he did not administer justice. If he has ever failed in the discharge of his duties, the power that placed him there is the power to remove him. Sir, to my certain knowledge, there was a numerously signed petition sent up to the president by Governor Shepley, urging him to remove Judge Peabody and discontinue the court, and, sir, the president never gave it any consideration, and I doubt if my friend Day, who was one of the principal movers of it, ever received any reply to it from the president.

But, sir, if Judge Peabody had no right to receive a military appointment, how is it that Judges Howell, Handlin and Hiestand had such rights? They are all loyal men; but unless Peabody had a right to receive a military appointment, it is difficult to see why they have one. If the auditor under the military appointment was false to his trust, and made improper payments of the money, then he is liable as much as Judge Peabody or anybody else.

There is a suit already instituted against Judge Peabody by Mr. Auditor before his honor Judge Durell, for the recovery of this money, and whether his honor decides for or against the State of Louisiana, really makes very little difference, as the case will be likely to go to the Supreme Court of the United States before it is settled. Now, sir, it is a little significant that the counsel defending Judge Peabody in the suit, the Hon. Christian Roselius and William H. Hunt, one of them in particular, Mr. Roselius, has always contended that the military had no right to appoint. It is a little significant, I say, that Roselius, the politician—Roselius, the lawyer, should defend a case against his own arguments that the military had no right to appoint. But when the case is decided by the Supreme Court of the United States the question will be settled.

I am reminded that a word used by me in the early part of my remarks is liable to be misunderstood. In using the term minion I used it respectfully and not in any opprobrious sense, as applicable only to persons appointed by the president to carry on the government in the States reclaimed from the rebel arms; and as the term is liable to be misunderstood, I retract it. As to any opinion I may have of Gov. Shepley in his political course, that is a matter of my own. As to the action of the auditor I have my own opinion, as I have in regard to the action of the present auditor. As to the judges, I have my own opinions, too. I make no distinction whether Gov. Hahn appoints them as military or civil governor. I hold that he has no such power to appoint, except that derived from the president of the United States. The constitution of 1852 gives no such power. That of 1864 only gives power to appoint, subject to the ratification of the Senate, just as Judge Durell was appointed by the president of the United States and afterwards ratified by the Senate. And I respectfully submit, that if the appointment had gone over one session of the Senate without confirmation, he would have ceased to be a judge of the United States Court.

But, sir, I come not here to uphold one side against the other. I come here to oppose the auditor's report from beginning to end. I do not desire to investigate it. It is not our business to investigate it. The question is between the officers and the president and Congress of the United States, and when the question comes up under the laws it will be time enough to investigate it. They are not responsible to us and we cannot bring them to an account for their actions. All we can do, at most, is to inform the president of their acts. They are responsible only to him and not to us, and to-morrow if you should elect or appoint a governor, and he should refuse to take upon himself, in addition to his duties as civil governor, the additional responsibilities of a military governor, he would be superceded by a military governor appointed by the president.

Now, sir, as to the question whether a man is a citizen or not, I contend that it makes no difference whatever.

Mr. AUSTIN Mr. President, I rise to a point of order. The gentleman is not discussing the point.

PRESIDENT—He is in order and will proceed.

Mr. HENDERSON—Mr. President, I intended to spare the committee, but I will read the first and second article of their report:

Your committee are of opinion that we should not interfere with the military powers, and therefore are unanimous in saying that inasmuch as the late auditor of public accounts, the Hon. S. H. Torrey, has issued warrants only by authority of the military governor, Gen. Shepley, he is not only excusable but justifiable.

As to the Hon. R. K. Howell and the Hon. A. M. Buchanan, your committee are of opinion that they have drawn their salary according to the constitution and laws of the State of Louisiana, and that the opinion of our worthy auditor, the Hon. A. P. Dostie, "that rebellion had terminated the existence of the Supreme Court," is unfounded and contrary to the prevailing opinion of all loyal citizens of Louisiana—"*That the State has never been out of the Union.*"

Now, sir, I contend that as Peabody was appointed chief justice, he had a right to accept the appointment, and having accepted, he had a right to his pay as such, on his own warrant. Whether he had anything to do or not, is not the question. If he had not, it was not his fault. We have nothing to do with the matter whatever. It is a question between the military and civil power, and we cannot decide it.

Now, sir, my friend from the Second District [Mr. Hills] made a very proper motion when he moved to postpone action on it indefinitely, but it was carried against him almost unanimously. I think it is unjust to take up any judge and condemn him without giving him any hearing as is done by this report, when it excuses all who are present in this city and condemns the very one who is not here to defend himself. This is unfair.

We are elected here as a civil body, for the purpose of framing a constitution for the State of Louisiana. We have no right to put censure upon Judge Peabody or any one else. Sir, it was the president of the United States that appointed him, and, sir, a delegation has been sent on from here by a large majority endorsing his renomination, and if we cast our votes for the report we cast a reflection upon the president, whom we have so heartily endorsed, and stultify ourselves.

Mr. MONTAMAT—Mr. President, before I shall cast my vote against this report, I would ask for information from the committee. They say that no Supreme Court was appointed. I wish to ask if the military authority ever did appoint Judge Peabody as chief justice of the Supreme Court. I merely wish to know, not whether a court was appointed, but if he was appointed.

PRESIDENT—He was appointed.

Mr. ABELL—I rise, Mr. President, to make but one or two observations, and I will state upon my own knowledge that Judge Peabody was appointed chief justice of the Supreme Court of this State. I make these remarks because the judge is absent. If he were here I trust he would be above suspicion. It was clamored about the streets about the time that he was appointed that the Supreme Court was to be erected in the State, and that in consequence the appointment of these judges would be necessary, and it was supposed that in a few days the court would be in operation. He was appointed chief justice, and he was expecting from day to day and from week to week that he would be called to the bench. I will go further: Judge Peabody had made arrangements in his own court to so arrange his business that he could attend to the duties of either. He was to attend at the Provisional Court at an earlier hour and adjourn in time for the other.

Now, sir, it is immaterial whether he was a citizen of this State or of any other State. This State was under the military power, and he was appointed by the military power. He received his appointment first, as the other judges received their's in this department, and I believe he was entitled to his pay. If any judge is appointed, and accepts his appointment, and does not go to the bench for six months, through no fault of his own, he is not deprived of his salary. So far as Judge Peabody and myself are concerned, sir, I do not defend him on account of any feeling for him personally. There are no two men in the United States that differ more widely than we do in politics, or at least in that part of politics that has the "nigger" in it. But, sir, I contend that justice ought to be done to every man, and I do not see the justice, sir, of condemning Judge Peabody in this report. I do not believe that he, sir, would be guilty of or accessory to an act of injustice to any man, and I consider that he has been presented to the country in a shamefully unjust manner, and I think it is the duty of this Convention to so far look into this matter as to place him right before the country, and I trust that this body will do so.

As to that part of the report that relates to Judge Howell and Judge Buchanan, I think it is most shameful to bring the matter before the country in this manner. It must have been evident to the committee and to every one else. It was something, as Webster said of the election of Gen. Taylor to the Presidency, "It was the worst selection that could have been made." I think it as unjust to those gentlemen as it is to Judge Peabody, because he stands as fair on the record as either of them, and they stand as fair as anybody can stand. I have not, Mr. President, stood up here vindicating Judge Peabody merely because I differed with the gentlemen who offered the report, or to show it the world that I did differ with them, but because I think it due to Judge Peabody and also to ourselves, to pass here a resolution justifying him in receiving the appointment from the military authorities and in receiving his salary.

Mr. THORPE—Mr. President, I desire to say one word in regard to my action in this matter. If we undertake to review the military government of this State, we will certainly get ourselves into a great deal of trouble, and take hold of a matter that really does not concern us. Whatever may be my personal opinion of the matter of paying Judge Peabody, I think it was done under military sanction; therefore we have nothing to do with it. I will state a little personal experience in that matter, which may be better than a long speech. While I was acting as surveyor, under Gen. Butler, he sent me a special order to do a certain thing, and I did it. The party sued me before a court and judgment was passed and is now recorded against me for doing what Gen. Butler specifically ordered me to do in writing. The absurdity of this need not be discussed. The military power has rescued the city and restored it to the old flag, and I do not believe that the history of the world can furnish an example of a military government so just and generally unexceptionable as that under the administration of Gens. Butler, Shepley and Banks. Therefore I move to lay the whole subject on the table.

Mr. CUTLER—In one of our school books —I believe Murray is the author—I used to read that knowledge is power—the philosopher's stone—the true alchemy which turns everything it touches to gold—the sceptre that gives us our dominion over nature—the key which unlocks the store-house of creation and opens to our view the treasures of the universe. And, sir, with this knowledge, let us not have facts smothered. Who made this report? Your humble servants, by your voice and will. Who caused this subject to be raised in this Convention and why was it demanded by our speakers —these sublime orators—these stars of this Convention—why? [Applause.] Because, sir, this Convention ordered it. I am one of that committee, and regretted much, sir, when you placed my name upon it.

But the auditor made his report, and in defence of the auditor, I say to you, that you have no right to call upon him for his report; but when you did, you found that he made it like a man—a man of honor, intelligence and respectability. [Applause.] When that report *was* made you wanted further investigation. You would not rest satisfied then. You want to rest *now*, do you? But no, a resolution must be offered, and the president must be required to appoint a committee of five, for the purpose of making a report to this Convention upon the auditor's report; I happened to be one of the unfortunate victims upon that committee. Now, sir, do you propose to say, after this explanation, that there is any ground for shame in using the names of the men which you called upon the auditor to produce? By no means; no honest man could say so. In discharge of our duties as a committee, what else should we do but to take the auditor's report, section by section, and ascertain what it was necessary to report to the Cicero of this Convention. [Laughter.] Now, sir, when the gentleman from the Second [Mr. Henderson] arose and said that he wanted no better cudgel with which to break the committee's heads than their own report, I hurl back upon him this assertion, that his own argument upon the premises assumed is the only cudgel I want to cut his throat entirely. As to my learned friend from—[A voice, "the Fifth,"] yes, from the Fifth [Mr. Abell]—I have heard it announced times enough to remember it—as to his taking the part of the learned Judge Peabody, I have not the the slightest objection; but why did he not speak upon the report of the auditor, as well as upon the report of the committee, and do justice to all. He is wrong in assuming that the committee brought this matter before the Convention.

Permit me to say that we did not censure the auditor. We say that under all the circumstances, of this Convention calling upon him to report, we find no serious objection to the manner and form in which he has seen proper to present this report. We went further, and, although he stated much in his report about Confederate money, we, as a committee, thought it proper to simply say—and I dare say there is not a loyal member upon this floor who would say otherwise — "we considered it trash." [Applause] What more would you have? We were compelled to report in discharge of our duty. "Your committee are of opinion that military power should not be interfered with." I beg to be distinctly understood, that by reference to these powers vested in Gen. Shepley, and him alone, as military governor, in regard to the action of the auditor, "your committee are of the opinion that he was not only excusable, but justifiable." You will all remember that when this report was before us it contained a slight reflection upon the conduct of the former auditor. No man should ever do another a personal injury, but should exonerate him from blame when deserving of it, and, therefore, we believe, that, inasmuch as the military governor of the State ordered the Hon. S. H. Torrey to issue these warrants, he could not resist that power, and therefore is to be excused.

Now, gentlemen, as to this very tender subject, touched upon with such ridicule—with the feeling of scorn—as to the epistle read by my friend from the Third, [Mr. Harnan] perhaps penned by himself and perhaps by some one else—God only knows, I do not—let me say that it does not touch the subject, and that it is foreign to the issue—both are in bad taste and spirit.

The president of the United States in issuing his great emancipation proclamation, recognized Louisiana as a State. Gen. Banks when he called upon the good people of the State of Louisiana to come forward and vote for each one of you, recognized this as the State of Louisiana, not a territory or a conquered province. Since this is the case let me ask if the report is not correct. The Hon. Judge Howell was elected to the judgeship of the Third District Court in the year 1861, and before this unholy rebellion assumed its present formidable position. He was elected by the people of his district, and was no creation of the military power or any civil appointment. The same argument applies to Judge Buchanan, and no man who knows the history of the past, or who is disposed to be just, will dispute the facts. Being then elected by the people in times of peace, let me ask where the man is who can put his hand upon his heart and say that he has never taken the oath to this,—I was about to say to this infernal Confederate government. There are a few exceptions, through powerful influences, but a majority of this body, and of every body or person of official capacity was, by the orders of the commanding general of this department, under Confederate rule, compelled to take the damnable oath of allegiance to the Confederate States against the United States of America. All persons in office necessarily had to conform to that damnable rule. Nevertheless, some benefit resulted, for a few maintained their offices, doing justice. No sooner did Gen. Butler come here, than he issued his proclamation, that any one voluntarily coming forward and renewing his oath of allegiance, would retain his position uninterrupted and unmolested. This was not treating us as a province or a territory, but most assuredly as a State again within the United States, whose protection had been suspended during rebel rule. Judge Howell bravely and nobly came forward then and renewed his oath of allegiance—early too, quite early. I know, for I was among the earliest, and he preceded me. When that was done, he was not appointed to office—there is where you are mistaken. When he renewed his old allegiance, he merely continued in the office to which the people had elected him. Why, then, is this censure by the gentleman from the Fifth and others, upon one who is as good and loyal a lawyer and man as ever stood upon Louisiana soil?

My friend (Mr. Abell) says that if Judge McCaleb had not resigned, he would have drawn *his* salary also. That statement is in keeping with the gentleman's position, for it happens that Judge McCaleb went into rebeldom and there died. He never renewed his allegiance, and how then is it possible that he could have drawn his salary? There are judges, perhaps, of the Supreme Court, as well as judges of the District Court of the State, who may have intruded their fingers into the city treasury, as somebody else did into the treasury of this State. So far as drawing salary as a judge is concerned, let me tell you that Gen. Butler was one of those stern, upright, honest and manly Union men who would not have allowed it. [Applause.] I want, sir, no greater test of loyalty than the cross-eye alone of Gen. Butler. [Great Applause.] Under all the circumstances I have detailed, can the loyalty of Judges Howell and Buchanan be questioned or their salaries withheld when they continue to perform the duties of their offices? I believe not, and believe that every conscientious man on this floor will say the same, though a prejudiced man may not. Again, if you are sent here to revise and amend the constitution of '52, you are not here as a people of a territory or conquered province, but as the sovereign people of a great State, one of that constellation which forms the United States. We see that the declaration of secession was a nullity and did not take the State out of the Union. [Applause.] Upon this basis we see that the auditor was mistaken in his opinion relative to the Supreme Court.

In the report of the committee they have not said that Judge Peabody was not appointed. By no means; but we have said that he was never chief justice of the Supreme Court of Louisiana, and I will prove it to you as clearly as the unclouded, brilliant rays of the meridian sun. The Constitution of 1852 says: "No person shall be eligible to any office of trust or emolument except justice of the peace." There is an express legal proposition, and now let us apply it. The president of the United States did grant to Judge Peabody a commission to go at once to the State of Louisiana. In the caption of this commission we find it stated that the civil law and the judges have been temporarily swept away by the rebellion—not destroyed—for the State existed, the courts existed, and the law existed. To prove that the law existed I will refer again to the document, which says that upon a trial, the forms of trial and forms of proceeding before your court shall conform as near as practicable to the proceedings of the District Courts of the United States and of the courts of the

State of Louisiana. No man on earth ever had the power that was granted to that judge. The Court of Queen's Bench and the Supreme Court of the United States sink into insignificance, for here this power is all granted to one man. With regard to his salary—have you ever seen, near Jackson Square, on the walls, "U. S. Provisional Court," and in the building the judge presiding there?

That is one office of emolument, is it not? How, then, is he entitled to a salary as chief justice, when the constitution says, no man in the State shall exercise but one office, except that of justice of the peace? This man, notwithstanding all the splendid power invested in him, stoops to preside over the Provost Court, which took the place of our recorders' courts. That makes two offices he held. What time had he then to act as chief justice of the Supreme Court of Louisiana? Let me ask you, then, as honorable men, not disposed to squander the money from the public treasury, if he was entitled to the salary of chief justice? I was United States attorney in the court of this very judge, but except the little spats that always are arising between parties in our respective positions, I never had any differences with him. My argument is founded on law, and the facts of the case. We have made a recommendation, but it casts no reflection upon either the auditor or the honorable judge. The trouble is not with the person, but with the court, for it is contrary to the principle of reconstruction, which are we advocating. Therefore, we simply request the president to withdraw this commission and recall this judge, though I believe that a necessity existed at one time for such a court. I know it no longer exists. Does not the appointment of judges supercede this provisional, temporary arrangement? We have, too, a district court to do anything which can be done in a United States court in Louisiana.

I believe that the president intended to have rebel property confiscated, but for all purposes of that kind the court was, to my personal knowledge, a failure. Fifty of sixty libels—gotten up and signed by G. D. Leamont, a man of eminent legal learning—were presented, but the court never did its duty, and we have failed to receive any benefit whatever from it. I once had two villainous capital cases there where the jury brought in a verdict of guilty—"*With or without capital punishment?*" asked the judge. "Guilty without any mitigating circumstances," was the response of the foreman. Defendant made a motion for a new trial, but those men will rot in jail before they are ever sentenced. I say it is time for us to have our own courts. Adopt the report, then, and do justice to yourselves, to the call you made upon your auditor and your committee, feeling sure that your recommendation will not be regarded as casting any reflections.

Mr. ABELL—I move the whole matter be adjourned until this day two weeks.

Mr. TERRY—The Convention will not be in session at that time, and I move the motion be laid on the table.

Mr. PRESIDENT—Before putting this vote I think it my duty to notice a remark which fell from our most worthy and able friend from the Second, (Mr. Henderson,) a remark, which, falling as it did in the heat of debate, I was glad to hear him so readily retract when called to his memory. I allude to the remark in connection with Gov. Shepley. From my connection with Gen. Shepley, as military commander of this city and military governor of this State, I can answer for him. There is no white man in the broad land of the United States who does not stand on an equal platform with the president of the United States, and no such man can be the President's minion. Gen. Shepley is an honorable gentleman. He has made mistakes in judgment, as what man has not, but in his character as a gentleman, he is a man who stands sans reproach.

[Terry's motion lost.

A rising vote was taken on the proposition to lay on the table—ayes 32, nays 32. There being a tie, the president voted in the negative, and the motion to lay on the table was lost.

On Mr. Abell's motion to postpone, a *viva voce* vote proved indecisive, when on rising vote the motion was lost—ayes 33, nays 39.]

Mr. TERRY—I move the adoption of the report.

[The ayes and nays were taken with the following result :]

YEAS—Messrs. Austin, Barrett, Baum, Beauvais, Bennie, Bofill, Burke, Collin, Cazabat, Crozat, Cutler, Decker, Duane, Duke, Dupaty, Ennis, Fish, Flagg, Foley, Gastinel, Geier, Healy, Hart, Heard, Hire, Howes, Kavanagh, Knobloch, Mann, Maurer, Mendiverri, Morris, Newell, Normand, O'Conner, Orr, Payne J., Paine J. T., Pintado, Purcell J., Pursell S., Schroeder, Schnurr, Seymour, Shaw, Spellicy, Stocker, Stumpf, Stiner, Stauffer, Taliaferro, Terry, Thorpe, Wenck and Wells—55.

NAYS—Messrs. Abell, Bell, Buckley, Cook J. K., Cook T., Dufresne, Flood, Fosdick, Gorlinski, Gruneberg, Harnan, Henderson, Hills, Maas, Mayer, Montamat, Murphy E., Murphy M. W., Poynot, Sullivan, Waters and Wilson—22.

[The report was adopted.]

Mr. BURKE—I move we adjourn until Wednesday, the 11th inst.

Mr. HILLS—I amend to Tuesday, the 5th inst.

[The motion was lost on rising vote—ayes 28, nays 44.

Mr. Burke's motion was also lost on rising vote--ayes 35, nays 49.]

Mr. MONTAMAT—I move we adjourn until 12 M., of Wednesday, the 6th inst.

[The motion was carried.]

WEDNESDAY, July 6, 1864.

The Convention met pursuant to adjournment, and the president being absent, on motion of Mr. Beauvais, Mr. Hills was called to the chair.

The secretary called the roll, and the following members answered to their names :

Messrs. Austin, Balch, Barrett, Baum, Beauvais, Bell, Bofill, Bromley, Buckley, Burke, Campbell, Collin, Cook J. K., Cook T., Crozat, Cutler, Davies, Duane, Dufresne, Edwards, Ennis, Flood, Foley, Geier, Gorlinski, Gruneberg, Gaidry, Healy, Harnan, Hart, Heard, Hills, Howes, Kavanagh, Knobloch, Maas, Mann, Maurer, Mayer, Mandiverri, Montamat, Morris, Murphy E., Murphy M. W., Newell, Normand, O'Conner, Payne J., Paine J. T., Pintado, Poynot, Purcell J., Pursell S., Schroeder, Schnurr, Shaw, Smith, Spellicy, Stocker, Stumpf, Stiner, Stauffer, Sullivan, Taliaferro, Terry, Wells, Wilson—67.

There being no quorum, the sergeant-at-arms was dispatched for absent members.

Mr. SHAW—I move a recess of fifteen minutes.

[The motion was carried.

At the expiration of the recess the House was again called to order and the roll called, when the following members answered their to names :]

Messrs. Austin, Balch, Barrett, Baum, Beauvais, Bell, Bofill, Bromley, Buckley, Burke, Campbell, Collin, Cook J. K., Cook T., Crozat, Cutler, Davies, Duane, Dufresne, Edwards, Ennis, Flood Foley, Fosdick, Fuller, Gastinel, Geier, Gorlinski, Gruneberg, Gaidry, Healy, Harnan, Hart, Heard, Hills, Hire, Howell, Howes, Kavanagh, Knobloch, Maas, Mann, Maurer, Mayer, Mendiverri, Montamat, Morris, Murphy E., Murphy M. W., Newell, Normand, O'Conner, Payne J., Paine J. T., Pintado, Poynot, Purcell J., Pursell S., Schroeder, Schnurr, Shaw, Smith, Spellicy, Stocker, Stumpf, Stiner, Stauffer, Sullivan, Taliaferro, Terry, Wells, Wilson—72.

Absent—Mr. President and Messrs. Abell, Ariail, Bennie, Bonzano, Brott, Cazabat, Decker, Duke, Dupaty, Fish, Flagg, Henderson, Lobdell, Millspaugh, Montague, Ong, Orr, Seymour, Thorpe, Thomas, Waters and Wenck—23.

Mr. BALCH—I move to adjourn.

[The motion was lost on a rising vote—yeas 25, nays 33.

After a further delay of half an hour, on motion of Mr. Smith, the Convention adjourned.]

THURSDAY, July 7, 1864.

The Convention met, pursuant to adjournment. Present, the Hon. E. H. Durell, president, and the following members :

Messrs. Abell, Austin, Balch, Barrett, Baum, Beauvais, Bell, Bennie, Bofill, Bromley, Buckley, Burke, Campbell, Collin. Cazabat, Cook J. K., Cook T., Crozat, Cutler, Davies, Decker, Duane, Dufresne, Edwards, Ennis, Fish, Flagg, Flood, Foley, Fosdick, Fuller, Gastinel, Geier, Gorlinski, Gruneberg, Gaidry, Healy, Harnan, Hart, Heard, Henderson, Hills, Hire, Howell, Howes, Kavanagh, Knobloch, Kugler, Maas, Mann, Maurer, Mayer, Mendiverri, Montamat, Morris, Murphy E., Murphy M. W., Newell, Normand, O'Conner, Ong, Orr, Payne J. T., Poynot, Pintado, Purcell J., Pursell S., Schroeder, Schnurr, Seymour, Shaw, Smith. Spellicy, Stocker, Stumpf, Stiner, Sauffer, Sullivan, Taliaferro, Terry, Thorpe, Waters, Wenck, Wells, Wilson—84.

The minutes of Saturday's and Wednesday's proceedings were read and adopted.

Mr. SHAW—Mr. President, before taking up the order of the day, in order to facilitate our work as much as possible, I move that a committee be appointed of five, to consist of the appointed members by the chair, to arrange and number the ordinances we have adopted, with instructions to correct mistakes and make any alterations in the language that may be deemed advisable, the committee to report in print as soon as possible.

[The motion was carried.]

PRESIDENT—The chair appoints Messrs. Shaw, Thorpe, Henderson. Cazabat and Smith.

Mr. SMITH—I have a resolution to offer to lie over till next Saturday.

Whereas, during the present rebellion individuals, as well as corporations and parishes, have issued a worthless paper currency, and forced its circulation on the poorer and only loyal classes of the community, therefore be it

Resolved, That a special committee of five be appointed to take into consideration the propriety of forming an article or articles to prevent the recurrence of the same in future, and to hold the property of whatever character, whether belonging to husband or wife, parishes or corporations for the redemption of the same, and that the committee be also instructed to submit to this Convention, for its approval or rejection, the draft of a petition to be sent to the Congress of the United States, asking them to empower the parishes of the State of Louisiana to apply the proceeds of sales of property of disloyal citizens for the purpose of redeeming the paper currency issued by them.

Mr. BURKE—I rise for information to a question of privilege. I find that we have ten enrolling clerks and four translating clerks. I wish simply to enquire by whom they were employed. It seems that they have been employed promiscuously by the committee, without the knowledge of the Convention or of the entire committee. I had a conversation with one of the committee on the subject and he told me he knew nothing at all about it. I have a list given me by the warrant clerk which shows the number I have stated. I move that a committee be appointed to investigate the matter and report the number of clerks necessary to do the business, in order that the public money may not be wasted by employing a lot of superfluous clerks.

Mr. TERRY—There are not only fourteen clerks, but twenty-two ; I have a list myself.

[The motion of Mr. Burke was lost.]

Mr. ABELL—Mr. President, I now move a reconsideration of the vote on the additional article relative to the mode of submitting the constitution to the people, offered by the gentleman from the Seventh District [Mr. Howell.]

Mr. MONTAMAT—I wish to read a report of the Finance Committee this morning, if the House will permit it :

REPORT OF THE FINANCE COMMITTEE OF THE CONSTITUTIONAL CONVENTION OF THE FUNDS FOR THE PAYMENT PER DIEM OF MEMBERS, SALARIES OF OFFICERS AND EMPLOYEES.

1864.		
June 25---Balance on hand in the State treasury........		$19,074 10
July 2---Paid warrant No. 81.....	$2,030 00	
July 2---Paid warrant No. 81.....	2,170 00	
July 2---Paid warrant No. 81.....	2,860 00	
July 2---Paid warrant No. 82.....	1,981 00	
July 2---Paid warrant No. 83.....	1,199 82---	$10,240 82
July 6---Balance on hand.......		$8,806 28
To which must be added the sum of........................		1,199 82
paid for salaries of employés, which properly belongs to expense account.		
The sum of $2328 08, being the balance on hand of the appropriation for contingent expenses, was paid out, that account fell short $1199 82, which was drawn from the appropriation for per diem and salaries, as stated above.		
Real balance.............		$10,006 10

The Convention being on the eve of adjourning, your committee respectfully recommend that a compensation be given to the following officers of this body :

J. E. Neelis, secretary, $500 ; L. O. Maureau, warrant clerk and clerk of Finance Committee, $250.

Respectfully submitted,
JOHN P. MONTAMAT,
Acting Chairman Finance Committee.
JOHN SULLIVAN,
L. P. NORMAND.

Mr. CAZABAT—I move that the reporters be included.

Mr. Waters—I move as an amendment that the members be allowed one thousand dollars each, in addition to their *per diem.*

[The recommendations of the committee, with the amendments, were laid on the table.]

Mr. Thorpe—I move that the president be added to the committee on arrangement.

Mr. Pursell—I have a report to make, accompanied by a resolution.

To the honorable the president and members of the Constitutional Convention:

Gentlemen—Your Committee on Contingent Expenses, have the honor to report the exhaustion of the amount of twenty-five thousand dollars, formerly appropriated, and ask for a further appropriation of five thousand dollars, and offer the following resolution:

Resolved, That the sum of five thousand dollars be and the same is hereby appro riated out of the general funds of the State, for the purpose of paying the contingent expenses of this Convention.

S. Pursell, Chairman.
John Payne,
John A. Newell,
James Duane,
Robt. B. Bell.

Mr. Duane—I move a suspension of the rules in order to act on it at once.

[The motion was carried.]

Mr. Stauffer—Mr. President, I rise to a point of order. I am informed that Mr. Knobloch, a member of this Convention, has never recorded his vote on the ordinance of emancipation. If he has not, I think that under our rules he should be required to vote.

President—The secretary will inform the gentleman whether Mr. Knobloch has voted.

Secretary—It will be impossible to give the information at this moment.

President—Very well. You can ascertain, and if Mr. Knobloch has not voted on that question he can do so to-morrow.

Mr. Austin—I have a resolution to offer as follows:

Resolved, That the members of this Convention, who went to Baltimore as delegates, be entitled to their per diem pay.

President—It lies over until Saturday.

Mr. Abell—I now move a reconsideration of the additional article offered by Judge Howell.

Mr. Smith—I move to lay that motion on the table.

Mr. Stocker—That motion should have been made yesterday: it is too late to-day. If there was no quorum yesterday, it was as much his fault as anybody's.

President—There having been no quorum present yesterday, it could not have been offered, and to-day is the first sitting day.

Mr. Sullivan—I call for the yeas and nays on that question.

[The question was decided by a rising vote—yeas 46, nays 27.

The motion to table was carried.]

President—The order of the day is now in order. Second reading of the report of the Committee on Public Education. The secretary will read the minority report of Mr. Sullivan as amended.

[The secretary commenced reading the report.]

Mr. Terry—Mr. President,in the haste of the moment, when that bill came up, I submitted an article as a substitute for the article two of the report, which was adopted. I hold in my hand a substitute for that article which, while it is essentially the same, expresses the idea more clearly than the one adopted, and I wish now to offer this in place of that, and therefore move it as a substitute for article two.

Art. 2. The Legislature shall establish free public schools throughout the State for the education of white children, and shall provide for their support by taxation laid upon property of white persons; and all moneys so raised shall be distributed to each parish in proportion to the number of white children contained therein, between such ages as shall be fixed by law.

The Legislature shall also establish free public schools throughout the State, for the education of colored children, and shall provide for their support by taxation laid upon property of colored persons; and all moneys so raised shall be distributed to each parish in proportion to the number of colored children contained therein, between such ages as shall be fixed by law.

It will be perceived that the purport of this article is precisely the same as that already adopted.

Mr. Hills—I second the motion of Mr. Terry.

Mr. Henderson—I have another substitute for both Mr. Terry's articles as follows:

Art. 2. The Legislature shall levy a special tax on the property of white persons owning property in the State, for the purpose of public schools for the education of white children, and money so arising shall not be otherwise appropriated.

The Legislature shall levy a special tax on colored persons in the State, and their property, for the purpose of public schools for the education of colored children, and money so arising shall not be otherwise appropriated.

Mr. DAVIES—I offer as a substitute for the whole article 1 of the majority report of the committee.

[The question was put on the adoption of Mr. Henderson's substitute, and a division being called for the substitute was adopted by the following vote: yeas 50, nays 19.]

Mr. HILLS—I wish to offer an additional article, viz:

All asylums for orphans containing over two hundred scholars, shall be considered public schools of the State.

[On motion to lay on the table the ayes and nays were called with the following result:]

YEAS—Messrs. Baum, Beauvais, Burke, Campbell, Collin, Cazabat, Cook J. K., Davies, Decker, Edwards, Ennis, Flagg, Flood, Gastinel, Geier, Gaidry, Hart, Heard, Hire, Howell, Kavanagh, Kugler, Maas, Mann, Mendiverri, Morris, Newell, Normand, Ong, Paine J. T., Pintado, Pursell S., Schroeder, Seymour, Shaw, Stumpf, Taliaferro, Wenck, Wells—39.

NAYS—Messrs. Abell, Austin, Balch, Barrett, Bell, Bennie, Bofill, Bromley, Buckley, Cook T., Crozat, Duane, Dufresne, Fish, Foley, Fosdick, Fuller, Gorlinski, Gruneberg, Healy, Harnan, Henderson, Hills, Howes, Knobloch, Maurer, Montamat, Murphy M. W., O'Conner, Orr, Poynot, Purcell J., Schnurr, Smith, Spellicy, Stocker, Stiner, Stauffer, Sullivan, Terry, Thorpe, Waters, Wilson—43.

Mr. SMITH—I move the previous question on the adoption of the article.

[The motion was lost.]

Mr. CAZABAT—Mr. President, I have an amendment to offer to the article:

No appropriation shall be made by the Legislature for the support of any private school or institution of learning whatever, but the highest encouragement shall be granted to public schools throughout the State.

Mr. SULLIVAN—I move to lay that on the table.

Mr. STOCKER—It is not in order: it was voted on last Saturday, and lost.

[The motion to table wast lost on a rising vote—yeas 36, nays 53.]

Mr. STOCKER—Mr. President, we certainly shall not vote on both sides of this question; for, last Saturday, when the yeas and nays were called on it, there were only seventy-five members present.

Mr. WILSON—Mr. President, I have had occasion to make a few remarks on nearly every subject of importance which has engaged the attention of this honorable body. But, now, at the close of our labors, it was my intention to simply record my vote, as I did not for a moment imagine that any efforts of mine would elucidate the points likely to arise at this late stage of proceedings.

The question of public education, however, has, within the past few days, assumed so many phases, that I think I would be direlict of duty did I not record my opinions thereupon. These opinions, Mr. President, are very plain. I believe that public schools should be secular; that nothing sectarian should be admitted therein; that no particular form of prayer, no particular form of worship should be impressed or forced upon the mind of any pupil, and that no share of the school fund should be distributed among the adherents of any particular church. Now, Mr. President, that is the platform upon which I stand, and I believe it is so plain, "that he, who runs, may read."

I believe every gentleman on this floor will agree with me, in according a large share of praise to Col. Thorpe for the eloquent word-picture drawn by him of the self-sacrificing Sisters of Charity. It was truly a masterpiece of oratorical art. His impassioned appeal for State aid to our Catholic Orphan Asylums required not the presence, even in imagination, of these fatherless and motherless, brotherless and sisterless children, with their ever-vigilant and never-tiring virgin guardians, whose life is one unceasing prayer, to strike a deep chord of sympathy in my heart; but, Mr. President, we must not forget that these sisters raise these orphan children in a faith which is not identified with the State, and it would not only be impolitic, but wrong to force the State to educate these children in that faith.

The school fund has been heretofore appropriated for the education of all children, regardless of creed; and did we force a change of that policy it would open the door to a feeling of religious acrimony which would sap the very foundation of our institutions, and end in the overthrow of that wise system which guarantees to the worshippers of every faith immunity from persecution. It was flight from religious persecution that brought Penn and a host of others to this country. I do not believe that I would be much in error were I to state that the giant republic of which we are citizens sprang from religious as well as political persecution, and that the glorious tree of liberty which to-day spreads its vigorous arms across the length and breadth of this land was planted by men who had to leave home and its sacred memories to avoid martyrdom for persisting in worshipping God according to the dictates of their own consciences.

With the history of the past before us, we should pause before giving State aid to sectarian schools. Edmund Burke has truly said that "Religion is the basis of civil society and the source of all good and of all comfort." But who shall decide for us what is true religion? For my part I believe that Christ's last commandment "Love one another," is a true enough precept upon which to build up the most beautiful fabric of faith. But Henry the Eighth, that great bad man, thought differently, and the fires of Smithfield not only consumed Barnes, Gerrard and Jerome, (Lutherans,) but Abel, Featherstone and Powell, (Roman Catholics,) and these men in their last agony objected, not so much to being burned to death for disagreeing with the flickering theology of the king, as for being sacrificed at the same time and in heretical company. One word more in connection with this part of the subject and I shall pass on. I believe that the greatest minds of the past, as well as the greatest minds of the present, have differed on religion, and when puny intellects debate such a question, contending that some particular mode of worship is correct, and, unless followed to the letter, the violator shall be eternally damned, I cannot help calling to mind that passage of Pope's, himself a Roman Catholic:

"For modes of faith, let graceless zealots fight—
His can't be wrong whose life is in the right:
In faith and hope the world will disagree,
But all mankind's concern is charity.
All must be false, that thwarts this one great end,
And all of God, that bless mankind or mend."

Col. Thorpe has asserted that men who oppose the proposition, to give a share of the school fund to these orphan asylumns, are narrow-minded, and urges upon them the necessity of expanding their comprehension. Were there a proposition before this body of a charitable character—a proposition to give aid to these Catholic Orphan Asylums to enable them to purchase the necessaries of life, I would vote in the affirmative, no matter how large the amount. But I hold that the school fund must not be given to any sectarian institutions. Public schools must be kept free from all religious influences, and were a proposition to be made hereafter to introduce even the Bible itself into any of the public schools, and I a member of the body into which such a proposition was introduced, I would most assuredly vote against granting permission.

In conclusion, I will say a few words in reference to the present system of public education. In the primary departments, I would suggest to teachers the propriety of not taxing the memory of children so much. I have known a teacher to give eight pages of spelling to a pupil to commit to memory, which was accomplished. But the pupil did not have time to learn the meaning of one-sixteenth of the words so committed, and a few days afterwards could not spell more than a dozen words on every page, and then he was doing very well, I thought. In the high school, or in connexion with it, I would suggest the establishment of a school of design, which would tend to develop any artistic taste the pupils might have, and create a passion for the fine arts.

Let us not be carried away by the eloquence of Col. Thorpe, to introduce into the organic law of our State the seeds of religious dissension—let us not follow the example of North Carolina and New Hampshire, and proscribe men for their religious tenets—but let us rather live in one harmonious brotherhood, according to every man the right to hold his religious and political tenets, and thus carry out the divine commandment which inculcates unbounded love for one another.

I will vote for Mr. Cazabat's amendment.

Mr. HENDERSON—It may seem singular to some gentlemen, Mr. President, that I have gone through such a radical change. A few days ago I desired to insert an article providing that no religious tenet should be taught in the public schools. I have been told by the President and members of this Convention that I had no second. All I have to say about the matter is that I am now on the reverse side of the question. The finger of scorn has been pointed at me, and it has been said that I wanted to discourage religion. That I was a scoffer who wanted to tear down religion and not to build it up. I repudiate such sentiments. I have no desire to destroy religious sentiment. I stand on the broad platform of Franklin and Jefferson, and other great men of former times, who have long since gone by the board. All the New England States have given money, and frequently other property, for the support of religious schools.

Mr. SMITH—Will the gentleman name the States.

Mr. HENDERSON—All of them.

Mr. SMITH—I say none of them have.

Mr. HENDERSON—Now, sir, I care not what you say. There will be found in all the New England States public schools, where prayer is made. Now, sir, a school where the teacher offers up prayer to God is a religious school, for before he gets through, he will have something to say, either about Jesus Christ, or the Virgin Mary, and these are the great questions which divide the Jews, the Protestants, and the Catholics. Man is more particular with regard to his religion than anything else on earth, and these schools are bound to be sectarian, if religion is taught in them at all. Sir, let a man teach a Presbyterian school, and a Methodist will not send his children to it any sooner than he would to a Roman Catholic. There is as great an aversion to schools of different denominations of Protestants, as between Protestants and Catholics. I am willing that no religious tenets shall be taught, but as the majority have decided against me, I desire that the door shall be opened wide enough for all. I don't want to see any discrimination used, and if the public money is to be used by one denomination, it should be used for the benefit of all. Give them all the same chance. I have been told that in New Orleans the asylums are under the charge of the Catholics. Other denominations have the same right to establish asylums and schools, and I would extend to them the same privileges and assistance. I care not whether the religion taught in their institutions is Protestant or Catholic. I am in favor of them both. If John Smith wants to send his children to a Catholic school that is supported by the State, it is no more than right that John Jones should, if he desires, be allowed to send his to a Protestant school supported by the State. It is as fair for one as for the other, and I am in favor of supporting both; so you see that instead of desiring to tear down religious institutions and destroying religious sentiments, I am in favor of building them up, not one denomination merely, but all of them.

We have in the United States at present no less than three hundred and sixty-five religious denominations—one for every day of the year—a sufficient variety, one would think, to gratify the taste of every one; and if we support one, where is the propriety of excluding any of the others? If we support one we should support all. Now, if you read the Bible in a school, it is a species of religion. If you begin with prayer, it is a species of religion; and if you tolerate anything of the kind, I can see no justice in excluding anything. It is impossible, perhaps, to exclude it entirely. In the case of the Gerard will it proved impracticable. He made a will leaving a large sum to found a school, and provided that no professors of any religious denomination should be employed as teachers.

The will was contested, and the Supreme Court of the United States decided that he had no right to leave the money under such restrictions, but it has been found impracticable to carry it out, for teachers who were not of some religious denomination could not be obtained, and they have been obliged to take Protestant teachers. Every man will say: I consider my duty to God higher than my duty to man, and religion will be taught in the schools. My object is, then, to prevent one set from teaching their own views to the exclusion of every other: I wish them all to stand on the same footing; and, as long as public opinion is in favor of teaching any, let all be taught. I would not allow a minority to oppress or do an injustice to the majority, or the majority to do an injustice to the minority. If yon open the door to religious instruction in the public schools, make it wide enough for all denominations to enter. Why, sir, so far as I am individually concerned, I espouse no religion: I am what is called a Deist; I am opposed to teaching religion at all in the public schools; but, sir, public opinion is against me; my own party is against me. Deists say: "Let them have their religious schools; let us have our own private opinions." The Catholics believe their own religion is paramount—the Protestants are equally as confident respecting their own, though more modest, perhaps, in their mode of expressing it, and they do no harm. But, if you allow religion to be taught, you must place all denominations on an equality. I will oppose no denomination; you may have as many as you please; but, make sure of one thing, that you are not ruled by priestcraft.

Henry VIII changed his religion as he changed his coat—on the score of public policy. Napoleon wanted no religion, but he wanted to be Pope—and to be Pope, he had to be elected by the bishops, and so he favored the Catholic religion from policy. You have your public schools, and the teachers will teach their own religion. Why, sir, is it that some of the northern colleges, supported by different denominations, are aided by the State? What is the harm done by it?

Mr. Hills—Mr. President, I rise to a point of order: I believe the gentleman has consumed his half hour.

Mr. Shaw—I move he be allowed to proceed.

Mr. Henderson—I thank the gentleman for his courtesy in making that motion, but will not detain the House longer, and will only say that, when the proper time comes, I shall vote no on the third reading of the report on Public Education.

Mr. Smith—Mr. President, I wish to say that the institutions the gentleman has pointed out, Wesleyan, Baptist, etc., are private institutions. They are not public institutions, and, sir, I am not afraid of contradiction in saying that the public school system of New England has nothing to do with sectarianism whatever. I think it best to let the private institutions take care of themselves, and if the public wants such institutions, let it pay for them, and let us keep the public schools and the funds of the public untouched by sectarian principles, and let the door of the public schools be open to children of every denomination, and thus every parent can avail himself of the right of sending his children there, if he pleases; if he does not wish to do so, it is his own business, and not ours. Let us have a place to educate the children of those who are not able to send them to a private school.

The institutions of the kingdom of Prussia are well known, and its system of education the best in the world, and I ask if there is any sectarian principle there? No; the door is open to every child who is willing to avail himself of it. Let us keep the public schools free from all sectarian institutions, to appropriate the funds, and allow no other influence to be brought to bear, and I shall go against, in every shape and form, one dollar of the public moneys being appropriated to private institutions. If they cannot take care of themselves, then, in God's name, let them go down.

Mr. Abell—Mr. President, I think I have done about as much speaking as falls to my share, but I wish to submit a very few remarks. I think that the object of the motion made by the gentleman from the Second, is one of the best that has been presented to this Convention. If he had been a little more restricted I should have voted for it with all my heart. If he had inserted "white" before "child," I should have been with him heart and soul; but without that qualifying word I will never support it, because I consider that it is for the interest of the negro as well as of the white, that the two races should be separated, and I hope this Convention will regard it as a sacred duty to do all within its power to keep the two classes apart. With regard to extending the public fund to these schools I have but a few words to say. If you see proper to extend the public fund to cover these charitable schools, there can be no conflict, as proposed in the clause offered by my worthy friend. It opens the lists to all who choose to step in and avail themselves of it; every denomination is embraced in the proposition of the gentleman from the Second, [Mr. Hills,] and no one need be jealous. In this city the Catholics have been in advance of the Protestants in respect to the schools. One of my parents was a Catholic and the other a Protestant, and I was raised a Protestant, and I think I have a predominance of that in my nature; but I possess so little religion that it is scarcely worth bragging about. I say if you establish a school containing two hundred scholars, of whatever denomination, it becomes the interest and duty of the State to throw its protecting arm around that institution. If there was no clause, I think, where so large a number of children absolutely dependent are found, it is the common interest of the State government, and the duty of every philanthropist and politician who looks to the true policy of the State, to take an interest in them and provide for their support. I am in favor of the resolution of the gentleman (Mr. Hills) and shall sustain it with a single qualification which I wish to see there, for the moment you bring the colored race in contact with the white race, you do them the greatest possible injury. We have already opened the way by which, through taxing the colored people, we have solved a part of the difficulty. With these remarks, Mr. President, I leave the question.

Mr. HILLS—Mr. President, I shall detain the Convention but a few moments. I have been forcibly reminded in listening to the amendment and remarks of my friend from the Fifth (Mr. Abell) of what a celebrated Persian poet said, that "If the ass of Christ were to make a journey to Mecca, he would come back an ass still." So it seems with the negro question and the sectarian question in this Convention. Wherever we send them, whether in the educational department or any other part of the constitution, the ass comes back an ass still, and the negro question is the negro question still; and so with the sectarian question. I say neither the negro nor the sectarian question has anything whatever to do with this clause which I have offered, and I will explain myself. In the first place, as to the point raised by Mr. Abell. If he will look at the clause already adopted, he will find that the public schools are separated, the colored from the white, and they are to be maintained by separate funds, the white schools by taxation of the whites and the colored schools by taxation of the colored people. The clause says that orphan asylums that number two hundred inmates shall be regarded as public schools. If they are white orphan asylums, they come under the head of white schools; if they are colored asylums, they come under the head of colored schools and are supported by the taxation of the property of the colored population, precisely as the other public schools. [Applause.]

Now, sir, as for sectarianism, I am not aware that an orphan asylum is a sectarian institution. I never regarded it as such. It may be that the majority of our charitable institutions are Catholic—it may be they are Presbyterian—I know not and care not, I simply propose by this measure to make a perpetual appropriation and fund for the support of these most desirable and useful institutions for the protection and care of orphan children. It is not a sectarian proposition, and it has not the taint or touch of sectarianism upon it, and no reasonable man who looks at it can accuse it of any such feature. By this proposition you simply require the Legislature to regard these orphan asylums as public schools and to make appropriations for them the same as though they were public schools, and in that way you create and secure a perpetual fund for their support, whether they be Roman Catholic or Protestant. They are all entitled to our benevolence and charity, and are the most useful and beneficent institutions that the State can possibly cherish, and do more to prevent crime than any other could; and every dollar that the State expends in their support saves money to our treasury by the prevention of pauperism, vagrancy and crime. Therefore, I say it is not sectarianism. It is simply a proposition to maintain perpetually these institutions, and I cannot see what objections gentlemen can raise to it.

Mr. HOWELL—Mr. President, the gentleman who has just taken his seat, has made reference to a Persian poet, and applied it to the remarks of the gentleman who preceded him on this floor.

Mr. HILLS—I beg your pardon, I applied it to these questions and not to the remarks of the gentleman.

Mr. HOWELL—I will apply it then to the measure which the gentleman presents for the action of this Convention. I contend, sir, that a public school is a public school, and a private school is a private school; that no resolution or ordinance of this Convention can make a private school a public school. You may declare as often as you please that a rose is a beet, but the rose is still a rose, notwithstanding. You may consider a private school a public school, but unless it gives up its condition as a private school it is still a private school. By declaring that an asylum shall be considered a public school, you take away the character of an asylum and place it under the direction of the public school system. You take it away from the managers of the asylum and put it under the control of the parties who are directed by law to control the public schools. What is the use of doing that? Those children, as inmates of the asylum, are counted in the distribution of the fund, and have a right to go to any of the public schools under the law; they have just as much right to go to the public schools while within the asylum, as they had when living at home before the death of their parents. You are doing either an inconsistency in declaring private schools to be public schools, or you are virtually dividing the school fund—the dmeasure against which I have been contending throughout, in this Convention. It is unjust to the tax-payer and to the citizen to give any number of children double advantage in this matter by any provision which you make. You do give the asylums a double advantage, for you continue them in their position as inmates of the asylum, and give them money from the public school fund for their education, because they have already been counted in the estimate by which the distribution is made.

PRESIDENT—The question is not on Mr. Hills' article, but on the substitute of Mr. Cazabat, striking that out.

Mr. HOWELL—All the speeches have been made on the first article, but I stand corrected.

Mr. CAZABAT—I have the right to close the debate.

Mr. M. W. MURPHY—I move to adjourn.

[The yeas and nays were ordered, and the motion lost, as follows:

YEAS—Messrs. Buckley, Burke, Edwards Waters—4.

NAYS—Messrs. Abell, Austin, Barrett, Bell, Bennie, Bofill, Campbell, Collin, Cazabat, Cook J. K., Cook T., Crozat, Cutler, Davies, Decker, Duane, Dufresne, Ennis, Fish, Flagg, Flood, Foley, Fosdick, Fuller, Gastinel, Geier, Gorlinski, Gruneberg, Gaidry, Healy, Harnan, Hart, Heard, Henderson, Hills, Hire, Howell, Howes, Knobloch, Kugler, Maas, Mann, Maurer, Montamat, Morris, Murphy M. W., Newell, Normand, O'Conner, Ong. Orr, Paine J. T., Pintado, Poynot, Purcell J., Pursell S., Schroeder, Schnurr, Shaw, Smith, Spellicy, Stocker, Stumpf, Stiner, Stauffer, Sullivan, Taliaferro, Terry, Wenck, Wells, Wilson—71.

The motion to adjourn was therefore lost.

Mr. CAZABAT—Mr. President, in vindication and support of my substitute to the additional article offered, to my great surprise, by the gentleman from the Second District, (Mr. Hills,) on the report of Public Education—I feel somewhat bound to make a few remarks. Since this question has been forced upon us, it becomes the duty of every member to be bold and fearless enough to oppose and defeat, if possible, such an unjust measure. I therefore call the attention of the Convention to the true character of said additional article, which, in my humble opinion, is calculated to produce more mischief than good. Are you prepared, gentlemen, to sanction, by your votes, the dangerous sectarian principle, more or less apparent in the clause offered by Mr. Hills, that "*all asylums for orphans, containing not less than two hundred inmates, shall be regarded as public schools?*"

Each and every one of us should, before casting his vote, reflect seriously upon this important subject, involving, now and hereafter, the welfare of society. I contend that if introduced or adopted in the organic law of the land, this new and strange article will most assuredly become, in the course of time, the source of the most fearful but now unforeseen evils to the good people of Louisiana.

It cannot be denied that the orphans' asylums, under the charge of those devoted self-sacrificing sisters of mercy, those angels of sublime charity, whose life is consecrated to the love of God, and the relief of suffering humanity, truly deserve the hearty support and assistance of the State, as *benevolent* and *charitable associations;* and permit me to observe here, that under this constitution, sufficient appropriations can and shall always be made by the Legislature for "*charitable purposes.*"

But when you ask more than you are entitled to, more than is already provided for by law, and granted by custom—when you attempt to place those private institutions on the same footing as our public schools, you are wrong to say the least; you are thereby doing a manifest injustice to your public schools, and I dare to proclaim openly that you will thus plant in the midst of your community, the seeds of sectarian education, and perhaps of dreadful religious war and persecution.

An article of a similar character was offered a short time ago to this Convention by Col. Thorpe, if I recollect right, and the purport thereof was a *pro rata* division of the public school funds, etc., etc.; but, fortunately, by the good sense of this honorable body, this unjust clause was defeated, and a second attempt is now made in another shape to revive the subject.

Sir, I care not what is your religious creed—I care not whether you are Christian, Jew or Protestant, Catholic or Methodist, you have the undisputed right to worship Almighty God according to the dictates of your conscience; but when you try, either directly or indirectly, to mix the "Church" with the "State," you are going too far—and such measure, if permitted, would be the first step of the most unsafe and dangerous policy.

Remember that religious fanaticism is more to be dreaded than a foreign enemy—more to be feared than the armies of the civilized world combined against our republic.

Let the sad experience of the past be a lesson for the future. Take heed, citizens of Louisiana! Let the bloody history of the last three years be a warning to you, now and forever! This cruel fratricidal conflict, this deplorable civil war is partly the culminating result of extreme *sectional* feelings and extreme *sectional* views; and, now, will you hesitate to avoid and prevent the introduction of *sectarian* views and *sectarian* feelings, and thereby the possibility of a religious war hereafter. (Great applause.)

Remember that the school-boy of to-day will become the citizen of to-morrow. It is therefore the sacred duty of the government to provide for the benefit of the rising generations, by a system of public education as perfect and as liberal as possible, in accordance with the progressive spirit of the age; but, above all, entirely divested of all sectarian doctrine and influence. What objections can be raised against our public schools? Are they not open equally to the rich and to the poor? Are they not the corner stone and nurseries of free and republican institutions? Are not the teachers of our public schools as loyal, as competent, as responsible and as respectable as those of your private and select institutions?

If so, you will cheerfully support as sensible and unprejudiced men my substitute, which, making a wise discrimination between private and public schools, provides that "*no appropriation shall be made by the Legislature for the support of any private school or institution of learning, of any denomination whatever, but the highest encouragement shall be granted to public schools throughout the State.*"

With these remarks, gentlemen, I submit the question to your honest convictions, and feel confident that the result of your decision will be in favor of the public schools.

[Mr. Cazabat's substitute was then adopted.]

YEAS—Messrs. Austin, Bennie, Bofill, Bromley, Burke, Campbell, Collin, Cazabat, Cook J. K., Davies, Decker, Edwards, Ennis, Fish, Flagg, Flood, Gastinel, Gaidry, Hart, Heard, Hire, Howell, Kugler, Maas, Mann, Maurer, Montamat, Morris, Newell, Normand, Ong, Paine J. T., Pintado, Poynot, Pursell S., Schroeder, Shaw, Smith, Spellicy, Stumpf, Stauffer, Taliaferro, Wenck, Wells, Wilson—45.

NAYS—Messrs. Abell, Barrett, Bell, Buckley, Cook T., Crozat, Cutler, Duane, Dufresne, Foley, Fosdick, Fuller, Geier, Gorlinski, Gruneberg, Healy, Harnan, Henderson, Hills, Howes, Knobloch, Murphy M. W., O'Conner, Orr, Purcell J., Schnurr, Stocker, Stiner, Sullivan, Terry, Thorpe, Waters—32.

The yeas and nays were ordered on the adoption of the report as a whole, on its second reading.

Mr. HOWELL—Under the rules no member can explain after the yeas and nays are called; therefore, I wish now to explain my vote on the report under consideration. It is not such a measure as I would make, and does not come up to my views, but inasmuch as we have spent so much time upon this question, I shall vote for its adoption, because I think it is better to take this than nothing at all.

Before the vote was announced, Mr. Spellicy changed his vote from "yes" to "no," and Mr. Gastinel from "no" to "yes."

The report was adopted by the following vote:

YEAS—Messrs. Austin, Barrett, Bell, Bennie, Bromley, Burke, Campbell, Cazabat, Cook J. K., Crozat, Davies, Edwards, Ennis, Fish, Flagg, Flood, Gastinel, Geier, Gorlinski, Hart, Henderson, Hills, Hire, Howell, Kugler, Maas, Mann, Maurer, Montamat, Morris, Newell, Normand, Ong, Paine J. T., Pursell S., Schroeder, Schnurr, Smith, Stumpf, Stauffer, Taliaferro, Wenck, Wells, Wilson—44.

NAYS—Messrs. Abell, Bofill, Buckley, Collin, Cook T., Cutler, Decker, Duane, Dufresne, Foley, Fosdick, Fuller, Gruneberg, Gaidry, Healy, Harnan, Heard, Howes, Knobloch, Murphy M. W., O'Conner, Orr, Pintado, Purcell J., Shaw, Spellicy, Stocker, Stiner, Sullivan, Terry, Thorpe, Waters—32.

Mr. SULLIVAN—I move to adjourn.

[The motion prevailed by a rising vote of 40 yeas to 32 nays, and the Convention adjourned till 12 M., Friday, July 8th, 1864.]

FRIDAY, July 8, 1864.

The Convention met, pursuant to adjournment, and was called to order by the president.

The secretary called the roll, and the following members answered to their names:

Messrs. Abell, Austin, Balch, Barrett, Baum, Beauvais, Bell, Bennie, Bofill, Bromley, Buckley, Burke, Campbell, Collin, Cazabat, Cook J. K., Cook T., Crozat, Cutler, Davies, Decker, Duane, Dufresne, Edwards, Ennis, Fish, Flagg, Flood, Foley, Fosdick, Fuller, Gastinel, Geier, Gorlinski, Gruneberg, Gaidry, Healy, Harnan, Hart, Heard, Henderson, Hills, Hire, Howell, Howes, Kavanagh, Knobloch, Kugler, Maas, Mann, Maurer, Mendiverri, Montamat, Morris, Murphy E., Murphy M. W., Newell, Normand, O'Conner, Orr, Payne J., Paine J. T., Pintado, Poynot, Purcell J., Pursell S., Schroeder, Schnurr, Seymour, Shaw, Smith, Spellicy, Stocker, Stumpf, Stiner, Stauffer, Sullivan, Taliaferro, Terry, Thorpe, Waters, Wenck, Wells, Wilson, and Mr. President—84.

The minutes of yesterday's proceedings were read and adopted.

Mr. DAVIES—Mr. President, I have a resolution to offer:

Be it resolved, That the Legislature of this State, during its next session, be instructed to order the authorities of this city to cause a bridge to be constructed on Claiborne street, across the new canal, belonging to the Canal and Banking Company.

PRESIDENT—The resolution must lie over.

Mr. MONTAMAT—Mr. President, I wish to offer a resolution:

An ordinance authorizing the city corporation of New Orleans to build a bridge over the Canal Carondelet, opposite Galvez street, similar to the one now at Broad street.

Be it ordained, That the city corporation of New Orleans be and is hereby authorized to build a bridge over the Canal Carondelet, opposite Galvez street, (similar to the one now built at the foot of Broad street,) in such manner as not to prevent the free ingress and egress of vessels; this ordinance to take effect from and after its passage.

PRESIDENT—It lies over until to-morrow. The order of the day—third reading of the report on education.

Mr. SULLIVAN—I have a rider to article 2.

Provided, That all institutions, of every denomination, comprising the mixed character of charity and asylums for orphans which educate children, shall be considered public schools of the State, and shall receive their pro rata of the school fund.

Mr. HEALY—I move its adoption.

Mr. STAUFFER—I move that it be laid on the table.

[The yeas and nays were called.]

Mr. STINER—I change my vote from "yes" to "no."

[The vote resulted as follows:]

YEAS—Messrs. Baum, Beauvais, Bennie, Bofill, Bromley, Burke, Campbell, Collin, Cook J. K., Davies, Edwards, Ennis, Flagg, Flood, Gastinel, Geier, Gaidry, Hart, Hire, Howell, Kugler, Maas, Morris, Newell, Normand, Payne J., Paine J. T., Pintado, Pursell S., Schroeder, Seymour, Shaw, Smith, Stumpf, Stauffer, Taliaferro, Wenck, Wells, Wilson—39.

NAYS—Messrs. Abell, Austin, Balch, Barrett, Bell, Buckley, Cook T., Crozat, Decker, Duane, Dufresne, Fish, Foley, Fosdick, Fuller, Gorlinski, Gruneberg, Healy, Harnan, Heard, Henderson, Hills, Howes, Kavanagh, Knobloch, Mann, Maurer, Montamat, Murphy E., Murphy M. W., Orr, Poynot, Purcell J., Schnurr, Spellicy, Stiner, Sullivan, Terry, Thorpe, Waters—40.

[The motion to lay on the table was lost.]

Mr. SULLIVAN—I move its adoption.

[The yeas and nays were called, with the following result:]

YEAS—Messrs. Abell, Austin, Balch, Barrett, Beauvais, Bell, Buckley, Cook T., Decker, Duane, Dufresne, Fish, Foley, Fosdick, Fuller, Gorlinski, Healy, Harnan, Heard, Henderson, Hills, Howes, Kavanagh, Knobloch, Murphy E., Murphy M. W., Orr, Purcell J., Schnurr, Spellicy, Stocker, Stiner, Sullivan, Terry, Thorpe, Waters—36.

NAYS—Messrs. Baum, Bennie, Bofill, Bromley, Burke, Campbell, Collin, Cook J. K., Crozat, Davies, Edwards, Ennis, Flagg, Flood, Gastinel, Geier, Gruneberg, Gaidry, Hart, Hire, Howell, Kugler, Maas, Mann, Maurer, Mendiverri, Montamat, Morris, Newell, Normand, Payne J., Paine J. T., Pintado, Poynot, Pursell S., Schroeder, Shaw, Smith, Stumpf, Stauffer, Taliaferro, Wenck, Wells, Wilson—44.

[The motion to adopt was lost.]

Mr. SMITH—I move the previous question on the adoption of the report as it passed its second reading.

[The motion was carried.

The ayes and noes were called on the adoption of the report with the following result:]

YEAS—Messrs. Austin, Barrett, Beauvais, Bell, Bennie, Bromley, Burke, Campbell, Collin, Cook J. K., Davies, Edwards, Ennis, Fish, Flagg, Flood, Gastinel, Geier, Gaidry, Hart, Henderson, Hills, Hire, Howell, Knobloch, Kugler, Maas, Mann, Mendiverri, Morris, Murphy E., Newell, Normand, Payne J., Paine J. T., Pintado, Poynot, Purcell J., Pursell S., Schroeder, Schnurr, Seymour, Smith, Stumpf, Stiner, Stauffer, Taliaferro, Wenck, Wells, Wilson, —50.

NAYS—Messrs. Abell, Balch, Baum, Bofill, Buckley, Cook T., Crozat, Decker, Duane, Dufresne, Foley, Fosdick, Fuller, Gorlinski, Gruneberg, Healy, Harnan, Heard, Howes, Kavanagh, Maurer, Montamat, Murphy M. W., O'Conner, Orr, Shaw, Spellicy, Stocker, Sullivan, Terry, Thorpe, Waters—32.

[The motion was carried and the report adopted on its third reading.]

PRESIDENT—The next business in order is the third reading of the report on Schedule.

[The secretary read the report.]

Mr. HENDERSON—Mr. President, I desire to offer an additional article:

Art. —. Common carriers, in all cases of contracts and quasi-contracts, offences and quasi-offences, where by law they are parties, may be liable in vindictive damages where, under the American and English jurisprudence regulating common carriers, such damages are legitimate and proper.

Mr. STAUFFER—I move to lay it on the table.

Mr. FOLEY—I move that the gentleman be instructed to write it in English.

Mr. HENDERSON—Mr. President, if the article is not English it is the fault of Louisiana legislators. In the code we have offences and quasi-offences, contracts and quasi-contracts. These are technical terms known to the jurisprudence of Louisiana, and, as such, their signification is well understood and determined, and they are the only words in the article that are not plain English. But, sir, the civil law in force in

Louisiana is clearly defective in this particular. Suppose the owner of a ferryboat attempts to take you across the river, and through his mismanagement you are drowned, your heirs can sue him and recover the actual damages which your loss may occasion to them, taking into consideration your means and circumstances. Come now to quasi-offences: when a house, on account of not being sufficiently well built, falls and kills you, the owner or builder is liable in damages, and the jury may assess actual damages. In other States they may, in either of the instances, assess punitive or vindictive damages. It is not necessary that they should stop at the actual damages, which can be computed as having accrued to the injured party, but they may assess damages at discretion sufficient to punish the party for his negligence and to warn others to beware of subjecting themselves to a like action. It is true, in some cases, vindictive damages have been given in our district courts, but they have always been reversed when carried to the Supreme Court, and that court has said, time after time, that common carriers are only liable in actual damages.

This is a state of things known only to the law of Louisiana. Here, men buy railroad tickets entitling them to seats in the street cars, and instead of sitting, generally stand. The companies have promised to give the public a certain thing. They have not done it, and yet if suit is brought against them, only actual damages can be recovered. Adopt this article and you have a remedy.

Mr. Howell—I do not know that this question really needs any discussion, but as we have in some of our proceedings adopted legislative measures, I do not know what the action of the Convention may be on what the gentleman is pleased to term his rider. The argument which he has made here might do very well before a jury or in a legislative hall, but here, I think it is out of place, and I beg to call the attention of the House to the language of the article itself. It is improperly called a rider. It has nothing whatever to do with the subject of the article. It tends to defeat nothing in the article, nor does it amend anything, but merely introduces new matter.

[Read:]

Common carriers, in all cases of contracts and quasi-contracts, offences and quasi-offences, where by law they are parties, may be liable in vindictive damages where, under the American and English jurisprudence regulating common carriers, such damages are legitimate and proper.

Now, what does that mean. It means that we shall provide that common carriers shall be liable in Louisiana just as they are in other States of the Union. If the Legislature sees the need of making such a law, well and good; but there is no necessity, whatever, for this Convention to proceed to the work of defining the laws regulating the liabilities of common carriers, and providing penalties for quasi-offences. Probably the gentleman forgets a case that recently occurred in which the Carrollton Railroad was mulct in damages to the amount of twenty-five thousand dollars for crippling a man on the road between here and Carrollton. If that was not vindictive damages I don't know what to call it. The directors of a railroad cannot properly be convicted of malice when their agents or employees manage the railroad so as to cripple some citizen. If they, themselves, are upon the railroad and direct the movements of the car, so as to produce that injury, they may, then, be guilty of malice; but if the damage done arise only from the acts of their agents, it is not the law that they shall be held as malicious in the performance or neglect of their duty. Apart from the merits—admitting the gentleman is right in his principles—it is a question which properly comes up in the Legislature, because our law has provided for these matters. It has provided already for the punishment of common carriers for neglect or malfeasance, and frequently judgments for large sums are rendered against common carriers, not only for actual damage done, but for consequential damages. I will agree with the gentleman, that it will be right and proper to enact such laws as to make all corporations responsible for all their acts, and make them responsible in such a manner as will secure the faithful performance of their duties. But, really, sir, this amending the statuary laws of the State, is a matter of legislation, and it is not to be incorporated in our constitution.

Mr. ABELL—I cannot see the propriety of inserting this rider in the constitution, and fully agree with the remarks of the last gentleman. It seems to me that there is not a single idea advanced that is not comprehended in our general laws on the subject. We have an article in the Code which almost covers everything that the gentleman has incorporated in his article. That says: "Every man shall be responsible for injury caused to another." The general principle is covered by laws already existing, and I consequently think that this proposition, if incorporated in the constitution, would be wholly inoperative.

Mr. HENDERSON—I am called upon to explain, and will first say that if the gentleman [Judge Howell] thinks this is already provided for, he is much mistaken. I think he takes a narrow-minded view of the matter.

Vindictive damages mean exemplary damages as punishment for non-discharge of duty. I refer the gentleman to the case of the Opelousas Railroad, and Mr. Hills, who sued for fifty thousand dollars damages. Judge Slidell said the railroad had no malice against Mr. H., and consequently the jury were wrong in giving their verdict for ten thousand dollars, and the remainder of the court held that actual malice must be shown. I would also refer him to the case of Roger Hearn, who undertook to carry mails and passengers, and would not take on board his boat a man whom he disliked. He was mulcted in two thousand and fifty dollars damages, though only two thousand were asked. Another case is that of a certain railroad company who refused to stop at a particular depot but carried a man on fifty yards further. In a suit he recovered four thousand five hundred doilars damages, and the verdict was affirmed by the Supreme Court, who said that the poor men who are obliged to live along the line of a railroad must be protected. [Applause.]

Angell on Carriers, and like works, are quoted in our courts as settling the law on that subject; but strange to say our courts declare that a man cannot recover vindictive damages against the employees of companies.

I have practiced law in this State for a long time, and knowing something of the matter, say that in cases where the jury have rendered exemplary damages, the Supreme Court have reduced the damages to merely nominal damages. Hence the reason I am in favor of the rider.

On the motion to adopt the rider the yeas and nays were called, and it was rejected by the following vote:

YEAS—Messrs. Balch, Bell, Bennie, Buckley, Campbell, Cook J. K., Cook T., Crozat, Duane, Flood, Foley, Gorlinski, Healy, Harnan, Henderson, Hills, Hire, Howes, Kavanagh, Murphy E., Murphy M. W., O'Conner, Orr, Paine J. T., Poynot, Smith, Stocker, Stiner, Terry, Thorpe, Wilson—31.

NAYS—Messrs. Abell, Austin, Barrett, Baum, Beauvais, Bofill, Bromley, Burke, Collin, Cutler, Davies, Decker, Dufresne, Edwards, Ennis, Fish, Flagg, Fuller, Gastinel, Geier, Gruneberg, Gaidry, Hart, Heard, Howell, Knobloch, Kugler, Maas, Mann, Maurer, Mendiverri, Montamat, Morris, Newell, Normand, Payne J., Pintado, Purcell J., Pursell S., Schroeder, Schnurr, Seymour, Shaw, Spellicy, Stumpf, Stauffer, Sullivan, Taliaferro, Waters, Wenck, Wells —51.

The report on Schedule was then adopted on its third reading.

The report on Ordinance was taken up on its third reading and read by the secretary.

REPORT OF THE COMMITTEE ON ORDINANCE.

To the honorable the president and members of the Constitutional Convention.

The undersigned, Committee on Ordinance, respectfully report as follows:

ORDINANCE.

Article 1. Immediately after the adjournment of the Convention, the governor shall issue his proclamation directing the several officers of this State, authorized by law to hold elections, or in default thereof such officers as he shall designate, to open and hold polls in the several parishes of the State, at the places designated by law, on the third Monday of July, 1864, for the purpose of taking the sense of the good people of this State in regard to the adoption or rejection of this constitution; and it shall be the duty of the said officers to secure the suffrage of all qualified voters. Each voter shall express his opinion by depositing in the ballot-box a ticket whereon shall be written "the constitution accepted," or, "the constitution rejected." At the conclusion of the said election, the officers and commissioners appointed to preside over the same shall carefully examine and count each ballot as deposited, and shall forthwith make due return thereof to the secretary of state in conformity to the provisions of law and usages in regard to elections.

Art. 2. Upon the receipt of said returns, or on the first Monday of August, if the returns be not sooner received, it shall be the duty of the governor, the secretary of state, the attorney general and the state treasurer, in the presence of all such persons as may choose to attend, to compare the votes at the said election for the ratification or rejection of this constitution, and if it shall appear at the close that a majority of all the votes given is for ratifying this constitution, then it shall be the duty of the governor to make proclamation of the fact, and thenceforth this constitution shall be ordained and established as the constitution of the State of Louisiana. But whether this constitution be accepted or rejected, it shall be the duty of the governor to cause to be published the result of the polls, showing the number of votes cast in each parish for and against the said constitution.

Art. 3. As soon as a general election can be held under this constitution in every parish of the State, without hostile molestation or interference, the governor shall, by proclamation, or in case of his failure to act, the Legislature shall, by resolution, declare the fact and order an election to be at a day fixed in said proclamation or resolution, and within sixty days of the date thereof, for officers of the State. The officers so chosen shall, on the fourth Monday after their election, be installed into office. The terms of office of the State officers elected on the 22d day of February, 1864, shall expire on the installation of their successors as herein provided for; but under no state of circumstances shall their term of office be construed as extending beyond the length of the terms fixed for said offices in this constitution. The officers elected under this article shall hold their offices for the terms prescribed in this constitution, counting from the second Monday of January next preceding their entering into office.

Art. 4. This constitution shall be published in English and French in the official journal of the Convention, from the period of its adjournment until the election for ratification or rejection on the third Monday of July, 1864.

Alfred Shaw,
M. D. Kavanagh,
A. Mendiverri,
O. H. Poynot.

Mr. Shaw—I have a rider to offer, and with the permission of the Convention I will state my reasons for it. The report of the Committee on Ordinance was drafted some days ago when it was expected this Convention would adjourn before the 4th of July, and consequently we fixed the third Monday in July for its ratification. That is too soon and I therefore offer the following rider:

Strike out of the fifth line of the first article, the word "third," and substitute the word "first," and in the sixth line strike out "July" and substitute "September," and also in the first line of the second article strike out the word "first" and insert "third," and in the second line of same article, strike out the word "August" and insert "September;" and further, insert after the word "office" in the eighth line of the third article, the words "and shall hold their offices for the terms prescribed in this constitution, counting from the second Monday of January next, preceding their entering into office, in case they do not enter into office on that date," and insert after the word "constitution," in the twelfth line of the same article, the words "and if not sooner held, the election of their successors shall take place on the first Monday of November, 1867, in all parishes where the same can be held, the officers elected on that date to enter into office on the second Monday of January, 1868;" and further, insert in the first line of the fourth article, after the word "in," the words "three papers to be selected by the president of the Convention, whereof two shall publish the same in English and French, and one in German;" and also insert in the third line of the same article, after the word "adjournment," the words "of the Convention" strike out in the same line the word "third," and insert "first," and in the fourth line strike out the word "July" and insert "September."

[The rider was adopted by a *viva voce* vote, and the report adopted on its third reading.]

President—That, gentlemen, closes all the reports on the Constitution. [Applause.] Now, when you adjourn — except to-morrow, which is for miscellaneous business —you will adjourn over to a certain day, in order to give the special committee you appointed yesterday on Arrangement and Form, time to present to you the Constitution as a whole for your decision thereupon; and speaking here, as your President, I should suppose that Tuesday next, sufficiently early; but that matter is left to yourselves. I think the Committee on Arrangement and Form, should have at least three days.

Mr. ABELL—As there is no miscellaneous business for to-morrow, I move to adjourn until Thursday next.

Mr. TERRY—I amend to to morrow, at 12 M.

[The motion was carried by a risin gvote of yeas 59, to nays 21, and the Convention adjourned until 12 M., Saturday, July 9th.]

SATURDAY, July 9th, 1864.

[The Convention met pursuant to adjournment. Present, the Hon. E. H. Durell, president, and the following members:]

Messrs. Abell, Austin, Balch, Barrett, Bell, Bennie, Buckley, Burke, Collin, Cook J. K., Crozat, Decker, Duane, Dufresne, Edwards, Ennis, Fish, Flood, Foley, Fosdick, Fuller, Gastinel, Geier, Gorlinski, Gruneberg, Healy, Harnan, Hart, Heard, Henderson, Hills, Hire, Howell, Howes, Knobloch, Kugler, Mann, Maurer, Mayer, Montamat, Murphy M. W., Newell, Normand, O'Conner, Pintado, Poynot, Pursell S., Schroeder, Schnurr, Seymour, Shaw, Smith, Spellicy, Stocker, Stumpf, Stiner, Sauffer, Sullivan, Taliaferro, Terry, Waters, Wenck, Wells, Wilson—65.

Mr. PURSELL—I move this Convention do adjourn until Thursday next, as I suppose there is no miscellaneous business for to-day, and the Committee on Arrangement cannot report before that time.

Mr. HILLS—I hope the Convention will *not* adjourn until Thursday next, as I am very anxious, in view of our already long protracted session and the lateness of the season, that we should complete our business. I would call upon the chairman of the Committee on Arrangement to state how long a time that committee will require to make their report, when I shall be in favor of an adjournment until that time. The chairman informed me this morning that they could be ready by Tuesday, and as it seems to me not right to adjourn until Thursday, I move that we do adjourn until Tuesday next.

Mr. SHAW—As chairman, I would state that we *can* report on Tuesday morning, but can make a fuller report by Wednesday.

PRESIDENT—I think the committee will require until Thursday next, without doubt.

Mr. Hills' motion to adjourn was lost on rising vote; yeas 30, nays 32.

Mr. HENDERSON—We cannot transact any business, and the only question that can come before us is that of adjournment. That question is lost, and I hope that gentleman will not be so anxious to adjourn, but wait until we have a quorum.

Mr. BALCH—I move we adjourn until Saturday next.

[Motion lost on rising vote; yeas 18, nays 30.

Mr. SULLIVAN—I move we adjourn until Friday next.

[The motion was lost on rising vote; yeas 15, nays 31.

Motion to adjourn until 12 M. of Thursday, the 14th inst., was then put and carried.]

THURSDAY, July 14, 1864.

[The Convention met, pursuant to adjournment. Present, the Hon. E. H. Durell, president, and the following members:]

Messrs. Abell, Austin, Balch, Barrett, Baum, Beauvais, Bell, Bennie, Buckley, Burke, Campbell, Collin, Cazabat, Cook J. K., Cook T., Crozat, Cutler, Davies, Decker, Duane, Dufresne, Dupaty, Edwards, Ennis, Fish, Flagg, Flood, Foley, Fosdick, Fuller, Gastinel, Geier, Gorlinski, Gruneberg, Healy, Harnan, Hart, Heard, Henderson, Hills, Hire, Howell, Howes, Kavanagh, Knobloch, Kugler, Maas, Mann, Maurer, Mayer, Mendiverri, Montamat, Morris, Murphy E., Murphy M. W., Newell, Normand, O'Conner, Ong, Orr, Payne J., Pintado, Poynot, Purcell J., Pursell S., Schroeder, Schnurr, Seymour, Shaw, Smith, Spellicy, Stocker, Stumpf, Stiner, Sullivan, Taliaferro, Terry, Thorpe, Thomas, Waters, Wenck, Wells, Wilson—83.

[The minutes of Friday's and Saturday's proceedings were read and adopted.]

Mr. ABELL—I rise for the purpose of asking that my friend, Mr. Stauffer, be excused for absence to-day, on account of sickness.

[No objection.]

Mr. HILLS—Mr. President, I would ask permission of the Convention to report verbally upon the matter of books belonging to the State library, at Baton Rouge. I have conferred with my associate, Judge Howell, on the subject, and we are both of opinion that the Convention has nothing to do with the return of those books. We are informed by the state librarian, that Maj. Gen. Banks has very kindly offered to see that they are transported to New Orleans, while Gov. Hahn has expressed his readiness to attend to the matter, if necessary. I ask that this committee be discharged, and that the thanks of the Convention be tendered to Maj. Gen. Banks and Gov. Hahn for their willingness in the premises. I make the motion to that effect.

[The motion was carried and the committee discharged.]

Mr. BELL—I have a resolution to offer:

Whereas, There exists an indebtedness resulting from the inauguration on the 4th of March, 1864, of the first free State officers of Louisiana, and other expenses incurred for the furtherance of free State government in Louisiana, amounting to about $10,000;

Therefore be it resolved, That the sum of ten thousand dollars be and is hereby appropriated for the payment of the same, which may be approved by a committee of seven, consisting of state auditor, state treasurer, secretary of state, and four members of this Convention, to be appointed by the president.

Mr. TERRY—I move that the rules be suspended for its adoption.

Mr. HENDERSON—I offer this substitute:

Whereas, A debt of ten thousand dollars has been created in the formation of the free State of Louisiana;

Therefore be it resolved, That said sum be paid out of the treasury of the State, upon the warrant of the governor of said State.

[Substitute accepted.]

Mr. SULLIVAN—Mr. President, if I am in order, I beg leave to say a few words on this subject. This bill, brought forward for our sanction by the honorable member from the Second District, if I understand it correctly, is that the Convention do appropriate the sum of ten thousand dollars from the State treasury to pay certain expenses incurred in the inauguration ceremonies held on the 4th of March last, in Lafayette Square. I am satisfied that this appropriation is not asked for to pay those expenses, as I am credibly informed that all the expenses incurred on that day was paid immediately after they were contracted for.

I am surprised that the gentleman should endeavor to cover his resolution by a falsehood. He cannot contradict what I state. It is stated to this body that this amount of money is needed to pay certain expenses to make it popular in this body, when I and every other member on this floor know full well it is asked for to pay the election expenses of the State officers elected on the 22d of February last—and for no other purpose—it is no use to deny it.

Who incurred these expenses? Was it the State authorities? No sir, it was not. Why bring it before this Convention? The parties who are responsible for these debts are the men who have been elevated by us to high and responsible offices in this State, and who up to this late day failed to pay the poor men they employed what they honestly earned.

Now, sir, in all conscience, I think, so far as this Convention is concerned, they have done a great deal for these officers, without further asking that the State treasury pay their election expenses. You may word your resolution in any way you choose, but I state it openly that this ten thousand dollars is for that purpose, and no other. You cannot throw dust in my eyes by the false wording of this resolution. You cannot mystify me in regard to this matter.

Gentlemen, you may have forgot what we have done already for the State officers. If you have, I have not. You have increased the salary of the lieutenant governor from eight dollars per day (paid him heretofore only during the sixty day session of the Senate as the presiding officer of that body) to the munificent sum of five thousand dollars per annum; and this, sir, a mere sinecure office. Next in order comes the secretary of state, from two to five thousand dollars, a clerical position that a boy sixteen years of age could fill very creditably; auditor of public accounts from four to five thousand dollars; state treasurer the same increase, and the attorney general from thirty-five hundred dollars to five thousand dollars. When the State under the Union flag numbered forty-eight parishes, it was not thought for a moment to increase these officers' salaries, but now I suppose their offices become more arduous and more difficult to fill.

I am sorry for the sake of the poor men

who have to wait up to this time for their hard-earned money. They know full well that the State is not responsible to them for their payment. They ought in justice and in honesty be paid by these men immediately after the election. By what right and by what authority were these men employed without having the means to pay them as soon as their work was completed? It will be a warning to them again who to trust in future.

I do not think it honest, just or right, for members of the Convention to vote away for electioneering purposes the money of the State, paid into the treasury by tax-payers to defray the expenses of the State government, to educate the children of the State, and to pay donations to State asylums, and for other charitable purposes.

If the gentlemen who have profited by that election only paid a portion of the yearly increase of their salaries, all the election bills could have been settled before this time; but no, sir, they do not intend to pay; the State, I suppose, must foot the bill for them

Why, sir, the Flanders party, or the conservative party, who were defeated in that election, with the same propriety has as good a right tó come into this Convention and ask that their election expenses be paid; and we, the members of this body, certainly ought to have our expenses also paid in the same manner. It is astonishing to me that the gentlemen did not ask for an appropriation of twenty-five thousand dollars to defray the election expenses of gentlemen who may desire to be candidates for the State Legislature in September next.

I intend to have the yeas and nays recorded on this resolution, so the people of this State may know who the delegates are in this Convention, who, by their votes, plunder the treasury of the State and squander the money of the people for such a purpose.

Mr. TERRY—Mr. President, I wish to submit a few words. I am sorry to differ from my friend from the same district; not only his constituents, but also mine, are the creditors in this case—poor, honest, hard working men. These are not, strictly speaking, the bills of the Executive Committee, as he says, but for inaugural expenses.

Mr. SULLIVAN—They are not: I deny it.

Mr. TERRY—The claims are for building the platform, the flowers, ropes, candles, &c., and I think it is no more than right that the State should pay the expenses of the inauguration. In one instance a bill of one hundred and fifty dollars was presented to me,---the bill of three hard working women--for mending of the flags, which some scoundrel defaced on the night of the 4th of March, for the detection of whom I, myself offered a reward. That bill, for the repairing of ten or twelve flags, remains unpaid to this day, and when these poor women called on me and told me that they had received no compensation, I was forced to put my hand into my own pocket and pay them. There are hard working men walking the streets of this city, tormenting me and other members of this Convention, asking when, for God's sake, shall they receive the little amounts which are their just dues. Pay these men. Why let money remain in the State treasury, when it can be put to a good use? We can give ten thousand dollars in charity: why not let charity begin at home, and pay those whom the State justly owes? There is no call to pay the expenses of the Flanders party, for they sent agents to the North who canvassed Pennsylvania, New York and Massachusetts, who received, I am informed, from thirty to thirty-five thousand dollars. Only seventeen or eighteen thousand of this amount was expended. This was raised by private subscription; whereas, on the contrary, the other party had no funds. I hope and am willing that the yeas and nays should be called on this question, for I wish to know who, here, were instrumental in establishing the Free state government in Louisiana, and the incurring of these trifling expenses incident to its inauguration, who will not vote to pay honest men their honest wages.

Mr. HENDERSON—Mr. President and gentleman, I do not pretend to know anything about the details of this bill, but I have suggested a substitute which the gentleman [Mr. Bell] has accepted. I do say this, however, that some twenty thousand dollars were sent to the Free State Committee, of which T. J. Durant was president. Thomas J. Durant aided the president of the United States, General Banks and Gov. Shepley, in his advice in the formation of a free State, and the money he received as president of the Free State Committee of Louisiana was intended for the purpose of forming a free State of Louisiana and not otherwise. [Applause.] Where is Thomas Durant now,—the head of that defunct free State party, for, thank God, it is dead, though it should have been buried ere this. He is in the North, while we stand here with cannon around us. Yet that man leaves (for the North) with the money of the Free State Committee in his pocket for the purpose of canvassing the North to defeat the prospective administration of this free State. The sum of ten thousand dollars has been expended in forming anew our State, and the payment of that small debt, no man in this Convention should hesitate about. Let us not imitate the example of our erring sister State, Mississippi, by repudiating our just debts.

Salmon Chase sent money here to help elect Flanders, and if he was here to-day, I would say to him, as I did to Colonell Higgins: "Sir, you belong to that portion of our party that seeks to destroy the Free State party and that would not allow the Free State party to concentrate upon President Lincoln as President. I respect Mr. Chase, for I knew his history long since, but when any one is conspiring against Mr. Lincoln, I am against him."

I beg you to be true to your instincts; let no small thing deceive you; let Louisiana be a star among the States, and be as Gen. Banks said: "Louisiana, the first returning State: her voice is for liberty," which will descend as your proudest heritage.

Mr. ABELL—Mr. President and gentlemen of the Convention, this is a second edition of that *large* sum of money—yes, gentlemen, of that LARGE sum of money! I hoped that the whole matter had gone under the table. If the people of Louisiana wished a free State constitution, I do not know what they needed this money for, and I hope it will burn the hand of every man who touches it. When it is publicly declared that this free State was got up by the use of "large sums of money," I think this is the most disgraceful matter that was ever brought into a deliberative body. What do *you* think, gentlemen? It is certainly a matter for serious reflection. Gentlemen want to tell you on this floor, when *people* only *hint* at it, that it is money and office which controls us. Even this did not satisfy them, but must bring up this matter. I protest, to-day, in the name of the sovereign people of Louisiana, against our having anything to do with this; against our contaminating our records more than we are forced to, because I consider that our action would be nothing short of that, and I defy any gentleman upon this floor to show otherwise. This money was used to corrupt the people, for the purpose of obtaining a free State government by bribery and corruption. What else has this "large sum of money" to do with the people of Louisiana? It is rich—rich, to bring into a deliberative body—to hold out to the world, that an attempt has been made to bribe the people of Louisiana against her own interest, for the gentleman does not tell you that it is for anything else. It *can* be for nothing else but to corrupt the people and buy representatives. *I* say it was for no other purpose, what do you say? [A voice, "no."] I would like to find who said "no," I would sit down and give him a chance to enlighten us. It is a reproach to the State of Louisiana to bring up this matter, and I hope this will canker the pocket of who ever has it, whether it be that of our fellow-citizens, Durant or Mr. Heath, rather than contaminate, in any shape, the State of Louisiana.

Mr. SMITH—Mr. President and gentlemen, in regard to this "large sum of money," I do not believe there is a man upon this floor who will refuse to pay just dues. As for the gentleman's assertion that some money has fallen into the hands of the defeated party, and that other money is to be used in buying up representatives, I do not believe it, for the people of Louisiana have already sent their representatives here and have honestly declared that Louisiana shall be a free State. If these expenses have been incurred in the inauguration of governor and other officers of this free State, in God's name let the State have magnanimity enough to come up and say that it is willing and able to defray the expenses incurred in inaugurating its first free State officers. [Applause.]

Mr. SULLIVAN—I have only a word to say, Mr. President. This bill is brought forward as for inauguration expenses, but I say positively to this Convention, that this money is asked for to pay the expenses of the last election. Why do not gentlemen come forward openly and state that? I hate to see this underhand work and wish to have the matter brought up openly, though upon the face of it the pretence advanced is a falsehood.

Mr. TERRY—Only a word, gentlemen. I have seen these bills myself and know about them. One item of a thousand dollars is for candles.

Mr. SULLIVAN—For the inauguration?

Mr. TERRY—Yes.

Mr. SULLIVAN—I deny it most positively.

Mr. TERRY—I can bring the proofs. Another item is for musicians, and another of one hundred and fifty dollars for repairing of flags.

Mr. BELL—I will state that these bills are now in the hands of Mayor Hoyt, amounting to over two thousand dollars, from the committee on which I was on.

[The rules were suspended—52 members rising.

Mr. Henderson's substitute was adopted.]

YEAS—Messrs. Austin, Barrett, Beauvais, Bell, Buckley, Burke, Collin, Cook T., Cook J. K., Crozat, Cutler, Davies, Duane, Edwards, Ennis, Fish, Flagg, Flood, Foley, Fuller, Gastinel. Geier, Gorlinski, Healy, Harnan, Hart, Henderson, Hire, Howes, Mann, Maurer, Mendiverri, Murphy E., Newell, Normand, O'Conner, Ong, Orr, Pintado, Poynot, Pursell S., Schroeder, Schnurr, Seymour, Shaw, Smith, Spellicy. Stocker, Stumpf, Stiner, Taliaferro, Terry, Thorpe, Thomas, Waters, Wenck, Wells, Wilson—58.

NAYS—Messrs. Abell, Balch, Decker, Dufresne, Heard, Howell, Kugler, Maas, Mayer, Montamat, Morris, Murphy M. W., Payne J., Sullivan—14.

Mr. HOWELL—I ask for a call of the House.

[The roll was called and no quorum present. After a short delay the quorum was re-established, and the vote taken again, with the following result:

YEAS—Messrs. Austin, Barrett, Beauvais, Bell, Buckley, Burke, Collin, Cook J. K., Cook T., Crozat, Cutler, Davies, Duane, Dupaty, Edwards, Ennis, Fish, Flagg, Flood, Foley, Fuller, Gastinel, Geier, Gorlinski, Healy, Harnan, Hart, Henderson, Hire, Howes, Mann, Maurer, Mendiverri, Murphy E., Murphy M. W., Newell, Normand, O'Conner, Ong, Orr, Pintado, Poynot, Purcell J., Pursell S., Schroeder, Schnurr, Seymour, Shaw, Smith, Spellicy, Stocker, Stumpf, Stiner, Taliaferro, Terry, Thorpe, Thomas, Waters, Wells, Wilson—64.

NAYS—Messrs. Abell, Balch, Decker, Dufresne, Heard, Howell, Kugler, Maas, Mayer, Montamat, Morris, Payne J., Sullivan, Wenck—14.

[The substitute was adopted.]

Mr. MONTAMAT—I beg leave to submit the report of the Committee on Finance:

REPORT OF THE FINANCE COMMITTEE.

Amount paid for per diem of members from 2d to July 9th, 1864	$7,800 00
Amount for salaries of officers	1,981 00
Amount for contingent expenses	2,411 25
	$12,192 25

Balance on hand, $1,124 03 belonging to contingent expense account.

Your committee recommend that they be authorized to draw from the general funds out of the treasury of the State the amount necessary for the payment of members, officers, employés and contingent expenses, until the end of the session.

Respectfully submitted,

JOHN T. MONTAMAT,
Acting Chairman Finance Committee.
New Orleans, July 8, 1864.

[The report was adopted.]

Mr. THORPE—Mr. President and gentlemen of the Convention, I wish to bring before you this morning, though I cannot say whether it is in order, a subject of very grave importance. If our action in this Convention is of any effect at all, it is not to write a constitution upon paper, but the practical action after we have got through with our work. I will, if the Convention will permit me, call attention fo a matter recently acted upon, which I here pronounce the grossest violation of the fundamental laws of this State—the establishment of our courts and of the cause that brought us here to represent the State of Louisiana. The facts are these: A negro woman sues her former master, before Judge Izard, for the value of certain articles of furniture, and judgment was given in her favor. The case was appealed to the Third District Court; the defence was, that the plaintiff, being a slave, had no rights in the court and could neither sue or be sued. The honorable judge of the Third District Court sustained the objection and dismissed the case. Attorney General Lynch—all honor to his name—with associate counsel, moved for a new trial, contending that the plaintiff had rights, but the court overruled the motion for a new trial and, without giving any written opinion, virtually decided that slavery and the Black Code still exist in Louisiana. I would state to you, gentlemen, that this honorable judge holds his position, first under President Lincoln's proclamation of emancipation; secondly, under martial law, and thirdly, under Gen. Banks' proclamation of January 11, 1863, in which we find the following language:

VI. The fundamental law of this State is martial law. It is competent and just for the government to surrender to the people, at the earliest moment, so much of military power as may be consistent with military operations.

Now, I am not prepared to make a speech on this subject, but I hold that this Convention has power to take this subject up and treat it as it deserves. If this trifling cannot be stopped, let us adjourn *sine die*, throw our constitution to the winds, and say we are not———

PRESIDENT—Does the gentleman address this Convention without presenting any conclusion?

Mr. THORPE—The resolution was to be offered by another gentleman. I apologize to the Convention and offer this:

Resolved, That all decisions of the courts of the State that declare slavery exists in the State, are contrary to the fundamental laws of the State, and are contempts of the emancipation ordinance passed by this Convention.

Mr. MONTAMAT—I move it be laid on the table.

YEAS—Messrs. Abell, Balch, Barrett, Beauvais, Buckley, Crozat, Cutler, Decker, Dufresne, Edwards, Fish, Fuller, Gastinel, Geier, Gruneberg, Healy, Heard, Howell, Knobloch, Maas, Mayer, Mendiverri, Montamat, Morris, Murphy M. W., Newell, Normand, Ong, Purcell J., Schnurr, Seymour, Stumpf, Sullivan, Thomas, Waters, Wenck, Wells, Wilson—38.

NAYS—Messrs. Austin, Bell, Bennie, Burke, Collin, Cook J. K., Cook T., Davies, Duane, Dupaty, Ennis, Flagg, Flood, Foley, Gorlinski, Harnan, Hart, Henderson, Hills, Hire, Howes, Kugler, Mann, Maurer, Murphy E., O'Conner, Orr, Payne J., Pintado, Poynot, Pursell S., Schroeder, Shaw, Smith, Spellicy, Stocker, Stiner, Taliaferro, Terry, Thorpe—40.

[Motion lost.]

Mr. HENDERSON—I would like to have the resolution divided so that I can vote yes upon the first clause, ending with "fundamental laws of this State," and no upon the remainder.

Mr. ABELL—I would ask this Convention if it is willing to give up all personal self-respect—is willing in the face of the people of Louisiana, to lay down all self-respect, and be led by those who are emphatically nothing but fanatics? If there ever was a thing that smelled and savored of fanaticism, it is now before the Convention. What, I ask, does this resolution propose? I say, first, with all respect to the gentleman who offered it, that it is the most silly one that could be or ever was laid down. Does not this attempt to make our incipient acts law seem to every honest and legal mind, the most extraordinary one that was ever undertaken on the face of the earth? I ask you, for the sake of your constituency, and your own self, to ponder well the question, as to whether we have made a constitution here—we, ourselves—much less one that has been ratified by the people? Is our ordinance the law of the land? Does, or can any man say, honestly, that this incipient constitution is yet the law of this State? Why, sir, you cannot go into the street and find a drayman who will say so. Until we and the people adopt it, it has no more power, efficiency, or binding effect than if it had not been done at all.

What was the case in the times of true liberty—when Jackson brought civil power into contempt? Judge Hall fined him a thousand dollars, and he had to pay it. I admit that the power here is now military power, and do not contest anything that it does, but submit to it, for it can collect all the negroes and keep them in a pen if that seems advisable. But we cannot enforce what we, civilly, have no right or power to: it is absurd, too foolish for the mind of any good or sensible man to receive it. No one knows that this Convention will ever ratify this Constitution. My private opinion is that the people will do so, for there are certain elements in it which I believe will cause them to, but until it is thus ratified, it is a dead letter, and I say boldly that we have no right to dictate to our courts. That is an undertaking to trammel them by this Convention, when it has no power. I look upon it as a contempt to the people of Louisiana,—making them slaves. If this Convention can thus dictate, the people of Louisiana are the greatest of all slaves—the most abandoned of all mankind—abandoned to abolitionists who have worried themselves into this Convention without any more right than the Chinese. It is an instance of slavery too degrading for us to contemplate, for when we trample upon the courts, we try to do one of the most wicked and absurd things ever attempted, and cease to be the representatives of the people.

What have we done? Why, sir, we have been in session a long time and have framed a constitution that we think to be some thing. But when an honest judge decides a point, bound by his sacred oath, it will not do for us to attempt to dictate, and if we do, we surrender civil liberty. What are the facts of this case? An upright, honest judge is accused of not recognizing the fact that a negro is upon the same footing as a white person. Now, gentlemen, honest men differ very materially in their views upon this subject. I say fearlessly, to-day, that the negro, according to the proclamation of President Lincoln, is as much a slave at this moment, in this parish, as he ever was, except that for military purposes, Gen. Banks has suspended the law. I believe that Gen. Banks is a good man and a great statesman, but I should be a slave and so would you, sir, to say that he is a perfect man,—which he does not claim himself. He has laid prostrate the old constitution. But though the law is thus superceded, not a solitary word or syllable did he strike from it. Now, if a judge, differing from his view of this subject, should not express his honest opinion while sitting upon the bench, and conscientiously called upon to do so, I should consider him a corrupt villain, unworthy of the bench. I believe President Lincoln's action to be illegal, and if I was upon the bench, so help me God, if my head was to fall, I would express that opinion when required. In regard to the opinion of Judge Lynch, the attorney general, whom I see before me now, I consider it wrong, and unworthy the State of Louisiana, and will never sanction any such doctrine. As a representative upon this floor, I contend that slavery is as much a feature of the law of Louisiana as ever,—not a particle different. These men have never been paid for their slaves, and no citizen can be divested of his property without receiving compensation. According to the president's proclamation, this parish and several others of the State, are excepted from its operation. Has Congress any power to liberate the slaves? No, sir, it has never assumed to have it. The people have the right to do what they consider proper, but until they choose to take this step, no other power this side of Heaven can do it. Every State, Indiana, Illinois, Ohio or New York, has also, in its sovereignty, the right to make itself a slave State Has Gen. Banks ever assumed to free the slaves here? No, he is too patriotic to thus lay the State prostrate and divest it of its sovereign rights which belong to it under the constitution of the land.

We stand here to-day to represent the State, and those who are the most zealous in this matter are those who have no right here. But we have not adopted this constitution and therefore have nothing to do with the affair.

Mr. Henderson—Mr. President and gentlemen of the Convention, this is a most serious question with which we have to deal. As may friend, Judge Neal, said: "With one stroke of the pen, I can send you to prison." So I say that we can abolish and have, by one stroke of the pen, abolished slavery in this State. But after we have done so, the question occurs as to what is the status of a human being. Now the Queen of Spain had Moorish blood in her veins. Who were these Moors, who for two hundred years occupied the country of Spain? The question comes home to ourselves and I will read from a book I hold in my hand, in order to show you. I read from Wheeler's law of slavery, p. 3, and want gentlemen here, who have Spanish blood in their veins, to know that the Moors have been declared slaves. I refer to the case of Hudgins against Wright 1 Hen. & Mumf. 134. Listen, you who are of Spanish blood, hear me and tremble!

Per cur. Tucker J., "From the first settlement of the colony of Virginia to the year 1778, October sessions, all negroes, Moors and mulattoes, except Turks and Moors in amity with Great Britain, brought into this country by sea or by land were slaves, and by the uniform declaration of our laws, the descendants of females remain slaves to this day, unless they can prove a right tq freedom by actual emancipation or by descent in maternal line from an emancipated female."

By the uniform declaration of our laws the descendants remain slaves to-day, unless they can prove their right to freedom by actual emancipation, or by descent in the maternal line from emancipated families. We do not, at this day, recognize the Moor or Chinese, as entitled to naturalization, because our law says, "every white person," and therefore the East Indian and Mexican are excluded as not coming within this term. What is the law of Spain in regard to the inhabitants of Spain or the Indian who occupied this soil before Columbus discovered America? The same as I have already read to you.

In my old State of Mississippi, we have the American Indian, Caucasian, and African blood all flowing in the veins of the same person, and this is also the case in my adopted State of Louisiana. I read from the same book, page five, where it says:

"In the Spanish and French West Indies, the following grades are distinguished: The first grade, that of the *mulatto*, which is the intermixture of a white person with a negro; the second are the *tercerones*, which are the production of a white person and a mulatto; the third grade are the *quarteroons*, being the issue of a white person and a quarteroon. Beyond this there is no degradation of color, not being distinguishable from white persons either by color or features.—Edwards' West Indies, book 4, chapter 1. Stevens' Harems of the West India Colonies Delineated, page 27."

Now, sir, according to the laws of Spain, from which the first white man came upon this soil, we find that after the fourth degree—no matter of what *color* a man may be—he is a white, and this is the law of all the slave States of this Union, with the exception of Louisiana and South Carolina. Now, to the point. I say now as before, not only as a member of this Convention, but as a lawyer, that Gen. Banks' military order, without the ratification of Abraham Lincoln, the commander-in-chief of the army and navy, is the law of the land until the commander-in-chief revokes it. [Applause.]

I have heard gentlemen here casting reflections upon the African, but never saying a word about the Indian. Let them go back to the case of Seville, which was the first decision under the old State of Louisiana, and we find the court declaring that there is no right of conquest which can consign an Indian to slavery. Look at Virginia, the first of the colonies to introduce slavery, and all her writers agree in saying, that slavery was not created, but sanctioned by municipal law; and Jefferson was right when he declared that slavery, whether of the black, Indian, white or mixed races, was contrary to the law of God.

After a careful perusal of Gen. Banks' order relative to slaves, I would ask if this decision in our own courts is not in conflict with it? Why, sir, Spain never abolished slavery, but the general who came upon her soil, and just so Gen. Banks has seen fit to abolish it here, and his act has been sanctioned for nearly the last two years. Now, to Judge Handlin, for whom I have the highest personal respect: I would say, in his presence, that his decision was not in accordance with this military order, and we must all sink or swim together on this question.

The Senate of the United States recently voted for the political equality of all the races, but on this point it differs from the House; but the time is fast approaching, and I have long foreseen its coming, when the constitution of the United States is to be reorganized, and all men, white, black or mixed blood, are to be declared citizens together.

I wish this resolution divided, for the action of this Convention has never adopted the ordinance of emancipation as part of the constitution, though it may be a statute, if so regarded by this Convention. Strike out the objectionable clause and it will be carried by a tremendous vote.

[A motion to adjourn over was lost.]

Mr. DURELL—Mr. President and gentlemen of the Convention, how hard it is for crime to die. I speak with humble tone, answering the learned arguments of my talented friend, who is stronger on this floor than I am; but I speak the sincere convictions of my soul. The gentleman who has been arraigned this day before this Convention represents the people in its judicial capacity. He is an honorable gentleman. He is a worthy gentleman, but in these troublous times he is not equal to the position he holds. He does not meet the occasion, when the occasion comes. Is this Convention to stultify itself? Are we to justify such a decision in the great national crisis through which we are passing. No, sir: organized as they have been by military order, the State courts are military courts. They derive their power from the military power; and the judge who does not acknowledge this fact should at once resign. Honesty is the best policy. There is not a district judge in the city of New Orleans who does not sit as a military judge. The military authority, in these troublous times, is the supreme power; and that power has declared that slavery no longer exists in Louisiana. Is it not a little singular that men are to be found who will still persist, even on this floor, in declaring that slavery still exists within this State. Go out into yonr streets and order your slave to perform your work; will he obey? Is there the means by which you can make him obey? Sir, the black is free. He occupies this position in the courts of Russia, of Her Majesty of Great Britain and of Napoleon III of France. We must not let prejudice blind us in these troublous and revolutionary times; we must accept the issue, and prove ourselves equal to it. Nothing goes backward in times of revolution. You must go with the current, or it will overwhelm you. I know the gentleman's views. I honor him. He is an excellent man. I know that every man who sits here believes that, in what he did, he acted sincerely. But, in these times, every man must be true to the cause. We are all sailing in the same boat.

Let any man tell me that slavery exists, and I will tell him that Heaven and the light of day proves the assertion false. [Applause.] Acknowledge the progress of events, and look not behind. Let your watchword be progress.

I am astonished that a gentleman, like my friend on my right, (Mr. Abell)—a gentleman so thoroughly acquainted with history and the law, should have failed, as he has failed, to understand the times. I should have expected that he, of all men, would have understood our position, for there are few so well versed in the history of the past and in the law, as he. But I have long since learned that those who hold on to the dead past go down with it, and sink forever. God's laws are certain. If any gentleman here wishes to hold on to the dead past, let him do so. If he goes down with it, he has no right to complain.

These are times of progress; we do away with the old and make all things new. We are to work no distinction of races, no distinction of color. The only distinction we are to make is, first, that which arises from necessity; after that, that which springs from intellect; and we must let every man, of whatever race, take his chance on that platform. There is not a slave within reach of the military order of the United States. There is not a man within reach of the military of the United States so black that its arm does not protect him in his freedom. He stands as free as you or I do. Such is the law of God, and you cannot change it. He has his rights, and, if he has intellect, he has a right to enter into the strife and business of this world, to rise or fall, according to the ability he may possess.

Mr. Cutler—Mr. President and gentlemen of the Convention, I hoped that the last speech of mine before this body had already been made, and I came here to-day for the purpose of hearing the report of the committee and of voting conscientiously for the constitution as a whole as we have adopted it, and then of hearing some member make a motion to adjourn *sine die*; but instead of that report, we have here a discussion, brought out by a resolution the most absurd, degrading and contemptible that was ever brought before a deliberative body. Now, sir, it is highly probable that among those who hold positions on this floor, there are some who will refuse to affix their signatures to this constitution. I hope not, sir. I would like for every member to sign it as we have adopted it. But, sir, I think it is exceedingly strange, while I do not impugn the motives of any gentleman, that there are all the time members who are disposed to introduce the seeds of discord, and to prevent, if possible, the signatures of all the members of this Convention from being affixed to this constitution. And, sir, I characterize the introduction of this resolution as the meanest and most contemptible act of the kind that has been attempted. I beg your attention for a few moments, while I discuss the legal and constitutional bearings which the matter presents. You have said in that resolution, or, rather by refusing to lay it on the table you have indicated that you will say, that the judge presiding in the Third District, and all judges hereafter, must decide that a certain portion of our work is already the organic law of the State, and must be so regarded even before it is submitted to the people. There must be a moral apprehension here. I do not think the members of this Convention are prepared to take that position, notwithstanding the fact that the honorable gentleman from the Third District and others have spoken with more ardor than reason on this floor, in favor of this ridiculous proposition.

Now, sir, in the first place, I hoped that the resolution would be tabled for the purpose of ending unprofitable discussion, so that we could go to work and adjourn this Convention; but I believe that many who voted not to table it, so voted for the purpose of voting it down on a direct vote

When the resolution was offered I from my seat announced that it was not only absurd and ridiculous, but without any foundation in common sense, law, reason or justice. Does the gentleman himself know what he offered? Does he know the meaning of it? Stop a moment, let me beg of you, and let us inquire what is does mean. You not only have to look at the organic law of Louisiana to ascertain, but you have to look to the great principles of the United States of America. We find that there are three great powers or elements of a republican government, and if you ignore the one you destroy the other two. There is the legislative department, the executive department, and the judiciary department. It was intended by the framers of the constitution that they should be separate and distinct from, and independent of, each other, in order that one might be a check upon the other. But it would seem by your pretentious vote on that damnable resolution offered here to-day that you want this Convention to disgrace itself by destroying the independence of the judiciary and dictating to one of the judges what shall be his decision. You say to the district judges of the State that if they decide that slavery has an existence within the State, they shall be subject to the censure of this august body for presuming to decide without acknowledging its acts as the organic law of the land. Is there not something absurd and ridiculous in this? Why, the emancipation ordinance is not yet a part of the organic law of the State. The assertion that it is, is false as hell. We have adopted no organic law; no organic law has been adopted by this Convention as yet. He who says there has is either crazy or a fool. Where is your constitution? If you go on in this way where will it be? It will be where the dungeon is that has been pictured for my friend Abell to tumble in. I am telling you what is the sentiment of the honorable people of Louisiana in my humble conviction, and let me tell you that if you undertake to dictate to one of those three great fundamental branches of government you will be doing that which you have no right to do, and which better be let alone. You should first have a law for the judiciary to execute. When the Convention for the revision and amendment of the constitution affixes its signatures to that instrument, which I hope in God's name you will all do, let it go forth to the peopl, let it be adopted, and when it is adopted will you tell me what will be adopted? I can tell you that you will have only the constitution of 1852 revised and amended. You will have nothing else. That is all we met for. We were called together to revise and amend that constitution—it is all we can do. It is all the people sent us here for. Well, sir, that is not done. Then why is this cowardly attack made on the judiciary, by the presiding officer of this Convention and his friend, Col. Thorpe? [Hisses and applause.] That the judge is, as is pretended, a military judge, is as false as the other proposition. Now, sir, I would have given something to have heard arguments on the other side of this question. There is a difference between *argument* and *assertion*. We have heard plenty of the one but none of the other. In the first place the gentleman who exhibits the enormous amount of courage requisite to get up before this body and waste the time of this Convention, in an attempt to destroy the independence of the judiciary, reads from a newspaper. Now, sir, newspapers are not always correct. They are sometimes wrong, and very often right. Now, sir, take the facts and the case in question amounts to this: one of our justices decided some case in favor of a woman who had been a slave. The case was appealed. On the trial of the case, there was appearance by counsel on the part of both parties, and the question arose as to the status of the slave, and the court held that the civil law deprived this woman from standing in judgment, and, sir, the decision was just as correct as the principles of Almighty God. Will any man dispute that slavery did exist in Louisiana? [No.] When was slavery abolished in Louisiana? It is very true, sir, that the president of the United States did issue his proclamation abolishing it in several States in rebellion; but, sir, he specially excepted certain parishes in Louisiana, and Orleans is one of the excepted parishes. Go read your proclamations and you will find that I am correct, and that the decision is based upon solid foundations. The commanding general of this department has never abolished slavery. There is no such power vested in him, even were he disposed to abolish slavery any where, and he has never attempted it. It is strange to me that you can come to such a conclusion. Let me state a proposition: Gen. Banks ordered the election for this Convention, did he not? [Yes.] Well what did he order it for? Was it to abolish slavery? There was no need of that if he had already abolished it himself. Did he order it as a military Convention? (Yes.) He did? Then we are a military Convention, are we? For God's sake then let us go home and put on our military coats at once and do our duty. We do not look like military men here We do not act like military men. If we are military men we have no business here. This is no place for military men. We are not a military Convention, sir, and we are not here by virtue of military orders exclusively, but by the orders of the loyal people of Louisiana. Why, sir, does it not appear evident enough to every gentleman here that we have never emancipated the slaves, and yet the worthy president of this Convention told us, when we passed the report of the Committee on Emancipation, that that act was a part and parcel of the law of the land. How come it so? We did not make it so. If it was so before, there was no necessity for us to take any action on the question, and we have been making asses of ourselves for nothing. Does not the worthy president of this body feel ashamed of himself when he reflects on the absurdity of the position in which he has voluntarily placed himself? He told you the slaves were free. We have not made them free. If they were free before, we have only been doing a great deal of work for which there was no necessity, and our provision for the emancipation of the slaves is mere nonsense. The argument that it required all this formality to set free a parcel of negroes that were free before is too absurd and ridiculous to be entertained for a moment. Why, sir, the commanding general himself told you, if I mistake not, that the emancipation of the slaves was the noble work of the noble people of Louisiana. Then, if it required us to do the work, what do you mean when you say that slavery was already abolished? Such an argument is, to say the least, extremely foolish, I care not in what light you place it.

Why, sir, where is the man that doubts that we are going to abolish slavery? It will be done in September, when the people vote on the constitution which we shall submit to them. Now, all know that I am one of the first who told you that I was in favor of immediate emancipation. We agreed on that with a very few exceptions, and we passed an ordinance. And many of us affixed our signatures to it, and yet you tell us to day that it was previously abolished. Why, sir, with your own words you choke yourself.

Until that act is finally passed your negroes may visit the Queen of Spain and of England. But that has nothing to do with the question of their emancipation. The question is, are they slaves here in the eye of the law, or are they free. Not whether they shall be made voters, nor shall they be free. Now, sir, it is contended against every principle of law, reason and justice, that this has already been done by the commanding general, and you propose to censure an honest judge for not so deciding. You are about to censure an honorable man, who stands with his hands tied, unable to defend himself. He cannot tell you why he rendered such a decision. He has to depend on the honesty and integrity of this Convention. Now, sir, was he not right when he decided that the status of that woman was not such as to permit her to stand in judgment before a court of this State? Why, sir, I need hardly repeat that the ordinance of emancipation will not become a part of the fundamental law of the State until it has been passed upon by the people. When that is done and the ordinance ratified, slavery will cease to exist in New Orleans.

My learned and esteemed friend who by the votes of the people was promoted to the office of attorney general, was called upon to give his opinion on the status of the negro, and was perfectly right when he reported back by letter that the status had been fixed by the proclamation of the president. The gentleman in view of the prospect that they had a right to stand before the court, appeared in court in the case in question, as their advocate, and contended that they had rights under the civil law, as though they were free. Sir, is it to be expected that any man of common sense would not know better when he came to look at the matter in its true light?

It is true that slaves have their rights in the criminal courts, as the slave courts are abolished and slavery ignored by military orders, but our ordinance is not yet finally passed, and cannot be law until it is, and the laws recognizing slavery are not yet abrogated, and let me ask how any one can be guilty of acting in contempt of a political body by refusing to recognize as a law, what they themselves have never made a law.

Are the laws of the State respecting slaves abrogated or repealed? Until they are, the judge who would decide contrary to law by so considering them, would be censurable indeed.

One gentleman who has preceded me (Mr. Durell) has said, "If you think slavery exists, go out into the streets and see if you can get your slave to obey you." This is mere nonsense; who has contended that it could be done? The question is one merely of legal right under the constitution and laws, and I hold, sir, that slavery has not yet been wiped out by the final and conclusive action of the people or by this Convention. This must be done before slavery ceases to exist in this part of the State. There is no use, sir, in your getting so far in advance as to tumble down and break your own neck. Let the Convention adopt the constitution; let it go to the people and let them adopt it and slavery is wiped out throughout the length and breadth of the land, and the parish of Orleans will not be excepted, either in a criminal, civil, or constitutional point of view. Notwithstanding all the arguments of men in courts or in this Convention, it will not be wiped out sooner than the day that the people adopt this constitution, or, this ordinance of emancipation. If I am wrong on this question get up and reply to me with reason; do not get up and get off a string of flowing assertions, but tell us, if you please, that the laws of the State have been abrogated, and prove it, or repealed by the action of any body of men, and prove it. When you do that, I'll turn the tables and vote with you; but you must first convince me that you are right and I am wrong. Now, in conclusion, you are about to cast your votes, gentlemen. I appeal to your reason and sense of justice, to vote down this proposition, founded as it is in injustice and absurdity, and I must say, *cowardice.*

Now, if there is any question that has not been discussed, that is necessary to a fair and honest vote to uphold the dignity of the judiciary, the ability and dignity of this Convention, and of the constitution and laws of this State, let us discuss it at once and vote down this proposition. Let us at once crush out this disposition to attempt to destroy men while we ought to be at work doing our duty. Let us crush out this disposition to do dirty work which is alike disgraceful to the judge, and every member who takes part in it. Let it go forth that while we are opposed to slavery, we are in favor of maintaining the laws until they are abrogated or repealed. For God's sake do not let it go forth that this Convention assembled here in the name of the loyal people of Louisiana, in the middle of the nineteenth century, holds the judiciary responsible for bad laws. Let it not be said that in Louisiana we have a Convention which censures judges because their decisions are in violation of its own ordinances not yet passed.

With these remarks, gentlemen, I am done, and will only say the subject is before you—consider it well and vote as you please. I care not, vote for it or vote against it; but vote like honest men.

Mr. GASTINEL—I move we adjourn.

[The motion was carried, and the Convention adjourned.]

FRIDAY, July 15, 1864.

[The Convention met pursuant to adjournment. Present, the Hon. E. H. Durell, and the following members:]

Messrs. Abell, Austin, Balch, Barrett, Baum, Beauvais, Bell, Bennie, Bofill, Buckley, Burke, Campbell, Collin, Cazabat, Cook J. K., Cook T., Crozat, Cutler, Davies, Decker, Duane, Dufresne, Dupaty, Edwards, Ennis, Fish, Flagg, Flood, Foley, Fuller, Gastinel, Geier, Gorlinski, Gruneberg, Gaidry, Healy, Harnan, Hart, Heard, Henderson, Hills, Hire, Howell, Howes, Kavanagh, Knobloch, Kugler, Maas, Mann, Maurer, Mayer, Mendiverri, Montamat, Morris, Murphy E., Murphy M. W., Newell, Normand, O'Conner, Payne J., Paine J. T., Pintado, Poynot, Purcell J., Pursell S., Schroeder, Schnurr, Shaw, Smith, Spellicy, Stocker, Stumpf, Stiner, Sullivan, Taliaferro, Terry, Thorpe, Thomas, Waters, Wenck, Wells, Wilson—83.

[The minutes of yesterday's proceedings were read and adopted.

On motion of Mr. Flagg, Mr. Seymour was excused for non-attendance.]

Mr. MONTAMAT—I wish to offer the following resolution:

Resolved, That the Finance Committee be, and is hereby authorized, to draw from the treasury of the State, (from all moneys not otherwise appropriated,) any amount necessary for the payment of members, officers, employés, and contingent expenses of this Convention.

[Adopted.]

Mr. SMITH—I submit the following:

Resolved, That in view that this Convention has adopted an article separating taxation, for the benefit of education, under two distinct heads—one for the education of the white and the other for the education of the colored children—it becomes necessary, in order to avoid difficulty in the future, that it should also define what degree of blood constitues a colored person.

Mr. MONTAMAT—I move it be laid upon the table.

[Motion lost on rising vote—yeas 30, nays 33.]

Mr. SMITH—I simply offer this resolution, because I know that if an assessor goes to many families and assesses them as colored people, he will be liable to have the top of his head shot off. Since we have passed this law, we must define it and have it understood whether a fourth, seven-eighths or any other proportionable intermixture, is to cause a man to be considered as white or black. Now is the time to settle the question, though it is a *mixed* one, any way.

Mr. HENDERSON—Mr. President, if this Convention refuses to arrange and settle this question of color by a constitutional proviso, or if the Legislature under this constitution refuses to do it, I will be one of the first to call upon Gen. Banks to fix by a military order what is white and what is black under the law of the land. In the case of Spaulding, one of the first lawyers of St. Louis, who sent a child, a slave, to New Orleans, and who was taken back again to St. Louis, a suit was brought against the owners of the boat for carrying a slave without the permission of the master. A verdict was rendered against the defendants and it went before the Supreme Court, whereas, the child, from appearance, could not be said to have colored blood, the judgment of the lower court was reversed. The court decided that it was an abominable law that compelled a steamboat to be responsible when the suspected person had a fair complexion, clear blue eyes and all the signs of pure white blood, and that a suit should not be brought when it was necessary to go back and trace his descent to see if he was colored and a slave. This shows the necessity of some action in the matter on our part, fixing this question so as to avoid future difficulty. We represent the people, and they should be the first to accomplish this for a class under the present circumstances not able to protect itself. I know these things are difficult, but not the less important. I do not believe in going back to trace the pedigree; but I am in favor of declaring the person white if he have the Caucasian color and cast of features, and we must settle this thing sometime or other.

In regard to the moral effect, you may encourage it in your families or not, as you please. If I don't choose to invite the governor of this State, he cannot be rereceived as a guest. If he does not choose to invite me, I cannot be received as a guest. So with the colored people; give them the rights that belong to them and they may rise in the social and political scale, but at the same time they can never rise superior to the white race and occupy his place as governor, member of the Legislature, or justice of the peace. I ask the gentleman to show a single instance where this has occurred anywhere. The law of Mississippi, inserted as a part of the constitution, says the Indian shall have all the rights, immunities and privileges of a white man. There are men who say that war, rebellion and emancipation are nothing, but to fix the status of the freemen is the most troublesome thing we have to do. When I say to a colored man, "I elevate you to the white man," I do not dishonor the white man, or take him down to the level of the colored man. I know one gentleman came with a fair and rosy complexion, and yet afterwards, I heard a Southern man say that he was a mulatto; but that individual has as good French blood as Napoleon, to-day. It was merely by the change of his complexion owing to the change of climate, for I knew him when he was fair and when he was brown. I am in favor of letting the father and mother testify to fix the status of the child, as is the practice in England, and from that there is no appeal; but to bring witnesses from the streets to tell their different stories, leads to injustice and uncertainty. I hope the Convention will seriously consider this matter and make it a part of the constitution, or pass it in the shape of an ordinance. If it is not done, and the Legislature fails to do it, there will be a military order, especially in New Orleans, as to the status of this class. Let us do it, and we shall do ourselves honor and credit, and accomplish that which Congress has failed to peform. As to the elective franchise of this people, that is outside matter, and we have passed a law on that question already, but the status we ought to fix, fully, clearly and distinctly, so that he who runs may read and understand.

[Resolution rejected—ayes 23, nays 47.]

Mr. MONTAMAT—I call up my ordinance.

[Secretary read the following:]

An ordinance authorizing the city corporation of New Orleans to build a bridge over the Canal Carondelet opposite Galvez street, similar to the one now at Broad street.

Be it ordained, That the city corporation of New Orleans be, and is hereby authorized to build a bridge over the Canal Carondelet, opposite Galvez street, (similar to the one now built at the foot of Broad street) in such manner as not to prevent the free ingress and egress of vessels; this ordinance to take effect from and after its passage.

[Tabled by rising vote—ayes 32, nays 19.]

Mr. SMITH—I call up my resolution.

[The secretary read:]

Whereas, During the present rebellion, individuals as well as corporations and parishes have issued a worthless paper currency and forced its circulation on the poorer and only loyal class of the community;

Therefore be it resolved, That a special committee of five be appointed to take into consideration the propriety of framing an article or articles to prevent the recurrence of the same in future, and to hold the property, of whatever character, whether belonging to husband or wife, parishes or corporations, for the redemption of the same, and that the committee be also instructed to submit to this Convention, for its approval or rejection, the draft of a petition to be sent to the Congress of the United States, asking them to empower the parishes of the State of Louisiana to apply the proceeds of sales of property of disloyal citizens for the purpose of redeeming the paper currency issued by them.

Mr. SMITH—Mr. President, I wish to state, as I have before, that this money has been forced upon the poor classes of the people, as the laborers, the butchers, and mechanics, who would not receive Confederate money. I wish it understood, that this money was not issued for the purpose of sustaining the rebellion in any form, but it was necessary to have some kind of currency. It is not in the hands of rich but of poor men, and I call upon the Convention to adopt some measure tending to redeem it.

[The resolution was adopted on rising vote—ayes 39, nays 22.]

Mr. HOWELL—I ask for a call of the House.

[The secretary called the roll; seventy-eight members responded.]

[The secretary read:]

Resolved, That all decisions of the courts of the State that declare slavery exists in the State, are contrary to the fundamental laws of the State, and are contempts of the emancipation ordinance passed by this Convention.

Mr. ABELL—The subject is one of vital importance. If that resolution is carried by this House I consider that we have the most mercenary judiciary that the world ever saw. We shall decide that a judicial officer must give his decisions in accordance with the dictates of this body; that a judge, however honest, may be stricken down without notice and without charge. The question was warmly debated yesterday; my friend, Henderson, indulged again in one of his Ciceronian flights; he was extremely eloquent, I have no doubt; so much so indeed that I was not able to understand what he meant, and I must confess that, much as he has spoken on this floor, it is very seldom that I am able to understand what he means. And the president of this Convention saw proper to take the floor to indulge in some elevated flights on the question, but I think my learned friend (Mr. Cutler) has pretty effectually demolished the finely expressed argument; but as he saw proper to allude to me personally, I suppose it would, if I should be a little plain in my remarks, be nothing more than "tit for tat." The president saw fit to address the men, who reverences the law and is determined to be governed by it in spite of the wishes or the dictation of others, in language which I must deem metaphysical. The language was to the effect that he who lagged behind, his head must come off. If he meant to imply that my head must come off for defending Louisiana, then all I have to say is, "here's a head, and heart with it, for Louisiana;" but I do not suppose he intended to be understood literally; surely if he does he is the wildest man on this floor. We have seen examples of men going ahead—Robespierre went ahead with a power that I am not capable of—with a power that the president does not possess, even had he the desire to go ahead as Robespierre did.

I am opposed, Mr. President, to laying the old aside until we see how the new will stand trial. I may be behind, and my head may come off for being behind. I have but one head, and if it is to come off it will only rob me of a few years, and it would rob me also of a great many inconveniences.

One gentleman informed us, Mr. President, early in the session, that the North expected us to do a certain thing, and to do it quickly, or else the North was to do something. What was it, Col. Thorpe? Were they to take us by the ears, or to boot us a little? One gentleman shakes over our heads large quantities of rope and tells us that we could not set here three hours if it were not for the military forces that are protecting us. I agree with him. I don't believe we could sit here two hours and a quarter if the military were removed, and I told the gentleman that he would be getting North to get out of the way of the rope. Another gentleman comes in here with large sums of money to be used in making Louisiana a free State. What does he want with it? Would he corrupt the people in order to make a free State? If they want a free State, they will make it without the money, and there is no need of buying them. And here comes another gentleman, no other than the president of this Convention, and he tells us that heads are now to come off. Why is it thus? Why is it, gentlemen, that you are threatening us with the North, and with ropes, and now with the guillotine? Do you bring in here large sums of money to destroy the great State of Louisiana? Do you propose with it to bribe the State and corrupt her people? Do you propose to bribe a portion with your large sums of money, and to take off heads in order to frighten the balance into your ranks? If that is your strategy, here's one that won't be frightened. Here's one that you can't scare. I call upon you, gentlemen, to explain yourselves. Tell me why all this from the other side of the House? Why all these threats of the North? Why these ropes, and why these large sums of money? Why are they brought in here, if not to corrupt and scare the people?

I give my friend Hills great credit for truthfulness. I believe him to be as truthful a man as there is on this floor, and I agree with him perfectly when he tells us that we could not stay here without the troops. Yes, sir, if the troops were withdrawn to-day, you would see a great scattering here, nothwithstanding the ropes, the money and the beheading.

These things should be looked into by this Convention. They do us no credit. It would have been for the good of the country to have had these things investigated. As to the North, I don't think the Convention is afraid of anything from that quarter. It is a long way off, in the first place, and in the next place I don't believe there are five hundred abolitionists who have showed their faith by their works. My friend there (Mr. Hills) did, I understand, enlist in the great army of the United States, and marked his trunk, "*On to Richmond*," and now he is found in this Convention—and from a district in which he does not reside.

I believe the president of this Convention showed a great deal of patriotism, and I believe he can go a little further into modern antiquity than I can, but I am not as patriotic as he is. It is but little more than two years ago that he wanted to raise a regiment—at least, I saw it so stated in the papers, and the papers always tell the truth. But he got up here before you yesterday and I expected him to produce clauses of the constitution to fortify the position that he took that "niggers" were citizens; but, sir, he did not do as well as my friend Terry, who quoted from an old tract that I used to hear when I was a boy; nor as my friend from the Second, (Mr. Hills,) who read from a scrap torn out of Helper's Impending Crisis. I had cited section and clause, and my friend comes here with his mouth full of broad assertions, and when I ask him for his authority he is unable to produce it, but can only reply "Oh, sir, it is printed." I do not say that this was the exact language, but the reply was to that effect. No clause was cited to show what right any man had to liberate slaves. No man, sir, has such a right. It is true that a military commander can do it. He may liberate the property—he may take my last dollar from my pocket. He has the power. With thousands of armed men at his command he can do anything he pleases, but that does not make it right.

I stand upon this floor to-day, sir, to

deny the right unless it is given by the constitution, the great charter of our liberties. I expected you to show by that instrument the right of the president to liberate slaves. You have not done it. You have not showed by what right the president can liberate the negro of the sovereign people of one of the States. You cannot do it. There is no power granted to the president, then to divest men of their property without compensation. Those who hold the contrary opinion necessarily ignore the constitution and the laws. I admit that military orders must be obeyed. The judge is a great lawyer, and I ask him, cannot a title be in abeyance and be as good in law as it was before? If it is a military necessity, titles can be put in abeyance by military authority, and the title to the negro is as good to-day as any title under the English law, because, as you know, Mr. President, there is no power to divest that title except it be given in the constitution of the United States.

The president yesterday declared that it was a self-evident fact that the negro was free because you see him going at large in the streets and beyond the power and control of their masters. Suppose they are, that proves nothing. The question is whether they have a legal right and title to their freedom; and you, Mr. President, and you, gentlemen of the Convention, know that they have not. They are held as slaves, under titles of the highest sanctity and antiquity. Why was it that Paul plead to the Romans that he was a Roman, free-born and not a slave? No, sir, we did not create slavery—we are not responsible for it. If we had brought the negroes here and made them slaves, I would say at once, gentlemen of the Convention, I give my voice for their immediate liberation.

But, sir, of all things that have been presented to this Convention, I pronounce the resolution of the gentleman from New York the most unprecedentedly ontrageous. Why, sir, it says that the judiciary, this high and fundamental branch of the government, shall be dependent on the will of the executive. That unless the judges fawn and flatter the minions of power, they shall be displaced and others appointed who will do the bidding of their masters. They must fawn like dogs at their master's feet or off goes their heads. To-day, sir, I see a gentleman who has been an honor to the bench cashiered—and to-day, sir, I would rather be that man than the man who cashiered him. I would consider it an honor, sir, for such a cause to be censured. But, sir, the act is unprecedented and without the shadow of authority. Could you, Mr. President, as judge of the United States District Court, be turned out by the president of the United States to-morrow. Oh, no, not at all, because there are laws that protect you in the enjoyment of the office that you possess. The constitution gives no one the power to remove you during good behavior, and it cannot be done.

I have argued to-day that slavery exists in Louisiana as much as it did ten years ago, and an honest judge is bound to so decide. Sir, the judge who has been cashiered is one of the most intense anti-slavery men that I have ever known, and yet he has shown that with all his zeal he has the power to discriminate between what is the law and what he would desire might be law; and, sir, he has my respect and esteem for the independence he has manifested in deciding against his own feelings what he believed to be the law. I should have been bound to decide the same way, because the president, with all his eloquence and learning—and yesterday he delivered one of the most pertinent and eloquent arguments that has been delivered on this floor—while he tells us that the negro is upon an equality with the white because he is as intelligent—makes those who are more intelligent, above whites who have less intelligence; and, consequently, by his own argument, they are not on an equality at all, and the saying that all men are equal is, by his own argument, false.

I have heard it said that if a man lay down with dogs, he would get up a dog. This is not true, but it would not be at all strange if he should get up with fleas. I do not believe that the negro is the equal of the white man; the finger of God is upon him; look at his flat head and flat nose and at his extended heel, and those who worship him I congratulate with the idea that they will require no perfume in the temples where they worship.

One remark made by the president I must notice, in conclusion; he remarked that I was unworthy of my position. Let my constituents speak for me. They are the best judges of that question. Out of five hundred and fifteen votes I received four hundred and forty-six, and my competitor sixty-nine. I am willing to leave the question whether I have performed the duty they send me here to perform with them, and to abide the result of their decision.

PRESIDENT—The gentleman is entirely mistaken. I never said that the gentleman was unworthy. On the contrary, I have always said that he was one of the most worthy gentlemen on this floor. I never made that remark respecting him. It did not apply to him.

Mr. ABELL—I am glad to be informed that I misunderstood the president. I understood the remark to apply to myself, and am glad to learn that I was in error.

Mr. THORPE—If proper, I would like to call up my resolution of yesterday. I do not care to have it spoken on but would like to have a vote of the Convention upon it.

Mr. THORPE—By usage I have the right to conclude, but if any one else wishes to speak I am willing to listen. The resolution which I brought before this Convention, and which I conceive to involves one of the most important principles that can be called up for our action, has been denounced, in two or three instances, in language not only unparliamentary, but, I will say entirely ungentlemanly. I have never listened to language that, without being personally offensive, was so coarse and offensive, in a deliberative body, as has been applied to the character of this resolution.

[In consequence of members speaking to the president and there being confusion on the floor, Mr. Thorpe took his seat.]

Mr. SMITH—As Mr. Thorpe has nothing more to say I wish to offer a few words.

Mr. THORPE—I wish to close the debate. I have listened with great respect to the other side ; I am entitled to the same consideration. I have particularly listened to Mr. Abell with attention, but he is now leaving his seat ; I desire that he remain in his place—I wish to reply to him.

PRESIDENT—I know of no rule to compel a gentleman to occupy his seat. You have the floor.

Mr. THORPE—Mr. President, when I entered this Convention, on the very first day after its organization, the honorable gentleman, who has been so conspicuous in this body for the advocacy of his pro-slavery doctrines, in the surprise and symplicity of my honesty, I called him to order, and expressed my extreme astonishment that a gentleman who was learned in the law, and had arrived at the years of discretion, and understood the meaning of words, would take the iron-clad oath and come into this Convention and advocate the doctrine he did on this floor. The honorable gentleman stated that he had become so accustomed to the taking of oaths that he was willing to take one two or three times a day and treated the subject with a great deal of levity. I am sorry to say—

Mr. ABELL—I said I had no objection to those patriotic gentlemen who chose to do so, taking the oath thus often.

Mr. THORPE—I am sorry to say that my subsequent experience of the gentleman's ideas of taking an oath have been confirmed, and that he seems to me to attach very little solemnity and responsibility to so solemn an act. I consider that it is logical, truthful and legal to say that there is not a member in this Convention that can stand up here and say one word in favor of slavery and be consistent with his iron-clad oath. (Applause.) I say that every single word said here in favor of slavery, under the peculiar circumstances by which we were called together, is a violation of a solemn contract we made with our government, Gen. Banks, Mr. Lincoln and our God. If this is the language of a slave, it is the language of honesty so far as regards this Convention, and I say that gentlemen who support such ideas as I have heard advanced here this morning and throughout this Convention, should not have staid in this Convention, but left it before it was organized.

The gentleman talks about the constitutional rights of Louisiana. Now, what is the history of her constitutional rights so far as Louisiana is concerned? Louisiana, by an intended solemn act, assumed to be an independent State and passed the ordinance of secession. She seized on the forts, arsenal, mint, and other property belonging to the United States, confiscated it and sold, and appropriated them to herself, and she was, to all intents and purposes, so far as her acts could do such a thing, out of the Union? Was not the State in open rebellion? So far as the United States is concerned, she was no more a part or parcel of the Union than is the Island of Japan or Great Britain. But in the course of time the forts below here were passed and the fleet of Admiral Farragut came up the river, and again was Louisiana placed under the American flag; and I ask Mr. Abell, or any other pro-slavery gentleman here, where were the constitutional rights of Louisiana when that fleet arrived here and took possession of the city? I contend she had abrogated every right, and there is not a lawyer who is acquainted with the law of nations who will not support this view. All the rights we have in this matter we have received from the government; and the Constitution of Louisiana and its sovereignty is a thing this Convention knows nothing about. Slavery was abolished, first by the United States government by the proclamation of the president, excepting some few parishes in this State; secondly, by various acts of Congress; and lastly, by a special order and proclamation of the commanding general of this department. When we met in this Convention and took the iron-clad oath, we separated ourselves forever, so far as members of this Convention are concerned, from that question of slavery, and every word said here in defence or advocacy of slavery, or the payment of loyal slaveholders, has been out of place, and the president would have been justified in ruling everything of the kind as out of order. The proposition I brought before the Convention was certainly a very simple one. It was that every decision that should be rendered by a judge, that slavery still existed in this State, was in contravention of the fundamental law. I don't say the law of Louisiana, but the fundamental, supreme law of the land. If we pass an ordinance of emancipation, and the judiciary declare slavery still exists, it makes our action a farce.

I have heard a good deal here in self-laudation of lawyers. Well, the law is a great thing for the legal expression of the opinion of the public will. The first laws enacted of which we have any record, were given forth by God Almighty on Mount Sinai, and to these ten commandments there has not been added one necessary word since they were printed thousands of years ago on that page of stone. What the gentlemen means by law, I fear is the machinery of law necessary for the guidance of the courts. There must be rules observed, and some principles of action with regard to details observed; but that is not law, it is the mechanical part of law. The great lawyser is the man who sees beyond this and can look through all the extraneous circumstances to the great principles involved; and the greatest of all lawyers and judges is he who can sit on the bench, go all through these accumulations of legal rubbish and come to a decision in favor of humanity and human rights. While I have the highest respect for Judge Handlin and personally regard him as an accomplished gentleman, I also say from my knowledge of his mind, learned from frequent conversations, that the decision he rendered took me by surprise—startled me almost as much as would a voice descending from the clouds. Mr. Abell says he envies him his position. I do not. I say, when a judge appointed in these peculiar times, and a person suddenly made free from human bondage comes into court and asks justice at his hands, it was demanded of a person who is equal to these times, to have at least made a decision, even if it strained the law in favor of freedom and humanity, instead of going back to the authority of a dead constitution and to the Black Code of a defunct State.

I have been called a citizen of New York, and other gentlemen have been sneeringly called citizens of other States.

of there is anything small, contemptible and illiberal, it is exhibited by those who stand up in this Convention and make such distinctions. I contend it is this sectionality—this dwelling on local distinctions, that is the foundation of secession and the father of rebellion. I have no objection to being called a citizen of New York; it is the largest and most powerful State in the Union, and I see by the official record that this Empire State of New York has put a force of 300,000 men in the field to defend our flag and restore the Union. But I am not a citizen of the State of New York. I am a citizen of the United States. [Applause.]

Now let me on their own narrow plat form come to my claims of being a Louisianian. Mr. Cutler is great on his claims of a Louisianian. I should like the gentleman to tell me how long he has lived here and what State he came from, in order to establish the basis of his claims to such exclusive State excellence.

Mr. Cutler—Twenty years; longer than you have, sir.

Mr. Thorpe—Gentlemen, I must here be a little personal to defend myself. I came to Louisiana twenty-seven years ago. [Applause.] I came to this State when the Second District was really the entire city of New Orleans. I married in the State of Louisiana and my family were born in the State of Louisiana, and before this gentleman was in the State. I was among the first to organize and found your public school system, and the first order for public school books sent to the North, I am justified in saying, was written by my hand and signed by my name. Three times in this State I have been offered a nomination for Congress, and this in one of the most intelligent and influential districts; and when one of our State conventions met at Baton Rouge, it did me the honor to nominate me for State superintendent of public education, and I was the only man in Louisiana that was ever thus nominated to a State office by acclamation. Why did I leave Louisiana after a residence of twenty years? Not because I had ceased to take an interest in the State, but circumstances over which I had no control led me away, and when it was rumored in the North that the old State of Louisiana was going to join this fearful rebellion, I said "No, I know the people better, and will stake my life on the Union sentiment of the majority." When the secession ordinance was passed, my head was bowed in the dust, and it was subsequently shown that the majority of the people here were in favor of the Union. Yet, I am charged by a pro-slavery gentleman with being a New Yorker. It is the bigoted spirit that makes this charge, that cheated Louisiana out of her sovereignty, and for a time dragged her down into the sloughs of rebellion. When the announcement was made that Louisiana was once more under the flag, as soon as it was possible to get back to Louisiana, I came back. Under Gen. Butler's orders I restored five miles of the levee that I found in smoking ruins. I made the previously repulsive looking drains of the city as attractive and perfect as the canals of Venice; and for the first time rendered them efficient for the quick drainage of the city. I took from the bed of the Mississippi earth enough and piled it up on the levee, to make an increase of real estate officially valued by the comptroller, even in these troublous times, at six hundred thousand dollars. I thoroughly cleaned the city and made it the admiration of strangers and the comfort of the citizens. I took the rooms of justice in the old buildings opposite Jackson Square, which were unsightly to look at and unfit for habitation, and transferred them into tasteful halls and fit abodes for justice. All this useful work and much more was done under my supervision. The gentleman wishes to know how long I was absent from the State, I will tell him seven years; but away or here, has the gentleman who has questioned me any better claims to be considered a Louisianian than myself? [Applause.]

I saw years ago approaching the storm of rebellion which has swept over the country. That clould at first was no larger than a man's hand, but it gradually spread all over the horizon and the result is that Louisiana has no more the possession of slavery than Massachusetts or New York.

Will you say to me, that slavery is abolished and the act of emancipation passed, and yet a judge can get up and decide that slavery still exists? I ask you what would be the effect of such a decision in any other free State? In the North should a decision be rendered that slavery existed, the judge would be treated as he should be here, as incompetent to sit on the bench. But I thank God we have an able and patriotic chief executive of the State, [applause] and that he did his duty. All glory and honor to that governor! I am glad that he came to this State a poor, humble child. While many men born under this flag and cherished by our free institutions are betraying those institutions and flag, I thank God that among the adopted citizens of the State there stands one who has been firm and consistent in the performance of his duty, one whose name will be immortal on the tablets of the State of Louisiana. I say to-day that Michael Hahn is the most distinguished, prominent and eminent, and the most to-be-honored man in the State of Louisiana. [Applause.] He has done more to redeem Louisiana from the curse of slavery, and to put in operation the act of emancipation than any other man. He has told the judiciary that they cannot foreswear themselves: that they must take things as they find them, and be equal to the occasion. If they hold courts they are all the creatures of the military power which has declared that slavery does not exist, and they must give their decisions in accordance with that power or be removed from the bench. We may honor the soldier who charges on the enemy; we may shed tears over the man who falls in the defence of his country, but it does not require half the principle or moral courage to do these things that Michael Hahn showed yesterday in making that decision of removal and settling forever this question of freedom to the State. [Applause.]

A few more words and I am done. I want the yeas and nays on this question. I want to see if there is a man in this Convention who is inconsistent enough to sign the ordinance of emancipation and then dare to vote against this resolution. Let us know by this vote how honest and sincere men of this Convention are. I have considerable suspicion that some of you are not altogether sincere in your protestations in favor of freedom. I have been forced to believe that behind some very nice words, other feelings than emancipation may lurk. Mr. Abell does not come in this category, but there are able men here, who have been making promises they might break, and who are prepared but for this resolution I have introduced to go out before the people and instead of presenting to them freedom and the free State of Louisiana, are prepared to give their constituents what would be like the apple of the Dead Sea, fair and beautiful on the outside, but within, filled wtth bitterness and ashes. I have heard enough to satisfy me there were men in the Convention who gloried in the fact that a judiciary, perhaps deceived and mistaken in their views, was prepared to go forth and sit on the bench and crush down this State under the heel of slavery. I am prepared to believe that the slaveholder, or rather the rebel, a man that hates freedom and hates this government, that we meet in the street every day and in social intercourse, the men that smile and smile and yet would murder, have chuckled over the prospect that our emancipation act would become a dead letter and our labor trampled upon and disregarded.

I am not to be driven from my position by either ridicule or sarcasm. The gentleman talks about ropes and of our not remaining here two hours but for the Federal troops, and seems to speak of it with a kind of exultation at the fact. If such is the case, look at the precipice upon which you stand. If the Confederates were to come in here to-morrow those who have consistently surported the act of emancipation and advocated the free State movement would fare the best, and from what I know personally of Jeff. Davis in years gone by, I would rather go before him as an open emancipationist and an enemy to slavery than one of the men of this Convention who, while they have voted for the ordinance of emancipation, are willing to leave, through votes and speeches, something behind that they can build upon when the hour of execution shall come. I believe Jeff. Davis would say to us: "We can trust you, honest men; go your way; but those men who belong on both sides we will hang." [Applause.] Gentlemen, you need not fear being hung if you are honest, if the Confederates ever come back, and I will tell you why. We are no abolitionists in the sense Mr. Abell would represent us; we are no under ground railroad people who are supporting these principles against the laws of the State. We do not proclaim universal emancipation to the people in defiance of the statutory law of the State. We have swept away these chains; we are disenthralled, and are violating no law, and are only advocating humanity. Human history would afford no precedent that would take from this Convention an honest advocate of human freedom and execute him for his principles because he had done all above board and kept nothing back; but these half-way men who are afraid to go the whole length of this grand movement and are unwilling to trust human nature as God made it, and set it going in the world; these men who are afraid to meet the exigencies of the times and lag behind in this hour of revolution, they are the men, Mr. President, as you said yesterday, that will be crushed by the wheels of the Juggernaut that follows in our rear. I tell you to-day, gentlemen, who are to go before the people of this State for offices? I would not give my chance as a fair open exponent of this emancipation act, to get the votes of the working men of this State who are the mass of voters and who have been elevated by the act of emancipation, for you, with your pro-slavery doctrines and affinities when you come to discuss before people. I say, gentlemen, that we should have jumped, as one man, to his act of emancipation and when any judiciary shall dare to say that the call that brought us together is not the fundamental law of the land, our indignation should have been immense, and our surprise overwhelming.

If it is the wish of the Convention, I will accept Mr. Henderson's amendment to my resolution, and I hope the yeas and nays will be demanded, and that the resolution will be put in the emancipation ordinance.

[The yeas and nays were called for and the resolution adopted by the following vote:]

YEAS — Messrs. Austin, Barrett, Baum, Beauvais, Bell, Bennie, Bofill, Burke, Collin, Cazabat, Cook J. K., Cook T., Crozat, Davies, Duane, Dupaty, Ennis, Fish, Flagg, Flood, Foley, Fuller, Geier, Gorlinski. Gaidry, Healy, Harnan, Hart, Henderson, Hills, Hire, Howes, Kavanagh, Kugler, Maas, Mann, Maurer, Murphy E., Murphy M. W., Newell, Normand, O'Conner, Payne J., Paine J. T., Pintado, Poynot, Pursell S., Schroeder, Schnurr, Smith, Spellicy, Stocker, Stiner, Taliaferro, Terry, Thorpe, Thomas, Wenck—58.

NAYS—Messrs. Abell, Balch, Buckley, Campbell, Cutler, Decker, Dufresne, Edwards, Gastinel, Gruneberg, Heard, Howell, Knobloch, Mayer, Mendiverri, Montamat, Morris, Sullivan, Waters, Wells, Wilson—21.

[On motion, the Convention then adjourned until 12 M., Saturday, July 16th.]

SATURDAY, July 16, 1864.

[The Convention met, pursuant to adjournment. Present, the Hon. E. H. Durell, president, and the following members:]

Messrs. Abell, Austin, Barrett, Baum, Beanvais, Bell, Bennie, Buckley, Burke, Campbell, Collin, Cook J. K., Cook T., Crozat, Cutler, Davies, Decker, Duane, Dufresne, Dupaty, Edwards, Ennis, Fish, Flagg, Flood, Foley, Fuller, Gastinel, Geier, Gorlinski, Gruneberg, Gaidry, Healy, Harnan, Hart, Heard, Henderson, Hills, Hire, Howell, Howes, Kavanagh, Knobloch, Kugler, Maas, Mann, Maurer, Mayer, Montamat, Morris, Murphy M. W., Newell, Normand, O'Conner, Orr, Paine J., Pintado, Poynot, Purcell J., Pursell S., Schroeder, Schnurr, Seymour, Shaw, Smith, Spellicy, Stocker, Stumpf, Stiner, Sullivan, Taliaferro, Terry, Thorpe, Thomas, Waters, Wenck, Wells, Wilson—80.

[The minutes of yesterday's proceedings were read and adopted.]

PRESIDENT—I appoint on the special committee raised by Mr. Smith's resolution of yesterday, relative to worthless currency, the following members, viz: Messrs. Smith, O'Conner, Balch, T. Cook and Poynot.

[The secretary read:]

NEW ORLEANS, July 16, 1864.

To the secretavy State Convention:

SIR—I hereby resign my seat in the State Constitutional Convention.

It seems to me that the session is being uselessly prolonged at a great expense to the public. I do not countenance the proceedings. Having received an appointment under the government, I wish to attend to my proper duties.

Respectfully,

I am your obedient servant,

J. T. PAINE.

Mr. THORPE—I consider that an insult to the dignity of this Convention, and shall move the gentleman's expulsion for the indignity offered in the language and address of his resignation.

Mr. SMITH—I understand that the objection he offers is that he has received an appointment under the government.

Mr. HILLS—I move that the resignation be accepted.

Mr. WATERS—I second the motion that he be expelled.

Mr. THOMAS—I second that.

Mr. STOCKER—Mr. President, the communication seems to be addressed to the secretary of the Convention. I for one am not willing to acknowledge that the secretary can accept a resignation.

Mr. HILLS—I offer a substitute: that the sergeant-at-arms be sent for Mr. Paine, and that he be compelled to take his seat until he makes his resignation in due form.

Mr. SULLIVAN—I move to lay that on the table.

[The motion was carried.]

Mr. WILSON—I offer the following as a substitute for Mr. Thorpe's motion:

Resolved, That J. T. Paine, of East Feliciana, is an unfit person to receive any employment from the government, on account of the disrespect offered to this Convention.

[The yeas and nays were called on its adoption with the following result:]

YEAS—Messrs. Austin, Burke, Collin, Cook T., Davies, Dupaty, Ennis, Flagg, Flood, Foley, Gorlinski, Gaidry, Harnan, Newell, Normand, Schroeder, Seymour, Smith, Taliaferro, Thorpe, Thomas, Wells, Wilson—23.

NAYS—Messrs. Abell, Barrett, Beauvais, Bell, Bennie, Buckley, Cook J. K., Crozat, Cutler, Duane, Dufresne, Edwards, Fish, Fuller, Gastinel, Geier, Gruneberg, Healy, Hart, Heard, Henderson, Hills, Hire, Howell, Howes, Knobloch, Kugler, Maas, Mann, Maurer, Mayer, Montamat, Morris, Murphy M. W., O'Conner, Orr, Pintado, Poynot, Purcell J., Pursell S., Schnurr, Shaw, Spellicy, Stocker, Stumpf, Stiner, Sullivan, Terry, Waters, Wenck—50.

[The substitute was lost.]

Mr. THORPE—I withdraw my motion to expel, if my seconder will consent.

Mr. STOCKER—I seconded it and consent.

Mr. HARNAN—Then I renew the motion. The gentleman has been drawing his pay here for a long time without rendering any service; for a long time before the resolution cutting off per diem for absence, he did not come into this hall, and since that, when he has answered to his name he has taken the first opportunity to step out of doors. I want to see this question put to a vote.

Mr. HENDERSON—I do not desire to see any action taken by this body that shall show any want of self-respect. It is not long since a gentleman sent in his resignation and it was accepted by this Convention against my vote, and I then stated that I should oppose the acceptance of any other resignation. The Convention is near its adjournment and we should require every member to remain in his seat. I want seventy-six members to sign the constitution.

But there is another question involved here, and that is, have we the right to expel a member without giving him an opportunity to be heard in his defence before the House. I contend that we have not, and if we are to expel him we must first bring him here and hear his defence.

Mr. ABELL—Mr. President and gentlemen: I would not like to deprive the people of a representative, and when a gentleman on account of some little misfortune fails in the discharge of his duty, I am willing to overlook that. The gentleman appears to have been all right until he got this office from the Governor. [Applause.] I shall vote, sir, for his expulsion, for I consider that he has been very disrespectful towards the president and members of this Convention. If a gentleman should get a little tight and come here, I could overlook it, but when a member deliberately tells this Convention that "all business *was* going on well, but now I have got an office from the Governor, I think the Convention is sitting too long," &c. I think it an insult not to be overlooked.

Mr. HENDERSON—Let Mr. Thorpe prefer charges against this gentleman. I am astonished that he should proceed in this *ex parte* manner. It is illegal, unwarrantable and unjust to expel a man without a trial, and therefore I ask that charges be preverred against him, and he be tried upon them.

Mr. WILSON—I think that Mr. Paine has acted with gross discourtesy to this Convention in addressing his resignation to the secretary. If the gentleman has received an appointment from the governor and thereupon concludes that we are wasting the public money and our own time in attending to what we consider our honest business, I think we should vote for his expulsion. [Applause.] I also think that a man sufficiently ignorant to address a resignation to the secretary of this Convention, overlooking the president and members, should be treated with no courtesy, at least beyond that which the laws of every Contion and Legislature grant. I, for one, will vote for his expulsion.

PRESIDENT—I will put the question with merely a remark. I do not consider the addressing of the gentleman's note to Mr. Secretary, an intentional insult to the Convention, but regard it as proceeding from want of information in regard to such subjects. I do think that according to parliamentary rules, every man, before being visited with so severe a punishment as is proposed in this resolution, should be heard in his own defence.

Mr. HENDERSON—Mr. President, can this House expel a member without charges being preferred against him, or without a two-thirds vote in favor of expulsion?

PRESIDENT—That is a very proper question for a member to put to the president of this body. This body has its power in its own hands; but giving you my opinion on the parliamentary laws with regard to this question, I think that under that law no member can be expelled by a sudden vote, but that he has a right to be heard at the bar in his own defence. Therefore, I shall decide that this question which I am now called upon to put, is out of order, and that the proper motion is, that the sergeant-at-arms shall bring that gentleman before the bar of this Convention. If you think that he has offered an insult to the Convention, you can thus bring him here to answer for it. I shall not put the question unless some gentleman appeals from the decision of the chair and the chair is overruled.

[The president called Mr. Sullivan to the chair.]

Mr. BEAUVAIS—I move we adjourn.

[Motion carried and Convention seperated until 12 M. of Monday, the 18th inst.

MONDAY, July 18, 1864.

[The Convention met pursuant to adjournment. Present, the Hon. E. H. Durell, president, and the following members:]

Messrs. Abell, Austin, Balch, Barrett, Baum, Beauvais, Bell, Bennie, Buckley, Burke, Campbell, Collin, Cazabat, Cook J. K., Cook T., Cutler, Davies, Decker, Duane, Dufresne, Dupaty, Edwards, Ennis, Fish, Flagg, Flood, Foley, Fosdick, Fuller, Gastinel, Geier, Gorlinski, Gruneberg, Healy, Harnan, Hart, Heard, Henderson, Hills, Hire, Howell, Howes, Kavanagh, Knobloch, Kugler, Maas, Mann, Maurer, Mayer, Mendiverri, Montamat, Morris, Murphy E., Murphy M. W., Newell, Normand, O'Conner, Ong, Orr, Payne J., Pintado, Poynot, Purcell J., Pursell S., Schroeder, Schnurr, Seymour, Shaw, Smith, Spellicy, Stocker, Stumpf, Stiner, Stauffer, Sullivan, Taliaferro, Terry, Thorpe, Thomas, Waters, Wenck, Wells, Wilson—84.

[Messrs. Crozat and Bofill were excused.

The minutes of yesterday's proceedings were read and adopted.

Mr. Montamat was called to the chair.]

PRESIDENT DURELL—I wish to make an explanation. I was extremely sorry that my remarks made on Thursday last, with regard to the decision of the learned gentleman who lately presided over the Third District Court of New Orleans, were somewhat misapplied, and considered to be rather personal, and pointed at his act as a judicial officer. I am a man swift to do right, when I am informed that, inadvertently, I have done a wrong. Never in my life, did I willingly and knowingly offer an insult to any man. Therefore, I will say, here, in my place on this floor, that with regard to that gentleman, I have been acquainted with him for some fifteen years, and in all of my acquaintance with him, I have found him a man of high honor and integrity, and when I saw the announcement of his appointment to that bench I, for one, felt extremely pleased thereat. To show the gentleman how easily a man's words may be turned aside in the heat of debate, here is my friend on my right, (Mr. Abell,) at whose side I love to speak, who thought that my remarks were, on that day, injurious to him; but I esteem a man who upholds on every occasion his side of a cause; who upholds his side of the question and acts honestly and fearlessly before the people and the country. Therefore, when I heard the gentleman rise in his place and say I had cast a reflection upon his high worthiness, I rose from my chair and said I esteemed no man on this floor more worthy than my friend, and if I have said anything either on this floor or in my place questioning the integrity and strict honesty of any gentleman here, I will say that I most assuredly did not mean it. There was another phase of the matter I was speaking of, but with regard to *that*, I hold an honest, firm and fixed position.

I was extremely sorry to see on this morning, that another gentleman who has been an ornament to our legal profession—whose integrity no man can question, and from whose decision no man ever went forth without being satisfied that that decision was founded upon his best knowledge of the law and most assuredly bore the stamp of his own most true and honest conscience—I was sorry to hear, I say, that this gentleman, (Judge Howell,) the judge of the Twelfth District Court, had tendered his resignation, founded, I was told, upon the action of the governor and upon the action of this Convention with regard to the great question of slavery, which is at the bottom of this whole revolution—for it is a revolution.

Judge Howell—I call the gentleman to order. My acts as a judge are not to be called in question here.

Mr. Durell—I call the acts of no man in question. I was extremely sorry at being obliged to defend my position, for I wish to state on this floor that it is impossible for me to question the integrity or honesty of either of these gentlemen, knowing them as well as I do, and I believe that either of them are incapable of giving a decision which was not perfectly true and right. After having done justice to the gentleman, whose motives I cannot question, and now speak to put myself right on record, I wish to be honestly understood by this Convention, and wish gentlemen to understand my motives. I wish to show you that it is impossible, as I believe, that my motives should be otherwise than those I think founded in the right. They may be erroneous; my action may be erroneous, but I do not wish you to mistake me.

I will start with this proposition: I know very well that there is some who will consider it an erroneous one, but I consider the act, or ordinance as it is called now, placed at the head of the charter of our rights, the constitution which we have formed, which declares slavery to be forever abolished in this State, to be the law of the land. I said that in my place, and said so honestly. I consider it already adopted. Slavery, then, being the foundation of all our troubles, we felt that to do away with that was to do away with our troubles, and I consider, however high a man may be, however great may be his integrity and honesty, however desirous to serve his country, that if that man goes contrary to this great measure, the power that can remove him should. I say he stands in the way of this great progress and should turn aside. I deny that the judiciary should be entirely independent. All know that the judiciary should not be called in question, and it is a thing I would never do; but there are times when the country is striving for its life, when its whole existence hangs upon a thread, and that is the case at the present time. However high the judiciary may be, if they falter upon that occasion, either through weakness of ability, or through what they consider extreme delicacy of conscience or heart, they should stand aside. I am a man, who, when the time comes, will give my flesh, my blood, my bones, my marrow and all. Therefore I have come here to do what I think is right to the very honorable gentleman who lately presided over the Third District Court, for a more honorable man in his life, a more learned man, for he is extremely so, and a more courteous man, I never met with, and my friend here will bear me out in this remark. But I want not only to do what is right to him, if he misunderstood my words, but to place myself in my proper position in regard to this thing. I do not wish to be misunderstood, and will say further, that I am glad that this State, now struggling for its existence and to get back to its normal state, has a military governor, a young, rising man, who fills a place among those men who have flourished in the present day and died prior to him, having nerve and straight-forwardness enough to do that most severe act which he felt to be his duty. This is no reflection upon either Judge Handlin or the other gentleman. The judge of the Second District Court, giving his decision boldly and honestly, taking the consequences, stands higher this day than ever before. Let him stand on that rock and take his chance. With these few words, I thank you, gentlemen, for your courtesy.

Mr. Abell—You all remember that on Thursday or Friday last, I made some statements with regard to the language of our president, and you will all bear me witness that no sooner had he said that he did not refer to me than I at once withdrew. I wish to go further, Mr. President, in regard to this matter, and say that, having stood in the minority on this floor on many occasions, that the minority has received from the president of this Convention every consideration that the majority has, and that I believe the minority has less right to complain to-day than the majority—if necessary I think I can show various instances. I will go one step further still and say that with regard to the imputations cast upon the president of this body, whatever may have been his language, I believe, from what I have seen of him, that he is incapable of doing any man injustice intentionally. He is like myself, extremely warm and zealous upon the point he espouses, and I must do him the justice to say that he entertains his opinions in a honest and candid spirit.

But there is one more point, which is this: On last week I stood up here and condemned the removal of Judge Handlin in terms unqualified, and I now say that he was right, or that we stultify ourselves. If these colored people are already free—hear me you hirelings—why are we struggling to-day to free this people? If they are really free, now then are we a most worthless and insignificent set of men. We would never think of bringing in a bill to free the whites, for they are already free; therefore, on the same principle, I say. great God, hear me, that we are not struggling to free a people who have already their freedom.

Mr. Thomas—Mr. President and gentlemen, I have a resolution I wish to offer in regard to the salary of the adjutant general of this State. It is this:

Resolved, That the adjutant general shall receive a salary at the rate of three thousand dollars per annum from the time of his entering into office and until otherwise provided by law.

Before the question is put, I would like to make an explanation with regard to the office of adjutant general. In times of peace, it has always been considered more of an honorary office, than anything else. The salary as now fixed by law is five hundred dollars *per annum*, but though a sinecure before, the labors of the station, if performed at all, are very arduous. They require the constant employment of the person filling it, and as for the gentleman who now fills it, he has to my personal knowledge, for the purpose of placing the militia of this State upon the same war footing that the North has placed their militia; do we not all know of—have we not all seen the militia of Pennsylvania and New York hurling back the invading hosts from their own soil and that of Maryland? He has, I say, in order to place the militia of this State upon the same footing, been to Washington laboring with the secretary of war, to secure the aid of the government of the United States, to carry this measure more perfectly into effect. Yet this has been done while he receives a salary of but five hundred dollars a year! I think, Mr. President, that as long as this rebellion lasts; as long as there shall be an immediate necessity for the training of our State militia, we ought to have a gentleman who is a soldier in this office; that this will require his constant attention, and that he should receive at least, a salary of three thousand dollars *per annum.* I have fixed at this moderate sum, though I, for one, believe it should be more; that would be satisfactory to the gentleman who holds the office, I doubt not, who should, in my opinion, receive it.

[Resolution adopted unanimously.

The secretary read the following communication:]

New Orleans, La., July 18th, 1864.

To the president and members of the State Constitutional Convention:

In explanation of my communication of July 10th, I have to say that it was designed to be presented to the Convention *through* the secretary, and not *to* the secretary for action.

In apologizing for the inadvertency, allow me to say that I mean no disrespect to the Convention or any member of it.

I again respectfully tender my resignation as a member of the Convention, and urge that it may be accepted.

Respectfully,

I am your obedient servant,

J. T. Paine.

Mr. Henderson—On the very eve of adjournment, no gentleman who undertakes to resign, whether or not he holds an important office, ought to be permitted so to do, and I will be the last to consent to his retiring. I stated on a former occasion of this kind, making, I believe, some reflections, that on any future occasion I would not consent to the receiving of any resignation. I mean no disrespect, but do say, that every member here now, should remain until the completion of our work, and therefore I ask that this resignation be rejected.

[Resignation rejected on rising vote; yeas 17, nays 49—on question of adoption.]

Mr. Smith—I beg leave to present a resolution, which I believe of much importance:

In view of the different degrees of blood in that portion of the population of Louisiana denominated "colored," comprehending the pure African, to those apparently white, it becomes imperative on this Convention that it should define as clearly as possible the status of a "colored" person;

Therefore be it resolved, That a committee of five, of which the honorable president shall be chairman, be appointed by the chair, to take this matter into consideration, and to report by resolution or otherwise, at the earliest opportunity to this Convention, defining what degree of blood shall constitute a "person of color."

Without some action the school fund cannot be rightly applied.

Mr. Balch—I offer the following important resolution:

Resolved, That the sum of five hundred dollars is hereby appropriated to Judge J. N. Carrigan, state librarian, for services rendered by him in furnishing books and documents to this Convention.

[The resolution was adopted on a rising vote—yeas 38, nays 22.]

Mr. Terry—I offer the following:

Whereas, It is desirable that the work of this Convention should be completed without unnecessary delay, be it

Resolved, That all motions relating to the adoption of the constitution or any part thereof, shall be put to vote without debate.

[Laid on the table.]

Mr. Austin—I call up my resolution:

Resolved, That the members of this Convention, who went to Baltimore as delegates, be entitled to their per diem pay.

Mr. Beauvais—I move its adoption.

[The motion was carried.]

Mr. Shaw—The Committee on Arrangement of Constitution beg leave to report as follows:

The undersigned, special Committee on Form and Arrangement, beg leave respectfully to report that they have carefully collated the several parts and provisions of the constitution submitted to them, and made the arrangement and disposition of them, which is submitted in the accompanying printed draft for the action of the Convention. We have made such corrections of phraseology as seemed to your committee best adapted to carry out the intentions of the Convention without change of the sense, except where arising from evident mistake or conflict between the several provisions.

In the legislative report we have corrected errors of apportionment as follows:

The report of the Legislative Committee, as submitted, gave the city 44 members and the country 74, making a total of 118 members in the lower House. This number of members would give one representative to say 3030 white inhabitants. Each parish is to have at least one representative. Let us apply this calculation to the country parishes:

Parishes.	White Population.	Delegates.	Excess of Population.	Total Delegates.	The Report Gives.
Ascension	3,940	1	910	1	1
Assumption	7,189	2	1,129*	3	2
Avoyelles	5,908	1	2,878	2	2
Baton Rouge, E	6,944	2	884	2	2
Baton Rouge, W	1,859	1	2,870*	1	1
Bienville	5,900	1	318	2	2
Bossier	3,348	1	1,703*	1	1
Caddo	4,733	1	1,422*	2	2
Calcasieu	4,452	1		2	2
Caldwell	2,888	1	1,094	1	1
Carroll	4,124	1	2,462	1	2
Catahoula	5,492	1	2,936*	2	2
Claiborne	8,996	2		3	3
Concordia	1,242	1	1,747*	1	1
DeSoto	4,777	1	1,054	2	2
Feliciana, E	4,081	1		1	1
Feliciana, W	2,036	1		1	1
Franklin	2,758	1	763	1	1
Iberville	3,793	1	2,337*	1	1
Jackson	5,367	1	875	2	2
Jefferson	9,965	3	1,279*	3	3
Lafayette	4,309	1	1,440*	2	2
Lafourche	7,500	2	90	3	2
Livingston	3,120	1		1	1
Madison	1,640	1	754	1	1
Morehouse	3,784	1	246	1	1
Natchitoches	6,396	2		2	2
Ouachita	1,887	1	1,613*	1	1
St. Landry	10,703	3		4	3
Plaquemines	2,595	1	1,064	1	1
Point Coupee	4,094	1		1	2
Rapides	9,711	3	621	3	3
Sabine	4,115	1	1,085	1	2
St. Bernard	1,771	1		1	1
St. Charles	938	1		1	1
St. Helena	3,413	1	383	1	1
St. James	3,348	1	318	1	1
St. John Baptiste	3,037	1	7	1	1
St. Martin	5,005	1	1,975*	2	2
St. Mary	3,508	1	478	1	1
St. Tammany	3,153	1	123	1	1
Tensas	1,475	1		1	1
Terrebonne	5,234	1	2,204*	2	2
Union	6,641	2	581	2	2
Vermillion	3,001	1		1	1
Washington	2,996	1		1	1
Winn	5,481	1	2,451*	2	2
Total		59		74	74

Those marked [*] being the fifteen largest surpluses, are allowed an extra representative each, in order to make up the 74.

From these calculations it is evident that
Assumption should have "3" instead of 2.
Carroll " " "1" instead of 2.
Lafourche " " "3" instead of 2.
St. Landry " " "4" instead of 3.
Point Coupée " " "1" instead of 2.
Sabine " " "1" instead of 2.

After the passage of the third article of the Legislative Department as it now stands, the Convention adopted a later period for ratification than that originally contemplated, making it almost if not quite impracticable to carry out, without so correcting the phraseology as to provide for an election of a General Assembly on the day of ratification, which correction has been accordingly made.

Such adaptations of phraseology have been made as to make the time of service of half the Senate coterminous with the first House of Representatives; of the other half with the second House of Representatives, and so on.

The provision giving the Legislature power at its discretion to pass laws extending suffrage has been transposed from under the title of General Provisions to the place where it was originally offered in the Legislative Department, reinserting the word "other" to make it bear its proper relation to the preceding paragraphs.

We have made numerous verbal alterations and transpositions of articles and phrases, keeping in view the carrying out of the intentions of the Convention, and the prevention of any clashing of the several provisions, or of their interpretation. As the action of the Convention upon the instrument now submitted will be final, and conclusive as to the wording of the instrument, to prevent incongruity or conflict of interpretation, whether arising from error or omission on the part of your committee, or imperfect consideration on the part of the Convention itself, we recommend that the Convention take sufficient time for each member to read and carefully consider each article as now reported.

In the printed copy submitted, the following words are omitted in article 138; the Convention will consider the words as inserted in taking action thereon:

"And that the municipal corporation of the city of New Orleans shall be prohibited from adjudicating, selling by sealed proposals, or in any manner contracting for the working or completing of any public works under their supervision and control."

The attention of your committtee has been frequently called by members of the Convention and other citizens, to articles deemed inappropriate and inadmissible to adopt as part of the organic law; some of which had been adopted after protracted debate and apparently full consideration. We have considered such questions as beyond the province of your committee, and that amendment could only come in the form of riders or substitutes on the final reading and adoption.

E. H. Durell,
Alfred Shaw,
Charles Smith,
A. Cazabat,
T. B. Thorpe,
John Henderson, Jr.

CONSTITUTION OF THE STATE OF LOUISIANA.

PREAMBLE.

We, the people of the State of Louisiana, do ordain and establish this Constitution.

TITLE I.

EMANCIPATION.

Article 1. Slavery and involuntary servitude, except as a punishment for crime, whereof the party shall have been duly convicted, are hereby forever abolished and prohibited throughout the State.

Art. 2. The Legislature shall make no law recognizing the right of property in man.

TITLE II.

DISTRIBUTION OF POWERS.

Art. 3. The powers of the government of the State of Louisiana shall be divided into three distinct departments, and each of them shall be confined to a separate body of magistracy, to-wit: those which are legislative to one, those which are executive to another, and those which are judicial to another.

Art. 4. No one of these departments, nor any person holding office in one of them, shall exercise power properly belonging to either of the others, except in the instances hereinafter expressly directed or permitted.

TITLE III.

LEGISLATIVE DEPARTMENT.

Art. 5. The legislative power of the State shall be vested in two distinct branches, the one to be styled "the House of Representatives," the other "the Senate," and both "the General Assembly of the State of Louisiana."

Art. 6. The members of the House of Representatives shall continue in service for the term of two years from the day of the closing of the general elections.

Art. 7. Representatives shall be chosen on the first Monday in November every two years, and the election shall be completed in one day. The General Assembly shall meet annually on the first Monday in January, unless a different day be appointed by law, and their sessions shall be held at the seat of government. There shall also be a session of the General Assembly in the city of New Orleans, beginning on the first Monday of October, eighteen hundred and sixty-four; and it shall be the duty of the governor to cause a special election to be held for members of the General Assembly, in all the parishes where the same may be held with safety to the electors, on the day of the election for ratification or rejection of this Constitution—to be valid in case of ratification; and in other parishes or districts he shall cause elections to be held as soon as it may become practicable, to fill the vacancies for such parishes or districts in the General Assembly. The term of office of the first General Assembly shall expire as though its members had been elected on the first Monday of November, eighteen hundred and sixty-three.

Art. 8. Every duly qualified elector under this constitution shall be eligible to a seat in the General Assembly: *Provided*, that no person shall be a representative or senator unless he be, at the time of his election, a duly qualified voter of the representative or senatorial district from which he is elected.

Art. 9. Elections for the members of the General Assembly shall be held at the several election precincts established by law.

Art. 10. Representation in the House of Representatives shall be equal and uniform, and shall be regulated and ascertained by the number of qualified electors. Each parish shall have at least one representative. No new parish shall be created with a territory less than six hundred and twenty-five square miles, nor with a number of electors less than the full number entitling it to a representative; nor when the creation of such new parish would leave any other parish without the said extent of territory and number of electors. The first enumeration by the State authorities, under this constitution, shall be made in the year eighteen hundred and sixty-six, the second in the year eighteen hundred and seventy, the third in the year eighteen hundred and seventy-six; after which time the General Assembly shall direct in what manner the census shall be taken, so that it be made at least once in every period of ten years for the purpose of ascertaining the total population, and the number of qualified electors in each parish and election district; and in case of informality, omission or error, in the census returns from any district, the Legislature shall order a new census taken in such parish or election district.

Art. 11. At the first session of the Legislature after the making of each enumeration, the Legislature shall apportion the representation amongst the several parishes and election districts on the basis of qualified electors as aforesaid. A representative number shall be fixed, and each parish and election district shall have as many representatives as the aggregate number of its electors will entitle it to, and an additional representative for any fraction exceeding one-half the representative number. The number of representatives shall not be more than one hundred and twenty, nor less than ninety.

Art. 12. Until an apportionment shall be made, and elections held under the same, in accordance with the first enumeration to be made, as directed in article 10. the representation in the Senate and House of Representatives shall be as follows:

For the parish of Orleans, forty-four representatives, to be elected as follows:

First Representative District		3
Second do.		5
Third do.		7
Fourth do.		3
Fifth do.		4
Sixth do.		2
Seventh do.		3
Eighth do.		3
Ninth do.		4
Tenth do.		8
Orleans, Right Bank		2
For the parish of	Livingston	1
do.	St. Tammany	1
do.	Pointe Coupée	1
do.	St. Martin	2
do.	Concordia	1
do.	Madison	1
do.	Franklin	1
do.	St. Mary	1
do.	Jefferson	3
do.	Plaquemines	1
do.	St. Bernard	1
do.	St. Charles	1
do.	St. John the Baptist	1
do.	St. James	1
do.	Ascension	1
do.	Assumption	3
do.	Lafourche	3
do.	Terrebonne	2
do.	Iberville	1
do.	West Baton Rouge	1
do.	East Baton Rouge	2
do.	West Feliciana	1
do.	East Feliciana	1
do.	St. Helena	1
do.	Washington	1
do.	Vermillion	1
do.	Lafayette	2
do.	St. Landry	4
do.	Calcasieu	2
do.	Avoyelles	2
do.	Rapides	3
do.	Natchitoches	2
do.	Sabine	1
do.	Caddo	2
do.	DeSoto	2
do.	Ouachita	1
do.	Union	2
do.	Morehouse	1
do.	Jackson	2
do.	Caldwell	1
do.	Catahoula	2
do.	Claiborne	3
do.	Bossier	1
do.	Bienville	2
do.	Carroll	1
do.	Tensas	1
do.	Winn	2
	Total	118

And the State shall be divided into the following senatorial districts: All that portion of the parish of Orleans lying on the left bank of the Mississippi river shall be divided into two senatoriol districts; the First and Fourth Districts of the city of New Orleans shall compose one district and shall elect four senators; and the Second and Third Districts of said city shall compose the other district, and shall elect three senators.

The parishes of Plaquemines, St. Bernard and all that part of the parish of Orleans on the right bank of the Mississippi river shall form one district, and shall elect one senator.

The parish of Jefferson shall form one district, and shall elect one senator.

The parishes of St. Charles and Lafourche shall form one district, and shall elect one senator.

The parishes of St. John the Baptist and St. James shall form one district, and shall elect one senator.

The parishes of Ascension, Assumption and Terrebonne shall form one district, and shall elect two senators.

The parish of Iberville shall form one district, and shall elect one senator.

The parish of East Baton Rouge shall form one district, and shall elect one senator.

The parishes of West Baton Rouge, Point Coupée and West Feliciana shall form one district, and shall elect two senators.

The parish of East Feliciana shall form one district, and shall elect one senator.

The parishes of Washington, St. Tammany, St. Helena and Livingston shall form one district, and shall elect one senator.

The parishes of Concordia and Tensas shall form one district, and shall elect one senator.

The parishes of Madison and Carroll shall form one district, and shall elect one senator.

The parishes of Morehouse, Ouachita, Union and Jackson shall form one district, and shall elect two senators.

The parishes of Catahoula, Caldwell and Franklin, shall form one district, and shall elect one senator.

The parishes of Bossier, Bienville, Claiborne and Winn shall form one district, and shall elect two senators.

The parishes of Natchitoches, Sabine, DeSoto and Caddo shall form one district, and shall elect two senators.

The parishes of St. Landry, Lafayette and Calcasieu shall form one district, and shall elect two senators.

The parishes of St. Martin and Vermillion shall form one district, and shall elect one senator.

The parish of St. Mary shall form one district, and shall elect one senator.

The parishes of Rapides and Avoyelles shall form one district, and shall elect two senators.

Art. 13. The House of Representatives shall choose its speaker and other officers.

Art. 14. Every white male who has attained the age of twenty-one years, and who has been a resident of the State twelve months next preceding the election, and the last six months thereof in the parish in which he offers to vote, and who shall be a citizen of the United States, shall have the right of voting.

Art. 15. The Legislature shall have power to pass laws extending suffrage to such other persons, citizens of the United States, as by military service, by taxation to support the government, or by intellectual fitness, may be deemed entitled thereto.

Art. 16. No voter, on removing from one parish to another within the State, shall lose the right of voting in the former until he shall have acquired it in the latter. Electors shall in all cases, except treason, felony or breach of the peace, be privileged from arrest during their attendance at, going to, or returning from elections.

Art. 17. The Legislature shall provide by law that the names and residence of all qualified electors shall be registered in order to entitle them to vote; but the registry shall be free of cost to the elector.

Art. 18. No pauper, no person under interdiction, nor under conviction of any crime punishable with hard labor, shall be entitled to vote at any election in this State.

Art. 19. No person shall be entitled to vote at any election held in this State except in the parish of his residence, and, in cities and towns divided into election precincts, in the election precinct in which he resides.

Art. 20. The members of the Senate shall be chosen for the term of four years. The Senate, when assembled, shall have the power to choose its own officers.

Art. 21. The Legislature, in every year in which they apportion representation in the House of Representatives, shall divide the State into senatorial districts.

Art. 22. No parish shall be divided in the formation of a senatorial district, the parish of Orleans excepted. And whenever a new parish shall be created, it shall be attached to the senatorial district from which most of its territory was taken, or to another contiguous District, at the discretion of the Legislature; but shall not be attached to more than one district. The number of senators shall be thirty-four; and they shall be apportioned among the senatorial districts according to the electoral population contained in the several districts: *Provided*, that no parish be entitled to more than seven senators.

Art. 23. In all apportionments of the Senate, the electoral population of the whole State shall be divided by the number thirty-four, and the result produced by this division shall be the senatorial ratio entitling a senatoraial district to a senator. Single or contiguous parishes shall be formed into districts, having a population the nearest possible to the number entitling a district to a senator; and if in the apportionment to make a parish or district fall short of or exceed the ratio, then a district may be formed having not more than two senators, but not otherwise. No new apportionment shall have the effect of abridging the term of service of any senator already elected at the time of making the apportionment. After an enumeration has been made as directed in the 10th article, the Legislature shall not pass any law until an apportionment of representation in both Houses of the General Assembly be made.

Art. 24. At the first session of the General Assembly, after this constitution takes effect, the senators shall be equally divided by lot, into two classes: the seats of the senators of the first class shall be vacated at the expiration of the term of the first House of Representatives; of the second class at the expiration of the term of the second House of Representatives; so that one-half shall be chosen every two years, and a rotation thereby kept up perpetually. In case any district shall have elected two or more senators, said senators shall vacate their seats respectively at the end of the term aforesaid, and lots shall be drawn between them.

Art. 25. The first election for senators shall be held at the same time that the election for representatives is held; and thereafter there shall be elections of senators at the same time with each general election of representatives, to fill the places of those senators whose term of service may have expired.

Art. 26. Not less than a majority of the members of each House of the General Assembly shall form a quorum to do business; but a smaller number may adjourn from day to day, and shall be authorized by law to compel the attendance of absent members.

Art. 27. Each House of the General Assembly shall judge of the qualifications, elections and return of its members; but a contested election shall be determined in such a manner as shall be directed by law.

Art. 28. Each House of the General Assembly may determine the rules of its proceeding, punish a member for disorderly behavior, and, with a concurrence of two-thirds, expel a member; but not a second time for the same offence.

Art. 29. Each House of the General Assembly shall keep and publish weekly a journal of its proceedings; and the yeas and nays of the members on any question shall, at the desire of any two of them, be entered on the journal.

Art. 30. Each House may punish, by imprisonment, any person not a member, for disrespectful and disorderly behavior in its presence, or for obstructing any of its proceedings. Such imprisonment shall not exceed ten days for any one offence.

Art. 31. Neither House, during the sessions of the General Assembly, shall, without the consent of the other, adjourn for more than three days, nor to any other place than that in which they may be sitting.

Art. 32. The members of the General Assembly shall receive from the public treasury a compensation for their services, which shall be eight dollars per day, during their attendance, going to and returning from the sessions of their respective Houses. The compensation may be increased or diminished, by law, but no alteration shall take effect during the period of service of the members of the House of Representatives by whom such alteration shall have been made. No session shall extend to a period beyond sixty days, to date from its commencement, and any legislative action had after the expiration of the said sixty days, shall be null and void. This provision shall not apply to the first Legislature which is to convene after the adoption of this constitution.

Art. 33. The members of the General Assembly shall in all cases, except treason, felony, breach of the peace, be privileged from arrest during their attendance at the sessions of their respective Houses, and going to or returning from the same; and for any speech or debate in either House shall not be questioned in any other place.

Art. 34. No senator or representative shall, during the term for which he was elected, nor for one year thereafter, be appointed to any civil office of profit under this State, which shall have been created, or the emoluments of which shall have been increased during the time such senator or representative was in office, except to such offices as may be filled by the election of the people.

Art. 35. No person, who at any time may have been a collector of taxes, whether State, parish or municipal, or who may have been otherwise entrusted with public money, shall be eligible to the General Assembly, or to any office of profit or trust, under the State government, until he shall have obtained a discharge for the amount of such collections, and for all public moneys with which he may have been entrusted.

Art. 36. No person, while he continues to exercise the functions of a clergyman of any religious denomination whatever, shall be eligible to the General Assembly.

Art. 37. No bill shall have the force of a law until, on three several days, it be read over in each House of the General Assembly, and free discussion allowed thereon; unless in case of urgency, four-fifths of the House, where the bill shall be pending, may deem it expedient to dispense with this rule.

Art. 38. All bills for raising revenue, shall originate in the House of Representatives; but the Senate may propose amendments, as in other bills: *Provided*, they shall not introduce any new matter, under the color of an amendment, which does not relate to raising revenue.

Art. 39. The General Assembly shall regulate, by law, by whom, and in what manner, writs of election shall be issued to fill the vacancies which may happen in either branch thereof.

Art. 40. The Senate shall vote on the confirmation or rejection of the officers, to be appointed by the governor with the advice and consent of the Senate, by yeas and nays; and the names of the senators voting for and against the appointments, respectively, shall be entered on a journal to be kept for that purpose, and made public at the end of each session, or before.

Art. 41. Returns of all elections for members of the General Assembly shall be made to the secretary of state.

Art. 42. In the year in which a regular election for a senator of the United States is to take place, the members of the General Assembly shall meet in the hall of the House of Representatives on the second Monday following the meeting of the Legislature, and proceed to said election.

TITLE IV.

EXECUTIVE DEPARTMENT.

Art. 43. The supreme executive power of the State shall be vested in a chief magistrate, who shall be styled the governor of the State of Louisiana. He shall hold his office during the term of four years, and, together with the lieutenant governor, chosen for the same term, be elected as follows: The qualified electors for representatives shall vote for governor and lieutenant governor at the time and place of voting for representatives; the returns of every election shall be sealed up and transmitted by the proper returning officer to the secretary of state, who shall deliver them to the speaker of the House of Representatives on the second day of the session of the General Assembly then to be holden. The members of the General Assembly shall meet in the House of Representatives to examine and count the votes. The person having the greatest number of votes for governor shall be declared duly elected; but if two or more persons shall be equal and the highest in the number of votes polled for governor, one of them shall immediately be chosen governor by joint vote of the members of the General Assembly. The person having the greatest number of votes polled for lieutenant governor shall be lieutenant governor; but if two or more persons shall be equal and highest in the number of votes polled for lieutenant governor, one of them shall be immediately chosen lieutenant governor by joint vote of the members of the General Assembly.

Art. 44. No person shall be eligible to the office of governor or lieutenant governor who shall not have attained the age of thirty years, and been a citizen and resident within the State for the period of ten years next preceding his election.

Art. 45. The governor shall enter on the discharge of his duties on the second Monday of January next ensuing his election, and shall continue in office until the Monday next succeeding the day that his successor shall be declared duly elected, and shall have taken the oath or affirmation required by the constitution.

Art. 46. No member of Congress, minister of any religious denomination, or any person holding office under the United States government, shall be eligible to the office of governor or lieutenant governor.

Art. 47. In case of impeachment of the governor, his removal from office, death, refusal or inability to qualify, resignation or absence from the State, the powers and duties of the office shall devolve upon the lieutenant governor for the residue of the term, or until the governor, absent or impeached, shall return or be acquitted. The Legislature may provide by law for the case of removal, impeachment, death, resignation, disability or refusal to qualify, of both the governor and the lieutenant governor, declaring what officer shall act as governor, and such officer shall act accordingly, until the disability be removed, or for the remainder of the term.

Art. 48. The lieutenant governor or officer discharging the duties of governor, shall, during his administration, receive the same compensation to which the governor would have been entitled had he continued in office.

Art. 49. The lieutenant governor shall, by virtue of his office, be president of the Senate, but shall have only a casting vote therein. Whenever he shall administer the government, or shall be unable to attend as president of the Senate, the senators shall elect one of their own members as president of the Senate for the time being.

Art. 50. The governor shall receive for his services a compensation of eight thousand dollars per annum, payable quarterly, on his own warrant.

Art. 51. The lieutenant governor shall receive for his services a salary of five thousand dollars per annum, to be paid quarterly.

Art. 52. The governor shall have power to grant reprieves for all offences against the State, and, except in cases of impeachment, shall, with the consent of the Senate, have power to grant pardons, remit fines and forfeitures, after conviction. In cases of treason, he may grant reprieves until the end of the next session of the General Assembly, in which the power of pardoning shall be vested.

Art. 53. He shall be commander-in-chief of the militia of this State, except when they shall be called into the service of the United States.

Art. 54. He shall nominate, and, by and with the advice and consent of the Senate, appoint all officers whose offices are established by the constitution, and whose appointments are not herein otherwise provided for: *Provided*, however, that the Legislature shall have a right to prescribe the mode of appointment to all other offices established by law.

Art. 55. The governor shall have power to fill vacancies that may happen during the recess of the Senate, by granting commissions which shall expire at the end of the next session thereof, unless otherwise provided for in this constitution; but no person who has been nominated for office and rejected by the Senate, shall be appointed to the same office during the recess of the Senate.

Art. 56. He may require information, in writing, from the officers in the executive department upon any subject relating to the duties of their respective offices.

Art. 57. He shall, from time to time, give to the General Assembly information respecting the situation of the State, and recommend to their consideration such measures as he may deem expedient.

Art. 58. He may, on extraordinary occasions, convene the General Assembly at the seat of government, or at a different place if that should have become dangerous from an enemy, or from epidemic; and, in case of disagreement between the two Houses as to the time of adjournment, he may adjourn them to such time as he may think proper, not exceeding four months.

Art. 59. He shall take care that the laws are faithfully executed.

Art. 60. Every bill which shall have passed both Houses shall be presented to the governor; if he approves, he shall sign it, if not, he shall return it with his objections to the House in which it originated, which shall enter the objections at large upon its journal, and proceed to consider it; if, after such consideration, two-thirds of all the members elected to that House shall agree to pass the bill, it shall be sent, with the objections, to the other House, by which it shall be likewise considered, and if approved by two-thirds of the members elected to that House, it shall be a law; but in such cases the vote of both Houses shall be determined by yeas and nays, and the names of the members voting for or against the bill shall be entered on the journal of each House respectively. If any bill shall not be returned by the governor within ten days (Sundays excepted) after it shall have been presented to him, it shall be a law in like manner as if he had signed it; unless the General Assembly, by adjournment, prevent its return.

Art. 61. Every order, resolution or vote, to which the concurrence of both Houses may be necessary, except on a question of adjournment, shall be presented to the governor, and before it shall take effect, be approved by him, or, being disapproved, shall be repassed by two-thirds of the members elected to each House of the General Assembly.

Art. 62. There shall be a secretary of state who shall hold his office during the term for which the governor shall have been elected. The records of the State shall be kept and preserved in the office of the secretary; he shall keep a fair register of the official acts and proceedings of the governor, and when necessary shall attest them; he shall, when required, lay the said register, and all papers, minutes and vouchers relative to his office, before either House of the General Assembly, and shall perform such other duties as may be enjoined on him by law.

Art. 63. There shall be a treasurer of the State, and an auditor of public accounts, who shall hold their respective offices during the term of four years.

Art. 64. The secretary of state, treasurer of state and auditor of public accounts shall be elected by the qualified electors of the State; and in case of any vacancy caused by the resignation, death or absence of the secretary, treasurer or auditor, the governor shall order an election to fill said vacancy.

Art. 65. The secretary of state, the treasurer and the auditor shall receive a salary of five thousand dollars per annum each.

Art. 66. All commissions shall be in the name and by the authority of the State of Louisiana, and shall be sealed with the State seal and signed by the governor.

Art. 67. The free white men of the State shall be armed and disciplined for its defence; but those who belong to religious societies whose tenets forbid them to carry arms, shall not be compelled so to do, but shall pay an equivalent for personal services.

Art. 68. The militia of the State shall be organized in such manner as may be hereafter deemed most expedient by the Legislature.

TITLE V.

JUDICIARY DEPARTMENT.

Art. 69. The judiciary power shall be vested in a Supreme Court, in such inferior courts as the Legislature may, from time to time, order and establish, and in justices of the peace.

Art. 70. The Supreme Court, except in cases hereafter provided, shall have appellate jurisdiction only; which jurisdiction shall extend to all cases when the matter in dispute shall exceed three hundred dollars; to all cases in which the constitutionality or legality of any tax, toll or impost whatsoever, or of any fine, forfeiture or penalty imposed by a municipal corporation, shall be in contestation; and to all criminal cases on questions of law alone whenever the offence charged is punishable with death or imprisonment at hard labor, or when a fine exceeding three hundred dollars is actually imposed.

Art. 71. The Supreme Court shall be composed of one chief justice and four associate justices, a majority of whom shall constitute a quorum. The chief justice shall receive a salary of seven thousand five hundred dollars, and each of the associate justices a salary of seven thousand dollars, annually, until otherwise provided by law. The court shall appoint its own clerks.

Art. 72. The Supreme Court shall hold its sessions in New Orleans from the first Monday in the month of November to the end of the month of June, inclusive. The Legislature shall have the power to fix the sessions elsewhere during the rest of the year; until otherwise provided the sessions shall be held as heretofore.

Art. 73. The Supreme Court, and each of the judges thereof, shall have power to issue writs of *habeas corpus*, at the instance of all persons in acutual custody under process, in all cases in which they may have appellate jurisdiction.

Art. 74. No judgment shall be rendered by the Supreme Court without the concurrence of a majority of the judges comprising the court. Whenever the majority cannot agree, in consequence of the recusation of any member of the court, the judges not recused shall have power to call upon any judge or judges of the inferior courts, whose duty it shall be, when so called upon, to sit in the place of the judge or judges recused, and to aid in determining the case.

Art. 75. All judges, by virtue of their office, shall be conservators of the peace throughout the State. The style of all process shall be "the State of Louisiana." All prosecutions shall be carried on in the name and by the authority of the State of Louisiana, and conclude against the peace and dignity of the same.

Art. 76. The judges of all courts within the State shall, as often as it may be advisable so to do, in every definitive judgment, refer to the particular law in virtue of which such judgment may be rendered, and in all cases adduce the reasons on which their judgment is founded.

Art. 77. The judges of all courts shall be liable to impeachment; but for any reasonble cause, which shall not be sufficient ground for impeachment, the governor shall remove any of them, on the address of a majority of the members elected to each House of the General Assembly. In every such case the cause or causes for which such removal may be required shall be stated at length in the address, and inserted in the journal of each House.

Art. 78. The judges both of the Supreme and inferior courts shall receive a salary which shall not be diminished during their continuance in office; and they are prohibited from receiving any fees of office or other compensation than their salaries for any civil duties performed by them.

Art. 79. The judges of the SupremeC ourt shall be appointed by the governor, by and with the advice and consent of the Senate, for a term of eight years; the judges of the inferior courts for a term of six years.

Art. 80. The clerks of the inferior courts shall be elected by the qualified voters of their several districts, and shall hold their offices during a term of four years.

Art. 81. The Legislature shall have power to vest in clerks of courts authority to grant such orders, and do such acts as may be deemed necessary for the furtherance of the administration of justice, and in all cases the powers thus granted shall be specified and determined.

Art. 82. The jurisdiction of justices of the peace shall not exceed, in civil cases, the sum of one hundred dollars, exclusive of interest, subject to appeal in such cases as shall be provided for by law. They shall be elected by the qualified voters of their several districts, and shall hold their office during a term of two years. They shall have such criminal jurisdiction as shall be provided by law.

Art. 83. There shall be an attorney general for the State, and as many district attorneys as the Legislature shall find necessary. The attorney general shall be elected every four years, by the qualified voters of the State. He shall receive a salary of five thousand dollars per annum, payable on his own warrant quarterly. The district attorneys shall be elected by the qualified voters of their respective districts, for a term of four years. They shall receive such salaries as shall be provided by the Legislature.

Art. 84. A sheriff and a coroner shall be elected in each parish by the qualified voters thereof, who shall hold their offices for the term of two years. The Legislature shall have the power to increase the number of sheriffs in any parish. Should a vacancy occur in either of these offices subsequent to an election, it shall be filled by the governor, and the person so appointed shall continue in office until his successor shall be elected and qualified.

TITLE VI.

IMPEACHMENT.

Art. 85. The power of impeachment shall be vested in the House of Representatives.

Art. 86. Impeachments of the governor, lieutenant governor, attorney general, secretary of state, state treasurer, auditor of public accounts, and the judges of the inferior courts, justices of the peace excepted, shall be tried by the Senate; the chief justice of the Supreme Court, or the senior judge thereof, shall preside during the trial of such impeachment. Impeachments of the judges of the Supreme Court shall be tried by the Senate. When sitting as a court of impeachment, the senators shall be upon oath or affirmation, and no person shall be convicted without the concurrence of a majority of the senators elected.

Art. 87. Judgments in case of impeachment shall extend only to removal from office, and disqualification from holding any office of honor, trust or profit under the State; but the convicted parties shall, nevertheless, be subject to indictment, trial and punishment, according to law.

Art. 88. All officers against whom articles of impeachment may be preferred, shall be suspended from the exercise of their functions during the pendency of such impeachment; the appointing power may make a provisional appointment to replace any suspended officer until the decision of the impeachment.

Art. 89. The legislature shall provide by law for the trial, punishment, and removal from office of all other officers of the State by indictment or otherwise.

TITLE VII.

GENERAL PROVISIONS.

Art. 90. Members of the General Assembly and all officers, before they enter upon the duties of their offices, shall take the following oath or affirmation:

"I, (A B) do solemnly swear (or affirm) that I will support the constitution and laws of the United States. and of this State, and that I will faithfully and impartially discharge and perform all the duties incumbent on me as ——, according to the best of my abilities and understanding, so help me God!"

Art. 91. Treason against the State shall consist only in levying war against it, or in adhering to its enemies, giving them aid and comfort. No person shall be convicted of treason, unless on the testimony of two witnesses to the same overt act, or his own confession in open court.

Art. 92. The Legislature shall have power

to declare the punishment of treason; but no attainder of treason shall work corruption of blood or forfeiture, except during the life of the person attainted.

Art. 93. Every person shall be disqualified from holding any office of trust or profit, in this State, and shall be excluded from the right of suffrage, who shall have been convicted of treason, perjury, forgery, bribery or other high crimes or misdemeanors.

Art. 94. All penalties shall be proportioned to the nature of the offence.

Art. 95. The privilege of free suffrage shall be supported by laws regulating elections, and prohibiting, under adequate penalties, all undue influence thereon from power, bribery, tumult, or other improper practice.

Art. 96. No money shall be drawn from the treasury but in pursuance of specific appropriation made by law; nor shall any appropriation of money be made for a longer term than two years. A regular statement and account of the receipts and expenditures of all public moneys shall be published annually, in such manner as shall be prescribed by law.

Art. 97. It shall be the duty of the General Assembly to pass such laws as may be proper and necessary to decide differences by arbitration.

Art. 98. All civil officers for the State at large shall be voters of, and reside within the State; and all district or parish officers shall be voters of, and reside within their respective districts or parishes, and shall keep their offices at such places therein as may be required by law.

Art. 99. All civil officers shall be removable by an address of a majority of the members elected to both Houses, except those the removal of whom has been otherwise provided by this Constitution.

Art. 100. In all elections by the people, the vote shall be taken by ballot; and in all elections by the Senate and House of Representatives, jointly or separately, the vote shall be given by yeas and nays.

Art. 101. No member of Congress, nor person holding or exercising any office of trust or profit under the United States, or under any foreign power, shall be eligible as a member of the General Assembly, or hold or exercise any office of trust or profit under the State.

Art. 102. None but citizens of the United States shall be appointed to any office of trust or profit in this State.

Art. 103. The laws, public records, and the judicial and legislative written proceedings of the State, shall be promulgated, preserved, and conducted in the language in which the constitution of the United States is written.

Art. 104. No power of suspending the laws of this State shall be exercised, unless by the Legislature or by its authority.

Art. 105. Prosecutions shall be by indictment or information. The accused shall have a speedy public trial, by an impartial jury of the parish in which the offence shall have been committed. He shall not be compelled to give evidence against himself; he shall have the right of being heard, by himself or counsel; he shall have the right of meeting the witnesses face to face, and shall have compulsory process for obtaining witnesses in his favor. He shall not be twice put in jeopardy for the same offence.

Art. 106. All persons shall be bailable by sufficient sureties, unless for capital offences, where the proof is evident or presumption great; or, unless after conviction for any offence or crime punishable with death or imprisonment at hard labor. The privilege of the writ of *habeas corpus* shall not be suspended, unless, when in cases of rebellion or invasion, the public safety may require it.

Art. 107. Excessive bail shall not be required; excessive fines shall not be imposed, nor cruel and unusual punishments inflicted.

Art. 108. The right of the people to be secure in their persons, houses, papers and effects, against unreasonable searches and seizures, shall not be violated; and no warrants shall issue but upon probable cause, supported by oath or affirmation, and particularly describing the place to be searched and the person or thing to be seized.

Art. 109. No *ex post facto* or retroactive law, nor any law impairing the obligations of contracts, shall be passed, nor vested rights be divested, unless for purposes of public utility, and for adequate com ensation previously made.

Art. 110. All courts shall be open; and every person, for any injury done him, in his lands, goods, person, or reputation, shall have remedy by due course of law, and right and justice administered without denial or unreasonable delay.

Art. 111. The press shall be free; every citizen may freely speak, write and publish his sentiments on all subjects—being responsible for an abuse of this liberty.

Art. 112. The Legislature shall not have power to grant aid to companies or associations of individuals, except to charitable associations, and to such companies or associations as are and shall be formed for the exclusive purpose of making works of internal improvement, wholly or partially within the State, to the extent only of one-fifth of the capital of such companies, by subscription of stock or loan in money or public bonds; but any aid thus granted shall be paid to the company only in the same proportion as the remainder of the capital shall be actually paid in by the stockholders of the company; and, in case of loan, such adequate security shall be required, as to the Legislature may seem proper. No corporation or individual association, receiving the aid of the State as herein provided, shall possess banking or discounting privileges.

Art. 113. No liability shall be contracted by the State as above mentioned, unless the same be authorized by some law for some single object or work, to be distinctly specified therein, which shall be passed by a majority of the members elected to both Houses of the General Assembly; and the aggregate amount of debts and liabilities incurred under this and the preceding article shall never, at any time, exceed eight millions of dollars.

Art. 114. Whenever the Legislature shall contract a debt exceeding in amount the sum of one hundred thousand dollars, unless in case of war, to repel invasion, or suppress insurrection, they shall, in the law creating the debt, provide adequate ways and means for the payment of the current interest and of the principal when the same shall become due. And the said law shall be irrepealable until principal and interest are fully paid and discharged, or unless the repealing law contains some other adequate provision for the payment of the principal and interest of the debt.

Art. 115. The Legislature shall provide by law for all change of venue in civil and criminal cases.

Art. 116. The Legislature shall have the power to license the selling of lottery tickets and the keeping of gambling houses; said houses in all cases shall be on the first floor and kept with open doors; but in all cases not less than ten thousand dollars per annum shall be levied as a license or tax on each vendor of lottery tickets, and on each gambling house, and five hundred dollars on each tombola.

Art. 117. The Legislature may enact general laws regulating the adoption of children, emancipation of minors, changing of names, and the granting of divorces; but no special laws shall be enacted relating to particular or individual cases.

Art. 118. Every law enacted by the Legislature shall embrace but one object, and that shall be expressed in the title.

Art. 119. No law shall be revived or amended by reference to its title; but in such case the act revived, or section amended, shall be re-enacted and published at length.

Art. 120. The Legislature shall never adopt any system or code of laws by general reference to such system or code of laws; but in all cases shall specify the several provisions of the laws it may enact.

Art. 121. Corporations shall not be created in this State by special laws except for political or municipal purposes; but the Legislature shall provide by general law for the organization of all other corporations, except corporations with banking or discounting privileges, the creation, renewal or extension of which is hereby prohibited.

Art. 122. In case of the insolvency of any bank or banking association, the bill holders thereof shall be entitled to preference in payment over all other creditors of such bank or association.

Art. 123. No person shall hold or exercise, at the same time, more than one civil office of trust or profit, except that of justice of the peace.

Art. 124. Taxation shall be equal and uniform throughout the State. All property shall be taxed in proportion to its value, to be ascertained as directed by law. The General Assembly shall have power to exempt from taxation property actually used for church, school or charitable purposes. The General Assembly shall levy an income tax upon all persons pursuing any occupation, trade or calling, and all such persons shall obtain a license, as provided by law. All tax on income shall be pro rata on the amount of income or business done.

Art. 125. The Legislature may provide by law in what case officers shall continue to perform the duties of their offices until their successors shall have been inducted into office.

Art. 126. The Legislature shall have power to extend this constitution and the jurisdiction of this State over any territory acquired by compact, with any State, or with the United States, the same being done by consent of the United States.

Art. 127. None of the lands granted by Congress to the State of Louisiana for aiding in constructing the necessary levees and drains, to reclaim the swamp and overflowed lands of the State, shall be diverted from the purposes for which they were granted.

Art. 128. The Legislature shall pass no law excluding citizens of this State from office for not being conversant with any language except that in which the constitution of the United States is written.

Art. 129. No liability, either State, parochial or municipal, shall exist for any debts contracted for, or in the interest of the rebellion against the United States government.

Art. 130. The seat of government shall be and remain at New Orleans, and shall not be removed without the consent of a majority of both Houses of the General Assembly.

Art. 131. The Legislature may determine

the mode of filling vacancies in all offices for which provision is not made in this constitution.

Art. 132. The Legislature shall pass no law requiring a property qualification.

TITLE VIII.

CORPORATION OF THE CITY OF NEW ORLEANS.

Art. 133. The citizens of the city of New Orleans shall have the right of appointing the several public officers necessary for the administration of the police of said city, pursuant to the mode of elections which shall be prescribed by the Legislature; *Provided*, that the mayor and recorders shall be ineligible to a seat in the General Assembly; and the mayor and recorders shall be commissioned by the governor as justices of the peace, and the Legislature may vest in them such criminal jurisdiction as may be necessary for the punishment of minor offences, and as the police and good of said city may require.

And that the city of New Orleans shall maintain a police which shall be uniformed with distinction of grade, to consist of permanent citizens of the State of Louisiana, to be selected by the mayor of the city, and to hold office during good behavior, and removable only by a police commission composed of five citizens and the mayor, who shall be president of the board. The commission to be appointed by the governor of the State for the term of two years, at a salary of not less than one thousand dollars per annum; a majority of whom shall remove for delinquencies. Members of the police when removed shall not again be eligible to any position on the police for a term of one year.

Interfering or meddling in elections in any manner will be a sufficient cause for instant dismissal from the police by the board.

The chief of police shall give a penal bond in the sum of ten thousand dollars; lieutenants of police, five thousand dollars; sergeants and clerks, each three thousand dollars; corporals, two thousand dollars; and privates one thousand dollars; with good and solvent security, as the law directs, for the faithful performance of their duties.

The various officers shall receive a salary of not less than the following rates:

The chief of police........	$250	per	month.
The lieutenants of police..	150	do.	do.
The sergeants of police....	100	do.	do.
The clerks of police......	100	do.	do.
The corporals of police...	90	do.	do.
The privates(day and night) each..................	80	do.	do.

TITLE IX.

LABOR ON PUBLIC WORKS.

Art. 134. The Legislature may establish the price and pay of foremen, mechanics, laborers and others employed on the public works of the State or parochial or city governments: *Provided*, That the compensation to be paid all foremen, mechanics, cartmen and laborers employed on the public works, under the government of the State of Louisiana, city of New Orleans, and the police juries of the various parishes of the State, shall not be less than as follows, viz: Foremen, $3 50 per day; mechanics, $3 00 per day; cartmen, $3 50 per day; laborers, $2 00 per day.

Art. 135. Nine hours shall constitute a day's labor for all mechanics, artizans and laborers employed on public works.

TITLE X.

INTERNAL IMPROVEMENTS.

Art. 136. There shall be appointed by the governor a state engineer, skilled in the theory and practice of his profession, who shall hold his office at the seat of government for the term of four years. He shall have the superintendence and direction of all public works in which the State may be interested, except those made by joint stock companies or such as may be under the parochial or city authorities exclusively and not in conflict with the general laws of the State. He shall communicate to the General Assembly, through the governor, annually, his views concerning the same, report upon the condition of the public works in progress, recommend such measures as in his opinion the public interest of the State may require, and shall perform such other duties as may be prescribed by law. His salary shall be four thousand dollars per annum. The mode of appointment, number and salary of his assistants shall be fixed by law. The state engineer and assistants shall give bonds for the performance of their duties as shall be prescribed by law.

Art. 137. The General Assembly may create internal improvement districts, composed of one or more parishes, and may grant a right to the citizens thereof to tax themselves for their improvements. Said internal improvement districts, when created, shall have the right to select commissioners, shall have power to appoint officers, fix their pay and regulate all matters relative to the improvements of their districts, provided such improvements will not conflict with the general laws of the State.

Art. 138. The General Assembly may grant aid to said districts out of the funds arising from the swamp and overflowed lands, granted to the State by the United States for that purpose or otherwise.

Art. 139. The General Assembly shall have the right of abolishing the office of state engineer, by a majority vote of all the members elected to each branch, and of substituting a board of public works in lieu thereof, should they deem it necessary.

TITLE XI.

PUBLIC EDUCATION.

Art. 140. There shall be elected a superintendent of public education, who shall hold his office for the term of four years. His duties shall be prescribed by law, and he shall receive such compensation as the Legislature may direct: *Provided*, that the General Assembly shall have power by a vote of a majority of the members elected to both Houses, to abolish the said office of superintendent of public education, whenever, in their opinion, said office shall be no longer necessary.

Art. 141. The Legislature shall levy a special tax on the property of all white persons owning property in the State, for the purpose of public schools for the education of white children, and money so arising shall not be otherwise appropriated.

The Legislature shall levy a special tax on colored persons in the State and their property for the purpose of public schools for the education of colored children, and money so arising shall not be otherwise appropriated.

Art. 142. The general exercises in the common schools shall be conducted in the English language.

Art. 143. A university shall be established in the city of New Orleans. It shall be composed of four faculties, to-wit: one of law, one of medicine, one of the natural sciences, and one of letters; the Legislature shall provide by law for its organization and maintenance.

Art. 144. the proceeds of all lands heretofore granted by the United States to this State for the use or purpose of the public schools, and of all lands which may hereafter be granted or bequeathed for that purpose, and the proceeds of the estates of deceased persons to which the State may become entitled by law, shall be and remain a perpetual fund on which the State shall pay an annual interest of six per cent., which interest together with the interest of the trust funds, deposited with the State by the United States, under the act of Congress, approved June 23, 1836, and all the rents of the unsold lands shall be appropriated to the purpose of such schools and the appropriation shall remain inviolable.

Art. 145. All moneys arising from the sales which have been, or may hereafter be made of any lands heretofore granted by the United States to this State for the use of a specific seminary of learning, or from any kind of a donation that may hereafter be made for that purpose, shall be and remain a perpetual fund, the interest of which at six per cent. per annum shall be appropriated to the promotion of literature and the arts and sciences, and no law shall ever be made diverting said funds to any other use than to the establishment and improvement of said seminary of learning: and the General Assembly shall have power to raise funds for the organization and support of said seminary of learning in such manner as it may deem proper.

Art. 146. No appropriation shall be made by the Legislature for the support of any private school or institution of learning whatever, but the highest encouragement shall be granted to public schools throughout the State.

TITLE XII.

MODE OF REVISING THE CONSTITUTION.

Art. 147. Any amendment or amendments to this constitution may be proposed in the Senate or House of Representatives, and if the same shall be agreed to by two-thirds of the members elected to each House, such proposed amendment or amendments shall be entered on their journals, with the yeas and nays taken thereon, and the secretary of state shall cause the same to be published, three months before the next general election for representatives of the State Legislature, in at least one newspaper in French and English, in every parish in the State in which a newspaper shall be published; and such proposed amendment or amendments shall be submitted to the people at said election; and if a majority of the voters at said election shall approve and ratify such amendment or amendments, the same shall become a part of the constitution. If more than one amendment be submitted at a time, they shall be submitted in such manner and form, that the people may vote for or against each amendment separately.

TITLE XIII.

SCHEDULE.

Art. 148. The constitution adopted in 1852 is declared to be superceded by this constitution; and in order to carry the same into effect, it is hereby declared and ordained as follows:

Art. 149. All rights, actions, prosecutions, claims and contracts, as well of individuals as of bodies corporate, and all laws in force at the time of the adoption of this constitution, and not inconsistent therewith, shall continue as if the same had not been adopted.

Art. 150. In order that no inconvenience may result to the public service from the taking effect of this constitution, no officer shall be superceded thereby; but the laws of this State relative to the duties of the several officers, executive, judicial and military, except those made void by military authority, and by the ordinance of emancipation, shall remain in full force, though the same be contrary to this constitution, and the several duties shall be performed by the respective officers of the State, according to the existing laws, until the organization of the government under this constitution, and the entering into office of the new officers to be appointed under said government, and no longer.

Art. 151. The Legislature shall provide for the removal of all causes now pending in the Supreme Court or other courts of the State under the constitution of 1852, to courts created by or under this constitution.

TITLE XIV.

ORDINANCE.

Art. 152. Immediately after the adjournment of the Convention, the governor shall issue his proclamation directing the several officers of this State, authorized by law to hold elections, or in default thereof such officers as he shall designate, to open and hold polls in the several parishes of the State, at the places designated by law, on the first Monday of September, 1864, for the purpose of taking the sense of the good people of this State in regard to the adoption or rejection of this constitution: and it shall be the duty of said officers to receive the suffrages of all qualified voters. Each voter shall express his opinion by depositing in the ballot-box a ticket whereon shall be written "The Constitution accepted," or, "The Constitution rejected." At the conclusion of the said election, the officers and commissioners appointed to preside over the same shall carefully examine and count each ballot as deposited, and shall forthwith make due return thereof to the secretary of state, in conformity to the provisions of law and usages in regard to elections.

Art. 153. Upon the receipt of said returns, or on the third Monday of September, if the returns be not sooner received, it shall be the duty of the governor, the secretary of state, the attorney general and the state treasurer, in the presence of all such persons as may choose to attend, to compare the votes at the said election for the ratificatien or rejection of this constitution; and if it shall appear at the close, that a majority of all the votes given is for ratifying this constitution, then it shall be the duty of the governor to make proclamation of the fact, and thenceforth this constitution shall be ordained and established as the constitution of the State of Louisiana. But whether this constitution be accepted or rejected it shall be the duty of the governor to cause to be published the result of the polls, showing the number of votes cast in each parish for and against this constitution.

Art. 154. As soon as a general election can be held under this constitution in every parish of the State, without hostile molestation or interference, the governor shall, by proclamation, or in case of his failure to act, the Legislature shall, by resolution, declare the fact, and order an election to be held on a day fixed in said proclamation or resolution, and within sixty days from the date thereof, for governor, lieutenant governor, secretary of state, auditor, treasurer, attorney general and superintendent of education. The officers so chosen shall, on the fourth Monday after their election, be installed into office; and shall hold their offices for the terms prescribed in this constitution, counting from the second Monday in January next preceding their entering into office in case they do not enter into office on that date. The terms of office of the State officers elected on the 22d day of February, 1864, shall expire on the instalation of their successors as herein provided for; but under no state of circumstances shall their term of office be construed as extending beyond the length of the terms fixed for said offices in this constitution; and, if not sooner held, the election of their successors shall take place on the first Monday of November, 1867, in all parishes where the same can be held, the officers elected on that date to enter into office on the second Monday in January, 1868.

Art. 155. This constitution shall be published in three papers to be selected by the president of the Convention, whereof two shall publish the same in English and French, and one in German, from the period of the adjournment of the Convention until the election for ratification or rejection on the first Monday of September, 1864.

President—If the Convention accepts the recommendation of the committee, any rider, amendment or change to the report will be in order whenever the Convention sees fit. If the Convention does not accept that recommendation, anything of that kind will be in order at once.

Mr. Sullivan—Mr. President, in the report of the Committee on Form and Arrangement, I have discovered a very serious omission. According to the report of the committee, they have totally omitted the amendment which I offered on the 59th day of the session of the Convention, which was unanimously carried by this Convention and added to the second article of the internal improvement. It reads thus:

And that the municipal corporation of the city of New Orleans shall be prohibited from adjudicating, selling by sealed proposals, or in any manner contracting for the working or completing of any of the public works under their supervision and control.

Now, sir, I consider this amendment, as unanimously passed on that day, is one of the most important ordinances passed during the session of this Convention, and why the committee did not insert it in the constitution is the most remarkable piece of assumption on their part that I ever heard of. When I discovered the discrepancy, I inquired of the Hon. E. H. Durell, the president of this body, the reason why it was stricken out of the report by the committee; he answered by telling me that it had no right to go into the constitution. I tell the honorable president of this body that he has no right to say what shall go into the constitution and what portion of an ordinance passed in this body shall not go into it; he has no right as chairman of that committee to refuse to insert this amendment of mine in the constitution. I repeat, he has no right to set up his opinion against the unanimous will of this body.

I shall require and insist that this amendment is a part and a parcel of this constitution. It cuts off forever the infamous system of contracting. It must be inserted in the constitution; and I believe it is the unanimous wish of this Convention that it shall be inserted in the constitution—not stricken out, although contrary to the wish of the honorable president of this body.

Mr. Abell—I rise to a question of privilege. I have received from Dr. Dostie a communication, which professes to be confidential, soliciting my vote, which belongs to the people of the State. I wish simply to have it read for the consideration of this Convention, as it seems to me like the "large sums of money."

[The secretary read the following:

[Confidential.]

New Orleans, July 15th, 1864.

Dear Sir—I entertain so strong an aversion to the incorporation into the "organic law" of the words "white," "black" and "color," that I am induced in this confidential note, (accompanied by a proposed "rider") to ask you to consider the propriety of altering the language of certain portions of the new constitution, so as to harmonize with the principle contained in this proposed "rider." Many members of the Convention have had the kindness to say to the governor and myself, that they will do what they can to expunge the obnoxious words from the militia and educational bills, before the question of final adoption, as a whole, comes up.

Very respectfully yours,
A. P. Dostie.

Art. —. The Legislature shall provide for the education of all children of the State, between the ages of six and eighteen years, by maintenance of free public schools.

Art. —. A university, composed of a law school, a medical school, and a collegiate school, combining therewith the State seminary of learning, shall be established and maintained.

Art. —. All moneys arising from grants, donations, or other sources, for educational purposes, shall be and remain a perpetual fund, the interest of which, at seven per cent. per annum, shall be appropriated exclusively to said purposes.

Mr. Abell—When a man addresses me in that way, he addresses the people of the State, and I believe that King Charles got his head cut off for interfering in that manner; besides which a president of the United States has set a warning example. An official should not attempt to dictate in this way, but as I think that there is a good deal to be said by way of apology for Dr. D., I shall offer no resolution in regard to the matter.

Mr. Shaw—Mr. President and gentlemen, I have to take notice of what the gentleman, [Mr. Sullivan] has said. It was not half an hour ago,—before the meeting of this Convention,—that this committee assured that gentleman that his article would be submitted as passed. They did so, and also called attention in their side report, to the fact that the draft, as submitted, and now in the secretary's hand, contains it. He heard it read, and knows the fact, and I characterize his remarks, in the very language he used toward the action of the committee, as a "ridiculous piece of assumption."

Mr. Cazabat—I move we proceed with our work, the adoption of the constitution of Louisiana, as a whole.

[Seconded.]

Mr. Abell—I move it be made the special order of the day for Thursday next.

[Seconded.]

Mr. HENDERSON—I see no occasion for postponement. Let the articles be taken up *seriatim*, when, if any gentleman chooses to offer a rider, substitute or amendment, he can do so, and we can pass upon the subject at once; otherwise we shall never get through. I am as willing to act at this time as any other, and I wish every article to be fully discussed, if necessary, and then acted upon. I think the gentleman is out of order.

Mr. ABELL—I think the gentleman is entirely mistaken, and that by postponement until Thursday next, we can dispose of any riders, &c., which may be offered, in ten minutes. I think it due to the Convention and justice, that I may have time to consider whether I approve or disapprove of the constitution, as it now stands.

Mr. STINER—I move Mr. Abell's motion be laid on the table.

[Motion lost on rising vote; yeas 20, nays 46.

Mr. Abell's motion was then carried:]

YEAS—Messrs. Abell, Austin, Barrett, Baum, Beauvais, Bell, Buckley, Burke, Collin, Cook J. K., Cutler, Decker, Dufresne, Dupaty, Edwards, Gastinel, Gruneberg, Healy, Harnan, Kavanagh, Knobloch, Maas, Maurer, Mayer, Mendiverri, Montamat, Murphy M. W., Normand, O'Conner, Orr, Pintado, Schroeder, Schnurr, Seymour, Shaw, Stumpf, Sullivan, Thomas, Waters, Wenck—40.

NAYS—Messrs. Balch, Cazabat, Cook T., Davies, Duane, Ennis, Fish, Flagg, Flood, Foley, Fuller, Geier, Gorlinski, Hart, Heard, Henderson, Hills, Hire, Howes, Mann, Morris, Murphy E., Newell, Ong, Payne J., Poynot, Pursell S., Smith, Spellicy, Stocker, Stiner, Stauffer, Taliaferro, Terry, Thorpe, Wells, Wilson.—37.

Mr. BELL—I beg leave to submit the following:

Resolved, That the following officers of this Convention receive the following sums, respectively, as extra compensation, viz:

Sergeant-at-arms	$250 00
Reporters, each	200 00
Door-keeper	100 00
Assistant sergeants-at-arms, each	100 00
Messengers, each	50 00

[The resolution was on motion laid on the table.]

Mr. AUSTIN—I offer the following resolution with a preamble:

Whereas, The perpetuity of our national government is now imperiled by a stupendous rebellion against the constitution and laws of our common country, originated, supported and carried on by wicked and designing men, for the purpose of establishing a despotic oligarchy, based upon human slavery, an institution reprobated and abhorred by the civilized world and common humanity;

And whereas, The stability of republican institutions as well as the liberty of the people, requires that the government of the United States should be preserved intact, and its laws executed throughout the whole domain;

And whereas, The period of election for president and vice-president of the United States is now approaching and near at hand; therefore be it

Resolved, That owing to the existing rebellion and the present condition of our national affairs, any change in the policy of the executive department of the government will embarrass and delay the vigorous prosecution of the war, and be productive of the most disastrous results.

Be it further resolved, That we recognize in Abraham Lincoln a wise president, true patriot and able statesman, who has been tried in the scales and not found wanting, whose past administration is a credit to himself and an honor to the country, and whose policy for the suppression of the rebellion meets our entire approbation. That we also recognize in Andrew Johnson a wise statesman, endowed with wisdom, patriotism and integrity, and in every way most worthy of the full confidence of the people; therefore,

Be it further resolved, That we most cordially endorse the action of the National Convention lately held at Baltimore, and will give to the nominees thereof our hearty support, and use every honorable means to secure their election.

Mr. DAVIES—I offer an amendment:

Resolved, That Ben Butler is the greatest man in the United States. [Laughter.]

Mr. ABELL—I was born close to Mr. Lincoln, though perhaps some of you didn't know it, and consider him a very honest old man. I can't say exactly whether I shall vote for him or not. I think that when elected he was a sound lawyer and a right good rail-splitter. If we have him for president and a tailor for vice-president I think that when we get them in the White House we shall have a fine family. It seems to me it will be like a man's going into a jeweller's shop, knowing nothing about the business, and undertaking to mend a watch—he will spoil the whole concern. I *rather think* I shall not vote for the resolution.

Mr. SMITH—Mr. President, I only wish to say a word. I am a mechanic myself, and I would ask the gentleman, if because Andrew Johnson was a tailor he objects to hi being nominee for president of the United States? [Tremendous applause.] I ask any man here if our institutions do not furnish such guarantees to the poor man that any of them may aspire to the highest office in this government? [Enthusiastic applause.] But, I say, that to-day the status of the Southern Confederacy is—a man is a slaveholder!

The speech was a burlesque, and I am sorry that the gentleman introduced the idea that because a man is a mechanic he is unfit to hold the highest office in this government. [Applause.] Throughout this whole session the gentleman has advocated a salary of ten thousand dollars and a life tenure for judges, simply because he is a lawyer. But I say that the most exalted office in this country is open alike to the rich and the poor—the mechanic and the lawyer—and that any man who is honest, worthy and industrious, is just as fit for it any other.

Mr. ABELL—Gentlemen see proper to reiterate the assertion used so frequently from the earlier days of our session, that we could not stay here without the military forces of the United States to protect us. I ask, then, in God's name, who are we representing? Are we representing the people of Louisiana? If they wanted us here they would let us stay here. If they don't want us here, why are we here, and who are we representing?

As far as Mr. Lincoln's administration is concerned, I believe that he has done the best he could. He is a great and noble man. He has, it is true, made some failures; but the best men make failures sometimes, and I don't know that he has made more than any other man would have made. I am opposed to the prolongation of this fratricidal war. It is continued by a set of army followers and contractors, who are enriching themselves on the blood of the people. They are the men that are howling for the war in order to increase their ill-gotten gains. If they and the politicians were out of the way, all obstacles to the termination of the contest would soon be removed and we should have peace within half a year. And for one, I will cast my vote for no man for president unles he comes with the olive branch.

If he wants more blood he cannot get my vote. I am opposed to this damnable pack of army followers, contractors and politicians who are continually crying for blood; and I shall give no vote which shall tend to assist them in carrying out their designs at the expense of the people.

You all know that I give Mr. Lincoln credit for faithfulness, and I expect he has sense. We are frequently mistaken in our estimates of others. People generally have a holy horror of the Mormons. They are believed to be the worst kind of people—thieves, murderers, and I don't know what not—but, sir, I lived among them for six years in California and found them as candid a people as the Catholics. Mr. Lincoln was mistaken in his ideas of the war when he said that he would end the war in three months. It has now been going on for three years, and who can tell us when the end will be.

I have never before heard, Mr. President, such a speech as that delivered on this floor by Col. Thorpe on Friday. I thought the speech of my friend who is in favor of the *poor man* was bad enough, but this puts that entirely in the shade. He told us that he had built six court-houses, swept out seven others, and many other things. When did he build them? Tell me and I will go and show you that he has been paid for it. I will show you his receipt for the money he got for it. Where are the wharves that he built, and the levees—where are they? I have been up and down the river and cannot find them. Where are the court-houses he built? I have seen some that have stood for half a century, but no others. What would you think of me, gentlemen, if I should stand up here and boast of work I had done for my constituents, and that they had paid me for?

If he has swept out court-houses he has been paid for it. I cannot look upon that as any evidence of extraordinary patriotism. I don't see where such a claim comes in. We are all for making all the money we can, and if the gentleman's peculiar talents enable him to make more money in sweeping out court-houses than in any other way—very well; but it does not look very well for him to lug his dirty court-houses in here, and base his claims to being a Louisianian and a patriot on his services in sweeping them out. If he has built any —and I don't believe he has—if he has renovated any, I will show you his receipt for his pay for it. He is a gentleman that has come here to build up a great State, and it must be a free State. Yes, sir, it must be a free State, regardless of the wishes of the people. He is one of those gentlemen who are willing to sacrifice every right—of his neighbor—to make Louisiana a free State. Yes, sir, these men want to strike out color from the constitution, and raise the negro—the "beloved nigger,"—to the level of the white, or to degrade the whites to the level of the negroes. They are ready, even, to blot out the judiciary to carry out their fanatic purposes. No man shall dare to give his decisions according to the laws of the land, fearlessly and without regard to their dictation, but off must come his head, and when this is the case we have no judiciary, for no man will accept a position on the bench—unless he be a servile wretch, unworthy the position—unless he enters it untrammeled, free to interpret the laws without dictation. The dignity of the position is gone when its exercise is dependent on another branch of the government, and to-day we stand without a judiciary; and, sir, if what has been done here were done within the realms of Queen Victoria, a rebellion would be the consequence. Such an act has never been known in England since the days of James II. From the commencement of the reign of James the II, dates the independence of the English judiciary; from that time to this there has never been any interference with it. I know, sir, that Gov. Hahn is a good man. I believe him to be an honest, upright and earnest man; but, sir, his zeal need not have carried him so far. There could have been no reflection upon him had he said to Judge Handlin: "You have acted honestly. I admire you for it, though I cannot agree with you." I believe you, Mr. President—I believe every honorable gentleman here—knows that the judiciary should be independent of the executive, that the judge should go on and do his duty fearlessly and faithfully, without dictation from any one. When we had military power here they did it. We had no such interference as has been witnessed here in the removal of Judge Handlin. Our civil rights were maintained. The laws were enforced through the courts. We had better return to the military power; then we should have something certain—something that we could depend on.

Do you tell us that this people is free when a judge, for deciding independently, must have his head struck off? Is that what you call freedom? If so, you have strange names for things in these times. Had I been in Judge Handlin's place I should have been bound to decide as he did—at any rate, I should have decided independently—for the constitution which you charge him with violating has not yet been made the law of the land—it is not yet adopted as a whole by this body, and after we shall have adopted it, it must, in order to be made law, be ratified by the people. Until that is done no man has a right to say that the negroes are free.

I have once remarked that I should oppose anything like politics in our discussions. I have not changed my position. I shall oppose these resolutions. I do not intend to tie myself to any man. I shall vote for the one I consider the best man, independent of every other consideration. I will stand by the rights of the people and the good of the country, as far as I understand it; and if I am wrong, God knows, I am honestly so, and, I care not what may be the consequences, I shall stand up boldly and honestly in defence of the principles I believe to be right. I intend to know what is right and to stand by it; and, sir —as I can see no reason for introducing these resolutions into this body, as I think them uncalled for and unnecessary—I shall vote against them.

[The ayes and noes were called.]

Mr. AUSTIN—Mr. President, so far as Lincoln is concerned, I shall vote for the resolution, yes; so far as Johnson is concerned, I shall vote no.

Mr. HARNAN—I move that those who are absent be brought in and required to record their votes on this question.

Mr. BAUM—I change my vote from no to yes.

[The vote resulted as follows:]

YEAS—Messrs. Austin, Barrett, Baum, Beauvais, Bell, Bennie, Burke, Cazabat, Cook J. K., Cook T., Davies, Duane, Dupaty, Edwards, Ennis, Fish, Flagg, Flood, Foley, Fuller, Geier, Gorlinski, Healy, Harnan, Henderson, Hills, Hire, Howes, Mann, Montamat, Morris, Murphy E., Murphy M. W., Newell, Normand, O'Conner, Orr, Payne J., Pintado, Poynot, Purcell J., Pursell S., Schroeder, Schnurr, Seymour, Shaw, Smith, Spellicy, Stocker, Stumpf, Stiner, Stauffer, Sullivan, Taliaferro, Terry, Thorpe, Thomas, Wenck, Wells, Wilson—60.

NAYS — Messrs. Abell, Balch, Buckley, Collin, Cutler, Decker, Dufresne, Gastinel, Gruneberg, Hart, Heard, Howell, Kavanagh, Knobloch, Maas, Maurer, Mayer, Mendiverri, Ong, Waters—20.

[The resolutions were adopted.]

Mr. MONTAMAT—I move to adjourn.

Mr. THORPE—Mr. President, and gentlemen of the Convention, I trust you will give me your attention for one moment while I offer an ordinance to send representatives to the present Congress next fall:

AN ORDINANCE TO PROVIDE FOR AN ELECTION TO FILL VACANCIES IN THE REPRESENTATION OF THE STATE OF LOUISIANA IN THE XXXVIIITH CONGRESS.

Section 1. *Be it ordained by the people of the State of Louisiana in Convention assembled*, That an election shall be held by the qualified electors of the State of Louisiana on the first Monday of September, 1864, for representatives in the Congress of the United States of America, to fill the vacancies now existing in the XXXVIIIth Congress, and to serve until the end of the term of the said Congress.

Sec. 2. *Be it further ordained*, That until otherwise directed by law the State shall be divided into five Congressional Districts as follows, and the qualified electors of each District shall choose one representative:

The First Congressional District shall comprise the parishes of St. Bernard and Plaquemines, the right bank of the parish of Orleans, the Ninth, Eighth, Seventh, Sixth, Fifth Representatives Districts of the parish of Orleans, and that portion of the Fourth Representative District of the parish of Orleans which is included between St. Louis, Rampart and Canal streets, and the Lake Pontchartrain.

The Second Congressional District shall comprise that portion of the Fourth Representative District of the parish of Orleans, which is included between St. Louis, Rampart and Canal streets and the Mississippi river; the Third, Second and First Representative Districts of the parish of Orleans, and that portion of the Tenth Representative District of the parish of Orleans which is known and designated by existing statutes as the Tenth Ward of the city of New Orleans.

The Third Congressional District shall comprise that part of the Tenth Representative District of the parish of Orleans which is known and designated as the Eleventh Ward of the city of New Orleans; and the parishes of Jefferson, Washington, St. Tammany, St. Helena, Livingston, St. Charles, St. John the Baptist, St. James, Ascension, East Baton Rouge, East Feliciana, West Feliciana, Terrebonne and Lafourche.

The Fourth Congressional District shall comprise the parishes of Natchitoches, Sabine, Rapides, Calcasieu, St. Landry, Vermillion, Avoyelles, Point Coupée, Lafayette, St. Martin, West Baton Rouge, Iberville, Assumption and St. Mary.

The Fifth Congressional District shall comprise the parishes of Bossier, Claiborne, Union, Morehouse, Carroll, Bienville, Jackson, Ouachita, Caldwell, Franklin, Madison, Tensas, Concordia, Catahoula, Winn, Caddo and DeSoto.

Sec. 3. *Be it further ordained*, That the several officers of the State, authorized by law to hold elections, or in default thereof, such officers as the governor shall designate or authorize, shall open and hold polls in the several congressional districts of the State, to choose representatives as aforesaid. At the conclusion of the said election, the officers and commissioners presiding over the same shall carefully examine and count each ballot as deposited, and shall forthwith make due return thereof to the secretary of state in conformity to the provisions of law and usages in regard to elections.

Sec. 4. *Be it further ordained*, That upon the receipt of said returns, or on the third Monday of September, if the returns be not sooner received, it shall be the duty of the governor, jointly with the secretary of state and the judge of one of the district courts of the State, in the presence of all such persons as may choose to attend, to proceed to ascertain from the said returns, the persons duly elected, a certificate of which shall be entered on record by the secretary of state, and signed by the governor, and a copy thereof, subscribed as aforesaid, shall be delivered to the person so elected, and another copy transmitted to the House of Representatives of the Congress of the United States, directed to the speaker thereof.

Sec. 5. *Be it furth r ordained*, That this ordinance shall be in force and take effect from and after its passage, and shall have the force and effect of a statue of the State.

Done in Convention, at the city of New Orleans, on the —— day of July, 1864.

Mr. MONTAMAT—I move it be printed and laid over till next Wednesday.

[The motion was carried.]

Mr. ABELL—I move to adjourn till next Wednesday.

[The motion was carried and the Convention adjourned.]

WEDNESDAY, July 20, 1864.

[The Convention met pursuant to adjournment. Present, the Hon. E. H. Durell, president, and the following members :]

Messrs. Abell, Austin, Barrett, Baum, Beanvais, Bell, Bennie, Bofill, Buckley, Burke, Collin, Cazabat, Cook J. K., Cook T., Crozat, Cutler, Decker, Duane, Dufresne, Dupaty, Edwards, Ennis, Fish, Flagg, Flood, Foley, Fuller, Gastinel, Geier, Gorlinski, Gruneberg, Gaidry, Healy, Harnan, Hart, Heard, Henderson, Hills, Hire, Howell, Howes, Kavanagh, Knobloch, Kugler, Maas, Mann, Maurer, Mendiverri, Montamat, Morris, Murphy E., Murphy M. W., Newell, Normand, O'Conner, Ong, Orr, Payne J., Pintado, Poynot, Purcell J., Pursell S., Schroeder, Schnurr, Seymour, Shaw, Smith, Spellicy, Stocker, Stumpf, Stiner, Stauffer, Sullivan, Taliaferro, Terry, Thorpe, Thomas, Waters, Wenck, Wells, Wilson—82.

[The minutes of last Monday's proceedings were read and adopted.]

Mr. CAZABAT—Mr. President, I wish to offer a resolution. That we proceed at once to adopt the constitution as a whole, without any argument, or the introduction of any subject which is not connected with the adoption of the Constitution, as a whole.

Mr. ABELL—I am opposed to that.

Mr. SULLIVAN—There are several inaccuracies in it.

PRESIDENT—Out of order. The Convention has decided that the matter should be deferred till Thursday next.

Mr. TERRY—I move a reconsideration.

Mr. MONTAMAT—I move to lay that motion on the table.

PRESIDENT—The order of the day—report of the special Committee on Currency.

Mr. SMITH—The committee is ready to report, Mr. President. The secretary has the report.

[The secretary read :]

To the honorable president and members of the Constitutional Convention of Louisiana :

GENTLEMEN — The undersigned, a committee appointed by your honorable body for the purpose of taking into consideration the propriety of providing for the redemption of a worthless paper currency, issued and forced upon the poor and only loyal class of the population of Louisiana since the outbreak of the rebellion, by private individuals, as well as by corporations and parochial authorities in the different sections and localities of the State, most respectfully beg leave to report that we have duly weighed the subject matter contained in the resolution submitted to our consideration, and, being fully convinced that some action should be taken in the matter by this Convention, beg leave to offer the following article as the result of our deliberations, to be incorporated as one of the ordinances of the constitution :

Art. —. That the property of all individuals, firms and companies, the taxable property situated in all villages, towns, cities and parishes, shall be liable and held responsible for the redemption in current funds of the United States, for all notes issued as a circulating medium during the present rebellion, to the extent of the amount issued by such individual, firm, company, village, town, city or parish respectively, recoverable before any court of competent jurisdiction, in due process of law.

CHARLES SMITH,
JOS. H. BALCH,
O. H. POYNOT,
TERENCE COOK,
P. K. O'CONNER.

Mr. SMITH—I wish gentlemen to understand that I do not own one dollar of that money.

Mr. BURKE—I understood you had twenty-five thousand dollars of it.

Mr. SMITH—I would ask the gentleman who issued this money ?

Mr. BURKE — Rebels, sir ; four or five rebels.

Mr. SMITH—Who has it now ?

Mr. BURKE—Rebels.

Mr. SMITH—Then the parish of St. John

the Baptist is an exception to the other parishes of the State. In every other parish of this State the money is in the hands of poor people. The money was not issued for the purpose of aiding the rebellion. The people would not take Confederate money and this was issued to take its place. They took it because they knew the parties who issued it were responsible, and they supposed their property would be bond for it. Now most of the money is in the hands of these poor people—artizans and mechanics—and having given value received for it, they ought to have some remedy against the parties who issued it, and who by refusing to redeem it have made a great many thousands of dollars themselves. There may be ten or fifteen thousand dollars of this money in the hands of parties in New Orleans.

Mr. BURKE—The money is in New Orleans. That raised in St. John the Baptiste was raised to clothe, arm and equip rebel soldiers. That is what it was issued for, and that is what was done with it.

Mr. SMITH—If there are a few thousand here, that signifies nothing. There is no question in my mind that the poor men who have given a fair equivalent should have their pay ; and even if the rebels, who issued the money and got an equivalent for it, should have to pay a few thousand to speculators or bankers in New Orleans, I don't know that any particular harm would be done by it. I don't know as there would be any harm in taking a few thousands from the rebels who have made largely by refusing to redeem it, and giving it to speculators who hold their promises to pay. Now they own property enough, but you ask one of them to redeem one of those notes and he will laugh at you.

Mr. MONTAMAT—Mr. President, I believe that rich people in New Orleans have got all this money. I see it spread out in all the shop windows of the brokers and Jews all over town. I don't know how it come there, but I see it there.

Mr. BURKE—I can tell you how it came there. It was brought down here and sold to uniform and equip rebels to meet General Butler when he was advancing on New Orleans. Soldiers from St. John were uniformed and equipped with the money so raised, and so were soldiers from other parishes. Then it was issued against the wishes of the people and without their knowledge, by some four or five men, and I don't believe that there are two loyal men in this house that will vote in favor of the report. The stuff is spurious any how, and the rebels want us to sustain the report so that they can make something out of what they have on hand—but it is worthless, and let us wipe it out entirely.

Mr. CUTLER—I wish to inquire for information before I cast my vote on this question. I am disposed to do something if it is poor men who are to receive this money, but I must say that without further explanation from the learned chairman of the committee who made this report, it will be impossible for me to cast my vote for it. Let me call the attention of the gentleman to an article of our constitution already adopted. He will find by reading article 129, that "no liability, either parochial, State or municipal, shall exist for any debts contracted for, or in the interest of the rebellion against the United States government."

Now, having adopted that article of the constitution, we cannot adopt this report. We have prohibited ourselves from taking any such action, for it is clearly in conflict with the constitutional provision. This is why I ask the information. I wonder that so learned and intelligent a gentleman as the member from St. Mary's should bring in a report in conflict with another portion of our work ; and if it is not in conflict with that article, I would like to vote for it, or if the gentleman will make a report in harmony with that article, I will cheerfully vote for it.

Mr. ABELL—Mr. President, I do not attach as much importance to this matter as my friend from St. Mary's, (Mr. Smith) does. I do not consider it as important a matter by any means as the matter which you have already acted upon on this floor, in which you have taken millions of property from loyal citizens in these hard times, without making them any compensation whatever. I think, sir, we should reject this matter without any disagreeable compunctions at all; let it go as one of the necessary evils of the state into which we are thrown by the war.

Mr. SMITH—I wish to state what I know relative to the parish of St. Mary, and I presume what is true of St. Mary is true of most, if not all the other parishes where this money was issued. Men who were loyal never issued any of this money. Point me out a parish where the police jury were loyal and I will point you to a parish that issued no money. No, sir, in a parish that issued money, you cannot point me to a police juror who was in favor of the United States. The laborers and mechanics were not willing to trust the Confederacy; they would not take Confederate notes. They had no faith in them, and it was in consequence of this fact that the parishes and individuals issued money to meet the local demand. The people accepted this paper the more readily because they knew it was issued by responsible parties—by parties who had property with which to redeem it. They preferred something with a tangible and visible basis to Confederate notes, and it is these laboring men—these loyal mechanics and laborers on whom the loss must fall, if no provision is made to enable them to realize the amount of their claims out of the property on the credit of which they accepted the stuff. These men must be punished for their loyalty unless you enable them to reach this property by such a provision as is proposed. The greater part of this money—seven-eighths of it at least—is now in the hands of these poor men. What matters it if a small portion of it is in the hands of Jews and speculators, justice demands that these laborers shall be paid their hire; and what harm will it be if a few Jews and speculators should make something by it, would the money be any the less good to the nation in their hands than in the hands of rebels who should be forced to pay these claims for which they have already got value received. I hope, sir, this resolution will pass, and I think every truly loyal man ought to vote for it.

[A rising vote was taken on the motion to reject; yeas 40, nays 20. The article was rejected.]

Mr. CUTLER—I have a resolution designed to do justice to one portion of the employees of this Convention, and in offering it it pleases me to bear testimony to the efficiency, promptness and faithfulness of the officers to whom it refers. I think it but just and right, sir, as it is consistent with long established custom, where the officers of a body like this, are efficient and faithful, to manifest our appreciation of their services by granting them an additional pecuniary compensation as an acknowledgment on our part of our appreciation of their services, and in offering this I mean no disparagement to the other departments, all of which have, so far as I am able to testify, performed their duties faithfully, and ought and probably will receive similar tokens of our appreciation of their services, all in due time.

The resolution is this:

Resolved, That the sum of one thousand dollars be and the same is hereby appropriated out of any moneys in the treasury of the State, not otherwise appropriated, for the purpose of paying the secretary of this Convention and his two assistants, for extra services rendered this Convention, and that the same be paid on their own warrants, as follows: To John E. Neelis, secretary, five hundred dollars; to S. G. Hamilton and Phillip Winfree, assistant secretaries, two hundred and fifty dollars each.

Mr. MONTAMAT—I move to amend by adding the following:

Be it further resolved, That the sum of two hundred and fifty dollars be and is hereby appropriated from the general funds in the State treasury, not otherwise appropriated, to L. O. Maureau, warrant clerk, payable on his own warrant, as extra compensation for extra services rendered.

Mr. CUTLER—I accept the amendment.

Mr. WATERS—I move to lay it on the table.

[The motion to table was lost and the resolution adopted.]

Mr. HENDERSON—I move to suspend the rules in order to act upon a motion to reconsider our vote on letting the final action on the constitution lie over until Thursday. I think we had better get through with our work at once, and the action can be taken to-day as well as at any subsequent time.

[A motion to lay the motion of Mr. Henderson was made, and on putting the question the chair decided it carried, whereupon a division was called when it appeared that the motion to table was lost—36 members voting yea, and 42 no.]

Mr. ABELL—Gentlemen are preparing some riders, I have no doubt, and are not ready to take up the matter to-day. You have promised once, by your votes, to let the subject lie over till Thursday, and you now propose to take us by surprise, by forcing us to a vote at once. For my own part I don't propose to offer any riders. I have not a single one to propose nor do I propose to raise a single objection, but I think it is but due to common justice that you should let the matter lie over as you have promised to do, till Thursday, to give those who propose to offer riders, the opportunity which you have promised they should have. I believe such a mode would be more satisfactory than any other that can be adopted, and hope it will prevail.

Mr. CUTLER—Mr. President, I have a remark or two to make on this question. I never have, nor do I ever expect to be, with the minority of this Convention in regard to the adoption of this constitution. I am in favor of its adoption. But I think it to be only fairness that inasmuch as on last Monday it was made the special order of the day for Thursday, and this day was set apart for the consideration of Col. Thorpe's resolution in regard to districting the State, that we should take up that bill. It is now half-past one o'clock, and if we should take up the constitution to-day, we cannot go through with it, though I believe we should not require more than a day to do so, if we wait till the time we have already fixed for it.

Now I do not believe in favoring majorities simply because they are majorities, nor do I believe in opposing minorities, and as we have fixed to-morrow as the day on which we will take it up, I think it is but due to the minority that we abide by our previous action, and wait till that time before we take it up. I think such a course will be more satisfactory to all parties, and there can surely nothing be gained by pursuing a different course.

Mr. HENDERSON—Mr. President, the question of adopting this constitution is of more importance than the consideration of sending members to Congress; for without it, we can have no members to Congress. The question of re-districting the State, &c., can be disposed of in a very few minutes, but after this Convention has had a whole day in which to carefully investigate this constitution as amended, it would be better to take it up at once and adopt it as a whole without taking it up section by section.

The last proclamation of President Lincoln has been misunderstood by some members of this body, who think he says: "Come into the Union with or without slavery." He does not say any such thing, but is misunderstood, and that to-day is our time of action. Every question has been discussed and passed its third reading and we have now come to a final action. Errors have been pointed out by the committee and corrected. Of course, my friend on my right, (Mr. Abell), sees errors from Alpha to Omega, for he cannot agree with this constitution any way. Why does he seek to postpone action now? Because he is for slavery, come weal or woe. The language of the gentleman on my left, (Mr. Cutler,) in regard to offering riders, &c., does not show any ground for postponement, and I submit, as a matter of policy, that unless this constitution is at once adopted as a whole, we shall have the constitution of 1852 at last, and not that of 1864. Get through with this and then bring up the ordinance.

Certain officers who have control of the treasury have something to say. Having finished the constitution, our sitting here longer is attended with great expenditure. We have now nothing else to do but to approve or disapprove it as a whole. In regard to the matter relating to contracts of the corporation of New Orleans, let that be brought up and decided upon at once.

Mr. ABELL—Mr. President and gentlemen, I certainly have no right to oppose this matter. The gentleman, (Mr. Henderson,) has seven amendments to offer, but I have none and don't expect to have any. Still I think that in fairness we should have an opportunity to consider of this report. I say also that the language of the president's last proclamation requires consideration, and that if we adopt it we had better dissolve. But we are an assemblage of the people of the State, as far as the Federal arms have gone, and in the making of the organic laws of the State are independent of the president. We have made a constitution, some parts of which have been framed in haste, which the committee have examined and corrected—requiring a week in which to do so—so that it is not unreasonable for us to ask for two days in which to weigh over the whole as revised.

[Motion to lay on the table the motion for reconsideration lost.]

Mr. Abell—I move to amend by inserting in the following section "fourth" after "fifth," and striking out all after "Orleans."

Sec. 2. *Be it further ordained*, That until otherwise directed by law the State shall be divided into five congressional districts as follows, and the qualified electors of each district shall choose one representative:

The First Congressional District shall comprise the parishes of St. Bernard and Plaquemines, the right bank of the parish of Orleans, the Ninth, Eighth, Seventh, Sixth, Fifth Representative Districts of the parish of Orleans, and that portion of the Fourth Representative District of the parish of Orleans which is included between St. Louis, Rampart and Canal streets, and the Lake Pontchartrain.

Mr. Cazabat—I move that be laid on the table.

[Motion carried on rising vote—yeas 44, nays 33.]

Mr. Howell—Mr. President, it is a part of my nature to reverence law, and not only to reverence and respect it, but to obey it. Whenever a law is once established by the people, whether it be a bad or a good law, it is a part of the duty of every good citizen to obey that law until it is amended or repealed. It is that principle, sir, that has always guided my actions during my whole life since I have arrived at the age of discretion. Whatever may be the opinion of individuals, I profess, sir, to be guided by that principle in all cases. It has been the rule of my action in this Convention, and so long as my reason is spared, shall ever be the rule of my action. Upon that principle I now rest my views against this ordinance. [Applause.]

Whatever may be the consequences to my individual person for the expression of my sentiments or the casting of my votes here, I claim the right to express my views and give my votes, and I am willing to take the consequences. I willingly leave the judgment of my conduct to my fellow-citizens and posterity. I care not for the expressions private or public that may be made, I care not for the vindictive charges that may be made, I shall pursue the even tenor of my course, guided by my own convictions.

Now, sir, as the reason of my opposition to this ordinance, let me call the attention of this Convention to a document which I presume is not yet abrogated—is not yet obsolete, and which is the highest authority in this government, the highest authority on this earth, to sustain which is this mighty struggle carried on. It is, sir, for the protection of this constitution of the United States that the army of the country is fighting. Section 4 reads: "The times, places and manner of holding elections for senators and representatives, shall be prescribed in each State by the Legislature thereof." That is an article in the constitution of the United States, and I presume this Convention does not contend it is either amended or abrogated. Every man here is under a solemn and specific oath to support the constitution of the United States. This ordinance professes to fix the time for holding the election for representatives to Congress. The question is: are we the Legislature of Louisiana? [Cries of "no, no."] Is it properly within our province? I trust a majority will answer no on the question of the adoption of this ordinance.

Mr. Thomas—Mr. President, this is a question in which I have always felt the deepest interest, and it is one, sir, that much affects the people of Louisiana. It is of the most vital importance that we should be recognized and represented in the Congress of this nation if we intend to remain a part and parcel of this great government. [Applause.] In 1862, the then military governor of this State, could call an election for representatives to the Congress of the United States, but in 1863 that call was not made, and to-day with all our power, with the loyalty that Louisiana has shown to the Union, we are without any representation in Congress, and the people of the North do not yet know, in the mass, whether we have any districts in Louisiana that are strictly loyal to the government. I know these things. I have seen them and told them in the past two months. On many occasions and by many prominent men holding high positions in the government, I have been asked: "Why are you not represented in Congress? Is it because you have no loyal men?" I said no, but the masses could not understand and fully appreciate that. This is a question therefore that demands our most serious consideration. If we have the power and right to say that an election shall soon be held, that we, representing the people of Louisiana, shall have our representatives in the Congress of the United States, I say in the name of God let us do it! [Applause.]

Let us have our men there that will advocate the interests of Louisiana. The question, then, is confined to this: have we a right to divide the State of Louisiana into electoral districts and order an election? There is but one law that forbids it, and that is the one quoted by the gentleman who has just addressed the Convention. In the constitution of the United States the word "Legislature" is used. Have we power to perform the functions of the Legislature? Can we enact a law? If not, then, gentlemen, I tell you, nine-tenths of your labor here is all in vain. If you come to any other conclusion, what becomes of the ordinance of emancipation? What becomes of all the laws we have enacted if they have not the force of laws? For one, I believe that the Convention can exercise any power which a Legislature might. I believe we may enact any law that any Legislature could enact, over and above the constitution. Why, sir, is not that authority—is not the lesser included in the greater? We have come here, delegated by the people, to make the fundamental law; and can we not pass an ordinary statute and provide what the law shall be until the Legislature otherwise provides? Most clearly we can, to my mind, and have the right. As to the remarks that have been made by the last gentleman on the floor, that the law should be reverenced and respected until it is changed, let me say to the gentleman who utters such sentiments, that no man has a higher regard for the law than he who now addresses this Convention. I know that, in these times, there are many words and phrases in the constitution of the United States, which were written and placed there, that might have been more explicit. It is only that the Legislature of the State may provide the times and places for the election of senators and representatives. It might have gone on and said a Convention of the people, and it has never been denied. It cannot be successfully controverted that the people, in their majesty and might, in Convention assembled as we are, have a right to pass any law they choose. We are legally here to enact the law of the land, and we are the people themselves, and every act we do is the act of the people themselves. Then why, I ask, have we not the authority? I say we have, and let us use it. Let Louisiana send some good men to the Congress of the United States, who may attend to her interests. She has many interests, and, if we sit here idle without any exertion, we shall soon be left out and all we have done here will be ignored. If we study our own interests, let us have a representation in Congress at its next meeting; and let Louisiana cast her vote for president, and come back and become, as she rightfully belongs, one of that bright galaxy of the stars of the Union.

Mr. Cazabat—Mr. President: I have uniformly expressed and entertained the opinion that the powers of this Convention are limited, because it was convened for the sole and exclusive purpose of amending and revising the constitution of Louisiana.

I am therefore inclined to conclude that the view taken by Judge Howell in regard to this question is correct and proper. But this question is one of great import, and as we have no Legislature in session at present, the proposed ordinance becomes a matter of necessity and policy; otherwise we must be deprived and prevented from sending senators and representatives to the next national Congress.

Section 4, article 1, of the constitution of the United States, conceded to be the supreme law of the land, declares that "*the times, places, and manner of holding elections for senators and representatives shall be prescribed in each State by the Legislature thereof*," &c.

But you will admit that the anomalous condition of affairs produced in this country by the rebellion, never was contemplated or provided for by the wise minds who framed that Constitution.

This Convention can be considered to all intents and purposes the Legislature, or law making power of the State ; nay more, it is the creating power that brings the Legislature into existence, and if the Legislature, the mere creature of the Convention, is empowered to provide for elections to Congress, is not the same power and authority granted by implication to this Convention.

In my humble opinion it becomes the duty and right of this body, under the circumstances, to proceed in this matter, and take the necessary steps to secure, if possible, the State representation in the next Congress, in order to let Louisiana resume her place into the Union, as "*the first returning State, whose voice is Liberty*," If this measure is adopted, it will no doubt be sanctioned and cheerfully approved by all loyal citizens; if, on the contrary, it is rejected and defeated, it will give the utmost encouragement and satisfaction to the spirit of opposition that seems to prevail here and elsewhere.

Mr. Durell—Mr. President and gentlemen of the Convention, I will not detain you long. I merely wish to answer in a few words, the argument of my most learned friend on the left, (Mr. Howell,) who holds a judicial position, and what he says carries great weight with it. The gentleman has read a clause from the constitution of the United States which says that the time, place and manner of holding the elections for senators and represntatives shall be prescribed in each State by the Legislature thereof. Now, what is the meaning of the word "Legislature ?" It is the law-making power for the time being—nothing else. [Applause.] I would ask the gentleman if we have a Legislature—if we are not now coming back to our normal state and to the Union—if we are not re-creating the State of Louisiana ? I would ask that gentleman if, when a territory passess from its territorial condition into the full grown condition of a State, the constitutional assembly called together to represent the people in their majesty, to form a constitution for the future State, does not at the same time determine when the representatives shall be elected and when the Legislature shall come together and when it shall elect senators of the U- S.? If it has not been the case even before the Legislature has assembled in a new State, that the constitution of that State was accepted by the government of the United States on one day and two senators representing the new State entered the senatorial chamber on the next ? Let us then not deceive ourselves ; let us take the word according to its meaning. It means that we have the power to determine the time, when and where the senators and representatives shall be elected. No one can misunderstand that ; a child can comprehend it. The principle laid down by the gentleman would ignore the action of the Senate in regard to three-fourths of the territories which have been erected into States, since the first adoption of the constitution. The gentleman could have given it small consideration when he made the remark. This Convention represents the people and is the highest legislative body that can meet together upon the soil of Louisiana. It has the power, in as far as it keeps within a true republican form of government as secured by the constitution, to do just what it pleases. It is answerable for it merely in the individual capacity of its members when it dissolves and they go back to the people.

Mr. Henderson — Mr. President, the learned gentleman who has just spoken, has very appropriately and truly said, that States have been admitted into the Union one day and the next day senators have taken their seats. I will tell my friend, Mr. Howell, of a stronger case. The State of Iowa asked for admission into the Union, and her senators and representatives were received before the constitution was placed before the people for ratification. That constitution was rejected, but the senators retained their seats.

In regard to the language of the constitution, the time, place and manner of holding elections are three distinct things; and when the question came up before Congress whether a State could divide itself into districts, it was discussed and admitted that the division into districts had nothing to do with time, place or manner, and was a matter to be left with the State. As respects our action here on these matters, no objection was made to that upon the Baltimore Convention. It was considered a political necessity, because we had no Legislature and the delegates were received from the Convention not from the Legislature. I maintain we have a right to insert this ordinance for the time being; there being no Legislature we take its place, and this is the doctrine of Gov. Hahn and Gen. Banks.

Mr. SHAW—I believe if this bill is passed, it should not be passed to-day, but should be well examined. We can take it up at any time when the House is not ready to act upon any other matter.

The argument, thus far, has been principally in regard to the *power* of this body to pass this bill, as it has been contended that under the constitution of the United States, only the Legislature has power to fix the time, place, &c.. of election to Congress. We must go back and ascertain what is the meaning, technical and legal, of the term "Legislature." The House and Senate do not constitute, alone, the Legislature, but the concurrence of the executive is necessary, except after a veto by the latter. The constitution of the United States does not fix what shall be the form of the legislative body, and therefore we can adopt any that we please, as long as we adhere to a republican form of government. No General Assembly is in existence in this State, and we must take such an interpretation of the word "Legislature," as will, in all probability, meet the intention of the framers of the constitution. That, as our learned president has said, means the law-making power of the State for the time being, which happens to be now the Convention of Louisiana. Certainly we can postpone it. I do not consider it of such wonderful moment whether we do it now, but yet, as in regard to any other good thing, there is no use of postponing it.

This brings us to consider the powers of this Convention, and to the question, whether, because in the order calling this Convention, certain reasons were given for doing so, our authority is thereby limited? I contend that when we were called together—no matter how or by whom—we were elected by the people of Louisiana and are a Convention with all the powers of a representative body. Because the order stated that we were called to revise and amend the constitution of Louisiana, we are not the less the representatives of the people of this State, and we must find our powers in what the conventions of the people have formerly done. Now, sir, they have in a multitude of cases, acted upon their inherent legislative power as subordinate to the power of making a constitution. If a convention has the right to make a constitution, has it not much more the lesser right of passing a statute? A constitution, when ratified, is irrepealable, except in a certain form, whereas a statute can be repealed by a Legislature three months afterwards. I undertake to say, that few conventions have sat in the United States which have not, in one form or another, exercised this inherent legislative power. So much for the *right* of this Convention to pass the ordinance in question.

I claim that the question is not in relation to this, but in regard to the amendment which has been offered. Mr. Abell desires that the whole of the Fourth Representative District shall be included in the First Representative District, as was formerly the case. In 1851 Louisiana was divided into four congressional districts, but under the apportionment made by Congress in 1861 it was enacted that the State of Louisiana should have five. Is it any reason that because Louisiana is entitled to five districts that the district of the gentleman (Mr. Abell) is to be entitled to the same territorial extent before? Is one-fifth to be as large as one-fourth?

Mr. Abell—Another parish, as I understand, belonged to our district, and, if so, the cutting of it off would be curtailing it illiberally.

Mr. Shaw—Instead of curtailing your rights this is in fact increasing them. The greater the territorial extent of a congressional district, the greater will be its population and number of voters, and the less the power and representation of each individual voter. But the gentleman is mistaken. No parish has been cut off; only such portion of the Fourth (State) Representative District as was necessary to equalize the population.

Mr. Cutler—Mr. President and gentlemen, this matter is one of serious importance, in my opinion, and deserves the careful consideration of every member of this Convention. I do not know but that I shall vote for the entire bill; I do not know but that I shall vote against it; at any rate I want time to consider it, as every member of this Convention must, to compare votes, lines, &c., and see where we stand. Under these circumstances, I suggest—that it would be justice towards all of us, to allow time for consideration that we may not vote hastily—that we postpone —not until to-morrow, because then comes up the adoption of the constitution as a whole—but until Saturday next; I therefore now make that motion.

Mr. Montamat—Mr. President and gentlemen, I am in favor of this ordinance; for, although some gentlemen say that we have no right to legislate, I contend that we have and have already done so. I, for my part, want to see Louisiana represented in the next Congress; we of the First District mean to run my friend, (Mr. Abell) and elect him too, to protect the interests of Louisiana and have the owners of slaves compensated. [Applause.]

[Mr. Cutler's motion was carried.]

Mr. Beauvais—I move we adjourn to 12 m. of Thursday, the 21st inst.

[The motion was carried.]

Thursday, July 21, 1864.

[The Convention met pursuant to adjournment, and was called to order by the president. The secretary called the roll and the following members answered to their names:]

Messrs.—Abell, Austin, Barrett, Baum, Beauvais, Bell, Bennie, Bofill, Buckley, Burke, Campbell, Collin, Cazabat, Cook J. K., Cook T., Crozat, Cutler, Davies, Decker, Duane, Dufresne, Dupaty, Edwards, Ennis, Fish, Flagg, Flood, Foley, Fosdick, Fuller, Gastinel, Geier, Gorlinski, Gruneberg, Gaidry, Healy, Harnan, Hart, Heard, Henderson, Hills, Hire, Howell, Howes, Kavanagh, Knobloch, Kugler, Maas, Mann, Maurer, Mayer, Mendiverri, Montamat, Morris, Murphy E., Murphy M. W., Newell, Normand, O'Conner, Ong, Orr, Payne J., Pintado, Poynot, Purcell J., Pursell S., Schroeder, Schnurr, Seymour, Shaw, Smith, Spellicy, Stocker, Stumpf, Stiner, Stauffer, Sullivan, Taliaferro, Terry, Thorpe, Thomas, Waters, Wenck, Wells, Wilson—86.

[The minutes of yesterday's proceedings were read and adopted.]

President—The order of the day is the constitution as reported by the Committee on Arrangement. The secretary will read it, pausing at the close of each article to give gentlemen an opportunity for any riders which they may propose to offer.

[The secretary read the preamble, viz:]

We, the people of the State of Louisiana, do ordain and establish this constitution.

Mr. Henderson—I offer the following as a substitute. I merely desire to insert the boundaries of the State:

We, the representatives of the people of the State of Louisiana in Convention assembled, do define the boundaries of said State to be as follows: Beginning at the mouth of the river Sabine, thence by a line to be drawn along the middle of said river, including all its islands, to the thirty-second degree of latitude, thence due north to the northernmost part of the thirty-third degree of north latitude; thence along the said parallel of latitude to the river Mississippi; thence down the said river to the river Iberville and from thence along the middle of said river and Lakes Maurapas and Pontchartrain to the Gulf of Mexico; thence bounded by the said Gulf to the place of beginning, including all islands within three leagues of the coast—and do ordain and establish this constitution.

Mr. Beauvais—Mr. President, I rise to a point of order; in my opinion it is too late now to offer any changes, as I understand a committee was appointed not for the purpose of making any changes in the constitution, but of fixing the different articles under their proper titles. Now, sir, under our rules, we have decided to adopt or we have adopted the different parts of the constitution, and I think it too late now to alter or change it. We must either adopt or reject it as it now stands, and although I would be glad to change some parts of it, I do not think we have a right at this stage of the proceedings to open up questions that have been settled under the rules we have adopted after long and tedious debate. If we do this I see no prospect of our adjournment for the next two months.

PRESIDENT—The gentleman's remarks are addressed to the good sense of this Convention. But he is wrong in supposing that it is too late now to take any other action than to adopt or reject as a whole. It is customary to amend by way of a rider until the last moment, and if the Convention shall choose to sit here for two or four months it is their right to do so, and neither you nor I can help it.

Mr. BAUM—I move its rejection.

Mr. CUTLER—Mr. President——

Mr. HILLS—I move the previous question.

[The motion was carried and the substitute of Mr. Henderson rejected.

Articles 1 to 6 inclusive, were read and adopted, without amendment or debate.

The secretary read :]

Art. 7. Representatives shall be chosen on the first Monday in November every two years, and the election shall be completed in one day. The General Assembly shall meet annually on the first Monday in January, unless a different day be appointed by law, and their sessions shall be held at the seat of government. There shall also be a session of the General Assembly in the city of New Orleans, beginning on the first Monday of October, eighteen hundred and sixty-four; and it shall be the duty of the governor to cause a special election to be held for members of the General Assembly, in all the parishes where the same may be held with safety to the electors, on the day of the election for ratification or rejection of this constitution—to be valid in case of ratification; and in other parishes or districts he shall cause elections to be held as soon as it may become practicable, to fill the vacancies for such parishes or districts in the General Assembly. The term of office of the first General Assembly shall expire as though its members had been elected on the first Monday of November, eighteen hundred and sixty-three.

Mr. CUTLER — I desire to propose an amendment. I think it improper to allude to the war or rebellion in the constitution, and therefore move to strike out "with safety to the electors."

Mr. SHAW—I second the motion.

[The motion was carried.

Articles 8, 9, 10 and 11, were adopted without amendment or debate.]

Art. 12. Until an apportionment shall be made, and elections held under the same, in accordance with the first enumeration to be made, as directed in article 10, the representation in the Senate and House of Representatives shall be as follows :

For the parish of Orleans, forty-four representatives, to be elected as follows :

First Representative District		3
Second	do.	5
Third	do.	7
Fourth	do.	3
Fifth	do.	4
Sixth	do.	2
Seventh	do.	3
Eighth	do.	3
Ninth	do.	4
Tenth	do.	8
Orleans, Right Bank		2
For the parish of Livingston		1
do.	St. Tammany	1
do.	Pointe Coupée	1
do.	St. Martin	2
do.	Concordia	1
do.	Madison	1
do.	Franklin	1
do.	St. Mary	1
do.	Jefferson	3
do.	Plaquemines	1
do.	St. Bernard	1
do.	St. Charles	1
do.	St. John the Baptiste	1
do.	St. James	1
do.	Ascension	1
do.	Assumption	3
do.	Lafourche	3
do.	Terrebonne	2
do.	Iberville	1
do.	West Baton Rouge	1
do.	East Baton Rouge	2
do.	West Feliciana	1
do.	East Feliciana	1
do.	St. Helena	1
do.	Washington	1
do.	Vermillion	1
do.	Lafayette	2
do.	St. Landry	4
do.	Calcasieu	2
do.	Avoyelles	2
do.	Rapides	3
do.	Natchitoches	2
do.	Sabine	1
do.	Caddo	2
do.	De Soto	2

For the Parish of	Ouachita	1
do.	Union	2
do.	Morehouse	1
do.	Jackson	2
do.	Caldwell	1
do.	Catahoula	2
do.	Claiborne	3
do.	Bossier	1
do.	Bienville	2
do.	Carroll	1
do.	Tensas	1
do.	Winn	2
Total		118

And the State shall be divided into the following senatorial districis: All that portion of the parish of Orleans lying on the left bank of the Mississippi river shall be divided into two senatorial districts; the First and Fourth Districts of the city of New Orleans shall compose one district, and shall elect four senators; and the Second and Third Districts of said city shall compose the other district, and shall elect three senators.

The parishes of Plaquemines, St. Bernard and all that part of the parish of Orleans on the right bank of the Mississippi river shall form one district, and shall elect one senator.

The parish of Jefferson shall form one district, and shall elect one senator.

The parishes of St. Charles and Lafourche shall form one district, and shall elect one senator.

The parishes of St. John the Baptist and St. James shall form one district, and shall elect one senator.

The parishes of Ascension, Assumption and Terrebonne shall form one district, and shall elect two senators.

The parish of Iberville shall form one district, and shall elect one senator.

The parish of East Baton Rouge shall form one district, and shall elect one senator.

The parishes of West Baton Rouge, Point Coupée, and West Feliciana shall form one district, and shall elect two senators.

The parish of East Feliciana shall form one district, and shall elect one senator.

The parishes of Washington, St. Tammany, St. Helena and Livingston shall form one district and shall elect one senator.

The parishes of Concordia and Tensas shall form one district, and shall elect one senator.

The parishes of Madison and Carroll shall form one district, and shall elect one senator.

The parishes of Morehouse, Ouachita, Union and Jackson shall form one district, and shall elect two senators.

The parishes of Catahoula, Caldwell and Franklin shall form one district, and shall elect one senator.

The parishes of Bossier, Bienville, Claiborne and Winn shall form one district, and shall elect two senators.

The parishes of Natchitoches, Sabine, DeSoto and Caddo shall form one district, and shall elect two senators.

The parishes of St. Landry, Lafayette and Calcasieu shall form one district, and shall elect two senators.

The parishes of St. Martin and Vermillion shall form one district, and shall elect one senator.

The parish of St. Mary shall form one district, and shall elect one senator.

The parishes of Rapides and Avoyelles shall form one district, and shall elect two senators.

Mr. Shaw—I move to change the representation of the senatorial districts of the parish of Orleans so that the district composed of the First and Fourth Districts of the city of New Orleans shall elect *five* instead of four senators, and the district composed of the Second and Third Districts shall elected *four* ir stead of three senators.

Mr. Foley—I move the adoption of the rider.

[The motion was carried.

Article 13 was adopted as reported.

The secretary read:]

Art. 14. Every white male who has attained the age of twenty-one years, and who has been a resident of the State twelve months next preceding the election, and the last six months thereof in the parish in which he offers to vote, and who shall be a citizen of the United States, shall have the right of voting.

Mr. Cutler—Mr. President, I have no rider prepared in writing, but I desire to speak to you and the Convention on the propriety of making a change in this article. This requires a man not only to live one year in the State, but six months in one particular parish before he can vote. Now, I think it is enough if he has been a year in the State. If he is a voter in the State, he ought to be allowed to vote anywhere in the State.

Mr. Abell—That would allow the country parishes to send in voters to carry elections in New Orleans.

Mr. Cutler—It will require a residence long enough to defeat that. Say three months. I move to strike out six months from the article and insert three.

Mr. Abell—That will do. I second the motion.

Mr. SULLIVAN—I move to lay the rider on the table.

[The motion was lost on a rising vote—35 ayes, 42 noes.]

Mr. SULLIVAN—Mr. President, this is outrageous; this will allow people to come in here by hundreds from all the surrounding parishes to vote at our elections in the city. If you don't like six months make it at least three. I would not object to that.

Mr. CUTLER—That was my motion.

[Mr. Cutler's amendment was carried.

Articles 15 and 21 were adopted as reported without debate.

The secretary read,]

Art. 22. No parish shall be divided in the formation of a senatorial district, the parish of Orleans excepted. And whenever a new parish shall be created, it shall be attached to the senatorial district from which most of its territory was taken, or to another contiguous district, at the discretion of the Legislature; but shall not be attached to more than one district. The number of senators shall be thirty-four; and they shall be apportioned among the senatorial districts according to the electoral population contained in the several districts: *Provided*, that no parish be entiled to more than seven senators.

Mr. SHAW—I have a rider to this article to make it correspond with the change we have made, which gives the parish of Orleans nine senators. In the last line change seven to nine.

[The rider was adopted.

The secretary read:]

Art. 23. In all apportionments of the Senate, the electoral population of the whole State shall be divided by the number thirty-four, and the result produced by this division shall be the senatorial ratio entitling a senatorial district to a senator. Single or contiguous parishes shall be formed into districts, having a population the nearest possible to the number entitling a district to a senator; and if in the apportionment to make a parish or district fall short of or exceed the ratio, then a district may be formed having not more than two senators, but not otherwise. No new apportionment shall have the effect of abridging the term of service of any senator already elected at the time of making the apportionment. After an enumeration has been made as directed in the 10th article, the Legislature shall not pass any law until an apportionment of representation in both Houses of the General Assembly be made.

Mr. SHAW—I have a rider to offer to this also, for the same reason as to the last article. We have added two senators to the parish of Orleans, so that now we have provided for the election of thirty-six instead of thirty-four. I therefore move to strike out thirty-four and insert thirty-six in this article.

[The motion was carried.

Articles 24 to 43 were adopted without amendment or debate.

The secretary read:]

Art. 44. No person shall be eligible to the office of governor or lieutenant governor who shall not have attained the age of thirty years, and been a citizen and resident within the State for the period of ten years next preceding his election.

Mr. FOLEY—I move to strike out "ten" and insert "five."

Mr. SULLIVAN—That is out of order. It is new matter.

Mr. FLOOD—I amend to two years.

Mr. BAUM—I move its rejection.

[The motion to reject was lost, and Mr. Foley's motion carried. Mr. Flood's not having been seconded, was not put to the House.

Articles 45 and 46 were adopted without debate or amendment.

The secretary read:]

Art. 47. In case of impeachment of the governor, his removal from office, death, refusal or inability to qualify, resignation or absence from the State, the powers and duties of the office shall devolve upon the lieutenant governor for the residue of the term, or until the governor, absent or impeached, shall return or be acquitted. The Legislature may provide by law for the case of removal, impeachment, death, resignation, disability or refusal to qualify, of both the governor and the lieutenant governor, declaring what officer shall act as governor, and such officer shall act accordingly, until the disability be removed, or for the remainder of the term.

Mr. HENDERSON—I move to strike out the word "residue," and insert "remainder," in order to correspond with the last line.

[The motion was lost.

The secretary read.]

Art. 67. The free white men of the State shall be armed and disciplined for its defence; but those who belong to religious societies whose tenets forbid them to carry arms, shall not be compelled so to do, but shall pay an equivalent for personal services.

Mr. CUTLER—I move as a rider that the words "free white men" be struck out and the words "all able-bodied men" be substituted therefor.

[The motion was carried by a rising vote of 51 ayes to 18 noes.]

Mr. SHAW—There is a further rider necessary to this article, which I hope will be presented.

Mr. SMITH—Mr. President, I have a rider to offer. I propose to substitute for the whole article the following, viz:

All able-bodied male residents between the ages of eighteen and forty-five years, (except subjects of foreign powers who have never voted in the United States nor declared their intention to become citizens,) shall be enrolled in the militia, and subject to military service according to law.

Mr. SULLIVAN—I move to lay that on the table.

[The motion was carried.]

Mr. CUTLER—I have another rider. The article as it now stands reads:

All able-bodied men of the State shall be armed and disciplined in its defence, etc. Now, I move to strike out all after the word defence.

[The motion was carried on a rising vote—ayes 58, noes 11.]

Mr. HARNAN—Mr. President, members don't know what they are voting for.

Mr. SEYMOUR—I move the ante-rooms be closed.

Mr. SULLIVAN—That's right. Leave out the whisky.

[Articles 68 to 78 were adopted without amendment or debate.

The secretary read:]

Art. 79. The judges of the Supreme Court shall be appointed by the governor, by and with the advice and consent of the Senate, for a term of eight years; the judges of the inferior courts for a term of six years.

Mr. SULLIVAN—I offer the following rider:

And that the judges of the Supreme Court be elected by the people for the term of eight years. Also that the judges of the inferior courts be elected by the people of their several districts for the term of six years, and that it shall be the duty of the Legislature to fix the time for holding elections for all judges, at a time which shall be different from that fixed for all other elections.

Mr. CUTLER—Mr. President, I have but this to say: when a section or article of this constitution has been submitted to this body upon its third reading, and has been adopted, the nature and character is to offer some matter that has not already been passed upon. It must be some new subject—some new matter. The honorable gentleman has offered a rider of precisely the same form and nature as the substitute he submitted in regard to the election of the judiciary, and that was passed upon. It is entirely out of order for any question that has been passed upon to come up again in the same language as a rider, and it cannot be introduced. This is certainly right; it is parliamentary and in accordance with common sense. If the gentleman has a rider, embracing new matter, let us hear it.

[The rider was lost.

No riders were offered to the succeeding articles up to article 106.]

Art. 106. All persons shall be bailable by sufficient sureties, unless for capital offences, where the proof is evident or presumption great; or, unless after conviction for any offence or crime punishable with death or imprisonment at hard labor. The privilege of the writ of *habeas corpus* shall not be suspended, unless, when in cases of rebellion or invasion, the public safety may require it.

Mr. HENDERSON—I offer the following rider:

All persons shall be bailable, by sufficient sureties, except for capital offences, where the proof is evident or presumption great; and this right of bail shall take place on appeal to the Supreme Court.

Mr. ABELL—I move to lay it on the table.

[Carried.

No riders were offered to the succeeding articles up to article 116.]

Art. 116. The Legislature shall have the power to license the selling of lottery tickets and the keeping of gambling houses; said houses in all cases shall be on the first floor and kept with open doors; but in all cases not less than ten thousand dollars per annum shall be levied as a license or tax on each vendor of lottery tickets, and on each gambling house, and five hundred dollars on each tombola.

Mr. DAVIES—I move to strike out all after "gambling houses" and insert "and insurance offices."

Mr. BEAUVAIS—I move to lay it on the table.

[Carried.]

Mr. CAZABAT—I move to strike out "and five hundred dollars on each tombola."

Mr. SULLIVAN—I move to lay it on the table.

[Carried.]

Mr. AUSTIN—I move to strike out the whole article.

Mr. SULLIVAN—I move to lay it on the table.

[Carried.]

Art. 117. The Legislature may enact general laws regulating the adoption of children, emancipation of minors, changing of names and the granting of divorces; but no special laws shall be enacted relating to particular or individual cases.

Mr. STAUFFER—I move to strike out all after the word "divorces."

Mr. SULLIVAN—I move to lay it on the table.

[Carried.

No riders were offered to the succeeding articles up to art. 122.]

Art. 122. In case of the insolvency of any bank or banking association, the bill holders thereof shall be entitled to preference in payment over all other creditors of such bank or association.

Mr. SMITH—I move to insert after the word "shall" the word "not."

Mr. BELL—I move to lay it on the table.

[Carried.]

Art. 123. No person shall hold or exercise, at the same time, more than one civil office of trust or profit, except that of justice of the peace.

Mr. KAVANAGH—I move to strike out "except that of justice of the peace."

[Laid on the table.

No riders were offered to the succeeding articles up to art. 130.]

Art. 130. The seat of government shall be and remain at New Orleans, and shall not be removed without the consent of a majority of both Houses of the General Assembly.

Mr. HILLS—I move to strike out "majority" and insert "three-fourths."

Mr. WENCK—I move to lay it on the table.

[Carried—yeas 40, nays 26.]

Mr. WATERS—I move a recess of fifteen minutes.

[Lost.]

Art. 133. The citizens of the city of New Orleans shall have the right of appointing the several public officers necessary for the administration of the police of said city, pursuant to the mode of elections which shall be prescribed by the Legislature; provided that the mayor and recorders shall be eligible to a seat in the General Assembly; and the mayor and recorders shall be commissioned by the governor as justices of the peace, and the Legislature may vest in them such criminal jurisdiction as may be necessary for the punishment of minor offences, and as the police and good of said city may require.

And that the city of New Orleans shall maintain a police which shall be uniformed with distinction of grade, to consist of permanent citizens of the State of Louisiana, to be selected by the mayor of the city, and to hold office during good behavior, and removable only by a police commission composed of five citizens and the mayor, who shall be president of the board. The commission to be appointed by the governor of the State for the term of two years, at a salary of not less than one thousand dollars each per annum; a majority of whom shall remove for delinquencies. Members of the police when removed shall not again be eligible to any position on the police force for a term of one year.

Interfering or meddling in elections in any manner will be a sufficient cause for instant dismissal from the police by the board.

The chief of police shall give a penal bond in the sum of ten thousand dollars; lieutenants of police, five thousand dollars; sergeants and clerks, each, three thousand dollars; corporals, two thousand dollars; and privates one thousand dollars; with good and solvent security, as the law directs, for the faithful performance of their duties.

The various officers shall receive a salary of not less than the following rates:

The chief of police	$250	per month.
The lieutenants of police ..	150	do.
The sergeants of police ...	100	do.
The clerks of police	100	do.
The corporals of police ...	90	do.
The privates (day and night) each	80	do.

Mr. ORR—Mr. President, I intend to offer a rider to this article, and wish to make a few explanatory remarks. When this police bill came up I offered an amendment, which was adopted and became a part of the police bill. The committee appointed to arrange these matters have seen proper to place the amendment in another portion of the constitution. I contend they have no such right, and cannot separate the bill. When an amendment is carried and adopted on its third reading it becomes a part of that bill and must remain so.

Mr. CAZABAT—I move to insert after the words "not less than the following rates," the words "unless otherwise provided by law."

Mr. SULLIVAN—I move to lay it on the table.

[Carried.]

Mr. CUTLER—Mr. President, as chairman of that committee, I was the author of this bill. Now, as a *bill*, I contend, sir, this Convention could do nothing better; the Legislature of the State could pass no better *bill*, save and except with the addition of the amendment I am about to offer. I move to strike out all after "the faithful performance of their duties."

I mean no disrespect to my brother members of the committee—I mean no disrespect to Mr. Orr, who moved the amendment. It was carried and put to this article, but the committee did not affix it thereto. I voted against the entire bill, because you have fixed the prices of cartmen and other men, worthy in their place, but a business with which we have nothing whatever to do. The bill, as a constitutional provision, I believe to be generally a proper and righteous one, but fixing all salaries by this constitutional Convention of municipal officers, and more especially of the good and honest laboring men on the public works, is a duty never imposed upon us, and that is the reason, sir, I voted against the entire bill since Mr. Orr's amendment was attached. Now, I discover on examining this report of the Special Committee, that you have not embraced Mr. Orr's bill. It was adopted by this Convention, and Mr. Orr has a right to complain; but, sir, with all his complaints and with all he might say, I am directly and bitterly opposed to such a proceeding.

PRESIDENT—Is not article 134 Mr. Orr's bill?

Mr. CUTLER—Yes, it is, but it is in a separate article. My motion is to strike out all after "duties."

Mr. ABELL—Mr. President, I think the police bill as reported by this committee and adopted, just exactly what it ought to be. If you wish to have the constitution adopted, let this remain as it is. If you strike out this, you will also strike off two or three thousand votes for this constitution.

[Mr. Cutler withdrew his motion.]

Art. 134. The Legislature may establish the price and pay of foremen, mechanics, laborers and others employed on the public works of the State or parochial or city governments.

Provided, That the compensation to be paid to all foremen, mechanics, cartmen and laborers employed on the public works, under the government of the State of Louisiana, city of New Orleans and the police juries of the various parishes of the State, shall not be less than as follows, viz: Foremen, $3 50 per day; mechanics, $3 00 per day; cartmen, $3 50 per day; laborers, $2 00 per day.

Mr. SULLIVAN—I offer the following:

Strike out all previous to the word *provided.*

[Laid on the table.]

Mr. TERRY—I move to substitute "shall" for "may" in the first line.

Mr. WENCK—I move to lay it on the table.

[Carried by the following vote:]

YEAS—Messrs. Abell, Austin, Barrett, Baum, Beauvais, Bennie, Burke, Campbell, Cazabat, Crozat, Cutler, Davies, Decker, Edwards, Ennis, Fish, Flagg, Fuller, Gastinel, Gruneberg, Heard, Henderson, Kavanagh, Knobloch, Kugler, Mann, Mayer, Newell, Normand, Ong, Pintado, Pursell S., Schnurr, Seymour, Shaw, Stumpf, Stiner, Stauffer, Taliaferro, Wenck, Wells, Wilson—42.

NAYS—Messrs. Bell, Bofill, Buckley, Collin, Cook J. K., Cook T., Duane, Dufresne, Flood, Foley, Fosdick, Geier, Gorlinski, Gaidry, Healy, Harnan, Hart, Hills, Hire, Howes, Maas, Maurer, Mendiverri, Montamat, Morris, Murphy E., Murphy M. W., O'Conner, Orr, Payne J., Poynot, Schroeder, Smith, Spellicy, Stocker, Sullivan, Terry, Thorpe, Thomas, Waters—40.

Mr. WELLS—I move to strike out the whole title.

[The yeas and nays being ordered, the roll was called, and the motion lost by the following vote:]

YEAS—Messrs. Austin, Beauvais, Bennie Crozat, Cutler, Decker, Edwards, Fish, Flagg, Fuller, Heard, Kavanagh, Kugler, Mann, Newell, Ong, Pursell S., Seymour,

Shaw, Taliaferro, Thorpe, Wenck, Wells, Wilson—24.

NAYS—Messrs. Abell, Barrett, Baum, Bell, Bofill, Buckley, Burke, Campbell, Collin, Cazabat, Cook J. K., Cook T., Davies, Duane, Dufresne, Duke, Dupaty, Ennis, Flood, Foley, Fosdick, Gastinel, Geier, Gorlinski, Gruneberg, Gaidry, Healy, Harnan, Hart, Henderson, Hills, Hire, Howes, Knobloch, Maas, Maurer, Mayer, Mendiverri, Montamat, Morris, Murphy E., Murphy M. W., Normand, O'Conner, Orr, Payne J., Pintado, Poynot, Schroeder, Schnurr, Smith, Spellicy, Stocker, Stumpf, Stiner, Stauffer, Sullivan, Terry, Thomas, Waters —60.

[Before the vote was announced, Messrs. Collin, Burke and Hire changed their votes from "yes" to "no."

The previous question was then moved and carried.

On a motion to adjourn, the yeas and nays were called :]

YEAS—Messrs. Campbell, Collin, Cook J. K., Dufresne, Dupaty, Flagg, Gaidry, Harnan, Knobloch, Mayer, Mendiverri, Murphy M. W., Newell, O'Conner, Orr, Pintado—16.

NAYS—Messrs. Abell, Austin, Barrett, Baum, Beauvais, Bell, Bennie, Bofill, Buckley, Burke, Cazabat, Cook T., Crozat, Cutler, Davies, Decker, Duane, Edwards, Ennis, Fish, Flood, Foley, Fosdick, Fuller, Gastinel, Geier, Gorlinski, Gruneberg, Healy, Hart, Heard, Henderson, Hills, Hire, Howes, Kavanagh, Kugler, Maas, Mann, Maurer, Montamat, Morris, Murphy E., Normand, Ong, Payne J., Pursell S., Schroeder, Schnurr, Seymour, Shaw, Smith, Spellicy, Stocker, Stumpf, Stiner, Stauffer, Sullivan, Taliaferro, Terry, Thorpe, Thomas, Waters, Wenck, Wells, Wilson—66.

[The motion was therefore lost.]

Art. 136. There shall be appointed by the governor a state engineer, skilled in the theory and practice of his profession, who shall hold his office, at the seat of government, for the term of four years. He shall have the superintendence and direction of all public works in which the State may be interested, except those made by joint stock companies or such as may be under the parochial or city authorities exclusively and not in conflict with the general laws of the State. He shall communicate to the General Assembly, through the governor, annually, his views concerning the same, report upon the condition of the public works in progress, recommend such measures as in his opinion the public interest of the State may require, and shall perform such other duties as may be prescribed by law. His salary shall be four thousand dollars per annum. The mode of appointment, number and salary of his assistants shall be fixed by law. The state engineer and assistants shall give bonds for the performance of their duties as shall be prescribed by law.

Mr. HILLS—I move to strike out "four thousand dollars per annum" and insert "five thousand dollars per annum until otherwise provided by law."

[A motion to table was lost by a vote of 51 nays to 9 yeas, and the rider adopted.

The following article was read :]

Art. 137. The General Assembly may create internal improvement districts, composed of one or more parishes, and may grant a right to the citizens thereof to tax themselves for their improvements. Said internal improvement districts, when created, shall have the right to select commissioners, shall have power to appoint officers, fix their pay and regulate all matters relative to the improvements of their districts: *Provided*, such improvements will not conflict with the general laws of the State.

And that the municipal corporation of the city of New Orleans shall be prohibited from adjudicating, selling by sealed proposals, or in any manner contracting for the working or completing of any public works under their supervision and control.

Mr. STAUFFER—I offer a rider to strike out all after "State."

Mr. SMITH—As a member of the committee, I voted to strike out the same portion of the article, as I see no good in it, for it certainly cuts off the city of New Orleans from doing anything and drives out competition. I am a mechanic and know that if you take away this power to contract, you throw everything into the hands of a very peculiar set of individuals. This amendment does not cure any evil, for the city must still employ foremen, who will in turn, put in their relatives, and thus the evil, instead of being cured, is made worse than before. Let the city have this power, and oblige her to make men fulfill their agreements in the spirit of their contracts. [Applause.]

Mr. SULLIVAN—Mr. President, the committee will please be so kind as to hear me whilst I give a word or two of explanation on this subject. This amendment which I offered in regard to contracts, and which was unanimously passed by this body some time ago, and which was ordered to be inserted in the second article of internal improvements, and should have been placed in article 137 of the printed report of the Committee on Form and Arrangement, but was altogether left out by this committee for some reason best known to themselves, consequently the members have not before them in the printed report this amendment of mine which was passed.

The object I had in having this amendment a part of the constitution of this State, was for the sole purpose of giving more work to the laboring classes of this city, and also that the tax-payer would be benefitted by their work. Not for the purpose of fostering a band of vampire contractors who have been years past sucking the money of the people from the treasury, without giving in return hardly any benefit either to the working men or to the taxpayers of the city.

The member from St. Mary (Mr. Smith) upholds the contract system. I do not. If that gentleman had lived in this city as long as I have, he would entertain far different opinions from what he now expresses. I am well acquainted with the manner that the contract system worked for years back in this city. I know every twist and turn of its rascality. For the sake of illustration: let the city sell a contract to-morrow, the contractor will put to work about ten men, where the city doing its own work would employ one hundred. It would cost the city as much money for the work done by these ten men on contract work, as the city itself would expend by the employment of one hundred men; so that by this contract system the city loses the labor of ninety men, thereby depriving the families of those poor men of their necessary support from the want of employment.

For this reason I am not in favor of contracting. I am its enemy; because I want to see right and justice done to the laboring man. I never want to see a contract for the completing of any of the public works of the city given out or sold. Let the city do its own work; let there be laborers, mechanics, cartmen and foremen employed to see that the work is properly done. Let this system be pursued by the city authorities and there shall be at all times plenty of work for the laboring classes and a sufficiency of money left in the treasury to pay them.

Mr. GORLINSKI—Mr. President, as chairman of the committee, I opposed Mr. Sullivan's amendment, because I thought it opened the door to speculation by the city. I still think so, and shall act accordingly.

Mr. STAUFFER—Mr. President. I differ entirely from the gentleman who offered this amendment, and think we have just as good a right to say that no private individual shall have a right to contract with me in regard to building or anything else. I consider the city as an indivdual, having as such a perfect right to enter into any of the contracts set forth. I do *not* not consider all men to be thieves and robbers, as the gentleman (Mr. Sullivan) does, but go upon the principle of considering a man honest until I find him out to be a rascal—up to which time I believe I have no right to judge him. In my opinion, the corporation has a right to let out contracts, and that if it is not allowed to, the municipal expenses will be twenty-five thousand dollars, when under contract system they would not be ten thousand. If there is any swindling, the city can look after the matter, and if it does not choose to do so, *it* must suffer—not the State.

Mr. CUTLER—Mr. President, this amendment has been changed since first offered, after deliberation. As to municipal regulations, they do not concern us, as all that we have to do is to fix the organic law. I am inclined to think we had better wipe out the words in question. [Applause.]

[Mr. Stauffer's motion carried.

The next article was read:]

Art. 138. The General Assembly may grant aid to said districts out of the funds arising from the swamp and overflowed lands, granted to the State by the United States for that purpose or otherwise.

Mr. CAMPBELL—I offer a rider:

Provided, That the city of New Orleans shall comprise one internal improvement and drainage district, and appropriations made for that purpose shall be paid into the treasury of the city of New Orleans.

Mr. BEAUVAIS--I move it be laid on the table.

PRESIDENT—This proviso belongs properly to article 137. Any gentleman acquainted with New Orleans knows the inconvenience of having it divided into three draining districts.

[Mr. Beauvais' motion carried, on division called: ayes 34, nays 31. Some dissatisfaction arising in regard to the vote, it was taken again, resulting: ayes 46, nays 21.]

PRESIDENT—I will say, *en passant*, that I cannot see how any gentleman living in New Orleans could have voted to lay that rider on the table.

[On article 139 there was no discussion. The following article was read.]

Art. 140. There shall be elected a superintendent of public education, who shall hold his office for the term of four years. His duties shall be prescribed by law, and he shall receive such compensation as the Legislature may direct, provided, that the General Assembly shall have power by a vote of the majority of the members elected to both Houses, to abolish the said office of superintendent of public education, whenever in their opinion said office shall be no longer necessary.

Mr. TERRY—I have a rider,—to strike out "such compensation as the Legislature may direct," and insert "a compensation of three thousand dollars *per annum*.

Mr. HEALY—I move that be laid on the table.

[Motion carried.]

Mr. BEAUVAIS—I offer a rider, the same as the last,—inserting, however, "five" in place of "three" thousand.

[Laid on the table.]

Mr. FISH--I offer a rider,--insert after the word receive, the words "a salary of four thousand dollars per annum," striking out the words "such compensation as the Legislature may direct."

[Motion to table lost on a rising vote—ayes 24, nays 49.

[Rider adopted.]

Mr. HILLS—I move to strike out "and who shall receive such compensation as the Legislature shall direct."

[Carried.

Secretary directed to read article 141.]

Mr. PURSELL--I have a rider to article 140.

PRESIDENT—Too late.

Mr. PURSELL—I appeal from the decision of the chair.

Mr. CUTLER—The gentleman had the floor and should be heard.

PRESIDENT—What is he to be heard upon? There is no question before the House.

Mr. Secretary read article 141.

Mr. PURSELL—I appeal, and insist upon it.

PRESIDENT—Sergeant-at-arms keep order. I shall be obliged to arrest you, sir.

Mr. PURSELL—Very well, sir, but I appeal.

Mr. STAUFFER—Every man of this Convention has a right to be heard. I insist upon that.

Mr. PURSELL—I insist upon my appeal.

PRESIDENT—Sergeant-at-arms, take that gentleman into custody.

Mr. CUTLER—He has a right to his appeal.

PRESIDENT—I will arrest you, too, sir, if you do not keep order.

[A motion to adjourn having been made, the president declared the Convention adjourned until 12 M., of Friday, the 22d inst., amid loud cries of "no adjournment," "division," &c.

The president having left the chair without directing a division, Mr. Fish was called to the chair, and on putting the motion to adjourn again, to the House, it was clearly carried, and the Convention adjourned.]

FRIDAY, July 22, 1864.

[The Convention met pursuant to adjournment. Present, the Hon. E. H. Durell, president, and the following members :]

Messrs. Abell, Austin, Barrett, Baum, Beauvais, Bell, Bennie, Bofill, Buckley, Burke, Campbell, Collin, Cazabat, Cook J. K., Cook T., Crozat, Cutler, Davies, Decker, Duane, Dufresne, Dupaty, Edwards, Ennis, Fish, Flagg, Flood, Foley, Fosdick, Fuller, Gastinel, Geier, Gorlinski, Gaidry, Gruneberg, Healy, Harnan, Hart, Heard, Henderson, Hills, Hire, Howes, Kavanagh, Knobloch, Kugler, Maas, Mann, Maurer, Mayer, Mendiverri, Montamat, Morris, Murphy E., Murphy M. W., Newell, Normand,

O'Conner, Ong, Orr, Payne J., Poynot, Purcell J., Pursell S., Schroeder, Schnurr, Seymour, Shaw, Smith, Spellicy, Stocker, Stumpf, Stiner, Stauffer, Sullivan, Taliaferro, Terry, Thorpe, Thomas, Waters, Wenck, Wells, Wilson—84.

[The minutes of yesterday's proceedings were adopted.]

PRESIDENT—Gentlemen : I rise to a question of personal privilege. My attention has been called to an article which appears in this morning's Times, headed "*Great time in Convention*," etc. I rise to denounce it as a most infamous libel upon myself and upon this Convention.

Mr. STAUFFER—Mr. President, I have a resolution to offer upon this matter.

Resolved, That the sergeant-at-arms be ordered to take immediate possession of the paper called the New Orleans Times and that the publication of the paper be suspended until its responsible editor, Thomas P. May, Esq., appear before this Convention and purge himself of the *libel* he has published in the issue of this date regarding the proceedings of this Convention of the 21st of July, 1864.

Mr. TERRY—I move its adoption.

Mr. HILLS—I move to lay it on the table.

Mr. ABELL—I second the motion.

[The yeas and nays were called.]

YEAS—Messrs. Abell, Baum, Bofill, Buckley, Campbell, Cazabat, Decker, Dufresne, Edwards, Ennis, Fish, Fosdick, Gastinel, Gorlinski, Gruneberg, Hart, Heard, Hills, Kavanagh, Knobloch, Mann, Maurer, Morris, Murphy E., Murphy M. W., Ong, Orr, Poynot, Shaw, Stumpf, Sullivan, Waters—32

NAYS—Messrs. Austin, Barrett, Beauvais, Bell, Bennie, Burke, Collin, Cook J. K., Cook T., Crozat, Cutler, Davies, Duane, Dupaty, Flagg, Flood, Foley, Fuller, Geier, Healy, Harnan, Henderson, Hire, Howes, Kugler, Maas, Mayer, Montamat, Newell, Normand, O'Conner, Payne J., Pursell S., Schroedor, Schnurr, Seymour, Smith, Spellicy, Stocker, Stiner, Stauffer, Terry, Thorpe, Thomas, Wenck, Wells, Wilson—47.

[The motion to lay on the table was lost.]

Mr. HENDERSON—Mr. President, I desire to—

Mr. MONTAMAT—I move the previous question.

Mr. HENDERSON—A man that will move to lay on the table now, is not a gentleman. Sir, we are not without precedent, and if the gentleman wants to learn something before he leaves this Convention he may have an opportunity of learning something he has never thought of heretofore. Now, Mr. President, we have gone on here and permitted papers of secession tendencies to be received here; but, sir, when it comes to this, when a man publishes infamous lies respecting this Convention and its proceedings, let us bring him here and let him give an account of himself. What has this man, Thomas P. May, done that we introduce this resolution? In the first place, he has told us that our president was drunk. I want him to be brought here to substantiate the charge. That paper has, until recently, been very cautious not to say anything. I have my private opinions as to who are its owners, although the name of Thomas P. May is at its head; and I say, to-day, that I believe we have an enemy among us in the person of Salmon P. Chase. Yes, sir, Salmon P. Chase attempted, through the power he held in his hands as secretary of the treasury, to be a rival of our president. And I believe that C. A. Weed, who is one of the owners of that paper, is nothing more than a Chase man, to-day. I believe, sir, that an editor may write and publish what he pleases, provided that he is responsible for what he publishes. Now, sir, he has not published our proceedings, but he has published some false statements respecting our president and this Convention. I suppose, sir, that I am the man that was struck. Why, sir, when the president declared the Convention adjourned we were nothing but private individuals. We were no longer a Convention. I started home. When I reached the door I had a right to go out. The door-keeper told me I could not go, and attempted to stop me; but sir, I refused to be stopped and went out as I had a right to do. Now, sir, I would like to see the man that had the boot applied to him. I don't think there was such a man. I have only heard of him through the Times. This may be all intended as a matter of ridicule and sport, but it certainly does not have that appearance.

But how are we to reach this case. I believe that the modern decisions only go so far as to exclude the reporter of the obnoxious sheet from the House.

Mr. CAZABAT—I have listened attentively

to the remarks of the gentleman, but notwithstanding the great respect I have for our president, I still have a higher respect for the freedom of speech and freedom of the press. Sir, it makes no difference to me whether the remarks in the Times are just and true, or whether they are entirely without foundation. I am an advocate of a free press and of free speech, and, sir, we have already adopted an article in the constitution which expresses my views and sentiments fully on the subject. I will read it:

"Art. 111. The press shall be free; every citizen may freely speak, write and publish his sentiments on all subjects—being responsible for an abuse of this liberty."

Yes, sir, this Convention is nothing but the creature of the people, and each and all of us are subject to the criticism of the public press, and of each and every one of them, no matter how humble or how high his station. I, sir, believe that the ruling of our worthy president was proper and correct, but even if incorrect, the gentlemen who attempted to disturb this Convention should have quietly submitted to the decision of the chair and were not justified in pursuing the course they adopted.

Mr. Montamat—Mr. President: I now wish to reply in a few words to Mr. Henderson. I did'nt move to lay on the table. I voted against it. Mr. Henderson is one of the most disorderly members in this House. He is always throwing stones into my garden.

Mr. Abell—I know the statement in the Times to be false, for I had the honor of walking with the president myself, to one of the most distinguished galleries of art in this city after the adjournment last evening, and if there was anything out of the usual course in his condition I should have perceived it. I therefore wish to protest against the truth of the Times' article, but I really think it would be giving that paper too much distinction and making too much of a small matter to notice it further than to denounce it as false. I shall therefore vote against the resolution.

Mr. Cutler—Mr. President and gentlemen of the Convention: I have a substitute for this resolution, but before offering it, it may be well for me to make a few remarks, to which I beg your attention. I am convinced, sir, that we are here for the purpose of doing justice to all classes of men within the sphere of our action, and that Mr. May is amenable to this body, although the constitution of the United States as well as that of our State reads thus: "The press shall be free. Every citizen may freely speak, write and publish his sentiments on all subjects, being responsible for an abuse of this liberty."

There being, on this particular occasion, no question in my mind, that there was not only an abuse of this privilege, but a serious outrage on the part of the editor of the Times. We have then a constitutional provision, that although a man may freely speak and write, yet he is responsible for any wrong he may commit. If this is true, sir, when he abuses an indivdual, how much greater the responsibility when this body is assailed, not because of us who are the members of it, but, sir, it is a political body and has a political existence. It is because of this political existence that the papers which publish our proceedings should disseminate the truth, and nothing but the truth. [Applause.] Now, sir, I was an eye-witness to the transactions which took place here yesterday, and I freely assert that in the Halls of Congress many scenes far more reprehensible have been enacted, and acts in themselves far worse been committed, not only by the speaker of the House and the president of the Senate, but by the members of both representative houses. I dare say, that there never was a deliberative body, composed of as many members, and gathered from as many different sources, sitting either in any State of this Union, or in any portion of the civilized world, in which there were fewer instances of party wrangling and discord. The matter of yesterday was a consequence naturally resulting from a difference of opinion, of which I, to some extent, may have been the cause. The president, influenced by reasons which to him seemed just and proper, was indisposed to put the motion at that particular moment, and he decided that it was out of order. This was perfectly within the scope of the president's authority. And again, when the gentleman [Mr. Purcell,] appealed from the decision of the chair, the president was perhaps still indisposed to put the motion. This, also, was a matter between him and the Convention.

Now, as an eye-witness, I beg leave to state, that every word and sentence in that paper (exhibiting a copy of the Times) this morning, is a corrupt and base falsehood!

In the first place the president may have been correct in his decision: he told me that he did not see the gentleman, which is of itself a sufficient explanation. I may have been wrong in making my motion, and the fifteen or twenty members who seconded me may have also been wrong in doing so. But, be it right or be it wrong, does it amount to anything so extraordinarily disgraceful, as it has been construed to be by the enlightened copperhead editor of the Times? [Applause.] I say, sir, that these are trying times! The nearer the rebels get to this city, the prouder the copperheads become. It is time to put them down, and the nearer they come the louder they shall hear my voice raised against them. If it had not been for the news placarded upon the Times' bulletin board yesterday, I do not believe that either the editor or reporter of that paper would have dared to insert this foul slander. My doctrine is to let the copperheads, rattlesnakes and rebels go down to hell together! [Applause.] Upon this Convention the whole public eye is cast, and when we have small wranglings or controversies in good humor, without any bad results, no paper should dare to publish such a villifying lie and slander in relation to it. We can get along, and conclude this great and noble work of making a constitution, but if we are to have the press against us, abusing its power and privilege, then I say it is time to suppress that press.

But let us give every man a fair chance of being heard. I know the language in question to be false,—it is a calumny,—but still give every one a fair trial. Let its author be heard. I have no doubt but that Mr. May is a man, and if I had taken his position, I would show myself to be a man. Let him be sent for; let him come into this Convention and disclaim any intention of offering us an insult. When he does that, he should, in my opinion, be excused,—but if he does not—then suppress his paper. [Applause.] I believe this is due to the dignity of the State, and were I the commanding general, with my limited knoweldge, I think that this paper (again exhibiting the Times) would not to-day issue an afternoon edition. [Applause.] This is not only a blow at us as members, but it shows a disposition to thwart the noble ends and purposes for which we are congregated here. [Applause.] Considering this critical juncture in national affairs, I denounce it as one of the most high-handed outrages that could have been committed by any paper or editor upon a legislative body, and therefore justifying the immediate action of this body. I offer then this substitute:

Resolved, That Thomas P. May, editor of the New Orleans Times, be brought before this Convention forthwith by the sergeant-at arms, and that he be required to purge himself of the contempt and libel on this body as published in the issue of July 22d, 1864, or that he be otherwise dealt with as the Convention may deem proper and just.

If he apologizes, we will excuse him, for I believe that the proper feelings of humanity exist in the heart of every man here; but if there is a refusal to apologize, then stop all such libels during the existence of this Convention. It has been said that "we have no power to do this." That is a very strange doctrine. Suppose, sir, a a party of disorderly persons, copperheads, if you please, should combine to disturb by noise, or otherwise this Convention. Could not, or would not the president direct the sergeant-at-arms to arrest them and bring them before this Convention for punishment? For the power exists to send out and take any man who interrupts our proceedings or runs counter to them. We have a right to do this by resolution, and if upon trial the offender is found guilty, the president has the power to sentence him to imprisonment. This power is not only vested in the Congress of the United States, and in the Legislature of every State, but in this body, and without it we would be a laughing-stock and scorn and unworthy of making a constitution.

Mr. ABELL—I deny that Congress even has any such power as is claimed here, and I say, sir, it is beneath the dignity of this body to carry it any further. We should not dignify so small a matter by any further action than a denial of its truth, as we have already done.

These gentlemen, who are so anxious for some action, wish to prolong the session of this body.

[The substitute offered by Mr. Cutler was adopted.]

[The order of the day was then taken up. Article 141 of the constitution.]

Art. 141. The Legislature shall levy a special tax on the property of all white persons owning property in the State, for the purpose of public schools for the education of white children, and money so arising shall not be otherwise appropriated.

The Legislature shall levy a special tax on colored persons in the State and their property for the purpose of public schools for the education of colored children, and money so arising shall not be otherwise appropriated.

Mr. TERRY—I offer the following rider for the whole article:

The Legislature shall provide for the education of all children in the State between the ages of six and eighteen years, by maintenance of free public schools by taxation or otherwise.

Mr. SULLIVAN—I move to lay it on the table.

[The yeas and nays were ordered and the motion lost, as follows:]

YEAS—Messrs. Abell, Bofill, Buckley, Campbell, Crozat, Decker, Dufresne, Edwards, Fuller, Gastinel, Geier, Gruneberg, Heard, Henderson, Knobloch, Maas, Mayer, Mendiverri, Montamat, Morris, Murphy M. W., Newell, Normand, Ong, Orr, Pursell S., Sullivan, Thomas, Waters—29.

NAYS—Messrs. Austin, Barrett, Baum, Beauvais, Bell, Bennie, Burke, Collin, Cazabat, Cook J. K., Cook T., Cutler, Davies, Duane, Dupaty, Ennis, Fish, Flagg, Flood, Foley, Fosdick, Gorlinski, Healy, Harnan, Hart, Hills, Hire, Howes, Kavanagh, Kugler, Mann, Maurer, Murphy E., O'Conner, Payne J., Poynot, Schroeder, Schnurr, Seymour, Shaw, Smith, Spellicy, Stocker, Stumpf, Stiner, Stauffer, Terry, Thorpe, Wells, Wilson—50.

Mr. DUANE—I move the previous question.

[Carried, and the yeas and nays called on the adoption of the rider.]

Mr. ABELL—I denounce it as disgraceful, and those who change this provision as hirelings. I vote "no" in the name of the State.

The rider was adopted by the following vote:]

YEAS — Messrs. Austin, Barrett, Baum, Beauvais, Bell, Bennie, Burke, Collin, Cazabat, Cook J. K., Cook T., Crozat, Cutler, Davies, Duane, Dupaty, Ennis, Fish, Flagg, Flood, Foley, Fosdick, Geier, Gorlinski, Healy, Harnan, Henderson, Hills, Hire, Howes, Kavanagh, Mann, Maurer, Murphy E., Newell, Normand, O'Conner, Payne J., Poynot, Purcell J., Schroeder, Shaw, Smith, Spellicy, Stocker, Stumpf, Stiner, Stauffer, Terry, Thorpe, Thomas, Wells, Wilson—53.

NAYS—Messrs. Abell, Bofill, Buckley, Campbell, Decker, Dufresne, Edwards, Fuller, Gastinel, Gruneberg, Hart, Heard, Knobloch, Kugler, Maas, Mayer, Mendiverri, Montamat, Morris, Murphy M. W., Ong, Orr, Pursell S., Schnurr, Seymour, Sullivan, Waters—27.

[No riders were offered to article 142.

The secretary read article 143.]

143. A university shall be established in the city of New Orleans. It shall be composed of four faculties, to-wit: one of law, one of medicine, one of the natural sciences, and one of letters; the Legislature shall provide by law for its organization and maintenance.

Mr. SMITH—I move to strike out "in the city of New Orleans" and insert "located by the Legislature.

Mr. FOLEY—I move to lay it on the table.

[The motion to table was carried.

No riders were offered to articles 144 and 145.

The secretary read article 146.]

Art. 146. No appropriation shall be made by the Legislature for the support of any private school or institution of learning whatever, but the highest encouragement shall be granted to public schools throughout the State.

Mr. FOLEY—I move the article be stricken out.

Mr. SMITH—I move to lay that on the table.

[Carried—yeas 54, nays 12.

The secretary read article 147.]

Art. 147. Any amendment or amendments to this constitution may be proposed in the Senate or House of Representatives, and if the same shall be agreed to by two-thirds of the members elected to each House, such proposed amendment or amendments shall be entered on their journals, with the yeas and nays taken thereon, and the secretary of state shall cause the same to be published, three months before the next general election for representatives of the State Legislature, in at least one newspaper in French and English, in every parish in the State in which a newspaper shall be published; and such proposed amendment or amendments shall be submitted to the people at said election; and if a majority of the voters at said election shall approve and ratify such amendment or amendments, the same shall become a part of the constitution. If more than one amendment be submitted at a time, they shall be submitted in such manner and form, that the people may vote for or against each amendment separately.

Mr. BEAUVAIS—I move to strike out "two-thirds," and insert "a majority."

Mr. FOLEY—I move to lay it on the table.

[The motion to table was lost, and the rider adopted.

No riders were offered up to article 154.]

Art. 154. As soon as a general election can be held under this constitution in every parish of the State, without hostile molestation or interference, the governor shall, by proclamation, or in case of his failure to act, the Legislature shall, by resolution, declare the fact, and order an election to be held at a day fixed in said proclamation or resolution, and within sixty days from the date thereof, for governor, lieutenant governor, secretary of state, auditor, treasurer, attorney general, and superintendent of education. The officers so chosen shall, on the fourth Monday after their election, be installed into office; and shall hold their offices for the terms prescribed in this constitution, counting from the second Monday of January next preceding their entering into office in case they do not enter into office on that date. The terms of office of the State officers elected on the 22d day of February, 1864, shall expire on the installation of their successors as herein provided for; but under no state of circumstances shall their term of office be construed as extending beyond the length of the terms fixed for said offices in this constitution; and, if not sooner held, the election of their successors shall take place on the first Monday of November, 1867, in all parishes where the same can be held, the officers elected on that date to enter into office on the second Monday of January, 1868.

Mr. SHAW—I move as a rider to strike out "without hostile molestation or interference."

[The motion was adopted.

No rider was offered to article 155.]

Mr. ABELL—I move the rejection of the constitution, it not being in conformity with the wish of the people.

[The motion was not seconded.

On the motion to adopt the constitution as a whole, the yeas and nays were called.

During the calling of the roll the following members explained their vote:]

Mr. ABELL—Mr. President and gentlemen of the Convention: The occasion is most important. I desire, sir, to give my reasons for the vote I am about to cast upon the adoption or rejection of the constitution as a whole. My views are before the country, and I will be brief now.

In this constitution I find much to admire. A more permanent Judiciary; by making it appointive; a more certain protection to person and property, by a permanent instead of a time-serving police; and other salutary amendments too numerous to mention here, meet my entire approbation.

But, Mr. President, there are objections which preponderate in my mind. I view the emancipation act, and the act authorizing the Legislature to extend suffrage, as destructive of the best interests of the people and State of Louisiana, and dangerous to its safety.

I look upon the emancipation ordinance as the most vital stroke at the life of the nation. By this unfortunate act you virtually say to the loyal men of the fourteen slave States, that the reward or *penalty* of loyalty is to be despoiled of their property against their will and without compensation, and no one is so simple as to suppose that the loyal men of those States will lay down their arms to be robbed of that property they have acquired under the guarantee of the parent government.

We virtually tell them to fight to the knife, and the knife to the hilt, or be despoiled.

I vote No, no, no.

Mr. BELL—With all my heart, I vote yes.

Mr. CAZABAT—Mr. President, believing that this free State constitution is calculated to benefit the people of Louisiana, I record my vote in favor of its adoption as a whole, and vote yes.

Mr. DUANE—As the noblest act of my life, I vote yes. [Applause.]

Mr. DUFRESNE--In the name of Louisiana, I vote no.

Mr. HEARD—There are certain things in this constitution which I have opposed upon principle; but, sir, there are so many good features in the constitution, that I think if it is adopted as a whole, under the present circumstances, the people of Louisiana will be better off, and I vote yes. [Applause.]

Mr. MENDIVERRI—Before I vote, I wish to give my reasons, and ask that my colleague be allowed to read.

Mr. MONTAMAT—I move it be spread on the minutes without being read.

[This being objected to, it was read by the secretary, as follows:]

Mr. MENDIVERRI—Mr. President and gentlemen of the Convention: the question of slavery, which is the prime cause of the desolating war now in existence, is one of the most embarrassing that can present itself to the consideration of the statesman; and yet more so is it to one who is entrusted by his constituents to a legislative assembly, charged with the intricate duty of reforming and amending the constitution of a State as renowned as that of Louisiana, in order that the fundamental laws of said State may be in harmony with the requirements of the age—of an enlightened civilization. Whilst on the other hand, the momentous interests growing out of and established under the shadow of an institution essentially vicious, merits respect, although as approved and authorized by the supreme code of the country, it has given rise to certain usages, customs and traditions, from which it is impossible to be divested.

A retrospective glance at the past will enable us to judge better of the present, and determine with greater prudence what may be necessary for the future.

Four years ago the State of Louisiana was one of the most prosperous commercial countries on the globe; not only the necessaries of life, but also the luxuries and superfluities thereof reigned everywhere in abundance throughout the whole extent of its territory.

The greatness of our resources and the prolific character of our soil, attracted hither annually thousands of inhabitants from the old world, who, by their labor and perseverance constantly augmented the power and wealth of the country; the State was aggrandized; in a word, we lived under the sweet reign of prosperity.

What were the causes that produced this wonderful fertility? There is nothing concealed or difficult of explanation about them.

The principal cause of our power simply consisted in the great fertility of our soil, our valuable and desirable products, which were exchanged for those of foreign nations, thus bringing back to us every species of commodity that could contribute to our wants and well being. Thus, then, are we indebted to agriculture, which is the true and only inexhaustible fountain of public or private wealth, and this agriculture, thus to speak, was the labor of negro slaves.

We are now groaning under the painful weight of a cruel and desolating war. The immense deposits of merchandise which formerly constituted our pride, have long since disappeared; our wharves are deserted; our streets are solitary; sadness reigns where late was happiness and joy; and in whatever way we turn our eyes, we behold horrid misery, where of late was plentiful abundance. Clouds and darkness are above us, which become more dense and dark as we gaze upon the horizon of the future.

And what is the cause of this profound difference—this change so radical and so repulsive? It is not necessary to attribute to unknown causes, or to seek in obscurity for that which presents itself before us in the clearest light. It is the insecurity which war has substituted for peace; it is because idleness struts about insolently where before was seen the most laborious diligence and industry; it is because the interest of the few has usurped the place of the many and better class; agricultural labor has ceased from causes known to everybody, the explanation of which would become odious; with it also have productions, commerce and happiness disappeared.

No one having the least knowledge of the circumstances by which we are surrounded, can deny the truth of this reasoning, and no one admitting it but will desire to ameliorate the sad condition in which we find ourselves. In this situation, the people of Louisiana, struggling with sorrow and misery, have asked themselves in tones of bitter anguish, if the evils which menace them in the future may not be greater than those of the present; and have enquired if if there be not, in our social organization, some hidden vice which is corroding and killing it in the bud.

In this situation, I say, the people of Louisiana have called together a Convention, charging it with the emendation and reformation of its fundamental laws, in the hope that the evils under which they have suffered may cease and the lost prosperity be regained, placing for its foundation justice and right. Thus, then, the Convention has met together for the purpose of reconciling discordant ideas--to confirm diverse interest and to form a complete whole out of regular and separate elements, at present scattered and heterogeneous. It has not assembled together for the purpose of passing judgment on the past, and spending its time in declamations of doubtful utility: its purpose is to ameliorate the present and give security against the dangers of the future; to constitute, to legislate, and firmly establish. Its purpose is to build up—not to destroy.

Imbued with these sentiments, the first question that presents itself for your examination, is that of slavery! This is, undoubtedly, the veritable worm that is gnawing the vitals and destroying the happiness of our people. Slavery is an institution equally repugnant to right and conscience, that is to say, to public as well as to private opinion; slavery, considered in the light of religion and philosophy, is a crime. Considered in a political point of view, it is a leprosy upon society; we recognize this truth, and no one desires more sincerely than myself to see every vestage of it disappear from our soil.

But in expressing this desire, I naturally and irresistibly ask myself the question, can slavery be immediately suppressed, under existing circumstances?

Perfect right, and the heart, answer *yes!* Whilst on the other hand, reason, conscience, equity, humanity, civilization, the interests of the slaves themselves even—exclaim aloud, *no!* Among us the slave has been deprived of his rights as a man; he has been classed by the State as a CHATTEL.

The inevitable result of such an iniquitious institution has been that the condition of slavery finds itself blended with our wealth, and consequently with our power and happiness. This is unfortunate. Pronounce immediate abolition, the negro will be free; ignorant of the true signification of the word "liberty," he will interpret for another word "license." Liberty, according to his comprehension, would be idleness, idleness would become misery, and misery degenerate into crime.

These are not gratuitous suppositions. Look at the West Indies, the English and French Antilles; look at Hayti, where within a few months past a drama was enacted near the very gates of the capital, that would put cannibals to the blush; in fact look at the sad spectacle now presented to us in our own Louisiana.

The negro, I repeat, has not been considered among us as *a man*, but as a thing—a CHATTEL, he has not received the least moral or intellectual education, much less a political one; the negro, so to speak, is not apt to enjoy a liberty he cannot comprehend. To make him free without this previous preparation is absurd, as he is not prepared by any qualification—it is to ask him to perform a great work, whilst depriving him of the necessary implements to accomplish it; it is, in a word, taking the beginning for the end.

And when from a human being, susceptible of being elevated to the level of a civilization required by the present age, through the medium of education and labor properly directed, you have made, not only a useless, but a vicious being—a being not comprehending the sacred obligation of "gaining his bread by the sweat of his brow"—shall we have discharged the obligations which religion, humanity and justice demand? *No!*

We shall have but taken him from the hands of a master, although it may be for his own interest, care and protection, in order to transfer him to vice and ignorance and unbridled passions, to a tyrant a thousand times worse than the first—to dire misery! and, to speak with truth and candor, between that slavery which affords protection, food and clothing, and that slavery which destroys by cold and hunger, I greatly prefer the former.

To suppress slavery suddenly and at a simple blow, is to destroy one abomination through the medium of another abomination. To cast down this domestic institution now, is to deprive the whole people of the means of existence.

And why should the interests and condition of four hundred thousand negroes prevail over and occupy our whole care, to the neglect and ruin of the interest and condition of 800,000 white persons! and when we behold the misery which our ruinous civil war has engendered, and is now causing in Europe, we should pause and consider what confusion, and endless evils would be brought upon the world, by an act, praiseworthy in itself, but iniquitous in its rash precipitation, because it will necessarily cause the agricultural products of our State, a State larger than many of the kingdoms of the old world, to be forever withdrawn from the commerce of the world. For, when we have nothing to offer to foreign nations and others in exchange, how are we to support ourselves? How can the closed channel of emigration be reopened? How can plenty be brought forth from the dried-up fountains of our wealth? And how can the lost happiness be brought back to our beloved country?

Let us suppress the abominable institution of slavery. Let us suppress it at an early period—but let us suppress it in such a manner as to remove afar off incalculable evils, and produce benefits to the slave, the master, and to the whole State.

In this way alone can the Convention fulfill the mission which it was called upon to perform, in this manner it will prove itself worthy of giving laws to a sovereign and independent people, who will approve of their acts, seeing they are marked with the seal of true philanthropy and with a sincere desire to labor for the happiness of the community.

By this proposition I seek to avoid both extremes, in this delicate and painful matter; inaction is as criminal as precipitate haste; to find a just medium wherein reason and justice reside, and abandon all visionary theories; as well those which deny right and justice to the whole human race, as well as those who seek to ignore the circumstances by which we are surrounded.

Gradual emancipation will, in my estimation, be the best method to bring about a consummation so devoutly to be wished—the interest of both masters and slaves.

Let us declare that slavery shall be abolished at the period of ten years, with a compensation to loyal owners; let a generation pass, and the generation then on the stage of action, educated by a wise and intelligent government, will know how to appreciate and put in practice the benefits of a liberty, which, if untimely conceded to to them, would be a sword in the hands of a child.

Prohibit the further acquisition of slaves, and that will destroy the immorality of the traffic, concede to them the enjoyment of the civil law, let their marriages and those of their children be legitimate, and that will open their hearts to the sweet ties of family affection, and with it, the whole circle of virtues of every description.

Digest laws for the punishment of the slaves, without leaving it to the discretion of the masters and slaves. Let colleges be established by the State, where the future freedmen may open their eyes upon the light of truth and religion, and be instructed in the most useful elementary branches.

Let labor be decreed as the fudamental law, and prosecute idleness and vagrancy to the utmost limit.

Finally, let the laws be digested in the most humane manner, and easy of execution, and when the hour of liberty is proclaimed to the slave, those who are now pariahs and outcasts, will then be useful men; and we, without having destroyed any individual interest or right of property, we have increased the value of all, without the least infringement upon justice—we will have resolved the most difficult problem of modern times, and at the same time satisfied the exigencies of equity and just rights.

To work in any other manner, would be to wander in a path strewn with errors and watered with tears, and destroy ourselves beyond all hope of redemption.

Mr. MONTAMAT—I have some objections to several of the articles in this constitution, but I am willing that the people of Louisiana shall decide whether they will accept or reject it. I vote "yes."

Mr. MORRIS—I have a particular objection to article 134, as well as to article 100, which should read "*viva voce*," instead of yeas and nays, but I vote "yes" on the adoption as a whole.

Mr. E. MURPHY—I have been a citizen of Louisiana for 48 years, and have always been a slave-holder, but with all my heart I vote "yes." [Applause.]

Mr. O'CONNER—I am not in favor of secession and am in favor of the free State party that sent me here, therefore I vote "yes."

Mr. ORR—I am in favor of emancipation —immediate emancipation. I voted for that measure in this Convention and I have signed the ordinance of emancipation, but the Committee on Arrangement to whom this constitution was submitted, have seen proper to change, and I contend in an unwarrantable manner, certain articles of this constitution that have been passed on their third reading, and became a part of the constitution. They took away amendments to bills and made separate sections of them, thereby exposing the bills to defeat, and I am afraid it was done for that purpose. Now, Mr. President, I consider their action unwarrantable—that they went beyond the power conferred upon them by this Convention, and although I favor emancipation and will vote for it to-morrow should it come up before the people, and sign anything in regard to immediate emancipation, certain clauses and certain parts of this constitution are objectionable in my view. One is, granting to the Legislature the right to confer upon the colored race the right of suffrage in this State. The change of parts of the constitution is another. I am therefore constrained against my own wishes under these circumstances to vote "no."

Mr. POYNOT—I have been since the organization of this Convention in favor of an elective judiciary, but having failed in carrying out my promise to my constituents, in their name, on the adoption as a whole, I vote "yes."

Mr. SMITH—Believing the slave-holding portion of Louisiana is eminently disloyal, for the safety of the only free government on the face of God's earth and the honor of the flag of our Union, I vote "yes." [Applause.]

Mr. STOCKER—As so many gentlemen have explained their votes, it may be expected of me; but, sir, after thinking over the matter seriously—for it is a matter upon which I have reflected deeply—I cannot find I have any explanation to make, and therefore I vote yes.

Mr. STUMPF—I was in favor of compensating the loyal slave owners, but as that has been denied I vote no.

Mr. SULLIVAN—I vote no.

Mr. TERRY—I came here elected on the free State ticket and advocating a free State the same as my able colleague [Mr. Sullivan]. Though I must say I am not here to force my own individual voice on this Convention. I have always tried to ascertain the views of my constituents, and it is a most singular thing that while the gentleman comes from the same district as myself and his constituents are the same as mine—mine sustain me in supporting the adoption of this constitution and for the welfare of Louisiana, and to aid in the practical reconstruction of the Union. I vote "yes" in their name.

Mr. WENCK—I endorse fully the act of emancipation and support it with all my heart, although some of the articles have met with my opposition. I vote "yes."

Mr. WELLS—I am opposed to everything in the constitution that belongs to the General Assembly; but, sir, for the welfare of my native State and maintenance of the republican government that flag represents, I cast my vote for the entire constitution [Applause.]

Mr. WILSON—Mr. President and gentlemen of the Convention: the police and laborers' bill, and the article 67 in Executive Department, title IV, which empowers the

State of Louisiana to draft into the militia of the State citizens of foreign powers, meet with my disapprobation.

But, in view of the great fact, that our constitution, made and adopted by us, overthrows and annulls the black code and the damning principle of slavery—the formal cause of this rebellion—and gives to the oppressed a home and an asylum, regardless of race or color, I vote for the constitution as a whole.

Mr. HILLS—Before the vote is declared, I move that the president of the Convention be requested to cast his vote, and that all members not present also have an opportunity to record their votes on the adoption of this constitution.

Mr. THOMAS—I amend by substituting "required."

Mr. HILLS—I accept the amendment.

[Carried.

Mr. Newell, on showing authority from Mr. Taliaferro, who was absent from illness, to vote yes on the adoption of the constitution, recorded the vote of that gentleman.

The president then announced the adoption of the constitution by the following vote:]

YEAS—Messrs. Austin, Barrett, Baum, Beauvais, Bell, Bennie, Burke, Collin, Cazabat, Cook J. K., Cook T., Crozat, Cutler, Davies, Duane, Dupaty, Edwards, Ennis, Fish, Flagg, Flood, Foley, Fuller, Geier, Gorlinski, Healy, Harnan, Hart, Heard, Henderson, Hills, Hire, Howes, Kavanagh, Kugler, Mann, Maurer, Montamat, Morris, Murphy E., Murphy M. W., Newell, Normand, O'Conner. Ong, Payne J., Poynot, Purcell J., Pursell S., Schroeder, Schnurr, Seymour, Shaw, Smith, Spellicy, Stocker, Stiner, Stauffer, Taliaferro, Terry, Thorpe, Thomas, Wenck, Wells, Wilson and Mr. President—66.

NAYS—Messrs. Abell, Bofill, Buckley, Decker, Dufresne, Gastinel, Gruneberg, Gaidry, Knobloch, Maas, Mayer, Mendiverri, Orr, Stumpf. Sullivan, Waters—16.

PRESIDENT—Gentlemen, no greater glory can a man accomplish than giving liberty to his fellow man. I vote yes. [Enthusiastic applause.] The constitution of Louisiana is adopted as a whole, in Convention, this 22d of July, 1864. [Applause and ringing cheers.]

Mr. MONTAMAT—I move that the Enrolling Committee be instructed to have the constitution enrolled by to-morrow at 12 o'clock.

PRESIDENT—I will state to the Convention that under its resolution, the pen with which the ordinance of emancipation was signed is to be presented to Major Gen. Banks to-morrow, when we adjourn. With regard to the Enrolling Committee, I have no doubt they will compel their clerks to labor faithfully, whether the constitution can be enrolled by 12, to-morrow, or not.

[Mr. Montamat's motion was carried.]

Motion to adjourn.]

PRESIDENT—Before I declare the vote, I will state to the Convention, that under the power confided to me by article 155, I appoint the True Delta newspaper, the Era newspaper, and the German Gazette newspaper, as the three papers to be selected by the president of the Convention—of which number the two first shall publish the constitution in English and French, and the latter in German from the period of the adjournment of the Convention until the election for the ratification or rejection of this constitution, on the first Monday of September, 1864.

[A motion to adjourn was carried.]

SATURDAY July 23, 1864.

[The Convention met pursuant to adjournment, and was called to order by the president. After prayer by the Rev. Mr. Strong, the secretary called the roll, and the following members answered to their names:]

Messrs. Abell, Austin, Balch, Barrett, Baum, Beauvais, Bell, Bennie, Buckley, Burke, Campbell, Collin, Cazabat, Cook J. K., Cook T., Cutler, Davies, Decker, Duane, Dufresne, Dupaty, Edwards, Ennis, Fish, Flagg, Flood, Foley, Fosdick, Fuller, Gastinel, Geier, Gorlinski, Gruneberg, Healy, Harnan, Hart, Heard, Henderson, Hills, Hire, Howes, Kavanagh, Kugler, Maas, Mann, Maurer, Mayer, Mendiverri, Montamat, Morris, Murphy E., Murphy M. W., Newell, Normand, O'Conner, Ong, Orr, Payne J., Pintado, Poynot, Purcell J., Pursell S., Schroeder, Schnurr, Seymour, Shaw, Smith, Spellicy, Stocker, Stumpf, Stiner, Stauffer, Sullivan, Taliaferro, Terry, Thorpe, Thomas, Waters, Wenck, Wells, Wilson—82.

[Messrs. Crozat, Bofill and Knobloch were excused for non-attendance.

In obedience to a resolution of yesterday, the sergeant-at-arms presented Thomas P. May, Esq., at the bar of the Convention accompanied by his counsel, Hon. J. S. Whitaker, and Major W. W. Howe, acting assistant adjutant general of the staff of the major general commanding the department.]

PRESIDENT—Mr. Thomas. P. May, you have been brought to the bar of this Convention this day, under and by authority of the following resolution, adopted by this Convention, July 22, 1864.

"*Resolved*, That the sergeant-at-arms be ordered to take immediate possession of the paper called the New Orleans Times, and that the publication of the paper be suspended until its responsible editor, Thomas P. May, Esq., be brought before this Convention, and purge himself of the libel he has published in the issue of this day, regarding the proceedings of this Convention on the 21st July, 1864."

What, sir, have you to say in response thereto?

Mr. MAY—I am here with the provost marshal, to obey a military order issued by Major Gen. Banks, and not in obedience to the resolution of this Convention. At the proper time, in the proper place, and in pursuance of the forms of law, I will answer to any charge made against me or my paper, the Times. That is my answer.

Mr. HENDERSON—I move, sir, that that be treated as an additional contempt of this body. We are in a civil tribunal, and I am astonished that a gentleman who occupies such a position in the State of Louisiana should come and offer such a reply. Therefore I move that charges be preferred against him, and that he be brought before this body for their action.

Mr. ABELL—Mr. President, it seems to me we have been here a long time, and I believe it is the interest of the public as well as the desire of the members of this Convention, and all the authorities in power, that we should bring this Convention to a close. I desire that our labors should be completed this day, but as this question has come up, I will repeat what I said yesterday, that I think we give this matter more importance than it really deserves. Any journal of the State has a right to fairly criticise our proceedings, no doubt, but certainly, sir, there is a point at which it should stop, and that the Times has exceeded its right, I have but very little doubt. But we must remember, Mr. President, that if we have been a little severely chastised, it may be we have sometimes been spared when we deserved it. Therefore let us waive the whole matter, and I move that the whole thing be postponed indefinitely. I think it will equally well subserve the ends of justice and guard the interests of the State and the honor of the members and the Convention as a body.

Mr. FOLEY—I move to lay that motion on the table.

[The yeas and nays were ordered, and the motion to table was carried by the following vote:]

YEAS—Messrs. Austin, Barrett, Beauvais, Bell, Bennie, Burke, Collin, Cook T., Cutler, Davies, Duane, Dupaty, Edwards, Ennis, Flagg, Flood, Foley, Fuller, Healy, Harnan, Hart, Henderson, Hire, Howes, Maas, Mann, Murphy E., Newell, Normand, O'Conner, Payne J., Poynot, Pursell S., Schroeder, Schnurr, Seymour, Smith, Spellicy, Stocker, Stumpf, Stiner, Stauffer, Taliaferro, Terry, Thomas, Wells, Wilson—47.

NAYS — Messrs. Abell, Balch, Baum, Buckley, Campbell. Cazabat, Cook J. K., Decker, Dufresne, Fish, Fosdick, Geier, Gorlinski, Gruneberg, Heard, Hills, Maurer, Mayer, Mendiverri, Montamat, Morris, Murphy M. W., Ong, Orr, Pintado, Purcell J., Shaw, Sullivan, Thorpe, Waters, Wenck —31.

Mr. CAZABAT—Mr. President, this attempted trial seems to me rather a strange and novel proceeding; for my part, sir, I am opposed to it from beginning to end, and protest against the action of the Convention in the premises.

The article published in the New Orleans Times, of which Mr. Thomas P. May is the ostensible and responsible editor and proprietor, was perhaps calculated to create a wrong sensation and impression upon the public mind, both at home and abroad, in regard to the conduct of our honorable president, but since said article has been already denounced emphatically as "*a most infamous and malicious libel*," it seems to me the Convention should deem this sufficient and satisfactory.

So far as the remarks of that newspaper are concerned, they were in my humble opinion uncalled for, unbecoming and unfounded in fact; but, sir, when a fellow-citizen, no matter what may be his position in life, the lowest or the most exalted, is brought at the bar of this Convention, to be made responsible *here* for the bold and fearless public expression of his sentiments or opinions, true or false, right or wrong, it matters not, I must say at once, without the least hesitation, that you are assuming, indeed, a most extraordinary, illegal and dangerous power, you are going entirely too far beyond your province, and I am ready and willing to stand upon this floor, solitary and alone, if necessary, against the majority, to sustain, vindicate and defend as far as possible with my humble voice, the great fundamental principles of liberty which I admire and cherish, and these are "*the freedom of speech and the freedom of the press.*" [Great applause].

In the first place, gentlemen, you ought to know and remember that the great theory and practice of all republican government, wisely requires that each of the three departments—executive, legislative and judiciary—should be kept as distinct and separate as possible. This principle has been duly observed in the new constitution.

If the individual who makes the law is empowered, at the same time, either to decide or execute the same, there is at once an end to freedom. As members of this Convention, as framers of the new constitution, you are in the truest sense of the word, the supreme law-makers of Louisiana; if so, how can you assume the triple and unconstitutional power of making, deciding and enforcing the law?

Can this Convention, which has nearly completed the organic law of the land, deny to any citizen the right of appealing to courts of justice for redress, a right sanctioned and recognized by the very constitution framed by yourselves?

Will this Convention, by such an unjust, harsh and illegal course, make itself unworthy of the high and respectable position it should occupy, at least before the friends of liberty.

Will you pretend to be at the same time the law makers, the law expounders, and the law enforcers in this case?

Where is your authority for such summary proceeding? What right have you to try a citizen for an alleged violation of the law?

Will you be the accusers, the witnesses, the prosecutors, the judges, and what else?

If the gentleman has been willfully disrespectful in his language towards the worthy and beloved president of this Convention, if any member feels offended at the article in question, if Mr. Thomas P. May has, as you contend, violated the law of his country, if he has abused the freedom of the press, go and appeal to the courts of justice and bring a regular suit for libel.

There is the proper place, and there only, at the proper time, in pursuance of the forms and rules of law you can make him responsible for any charge brought against him or his paper, the Times.

Otherwise, gentlemen, you are assuming too much power, as you are without jurisdiction, and instead of respect your course will be calculated to bring contempt upon this body.

Now let us refer to the law applicable to this case. The article 110 of the new constitution provides that "*all courts shall be open; and every person for any injury done him in his property, person and reputation, shall have remedy by due course of law,*" &c., &c.

We have also adopted article 111 in the same constitution, which expressly declares that "*the press shall be free; every citizen may freely speak, write and publish his sentiments on all subjects, being responsible for an abuse of this liberty.*"

Responsible to whom? Responsible only to the aggrieved and complaining party; responsible only before the duly authorized tribunals of the State of Louisiana; responsible only before a court of competent jurisdiction in the case, to be tried according to law by an impartial jury.

Such is the doctrine recognized by the fundamental law of the land made by this Convention, I mean the free State constitution, framed, no doubt, with some imperfections and shortcomings, but which, I trust, will be ratified by the people, because it will, I believe, benefit Louisiana.

It then becomes our sacred duty to be the first to respect the law placed in said constitution.

If it is not yet the law of the land, because it has not been adopted by the people; then the constitution of 1852 which contains the same provision in regard to the freedom of the press, is still in force and existence. If every citizen has the right to freely speak and publish his sentiments on all subjects, how much more should a newspaper be permitted to criticize to the fullest extent the acts of the public servants of Louisiana, the mere creatures of the sovereign people!

The press claims justly the privilege to discuss public measures, and the acts of public men,--the press should be maintained by all true lovers of free government in the right to criticize freely, on all occasions, and under all circumstances, the proceedings of deliberative bodies, *pro bono publico*, for the public good.

The right of a journalist should be held as sacred, as necessary and as imprescriptable as the right of the legislator.

Call me "secesh," "copperhead sympathiser," or whatever you please, the record here will show that I was the first man in this Convention to raise my voice on behalf of immediate and unconditional emancipation, in accordance with the spirit of the immortal proclamation of PresidentLincoln.

Besides, the first and second articles of your free State constitution are principally due to myself and the chairman of the committee on emancipation. But, sir, when you bring before this body a resolution, which, if passed, will abridge or destroy the freedom of speech and of the press, I, for one, never can, and never will sanction it, or countenance it by my vote or voice. [Applause].

Mr. Hills—Mr. President: I, sir, from the first, have been oppossed to any action in this matter. When the proposition was made yesterday in regard to it, I moved to lay it upon the able. My views of the subject have undergone no change. I think it unbecoming and unworthy of the dignity of this body to take any official notice of the publication. I am not here, sir, to defend that publication or its statements. The honored president of this Convention arose in his seat yesterday, and characterized it as an infamous libel upon himself and upon the Convention. Other members of the Convention also characterized it in equally strong terms, and it seems to me the matter should have ended there. A man, sir, who publishes a malicious falsehood about others, and who goes forth with the falsehood and slander branded upon his forehead, is already sufficiently punished. The mark upon him is not less than that upon Cain, the first murderer. The great fact was told us that a "good name in man and woman is the immediate jewel of their souls." I say when that statement was characterized as a calumny, an infamous libel and a slander, and was fastened upon its author as such, that the matter should have ended, and the Convention should have taken no further notice of it. It is purely a personal matter, and I take it we are not here to settle the private quarrels of any member of this Convention. If the president feels he has not been sufficiently avenged by branding that slander as it deserved, then he has a legal remedy in the courts. If that member who is so pathetically described in the article as having received the application of the boot, feels he is agrieved, he, too, has his remedy against the individual who inflicted that blow. (Applause and laughter.) It seems to me, gentlemen, this is trifling away our time, trifling away the money of the people, trifling with our own dignity, and I am opposed to the whole proceedings from beginning to end, and I shall oppose it and vote against it in every form and shape whatever.

Mr. Smith—Mr. President: I say I am not opposed to these proceedings. I have seen the effects of the publication of that paper ever since the Convention first convened. Show me a single paragraph in that paper that has said anything in favor of this Convention. Is this the first legally constituted body since this State was precipitated into open, armed rebellion, by men whose object it was to break up the Government of the United States? Do we represent the people, or do we not? Here is an infamous libel, not on one individual, but from the honored president of this Convention to every member. I see no "black eyes;" no man to whom the "boot was applied." I see no "broken chairs," and every member will bear me out when I assert it is false—every word of it. [Applause.]

Now, sir, this thing has gone into print, and the paper has gone broadcast all over the land, and do you tell me, gentlemen, that it requires no action? Do you tell me, when men raise their voices and utter things of that kind to lower this Convention in the minds of the people and the government, that it should not be noticed, and that, too, when it has been more than once asserted that every sympathy here was with the other side? I, for one, will never vote to pass it over, and I am for action, and immediate action upon it. [Applause.]

Mr. HENDERSON — Mr. President: this question is one of the most important that has ever come before this body. It has been said that because this man belongs to the editorial corps he has a right to say anything he pleases, and should not be held responsible for what he says. Sir, but a few weeks since, the Picayune and a French paper published a so-called proclamation of the president, which turned out to be spurious. Nevertheless such was the offence committed that these two papers were suppressed by military authority. Mark you, there is a long distance between Washington and New Orleans, and those papers may have published it innocently. They had a right to publish it, but by the same law that conferred the right they were responsible for their publication. We find an illustration of the doings of Copperheads in the case of Gen. Dix, who enforced the military order of the president of the United States. We have another Copperhead enemy, in my estimation far more infamous, in Mr. May, editor of the *Times*. In a free State where there is no rebellion—no martial law declared, if the president deems it necessary, he may stop a paper because of libel, as was done, but how much ground there is for doing it when the man in the disguise of hypocrasy pretends to be a free State man and publishes things that hinder the progress of a free State more than the army of Jeff. Davis. Sir, had I the military authority, he would not appear before this Convention. I would send him to Dixie. [Cheers.] As to his position as a writer, there is no one in this community who respects him more highly in that capacity than myself. The editorial articles of that paper indicate ability, whether he be the actual writer or some one else. My rule of action is this: when a man high in position and great in power violates the law, his offence is aggravated according to his superior advantages. In regard to this, gentlemen, look at this morning's *Times*. He comes out this morning in an article on the freedom of the press, without referring to the facts of yesterday. There is nothing extenuating, but only adding insult to injury. He says he has a right to criticise a public body. What member opposes that right? But when he endeavors to make capital for Louis Napoleon, for Queen Victoria and for Jeff. Davis, he is unworthy of being an editor, and I hope the president of the United States will remove him from the office he holds, and send both him and his paper beyond the Federal lines. [Applause.]

I have said all I wish to say. Personally, I have not much knowledge of the gentleman. At the first I said if he was present and stated that the president was incapable of performing his duties and also made a wrong decision, all of which I will swear is false—for the president was correct according to parliamentary usage—I would personally denounce him as a libeler and a liar. [Applause.] I use the terms in a political sense, and mean to cast no reflection upon him as a man. But I look upon him as a public officer and the publisher of a paper that purports to be a free State organ, yet Jeff. Davis never published anything stronger than the doctrine of the gentleman on yesterday morning.

Mr. CUTLER—Mr. President, and gentlemen of the Convention: I had not the distinguished honor of being present this morning, when the prisoner at the bar made his explanation to you and to this Convention. But I have been informed of the nature, character and extent of his apology, and heartily concur with what has been heretofore remarked—that instead of its being an apology, it was a second contempt of the authority of this Convention. [Applause.] Mr. President, I admit that this is a very grave and important question, and one deserving the serious consideration of every member of this Convention before the final action is taken thereon. The reasons why I take this view of the subject are simply these: that some three years ago this State and its laws were swept away, and now when Louisiana is trying to return to that government which is her proper source of origin, it is, in my estimation, highly improper for any man who pretends to maintain a character and position for loyalty, to thwart the slightest measure tending to that end. On this important question, on this important occasion, and on this all-important day, which is, I hope, to be the last meeting of this body, the question presented is, shall the acts and the authority of this Convention be treated with contempt by any person in the State of Louisiana, or within the Federal lines? [Cries of "No!" "No!"]

To Mr. Thomas P. May, in his character as a man and as a gentleman, I have not the slightest objection and no fault to find; but he is responsible as the ostensible editor of the Daily Times newspaper. He has published a scurrilous falsehood and a set of lies, infamous in their character, and pernicious in their influence against the action of this Convention. If this was only to affect us individually, I would not, so far as I am concerned, care a straw; I would not raise my voice to-day if this was the case; but it affects the character of this body most immediately, and throws a great obstacle in the way of the adoption of the labors of this Convention by the people of Louisiana. Besides it is in bad taste. Suppose, sir, that the immortal, the unparalleled and unequalled Grant was to be on this day, or had on yesterday been announced as having taken Richmond, (and the day is not far distant when that will be so announced,) [applause] and the Times had been disposed to publish that news to the people, let me ask you if it would have appeared in larger letters than did the disgraceful article in yesterday morning's issue? Was not that slander as emphatic and as largely displayed as would have been the eulogy and praise of Grant after the capture of Richmond? [Cries of "yes," "yes."] I do not know but that the characters used in the condemnation and denunciation of this Convention, while discharging its duty, were larger than they would have been on the occasion alluded to. Then, sir, it is necessary for us faithfully and impartially to discharge our duty.

We must first inquire has this body the right to act as we propose? Is there any law by which the president of this body can arrest Mr. Thomas P. May, the author of that scurrilous article and libel, or is there no such authority? We find that Gen. Banks, in his attempt to re-frame this State, both by force of arms and by reproducing civil authority, has called forth this body and empowered us to aid and assist in restoring this State to the Union. Now, let me say to you, that if there is any obstacle thrown in the way of this general progress, whosoever does so must be put out of the way. It has been said by the gentleman from St. Mary's, (Mr. Smith,) with perfect candor and correctness, that since this Convention has been assembled, it has been the misfortune of the members of this body to read daily in that paper, (the Times) harsh epithets, inuendoes and improper insinuations against the acts and conduct of this assemblage. If it is to go forth to the people of Louisiana, and the entire loyal population of the United States that this Convention is a set of drunken men, who on a certain day committed outrages the most disgraceful—all this is to be published in large letters in the Times—it will certainly carry with it, if not contradicted, a kind of reputation which will redound to our injury and the injury of the great cause in which we are all engaged. Suppose a hundred secessionists and rebels should daily assemble about this hall, and that the president of this Convention on account of the noise and confusion, should send out and arrest them. That act would be justified by the very nature of the case, through the exercise of the power vested in every deliberative body. Well, sir, what is a small disturbance created by fifty or a hundred men in the street? It is con fined to the surrounding walls, and by closing the doors and windows we could exclude the noise and go on with our great work. Therefore, if the power of this body can be exercised to suppress an abuse of this kind, how much greater is the power and how much greater is the necessity for its exercise, when, with a dagger, a villain seeks to cut the very heart strings of the constitution we are trying to adopt.

The publication comes forth, scandalous and libelous, a tissue of falsehood from beginning to end—of a character most contemptible, and, allow me the word, most damnable. I was astonished that any man who pretends to loyalty, could descend so low and so far forget himself as to be the author of, or sanction the publication of, the document published in the copperhead *Times* of the 22d inst. "He that is not for us is against us," I mean, against the great cause in which we are all engaged. "No man," in the language of Jesus Christ, "can worship God and mammon" at the same time; he must be on the side of the Lord or the devil; there are but two to serve, and there is no middle ground. Although the rebels may capture Baltimore and Washington, thus intimidating some men, there are but two sides still—a man must either support the government of the United States or violate his oath of allegiance and go down to rebeldom and disgrace. However loyal this editor may be, whatever may have been his previous conduct, however high his position in the government of the United States, matters not. These are trying times, when the country needs the benediction of Almighty God, the humble confession of every sinner and his prayer to the Giver of all good that a blessing may rest upon our labors. Therefore, I say, sir, that when this is the condition of affairs, the publication of such atrocious falsehoods was a high-handed piece of injustice and that it was an ungodly wrong thus to attempt the striking of a death-blow to the purposes and ends of this Convention, and the designs of Major General Banks in calling it.

Would it not have been better for Mr. Thos. P. May to have inserted in his paper something like this—and it would have been true: "In the Convention yesterday there was a little farce—a little quarrel—arising out of the fact that some of the members opposed the president while the president in turn opposed the members, resulting finally in rather a disorderly adjournment?" That would not have harmed our noble cause, nor struck a death-blow with a sledge hammer at the gentlemen of this body and the loyal people of Louisiana. Now, sir, he has lied, and with his eyes open has perpetrated a foul slander and libel, not against an individual merely, but against every member of this Convention, by printing that which is known to be a base falsehood. Not only has the *Times* propagated this here in the city of New Orleans, but abroad—thus bringing the great State of Louisiana into contempt before the authorities of the general government and the good people of our nation. Then, gentlemen, do you tell me that when this man is brought into this body, by the power of the law which surrounds us, and he refuses to offer an excuse, but folds his arms and tells you in an insulting manner that he is here by the order of Major Gen. Banks—and not for the purpose of answering to anything we may charge him with? If that does not amount to a second contempt to the authority of this body, tell me what could? Does it not? [Cries of "yes," "yes."] Instead of acting as he has, what should he have done? There was an excuse for him; there is none now. Had he proposed an apology, I would have tried to have been the first to take his hand and pardon him, because I was, perhaps, the most severe against him on yesterday. When he entered this hall, he should have done so with due respect—not that we are Almighty God or his disciples, but because we hold a great power vested in us by the government of the United States and sanctioned by the people. [Applause.] If he had then arisen and said: "Mr. President and gentlemen—I am not the author of the few lines which appeared in my paper"—

which I believe would have been true, for I think he writes but little himself. "I know nothing personally of the transaction in this Convention, on yesterday, but some of my employées, of whom I have many, may have done this in a spirit of prejudice, with a disposition to injure this body, and I, as the responsible editor of the Times, offer to you, sir, and this Convention my heartfelt regrets." Had he done this like a man, he would have been cordially received and pardoned, but when he comes here and bids defiance to this body, it is as much as to say—"Here you are a mere contemptible set of beings, so continuously drunk and ignorant, so without principles or consideration—that you are beneath my notice. I will not even condescend to inform you that I am ready to apologize at all." I say that such a man should be dealt with in the severest manner; the president of the United States should be made cognizant as to whom he has made sub-treasurer; that the president of the United States and his cabinet ought to know who is interfering with the proud progress of this Convention. [Enthusiastic applause.] They ought to know who it is that is throwing obstacles in the way of our armies—in the way of the success of our country and in the way of the returning people of Louisiana.

There is but one way in which to do all this. Offer your resolutions to this effect and thus do justice to God, to man, and to yourselves. Let this man, May, know that this is a sacred body; that here, the great God has not refused his eye; that we have done works worthy the consideration of this State; yes, I repeat it, worthy of the consideration of the people of this State and of the people of every country on the face of the earth. [Applause.] We are not perfect beings, for no man, though created by God in his own image, is perfect, but notwithstanding we, on yesterday, finished a Constitution, which I firmly believe will be acceptable to the people of the State and acceptable to the Congress of the United States. Then we have put the honest, loyal people of Louisiana in their true position. Let the rest go into rebeldom, and there remain.

God knows that if I had been the commanding general of this department, though I cannot claim one-tenth part of his capacity, that no evening edition of the Times should have been issued on yesterday, nor any morning edition to-day. When we find a man who pretends not only to be loyal but the embodiment of loyalty, previous to election, and then find him abandoning his platform as soon as his friends are defeated, and opposing the very ends which he undertook to subserve, simply because they are not promoted to some position—we find in that man a character deeply stained with rebelism. Now, sir, if this be so, is it proper for this Convention to allow itself to be thus defamed? If this publication was true, my voice would not have been raised against it on yesterday, nor would it again to-day, because I fear the truth, if it is against me, while my disposition is to try to be right, and when right I fear neither man nor devil. Then, sir, having been here on yesterday, and knowing as does every other member of this Convention and every man outside, that this publication was a falsehood from beginning to end, I denounce its author and demand the punishment of Mr. Thomas P. May, for contempt of this Convention.

There must have been a motive, an incentive in the publication of that article. Was it to promote the interest of the general government or the State? No, sir! It could not have been. It was to throw obstacles in the way of our work. It was perhaps to give a blow indirectly to the military and civil powers that be. It meant to tell the people of this State that this Constitution is corrupt and not to be voted for. That, sir, certainly was the intent and meaning of this publication.

Let us, in conclusion, do justice; let us have no rashness or unfairness. We have, gentlemen, the power to act upon this. We are not only a Convention of the State of Louisiana, but a military power,—created and emanating from no other source than the military power, and existing by virtue of civil authority of the government of the United States. The president of the United States, having then vested us with this power,—there has never been such power vested in any legislative or deliberative body on the face of the earth as in this, unless it was in the Arkansas and Missouri Conventions, which were brought about in the same manner,—the loyal people of this State, within the Federal lines, have sent us here, thus embodying themselves. What more power do you want in a matter of this kind than that power which is inherent in the people? In this very hall, yes, in this very hall, during the session of the Secession Convention of 1861, I was sitting in that very gallery, when a gentleman entered, bearing an American flag. What was the result? It was such a contempt in the eyes of that august body of rebels that they instantly arrested and incarcerated him in prison. [Cries of "yes!" "That is so."] Then I do not lie as the Times does. [Laughter.] If you want nothing but an example of legislative power—there it is. If there is any such thing as the preservation of the dignity of this Convention, let us exercise our power now, and not postpone it until to-morrow, Monday, or any other day. Do it now! Let the States of Massachusetts, New York, Connecticut, and all the rest understand that we are the people's loyal Convention, and determined to do our duty. [Applause.]

What is the remedy? There is but one. Let that man go scot free to scandalize this Convention, to-morrow, and until this constitution goes before the people for its adoption or rejection. Let him go on with his paper; it necessarily has its influence and may result in the defeat of all our noble plans. It may have this tendency, for it is confederated with rebels and disloyal traitors, rattlesnakes and devils, to thwart our ends. Whenever there is a wrong there is a remedy. *Send Thomas P. May to jail!* Let him know that he lives in a land of liberty, but must not abuse that liberty. [Great Applause.] Suppress that infamous, lying paper—that is proper, also. Do it, I say, and when that is done, we shall have no more copperhead editorials or infamous libels. Again,—do not stop there,—but request the military authorities to ask the president of the United States to withdraw the commission under which he holds office, and remove him from the position which he now disgraces. [Great applause.]

I do not wish to be considered too severe upon a private individual. No! I am only severe upon public acts. God save me from going down so low in the scale of intellect as to persecute any man on account of his private acts. I would not, like miscreants, stab a man in the back, nor punish severely the private acts of the editor of the Times, for I say not a word against any other than public acts. It would be unfair, unjust, and unreasonable, as well as opposed to good policy, for this Convention to adjourn without letting the papers of this town—whether rebel, copperhead, or otherwise—know that this Convention has been a Union one, working with the purpose of perpetuating this Union, and also for the purpose of liberating this State from the power of the rebels. Do this and you will do justice—you will commit no injustice; but do it at once!

I now call upon the president of this body to arraign at its bar Thomas P. May. It now, sir, (addressing the president,) becomes your solemn duty, in the name of our nation, our liberty, and the vindication of character, to inform Mr. May of his wrong and then to sentence him to the necessary penalty—certainly, not less than imprisonment until the end of the Convention—the suppression of his paper until the Convention adjourns *sine die.*

Mr. TERRY—I move the previous question.

[The motion was carried.]

Mr. ABELL—I rise to a question of order. The question is this: the gentleman in his answer declares that he appears here under orders from a higher power than we have, and we have never inquired what that authority is.

PRESIDENT—I have it on my desk and will read it.

[Read.]

HEADQUARTERS DEPARTMENT OF THE GULF,
New Orleans, 23d July, 1864.

The provost marshal general is directed, upon receipt of this order, to take such measures as may be necessary to enable Mr. DeCoursey, sergeant-at-arms of the Constitutional Convention, to bring before that Convention Thomas P. May, Esq., assistant treasurer of the United States, and proprietor and publisher of the New Orleans Times newspaper, to answer to that body for an infringement of its privileges as a representative assembly of the people of Louisiana.

This order will be executed immediately.

N. P. Banks,
Maj. Gen. Commanding.

Official: W. W. Howe,
Major and A. A. A. Gen.

Under that order Mr. May appears here in the custody of the sergeant-at-arms of this Convention. Gen. Banks, as it was his duty to do, as a loyal citizen and a loyal general, has given his aid to enforce the civil power of this Convention. What further action do you choose to take?

Mr. Abell—I insist that Mr. May is bound to plead to this in some way.

Mr. Cutler—He has plead.

Mr. Thomas—I wish to offer some resolutions, viz:

Whereas, Thos. P. May, Esq., editor and proprietor of the newspaper called the New Orleans Times, published in the city of New Orleans, has, within the past six months, published articles in said paper which, in the opinion of this Convention, were disloyal in their sentiments to the government, and many of which were in contempt of this Convention; and

Whereas, In the issue of said paper of the 22d of July, a gross libel was published upon the president and members of this Convention, and upon being brought to the bar thereof has refused to purge himself in any manner of said libel and contempt; therefore be it

Resolved, That Thos. P. May, Esq., for said contempt, committed upon the president and members of this Convention, in publishing in said newspaper said libel, shall be imprisoned in the parish prison of the parish of Orleans for the space of ten days, unless this Convention sooner adjourns; and that the sergeant-at-arms be directed and authorized to carry this resolution into effect.

Be it further resolved, That the military authorities of this department be respectfully requested by this Convention to suppress the publication of said newspaper.

Be it further resolved, That the president of the United States be respectfully requested by this Convention to remove the said Thos. P. May, Esq., from the office of assistant treasurer of the United States, in New Orleans, that he now holds.

Mr. Terry—I move the previous question.

[The motion was carried and the resolutions adopted by the following vote:]

Yeas—Messrs. Austin, Barrett, Baum, Beauvais, Bell, Bennie, Burke, Collin, Cook J. K., Cook T., Cutler, Davies, Duane, Dupaty, Edwards, Ennis, Flagg, Flood, Foley, Fuller, Healy, Hart, Henderson, Hire, Howes, Maas, Maurer, Murphy E., Newell, Normand, O'Conner, Payne J., Poynot, Purcell J., Pursell S., Schnurr, Seymour, Smith, Spellicy, Stocker, Stiner, Stauffer, Taliaferro, Terry, Thorpe, Thomas, Wenck, Wells, Wilson—49.

Nays—Messrs. Abell, Balch, Buckley, Campbell, Cazabat, Decker, Dufresne, Fish, Fosdick, Gastinel, Geier, Gorlinski, Gruneberg, Harnan, Heard, Hills, Kavanagh, Mann, Mayer, Mendiverri, Montamat, Morris, Murphy M. W., Ong, Orr, Pintado, Schroeder, Shaw, Stumpf, Sullivan, Waters—31.

President—Mr. Secretary, you will hand the sergeant-at-arms a certified copy of these resolutions. Mr. Sergeant-at-arms you will carry this order of the Convention into effect.

Mr. Abell—Mr. President, I think we have now done all that is necessary in this matter.

Mr. Thorpe—Mr. President, I have a resolution to offer:

Resolved, That until otherwise fixed by the Legislature, the salary of the private secretary of the governor shall be twenty-five hundred dollars per annum, and the salary of the chief clerk of the secretary of state shall be two thousand dollars per annum, payable by the auditor of public accounts, quarterly, on their own warrants, and to take effect from the 4th of March, 1864.

[The resolution was adopted on a rising vote—47 yeas to 18 nays.]

Mr. Thomas—I have a resolution to offer in regard to business which will necessarily be unfinished at the time of the adjournment of this Convention. It is to provide for a committee to audit the bills which will necessarily be incurred after we adjourn.

Resolved, That all bills, indebtedness and unsettled accounts of this Convention accruing at, or after its adjournment, shall be referred to a special auditing committee, to be composed of five members to be appointed by the president. No bills shall be paid without being examined, audited and approved by a majority of said committee; and bills so audited and approved shall be paid on the warrant of the president on the treasurer of the State, out of any moneys in the treasury of the State not otherwise appropriated.

PRESIDENT—I appoint on the committee Messrs. Thomas, Montamat, Barrett, Crozat and Buckley.

Mr. WELLS—I have a resolution to offer :

Resolved, That the reporters of this Convention each receive from the funds in the public treasury not otherwise appropriated, the sum of five hundred dollars, as extra compensation for their arduous labor during this Convention, and for the necessary work to be performed after the adjournment of this body—said sums to be drawn upon their own warrants.

Mr. MONTAMAT—I have a substitute :

Resolved, That the following employés of the Convention shall receive the following compensation, to be paid out of the funds of contingent expenses of this Convention :

Sergeant-at-arms	$200 00
Chief of enrolling clerks	100 00
Enrolling clerks, (each)	100 00
Postmaster	50 00
Doorkeeper	100 00
Messengers, (each)	25 00
Reporter and assistants, (each)	200 00

Mr. STINER—I move as an amendment :

Resolved, That the sum of two hundred and fifty dollars each, be paid to Messrs. Matthew Whilldin and J. N. Russ, reporters, for services rendered to this Convention.

Mr. MONTAMAT—I accept the amendment.

Mr. SMITH—I move the adoption of the substitute.

Mr. SULLIVAN—I move the policemen be included for fifty dollars each.

[The resolution, with Mr. Stiner's amendment, was adopted.]

Mr. ABELL—One of the reporters, Mr. Gallup, has performed very arduous duties. It is with the knowledge of the president and under his direction that he has performed the duties of the official reporter, during the greater part of the session, in addition to his duty as assistant reporter ; I therefore offer the following :

Whereas, During the absence of the official reporter the duty of reading and revising the manuscripts and proofs, the compilation of the debates and other duties of the position, have been performed under the direction of the president, by H. A. Gallup, Esq., assistant reporter, in addition to his duties as such—

Resolved, That for such services so rendered H. A. Gallup receive, in addition to his salary as assistant reporter, the same compensation as is provided for the official reporter for such time as may be found due by the president, to be paid on the warrant of the president out of any money in the treasury not otherwise appropriated.

Mr. CUTLER—We should do justice to everybody. There are certain men, employés of this Convention, who have done their duty faithfully. Let them be paid for it. This resolution is very clear. Mr. Gallup has done other duty, not within the scope of his position as assistant reporter for which he is paid, and it is due that, for such duty, he be paid the amount provided for the performance of that duty ; but we must not stop here. To officers who have been faithful, we must give as a token of our appreciation of their services a *bonus* in addition to any pay that may be due them for services rendered, and after we pass this resolution and provide a liberal *bonus* for each of the reporters, "sergeant-at-arms ! do your duty," should come in, and he has done his duty well and faithfully. A resolution should be passed making liberal appropriations for all these officers, but that should not interfere with this, which is a mere resolution to pay the *per diem* provided for certain services to the officer who has performed them, for the time during which he has performed them, and you all know that they could not have been performed more faithfully or satisfactorily than he has performed them.

Mr. ABELL—The resolution as offered by me is a very simple one. It simply provides that Mr. Gallup shall receive the *per diem* of the official reporter in addition to his own, for the time that he has done the work of both. That the work has been performed and faithfully performed every member here can testify, and the president knows the time that Mr. Gallup has done it, for he himself entrusted the papers to him, and it is certainly a rightful claim upon this Convention for the pay as provided in this resolution.

Mr. MONTAMAT—That would give Gallup about two thousand dollars in addition to what he has got already.

Mr. ABELL—It makes little difference what it would give him. It is a mere matter of compensation. If he has done the work he is entitled to the compensation.

Mr. MONTAMAT—I understand that the

other assistants have done the same duty a part of the time too.

PRESIDENT—You can, if you choose, make a similar resolution respecting them.

Mr. MONTAMAT—I move that the other reporters and the police be included.

PRESIDENT—I shall decide that the amendment is not german to the question.

[The resolution was adopted by a rising vote—45 yeas to 15 nays.]

Mr. WATERS—Mr. President, I now move that the reporter and each of the assistants receive five hundred dollars.

[The motion was carried by a rising vote —39 yeas to 33 nays.

Mr. Thorpe's resolution re-districting the State was taken up and adopted without discussion.]

Mr. CUTLER—I now move that the sergeant-at-arms receive five hundred dollars as extra compensation.

Mr. HILLS—I amend by adding and his assistants two hundred dollars each.

[The motion was carried.]

Mr. THORPE—As chairman of the Committee on Enrollment, I wish to report progress as far as the enrollment of the constitution is concerned. I would say that the enrolling clerks went to work and worked all night and have produced the entire constitution enrolled, but the committee have not yet had time to read it over and compare it with the constitution as adopted, and consequently are not prepared to report it.

PRESIDENT—Several of these motions for extra compensation are not in due form—a mere motion that this Convention appropriate a certain sum with nothing further, can never be paid. The resolution must appropriate the money and set aside a sum in the treasury to pay it, or provide that it shall be paid out of any money not otherwise appropriated. Gentlemen can reduce their resolutions to writing and they can be acted on on Monday.

[On motion the Convention adjourned till Monday at 12 o'clock.]

MONDAY, July 25, 1864.

[The Convention met, pursuant to adjournment, and was called to order by the president. The secretary called the roll, and the following members answered to their names :]

Messrs. Abell, Austin, Balch, Barrett, Baum, Beauvais, Bell, Bofill, Buckley, Burke, Campbell, Collin, Cazabat. Cook J. K., Cook T., Crozat, Cutler, Davies, Decker, Duane, Dufresne, Duke, Dupaty, Edwards, Ennis, Fish, Flagg, Flood, Foley, Fosdick, Fuller, Gastinel, Geier, Gorlinski, Gruneberg, Healy, Harnan, Hart, Heard, Henderson, Hills, Hire, Howes, Kavanagh, Knobloch, Kugler, Maas, Mann, Maurer, Mendiverri, Montamat, Morris, Murphy E., Murphy M. W., Normand, O'Conner, Orr, Payne J., Pintado, Poynot, Purcell J., Pursell S., Schroeder, Schnurr, Seymour, Shaw, Smith, Spellicy, Stocker, Stumpf, Stiner, Stauffer, Sullivan, Terry, Thorpe, Thomas, Waters, Wenck, Wells, Wilson—80.

[The day's proceedings were then opened with prayer by the Rev. Mr. Strong.

The minutes of yesterday's proceedings were read.]

Mr. CUTLER—Mr. President, if I am not laboring under a mistake, the minutes are not entirely correct, so far as to the appropriations to officers and employés are concerned. I remember that several resolutions were offered, several amendments were made, and I believe several substitutes, only a part of which were regularly drawn up and passed. I recollect that you stated that such of the resolutions as were not drawn up in writing, with a provision appropriating certain moneys in the treasury for their payment, could not be paid and should be offered over on Monday. I proposed that they should be immediately reduced to writing and finally acted upon, but a motion to adjourn was made and there the matter rests. That being the condition in which the matter now stands, I have a resolution which I think will remedy the difficulty, and which embraces all the cases not in due form Saturday, and I desire to correct the minutes.

Mr. MONTAMAT—Mr. President : For my part, I shall oppose the motion. I offered a substitute in writing, properly framed, and it was passed. We cannot alter it without a reconsideration of the vote adopting it. If the secretary will read it you will see that it is right, and it has passed this Convention. Now, if the gentleman wants to repeal it, he must get a reconsideration. If he cannot do this, it will remain in force, and his resolution will not affect it—and, on my part, I will not move a reconsideration, for I am satisfied with it as it stands.

Mr. HENDERSON—I remember that the president remarked on Saturday, just after my friend Judge Cutler moved that the sergeant-at-arms receive five hundred dollars, and the motion had been carried, that the motion, being merely that a certain officer receive so much money, and being carried in that form, nothing could be framed on it, that in order to make the resolution effective, the words " out of any money in the treasury not otherwise appropriated" should have been added. On the other hand, Mr. Waters, after his motion had been put and carried, reduced it to writing in proper form, and consequently the money, under that resolution was properly appropriated. The president stated as to other moneys for which the motions were not made in proper form that they could come up in proper form on Monday. That is my recollection of the matter.

Mr. CAZABAT—Mr. President: In connection with this subject I beg leave to say it is not within my knowledge that the amount of contingent expenses of this Convention will exceed fifty or a hundred thousand dollars. But, sir, it makes no difference in the principle, whether they reach one thousand or fifty thousand, if a bill which is due is presented.

PRESIDENT—Are you speaking to the correcting of the minutes?

Mr. CAZABAT—No, sir.

Mr. CUTLER—Mr. President——

Mr. WELLS—Mr. President: I understand——

PRESIDENT—Mr. Cutler has the floor.

Mr. CUTLER—Mr. President, my motion was to correct the minutes.

PRESIDENT—I believe the minutes are correct. There were two or three motions to pay different sums of money to different officers without making any appropriation out of which such sums could be paid. I therefore stated that a mere motion that a certain officer should receive a certain sum of money, without stating the source from which that money was to be obtained—that the resolution, without containing the usual clause, "out of such money in the treasury as is not otherwise appropriated," would be nugatory, and that the treasurer would not pay it, and that the resolution as adopted would be of no effect.

Mr. THORPE—I made a verbal appropriation which does not appear in the minutes at all.

[The question on the adoption of the minutes was put to the House, and they were adopted without amendment.]

Mr. CUTLER—I may very readily accept the explanation of the president as the correct one, and in order that the officers in whose favor resolutions not in proper form were passed on Saturday may receive the money as we intended they should, and to compensate a few others with respect to whom no action has yet been taken, I offer the following resolution:

Resolved, That the following named officers of this Convention, and others, receive as extra compensation the following sums from the treasury of the State, on the warrant of the president, from money not otherwise appropriated:

To Hon. J. N. Carrigan, state librarian	$500 00
To each of the reporters	500 00
To the sergeant-at-arms	500 00
To each of the deputy sergeants-at-arms	100 00
To the post-master	150 00
To the door-keeper	300 00
To the chief enrolling clerk	100 00
To each enrolling clerk	100 00
To each messenger	50 00
To three porters, each	50 00
To four policemen, each	100 00
To J. N. Russ, of the State Gazette, M. Whilldin and T. H. Draper, of the True Delta, (reporters,) each	250 00

Most of this bill has already been passed so far as the figures are concerned, and hence the necessity of appropriating the funds. Certainly there is no man here who can doubt the propriety of paying men extra wages for arduous services like those of the employés of this body, and I must say for one, that I have never seen more faithful men. We have been particularly fortunate in our selection of employés. The will of the president has been carried out to the very letter. Then, sir, it is proper for us to vote them some extra compensation. I am willing to admit that the compensation proposed is too low, but it would certainly be unfair for us to give one extra and not another. I do not believe there is a man here who will oppose this view. My opinion is that the reporters are entitled to more than five hundred dollars each for their ordinary services in addition to anything that is due for extra services, and for which payment is provided in a resolution passed on Saturday. Their work has been faithfully performed. They have been punctually and constantly at their posts and prompt in the execution of their duty. I think the sergeant-at-arms is entitled to more. He has done his duty as few men could have done it. I know there is no gentleman here who is opposed to the payment of extra compensation to the enrolling clerks. When a man does extra work—when he consumes the mid-night oil or the gas light, while we are out enjoying ourselves—he is entitled to extra pay, and we find them put down at one hundred dollars each. The president of the Convention and the chairman of the Committee on Enrollment to decide how many there is of them.

Mr. TERRY—There are twenty-two.

Mr. CUTLER—The chairman of the committee informs me that there are seven enrolling clerks and several translating clerks employed. God knows how many there are altogether, I don't. But let the president and the chairman of the committee settle that question.

Mr. MONTAMAT—I want to amend as to the reporters—three hundred dollars each.

[The motion was not decided.

Mr. Cutler's resolution was put to vote, and adopted on rising vote; 67 yeas to 7 nays.]

Mr. MONTAMAT—I wish my vote to be recorded against that resolution. It is a robbery of the State.

Mr. FISH—Mr. President, I desire to offer for the action of this Convention the following preamble and resolutions:

Whereas, A Convention, claiming to act in the name of the State of Louisiana, did, on the 26th day of January, 1861, pass an ordinance entitled "An ordinance to dissolve the union between the State of Louisiana and other States united with her under the compact entitled 'The Constitution of the United States of America,'" therein declaring and ordaining the repeal of "all laws and ordinances by which the State of Louisiana became a member of the Federal Union," and absolving "her citizens from all allegiance to said Government;"

And whereas, Such ordinance of secession was based upon an unfounded assumption of State sovereignty, and a perverted theory of State rights, and brought about in the interest of slavery; therefore be it

Resolved, That we the people of Louisiana in Convention assembled, do solemnly denounce the doctrines of "State rights" and State sovereignty (interpreted as they have been into a justification of secession) as utterly subversive of our form of government, and tending to confusion, anarchy and national destruction.

Resolved, That we hold and maintain that our primary allegiance is due to the government of the United States; that the constitution and laws of the United States are the supreme law of the land, anything in the constitution or laws of any State to the contrary notwithstanding; that no State convention, whether fairly representing the people or not, has any right, power or authority to absolve us from that allegiance, and that, consequently, the act commonly called the "Ordinance of Secession" is, and always has been, null and void.

Resolved, That having legally abolished the institution of slavery in this State, as an evil in itself and a constant source of national disturbance and danger, and desiring for the same reasons to see it legally abolished throughout the country, we are in favor of so amending the constitution of the United States as to secure this object.

Mr. President, in offering these resolutions, I know that I am introducing a matter calculated to provoke debate, but I desire to see them adopted without debate.

Mr. FOLEY—I move the previous question.

Mr. ABELL—I desire to explain my vote on these resolutions. I wish it distinctly understood by the members of this Convention and by the people, that I am unqualifiedly opposed to the political dogma that the people are slaves to the government. On the contrary, I believe in the sovereignty of the people, and therefore I shall vote emphatically against these resolutions.

Mr. FOLEY — Endorsing most heartily every word of the preamble and resolutions, I vote yes.

Mr. HENDERSON—I vote for these resolutions on the ground that I am bound to be subservient either to the government of the United States or the so-called Confederate government. As my mind and heart are with the government of the United States, and not in favor of a dissolution of the Union, I vote yes.

Mr. STOCKER—I vote yes, without any qualifications whatever.

Mr. STUMPF—I vote yes. While I live I am ready to die for the United States.

Mr. BUCKLEY—Mr. President, I ask if it takes the rights away from the States.

PRESIDENT—The gentleman must construe it for himself.

Mr. BUCKLEY—I vote yes.

[The resolutions were adopted by the following vote:]

YEAS—Messrs. Austin, Barrett, Baum, Beauvais, Bell, Bofill, Buckley, Burke, Campbell, Collin, Cazabat, Cook T., Crozat, Cutler, Davies, Duane, Duke, Dupaty, Edwards, Ennis, Fish, Flagg, Flood, Foley, Fosdick, Fuller, Geier, Gorlinski, Healy, Harnan, Hart, Henderson, Hills, Hire, Howes, Kavanagh, Kugler, Mann, Maurer, Montamat, Morris, Murphy E., Normand, O'Conner, Orr, Payne J., Pintado, Poynot, Purcell J., Pursell S., Schroeder, Schnurr, Seymour, Shaw, Smith, Spellicy, Stocker, Stumpf, Stiner, Stauffer, Sullivan, Terry, Thorpe, Thomas, Waters, Wenck, Wells, Wilson—68.

NAYS—Messrs. Abell, Balch, Decker, Dufresne, Gruneberg, Maas, Mendiverri, Murphy M. W.—8.

Mr. ABELL—Mr. President, it is said that five would have saved Sodom and Gomorrah. I certainly think eight will save the sovereign people.

Mr. THOMAS—Mr. President, I have a resolution which I desire to offer. I see that it is provided in the constitution we are about to present to the people, that "Every white male who has attained the age of twenty-one years, and who has been a resident of the State twelve months next preceding the election, and the last three months thereof in the parish in which he offers to vote, and who shall be a citizen of the United States, shall have the right of voting." I have a resolution to offer on the subject matter of this article, and in offering it will merely explain the reasons why I offer it. We are about to submit this constitution to the people of the State. Every man born in the United States before the war broke out is a citizen of the United States. Jeff. Davis, John Slidell and Judah P. Benjamin are citizens of the United States, and so are thousands of other rebels now within the limits of the State of Louisiana. Do we desire now to submit the constitution to rebels or only to loyal men? It would be worse than folly to submit it to rebels or to have it liable to be defeated by rebel votes. We must not submit it to traitors that are now in the land; let us rather submit it to those whom we represent—men whom we represent and whom we know to be loyal to the government. In order to effect this, I offer the following:

AN ORDINANCE DEFINING THE QUALIFICATIONS OF VOTERS.

SECTION 1. *Be it ordained by the people of the State of Louisiana in Convention assembled,* That until otherwise provided by law, all commissioners, or other officers or persons presiding over elections held in this State, shall require that each voter shall possess the qualifications defined in the constitution as adopted and submitted by this Convention, and shall have declared his allegiance to the United States government according to the provisions of the president's proclamation of December the 8th, 1863.

SEC. 2. *Be it further ordained,* That the executive officers of the State be charged with the execution of this ordinance, and the providing of such details and instructions as may be necessary to carry the same into effect.

SEC. 3. *Be it further ordained,* That this ordinance shall have the force and effect of law from and after its passage until hereafter repealed or modified by the Legislature of the State.

Mr. FOLEY—On its adoption I move the previous question.

[The previous question was carried, and the ordinance adopted.]

Mr. FOSDICK—I wish to offer a preamble and resolutions:

Whereas, The adoption of article 36 of the constitution, excluding ministers of every persuasion or calling from a seat in the Legislature of this State is liable to a misconstruction, be it therefore

Resolved, That the adoption of said article was intended solely to separate the holy calling of the ministry from the arena of politics, believing by such a course we are furthering the true interests of the gospel.

Resolved, That the sum of $1000 be paid on the warrant of the president of this Convention out of any moneys in the State treasury not otherwise appropriated, to be by him distributed among the clergy who have officiated by prayer during the session of this Convention.

Mr. MONTAMAT—I move to lay that on the table.

[The ayes and noes were called.]

Mr. ABELL—I believe it my duty and the duty of this Convention to recognize christianity, and therefore on the question of laying on the table, I vote no.

Mr. HARNAN—I pay my preacher myself, and I don't want to be at any expense to the public to pay preachers who were introduced here against the wishes of a part of this Convention. I believe the preachers were the great cause of this war. I vote yes.

Mr. STOCKER—Mr. President, it certainly will be remembered by yourself, as well as others, that when the gentleman introduced the article in his report, that I raised my voice against it; I then said that it was a direct insult to the clergy. I now think this looks like knocking a man down with a cudgel and then making an apology for it. I vote yes.

[The motion to table was lost by the following vote:]

YEAS—Messrs. Collin, Davies, Dupaty, Edwards, Gastinel, Healy, Harnan, Hart, Kugler, Montamat, Murphy M. W., Normand, Schnurr, Seymour, Stocker, Stumpf, Sullivan, Waters Wenck—19.

NAYS—Messrs. Abell, Austin, Balch, Barrett, Baum, Beauvais, Bell, Bennie, Bofill, Buckley, Burke, Campbell, Cazabat, Cook T., Crozat, Cutler, Decker, Duane, Dufresne, Duke, Ennis, Fish, Flagg, Flood, Foley, Fosdick, Fuller, Geier, Gorlinski, Gruneberg, Henderson, Hills, Hire, Howes, Kavanagh, Maas, Mann, Maurer, Mendiverri, Morris, Murphy E., O'Conner, Orr, Payne J., Pintado, Poynot, Purcell J., Pursell S., Schroeder, Shaw, Smith, Spellicy, Stiner, Stauffer, Terry, Thorpe, Thomas, Wells, Wilson—58.

Mr. FOLEY—I move the previous question.

Mr. BOFILL—I have an amendment:

Provided, The Rev. Mr. —— (Reporters *did not understand the name*) shall not be entitled to his proportion.

Mr. MONTAMAT—He is not a priest. He has been silenced.

[On motion the amendment was tabled.]

Mr. STAUFFER—I have a substitute:

Resolved, That the thanks of this Convention are due, and hereby tendered, to those ministers of the gospel who have officiated during its sessions.

[A rising vote on tabling the substitute resulted in a tie, 29 members voting for and 29 against the motion. The president gave the casting vote in the affirmative and the substitute was tabled.

The resolution of Mr. Fosdick was then adopted on a rising vote—56 yeas and 20 nays.]

Mr. HARNAN—Mr. President, I shall vote against the proceedings of this Convention.

Mr. SHAW—It seems to me, Mr. President, that it is necessary for us to provide for the completion of our work after adjournment.

Mr. HARNAN—Mr. President, I tender my resignation.

Mr. SHAW—I have some resolutions, Mr. President, which I think are necessary to provide for winding up our business as follows:

Resolved, That such officers and employés of the Convention as may be necessary for the completion of its work shall, after adjournment, be under the direction of the chairman of the Committee on Enrollment and the president of the Convention, and the services of all officers and employés not required by said president or chairman, or either of them, shall be discontinued and they shall have power to discharge any of said officers for want of promptness, or on account of the completion of their work.

Resolved, That after adjournment any of the standing committees may perform such duties as may have been assigned them by the rules or resolutions of the Convention, and which may be necessary for winding up and perfecting the work of the Convention, and the president shall require any such duties to be performed by such committees if deemed by him necessary in case of their neglect.

[The resolutions were adopted.]

Mr. CUTLER—Mr. President, I have a resolution to offer:

Resolved, That the salary of the clerk of the treasurer and the chief clerk of the auditor of public accounts of the State of Louisiana, shall be three thousand dollars per annum, until otherwise provided by law. This resolution to take effect from its passage.

[On motion the resolution was tabled.]

Mr. CUTLER—I have another resolution to offer which I hope will meet the approbation of this body, and I hope you will give me your attention while I read it:

Resolved, That when this Convention adjourns, it shall be at the call of the president, whose duty it shall be to reconvoke the Convention for any cause, or in case the constitution should not be ratified, for the purpose of taking such measures as may be necessary for the formation of a civil government for the State of Louisiana. He shall also, in that case, call upon the proper officers of the State to cause elections to be held to fill any vacancies that may exist in the Convention, in parishes where the same may be practicable.

Resolved, That in case of the ratification of the constitution, it shall be in the power of the Legislature of the State, at its first session, to reconvoke the Convention, in like manner, in case it should be deemed expedient or necessary, for the purpose of making amendments or additions to the Constitution that may, in the opinion of the Legislature, require a reassembling of the Convention, or, in case of the occurrence of any emergency requiring its action.

Resolved, That no per diem of members shall be allowed during the adjournment.

These resolutions, Mr. President, are offered for the purpose of taking into consideration now, our future action. It is my opinion and the opinion of many of us, that when this Convention adjourns it should adjourn over to a certain day, and of course without pay, and it is now our duty to act upon these resolutions, and say whether, when we adjourn we shall adjourn *sine die*, or whether we shall adjourn to a certain time.

I am very sorry that the major general commanding the department has not waited upon us to-day. I am very much afraid we shall be disappointed in making him a tender of the pen with which the ordinance of emancipation was signed in token of our appreciation of his efforts in behalf of the restoration of the State. Therefore it may be possible that when we adjourn to-day, we should adjourn to another day for the purpose of making that presentation and signing the constitution. But that is not the object of the resolutions. My object in offering them is that we may keep a watchful eye over the work of the people, and when this work is completed there will be no longer any necessity for the existence of this body, but until it is done, until the constitution is adopted, until the people have ratifying it, there should be a remedy in case its enemies should be likely to prove successful in defeating it.

Mr. ABELL—Mr. President——

Mr. HENDERSON—Mr. President——

Mr. FOLEY—I move the previous question.

Mr. ABELL—I have but a word to say, which is this: that I think the duties of this body will be done when they have signed the constitution. And now I will say to my learned friend there, that when I die, I wish to be buried and not to be suspended like the corpse of Mahomet. As soon as our duties are completed I think we ought to go out of existence as a Convention. I believe we are defunct as a Convention as soon as the object for which we were called together is accomplished.

I shall oppose these resolutions on two grounds: *first*, because I think we have discharged our duty and have no power to go further. Should a majority of this body do so, it will only be for the purpose of further misrepresenting the people. If they don't adopt this constitution they will ignore us. If they approve our work they will have no further use for us. Therefore, I say when we have signed the constitution, a good, honest constitution, as I grant it is in many respects, let us cease to exist as a Convention, and let the people, if they ignore us by rejecting our work, elect servants who will represent their views more faithfully. If we have been faithful, and the people think so, they will re-elect us.

Mr. FOLEY—I move the previous question.

[The motion was carried and the ayes and nays called on the adoption of the resolutions, with the following result:]

YEAS — Messrs. Austin, Balch, Barrett, Baum, Beauvais, Bell, Burke, Collin, Cazabat, Cook T., Crozat, Cutler, Davies, Duane, Dufresne, Duke, Dupaty, Edwards, Ennis, Fish, Flagg, Flood, Foley, Fuller, Geier, Gorlinski, Gruneberg, Hart, Henderson, Hire, Howes, Kavanagh, Kugler, Maas, Mann, Maurer, Morris, Murphy E.,

Normand, O'Conner, Orr, Payne J., Pintado, Poynot, Purcell J., Pursell S., Schroeder, Schnurr, Seymour, Shaw, Smith, Spellicy, Stocker, Stumpf, Stiner, Stauffer, Terry, Thorpe, Thomas, Waters, Wells, Wilson —62.

NAYS—Messrs. Abell, Bofill, Buckley, Campbell, Decker, Fosdick, Gastinel, Healy, Hills, Mendiverri, Montamat, Murphy M. W., Sullivan, Wenck—24.

Mr. THORPE—Mr. President, as chairman of the Committee on Enrollment, I have the honor to report the constitution enrolled.

PRESIDENT—The president will sign it. I will now answer a question propounded to me by one of the honorable gentlemen, and I intended to have answered it at the time. The constitution having already been adopted by a large majority requires only the signature of the president and secretary by way of authentication.

Mr. BOFILL—I move the roll be called, and that members sign as their names are called.

[The secretary proceeded to call the roll. As the names were called several members expressed their reasons, as follows :

Mr. ABELL—Mr. President, I desire now to state the reasons why I will not sign that constitution. I think there are one or two provisions in it which are against every interest in the State and every principle of justice.

Mr. ORR—I am compelled to decline.

Mr. MENDIVERRI—Under my honest convictions of what is politic, right and just, I am compelled to decline.

Mr. SMITH—If it hangs me to-morrow I will sign it.

Mr. WATERS—I decline to sign it.

[After the roll had been gone through, the president announced that sixty-one members had signed the constitution.]

Mr. THORPE—I now move that the constitution be deposited in the office of the secretary of state, and that members who have not signed may be allowed to affix their signatures to it there.

Mr. MONTAMAT—I move as an amendment that it be left in the hands of the committee appointed on Saturday.

[Mr. Thorpe's motion was put and carried.]

Mr. FOSDICK—I have a resolution to offer.

Resolved, That the thanks of this Convention are eminently due, and are hereby tendered to the Hon. E. H. Durell, for the courteous, just and dignified manner with which he has presided over our deliberations.

[The president called Mr. Shaw to the chair.]

Mr. FOSDICK—My object in offering the resolution is explained in the resolution itself. I offer them from the fact that I opposed his election, and as his opponent in that election, I am willing to bear testimony to the dignified manner in which he has performed his duties as our presiding officer.

Mr. CAZABAT—Mr. President and gentlemen of the Convention, I have seconded the resolution offered by Mr. Fosdick. If I have been one of the first to raise my voice in behalf of the freedom of the press and in vindication of liberty, I shall not be the last to raise my voice when it is proposed to testify our respect to the worthy president of this body. He has presided over our deliberations with a patience, urbanity and dignity deserving of our highest commendation, and I trust, sir, that this resolution will be carried without a dissenting voice.

Mr. ABELL—I wish to make a remark to the resolution, Mr. President, before it is put to vote. I approve that resolution most heartily, and I wish in a word or two to explain my reasons, because some gentlemen might otherwise think that I was opposed to it. To the gentlemen here, Mr. President, and to yourself, it is well known that the honorable president and myself have differed on almost every important question that has been presented to this body for consideration, at least on the questions of highest importance, in my estimation ; but, sir, no difference of opinion will induce me to do injustice to any man. I may, in the heat of debate, have said things that I ought not to have said ; but, sir, I believe from my heart that no man ever presided over a deliberative body with more faithfulness of purpose than he has. I voted against him for another gentleman whom I liked, from first to last ; but, sir, I award to him but that which is his due, when I say that no man, who has any respect for himself, can say that Judge Durell has not presided over the deliberations of this body with dignity, impartiality, faithfulness and candor.

I am not a man to seek the favor of great men, sir. I care as little for great men, sir, as anybody; and now, sir, I only want to award to Judge Durell the justice that is due to him. I have stood upon questions on this floor in the minority, and in behalf of the minority, I must say, in justice to Judge Durell, that if there was on his part any departure from the strict rules which govern parliamentary bodies, it was always such as to favor the minority in making a full and fair expression of their views. He has been indulgent to the minority and I thank him for it.

I must also thank the members of the Convention for their great indulgence to me in this Convention; and in conclusion, will only remark, that I hope the vote on the adoption of the resolution will be unanimous.

Mr. Hills—Mr. President: As one of the members of this Convention who voted against our honored president, I deem it proper to express my hearty approval of the resolution of thanks offered by my colleague from the Second, [Mr. Fosdick]. I cheerfully bear witness to the uniform dignity and impartiality with which he has presided over the deliberations of this body, and to the courtesy which he has extended towards the members. In that description of wonderful and surpassing beauty which Homer gives of the formation of the shield of Achilles, we read that the divine artizan cast into his furnace impenetrable brass and tin, and precious gold and silver, and having formed a five-fold shield both large and solid, he ornamented it all over with many curious works with cunning skill. "On it he wrought the earth and the heaven and the sea, the unwearied sun and the full moon, and on it, also, he represented all the constellations with which heaven is crowned."

Sir, in forming this constitution we have cast into the furnace principles of everlasting truth and justice, more enduring than impenetrable brass, or tin, or precious gold and silver We have ornamented our work with liberty—a principle more lasting than the earth, or the heaven, or the sea, the unwearied sun and the full moon, or all the constellations with which heaven is crowned, and in the name of Liberty we go forth sheltered by a stronger than the five-fold shield of Achilles, which the enemies of freedom and justice will in vain assail.

Mr. Abell—I call the gentleman to order. He is not speaking to the question; I insist he shall confine his remarks to the resolution of thanks.

Mr. Hills—It was unnecessary for the gentleman to call me to order, for I had concluded all that I had to say in behalf of of the divine principle of liberty which is always so offensive to my friend from the Fifth District [Mr. Abell].

I have simply to say, in conclusion, that in this great and noble work which we have performed, we have found in our presiding officer a steady, earnest and consistent friend, ready at all times to do full justice to every member on this floor, and I repeat that I shall most cheerfully support the resolution under consideration. [Applause.]

Mr. Stocker—Mr. President, I have but few words to say, and will detain you but a very few minutes, and I hope gentlemen will grant me the same privilege they have granted Mr. Abell. I, too, was one who opposed the election of the president to the seat which he occupies in this Convention, and I desire to say, that the gentleman who introduced that resolution only anticipated me, for I had a resolution to the same effect written and endeavored to present it, but he caught the president's eye first and was assigned the floor. And although I opposed his election. I must say, that I am very glad, as matters have gone, that he was elected, and the resolution of the gentleman meets my most hearty approval. Now, sir, my friend, Mr. Abell, has tendered his thanks to this Convention for the courtesy that has been shown to him. I have not made a calculation myself, but I have a son about fifteen years of age who is very quick at figures, and he has entered into a minute calculation as to what the indulgence extended to Mr. Abell has cost the State, and he figures it up at $61,962 16—a pretty round sum.

Mr. Abell—I call the gentleman to order. If I have cost one hundred thousand dollars I have benefitted the State ten millions, but that has nothing to do with this question.

President [Mr. Shaw.]—Gentlemen will please confine their remarks to the question.

Mr. Abell—The question how much I cost the State has nothing to do with the question under debate. I was sent here by my constituents of the Fifth Ward; I represent them——

Mr. Stocker—As I was saying a minute calculation of the time that the gentleman has occupied——

Mr. Abell—Let him speak to the question. What I object to is the large sums of money he is trying to bring in here——

Mr. Thomas—The gentleman is out of order.

President—The chair appeals to the gentleman from the Fifth to keep order himself. There must necessarily be some freedom of discussion.

Mr. Stocker—Since it is so disagreeable to the gentleman to see how much he has cost the State, and to see the figures which foot up to the amount of $61,962.16——

Mr. Abell—[rising and starting towards the other side of the room where Mr. Stocker was speaking].—If he says that again I will knock him down.

Mr. Stocker—I will not carry the computation any further, and will only say in conclusion that I take great pleasure in indorsing the resolution under discussion, as I do with all my heart.

Mr. Montamat—I agree with the remarks of my colleague fiffrom the th. The position of the president is a very onerous one. I, for my part, would not take it for a hundred dollars a day. Though I don't agree with my colleague in regard to his reasons for not signing the constitution, because I believe it to be a good one, just as good as ever was made in the State of Louisiana, and I desire to leave the people to vote on it themselves. But I believe that Judge Durell has acted impartially towards every member of this Convention and particularly towards my old friend, Abell, the old Kentucky horse.

[The question was put, and the resolution adopted.]

Mr. Shaw [to Mr. Durell].—Mr. President, it now becomes my duty to communicate to you the following resolution which has just been unanimously adopted by this Convention. [Read the resolution.]

Mr. Cutler—Gentlemen of the Convention, I propose before the president replies that we stand and give three cheers for the president of this Convention.

[Three cheers were given as proposed.]

Mr. Montamat—Mr. President, before we adjourn I call on my friend the governor to give us a speech.

Mr. Hills—Let us first hear the president in reply.

President — Gentlemen, I rise with profound emotion to respond to the compliment you have this day paid me. But this is not a time for humility. I will say that I know, and that you know, that I have performed my duties as your president to the best of my ability, and with a good conscience. I will say further, that I know, and that you know, that all of you, sitting upon that floor as members of this great Convention—the representative of the majesty of the people of Louisiana—have performed your several duties to the best of your abilities, with a good conscience.

This Convention, assembled in these troublous times, has had a hard and most dangerous work to perform. Starting, in the honesty of your purpose, and firm in the truthfulness of your acts, you have done that which no convention or legislative body before assembled—as far as history speaks of these matters—has ever performed. [Applause.]

This Convention has proved itself to be an honest, true and hard-working Convention. Its honesty is proved by the fact that it has had no leaders upon the floor; but every man has acted independently for himself, and has done that which he has thought it was his duty to do. [Cheers.] As a larger proof of the honesty and truthfulness of this Convention, it adopted, immediately on its first sitting, the number seventy-six for its quorum ; a number which would have been its quorum had every parish in the State been represented on this floor ; and you have abided by that quorum, therein showing and proclaiming to the State, and to our sister States, that you have acted for the people and under the people.

Now, gentlemen, what have you done? Your first great work—and I do not wish to say anything that may be displeasing to the ears of any gentleman upon this floor, because I know there are gentlemen on this floor who disagree with the majority in this matter, and disagree honestly and truly, and I question no man's motives—I say, the first great work you did, was to give freedom to the slave. [Great applause.] And I say, that this work is the crown and glory of this Convention. That act is the commencement of a new era in civilization. That act is the dividing line between the old and worn out past and the new and glorious future, and will be imitated sooner or later by every one of our Southern sisters now groaning under the incubus of secession. [Applause.]

Then you have fixed the true basis of representation, resting it upon the free voter, and upon the man—he who works honestly and gains his bread, as God said to Adam, by the sweat of his brow. [Cheers.]

You have gone still farther and adopted the true principle and foundation, that of all civilization in every age, among a free people, which is this : a common education to every child of the soil. You have laid deep and enduring the civilization of men and of women who differ not from us except in as far as the sun has beat down more heavily upon their skins and made them black, instead of white. [Loud cheers.] You have accomplished a work which, at this time, may not be appreciated in its height and depth—in the length and breadth of it ; but you have accomplished a work which will assert its importance hereafter. Look over the constitutions of your sister States from the time of the first compact between the original thirteen colonies down to this time, and you will find no such provisions giving protection to the poor against the rich, and giving the rich all that belongs to them. [Applause.]

You have introduced certain policies into the constitution which may be questioned, but no man who is a philosopher—no man who is a statesman, who will contemplate them, reflect upon them and study out their full meaning, will come to any other conclusion than that of the majority of this Convention. I speak, in the first place, with regard to that feature in our constitution, and I am very glad to see before me the member that introduced it, (Mr. Sullivan,) for it is a crown to his head, which takes the police of our great city out of the politics of our city. In modern times the tendency of population is to gather together in cities and to build up vast conglomerate populations. We must depend upon those who watch over us, for protection during the night as during the day, and such men should be independent of political change.

This is the great problem, whose solution has been sought for the last fifty years in England, in France, in Austria and in Germany, and you have solved it. [Applause.]

I come now, gentlemen, to the second extraordinary feature of the constitution. It is this : you have shown yourselves capable of grasping the strength and the weaknesses of humanity. You have not feared to meet the issue—you have proved yourselves willing to acknowledge vice and refused to ignore it. Every man within the hearing of my voice, and that eloquent man of God, (Dr. Newman,) who talks to his people as a true disciple and a master, knows that there are certain vices planted within the human breast, which will always remain there, as long as man is man—for what reason we know not, except that God is wise, and his ways are past finding out—those vices have existed from the beginning and will exist to the end—and it is the duty the first duty of legislators, not to ignore them, but to acknowledge, grapple with and rule them. You have put the gambling article into the constitution, and, from report, I suppose that article will be more criticised and questioned than any other; but you are supported by the writings of the philosophers and by the judgment of the most eminent of the political writers of Europe.

This constitution was formed, not in times of peace, when we could meet in quietude, not in the midst of our friends who were aiding and assisting us, but in a time of war, and I know that, outside of this hall, an immense pressure has been brought to bear against it by those who go about in sheep's clothing, covering the wolf's hide, but you have proved too strong for them. You have proved too courageous for them. You have exhibited courage in this matter superior to the courage of the soldier on the field who marches bravely up to the cannon's mouth. You are civil soldiers, and if you fail the doom of the hangman is your doom. Therefore, I say, that no man with the panoply of war upon his back can exhibit a courage superior to that which you have exhibited sitting on that floor. [Applause.]

With these remarks, gentlemen, I will conclude, wishing you every prosperity of life, wishing you true happiness, wishing, above all things that we, before our eyes are closed in death, may see our beloved country united as it was in the beginning, with that glorious flag floating over every inch of land from the Canadas to the Gulf —from the Atlantic to the Pacific, and our nation the strongest, the most just and the most pure that God's sun ever shown upon. [Applause.]

[Governor Hahn was then loudly called for, and on coming forward, spoke as follows :]

Mr. President ard gentlemen of the Convention: Although I have appeared before many an audience in my life—although I have been in high and dignified bodies, I must say that this demonstration of your approval of my public conduct enters more deeply into my heart, than any other evidence of approval I have received. I owe much to you, and my fellow-citizens of Louisiana, for the high and dignified position in which I have been placed. Fellow-citizens, there is but one position which I would be proud to fill beyond that of governor of the State, and that is, I would like to have been a member of this Convention. [Applause.] And I frequently felt so, and expressed myself to many of you, that I would any day have given up the executive which I hold for the proud honor of having my name stamped with those noble and liberal principles which shine out so prominently in the admirable constitution you have this day signed. [Great applause.]

Fellow-citizens: You have this day concluded a noble work. Educated with strong prejudices, living in a community of singular institutions, you have seen your country about to be separated, and, like true patriots, you have cast aside your early prejudices--you have thrown aside your property and have boldly and manfully come forward in the true spirit of the American, and said: "Let us lose all this rather than lose our country." [Cheers.] And, gentlemen, you will not lose your country. The guns that to-day boom over Atlanta and Petersburg will accomplish the work for which they were designed. [Applause.] This Union of States—created not by man, but by the finger of Almighty God—cannot be divided. [Loud cheers.] Macaulay, in his History of England, truly, says, that "England has frequently been visited by blessings in the guise of disasters." So, fellow-citizens, it may be with us in this apparently great disaster to our country, of a division among its people; but we are going through a system of purification, and when we rid ourselves of the rubbish and the obstacles in the path of true republicanism, our country will stand out brighter and more glorious, and more powerful than any upon which the light of Heaven has ever fallen. [Applause.] We will then not only have secured the blessings of liberty to ourselves and our posterity in this country, but we will be in a position to say that these principles shall prevail all along our boundries. [Great applause.]

Fellow-citizens: I am satisfied that the constitution that you have made will not only meet with a warm response and an overwhelming approval from the loyal people of Louisiana, but that it will come up to the expectations of all loyal men all over this great country. [Applause.]

I thank you for the many evidences of your hearty co-operation with the executive of the State during the months you have been in session, and I think that this is probably the only Convention that has ever been held in the United States in which every member of the Convention was upon terms of the utmost friendship and cordiality with the executive. [Applause.] I feel that I enjoy the friendship and the confidence of every single member in this Convention. [Cheers and cries of "yes," "yes."] I have never sought unduly to impress my views upon you, except upon great occasions when I thought the duty of the humblest citizen required him to advise with his fellow-citizens. I have used no power or influence within my peculiar control to modify or operate upon a single provision in that constitution. I was placed in the office which I now fill much against my own inclinations, and I now state to you that as soon as the constitution is ratified, and this Union is restored, my highest ambition will be to give up that office and to retire into private life with your approbation, and the approbation of my fellow-citizens. [Prolonged applause.]

[A motion was made to adjourn.]

President—The proceedings will be closed with prayer by Rev. Dr. Newman.

[The Rev. Dr. Newman then came upon the platform and offered up a prayer, in language as follows:]

O God! we thank thee that we have lived to see this day,—a day destined to live not only while our memories shall endure, but destined to live in the memories of mankind to the latest generations of time.

We thank thee that during the long and laborious session of this Convention, thy servants have been preserved in body and in mind, and that death has not invaded their circle. We thank thee that reason has maintained her sovereign reign: that their mental powers remain unimpaired; and we rejoice, that at the consummation of their work, with thy benediction abiding on them, they return to the privacy of life and to the various vocations to which thy providence has called them.

Great Father of the Universe! accept our united thanksgiving for the constitution which this Convention has adopted—for the sublime principles of Divine, natural and political justice incorporated therein, and especially that it prohibits slavery and raises the banner of freedom over an enfranchised people.

Great Source of Knowledge! we thank thee that the common intellect, throughout the State, has been emancipated; that the advantages of education are proffered to all; and that without respect of color or circumstances, the children of this and of future generations, are to be instructed in those natural and changeless laws which lead our thoughts up from "nature to nature's God."

Command thy blessing on this instrument of legislation. Are there errors in it? O! remember "to err is human." Suffer not such errors to work out evil to the commonwealth, but according to thy high prerogative, by thine unerring Providence bring good out of the evil.

We beseech thee, prepare the minds of the people for its comprehension and their hearts for its affectionate support.

Be thou the guardian of this fair State, which on this day is born again, and enters on a new, better, higher life of virtue and power, of wealth and glory. Deliver her soil from the last rebel footstep. Over her broad plantations and populous towns extend the shield of thy protection; and re-establish liberty and union, law and order throughout her borders.

Graciously bless our chief executive, and grant our governor all that intellectual power and all that favor with the people which will enable him to discharge his ardous and responsible duties with credit to himself, honor to the State and glory to thine exalted name. And may the State over which he is called to preside, rise in beauty and power among the sister States of our glorious Union, having all her channels of trade re-opened and pouring forth her vast resources of wealth and power in unprecedented profusion.

Command thy blessing on thy servant the president of this Convention. Preserve his valuable life to the country and to the State. Preserve his mental powers unimpared, and grant that in the future as in the past, he may subserve the nation's good and the interests of mankind.

Graciously remember thy servants who shall separate this day. Whatever may betide them ; whatever joys may be strown in their pathway ; whatever sorrows they may be called upon to endure, O! be thou to each a father and a friend : pardon, we beseech thee, the sins of one and all ; regenerate all hearts ; that they may rise and shine in the resurrection of the just and be received into the habitations of the blessed at thy right hand.

Infinite in thy mercies and unmeasured in thy love, answer us for all the employés of the Convention and for all associated therewith.

Honor with thy sustaining and illuminating presence the president of these United States.

Remember Grant and Sherman, to crown them with victory. May Atlanta fall and Richmond surrender ; and, great God, grant that ere many suns shall rise, the last rebel shall be subdued and righteousness and peace and order be restored to our beloved country. In these, our humble requests, answer us, most merciful Father. In all of life's duties be thou our guide. Bring us down to our silent graves with the composure of Christians and with the calmness of a well-grounded hope in Jesus Christ. And O, when the great day of retribution shall have dawned, when the archangel's trumpet shall awake the slumbering millions of mankind, from the depths of the ocean and from the tombs of the earth, grant we may all receive the welcome plaudit, "Well done, good and faithful servant, enter into the joy of thy Lord."

And may the grace of our Lord Jesus Christ, the love of God the Father and the communion of the Holy Spirit abide with your hearts forever. Amen.

[Upon motion, the Convention then adjourned, subject to the call of the president.]

CONSTITUTION OF THE STATE OF LOUISIANA.

ADOPTED IN CONVENTION, JULY 23, 1864.

PREAMBLE.

We, the people of the State of Louisiana, do ordain and establish this Constitution.

TITLE I.

EMANCIPATION.

Article 1. Slavery and involuntary servitude, except as a punishment for crime, whereof the party shall have been duly convicted, are hereby forever abolished and prohibited throughout the State.

Art. 2. The Legislature shall make no law recognizing the right of property in man.

TITLE II.

DISTRIBUTION OF POWERS.

Art. 3. The powers of the government of the State of Louisiana shall be divided into three distinct departments, and each of them shall be confined to a separate body of magistracy, to-wit: those which are legislative to one, those which are executive to another, and those which are judicial to another.

Art. 4. No one of these departments, nor any person holding office in one of them, shall exercise power properly belonging to either of the others, except in the instances hereinafter expressly directed or permitted.

TITLE III.

LEGISLATIVE DEPARTMENT.

Art. 5. The legislative power of the State shall be vested in two distinct branches, the one to be styled "the House of Representatives," the other "the Senate," and both "the General Assembly of the State of Louisiana."

Art. 6. The members of the House of Representatives shall continue in service for the term of two years from the day of the closing of the general elections.

Art. 7. Representatives shall be chosen on the first Monday in November every two years, and the election shall be completed in one day. The General Assembly shall meet annually on the first Monday in January, unless a different day be appointed by law, and their sessions shall be held at the seat of government. There shall also be a session of the General Assembly in the city of New Orleans, beginning on the first Monday of October, eighteen hundred and sixty-four; and it shall be the duty of the governor to cause a special election to be held for members of the General Assembly, in all the parishes where the same may be held, on the day of the election for ratifica tion or rejection of this Constitution—to be valid in case of ratification; and in other parishes or districts he shall cause elections to be held as soon as it may become practicable, to fill the vacancies for such parishes or districts in the General Assembly. The term of office of the first General Assembly shall expire as though its members had been elected on the first Monday of November, eighteen hundred and sixty-three.

Art. 8. Every duly qualified elector under this constitution shall be eligible to a seat in the General Assembly: *Provided*, that no person shall be a representative or senator unless he be, at the time of his election, a duly qualified voter of the representative or senatorial district from which he is elected.

Art. 9. Elections for the members of the General Assembly shall be held at the several election precincts established by law.

Art. 10. Representation in the House of Representatives shall be equal and uniform, and shall be regulated and ascertained by the number of qualified electors. Each parish shall have at least one representative. No new parish shall be created with a territory less than six hundred and twenty-five square miles, nor with a number of electors less than the full number entitling it to a representative; nor when the creation of such new parish would leave any other parish without the said extent of territory and number of electors. The first enumeration by the State authorities, under this constitution, shall be made in the year eighteen hundred and sixty-six, the second in the year eighteen hundred and seventy, the third in the year eighteen hundred and seventy-six; after which time the General Assembly shall direct in what manner the census shall be taken, so that it be made at least once in every period of ten years for the purpose of ascertaining the total population, and the number of qualified electors in each parish and election district; and in case of informality, omission or error, in the census returns from any district, the the Legislature shall order a new census taken in such parish or election district.

Art. 11. At the first session of the Legislature after the making of each enumeration, the Legislature shall apportion the representation amongst the several parishes and election districts on the basis of qualified electors as aforesaid. A representative number shall be fixed, and each parish and election district shall have as many representatives as the aggregate number of its electors will entitle it to, and an additional representative for any fraction exceeding one-half the representative number. The number of representatives shall not be more than one hundred and twenty, nor less than ninety.

Art. 12. Until an apportionment shall be made, and elections held under the same, in accordance with the first enumeration to be made, as directed in article 10. the representation in the Senate and House of Representatives shall be as follows:

For the parish of Orleans, forty-four representatives, to be elected as follows:

First Representative District............3
Second do. 5
Third do. 7
Fourth do. 3
Fifth do. 4
Sixth do. 2
Seventh do. 3
Eighth do. 3
Ninth do. 4
Tenth do. 8
Orleans, Right Bank..................2
For the parish of Livingston............1
do. St. Tammany.............1
do. Pointe Coupée............1
do. St. Martin................2
do. Concordia 1
do. Madison 1
do. Franklin 1
do. St. Mary..................1
do. Jefferson 3
do. Plaquemines..............1
do. St. Bernard...............1
do. St. Charles...............1
do. St. John the Baptist.......1
do. St. James.................1
do. Ascension................1
do. Assumption 3
do. Lafourche................3
do. Terrebonne 2
do. Iberville 1
do. West Baton Rouge........1
do. East Baton Rouge.........2
do. West Feliciana............1
do. East Feliciana............1
For the Parish of Washington............1
do. St. Helena................1
do. Vermillion 1
do. Lafayette 2
do. St. Landry................4
do. Calcasieu 2
do. Avoyelles 2
do. Rapides..................3
do. Natchitoches..............2
do. Sabine 1
do. Caddo 2
do. DeSoto 2
do. Ouachita 1
do. Union 2
do. Morehouse 1
do. Jackson..................2
do. Caldwell.................1
do. Catahoula................2
do. Claiborne 3
do. Bossier..................1
do. Bienville 2
do. Carroll..................1
do. Tensas..................1
do. Winn 2

Total..............118

And the State shall be divided into the following senatorial districts: All that portion of the parish of Orleans lying on the left bank of the Mississippi river shall be divided into two senatorial districts; the First and Fourth Districts of the city of New Orleans shall compose one district and shall elect five senators; and the Second and Third Districts of said city shall compose the other district, and shall elect four senators.

The parishes of Plaquemines, St. Bernard and all that part of the parish of Orleans on the right bank of the Mississippi river shall form one district, and shall elect one senator.

The parish of Jefferson shall form one district, and shall elect one senator.

The parishes of St. Charles and Lafourche shall form one district, and shall elect one senator.

The parishes of St. John the Baptist and St. James shall form one district, and shall elect one senator.

The parishes of Ascension, Assumption and Terrebonne shall form one district, and shall elect two senators.

The parish of Iberville shall form one district, and shall elect one senator.

The parish of East Baton Rouge shall form one district, and shall elect one senator.

The parishes of West Baton Rouge, Point Coupée and West Feliciana shall form one district, and shall elect two senators.

The parish of East Feliciana shall form one district, and shall elect one senator.

The parishes of Washington, St. Tammany, St. Helena and Livingston shall form one district, and shall elect one senator.

The parishes of Concordia and Tensas shall form one district, and shall elect one senator.

The parishes of Madison and Carroll shall form one district, and shall elect one senator.

The parishes of Morehouse, Ouachita, Union and Jackson shall form one district, and shall elect two senators.

The parishes of Catahoula, Caldwell and Franklin, shall form one district, and shall elect one senator.

The parishes of Bossier, Bienville, Claiborne and Winn shall form one district, and shall elect two senators.

The parishes of Natchitoches, Sabine, DeSoto and Caddo shall form one district, and shall elect two senators.

The parishes of St. Landry, Lafayette and Calcasieu shall form one district, and shall elect two senators.

The parishes of St. Martin and Vermillion shall form one district, and shall elect one senator.

The parish of St. Mary shall form one district, and shall elect one senator.

The parishes of Rapides and Avoyelles shall form one district, and shall elect two senators.

Art. 13. The House of Representatives shall choose its speaker and other officers.

Art. 14. Every white male who has attained the age of twenty-one years, and who has been a resident of the State twelve months next preceding the election, and the last three months thereof in the parish in which he offers to vote, and who shall be a citizen of the United States, shall have the right of voting.

Art. 15. The Legislature shall have power to pass laws extending suffrage to such other persons, citizens of the United States, as by military service, by taxation to support the government, or by intellectual fitness, may be deemed entitled thereto.

Art. 16. No voter, on removing from one parish to another within the State, shall lose the right of voting in the former until he shall have acquired it in the latter. Electors shall in all cases, except treason, felony or breach of the peace, be privileged from arrest during their attendance at, going to, or returning from elections.

Art. 17. The Legislature shall provide by law that the names and residence of all qualified electors shall be registered in order to entitle them to vote; but the registry shall be free of cost to the elector.

Art. 18. No pauper, no person under interdiction, nor under conviction of any crime punishable with hard labor, shall be entitled to vote at any election in this State.

Art. 19. No person shall be entitled to vote at any election held in this State except in the parish of his residence, and, in cities and towns divided into election precincts, in the election precinct in which he resides.

Art. 20. The members of the Senate shall be chosen for the term of four years. The Senate, when assembled, shall have the power to choose its own officers.

Art. 21. The Legislature, in every year in which they apportion representation in the House of Representatives, shall divide the State into senatorial districts.

Art. 22. No parish shall be divided in the formation of a senatorial district, the parish of Orleans excepted. And whenever a new parish shall be created, it shall be attached to the senatorial district from which most of its territory was taken, or to another contiguous district, at the discretion of the Legislature; but shall not be attached to more than one district. The number of senators shall be thirty-six; and they shall be apportioned among the senatorial districts according to the electoral population contained in the several districts: *Provided*, that no parish be entitled to more than nine senators.

Art. 23. In all apportionments of the Senate, the electoral population of the whole State shall be divided by the number thirty-six, and the result produced by this division shall be the senatorial ratio entitling a senatorial district to a senator. Single or contiguous parishes shall be formed into districts, having a population the nearest possible to the number entitling a district to a senator; and if in the apportionment to make a parish or district fall short of or exceed the ratio, then a district may be formed having not more than two senators, but not otherwise. No new apportionment shall have the effect of abridging the term of service of any senator already elected at the time of making the apportionment. After an enumeration has been made as directed in the 10th article, the Legislature shall not pass any law until an apportionment of representation in both Houses of the General Assembly be made.

Art. 24. At the first session of the General Assembly, after this constitution takes effect, the senators shall be equally divided by lot, into two classes; the seats of the senators of the first class shall be vacated at the expiration of the term of the first House of Representatives; of the second class at the expiration of the term of the second House of Representatives; so that one-half shall be chosen every two years, and a rotation thereby kept up perpetually. In case any district shall have elected two or more senators, said senators shall vacate their seats respectively at the end of the term aforesaid, and lots shall be drawn between them.

Art. 25. The first election for senators shall be held at the same time that the election for representatives is held; and thereafter there shall be elections of senators at the same time with each general election of representatives, to fill the places of those senators whose term of service may have expired.

Art. 26. Not less than a majority of the members of each House of the General Assembly shall form a quorum to do business; but a smaller number may adjourn from day to day, and shall be authorized by law to compel the attendance of absent members.

Art. 27. Each House of the General Assembly shall judge of the qualifications, elections and return of its members; but a contested election shall be determined in such a manner as shall be directed by law.

Art. 28. Each House of the General Assembly may determine the rules of its proceeding, punish a member for disorderly behavior, and, with a concurrence of two-thirds, expel a member; but not a second time for the same offence.

Art. 29. Each House of the General Assembly shall keep and publish weekly a journal of its proceedings; and the yeas and nays of the members on any question shall, at the desire of any two of them, be entered on the journal.

Art. 30. Each House may punish, by imprisonment, any person not a member, for disrespectful and disorderly behavior in its presence, or for obstructing any of its proceedings. Such imprisonment shall not exceed ten days for any one offence.

Art. 31. Neither House, during the sessions of the General Assembly, shall, without the consent of the other, adjourn for more than three days, nor to any other place than that in which they may be sitting.

Art. 32. The members of the General Assembly shall receive from the public treasury a compensation for their services, which shall be eight dollars per day, during their attendance, going to and returning from the sessions of their respective Houses. The compensation may be increased or diminished, by law, but no alteration shall take effect during the period of service of the members of the House of Representatives by whom such alteration shall have been made. No session shall extend to a period beyond sixty days, to date from its commencement, and any legislative action had after the expiration of the said sixty days, shall be null and void. This provision shall not apply to the first Legislature which is to convene after the adoption of this constitution.

Art. 33. The members of the General Assembly shall in all cases, except treason, felony, breach of the peace, be privileged from arrest during their attendance at the sessions of their respective Houses, and going to or returning from the same; and for any speech or debate in either House shall not be questioned in any other place.

Art. 34. No senator or representative shall, during the term for which he was elected, nor for one year thereafter, be appointed to any civil office of profit under this State, which shall have been created, or the emoluments of which shall have been increased during the time such senator or representative was in office, except to such offices as may be filled by the election of the people.

Art. 35. No person, who at any time may have been a collector of taxes, whether State, parish or municipal, or who may have been otherwise entrusted with public money, shall be eligible to the General Assembly, or to any office of profit or trust, under the State government, until he shall have obtained a discharge for the amount of such collections, and for all public moneys with which he may have been entrusted.

Art. 36. No person, while he continues to exercise the functions of a clergyman of any religious denomination whatever, shall be eligible to the General Assembly.

Art. 37. No bill shall have the force of a law until, on three several days, it be read over in each House of the General Assembly, and free discussion allowed thereon; unless in case of urgency, four-fifths of the House, where the bill shall be pending, may deem it expedient to dispense with this rule.

Art. 38. All bills for raising revenue, shall originate in the House of Representatives; but the Senate may propose amendments, as in other bills: *Provided*, they shall not introduce any new matter, under the color of an amendment, which does not relate to raising revenue.

Art. 39. The General Assembly shall regulate, by law, by whom, and in what manner, writs of election shall be issued to fill the vacancies which may happen in either branch thereof.

Art. 40. The Senate shall vote on the confirmation or rejection of the officers, to be appointed by the governor with the advice and consent of the Senate, by yeas and nays; and the names of the senators voting for and against the appointments, respectively, shall be entered on a journal to be kept for that purpose, and made public at the end of each session, or before.

Art. 41. Returns of all elections for members of the General Assembly shall be made to the secretary of state.

Art. 42. In the year in which a regular election for a Senator of the United States is to take place, the members of the General Assembly shall meet in the hall of the House of Representatives on the second Monday following the meeting of the Legislature, and proceed to said election.

TITLE IV.

EXECUTIVE DEPARTMENT.

Art. 43. The supreme executive power

of the State shall be vested in a chief magistrate, who shall be styled the governor of the State of Louisiana. He shall hold his office during the term of four years, and, together with the lieutenant governor, chosen for the same term, be elected as follows: The qualified electors for representatives shall vote for governor and lieutenant governor at the time and place of voting for representatives; the returns of every election shall be sealed up and transmitted by the proper returning officer to the secretary of state, who shall deliver them to the speaker of the House of Representatives on the second day of the session of the General Assembly then to be holden. The members of the General Assembly shall meet in the House of Representatives to examine and count the votes. The person having the greatest number of votes for governor shall be declared duly elected; but if two or more persons shall be equal and the highest in the number of votes polled for governor, one of them shall immediately be chosen governor by joint vote of the members of the General Assembly. The person having the greatest number of votes polled for lieutenant governor shall be lieutenant governor; but if two or more persons shall be equal and highest in the number of votes polled for lieutenant governor, one of them shall be immediately chosen lieutenant governor by joint vote of the members of the General Assembly.

Art. 44. No person shall be eligible to the office of governor or lieutenant governor who shall not have attained the age of thirty-five years, and been a citizen and resident within the State for the period of five years next preceding his election.

Art. 45. The governor shall enter on the discharge of his duties on the second Monday of January next ensuing his election, and shall continue in office until the Monday next succeeding the day that his successor shall be declared duly elected, and shall have taken the oath or affirmation required by the constitution.

Art. 46. No member of Congress, minister of any religious denomination, or any person holding office under the United States government, shall be eligible to the office of governor or lieutenant governor.

Art. 47. In case of impeachment of the governor, his removal from office, death, refusal or inability to qualify, resignation or absence from the State, the powers and duties of the office shall devolve upon the lieutenant governor for the residue of the term, or until the governor, absent or impeached, shall return or be acquitted. The Legislature may provide by law for the case of removal, impeachment, death, resignation, disability or refusal to qualify, of both the governor and the lieutenant governor, declaring what officer shall act as governor, and such officer shall act accordingly, until the disability be removed, or for the remainder of the term.

Art. 48. The lieutenant governor or officer discharging the duties of governor, shall, during his administration, receive the same compensation to which the governor would have been entitled had he continued in office.

Art. 49. The lieutenant governor shall, by virtue of his office, be president of the Senate, but shall have only a casting vote therein. Whenever he shall administer the government, or shall be unable to attend as president of the Senate, the senators shall elect one of their own members as president of the Senate for the time being.

Art. 50. The governor shall receive for his services a compensation of eight thousand dallars per annum, payable quarterly, on his own warrant.

Art. 51. The lieutenant governor shall receive for his services a salary of five thousand dollars per annum, to be paid quarterly.

Art. 52. The governor shall have power to grant reprieves for all offences against the State, and, except in cases of impeachment, shall, with the consent of the Senate, have power to grant pardons, remit fines and forfeitures, after conviction. In cases of treason, he may grant reprieves until the end of the next session of the General Assembly, in which the power of pardoning shall be vested.

Art. 53. He shall be commander-in-chief of the militia of this State, except when they shall be called into the service of the United States.

Art. 54. He shall nominate, and, by and with the advice and consent of the Senate, appoint all officers whose offices are established by the constitution, and whose appointments are not herein otherwise provided for: *Provided*, however, that the Legislature shall have a right to prescribe the mode of appointment to all other offices established by law.

Art. 55. The governor shall have power to fill vacancies that may happen during the recess of the Senate, by granting commissions which shall expire at the end of the next session thereof, unless otherwise provided for in this constitution; but no person who has been nominated for office and rejected by the Senate, shall be appointed to the same office during the recess of the Senate.

Art. 56. He may require information, in writing, from the officers in the executive department upon any subject relating to the duties of their respective offices.

Art. 57. He shall, from time to time, give to the General Assembly information respecting the situation of the State, and recommend to their consideration such measures as he may deem expedient.

Art. 58. He may, on extraordinary occasions, convene the General Assembly at the seat of government, or at a different place if that should have become dangerous from an enemy, or from epidemic; and, in case of disagreement between the two Houses as to the time of adjournment, he may adjourn them to such time as he may think proper, not exceeding four months.

Art. 59. He shall take care that the laws are faithfully executed.

Art. 60. Every bill which shall have passed both Houses shall be presented to the governor; if he approves, he shall sign it, if not, he shall return it with his objections to the House in which it originated, which shall enter the objections at large upon its journal, and proceed to consider it; if, after such consideration, two-thirds of all the members elected to that House shall agree to pass the bill, it shall be sent, with the objections, to the other House, by which it shall be likewise considered, and if approved by two-thirds of the members elected to that House, it shall be a law; but in such cases the vote of both Houses shall be determined by yeas and nays, and the names of the members voting for or against the bill shall be entered on the journal of each House respectively. If any bill shall not be returned by the governor within ten days (Sundays excepted) after it shall have been presented to him, it shall be a law in like manner as if he had signed it; unless the General Assembly, by adjournment, prevent its return.

Art. 61. Every order, resolution or vote, to which the concurrence of both Houses may be necessary, except on a question of adjournment, shall be presented to the governor, and before it shall take effect, be approved by him, or, being disapproved, shall be repassed by two-thirds of the members elected to each House of the General Assembly.

Art. 62. There shall be a secretary of state who shall hold his office during the term for which the governor shall have been elected. The records of the State shall be kept and preserved in the office of the secretary; he shall keep a fair register of the official acts and proceedings of the governor, and when necessary shall attest them; he shall, when required, lay the said register, and all papers, minutes and vouchers relative to his office, before either House of the General Assembly, and shall perform such other duties as may be enjoined on him by law.

Art. 63. There shall be a treasurer of the State, and an auditor of public accounts, who shall hold their respective offices during the term of four years.

Art. 64. The secretary of state, treasurer of state and auditor of public accounts shall be elected by the qualified electors of the State; and in case of any vacancy caused by the resignation, death or absence of the secretary, treasurer or auditor, the governor shall order an election to fill said vacancy.

Art. 65. The secretary of state, the treasurer and the auditor shall receive a salary of five thousand dollars per annum each.

Art. 66. All commissions shall be in the name and by the authority of the State of Louisiana, and shall be sealed with the State seal and signed by the governor.

Art. 67. All able-bodied men in the State shall be armed and disciplined for its defence.

Art. 68. The militia of the State shall be organized in such manner as may be hereafter deemed most expedient by the Legislature.

TITLE V.

JUDICIARY DEPARTMENT.

Art. 69. The judiciary power shall be vested in a Supreme Court, in such inferior courts as the Legislature may, from time to time, order and establish, and in justices of the peace.

Art. 70. The Supreme Court, except in cases hereafter provided, shall have appellate jurisdiction only; which jurisdiction shall extend to all cases when the matter in dispute shall exceed three hundred dollars; to all cases in which the constitutionality or legality of any tax, toll or impost whatsoever, or of any fine, forfeiture or penalty imposed by a municipal corporation, shall be in contestation; and to all criminal cases on questions of law alone whenever the offence charged is punishable with death or imprisonment at hard labor, or when a fine exceeding three hundred dollars is actually imposed.

Art. 71. The Supreme Court shall be composed of one chief justice and four associate justices, a majority of whom shall constitute a quorum. The chief justice shall receive a salary of seven thousand five hundred dollars, and each of the associate justices a salary of seven thousand dollars, annually, until otherwise provided by law. The court shall appoint its own clerks.

Art. 72. The Supreme Court shall hold its sessions in New Orleans from the first Monday in the month of November to the end of the month of June, inclusive. The Legislature shall have the power to fix the sessions elsewhere during the rest of the year; until otherwise provided the sessions shall be held as heretofore.

Art. 73. The Supreme Court, and each of the judges thereof, shall have power to issue writs of *habeas corpus*, at the instance of all persons in acutual custody under process, in all cases in which they may have appellate jurisdiction.

Art. 74. No judgment shall be rendered

by the Supreme Court without the concurrence of a majority of the judges comprising the court. Whenever the majority cannot agree, in consequence of the recusation of any member of the court, the judges not recused shall have power to call upon any judge or judges of the inferior courts, whose duty it shall be, when so called upon, to sit in the place of the judge or judges recused, and to aid in determining the case.

Art. 75. All judges, by virtue of their office, shall be conservators of the peace throughout the State. The style of all process shall be "the State of Louisiana." All prosecutions shall be carried on in the name and by the authority of the State of Louisiana, and conclude against the peace and dignity of the same.

Art. 76. The judges of all courts within the State shall, as often as it may be advisable so to do, in every definitive judgment, refer to the particular law in virtue of which such judgment may be rendered, and in all cases adduce the reasons on which their judgment is founded.

Art. 77. The judges of all courts shall be liable to impeachment; but for any reasonble cause, which shall not be sufficient ground for impeachment, the governor shall remove any of them, on the address of a majority of the members elected to each House of the General Assembly. In every such case the cause or causes for which such removal may be required shall be stated at length in the address, and inserted in the journal of each House.

Art. 78. The judges both of the Supreme and inferior courts shall receive a salary which shall not be diminished during their continuance in office; and they are prohibited from receiving any fees of office or other compensation than their salaries for any civil duties performed by them.

Art. 79. The judges of the SupremeCourt shall be appointed by the governor, by and with the advice and consent of the Senate, for a term of eight years; the judges of the inferior courts for a term of six years.

Art. 80. The clerks of the inferior courts shall be elected by the qualified voters of their several districts, and shall hold their offices during a term of four years.

Art. 81. The Legislature shall have power to vest in clerks of courts authority to grant such orders, and do such acts as may be deemed necessary for the furtherance of the administration of justice, and in all cases the powers thus granted shall be specified and determined.

Art. 82. The jurisdiction of justices of the peace shall not exceed, in civil cases, the sum of one hundred dollars, exclusive of interest, subject to appeal in such cases as shall be provided for by law. They shall be elected by the qualified voters of their several districts, and shall hold their office during a term of two years. They shall have such criminal jurisdiction as shall be provided by law.

Art. 83. There shall be an attorney general for the State, and as many district attorneys as the Legislature shall find necessary. The attorney general shall be elected every four years, by the qualified voters of the State. He shall receive a salary of five thousand dollars per annum, payable on his own warrant quarterly. The district attorneys shall be elected by the qualified voters of their respective districts, for a term of four years. They shall receive such salaries as shall be provided by the Legislature.

Art. 84. A sheriff and a coroner shall be elected in each parish by the qualified voters thereof, who shall hold their offices for the term of two years. The Legislature shall have the power to increase the number of sheriffs in any parish. Should a vacancy occur in either of these offices subsequent to an election, it shall be filled by the governor, and the person so appointed shall continue in office until his successor shall be elected and qualified.

TITLE VI.

IMPEACHMENT.

Art. 85. The power of impeachment shall be vested in the House of Representatives.

Art. 86. Impeachments of the governor, lieutenant governor, attorney general, secretary of state, state treasurer, auditor of public accounts, and the judges of the inferior courts, justices of the peace excepted, shall be tried by the Senate; the chief justice of the Supreme Court, or the senior judge thereof, shall preside during the trial of such impeachment. Impeachments of the judges of the Supreme Court shall be tried by the Senate. When sitting as a court of impeachment, the senators shall be upon oath or affirmation, and no person shall be convicted without the concurrence of a majority of the senators elected.

Art. 87. Judgments in case of impeachment shall extend only to removal from office, and disqualification from holding any office of honor, trust or profit under the State; but the convicted parties shall, nevertheless, be subject to indictment, trial and punishment, according to law.

Art. 88. All officers against whom articles of impeachment may be preferred, shall be suspended from the exercise of their functions during the pendency of such impeachment; the appointing power may make a provisional appointment to replace any suspended officer until the decision of the impeachment.

Art. 89. The Legislature shall provide by law for the trial, punishment, and removal from office of all other officers of the State by indictment or otherwise.

TITLE VII.

GENERAL PROVISIONS.

Art. 90. Members of the General Assembly and all officers, before they enter upon the duties of their offices, shall take the following oath or affirmation:

"I, (A B) do solemnly swear (or affirm) that I will support the constitution and laws of the United States, and of this State, and that I will faithfully and impartially discharge and perform all the duties incumbent on me as ——, according to the best of my abilities and understanding, so help me God!"

Art. 91. Treason against the State shall consist only in levying war against it, or in adhering to its enemies, giving them aid and comfort. No person shall be convicted of treason, unless on the testimony of two witnesses to the same overt act, or his own confession in open court.

Art. 92. The Legislature shall have power to declare the punishment of treason; but no attainder of treason shall work corruption of blood or forfeiture, except during the life of the person attainted.

Art. 93. Every person shall be disqualified from holding any office of trust or profit, in this State, and shall be excluded from the right of suffrage, who shall have been convicted of treason, perjury, forgery, bribery or other high crimes or misdemeanors.

Art. 94. All penalties shall be proportioned to the nature of the offence.

Art. 95. The privilege of free suffrage shall be supported by laws regulating elections, and prohibiting, under adequate penalties, all undue influence thereon from power, bribery, tumult, or other improper practice.

Art. 96. No money shall be drawn from the treasury but in pursuance of specific appropriation made by law; nor shall any appropriation of money be made for a longer term than two years. A regular statement and account of the receipts and expenditures of all public moneys shall be published annually, in such manner as shall be prescribed by law.

Art. 97. It shall be the duty of the General Assembly to pass such laws as may be proper and necessary to decide differences by arbitration.

Art. 98. All civil officers for the State at large shall be voters of, and reside within the State; and all district or parish officers shall be voters of, and reside within their respective districts or parishes, and shall keep their offices at such places therein as may be required by law.

Art. 99. All civil officers shall be removable by an address of a majority of the members elected to both Houses, except those the removal of whom has been otherwise provided by this constitution.

Art. 100. In all elections by the people the vote shall be taken by ballot; and in all elections by the Senate and House of Representatives, jointly or separately, the vote shall be given *viva voce*.

Art. 101. No member of Congress, nor person holding or exercising any office of trust or profit under the United States, or under any foreign power, shall be eligible as a member of the General Assembly, or hold or exercise any office of trust or profit under the State.

Art. 102. None but citizens of the United States shall be appointed to any office of trust or profit in this State.

Art. 103. The laws, public records, and the judicial and legislative written proceedings of the State, shall be promulgated, preserved, and conducted in the language in which the constitution of the United States is written.

Art. 104. No power of suspending the laws of this State shall be exercised, unless by the Legislature or by its authority.

Art. 105. Prosecutions shall be by indictment or information. The accused shall have a speedy public trial, by an impartial jury of the parish in which the offence shall have been committed. He shall not be compelled to give evidence against himself; he shall have the right of being heard, by himself or counsel; he shall have the right of meeting the witnesses face to face, and shall have compulsory process for obtaining witnesses in his favor. He shall not be twice put in jeopardy for the same offence.

Art. 106. All persons shall be bailable by sufficient sureties, unless for capital offences, where the proof is evident or presumption great; or, unless after conviction for any offence or crime punishable with death or imprisonment at hard labor. The privilege of the writ of *habeas corpus* shall not be suspended, unless, when in cases of rebellion or invasion, the public safety may require it.

Art. 107. Excessive bail shall not be required; excessive fines shall not be imposed, nor cruel and unusual punishments inflicted.

Art. 108. The right of the people to be secure in their persons, houses, papers and effects, against unreasonable searches and seizures, shall not be violated; and no warrants shall issue but upon probable cause, supported by oath or affirmation, and particularly describing the place to be searched and the person or thing to be seized.

Art. 109. No *ex post facto* or retroactive law, nor any law impairing the obligations of contracts, shall be passed, nor vested rights be divested, unless for purposes of public utility, and for adequate compensation previously made.

Art. 110. All courts shall be open; and

every person, for any injury done him, in his lands, goods, person, or reputation, shall have remedy by due course of law, and right and justice administered without denial or unreasonable delay.

Art. 111. The press shall be free; every citizen may freely speak, write and publish his sentiments on all subjects—being responsible for an abuse of this liberty.

Art. 112. The Legislature shall not have power to grant aid to companies or associations of individuals, except to charitable associations, and to such companies or associations as are and shall be formed for the exclusive purpose of making works of internal improvement, wholly or partially within the State, to the extent only of one-fifth of the capital of such companies, by subscription of stock or loan in money or public bonds; but any aid thus granted shall be paid to the company only in the same proportion as the remainder of the capital shall be actually paid in by the stockholders of the company; and, in case of loan, such adequate security shall be required, as to the Legislature may seem proper. No corporation or individual association, receiving the aid of the State as herein provided, shall possess banking or discounting privileges.

Art. 113. No liability shall be contracted by the State as above mentioned, unless the same be authorized by some law for some single object or work, to be distinctly specified therein, which shall be passed by a majority of the members elected to both Houses of the General Assembly; and the aggregate amount of debts and liabilities incurred under this and the preceding article shall never, at any time, exceed eight millions of dollars.

Art. 114. Whenever the Legislature shall contract a debt exceeding in amount the sum of one hundred thousand dollars, unless in case of war, to repel invasion, or suppress insurrection, they shall, in the law creating the debt, provide adequate ways and means for the payment of the current interest and of the principal when the same shall become due. And the said law shall be irrepealable until principal and interest are fully paid and discharged, or unless the repealing law contains some other adequate provision for the payment of the principal and interest of the debt.

Art. 115. The Legislature shall provide by law for all change of venue in civil and criminal cases.

Art. 116. The Legislature shall have the power to license the selling of lottery tickets and the keeping of gambling houses; said houses in all cases shall be on the first floor and kept with open doors; but in all cases not less than ten thousand dollars per annum shall be levied as a license or tax on each vendor of lottery tickets, and on each gambling house, and five hundred dollars on each tombola.

Art. 117. The Legislature may enact general laws regulating the adoption of children, emancipation of minors, changing of names, and the granting of divorces; but no special laws shall be enacted relating to particular or individual cases.

Art. 118. Every law enacted by the Legislature shall embrace but one object, and that shall be expressed in the title.

Art. 119. No law shall be revived or amended by reference to its title; but in such case the act revived, or section amended, shall be re-enacted and published at length.

Art. 120. The Legislature shall never adopt any system or code of laws by general reference to such system or code of laws; but in all cases shall specify the several provisions of the laws it may enact.

Art. 121. Corporations shall not be created in this State by special laws except for political or municipal purposes; but the Legislature shall provide by general law for the organization of all other corporations, except corporations with banking or discounting privileges, the creation, renewal or extension of which is hereby prohibited.

Art. 122. In case of the insolvency of any bank or banking association, the bill holders thereof shall be entitled to preference in payment over all other creditors of such bank or association.

Art. 123. No person shall hold or exercise, at the same time, more than one civil office of trust or profit, except that of justice of the peace.

Art. 124. Taxation shall be equal and uniform throughout the State. All property shall be taxed in proportion to its value, to be ascertained as directed by law. The General Assembly shall have power to exempt from taxation property actually used for church, school or charitable purposes. The General Assembly shall levy an income tax upon all persons pursuing any occupation, trade or calling, and all such persons shall obtain a license, as provided by law. All tax on income shall be pro rata on the amount of income or business done.

Art. 125. The Legislature may provide by law in what case officers shall continue to perform the duties of their offices until their successors shall have been inducted into office.

Art. 126. The Legislature shall have power to extend this constitution and the jurisdiction of this State over any territory acquired by compact, with any State, or with the United States, the same being done by consent of the United States.

Art. 127. None of the lands granted by Congress to the State of Louisiana for aid.

ing in constructing the necessary levees and drains, to reclaim the swamp and overflowed lands of the State, shall be diverted from the purposes for which they were granted.

Art. 128. The Legislature shall pass no law excluding citizens of this State from office for not being conversant with any language except that in which the constitution of the United States is written.

Art. 129. No liability, either State, parochial or municipal, shall exist for any debts contracted for, or in the interest of the rebellion against the United States government.

Art. 130. The seat of government shall be and remain at New Orleans, and shall not be removed without the consent of a majority of both Houses of the General Assembly.

Art. 131. The Legislature may determine the mode of filling vacancies in all offices for which provision is not made in this constitution.

Art. 132. The Legislature shall pass no law requiring a property qualification for office.

TITLE VIII.

CORPORATION OF THE CITY OF NEW ORLEANS.

Art. 133. The citizens of the city of New Orleans shall have the right of appointing the several public officers necessary for the administration of the police of said city, pursuant to the mode of elections which shall be prescribed by the Legislature; *Provided*, that the mayor and recorders shall be ineligible to a seat in the General Assembly; and the mayor and recorders shall be commissioned by the governor as justices of the peace, and the Legislature may vest in them such criminal jurisdiction as may be necessary for the punishment of minor offences, and as the police and good of said city may require.

The city of New Orleans shall maintain a police which shall be uniformed with distinction of grade, to consist of permanent citizens of the State of Louisiana, to be selected by the mayor of the city, and to hold office during good behavior, and removable only by a police commission composed of five citizens and the mayor, who shall be president of the board. The commission to be appointed by the governor of the State for the term of two years, at a salary of not less than one thousand dollars per annum; a majority of whom shall remove for delinquencies. Members of the police when removed shall not again be eligible to any position on the police for a term of one year.

Interfering or meddling in elections in any manner will be a sufficient cause for instant dismissal from the police by the board.

The chief of police shall give a penal bond in the sum of ten thousand dollars; lieutenants of police, five thousand dollars; sergeants and clerks, each three thousand dollars; corporals, two thousand dollars; and privates one thousand dollars; with good and solvent security, as the law directs, for the faithful performance of their duties.

The various officers shall receive a salary of not less than the following rates:

The chief of police........	$250	per	month.
The lieutenants of police..	150	do.	do.
The sergeants of police....	100	do.	do.
The clerks of police......	100	do.	do.
The corporals of police...	90	do.	do.
The privates (day and night) each..................	80	do.	do.

TITLE IX.

LABOR ON PUBLIC WORKS.

Art. 134. The Legislature may establish the price and pay of foremen, mechanics, laborers and others employed on the public works of the State or parochial or city governments: *Provided*, That the compensation to be paid all foremen, mechanics, cartmen and laborers employed on the public works, under the government of the State of Louisiana, city of New Orleans, and the police juries of the various parishes of the State, shall not be less than as follows, viz: Foremen, $3 50 per day; mechanics, $3 00 per day; cartmen, $3 50 per day; laborers, $2 00 per day.

Art. 135. Nine hours shall constitute a day's labor for all mechanics, artizans and laborers employed on public works.

TITLE X.

INTERNAL IMPROVEMENTS.

Art. 136. There shall be appointed by the governor a state engineer, skilled in the theory and practice of his profession, who shall hold his office at the seat of government for the term of four years. He shall have the superintendence and direction of all public works in which the State may be interested, except those made by joint stock companies or such as may be under the parochial or city authorities exclusively and not in conflict with the general laws of the State. He shall communicate to the General Assembly, through the governor, annually, his views concerning the same, report upon the condition of the public works in progress, recommend such measures as in his opinion the public interest of the State may require, and shall perform such other duties as may be prescribed by law. His salary shall be five thousand dollars per annum, until otherwise provided by law. The mode of appointment, number and salary of his assistants shall be fixed by law. The state engineer and assistants shall give bonds for the performance of their duties as shall be prescribed by law.

Art. 137. The General Assembly may create internal improvement districts, composed of one or more parishes, and may grant a right to the citizens thereof to tax themselves for their improvements. Said internal improvement districts, when created, shall have the right to select commissioners, shall have power to appoint officers, fix their pay and regulate all matters relative to the improvements of their districts, provided such improvements will not conflict with the general laws of the State.

Art. 138. The General Assembly may grant aid to said districts out of the funds arising from the swamp and overflowed lands, granted to the State by the United States for that purpose or otherwise.

Art. 139. The General Assembly shall have the right of abolishing the office of state engineer, by a majority vote of all the members elected to each branch, and of substituting a board of public works in lieu thereof, should they deem it necessary.

TITLE XI.

PUBLIC EDUCATION.

Art. 140. There shall be elected a superintendent of public education, who shall hold his office for the term of four years. His duties shall be prescribed by law, and he shall receive a salary of four thousand dollars per annum until otherwise provided by law: *Provided*, that the General Assembly shall have power by a vote of a majority of the members elected to both Houses, to abolish the said office of superintendent of public education, whenever, in their opinion, said office shall be no longer necessary.

Art. 141. The Legislature shall provide for the education of all children of the State, between the ages of six and eighteen years. by maintenance of free public schools by taxation or otherwise.

Art. 142. The general exercises in the common schools shall be conducted in the English language.

Art. 143. A university shall be established in the city of New Orleans. It shall be composed of four faculties, to-wit: one of law, one of medicine, one of the natural sciences. and one of letters; the Legislature shall provide by law for its organization and maintenance.

Art. 144. the proceeds of all lands heretofore granted by the United States to this State for the use or purpose of the public schools, and of all lands which may hereafter be granted or bequeathed for that purpose, and the proceeds of the estates of deceased persons to which the State may become entitled by law, shall be and remain a perpetual fund on which the State shall pay an annual interest of six per cent., which interest together with the interest of the trust funds, deposited with the State by the United States, under the act of Congress, approved June 23, 1836, and all the rents of the unsold lands shall be appropriated to the purpose of such schools and the appropriation shall remain inviolable.

Art. 145. All moneys arising from the sales which have been, or may hereafter be made of any lands heretofore granted by the United States to this State for the use of a specific seminary of learning, or from any kind of a donation that may hereafter be made for that purpose, shall be and remain a perpetual fund, the interest of which at six per cent. per annum shall be appropriated to the promotion of literature and the arts and sciences, and no law shall ever be made diverting said funds to any other use than to the establishment and improvement of said seminary of learning: and the General Assembly shall have power to raise funds for the organization and support of said seminary of learning in such manner as it may deem proper.

Art. 146. No appropriation shall be made by the Legislature for the support of any private school or institution of learning whatever, but the highest encouragement shall be granted to public schools throughout the State.

TITLE XII.

MODE OF REVISING THE CONSTITUTION.

Art. 147. Any amendment or amendments to this constitution may be proposed in the Senate or House of Representatives, and if the same shall be agreed to by a majority of the members elected to each House, such proposed amendment or amendments shall be entered on their journals, with the yeas and nays taken thereon. Such proposed amendment or amendments shall be submitted to the people at an election to be ordered by said Legislature, and held within ninety days after the adjournment of the same, and after thirty day's publication according to law; and if a majority of the voters at said election shall approve and ratify such amendment or amendments, the same shall become a part of the constitution. If more than one amendment be submitted at a time, they shall be submitted in such manner and form, that the people may vote for or against each amendment separately.

TITLE XIII.

SCHEDULE.

Art. 148. The constitution adopted in 1852 is declared to be superceded by this constitution; and in order to carry the same into effect, it is hereby declared and ordained as follows:

Art. 149. All rights, actions, prosecutions, claims and contracts, as well of individuals as of bodies corporate, and all laws in force at the time of the adoption of this constitution, and not inconsistent therewith, shall continue as if the same had not been adopted.

Art. 150. In order that no inconvenience may result to the public service from the taking effect of this constitution, no officer shall be superceded thereby; but the laws of this State relative to the duties of the several officers, executive, judicial and military, except those made void by military authority, and by the ordinance of emancipation, shall remain in full force, though the same be contrary to this constitution, and the several duties shall be performed by the respective officers of the State, according to the existing laws, until the organization of the government under this constitution, and the entering into office of the new officers to be appointed under said government, and no longer.

Art. 151. The Legislature shall provide for the removal of all causes now pending in the Supreme Court or other courts of the State under the constitution of 1852, to courts created by or under this constitution.

TITLE XIV.

ORDINANCE.

Art. 152. Immediately after the adjournment of the Convention, the governor shall issue his proclamation directing the several officers of this State, authorized by law to hold elections, or in default thereof such officers as he shall designate, to open and hold polls in the several parishes of the State, at the places designated by law, on the first Monday of September, 1864, for the purpose of taking the sense of the good people of this State in regard to the adoption or rejection of this constitution: and it shall be the duty of said officers to receive the suffrages of all qualified voters. Each voter shall express his opinion by depositing in the ballot-box a ticket whereon shall be written "The Constitution accepted," or, "The Constitution rejected." At the conclusion of the said election, the officers and commissioners appointed to preside over the same shall carefully examine and count each ballot as deposited, and shall forthwith make due return thereof to the secretary of state, in conformity to the provisions of law and usages in regard to elections.

Art. 153. Upon the receipt of said returns, or on the third Monday of September, if the returns be not sooner received, it shall be the duty of the governor, the secretary of state, the attorney general and the state treasurer, in the presence of all such persons as may choose to attend, to compare the votes at the said election for the ratificatien or rejection of this constitution, and if it shall appear at the close, that a majority of all the votes given is for ratifying this constitution, then it shall be the duty of the governor to make proclamation of the fact, and thenceforth this constitution shall be ordained and established as the constitution of the State of Louisiana. But whether this constitution be accepted or rejected it shall be the duty of the governor to cause to be published the result of the polls, showing the number of votes cast in each parish for and against this constitution.

Art. 154. As soon as a general election can be held under this constitution in every parish of the State, the governor shall, by proclamation, or in case of his failure to act, the Legislature shall, by resolution, declare the fact, and order an election to be held on a day fixed in said proclamation or resolution, and within sixty days from the date thereof, for governor, lieutenant governor, secretary of state, auditor, treasurer, attorney general and superintendent of education. The officers so chosen shall, on the fourth Monday after their election, be installed into office; and shall hold their offices for the terms prescribed in this constitution, counting from the second Monday in January next preceding their entering into office in case they do not enter into office on that date. The terms of office of the State officers elected on the 22d day of February, 1864, shall expire on the instalation of their successors as herein provided for; but under no state of circumstances shall their term of office be construed as extending beyond the length of the terms fixed for said offices in this constitution; and, if not sooner held, the election of their successors shall take place on the first Monday of November, 1867, in all parishes where the same can be held, the officers elected on that date to enter into office on the second Monday in January, 1868.

Art. 155. This constitution shall be published in three papers to be selected by the president of the Convention, whereof two shall publish the same in English and French, and one in German, from the period of the adjournment of the Convention until the election for ratification or rejection on the first Monday of September, 1864.

(Signed)

E. H. DURELL, President of the Constitutional Convention of the State of Louisiana.

O. W. AUSTIN,
JOHN T. BARRETT,
JOSEPH G. BAUM,
RAPHAEL BEAUVAIS,
ROBERT BRADSHAW BELL,
YOUNG BURKE,
EMILE COLLIN,
A. CAZABAT,
TERRENCE COOK,
F. M. CROZAT,
R. KING CUTLER,
JOHN L. DAVIES,
JAMES DUANE,
JOSEPH DUPATY,
H. C. EDWARDS,
JAMES ENNIS,
W. R. FISH,
G. H. FLAGG,
PATRICK HARNAN,
EDMOND FLOOD,
JOHN FOLEY,
G. A. FOSDICK,
JAMES FULLER,
GEORGE GEIER,
JOS. GORLINSKI,
JEREMIAH J. HEALY,
JOS. H. BALCH,
EDWARD HART,
THOMAS ONG,
JOHN HENDERSON, JR.,
ROBERT W. BENNIE,
ALFRED C. HILLS,
JOHN SULLIVAN,
WILLIAM H. HIRE,
GEORGE HOWES,
M. D. KAVANAGH,
P. A. KUGLER,
WILLIAM DAVIS MANN,
XAVIER MAURER,
JOHN P. MONTAMAT,
ROBERT MORRIS,
EDWARD MURPHY,
M. W. MURPHY,
LUCIEN P. NORMAND,
P. K. O'CONNER,
JOHN PAYNE,
EUDALDO G. PINTADO,
O. H. POYNOT,
JOHN PURCELL,
SAMUEL PURSELL,
J. B. SCHROEDER,
MARTIN SCHNURR,
WILLIAM H. SEYMOUR,
ALFRED SHAW,
CHARLES SMITH,
JOHN A. SPELLICY,
WILLIAM TOMPKINS STOCKER,
J. H. STINER,
C. W. STAUFFER,
J. RANDALL TERRY,
T. B. THORPE,
JOHN BUCKLEY, JR.,
JOHN W. THOMAS,
ERNEST J. WENCK,
W. H. WATERS,
THOMAS M. WELLS,
JOSEPH HAMILTON WILSON,
JOHN A. NEWELL,
ROBERT W. TALIAFERRO,
M. F. BONZANO,
H. MILLSPAUGH,
LOUIS GASTINEL,
JOSEPH V. BOFILL,
BENJAMIN H. ORR,
GEO. F. BROTT,
JOHN K. COOK,
H. MAAS.

JNO. E. NEELIS, Secretary.

www.ingramcontent.com/pod-product-compliance
Lightning Source LLC
LaVergne TN
LVHW021056110826
845150LV00001B/91

* 9 7 8 1 4 2 5 5 6 6 5 5 5 *